proxibid®

# It's all in the marketplace™

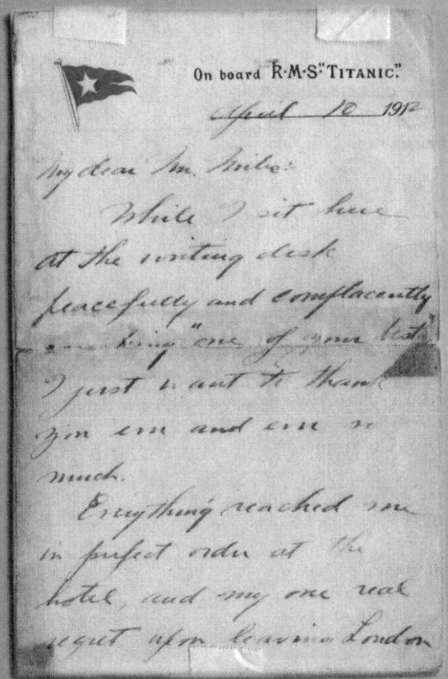

On board R.M.S. "Titanic."

April 10 1912

My dear Mr. [illegible]:

While I sit here at the writing desk peacefully and complacently [illegible] "one of your best" I just want to thank you ever and ever so much.

Everything reached me in perfect order at the hotel, and my one real regret upon leaving London was that I was unable to get down to Great Queen Street so as to bid you good-bye.

If you ever come to America try and come to Minneapolis where I shall be ever too glad to try and make your visit pleasant as well as interesting.

Thanking you again for your remembrance

Yours very sincerely

[illegible] Snyder

*Rare Titanic handwritten letter offered on Proxibid, March 2 by Philip Weiss Auctions*

**www.proxibid.com/antiques**

The largest, most trusted online real auction marketplace, Proxibid is easy to use and trusted by thousands of bidders worldwide.

**Need help getting started?** Contact us toll-free: 877-505-7770 or email: info@proxibid.com

Randolph S
500·121

# ANTIQUES & COLLECTIBLES

## 2013 PRICE GUIDE • 29th Edition

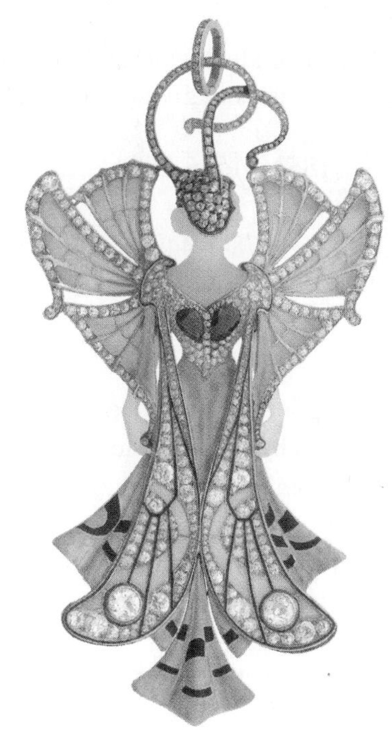

Published by

Krause Publications, a division of F+W Media, Inc.
700 East State Street • Iola, WI 54990-0001
715-445-2214 • 888-457-2873
www.krausebooks.com

To order books or other products call toll-free 1-800-258-0929
or visit us online at www.krausebooks.com or www.Shop.Collect.com

ISSN: 1536-2884

ISBN-13: 978-1-4402-3206-0
ISBN-10: 1-4402-3206-7

Cover Design by Sharon Bartsch and Jana Tappa
Designed by Marilyn McGrane
Edited by Eric Bradley

Printed in the United States of America

**Front cover, clockwise from top:**
Chinese export porcelain dish in Famille Rose, circa 1850-1900, 5-1/2" h., $215 (Heritage Auctions)
Wildflower water pitcher, Adams & Co., fourth quarter 19th c., 8-3/4" h., 5-1/4" dia. rim, $69 (Green Valley Auctions)
European 18k gold, amethyst, rose diamond, and purple enamel necklace, circa 1890s, 24" with chain, $6,500 (Steve Fishbach Collection; Linda Lombardo photo)
Poplar two-part glazed corner cupboard, Middle Atlantic states, early 19th c., 85" h. x 42-1/2" w. x 23" d. to corner, $1,778 (Skinner, Inc.)
"The Public Library" oil on canvas by Guy Carleton Wiggins, signed lower right, 29-1/2" x 23-1/4" framed, $17,250 (Morphy Auctions)
**Back cover:**
Tiffany pastel tulip candlestick, signed on underside "1845 L.C. Tiffany-Favrile," 16" t., $6,612 (James D. Julia Auctioneers)
Superman lunchbox, Adco, 1954, $16,500

# Table of Contents



## Listings

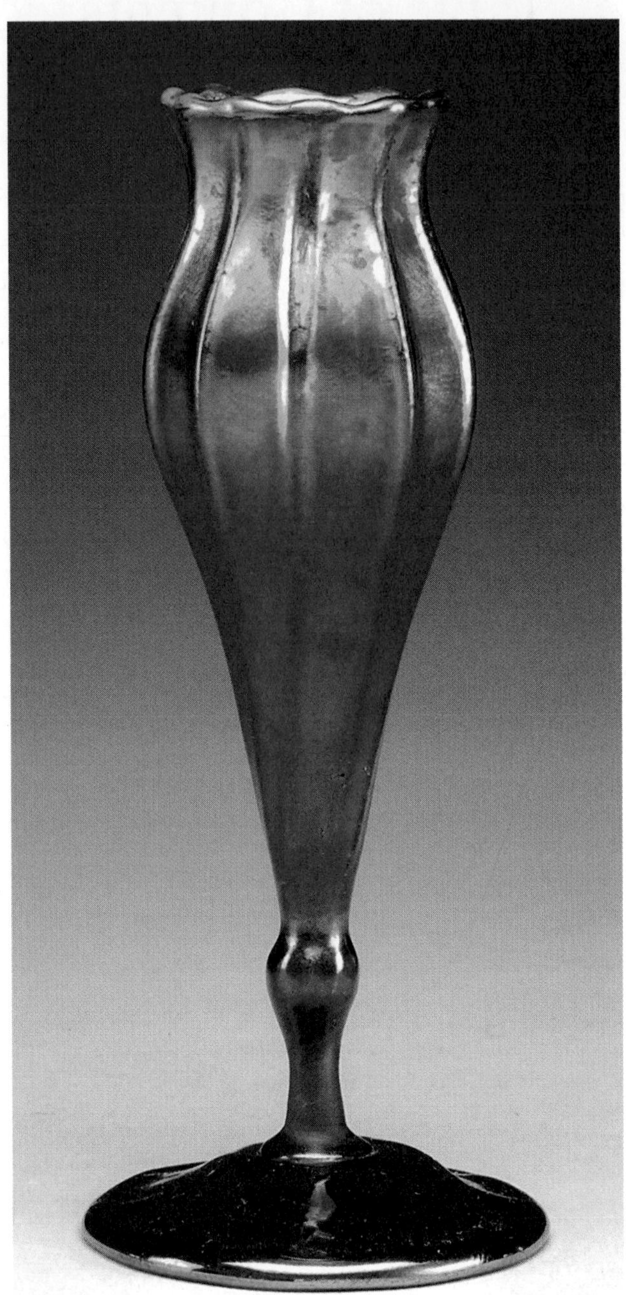

Tiffany Studios mini flower-form vase, $2,400. More details on page 574.
*James D. Julia, Inc.*

# Introduction

What a difference a year can make.

You don't have to look hard to see antiques are chic. Suddenly, the mainstream has discovered the passion, design and dollars behind the American antiques market in a way never before seen on television, in movies and even online. Cable and broadcast television networks now produce 30 different antiques-themed television programs, with more to come. Young people are holding "type ins" in New York, at which people meet up to share details on their vintage typewriter models and clack away while curious onlookers sip lattes. Antiques shows and flea markets are seeing the largest crowds in more than a decade at events big and small.

*Eric Bradley*

While it's true most of the dollars in the trade are changing hands at auction rather than events or collecting club functions, new technologies are making it easier to buy and collect and research. For collectors and investors, quality (as defined by rarity and condition) has emerged as the primary qualifier for values and prices. As such, there has never been a better time to be a dealer and investor in antiques. Fantastic items are appearing on the market every year, as the public gains a greater awareness of how profitable and important antiques and collectibles can be to their pocketbooks and the nation's cultural history. It's a renaissance of sorts, occurring at the intersection of low prices and appreciation.

In this year's edition, we've expanded and updated the most popular sections and added new ones, too. The glass section is the most comprehensive in years, and additions of bronze and fine art, with a special emphasis on Asian art, round out the year's top sales. You'll notice special attention is drawn to the very best items pursued by collectors and investors as Top Lots. Also new this year is a section on collectibles produced by The Franklin Mint, which will soon celebrate its 50th anniversary.

A special treat for collectors: new and expanded sections on books and magazines and ephemera, most notably postcards.

A book of this magnitude is a team project and much thanks is owed to editors Mary Sieber, Paul Kennedy, Karen Knapstein of Antique Trader magazine, designer Marilyn McGrane and author Donald-Brian Johnson. Ever the professionals, they work year round to make this book the best it can be. Their passion, patience, hard work and great ideas are always focused on one goal: selecting the topics, images and features our readers will find the most fascinating.

We hope you enjoy the results. As always, we welcome your thoughts and comments on this and future editions. Feel free to reach out at ATpriceguide@fwmedia.com.

---

**ERIC BRADLEY** is the editor of *Antique Trader* magazine, AntiqueTrader.com and the Antique Trader blog. He is the author of *Antique Trader Antiques and Collectibles Price Guide*, America's No. 1-selling guide to the antiques and collectibles market. An award-winning investigative journalist with a degree in economics, Bradley has written hundreds of articles about antiques and collectibles and has made several media appearances as an expert on the antiques market. His work has received press from *The New York Times* and *The Philadelphia Inquirer*, and most recently he has been a featured guest speaker on the topic of investing in antiques at MoneyShow San Francisco on MSN Money and Nasdaq.com.

Antique Trader®

# About AntiqueTrader.com

We think you'll be impressed with the new layout, sections and information in this year's annual. Because the antiques world (like everything else) is constantly changing, I invite you to visit AntiqueTrader.com and make it your main portal into the world of antiques.

Like our magazine, AntiqueTrader.com's team of collectors, dealers and bloggers share information daily on events, auctions, new discoveries and tips on how to buy more for less. Here's what's you'll find at AntiqueTrader.com.

- Free eNewsletters: Get a recap of the world of antiques sent to your inbox every week.
- Free Classified Ads: Discover inventory (great and small) from around the world offered to buy, sell or trade.
- Exclusive video: See what's going on with the stars of your favorite shows — "Antiques Roadshow," "American Pickers," "Pawn Stars," "Cash & Cari," "Storage Wars" and more!
- Expert Q&A columns: Learn how to value and sell your collections online and for the best prices.
- The Internet's largest free antiques library: Dig into more than 10,000 articles of research, show reports, auction results and more.
- Blogs: Get vital how-to information about topics that include selling online, buying more for less, restoring pieces, spotting fakes and reproductions, displaying your collections and finding hidden gems in your town!
- Show Guides: Check out the largest online events calendar in the world of antiques, with links to more than 1,000 shows worldwide.

Hubley cast-iron Bathing Beauties doorstop, design by Fish........................ **$10,350**
*Bertoia Auctions*

Hubley cast-iron Messenger Boy doorstop, design by Fish ................................ **$8,050**
*Bertoia Auctions*

# Advertising

Thousands of advertising items made in various materials, some intended as gifts with purchases, others used for display or given away for publicity, are actively collected.

Before the days of mass media, advertisers relied on colorful product labels and advertising giveaways to promote their products. Containers were made to appeal to the buyer through the use of stylish lithographs and bright colors. Many of the illustrations used the product in the advertisement so that even an illiterate buyer could identify a product.

Advertisements were put on almost every household object imaginable and became constant reminders to use the product or visit a certain establishment.

TOP! LOT!

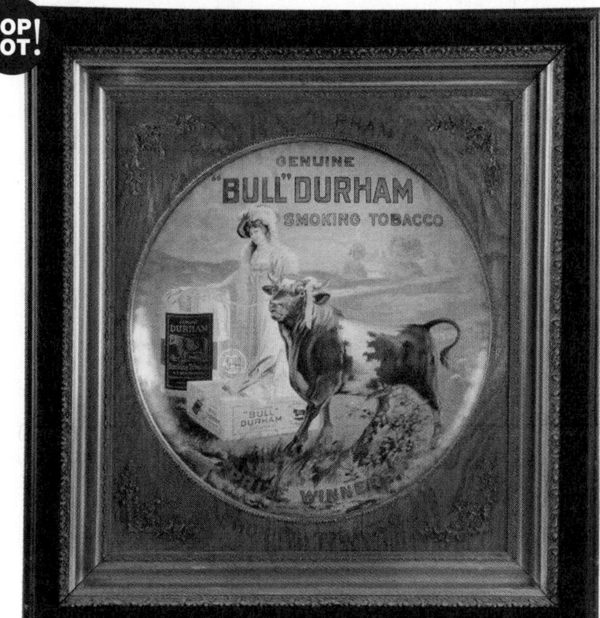


Charger, Bull Durham smoking display, scarce, original 24" round charger set in its original period, ornate wood frame with Bull Durham Smoking Tobacco name lightly embossed in the wood, Blackwell Manufacturing Co. added a heavy wood protective border frame with original label on back.......................................................................................**$4,600**

Rodeo cowboy advertising poster, circa 1930s, framed: 34-1/4" by 29"..................................**$105**

Hires Rootbeer bottles and case, circa early 1900s, original small wood crate advertising "Hires Rootbeer Stands for Health" with 12 original embossed bottles, not usually found complete, 7-1/2" x 5"...................................**$180**

Tins, group of three promoting Canadian Circus Marshmallows, upright round tins with hats (the lids of the tins) on cat, dog and monkey animal characters, each 7". ................................**$575**

*All images courtesy Dan Morphy Auctions*

Coca-Cola cardboard sign, circa 1950s image of girl holding fishing pole and reaching for a bottle of Coke, original frame, framed: 29" x 18".......................... **$287**

Bowey's Chocolate store canister, 10-pound square tin with screw top promoting Bowey's Hot Chocolate Powder, manufactured in Chicago, 10-1/2" .................. **$160**

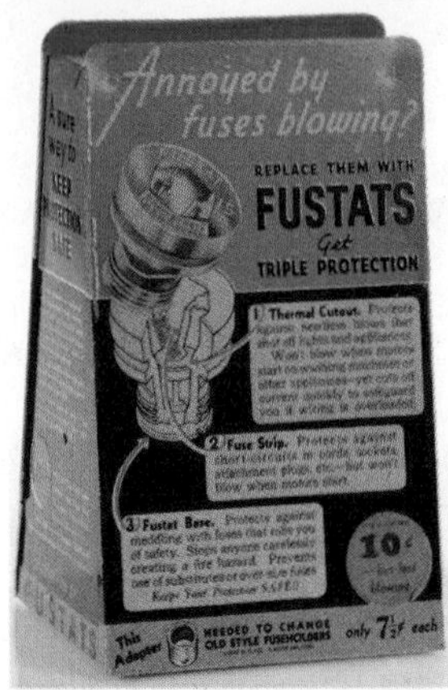


Fustat Fuses, metal store counter dispenser display with product images and descriptive copy on front and back, 11-1/2"............... **$80**

M'Gregor Happy Foot display, figural papier-mâché smiling foot for McGregor Socks, 17"....... **$1,000**

Campbell's Soup porcelain sign, classic image of Campbell's Tomato Soup can, soup can-shape curved porcelain, 22-1/2". **$1,400**

Merrick's Round Spool Cabinet, Merrick's Spool Cotton oak spool cabinet with curved glass, contains original thread spools, 20". ...................................... **$1,265**

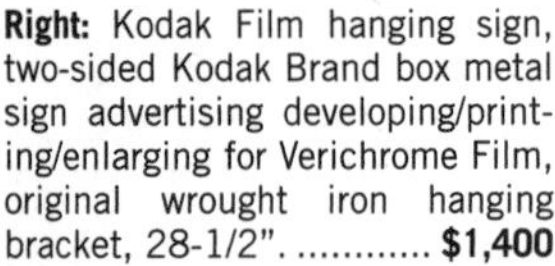

**Right:** Kodak Film hanging sign, two-sided Kodak Brand box metal sign advertising developing/printing/enlarging for Verichrome Film, original wrought iron hanging bracket, 28-1/2". ............ **$1,400**

**Far right:** Match holder, DeLaval, scarce variation of die-cut embossed tin litho of DeLaval's separating machine, 6-1/4". ...... **$184**

Andy Gump Thrift Bank, tobacco pocket tin with coin slot on top; General Thrift Product Co., Chicago, images of Andy Gump and his family on both sides, 4-1/2" ...... **$190**

Dispenser, National Biscuit counter display, embossed lettering on glass, metal lid not original, 10". ...... **$126**

**Right:** Tin, Farmers Pride Brand Steel Cut Coffee, manufactured by Hulman & Company in Terre Haute, Ind., can is full and unopened, 6". ...... **$750**

Ever-Ready Shaving Brushes store counter, case with 10 Ever-Ready brushes and six packs of razor blades, metal case has glass lift lid with a die-cut marquee, 10-1/2". ...... **$5,750**

# Asian Art & Antiques

Andrew Stramentov

Art and antiques from China, Japan, Korea, the Pacific Rim, and Southeast Asia have fascinated collectors for centuries because they are linked with the rich culture and fascinating history of the Far East. Their beauty, artistry, and fine craftsmanship have lured collectors through the ages. The category is vast and includes objects ranging from jade carvings to cloisonné to porcelain to bronze figures. Prices for Asian antiques and art fluctuate considerably depending on age, condition, decoration, etc.

Investors have long sought antiques and fine objects to safeguard their earnings. The lingering global economic uncertainties mean new markets are prime for new collectors and fresh cash. As the Asian market soars and contemporary artists become ever more collectible, auction houses are developing these two key divisions to capitalize on the globalization of the antiques market. Bonhams recently added Andrew Stramentov, Senior Specialist of Contemporary Art. He shares his advice for those seeking a haven for either their passion for art or their nest egg.

**Q:** Is this a good time for U.S. investors to jump into the Asian market to make strategic purchases of Asian art and antiques?

**A:** The art market is at times unpredictable and the decision to collect is a very personal one. The market for Asian works of art is strong and continues to grow in popularity.

Both Eastern and non-Eastern collectors are passionate and dedicated to collecting the best examples of Chinese art, whether it is Imperial objects or contemporary paintings. There has been a long history of trade between East and West, from the silk route to the spice road, and this is simply an extension of that. Tastes are becoming more refined and diversified as people discover art forms, be it from the wealth of new galleries opening – both Western and local – or new or existing museums.

Q: What are some of the contemporary Asian artists buyers should seek out when looking to collect Asian art?

A: The established artists that the current market is interested in are artists like Zao Wou-Ki and Chu Teh-Chun, who are both late career artists but have produced a wealth of fabulous work, which very much encapsulates the Eastern philosophies within their oeuvre while clearly being influenced by the best of European art.

Q: If a client was interested in investing in fine Asian art, which purchases, artists, mediums (ceramics, jade, paintings, contemporary sculpture) or eras would you suggest?

A: Buy with your heart, not what you think will give you a return when you sell it. Seek advice from people you trust and most of all, if you see something and you like it, read about the artist. You can discover as much in books and the Internet as you can in museums. If you buy something, spend time with it.

***Eric Bradley***

Statue, Southeast Asian bronze figure of Parvati, likely Chola, seated pose with conical headdress, serene expression, body draped with multiple necklaces and strands of beads, wearing a dhoti with repetitive raised pattern, 14" h. .......... **$26,000**

Huanghuali altar table, late 20th c., floating panel top fitted into mitered, mortise and tenoned frame with upturned ends over shaped, beaded apron joined to legs carved with a sword-edge pattern and joined to paired oval stretchers, 33-3/4" x 59-3/4" x 16-3/8" ............**$17,500**
*Bonhams*

Huanghuali brush pot with hardstone inlay, 18th/19th c., inlay late Qing/Republic period, cylindrical section in dark wood with whorls to the grain surrounding an interior metal lining; sides with ivory and hardstone inlaid tableau of 18 luohan engaged in various pursuits in a garden setting; base bears six-character Qianlong mark in mother-of-pearl, 9-1/2" dia. ....................................**$17,500**
*Bonhams*

TOP! LOT!

Jade and hardstone-inlaid lacquered wood panel of kingfishers and wisteria, 19th c., dark yellow lacquer ground inlaid with colored stones to depict two birds roosting on flowering wisteria hanging from gnarled vines of carved wood that continue as the frame around the panel, reversed by shiny black lacquer on the flat wood ground, patinated metal bail hanging device, 34" x 50-1/2"..............**$338,500**
*Bonhams*

Rare pair of zitan and hongmu recessed leg altar tables, 18th/19th c., each with two-board top set into mitered, mortise and tenoned frame with molded veneer edge joined to recessed solid legs cut at top to receive carved apron of peony blossoms and foliage rendered in high relief, repeated on side panels tongue-and-grooved into side of legs and slab feet, 35-1/4" x 91-1/8" x 19-1/8" ............................................................**$2,714,500**
*Bonhams*

Chinese celadon porcelain bowl, Qing dynasty, artist unknown, 7-3/4" dia........................ **$350**

Champlevé enamel-decorated bronze Kannon, Meiji/Taisho period, depicted in raiment and standing on lotus pedestal, brocade-patterned robes and waisted plinth with colored enamel accents repeated on separately cast openwork mandorla, adorned with two diadems fronted by image of small seated Buddha, 30-3/4" ........................ **$5,000-$7,000**
*Bonhams*

Carved zitan and hongmu throne chair, 19th c., three-part top rail set off with leaf and scroll work edge framing a recessed central panel carved with clouds and a central bat above three carved panels featuring profiled dragons flanking a central five-clawed dragon, each below a specific trigram medallion set into a network of scrolling clouds, lower sections captured with more clouds and trigrams above a caned hard seat, exterior side panels rendered with bats and scattered clouds over a pierced waisted frame with cloud collar corner brackets carved into hipped cabriole legs resting on single balls and joined to a separately carved humpback stretcher frame, 40-3/8" x 40-1/2" x 29-1/4" ............ **$1,022,500**
*Bonhams*

Qi Baishi (1863-1957), album of various subjects, nine paintings of double leaves, ink or ink and color on paper: a) bird on blossoming branch, signed Huang Jiping Laoren, with one seal reading Jieshanweng; b) children playing with arrows, signed Sanbaishiyin Fuweng, with one seal reading Azhi; c) bird on lotus stalk, signed Laoping, with one seal reading Baishiweng; d) sailing alone, signed Sanbaishiyin Fuweng Baishi, with two seals reading Azhi and Muren; e) landscape, signed Baishi, with two seals reading Muren and Muren; f) misty landscape, signed Baishi Huang, with a seal reading Baishiweng; g) old man picking his ear, signed Huang with one seal reading Muren; h) painting in house among trees, signed Qi Huang with two seals reading Muren and Baishiweng; i) plum blossom, signed Baishi, "painted at Jiping Tang" with one seal reading Muren; with additional leaf of calligraphy by Lou Shibai (b. 1918) with a four-character inscription dated xinwei 1991, 9-3/8" x 14-1/8" each double leaf ................................ **$506,500**
*Bonhams*

Cast bronze seated figure of Amitabha Buddha, Ming dynasty, coiffure of circular ushnisha in crisply cast curls surrounding prominent secondary urna, pendulous earlobes framing full square face, loose-fitting robes tied at mid-waist with hems of incised lotus and flower decoration open to reveal a chest centered by small svastika, hands with incised cakra on the palm held in dhyanamudra upon folded legs in dhyanasana posture of meditation, seated upon an unsealed multi-petaled lotus throne with stylized leaf and vines cast en suite; all exterior surfaces showing traces of red and gilt lacquer, 29" ................................ **$578,500**

*Bonhams*

Pair of spinach jade rectangular plaques with gilt and silver-painted decoration, late Qing/Republic period, each mottled dark green plaque painted with a phoenix standing beneath a wutong tree surrounded by peony blossoms and other birds rendered in shades of gilt and russet pigment, also used on reverse to paint a cloud-filled Daoist paradise peopled with male and female immortals, their heads highlighted in silver and black pigment, 13-1/2" x 10" ea. ........................................................ **$3,000-$5,000**

*Bonhams*

He Tianjian (Chinese, 1891-1977) landscape, watercolor and ink on silk, 33" x 15-3/4" ........................................................ **$9,560**

Chinese export silver footed salt, Wang Hing & Co., Hong Kong and Canton, China, circa 1875-1925, flower blossom form raised on three flower and stem legs, marks: WH, 2-5/8" x 2" dia., 1.00 troy oz............................ **$89**

Pair of Dehua porcelain figures of Magu, late Qing/Republic period, facing pair each depicting Daoist divinity with lingzhi fungus branch in one hand, standing next to deer balancing basket of blossoms on its back, both supported on a faceted rocky plinth, 15-1/2" ...................................................... **$5,000-$7,000**
*Bonhams*

Group of five Asian brushes, largest 21-1/2" l. . **$239**

Chinese export silver center bowl, maker unknown, China, circa 1900, octagonal reticulated bowl in chinoiserie motif with removable silver liner, chop mark, 8-1/4" dia., 39.6 troy oz. ............................ **$4,687**

Rare huanghuali clothes rack, yijia, Qing dynasty, composed of paired rectangular beaded uprights mitered and tenoned into a horizontal top rail terminating into separately carved open-mouth dragon head terminals over pierced dragon spandrels tenoned into the side of the uprights set into solid bases carved with dissolved zoomorphic birds to front and back, fitted with upright spandrels carved with dragons in clouds over lishui, mortise and tenoned into molded rails that support a central section fitted with three horizontal stretchers all carved with beaded edges and mitered, mortise and tenoned into a vertical short post carved with lotus finials at each end, central panel of full front four-clawed dragon in clouds treading on crashing waves and rock work flanked by two profiled dragons enclosed by a beaded frame, the lower two rails fitted with elaborate dragon spandrels echoing the vertical spandrels at the foot and under the top rail; 56-3/4" x 53-1/2" x 16-1/4" .. **$338,500**
*Bonhams*

Chinese pocket sundial, circa 19th c., consisting of paper register, compass and brass folding vane, wood two-piece circular box, lift-off top, inner paper in top lid, 2-1/2" ................................................... **$537**

Solid nephrite jade bear, largest jade sculpture known of its time, dating back from the Warring State to Eastern Han dynasty (475 B.C-220 A.D), made for a significant figure/ruler with whom it was buried, extensive calcification due to centuries of extended burial. White and green translucent jade behind the surface calcification around feet and other areas, cup-shaped opening on top of head, possibly made as a stand or base for an object such as a flag pole, table, or bell stand. High relief designs include "S," cornered "L" and "Z" shapes. (The bear currently is the national symbol for the Federal Republic of Russia.) Includes analytical report concluding that the artifact is original, as well as certificate of authenticity from the Beijing Wenzhenyuan Relic Identification Consulting Co.; 14" h. x 7-1/2" w., 40.25 lbs. Provenance: Purchased by a private New York estate in 1998.................................................. **$7,050,000**
*Elite Decorative Arts*

Two carved huanghuali veneer fragments, 18th c., each a rectangular section from a larger composition now mounted together in a single frame, upper section carved with five-clawed dragon facing front as it grasps a flaming jewel amidst swirling clouds, lower panel of spiraling waves and clouds scrolls to the right of a partial faceted rock, each fragment laid onto a pieced wood back, 45-5/8" x 32" ....**$8,000-$12,000**
*Bonhams*

Chinese hardstone censor on carved wooden stand, 20th c., 6-3/4" h.......................................**$23,750**

◀Pair of Chinese hardwood arm chairs, Qing dynasty, woven cane seats laid over board, square straight legs and arms, carved medallion to center of back rails, 34-1/4" x 21" x 18".................................. **$3,000**
*Boss Star Collection*

# Autographs

In *The Meaning and Beauty of Autographs,* first published in 1935 and translated from German by David H. Lowenherz of Lion Heart Autographs, Inc. in 1995, Stefan Zweig explained that to love a manuscript, we must first love the human being "whose characteristics are immortalized in them." When we do, then "a single page with a few lines can contain the highest expression of human happiness, and... the expression of deepest human sadness. To those who have eyes to look at such pages correctly, eyes not only in the head, but also in the soul, they will not receive less of an impression from these plain signs than from the obvious beauty of pictures and books."

John M. Reznikoff, founder and president of University Archives, has been a leading dealer and authority on historical letters and artifacts for 32 years. He described the current market for autographs as "very, very strong on many fronts. Possibly because of people being afraid to invest in the market and in real estate, we are seeing investment in autographs that seems to parallel gold and silver."

Reznikoff suspects that Civil War items peaked after Ken Burns' series but that Revolutionary War documents, included those by signers of the Declaration of Independence and the Constitution are still undervalued and can be purchased for under $500.

Currrently, space is in high demand, especially Apollo 11. Pop culture, previously looked at as secondary by people who dealt in Washingtons and Lincolns, has come into its own. Reznikoff anticipates continued growth in memorabilia that includes music, television, movies and sports. Babe Ruth, Lou Gehrig, Ty Cobb and Tiger Woods are still good investments but Reznikoff warns that authentication is much more of a concern in sports than in any other field.

The Internet allows for a lot of disinformation and this is a significant issue with autographs. There are two widely accepted authentication services: Professional Sports Authenticator (PSA/DNA) and James Spence Authentication (JSA). A dealer's reliability can be evaluated by seeing whether he is a member of one or more of the major organizations in the field: the Antique Booksellers Association of America, UACC Registered Dealers Program and the National Professional Autograph Dealers Association (NPADA), which Reznikoff founded.

There is an additional caveat to remember and it is true for all collectibles: rarity. The value of an autograph is often determined less by the prominence of the signer than by the number of autographs he signed.

***Zac Bissonnette***

Chuck Berry, white Signature Series electric guitar with Chuck Berry logo and image on the body, signed on the pick guard. ........................................ **$478**
*Heritage Auction Galleries*

Alex Rodriguez, 8" x10" photo depicts the day he signed with the Yankees. .......................... **$179**
*Heritage Auction Galleries*

Color photograph signed by all seven members of the Columbia Space Shuttle mission STS-107, an official NASA lithograph showing each member of the crew in a space suit. Signed in the image, above the relevant portrait. Crew biographies printed on the back, approximately 8" x 10". ........................................................ **$8,500**
(All seven crewmembers died when Columbia was destroyed on re-entry on Feb. 1, 2003.)
*Swann Auction Galleries*

Christopher "Kit" Carson, carte-de-visite portrait by Brady, showing the soldier and frontiersman in civilian attire. Signed on the mount below the image. Photographer's full imprint on back. Approximately 3-1/4" x 2-1/4" (image), corners and top edge trimmed, minor scattered soiling. ........................................... **$28,000**
*Swann Auction Galleries*

Custer's Own Portrait of Officers of the Seventh Cavalry, photograph inscribed and signed "G.A.C." twice, in ink and pencil. An albumen print group portrait (by Orlando S. Goff), showing Custer and the officers under his command and their wives. On the mount below the image, Custer has written, in ink, the name of each person in the group, adding, in pencil, "Names written in the order of the persons in the picture. G.A.C." On the back, in pencil, he notes, "Our house at Fort Lincoln, Dakota." Approximately 5" x 7-1/4" (image), 8" x 10" overall; minor toning at edges of mount, scattered minor foxing on verso. (Fort Lincoln, N.D., November 1873) ............................. **$20,000**
*Swann Auction Galleries*

Frank Sinatra, 2-1/2" x 2" autograph, cut, framed along with a color 8" x 10" photo.................... **$143**
*Heritage Auction Galleries*

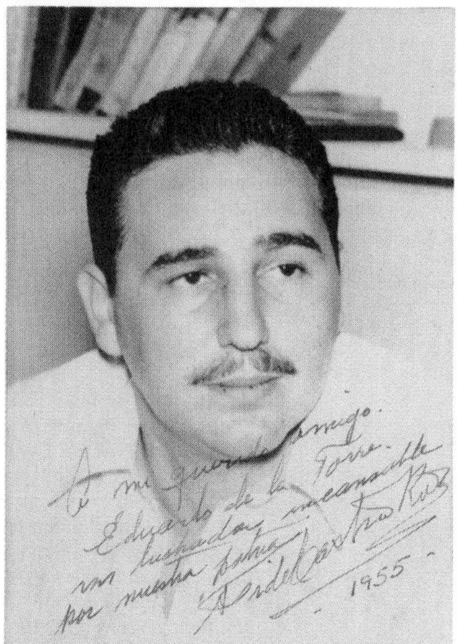


Fidel Castro, photograph signed, "Fidel Castro Ruz," and inscribed: "To my dear friend / Eduardo de la Torre, / a tireless fighter / for our country / 1955," in Spanish, bust portrait showing the young revolutionary clean-shaven except for a mustache. Signed in the image at bottom. Approximately 7" x 5"; slight silvering along top edge; owner's ink stamp on back: "Propiedad de Gaston Bernal." Castro was arrested in 1953 and sentenced to 15 years in prison for his part in an ill-fated attack on the Batista regime. He was released in 1955 and almost immediately went to Mexico and the United States to revive his movement, raise money and recruit supporters. This photo dates from that trip.................................... **$3,000**
*Swann Auction Galleries*

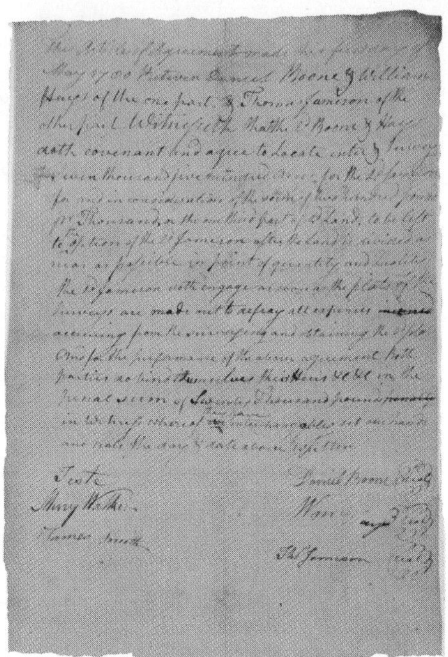

This Article of Agreement made this first day of May 1780 between Daniel Boone & William Hays of the one part & Thomas Jamison of the other part Witnesseth that the sd Boone & Hays doth covenant and agree to locate enter & survey Fifteen thousand five hundred acres for the sd Jamison for and in consideration of the sum of two hundred pounds per Thousand, or the one third part of sd Land, to be left to option of the sd Jamison after the land is divided as near as possible in point of quantity and quality the sd Jamison doth engage as soon as the plots of the surveys are made out to repay all expences accruing from the surveying and obtaining the sd plots And for the performance of the above agreement both parties do bind themselves their Heirs &c &c in the penal sum of Twenty Thousand pounds in witness whereof we have interchangeably set our hands and seals the day & date above written

Teste
Mary Walker
Thomas Smith

Daniel Boone (Seal)
Wm Hays (Seal)
Th Jamison (Seal)

Daniel Boone signed surveying agreement, 1780 ............................................................**$13,146**

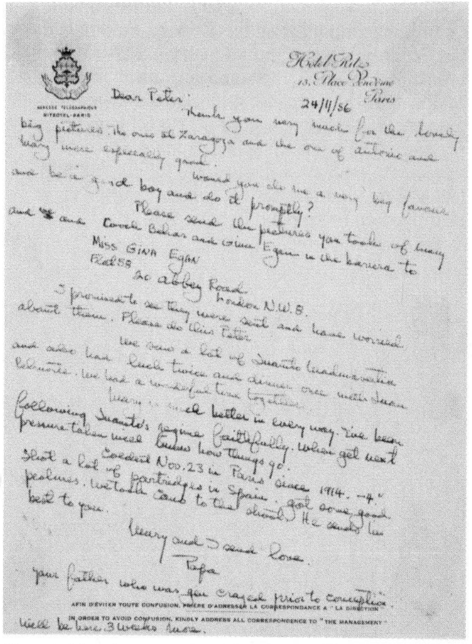

ADRESSE TELEGRAPHIQUE RITZOTEL-PARIS

Hotel Ritz
15, Place Vendôme
Paris
24/11/56

Dear Peter:

Thank you very much for the lovely big pictures. The ones of Zaragoza and the one of Antonio and Mary were especially good.

Would you do me a very big favour and be a good boy and do it promptly?

Please send the pictures you took of Mary and and Carol Bakas and Gina Egan in the barrera to

Miss Gina Egan
Flat 58
20 Abbey Road
London N.W.8

I promised to see they were sent and have worried about them. Please do this Peter.

We saw a lot of Juanito Quintana and also had lunch twice and dinner once with Juan Belmonte. We had a wonderful time together.

Mary is much better in every way. I've been following Juanito's regime faithfully.

Shot a lot of partridges in Spain.

Mary and I send love.

Papa

AFIN D'EVITER TOUTE CONFUSION, PRIERE D'ADRESSER LA CORRESPONDANCE A "LA DIRECTION"
IN ORDER TO AVOID CONFUSION, KINDLY ADDRESS ALL CORRESPONDENCE TO "THE MANAGEMENT"

Will be here 3 weeks more.

Ernest Hemingway signed letter, 1956, discussing bull fighting, hunting, Spain. ....................... **$2,868**

George Armstrong Custer, 1868, letter to Captain W.J. Lough, concerning the alleged poor treatment of Custer's horses, Phil and Mack, under Lough's care. Custer writes in part: "I do not want him kept from his regular full account of work merely because he shys . . . I certainly do not intend to pay for any time not even a day that my horse does not receive the work and care on the track which I intended he should . . . I distinctly told you that I did not want my horses taken outside the track enclosure and I still desire that except for shoeing." Four pages, written on a single folded sheet; soiling on terminal page, vertical fold through signature, small stain through text on terminal page. With Captain Lough's letter in response to Custer, defending his work........................... **$7,200**
*Swann Auction Galleries*

In Congress March 20. 1776

Resolved That the committee of safety of the colony of New Jersey be desired to remove the prisoners from Trenton to such place or places in that colony as may be thought convenient, at a proper distance from the Sea and post roads, subject to the regulations formerly made respecting prisoners.

Resolved That all officers prisoners, who shall refuse to subscribe the parole ordered by Congress, be committed to prison

Extract from the minutes
Chas Thomson secy

By order of Congress
John Hancock President

John Hancock signed document, 1776........**$13,145**

George Herbert Walker Bush and Mikhail Sergeyevich Gorbachev, photo signed by both, showing each with one arm around the other and smiling at the 10-year-anniversary celebrations of the fall of the Berlin Wall. Approximately 11-1/2" x 8" overall. ................ **$700**
*Swann Auction Galleries*

Hans Christian Andersen, signed, "H.C. Andersen," carte-de-visite portrait by Georg E. Hansen, showing the Danish fairytale author seated at a desk holding an open book. Signed on the mount at bottom. Approximately 3-1/2" x 2-1/4" (image), framed. **$2,600**
*Swann Auction Galleries*

# Banks

Banks with no mechanical action are known as still banks. The first still banks were made of wood or pottery or from gourds. Redware and stoneware banks, made by America's early potters, are prized possessions of today's collectors.

Still banks reached a golden age with the arrival of cast iron banks, which were often ornately painted to enhance their appeal. During the cast iron era, banks and other businesses used the still bank as a form of advertising.

The tin lithograph still bank, also a tool for advertising, reached its zenith from 1930 to 1955 and often resembled the packaging of the product.

Banks that display some form of action while accepting a coin are considered mechanical banks. These banks date back to ancient Greece and Rome, but the majority of collectors are interested in those made between 1867 and 1928 in Germany, England, and the United States. Approximately 2,000-3,000 types and varieties of mechanical banks were made in the early period.

More than 80 percent of all cast iron mechanical banks produced between 1869 and 1928 were made by J. E. Stevens Co., Cromwell, Connecticut. Tin banks are usually of German origin.

Original early mechanical and cast-iron still banks are in great demand with collectors. Their scarcity has caused numerous reproductions of both types, and the novice collector is urged to exercise caution.

Cast iron "Uncle Remus" mechanical bank, Kyser & Rex, highlights to base, 5-3/4" l. ................**$26,400**
*Morphy Auctions*

Cast iron apple still bank, Kyser & Rex, 5-1/2" l. ............................................................ **$1,200**
*Morphy Auctions*

Cast iron "Darktown Battery" mechanical baseball bank, J. & E. Stevens Co., Cromwell, Connecticut, late 19th c., original painted surface, coin trap marked "Patented February 2 1875," 7-1/4" h., 9-3/4" l. ............................................................ **$2,726**
*Skinner, Inc.*

Brass "Cat and Mouse" mechanical bank, J. & E. Stevens Co., Cromwell, Connecticut ..... **$8,050**
*Bertoia Auctions*

Cast-iron safe-shape still bank with bust of Grover Cleveland ....................................**$11,500**
*Bertoia Auctions*

Cast iron building still bank with eagle finial, American, late 19th c., cast with two chimneys, original red and gold paint, 9-3/4" h. x 5-1/4" w. x 5" d. ............ **$1,896**
*Skinner, Inc.*

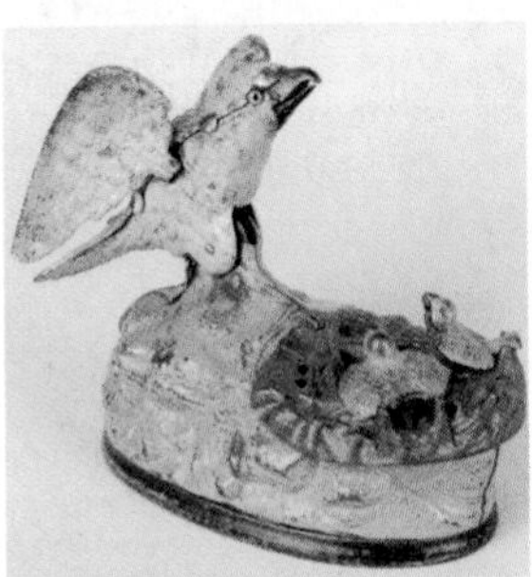

Cast iron "Eagle and Eaglets" mechanical bank, J. & E. Stevens Co., Cromwell, Connecticut, includes bellows, 8" l. ........... **$720**
*Morphy Auctions*

Cast iron "Mammy With Spoon" mechanical bank, Kyser & Rex, blue dress variation, 7-1/2" t. ..................................... **$2,400**
*Morphy Auctions*

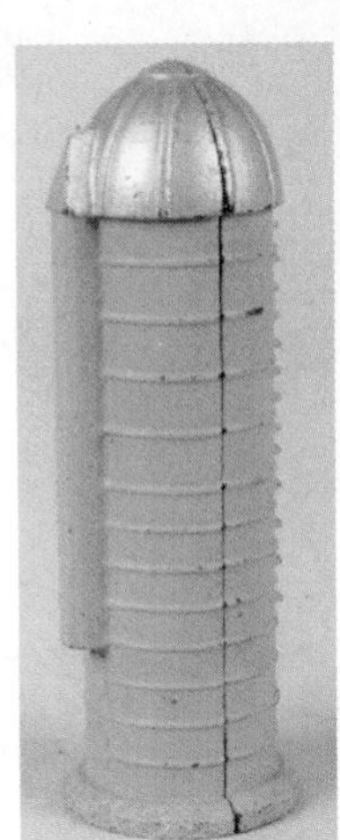

Cast iron "Marietta Silo" still bank, 5-1/2" t. ................ **$1,140**
*Morphy Auctions*

Cast iron "Humpty Dumpty" mechanical clown bank, Shepard Hardware Co., Buffalo, New York, c. 1884, base with maker's name and patent dates for United States, Canada, and England, 7-3/4" h............**$1,304**
*Skinner, Inc.*

Polychrome cast iron mechanical "New Bank," American, late 19th c., gilt mechanical guard, painted red and green with blue and white accents, 6-1/4" h. ........... **$1,659**
*Skinner, Inc.*

Cast iron "Trick Dog" mechanical bank, Shepard Hardware Co., Buffalo, New York, c. 1888, polychrome painted, bottom marked "PAT. JULY 31 1888," 7-5/8" h., 2-7/8" w., 8-3/4" l. ......... **$1,304**
*Skinner, Inc.*

Large Independence Hall still bank, Enterprise Manufacturing Co., Philadelphia, for the 1876 Centennial Exposition, copper/bronze-toned paint, 10-1/4" h. x 9-3/8" w. x 8" d. ............. **$1,422**
*Skinner, Inc.*

Four cast iron bank building banks, J. & E. Stevens Co., Cromwell, Connecticut, late 19th c., three "Hall's Excelsior Bank" mechanical banks, each with carved and painted wood cashier in roof, large "crown" still bank, 5-1/8"-5-3/8" h. ........................................................ **$1,659**
*Skinner, Inc.*

Small Independence Hall still bank, Enterprise Manufacturing Co., Philadelphia, commemorating the 1876 Centennial Exposition, copper/bronze-toned paint, 9" h. x 6-3/4" w. x 6-1/4" d. ........................................ **$948**
*Skinner, Inc.*

Four small cast iron still banks, J. & E. Stevens Co., Cromwell, Connecticut, 1870-1880, two "crown" banks and two "cupola" banks, 3-1/2"-4-1/4" h.... **$1,007**
*Skinner, Inc.*

Painted cast iron "Uncle Tom" mechanical bank, Kyser and Rex, Philadelphia, c. 1885, original paint, 5-1/2" h.................. **$889**
*Skinner, Inc.*

Cast iron "Safety Deposit" still bank, 6" t........................... **$90**
*Morphy Auctions*

# Barbie

At the time of her introduction in 1959, no one could have guessed that this statuesque doll would become a national phenomenon and eventually the most famous girl's plaything ever produced.

Over the years, Barbie and her growing range of family and friends have evolved with the times, serving as an excellent mirror of the fashion and social changes taking place in American society. Today, after more than 50 years of continuous production, Barbie's popularity remains unabated among both young girls and older collectors. Early and rare Barbies can sell for remarkable prices, and it is every Barbie collector's hope to find a mint condition #1 Barbie.

For more information on the Barbie doll, see *Warman's Barbie Doll Field Guide* by Paul Kennedy.

Bubblecut Barbie, introduced 1961, rounded hairstyle, blonde, brunette, or titian (red) hair, red jersey one-piece swimsuit, matching red open toe heels and a gold wrist tag, mint in box ....... **$1,400**

Ponytail #2 Barbie, no holes in feet, produced in blond and brunette hair, mint in box..... **$7,000**

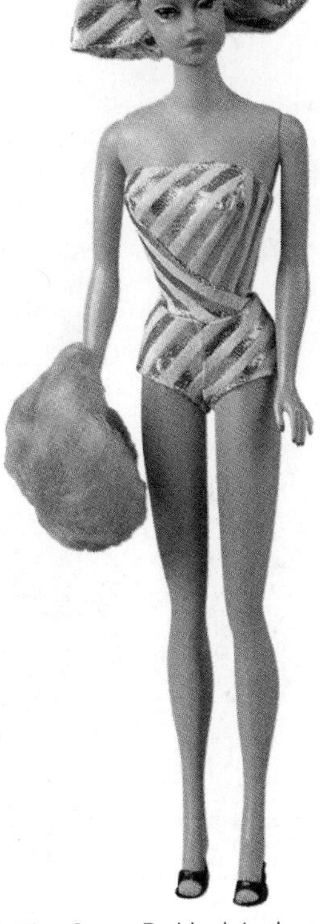

Fashion Queen Barbie, introduced 1963, original packaging included three wigs, mint in box........ **$500**

►Miss Barbie, introduced 1964, with "sleep eyes" that open and close, mint in box ........................................................................**$1,200**

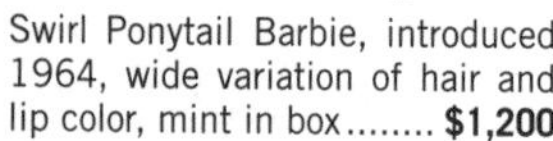

Swirl Ponytail Barbie, introduced 1964, wide variation of hair and lip color, mint in box........ **$1,200**

American Girl Barbie, introduced 1965, bendable leg, first issued in 1965, mint in box ........... **$1,900**

Twist 'N Turn Barbie (also known as TNT), introduced 1967, with bendable waist, mint in box. **$500**

Color Magic Barbie, introduced 1966, includes Color Magic liquid changer A and B, sponge applicator with pink handle, and instruction booklet allowing hair, swimsuit, and headband colors to change back and forth between two alternatives; when swabbed with color changing solution, Golden Blonde hair changed to Scarlet Flame, and Midnight changed to Ruby Red. The yellow and green swimsuit changed to red and burgundy, as did Barbie doll's matching headband, mint in box................................ **$3,500**

Talking Barbie, introduced 1968, with Twist 'N Turn body and pull-string talking feature, mint in box ........................................ **$425**

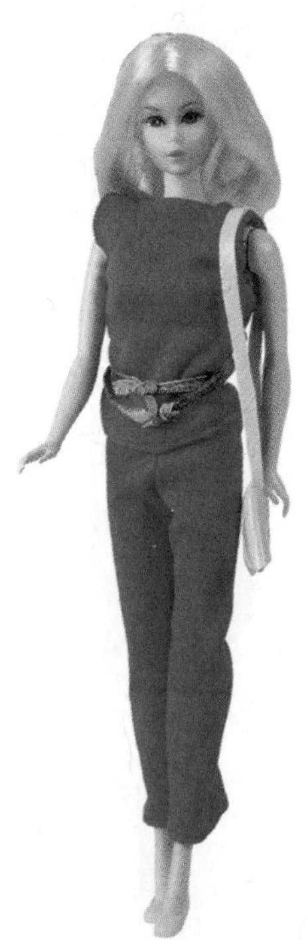

Walk Lively Barbie, introduced 1971, packaged with special stand that allowed her to walk and swing her arms, mint in box. **$225**

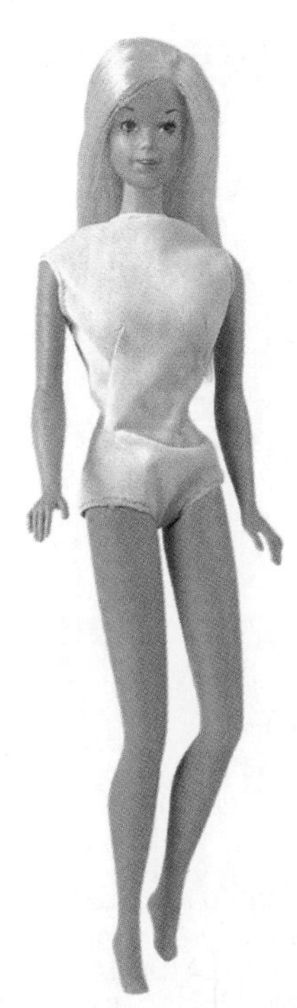

Mailbu Barbie (also known as The Sun Set) introduced in 1971, mint in box .......................... **$60**

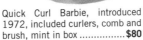

Talking Busy Barbie, introduced 1972, with gripping hands and twist 'n turn waist, mint in box ........................................ **$300**

Quick Curl Barbie, introduced 1972, included curlers, comb and brush, mint in box ................ **$80**

Free Moving Barbie, introduced 1974, with lever on back to swing arms and upper torso, mint in box ........................................ **$100**

Montgomery Ward 100th Anniversary "Original Barbie" reissue, released in 1972 to commemorate Montgomery Wards' 100 years in business, with reproduction Barbie dressed in black-and-white swimsuit of an early Ponytail, sold in a sparsely illustrated pink box under the name "The Original Barbie"; dolls ordered through the store's catalog were shipped in plain boxes, mint in box ...... **$800**

Sweet 16 Barbie, introduced 1974, accessories include scented sticker barrettes, mint in box.................................. **$125**

Supersize Barbie, introduced 1977, 18" alternative to the standard 11-1/2" size, mint in box ......................................... **$200**

Miss America Barbie, introduced 1974, mint in box **$75**

Superstar Barbie, introduced 1977, mint in box.................... **$70**

Kissing Barbie, introduced 1979, a mechanism on Barbie doll's back, when pushed, triggered the pucker motion and kissing sound, included lipstick, mint in box. **$65**

# The Best of Barbie
## *A Rare Sight to See*

During the past two decades, Sandi Holder's Doll Attic in Union City, Calif., has handled some of the rarest Barbie dolls and accessories. Holder has auctioned one-of-a-kind items, prototypes, Japanese fashions, store exclusives, and items many didn't even know existed until they surfaced at Doll Attic.

Consider this: Doll Attic sold a pristine #1 Blond Ponytail Barbie doll for $25,527 in 2003. That amazing doll, which sold for $3 in 1959, still holds the world record for the highest amount ever paid for a Barbie. Three years later she sold an exquisite example of #1 Blond Ponytail Barbie in Pink Silhouette box, wearing a Barbie-Q fashion outfit, for $25,147. Also in 2006, she sold one of her all-time favorite items: a Barbie and Ken Dressed Doll Assortment store display from 1963. It was the first time Holder had seen something like this in person. That incredible display holding six dolls sold for $19,144. When you consider that the display originally sold for $70.50, you quickly realize just how passionate people can be when it comes to Barbie doll rarities.

In the following pages we showcase an exceptional array of rare dolls and accessories that have sold at Doll Attic over the years. Some items have survived the test of time in unparalleled condition; some were never massed produced; and others come from far-flung places. Some have sold for astounding prices. All, however, hold a special place in Barbie doll history.

This pristine #1 Blond Ponytail Barbie doll set a world record when it sold for $25,527 in 2003.

What would you pay for a rare Barbie doll dress? How about $5,000? That's exactly what this near-mint, incredibly rare Japanese version of the classic 1960's Let's Dance dress sold for at auction.

This showcase Brunette #1 Ponytail Barbie doll is a grand example of a mint-in-box beauty. She features all original makeup, a hint of smoky eye shadow, dark pointed eyebrows and awesome orangey-red lips. She is complete with copper tubes in feet, original stand, booklet, heels, and sunglasses. Even the box is beautiful, still bearing the $3 price sticker on an end flap. No wonder this mint-in-box Barbie doll sold for nearly $14,000 at auction.

Barbie doll first demonstrated her cooking skills outdoors at her very own barbecue, and with great results. This exquisite example of a #1 Blond Ponytail Barbie in Pink Silhouette box, wearing a 1959 Barbie-Q outfit (#962), sold at a Doll Attic auction for $25,147 in 2006.

A stunning example of a European version of a Platinum Swirl Ponytail Barbie, this factory mint doll came dressed in the Fashion Queen swimsuit. In never-removed-from-box condition, she sold for nearly $3,000 at auction in 2007.

This Japanese Dressed Box Brunette Bubblecut Orange Blossom (#987) is in mint condition. The beauty included a Japanese fashion booklet and very rare Japanese pedestal stand, with the Barbie logo embossed in gold on pedestal base. This doll sold for $5,000 in a 2007 auction.

In a Pink Silhouetted Dressed Box, this #3 Ponytail Barbie doll wears a mint condition "Solo in the Spotlight" fashion outfit. But what makes her extremely rare is the factory bun in her ponytail. She also has perfect ringlet curls on her bangs. This eye-popping beauty sold for more than $5,500 at a 2007 auction.

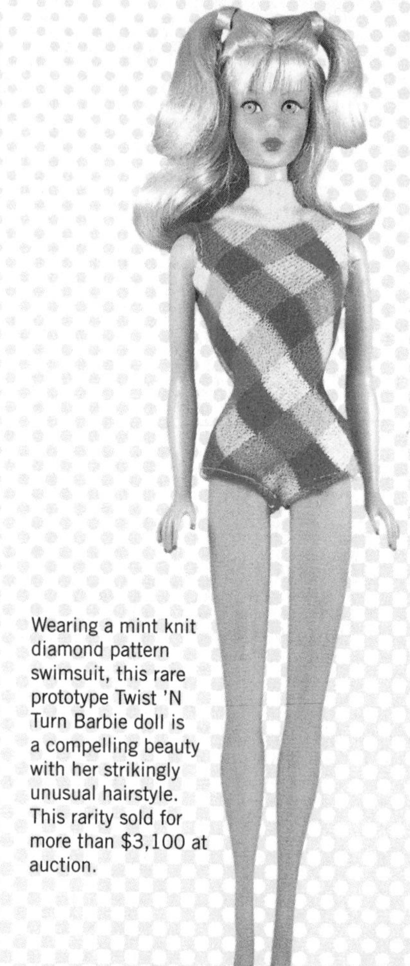

Wearing a mint knit diamond pattern swimsuit, this rare prototype Twist 'N Turn Barbie doll is a compelling beauty with her strikingly unusual hairstyle. This rarity sold for more than $3,100 at auction.

When Barbie entertains, collectors pay attention—especially when it comes to the vintage, never-removed-from-box 1965 Barbie's Hostess Set (#1034). The set includes many easy-to-lose pieces, making this set extremely valuable to collectors. The original price tag reads $6.88 on the box, but this pristine find, with its 46-piece Cook 'N Serve set and two fashion ensembles, sold for nearly $9,000 at auction.

Originally marketed by Mattel to retailers, this Barbie and Ken Dressed Doll Assortment store display (#909) from 1963 is an incredible piece. The display originally sold as two units with six dolls in each unit. Each unit was an easel-backed 16" x 31" corrugated display that held six dolls and originally sold for $70.50. The availability of this item was limited. From top row, left to right: #6 Redhead Ponytail dressed in Garden Party fashion outfit; Ken in Time for Tennis outfit; Ash Blond Bubblecut Barbie doll wears a Nighty Negligee. On the bottom row (from left): Brunette Bubblecut Barbie doll dressed in American Airlines fashion outfit; Ken in Casuals outfit, a painted hair brunette doll in pristine condition, including car keys in booklet cello; and blond Bubblecut Barbie doll dressed in Mood for Music fashion outfit. This rare store display brought $19,144 in a 2006 auction.

Rare beauty could be defined by this spectacular doll, #6 Lemon Blond Ponytail Japanese Dressed Box Barbie doll wearing a Resort Set (#963) fashion outfit. She has a face that is stunning with perfect pinkish-coral lips, great eyebrows, sultry blue eyes, and blue eyeliner. Her silky, lemon blond hair is pristine with original topknot and full, soft curly bangs. The red, white, and blue nautical themed Resort Set outfit includes a red sailcloth jacket with middy collar, patch pockets, and white trim top, a knit navy/white horizontal striped sleeveless shell and white "cuffed" sailcloth shorts. This extremely rare doll in beautiful condition sold for more than $8,500 at auction.

# Baseball

Baseball was reputedly invented by Abner Doubleday as he laid out a diamond-shaped field with four bases at Cooperstown, New York. A popular game from its inception, by 1869 it was able to support its first all-professional team, the Cincinnati Red Stockings. The National League was organized in 1876, and though the American League was first formed in 1900, it was not officially recognized until 1903.

Today, the "national pastime" has millions of fans, and collecting baseball memorabilia has become a major hobby with enthusiastic collectors seeking out items associated with players such as Babe Ruth, Lou Gehrig, and others who became legends in their own lifetimes.

For more information on memorabilia and baseball cards, see *Standard Catalog of Baseball Cards (2012)*, 21st Edition, by Bob Lemke.

Hall of Fame and 500 Home Run Club member Eddie Mathews' rookie jersey with the Boston Braves.............................. **$71,100**
*Heritage Auctions*

Before all of the renovations and eventual new stadium for the New York Yankees was this original 1923 Yankee Stadium seat.................................. **$1,554**
*Heritage Auctions*

In 1969, the New York Mets stunned the baseball world by winning the World Series, and pitcher Tom Seaver was a big reason why. The righty went 25-7 en route to winning the Cy Young award in 1969. This jersey from the Seth Swirsky Collection is the perfect memento for that season. ........................... **$47,800**
*Heritage Auctions*

The New York Yankees were in the midst of their World Series binge in 1998, which would be the second of four titles in a five-year run for the team (1996-2000). The ring's significance and Yankee ties helped it sell. ........................................... **$26,290**
*Heritage Auctions*

The most famous trading card in history – the 1909-11 T206 Honus Wagner. It's speculated the card was pulled from the original set because Wagner was not fond of targeting tobacco toward kids. This example, graded PSA 3, sold in a Goodwin and Co. auction in 2012................................................ **$1.2 million**

1930s Play Baseball gumball machine ......... **$2,032**
*Heritage Auctions*

This is the ball that rolled through Bill Buckner's legs that scored Mookie Wilson and led to the New York Mets come-from-behind victory in Game 6 of the 1986 World Series. The Mets would go to win the Series in seven games. Part of the Seth Swirsky Collection.................................................. **$418,500**
*Heritage Auctions*

◄1910-11 T3 Turkey Red Cabinets Ty Cobb 39, with a checklist back, graded SGC 60................ **$10,755**
*Heritage Auctions*

Famous T206 Sherry Magie (Magee) error card – the highest graded example to date at SGC 80...**$80,077**
*Goodwin and Co.*

1911 Philadelphia Athletics World Championship plate.........................**$364**
*Grey Flannel*

Rookie jersey of Hall of Famer Reggie Jackson, from his 1967 season with the Kansas City A's.....**$28,298**
*Grey Flannel*

Circa 1910 Boston Red Sox pennant, from the personal collection of Ted Williams. .................. **$2,100**
*Hunt Auctions*

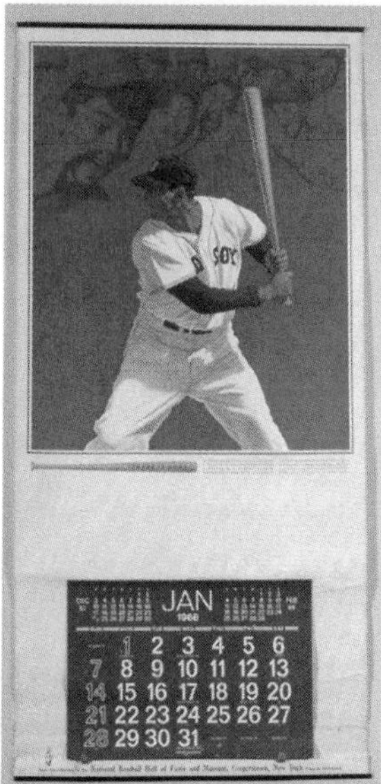


1968 Ted Williams artwork calendar, 16" x 32" color lithograph calendar featuring an image of Ted Williams batting at the top, from the personal collection of Ted Williams. ............................... **$225**
*Hunt Auctions*

Ted Williams collectible plate featuring painting by Carlo Beninnati, from the personal collection of Ted Williams. .......................... **$229**
*Hunt Auctions*

Scarce "Nuf Ced" McGreevy souvenir shot glass, circa1900-1915, from the personal collection of Ted Williams. ........................ **$3,200**
*Hunt Auctions*

Vintage Ted Williams souvenir pinback button, circa 1940s, from the personal collection of Ted Williams..................................**$85**
*Hunt Auctions*

Ted Williams signed black-and-white photo, from the personal collection of Ted Williams.... **$350**
*Hunt Auctions*

Cap worn by Jose Canseco in a 1993 game in which the ball bounced off his head for a home run. ............................................................ **$11,950**

*Heritage Auctions*

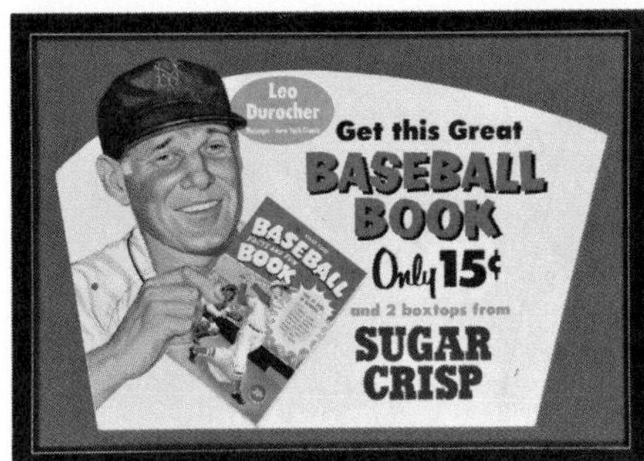


1955 "Sugar Crisp" die-cut display featuring Leo Durocher, 31" x 20"........................................ **$299**

*Legendary Auctions*

Pair of 1961-62 Los Angeles Dodgers bobbin' heads, 6-1/2" t.......................................................... **$538**

*Legendary Auctions*

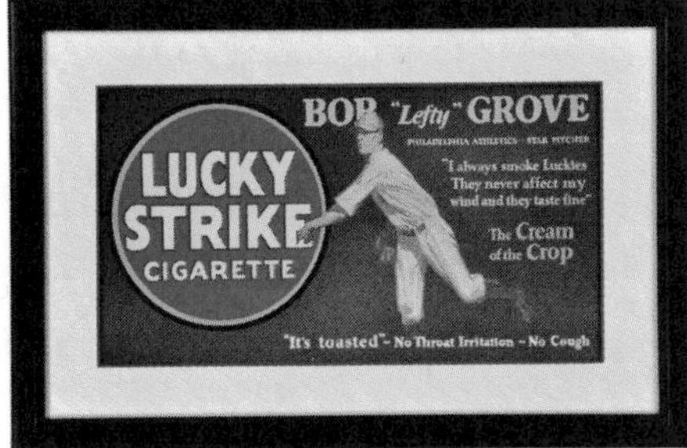


1928 Lefty Grove "Lucky Strike" trolley car ad sign, 11" x 21"................................................ **$8,963**

*Legendary Auctions*

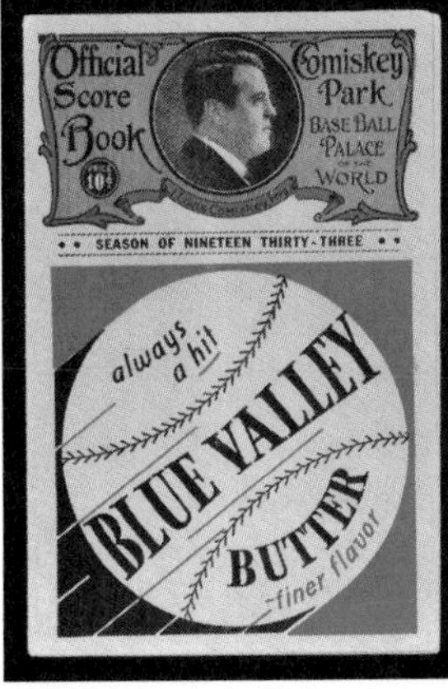


1933 inaugural Major League Baseball All-Star Game program in Chicago.......................... **$837**

*Legendary Auctions*

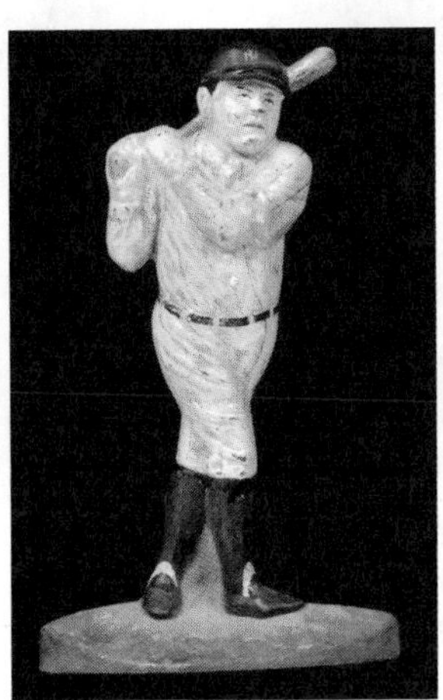

1920s Babe Ruth cast iron door stop, 9" t. and 5" w., 2 lbs.. **$329**

*Legendary Auctions*

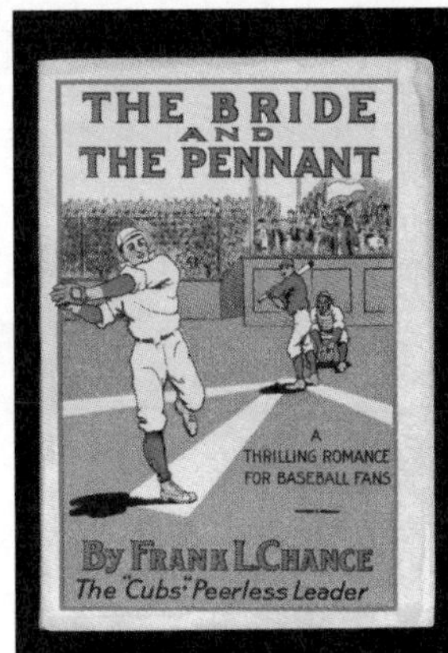


Scarce 1910 *The Bride and the Pennant* softcover book by Frank Chance. ............................ **$329**

*Legendary Auctions*

1920 Ty Cobb candy box. Sold as a lot of four with large box (G-VG), small box (VG), cardboard advertising display (EX-MT) for store shelves, and very rare candy wrapper. .......................................... **$6,000**
*Lelands*

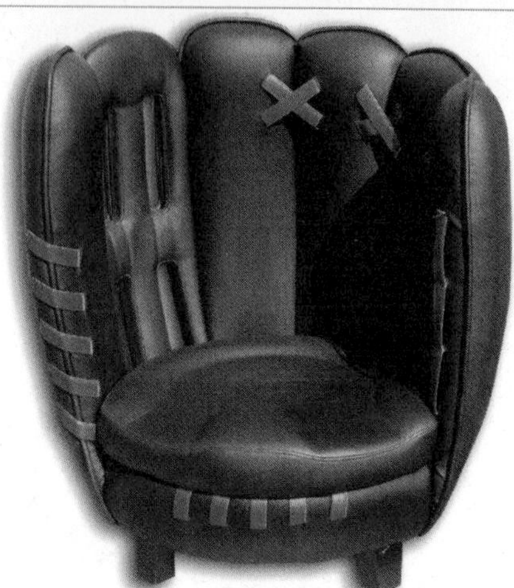

Budweiser beer giant leather baseball glove chair, 3' t. .......................................................... **$2,500**
*Lelands*

Babe's rookie card, 1916 M101-5 blank back Babe Ruth rookie card, graded SGC 70 .............**$107,550**
*Heritage Auctions*

1953-1955 Yankee Stadium Dormand postcard featuring the photography of Louis Dormand......... **$180**
*Lelands*

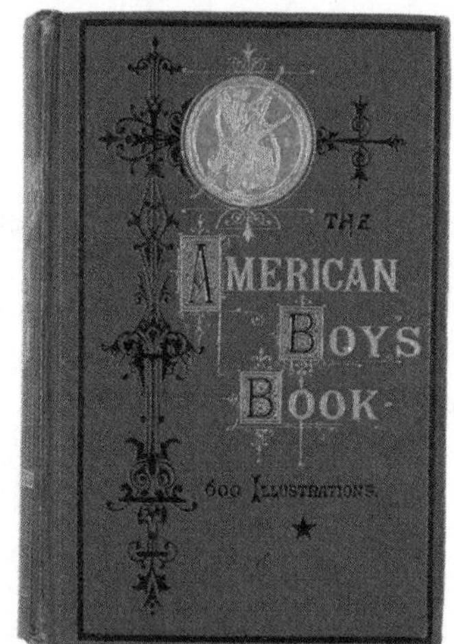


1864 *American Boy's Book of Sports and Games*, the first book to feature a color plate relating to baseball. ............................................................... **$593**
*Robert Edward Auctions*

◄1914 Boston Braves World Series press pin issued for the 1914 World Series against the Philadelphia Athletics .................................................. **$5,288**
*Robert Edward Auctions*

Circa 1885 Base Ball board game issued by J. Ottmann Lith. Co. .............................................. **$474**
*Robert Edward Auctions*

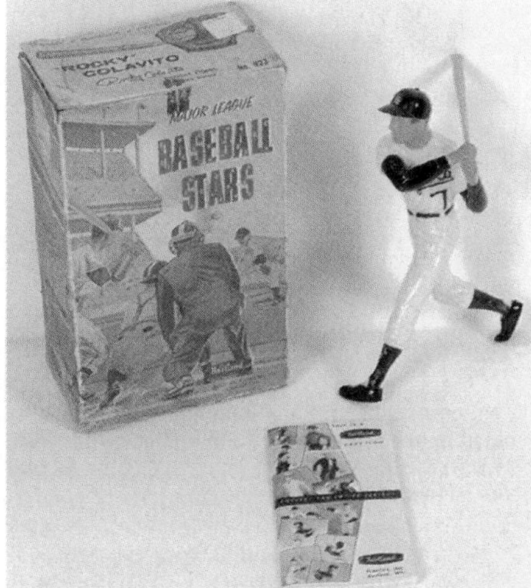


Original Hartland statues remain coveted pieces of sports memorabilia. Rocky Colavito example with original box .................................................. **$593**
*Robert Edward Auctions*

Original watercolor-on-board painting of Roberto Clemente created by Dick Perez in 1981 for the Perez-Steele Hall of Fame postcard set, signed by the artist in the lower center, 14" x 17" ..................... **$5,925**
*Robert Edward Auctions*

1912 H813 Boston Garter Eddie Collins set, one of the rarest in existence, with just 16 cards in the set and featuring beautiful artwork. .................**$29,625**
*Robert Edward Auctions*

Charles Conlon was the prominent sports photographer of the early 20th century. His photos have become the iconic images for many of baseball's legends. Joe Jackson original Type 1 photo.......**$32,588**
*Robert Edward Auctions*

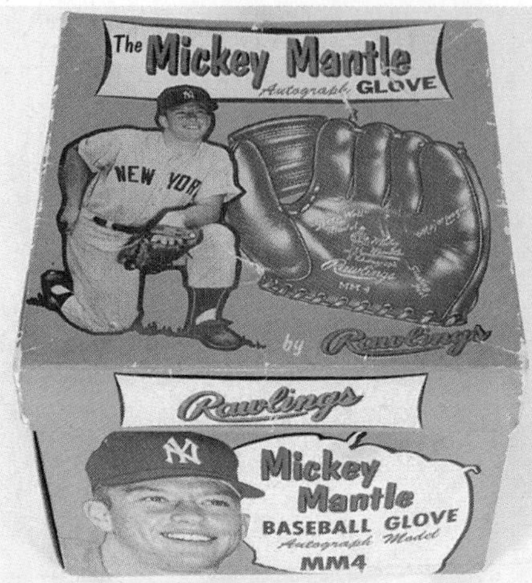


Rare original box that housed a 1954-1956 Mickey Mantle Rawlings model "MM4" glove, 8-1/4" x 8-1/4" x 6-1/2" and features some great images of The Mick. ................................................ **$3,555**
*Robert Edward Auctions*

1948 Babe Ruth figural desk clock produced shortly after the Babe's death with the intent to be awarded as a punch board prize, approximately 12" x 11" x 5"........................................................ **$3,346**
*Heritage Auctions*

Pair of 1930s Babe Ruth and Lou Gehrig stadium souvenir pin backs complete with original charms and ribbons....................................................... **$436**
*SCP Auctions*

First bronze statue of Babe Ruth and Lou Gehrig ever created by renowned artist Palmer Murphy in 1994, only statue of its kind................................. **$2,500**
*Robert Edward Auctions*

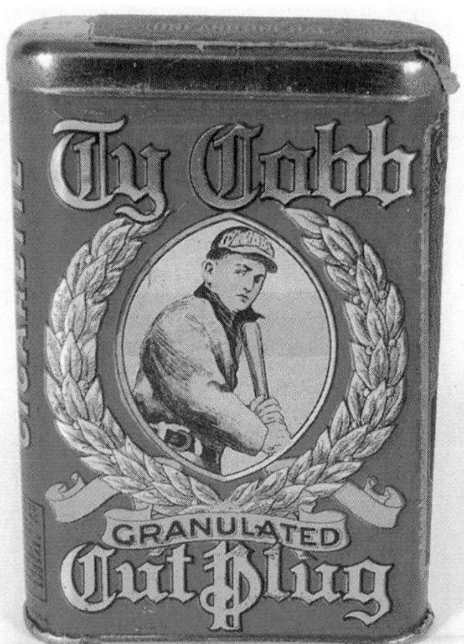


1912 Ty Cobb tobacco tin has been a hot seller in the past year, with one example showing up inside the walls of a house during renovation. This example is the finest known to date, with the original tax stamp paper strip still attached. ..........................**$88,875**
*Robert Edward Auctions*

Game-used cap worn by Babe Ruth in the 1930s and by David Wells in which he pitched for the Yankees in 1997 ...................................................... **$537,278**
*SCP Auctions*

Cap worn by Bobby Thomson during his historic "Shot Heard 'Round the World," the home run that clinched the National League pennant in 1951 for the New York Giants over the Brooklyn Dodgers. ...... **$173,102**
*SCP Auctions*

**TOP LOT!**

1920 New York Yankees jersey was worn by Babe Ruth, the earliest jersey of his known to exist and now the highest-selling piece of sports memorabilia on record. .................................................. **$4.4 million**
*SCP Auctions*

# Baskets

The American Indians were the first basket weavers on this continent and, of necessity, the early Colonial settlers and their descendants pursued this artistic handicraft to provide essential containers for berries, eggs, and endless other items to be carried or stored.

Rye straw, split willow and reeds are but a few of the wide variety of materials used. Nantucket baskets, plainly and sturdily constructed, along with those made by specialized groups, would seem to draw the greatest attention to this area of collecting.

Avoid displaying baskets in a kitchen area. The combination of grease and fluctuating temperatures can ruin a basket's patina. High humidity should be avoided, also.

Two Shaker baskets, second half 19th c., small cat's head example together with a larger cheese basket. The first 8" h., 8" dia.; cheese basket of flat, open weave, 8-1/2" h. x 23" dia. ............................ **Pair $400-$500**
*James D. Julia, Inc.*

Group of eight woven baskets, late 18th/early 19th c., including five circular carrying baskets, one with handle branded "T. WARD" and one large example with swing handle. Square basket with double swing handle and with hinged lid. Small feather basket with lid and a conical example with a single C-form handle. Largest measures 16-1/2" dia.; feather basket 21" h.; smallest 9" dia. ............................ **$202**
*James D. Julia, Inc.*

Vermont blue painted salmon creel, strapped-on wood lid with center hole, painted in a dark blue color, make-do rawhide and wood latch,10-1/4" h., 16-1/2" w., 11-1/2" d. ............................................ **$531**
*James D. Julia, Inc.*

Two palm leaf baskets, first quarter 20th c., Vermont. These baskets originated with Ms. Alta Davis in the early 1900s, who formed a group of women called the "Dover Bees." These baskets are woven from palm leaves that the group imported from the islands. Examples were sold through the Arts and Crafts Society of Boston up until the early 1920s. First example, in the form of a sombrero, fitted with a circular lid, 9-1/2" dia. Second example with round rim and rippled square tapering sides, 6" h., 9-1/2" dia. .. **$115**
*James D. Julia, Inc.*

Shenandoah Valley of Virginia painted rib-type woven splint miniature basket, white oak, finely woven bulbous kidney form with vertical wrapped rim and low arched handle, outstanding original dry dark-green painted surface. Probably Rockbridge or Augusta County, fourth quarter 19th c., 3-1/2" h. overall, 2-1/2" h. rim, 3-3/8" dia. rim..................... **$1,955**
*Jeffrey S. Evans & Associates*

"Buttocks" basket, New England, second half 19th c., large example of typical form with bentwood handle, retains original surfaces, 16-1/2" h., 21-1/2" l., 20" w. ......................................................... **$202**
*James D. Julia, Inc.*

Three New England baskets, late 19th/early 20th c., American, including a small buttocks basket, 5-1/2" h.; a round splint basket in green paint with steamed handle, 9-1/4" h.; a small Shaker square sewing box with lid with mark of "Sabbathday Lake, Maine," 2-3/4" h., 5" square. ........................ **Lot $300-$500**
*James D. Julia, Inc.*

Shenandoah Valley of Virginia rib-type woven splint miniature basket, white oak, very finely woven rectangular form with delicate wrapped double rim and high arched handle featuring X-form wraps, additional iron tack securing each handle to rim, late 19th/early 20th c., 3-1/2" h. overall, 1-3/4" h. rim, 2-1/2" w., 3-5/8" l. .................................................. **$1,150**
*Jeffrey S. Evans & Associates*

Shenandoah Valley of Virginia decorated woven splint basket, white oak and ash, small rectangular form with a low arched handle featuring carved exterior rim notches and V-wrapped rim. Original polychrome "rail fence and X" decoration on dry natural surface. Floyd or Patrick County, Virginia. First quarter 20th c., 9-1/2" h. overall, 6" h. rim, 8-1/2" w., 10-1/4" l. ........................................................... **$3,738**
*Jeffrey S. Evans & Associates*

Shenandoah Valley of Virginia woven splint work basket, white oak, unusual long low form with wrapped rim, open-weave bottom, and high arched handle. Provenance: Estate of Viola Hinkel Andes Fearneyhough Beahm, Greenmount, Rockingham County, Virginia. Family tradition indicates that John H. Fearneyhough (1852-1927) made this basket for his wife, Viola Henkel Fearneyhough (1890-1980). Mrs. Fearneyhough took in laundry, and this basket was used to transport ironed linens and clothing. 15-1/2" HOA, 7" h. rim, 15" w., 43" l. .............................. **$184**
*Jeffrey S. Evans & Associates*

Shenandoah Valley of Virginia or West Virginia pulled rod basket, white oak, circular "skeleton" form with complex Madeira rim and foot joined by tripartite open ribs, high arched handle with penciled initials on top. Probably Rockingham or Highland County, Virginia, or Pendleton County, West Virginia. Late 19th/first quarter 20th c., 12" h. overall, 7" h. rim, 10" dia. ........................................................... **$863**
*Jeffrey S. Evans & Associates*

Woven splint low basket, white oak, very finely woven circular form with X-wrap rim and two arched rim handles, fine kick-up bottom, by one of the Nichols family of basketmakers, Page County, Virginia. First half 20th c., 3" h. rim, 7-1/2" dia. ................ **$345**
*Jeffrey S. Evans & Associates*

Numerous members of the Nichols (sometimes spelled Nicholson) family were well known basket makers in Page County, Virginia, in the 19th and 20th centuries, including brothers Henry (1873-1935), Howard (I) (1870-1937), and Casper (b.c. 1880), in addition to Howard (II) (b.?-1937). Upon their deaths, the local newspaper referred to them individually as "one of the celebrated basket makers of the county," "an expert basket maker by trade," "well known maker of baskets," and "almost every size basket known on the market has been made by Howard Nichols."

*Jeffrey S. Evans*

Shenandoah Valley of Virginia woven splint low basket, white oak, heavy circular form with X-wrap rim and two high arched bentwood handles, domed kick-up bottom, probably northern Blue Ridge Mountains. Late 19th/early 20th c., 5-1/4" h. overall, 3-1/4" h. rim, 7-1/2" dia. .......................................... **$161**

*Jeffrey S. Evans & Associates*

Virginia decorated rib-type woven splint diminutive basket, white oak with red and blue-green staining, very finely woven bulbous kidney form with wrapped double rim and arched handle. Mid-20th c., 5" h. overall, 3-1/4" h. rim, 4-1/2" w., 5-1/4" l........ **$196**

*Jeffrey S. Evans & Associates*

Shenandoah Valley of Virginia painted woven splint flower basket, white oak, low form with turned up sides, X-wrap rim, high arched handle and kick-up bottom. Possibly by a member of the Nichols family of basket makers, Page County, Virginia. First quarter 20th c., 7-3/4" h. overall, 3" h. side rim, 8-1/4" w., 11-1/4" l. ................................................. **$374**

*Jeffrey S. Evans & Associates*

Virginia rib-type woven splint basket, white oak, bulbous kidney form with wrapped double rim, high arched handle and complex rim/handle support. Late 19th/early 20th c., 9-1/2" h. overall, 5-1/2" h. rim, 9-1/2" w., 10-1/2" l. .................................. **$104**

*Jeffrey S. Evans & Associates*

Two Shenandoah Valley of Virginia woven baskets, white oak, comprising a splint example with high handle, 12-1/2" h. overall, 8-1/4" dia. rim; and a pulled rod example made without a handle, 5-1/2" h., 8-1/4" dia. Family history indicates John H. Fearneyhough as maker, Greenmount, Rockingham County, Virginia. First quarter 20th c. .............................. **$184**

*Jeffrey S. Evans & Associates*

Two Shenandoah Valley of Virginia woven splint egg baskets, white oak, each of circular form with X-wrap rim, high arched handle and kick-up bottom. Possibly by a member of the Nichols family of basket makers, Page County, Virginia. First half 20th c., 9" and 9-1/4" h. overall, 9" dia...... **$150**
*Jeffrey S. Evans & Associates*

Virginia rib-type woven splint basket, white oak, exaggerated kidney form with wrapped double rim and high arched handle. First half 20th c., 11" h. overall, 5-1/2" h. rim, 9" w., 10" l. ............................ **$69**
*Jeffrey S. Evans & Associates*

Shenandoah Valley of Virginia woven splint basket, white oak, deep circular form with X-wrap rim, made without a handle, kick-up bottom. First quarter 20th c., 5-3/4" h., 10" dia. .................................... **$81**
*Jeffrey S. Evans & Associates*

Mid-Atlantic rib-type woven splint basket, white oak, bulbous kidney form with wrapped rim and tripartite low arched handle. First half 20th c., 6-1/2" h. overall, 4" h. rim, 7-3/4" w., 8" l. .......................... **$92**
*Jeffrey S. Evans & Associates*

Virginia woven splint basket, white oak, circular slant wrapped rim and square open-weave bottom with a flattened-arch handle featuring carved interior rim notches. First quarter 20th c., 13" h. overall, 8" h. rim, 11-1/2" dia............................................ **$92**
*Jeffrey S. Evans & Associates*

# Bells

Bells—one of the oldest forms of art—hearken back centuries to ancient civilizations long gone. They are steeped in mystery, surrounded by legends of special powers ranging from thwarting demons to invoking curses and lifting spells.

In general, bells were most often used as a signal, marking significant points of ritual, calling to worship, tolling the hours, announcing events, and helping communities to rejoice, mourn, or send warning. Their power was at one time extremely significant to many religions. Bells have also been treasured as patriotic symbols and war trophies.

Most cultures today have turned these utilitarian objects into works of art with respect to shape, materials, and ornamentation. Created of porcelain, wood, metal, china, crystal, and other materials, the melodious chimers are a double joy for collectors because they are both lovely to hear and to look at.

American silver plate dinner bell, Gorham Manufacturing Company, Providence, Rhode Island, circa 1900, marks: G.MFG (anchor), 046, 5 h. x 2-1/2" dia. .......................................... **$359**
*Heritage Auction Galleries*

American silver dinner bell, Tiffany & Co., New York, New York, circa 1888, marks: TIFFANY & CO., 9993 M 7353, STERLING-SILVER, 5" h. x 4-3/4" w. ................................................................. **$5,975**
*Heritage Auction Galleries*

►American silver dinner bell, Towle Silversmiths, Newburyport, Massachusetts, 20th c., marks: (lion on T), STERLING 7405, B, 4-1/2 x 2-3/8" ...... **$287**
*Heritage Auction Galleries*

Danish silver dinner bell, Georg Jensen Silversmithy, Copenhagen, Denmark, circa 1930, marks: GEORG JENSEN (within beaded oval), STERLING, DENMARK, DESSIN (intertwined GA), 148, 3-1/4" h. ..........**$263**
*Heritage Auction Galleries*

Mexican silver dinner bell, William Spratling, Taxco, Mexico, circa 1960, marks: WILLIAM SPRATLING, TAXCO MEXICO, script WS 925, 4-1/2" h. x 3-1/8" w............................................................ **$2,390**
*Heritage Auction Galleries*

Mexican silver dinner bell, William Spratling, Taxco, Mexico, circa 1940, marks: SPRATLING MADE IN MEXICO (circling) WS, SPRATLING SILVER, 3-3/8 x 1-3/4 x 1-5/8" ..................**$717**
*Heritage Auction Galleries*

American silver répoussé bell, Mark of Mauser, New York, circa 1900, body entirely repousse, handle plain tear drop shape, 4" h...................................... **$168**
*Heritage Auction Galleries*

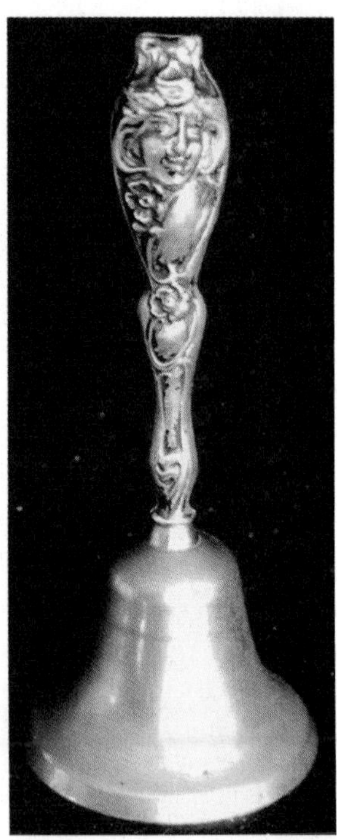

Art Nouveau bell with sterling handle, unmarked, 5-1/2" h.**$150**
*Arus Auctions and LiveAuctioneers.com*

Pennsylvania railroad hand bells (two), late 19th c., 7" h. and 6" h. .............................................. **$178**
*Pook & Pook, Inc.*

Waterford Bicentennial Anniversary bell (1976), crystal, hand-cut, excellent condition, marked Waterford, 4" h., 3" w. ...................................................... **$30**
*Seized Asset Auctioneers and LiveAuctioneers.com*

Waterford Crystal bell, dated 1998, from "Songs of Christmas" collection, "Hark the Herald Angels Sing," with original Waterford Crystal label, 5-1/4" h. ......... **$20**
*Professional Appraisers & Liquidators LLC and LiveAuctioneers.com*

Gorham silver table bell, circular, interior gilt, cast scrolled handle topped with child's bust, flower heads below handle, 3" h., 2.4 oz ....................................... **$200**
*Dan Morphy Auctions LLC and LiveAuctioneers.com*

Fenton glass bell, "Woodland Frost," 6" h. ........................ **$15**
*Martin Auction Co. and LiveAuctioneers.com*

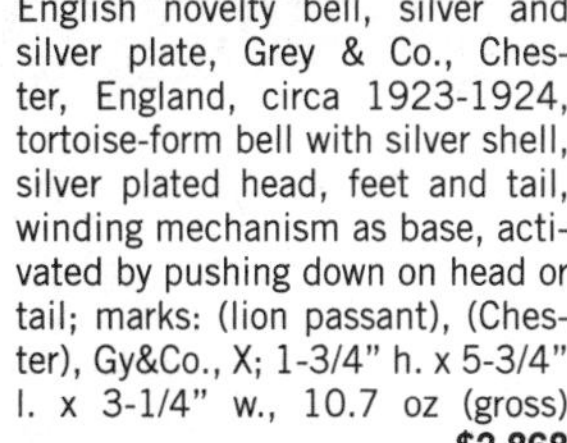

English novelty bell, silver and silver plate, Grey & Co., Chester, England, circa 1923-1924, tortoise-form bell with silver shell, silver plated head, feet and tail, winding mechanism as base, activated by pushing down on head or tail; marks: (lion passant), (Chester), Gy&Co., X; 1-3/4" h. x 5-3/4" l. x 3-1/4" w., 10.7 oz (gross) ...................................... **$2,868**
*Heritage Auction Galleries*

# Books & Magazines

## Little Golden Books

Western Publishing Company, Inc., one of the largest printers of children's books in the world, began in Racine, Wisconsin when Edward Henry Wadewitz purchased the West Side Printing Company in 1907. In 1910, the name was changed to Western Printing and Lithographing Company.

By its seventh year, sales had topped $127,000. Wadewitz was approached by the Hamming-Whitman Publishing Company of Chicago to print its line of children's books. Unable to pay its bills, Hamming-Whitman left Western with thousands of books in its warehouse and in production. Trying to cut its losses, Wadewitz entered Western into the retail book market for the first time. It proved so successful that the remaining Hamming-Whitman books were liquidated.

After acquiring Hamming-Whitman on Feb. 9, 1916, Western formed a subsidiary corporation called Whitman Publishing Company. Whitman grossed more than $43,500 in children's book sales in its first year. Sam Lowe joined the Western team in 1916. Lowe sold Western and Whitman on the idea of bringing out a 10-cent children's book in 1918.

By 1928, sales were more than $2.4 million. Western was able to keep its plant operational during the Depression years (1929-1933) by introducing a jigsaw puzzle and a new series of books called Big Little Books.

Western formed the Artists and Writers Guild Inc. in the 1930s to handle the development of new children's books. This company, located on Fifth Avenue in New York City, had an immense hand in the conception of Little Golden Books.

In 1940, Sam Lowe left the company and George Duplaix replaced him as head of the Artists and Writers Guild. Duplaix came up with the concept of a colorful children's book that would be durable and affordable to more American families than those being printed at that time. The group decided on 12 titles to be released at the same time. These books were to be called Little Golden Books. The books sold for 25 cents each. In September 1942, the first 12 titles were printed and released to stores in October.

***The First 12 Little Golden Books***

1 Three Little Kittens
2 Bedtime Stories
3 The Alphabet A-Z
4 Mother Goose
5 Prayers for Children
6 The Little Red Hen
7 Nursery Songs
8 The Poky Little Puppy
9 The Golden Book of Fairy Tales
10 Baby's Book
11 The Animals of Farmer Jones
12 This Little Piggy

Within five months, 1.5 million copies of the books had been printed and they were in their third printing. They became so popular with children that by the end of 1945, most of the first 12 books had been printed seven times. When the books were first released, they were sold mainly in book and department stores. From there, they moved into variety, toy, and drug stores, and finally in the late 1940s, to something new called the supermarket.

Sales of Little Golden Books were doing so well that in 1944, Simon & Schuster decided to create a new division headed by George Duplaix, called Sandpiper Press. Duplaix hired Dorothy Bennett as the general editor. She was responsible for many of the subjects used in Little Golden Books through the mid-1950s.

In 1952, on the tenth anniversary of Little Golden Books, approximately 182,615,000 Little Golden Books had been sold. In their eleventh year, almost 300 million Little Golden Books had been sold. More than half of the titles printed by 1954 had sold more than a million copies each.

Little Golden Books have been printed in more than 42 countries. In 1982, Little Golden Books were 40 years old and more than 800 million books had been sold. On Nov. 20, 1986, the one billionth Little Golden Book was printed in the United States, *The Poky Little Puppy.*

Little Golden Books are still published today.

For more information on Little Golden Book, see *Warman's Little Golden Books Identification and Price Guide* by Steve Santi.

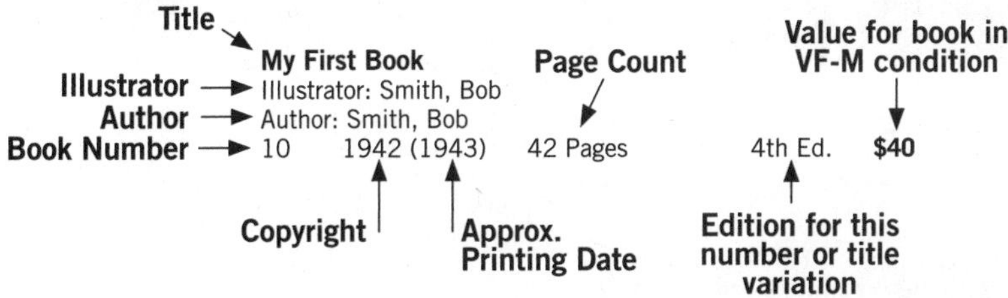


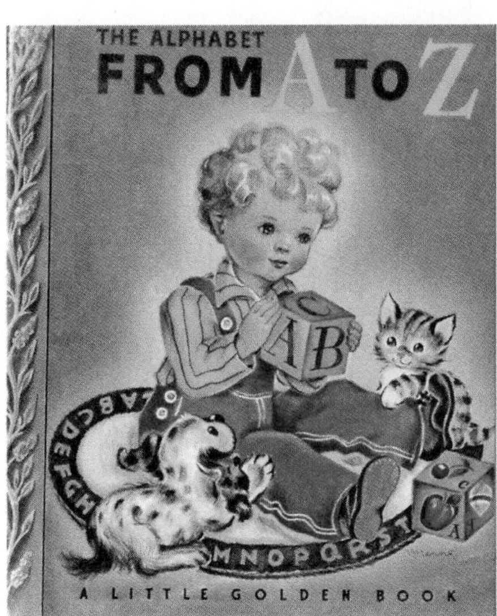


**Alphabet From A-Z, The**
Illustrator: Blake, Vivienne
3 1942 42 Pages 1st Ed. **$50**
Four-Color and Black & White
Blue Spine with Dust Jacket **$50-$200**
3 1942 (1950) 42 Pages 18th Ed. **$16**
Four-Color and Black & White Golden Paper Spine. Song added to last page.

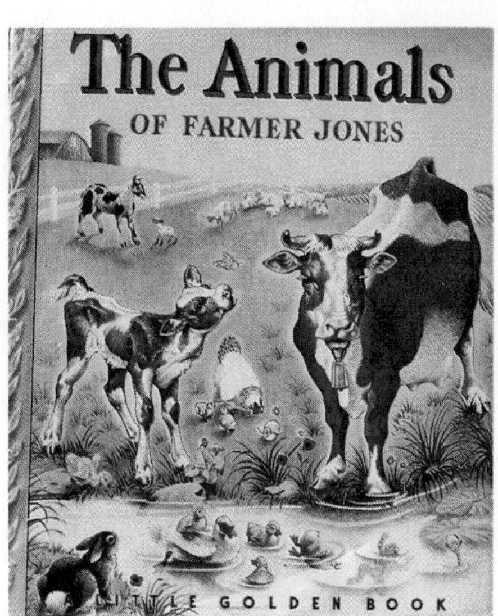


**Animals of Farmer Jones, The**
Illustrator: Freund, Rudolf
Author: Gale, Leah
11 1942 42 Pages 1st Ed. **$50**
Four-Color and Black & White
Blue Spine with Dust Jacket **$50-$200**
11 1942 (1943) 24 Pages 1st Ed. **$22**
Four-Color and Black & White Blue Spine Blue Spine with Dust Jacket **$40-$100**
11 1942 (1947) 42 Pages 10th Ed. **$15**
Four-Color and Black & White
Golden Paper Spine

**Bedtime Stories**
Illustrator: Tenggren, Gustaf
Author: Misc. Authors
2 1942 42 Pages 1st Ed. **$50**
Four-Color and Black & White
Blue Spine with Dust Jacket **$50-$150**
Five Stories: Chicken Little, The Three Bears, The Three Little Pigs, Little Red Riding Hood, The Gingerbread Man
2 1942 (1955) 28 Pages 21st Ed. **$12**
Four-Color. Foil Spine
Three Stories: The Gingerbread Man, Chicken Little, Little Red Riding Hood

**Baby's Book**
Illustrator: Smith, Bob
Author: Smith, Bob
10 1942 42 Pages 1st Ed. **$50**
Four-Color and Black & White
Blue Spine with Dust Jacket **$75-$300**

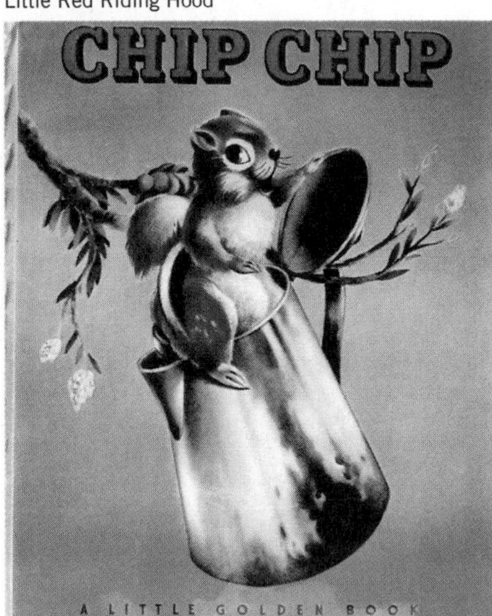


**Chip Chip**
Illustrator: Carbe, Nino
Author: Wright, Norman
28 1947 42 Pages 1st Ed. **$25**
Four-Color and Black & White
Blue Spine with Dust Jacket **$50-$150**

**Circus Time**
Illustrator: Gergely, Tibor
Author: Conger, Marion
31 1948 42 Pages 1st Ed. **$20**
Four-Color and Black & White
31 1948 (1950) 42 Pages 7th Ed. **$16**
Four-Color and Three-Color. Golden Paper Spine
31 1948 (1952) 28 Pages 9th Ed. **$12**
Four-Color. Foil Spine

**Counting Rhymes**
Illustrator: Malvern Corrine
12 1946 42 Pages 1st Ed. **$25**
Four-Color and Black & White
Blue Spine with Dust Jacket **$50-$100**
12 1942 (1948) 28 Pages 4th Ed. **$16**
Four-Color. Golden Paper Spine

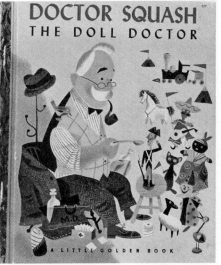

**Day in the Jungle, A**
Illustrator: Gergely, Tibor
Author: Lowrey, Janet Sebring
18 1943 42 Pages 1st Ed. **$35**
Four-Color and Black & White
Blue Spine with Dust Jacket **$50-$150**
18 1943 (1946) 42 Pages 3rd Ed. **$27**
Four-Color and Black & White
Blue Spine with Dust Jacket **$50-$125**
A couple pictures were modified.
18 1943 (1951) 42 Pages 9th Ed. **$20**
Four-Color and Black & White. Golden Paper Spine
Pictures are back to original.

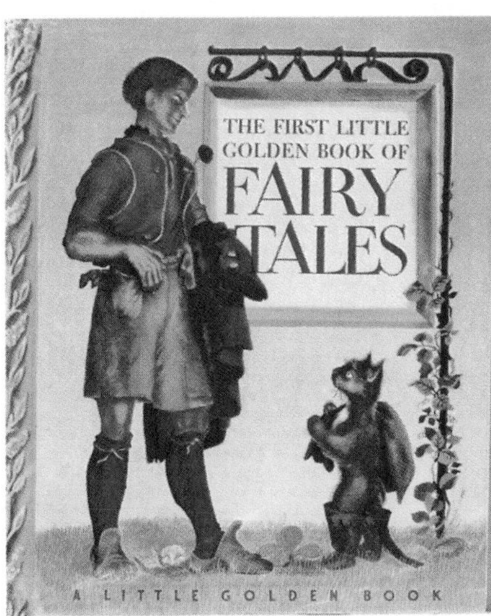


**First Little Golden Book of Fairy Tales, The**
Illustrator: Elliott, Gertrude
9 1946 24 Pages 1st Ed. **$20**
Four-Color and Black & White
Blue Spine with Dust Jacket **$50-$100**
Three stories: Jack and the Beanstalk, Puss in Boots, Sleeping Beauty
9 1946 (1947) 42 Pages 2nd Ed. **$16**
Four-Color and Black & White. Golden Paper Spine

**Golden Book of Birds, The**
Illustrator: Rojankovsky, Feodor
Author: Lockwood, Hazel
13 1943 42 Pages 1st Ed. **$25**
Four-Color and Black & White
Blue Spine with Dust Jacket **$50-$150**
13 1943 (1948) 42 Pages 4th Ed. **$20**
Four-Color and Black & White. Golden Paper Spine

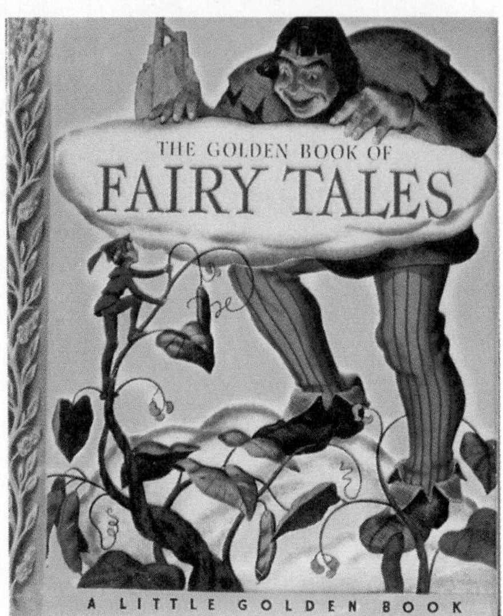


**Golden Book of Fairy Tales, The**
Illustrator: Hoskins, Winfield
9 1942 42 Pages 1st Ed. **$50**
Four-Color and Black & White
Blue Spine with Dust Jacket **$50-$200**
Four stories: Jack and the Beanstalk, Cinderella, Puss in Boots, Sleeping Beauty
9 1942 (1943) 24 Pages 1st Ed. **$22**
Four-Color and Black & White
Blue Spine
Three stories: Jack and the Beanstalk, Puss in Boots, Cinderella
Blue Spine with Dust Jacket **$40-$100**
Four-Color and Black & White

**Golden Book of Flowers, The**
Illustrator: Hershberger
Author: Witman, Mabel
16 1943 42 Pages 1st Ed. **$30**
Four-Color and Black & White
Blue Spine with Dust Jacket **$50-$150**

**Hansel and Gretel**
Illustrator: Weihs, Erika
Author: Bros. Grimm
17 1945 42 Pages 1st Ed. **$30**
Four-Color and Black & White
Blue Spine with Dust Jacket **$50-$150**
17 1945 (1952) 28 Pages 8th Ed. **$14**
Four-Color and Three-Color. Cover art by Eloise Wilkin.

**Little Red Hen, The**
Illustrator: Freund, Rudolf
Author: Potter, Marion
6 1942 42 Pages 1st Ed. **$50**
Four-Color and Black & White
Blue Spine with Dust Jacket **$50-$200**
6 1942 (1949) 42 Pages 12th Ed. **$15**
Four-Color and Three-Color

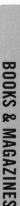

**Little Red Hen, The**
Illustrator: Freund, Rudolf
Author: Potter, Marion
6 1942 (1952) 28 Pages 13th Ed. **$25**
Four-Color and Three-Color
Foil Spine

**Mother Goose**
Illustrator: Elliott, Gertrude
Author: Fraser, Phyllis
4 1942 42 Pages 1st Ed. **$50**
Four-Color and Black & White
Blue Spine with Dust Jacket **$50-$200**
4 1942 (1943) 24 Pages 4th Ed. **$20**
Four-Color and Black & White
Blue Spine
Abridged for the war.
Blue Spine with Dust Jacket **$40-$100**
4 1942 (1953) 28 Pages 22nd Ed. **$12**
Four-Color and Three-Color
Foil Spine

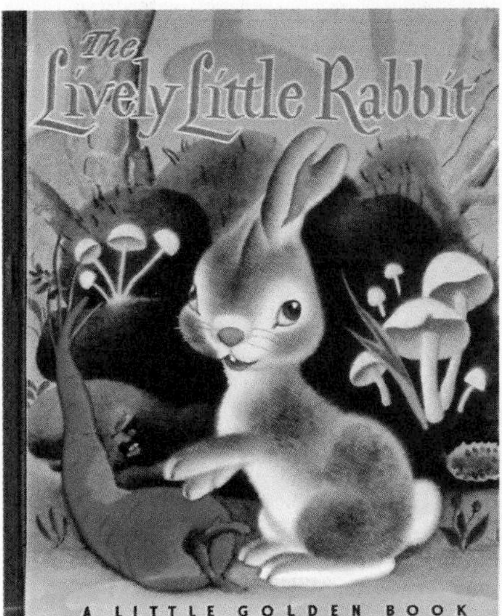


**Lively Little Rabbit, The**
Illustrator: Tenggren, Gustaf
Author: Ariane
15 1943 42 Pages 1st Ed. **$35**
Four-Color and Black & White
Blue Spine with Dust Jacket **$50-$150**
15 1943 (1943) 24 Pages 1st Ed. **$22**
Four-Color and Black & White. Blue Spine, War Edition
Blue Spine with Dust Jacket **$50-$100**
15 1943 (1948) 42 Pages 10th Ed. **$15**
Four-Color and Black & White. Golden Paper Spine
Sleeping owl picture dropped from book.
15 1943 (1951) 42 Pages 14th Ed. **$14**
Four-Color, Foil Spine. Song added to last page.

**Lively Little Rabbit, The**
Illustrator: Tenggren, Gustaf
Author: Ariane
15 1943 (1954) 28 Pages 15th Ed. **$15**

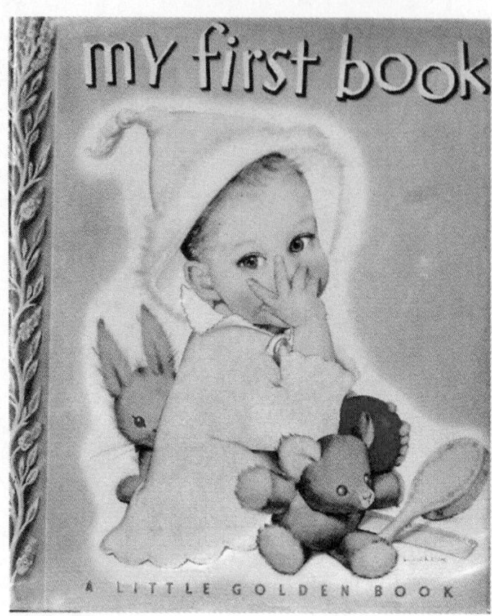


**My First Book**
Illustrator: Smith, Bob
Author: Smith, Bob
10 1942 (1943) 42 Pages 4th Ed. **$40**
Four-Color and Black & White
Blue Spine with Dust Jacket

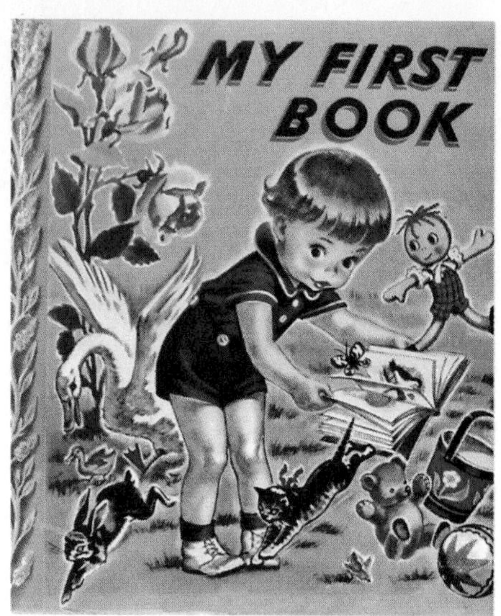


**My First Book**
Illustrator: Smith, Bob
Author: Smith, Bob
10 1942 (1947) 42 Pages 8th Ed. **$20**
Four-Color and Black & White
Gold Paper Spine
Laddie the dog's name changed to Bow-wow.

**My First Book of Bible Stories**
Illustrator: Ferand, Emmy
Author: Walton, Mary Ann
19 1943 42 Pages 1st Ed. **$40**
Four-Color and Black & White
Blue Spine with Dust Jacket **$60-$175**

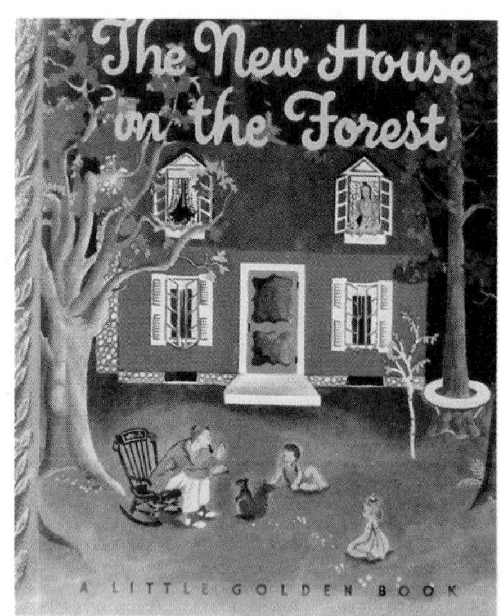


**New House in the Forest, The**
Illustrator: Wilkin, Eloise
Author: Mitchell, Lucy Sprague
24 1946 42 Pages 1st Ed. **$40**
Four-Color and Black & White
Blue Spine with Dust Jacket **$50-$175**

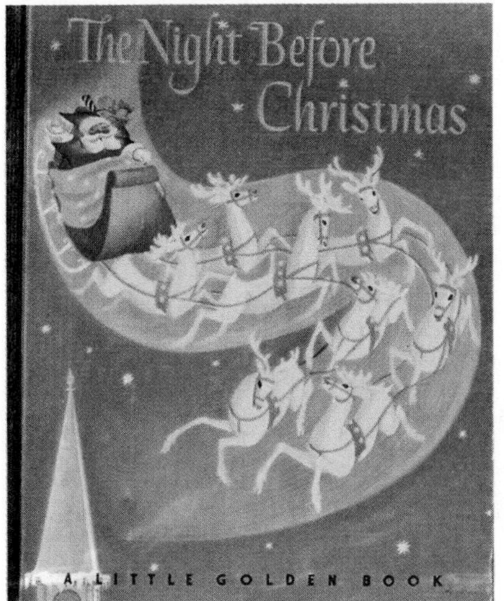


**Night Before Christmas, The**
Illustrator: DeWitt, Cornelius
Author: Moore, Clement C.
20 1946 42 Pages 1st Ed. **$25**
Blue spine; never printed with dust jacket.
20 1946 (1948) 42 Pages 3rd Ed. **$22**
Four-Color and Black & White
Golden Paper Spine, Two songs added.

**Night Before Christmas, The**
Illustrator: Malvern, Corinne
Author: Moore, Clement C.
20 1949 28 Pages 1st Ed. **$15**
Four-Color
Gilded cover and pages.

**Night Before Christmas, The**
Illustrator: Malvern, Corinne
Author: Moore, Clement C.
20 1949 (1951) 28 Pages 5th Ed. **$18**
Four-Color, Foil Spine
Gilded cover and pages.

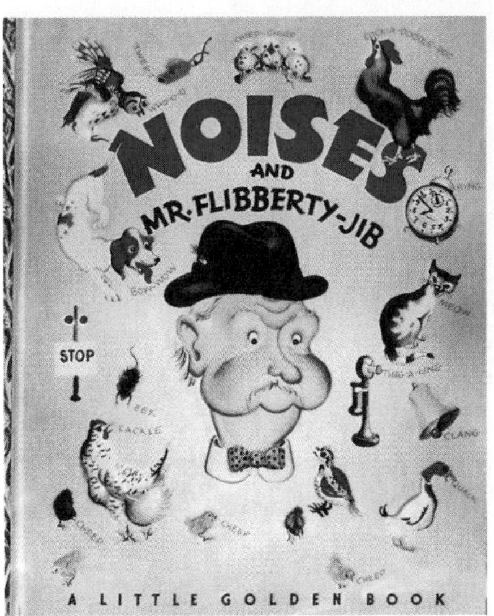


**Noises and Mr. Flibberty-Jib**
Illustrator: Wilkin, Eloise
Author: Wilkin, Eloise
29 1947 42 Pages 1st Ed. **$40**
Four-Color and Black & White
Gold Paper Spine

**Nursery Songs**
Illustrator: Malvern, Corinne
Author: Gale, Leah
7 1942 42 Pages 1st Ed. **$40**
Four-Color and Black & White
Blue Spine with Dust Jacket **$50-$200**

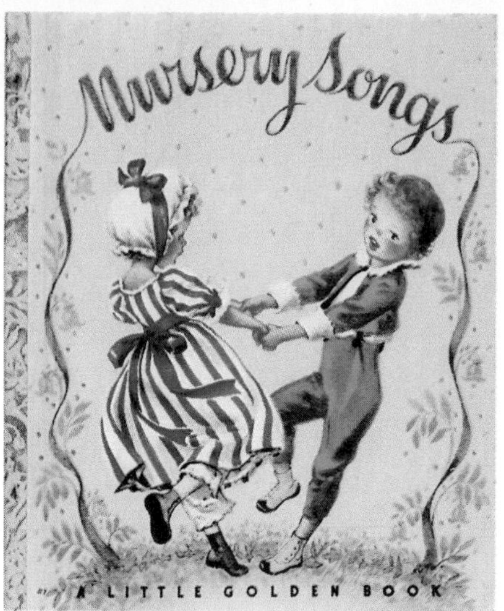


**Nursery Songs**
Illustrator: Malvern, Corinne
Author: Gale, Leah
7 1942 (1949) 42 Pages 15th Ed. **$15**
Gold Paper Spine

**Nursery Tales**
Illustrator: Masha
14 1943 42 Pages 1st Ed. **$25**
Four-Color and Black & White
Blue Spine with Dust Jacket **$50-$150**
14 1943 (1951) 42 Pages 9th Ed. **$20**
Four-Color and Black & White
Golden Paper Spine. Song added to last page.

**Poky Little Puppy, The**
Illustrator: Tenggren, Gustaf
Author: Lowrey, Janet Sebring
8 1942 42 Pages 1st Ed. **$50**
Four-Color and Black & White
Blue Spine with Dust Jacket **$50-$200**
8 1942 (1950) 42 Pages 21st Ed. **$15**
Four-Color. Golden Paper Spine
8 1942 (1950) 28 Pages 22nd Ed. **$10**
Four-Color. Foil Spine

**Prayers for Children**
Illustrator: Dixon, Rachel Taft
5 1942 42 Pages 1st Ed. **$40**
Four-Color and Black & White
Blue Spine with Dust Jacket **$50-$200**
5 1942 (1948) 42 Pages 12th Ed. **$15**
Four-Color and Black & White. Golden Paper Spine
Prayer "Till the victory is ours" changed to "Good Night."
5 1942 (1950) 42 Pages 18th Ed. **$12**
Four-Color and Three-Color
Golden Paper Spine. Song added to last page.
5 1942 (1950) 42 Pages 19th Ed. **$10**
Four-Color and Three-Color. Golden Paper Spine
Song on last page given solid background.

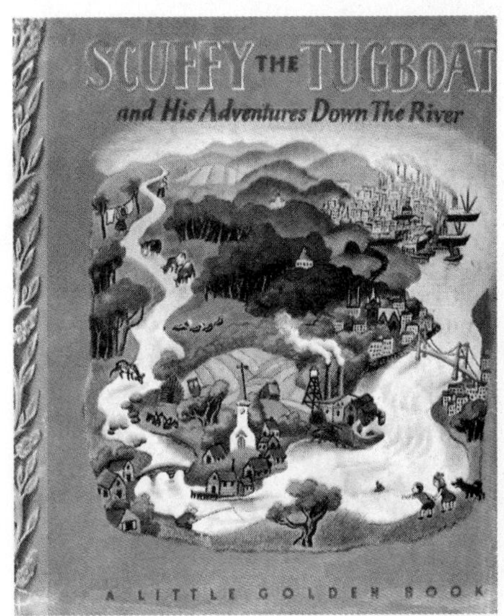


**Scuffy the Tugboat**
Illustrator: Gergely, Tibor
Author: Crampton, Gertrude
30 1946 42 Pages 1st Ed. **$25**
Four-Color and Black & White
Blue Spine with Dust Jacket **$50-$150**
30 1946 (1951) 42 Pages 9th Ed. **$18**
Four-Color, Foil Spine

**Shy Little Kitten, The**
Illustrator: Tenggren, Gustaf
Author: Schurr, Kathleen
23 1946 42 Pages 1st Ed. **$25**
Four-Color and Black & White
Blue Spine with Dust Jacket **$50-$150**
23 1946 (1949) 28 Pages 5th Ed. **$12**
Four-Color, Golden Paper Spine

**Story of Jesus, The**
Illustrator: Lerch, Steffie
Author: Alexander, Beatrice
27 1946 42 Pages 1st Ed. **$25**
Four-Color and Black & White
Blue Spine with Dust Jacket **$50-$150**
27 1946 (1949) 42 Pages 6th Ed. **$18**
Four-Color and Three-Color
Golden Paper Spine

**Taxi That Hurried, The**
Illustrator: Gergely, Tibor
Author: Mitchell, Lucy Sprague; Simonton
25 1946 42 Pages 1st Ed. **$25**
Four-Color and Black & White
Blue Spine with Dust Jacket **$50-$150**
25 1946 (1951) 42 Pages 6th Ed. **$8**
Four-Color and Black & White
Golden Paper Spine
25 1946 (1951) 28 Pages 10th Ed. **$8**
Four-Color. Foil Spine
25 1946 (1963) 24 Pages 13th Ed. **$5**
Four-Color. Foil Spine

**Three Little Kittens**
Illustrator: Masha
1 1942 42 Pages 1st Ed. **$50**
Four-Color and Black & White
Blue Spine with Dust Jacket **$50-$200**
1 1942 (1946) 24 Pages 9th Ed. **$30**
Four-Color and Black & White. Blue Spine
"To Albert" no longer written above clothsline.
Blue Spine with Dust Jacket **$40-$100**
1 1942 (1951) 42 Pages 17th Ed. **$20**
Four-Color and Three-Color. Golden Paper Spine
Song added to last page.
1 1942 (1952) 28 Pages 19th Ed. **$12**
Four-Color and Three-Color. Foil Spine
Song on page 4.

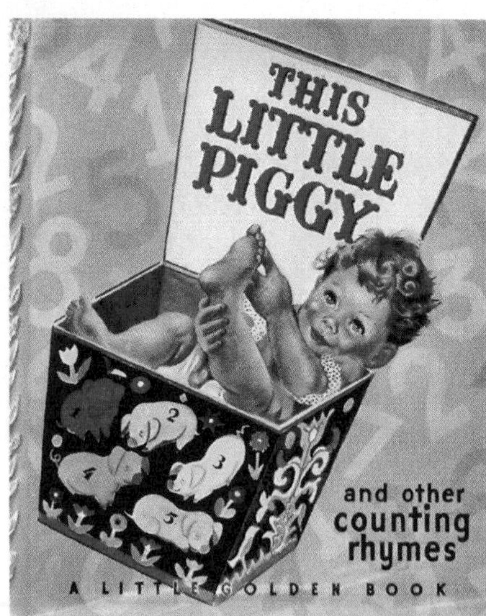


**This Little Piggy and Other Counting Rhymes**
Illustrator: Paflin, Roberta
12 1942 42 Pages 1st Ed. **$60**
Four-Color and Black & White
Blue Spine with Dust Jacket **$60-$250**

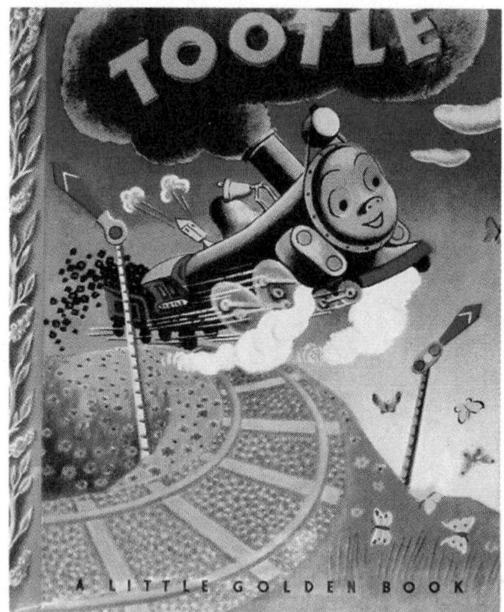


**Tootle**
Illustrator: Gergely, Tibor
Author: Crampton, Gertrude
21 1945 42 Pages 1st Ed. **$30**
Four-Color and Black & White
Blue Spine with Dust Jacket **$50-$175**

## Paperbacks

The first mass-market, pocket-sized, paperback book printed in the U.S. was an edition of Pearl Buck's *The Good Earth*, produced by Pocket Books in late 1938, sold in New York City.

At first, paperbacks consisted entirely of reprints, but publishers soon began publishing original works. Genre categories began to emerge, and mass-market book covers reflected those categories. Mass-market paperbacks had an impact on slick magazines (slicks) and pulp magazines. The market for cheap magazines diminished when buyers went to cheap books instead. Authors also turned from magazines and began writing for the paperback market. Many pulp magazine cover artists were hired by paperback publishers to entice readers with their alluring artwork. Several well-known authors were published in paperback, including Arthur Miller and John Steinbeck, and some, like Dashiell Hammett, were published as paperback originals.

For more information and details on condition grades (values here are in three grades: good, very good and fine), consult *Antique Trader Collectible Paperbacks Price Guide* by Gary Lovisi, or visit www.gryphonbooks.com.

*Warped Women* by Janet Pritchard, Uni Book #9, 1951, digest-size paperback. ....................$12-35-100

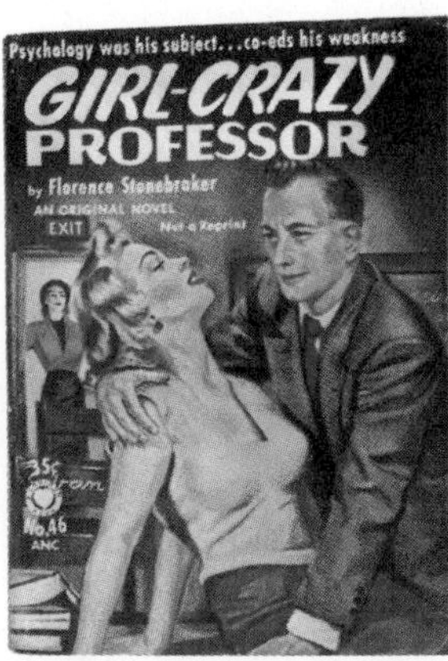


*Girl-Crazy Professor* by Florence Stonebraker, Croydon Book #46, 1953, digest-size paperback. .................... $9-22-55

*Dance-Hall Dyke* by Toni Adler, Playtime Book #699-S, 1964. Cover art by Robert Bonfils. .................... $12-25-55

*A Dame Gets Hers* by Duke Nolan, Scion Books, 1952, UK digest-size paperback. .........$15-55-125

*Office Hussy* by John Hunter, Star Novels #767, 1957, digest-size paperback.................. $12-35-75

*Sin Street* by Dorine Manners, Pyramid Book #21, 1950. .................... $9-22-50

*Rock 'N Roll Gal* by Ernie Weatherall, Beacon Book #B379, 1957. Cover art by Owen Kampen. ................................ **$12-28-65**

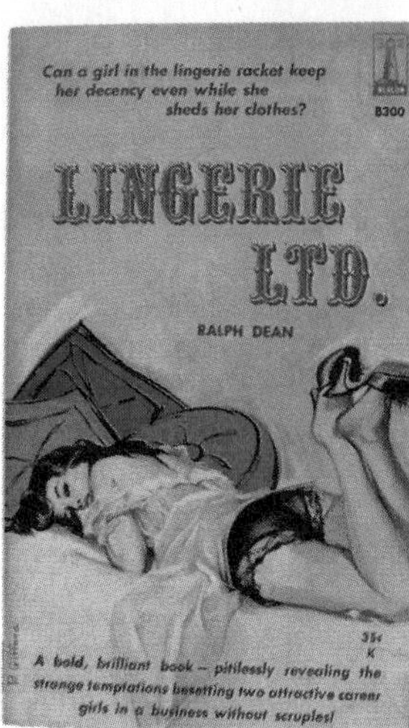


*Lingerie Ltd.* by Ralph Dean, Beacon Book #B300, 1960. Cover art by R. Gifford. ............... **$9-15-35**

*Knock On Any Head* by Frank S. Miller, Vega Book #V-19, 1962. ................................... **$7-15-40**

*Invasion of the Nymphomaniacs* by Sean O'Shea, Belmont Book #B50-798, 1967. ........ **$9-15-35**

*I Made My Bed* by Celia Hye, Beacon Book #B188, 1958. **$7-15-35**

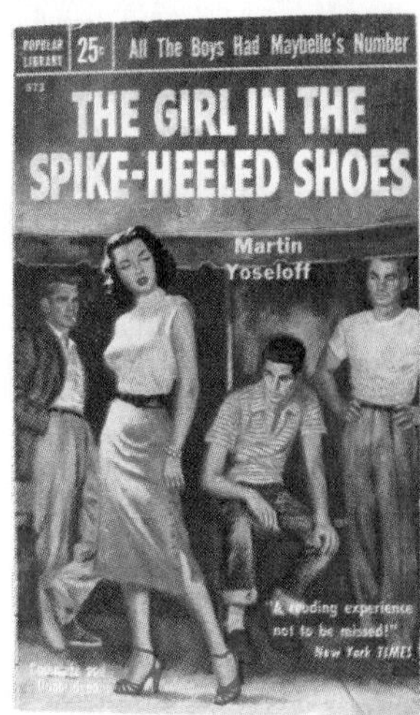


*The Girl in the Spike-Heeled Shoes* by Martin Yoseloff, Popular Library #573, 1954...... **$5-15-28**

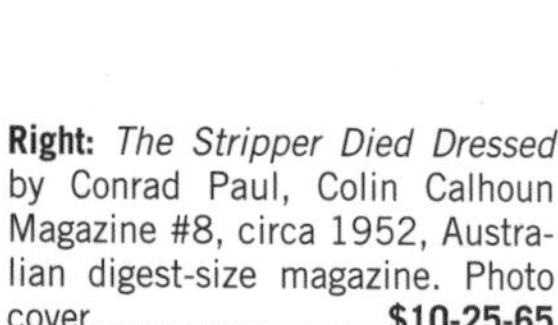

**Right:** *The Stripper Died Dressed* by Conrad Paul, Colin Calhoun Magazine #8, circa 1952, Australian digest-size magazine. Photo cover. ........................ **$10-25-65**

**Far right:** *This Way For Hell* by Spike Morelli, Leisure Library #7, 1952. Cover art by Reginald Heade. ...................... **$12-30-65**

# Cookbooks

Whether you're just starting a collection or are a seasoned connoisseur of culinary literature, this section is a valuable resource for identifying, pricing and learning about 20th-century American cookbooks published from the late 1800s up to about the 1970s—a large slice of publishing history filled with rich examples of culinary art, culture, trends, humor and, of course, recipes for some great food.

The best advice for collecting cookbooks is probably true for collecting anything—collect what you find interesting, meaningful, fun or important. Let your collection be an expression of your interest, not just the value the marketplace puts on your books.

Try to buy books with dust jackets whenever possible. A dust jacket not only protects the book, but it often provides hard-to-find information about the author or the cookbook itself. Dust jackets are often missing from older cookbooks and, when intact, instantly add value.

Buy the best condition you can afford. Buying a book in "cooking copy" condition is a good idea only if you intend to use it in the kitchen, or consider it a "placeholder" in your collection.

Store your cookbooks out of the kitchen, out of the basement, and out of the attic. Even the cleanest kitchens tend to be a challenging environment for a book (grease, smoke, moisture, humidity, etc.) A lot of great old books have been ruined by insects, moisture, heat, and other effects of improper storage.

If you intend to use the cookbooks you purchase, consider buying the best copy you can afford and buying another one in marginal shape for the kitchen.

Buy from reputable dealers who know cookbooks, know how to describe them, and offer a money-back satisfaction guarantee.

Focus your collection on a particular sub-category or passion. This might be anything from a collection of cookbooks from your region to a collection about confections, cakes, or cocktails. From a buyer's point of view, focused and complete collections are more desirable than a disparate gaggle of books. From a collector's perspective, it will make your treasure hunting more manageable.

For more information on cookbooks, see *Antique Trader Collectible Cookbooks Price Guide* by Patricia Edwards and Peter Peckham.

1926
**104 Prize Radio Recipes**
Allen, Ida Bailey
J. H. Sears & Co.
Hardcover
126 pages
A series of 24 radio addresses by Allen are reproduced here with the recipe contest prize-winning recipes. Illustrative look at how radio shows shaped the thinking of the American homemaker
Value: **$31-$56**

1958
**1001 Ways to Please a Husband**
Waldo, Myra
Van Nostrand
Hardcover
Value: **$53-$94**

1933-1939
**All About Home Baking**
General Foods
General Foods
Hardcover
144 pages
Highly illustrated with charming period color illustrations and black-and-white, step-by-step photos. Also available as soft cover
Value: **$20-$36**

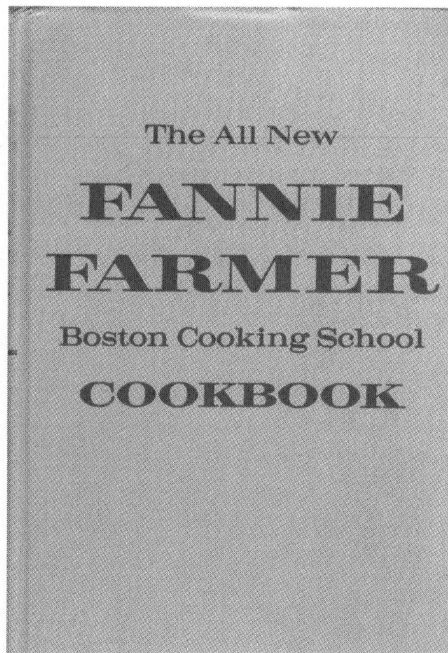

1959
**All New Fannie Farmer Boston Cooking School Cookbook, The**
Perkins, Wilma Lord (editor)
Little, Brown and Co.
Hardcover
596-plus pages
10th Edition. First printing of the 1959 edition. 596 pages plus blank pages for notes and recipes. Illustrations by Alison Mason Kingsbury. There are several other printings of the 10th edition, but contents are identical.
Value: **$60-$106**

1954
**Ann Pillsbury's New Cook Book**
Pillsbury, Ann
Arco
Hardcover
144 pages
Value: **$32-$56**

1880
**Appledore Cook Book, The**
Parloa, Maria
Andrew F. Graves
Hardcover
240 pages
Second edition
Value: **$105-$188**

1944
**Better Homes & Gardens Cook Book**
Better Homes and Gardens
Meredith
Hardcover binder
The desirable wartime edition of the Better Homes and Gardens De-Luxe Edition Cook Book, complete with the Wartime Supplement in separate wrapper
Black-and-white and color photos Blue tabs with lettered indexing
Value: **$69-$123**

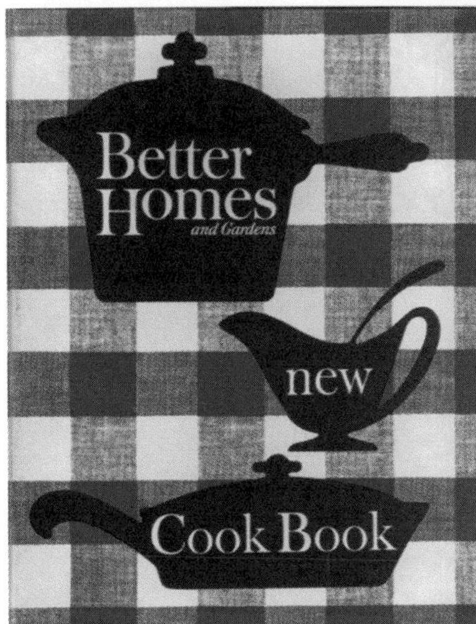


1962-1965
**Better Homes and Gardens New Cook Book**
Editors of Better Homes and Gardens
Meredith Publishing
Hardcover binder
Yellow tabs
Value: **$41-$73**

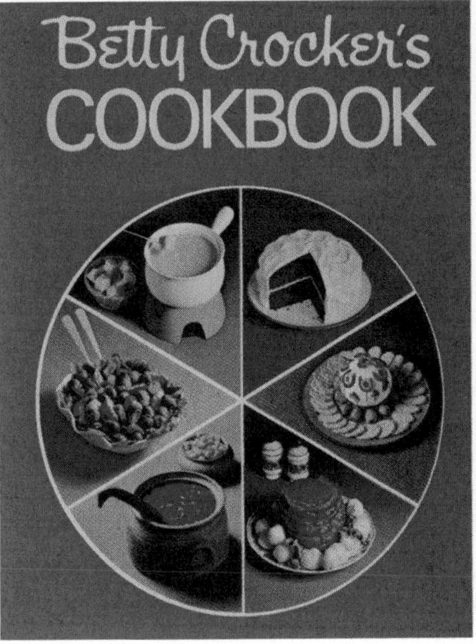


1969
**Betty Crocker's Cookbook**
Crocker, Betty
Golden Press
Hardcover or binder
480 pages
Also known as the "pie" cover as a reference to the graphic shape
Value: **$63-$112**

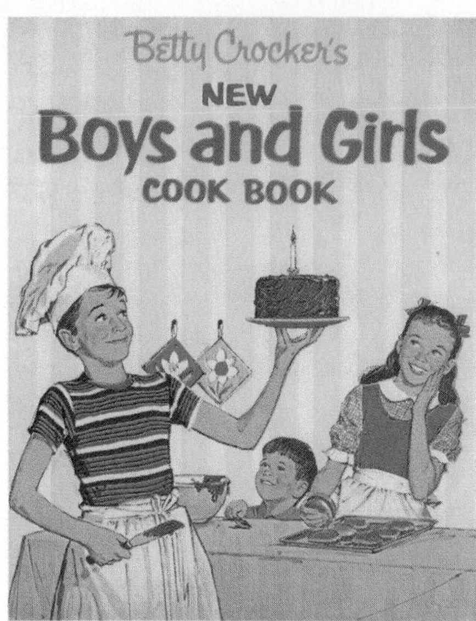


1965
**Betty Crocker's New Boys and Girls Cook Book**
Crocker, Betty
Golden Press
Hardcover, wire bound
156 pages
Illustrations by Gloria Kamen. Color and black-and-white photos and illustrations
Value: **$25-$44**

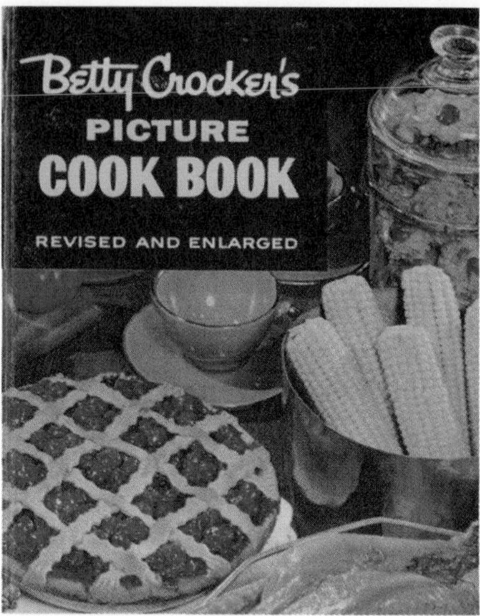


1956
**Betty Crocker's Picture Cook Book**
Crocker, Betty
McGraw Hill
Hardcover
472 pages
Revised and enlarged 2nd edition. Same contents as gray cover. Available in hardcover or binder
Value: **$70-$124**

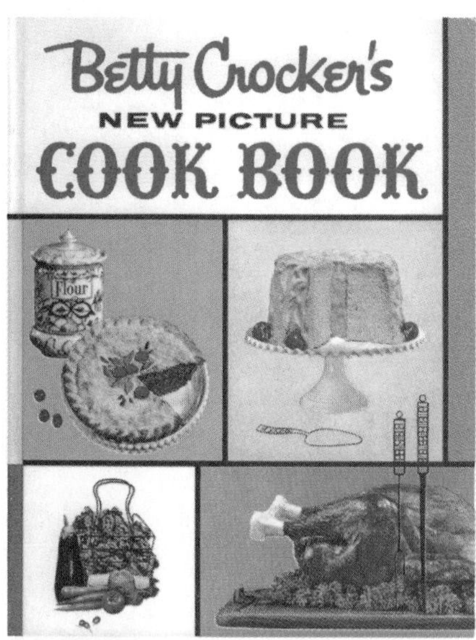


1961-1968
**Betty Crocker's New Picture Cook Book**
Crocker , Betty
McGraw-Hill
Hardcover binder
454 pages
Available in hardcover or binder edition. Binders command slightly higher prices.
Value: **$90-$161**

1904
**Boston Cooking-School Cook Book, The**
Farmer, Fannie Merritt
Little, Brown and Co.
Hardcover
Unclear if this is considered the 2nd edition or a modified first edition. Revised with an appendix of 300 recipes and an addendum of 60 recipes.
666 pages plus 20 pages of advertising
Value: **$88-$156**

1923
**Cakes and Pastries**
Carney, Cleve
Calumet
Hardcover
58 pages
270 pastry recipes for professional bakers. Recipes are for large quantities. Exceptional color plates. Additional pages for recording recipes
Value: **$88-$156**

1954-1960
**Cooking Magic or Fabulous Foods Binder Set**
De Proft, Melanie (editor)
Culinary Arts
Hardcover binder plus 24 booklets
Complete set of 24 booklets in two, red-and-white, 3"-thick, binders. The name on the binders alternated between Cooking Magic, Fabulous Foods and Cooking Magic Fabulous Foods. No matter the name, the contents are the same. Binders must be complete and in excellent condition to command the following prices.
Individual booklet values: French, Italian, and Creole—**$15-20. Others $3-$10**
Value: **$137-$244**

1940s
**Culinary Arts Institute Encyclopedia of Cooking and Homemaking, The**
Berolzheimer, Ruth (editor)
Culinary Arts Institute
Hardcover binder and 20 booklets
48 pages
Each booklet was printed in a variety of possible colors, including red, green, orange, aqua and blue. The binder is brown with removable binding wires. Individual booklet prices range from **$7-$15. Binder is difficult to find in acceptable condition.**
Also look for the companion box containing the entire set titled American Encyclopedia of Cooking and Homemaking. Note that binder must be in exceptional condition to command these prices.
Value: **$102-$181**

1901
**Dining Room and Kitchen**
Townsend, Grace
Home Publishing Co.
Hardcover
527 pages
Revised edition of Dining Room and Kitchen, an economical guide in "Practical Housekeeping for the American Housewife containing the Choicest Tried and Approved Cookery Recipes"
Black-and-white engravings
Value: **$123-$219**

1950s
**Encyclopedia of Cooking in 24 Volumes, The**
Berolzheimer, Ruth
Culinary Arts Institute
Hardcover binder and 24 booklets
White binder has gold lettering and removable binding wires. Some binders include index on the spine. Binder is difficult to find in acceptable condition. Note: binder must be in exceptional condition to command these prices.
Individual booklet prices range from **$3-$15.**
Value: **$126-$225**

1949
**Esquire's Handbook for Hosts**
Editors of Esquire Magazine
Grosset & Dunlap
Hardcover
288 pages
Highly illustrated bachelor guide to cocktails, food and etiquette. Design and Typography by A. P. Tedesco. Witty and stylish
Value: **$41-$74**

1946-1950
**Fannie Farmer's Boston Cooking School Cook Book**
Perkins, Wilma Lord (editor)
Little, Brown
Hardcover
879 pages
8th Edition. Black-and-white illustrations
Value: **$34-$61**

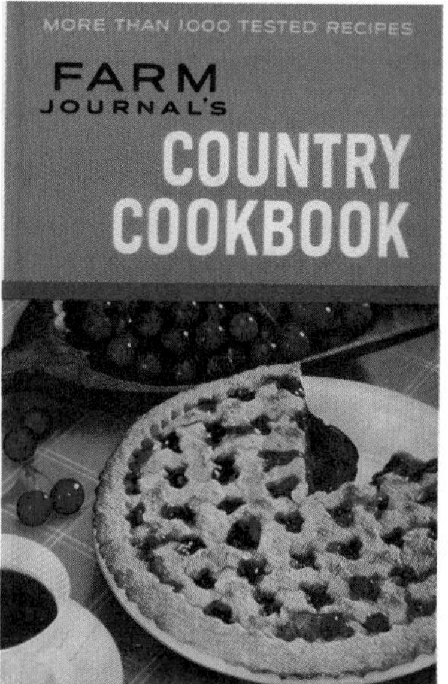


1959
**Farm Journal's Country Cookbook**
Nichols, Nell B. (editor)
Doubleday
Hardcover
Printed with several distinct covers. Showing "Deluxe Edition"
Value: **$41-$73**

1949
**Fireside Cook Book, The**
Beard, James
Simon and Schuster
Hardcover
Illustrations by Alice and Martin Provensen
Value: **$48-$86**

1944
**Good Housekeeping Cook Book, The**
Marsh, Dorothy B. (editor)
Rinehart & Co.
Hardcover
981 pages
Same contents as the second printing of the doily cover. Value: **$54-$96**

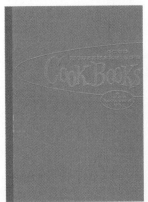

1958, 1959
**Good Housekeeping's Cook Books**
(20 Booklets Plus Binder)
Good Housekeeping editors
Good Housekeeping/Consolidated Books
Hardcover binder plus 20 booklets
Twenty separate Good Housekeeping recipe booklets, each with 68 pages, make up the chapters in this enormous classic. Each booklet is charming on its own and is notable for its exceptional period illustrations by various artists.
Spot color drawings, black and white and color photos
Value: **$88-$156**
White binder has gold lettering and removable binding wires. Some binders include index on the spine. Binder is difficult to find in acceptable condition. Note: binder must be in exceptional condition to command these prices.
Individual booklet prices range from **$3-$15.**

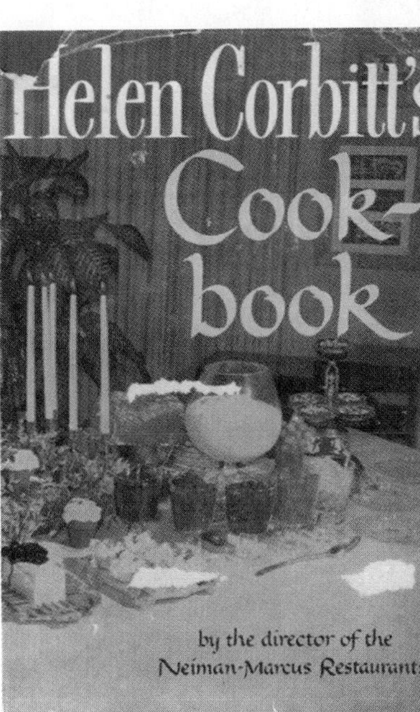


**Far left:**
1909
**Good Housekeeping Woman's Home Cook Book, The**
Curtis, Isabel Gordon (editor)
Reilly & Britton Co.
Hardcover
320 pages
Value: **$60-$106**

1957
**Helen Corbitt's Cookbook**
Corbitt, Helen
Riverside Press
Hardcover
Famous for the creation of superb recipes for the Zodiac Room of Neiman-Marcus in Dallas. Charming vintage illustrations
Value: **$16-$28**

**Home Queen Cook Book, The**
Author not noted
M. A. Donohue
Hardcover
608 pages
Subtitled *Two Thousand Valuable Recipes on Cookery and Household Economy, Table Etiquette, Toilet Etc.* Contributions came from over 200 "World's Fair Lady Managers, Wives of Governors, and other Ladies of Position and Influence." Most recipes include a reproduced signature. The book was published in time for the 1893 Chicago World's Fair. A short biography of Juliet Corson is included as an introduction to her position as the director of the exhibit of cooking schools at the Exposition.
The editor or author of this cookbook is not noted, and Julia's contribution is unclear, but the original printing (1893) is listed in Bitting as James Edson White and Mrs. M. L. Wanless [Anon.]
Value: **$102-$181**

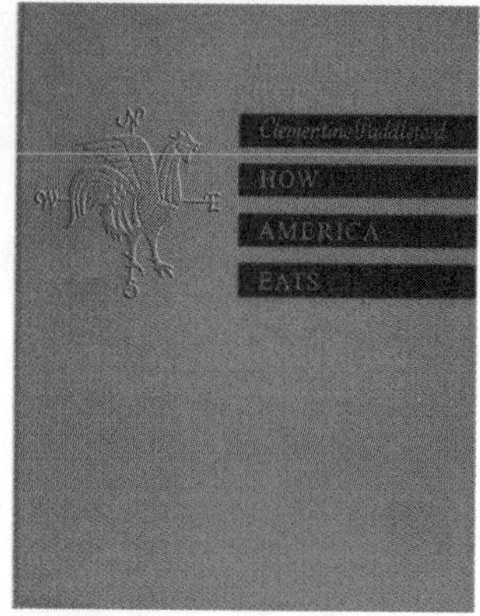


1960
**How America Eats**
Paddleford, Clementine
Charles Scribner and Sons
Hardcover
496 pages
Long considered one of the most thorough and interesting American regional cookbook compilations. Paddleford writes in a warm and engaging style, recounting stories of personal encounters with cooks around the country, faithfully penning their recipes and capturing their spirit.
Twelve years in the making, Paddleford's book is a charming read and an American treasure. Color and black and white photos
Value: **$67-$119**

1935-1941
**Household Searchlight Recipe Book**
Household Magazine, The
Hardcover
289-plus blank pages
1st through 14th editions have identical contents.
Thumb-indexed
Compiled and edited by: Migliario, Ida; Allard, Harriett; Titus, Zorada; and Nunemaker, Irene
Value: **$39-$69**

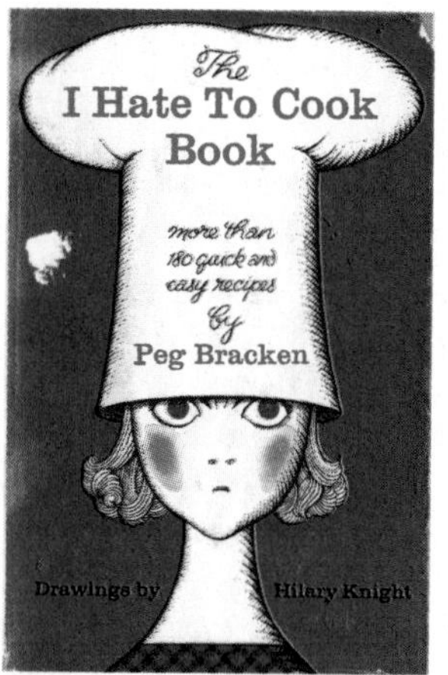


1963
**I Hate To Cook Book, The**
Bracken, Peg
Harcourt, Brace
Hardcover, but also available in paperback
176 pages
Illustrations by Hilary Knight
Value: **$32-$56**

1940
**Ida Bailey Allen's Money-Saving Cook Book**
Allen, Ida Bailey
Garden City Publishing
Hardcover
481 pages
Value: **$16-$28**

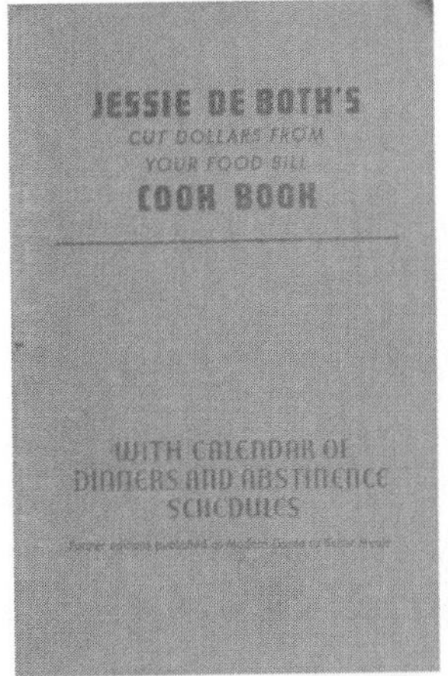


1942
**Jessie De Both's Cut Dollars From Your Food Bill Cook Book**
DeBoth, Jesse Marie
Consolidated Book Publishers Inc.
Hardcover
374 pages
With calendar of dinners and abstinence schedules. Formerly published as Modern Guide to Better Meals
Value: **$28-$50**

1943
**Joy of Cooking, The**
Rombauer, Irma S.
Bobbs-Merrill
Hardcover
1943 printing of the blue diamond cover—one of the most desirable editions. The 1946 printing with the same cover has slightly different contents.
Value: **$55-$98**

1963
**Ladies' Home Journal Cook Book**
Truax, Carol (editor)
Doubleday
Hardcover
728 pages
1st and second printing of this cookbook have the exact same contents. However, the covers are different, the endpapers have different illustrations and the first printing is thumb-indexed.
Value: **$45-$81**

1970
**Liberace Cooks!**
Liberace, Wladziu Valentino (with Truax, Carol)
Doubleday
Hardcover
225 pages
Wladziu Valentino Liberace
Part biography, part cookbook, it includes hundreds of recipes from Liberace's Polish and Italian roots. Color photos of Liberace cooking
Value: **$69-$123**

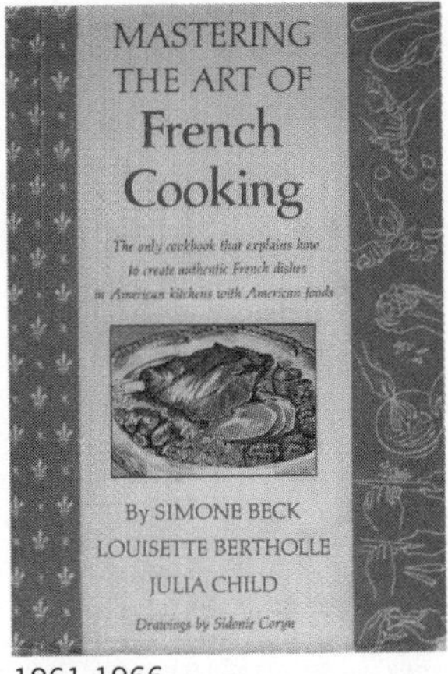


1961-1966
**Mastering the Art of French Cooking Volume One**
Child, Julia; Beck, Simone; Berthole, Louisette
Alfred A. Knopf
Hardcover
684 pages
Early printings do not indicate volume number. Book club reprints are slightly smaller, but still high quality printings.
Illustrations by Sidonie Coryn. Color jacket illustration by Gigot Rôti. Book and jacket design by Warren Chappell
Value: **$35-$62**

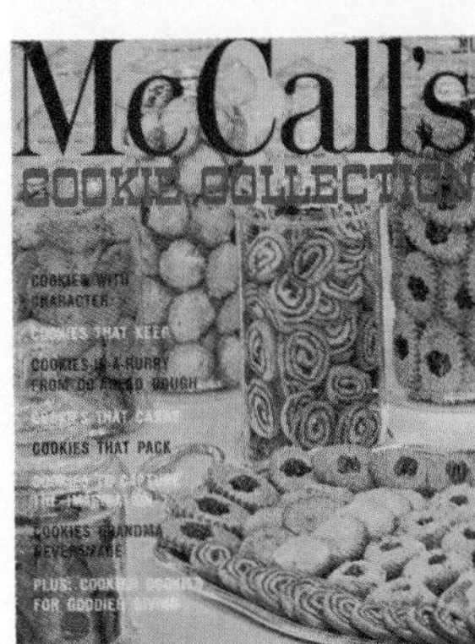


1965-1975
**McCall's Cookbook Series**
Editors of McCall's
Advance Publishers
Series of 18 (plus index) large-format, soft cover cookbooks. Originally available with a white plastic holder
Complete set with holder: **$95-$120**

1942
**Modern Family Cook Book, The**
Given, Meta
J. Ferguson
Hardcover
938 pages
First edition of The Modern Family Cook Book, thumb-indexed with red spray decoration on the book fore edges. Highly illustrated with color photos and black-and-white drawings, charts and tables
Value: **$46-$81**

1886
**Mrs. Rorer's Philadelphia Cook Book**
Rorer, Sarah Tyson
Arnold and Co.
Hardcover
581 pages plus ads
First edition
20 pages of advertisements at end of book
Value: **$60-$106**

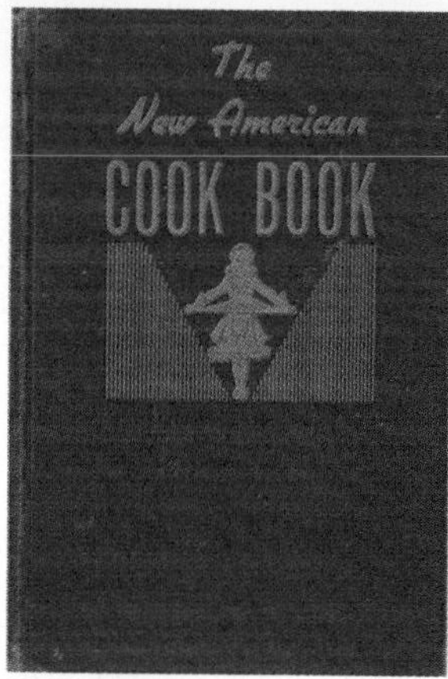


1941-1944
**New American Cook Book, The**
Wallace, Lily Haxworth
American Publishers
Hardcover
932 pages
Cover colors vary but contents are identical
1941-1944
Thumb-indexed. Color and black-and-white photos and illustrations
Value: **$49-$87**

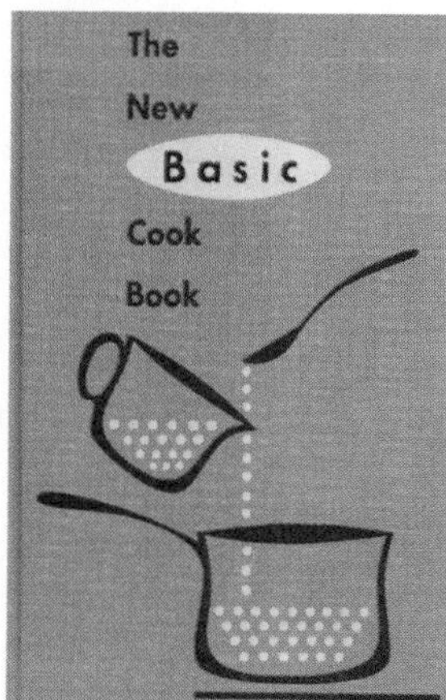


1957
**New Basic Cook Book, The**
Heseltine, Marjorie and Dow, Ula
Riverside Press
Hardcover
718 pages
Value: **$46-$81**

1959
**Pillsbury's Best 1000 Recipes: Best of the Bake-Off Collection**
Pillsbury, Ann (editor)
Consolidated Book Publishers
Hardcover
608 pages
Each recipe is a famous Bake-off prizewinner. Includes a history of the Bake-off, color and black-and-white photos of the dishes and illustrations by Suzanne Snider
Shown: Pictorial cover or dust jacket and cloth cover with gold lettering. Cloth cover is billed as the "deluxe edition" and is thumb-indexed. Also available as a souvenir leatherette edition presented to Bake-off winners.
Value: **$105-$188**

1969-1975
**Pooh Cook Book, The**
Ellison, Virginia H.
Dutton
Hardcover
120 pages
Charming little cookbook with many "pooh-isms." Every recipe is made with honey. Illustrated by Ernest H. Shepard
Recipes include: Poohanopiglet Pancakes, Popovers for Piglet, Fairy Toast and Hipy Papy Bthuthdth Thuthda Bthuthdy Cake.
Value: **$28-$49**

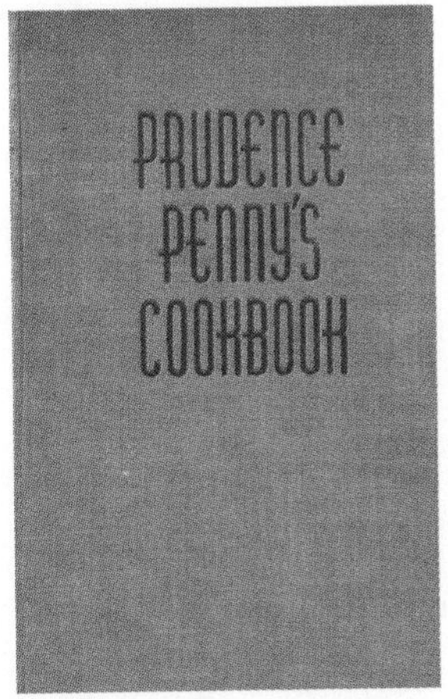


1939
**Prudence Penny's Cookbook**
Penny, Prudence
Prentice-Hall
Hardcover
385 pages
By Prudence Penny, Home Economics Editor of the Los Angeles Examiner
Adept black-and-white cartoon illustrations. Photo of and intro by the actor Leo Carillo
Value: **$52-$93**

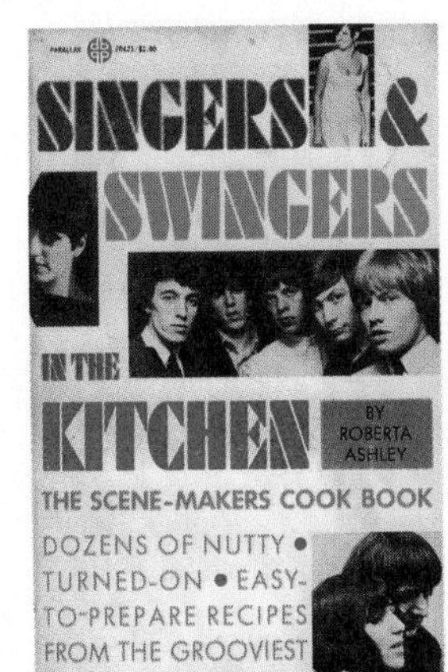


1967
**Singers & Swingers in the Kitchen**
Ashley, Roberta
Parallax
Soft cover
96 pages
Favorite recipes of '60s pop idols like Sonny and Cher, The Monkees, The Hermits, The Rolling Stones, Bobby Darin and many more. Black and white photos of celebrities throughout
Value: **$60-$106**

1950
**Spice Sampler, The**
Barber, Edith M.
Sterling Publishing
Hardcover
62 pages
Includes spice sample packets from John Wagner & Sons of Hatboro, Pa.
Cloth cover
Value: **$27-$48**

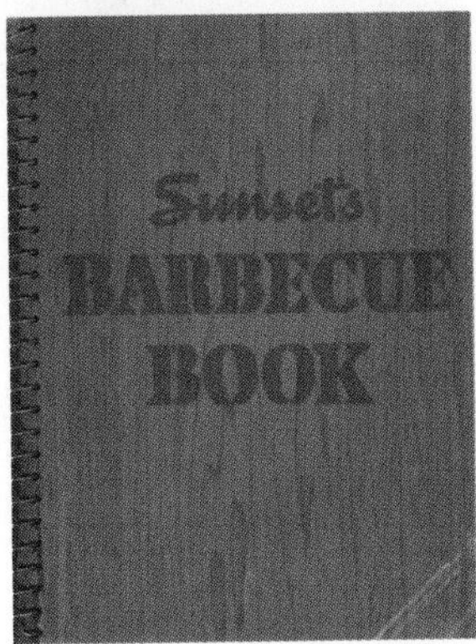


1938, 1939
**Sunset's Barbecue Book**
Sanderson, George and Rich, Virginia
Sunset
Hardcover, wood
72 pages
Likely the first book ever published on the subject of home barbecuing. Includes plans for barbecue building and recipes
The original edition has an actual wood cover. Later printings are faux printed to look like wood.
Value: **$49-$88**

1955
**Tooth Sweet**
Rosen, Ruth Chier
Rosen
Soft cover, plastic comb binding
140 pages
Available in two cover designs. Price shown for book with original box.
Value: **$31-$56**

1942, 1943
**Victory Binding of the American Woman's Cook Book Wartime Edition**
Berolzheimer, Ruth (editor)
Culinary Arts
Hardcover
816 pages plus wartime section
Printed in 1942 and 1943. The 1943 printing is more desirable and contains a full-page illustration and dedication to Gen. Douglas MacArthur. Both printings have 816 pages plus additional sections devoted to "Wartime Cookery."
Thumb-indexed. Color and black and white photos and illustrations
Value: **$88-$156**

1942, 1943
**Victory Binding of the American Woman's Cook Book Wartime Edition**
Berolzheimer, Ruth (editor)
Culinary Arts
Hardcover
816 pages plus wartime section
Printed in 1942 and 1943. The 1943 printing is more desirable and contains a full-page illustration and dedication to Gen. Douglas MacArthur. Both printings have 816 pages plus additional sections devoted to "Wartime Cookery."
Thumb-indexed. Color and black and white photos and illustrations
Value: **$88-$156**

1960
**Woman's Day Collector's Cook Book**
Woman's Day
E. P. Dutton
Hardcover
320 pages
Illustrations by Joseph Low. Chapter introductions by James Beard. Reprinted many times in different sizes and covers
Value: **$12-$21**

1938-1945
**Watkins Cook Book**
Allen, Elaine
Whitman
Soft cover, wire bound
Contents of each year are slightly different but covers are similar.
1938: 288 pages, includes a color bird's-eye view of Watkins buildings
1943: 4th edition, blue cover, 264 pages. No mention of the war but does have a chapter on economy desserts and one on economy meats and salads
1948: 288 pages
Wartime edition contains sections on sugar substitutes and "How to meet the butter shortage," and carries an increased value of 20-30 percent over that immediately below.
Value: **$28-$49**

1902
**Woman's Favorite Cook Book**
Gregory, Annie
Hardcover
578 pages
Embellished with many colored and photo engravings. Written by Annie Gregory "for 10 years chef of the Union League Club, Chicago, now of Grand Pacific Hotel," who was assisted by 1,000 homemakers. Many cosmetic recipes like creams, tooth powder, cure for rough skin, shampoos, recipe "to make a handsome throat," etc. Recipes attributed to contributors
Value: **$88-$156**

1900
**White House Cook Book, The**
Gillette, Mrs. F. L.; Ziemann, Hugo
Saalfield Publishing
Hardcover
590 pages
New and enlarged edition
590 pages plus two pages of advertisements for other Saalfield books
Engravings and photos of first ladies, and additional black-and-white illustrations
Value: **$53-$94**

1942-1946
**Woman's Home Companion Cook Book**
Kirk, Dorothy and Roberts, Willa (editors)
P. F. Collier & Son Corp.
Hardcover
952 pages
First edition is shown here in rare, original 1942 wartime dust jacket. 1942-1945 printings contain a short wartime postscript addressing the "inevitable food shortages." While this exact cookbook was reprinted many times between 1942 and 1955, only the first 1942 printing mentions Willa Roberts as the co-editor.
Color and black-and-white photos and illustrations
Value: **$67-$119**

# Magazines

The disposable nature of magazines makes them a rarity. Unlike a book, there are a multitude of reasons to collect a vintage magazine: writer, illustrator, and advertising.

For a lazy researcher, there is no controversy as to first edition. First appearances are in magazines, from Edgar Allan Poe to Jack London to Agatha Christie.

Most first appearances of the works of great authors were published in magazines. Many of these writers were also editors and publishers. Charles Dickens wrote and published *Household Words* with writer/editor Wilkie Collins in the 1850s. Edgar Allan Poe's first appearance in a magazine of national circulation was the anonymous publication of "The Visionary" in *Godey's Lady's Book* in January 1834. Poe was also an editor for *Graham's Magazine* where his first American detective story, "The Murders in the Rue Morgue," was published in April 1841. Poe's most famous poem, "The Raven," was published under the pseudonym of Quarles in *The American Review: A Whig Journal* in February 1845. Arguably, the world's most popular detective, Sherlock Holmes, made his first appearance in *Beeton's Christmas Annual of 1887* in Arthur Conan Doyle's "A Study in Scarlet." However, it was the publication of "A Scandal in Bohemia" in *The Strand Magazine* in July of 1891 that made Sherlock Holmes a household name and boosted the circulation of *The Strand*. When Doyle "killed" off Holmes in "The Final Problem," *The Strand* and Doyle were besieged with upset and outraged readers. Doyle was "forced" to create the "return of Sherlock Holmes" in "The Empty House" and the rest is literary history.

*Godey's Lady's Book* was edited by Sarah J. Hale. Mrs. Hale was the original author of the poem "Mary Had a Little Lamb." She was one of the first women to actually make a living as a writer/editor. *Godey's* was the fashion and household bible for the American woman in the 1800s. Mrs. Hale was one of the earliest champions of women's rights. During the Civil War, it was one of the most sought after smuggling operations for the women in the South. They *had* to get their *Godey's* fashions and recipes. Mrs. Hale brought Edgar Allan Poe to the American public. Her son had known Poe at West Point. Each issue of *Godey's* contained hand-colored fashions for women that were, for the most part, hand-tinted by women. The fashions were copied and then removed for framing. It is sometimes difficult to find an early issue of *Godey's* with all of the illustrations intact. Today, however, they are still sought after for their content, whether it be writers such as Poe or Civil War reenactment enthusiasts.

At the turn of the century, American magazines, especially the Hearst-owned *Cosmopolitan*, attracted not only authors such as Jack London, but began to feature important illustrators on their covers. Artists such as Harrison Fisher illustrated Hearst magazine covers exclusively under contract through the early 1930s until his death. The Fisher Girls rivaled the Gibson Girls created by artist Charles Dana Gibson. In 1886, Gibson sold his first drawing to John Ames Mitchell, the editor of the original *Life Magazine*, a weekly humor magazine, in January 1883. Gibson became the editor and publisher of *Life Magazine* after World War I. While well-known artists such as Maxfield Parrish, Coles Phillips and John Held Jr. illustrated *Life's* covers, a little-known artist, T.S. Sullivant, was drawing the cartoons. T.S. Sullivant (1854-1926) studied at the Pennsylvania Academy of Fine Arts. His mentor was A.B. Frost, who helped him connect with *Puck Magazine* and then onto *Judge* and *Life Magazine*. Out of all the aforementioned magazine artists/illustrators, Sullivant has probably had the most influence on our modern visual world. His cartoons of animals and cave people have been inspiring the animation artists of Disney and Warner since "Fantasia." The Disney

Godey's Lady's Book, June 1868, January-December 1868 (Civil War) .............. **$250**

Studio Library has Sullivant clippings that, in spite of computer-generated graphics, are still revered by Disney artists.

A German magazine called *Jugend* was the harbinger of Art Nouveau. Some of Aubrey Beardsley's earliest work was in *The Chap-Book*. *Vogue Magazine* featured the Art Deco illustrations of Helen Dryden, Georges Lepape, and Erte.

The third area of magazines that collectors cultivate is advertising. Magazine specialists call these people "rippers," after Jack. These are the people who cull vintage magazines for Cream of Wheat ads, Packard, Ford, and Ivory soap ads by artists such as Joseph Clement Coll, Jessie Willcox Smith, Coles Phillips, Maxfield Parrish (he did quite a few Colgate ads) and, of course, the king of ad collecting, Coca-Cola. Ad collectors are as stringent and exacting as author and illustrator collectors. If one page is missing from a magazine, it is returned, regardless of the fact that it does not have their coveted ad on that page.

Most of all, vintage magazines offer a wonderful opportunity for time travel. In the same day you can vicariously experience the San Francisco earthquake, follow the murderous trail of Jack the Ripper, cry for the children of the Donner Party or laugh at the wit of H.L. Mencken and Robert Benchley. You are on the scene in both words and pictures from a "now" point of view. The only thing you need to start your trip is the knowledge of what to collect.

For more information on collectible magazines, see *Antique Trader Vintage Magazines Price Guide* by Richard Russell and Elaine Gross Russell, www.sangraal-books.com.

***Richard Russell and Elaine Gross Russell***

*Appleton's Magazine*, December 1906.................................**$15**

*Atlantic Monthly*, March 1954 ............................................**$5**

*Ballyhoo*, 1932 ............ **$15-$20**

*Black Cat*, November 1895 ...**$50**

*Blue Book*, February 1917 (Edgar Rice Burroughs)....................**$65**

*The Bookman*, Christmas issue 1926................................**$125**

*Boy's Life,* March 1964 ......... **$20**

*Captain Billy's Whiz Bang,* February 1928 (Louise Brooks) ...... **$55**

*Collier's,* June 15, 1907 (Red Riding Hood) ............................ **$30**

*Cosmopolitan,* April 1934 (Ernest Hemingway, Fisher cover) ...... **$75**

*Country Gentleman,* May 1936 ............................................ **$45**

*Esquire,* October 1935.......... **$75**

*Everybody's Magazine,* July 1908 ........................................ **$30**

*Good Housekeeping,* June 1937 ........................................... **$45**

*Harper's Bazaar,* May 1937; unremarkable single issue without the fashion pattern ...................... **$10**

Unremarkable single issue with the fashion pattern ............... **$30**

*Life*, April 28, 1927 (John Held Jr. cover)............................**$45**

*McCall's*, July 1905.............**$25**

*The New Yorker*, Aug. 31, 1946 ..........................................**$75**

*Pictorial Review*, October 1932 ..........................................**$35**

*Popular Science*, June 1937....**$5**

*Puck*, June 12, 1915...........**$15**

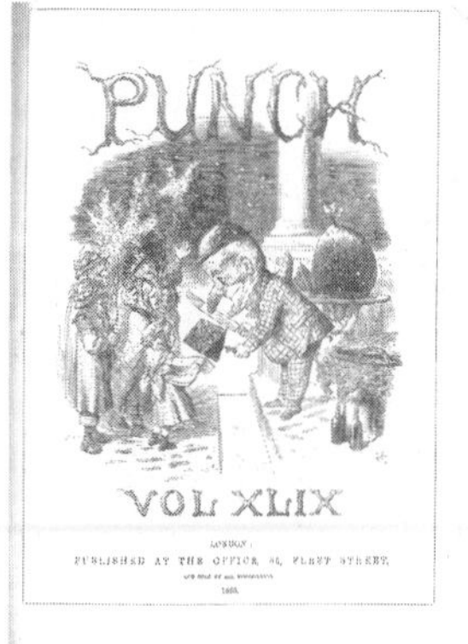


*Punch*, 1865, July-December 1865 (John Tenniel) ...........**$100**

*Radio News*, September 1919**$40**

*Redbook*, March 1933 ..........**$25**

*Saturday Evening Post,* Dec. 23, 1933 (P.G. Wodehouse, Leyendecker cover)........................ **$65**

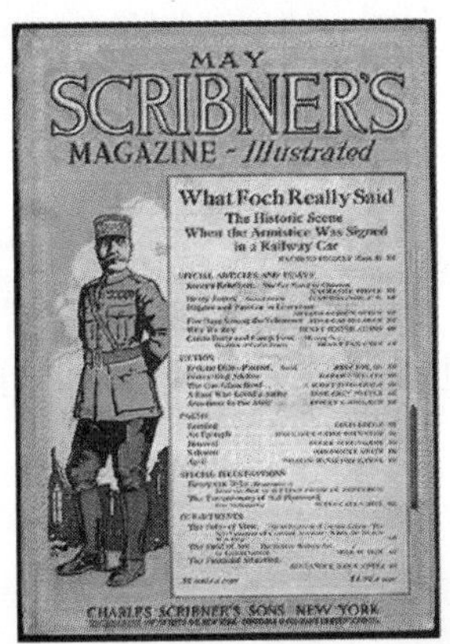


*Scribner's Magazine,* May 1920 .......................................... **$65**

*The Strand Magazine,* September 1904.................................. **$20**

*Vanity Fair,* October 1935 (The Lindberghs) ....... **$45**

*Vogue,* April 1, 1918 (George Plank Peacock cover) ................................................................ **$250**

*Woman's Home Companion,* December 1945 (Steinbeck's "Pearl")................................ **$75**

# Bookends

Once a staple in many homes, bookends serve both functional and decorative purposes. They not only keep a person's books in order, they look good while they're doing it.

Bookends are commonly made of a variety of metals – bronze, brass, pewter, or silver plate – as well as marble, wood, ceramic, and other natural or manmade materials. The art they feature represents many subjects, with wildlife, domesticated animals and pets, sports figures or items, nautical themes, and fantasy themes as favorites.

The value of an antique bookend is determined by its age, the material it is made from, what it represents, the company that created it, and how scarce it is.

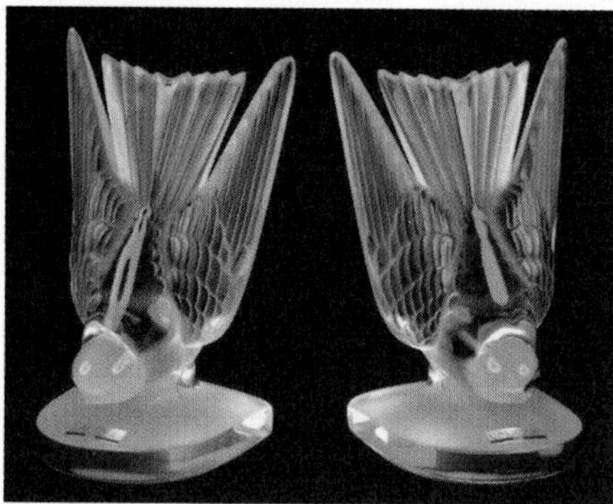

Pair of Lalique frosted glass bird bookends, 6-1/4" h. ........ **$475**
*Susanin's Auctions*

Pair of Jenning Brothers Lincoln bookends, patinated metal, after D. C. French's Lincoln Memorial, marked 2440, felt bottom, 7" h. x 4-3/4" x 4-1/2" ...... **$125**
*Burchard Galleries, Inc.*

Two gilt metal and reticulated hardstone bookends, 6-1/2" h. ........ **$190**
*Michaan's Auctions*

Studio, pair of figured wood bookends with natural edges, each approximately 6" x 5-1/2" x 4-3/4" **$300**
*Rago Arts and Auction Center*

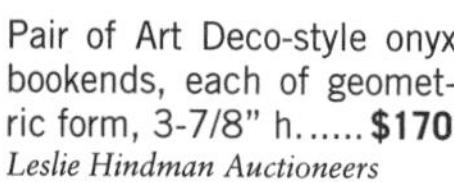

Pair of Art Deco-style onyx bookends, each of geometric form, 3-7/8" h. ...... **$170**
*Leslie Hindman Auctioneers*

Pair of bronze patinated spelter Dante bookends, 6-1/2" x 5-1/2" ... **$55**
*Saucon Valley Auction*

Cold-painted bronze bookends, Continental, each having an Arab rugmaker on an Oriental carpet, unmarked, each 5" h. x 4-3/4" w. ........................................ **$250**
*Cowan's Auctions*

Two pirate on treasure chest bookends, cast iron, 6" h., unmarked................................................ **$60**
*Central Street Antiques and Auction*

Pair of patinated metal bookends, Lincoln, J 2440, 7-1/4" t........................................................ **$60**
*Depew Auction Gallery*

Fine pair of wood-carved figural bookends, Don Quixote and Sancho Panza, tallest is 11-1/2" h. ......................... **$90**
*Stanton Auctions*

Pair of Ronson bookends, patinated metal with figural tigers on rocks, Ronson label remains on felt base of both, 7" h. x 7-1/2" x 5" .................................... **$100**
*Burchard Galleries, Inc.*

Pair of American bronzed metal bookends in the form of a Native American holding a bow before a teepee raised on a naturalistic base, 7-1/2" h. ........................................................................................ **$170**
*Leslie Hindman Auctioneers*

Two pairs of Rookwood white press molded art pottery bookends, elephant and dog motifs, 1926-1928, marks: RP, XXVI; XXVIII, 4-7/8" h. (dog), original Rookwood labels on elephants..... **$594**
*Heritage Auction Galleries*

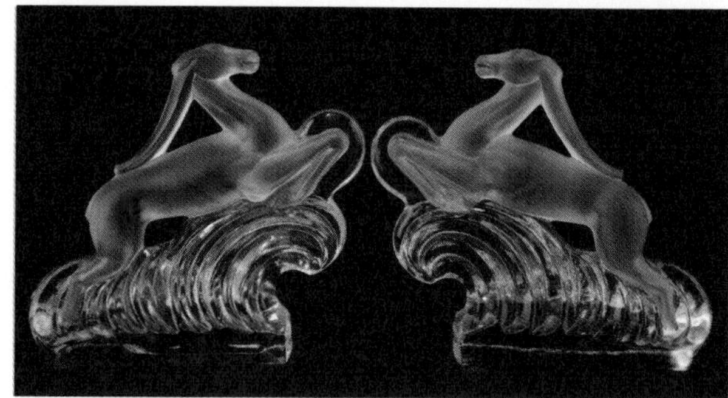

Pair of Steuben Art Deco clear and frosted glass gazelle bookends, circa 1930, engraved Steuben, 7-1/2" l. ............................ **$717**
*Heritage Auction Galleries*

Two pairs of bookends, 1970s, first in the form of Doric columns, metal, front of each reads "Associate / University of Southern California"; second in form of Lincoln Memorial, metal and brass, stamped on the back JB 2440 / D.C. French, 7" x 6" x 3" and 7" x 5" x 4" ........................................................................ **$1,315**
*Heritage Auction Galleries*

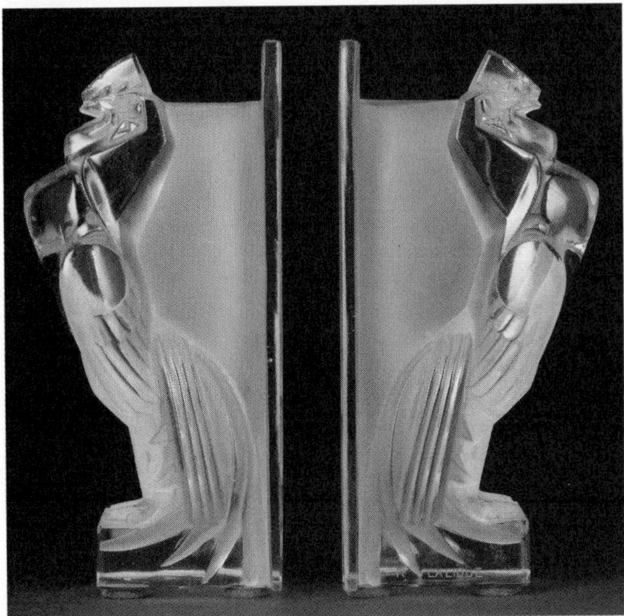

Pair of Lalique clear and frosted glass Coq Houdan bookends, circa 1929, engraved R. Lalique, France, 7-1/2" h. ..................................**$8,963**
*Heritage Auction Galleries*

Pair of Rookwood pottery geisha bookends, geisha wears light blue gown and purple head gear and sits against a wall with arms and legs crossed, marked on underside with Rookwood flame mark dated 1924, one bookend retains remnants of paper Rookwood label, 7-1/2" h............................................... **$345**
*James D. Julia, Inc.*

Rookwood pottery owl bookends in a shaded brown glaze, marked on underside with Rookwood flame mark dated 1946, 5-3/4" t............................ **$143**
*James D. Julia, Inc.*

▼Pair of Rookwood pottery rook bookends, 5-3/8" h. ................................................................... **$213**
*Pook & Pook, Inc.*

BOTTLES

# Bottles

Interest in bottle collecting, and high interest in extremely rare bottles, continues to grow, with new bottle clubs forming throughout the United States and Europe. More collectors are spending their free time digging through old dumps and foraging through ghost towns, digging out old outhouses (that's right), exploring abandoned mine shafts, and searching their favorite bottle or antique shows, swap meets, flea markets, and garage sales. In addition, the Internet has greatly expanded, offering collectors numerous opportunities and resources to buy and sell bottles with many new auction websites, without even leaving the house. Many bottle clubs now have websites providing even more information for the collector. These new technologies and resources have helped bottle collecting to continue to grow and gain interest.

Most collectors, however, still look beyond the type and value of a bottle to its origin and history. Researching the history of a bottle is almost as interesting as finding the bottle itself.

"The knowledge and experience of collectors in the hobby today is at a record pace," according to Jeff Wichmann, president of American Bottle Auctions. "It has not only brought a keener appreciation for the hobby, but apparently a bag full of money with it. Prices for the best of the best [have] never been greater, and as we continue to gain more experienced collectors, I see no limit in sight. It's still a very affordable hobby to pursue, but if the Tiffany of antique bottles is what you're looking for, you'd be advised to bring your checkbook and have a load of cash to cover it.

"It's not the addition of new offerings to the market as much as the limited availability of pieces that fit into that world of the very best," Wichmann said. "When a piece comes up, unlike even five years ago, it's now every [person] for himself. There has always been the average example and there always will be, but it's the one-known bitters or odd-colored historical flask that is finally getting its due respect."

For more information on bottles, see *Antique Trader Bottles: Identification & Price Guide*, 7th edition, by Mike Polak.

Doctor Fisch's Bitters – W.H. Ware – Patented 1866, golden amber, figural fish, 11-1/2", smooth base, applied top, 1866-1875.... **$250-$300**

## Bottle Resources

- *Bottles & Extras Magazine*, the official publication of the Federation of Historical Bottle Collectors, 816-318-0160
- *Antique Bottle & Glass Collector*, Jim Hagenbuch, editor, 215-679-5849
- Norman C. Heckler & Co., 79 Bradford Corner Rd., Woodstock Valley, CT 06282, 860-974-1634, www.hecklerauction.com
- Glass Works Auctions, PO Box 187, East Greenville, PA 18041, 215-679-5849 glswrk@enter.net
- American Bottle Auctions, 2523 J St., Suite 203, Sacramento, CA 95816, 800-806-7722, www.americanbottle.com
- International Perfume Bottle Association, www.perfumebottles.org, IPBA_membership@verizon.net
- Colonial Williamsburg's DeWitt Wallace Decorative Arts Museum, Williamsburg, Va., 800-447-8679

# Flasks Set World Records at Auction

It had been more than a decade since a record price was set for a collectible bottle, and then, within a few months of each other, two new record prices were set in 2010.

A bottle referred to as the "Firecracker flask," because the names John Adams and Thomas Jefferson were embossed on the medial ridge, set a world record for the highest selling bottle at auction in March 2010 when it sold for $100,620. In addition to Adams' and Jefferson's names, the light blue bottle also featured the date they both died: July 4, 1826. This example, manufactured by Kensington Glass Works, Philadelphia (1820-1840), is one of the few known in blue and is in excellent condition. The bottle was sold by Heckler Auctions of Woodstock, Conn.

But that record was smashed in October 2010, when a new world record of $176,670 was set for a General Jackson and Bust – J.R./Laird. S.C. Pitt. and Eagle Portrait flask, also sold by Heckler Auctions. The yellow green flask, manufactured by John Robinson Manufacturers of Pittsburgh, Pa. (1820-1840), was described as "extremely rare mold in an extremely rare color, perhaps unique. Particularly strong embossing."

The previous record, set in 1999, was $68,750 for a Bryant's cone-shaped bitters bottle sold by American Bottle Auctions of Sacramento, Calif.

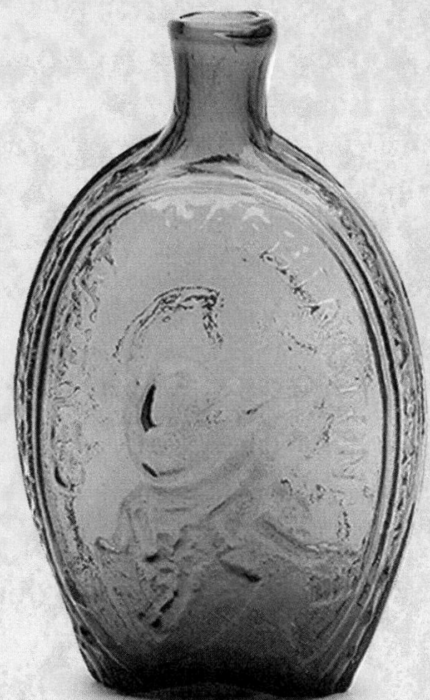

This "Firecracker flask" set a record when it sold for $101,620 at auction in March 2010. The record was subsequently broken by another flask, selling for $176,670 in October 2010.
*Heckler Auctions*

## BITTERS

Suffolk Bitters – Philbrook & Tucker – Boston, light golden yellow amber, 10-1/8", figural pig, smooth base, applied tapered collar top, 1865-1875 ... **$800-$900**

William Allen's Congress Bitters, deep blue aqua, 10-1/4", semi-cabin shape, smooth base, applied tapered collar top, 1865-1875......................... **$200-$225**

Brown's Celebrated Indian Herb Bitters – Patented – Feb 11 – 1868, clear glass with amethyst tone, 12-1/8", Indian queen, smooth base, sheared and ground lip, 1868-1875.............. **$20,000**

Kelly's Old Cabin Bitters – Patented 1863 – Kelly's Old Cabin Bitters – Patented 1863, amber, 9-1/4", log cabin shape, smooth base, applied top, 1863-1870 ........................... **$1,000-$1,100**

## BLACK GLASS

Black glass presentation stippled wine bottle, "A Present – From – George Aitken – to George Cairns – of Arme Cairns Aitken (thistle alongside a coat-of-arms) – 'Efflo Eseo' (large cornucopia)," dark olive amber, 10-1/4", Scotland 1835-1860 ......**$550-$600**

Black glass onion shape wine bottle, medium olive green, 6-7/8" x 5-1/2" dia., Dutch 1720-1750 ........ **$250-$300**

►Black glass triangular wine bottle (Masonic seal), deep olive amber, 9-3/8", Scotland 1845-1860, very rare ..................... **$2,300-$2,500**

Black glass mallet shape wine bottle, dark olive green, squat shape, 8-1/8", American 1790-1810 ................ **$225-$250**

## FIRE GRENADES

Fire grenade, "Barnum's Hand Fire – Ext. Diamond Pat.d – June 26th – 1869 – Diamond," 6-1/8", rough sheared lip, American 1870-1895..........**$100-$125**

Fire grenade, "Rockford –Kalamazoo – Automatic And – Hand Fire Extinguisher – Patent applied For," cobalt blue, 11", tooled lip, American 1875-1895 ........................................................**$500-$600**

Fire grenade, "Hayward's Hand Fire Grenade – S.F. Hayward – 407 Broadway – N.Y. – Patented Aug. – 8 –1871," medium lime green, 6-1/8", sheared and tooled lip, American 1872-1895............**$200-$250**

Fire grenade, "Hazelton's High Pressure Chemical Fire Keg," amber, 11", tooled lip, original metal neck band and swing handle, American 1875-1896 ..........................................................**$450-$500**

## FLASKS

Label under glass whiskey flask, image of Victorian woman, clear glass, 5-1/4", screw top lid, American 1895-1920 ........................................ **$350-$400**

Label under glass whiskey flask, image of Otto Wallin, Waukegan, Ill. with son, clear glass, 5-1/4", screw top lid, American 1895-1920 ...................... **$275-$300**

The Peerless – A. Fuhrberg - Prop – Anaheim, Calif., clear glass, pint, tooled top, American 1890-1915 ........................................................... **$250-$350**

Pumpkin seed flask and leather bag, "Hand Made Sour Mash – 7 Years Old," clear glass, 4-5/8", tooled top, American 1890-1910 ..................... **$125-$150**

## FOOD & PICKLE

Two Heinz sample jugs, "Heinz Tomato Chutney," 3"; "Prepared Mustard," 3", 1885-1920 ........................................................ **$75-$100**

◀Maple Sap & Boiled Cider – Vinegar – The CI Co LTD. – East Ridge NH., deep cobalt blue, quart, tooled top, American 1890-1910 .................................................................................. **$300-$350**

Willington cathedral pickle jar, deep blue aqua, 8-5/8", open pontil, rolled lip, American 1840-1860..................... **$2,100-2,300**

Three Heinz food bottles, 1885-1920, "Heinz's Keystone Chow Chow," 7-1/4" ................................................................................ **$200-$240**
"Heinz's Pickles," 11-1/4" ................................................. **$200-$240**
"Heinz's Cauliflower – Pickle," ........................................... **$200-$240**

## HAWAIIAN BOTTLES

**Left:** Hollister Drug Co. Ld – Honolulu, mid-1890s.........**$150-$200**

**Far left:** Rycroft – Arctic Soda Co., Ltd. – Rycroft's Old Fashioned Ginger Beer – Honolulu, T.H., 1917 .................................**$175-$300**

Hawaiian Rose Dairy – Wahiawa – Phone 2 Blue 329, 1930 .........................**$250-$300**

Consolidated Soda Water – Works Co. – Honolulu. H., 1895 ................................**$200-$300**

Siphon Co. LTD. – Honolulu, T. H. – Contents 35 Fl. Oz., 1935 ........................... **$1,800-$2,500**

## INK

Cone ink, deep olive green, 2-3/8", open pontil, tooled lip, American 1840-1860............ **$500-$550**

Inkwell, medium green, 2-1/2", American 1840-1860................................................ **$175-$200**

## PATTERN-MOLDED

Midwestern club bottle, blue aqua, 8-1/8", 36-broken-rib pattern swirled to right, American 1815-1835 .............. **$125-$150**

Midwestern pattern molded flask, medium yellow green, 6", 24-vertical rib pattern, American 1815-1835...... **$1,000-$1,100**

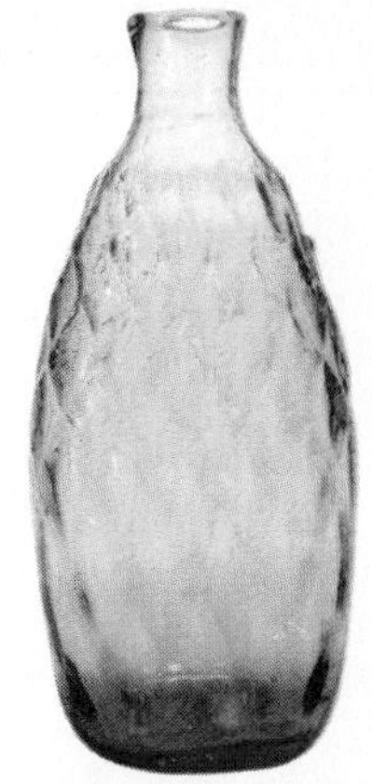

Fourteen-diamond pattern flask, pale blue green, 6-1/8", American 1815-1835............ **$250-$350**

**Right:** Rib pattern chestnut flask, medium amethyst, 5-7/8", 14-vertical rib pattern, European 1810-1830 .............. **$450-$500**

**Far right:** Pattern molded pocket flask, medium amethyst with overall diamond pattern, 5-3/8", American 1940s (possibly made by Emil Larson at Clevenger Brothers) ................................ **$200-$225**

## SODA

F & L Schaum – Baltimore – Glass Works, deep olive green, 7-1/4", American 1840-1860 ................................**$450-$475**

Geo. W. Hoffman – Allentown – PA, medium blue green, 7-1/8", American 1855-1865...**$90-$100**

J. Rother, black amethyst, 9", 10-pin shape, American 1855-1865 ............................**$6,500-$7,000**

M. Richardson – Lockport, blue aqua, 7-1/4", American 1840-1860..........................**$450-$500**

Keller & Velten – Louisville, KY., light green, 7-1/8", 10-sided, American 1860-1870.**$400-$500**

# Boxes

Boxes come in all shapes, sizes, and degree of antiquity—good news for the collector seeking a lifelong passion. Once early mankind reached the point where accumulation began, the next step was the introduction of containers designed especially to preserve those treasures.

Boxes have been created from every source material imaginable: wood, stone, precious metals, papier maché, porcelain, horn, and even shell. Among the most collectable:

**Snuff boxes.** These small, lidded boxes first came to favor in the 1700s. Although originally intended as "for use" items, snuff boxes are now prized for the elegant miniatures often painted on both the box exterior and interior.

**Pillboxes.** Like the snuffbox, these tiny boxes were as much in demand for their design as for their usefulness. Among the most desirable are 18th century pillboxes with enameled or repoussé (metal relief) decoration.

**Match safes.** In the days before safety matches, metal boxes with a striker on the base kept matches from inadvertently bursting into flame. Match safe material ranged from base metal to sterling silver. Although flat, hinged safes were the most common, novelty shapes, such as animal heads, also proved popular.

**Lacquered boxes.** Often classified as "Oriental" due to the 19th century fondness for decorating them with Asian motifs, lacquered boxes are actually found in almost every culture. Ranging anywhere from trinket- to trunk-sized, the common denominator is a highly polished, lacquered surface.

**Folk art boxes.** The diversity of available folk art boxes accounts for their modern collectability. Folk art boxes were often the work of untrained artisans, created solely for their own needs from materials readily at hand. Among the many choices: wallpaper boxes, decoupage boxes, and "tramp art" boxes. Fueled by the imagination and ingenuity of their makers, the selection is both fascinating and limitless.

Bird's-eye maple apple box, America, first half 19th c., square dovetailed box with canted sides joined by a flat bottom, old refinish, 3-1/2" h. x 8-1/4" w. x 8-1/4" d. .................................................. **$948**
*Skinner, Inc.*

Blue pictorial-printed covered bandbox, America, c. 1835, oblong form with sailing ship on cover and inscription "Prosperity to Our Commerce and Our Manufacturers," village scene depicted around sides, printed in blue, green, brown, and white varnishes, 12-1/2" .................................................. **$563**
*Skinner, Inc.*

◄Bittersweet-painted pine slide-lid trinket box, New England, last half 19th c., lid opens to a nail-constructed box, old painted surface, 3-1/4" h. x 6-1/2" w. x 4" d. .................................................. **$711**
*Skinner, Inc.*

"Circus" broadside-covered band box, America, early 19th c., oblong box with polychrome printed circus figures around sides, cover and interior, interior sides with large printed inscriptions "CIRCUS/RIVERS, DERIOUS & CO's," 9-1/2" h. x 11-1/2" w. x 14" l. .......................................... **$889**
*Skinner, Inc.*

Emile Galle faience smiling cat box and cover, yellow and blue figural with glass eyes, circa 1890, marks: G. R. (painted), 13-1/2" h........................... **$2,031**

Green-painted four-finger lap-seam box, America, 19th c., pine top and bottom and maple bentwood sides, slightly beveled fingers secured with copper tacks, box painted under cover rim and on bottom, 4-5/8" h., 12-1/4" dia.................................. **$770**
*Skinner, Inc.*

Franz Xavier Bergman cold-painted bronze box, pillow-form with two cats and three mice, Vienna, Austria, circa 1900, marks: (amphora-B), 5" l.... **$3,107**

Compass-decorated, polychrome-painted covered round storage box, possibly northern Europe, 19th c., lapped-seam box with laced splints joining nine fingers, cover painted red and centered with a large polychrome medallion, bottom painted black, 4-7/8" h., 14-1/2" dia............................................ **$593**
*Skinner, Inc.*

Continental enamel and 18k gold snuff box with blue and white scrolled enamel decoration to body and hinged lid, maker unknown, probably France, circa 1875, unmarked, 3-7/8" l., 4.1 oz.............. **$6,875**

Handmade marquetry music box, made by Sorrento of Italy, pl ays "Somewhere Out There," 6" sq., 3" h. ............................................................. **$310**

1920s Jack Norworth cigar box, lyricist of "Take Me Out to the Ball Game," baseball's greatest song, smiles from multiple images affixed to antique wooden box................................................ **$537**

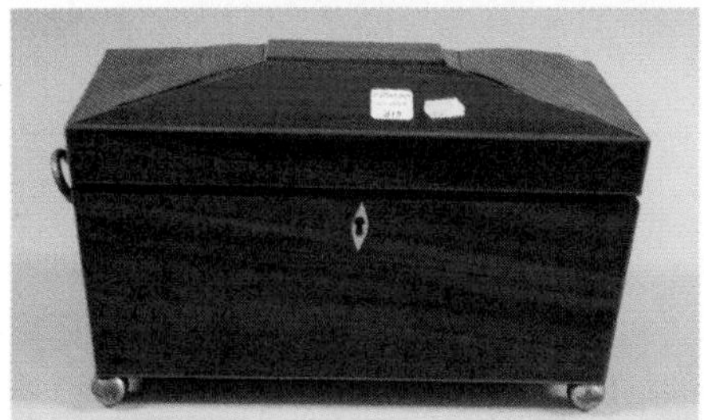

◀Mahogany veneer box-form tea caddy with brass ring handles and inlaid ivory escutcheon, raised on four ball feet, two interior compartments, 6-1/2" h. x 12" l. x 6" d. .............................................. **$237**
*Skinner, Inc.*

John Quincy Adams colorful patch box, produced in France for export to America, glass, pasteboard and embossed paper foil, hand-colored portrait under glass of "John Q. Adams" on cover of "book," back cover inscribed "Forget Me Not." ................ **$1,434**

◀Hand-painted Limoges box in the form of a leek, painted with bronze finished bow at hinge, marked "Limoges France/Paint Main P.V.," 6-1/4" l........ **$79**

Polychrome-painted carved pine box, America, 19th c., rectangular box with hinged lid decorated with relief-carved rosettes, geometric designs and borders, mustard, red, and black with black borders, 6-1/2" h. x 8-1/4" w. x 17" l. .................................... **$4,148**
*Skinner, Inc.*

Early red-painted pine box, probably New England, late 17th c., rosehead nail constructed box with pintle-hinged lid with molded and shaped edges, 3-3/4" h. x 6-3/8" w. x 4-1/2" d............................. **$2,015**
*Skinner, Inc.*

Red-painted pine slide-lid trinket box, New England, early 19th c., chamfered lid with carved finger-hold on dovetailed box with molded top edge and applied base molding, old surface, 3-1/4" h. x 5-1/2" w. x 4-1/2" d. ...................................................... **$948**
*Skinner, Inc.*

Tramp art-style document box, circa early 1900s, deep layering and carved feet, rows of carved layers all intact, 5" h. x 11" w. x 8-1/2" d. ............... **$281**

Polychrome-painted bride's box, northern Europe, late 19th c., oblong covered lapped-seam box, top painted with a gentleman hunter shooting a stag with a verse inscribed above the scene, sides decorated with floral borders, 7-1/2" h. x 13" w. x 19-1/2" l. .......... **$415**
*Skinner, Inc.*

Red-painted pine knife box, probably New England, early 19th c., canted sides on rectangular box with shaped divider with cut-out handle, 8-1/4" h. x 7-1/4" w. x 15" l........................................... **$356**
*Skinner, Inc.*

Three round painted lap-seam pantry boxes, America, 19th c., two larger boxes painted blue, one with the name "J. Burr" impressed on bottom, smallest painted green with faint penciled inscriptions on inside of lid, "Angie F------ ---- Maine" in period script, 2-5/8"-5-1/4" h., 6-1/2"-9-1/2" dia. ......................... **$504**
*Skinner, Inc.*

Tramp art-style pedestal box decorated with chip-carved accents resulting in 11 pyramids, ex. Wallach Collection, 6-3/4" h. x 11" w. x 7-1/2" d......... **$177**

# Ceramics

## Marc Bellaire

Born in Toledo in 1925, Marc Bellaire (Donald Fleischman) studied at the Chicago Academy of Art and Chicago Art Institute before moving to California in 1950 and beginning his association with early employer Sascha Brastoff.

The object shapes and placement of decoration on many Bellaire pieces show the Brastoff influence. A curved-edge central image is often the focal point of a design, echoing the curved edges of the object itself—whether ashtray, bowl, or rounded platter. Bold, contrasting color combinations were favored by both, as were metallic color accents. Themes, however, show a much greater variance: Brastoff's images are often romanticized and ethereal. Bellaire's fierce "Jungle Dancers," slyly smiling "Cotillion" women, and blank-faced "Mardi Gras" celebrants are darker, more knowing, and more exotic.

In the early 1950s, Bellaire branched out on his own, opening the Marc Bellaire Ceramics Studio in Culver City, California. While he produced artware in the Brastoff vein—platters, planters, and the like—the stylistic touch became distinctively Bellaire. Brastoff's figures, though often whimsical, generally retain normal proportions. Bellaire's, with arms and legs of exaggerated length, and bizarre or rudimentary features, at times resemble aliens or stick figures.

The effect is even more pronounced and startling in the three-dimensional figurines Bellaire produced to accompany such lines as "Mardi Gras" and "Jamaica." Here, the relationship to reality is intriguingly tenuous. While the images are clear, their details are minimal: the featureless "Mardi Gras" dancer's carnival mask or the ballooning sleeves and floppy straw hats of the "Jamaica" musicians. Bellaire's ease with the other-worldly came in particularly handy for his additional, large-scale design assignments in Hollywood, Las Vegas, and Disneyland.

Although not as universally recognized as the heavily promoted Brastoff, Bellaire's design influence was equally long-lasting. In fact, many amateur ceramists of the 1950s and 1960s owe their entire technique to Bellaire. After achieving his own success, he wrote numerous "how-to" articles for *Popular Ceramics*, allowing the general public to try its hand at bowls, vases, and other vessels featuring his characteristic elongated figures and colorful glazes.

Bellaire's later designs, until his death in 1994, focused on pots and vases in the Southwestern style, with little reference to his earlier work. His pieces can be identified by a full or partial signature on the object surface or reverse.

Heralded by *Giftware* magazine as one of the top 10 artware designers of the 1950s, Bellaire's work reflects the message he conveyed to budding craftsmen: "Creative expression must bring joy to its creator; without it, the work itself lacks joy."

MB 16: (left): "Balinese" double server with handle, 9" l. ....... **$125-$150**
(right): "Balinese" candleholders, 7-3/4" h. ....... **$250-$275/pr.**

MB 9: (left): "Beachcomber" ashtray, triangular, 11-3/4" l. ................................**$125-$150**
(right): "Beachcomber" shallow dish, 17-3/4" l. ..........**$225-$250**

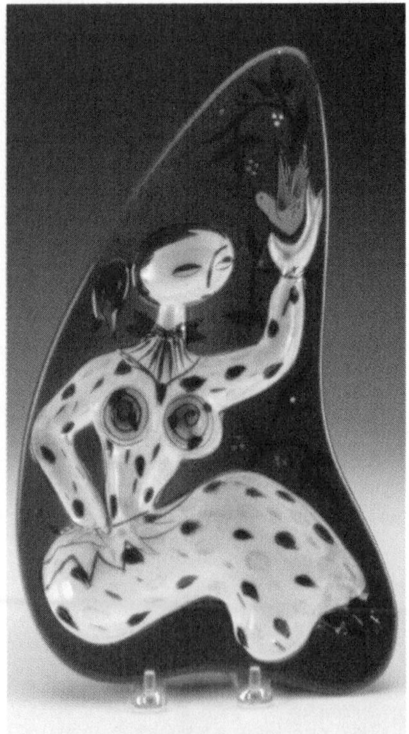

MB 11: "Grecian Woman" oversize vase, 11" h. ........................................................**$275-$300**

◀ MB 12: "Cotillion" freeform platter, lady holding bird, 12" l. ....................................................**$175-$200**

MB 20: (left): "Green Bird" bowl, 6-1/2 dia. **$50-$75** (right): "Green Bird" vase, 7-1/4" h......... **$175-$200**

MB 7: "Jamaica" musicians, tallest figure, 9" ...... **$625-$675 ea.**

"Birdcage" lamp for Rembrandt, 13-1/2" h. ............................................... **$500-$600**

"Bird Isle" boomerang-shaped covered dish, 11-1/2" l................................ **$175-$200**

"Jungle Dancer" platter, 18" l. ...... **$300-$325**

"Oriental" single-fold ashtray, 9-1/2" l. ................................................ **$75-$100**

"Oriental" vase, 15-3/4" h. ........... **$250-$275**

"Park Avenue Primitive" oblong dish, 15" l. ............................................... **$225-$250**

"Pastorale" ashtray, 14-1/2" l........ **$125-$150**

"Polynesian Star" square bottle vase, 7-1/2" h. ............................................... **$150-$175**

"Root Heads" triangular dish, 15-1/2" l. ............................................... **$250-$275**

◀MB 5: (left): "Mardi Gras" figure, standing, 11-1/4" h. ................................ **$400-$425** (right): "Mardi Gras" pillow vase, 7-1/4" h. ................................................ **$275-$300**

# Belleek

The name Belleek refers to an industrious village in County Fermanagh, Northern Ireland, on the banks of the River Erne, and to the lustrous porcelain wares produced there.

In 1849, John Caldwell Bloomfield inherited a large estate near Belleek. Interested in ceramics, and having discovered rich deposits of feldspar and kaolin (china clay) on his lands, he soon envisioned a pottery that would make use of these materials, local craftspeople and water power of the River Erne. He was also anxious to enhance Ireland's prestige with superior porcelain products.

Bloomfield had a chance meeting with Robert Williams Armstrong who had established a substantial architectural business building potteries. Keenly interested in the manufacturing process, he agreed to design, build, and manage the new factory for Bloomfield. The factory was to be located on Rose Isle on a bend in the River Erne.

Bloomfield and Armstrong then approached David McBirney, a highly successful merchant and director of railway companies, and enticed him to provide financing. Impressed by the plans, he agreed to raise funds for the enterprise. As agreed, the factory was named McBirney and Armstrong, then later D. McBirney and Company.

Although 1857 is given as the founding date of the pottery, it is recorded that the pottery's foundation stone was laid by Mrs. J.C. Bloomfield on Nov. 18, 1858. Although not completed until 1860, the pottery was producing earthenware from its inception.

With the arrival of ceramic experts from the (William Henry) Goss Pottery in England, principally William Bromley, Sr. and William Wood Gallimore, Parian ware was perfected and, by 1863, the wares we associate with Belleek today were in production.

With Belleek Pottery workers and others emigrating to the United States in the late 1800s and early 1900s, Belleek-style china manufacture, known as American Belleek, commenced at several American firms, including Ceramic Art Company, Colombian Art Pottery, Lenox Inc., Ott & Brewer, and Willets Manufacturing Co.

Throughout its Parian production, Belleek Pottery marked its items with an Irish harp and wolfhound and the Devenish Tower. The 1st Period mark of 1863 through 1890 is shown below. Its 2nd Period began with the advent of the McKinley Tariff Act of 1891 and the (revised) British Merchandise Act as Belleek added the ribbon "Co. FERMANAGH IRELAND" beneath its mark in 1891. Both the 1st and 2nd period marks were black, although they occasionally appeared in burnt orange, green, blue or brown, especially on earthenware items. Its 3rd Period begin in 1926, when it added a Celtic emblem under the 2nd Period mark as well as the government trademark "Reg No 0857," which was granted in 1884. The Celtic emblem was registered by the Irish Industrial Development Association in 1906 and reads "Deanta in Eirinn," and means "Made in Ireland." The pottery is now utilizing its 13th mark, following a succession of three black marks, three green marks, a gold mark, two blue marks and three green. The final green mark was used only a single year, in 2007, to commemorate its 150th anniversary. In 2008, Belleek changed its mark to brown. Early earthenware was often marked in the same color as the majority of its surface decoration. Early basketware has Parian strips applied to its base with the impressed verbiage "BELLEEK" and later on, additionally "Co FERMANAGH" with or without "IRELAND." Current basketware carries the same mark as its Parian counterpart.

The item identification scheme is that followed within the works by Richard K. Degenhardt: *Belleek The Complete Collector's Guide and Illustrated Reference* (both first and second edition). Additional information, as well as a thorough discussion of the early marks, is located in these works as well as on the Internet at Del E. Domke's Web site: http://home.comcast.net/~belleek_website.

The prices given are for items in excellent condition, i.e., no chips, cracks, crazing or repairs. On flowered items, however, minimal chips to the flowering are acceptable, to the extent of the purchaser's tolerance. Earthenware items often exhibit varying degrees of crazing due to the primitive bottle kilns originally utilized at the pottery.

*All Irish Belleek photographs used with permission, Rod Kearns, photographer.*

## AMERICAN BELLEEK

### *Marks:*

American Art China Works - R&E, 1891-95
AAC (superimposed), 1891-95
American Belleek Company - Company name, banner & globe
Ceramic Art Company - CAC palette, 1889-1906
Colombian Art Pottery - CAP, 1893-1902
Cook Pottery - Three feathers w/"CHC," 1894-1904
Coxon Belleek Pottery - "Coxon Belleek" in a shield, 1926-1930
Gordon Belleek - "Gordon Belleek," 1920-28
Knowles, Taylor & Knowles - "Lotusware" in a circle w/a crown, 1891-96
Lenox China - Palette mark, 1906-1924
Ott & Brewer - crown & shield, 1883-1893
Perlee - "P" in a wreath, 1925-1930
Willets Manufacturing Company - Serpent mark, 1880-1909
Cook Pottery - Three feathers w/"CHC"

### *Plates and Platters*

Ceramic Art Company plate, hand-painted in the center with a bust portrait of a young maiden holding a closed book and a stylus, wearing a white wrap on her head, a white gown and red shawl, wide claret border band decorated with an ornate gilt swag band with foliate scrolls and flower garlands, gilt rim band, artist-signed, ca. 1905, 10-1/2" dia. .................................. **$2,880**

## IRISH BELLEEK

### *Comports & Centerpieces*

Comport, Trihorse Comport, impressed "Belleek Co. Fermanagh," D37-I ........ **$3,400**

### *Figurines*

Boy and Shell, 9" h., D9-II .. **$3,000**

### *Tea Ware - Museum Display Patterns (Artichoke, Chinese, Finner, Five O'Clock, Lace, Ring Handle Ivory, Set #36 & Victoria)*

Muffin dish, cov., Artichoke Tea Ware, gilt trim, D720-I ........ **$2,000**

Plate, Ring Handle Ivory Ware plate, hand-painted Irish scene, unsigned but from the School of Eugene Sheerin, 7-1/2" dia., D823-II ........ **$1,800**

◀Tray, Lace Tea Ware, gilt decoration, designed as a wall hanging with pierced hanging holes at the top, 13" dia., D803-IV ........ **$4,800**

## *Tea Ware - Rare Patterns (Aberdeen, Blarney, Celtic [low & tall], Cone, Erne, Fan, Institute, Ivy, Lily [high & low], Scroll, Sydney, Thistle & Thorn)*

Celtic Candlestick, Low, painted and gilt, 4-3/4" h., D1511-VI ........................................ **$340**

Celtic Design creamer, Celtic Design tea ware, tall shape, multicolored, ("mystery" mark, 1st Period over Celtic Scroll, probably a transition from 1st to 2nd period), 4-1/2" h., D1442-II ........... **$400**

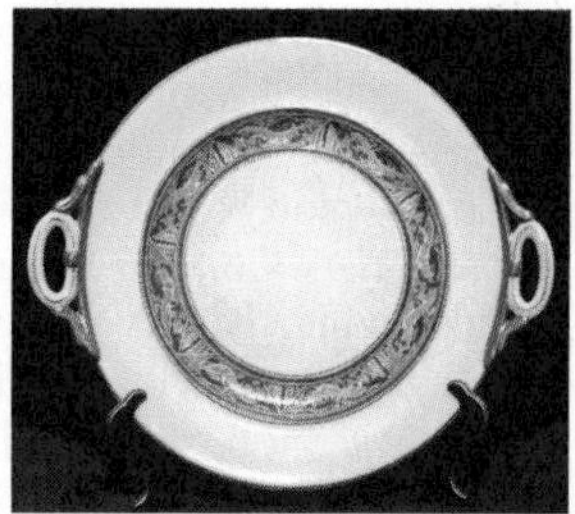

Celtic Design bread plate, Celtic Design tea ware, multicolored and gilt, D1425-III .................. **$600**

## *Tea Wares - Miscellaneous*

Celtic bowl of roses, hand-painted colors of dark pink, yellow, and green, D1510-VII....................... **$2,600**

Plate, pottery, Scenic Celtic Commemorative Plate, painted and gilded, D1553-V......................... **$800**

**Far left:** Plate, scenic center of Irish peasant homes with gilt scroll border, painted by former pottery manager Cyril Arnold, artist signed with "15 PA" following the signature, 8-1/2" dia., D1527-IV ......................... **$1,200**

**Left:** Wedding cup, three-handled, Shamrock pattern, hand-painted trim, D2105-II .......................... **$640**

# Bennington

Bennington wares, which ranged from stoneware to parian and porcelain, were made in Bennington, Vermont, primarily in two potteries, one in which Captain John Norton and his descendants were principals, and the other in which Christopher Webber Fenton (also once associated with the Nortons) was a principal. Various marks are found on the wares made in the two major potteries, including J. & E. Norton, E. & L. P. Norton, L. Norton & Co., Norton & Fenton, Edward Norton, Lyman Fenton & Co., Fenton's Works, United States Pottery Co., U.S.P. and others.

The popular pottery with the mottled brown on yellowware glaze was also produced in Bennington, but such wares should be referred to as "Rockingham" or "Bennington-type" unless they can be specifically attributed to a Bennington, Vermont factory.

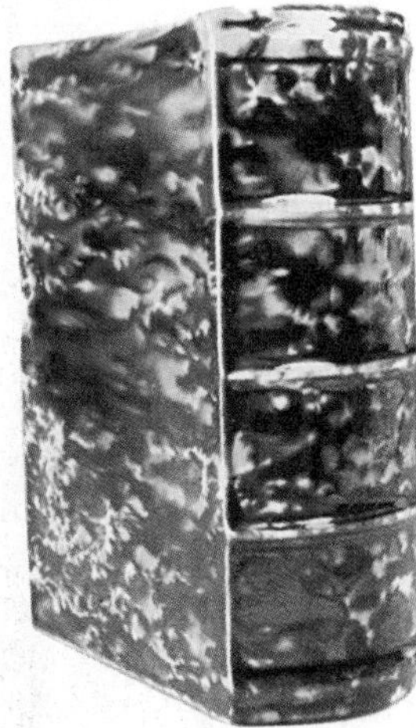

Book flask, binding marked "Departed Spirits G," Flint Enamel glaze, 5-1/2" h. ................. **$532**

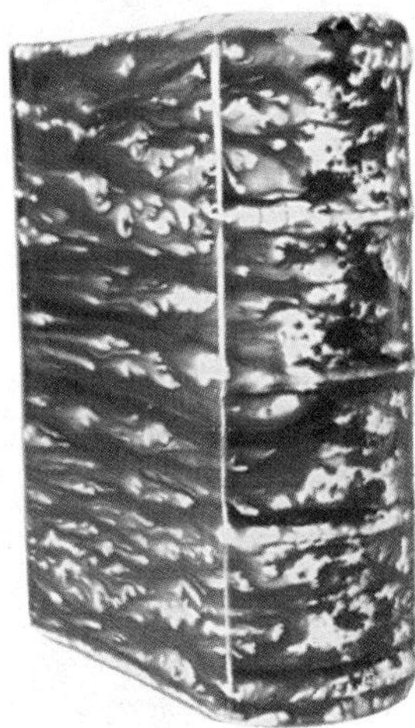

Book flask, noting lettering on binding, mottled brown and cream Rockingham glaze, 5-3/4" h. ........................................**$392**

Toby pitcher, figural seated Mr. Toby, dark brown mottled Rockingham glaze, unmarked, 6" h. ........................................ **$259**

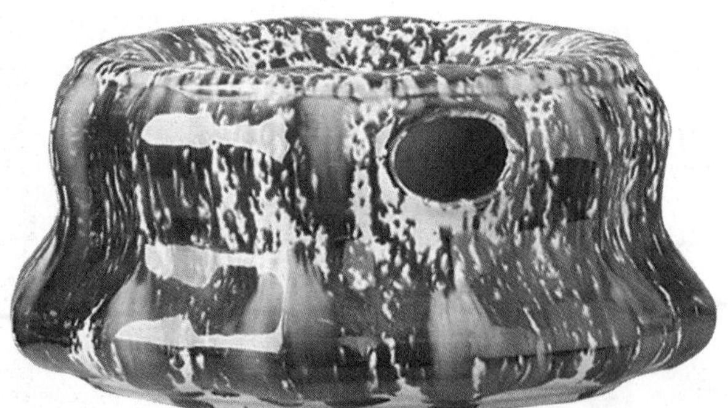

Cuspidor, short round waisted shape with side hole, Flint Enamel glaze, Type A impress mark on base, mid-19th c., 8" dia., 3-3/4" h. ...... **$144**

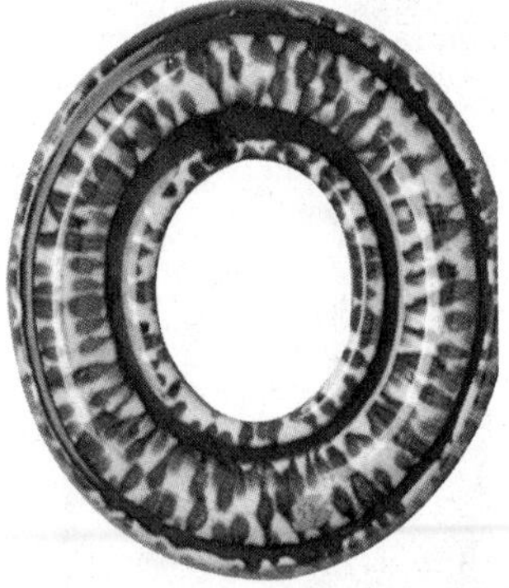

Picture frame, oval with wide ringed rounded sides, overall mottled Rockingham glaze, few underside flakes, mid-19th c., 8-3/4 x 9-3/4" ........................................ **$489**

# Delft

In the early 17th century, Italian potters settled in Holland and began producing tin-glazed earthenwares, often decorated with pseudo-Oriental designs based on Chinese porcelain wares. The city of Delft became the center of this pottery production and several firms produced the wares throughout the 17th and early 18th century. A majority of the pieces featured blue on white designs, but polychrome wares were also made. The Dutch Delftwares were also shipped to England, where eventually the English copied them at potteries in such cities as Bristol, Lambeth and Liverpool. Although still produced today, Delft peaked in popularity by the mid-18th century.

Bowl, scalloped rim on low lobed body, hand-painted with blue stylized flowers on a powder blue ground, England, mid-18th c., minor rim chips and glaze wear, 8-5/8" dia., 2" h. .................................. **$470**

Charger, round shallow dished form with narrow flanged rim, center with large rounded panel-sided reserve painted with leafy scrolls around center with stylized leafy blossom, border band decorated with small oval reserves decorated with scrolls, squiggles, blue initial or X under the bottom, Holland, 18th c., 13-3/4" dia. ................................................ **$460**

Plate, shallow dished form with wide flanged rim, the center h.p. in dark blue with large urn filled with fruit, fanned, feathery leaves, flowers, the border painted in dark blue with half-leaves alternating with squiggle bands, Holland, 18th c., tight hairline from rim nearly to center, 8-3/4" dia. .................................. **$230**

Tile, rectangular, decorated in blue and white with seaside scene of women standing on shore and sailing ships heading out to sea, after a painting by Hendrik Willem Mesdag, marked with Delft and other painted and impressed marks, late 19th/early 20th c., 7-7/8" x 10" ................................................ **$500**

# Doulton and Royal Doulton

Doulton & Company, Ltd., was founded in Lambeth, London, in about 1858. It operated there until 1956 and often incorporated the words "Doulton" and "Lambeth" in its marks. Pinder, Bourne & Company Burslem was purchased by the Doultons in 1878 and in 1882 became Doulton & Company Ltd. It added porcelain to its earthenware production in 1884. The "Royal Doulton" mark has been used since 1902 by this factory, which is still in operation. Character jugs and figurines are commanding great attention from collectors at the present time.

John Doulton, the founder, was born in 1793. He became an apprentice at the age of 12 to a potter in south London. Five years later he was employed in another small pottery near Lambeth. His two sons, John and Henry, subsequently joined their father in 1830 in a partnership he had formed with the name of Doulton & Watts. Watts retired in 1864 and the partnership was dissolved. Henry formed a new company that traded as Doulton and Company.

In the early 1870s the proprietor of the Pinder Bourne Company, located in Burslem, Staffordshire, offered Henry a partnership. The Pinder Bourne Company was purchased by Henry in 1878 and became part of Doulton & Company in 1882.

With the passage of time, the demand for the Lambeth industrial and decorative stoneware declined whereas demand for the Burslem manufactured and decorated bone china wares increased.

Doulton & Company was incorporated as a limited liability company in 1899. In 1901 the company was allowed to use the word "Royal" on its trademarks by Royal Charter. The well known "lion on crown" logo came into use in 1902. In 2000 the logo was changed on the company's advertising literature to one showing a more stylized lion's head in profile.

Today Royal Doulton is one of the world's leading manufacturers and distributors of premium grade ceramic tabletop wares and collectibles. The Doulton Group comprises Minton, Royal Albert, Caithness Glass, Holland Studio Craft and Royal Doulton. Royal Crown Derby was part of the group from 1971 until 2000 when it became an independent company. These companies market collectibles using their own brand names.

Ashtray, earthenware, advertising-type, low squared white shape with rounded corners with notches for cigarettes, the rounded sides printed with advertising for De Reszke Cigarettes, Burslem, ca. 1925, 5-1/2" w. .................................................. **$250**

Centerpiece, Vellum Ware, low oblong floral-decorated dish with crimped and ruffled sides curving up at one end to form a high curved handle molded with a figural gold drag-on, designed by Charles Noke, ca. 1895 .................................................. **$2,000**

Bowl, 16" dia., 9" h., a wide round pedestal base in brown and green supporting a wide, deep curved bowl decorated with a continuous band of large bright yellow tulips on dark green leaves and stems, ca. 1910 .................................................. **$3,600**

Bowl, 5-1/4" dia., Titanian Ware, shallow rounded shape hand-painted on the interior with flowers, designed by Percy Curnock, ca. 1920 ................ **$750**

Cracker jar, cov., Bewick Birds Series, barrel-shaped with a low molded rim and inset cover, the sides decorated with a design of Bewick birds perched in a leafy branch, done in the print and tint technique in shades of brown, blue, yellow, rose red, green and pale blue, Burslem, ca. 1905 ......................... **$500**

Dessert plate, bone china, rounded with low ruffled rim, hand-painted scene of a polar bear by a river, ca. 1890 .................................................. **$300**

Bowl, 8-7/8" d., 3-3/4" h., wide shallow rounded form, interior with transfer-printed polychrome fox hunt scenes, green vintage border with gilt trim, early 20th c. ............................................... **$125**

Cabinet plates, 10-1/4" d., each with a different English garden view within a narrow acid-etched gilt border, transfer-printed and painted by J. Price, ca. 1928, artist- signed, green printed lion, crown and circle mark, impressed year letters, painted pattern numbers "H3587," set of 12 .................... **$2,750**

Chocolate set: 8" h. cov. chocolate pot, 6-1/2" h. cov. water pot, creamer, sugar bowl and eight cups and saucers; bone china, each enamel decorated with relief-molded fox in various poses, crop-form handles, 20th c., England, the set................ **$650**

Pitcher, 11" h., Poplars at Sunset patt. ........... **$175**

Plate, 9-1/8" d., Peony patt., dark blue floral center with rectangular panels around the border, trimmed with red-dish rust and beige, ca. 1900 ........... **$65**

Plates, 9" d., slightly dished with scalloped rim, gilt-trimmed rim with polychrome leafy vines bordering brown enameled Shakespearean sites, retailed by Theodore B. Starr, New York City, Doulton, Burslem, late 19th c., set of 12 ................................ **$450**

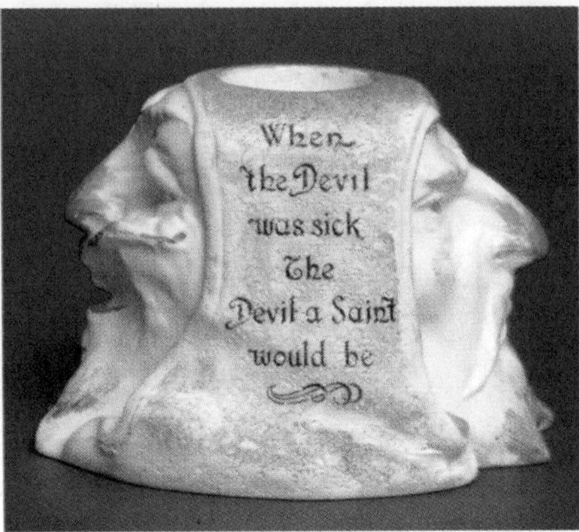


Match holder, bone china, figural, an upright oblong shape molded on one side with the smiling face of Mephistopheles and on the other side with his frowning face, the sides in blue inscribed with a motto, designed by Charles Noke, Burslem, ca. 1900 ............................................................... **$1,000**

Figure group, earthenware, limited edition tribute to George Tinworth, the oval brown base inscribed "The Tug of War," a green grassy mound with three dark blue frogs pulling against three brown mice, Model No. LW2, one of 150, designed by Martyn Alcock, Burslem, 2005, 5-1/2" l. .............................. **$600**

Napkin rings, each decorated with applied handmade colorful flowers, ca. 1935, a boxed set of four ............................................................... **$400**

◀ Ginger jar, covered, bulbous nearly spherical body with a domed cover, bright yellow ground painted in colorful enamels with a long-tailed bird-of-paradise flying among stylized pendent flowers and fruiting branches, Model No. 1256C, date code for December 1925, 10-3/4" h. ....................................... **$1,315**

Pitcher, Ruby Lustre, wide bulbous body tapering to a short cylindrical wide neck with spout, simple loop handle, hand-painted design of stylized dragons in the style of William de Morgan, ca. 1890...... **$1,500**

Teapot, covered, figural Old Salt model, the body in the image of a sailor mending a net, a mermaid forming the handle, designed by William K. Harper, introduced in 1989 ........................................... **$300**

Teapot, covered, Polar Bear Series, footed very wide squatty low body tapering to a flat rim and conical cover with disk finial, short angled spout and loop handle, overall crackled background with a center band of walking polar bears, ca. 1920s ............. **$90**

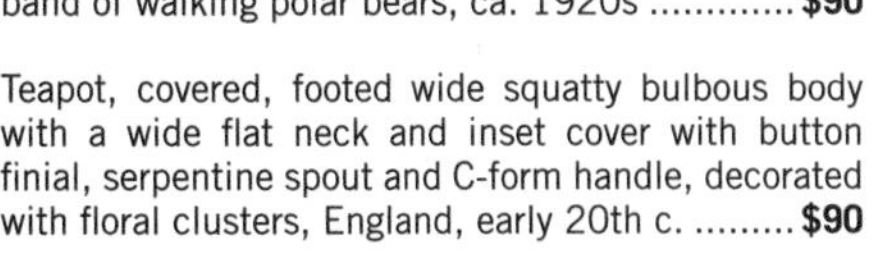

Teapot, covered, footed wide squatty bulbous body with a wide flat neck and inset cover with button finial, serpentine spout and C-form handle, decorated with floral clusters, England, early 20th c. ......... **$90**

Salt dip, small gilded ball feet supporting the squatty bulbous dish decorated with flowers on a pale blue ground, gilt rim band, with a salt spoon, ca. 1900 ................................................................ **$400**

Teapot, covered, figural Pirate and Captain model, designed by Anthony Cartlidge, limited edition of 1,500, introduced in 2003 ........................... **$300**

Teapot, covered, bone china, hand-painted with images of exotic birds and heavy gilt scroll trim, painted by Joseph Birbeck, ca. 1910 ...................... **$2,000**

Teapot, covered, figural Norman and Saxon model, designed by Anthony Cartlidge, limited edition of 1,500, introduced in 2003............................ **$300**

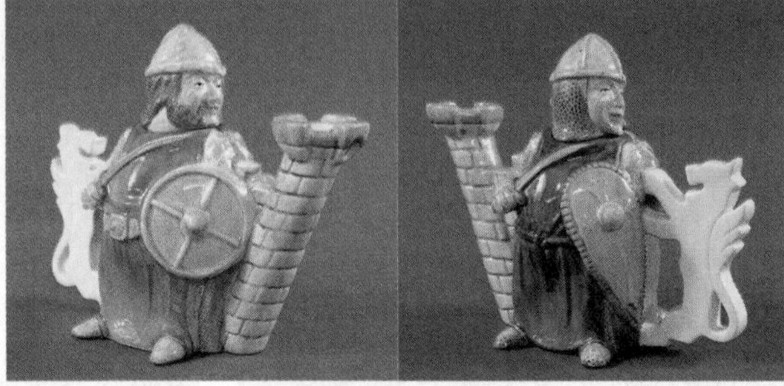

Tray, earthenware, rectangular with rounded corners and tab end handles, a tan border and scattered pink and yellow floral clusters around the interior, ca. 1895, 17" l............................................ **$400**

Tyg (three-handled mug), Vellum Ware, ornately scroll-molded cylindrical body decorated with a large panel of Spanish Ware floral decoration, three figural cherub handles, ca. 1895 ............................ **$800**

Vase, bone china, tall pedestal foot supporting the slightly tapering cylindrical body with a flared and ruffled rim, gold loop handles at the lower body, hand-painted white reserve with a colorful floral bouquet within a raised gilt border, the cobalt blue background further trimmed with ornate gold, ca. 1910...... **$600**

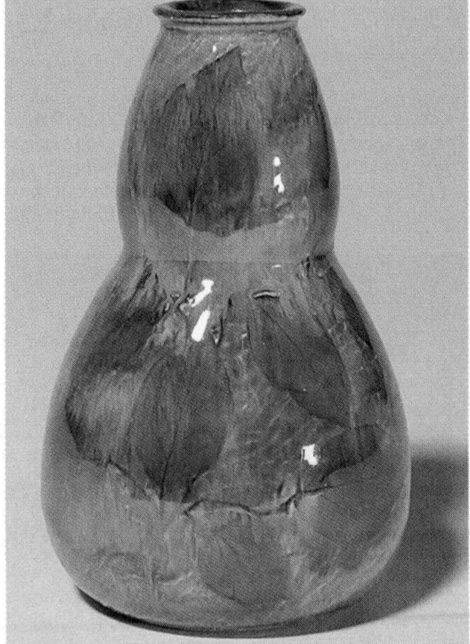

Vase, 5-7/8" h., Natural Foliage Ware, tapering gourd-form body, decorated with scattered brown leaves on a mottled green and yellow ground, impressed mark, Shape No. 7669.......................................... **$173**

Vase, 6" h., bone china, footed ovoid body with a short trumpet neck, dark yellow ground hand-painted with a large bird perched on a blossoming branch, designed by Arthur Eaton, ca. 1920 .......................................... **$400**

Vases, Vellum Ware, buff-colored, a scalloped foot below the wide bell-shaped body molded with a decoration of a frog and a mouse, a slender ringed neck with cupped rim, small loop shoulder handles, pr. ............................................ **$1,000**

Vases, 8" h., earthenware, cylindrical foot supporting the swelled cylindrical body with a wide flat mouth, printed with colorful stylized Art Deco florals hanging from the rim, ca. 1935, pr. ............................................................. **$400**

►Vase, 7" h., bone china, footed bulbous ovoid body tapering to a flaring trumpet-form neck flanked by gold loop handles, hand-painted in shades of blue with the scene of a large bear standing beside a rocky shoreline, ca. 1910 ........... **$1,200**

◄Vase, covered, Vellum exhibition-type, round foot and ringed pedestal in gold supporting the wide bulbous body with a small cylindrical gold neck with flaring rim and a low domed cover with knob finial, decorated in the Spanish style with colorful florals, ca. 1895 ......................... **$1,000**

Vase, 18-1/2" h., bulbous tulip-shaped body on a fluted pedestal base, the sides of the body finely hand-painted with a continuous pastoral and wooded landscape, high flaring and fluted mouth with a ruffled rim matches the base and molded to resemble folds of cloth with gilt-trimmed dark green panels alternating with gilt-trimmed pale green panels, attributed to Arthur Eaton, ca. 1880 .............................. **$4,560**

Whiskey decanter with stopper, figural bell, shaded dark to light brown, advertising Bells Whisky (sic), 1955, 10-1/2" h. ......................................... **$150**

Vase, bone china, footed gently flaring cylindrical body with a flat rim, hand-painted scene of a man and his dog in an autumnal landscape, designed by Harry Allen, ca. 1910 ................................... **$800**

Vase, bone china, footed tapering ovoid body with a small trumpet-form neck, dark blue ground hand-painted with white swans and trimmed with raised paste gold, designed by Fred Hodkinson, ca. 1910 .... **$1,000**

## CHARACTER JUGS

Night Watchman, large, D 6569, 7" h. ............ **$130**

Rip Van Winkle, large, D 6438, 6-1/2" h. ........**$115**

Apothecary, small, D 6574, 4" h........................ **$65**
Aramis, small, D 6454, 3-1/2" h. ..................... **$48**
'Arriet, miniature, D 6250, 2-1/4" h. ................ **$65**
Cap'n Cuttle "A", small, D 5842, 4" h. ............. **$95**
Dick Turpin, horse handle, small, D 6535, 3-3/4" h. ............................................................... **$60**
Don Quixote, miniature, D 6511, 2-1/2" h......... **$55**
Falstaff, small, D 6385, 3-1/2" h. .................... **$45**
Fortune Teller (The), miniature, D 6523, 2-1/2" h. ............................................................... **$375**
Gondolier, small, D 6592, 4" h...................... **$395**
Henry VIII, small, D 6647, 3-3/4" h.................. **$65**
Jarge, small, D 6295, 3-1/2" h....................... **$135**
Jockey, second version, small, D 6877, 4" h...... **$55**
John Peel, small, D 5731, 3-1/2" h. ................. **$60**
Lobster Man, small, D 6620, 3-3/4" h. ............. **$50**
Long John Silver, large, D 6335, 7" h. .............. **$90**
Lumberjack, small, D 6613, 3-1/2" h. .............. **$55**
Merlin, miniature, D 6543, 2-3/4" h.................. **$50**
Mine Host, large, D 6468, 7" h. ...................... **$105**
Mr. Micawber, miniature, D 6138, 2-1/4" h....... **$60**
Mr. Pickwick, miniature, D 6254, 2-1/4" h........ **$55**
Mr. Quaker, large, D 6738, 7-1/2" h. .............. **$650**
North American Indian, small, D 6614, 4-1/4" h. ............................................................... **$45**
Old Charley, tiny, D 6144, 1-1/4" h................... **$75**
Old Salt, miniature, D 6557, 2-1/2" h............... **$50**
Parson Brown "A", small, D 5529, 3-1/4" h. ..... **$63**
Pearly Queen, small, D 6843, 3-1/2" h. ............ **$60**
Pied Piper, large, D 6403, 7" h. ....................... **$75**
Poacher (The), small, D 6464, 4" h. ................. **$45**
Porthos, large, D 440, 7-1/4" h. ...................... **$90**
Red Queen (The), large, D 6777, 7-1/4" h....... **$125**
Robin Hood, 1st version, miniature, D 6252, -1/4" h. ............................................................... **$50**
Robin Hood, large, D 6205, 6-1/4" h. ............. **$125**
Robinson Crusoe, small, D 6539, 4" h. ............. **$60**
Sairey Gamp, miniature, D 6045, 2-1/8" h. ....... **$40**
Sancho Panza, large, D 6456, 6-1/2" h............. **$85**
Sancho Panza, small, D 6461, 3-1/4" h. ........... **$60**
Santa Claus, reindeer handle, large, D 6675, 1/4" h ............................................................... **$265**
Scaramouche, small, D 6561, 3-1/4" h........... **$525**
Sir Francis Drake, large, D 6805, 7" h. ........... **$105**
Sleuth (The), miniature, D 6639, 2-3/4" h. ....... **$65**
Snooker Player (The), small, D 6879, 4" h......... **$55**
Tam O'Shanter, small, D 6636, 3-1/4" h. .......... **$70**
Toby Philpots, small, D 5737, 3-1/4" h. ............ **$60**
Trapper (The), large, D 6609, 7-1/4" h............ **$125**
Ugly Duchess, small, D 6603, 3-1/2" h........... **$395**
Veteran Motorist, miniature, D 6641, 2-1/2" h. **$135**
Viking, small, D 6502, 4" h. ......................... **$150**
Walrus and Carpenter (The), miniature, D 6608, 2-1/2" h. ................................................ **$175**
Winston Churchill pitcher, large, D 6907, 7" h. **$135**
Witch (The), large, D 6893, 7" h. .................. **$290**

Sam Weller, large, D 6064, 6-1/2" h. ................**$80**

## KINGSWARE

This line of earthenware featured a very dark brown background often molded with scenes or figures trimmed in color and covered with a glossy glaze. All pieces in this line were designed by the leading Royal Doulton designer, Charles Noke.

Shaving mug, ovoid body with a flared rim and projecting brush spout, molded Friar portrait .................... **$1,500**

► Flask, figural, man wearing a top hat seated astride a large barrel, known as the Bacchus model, 8-1/2" h. .................................................................. **$3,000**

## LAMBETH ART WARES

Clock, stoneware, spherical case enclosing a round dial with Arabic numerals, ca. 1900 ........................ **$1,200**

Candlesticks, stoneware, funnel-shaped base tapering with a flaring drip pan centered by a tall cylindrical shaft with looped base handles, decorated with incised de signs trimmed in blue and brown, ca. 1872, 11" h., pr. .................. **$2,000**

Isobath, stoneware, a round domed foot supporting a wide cylindrical cup-shaped body with a side cup spout and a conical cover with knob finial, brown with blue band rim, the body and cover decorated with ornate large cream-colored floral and scrolling leaf panels, made for Thos. de la Rue, ca. 1893, 6" h.. **$500**

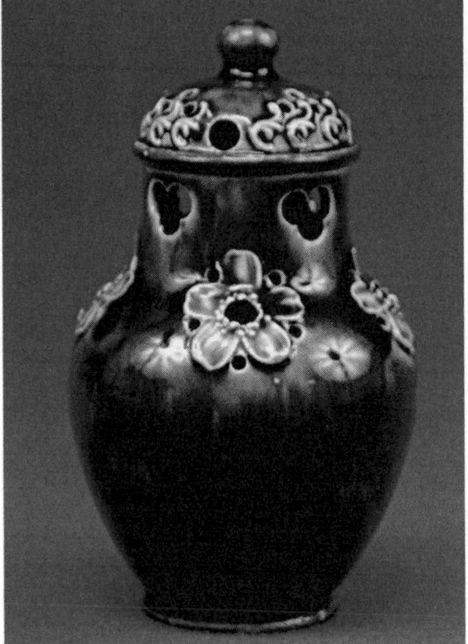

Potpourri jar, covered, stoneware, a bulbous ovoid body tapering to a wide cylindrical neck, the mottled bluish black ground applied around the shoulder with pierced blue flower blossoms below an upper band of pierced trefoils, the domed cover with a knob finial pieced with small holes separated with a thin molded scroll band, ca. 1900 ................................ **$1,500**

►Teapot, covered, Marqueterie Ware, spherical body with ribs around the lower half, short angled spout, squared handle, small domed cover, Doulton and Rix patent, ca. 1890. ...................................... **$2,000**

Jardinière, stoneware, squatty bulbous shape with a wide, low cylindrical neck, molded in high-relief with stylized long fish in green and brown swimming through large scrolling brown, grey and tan waves, designed by Mark Marshall, ca. 1900, 9" h...... **$2,000**

Pitcher, stoneware, tankard-style, flared base ring below the tall cylindrical body with a neck ring and short neck with rim spout, C-form handle, the main body applied and incised with a stylized scrolling blue and green foliate design, designed by George Tinworth, ca. 1880................................................... **$1,500**

CERAMICS

## BARLOW FAMILY DOULTON WARES

Jug, stoneware, footed ovoid body tapering to a cylindrical slightly flaring neck with pinched rim spout, strap handle, incised with a large scene of a huntsman, his horse and a fox, decorated by Hannah Barlow, ca. 1880 ..... **$2,000**

Cache pot, stoneware, bulbous ovoid form with a wide, short cylindrical neck, the sides incised with panels of horses framed by bold cobalt blue scrolling legs, tan neck, decorated by Hannah Barlow and Eliza Simmance, ca. 1885 ................................ **$2,000**

## TINWORTH DOULTON PIECES

►Menu holder, stoneware, figural, two white mouse musicians on a brown and blue molded round base, ti-tled "Harp and Concertina," ca. 1884, 4" h. **$3,000**

►Vase, stoneware, large ovoid body with a wide short cylindrical neck, applied and incised overall with ornate scrolling and leaf designs in dark blue, brick red, brown and blue, ca. 1880.... **$3,500**

▲Ewer, stoneware, footed tall ovoid body with a tall gently flaring neck with rim spout and large C-form handle, the base band incised with vertical pale blue lappets alternating with beaded bands on a dark blue ground below a white beaded band, the wide brown central band incised with a continuous scrolling band of pale green leaves and applied blue florettes, an upper thin white beaded band below the round shoulder incised with alternating dark green spear points and pale blue petals, the brown neck applied with blue florettes, ca. 1880 ................................................................ **$3,000**

# Fiesta

The Homer Laughlin China Company originated with a two-kiln pottery on the banks of the Ohio River in East Liverpool, Ohio. Built in 1873-'74 by Homer Laughlin and his brother, Shakespeare, the firm was first known as the Ohio Valley Pottery, and later Laughlin Bros. Pottery. It was one of the first white-ware plants in the country.

After a tentative beginning, the company was awarded a prize for having the best white-ware at the 1876 Centennial Exposition in Philadelphia.

Three years later, Shakespeare sold his interest in the business to Homer, who continued on until 1897. At that time, Homer Laughlin sold his interest in the newly incorporated firm to a group of investors, including Charles, Louis, and Marcus Aaron and the company bookkeeper, William E. Wells.

Under new ownership in 1907, the headquarters and a new 30-kiln plant were built across the Ohio River in Newell, West Virginia, the present manufacturing and headquarters location.

In the 1920s, two additions to the Homer Laughlin staff set the stage for the company's greatest success: the Fiesta line.

Dr. Albert V. Bleininger was hired in 1920. A scientist, author, and educator, he oversaw the conversion from bottle kilns to the more efficient tunnel kilns.

In 1927, the company hired designer Frederick Hurten Rhead, a member of a distinguished family of English ceramists. Having previously worked at Weller Pottery and Roseville Pottery, Rhead began to develop the artistic quality of the company's wares, and to experiment with shapes and glazes. In 1935, this work culminated in his designs for the Fiesta line.

For more information on Fiesta, see *Warman's Fiesta Identification and Price Guide* by Glen Victorey.

## Fiesta Colors

From 1936 to 1972, Fiesta was produced in 14 colors (other than special promotions). These colors are usually divided into the "original colors" of cobalt blue, light green, ivory, red, turquoise, and yellow (cobalt blue, light green, red, and yellow only on the Kitchen Kraft line, introduced in 1939); the "1950s colors" of chartreuse, forest green, gray, and rose (introduced in 1951); medium green (introduced in 1959); plus the later additions of Casuals, Amberstone, Fiesta Ironstone, and Casualstone ("Coventry") in antique gold, mango red, and turf green; and the striped, decal, and Lustre pieces. No Fiesta was produced from 1973 to 1985. The colors that make up the "original" and "1950s" groups are sometimes referred to as "the standard 11."

In many pieces, medium green is the hardest to find and the most expensive Fiesta color.

### Fiesta Colors and Years of Production to 1972

| | |
|---|---|
| Antique Gold—Dark Butterscotch | (1969-1972) |
| Chartreuse—Yellowish Green | (1951-1959) |
| Cobalt Blue—Dark Or "Royal" Blue | (1936-1951) |
| Forest Green—Dark "Hunter" Green | (1951-1959) |
| Gray—Light Or Ash Gray | (1951-1959) |
| Green—Often Called Light Green When Comparing It To Other Green Glazes, Also Called "Original" Green | (1936-1951) |
| Ivory—Creamy, Slightly Yellowed | (1936-1951) |
| Mango Red—Same As Original Red | (1970-1972) |
| Medium Green—Bright Rich Green | (1959-1969) |
| Red—Reddish Orange | (1936-1944 and 1959-1972) |
| Rose—Dusty, Dark Rose | (1951-1959) |
| Turf Green—Olive | (1969-1972) |
| Turquoise—Sky Blue, like the stone | (1937-1969) |
| Yellow—Golden Yellow | (1936-1969) |

## Fiesta Bottom Marks

Bottom of 6" bread plate in turquoise, showing "Genuine Fiesta" stamp.

An ink stamp on the bottom of a piece of Fiesta.

Examples of impressed Fiesta bottom marks.

Two different impressed marks on the bottoms of relish tray inserts.

Notice the different bottoms of two ashtrays. The top one has a set of rings with no room for a logo. The bottom ashtray has rings along the outer edge, opposite of the ring pattern on the ashtray above. The red example is an older example. The yellow ashtray with the logo can be dated to a time period after 1940.

Ashtray in cobalt blue. .............................. **$50-$59**

Cream soup cup in turquoise. .................... **$43-$49**

Covered onion soup bowl in yellow.......... **$635-$695**

Dessert bowl in medium green. ............... **$675-$748**

Footed salad bowl in red........................ **$415-$475**

4-3/4" fruit bowl in yellow. ........................ **$23-$27**

5-1/2" fruit bowl in rose............................ **$33-$39**

11-3/4" fruit bowl in ivory. ..................... **$295-$330**

Individual salad bowl in medium green. ...**$115-$130**

#1 mixing bowl in turquoise. ..................**$275-$299**

#2 mixing bowl in cobalt blue.................**$118-$147**

#3 mixing bowl in red. ...........................**$135-$158**

#4 mixing bowl in cobalt blue.................**$165-$185**

#5 mixing bowl in ivory. .........................**$225-$265**

#6 mixing bowl in red. ...........................**$282-$327**

#7 mixing bowl in yellow. .......................**$449-$589**

Very rare bowl lids in red ....................**$900-$1,100** light green .......**$800-$900** and yellow....... **$800-$900**

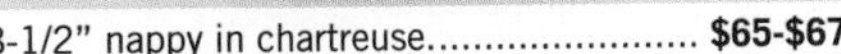

8-1/2" nappy in chartreuse........................ **$65-$67**

9-1/2" nappy in red. ................................. **$75-$81**

Bulb candleholder in yellow. ............................**$105-$130/pair**

Tripod candleholders in cobalt blue .............................**$575-$630/pair**, and red.......................................................................**$635-$699/pair**

Carafes in red....................................... **$295-$335**
and ivory.............................................. **$310-$320**

Comport in cobalt blue.......................... **$175-$195**

Covered casserole in rose........................ **$285-$300**

Sweets comport in cobalt blue. ................. **$85-$95**

Coffeepot in red.......... **$250-$275**

Demitasse coffeepot in yellow. ................................ **$450-$500**

Covered sugar in turquoise. .................................... **$49-$58**

Ring-handle creamer in rose. .................................. **$40-$50**

Ring-handle creamer and covered sugar bowl in medium green.
For the creamer ............................................................ **$120-$135**
For the sugar bowl ......................................................... **$195-$215**

Demitasse cup and saucer in light green....................... **$78-$80/set**

Eggcup in yellow........... **$56-$64**

Teacup and saucer in medium green...................... **$60-$70/set**

Tom & Jerry mug in medium green.........................**$125-$140**

Three mustards. In yellow...................................................**$270-$295**
In light green.........................................................................**$260-$280**
In turquoise ..........................................................................**$295-$320**

Marmalade jar in light green. .................**$325-$375**

Disk water pitcher in cobalt blue. ............**$155-$175**

Ice pitcher in ivory. ...............................**$140-$160**

Two-pint jug in rose...............................**$150-$160**

DripCut syrup pitcher in cobalt blue with a blue top, marked Fiesta. ...................................... **$420-$440**

10" plate in yellow. ................................. **$35-$45**

6" plate in gray. ...................................... **$10-$11**

9" plate in cobalt blue. ............................. **$17-$19**

Deep plate in cobalt blue. ......................... **$60-$70**

Top and side views of a cake plate in yellow. ...................................................... **$1,200-$1,300**

13" chop plate in rose. ............................ **$85-$90**

15" chop plate in red................................**$90-$100**
Yellow bud vase........................................ **$85-$92**

Oval platter in ivory.................................. **$45-$50**

Sauceboat in gray. .................................... **$70-$82**

Shakers in cobalt blue......................... **$30-$34/pair**

Medium teapot in red............................**$200-$230**

Utility tray in yellow. .... **$44-$48**

Relish tray and inserts in light green, as it would have come from the factory. .......................................................................... **$295-$310/set**

Tidbit tray in ivory, light green, and cobalt blue................. **$100-$200**

Water tumbler in red. ..... **$75-$85**

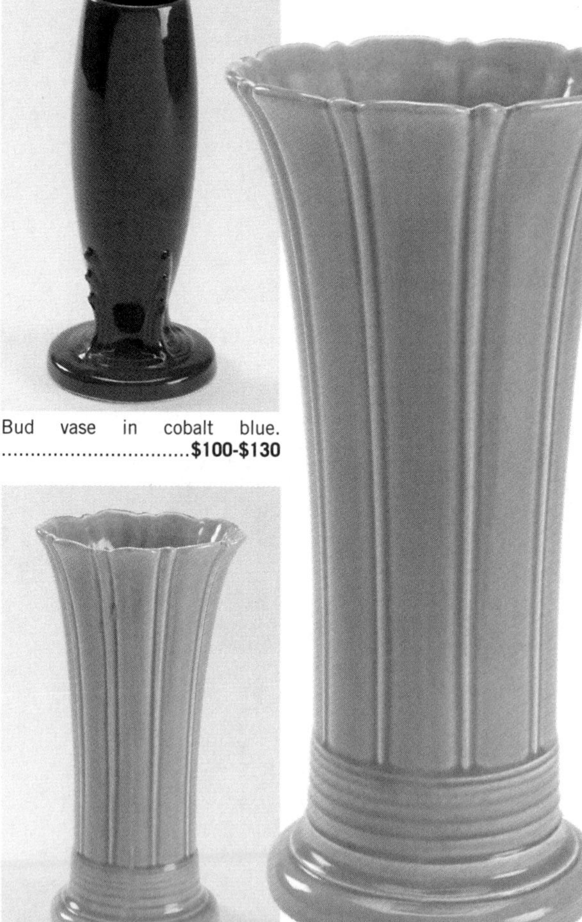

Bud vase in cobalt blue. ................................**$100-$130**

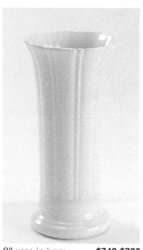

8" vase in ivory...........**$740-$780**

10" vase in light green. ................................**$900-$975**

12" vase in light green. ..........................**$1,100-$1,200**

# Franciscan Ware

A product of Gladding, McBean & Co. of Glendale and Los Angeles, California, Franciscan Ware was one of a number of lines produced by that firm over its long history. Introduced in 1934 as a pottery dinnerware, Franciscan Ware was produced in many patterns including Desert Rose, introduced in 1941 and reportedly the most popular dinnerware pattern ever made in this country. Beginning in 1942, some vitrified china patterns were also produced under the Franciscan name.

After a merger in 1963, the company name was changed to Interpace Corp., and in 1979 Josiah Wedgwood & Sons purchased the gladding, McBean & Co. plant from Interpace. American production ceased in 1984.

Coffee pot, Franciscan ware, Desert Rose pattern.................... **$10**

China set, Franciscan ware, Desert Rose pattern, approximately 50 pieces .......... **$80**

Platter and cookie jar, Franciscan Ware, Apple pattern, with hand-painted decoration, large round platter, 13-3/4" dia., with lidded cylinder cookie jar, 10-1/2" h. x 6-1/2" dia.......... **$70**

China set, Franciscan Ware, Desert Rose pattern, 51-piece set: teapot, coffee pot, creamer, covered sugar, eight cups, eight saucers, eight salad plates (8" dia.), eight dinner plates (10-1/2" dia.), eight bowls, gravy boat with attached stand, salt and pepper shakers, divided bowl (2-1/4" h. x 11" l.), vegetable bowl (2-1/2" h., 8-3/4" dia.), two platters (12-1/4" and 14-1/4" l.) ................................ **$150**

China set, Franciscan ware, Floral pattern, 11 pieces: covered sugar, five cups, five saucers ................. **$50**

Vases, Franciscan Ware, American, bottle neck sang de boeuf-colored vases marked GMB, each with original Franciscan Ware California paper label ......... **$80**

Milk pitcher, Franciscan Ware, Apple pattern, 6-3/4" h. x 7" w. ........................................................ **$20**

China set, Franciscan Ware, Woodside pattern, 56 pieces: 10 dinner plates, 10 salad plates, 10 bread and butter plates, 10 cups, 10 saucers, oval platter, gravy boat, oval vegetable bowl, coffee pot, creamer and covered sugar bowl ........................................................ **$325**

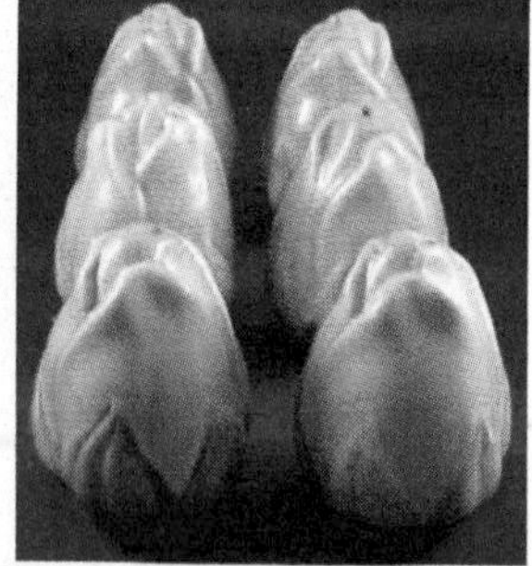

Salt and pepper shakers, Franciscan Ware, Dessert Rose pattern, three sets, shakers in shape of rose, 2-3/4" x 1-3/4" .............. **$5**

# Frankoma

John Frank started his pottery company in 1933 in Norman, Oklahoma. However, when he moved the business to Sapulpa, Oklahoma, in 1938, he felt he was home. Still, Mr. Frank could not know the horrendous storms and trials that would follow him. Just after his move, on November 11, 1938, a fire destroyed the entire operation, which included the pot and leopard mark he had created in 1935. Then, in 1942, the war effort needed men and materials so Frankoma could not survive. In 1943, John and Grace Lee Frank bought the plant as junk salvage and began again.

The time in Norman had produced some of the finest art ware that John would ever create and most of the items were marked either "Frank Potteries," "Frank Pottery," or to a lesser degree, the "pot and leopard" mark. Today these marks are avidly and enthusiastically sought by collectors. Another elusive mark wanted by collectors shows "Firsts Kiln Sapulpa 6-7-38." The mark was used for one day only and denotes the first firing in Sapulpa. It has been estimated that perhaps 50 to 75 pieces were fired on that day.

The clay Frankoma used is helpful to collectors in determining when an items was made. Creamy beige clay know as "Ada" clay was in use until 1953. Then a red brick shale was found in Sapulpa and used until about 1985 when, by the addition of an additive, the clay became a reddish pink.

Rutile glazes were used early in Frankoma's history. Glazes with rutile have caused more confusion among collectors than any other glazes. For example, a Prairie Green piece shows a lot of green and it also has some brown. The same is true for the Desert Gold glaze; the piece shows a sandy-beige glaze with some amount of brown. Generally speaking, Prairie Green, Desert Gold, White Sand, and Woodland Moss are the most puzzling to collectors.

In 1970 the government closed the rutile mines in America and Frankoma had to buy it from Australia. It was not the same so the results were different. Values are higher for the glazes with rutile. Also, the pre-Australian Woodland Moss glaze is more desirable than that created after 1970.

After John Frank died in 1973, his daughter Joniece Frank, a ceramic designer at the pottery, became president of the company. In 1983 another fire destroyed everything Frankoma had worked so hard to create. They rebuilt but in 1990, after the IRS shut the doors for nonpayment, Joniece, true to the Frank legacy, filed for Chapter 11 (instead of bankruptcy) so she could reopen and continue the work she loved.

In 1991 Richard Bernstein purchased the pottery, and the name was changed to Frankoma Industries. The company was sold again in 2005 to Det and Crystal Merryman. Yet another owner, Joe Ragosta, purchased the pottery in 2008.

Frankoma Pottery was closed for good in 2010 with a factory closeout auction in Oklahoma in 2011.

Book ends, Walking Ocelot on a two-tiered oblong base, black high glaze, Model No. 424, signed on reverse of tiered base "Taylor" denoting designer Joseph Taylor, pot & leopard mark on bottom, 7" l., 3" h., pr. ....**$1,900**

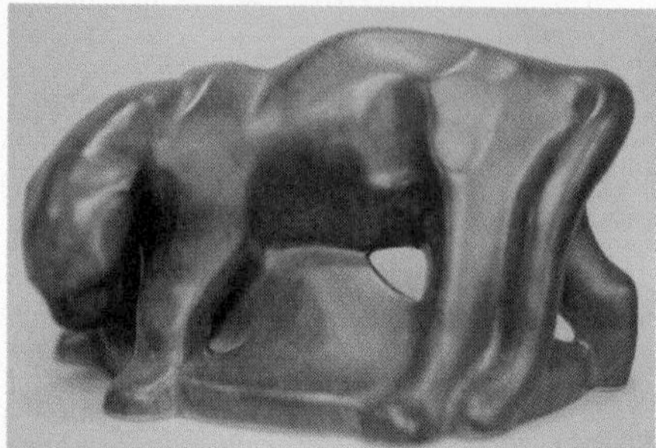

Book ends, model of leopard, Pompeian Bronze glaze, Model No. 431, 9" l., 5-1/2" h. ............... **$1,800/pr.**

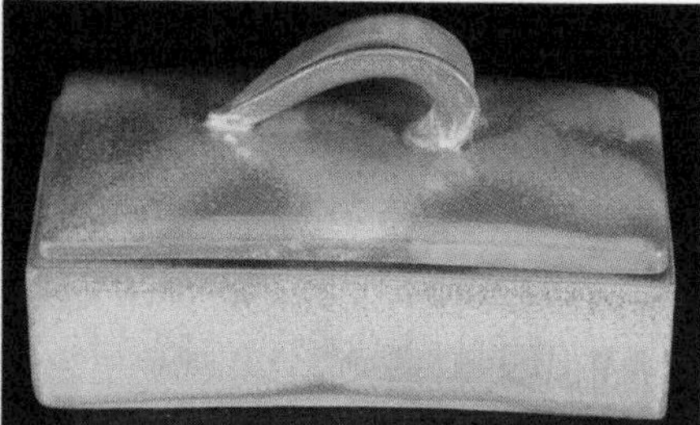

Cigarette box, covered, rectangular, cover with single raised and hard-to-find curved leaf handle, Bronze Green glaze, Ada clay, marked "Frankoma," 4 x 6-3/4", 3-1/2" h. ................................... **$175**

Ornament, "The ABCs of life," gift with purchase from Tulsa shopping mall, 1987, white background with sketch of three children, 3-1/2" dia. ........... **$69**

Bowl, shallow form, advertising "Oklahoma Gas Company - Golden Anniversary," 1956, Desert Gold, marked "Frankoma," 5-3/4" dia. ..................... **$186**

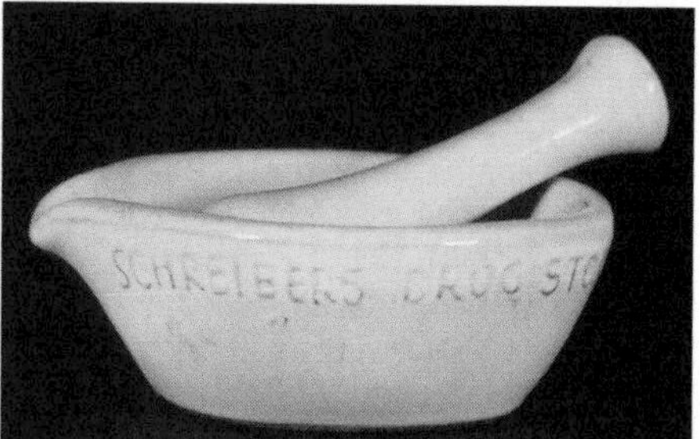

Mortar and pestle, advertising "Schreibers Drug Store," White Sand, marked "Frankoma," 3-1/4" ............................................................ **$145**

▲Sign, dealer teepee, Prairie Green, 1940s, marked "Frankoma," 6-1/2" h. .................................. **$725**

◀Teapot, covered, Wagon Wheel pattern, Desert Gold glaze, Sapulpa, Oklahoma, ca. 1942 ................. **$25**

## Fulper Pottery

From the "Germ-Proof Filter" to enduring Arts & Crafts acclaim—that's the unlikely journey of Fulper Pottery, maker of the early 20th-century uniquely glazed artware that's become a favorite with today's collectors.

Fulper began life in 1814 as the Samuel Hill Pottery, named after its founder, a New Jersey potter. In its early years, the pottery specialized in useful items such as storage crocks and drain pipes fashioned from the area's red clay. Abraham Fulper, a worker at the pottery, eventually became Hill's partner, purchasing the company in 1860. Renamed after its new owner, Fulper Pottery continued to produce a variety of utilitarian tile and crockery. By the turn of the 20th century, the firm, now led by Abraham's sons, introduced a line of fire-proof cookware and the hugely successful "Germ-Proof Filter." An ancestor of today's water cooler, the filter provided sanitary drinking water in less-than-sanitary public places, such as offices and railway stations.

In the early 1900s, Fulper's master potter, John Kunsman, began creating various solid-glaze vessels, such as jugs and vases, which were offered for sale outside the pottery. On a whim, William H. Fulper II (Abraham's grandson, who'd become the company's secretary/treasurer) took an assortment of these items for exhibit at the 1904 Louisiana Purchase Exposition—along with, of course, the Germ-Proof Filter. Kunsman's artware took home an honorable mention.

Since Chinese art pottery was then attracting national attention, Fulper saw an opening to produce similarly styled modern ware. Dr. Cullen Parmelee, who headed up the ceramics department at Rutgers, was recruited to create a contemporary series of glazes patterned after those of ancient China. The Fulper Vasekraft line of art pottery incorporating these glazes made its debut in 1909. Unfortunately, Parmelee's glazes did not lend themselves well to mass production; they did not result in reliable coloration. Even more to their detriment, they were expensive to produce.

In 1910, most of Parmelee's glazes disappeared from the line. A new ceramic engineer, Martin Stangl, was given the assignment of revitalizing Vasekraft. His most notable innovation: steering designs and glazes away from reinterpretations of ornate Chinese classics and toward the simplicity of the burgeoning Arts & Crafts movement. Among his many Vasekraft successes: candleholders, bookends, perfume lamps, desk accessories, tobacco jars, and even Vasekraft lamps. Here, both the lamp base and shade were of pottery; stained glass inserts in the shades allowed light to shine through.

Always attuned to the mood of the times, William Fulper realized that by World War I the heavy Vasekraft stylings were fading in popularity. A new and lighter line of Fulper Pottery Artware, featuring Spanish Revival and English themes, was introduced. Among the most admired Fulper releases following the war were Fulper Porcelaines: dresser boxes, powder jars, ashtrays, lamps, and other accessories designed to complement the fashionable boudoir.

Vase, flared bowl form glazed in auburn and mottled blue-green "famille Rose" glaze, stamped over glaze, 7" d., from the collection of Richard and Rita Chouinard .......... **$95**

Pair of two-handled vases, one in purple glaze with racetrack mark, the other in pink and green glaze with impressed mark/643, taller 7-1/2" h. .......... **$600**

Fulper Fayence, the popular line of solid-color, open-stock dinnerware eventually known as Stangl Pottery, was introduced in the 1920s. In 1928, following William Fulper's death, Martin Stangl was named company president. The artware that continued into the 1930s embraced Art Deco as well as Classical and Primitive stylistic themes. From 1935 onward, Stangl Pottery became the sole Fulper output. In 1978, the Stangl assets came under the ownership of Pfaltzgraff.

Unlike wheel-thrown pottery, Fulper was made in molds; the true artistry came in the use of exceptionally rich, color-blended glazes. Each Fulper piece is one-of-a-kind. Because of glaze divergence, two Fulper objects from the same mold can show a great variance. While once a drawback for retailers seeking consistency, that uniqueness is now a boon to collectors: each Fulper piece possesses its own singular visual appeal.

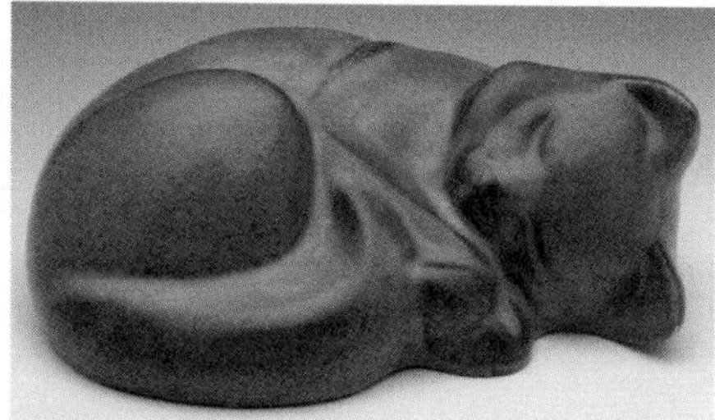

Sculpture, sleeping curled-up cat in blue matte glaze, marked, 9" w. by 3" h.................................. **$600**

Sculpture, reclining cat in tan, brown, and blue glaze, marked, 9-1/2" w. x 6" h. .......................... **$1,000**

Bookends, Ramses II book blocks in verte antique glaze, each marked with vertical racetrack logo with stylized letters, one bears Fulper label on Pharaoh's back, excellent original condition, 8-1/4" h...... **$650**

Bowl with matte mirrored black exterior lined with mulberry flambé interior, unmarked, excellent original condition, 3-1/2" h. x 10" w............................ **$70**

Bowl encircled by panels with peacock feather theme in yellow and blue flambé glaze, rectangular Fulper ink stamp, 5-3/4" h. x 10-1/2" w.................... **$300**

TOP LOT!

Mushroom-shaped table lamp with leaded glass inserts, Chinese blue flambé glaze, shade with vertical rectangular stamp, 19-1/2" h. x 14-1/2" w. .**$12,000**

Lamp, Arts & Crafts, mottled matte green glaze, mushroom shaped, original hardware except cord and plug, inset colored slag glass, marked with rectangle "Fulper" and circular "vasekraft" mark, "Patents pending in the United States and Canada and France and Germany," marked inside base, c.1915, 19" h. **$4,541**

Vase with yellow to brown flambé glaze, raised Fulper logo, excellent factory original condition, 6-3/4" h. **$160**

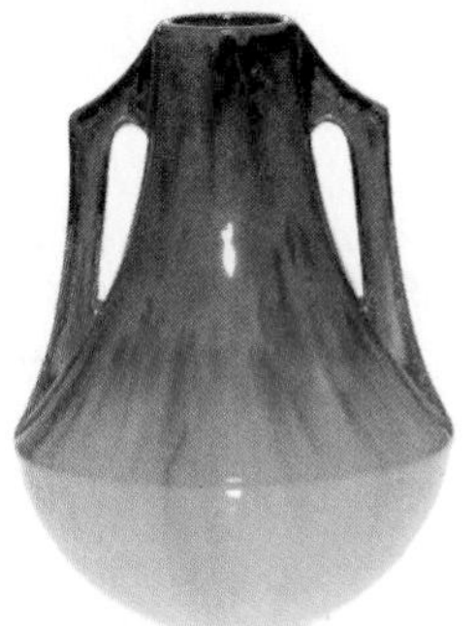

Vase with two handles, flambé glaze in blue, green, and taupe, die stamped with Fulper's incised mark, excellent condition, 9-1/2" h. **$275**

Vase, four-handled vase in Chinese blue flambé, unmarked, 13-1/2" h. x 11" w. **$550**

Vase, light blue and tan glaze, first paper label reads "Vasekraft - 61 - Edary Bowl Cat's Eye & Blue of Sky"; second paper label reads "Panama-Pacific Exposition San Francisco 1915 Highest Award to Fulper Pottery," 5-1/2" h. **$250**

Vase, matte glaze, 5" x 6" **$125**

Vase, buttressed, Chinese blue flambé glaze with blue "snowflake crystals," marked with impressed incised mark, in excellent original condition, 8-1/4" h. **$500**

Vase, gloss gray and black glazes dripped over matte dark green, Prang ink stamp (indicating a piece made to be sold through the Prang Art Supply Co. sales catalog), 8" h. **$450**

Ibis bowl, exterior glazed with green matte over blue matte, interior in glossy blue and green, mark obscured by thick glaze, moderate craze lines in bowl, 5-1/4" t. **$325**

# Grueby

Some fine art pottery was produced by the Grueby Faience and Tile Company, established in Boston in 1891. Choice pieces were created with molded designs on a semi-porcelain body. The ware is marked and often bears the initials of the decorators. The pottery closed in 1907.

GRUEBY

Bowl, small footring supporting the deep vertical and slightly uneven sides, wide flat rim, dappled green matte glaze, impressed mark, two pinhead-sized glaze pops, 3" dia., 4-1/4" h. .......................... **$805**

Bowl, wide low rounded sides and wide flat molded rim, overall medium-dark blue matte glaze, impressed mark, 5-3/8" dia., 1-7/8" h. ............................ **$345**

Candlestick, wide flat dished base with low vertical sides, centered by a tapering ringed shaft with ovoid socket with flattened flared rim, mottled yellow and brown matte glaze, circular tulip-style insignia, No. 227, glazed-over chip at top rim, 5-3/8" h. ...... **$460**

Paperweight, model of a scarab beetle, oval, matte blue glaze, impressed circular mark, some small glaze chips at base, 3-7/8" l. .................................. **$196**

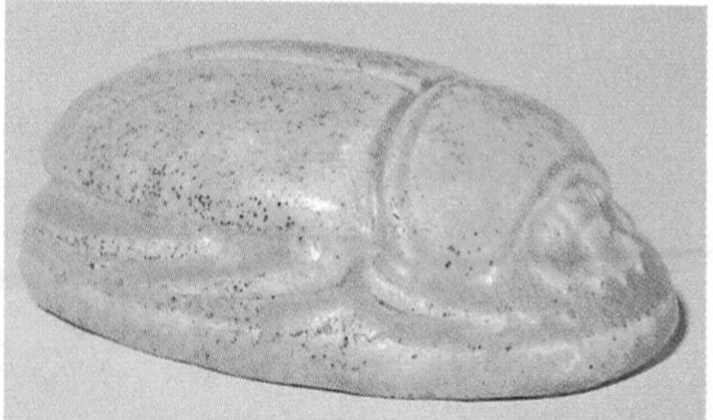

Paperweight, model of a scarab beetle, oval, matte oatmeal glaze, impressed circular mark, glaze peppering, 3-7/8" l. ........................................... **$345**

Plaque, rectangular, architectural-type, carved and modeled with a family of elephants in black against bluish grey ground, mounted in black box frame, two firing lines in body, restoration to one, small chip to one corner, stamped mark, 14" x 23"........................................................................................................ **$9,775**

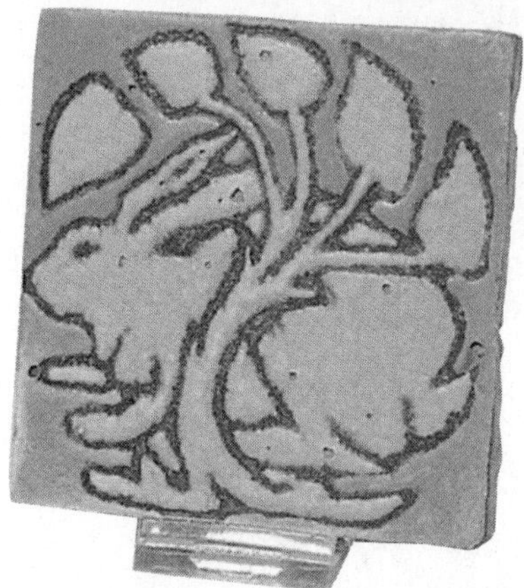

Tile, square, a large white rabbit crouched behind a small stylized leafy shrub in white, both outlined in dark blue against a pale blue ground, impressed tulip-style mark, burst glaze bubbles, some small edge nicks, 3-7/8" w. ............... **$690**

▲Vase, rare large form with bulbous body centered by a flaring cylindrical neck, tooled and applied with large wide pointed overlapping leaves, organic matte green glaze, couple of very minor edge nicks, by Marie Seaman, stamped round mark, 12-1/2" h., 8-1/4" dia...... **$11,500**

◀Vase, squatty bulbous form with wide flat mouth, molded around shoulder with seven flower buds alternating with seven wide leaves down the sides, mottled matte yellow glaze, unmarked, restoration to center of base, ca. 1908, 6-1/4" h. ............................................ **$5,288**

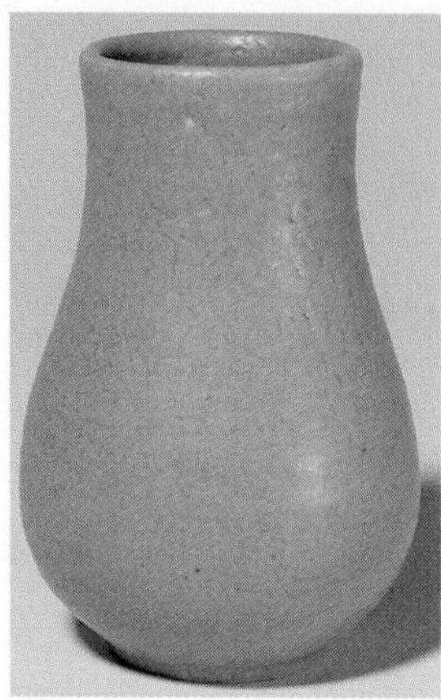

Vase, footed simple ovoid body tapering to a flat mouth, textured matte blue glaze, impressed Grueby mark , 6-3/4" h., ......................................**$690**

Vase, footed squatty bulbous lower body tapering to a wide cylindrical neck with molded rim, dark green matte glaze, 9-1/2" h. ..........**$1,265**

Vase, squatty bulbous base with angled shoulder to the tall gently flaring neck, tooled floral designs, dark matte green glaze, impressed tulip mark, 7-3/4" h. .......**$1,610**

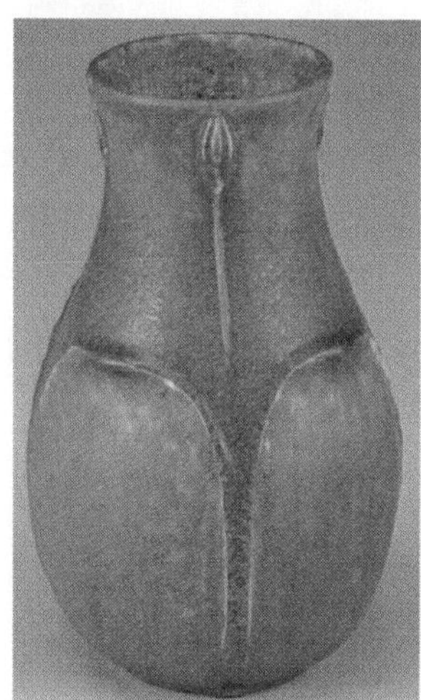

**Above:** Vase, bulbous ovoid body with wide rolled rim, crisply tooled with broad leaves up the sides, covered in a leathery dark green glaze, some highpoint nicks, circular mark, 5-1/2" h., 4-1/2" dia. ................................**$2,875**

**Above left:** Vase, ovoid body tapering to a wide gently flaring neck, tooled and applied with rounded leaves around the lower half with four buds up the sides, medium matte green glaze, small nick to one leaf edge, mark obscured by glaze, 7-1/2" h., 4-1/2" dia. ..............................................................**$2,875**

**Left:** Vase, swelled cylindrical body tapering to a short flared neck, matte green glaze with a number of pinhead burst bubbles, area of thin glaze on side, 12-1/2" h. ..............................................................**$1,265**

# Haeger

Sleek. Sinuous. Colorful and cutting edge. Timeless, trim of line, and, above all, thoroughly modern. That's the hallmark of Haeger Potteries. Since its 1871 founding in Dundee, Illinois, the firm has successfully moved from the utilitarian to the decorative. Whether freshly minted or vintage, Haeger creations continue to provide what ads called "a galaxy of exquisite designs. . . visual achievements symbolizing expert craftsmanship and pottery-making knowledge."

Today's collectors are particularly captivated by the modernistic Haeger output of the 1940s and '50s – from "panther" TV lamps and figurines of exotic Oriental maidens to chomping-at-the-bit statuary of rearing wild horses and snorting bulls. But the Haeger story began long before then, with the Great Chicago Fire of 1871.

Founder David Haeger had recently purchased a budding brickyard on the banks of Dundee's Fox River. Following the fire, his firm produced bricks to replace decimated Chicagoland structures. For the next 30 years, industrial production remained the primary emphasis of the Haeger Brick and Tile Company. It wasn't until 1914 that the company, now under the guidance of Edmund Haeger, noted the growing popularity of the Arts & Crafts movement and turned its attention to artware.

From the very beginning, Haeger was distinguished by its starry roster of designers. The first: J. Martin Stangl, former glaze wizard for Fulper. The design emphasis of Stangl and his early Haeger successors was on classically simple, uncluttered Arts & Crafts stylings. Haeger's roster of pots, jugs, vases, bowls, and candleholders all proved big hits with buyers.

An early zenith was reached with a pavilion at the 1934 Chicago World's Fair. In addition to home environment settings accented with Haeger, there was an actual working factory. Once fair-goers had viewed the step-by-step pottery production process, they could purchase a piece of Haeger on the way out. The World's Fair brought Haeger to America's attention – but its grandest days of glory were still ahead.

The year 1938 saw the promotion of Edmund Haeger's forward-thinking son-in-law, Joseph Estes, to general manager, the arrival of equally forward-thinking designer Royal Arden Hickman, and the introduction of the wildly popular "Royal Haeger" line.

The multi-talented Hickman, snapped up by Haeger after stays at J.H Vernon, Kosta Crystal, and his own Ra Art, quickly made his mark. Earlier Haeger figurals were generally of animals and humans at rest. Under the guidance of Hickman, and the soon-to-follow Eric Olsen, *motion* was key: leaping fish, birds taking wing, and a ubiquitous snarling black

Eric Olsen "Mountain Lion," 1950, the tail is hand-applied, 10" h. x 12" w. .......... **$200-$250**

panther. The energetic air of underlying excitement in these designs was ideally suited to the action-packed atmosphere of World War II, and the postwar new day that followed.

In 1944, Hickman left Haeger following a dispute over lamp production, returning only for occasional free-lance assignments. The 1947 arrival of his successor, Eric Olsen, coincided with the official celebration of Haeger's "Diamond Jubilee"; that's when much of the Olsen line made its debut. From towering abstract figural lamps to long-legged colts, self-absorbed stalking lions, and mystic pre-Columbian priests, his designs were ideal for the soon-to-be-ultra-current "1950s modern" décor.

Today, "The Haeger Potteries" continues as a family affair under the leadership of Joseph Estes' daughter, Alexandra Haeger Estes. And whether collectors favor the early Arts & Crafts pieces, the modernistic designs of the 1940s and '50s, or examples of today's output, one constant remains: This is artware collectors are eager to own. Retailer Marshall Field & Co. said it best in 1929: "Haeger Pottery will become an indispensible charm in your home!"

*Photos by Ben Aldis, except as noted. Reference materials and figurines courtesy of John Magon.*

"Thunder and Lightning,"walnut glaze, 1954, 17-1/2" h. A lively and rare figurine, as the horses jump through a stylized lightning bolt. .......................... **$300-$500**
*Figurine and photo courtesy of Ann Mulhollan*

"Large Bull" by Eric Olsen, Haeger red glaze, 1955, 8" h. x 18" l. The bull remained part of the Haeger line well into the 1970s. ........................ **$100-$150**

The famous Haeger panther, a Royal Hickman design, ebony glaze, 20" h. x 28" w. This large "Panther Lamp" with leopard shade, on a wood base, dates from the early 1940s. ............................ **$225-$275**

"Panther Tail Dragging," amber crystal glaze, 1949, 5-1/2" h. x 29" l. The tail of this Royal Hickman design was prone to breakage. In later versions, the tail curls up and makes contact with the back heel for greater stability. .......................................................................................................... **$225-$275**

"Colt," chartreuse and honey glaze, 1952, 14-1/2" l. Since the colt's legs are easily broken, most of these figures were attached to planters. Part of 1952's "Style by Jury" line................................**$125-$175**

*Figurine courtesy of John and Becky Howland*

"Lion Head Bookends" by Eric Olsen, chartreuse glaze, 1949, 7-1/2" h. x 6-1/4" w......... **$75-$125/pr**

"Indian," desert red glaze, 1950, 13" h. x 9-1/2" w. One of Haeger's rarest "western" figurines. **$225-$275**

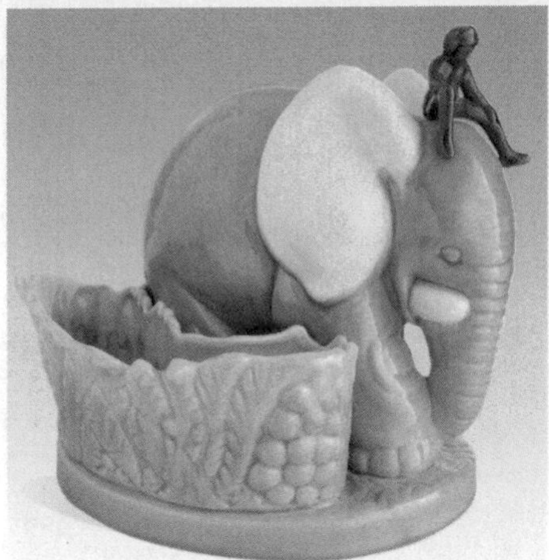

"Elephant Planter with Rider," chartreuse and honey glaze, 1949, 10" h. x 10" w.....................**$75-$125**

►Two from Haeger's "Pre-Columbian" line of the 1960s, both in an Etruscan ivory glaze. "Head of Priest," 12-1/2" h; "Armadillo," 8-1/2" h. x 15-1/2" l..................................................**$75-$125 ea.**

An Eric Olsen "Lion," desert red glaze, 1950, 6-1/2" h. x 16-1/2" l................................**$225-$275**

Eric Olsen "Buddha," green agate glaze, 1949, 10-1/2" h. x 7" w..................................**$125-$175**

"Temple Goddess" by Eric Olsen, ebony and chartreuse glaze, 1950, 12" h. x 7" w............**$75-$125**

◀Olsen's "Dragon Bowl," chartreuse and yellow glaze, 1949, 5" h. x 10" w.....................**$125-$175** Posed inside bowl, his "Jeweled Lady," chartreuse and honey glaze, 1948, 15-1/2" h............**$50-$100**

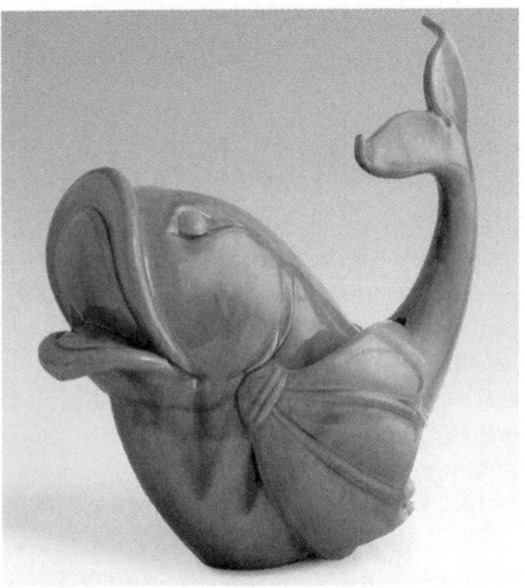

"Dolphin Planter" by Eric Olsen, jade crackle glaze, 1959, 19" h. x 17" w. The side fins were hand-applied. ............................................. **$200-$250**

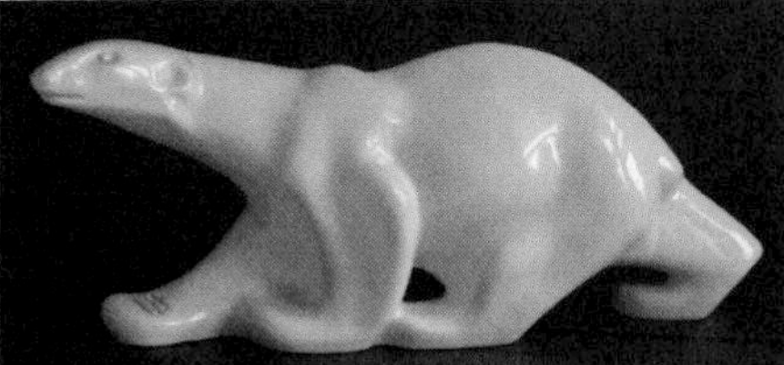

Eric Olsen's "Running Polar Bear," white glaze, 1949, 6-1/4" h. x 16" l. ......................... **$124-$175**

Royal Hickman's "Peasant Man & Woman" in a bronze red ("bloodstone") glaze, 1946, 16-1/2" h. Later versions were given a different glaze, and also abandoned the hand-applied potato in the Peasant Woman's dish, for simpler production. **$400-$500 pr.**

*Figurines courtesy of Steve Schoneck*

Olsen's "Bird Plaque" was one of a pair, each in a different high-flying pose. Ebony cascade glaze, 1959, 18" w. ............................................... **$50-$100**

Two very early Royal Hickman designs, dating from 1941, both in an Alice blue glaze.
"Sailor," 16" h. ..................................... **$175-$225**
"Anchor Vase," 10" h. .............................. **$50-$75**

"Comedy and Tragedy TV Lamp," ebony cascade glaze, 1957, 7" h. ................................ **$125-$175**

# Hall China

HALL CHINA (HALL) MADE IN U.S.A.

Founded in 1903 in East Liverpool, Ohio, this still-operating company at first produced mostly utilitarian wares. It was in 1911 that Robert T. Hall, son of the company founder, developed a special single-fire, lead-free glaze that proved to be strong, hard and nonporous. In the 1920s the firm became well known for its extensive line of teapots (still a major product), and in 1932 it introduced kitchenwares, followed by dinnerwares in 1936 and refrigerator wares in 1938.

The imaginative designs and wide range of glaze colors and decal decorations have led to the growing appeal of Hall wares with collectors, especially people who like Art Deco and Art Moderne design. One of the firm's most famous patterns was the "Autumn Leaf" line, produced as premiums for the Jewel Tea Company. For listings of this ware see "Jewel Tea Autumn Leaf."

Helpful books on Hall include *The Collector's Guide to Hall China* by Margaret and Kenn Whitmyer, and *Superior Quality Hall China-A Guide for Collectors* by Harvey Duke (An ELO Book, 1977).

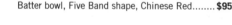

Batter bowl, Five Band shape, Chinese Red........ **$95**

Casserole, cov., Art Deco with chrome reticulated handled base.................................................. **$55**

Casserole with inverted pie dish lid, Radiance shape, No. 488, 6-1/2" dia., 4" h. .............................. **$60**

Coffeepot, cov., Terrace shape, Crocus pattern ................................................................ **$80**

Bean pot, cover, Sani-Grid (Pert) shape, Chinese Red ........... **$100**

Cookie jar, cover, Flareware ........................................ **$65**

Cookie jar, cover, Five Band shape, Meadow Flower pattern ........................................ **$325**

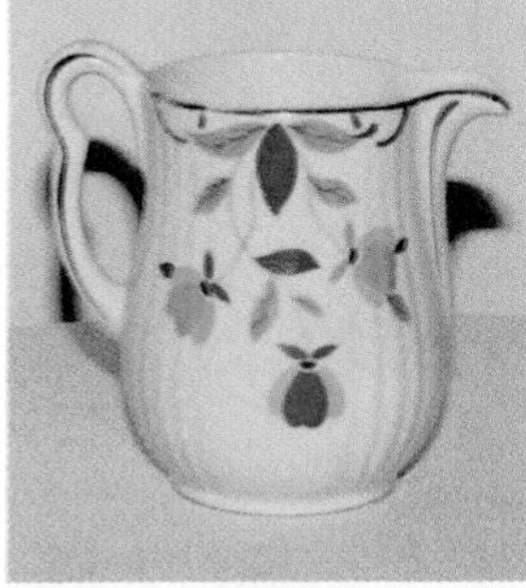
Creamer, Radiance shape, Autumn Leaf pattern................ **$45**

Humidor, cover, Indian decal, walnut lid ............................... **$55**

Leftover dish, covered, Zephyr shape, Chinese red ............ **$110**

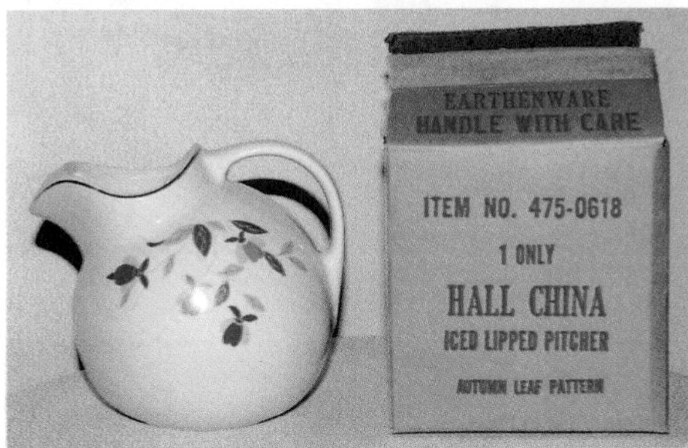

Pitcher, ball shape, Autumn Leaf pattern, 1978, with box ............. **$65**

Mug, Irish coffee, footed, commemorative, "Hall China Convention 2000" ......................... **$40**

Pitchers, Sani-Grid (Pert) shape, Chinese red, three sizes.................................................. **$35-$55**

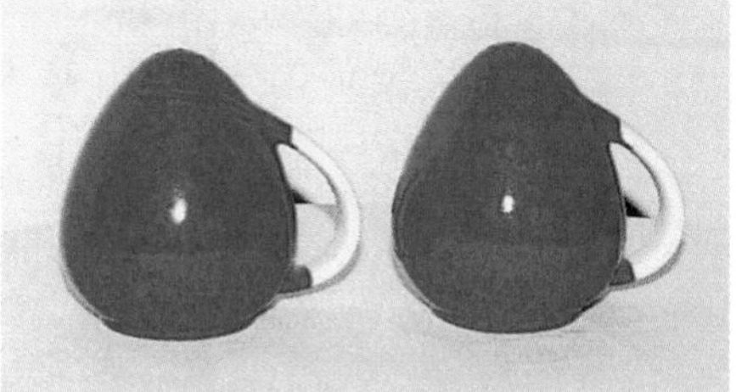
Salt and pepper shakers, Sani-Grid (Pert) shape, Chinese red. .................................................**$35/pr.**

Teapot, cover, Adele shape, Art Deco style, olive green .......................................................... **$200**

Teapot, cover, Aladdin shape, round opening for cover and insert, gold swag decoration ................ **$70-$75**

Teapot, cover, Aladdin shape, round opening with insert, marine bue ....................................... **$65-$75**

Teapot, cover, Aladdin shape, round opening with insert, maroon ........................................... **$65-$75**

Teapot, cover, Aladdin shape, with infuser, Serenade pattern ........................................................ **$350**

Teapot, cover, Aladdin shape, Wildfire pattern, with oval infuser, 1950s ........................................... **$75**

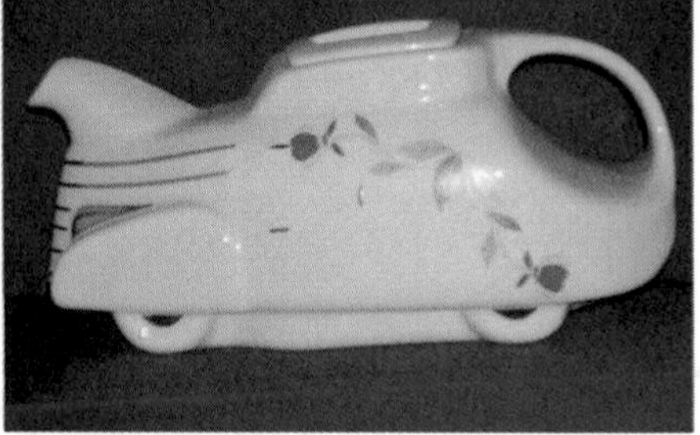

▲Teapot, cover, automobile shape, Autumn Leaf pattern, reissue for China Specialties with commemorative stamp on bottom, 1993 ........................... **$175**

◀Teapot, cover, birdcage shape, canary yellow with "Gold Special" decoration .............................. **$450**

Teapot, cover, donut shape, Orange Poppy pattern ........ **$450**

Teapot, cover, football shape, commemorative, "Hall 2000 Haul, East Liverpool, Ohio," ivory........... **$125**

Teapot, cover, Hook Cover shape, Cameo Rose pattern, part of a limited edition produced exclusively for China Specialties, Strongsville, Ohio, fewer than 500 made........ **$95**

Teapot, cover, Hook Cover shape, Chinese red ........ **$250**

Teapot, cover, Illinois shape, maroon with gold decoration ........ **$225**

Teapot, cover, Philadelphia shape, Chinese red. ........ **$250**

Teapot, cover, Morning Set shape, Blue Garden pattern........ **$350**

Teapot, cover, Lipton tea shape, mustard yellow ........ **$40**

Teapot, cover, Radiance shape, Acacia pattern ........ **$225**

Teapot, cover, Rutherford shape, ribbed, Chinese red ........ **$300**

Teapot, cover, star shape, turquoise with gold decoration ........ **$100-125**

Teapot, cover, Streamline shape, Fantasy pattern ........ **$400**

Teapot, cover, Sundial shape, Blue Blossom pattern ........ **$300**

Teapot, cover, Tea-for-Two shape, pink with gold decoration ........ **$150**

# Haviland

Over 60,000 chinaware patterns: Since its founding in 1840, that's the number totaled by the Haviland China Co. The company's story is a unique one. Although based in the United States, Haviland China produced its wares in the French porcelain capital of Limoges, exporting those products for sale domestically. Over the years, Haviland has become so closely identified with Limoges that many have used the terms interchangeably, or assumed Haviland was yet another of the numerous French firms that made Limoges their manufacturing base.

H&Co

Haviland &Co Limoges

The Haviland company was actually the result of its founder's quest for the "ideal" china. New York importer David Haviland was dissatisfied with the china then available for his clientele. Its varying coloration (never consistently white) and grainy, porous texture made it not only visually unappealing, but also unsuitable for long-term use.

Haviland's search led him to Limoges, already a busy hub of porcelain production, and home to over 40 manufacturing firms. The reason? The 1765 discovery of rare kaolin deposits in the Limoges vicinity. Kaolin was a necessary component of fine, hard paste porcelain. Blessed with abundant supplies of other necessities for porcelain manufacture (wood, water, and a willing work force), Limoges quickly gained renown for its superb product.

Impressed by the area's output—the porcelain had a pristine whiteness, as well as a smooth, non-porous finish—Haviland set up shop. The firm's dinnerware exports found immediate success, thanks to the delicate translucence of the ware and its exquisitely detailed decoration.

In the mid-19th century, at Haviland's peak of popularity, "fine dining" was a term taken seriously. Specific foods required specific serving dishes, and each course of a meal mandated its own type of tableware. Substituting a luncheon plate for a bread-and-butter plate was not only unthinkable, but in the worst possible taste. China cabinets in affluent homes were filled to overflowing, and much of that overflow was thanks to Haviland. Just a sampling from its vast dinnerware inventory includes: fish plates, bone plates, salad plates, chop plates, bon bon plates, and underplates; chocolate pots and coffee pots; bouillon cups, eggcups, and teacups; lemonade pitchers and milk pitchers; honey dishes and vegetable dishes; toast trays and celery trays; pudding sets and dessert sets; sauceboats and sauce tureens; broth bowls, soup bowls, and punch bowls. Imagine any conceivable fine dining need, and Haviland dinnerware was there to meet it.

Although dinnerware was its mainstay, Haviland also produced a multitude of other decorative yet useful porcelain housewares. Among them were dresser trays, hair receivers, ashtrays, and decorative baskets. A limited line of art pottery was also released from 1885 into the 1890s, utilizing the underglaze slip decoration technique known as "Barbotine." Developer Ernest Chaplet supervised this series for Haviland, in which pigments were combined with heavy white clay slip. The mixture, applied to the clay body of a piece, had the consistency of oil paint; the resulting finish had the texture of an oil painting.

Because various Haviland family members eventually branched out on their own, the porcelain markings are many. "H & Co." was the earliest, succeeded by such variations as "Haviland, France" and "Decorated by Haviland & Co." Theodore Haviland achieved much acclaim after forming his own firm in 1892, and those pieces are often marked "Theodore Haviland" or other variants of his name. (In 1941, the Theodore Haviland facility relocated to the United States.)

Haviland's overwhelming variety of available product, a necessity when first introduced, is a boon to today's avid porcelain collectors. Hunting down and accumulating a complete set of Haviland—even in a single dinnerware pattern—can (quite enjoyably) occupy a lifetime.

Haviland porcelain plate with hand-painted decoration, cobalt and gilt border, scene from Parsifal in center, inscribed on reverse (No 8) Parsifal, Evocation de Kundry, acte II, circa 1900, marks: Haviland, France; Haviland & Co., Limoges; 9" dia. ....................................................$237

Haviland Limoges coffee pot, 9-3/4" t. ....................................................$35

Seven Haviland porcelain dessert plates in Jewel pattern and associated covered tureen with applied flowers, France, 19th c., marks: Theodore Haviland France, Theodore Haviland Limoges France, Jewel; 8-1/2" dia....$84

Fifty-seven piece Haviland gilt polychrome porcelain service: covered serving dish, two-handled serving dish, rectangular two-handled platter, 10 teacups, 10 saucers, 12 fruit plates, 10 luncheon plates, 12 butter pats; France, 20th c., marks: Haviland & C. Limoges, H&G (over) L; 4-1/4" h. (covered serving dish)..............$418

Charles Field Haviland Limoges gilt cobalt blue porcelain covered tureen, patent date 1883, marks: CFH (over) GDM, 14 Aout 83, R.B.; 6-1/2" h. .................. **$131**

Comport, pedestal on three feet with ornate gold shell design, top with reticulated edge, peach and gold design around base and top, 9" dia. .............................. **$595**

Hair receiver, covered, squatty round body on three gold feet, hand-painted overall with small flowers in blues and greens with gold trim, mark of Charles Field Haviland ........................... **$225**

Four French cabinet plates painted with Napoleonic ladies, 19th c., one Haviland & Co., depicting Empress Josephine, signed A. SOUSTRE, 9-9/16" dia.; three matching with unsigned portraits identified on the reverse as Caroline Alurat, Mlle. Georges, and Dsse. de Montibello, 9-1/2" dia. .............................................................................. **$593**

*Skinner, Inc.*

Fish set: 13 pieces, each with a different fish in center, border in two shades of green design with gold trim, hand-painted scenes by L. Martin, mark of Theodore Haviland, 22" l. oval platter and 12 8 -1/2" dia. plates ........................................................................ **$2,750**

CERAMICS

# Hull Pottery

The A.E. Hull Pottery Company grew from the clay soil of Perry County, Ohio, in 1905. By the 1930s, its unpretentious line of ware could be found in shops and, more importantly, homes from coast to coast, making it one of the nation's largest potteries. Leveled by flood and ensuing fire in 1950, like a phoenix, Hull rose from the ashes and reestablished its position in the marketplace. Less than four decades later, however, the firm succumbed after eight bitter strikes by workers, leaving behind empty buildings, memories and the pottery shown in this volume.

Addis Emmet Hull founded A.E. Hull Pottery in July 1905. By the time the company was formed, the Crooksville/Roseville/Zanesville area was already well established as a pottery center. Hull constructed an all-new pottery, featuring six kilns, four of them large natural gas-fired beehive kilns.

The early years were good to Hull. In fact, after only two years of operation, Hull augmented the new plant by taking over the former facilities of the Acme pottery. By 1910, Hull was claiming to be the largest manufacturer of blue-banded kitchenware in the United States. By 1925 production reached three million pieces annually.

This early ware included spice and cereal jars and salt boxes. Some of these items were lavishly decorated with decals, high-gloss glazes or bands. This evolved into some early art ware pieces including vases and flowerpots. However, Hull could not keep up with the demand, especially the growing demand for artwares, which could be sold in five and dime stores. Hence, Addis Hull visited Europe and made arrangements to import decorative items from Czechoslovakia, England, France, Germany and Italy. To accommodate the influx of these items, Hull opened a facility in Jersey City, N.J. This arrangement continued until 1929, when import operations were discontinued.

In 1926 Plant 1 was converted to manufacture decorative floor and wall tiles, which were popular at the time. But by the time of Addis Hull's death in 1930, the company bearing his name was exiting the tile business. Plant 1, Hull's original, which had been converted to the now-discontinued line of tile production as well as being elderly, was closed in 1933.

When Addis Hull Sr. died in 1930, management of the works was passed to his son, Addis Hull Jr., who was involved in the formation of the Shawnee Pottery Company. By the late 1930s, Addis Junior left the family business and assumed the presidency of Shawnee.

World War II affected the entire nation, and Hull was no exception. This time period saw the production of some of Hull's most famous lines, including Orchid, Iris, Tulip and Poppy. Their airbrushed matte hues of pink, blue, green and yellow became synonymous with the Hull name. Sales of such wares through chain and dime stores soared.

The close of the decade saw the emergence of high-gloss glazed art pottery as the growing trend in decorative ceramics. Hull responded initially by merely changing the glaze applied to some of its earlier lines. Another significant

No. 210 Coronet vase, 9". .................................. **$15-$25**

development of the time was the growing influence of designer Louise Bauer on Hull's lines. First and most notable was her 1943 Red Riding Hood design, but also significant were her Bow-Knot and Woodland lines.

While the late 1940s and early 1950s saw the demise of long-time rivals Weller and Roseville, business at Hull flourished. This is particularly surprising given that on June 16, 1950, the pottery was completely destroyed by a flood, which in turn caused the kiln to explode, and the ensuing fire finished off the venerable plant.

A new plant officially opened on Jan. 1, 1952. With the new plant came a new company name – Hull Pottery Company.

Hull entered into dinnerware manufacture in the early 1960s at the behest of one of its largest customers, the J.C. Penney Company. Penney, whose offers to purchase Pfaltzgraff dinnerware were declined by the manufacturer, turned to Hull to create a competitive line. Hull's response to this was the new House 'n Garden line, which would remain in production until 1967 and would grow to 100 items.

During the 1970s and 1980s, the pottery was closed by no fewer than eight strikes, one of which lasted for seven weeks. The eighth and final strike by workers sounded the death knell for the pottery. In 1986, the Hull Pottery Company ceased business operations. For more information on Hull pottery, see *Warman's Hull Pottery Identification and Price Guide* by David Doyle.

Most of Hull's art pottery had different decorations on their fronts and rears, and this Blossom Flite console bowl is no exception. T10 Console bowl, 16-1/2". ........ **$100-$150**

B13 Butterfly basket, 8". ........ **$100-$150**

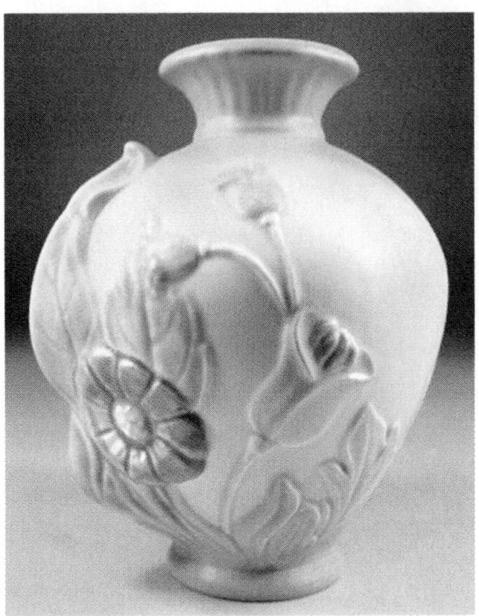

Bow-Knot and many other patterns from Hull's golden era were produced in multiple color combinations, as seen on this 6-1/2" B-4 vase. ........ **$250-$275**

B-18 Bow-Knot jardinière, 5-3/4". ........ **$225-$275**

No. 530/33 5" Calla Lily vase.................**$125-$150**

No. 540/33 6" Calla Lily vase. ...............**$125-$150**

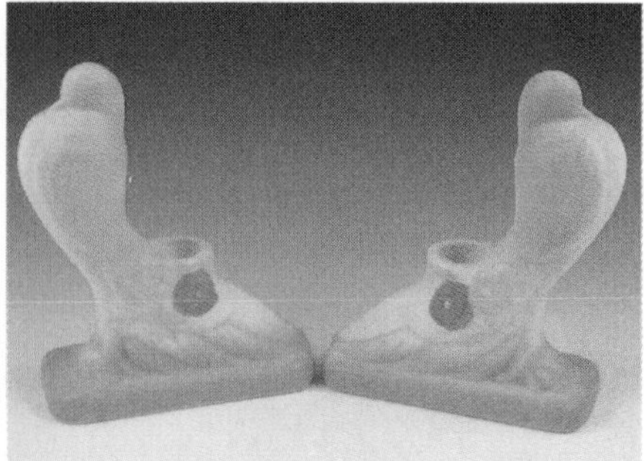

No. 117 Camellia 6-1/2" dove candleholders. ......................................................**$150-$200/pair**

No. 138 Camellia 6-1/4" vase. ...............**$125-$150**

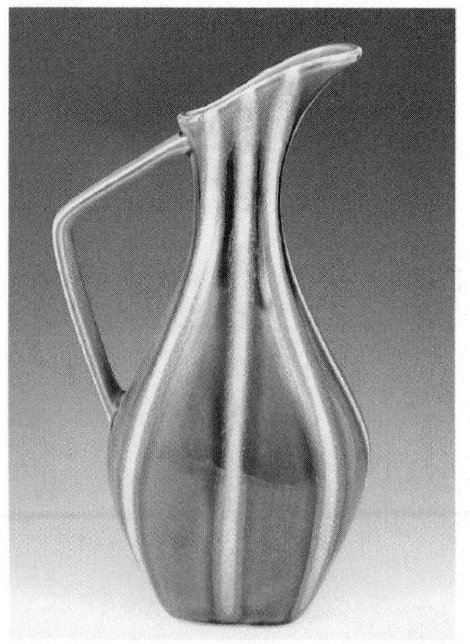

C56 Continental ewer, 12-1/2". ..............**$125-$200**

C46 Capri 4-1/2" x 8" flower bowl. ............ **$30-$40**

C67 Continental 4" candleholder/planter. ... **$20-$40**

This Crestone pitcher, mold number 349, is finished in a non-standard glaze. Experimental pieces such as this are highly sought after by collectors. .... **$40-$50**

B-8 Crescent cookie jar, 9-1/2"................. **$50-$75**

O-17 Debonair casserole. ......................... **$20-$30**

This experimental Dogwood piece was created for testing, but never entered mass production. ............................................. **No established value**

◄ No. 510 Dogwood vase, 10-1/2"......... **$300-$375**

Among Hull's Early Art stoneware offerings was this hanging basket in green, blue, and red high glaze. The unmarked basket measures 7-1/2" wide by 4-3/4" tall. ............................................**$75-$125**

A Hull Early Utility Ware stoneware bowl..... **$20-$30**

No. 77 Fantasy compote, 11-1/2" x 7-1/2". **$10-$20**

E-4 Ebb Tide ewer, 8-1/4"......................**$125-$175**

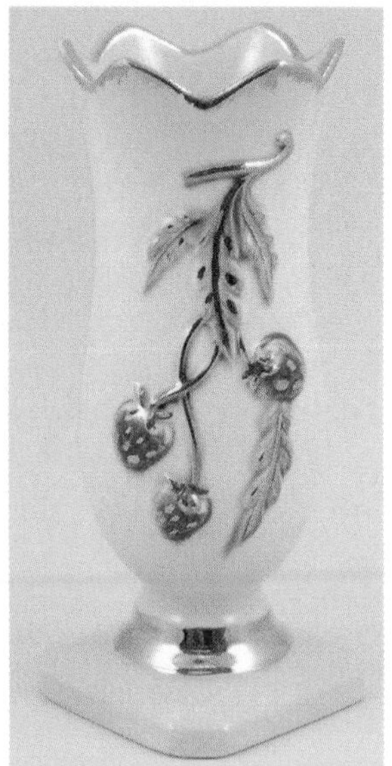

E-11 Ebb Tide basket, 16-1/2"........................................**$175-$225**

◄ This is a Fiesta No. 45 strawberry vase with gold trim, 8-1/2" x 4-1/2", marked Hull USA 45............................................... **$20-$40**

No. 44 and 45 Floral salt and pepper shakers, 3-1/2"............................................. **$10-$15 each**

No. 47 Granada vase, 9"........................... **$75-$100**

No. 216 Granada vase, 9"......................... **$50-$75**

A-18 Heritageware cookie jar. .................... **$25-$35**

F34 Imperial compote.............................. **$10-$20**

▶ No. 525 House 'n Garden jug................ **$12-$16**

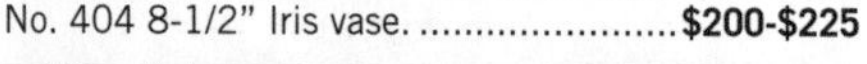

No. 404 8-1/2" Iris vase. .......................**$200-$225**

F81 Imperial twin swan planter, 10-1/2" x 8-1/4" x 5". ....................................................... **$30-$50**

Two of the more attractive Iris items are the No. 406 vase and 408 basket, both highly collectible. No. 406.......................... **$175-$200**
No. 408......................................................................... **$250-$275**

No. 418 Jubilee top hat basket, 8-3/4". .............................**$20-$40**

◀ This unmarked bulbous vase, 7-5/8" tall by 4-3/4" wide, is also part of the Lusterware line. Collectors should expect to pay **$50-$75** for an attractive example such as this.

▶ No. 7 8-1/2" Magnolia vase. ............................. **$125-$175**

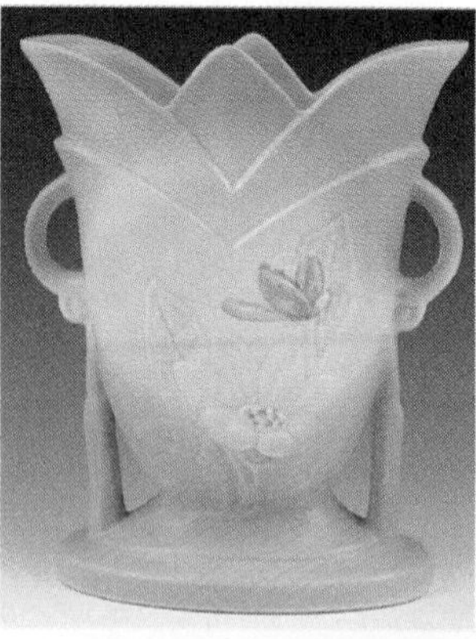

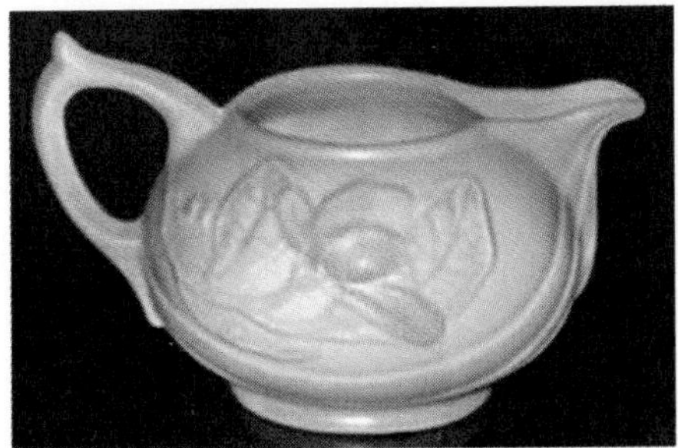

No. 24 Magnolia creamer, 3-3/4"............... **$50-$75**

No. 83 7-1/2" Mayfair hand and cornucopia vase. ............................................................ **$25-$40**

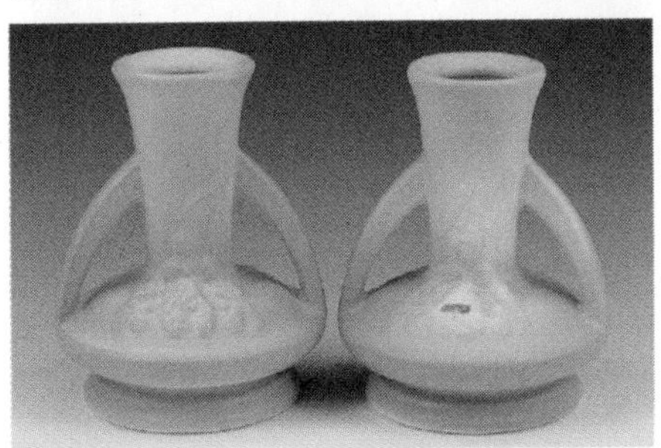

No. 315 4" Orchid candleholders.... **$125-$150 each**

No. 48 9" Mardi Gras vase....................... **$75-$100**

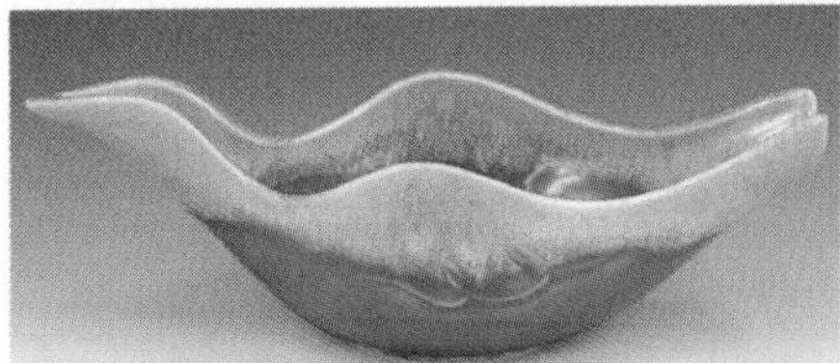

No. 814 11-1/2" Medley flower bowl.......... **$10-$15**

New Magnolia teapot, creamer and sugar bowl.
No. H-20 teapot .................................... **$150-$200**
No. H-21 creamer and H-22 sugar bowl **$40-$60 each**

The pair of 4" No. 315 Orchid candleholders provide a nice accent for the 13" console bowl. ................................ **$500-$700**

S-11 Parchment and Pine teapot, 6"...............................**$75-$125**

6-1/2" Pine Cone vase. ..........................**$150-$200**

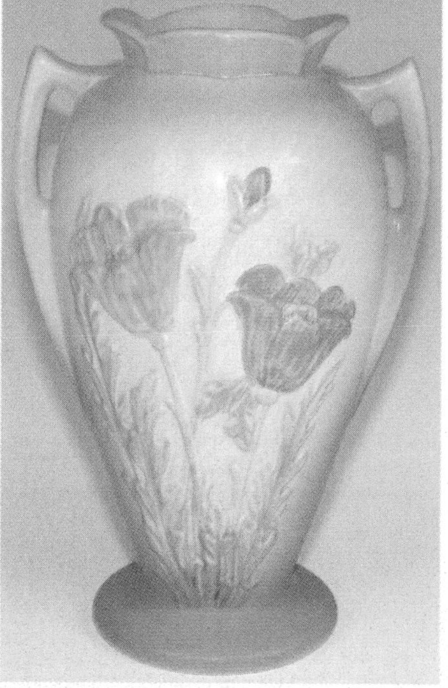

No. 607 Poppy vase...............................**$175-$225**

No. 540 Rainbow leaf serve-all. ................. **$35-$45**

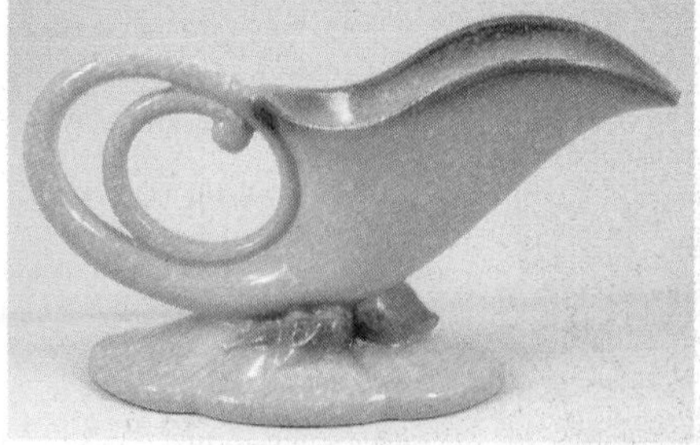

W10 Royal cornucopia, 11"....................... **$35-$50**

► R-12 7" Rosella basket......................**$225-$275**

S1 Serenade bud vase, 6-1/2".................. **$40-$60**

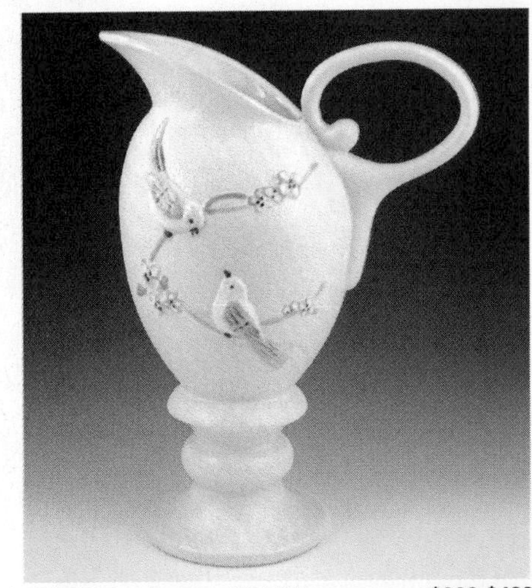

S13 Serenade ewer, 13-1/4".................**$300-$400**

S16 Serenade candleholders, 6-1/2"... **$50-$75 each**

No. 914 Tangerine two-quart ice jug........... **$25-$30**

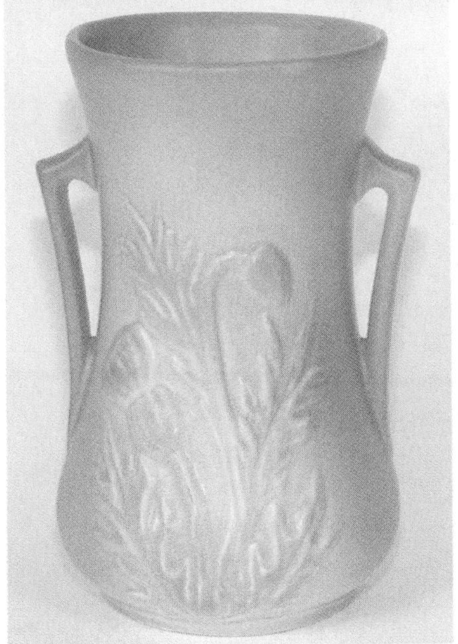

No. 52 Thistle vase, 6-1/2"....................**$125-$150**

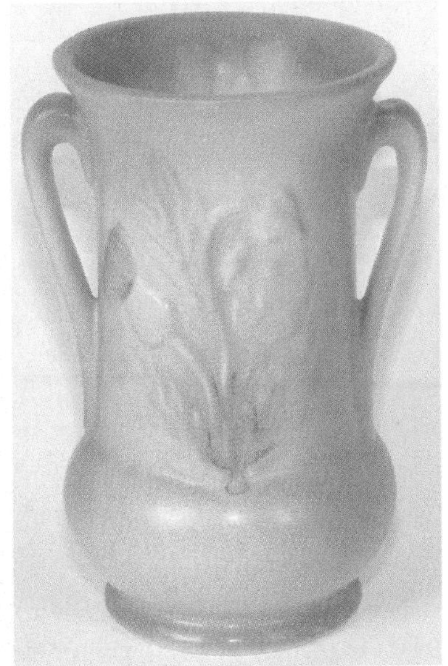

No. 53 6-1/2" vase...............................**$100-$125**

No. 9 Tokay planter, 5-1/2" x 6-1/2". ......... **$30-$50**

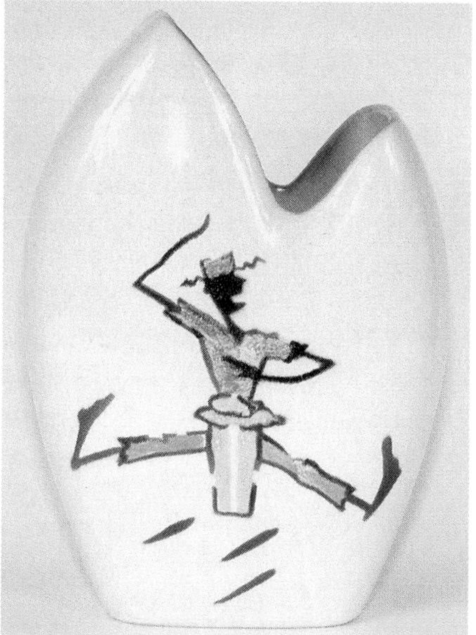
No. T53 Tropicana vase, 8-1/2". ............. **$325-$425**

No. 15 Tokay basket, 12"........................ **$150-$200**

No. 102 Tulip basket, 6"......................... **$125-$150**

◀ No. 115, 7" jardinière, ....................... **$275-$325**

No. 26 Vegetable pitcher, one quart. .......... **$40-$60**

L-6 Water Lily vase, 6-1/2"..................... **$100-$125**

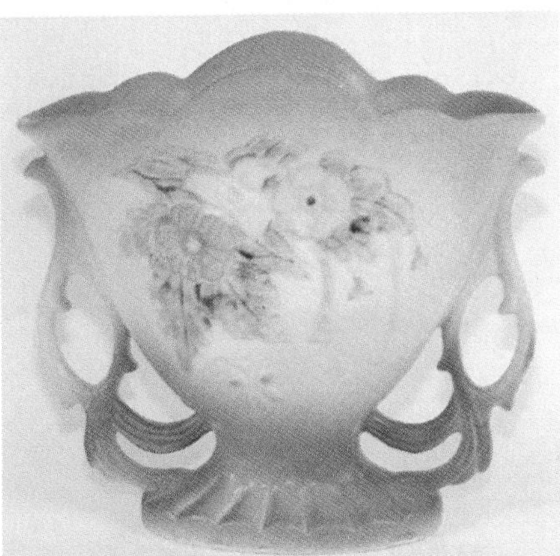
This 6-1/4-inch vase is from the Hull earlier "number series" produced during 1942-43. The pink and tan vase is marked "60-6-1/4"" and "Hull Art USA" on the bottom. .......................................... **$100-$150**

L-1 Water Lily vase, 5-1/2"........................ **$50-$75**

No. 54 Wildflower vase, 6-1/4". .............. **$150-$175**

W-21 Wildflower console bowl. ................ **$225-$250**

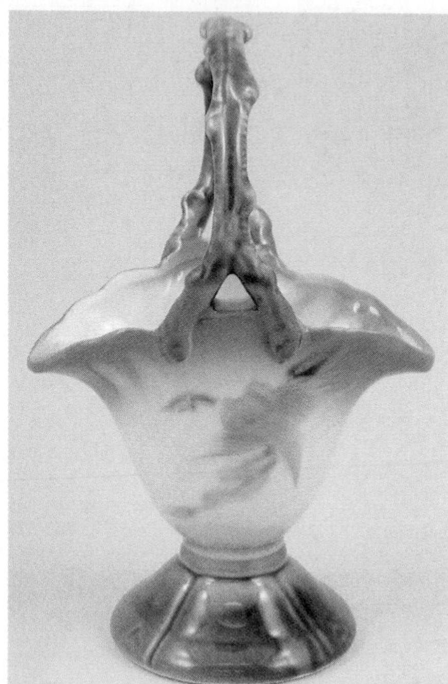
W9 Woodland Hi-Gloss basket, 8-3/4"..... **$200-$250**

W7 Woodland jardinière, 5-1/2".............. **$150-$200**

W28 Woodland sugar bowl, 3-1/2".......... **$150-$200**

W22 Woodland basket, 10-1/2"............. **$550-$650**

W30 Woodland Hi-Gloss candleholders, 3-1/2". ...................................................... **$125-$150 each**

# Ironstone

The first successful ironstone was patented in 1813 by C.J. Mason in England. The body contains iron slag incorporated with the clay. Other potters imitated Mason's ware, and today much hard, thick ware is lumped under the term ironstone. Earlier it was called by various names, including graniteware. Both plain white and decorated wares were made throughout the 19th century. Tea Leaf Lustre ironstone was made by several firms.

## GENERAL

Chamber pot, covered, Atlantic shape, all-white, T. & R. Boote .......................................... **$125-$150**

Sugar bowl, covered, Four Square Wheat shape, all-white, unmarked .......................................... **$80**

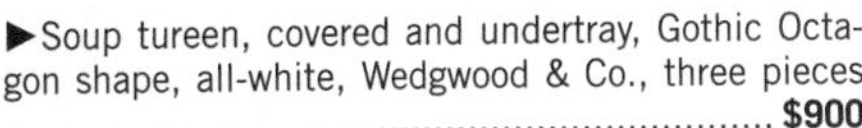

►Soup tureen, covered and undertray, Gothic Octagon shape, all-white, Wedgwood & Co., three pieces .......................................... **$900**

Compote, open, oval, President shape, all-white, John Edwards .......................................... **$350-$400**

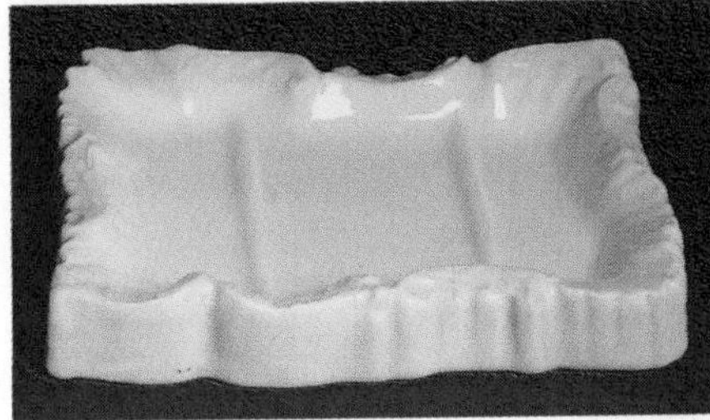

Soap slab, rectangular with molded scroll edges, all-white, marked "ELO" [East Liverpool, Ohio] .......................................... **$20-$30**

Syllabub cup, Hyacinth shape, all-white, Wedgwood & Co., ca. 1865 .............................................. **$45**

Teapot, covered, all-white, Plain Seashore shape, molded dolphin on handle and finial, by W. & E. Corn, ca. 1885..................................... **$125-$150**

Teapot, covered, Full Paneled Gothic shape, all-white, John Alcock, ca. 1850 ........................... **$275-$300**

Vegetable tureen, covered, Sydenham shape, all-white, T. & R. Boote, 1853..................... **$190-$240**

## TEA LEAF IRONSTONE

Butter dish, cover and insert, Chelsea pattern, Alfred Meakin, the set (minor flaws)............................ **$60**

Butter dish, cover and insert, Brocade pattern, Alfred Meakin, flanks inside base, chip on insert........ **$110**

Chamber pot, covered, Cable shape, Anthony Shaw ........ **$175**

Compote, open, square with rounded corners, pedestal base, H. Burgess ........ **$185**

Creamer and covered sugar bowl, child's, slant-sided shape, Mellor Taylor, pr. ........ **$100**

Creamer, Chinese shape, Anthony Shaw ........ **$410**

Mustache cup and saucer, Edge Malkin, professional rim repair ........ **$500**

Pitcher, 8" h., Blanket Stitch shape, Alcock ..... **$140**

Pitcher, 8" h., Square Ridged shape, Wedgwood ........ **$50**

Pitcher, water, Cable shape, Anthony Shaw, rare ........ **$1,200**

Punch bowl, Cable shape, Anthony Shaw ........ **$400**

Teapot, cover, Scroll shape, Alfred Meakin ....... **$160**

Toothbrush vase, cylindrical with molded handles near pedestal base, drain holes, no underplate, possibly by Shaw ........ **$850**

Wash bowl and pitcher set, Cable shape, Anthony Shaw, the set ........ **$225**

Cake plate, Empress pattern, Micratex by Adams, ca. 1960s ........ **$160**

Creamer, Maidenhair Fern pattern, T. Wilkinson **$150**

Chamber pot, open, King Charles pattern, Mayer ........ **$100**

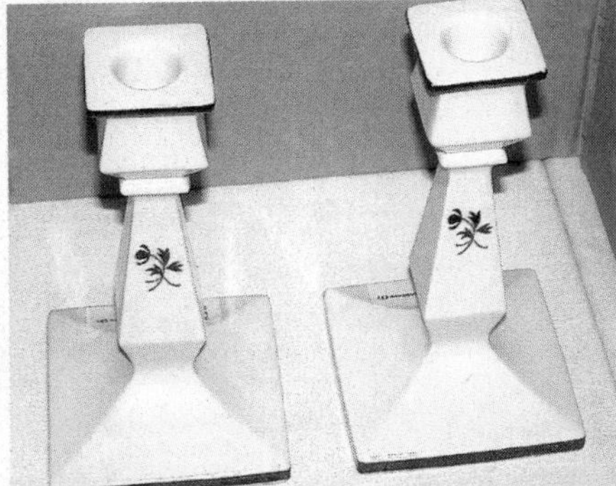

Candlesticks, square, Red Cliff, ca. 1970, pr. .. **$360**

Coffeepot, covered, Woodland pattern, W. & E. Corn, minor flaws ........ **$60**

Gravy boat with attached undertray, Empress pattern, Micratex by Adams, ca. 1960 ........ **$80**

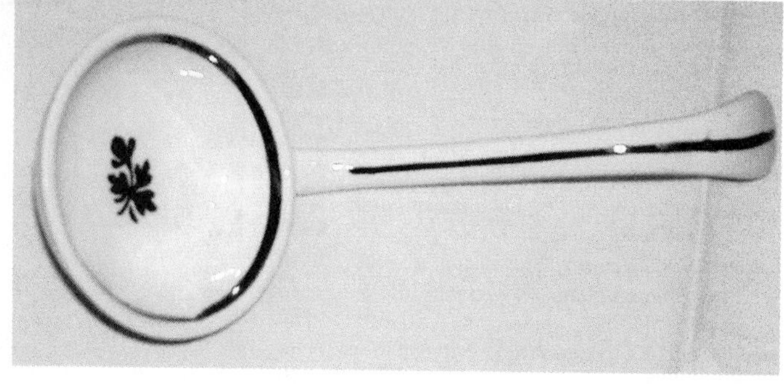

Ladle, sauce tureen-size, some crazing. .............................. **$200**

Platter, oval, Fleur-de-Lis Chain pattern, Wedgwood & Co., large............... **$50**

Salt and pepper shakers, Empress pattern, Micratex by Adams, ca. 1960s, pr. .............................. **$130**

Teapot, covered, Ginger Jar pattern, unmarked, repair to spout........................................................... **$60**

Vegetable dish, covered, Bullet pattern, A. Shaw, minor flaws....................................................... **$65**

Ironstone can darken with age, but it should never be cleaned with chlorine bleach, as it will destroy the glaze.

---

The tea leaf decoration probably originated from a superstition that finding a complete open tea leaf at the bottom of a tea cup would bring good luck.

Vegetable dish, covered, oval, Edge Malkin ........................................ **$325**

Wash bowl and pitcher set, Chrysanthemum pattern, H. Burgess, the set ........................ **$575**

## TEA LEAF VARIANTS

Chamber pot, covered, Pre-Tea Leaf pattern, Niagara shape, E. Walley ........................ **$1,050**

Coffeepot, covered, Wheat in Meadow shape, lustre band trim, Powell & Bishop ........................ **$325**

Creamer, Wrapped Sydenham shape, lustre bands and pinstripes, Edward Walley ........................ **$260**

Cup and saucer, handleless, Pre-Tea Leaf pattern, Niagara shape, E. Walley ........................ **$90**

Gravy boat, Scallops pattern, Sydenham shape, E. Walley ........................ **$250**

Mug, Gothic shape, paneled sides, lustre band, Livesley & Powell ........................ **$100**

Posset cup, Tobacco Leaf pattern, Tulip shape, Elsmore & Forster ........................ **$325**

Sauce tureen, covered, Gothic Cameo shape, lustre band trim, Edward Walley ........................ **$250**

Sauce tureen, cover, undertray and ladle, Moss Rose pattern, H. Burgess, the set ........................ **$375**

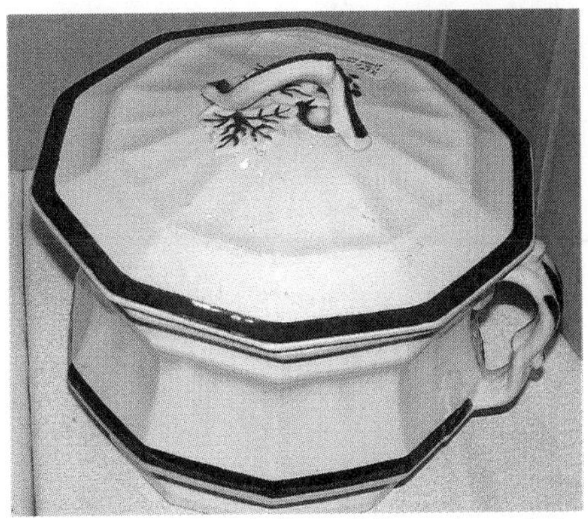

Chamber pot, covered, Grape Octagon shape, lustre band trim, E. Walley, minor flaws ........................ **$150**

Coffeepot, covered, Pinwheel pattern, Grape Octagon shape, E. Walley, slight crazing on cover .......... **$230**

Pitcher, 7-3/4" h., Laurel Wreath pattern, lustre trim, Elsmore & Forster, minor flaws ........................ **$325**

Vegetable dish, covered, Reverse Teaberry pattern, Portland shape, Elsmore & Forster ........................................................................ **$380**

Toothbrush vase, Teaberry pattern, Heavy Square shape, Clementson Bros., slight flaws .................................. **$1,350**

Teapot, covered, Teaberry pattern, Ring O' Hearts shape, J. Furnival ....................................... **$650**

Soap dish, cover and insert, Lily of the Valley shape, lustre band trim, chip inside lip, Anthony Shaw, the set........................................................... **$205**

Sugar bowl, covered, Quartered Rose shape, copper lustre bands and cobalt blue plumes, minor flaws, J. Furnival ................................................ **$180**

Syrup pitcher with hinged metal lid, Moss Rose pattern, George Scott ..................................... **$325**

Teapot, covered, Moss Rose pattern ................. **$100**

Teapot, covered, Quartered Rose shape, copper lustre bands and cobalt blue plumes, possibly J. Furnival ........................................................... **$225**

Vegetable dish, covered, Quartered Rose shape, copper lustre bands and trim and cobalt blue plumes, slight flaws ............................................... **$250**

Waste bowl, Gothic shape, Chelsea Grape pattern, minor flaws ..................................................... **$35**

# Limoges

Limoges is a magical word for those who love beautiful French porcelain. The word is synonymous with fine porcelain, but the name belongs to a special city in central France. Here, in the 18th and 19th centuries, a number of porcelain factories were established because deposits of the special clays required to produce true hard paste porcelain were located nearby.

The best known of these Limoges factories was founded by the Haviland family; however, there were many other firms that produced wares just as fine. All Limoges-made porcelain is high quality and worthy of collector interest.

Charger, large rounded shape with ornate scroll-molded gold border, hand-painted with a scene of two battling brown stags against a shaded ground with leaves in shades of yellow, green, and lavender, 13" dia. ........................ **$201**

Fish set: 11 x 24" oval fish tray, 12 matching 9-1/2" dia. plates, 7-1/4" l. sauceboat and underplate; each piece with scalloped rim and paneled sides, each hand-painted with a different game fish, lake landscape, andflower, bases marked "B.B. H. Limoges, France" ..................... **$1,668**

Punch set: punch bowl, base and 10 champagne-style stems; the footed bowl with deep rounded and flaring sides hand-painted around the sides with large gold leafy grapevines on stems against a pale blue shaded to white ground, on a matching base with large gold paw feet, the saucer-shaped matching stems with a wide shallow round bowl on a simple stem, mark of Tressemann & Vogt, Limoges, late 19th-early 20th c., bowl 16" dia., 7" h., base 3-1/2" h., stems each 3-1/2" h.................. **$1,035**

Tankard-type pitcher, gold and brown ringed base below slightly tapering cylindrical body with reddish brown D-form handle, painted with friar seated at tavern table, artist-signed, 14-1/2" h....... **$518**

Tea set: one-cup covered teapot, open sugar, creamer, and oblong tray; each piece painted with roses, gold wave scroll band around teapot and creamer neck, gold loop handles and teapot finial, marks of Gèrard, Dufraisseix & Abbot, Limoges, France, ca. 1900-1941 .................... **$900**

# Majolica

In 1851, an English potter was hoping that his new interpretation of a centuries-old style of ceramics would be well received at the "Great Exhibition of the Industries of All Nations" set to open May 1 in London's Hyde Park.

W.S. & S. vase with mask feet and handles, 12-1/2" t. ........................................ **$500+**

Potter Herbert Minton had high hopes for his display. His father, Thomas Minton, founded a pottery works in the mid-1790s in Stoke-on-Trent, Staffordshire. Herbert Minton had designed a "new" line of pottery, and his chemist, Leon Arnoux, had developed a process that resulted in vibrant, colorful glazes that came to be called "majolica."

Trained as an engineer, Arnoux also studied the making of encaustic tiles, and had been appointed art director at Minton's works in 1848. His job was to introduce and promote new products. Victorian fascination with the natural world prompted Arnoux to reintroduce the work of Bernard Palissy, whose naturalistic, bright-colored "maiolica" wares had been created in the 16th century. But Arnoux used a thicker body to make pieces sturdier. This body was given a coating of opaque white glaze, which provided a surface for decoration.

Pieces were modeled in high relief, featuring butterflies and other insects, flowers and leaves, fruit, shells, animals and fish. Queen Victoria's endorsement of the new pottery prompted its acceptance by the general public.

When Minton introduced his wares at Philadelphia's 1876 Centennial Exhibition, American potters also began to produce majolica.

For more information on majolica, see *Warman's Majolica Identification and Price Guide* by Mark F. Moran.

French asparagus covered barrel three piece, with under plate, strong color and detail, tray 14" l., barrel 11" l., 7-1/2" t., professional repair to leaf on barrel cover. ........................................................ **$800+**

Four begonia leaf on basket butter pats. ...**$275+ all**

Floral and basket-weave basket with bird perched on twig handle, bird missing beak, 8" t. ............ **$300+**

Bird on branch low cake stand, 8-3/4" dia. ...... **$60+**

Holdcroft footed bowl large pond lily, 11" dia. ............................................................ **$200+**

George Jones table centerpiece with putto riding dolphin atop shell and coral base while holding shell, rim chip to one shell and hairline to another, outstanding color and detail, 15" t., 13-1/2" w. (Collector tip: The company started operations in the early 1860s as George Jones in Stoke, Staffordshire, England, and in 1873 became George Jones & Sons Ltd.).....**$3,500+**

George Jones diamond-shaped cachepot, cobalt ground with bamboo borders, storks, water lilies and flowers in relief, outstanding color and detail, 11-1/2" l., 7" t. ............................... **$5,750+**

George Jones apple blossom full-size cheese keeper, strong color, hairline to cover, 12-1/2" t. ....................$2,500+

Etruscan maple leaf shallow compote, with early mark for Griffen, Smith and Hill, 9" diameter, 5-1/2" t. .................... $250

Morley & Co. mottled leaf comport (or compote), rim repair. (Morley & Co. Pottery was founded in 1879, Wellsville, Ohio, making graniteware and majolica.) .................... $110+

◀ Julius Dressler leaf tray with six eggcups, 13" w. (Collector tip: Julius Dressler, Bela Czech Republic, company founded 1888, producing faience, majolica and porcelain. In 1920, the name was changed to EPIAG. The firm closed about 1945.) ....................$70+ all

Samuel Lear water lily creamer and sugar, hairline crack to creamer, nicks to sugar lid. ................ $110+ pair

Wardle bird and fan covered butter dish, hairline crack to base, 8-1/2" dia. (Collector tip: Wardle & Co., established 1871 at Hanley, Staffordshire, England.) ............................................................. **$150+**

Bird and fan turquoise humidor, 5-1/2" t. ..... **$150+**

Hugo Lonitz cobalt ewer with swan atop cattails, strong color and detail, professional repair to handle, 15" t. (Collector tip: Hugo Lonitz operated in Haldensleben, Germany, from 1868-1886, and later Hugo Lonitz & Co., 1886-1904, producing household and decorative porcelain and earthenware, and metal wares. Look for a mark of two entwined fish.) ..........................................................**$1,200+**

Continental inkwell with cats on bicycles and floral design, professional leg and rim repair to base, 8-1/2" l. ...................................................... **$75+**

Holdcroft cobalt footed jardinière with ladies head handles and garland drapes, good color, professional rim repair, 11" w., 7" t. (Collector tip: Joseph Holdcroft majolica ware was produced at Daisy Bank in Longton, Staffordshire, England, from 1870 to 1885. Items can be found marked with "JHOLDCROFT," but many items can only be attributed by the patterns and colors that are documented to have come from the Holdcroft potteries.) .... **$400+**

Minton ram's head jardinière professional repair to rams heads, rim and base, good color, 14-3/4" t., 19-1/2" w. ............................................... **$1,500**

Palissy Ware jug with oak leaves, acorns and snake wrapped around jug with frog on spout, professional rim, handle and spout repair, 10" t. (Collector tip: In the style of Bernard Palissy, c. 1510-1590, the great French Renaissance potter.)........................**$1,100+**

Continental rabbit and tree stump figural match striker, base repair, 8" w. ............................ **$350+**

George Jones apple blossom and basket weave mug, good color and detail, 5-1/2" t. (Collector tip: The company started operations in the early 1860s as George Jones in Stoke, Staffordshire, England, and in 1873 became George Jones & Sons Ltd.).....**$2,000+**

Longchamp oyster plate, 8-3/4" dia. .............. **$300**

◀ French Faience-type oyster plate with floral center, 10-1/2" w. ............................................... **$110+**

HB Quimper large floral oyster platter, 14-1/2" dia. (Collector tip: Named for the earliest known firm producing hand-painted pottery in Brittany, France, founded in 1685 by Jean Baptiste Bousquet.) **$125+**

Brownfield pink hops and wheat pitcher with lavender ground, minor glaze nick and hairline, Bacall Collection, 6-1/2" t. (Collector tip: W. Brownfield & Son, Burslem and Cobridge, Staffordshire, England, 1850 to 1891.)........................................... **$2,300+**

Blackberry on bark pitcher, 7-1/2" t. ............ **$200+**

Etruscan pink sunflower syrup pitcher, good color. ............................................................ **$425+**

◀ Fielding fan and scroll with insect pitcher, turquoise ground, minor surface wear to pebble ground, 6-1/2" t. (Collector tip: Railway Pottery, established by S. Fielding & Co., Stoke, Stoke-on-Trent, Staffordshire, England, 1879.)................................ **$110+**

George Jones orchid pitcher with leaf handle, good color, professional handle repair, 7" t. ........**$1,000+**

Wild rose on yellow pebble ground pitcher, small rim chip, 7-1/4" t. ........................................... **$110+**

French Palissy Ware planter with fish, leaves and ferns, minor rim repair, good detail, 7" w., 5-1/2" t. ............................................................ **$400+**

Wedgwood Argenta sunflower and urn pitcher, hairline crack to handle, 8" t. (Collector tip: Founded by Josiah Wedgwood in 1759 at Burslem, Staffordshire, England.)................................................. **$275+**

Large Delphin Massier pink flamingo figural planter, great detail, 14-1/2" l., 10-1/2" t. .............**$1,000+**

Begonia on basket plate with cobalt rope edge, good color, 8" dia. ............................................ **$250+**

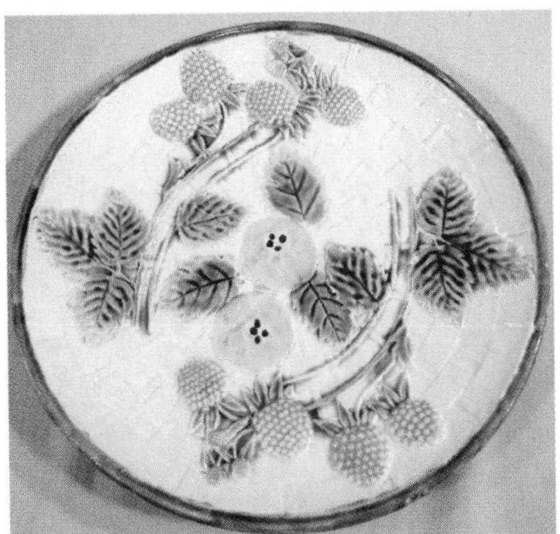

Etruscan basket-weave strawberry and apple plate with cobalt rim, 9-1/4" dia. (Collector tip: Made by Griffen, Smith and Hill of Phoenixville, Pa., 1879 to about 1890.) .............................................. **$75+**

Fielding morning glory wheat, ribbon and bow plate, minor rim nick, 8" dia. ................................. **$60+**

Samuel Lear floral and fan plate 8" dia. (Collector tip: Samuel Lear, Hanley, Staffordshire, England, 1877 to 1886.) .................................................... **$140+**

Wedgwood cobalt monkey on branch plate, professional repair to hairline crack, 8-1/2" dia. ........................................................................ **$850+**

Cobalt floral platter strong color, 13-1/4" w. ........**$250+**

Lavender covered game tureen with liner, good color, professional rim repair to base and rim of lid, 9" w. .......... **$750+**

Victoria Pottery Co. boar's head game tureen with brown ground trimmed in green, insert included, minor nick to handle, good detail, 12" w. (Collector tip: Victoria Pottery Co., Hanley, Staffordshire, England, 1895 to 1927.).......... **$200+**

Pair of Sarreguemines dolphin and shell vases, shape no. 949, one with professional rim repair, 14-1/2" t. (Collector tip: Named for the city in the Alsace-Lorraine region of northeastern France.)... **$600+ pair**

W.S. & S. vase with mask feet and handles, 12-1/2" t. .......... **$500+**

◀ Minton vase with basket-weave and applied floral motif, hairline, shape no. 1287, date code for 1870, good color, 6-3/4" t. (Thomas Minton founded his factory in the mid-1790s in Stoke-on-Trent, Staffordshire, England. His son, Herbert Minton, introduced majolica pottery—with glazes created by Léon Arnoux—at England's Great Exhibition of 1851.)**$700+**

# McCoy Pottery

McCoy

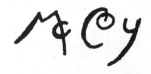

The first McCoy with clay under his fingernails was W. Nelson McCoy. With his uncle, W.F. McCoy, he founded a pottery works in Putnam, Ohio, in 1848, making stoneware crocks and jugs.

That same year, W. Nelson's son, James W., was born in Zanesville, Ohio. James established the J.W. McCoy Pottery Co. in Roseville, Ohio, in the fall of 1899. The J.W. McCoy plant was destroyed by fire in 1903 and was rebuilt two years later.

It was at this time that the first examples of Loy-Nel-Art wares were produced. The line's distinctive title came from the names of James McCoy's three sons, Lloyd, Nelson, and Arthur. Like other "standard" glazed pieces produced at this time by several Ohio potteries, Loy-Nel-Art has a glossy finish on a dark brown-black body, but Loy-Nel-Art featured a splash of green color on the front and a burnt-orange splash on the back.

George Brush became general manager of J.W. McCoy Pottery Co. in 1909. The company became Brush-McCoy Pottery Co. in 1911, and in 1925 the name was shortened to Brush Pottery Co. This firm remained in business until 1982.

Separately, in 1910, Nelson McCoy Sr. founded the Nelson McCoy Sanitary and Stoneware Co., also in Roseville. By the early 1930s, production had shifted from utilitarian wares to art pottery, and the company name was changed to Nelson McCoy Pottery.

Designer Sydney Cope was hired in 1934, and was joined by his son, Leslie, in 1936. The Copes' influence on McCoy wares continued until Sydney's death in 1966. That same year, Leslie opened a gallery devoted to his family's design heritage and featuring his own original art.

Nelson McCoy Sr. died in 1945, and was succeeded as company president by his nephew, Nelson McCoy Melick.

A fire destroyed the plant in 1950, but company officials—including Nelson McCoy Jr., then 29—decided to rebuild, and the new Nelson McCoy Pottery Co. was up and running in just six months.

Nelson Melick died in 1954. Nelson Jr. became company president, and oversaw the company's continued growth. In 1967, the operation was sold to entrepreneur David Chase. At this time, the words "Mt. Clemens Pottery" were added to the company marks. In 1974, Chase sold the company to Lancaster Colony Corp., and the company marks included a stylized "LCC" logo. Nelson Jr. and his wife, Billie, who had served as a products supervisor, left the company in 1981.

In 1985, the company was sold again, this time to Designer Accents. The McCoy pottery factory closed in 1990.

For more information on McCoy pottery, see *Warman's McCoy Pottery*, 2nd edition, by Mark F. Moran.

Two shoulder bowls in a windowpane pattern, 1920s, with shield marks, 8" and 9"................ **$75-$85 ea.**

Nelson McCoy Sanitary Stoneware six-gallon crock, 1910-1920, shield mark, came in various sizes from two to 50 gallons.................................**$100-$125**

Bean pot, 1950s, McCoy mark, 6" h. ......... **$65-$75**

Covered casserole, 1940s, McCoy USA, 6-1/2" dia. ............................................................ **$55-$65**

W.F. McCoy five-gallon crock, salt glaze with stenciled ink lettering: "W.F. McCoy Wholesale Dealer in Stoneware–Zanesville, O.," with impressed "5," late 1800s, 13" h...........**$1,200-$1,400 in mint condition**

Cherries and Leaves charger in glossy yellow, mid-1930s, unmarked, 11-1/4" dia...............**$550-$650**

Elephant and donkey pitchers (also called pitcher vases) in matte white, 1940s, NM USA mark, rare in any color.........................................**$300-$350 ea.**

Two parrot pitchers (also called pitcher vases), early 1950s, McCoy USA mark ........................ **$200-$225 ea.**

Ring Ware pitcher and three tumblers in glossy green (note color variations), 1920s, unmarked. Pitcher, 9" h. **$80-$100**
Tumblers, 4-1/4" h. **$80-$90 ea.**

Strap pitcher in glossy burgundy, late 1940s, McCoy mark ...................................................... **$75-$85**

McCoy flowerpot, ribbed with rose design, stoneware, 1920s, unmarked, 4" h., 5-1/2" dia. .............. **$30+**

Flowerpot in a skyscraper design, detached saucer, 1930s-40s, found in other colors, unmarked, 9" h., 10-1/2" dia. ............. **$75+**

Leaves and Berries flowerpot in matte brown and green, 5-1/2" dia. .................................... **$60-$70**

Garden Club pot and saucer in glossy yellow, late 1950s, McCoy USA mark, 8" h............. **$80-$90**

Three sizes of flowerpots in pale green, 1950s, McCoy USA mark, 7", 6-1/4", and 4-1/4" ............................. **$75-$100 ea.**

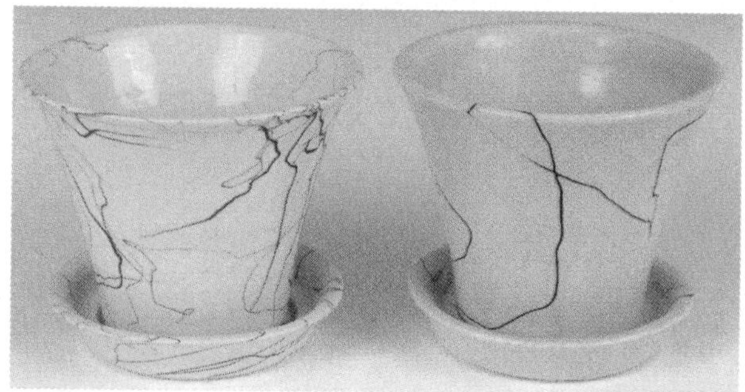
Two "Squiggle" pots and saucers in glossy yellow and matte pink, 1960s, McCoy USA mark, 5-1/2" h................................. **$50-$60**

Two jardinières with applied leaves and berries, late 1940s, McCoy USA mark, 7-1/2" h.**$200-$250 ea.**

Ivy jardinière in brown and green, early 1950s, unmarked, also found in a brighter glossy tan and green with matching pedestal, 8" h.................. **$350-$450**

Jardinière in a ring-ware design, stoneware, 1930s, unmarked, 9" h., 10" dia. opening................ **$100+**

Sunburst jardinière in a multicolored glaze, 1930s, unmarked, 6-3/4" h. ............**$50-$70**

Basket-Weave jardinière and pedestal, peach glaze, late 1930s, NM USA mark, 13" and 7-1/2" h. ........ **$250+ set**

Holly jardinière and pedestal in matte green, unmarked; jardinière, 7-1/2" dia.; pedestal, 13" h...................................... **$300-$350/pair**

Leaves and Berries jardinière and pedestal in matte brown and green; jardinière, 7-1/2" dia.; pedestal, 6-3/4" h. ....**$225-$275/pair**

Shoulder bowl in a windowpane pattern, 1920s, with shield mark and #4, 11" ........................ **$100-$125**

Penguin spoon rest, 1950s, 7" x 5-1/2" .. **$125-$175**

Five sizes of Stone Craft mixing bowls (called pink and blue) ranging in diameter from 7" to 14" (also a 5" size), mid-1970s, McCoy LCC mark. ..................................... **$225-$250 for complete set**

Two shoulder bowls in a windowpane pattern, 1920s, with shield marks, 8" and 9" ................ **$75-$85 ea.**

Ring ware covered butter or cheese crock, 1920s, shield mark "M." .................................... **$90-$110**

Pine Cone planter, mid-1940s, McCoy USA mark, 8" w., rare ................................................ **$500-$600**
(A slightly larger planter in rust glaze **$1,800-$2,000**)

Bird planting dish, 1950s, McCoy mark, 10" w. ............................................................ **$25-$35**

Elephant planter in matte aqua, attributed to McCoy, unmarked, 9" h., with attribution.................... **$100**

Large fish planter, found in other colors, 1950s, McCoy mark, 12" l.............................. **$1,200-$1,400**

Hummingbird planter in green, late 1940s, McCoy USA mark, 10-1/2" w. ........................... **$125-$150**

Parrot planter in matte white, 1940s, NM mark, 7-1/2" h........... **$70-$80**

Swan planting dish in rustic ivory and turquoise, 1950s, McCoy USA mark, 8-1/2" h. ........................................................ **$700-$800**

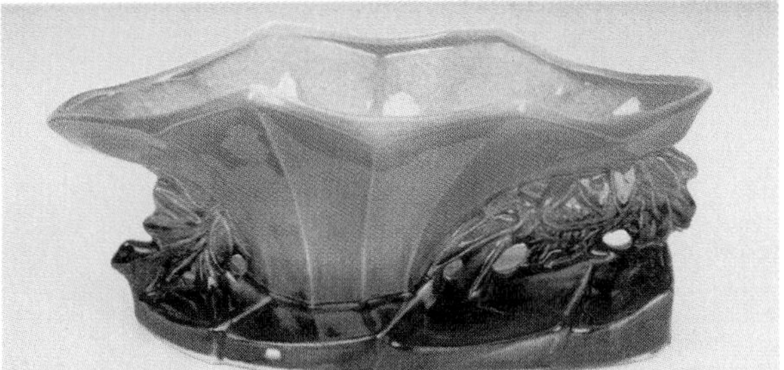

Large centerpiece planter, 1950s, McCoy USA mark, found in other colors, 12" l................ **$90-$110**

Sand dollar vase in matte white, stoneware, 1940s, unmarked, also found in pastel colors, and brown and green .....**$250-$300, depending on color**

Sunflower vase using same mold as lamp, 1950s, with unusual airbrush decoration, unmarked ................................**$450-$550**

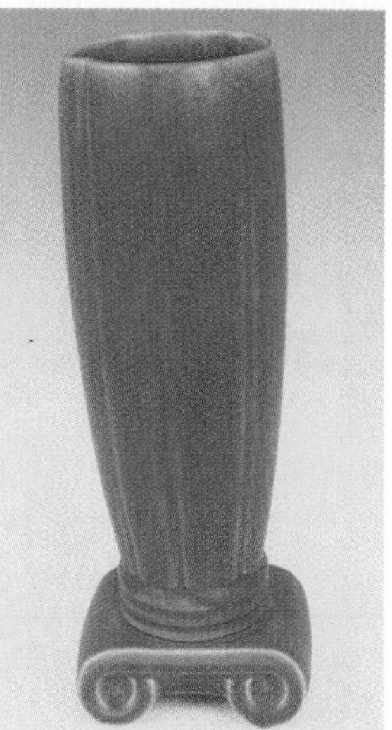

Tall scroll vase in matte green (often found in glossy tan-brown), late 1940s, USA mark, 14" h. ................................**$150-$200**

Apple wall pocket in gold trim, 1950s, unmarked, 7" l. ................................**$200-$225**

Shrimp vase in traditional colors, 1950s, McCoy USA mark, 9" h. ....................................... **$175+**

Floor vase in a blue onyx glaze, 24" h., unmarked.......**$700-$900**

Bird on sunflower wall pocket, can also stand as planter, McCoy mark, came in a variety of glaze combinations, 6-1/2" h.. **$60-$75**

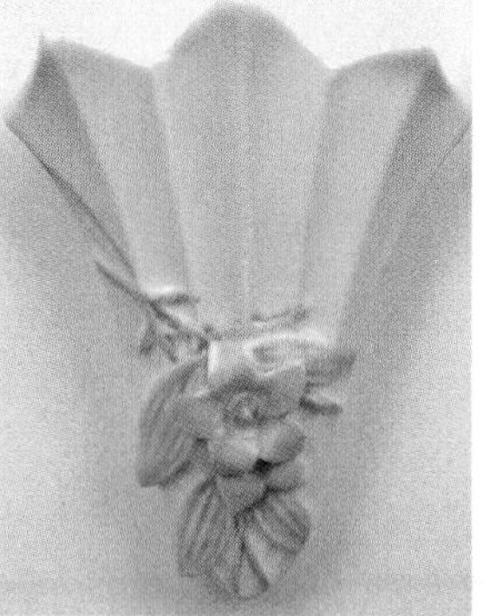

Blossomtime wall pocket in matte yellow, McCoy mark, 7-3/4" l. ..................................**$90-$110**

►Violin wall pocket in blue with gold trim, 1950s, McCoy USA and Shafer mark, 10" l......**$275-$325**

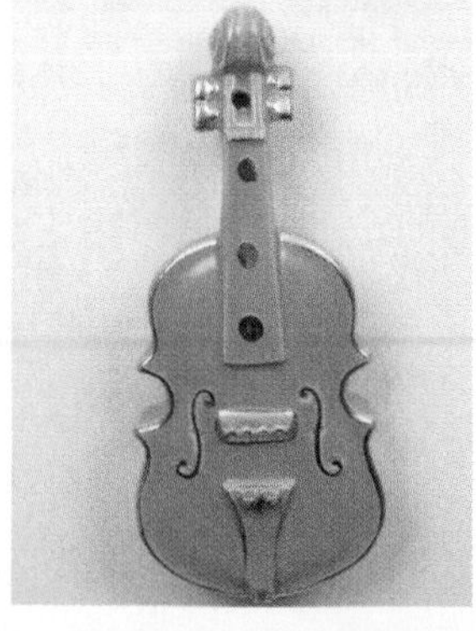

# Meissen

The secret of true hard paste porcelain, known long before to the Chinese, was "discovered" accidentally in Meissen, Germany, by J.F. Bottger, an alchemist working with E.W. Tschirnhausen. The first European true porcelain was made in the Meissen Porcelain Works, organized about 1709. Meissen marks have been widely copied by other factories.

Centerpiece, allegorical, flaring reticulated oblong top base with open end handles decorated overall with encrusted flowers and green leaves among gilt-trimmed scrolls, raised on ornate flower-encrusted pedestal with flower-painted scrolled cartouche above a group of children representing the Four Seasons around the scrolled base, blue crossed-swords mark, modeled by Leuteritz, ca. 1880, overall 17-3/8" h. .......... **$7,768**

Figure group, young mother in 18th c. costume seated holding her bare-bottomed toddler across her lap with a switch in her other hand, her young daughter pulling at her arm to dissuade her, on a round molded and gilt-trimmed base, blue crossed-swords mark, late 19th c., 10-1/4" h. .......... **$3,585**

Dinner service: 10 10" dia. dinner plates, nine cups and saucers, eight cream soup bowls, and eight under-plates; Blue Onion pattern, all marked with blue crossed swords, 19th c. .......... **$1,725**

Vase, footed bottle-form body tapering to a ringed neck with widely flaring rim, cobalt blue ground enameled in white in the Limoges style with a pair of amorous putti sitting on a leafy branch, one extending a floral wreath to a third in flight releasing a dove, gold banding at the foot, neck ring and rim, blue crossed-swords mark, probably designed by E.A. Leuteritz, ca. 1880, 6-5/8" h. .................... **$2,868**

Urn, flaring gadrooned foot joined by a white-beaded disk to the large ovoid urn-form body with gold gadrooning around the lower portion below the wide white central band hand-painted with large bouquet of colorful flowers, the tapering neck in deep pink below the heavy gold rolled and gadrooned rim, white and gold entwined serpent handles at each side, blue crossed-swords mark, late 19th c., 11" h. .................... **$518**

Vase, classic baluster-form, a fluted flaring base and pedestal with rings supporting the ovoid body with band of flutes below the wide cobalt blue body band decorated with large gilt and silver florals, ringed shoulder and short flaring neck with incurved molded rim flanked by long looped snake handles from rim to shoulder, gilt trim on base and body and new gilt trim on handles, late 19th c., 15-1/2" h. .................... **$2,300**

Vases, baluster form with entwined snake handles, cobalt blue ground, the mouth, collar and foot molded and trimmed with gilt, late 19th-early 20th c., blue crossed swords marks and incised and impressed numbers, mounted as lamps, 19" h. .................... **$2,990/pr.**

Teapot, covered, nearly spherical slightly tapering body decorated with robin's-egg blue ground, the flat cover with gold knob finial, short curved shoulder spout and pointed arch handle, each side centered by a hand-painted color scene of merchants haggling at quayside within a gold border, the cover with two smaller views, "Indianische Blumen" design under spout and on handle, blue crossed-swords mark, 1735-40, overall 4-1/4" l., 4-1/4" h. .................... **$4,780**

# Nippon

"Nippon" is a term used to describe a wide range of porcelain wares produced in Japan from the late 19th century until about 1921. It was in 1891 that the United States implemented the McKinley Tariff Act, which required that all wares exported to the United States carry a marking indicating their country of origin. The Japanese chose to use "Nippon," their name for Japan. In 1921 the import laws were revised and the words "Made in" had to be added to the markings. Japan was also required to replace the "Nippon" with the English name "Japan" on all wares sent to the United States.

Many Japanese factories produced Nippon porcelain, much of it hand-painted with ornate floral or landscape decoration and heavy gold decoration, applied beading and slip-trailed designs referred to as "moriage." We indicate the specific marking used on a piece, when known, at the end of each listing. Be aware that a number of Nippon markings have been reproduced and used on new porcelain wares.

Important reference books on Nippon include: *The Collector's Encyclopedia of Nippon Porcelain, Series One through Three*, by Joan F. Van Patten (Collector Books, Paducah, Kentucky) and *The Wonderful World of Nippon Porcelain, 1891-1921* by Kathy Wojciechowski (Schiffer Publishing, Ltd., Atglen, Pennsylvania).

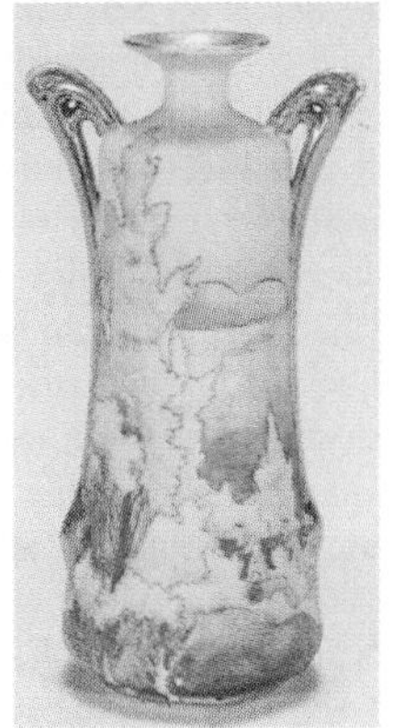

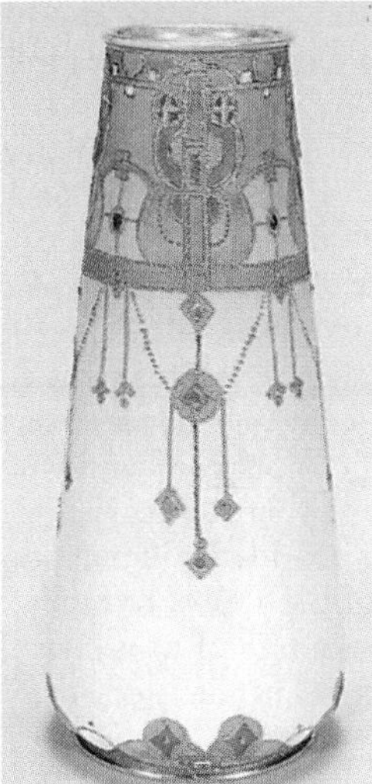

**Above left:** Humidor, covered, three square block feet supporting the wide slightly tapering cylindrical body with slightly tapering cover with large mushroom finial, the body decorated with a landscape of a man in a canoe with stag in green bushes on the shore, dark yellow to pale cream ground, the feet and top rim decorated with geometric decorative bands with stylized symbols, matching band around the cover, 7" h. **$575**

**Above center:** Vase, "sharkskin" technique, slender slightly tapering cylindrical body with a narrow shoulder centered by a short neck with widely flaring mouth, arched and pierced-loop gold shoulder handles, the sides hand-painted with a stylized landscape with tall trees in the foreground and small houses and a lake in the distance, done in pastel shades of blue, yellow, green, lavender and orange, purple Cherry Blossom mark, tiny glaze nick in the base, 7-1/8" h. **$230**

**Above right:** Vase, bulbous ovoid body tapering to a short flaring neck trimmed in gold and flanked by arched gold shoulder handles, the body centered by a large gold oval reserve painted with a full-length portrait of an exotic young woman standing in front of a peacock, surrounded by an overall gold lattice and pink rose decoration on the white ground, green Maple Leaf mark, minor gold wear, 5-3/4" h. **$432**

◀Vase, tapestry-type, tall gently tapering cylindrical body with a flat rim, the upper body decorated with a wide band of stylized geometric designs in shades of green, blue, rose red, and gold and faux jewels, gold beaded swags suspended down the sides, blue Maple Leaf mark, 9-1/2" h. **$1,150**

## Noritake

Although Noritake is the long-recognized identifier for a particular brand of fine china, the firm began life in 1904 as Nippon Gomei Kaisha. The "Noritake" moniker came from the company's location in the village of Noritake, Japan. Because it was a geographic designation, the firm had to wait until the 1980s before receiving permission to officially register "Noritake" as a trade name.

Prior to the 1900s, Japan's "closed" society meant that relatively few domestically produced items found their way past the country's borders. Japanese artware was prized as much for its rarity as for its skillful execution. In the late 1800s, the easing of economic sanctions and growing interaction with the West meant that the rest of the world could appreciate the artistry of Japan.

Noritake was developed by Morimura Brothers, a distributorship founded in 1876. In its earliest years, Morimura operated as an exporter, bringing traditional Japanese giftware (paper lanterns, china, and a variety of decorative curio items) to buyers on American shores. The company eventually embraced the goal of producing a line of fine china dinnerware that, while Japanese-made, would prove irresistible in styling and execution to Western consumers.

Noritake dinnerware debuted in 1904. In 1914, when the product was deemed ready for a larger audience, exports began. The first Noritake pieces were hand-painted with extensive gold trim, both costly and time-consuming to produce. Additionally, much of the decorative work was farmed out to independent artisans throughout the region. Quality varied due to the varying skills of individual freelancers.

With the onset of mass production in the 1920s, Noritake was able to achieve consistency in its output, expand productivity, lower costs, and increase brand name recognition.

From the 1920s until World War II, Noritake achieved its greatest prominence. The inventory fell into two overall categories: dinnerware and fancy ware. Dinnerware, as the name implies, encompassed products made specifically for the table—plates, bowls, tea sets, condiment holders, and the like. Fancy ware covered everything else, from wall pockets and vases to elaborately decorated display platters.

A major factor in Noritake's success was the Morimura brothers' early and aggressive use of advertising, cementing the brand in the minds of American buyers. Full-page Noritake ads graced major trade journals. Early on, the company also saw the value of such promotional efforts as premium tie-ins. During the 1920s, the Larkin Co., a New York mail-order distributor of various home and beauty products, offered buyers an assortment of Noritake china as a bonus when buying from the company's catalog. Among the most popular Larkin patterns was Azalea, still a favorite today.

The onset of World War II meant that, overnight, Noritake china was no longer available (or even welcome) in American homes. The company continued to produce china on a limited basis during the war, but only for domestic buyers.

During the American occupation of Japan (1945-1952), Noritake china became popular with servicemen stationed there; the company's increased production was one factor in assisting Japan along the road to economic recovery. The "Noritake China" name was, for a time, replaced with a more indeterminate "Rose China." The company indicated this was because the china was not yet at its pre-war level of quality; concerns about identifying the product too closely with a recent adversary may also have been a contributing factor.

In the years following the war, Noritake regained its previous worldwide reputation for quality. Whether lusterware of the 1920s, Art Deco stylings of the 1930s, or today's contemporary designs, Noritake porcelain reflects the artistic sensibilities of its creators, yet remains perfectly attuned to the specific cultural sensibilities of its intended audience.

Art Deco Noritake porcelain from the collection of Marilyn Derrin hit the auction block June 1-2, 2012, setting the standard for new values in the marketplace. The collection's primary focus was on Art Deco Noritake porcelain, but also included Nippon and Made In Japan export wares. This was the largest collection of its kind to come to the marketplace.

What follows is a selection of important lots from that sale. The pieces rarely seen on the market soared past any price guide expectations. The exceptional but more common pieces held their values, and the lesser examples hit peaks and valleys in their final pricing.

The sale was managed by A.H. Wilkens Auctions & Appraisals of Toronto. The prices here have been converted to U.S. dollars from Canadian dollars.

Art Deco Noritake flat powder, orange and green lustre with a lady in red fur coat................. **$181**

Noritake Art Deco vase, cream ground with over-gilded roses and stylized handles, red M-in-wreath, 6-1/8" h..................................... **$103**

Noritake clown dresser jar, red polka dot suit with yellow and green ruffled collar, green M-in-wreath, 5-3/4" h.............. **$1,821**

Rare Noritake figural dresser jar, girl with comb in her hair and shaded pink petal skirt, red M-in-wreath, 6-1/4" h.............. **$1,252**

Noritake figural dresser jar, girl seated on caramel lustre chair, green M-in-wreath, 6-7/8" h. ...................................... **$2,504**

Noritake four-piece figural condiment set, each piece a Betty Boop-style lady in orange and green, red M-in-wreath, 6-7/8" l. tray .................................. **$284**

Noritake dresser tray, "Suzie Skier" on lustre ground, red M-in-wreath, 8-1/4" ................................ **$683**

Noritake lustre portrait plate, woman in striped pilgrim hat, named Daisy, red M-in-wreath, 6-3/8" dia. ................................................................ **$1,138**

◀Japanese figural porcelain tea infusers in the form of children's heads, 2-1/2" h. ........................... **$58**

Noritake figural inkstand, clown's head and ruffled collar in caramel and matte green, English Spoke mark, 4-1/8" h. ............... **$2,277**

Noritake figural nightlight described as Polly Peachman in high lustre caramel dress and hat with black porcelain lamp base, 7-1/2" ........................... **$6,261**

Noritake pink porcelain dancer, Art Deco with gold accents in red glaze base, back stamp 33.056, 8"h. ............................... **$2,163**

Noritake sandwich plate, scalloped square plate with green lustre border, lady in gown at masquerade ball, red M-in-wreath, 7-5/8" ................................ **$455**

Rare Noritake figural nightlight, girl in pink dress with painted cherry blossoms holding bouquet of flowers, lamp base is extension of her skirt, green M-in-wreath, 9-1/2" h........................................ **$8,271**

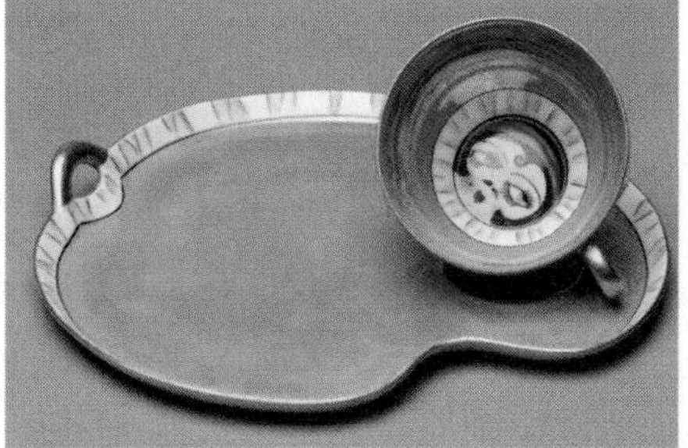

◀Noritake lustre toast and tea, purple lustre palette-shaped toast with Betty Boop-style teacup, green M-in-wreath, 8-1/2" l................................... **$170**

Noritake figural wall pocket, blue lustre ground with applied nude lady and butterfly, red M-in-wreath, 7-1/2" ................... **$569**

Noritake green lustre vase on tripod feet with painted Art Deco lady in gown with headdress, red M-in-wreath, 7-1/2" h...... **$1,480**

Rare Noritake Indian maiden dresser jar, finely molded seated figure in seafoam green dress and feather plumed hat, outstretched arms to hold a floral garland, octagonal base in black and gold stripes, green M-in-wreath, 10-1/4" h......................**$13,663**

## Paul Revere Pottery

S.E.G.

This pottery was established in Boston, Massachusetts, in 1906, by a group of philanthropists seeking to establish better conditions for underprivileged young girls of the area. Edith Brown served as supervisor of the small "Saturday Evening Girls Club" pottery operation, which was moved, in 1912, to a house close to the Old North Church where Paul Revere's signal lanterns had been placed. The wares were mostly hand decorated in mineral colors, and both sgraffito and molded decorations were employed. Although it became popular, it was never a profitable operation and always depended on financial contributions to operate. After the death of Edith Brown in 1932, the pottery foundered and finally closed in 1942.

Bowl, deep rounded sides with a wide flat rim, brown semi-matte ground decorated around the rim with a cuerda seca band of Greek key in taupe and ivory on white, signed "SEG - 10.12 - FL," 6" dia., 3" h. .......... **$1,116**

Bowl, bulbous ovoid body with a wide flat mouth, decorated around the top with a yellow band accented by flying scarabs in light green, streaky pale blue glaze, marked "S.E.G. - 05-1-14," crazing, 1914, 4 1/4" dia. .......... **$1,093**

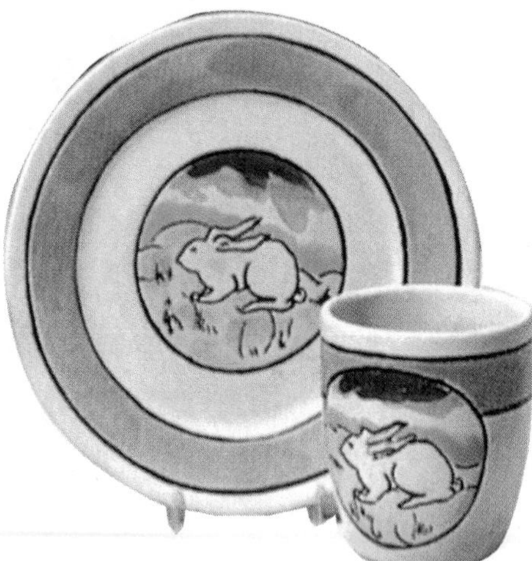

Breakfast set: child's, 7-1/2" dia. plate and 3-5/8" h. mug; each hand-painted with a circle enclosing a picture of a white rabbit lying on a green grassy mound, white and blue outer bands, initialed by the artist, early 20th c. .......... **$1,116**

Jardiniere, wide bulbous squatty body with a closed rim, yellow ground with a wide rim band in cuerda seca with black-outlined white lotus blossoms trimmed with yellow, stamped mark, firing lines around rim and base, two restored rim chips, 9" dia., 7" h. .......... **$1,495**

Plate, dinner, dark greyish blue ground decorated around the rim in cuerda seca with a band of stylized white lotus blossoms, signed "SEG - AM - 11-14," rim bruise, small chips to footring, 10" dia. .................................... **$646**

►Vase, simple ovoid body with a wide flat rim, dark bluish grey lower body, a wide shoulder band in cuerda seca decorated with a band of stylized oak leaves andacorns in green, brown and pale blue, inkstamped "SEG - AM - 12-17," 1917, 6-1/4" h., 3-3/4" dia. ..................... **$4,025**

Plates, luncheon, creamy white with a dark blue border band decorated with stylized white lotus blossoms, Saturday Evening Girls mark and dated 1910, set of 12, 8-1/2" dia. .................................. **$2,645**

Tea set: covered bulbous 4-3/4" h. teapot, 4-1/4" h. cylindrical creamer, 4" h. cylindrical covered sugar bowl, and 5-1/4" w. square tea tile; each decorated with a dark blue glaze with a border band of stylized white lotus blossoms, all marked with the Saturday Evening Girls mark and dated 1910, teapot cover cracked, glued chip on inner rim of teapot .............................. **$1,955**

# Red Wing Pottery

Various potteries operated in Red Wing, Minnesota, starting in 1868, the most successful being the Red Wing Stoneware Company, organized in 1877. Merged with other local potteries through the years, it became known as Red Wing Union Stoneware Company in 1906 and was one of the largest producers of utilitarian stoneware items in the United States.

After a decline in the popularity of stoneware products, an art pottery line was introduced to compensate for the loss. This was reflected in a new name for the company, Red Wing Potteries, Inc., in 1936. Stoneware production ceased entirely in 1947, but vases, planters, cookie jars, and dinnerware of art pottery quality continued in production until 1967, when the pottery ceased operation altogether.

For more information on Red Wing pottery, see *Warman's Red Wing Pottery Identification and Price Guide* by Mark F. Moran.

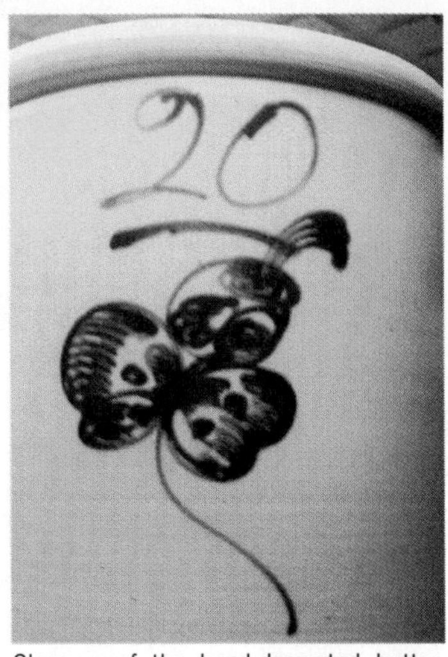


Close-up of the hand-decorated butterfly and flower on a 20-gallon salt-glaze crock.................. **$2,000-$2,500, signed**

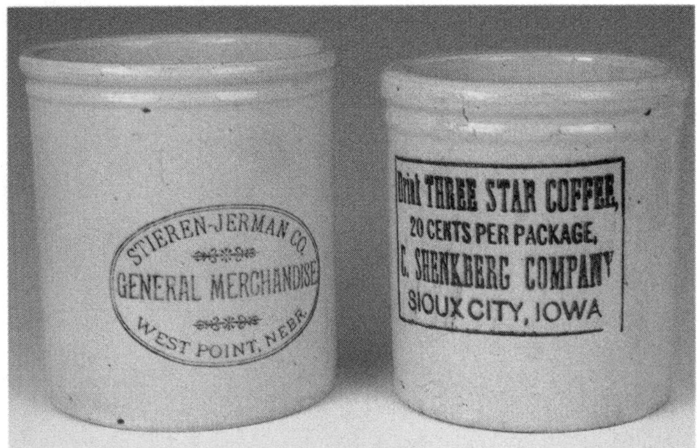


White stoneware advertising crocks 6-1/4" and 6" t., unmarked. ......... **$900-$1,200 ea.**

White stoneware advertising crocks 5" and 3-3/4" t., unmarked. ......... **$900-$1,200 ea.**

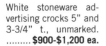

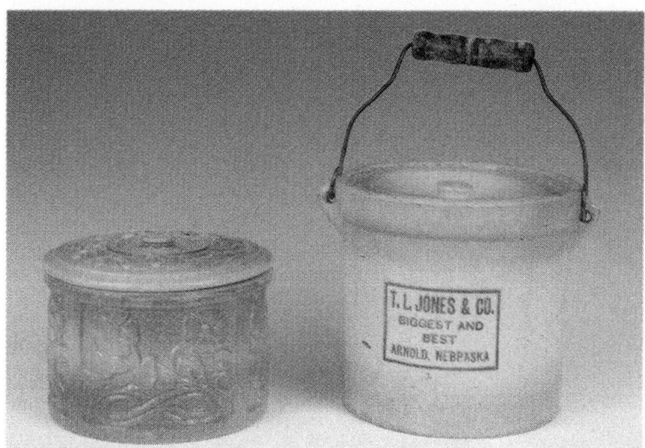


Blue and white covered butter crock in a daisy pattern, left, 4-1/2" t. with lid, 5-1/2" dia. .......................................... **$400+**
Blue and white bail-handle covered butter crock with advertising, 5-1/2" t. without handle.... **$500+**

Two-gallon crock with tilted birch leaves and oval stamp with "Minnesota Stoneware Company" (spelled out, commonly found as "Co."), 12" t. with lid, otherwise unmarked. ........................................**$1,500+**

Two-gallon white stoneware crock with tilted birch leaves, 10" t., impressed mark, "Minnesota Stoneware Co. Red Wing, Minn." ........................ **$70-$90**

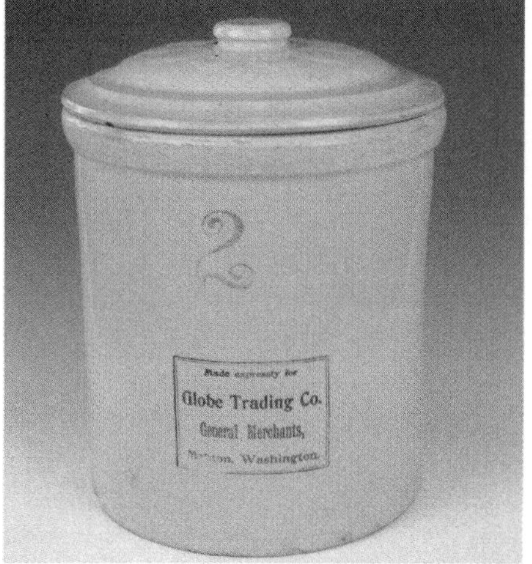


Two-gallon crock with Washington advertising and original lid, 12" t. with lid. .......................... **$2,500**

Two-gallon crock with both marks in red, 10" t. .................................................................. **$2,200**

White stoneware bail-handle butter crock with advertising (cover missing), left, 7-1/4" t. without handle, unmarked............ **$400+**
Sponge-decorated butter crock with lid, 7" t., unmarked... **$300+**

Three-gallon white stoneware crock with tilted birch leaves and original lid, and rarely seen "Minnesota Stoneware Company" oval mark, 10-3/4" t. without lid; lid, 11" dia. ........................................ **$900+**

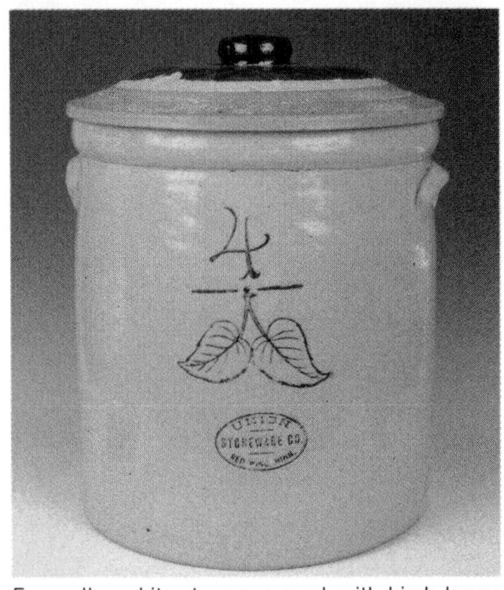


Four-gallon white stoneware crock with birch leaves called "elephant ears," and original lid, 11-1/2" t. without lid. ................................................ **$150+**

Five-gallon white stoneware crock with oval and large wing, the most commonly found size for crocks and jugs........................................................... **$70+**

Transitional five-gallon crock with hand-decorated blue-black number and "bowtie," circa 1900, the glaze on this crock is between white and tan, 13-1/4" t., unmarked................................. **$300+**

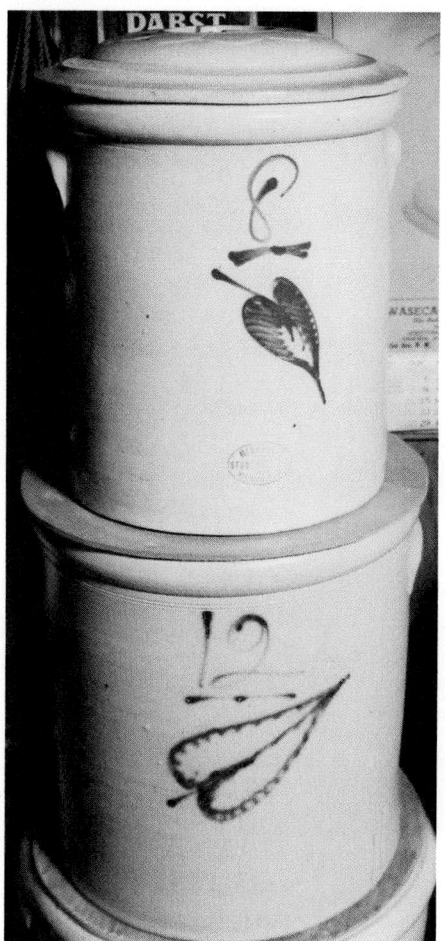


Eight-gallon transitional zinc-glaze crock with stamped Minnesota oval and hand-decorated birch leaf. ........................................................ **$3,500+**
Twelve-gallon salt-glaze crock with large hand-decorated birch leaf pointing up. ........................ **$2,500**

◀ Ten-pound butter crock with Osage, Iowa, advertising, 6-3/4" t., otherwise unmarked............... **$1,500**

Ten-gallon crock with Washington advertising that includes crockery. (Collector Tip: Strange as it may sound, it's unusual to find the word "crockery" on crockery.) ................................... **$1,500+ if perfect**

Fifteen-gallon salt-glaze crock with cobalt decoration of "bowtie" and double leaves, circa 1890, 18-1/2" t., unmarked. (Collector Tip: The leaves seen here are precursors to the stenciled or stamped birch-leaf decoration used on white hand-thrown stoneware made just a few years later.) ......................... **$800-$1,000**

White stoneware 20-pound butter crock with hand-decorated numbers, a transitional mark before stamping was regularly used, circa 1900, 8" t., 11-1/2" dia., raised mark on bottom, "Minnesota Stoneware Red Wing, Minn." ............................... **$800-$1,000**

White stoneware 20-pound butter crock with 4" wing, 7-1/2" t., 11-1/2" dia. ............................... **$1,000+**

Stoneware bread crock in glossy green glaze, also found with matte Brushed Ware surface, and in tan; lid missing, 11" t., 14" dia., rare..... **$2,800+ (as is);** with lid .................................................. **$4,000+**

Eighth-pint fancy jug with rare blue sponge decoration, 2-3/4" t. ......................................... **$1,800+**

Three brown-top mini jugs two with advertising and one a souvenir, each 4-1/4" t., found unmarked and with raised "R.W.S.W. Co." ........................................ **$250+ ea., with a high range of $800 depending on markings**

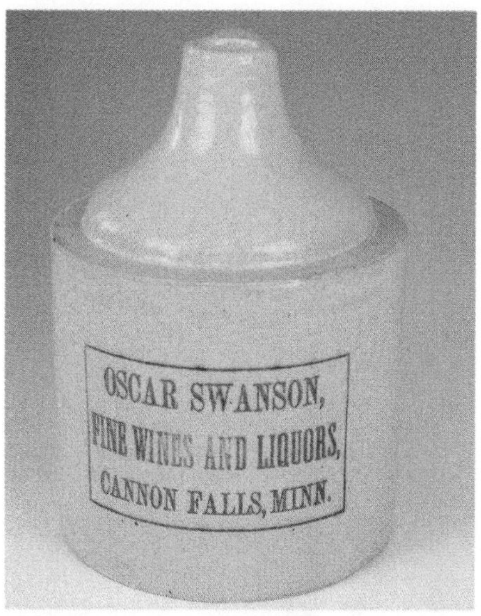


Half-gallon shoulder jug with Cannon Falls, Minn., advertising, 8-1/2" t., impressed bottom mark, "Minnesota Stoneware Co. Red Wing, Minn." ........ **$500+**

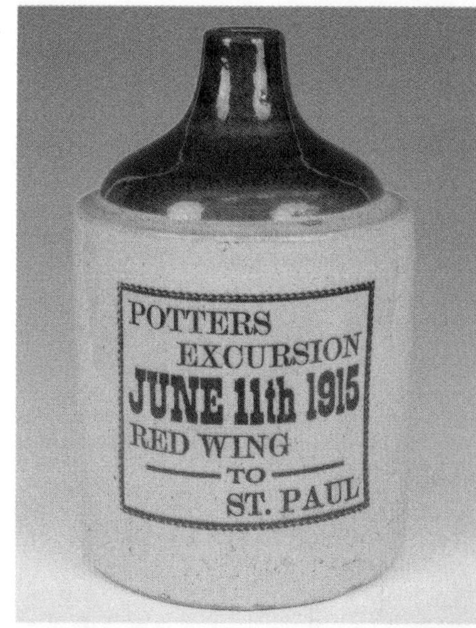


1915 Potters Excursion shoulder jug one gallon, 11" t. ........................................................ **$7,000+**

Wide-mouth, brown-top one-gallon jug left, with raised star on bottom, 10" t. .......................... **$75+**
Dome-top one-gallon jug with unglazed top, with raised letters, "Wm. R. Adams Microbe Killer," 10-1/2" t., unmarked................................. **$325+**

Two one-gallon white stoneware shoulder jugs with cobalt trim, with narrow and wide mouths, 11" and 10-1/4" t., both marked on bottom, "Minnesota Stoneware Co. Red Wing, Minn."........**$375-$450 ea.**

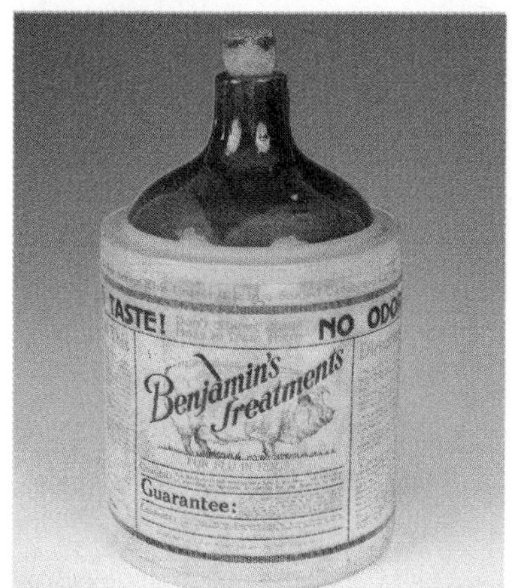

Blue and white "Greek Key" stoneware mixing bowls, complete set of seven, in sizes ranging from 6" to 12" dia., unmarked..................................... **6" to 10" size, $125+ ea.**
11" and 12" ............................................**$250-$300 ea.**

◀ One-gallon brown-top stoneware jug with rare original paper label, 11" t. ................................................... **$300+**

Red (pink) and blue banded ribbed stoneware mixing bowls, complete set of eight, in sizes ranging from 4-1/4" to 12" diameter, unmarked.......**$90-$110 ea.**

Sponge-decorated paneled mixing bowls, complete set of seven, in diameters of 5", 6-1/4", 7-1/2", 8", 9", 10" and 11", unmarked except for impressed size number. .........**5", $500+; other sizes, $125-$300 ea.**

Sponge-decorated yellow ware bowls; left, two sizes, with advertising, 1930s, 7-1/2" and 5-1/2" dia.; right, Saffron Ware covered casserole with advertising, 7-1/2" dia. without handles, ink-stamped, "Red Wing Saffron Ware."........................................................**$300-$400 ea.**

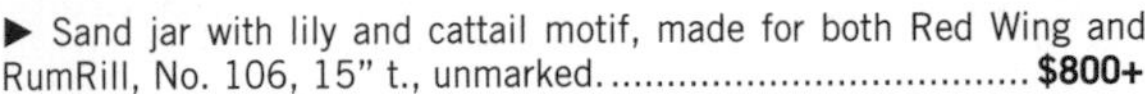

▶ Sand jar with lily and cattail motif, made for both Red Wing and RumRill, No. 106, 15" t., unmarked......................................**$800+**

Sponge-decorated pitchers, three sizes, two with advertising; left, with cherry band, 8-1/2" t. ...........**$1,800+**
Center, 9" tall ......................................................................................................................**$400+**
Right, squat jug, with advertising inside, "Compliments of Farmers Co-op Creamery Association—Hull, Iowa," 6-1/2" tall ..................................................................................................................**$1,500+**

# Rockingham Wares

The Marquis of Rockingham first established an earthenware pottery in the Yorkshire district of England around 1745, and it was occupied afterwards by various potters. The well-known mottled brown Rockingham glaze was introduced about 1788 by the Brameld Brothers and became immediately popular. It was during the 1820s that the production of true porcelain began at the factory, and it continued to be made until the firm closed in 1842. Since that time the so-called Rockingham glaze has been used by various potters in England and the United States, including some famous wares produced in Bennington, Vermont. Very similar glazes were also used by potteries in other areas of the United States including Ohio and Indiana, but only wares specifically attributed to Bennington should use that name. The following listings will include mainly wares featuring the dark brown mottled glaze produced at various sites here and abroad.

Creamer, tapering ovoid body with an undulating rim and wide arched spout, C-scroll handle, yelloware with overall mottled dark brown Rockingham glaze, 19th c., 5-1/2" h. .......................... **$44**

Flask, figural Mermaid design, dark brown glaze, ca. 1860, 8" h. ...................................... **$187**

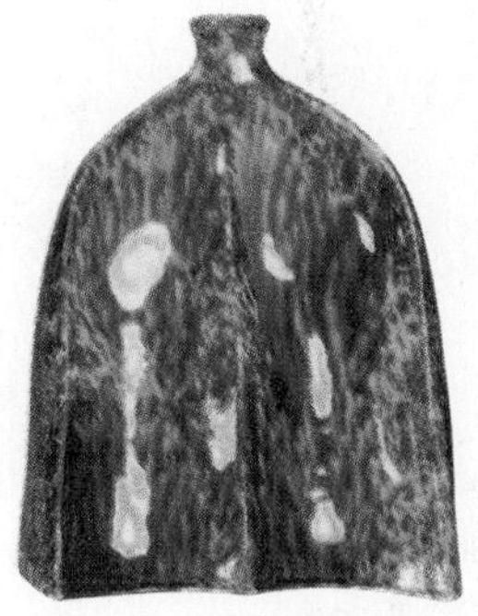

Foot warmer, wide flattened half-round form with two molded indentations on the top for feet, a small spout at the top end, overall mottled brown glaze, American-made, ca. 1860, underside crazing, small flakes in the glaze, 7" w., 10" h. ..................... **$230**

**Right:** Flask, flattened ovoid body with small neck, yellowware molded in relief with an oval reserve enclosing a half-length portrait of a man snorting snuff on each side, overall dark mottled brown Rockingham glaze, possibly Bennington, Vermont, or East Liverpool, Ohio, excellent condition, first half 19th c., 7-1/2" h. ...................................... **$248**

**Far right:** Flask, flattened ovoid shape tapering to a fluted neck and ringed mouth, molded on one side with the American Eagle and on the other with a morning glory vine, dark brown Rockingham glaze, No. G11-19, several old glaze chips, ca. 1840-60, pt. ...................................... **$308**

Inkwell, figural, modeled as a woman reclining asleep on an oblong rockwork base, yellowware with overall mottled dark brown Rockingham glaze, several old edge chips, reportedly made by the Larkin Bros. Company, Newell, West Virginia, ca. 1850-80, 3-7/8" h. .................................................................. **$101**

Jug, advertising-type, figural, model of a walking pig, impressed on the rear "Bieler's Ronny Club," yellowware with a mottled brown Rockingham glaze, original white porcelain stopper marked "Brookfield Rye Bieler," reportedly from Cincinnati, Ohio, ca. 1880-1900, 9-1/2" l., 5-1/4" h. ........................... **$1,232**

Model of a lion, recumbent animal raised on a deep rectangular base, mottled dark brown glaze, restoration to minor surface roughness along base, ca. 1860, 6-3/4 x 9" ........................................ **$303**

Pitcher, hound-handled, wide bulbous body with a flattened shoulder to the wide flared neck and wide arched spout, relief-molded with stag hunting scene, overall very dark brown glaze, possibly Bennington, Vermont, ca. 1850, 6-1/2" h.......................... **$144**

Pitcher, yellowware with overall mottled dark brown glaze, molded hound handle, wide baluster form shape molded in relief with eight panels of hanging game and fowl, a molded eagle under the wide spout, minor hairline in bottom, minor glaze wear, ca. 1850, 9-1/2" h. ................................................................ **$121**

Pitcher, hound-handled, flat-bottomed swelled cylindrical body with a flattened shoulder to the neck with a wide arched spout, the body molded in relief with a continuous hound and deer hunting scene, molded vine band around the neck, yellowware with overall dark brown Rockingham glaze, possibly West Troy Factory, Troy, New York, ca. 1860, excellent condition, 6-1/2" h. ............................................ **$275**

# Rookwood Pottery

Maria Longworth Nichols founded Rookwood Pottery in 1880. The name, she later reported, paid homage to the many crows (rooks) on her father's estate and was also designed to remind customers of Wedgwood. Production began on Thanksgiving Day 1880 when the first kiln was drawn.

Rookwood's earliest productions demonstrated a continued reliance on European precedents and the Japanese aesthetic. Although the firm offered a variety of wares (Dull Glaze, Cameo, and Limoges for example), it lacked a clearly defined artistic identity. With the introduction of what became known as its "standard glaze" in 1884, Rookwood inaugurated a period in which the company won consistent recognition for its artistic merit and technical innovation.

Rookwood's first decade ended on a high note when the company was awarded two gold medals: one at the Exhibition of American Art Industry in Philadelphia and another later in the year at the Exposition Universelle in Paris. Significant, too, was Maria Longworth Nichols' decision to transfer her interest in the company to William W. Taylor, who had been the firm's manager since 1883. In May 1890, the board of a newly reorganized Rookwood Pottery Company purchased "the real estate, personal property, goodwill, patents, trade-marks... now the sole property of William W. Taylor" for $40,000.

Under Taylor's leadership, Rookwood was transformed from a fledgling startup to successful business that expanded throughout the following decades to meet rising demand.

Throughout the 1890s, Rookwood continued to attract critical notice as it kept the tradition of innovation alive. Taylor rolled out three new glaze lines—Iris, Sea Green and Aerial Blue—from late 1894 into early 1895.

At the Paris Exposition in 1900, Rookwood cemented its reputation by winning the Grand Prix, a feat largely due to the favorable reception of the new Iris glaze and its variants.

Over the next several years, Rookwood's record of achievement at domestic and international exhibitions remained unmatched.

Early wares silver-overlaid Standard Glaze tri-corner pitcher by Edith Felten, 1893, with an elf sitting on a crescent moon, covered with Gorham silver in floral pattern, 8-3/4" x 7"..................... **$2,000-$4,000**

Throughout the 1910s, Rookwood continued in a similar vein and began to more thoroughly embrace the simplified aesthetic promoted by many Arts and Crafts figures. Production of the Iris line, which had been instrumental in the firm's success at the Paris Exposition in 1900, ceased around 1912. Not only did the company abandon its older, fussier underglaze wares, but the newer lines the pottery introduced also trended toward simplicity.

Unfortunately, the collapse of the stock market in October 1929 and ensuing economic depression dealt Rookwood a blow from which it did not recover. The Great Depression took a toll on the company and eventually led to bankruptcy in April 1941.

Rookwood's history might have ended there were it not for the purchase of the firm by a group of investors led by automobile dealer Walter E. Schott and his wife, Margaret. Production started once again. In the years that followed, Rookwood changed hands a number of times before being moved to Starkville, Mississippi, in 1960. It finally closed its doors there in 1967.

## ROOKWOOD MARKS

Rookwood employed a number of marks on the bottom of its vessels that denoted everything from the shape number, to the size, date, and color of the body, to the type of glaze to be used.

### *Company Marks:*

#### 1880-1882

In this early period, a number of marks were used to identify the wares.

1. "ROOKWOOD" followed by the initials of the decorator, painted in gold. This is likely the earliest mark, and though the wares are not dated, it seems to have been discontinued by 1881-1882.

2. "ROOKWOOD / POTTERY. / [DATE] CIN. O." In *Marks of American Potters* (1904), Edwin AtLee Barber states, "The most common marks prior to 1882 were the name of the pottery and the date of manufacture, which were painted or incised on the base of each piece by the decorator."

3. "R. P. C. O. M. L. N." These initials stand for "Rookwood Pottery, Cincinnati, Ohio, Maria Longworth Nichols," and were either painted or incised on the base.

4. Kiln and crows stamp. Barber notes that in 1881 and 1882, the trademark designed by the artist Henry Farny was printed beneath the glaze.

5. Anchor stamp: Barber notes that this mark is "one of the rarest."

6. Oval stamp.

7. Ribbon or banner stamp: According to Barber, "In 1882 a special mark was used on a trade piece... the letters were impressed in a raised ribbon.

8. Ribbon or banner stamp II: A simpler variation of the above stamp, recorded by Herbert Peck.

#### 1883-1886

1. Stamped name and date.
2. Impressed kiln: Appears only in 1883.

#### 1886-1960

Virtually all of the pieces feature the conjoined RP monogram. Pieces fired in the anniversary kilns carry a special kiln-shaped mark with the number of the anniversary inside of it.

#### 1955

A diamond-shaped mark that reads: "ROOKWOOD / 75th / ANNIVERSARY / POTTERY" was printed on wares.

#### 1960-1967

Occasionally pieces are marked "ROOKWOOD POTTERY / STARKVILLE MISS"; from 1962 to 1967 a small "®" occasionally follows the monogram.

### *Date Marks*

Unlike many of their contemporaries, Rookwood seems very early on to have adopted a method of marking its pottery that was accurate and easy to understand.

From 1882-1885, the company impressed the date, often with the company name, in block letters (see 1883-86, No. 1).

Although the date traditionally given for the conjoined RP mark is June 23, 1886, this marks the official introduction of the monogram rather than the first use.

Stanley Burt, in his record of the Rookwood at the Cincinnati Museum noted two pieces from 1883 (Nos. 2 and 3) that used the monogram. The monogram was likely designed by Alfred Brennan, since it first appears on his work.

From 1886 on, the date of the object was coded in the conjoined "RP" monogram.

1886: conjoined "RP" no additional flame marks.

1887-1900: conjoined "RP" with a flame added for each subsequent year. Thus, a monogram with seven flames would represent 1893.

1900-1967: conjoined "RP" with fourteen flames and a Roman numeral below the mark to indicate the year after 1900. Thus, a monogram with fourteen flames and the letters "XXXVI" below it signifies 1936.

### *Clay-Type Marks*

From 1880 until around 1895, Rookwood used a number of different colored bodies for production and marked each color with a letter code. These letters were impressed and usually found grouped together with the shape number, sometimes following it, but more often below it.

The letter "S" is a particularly vexing designation since the same initial was used for two other unrelated designations. As a result, it is particularly important to take into account the relative position of the impressed letter.

R = Red

Y = Yellow

S = Sage

G = Ginger

W = White

O = Olive

P = From 1915 on Rookwood used an impressed "P" (often found perpendicular to the orientation of the other marks) to denote the soft porcelain body.

### *Size and Shape Marks*

Almost all Rookwood pieces have a shape code consisting of three or four numbers, followed by a size letter. "A" denotes the largest available size, "F" is the smallest. According to Herbert Peck, initial designs were given a "C" or "D" designation so that variations could be made. Not every shape model, however, features a variation in every size.

### *Glaze Marks*

In addition to marking the size, shape and year of the piece, Rookwood's decorators also used a number of letters to designate the type of glaze to be used upon a piece. Generally speaking, these marks are either incised or impressed.

"S" = Standard Glaze to be used. (Incised.)

"L" = Decorators would often incise an "L" near their monogram to indicate that the light variation of the Standard Glaze was to be used. (Incised.)

"SG" = Sea Green Glaze to be used.

"Z" = from 1900-1904 designated any piece with a mat glaze. (Impressed.)

"W" = Iris Glaze to be used.

"V" = Vellum Glaze to be used; variations include "GV" for Green Vellum and "YV" for Yellow Vellum.

### *Other Marks*

"S" = If found away from the shape number, this generally indicates a piece that was specially thrown at the pottery in the presence of visitors. (Impressed.)

"S" = If this precedes the shape number than it denotes a piece that was specifically thrown and decorated from a sketch with a corresponding number. Because of the size and quality of pieces this letter has been found on, this probably signifies a piece made specifically for an important exhibition.

"X" = Rookwood used a wheel ground "x" to indicate items that were not of first quality. There has been some suggestion that decorators and salespersons might have conspired to "x" certain pieces that they liked, since this designation would reduce the price. Since there are a number of items that appear to have been marked for no apparent reason, there may be some truth to this idea. Unfortunately, as this idea has gained credence, many pieces with obvious flaws have been listed as "marked x for no apparent reason," and collectors should be cautious.

Generally, the mark reduces the value and appeal of the piece. Peck describes a variation of the "x" that resembles an asterisk as indicating a piece that could be given away to employees.

"T" = An impressed T that precedes a shape number indicates a trial piece.

➢ ⑤

▲ = These shapes (crescents, diamonds, and triangles) are used to indicate a glaze trial.

◆

"K1" and "K3" = c. 1922, used for matching teacups and saucers

"SC" = Cream and Sugar sets, c. 1946-50

"2800" = Impressed on ship pattern tableware

For more information on Rookwood, see *Warman's Rookwood Pottery Identification and Price Guide* by Denise Rago and Jonathan Clancy.

## SOME LINES OF NOTE

**Aerial Blue:** Commercially, this line was among the least successful. As a result, there are a limited number of pieces, and this scarcity has increased their values relative to other wares.

**Black Iris:** This line is among the most sought after by collectors, commanding significantly more than examples of similar size and design in virtually any other glaze. In fact, the current auction record for Rookwood—over $350,000—was set in 2004 for a Black Iris vase decorated by Kitaro Shirayamadani in 1900.

**Iris:** Uncrazed examples are exceptionally rare, with large pieces featuring conventional designs commanding the highest prices. Smaller, naturalistically painted examples, though still desirable, are gradually becoming more affordable for the less advanced collector.

**Production Ware:** This commercial and mass-produced artware is significantly less expensive than pieces in most other lines.

**Standard Glaze:** These wares peaked in the 1970s-1980s, and the market has remained thin in recent years, but regardless of the state of the market, examples of superlative quality, including those with silver overlay, have found their places in the finest of collections.

**Wax Mat:** This is among the most affordable of the hand-decorated lines.

Rare counter sign displays Rookwood flame mark with "Rookwood Pottery Starkville Miss" in block letters below, finished in a bright green glaze and marked on the back with the Rookwood flame mark, "R" and dated "LXV," 4-5/8" t..........**$708**
*James D. Julia, Inc.*

## EARLY WARES

Standard Glaze ewer decorated with green wheat against a green shading to orange background, marked on underside with Rookwood flame mark dated 1893 and artist initials "AMV" for Anna Marie Valentien, 6" t. x 5-1/2" dia. .......................... **$460**
*James D. Julia, Inc.*

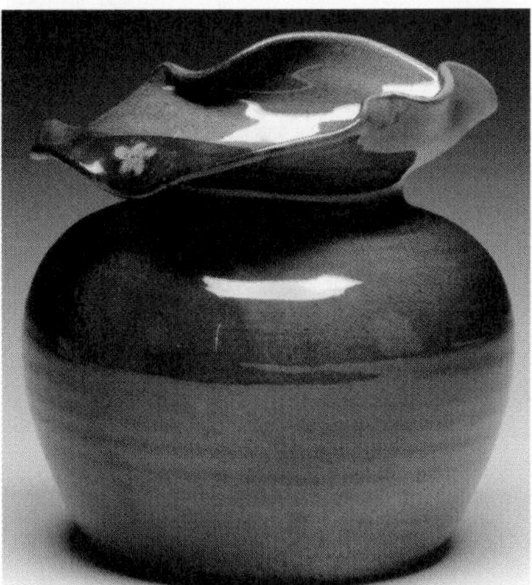

Early Standard Glaze pottery vase has bulbous body with flaring freeform lip decorated with a single tiny cluster of three flowers, finished in a speckled green shading to brown shading to tan, impressed on underside "Rookwood 1885 G272 C," 5-1/4" t. ....... **$287**
*James D. Julia, Inc.*

► Early chocolate pot of glazed beige clay, 1885, stamped ROOKWOOD/1885/251, 8" x 6-1/2" .......................................................... **$250-$350**

Standard Glaze planter decorated with green leaves, stems, and seed pods set against a dark brown background shading to orange, finished with three applied vertically ribbed handles, signed on the underside with Rookwood flame mark dated 1897 as well as artist initials "MN" for Mary Madeline Nourse, 6-1/2" t. x 10" dia. ................................................ **$517**
*James D. Julia, Inc.*

Standard Glaze pottery bowl has squat bulbous body with ruffled rim, decorated with leaves and stems against a green shading to brown background, signed on the underside with Rookwood flame mark dated 1891 and is artist signed with initials "SA" for Amelia Browne Sprague, 7" dia. ............................ **$287**
*James D. Julia, Inc.*

Limoges-style humidor with double-lid by Maria Longworth Nichols, 1882, painted with spiders and bats on a mottled ground, stamped ROOKWOOD/1882/MLN, 6" x 6" ................................ **$2,000-$3,000**

Early jug and stopper painted with white dogwood and star-shaped blossoms on a mottled indigo ground, 1885, stamped ROOKWOOD 1885, 14" x 6-1/2" ....................................................... **$800-$1,200**

Early tea caddy painted by A.R. Valentien with yellow chrysanthemums and a bee on a speckled olive green ground, 1885, stamped ROOKWOOD/1885/A.R.V./142/D, 5" x 3-1/2" ...................... **$600-$800**

Small Cameo ewer painted by an unidentified artist with a white rose, 1888, flame mark/40W/S/R, 6-1/4" x 4" .......................................... **$400-$600**

Standard Glaze chocolate pot composed and painted by Caroline Steinle with orange and brown nasturtium, 1899, flame mark/772/CS, 9" x 6-1/4" ........ **$850-$1,250**

Standard Glaze Light small pitcher painted by Emma Foertmeyer with roses, 1890, marked, 2-3/4" ........ **$200-$300**

Standard Glaze vase decorated with two yellow flowers with long green stems and leaves set against a dark brown background shading to green, marked on the underside with Rookwood flame mark dated 1902 with artist initials "MM" for Marianne Mitchell, 7" t. ........ **$324**

*James D. Julia, Inc.*

◀ Tiger Eye narrow vase painted by K. Shirayamadani with a cicada on a large lily pad, 1897, flame mark/589F/Japanese cipher, 7" x 3" ........ **$1,500-$2,500**

## MAT GLAZES

Z-Line jug embossed with swirls around shoulder and covered in a matte green glaze, 1905, flame mark/V/X, 7-3/4" x 4-1/2" .............................. **$550-$750**

Modeled Mat squat vessel by William Hentschel with green fish and sea plants on a brown and green butterfat ground, 1911, flame mark/XI/438/WEH, 6" x 8-3/4" ........................................... **$1,750-$2,500**

Incised Mat pitcher by William Hentschel with tooled dandelion leaves in dark blue on a stippled dark blue ground, with matte purple glaze at mouth, 1910, flame mark/X/668/WEH, 6-1/4" x 5-3/4" ........ **$800-$1,200**

Painted Mat small bulbous vase painted by C.S. Todd with roosters in polychrome on an indigo-to-red ground, 1911, flame mark/XI/1656F/C.S.T. 5-3/4" x 2-1/2" .......................................... **$8,000-$12,000**

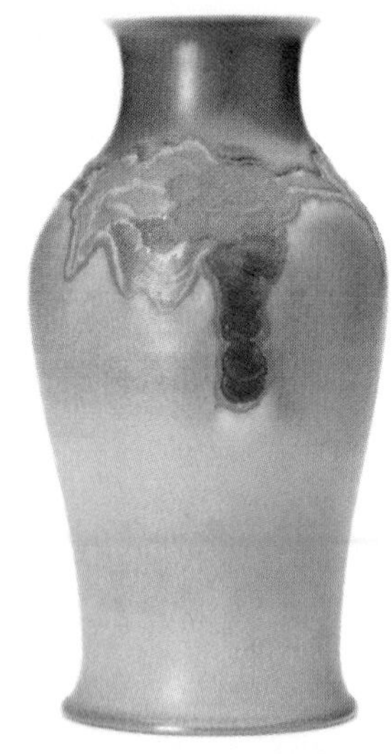

►Incised Mat vase by Charles Todd with purple grapes, green leaves, on a deep blue ground, 1920, flame mark/X/CAT/2301B, 13" x 8"... **$2,500-$3,500**

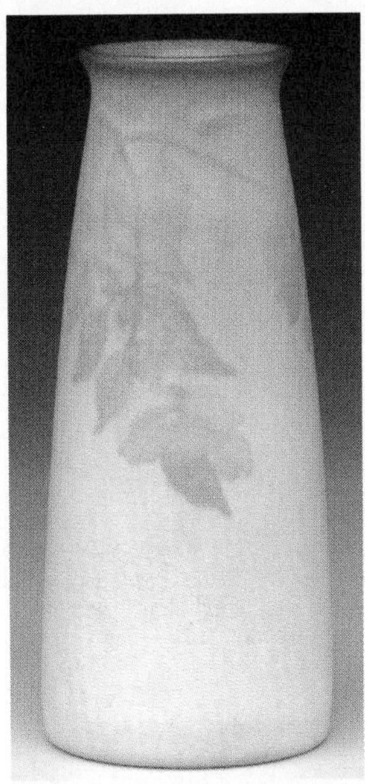

Vellum vase decorated with red bellflowers extending from green stems and leaves against a cream shading to gray background, signed on underside with the Rookwood flame mark and dated 1912 and carries the artist signature "MHM" for Mary Helen McDonald, 7-3/8" t. ............... **$402**
*James D. Julia, Inc.*

Unusual Vellum ovoid vase by Arthur Conant, 1916, painted with a repeated pattern of birds-of-paradise and exotic flowers in red, green and violet against a deep purple ground, with blue interior, flame mark/XVI/534D/V/ artist's cipher, 7-3/4" x 3-3/4" ........................... **$1,500-$2,000**

Ombroso squat vessel by William Hentschel with stylized flowers under a fine amber, green and brown butterfat glaze, 1915, flame mark/XV/95C/WEH, 4-3/4" x 7-1/2" ........**$2,000-$3,000**

Vellum vase painted by Kitaro Shirayamadani with tall pines by a brook in dark green, yellow and purple, 1910, flame mark/X/ 1665/artist's cipher, 11-1/2" x 6-1/2" ....... **$3,500-$5,000**

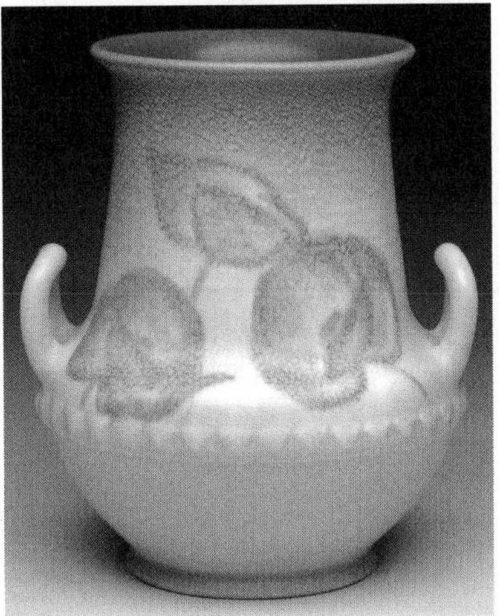

Mat finish vase by Kataro Shirayamadani, decorated with red poppies against a background of maroon shading to yellow shading to green, finished with two handles and a raised square tack head pattern around waist, interior finished with a shaded blue glaze, signed on underside with Rookwood flame mark "XL," "6492," and artist signed "KS," 7-1/8" t....... **$1,552**
*James D. Julia, Inc.*

## NEW PORCELAIN BODY

Butterfat bulbous vase by Lorinda Epply with exotic birds on trees, 1927, flame mark/XXVII/2914/LE, 8-1/4" x 6-1/2" .............................. **$2,000-$3,000**

Decorated Mat vase painted by M.H. McDonald with pink leaves on a turquoise butterfat ground, 1928, flame mark/XXVII/2182/MHM, 5-1/4" x 4" ........................................................ **$900-$1,300**

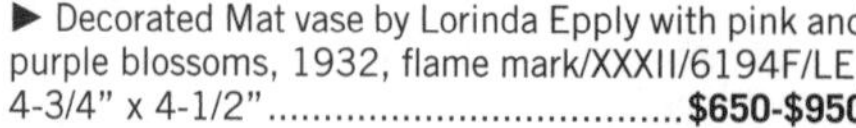

► Decorated Mat vase by Lorinda Epply with pink and purple blossoms, 1932, flame mark/XXXII/6194F/LE, 4-3/4" x 4-1/2" ................................... **$650-$950**

Decorated Mat three-legged center bowl decorated by Sallie Coyne with a wreath of blue leaves on a turquoise and green interior, 1922, flame mark/XXII/2632/SEC. 5-3/4" x 11" ............. **$750-$1,000**

Decorated Mat faceted jardinière painted by Elizabeth Lincoln with pine cones, 1926, flame mark/XXVI/2741/LNL, 4" x 5-1/2" .................. **$550-$750**

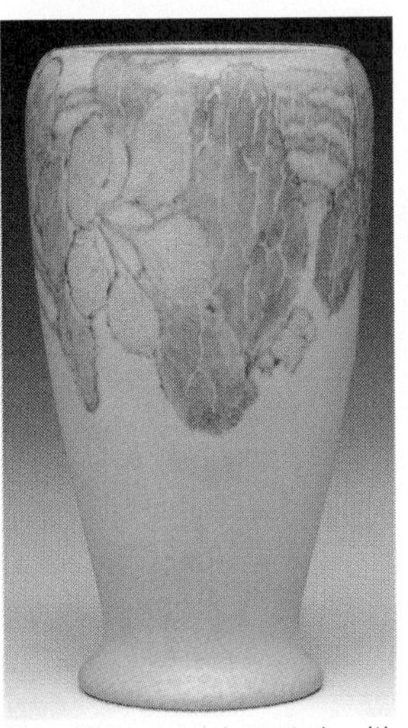

Wax Mat vase decorated with pink and yellow flowers with green foliage surrounding the upper half, set against a turquoise green background, signed on the underside with the Rookwood flame mark, stamped 1928, artist signed "CSE" for Sarah Elizabeth Coyne, 7-1/2" t. ................. **$575**
*James D. Julia, Inc.*

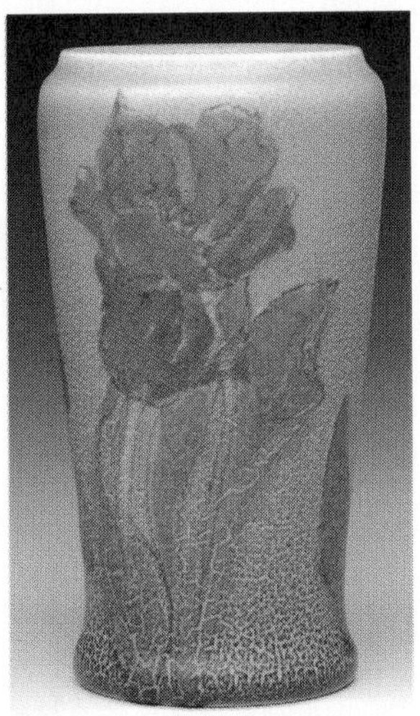

Wax Mat vase decorated with deep red flowers and green leaves against a mottled background, interior finished with a bright yellow glaze, marked on underside with Rookwood flame mark and dated 1925, artist signed "MHM" for Margaret Helen McDonald, 8" t. ........................................ **$649**
*James D. Julia, Inc.*

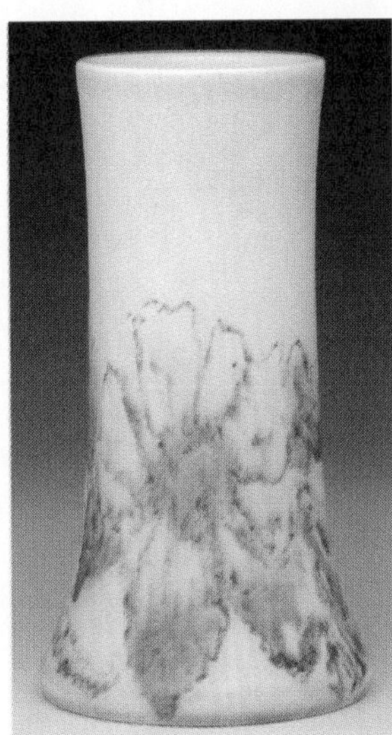

Wax Mat vase decorated with stylized yellow, green, and brown flowers against a shaded cream-colored background, signed on underside with the Rookwood flame mark and dated 1924, artist signed with the monogram for Elizabeth Barrett, 9" t......... **$531**
*James D. Julia, Inc.*

Later Mat/Mat Moderne vase by William Hentschel with white leaves on turquoise ground, 1929, flame mark/XXIX/927D/WEH, 9-1/4" x 7" .............. **$1,400-$1,900**

►Jewel Porcelain bulbous vase by Jens Jensen, 1944, decorated with pink cherries and cobalt leaves on a taupe ground, flame mark/XLIV/6872/artist's cipher, 9" x 8" ...................................................... **$500-$800**

Jewel Porcelain spherical vase painted by A. Conant with chrysanthemums in polychrome, 1919, marked, 5-1/2" .............................. **$800-$1,200**

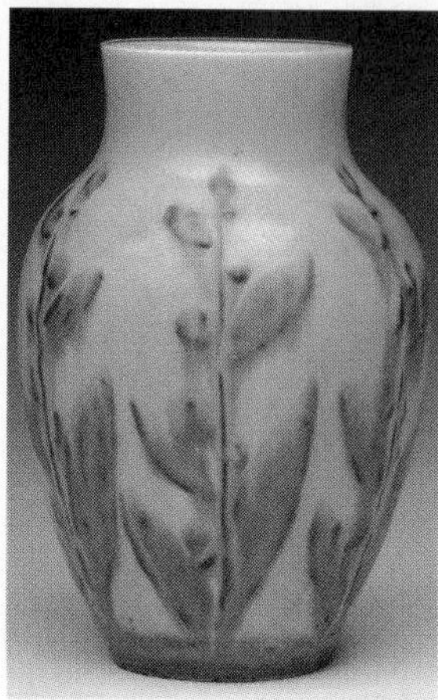

Jewel Porcelain vase decorated with brown and blue stylized flowers extending vertically from the foot of the vase, just past the shoulder, set against a light blue background, signed on underside with the Rookwood flame mark and dated 1928, artist signed, believed to be Elizabeth Barrett, 7-1/2" t. ............................ **$472**

*James D. Julia, Inc.*

Jewel Porcelain vase painted by M.H. McDonald with branches of oak leaves and acorns on a butterfat ground, 1936, flame mark/XXXVI/621/MHM, 10" x 6-1/4" ........................... **$1,750-$2,500**

▶Jewel Porcelain vase by Margaret McDonald, 1943, painted with red tulips on an ivory ground, flame mark/MHM, 5" ..**$450-$650**

Jewel Porcelain vase by K. Shirayamadani with an all-over, chintz-like pattern of cherry blossoms on a raspberry pink ground, 1922, flame mark/XXII/589F/artist's Japanese cipher, 7-1/2" x 3" ........................... **$3,000-$4,000**

## PRODUCTION WARES

Production candlesticks, 1919, covered in blue and turquoise matte glaze, flame mark/XVIV/822D, 6" ........................................................ **$150-$250**

Production urn impressed with a geometric pattern under a rich puce and green butterfat glaze, 1912, flame mark, 18" .............................. **$3,000-$4,000**

# Roseville Pottery

Roseville is one of the most widely recognizable of potteries across the United States. Having been sold in flower shops and drug stores around the country, its art and production wares became a staple in American homes through the time Roseville closed in the 1950s.

The Roseville Pottery Company, located in Roseville, Ohio, was incorporated on Jan. 4, 1892, with George F. Young as general manager. The company had been producing stoneware since 1890, when it purchased the J. B. Owens Pottery, also of Roseville.

The popularity of Roseville Pottery's original lines of stoneware continued to grow. The company acquired new plants in 1892 and 1898, and production started to shift to Zanesville, just a few miles away. By about 1910, all of the work was centered in Zanesville, but the company name was unchanged.

Young hired Ross C. Purdy as artistic designer in 1900, and Purdy created Rozane—a contraction of the words "Roseville" and "Zanesville." The first Roseville artwork pieces were marked either Rozane or RPCO, both impressed or ink-stamped on the bottom.

In 1902, a line was developed called Azurean. Some pieces were marked Azurean, but often RPCO. In 1904 at the St. Louis Exposition, Roseville's Rozane Mongol, a high-gloss oxblood red line, captured first prize, gaining recognition for the firm and its creator, John Herold.

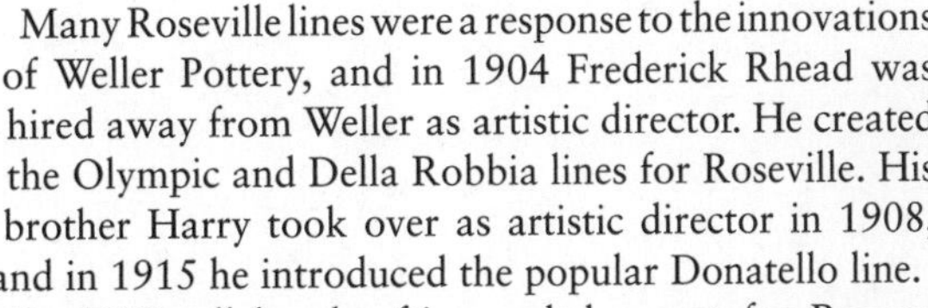

Many Roseville lines were a response to the innovations of Weller Pottery, and in 1904 Frederick Rhead was hired away from Weller as artistic director. He created the Olympic and Della Robbia lines for Roseville. His brother Harry took over as artistic director in 1908, and in 1915 he introduced the popular Donatello line.

By 1908, all handcrafting ended except for Rozane Royal. Roseville was the first pottery in Ohio to install a tunnel kiln, which increased its production capacity.

Frank Ferrell, who was a top decorator at the Weller Pottery by 1904, was Roseville's artistic director from 1917 until 1954. This Zanesville native created many of the most popular lines, including Pine Cone, which had scores of individual pieces.

Many collectors believe Roseville's circa 1925 glazes were the best of any Zanesville pottery. George Krause, who had become Roseville's technical supervisor, responsible for glaze, in 1915, remained with Roseville until the 1950s.

Company sales declined after World War II, especially in the early 1950s when cheap Japanese imports began to replace American wares, and a simpler, more modern style made many of Roseville's elaborate floral designs seem old-fashioned.

In the late 1940s, Roseville began to issue lines with glossy glazes. Roseville tried to offset its flagging artware sales by launching a dinnerware line—Raymor—in 1953. The line was a commercial failure.

Roseville issued its last new designs in 1953. On Nov. 29, 1954, the facilities of Roseville were sold to the Mosaic Tile Company.

For more information on Roseville, see *Warman's Roseville Pottery*, 2nd edition, by Denise Rago.

Blended fine majolica-type jardinière and pedestal set, the Nouveau-style jardinière with applied women's bust to two sides, unmarked, pedestal: 28", jardinière: 15" ........................................ **$1,500-$2,500**

## BOTTOM MARKS

There is no consistency to Roseville bottom marks. Even within a single popular pattern like Pine Cone, the marks vary.

Several shape numbering systems were implemented during the company's almost 70-year history, with some denoting a vessel style and some applied to separate lines. Though many pieces are unmarked, from 1900 until the late teens or early 1920s, Roseville used a variety of marks including "RPCo," "Roseville Pottery Company," and the word "Rozane," the last often with a line name, i.e., "Egypto."

The underglaze ink script "Rv" mark was used on lines introduced from the mid-to-late teens through the mid-1920s. Around 1926 or 1927, Roseville began to use a small, triangular black paper label on lines such as Futura and Imperial II. Silver or gold foil labels began to appear around 1930, continuing for several years on lines such as Blackberry and Tourmaline, and on some early Pine Cone.

From 1932 to 1937, an impressed script mark was added to the molds used on new lines, and around 1937 the raised script mark was added to the molds of new lines. The relief mark includes "U.S.A."

All of the following bottom mark images appear courtesy of Adamstown Antique Gallery, Adamstown, Pennsylvania.

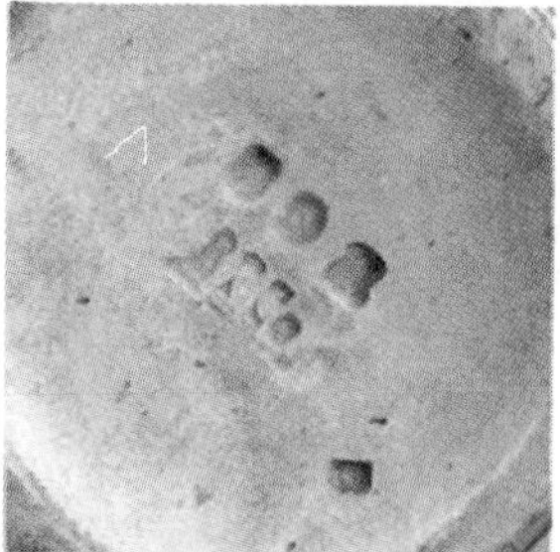

Impressed mark on Azurean vase, 8" h.

Raised mark on a Bushberry vase.

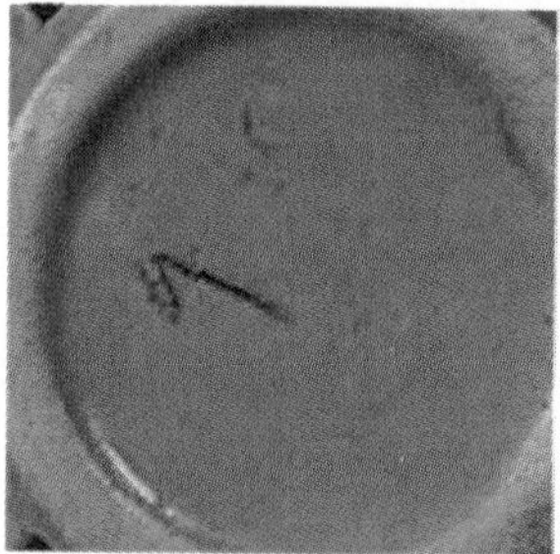

Ink stamp on a Cherry Blossom pink vase, 10" h.

Wafer mark on a Della Robbia vase, 10-1/2" h.

Gold foil label and grease pencil marks on an Imperial II vase, 10" h.

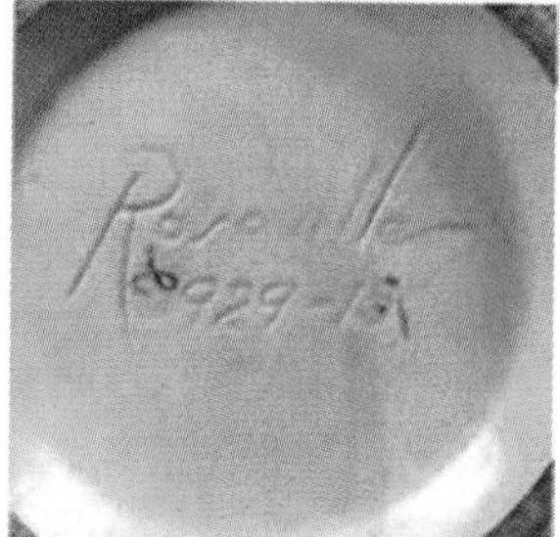

Impressed mark on an Iris vase.

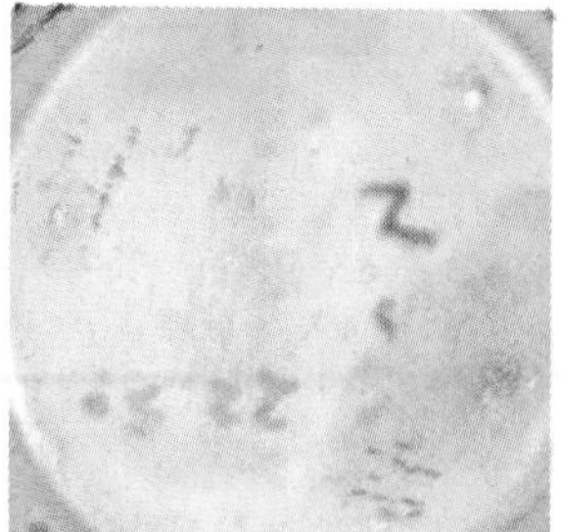

Ink stamps on a Wisteria bowl, 5" h.

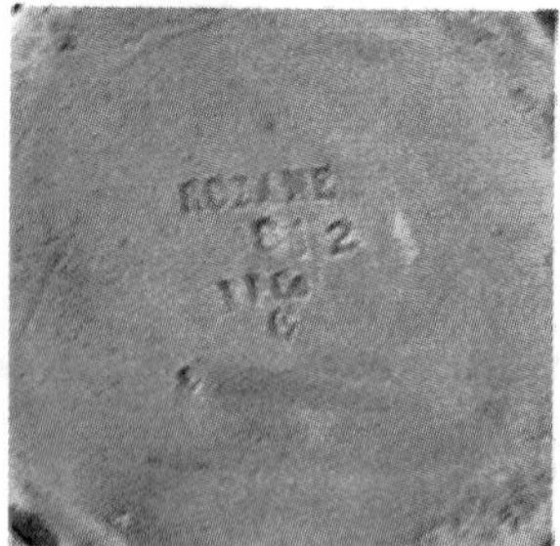


Impressed marks on a Rozane portrait vase, 13" h.

Pink Apple Blossom basket, 310-10", marked .................... **$150-$250**

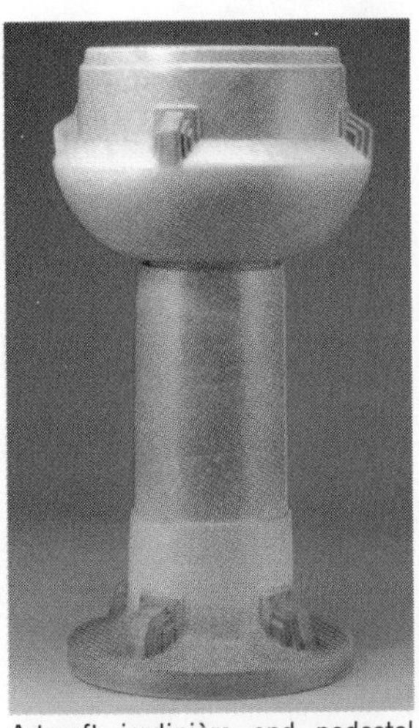

Artcraft jardinière and pedestal set, unmarked, 29" overall height ........................... **$2,500-$3,500**

Artwood green vase with pinecones, 1060-12", raised mark ................................ **$250-$300**

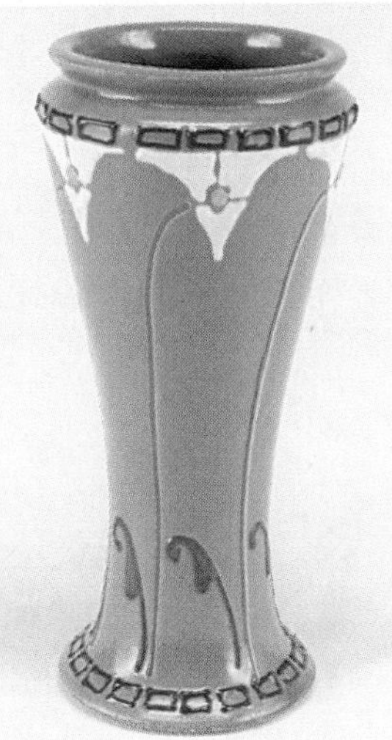

Aztec corseted vase with white flowers and blue leaves, unmarked, 8-1/4" x 4" ...**$400-$600**

Pink Baneda flaring vase, 604-7", unmarked .................**$400-$650**

Azurean two-handled vase beautifully painted by T.S. with clover blossoms, impressed 844/3/artist's initials on body, 4-1/4" x 3-3/4" .................**$650-$850**

Two Bittersweet vases, 885-10", in gray and yellow, both marked.................................... **$100-$150 ea.**

Blackberry basket, 336-8", unmarked, 8-1/2" x 5-1/2" .......... **$850-$1,250**

Blue Bleeding Heart vase, 974-12", raised mark .......... **$250-$375.**

Blended fine majolica-type jardinière and pedestal set, the Nouveau-style jardinière with applied women's bust to two sides, unmarked, pedestal: 28", jardinière: 15" .......... **$1,500-$2,500**

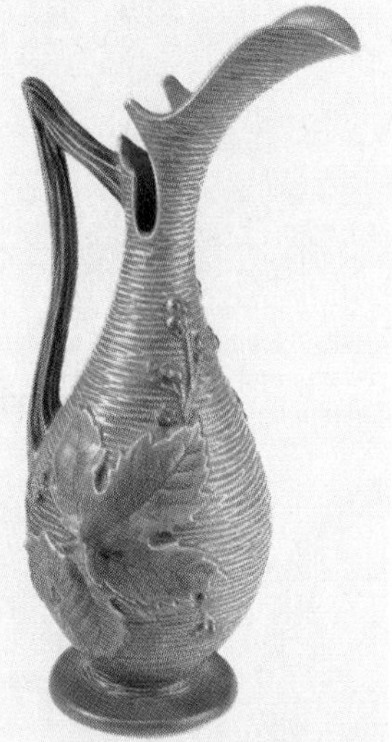

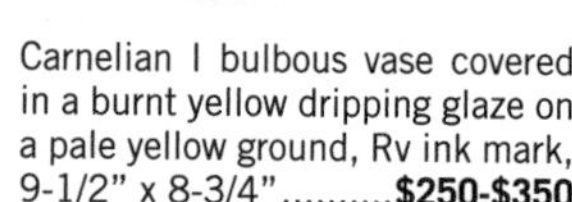

Carnelian I bulbous vase covered in a burnt yellow dripping glaze on a pale yellow ground, Rv ink mark, 9-1/2" x 8-3/4" .......... **$250-$350**

◀Brown Bushberry ewer, 3-15", raised mark .......... **$350-$450**

Carnelian II ribbed bowl covered in a fine deep red, green, and ochre dripping glaze, Rv ink mark, 4" x 10" .......... **$350-$450**

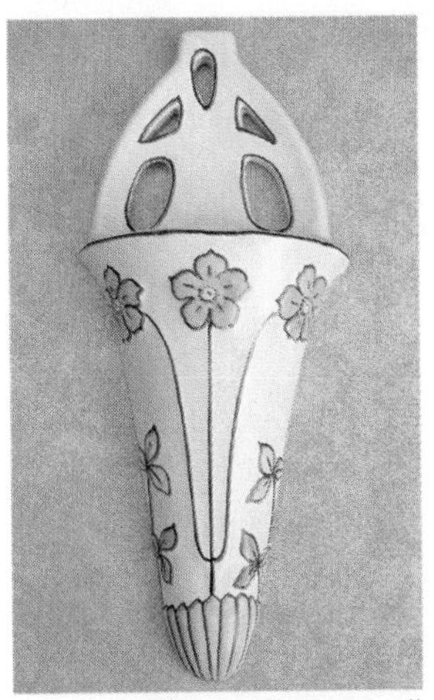

Ceramic Design Persian-type wall pocket decorated with pink flowers and green leaves, unmarked, 11" ........................... **$400-$600**

Pink Cherry Blossom ovoid vase with collared rim, 626-10", unmarked ...................... **$650-$850**

Blue Columbine vase, 27-16", raised mark ................ **$450-$650**

Green Clemana bulbous vase, 756-9", impressed mark ................................................. **$500-$700**

Green Clematis ewers, 18-15" and 17-10", raised marks ............................ **$200-$400 and $150-$250**

Brown Cosmos spherical footed basket, 357-10" .......................... **$200-$300**

Pink Cremona vase with lavender freesia, unmarked, 12-1/4" x 4" ...... **$250-$350**

Dahlrose wall pocket, unmarked, 10" x 6-3/4" .............. **$300-$400**

Pair of Dawn pink bookends, impressed mark, 5-1/4" x 4-1/4" x 4-1/2" ............................ **$450-$550/pr.**

Dogwood jardinière and pedestal set, unmarked, 28" overall height .................................... **$850-$1,250**

Della Robbia bulbous vase carved with daisies on a blue and gray ground, Rozane seal, 8" x 6-1/4" .................................................. **$12,500-$17,500**

Rare Donatello lidded powder box embossed with nudes playing instruments, unmarked, 2-1/4" x 4-1/2" ................................................ **$450-$650**

Egypto inkwell and cover of classical design, with a medallion of Caesar on the lid, a wreath of laurels, and columns and classical motifs around the drum base, Rozane wafer, 3-3/4" x 5" .......... **$750-$1,000**

◀Pair of Earlam faceted candlesticks, unmarked, 3-1/2" ................................................ **$300-$400**

Blue Falline vase, 649-8", foil label, 8-1/4" ........................................................ **$750-$1,000**

Brown Florentine jardinière and pedestal set, unmarked, 30" overall height ..................... **$600-$900**

Red Ferella flaring bowl with built-in flower frog, 87-8", foil label, store label, 9-1/2" d x 4-1/4" ........................................................ **$500-$750**

Blue Foxglove basket, 375-12", raised mark ........................................................ **$300-$400**

Green Freesia vase, 121-8", raised mark ...**$75-$150**

Brown Fuchsia vase, 903-12", impressed mark ....................................................... **$300-$400**

Futura faceted bowl, 188-8", unmarked, 4" x 8" ....................................................... **$350-$550**

Imperial II bulbous lamp base with embossed band around rim, covered in dripping pale green over pink glaze, paper label, 8-3/4" x 7-1/2".... **$1,000-$1,500**

Gray Gardenia jardinière and pedestal set, 603-10", both marked......................................... **$600-$900**

Brown Iris jardinière and pedestal, 647-10", raised mark ................................................ **$750-$1,150**

Two Ixia pink vases: one with collared rim (illegible mark) and one flaring, 852-6"; both have crisp molds, impressed marks; taller: 10-1/2" x 4-3/4" ........................................ **$275-$325/pr.**

Red Laurel vase, partial foil label, 9-1/4" x 6-1/4" ........................................ **$300-$350**

Jonquil basket, 328-9", paper label, 9"... **$500-$750**

Brown Lotus tapering vase, L3-10", raised mark ........................................ **$200-$350**

◀Green Luffa sand jar, 771-10" x 15", unmarked ........................................ **$750-$1,250**

Large white Ming Tree vase, 585-14", raised mark ........................................................ **$350-$500**

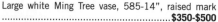

Brown Montacello bowl, unmarked, 3-1/2" x 13-1/2" ................................................ **$300-$500**

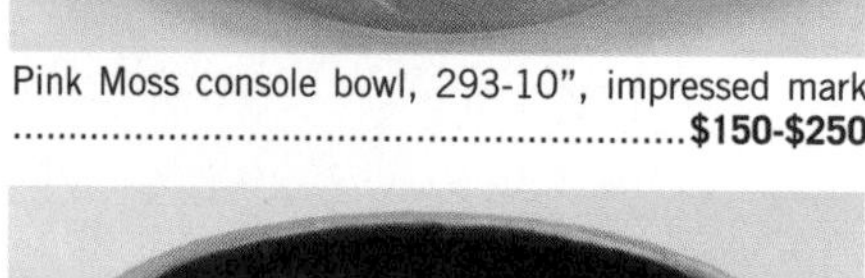

Pink Moss console bowl, 293-10", impressed mark ........................................................ **$150-$250**

Mostique low bowl, unmarked, 8-3/4" .......**$75-$150**

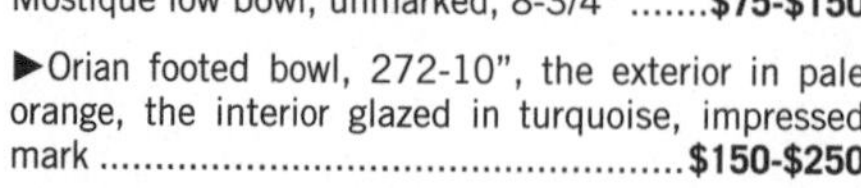

►Orian footed bowl, 272-10", the exterior in pale orange, the interior glazed in turquoise, impressed mark ................................................ **$150-$250**

Green Mock Orange basket, 911-10", impressed mark ................................................ **$200-$300**

White Morning Glory flaring vase, 726-8", foil label ........................................................ **$250-$350**

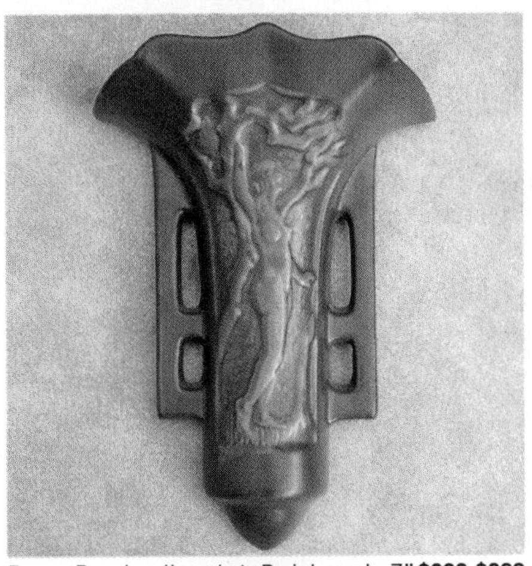

Brown Panel wall pocket, Rv ink mark, 7" **$600-$800**

Green Peony floor vase, 70-18", raised mark ........................................................ **$350-$500**

Blue Pine Cone basket, 338-10", impressed mark ........................................................ **$350-$500**

Brown Pine Cone ice-lip pitcher, #1321, impressed mark, 7-3/4" x 8 -/4"............................ **$400-$600**

Gray Poppy vase, 875-10", impressed mark ........................................................ **$275-$350**

◀Large and rare green Pine Cone urn, 912-15", impressed mark.................................. **$1,250-$2,250**

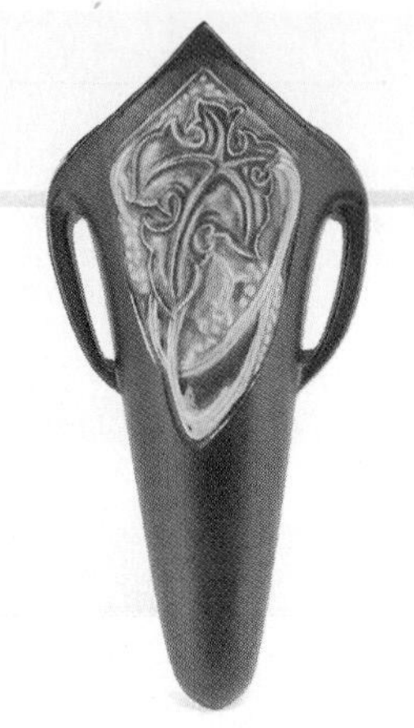

Rosecraft Vintage wall pocket, this example has pale decoration, Rv ink mark, 8" ..........................................**$350-$500**

Rozane tray painted with Myers with acorns, impressed/artist's marks, 13" x 8-1/2" ..............................................**$500-$750**

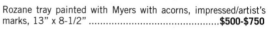

Orange Russco footed vase, unmarked, 7-1/2" x 7-1/2"......................**$200-$300**

Sunflower window box, unmarked, 3-1/2" x 11-1/2" ..............................................................**$1,000-$1,500**

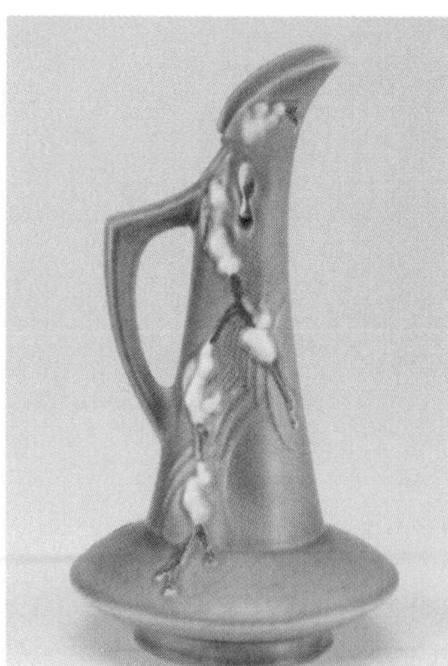

Green Snowberry ewer, ITK-10", raised mark ....................................**$100-$150**

Blue Tourmaline footed bowl, 241-12", unmarked....**$200-$300**

Pink Tuscany squat vessel, unmarked, 5-1/4" x 7-1/2" ...........**$100-$200**

Blue Velmoss II spherical vase, unmarked, 6-1/2" x 8-1/2" .................................................. **$350-$450**

Brown Water Lily cookie jar, 1-8, raised mark .................................................. **$250-$400**

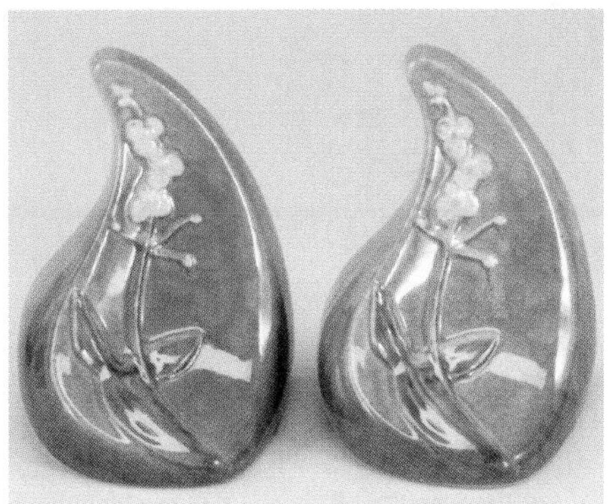

Brown Wincraft bookends with white flowers, 259-6", marked .......................................... **$150-$250/pr.**

Vista umbrella stand, unmarked. 20" x 9-1/2" .................................................. **$1,000-$1,500**

Brown White Rose bulbous vase, 991-12", raised mark .................................................. **$175-$275**

# R.S. Prussia

Ornately decorated china marked "R.S. Prussia" and "R.S. Germany" continues to grow in popularity. According to the Third Series of Mary Frank Gaston's Encyclopedia of R.S. Prussia (Collector Books, Paducah, Kentucky), these marks were used by the Reinhold Schlegelmilch porcelain factories located in Suhl in the Germanic regions known as "Prussia" prior to World War I, and in Tillowitz, Silesia, which became part of Poland after World War II. Other marks sought by collectors include "R.S. Suhl," "R.S." steeple or church marks, and "R.S. Poland."

The Suhl factory was founded by Reinhold Schlegelmilch in 1869 and closed in 1917. The Tillowitz factory was established in 1895 by Erhard Schlegelmilch, Reinhold's son. This china customarily bears the phrase "R.S. Germany" and "R.S. Tillowitz." The Tillowitz factory closed in 1945, but it was reopened for a few years under Polish administration.

Prices are high and collectors should beware of the forgeries that sometimes find their way onto the market. Mold names and numbers are taken from Mary Frank Gaston's books on R.S. Prussia.

This pink and white rose decorated urn with gold trim and opal jewels.............................. **$500**

The "Prussia" and "R.S. Suhl" marks have been reproduced, so buy with care. Later copies of these marks are well done, but quality of porcelain is inferior to the production in the 1890-1920 era.

Collectors are also interested in the porcelain products made by the Erdmann Schlegelmilch factory. This factory was founded by three brothers in Suhl in 1861. They named the factory in honor of their father, Erdmann Schlegelmilch. A variety of marks incorporating the "E.S." initials were used. The factory closed circa 1935. The Erdmann Schlegelmilch factory was an earlier and entirely separate business from the Reinhold Schlegelmilch factory. The two were not related to each other.

*Images courtesy Turkey Creek Auctions of Citra, Fla. and Woody Auction*

A selection of various R.S. Prussia marks.

Icicle mold chocolate pot with six matching cups and saucers, all decorated in a swan scene. **$3,750**

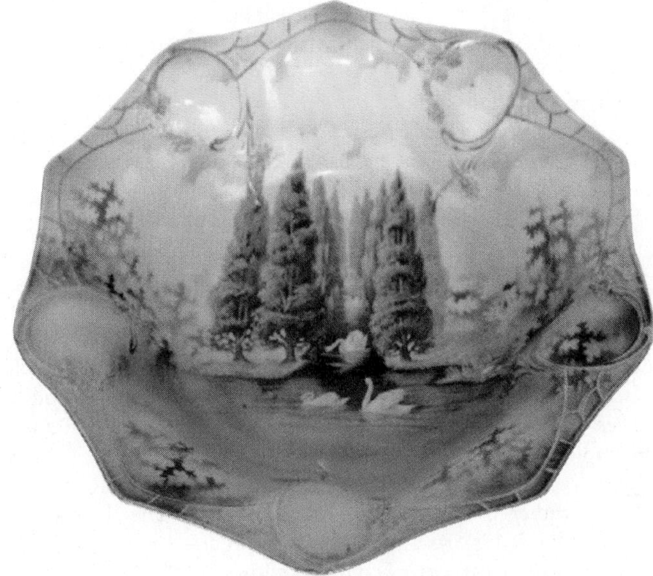

R.S. Prussia embossed bowl with swan and landscape design,10-3/4 inches in diameter. ............................ **$300**

Group of four porcelain serving pieces, including an R.S. Prussia hand-painted, two-handled pastry tray in "Poppies" decor, 1904-1908; a smaller R.S. Prussia fruit bowl, also in "Poppies" decor; a German polychromed and parcel-gilt porcelain berry bowl in the R.S. Prussia style; and an Altrohlau richly decorated porcelain berry bowl in "Peonies" decor, 1884-1909; the R. S. Prussia and Altrohlau examples all signed; the largest diameter is 11-3/8 inches. ............................ **$70**

# Hedi Schoop

Hedi Schoop (1906-1996) was one of the most popular (and most imitated) California ceramic artists of the 1940s and '50s. Born in Switzerland, Schoop spent her early years studying sculpture, fashion design, and acting. With her husband, famed movie composer Frederick Hollander, she fled Nazi Germany in the early 1930s, settling in Hollywood where his career flourished.

In her new environment, Schoop amused herself by creating plaster dolls, which she then painted and dressed in fashions of the day. A successful showing of the dolls at a Los Angeles department store prompted her to adapt these ideas to a more permanent medium: ceramics. Early slip-cast figures sold well from Schoop's small workshop, and a larger North Hollywood facility, "Hedi Schoop Art Creations," opened in 1940.

The impact was immediate, as evidenced by the praise lavished on her that year, in a *Los Angeles Times* ad for Barker Bros.:

*"We searched out the creator of these appealing flower and candle holders, and found a young lady from Switzerland, looking remarkably like her own wistful little flower girls. Her name is Hedi Schoop, and she creates the most charming pottery figures we've ever seen. She tells us she not only designs the pieces, but does all the molding and coloring, so that every piece is very much her own execution. Very whimsical and smart!"*

Schoop designed and modeled most of the figurines released by her company, and many came equipped for secondary uses — from flower-holders and wall pockets to candlesticks, soap dishes, and, with the advent of television, TV lamps. She was perhaps the most commercially successful California ceramics designer of the postwar period, and certainly the most ubiquitous. If a Schoop figure proved popular with consumers, an entire line of accompanying décor objects, such as planters, bowls, ashtrays, and candy dishes, would be built around it. At its busiest in the late 1940s, the studio produced more than 30,000 giftware items per year, and employed more than 50 workers.

Hedi Schoop figurines are largely representational and achieve their visual impact through overall shape and size, rather than through minute detailing. The figures are often caught in motion — arms extended, skirts aflutter, heads bowed — but that motion is fluid and unhurried. Rough and incised textures combine with smooth ones; colorful glossy glazes contrast with bisque. Her subjects — ethnic dancers, musicians, peasant boys and girls — are captured at a specific moment in time. A figurine by Hedi Schoop is a captivating still photo.

The broadly drawn features, soft colors, and rippling garments of Schoop's oversize figurines and planters made them easy to emulate. During the height of her career, similar designs were turned out by a variety of other California ceramic firms, usually run by former Schoop employees, including Ynez and Yona Lippen. The most successful was onetime Schoop decorator Katherine Schueftan, known professionally as Kay McHugh. Her ceramics, marked "Kaye Figurines," resulted in a unique 1942 court injunction prohibiting copying of the Schoop inventory. McHugh resurfaced in 1945 with a new line, "Kaye of Hollywood," featuring less Schoop-like figures; her ex-husband later utilized McHugh's designs for his own "Kim Ward" releases. No further court action is reported.

Due to look-alike styles by the numerous Schoop competitors, signature identification is an important means of object verification. While some pieces carried paper labels, most featured stamped or incised signatures, often with the additional words "Hollywood, Cal." or "California."

The Schoop factory was destroyed by fire in 1958. After collaborating for a time with The California Cleminsons, popular creators of decorative kitchenware, Schoop retired from ceramic design, focusing instead on painting, but her glamorous legacy lives on.

"Blue Dancers," 12-1/2" h. ............... **$275-$300/pr.**

"Tyrolean Girl" planter, 11-1/2" h. ............**$75-$100**

Apron dance pair in green, 7" h. ........ **$150-$175/pr.**

Pink "Phantasy Lady" figural vase and dual swirl candleholder, 12" h., 8-1/4" h. ..**$125-150; $25-$50**

"Veiled Lady" candy dish, 12" d. ............**$250-$275**

Oriental couple, with flower basket buckets, 12" h, 11" h. ........................................... **$175-$200/pr.**

Serving women, sculpted in profile, 14" h. ........................................................ **$250-$275/pr.**

▶1943's "Josephine," with a 1941 horse planter, 13" h., 10" h...................... **$225-$250; $125-$150**

Peasant couple. Woman, 13-1/2" h.; man, 14-1/2" h.................................................. **$175-$200/pr.**

Boy and girl pair, with real rope accents, 8-1/4" h., 9-1/4" h. ....................................... **$100-$125/pr.**

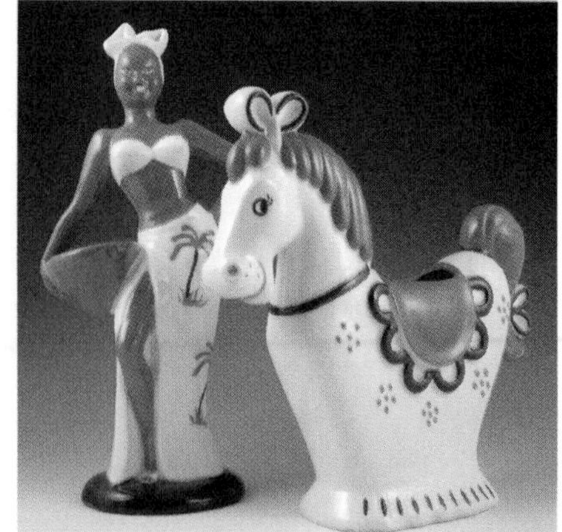

Rare "Temple Dancers," green with gold accents, 13" h. .................................................. **$350-$375/pr.**

"Siamese Dancers," dating from 1947. Man, 14-1/2" h.; woman, 14" h. ........................... **$300-$325/pr.**

"My Sister and I" Dutch couple, 11" h. **$175-$200/pr.**

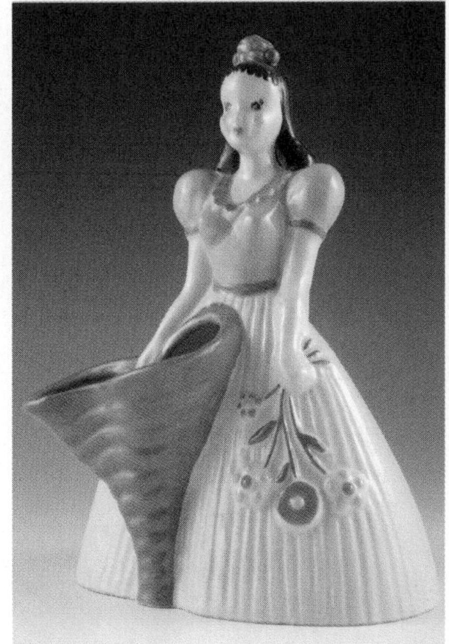

Flower girl, 9-1/2" h. ............................... **$50-$75**

◀Pink "Phantasy Ladies" with trailing skirts, 12" h. ....................................................... **$150-$175/pr.**

"Conchita," 12-1/2" h. .......................... **$150-$175**

Oval vase, with recessed front panel in a "curtained" border, 8-1/2" h. ................................. **$225-$250**

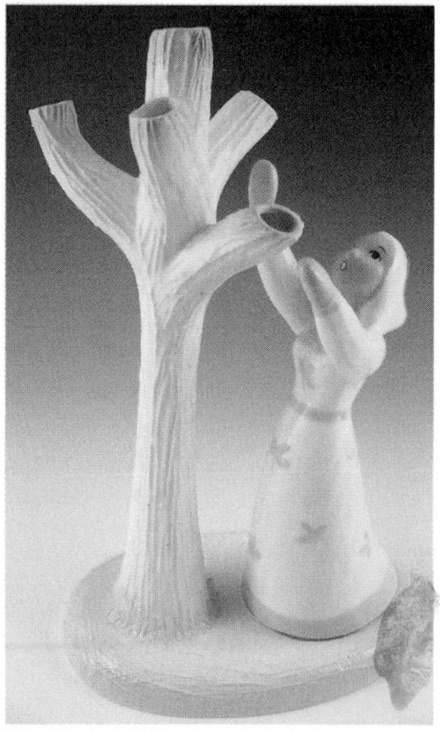

"Tree Planter," 12" h. When the individual tube planters are filled, the girl appears to be reaching for the blossoms above her. .............................. **$200-$225**

Seated white cat, 8" h. A reclining version was also available. ................................................ **$50-$75**

# Spatterware

Spatterware takes its name from the "spattered" decoration, in various colors, used to trim pieces hand painted with rustic center designs of flowers, birds, houses, etc. Popular in the early 19th century, most was imported from England.

Related wares, called "stick spatter," had freehand designs applied with pieces of cut sponge attached to sticks, hence the name. Examples date from the 19th and early 20th century and were produced in England, Europe, and America.

Some early spatter-decorated wares were marked by the manufacturers, but not many. Twentieth century reproductions are also sometimes marked, including those produced by Boleslaw Cybis.

Red and green rainbow spatterware bull's-eye plate, 19th c., 8-1/4" dia......................... **$119**
*Pook and Pook, Inc.*

Collection of rainbow spatterware, blue and red covered sugar, purple and blue cup and saucer, red and blue cup and saucer, and a red, bluew, and green waste bowl. ........................................ **$356**
*Pook and Pook, Inc.*

Red spatterware teapot with tulip, 19th c., 9" h., purple teapot with shed, 5-1/2" h. ................. **$356**
*Pook and Pook, Inc.*

Two spatterware plates, 19th c., purple dahlia and red tulip, 8-1/4" dia. .................................. **$652**
*Pook and Pook, Inc.*

# Spongeware

Spongeware's designs were spattered, sponged or daubed on in colors, sometimes with a piece of cloth. Blue on white was the most common type, but mottled tans, browns and greens on yellowware were also popular. Spongeware generally has an overall pattern with a coarser look than Spatterware, to which it is loosely related. These wares were extensively produced in England and America well into the 20th century.

Bowl, three bands of blue on white sponging alternating with two narrow white bands, minor surface wear, late 19th/early 20th c., 8-3/4" dia., 3-1/2" h..... **$88**

Butter crock, wide flat-bottomed cylindrical form, overall dark blue sponging on white with the printed word "Butter," excellent condition, 6-1/2" dia., 4-1/4" h. ............................................................ **$143**

◄Canister, cov., cylindrical with molded rim and inset flat cover, light blue fine overall sponging on cream, very tight hairline through bottom, stack mark on cover, late 19th/early 20th c., 7" h. ............ **$303**

Chamber pot, miniature, cream with overall light blue sponging, ca. 1900, 1-1/2" h........................... **$88**

Chamber set: washbowl and pitcher, round soap dish, shaving mug, and master waste jar with cover; cream background with overall coarse blue sponging, minor losses to pitcher, late 19th/early 20th c., pitcher 10" h. ........................................ **$546**

Charger, round dished form with overall dark blue sponging on white, minor wear, late 19th c., 10-1/8" dia. .................................................................. **$173**

Creamer, bulbous wide body tapering to a wide cylindrical neck with wide spout and loop handle with pointed thumb rest, the lower body molded in relief with a scene of a heron holding a snake in its beak in a garden setting, dark blue overall sponging on white, late 19th/early 20th c., 5-1/2" h. .................... **$495**

Harvest jug, beehive-shaped with high arched handle across the top above the short angled shoulder spout and round raised back shoulder opening, overall heavy blue sponging on white with the incised and blue-tinted name "A. Noland," long U-shaped glued crack on the back, rare, ca. 1860, 13" h. ................. **$688**

Pitcher, cylindrical body with molded rim and pointed rim spout, pointed scroll loop handle, overall dark blue sponging on white, minor interior stains, late 19th/early 20th c., 6-1/2" h. .......................... **$201**

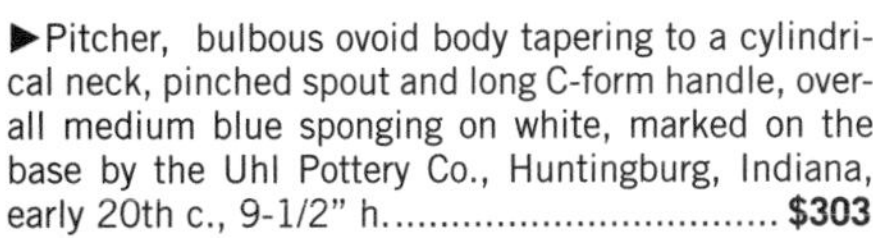

►Pitcher, bulbous ovoid body tapering to a cylindrical neck, pinched spout and long C-form handle, overall medium blue sponging on white, marked on the base by the Uhl Pottery Co., Huntingburg, Indiana, early 20th c., 9-1/2" h. ................................. **$303**

Pitcher, tall slightly tapering cylindrical body with a molded rim with pointed spout, C-form long handle, overall bold blue sponging on white, minor crazing in glaze, late 19th/early 20th c., 9" h. **$303**

Pitcher, cylindrical body with a flat rim and large pointed spout, small C-form handle, overall coarse banded blue sponging on white, early 20th c., 9" h. ............ **$403**

Pitcher, cylindrical body with flat rim and pointed spout, squared loop handle, overall fine medium blue sponging on white, flake on base, early 20th c., 9" h. ... **$288**

Pitcher, slightly tapering cylindrical body with pointed rim spout and small C-form handle, dark overall navy blue on white wavy design, hairline from rim near handle, late 19th/early 20th c., 9" h. ................................ **$176**

Pitcher, slightly tapering cylindrical body with pointed rim spout and small C-form handle, overall blue on white "chicken wire" design, tight T-shaped hairline in bottom rim up into the sides, late 19th/early 20th c., 9" h. ..... **$165**

Pitcher, swelled bottom below the cylindrical body with a pointed rim spout and angled loop handle, overall blue sponging on white, minor glaze flake at spout, late 19th/early 20th c., 9" h. ..... **$303**

Pitcher, paneled cylindrical form with rim spout and C-form handle, all over scattered large blue dot sponging on white, professional restoration to a large chip at spout and a couple of interior glaze flakes at rim, overall glaze crazing, late 19th/early 20th c. (second from left with three larger sponged pitchers), 9" h. ........................................................ **$143**

◀Pitcher, cylindrical with rim spout and C-form handle, medium blue repeating wavy vertical bands of sponging on white, interior rim flake near spout, 9" h. ......................................................... **$275**

Salt and pepper shaker, one-piece, ovoid body divided into two halves with two short spouts with metal caps, overall blue and brown sponging on white, some small cap dents, excellent condition, early 20th c., 3" h. ............................................................... **$154**

Whimsey, model of a standing pig, white Bristol glaze with scattered blue spots, some surface chipping, 5" l............................................................ **$303**

Toothbrush vase, footed baluster-form, wide dark blue on white sponged bands alternating with two narrow white bands, excellent condition, late 19th/early 20th c., 5" h...................................................... **$440**

Syrup jug, advertising-type, bulbous beehive-shaped with short rim spout and wire bail handle with black turned wood grip, overall blue sponging with lower oval reserve stenciled "Grandmother's Maple Syrup of 50 Years Ago," relief-molded vine design around top half, bottom molded in relief "Mfg'd by N. Weeks - Style XXX Pat. Pending - Akron, O.," surface chips on spout, late 19th/early 20th c., 5-1/4" h. ............................................................... **$495**

Washbowl and pitcher, bulbous ovoid pitcher tapering to a wide flaring neck, C-scroll handle, matching bowl with rolled rim, the pitcher with overall coarse blue sponging on white with a wide band in blue and white around the bottom, sponged rim and base bands on the bowl flank the wide blue and white bands, attributed to Red Wing, Minnesota, early 20th c., minor hairline and glaze flake on pitcher, pitcher 12" h. ............................................................... **$633**

CERAMICS

# Wedgwood

Reference here is to the famous pottery established by Josiah Wedgwood in 1759 in England. Numerous types of wares have been produced through the years to the present.

WEDGWOOD

## BASALT

Ewer, Classical urn-form body on a square foot and ringed and reeded pedestal, the body with a fluted lower body and narrow molded band below large molded grapevine swags, the angled shoulder with a cylindrical neck and high arched spout with the figure of a crouching satyr reaching around the base of the spout to grasp the horns of a goat mask below the spout, the loop handle issuing from the shoulders of the satyr, 19th c., 15-1/2" h... **$863**

Figure of a nude male, standing with legs crossed and playing a flute, leaning against a tall tree trunk with his cloak pinned at one shoulder and draping down around the stump, 19th c., 17-1/4" h.......... **$920**

## MISCELLANEOUS

Boston cup, Fairyland Lustre, a low cylindrical footring supporting the wide rounded bowl, the exterior decorated with the Leaping Elves pattern, yellowish brown upper sides decorated with fairing with transparent gold wing frolicking on a green and blue ground with mushroom, the upper section sprinkled with printed gold stars; the interior decorated with the Elves on a Branch pattern with two small elves perched on a prickly branch with black bat and bird around the leafy rim, base with the Portland Vase mark and "ZXXXX," 5-1/4" dia......... **$1,725**

Bowl, Fairyland Lustre, a narrow footring supports the deep rounded sides, exterior Poplar Tree pattern decorated with a fanciful landscape of stylized trees against a midnight blue lustre ground, interior decorated with the Woodland Elves V, Woodland Bridge pattern, some minor scratches on the interior, 10-3/4" dia., 4-3/4" h. ..................................... **$5,175**

Bowl, Fairyland Lustre, wide rounded shape, the interior decorated with the Garden of Paradise (Variation I) pattern with daylight lustre, the arch in the design is missing but the black pillars remain against a mother-of-pearl sky, two different idol figures appear in violet and the dancing beetle faces the opposite way, the green "Cake" tree with a companion tree with a curvaceious black trunk and copper brown foliage, the exterior with the Flight of Birds pattern printed in gold outline on a very dark green and blue lustre ground encircling the sides, the under rim and foot decorated with gold pebble and grass border, signed on the base, Pattern No. Z4968, 11" dia. ........................ **$4,600**

Bowl, Fairyland Lustre, footed deep octagonal shape decorated in the Willow pattern, the exterior in Coral and Bronze decorated with a printed gold Willow Ware style decoration, the interior with a Willow pattern in the bottom and a blue leafy band around the rim, Portland Vase mark and "Z5406," 8" w........ **$3,450**

Bowl, Fairyland Lustre, Woodland Elves VI pattern, a narrow footring supports the octagonal bowl, the exterior with a continuous design of tree trunks in dark bluish green and all the elves in brown on a flame lustre background of orange over crimson, the interior with the Ship and Mermaid pattern with a flame lustre center, Pattern No. Z5360, 8-1/2" dia., 4" h., ................................................................ **$7,475**

Bowl, Fairyland Lustre, footed octagonal form, the exterior in the Woodland Elves VI pattern, the Fiddler in Tree against a midnight blue lustre background, the interior decorated with the Ship and Mermaid pattern against a white lustre ground, some minor scratches to interior bottom, 8" w. ............................. **$4,600**

Bowl, Fairyland Lustre, footed octagonal shape, Fairy in a Cage pattern, the exterior with each side with a lacy gold border enclosing a landscape scene, the interior decorated with fantastic creatures in an exotic landscape, No. Z5125, 9-3/8" w., 4-1/2" h. ................................................................ **$3,450**

◀Bowl, miniature, Lustre Ware, footed octagonal shape, the exterior with a mottled orange lustre glaze decorated with various gold mythological beasts between gold rim and base bands, the dark blue mottled interior decorated with a stylized spider, 2-1/4" w. ................................................................ **$260**

Jar, covered, Fairyland Lustre, malfrey pot Shape No. 2312, bulbous ovoid body fitted with a domed cover, the exterior includes various patterns including Demon Tree, Roc Bird, Bat in the Demon Tree, Black Toad and Dwarf, Red Monkeys and the Scorpion with a long yellow tail and spines, a narrow dragon bead border around the base and rim of the collar, inside of collar decorated in the Pan-Fei border, the cover decorated with Owls of Wisdom with purple bodies and bright copper-colored faces, blue eyes and red pupils, the cover with a Red Fei border band and the Scorpion, cover also with a Pan-Fei border around the inside surrounding Elves on a branch in the center, Pattern No. Z-4968, 14" h. ........................**$57,500**

Vase, Fairyland Lustre, footed squatty bulbed base band below the tall slightly flaring cylindrical body, decorated with daylight lustre background with crimson and violet Imps crossing a red bridge with a light yellow top against green bushes, the sky in reddish pink and the river in deep blue with a yellow canoe, the bubbles boy and bat are black and the Roc bird is vermilion, the base band with a blue lustre background with a green flaming wheel border, the treehouse above the bridge with a green roof with yellow, red and black walls, signed on the base and numbered "Z4968," 17" h. ............................**$43,125**

Plates, Lustre decoration, octagonal with eight alternating panels of gold geometric designs alternating with panels showing Oriental men, the figures in gold against a dark blue lustre ground, Portland Vase mark and retailer mark for William H. Plummer and Co., New York, set of 12, 11" dia. .........................**$900**

Punch bowl, Fairyland Lustre, wide flaring foot supporting the wide deep rounded bowl, exterior decorated with the Lahore pattern featuring swags of brilliant colors and hanging lanterns, the interior decorated with three elephants, two of which have riders, a camel, a war horse with lancer and a flying goose in the center, all figures in black mother-of-pearl outlined in gold against a yellow lustre ground, Pattern Z5266, 11" dia., 5-5/8" h. .........................**$8,625**

Vase, Fairyland Lustre, Serpent Tree pattern, a flaring base tapering to a tall cylindrical body with a flaring rim, the abstract tree and landscape design in bright colors against a flame lustre sky, base signed, Pattern No. Z4968, 11" h. ...................................**$7,475**

# Weller Pottery

Weller Pottery was made from 1872 to 1945 at a pottery established originally by Samuel A. Weller at Fultonham, Ohio and moved in 1882 to Zanesville, Ohio.

Mr. Weller's famous pottery slugged it out with several other important Zanesville potteries for decades. Cross-town rivals such as Roseville, Owens, La Moro, and McCoy were all serious fish in a fairly small and well-stocked lake. While Mr. Weller occasionally landed some solid body punches with many of his better art lines, the prevailing thought was that his later production ware just wasn't up to snuff.

Samuel Weller was a notorious copier and, it is said, a bit of a scallywag. He paid designers such as William Long to bring their famous discoveries to Zanesville. He then attempted to steal their secrets, and, when successful, renamed them and made them his own.

After World War I, when the cost of materials became less expensive than the cost of labor, many companies, including the famous Rookwood Pottery, increased their output of less expensive production ware. Weller Pottery followed along in the trend of production ware by introducing scores of interesting and unique lines, the likes of which have never been created anywhere else, before or since.

In addition to a number of noteworthy production lines, Weller continued in the creation of hand-painted ware long after Roseville abandoned them. Some of the more interesting Hudson pieces, for example, are post-World War I pieces. Even later lines, such as Bonito, were hand painted and often signed by important artists such as Hester Pillsbury. The closer you look at Weller's output after 1920, the more obvious the fact that it was the only Zanesville company still producing both quality art ware and quality production ware.

For more information on Weller pottery, see *Warman's Weller Pottery Identification and Price Guide* by Denise Rago and David Rago.

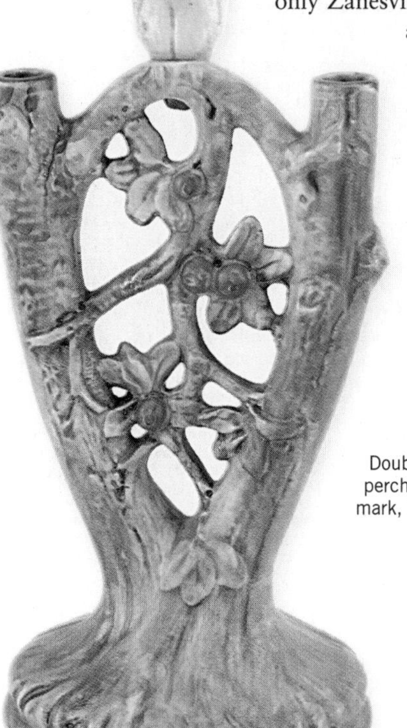

Double bud vase, Woodcraft, owl perched on the top, impressed mark, 14" x 7-1/2" ........ **$500-$750**

## MARKS

An important factor collectors should familiarize themselves with is the markings found on Weller pottery. There are many different markings found on pieces and here are some examples.

Incised script mark.

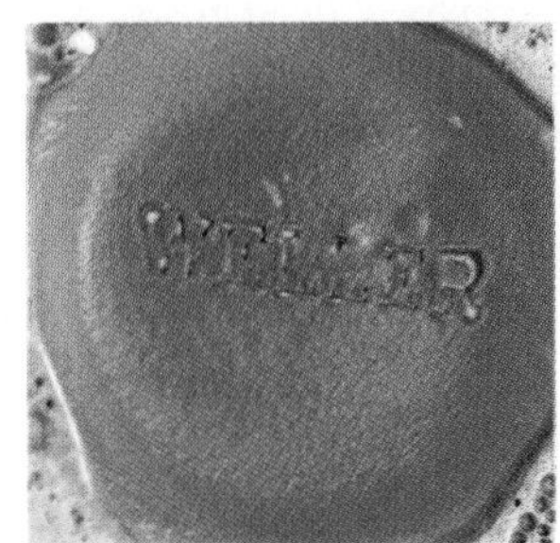

Impressed WELLER mark.

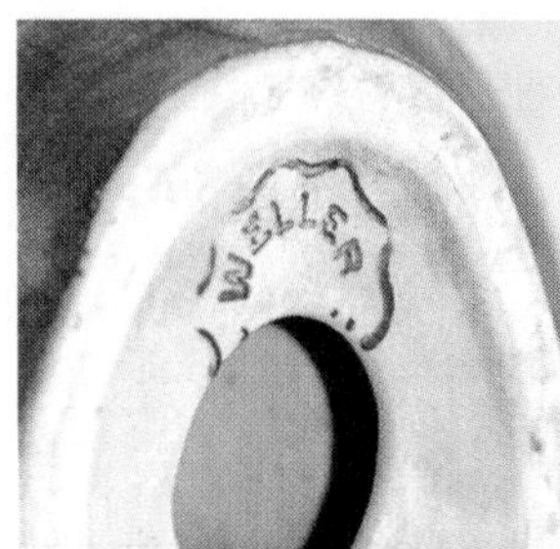

Ink stamp mark.

Incised script mark on a Patra vase.

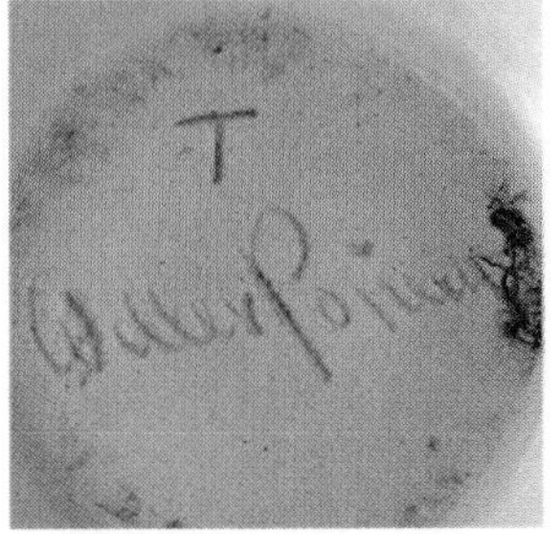
Incised script mark on a star vase.

Rhead Faience incised mark.

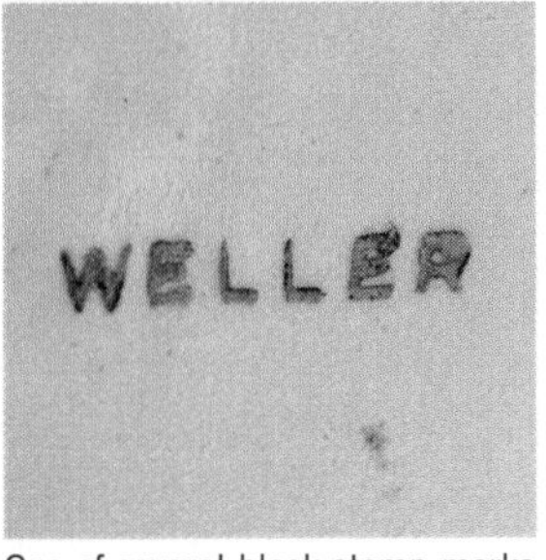

One of several black stamp marks used by Weller.

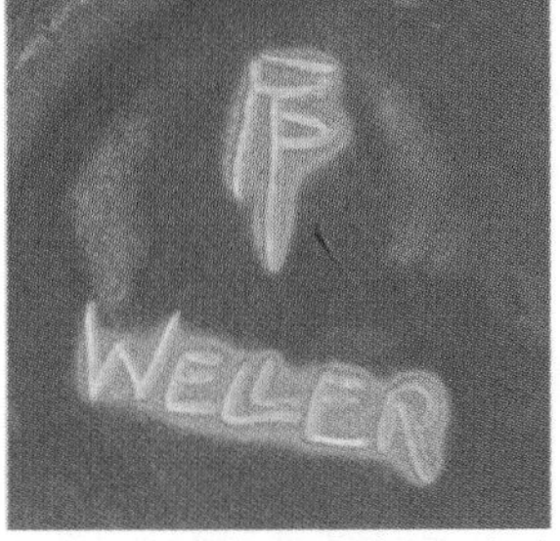

Another variation of the incised Rhead Faience mark.

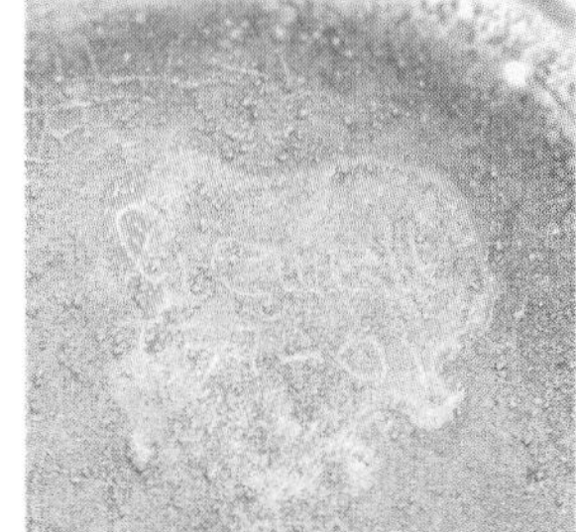
This is an example of the etched marking found on Clewell's metal-covered pieces; this particular piece was produced using a Weller blank.

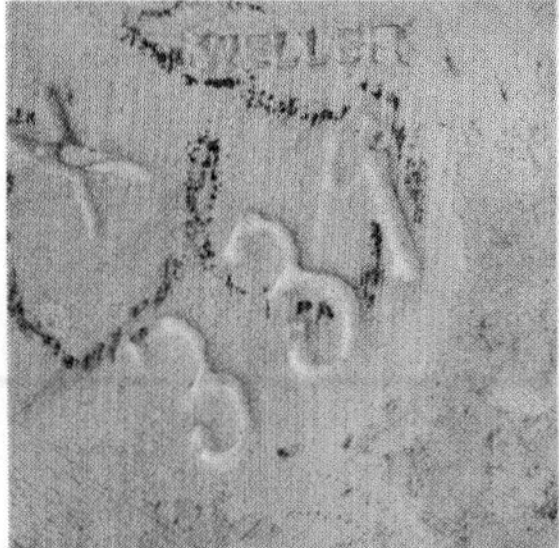
Impressed numerals found on several of their forms.

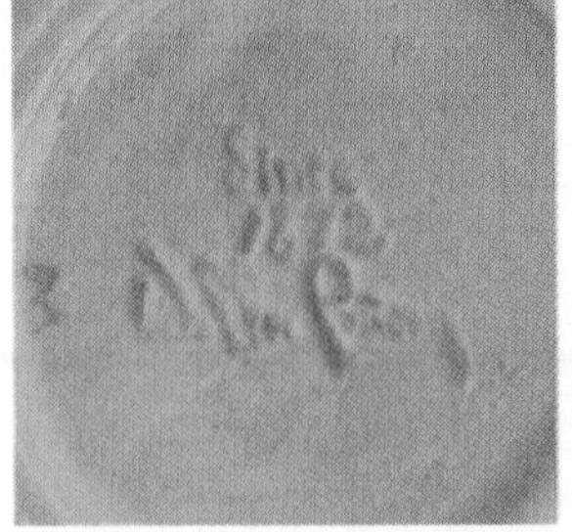
A very rare raised mark, found on a Stellar vase.

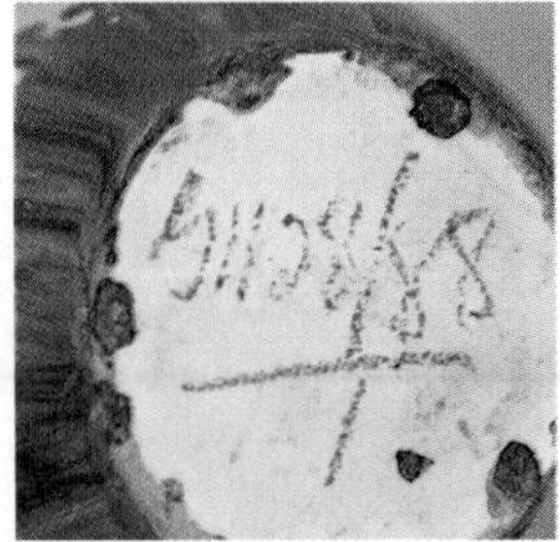
Occasionally a piece will be found with a sequence of numbers in crayon or pencil.

## EARLY ART WARE

Vase, Floretta, three-sided with grapes, impressed mark, 7" x 3-1/2" ....................... **$100-$150**

Vessel, Etna, squat, has two crossed handles, decorated with pink blossoms, impressed mark, 4-3/4" x 8-3/4" .............................. **$250-$350**

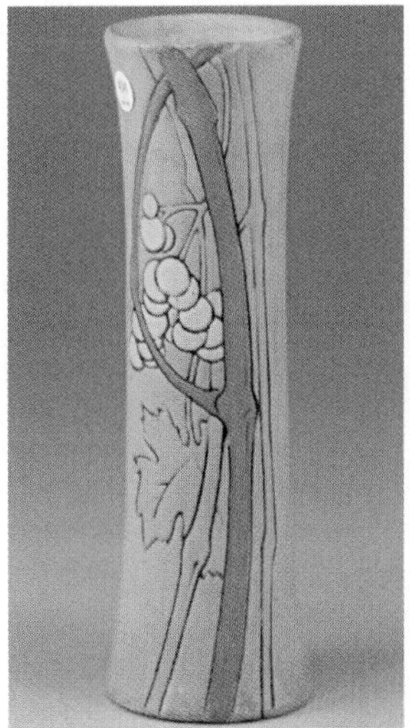

Vase, Etched Floral or Modeled Etched Matt, corseted, with berries, branches, and leaves on an ochre matt ground, unmarked, 13" x 4" .................... **$350-$500**

Bowl, Fru Russett, squat, with berries and leaves on a blue ground, 6-1/2" diameter ........................................................... **$500-$700**

Pillow vase, Hunter, painted with butterflies, incised mark and artist's initials, 5-1/4" ..... **$350-$500**

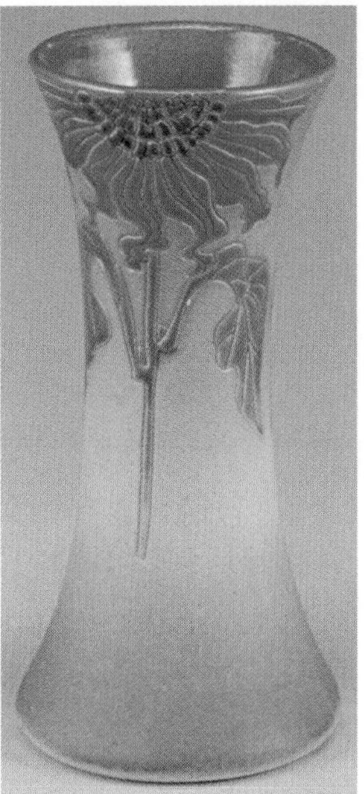

Ewer, Jap Birdimal, finely decorated by Rhead with trees and a geisha, incised Weller Faience Rhead G580, 10-3/4" x 7" **$1,000-$1,500**

◀Vase, Fudzi, corseted, decorated with sunflowers, one of the very few known marked examples of this line, impressed mark, 8-1/2" ................. **$1,000-$1,500**

Vase, Rhead Faience, yellow, handled, with a band of ducks, signed Weller Faience with impressed numbers B500, 500, full Rhead signature, which often indicates he decorated the piece himself, 8-1/2" ................ **$2,000-$3,000**

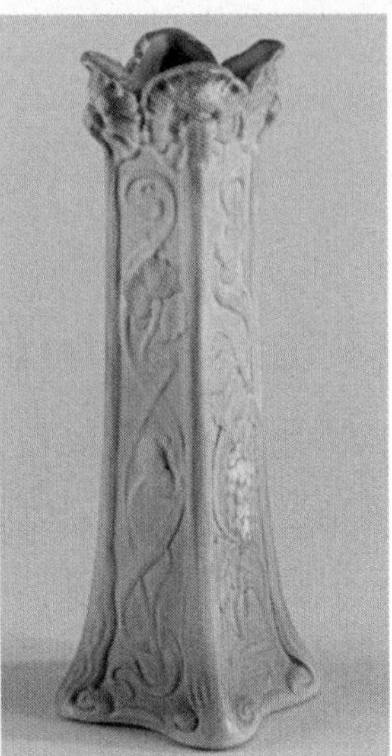

Vase, L'Art Nouveau, four-sided, with panels of poppies and grapes, unmarked, 11" x 3-1/4" ................................**$450-$650**

Vase, Louwelsa, ovoid, painted with gooseberries and leaves, impressed mark, 10-1/2" x 5-1/2" ................................**$150-$250**

Planter, Matt Green, rare, architectural form, ribbed bands on body and buttressed handles, unmarked, 7" x 10" ..................................................**$650-$950**

Biscuit jar, Turada, with an ivory foliate decoration on an indigo ground, impressed Turada mark, #615, 6-3/4" x 5-1/2"....................................**$250-$350**

Vase, Sicard, collared rim, decorated with swirling leaves, marked on body, 10"................ **$700-$1,000**

## MIDDLE PERIOD TO LATE ART WARE AND COMMERCIAL WARE

Bowl, Ardsley, flaring, stamped mark, 4-1/2" x 8" ............ **$250-$350**

Pair of candlesticks, Blue Drapery, stamped marks, 9-1/2" h ............ **$100-$200/pr.**

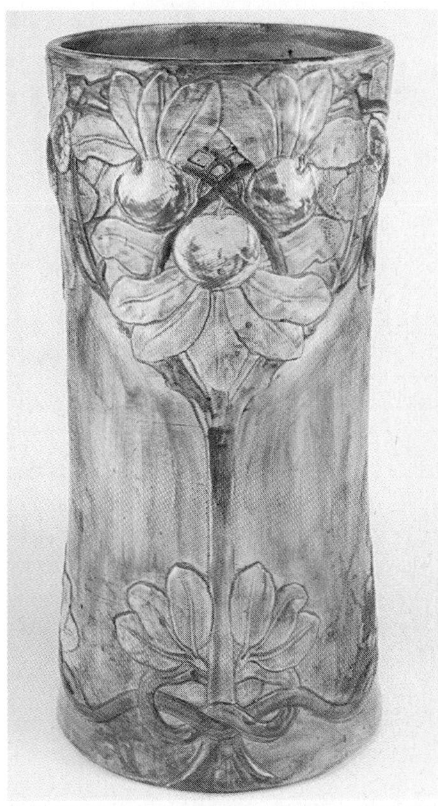

Umbrella stand, Baldin, brown, unmarked ............ **$1,000-$1,750**

Vase, Blue and Decorated, tapering, painted with berries and leaves, impressed mark, 13-1/2" x 4-1/4" ............ **$300-$500**

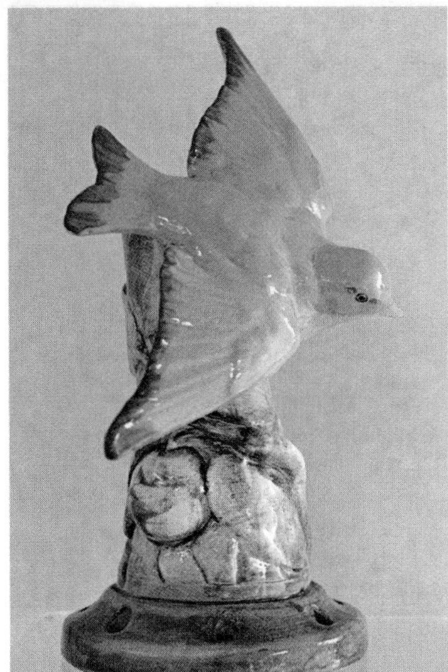

Flower frog, Brighton, flying bluebird and apple tree, unmarked, 9" ........ **$750-$1,000**

Vase, Burntwood, bulbous with morning glories; this example shows a weak mold, unmarked, 8-1/2" x 6" .......... **$200-$300**

Umbrella stand, Clinton Ivory, unmarked, 22-1/2" x 10" .......... **$500-$750**

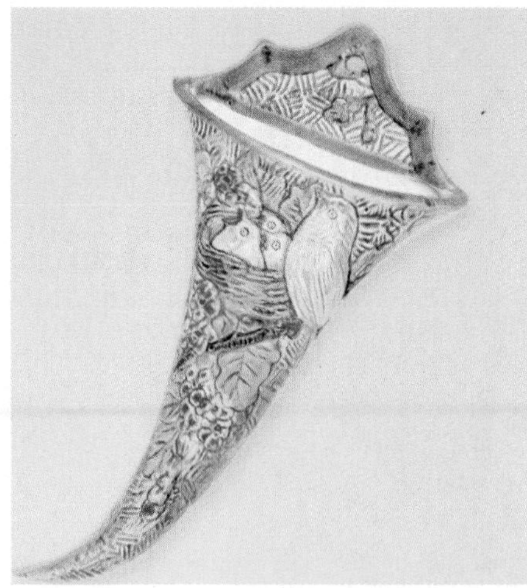

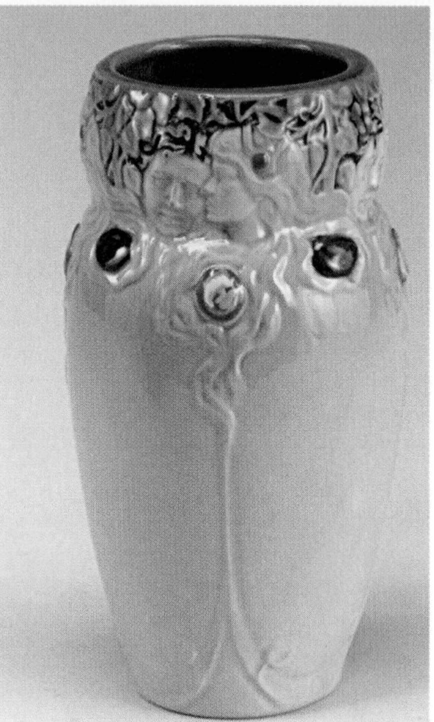

Fine vase, Jewell, embossed with men and women around the rim above a jeweled band, impressed mark, 10-3/4" x 5-1/2" .......... **$1,500-$2,000**

Figure, "Banjo Frog," Coppertone, 9" **$4,000-$5,000**

◀Wall pocket, Glendale, cornucopia shaped, stamped mark, 12" x 6" .......... **$450-$650**

Vase, Greora, flaring, incised mark, 11-1/2" x 7" ........................................................... **$300-$450**

Vase, Hudson, bulbous, two large handles, painted by Mae Timberlake with ivory and yellow roses, artist's mark only, 8" x 8" .............................. **$750-$1,000**

Jar, Selma, lidded, decorated with swans, impressed mark, 4-1/4"........................................ **$650-$950**

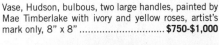

Vase, LaSa, large baluster, decorated with a mountains, tall trees, and a body of water, unmarked, 14" x 6-3/4" ........................................ **$1,500-$2,000**

◀Figure of a woman kneeling on rocks, Muskota/Flemish, unmarked, 7" .......................... **$350-$500**

Jardinière and pedestal, Marvo, brown, stamped mark, 32" overall................................ **$750-$1,250**

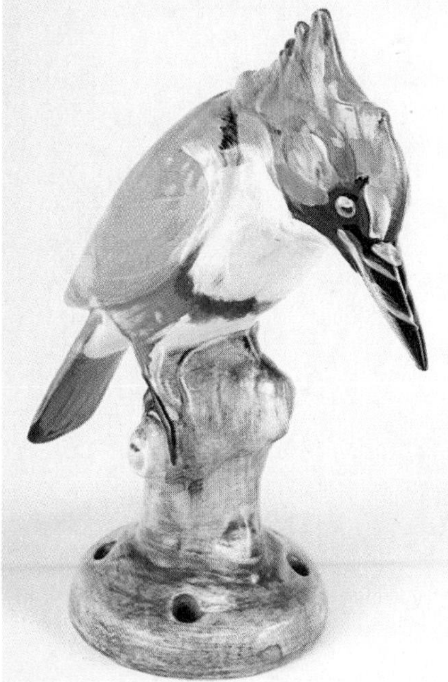

Flower frog, large, kingfisher, possibly Zona or Brighton, impressed mark, 9" x 7".................. **$200-$350**

Large planter, most likely from the Roma line, embossed with a band of fruit, flowers, and corn, unmarked, 11" x 13"................................ **$250-$350**

Silvertone corseted vase with irises, 5-1/2" .......................................................... **$350-$450**

Vase, Souevo, squat, with geometric design in black and white, unmarked, 4-1/2" x 7"........... **$100-$200**

# Chalkware

Chalkware figures are made of sculpted gypsum or cast from plaster molds and painted with watercolors. Portraying everything from whimsical animals to historical characters, chalkware was made from the late 18th century through the beginning of the 20th century, and again during the Great Depression. Early chalkware was often hollow and can be difficult to find unblemished.

Three pieces of chalkware, 19th/20th c., including two hollow cats, tallest 8-1/2" h. .................... **$207**
*Pook & Pook, Inc.*

Chalkware recumbent stag, 19th c., 10" h......... **$59**
*Pook & Pook, Inc.*

Large Pennsylvania chalkware cat, 19th c., original polychrome decorated surface, 14" h. .......... **$4,503**
*Pook & Pook, Inc.*

Two hollow chalkware animals, 19th c., spaniel and seated cat, 13-1/2" h. and 7-1/2" h. .............. **$267**
*Pook & Pook, Inc.*

Figural chalkware string holder, good condition, 8" t. .......... **$25**
*Showtime Auction Services*

Pennsylvania chalkware figure of a squirrel, 19th c., 6-1/2" h. .......... **$1,600**
*Pook & Pook, Inc.*

Chalkware Native American bust, "Iroqoi," very good condition, 14-1/2" t. .......... **$175**
*Showtime Auction Services*

19th c. chalkware bust of Native American warrior, signed on lower right, 20-1/2" t. x 12" w. .......... **$275**
*Showtime Auction Services*

Chalkware bull's head, painted brown, possibly trade stimulator, 12-1/4" h., imperfections and restorations............................................................ **$90**

*Conestoga Auction Company*

◀Molded chalkware pug dog, first quarter 20th c., the dog with an old painted surface and depicted in a studded collar in a lifelike stance, 13-1/2" h. x 5-1/2" w. x 16" l.......................................... **$125**

*New Orleans Auction Galleries, Inc.*

Fine seated chalkware cat, 19th c., salmon, mustard, and brown painted surface with a green rim base, overall very good condition, 10-1/4" h. ..................... **$17,000**

*Pook & Pook, Inc.*

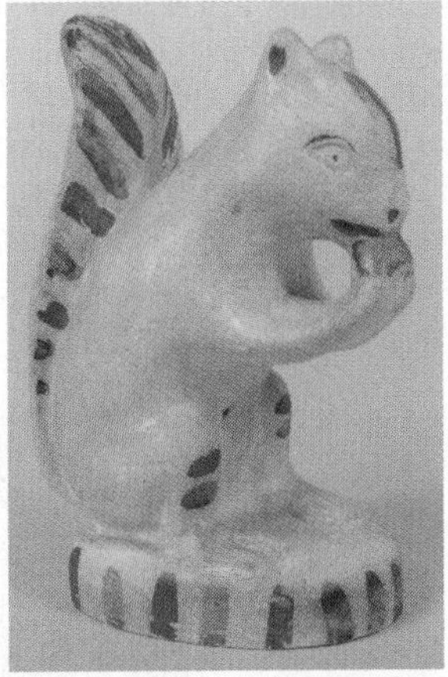

Seated squirrel with nut hollow cast chalkware, vertical tail painted with green and red accents, red on ears, nose, and mouth with black outlined eyes and green nut, red and green stripes on base, unmarked, 6"h. ........................................ **$650**

*Conestoga Auction Company*

Humphrey Bogart figure (Esco, 1973), unrestored with bright color and clean overall appearance, very fine+, 17" h., 7 lbs. ........ **$108**

***Note:*** *Esco Products, Inc. was established in the early 1970s in New York, producing plaster/chalkware statues of personalities from the world of entertainment, politics, and sports. The average statue stood about 17" tall and weighed 7-10 pounds. There were over 100 statues in the line, including several busts, wall faces, and custom-made specialty figures.*

*Heritage Auction Galleries*

# Christmas Collectibles

After World War II, decorating for the holidays became big business. Dad took care of the outside work, braving the elements to string colored lights along the eavestroughs. Mom's domain was indoors, with plenty of homemaking magazines eager to assist her.

From the late 1940s well into the 1970s, holiday edition "specials" of such publications trumpeted "The Most Memorable Christmas Issue Ever Produced!" and "The Most Famous Christmas Issue Of All!" Among the budget-friendly topics: "Start with What You Have at Christmas" and "'Expensive' Decorations—From the Dime Store!"

Decorations of the 1950s and '60s offer infinite interpretations of a standard cast of holiday characters: the Holy Family (with accompanying angels, shepherds, Wise Men, villagers, and animals); Santa, his elves, his wife, his reindeer (including Rudolph), and other assorted North Pole denizens; frisky "Frosty the Snowman" and friends; and Dickensian carolers. Among their numerous starring appearances: on holiday candy dishes, ashtrays, tea towels, drinking glasses, cookie plates, salt-and-peppers, and candleholders. The nativity was re-envisioned by artisans as diverse as Lladró ceramists and Zulu tribesmen. Glass and ceramic angels ranged from the willowy ethereal to the chubbily impish. There were Santa figurines, Santa bubble lights, plastic wall Santas, and even Santas that talked.

For collectors of vintage Christmas, that myriad of depictions is a bottomless treasure trove. No matter how much you collect, you will never run out of options. Best of all, holiday knickknacks remain extremely affordable, primarily because they were produced in such vast quantities. After the restrictions of World War II were eased, decorative Christmas items by such importers as Lefton, Napco, and Enesco flooded the market. Cheap but charming, these imports brightened many a mid-century home. Today, like individual sparkling snowflakes, they recapture — at least for a moment — the nostalgic appeal of a more innocent time.

Smiling Santas grace the cover of *Ideals*, 1950 holiday edition .......... **$20-$25**

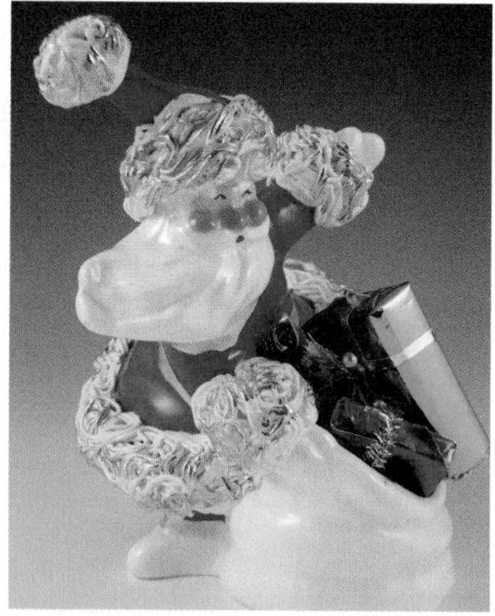

Spaghettiware standing Santa by Johanna, 7" h. .......... **$35-$40**

Papier-maché Santa (7" h., $40-$50), surrounded by two brush trees (Japan, 9" h., **$40-$50/pr.**) and two flocked reindeer (Japan, 7" h., **$10-$15/pr.**).

Bell-ringer Santa with light-up eyes, battery-operated, 13-1/2" h. ............................................ **$50-$75**

Santa and sleigh windup, with rocking action, "Jingle Bells" music box, and star bulb, 20" l..... **$125-$150**

Brad Keeler's Santa in sleigh, 8" h............ **$40-$50**

Holt-Howard Santa "Noel" candleholder, 5" h. x 10" l.......................................................... **$30-$35**

Plastic snowman light (7-1/2" h., **$15-$20**) and ceramic snowmen salt-and-peppers (Japan, 3" h., **$10-$15/pr.**).

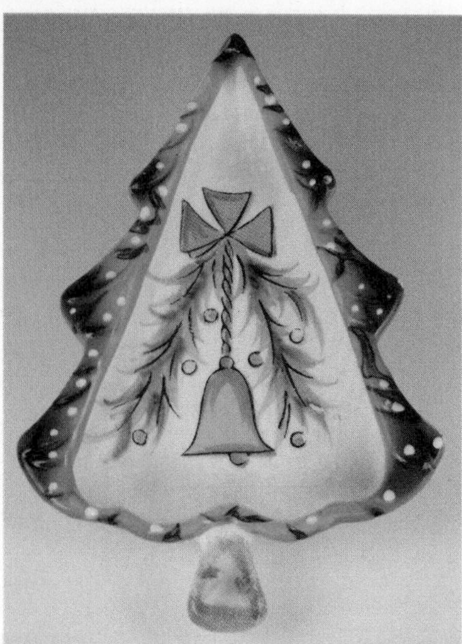

Holt-Howard ceramic "tree tray," 10" l. ...... **$10-$15**

Lefton bell girl trio, tallest figure 5" h.....**$45-$50/set**

Napco choir girl sings to a plastic reindeer, 4" h. ........................................................ **$10-$15 ea.**

►"Merry Kissmas" angel plate, 9-3/4" d.... **$25-$30**

Six-piece ceramic caroler set, marked "Briggs—Holland Mold," tallest section 10" h. .............**$75-$100**

Gurley candle carolers, 6" h. ................. **$10-$15/pr.**

"Noel" quartet, Japan, tallest piece 4-1/4" h. ........................................................**$40-$50/set**

Florence angel, 7" h. ..............................**$75-$100**

1940s large plastic angel with light-up wings, stand or wall-mount, music box plays "Silent Night," 14" h.......................................................**$100-$125**

Two Lefton tree-and-candle-toting angels (5" h., **$40-$45/pr.**) frame a central candle angel marked "1940" (4" h., **$15-$20**).

Three praying china angels in bright felt gowns, Japan, 3-1/2" h..................................... **$10-$15 ea.**

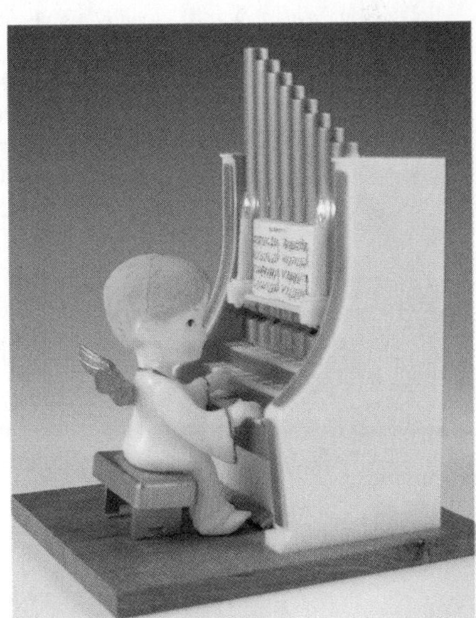

Battery-operated angel organist, Hong Kong, 6" h. ............................................................. **$15-$20**

# Civil War Collectibles

The Civil War began on April 12, 1861, at Fort Sumter, the Confederates surrendered at Appomattox Courthouse on April 9, 1865, and all official fighting ceased on May 26, 1865.

Between the beginning and end of the Civil War, the way wars were fought and the tools soldiers used changed irrevocably. When troops first formed battle lines to face each other near Bull Run Creek in Virginia on June 21, 1861, they were dressed in a widely disparate assemblage of uniforms. They carried state-issued, federally supplied, or brought-from-home weapons, some of which dated back to the Revolutionary War, and marched to the orders and rhythms of tactics that had served land forces for at least the previous 100 years. Four short years later, the generals and soldiers had made major leaps in the art of warfare on the North American continent, having developed the repeating rifle, the movement of siege artillery by rail, the extensive employment of trenches and field fortifications, the use of ironclad ships for naval combat, the widespread use of portable telegraph units on the battlefield, the draft, the organized use of African-American troops in combat, and even the levying of an income tax to finance the war.

For some Civil War enthusiasts, collecting war relics is the best way to understand the heritage and role of thousands who served. Collecting mementos and artifacts from the Civil War is not a new hobby. Even before the war ended, people were gathering remembrances. As with any period of warfare, the first collectors were the participants themselves. Soldiers sent home scraps of flags, collected minie-ball shattered logs, purchased privately marketed unit insignias, or obtained a musket or carbine for their own use after the war. Civilians wrote to prominent officers asking for autographs, exchanged photographs ("carte de visites") with soldiers, or kept scrapbooks of items that represented the progress of the conflict.

After the war, the passion for owning a piece of it did not subside. Early collectors gathered representative weapons, collected battlefield-found relics, and created personal or public memorials to the veterans. Simultaneously, surplus sales emerged on a grand scale. This was the heyday of Civil War collecting. Dealers such as Francis Bannerman made hundreds of Civil War relics available to the general public.

Following World War II, a new wave of collecting emerged. Reveling in the victories in Japan and in Europe, Americans were charged with a renewed sense of patriotism and heritage. At the same time, newspapers started to track the passing of the last few veterans of Civil War. As the nation paid tribute to the few survivors of the Rebellion, it also acknowledged that the 100-year anniversary of the war was fast upon them. In an effort to capture a sense of the heritage, Civil War buffs began collecting in earnest.

During the Civil War Centennial in the 1960s, thousands of outstanding relics emerged from closets, attics, and long-forgotten chests, while collectors eagerly bought and sold firearms, swords, and uniforms. It was during this time that metal detectors first played a large role in Civil War collecting, as hundreds donned headphones and swept battlefields

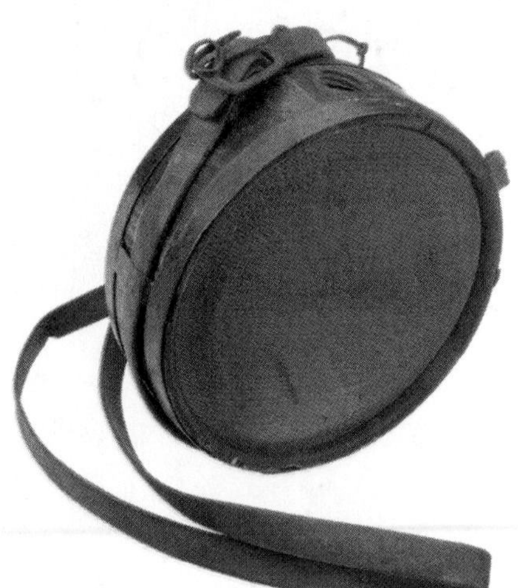

Even though the stopper is missing, the complete leather sling adds dramatically to the value of the Confederate-styled cedar canteen. .................................................... **$2,450-$3,200**
*Middle Tennessee Relics*

and campsites, uncovering thousands of spent bullets, buttons, belt plates, and artillery projectiles.

By the 1970s, as this first wave of prominent and easily recognized collectibles disappeared into collections, Civil War buffs discovered carte-de-visites, tintypes, and ambrotypes. Accoutrements reached prices that far outstretched what surplus dealers could have only hoped for just a few years prior. The demand for soldiers' letters and diaries prompted people to open boxes and drawers to rediscover long-forgotten manuscript records of battles and campaigns.

By the end of the 20th century, collectors who had once provided good homes for the objects began to disperse their collections, and Civil War relics reemerged on the market. It is this era of Civil War relic reemergence in which we currently live. The fabulous collections assembled in the late 1940s and early 1950s are reappearing.

It has become commonplace to have major sales of Civil War artifacts by a few major auction houses, in addition to the private trading, local auctions and Internet sales of these items. These auction houses handle the majority of significant Civil War items coming to the marketplace.

The majority of these valuable items are in repositories of museums, universities, and colleges, but many items were also traded between private citizens. Items that are being released by museums and from private collections make up the base of items currently being traded and sold to collectors of Civil War material culture. In addition, many family collections collected over the years have been recently coming to the marketplace as new generations have decided to liquidate some of them.

Civil War items are now acquired by collectors in the same fashion as any material cultural item. Individuals interested in antiques and collectibles find items at farm auction sales, yard sales, estate sales, specialized auctions, private collectors trading or selling items, and the Internet and online auction sales.

Provenance is important in Civil War collectibles – maybe even more important than with most other collectibles. Also, many Civil War items have well-documented provenance as they come from family collections or their authenticity has been previously documented by auction houses, museums or other experts in the field.

For more information on Civil War memorabilia, see *Warman's Civil War Collectibles Identification and Price Guide*, 3rd edition, by Russell L. Lewis.

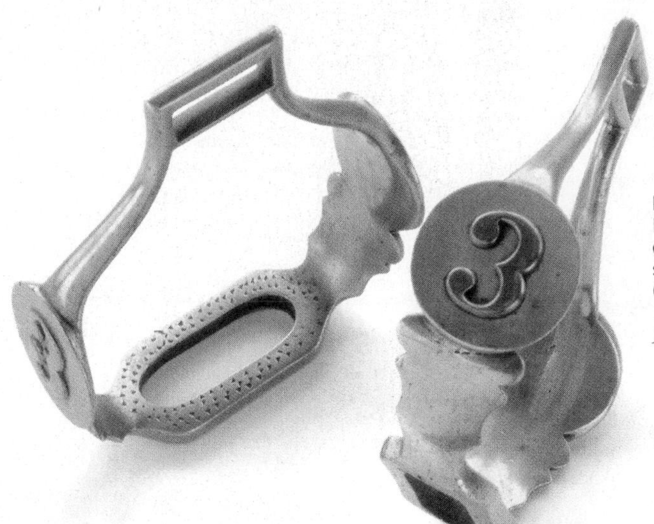


Pair of brass Civil War stirrups. Heavy cast brass stirrups, each embellished on both sides with a high-relief "3". Generally very good condition. .................................. **$600**

*James D. Julia Auctioneers*

Accoutrements lot consists of a Model 1874 pistol cartridge pouch with U.S. embossed on the flap. The inside exhibits a modification to the Civil War cap pouch made by the Ordnance Department. A Civil War item found modified for the Indian Wars period.................................. **$805**
*James D. Julia Auctioneers*

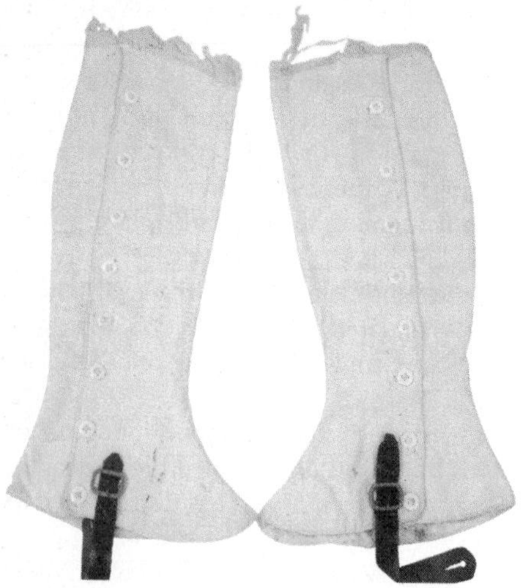

Leggings or "gaiters" were worn to protect the lower portion of a soldier's trousers. They figured prominently into the uniform of Zouaves and Chasseurs. ........................................................ **$695-$1,000**
*S.E.L.L. Antiques/Paul Goodwin*

U.S. artillery fuse pouch and belt, with flap marked "Watertown Arsenal, 1863"............... **$1,000-$1,250**
*James D. Julia Auctioneers*

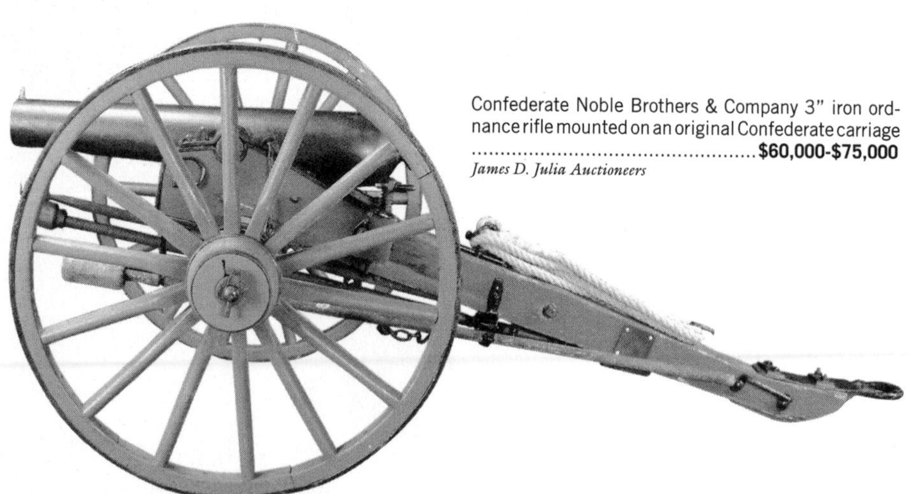

Confederate Noble Brothers & Company 3" iron ordnance rifle mounted on an original Confederate carriage ................................................ **$60,000-$75,000**
*James D. Julia Auctioneers*

This rare officer's-grade sword belt plate was made for troops from Ohio.............................. **$2,800-$3,000**
*S.E.L.L. Antiques/Paul Goodwin*

Excavated, large oval, die-struck, Breckenridge pattern, C.S. waist belt plate................. **$2,850-$3,350**
*Middle Tennessee Relics*

U.S. Navy 150 lb. Parrott chilled nose bolt with brass sabot, excavated. Fired from a U.S. Navy 8" Parrott at Fort Moultrie, South Carolina, during the blockade and bombardment of Charleston, South Carolina. ................................................... **$4,500-$5,000**
*James D. Julia Auctioneers*

U.S. 8" incendiary shell, non-excavated with original 1859-dated water cap fuse.............. **$1,600-$1,750**
*James D. Julia Auctioneers*

Confederate 12 lb. Bormann-fused cannon ball on original wooden howitzer sabot, non-excavated ................................................... **$3,000-$3,400**
*James D. Julia Auctioneers*

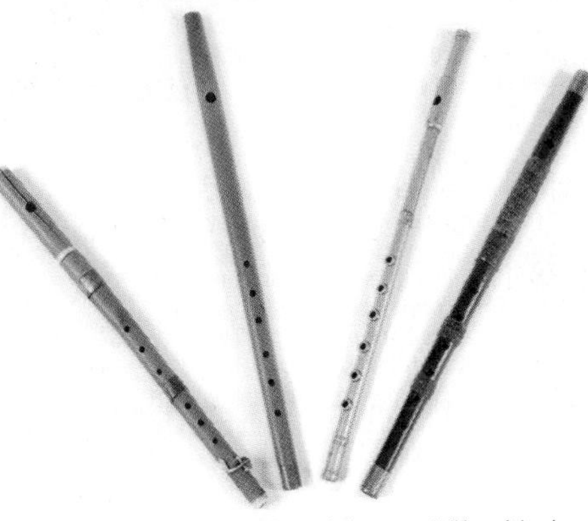

Four Union fifes. From left to right: wood fife with six finger stops and brass key (14-1/2" l.), $250; wooden fife with six finger holes used by James W. Goram, Co. G, United States Sharpshooters (16-1/2" l.), $1,200; nickel-plated brass flute with six finger holes (16-1/4" l.), $225; wooden fife with one brass ring on each end (17" l.).......................................... **$200**
*Wisconsin Veterans Museum*

Snare drum and single drumstick. Drum is 16-1/2" in dia. and 14-1/2" t. with Maryland state seal painted on the side. The drumstick was found on Rowley Farm near Williamsburg, Va., easily associated with the Confederacy ................................ **$8,000-$20,000**
*Wisconsin Veterans Museum*

Confederate 1st National lance pennon made from polished cotton and hand-sewn. The field measures 11-7/8" on its hoist by 16-3/4" to 17" to the points of the swallowtail and 11-3/4" to the cut of the swallowtail, and is composed of three horizontal 4" wide bars............................................**$10,000-$13,500**
*James D. Julia Auctioneers*

Thirty-four-star (1861-1863), U.S. national color of famous New York Battery that fought at Gettysburg. Tiffany & Co., all silk, U.S. national color of the 4th Independent Battery New York Volunteer Artillery. It is likely that this flag served with the unit during its 1862 and 1863 campaigns. For its age, as a silk flag, this national color is in remarkably good condition, with only minor damage to the fly end due to service wear and a cracking separation starting where the flag was once folded in half. The flag has been professionally framed, and only minor water staining is noticeable in the upper pair and central stripes...**$40,250**
*James D. Julia Auctioneers*

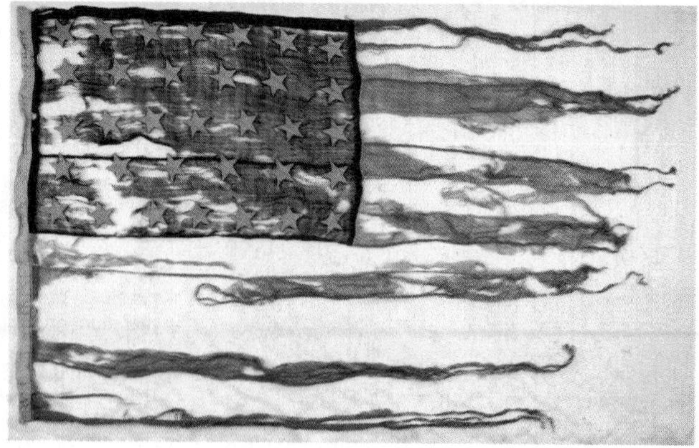

The first American flag captured. "This flag was hauled down by secessionists on January 12, 1861, fully three months before the firing on Fort Sumter, and so far as known was the first United States flag so desecrated in the Great Conflict" reads the provenance from the Soldier and Sailors Memorial, where this flag has been since 1912 just being de-accessed in 2007. Much of the stripes are worn and missing; however, the canton is fairly complete with all 33 stars. The hoist is sound. Markings on hoist are very good. Attached pennant is intact with one approx. 2" x 2" hole and several large stains..........**$33,350**
*James D. Julia Auctioneers*

Confederate 1862 contract battle flag of the 4th Tennessee Infantry, made by New Orleans contractor Henry Cassidy and delivered to the Confederate Army of the Mississippi (afterward the Confederate Army of Tennessee) ........ **$115,000-$125,000**

*James D. Julia Auctioneers*

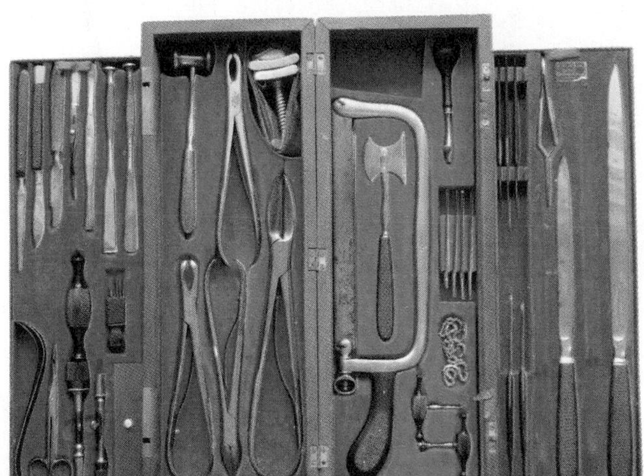

A Civil War military issue set by Kolbe, Philadelphia, marked "U.S.A., Hosp. Dept." for amputation and major bone surgery ........ **$15,500**

*Dr. Michael Echols*

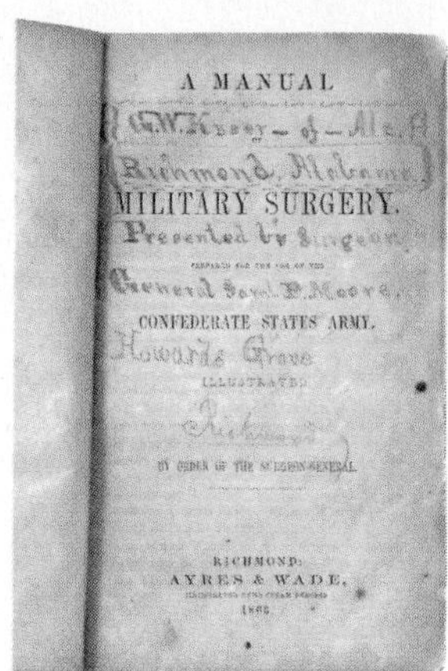

*A Manual of Military Surgery,* by Samuel Moore, M.D., Richmond: Ayres & Wade, 1863. With 30 plates and 174 figures, this was the first of only two illustrated military surgical manuals to have been compiled and printed in the Confederacy. During the Civil War, Dr. Moore was the surgeon general of the Confederate States Army Medical Department. ....... **$4,500**
*Dr. Michael Echols*

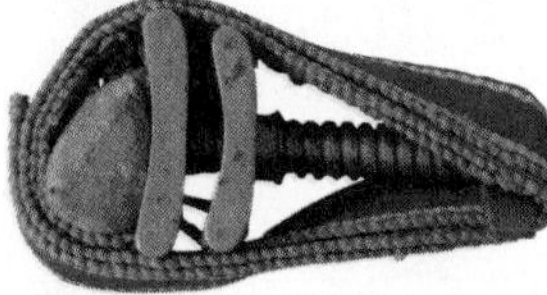

Tourniquet, petit brass screw frame, fabric strap, maker ................................**$200-$270**
*Dr. Michael Echols*

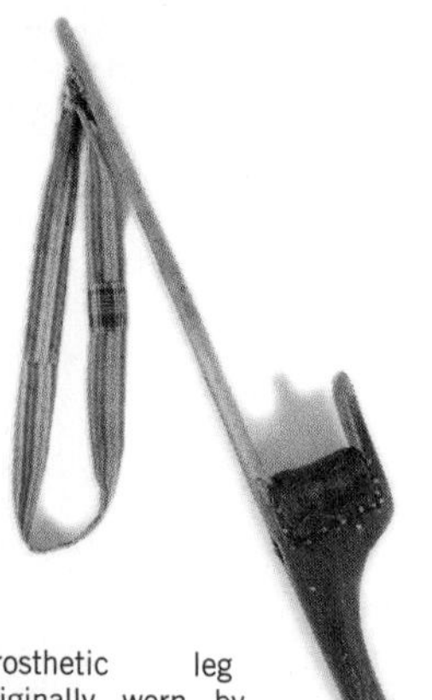

Prosthetic leg originally worn by soldier injured Feb. 7, 1865 at Hatcher's Run. The soldier had his right leg amputated below the knee at a hospital in Baltimore, Maryland. ................................**$1,150**
*Wisconsin Veterans Museum*

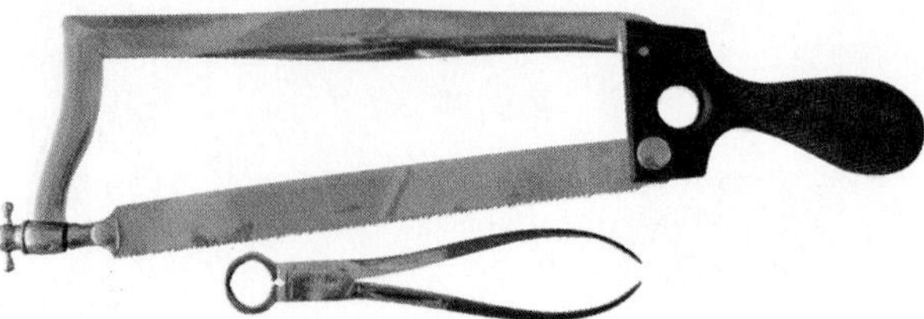

Bone saw, by Hernstein, with bone forceps, saw only...........**$200-$350**
*Dr. Michael Echols*

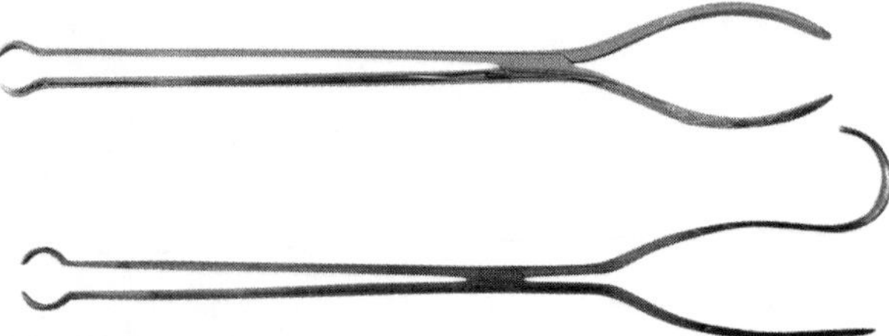

Bullet forceps, early curved handle, later straight................**$100-$280**
*Dr. Michael Echols*

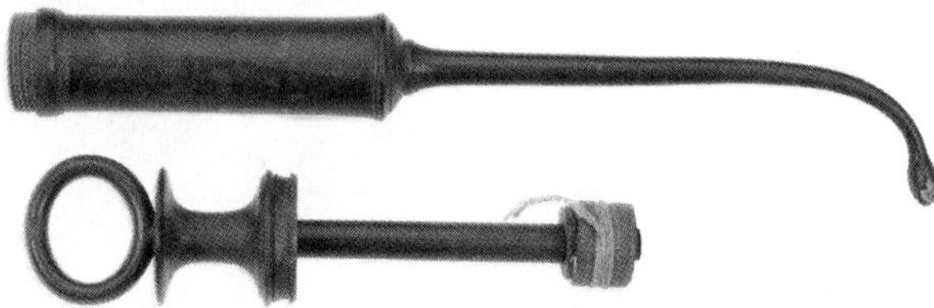

Gutta percha irrigation syringe ................................................... **$190**
*S.E.L.L. Antiques/Paul Goodwin*

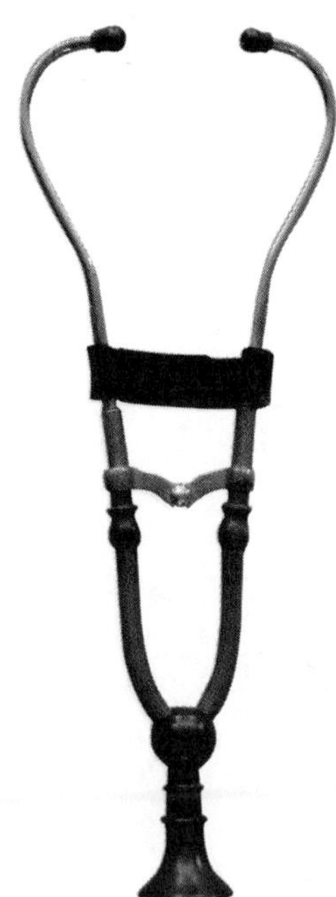

Cammann Binaural stethoscope, unusual for Civil War...**$300-$600**
*Dr. Michael Echols*

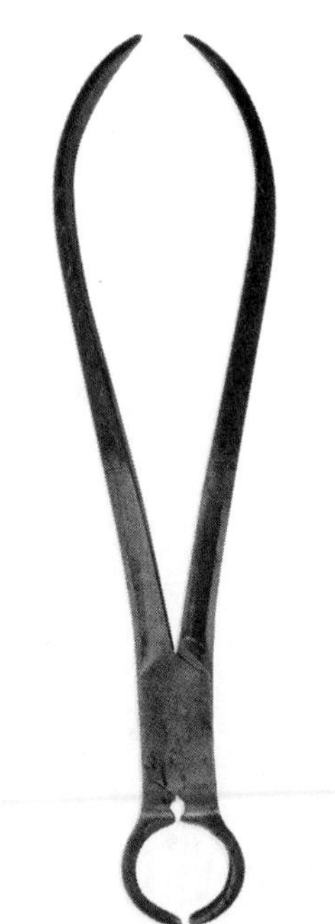

Bone cutting forceps, end cutting, U.S.A. Hosp. Dept. ............ **$200**
*Dr. Michael Echols*

Rank and branch of service as well as unit designation were often attached on an officer's epaulettes. This pair denotes that the owner was a U.S. colonel of the 2nd Infantry (state unknown). .... **$1,800**

*Tommy Haas/Paul Goodwin*

This is a privately purchased combination identification and corps badge belonging to William A. Craven, Co H, 8th Wisconsin Infantry Regiment. The top portion of the badge–the moon and star–is the only decorative element.... **$2,200**

*Wisconsin Veterans Museum*

Civil War-period thermoplastic inkwell.............................. **$55-$85**

*Middle Tennessee Relics*

Wooden folding cylindrical writing case. Case is made of slatted wood backed with tarred canvas with a tarred canvas liner, which surrounds a small tin open-sided cylinder measuring 8" l. x 1-1/4" dia. Inside the case is a small mechanical pencil marked "Eagle Pencil Co./New York," a rosewood and glass screw tip ink well, and two cancelled two-cent Civil War period Internal Revenue stamps. Written in pencil on the outside of the wooden case is "John H. Bishop/This was made in Civil War for the war of the rebellion." There is a John H. Bishop listed as a private in the 7th CT. Inf......... **$575**

*James D. Julia Auctioneers*

Checkerboard possibly related to famous Colonel Ellsworth. This 15-1/2" x 15-1/2" handmade 19th c. checkerboard is a highly collectible form of folk art and documentation on the reverse reads, "This checkerboard was once the property of the club that occupied this room. 1860?-1862 known as the Ellsworth Associates. Fifteen of its members out of sixteen enlisted in the Union Army presented by Comrade J.E. ?" (Last name ends in "ALK," but the first two or three letters cannot be discerned). It is possible that this may relate to the famous Col. Ellsworth, who was the first Union fatality of the Civil War. ........................................................................................ **$690**

*James D. Julia Auctioneers*

Civil War tinware, from mugs to coffee boilers ......... **$65-$200 ea.**

*Wisconsin Veterans Museum Collection*

Colt Model 1849 pocket revolver, .31 caliber, serial number 1798xx, with a hand engraved inscription on the back strap that reads, "F.M. Hewett, 3d S.C. Inf." ........ **$3,500-$4,000**

*James D. Julia Auctioneers*

Historic First Model LeMat revolver captured from the Confederate ironclad Atlanta. Serial number 7. First Model LeMat revolver serial number 7. LeMat revolvers were invented by Dr. Jean Alexandre Francois LeMat of New Orleans. The LeMat revolver is a .42 caliber cap and ball black powder revolver that featured a rather unusual secondary 16-gauge smoothbore barrel capable of firing grapeshot. The First Model LeMats were produced in Paris in 1862. All iron, these revolvers had checkered walnut two-piece grips. This is also the lowest serial number known on any LeMat. On the right side of the grip is a small silver plate, affixed with two pins and engraved "ATLANTA." Documentary evidence for the inventory of this Confederate ironclad ship lists three LeMat revolvers. Only two other documented LeMat revolvers exist with Confederate naval usage. ........ **$166,750**

*James D. Julia Auctioneers*

Forage cap of Sgt. A. W. Burrell, 107th NY Volunteers. The insignia on this hat, "K 107," representing Company K 107th NY, has been individually sewn into place. This hat has the patented vent that is also attached to crown of this hat. This patent device is commonly excavated in Union winter camps of the winter of 1862-1863 and battlefields after that date. Accompanying this forage cap is a photograph of Sgt. Burrell in civilian dress along with a tag that states that this is his hat and he died in a Philadelphia hospital during the Civil War. ........ **$14,950**

*James D. Julia Auctioneers*

Union officer's slouch hat of the 28th Pennsylvania Infantry. This black felt officer's slouch has an embroidered 28th Infantry hat insignia on front, officer's hat cord, ostrich plume, and a star inside a star Corps badge. This Corps badge is quite rare designating 12th and 20th Army Corps. Edge of hat is bound in 7/16" cloth binding. Interior of hat is red silk with a "Rochet, Paris" maker's label. Lining is bound by a 2-1/4" patent leather sweatband. ........ **$21,275**

*James D. Julia Auctioneers*

SLC Civil War Mem 442
Union brigadier general's double-breasted frock coat, gold brocade belt, and sash .... **$17,500-$20,000**
*Tommy Haas/ Paul Goodwin*

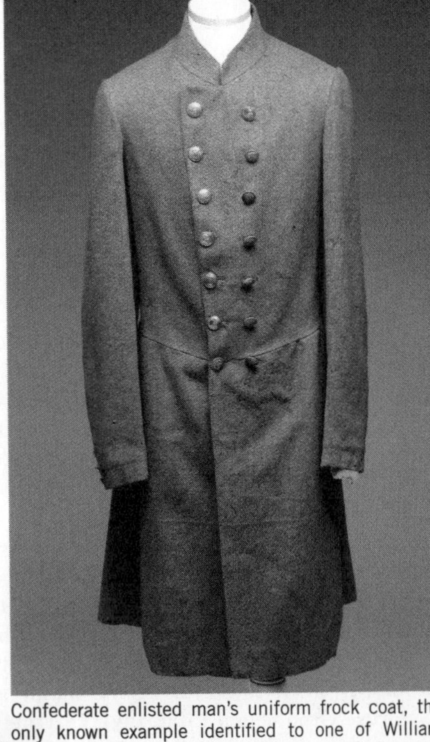

Confederate enlisted man's uniform frock coat, the only known example identified to one of William Quantrell's Raiders. This is probably the only surviving identified coat from one of Quantrell's men. James S. Milliken was a private under Quantrell and, according to newspaper articles, one of the youngest of Quantrell's men. Private Milliken was born Jan. 18, 1849 in Floyd, West Carroll Parish, Louisiana, and enlisted with Quantrell's Missouri Minutemen at the age of 14 in 1863. He died at Lake Providence, Louisiana, at age 79. Letter of authentication by Les Jensen states, "This frock coat is an original and very good example of a Confederate Enlisted frock coat...it is, to my knowledge, the only surviving coat worn by one of Quantrell's men."......................**$28,750**
*James D. Julia Auctioneers*

Confederate uniform jacket and pants. This important lot includes a handmade uniform jacket with provenance to Private Matthew Reynolds of GA. Both the jacket and the pants have been extensively examined by noted Confederate uniform expert Les Jensen. It was Jensen's conclusion that although the jacket has a number of nonstandard features and postwar modifications, it is likely to have been the jacket worn by Matthew Reynolds. Private Matthew Reynolds was found in the National Archives as a member of Company K, 20th Georgia Infantry in 1864. He served in a local defense unit. This jacket, according to Jensen, was most likely worn by Reynolds during the Civil War............................ **$11,500**
*James D. Julia Auctioneers*

# Clocks

The measurement and recording of time has been a vital part of human civilization for thousands of years, and the clock, an instrument that measures and shows time, is one of the oldest human inventions.

Mechanical, weight-driven clocks were first developed and came into use in the Middle Ages. Since the 16th century, Western societies have become more concerned with keeping accurate time and developing timekeeping devices that were available to a wider public. By the mid-1600s, spring-driven clocks were keeping much more accurate time using minute and seconds hands. The clock became a common object in most households in the early 19th century.

Clocks are a prime example of form following function. In its earliest incarnations, the functionality of a timepiece was of paramount importance. Was it telling the time? More importantly, was it telling the *correct* time? Once those basic questions had been answered, designers could experiment with form. With the introduction of electronics in the 20th century, almost all traditional clockwork parts were eliminated, allowing clocks to become much more compact and stylistically adaptable.

In lavish Art Deco styles of the 1920s and '30s, clocks featured the same attention to exterior detail as a painting or sculpture. Fashioned of materials ranging from exotic woods to marble, bronze, and even wedges of Bakelite, Art Deco clocks were so lovely that it was actually an unexpected bonus if they kept perfect time. The Parisian firm, Leon Hatot, for instance, offered a clear glass stunner with hands and numerals of silver.

For the budget-conscious, particularly during the 1930s Depression years, inexpensive novelty clocks found favor. Prominent among these were molded-wood clocks by Syroco (Syracuse Ornamental Company). Offering the look of hand-carving at a fraction of the cost, Syroco clocks featured an interior mechanism by Lux.

Also popular: affordable clocks ideally suited for a specific room in the home, such as the Seth Thomas line of kitchen-ready "Red Apple" clocks. Other companies specialized in attractively priced clocks with added whimsy. Haddon's "Ship Ahoy" clock lamp had a sailboat rocking on its painted waves, while MasterCrafters ceramic clocks replicated a pendulum effect with moving figures, such as children on swings or old folks in rocking chairs. Another best-seller, still in production today, is the "Kit-Cat Clock" with pendulum tail and hypnotic moving eyes.

And possessing an irresistible kitschy charm: "souvenir" clocks from locales as diverse as New York and Las Vegas. What better way to travel back in time than with a "Statue of Liberty Clock" (complete with glowing torch) or a sparkly Vegas version with casino dice marking the hours?

After the production restraints of World War II, postwar clock designers found inspiration in fresh shapes and materials. Among the most unusual: "clock lamps" by San Francisco's Moss Manufacturing. These Plexiglas eye-poppers exhibit a mastery of multi-purposing. They tell time. They light up. They hold flowers. Many even include a rotating platform: flick the switch, and a ceramic figurine (often by a prominent design name, such as deLee, Hedi Schoop, or Lefton) begins to twirl.

Equally modern yet less over-the-top were fused glass clocks by Higgins Glass Studio of Chicago. Although artisans such as Georges Briard also designed glass clocks, those by Michael and Frances Higgins are among the mid-century's most innovative. Clocks were a natural outgrowth for these pioneers of practical design, whose decorative housewares ran the gamut from cigarette boxes to candleholders.

According to Michael Higgins, "We try to make things which may be thought beautiful. But we are not ashamed if our pieces are useful. It makes them easier to sell."

A 1954 Higgins clock for GE, featuring ball-tipped rays radiating outward on the glass face, is as unexpectedly glorious as an alien sun. A later line of glass-on-glass clocks was created for Haddon during the Higgins' stay at Dearborn Glass Company. The hours are indicated by colorful glass chunks fused to a vibrantly patterned glass slab. While *from* the mid-century, a Higgins clock is not *of* the mid-century. Simplicity and clarity of line, coupled with a bold use of color, make Higgins clocks right at home in any age.

There's no time like the present to explore the limitless treasure trove of mid-20th century clocks. Which will be your favorite? Only time will tell.

## Antique Clocks

TOP! LOT!

**Far left:** The Burkholder family carved walnut tall case clock, George Hoff, Lancaster, Pennsylvania, late 18th century, the scrolled cresting terminating in carved rosettes above the 14" white-painted, polychrome, and gilt dial with moon's age indicator in the arch, and floral spandrels, with hands indicating the date, hours, minutes, and seconds, inscribed "George Hoff/Lancaster," and brass eight-day weight-driven movement, with three turned wooden finials, three keys, winder, pendulum, and two brass-cased lead weights, original surface, 98" h. According to family history, this clock descended to John Burkholder (1803-1843) and then to the current owner through six generations of the Burkholder family, farmers in Lancaster County, Pennsylvania. ................ **$11,258**
*Skinner, Inc.*

**Left:** Tiger maple tall case clock, David Wood, Newburyport, late 18th/early 19th century, the hood with pagoda top centering an applied carved heart, with white-painted and polychrome iron dial showing the moon's age, second hand, and calendar aperture, inscribed "David Wood/Newburyport," with brass eight-day weight-driven movement, refinished, 84" h. ................................. **$5,925**
*Skinner, Inc.*

Classical carved mahogany and mahogany veneer shelf clock, manufactured for George Mitchell by Atkins and Downes, Bristol, Connecticut, c. 1825, the eagle cresting above two engaged columns flanking the gilt and white-painted dial with Arabic numerals, wooden weight-driven 30-hour movement, above an eglomise panel showing a landscape with building, 29-1/2" t. x 16-3/4" w. ........................................ **$356**

*Skinner, Inc.*

Mahogany shelf clock, J.C. Brown, Bristol, Connecticut, the door with eglomise mat and reverse-painted tablet showing the White House, opens to a painted zinc dial signed "JC Brown, Bristol CT. US," with spring-driven brass movement marked "Forestville Mfg, Bristol, CT," the base with applied ripple molding, 15" h. x 9 w. x 4" d. ........................................ **$551**

*Skinner, Inc.*

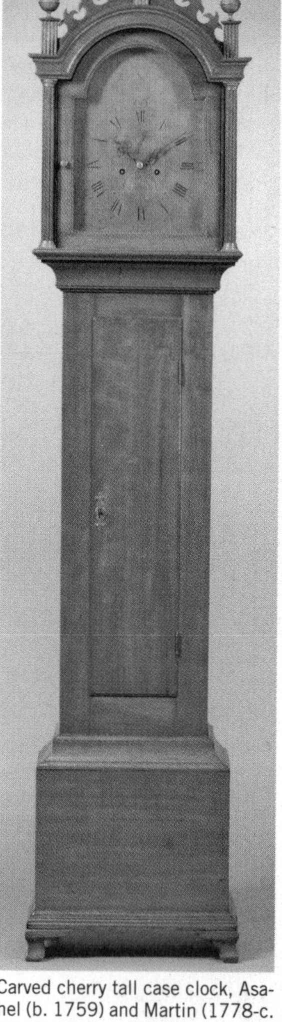

Carved cherry tall case clock, Asahel (b. 1759) and Martin (1778-c. 1830) Cheney, Putney, Vermont, 1798-1803, the engraved brass tombstone dial with a rampant lion in the arch, floral spandrels, second hand and calendar aperture, signed "Asahel Cheney/Putney," with eight-day brass weight-driven movement, refinished, 90" h. Provenance: Douglas Marland Collection, Windsor House, New Canaan, Connecticut; Bernard and S. Dean Levy, New York City, 1993; purchased by the current owners from the preceding. Exhibitions: The Best the Country Affords: Vermont Furniture, 1765-1850, The Bennington Museum, Bennington, Vermont, 1995. ........................................ **$11,850**

*Skinner, Inc.*

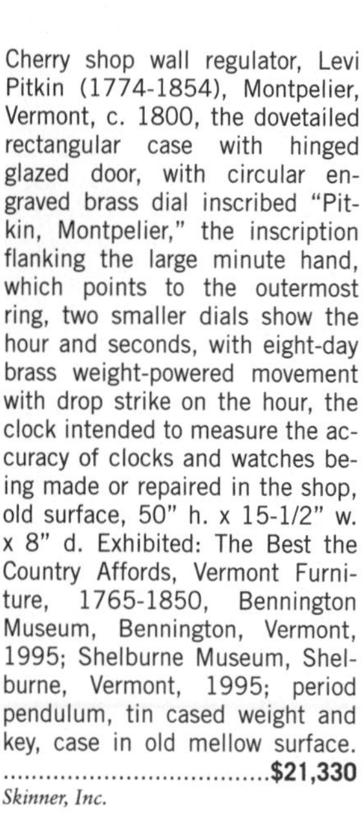

TOP LOT!

Cherry shop wall regulator, Levi Pitkin (1774-1854), Montpelier, Vermont, c. 1800, the dovetailed rectangular case with hinged glazed door, with circular engraved brass dial inscribed "Pitkin, Montpelier," the inscription flanking the large minute hand, which points to the outermost ring, two smaller dials show the hour and seconds, with eight-day brass weight-powered movement with drop strike on the hour, the clock intended to measure the accuracy of clocks and watches being made or repaired in the shop, old surface, 50" h. x 15-1/2" w. x 8" d. Exhibited: The Best the Country Affords, Vermont Furniture, 1765-1850, Bennington Museum, Bennington, Vermont, 1995; Shelburne Museum, Shelburne, Vermont, 1995; period pendulum, tin cased weight and key, case in old mellow surface. ........................................ **$21,330**

*Skinner, Inc.*

Carved cedar tall case clock, John Bailey, Hanover, Massachusetts, c. 1780, with a engraved brass tombstone dial inscribed John Bailey Hanover in the arch, with seconds indicator, brass eight-day weight-powered movement with skeletonized plates, 83" h. A partial label mounted inside the drawer reads in part, "This pine [sic] high clock was made in Hanover, Massachusetts, by John Bailey, who was born August 6, 1751, and was one of the first clocks made by him. The history of Hanover speaks of his having made his first clock at the age of eleven years, 'which (in 1893) is still keeping good time.' This clock was purchased of John Bailey by Thomas Rose, who was deacon of the first church of Hanover and also selectman of the town... from Mr. Magner [likely an early 20th century owner] it was purchased by Henry D. Sleeper for Mr. George F.---, W---town, Pennsylvania." ........................ **$3,555**
*Skinner, Inc.*

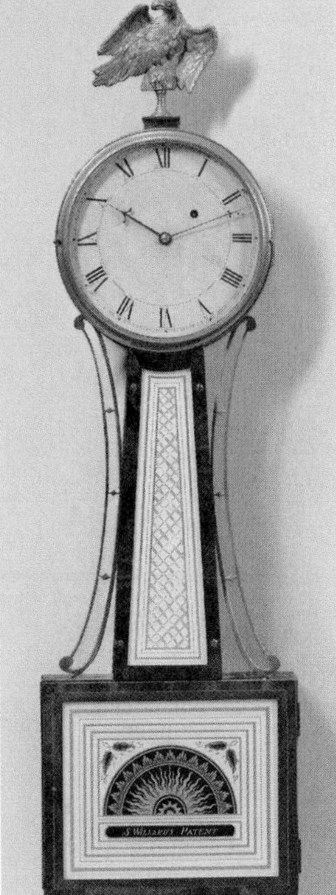

Pine dwarf clock, Joshua Wilder, Hingham, Massachusetts, c. 1815, with brass weight-driven time and strike movement, refinished, 53-1/2" h. An old label on the interior reads "LA DOUGLAS, dealer in ANTIQUE CLOCKS and BRIC-A-BRAC, Hingham, Massachusetts." ........................ **$4,740**
*Skinner, Inc.*

**Above center:** Federal gilt gesso and mahogany patent timepiece, attributed to Aaron Willard, Jr., Boston, Massachusetts, c. 1812-'15, with eight-day brass weight-driven movement with T-bridge, eglomise tablets appear to be original, 43" h................. **$6,518**
*Skinner, Inc.*

**Left:** Mahogany inlaid patent timepiece, Simon Willard, Roxbury, Massachusetts, c. 1805-'08, 32-1/4" h. ...................... **$2,252**
*Skinner, Inc.*

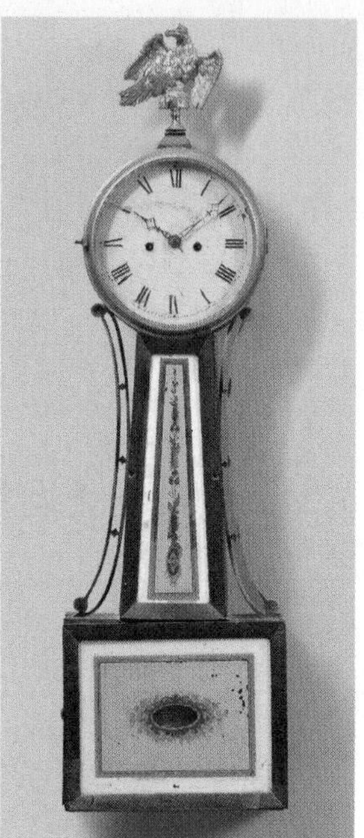

Mahogany striking patent timepiece, Boston, Massachusetts, c. 1830, with mustard yellow and red eglomise tablets, 29-1/4" without finial.................. **$3,851**
*Skinner, Inc.*

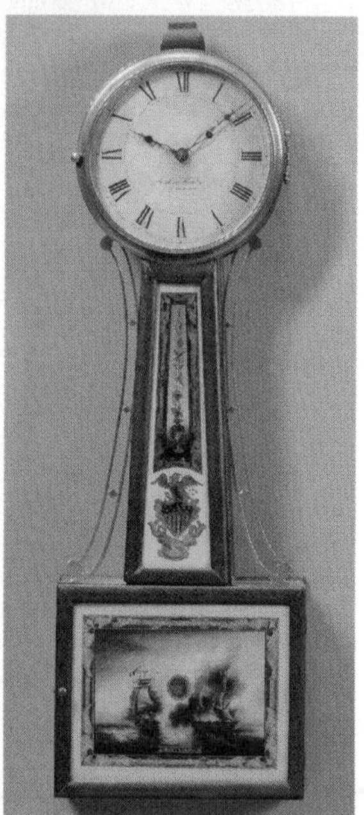

Mahogany patent timepiece, possibly Joshua Wilder, Massachusetts, c. 1820, the tablets showing the sea battle "Hornet & Penguin," without finial 30" h. ......... **$1,067**
*Skinner, Inc.*

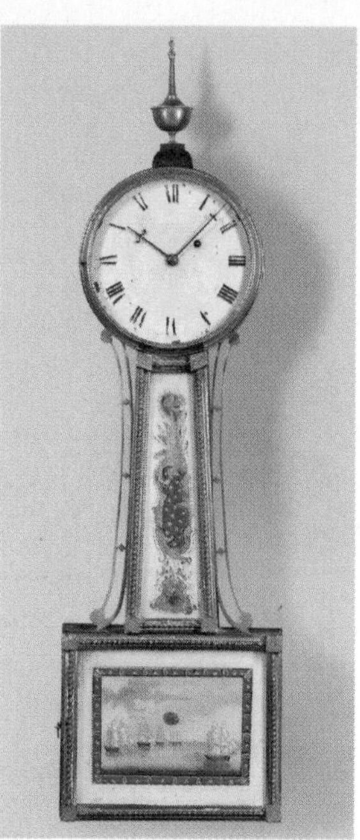

Federal mahogany and gilt gesso patent timepiece, Massachusetts, c. 1815-'20, the painted iron dial with Arabic numerals, and brass eight-day weight-driven movement, the lower tablet showing a ship battle, 34-3/4" h...... **$1,778**
*Skinner, Inc.*

Federal inlaid mahogany tall case clock, Roxbury, Massachusetts, the white-painted iron tombstone dial with painted floral spandrels, second hand and calendar aperture, lettered "S. Willard," with brass eight-day weight-driven movement, the case with brass stop-fluting and inlaid stringing, old surface, 91-1/4" h. .... **$4,740**
*Skinner, Inc.*

◀Mahogany carved lyre-front wall timepiece, John Sawin, Boston, Massachusetts, c. 1830, refinished, 41" h. .................. **$1,778**
*Skinner, Inc.*

Federal mahogany inlaid tall case clock, probably New England, c. 1810, the white-painted iron tombstone dial with polychrome and gilt designs of anchor in the arch and floral spandrels, second hand and calendar aperture, and brass eight-day weight-driven movement, 91-1/2" h. ..... **$7,110**
*Skinner, Inc.*

**Above left:** Mahogany shelf timepiece, attributed to Aaron Willard, Boston, Massachusetts, c. 1820-'25, with concave dial, eight-day time only movement, 36" h. .......... **$2,133**
**Above right:** Mahogany shelf timepiece, attributed to Aaron Willard, Boston, c. 1820-'25, the concave iron dial with eight-day movement and recoil escapement, 36" h. .......... **$5,333**
*Skinner, Inc.*

Mahogany veneer pillar and scroll shelf clock, Samuel Terry, Bristol, Connecticut, c. 1827-'29, with wooden weight-driven 30-hour movement, 30-1/4" h. ........ **$796**
*Skinner, Inc.*

Acorn shelf clock, Forestville Manufacturing Company, Bristol, Connecticut, c. 1847, with eight-day time and strike fusee movement, 24-1/4" h. .......... **$2,573**
*Skinner, Inc.*

◀Majolica pottery clock, attributed to D.F. Haynes Chesapeake Pottery Co., or Haynes, Bennett & Co., Baltimore, Maryland, late 19th century, dark green glazed majolica round clock case on a rectangular plinth ornamented with leaf devices and lion masks and with molded oak leaves, acorns, flower blossoms, and beading in relief, white-glazed ceramic clock face with gilt highlights,12" h. x 10-3/4" w. x 4-1/4" d. ...... **$551**
*Skinner, Inc.*

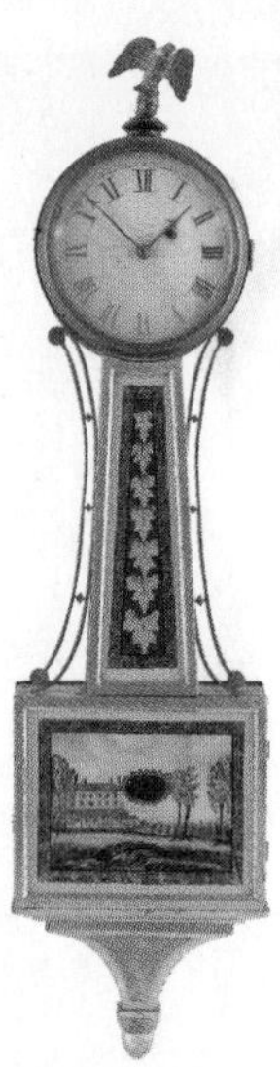

New England banjo clock, ca. 1815, 39" h. .................. **$1,067**
*Pook & Pook, Inc.*

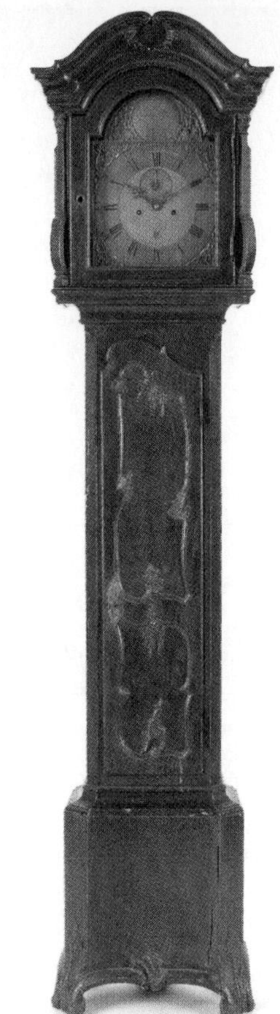

George II painted tall case clock, mid-18th century, the eight-day works with brass face, inscribed Aylmer Stopes London, in an associated case retaining an old faux oak graining, 92" h.......... **$1,304**
*Pook & Pook, Inc.*

French repeating carriage clock, late 19th century, signed Aiguilles, 6" h...................... **$415**
*Pook & Pook, Inc.*

Massachusetts Chippendale mahogany tall case clock, ca. 1800, with an eight-day moon phase works and Roxbury case, 91" h..... **$3159**
*Pook & Pook, Inc.*

Ornate Black Forest cuckoo clock with fox chasing fowl, 37" h. ..................................... **$4,800**
*Pook & Pook, Inc.*

Reading, Pennsylvania Federal cherry tall case clock, ca. 1810, the broken arch bonnet with pinwheel rosettes and original urn finials enclosing an eight-day works with moon phase, signed Daniel Oyster Reading, above a line inlaid case with fan apron, 95-1/4" h... **$2,800**
*Pook & Pook, Inc.*

English lantern clock by Richard Rayment, Bury Street Edmonds, ca. 1700, 15-1/2" h. Rayment is one of England's most respected lantern clock makers. Provenance: Descended in a Philadelphia family from the 18th century to the present owners. ............... **$4,503**
*Pook & Pook, Inc.*

English mahogany lyre form bracket clock, ca. 1810, signed Robert Best, London, 17" h. ....................................... **$2,844**
*Pook & Pook, Inc.*

George III mahogany bracket clock made by Ellicott, London, late 18th century, with a fully engraved back plate, porcelain dial and extensive ormolu mounts, 18" h. ....................................... **$7,110**
*Pook & Pook, Inc.*

English oak tall case clock, ca. 1795, the brass face works inscribed Edward Dodswell, East Bourne, 77" h. ................ **$1,422**
*Pook & Pook, Inc.*

TOP LOT!

Important Philadelphia Queen Anne walnut tall case clock, mid-18th century, the sarcophagus bonnet with ball and spire finials and open fretwork enclosing an eight-day works with brass face, signed Edw. Duffield, Philadelphia, above a case with an arched door and bracket feet. This clock, from one of Philadelphia's earliest and best known makers, remains in a remarkable state of preservation with its original finials, fretwork, full sarcophagus, and feet, as well as an old dry surface, 101" h. Provenance: A New Jersey Educational Institution. ......**$118,500**
*Pook & Pook, Inc.*

Massachusetts Federal mahogany and giltwood banjo timepiece, ca. 1815, the dial, signed Aaron Willard Boston, 40" h. ............. **$593**
*Pook & Pook, Inc.*

Commemorative Admiral Dewey gingerbread clock, top crest with a relief bust of Dewey flanked by press decoration of crossed American flags with cannonballs and columns, side pieces with press decoration of cannon and flag and the bottom decoration with anchor and star, original decorated glass with a destroyer and flags in gold, original pendulum with casting of eagle and flags with cannons; clock made by Ingraham Company with strike movement, original finish, 23" h. x 14" w., no key. Provenance: From a coastal New Jersey home. ...................... **$172**
*James D. Julia, Inc.*

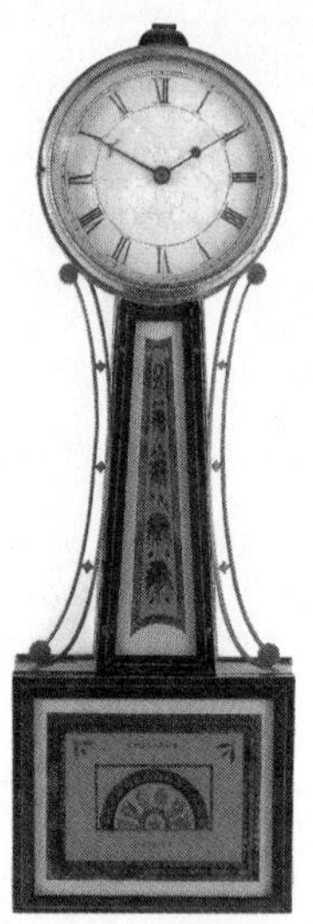

Willard's patent mahogany banjo clock, ca. 1810, 29-3/4" h. **$1,541**
*Pook & Pook, Inc.*

Philadelphia Federal mahogany tall case clock, ca. 1820, the case probably from the workshop of Joseph Barry & Son, the broken arch bonnet enclosing an eight-day works with moon phase and painted face, inscribed John Townsend Jr. Philad, over a case with chamfered corners, 96" h. ................. **$5,688**
*Pook & Pook, Inc.*

◄Classical Revival carved mahogany tubular chime tall case clock, 1900-'10, Schwarzwald, Germany, brass movement stamped with the maker's name, Math. Bauerle, Saint Georgem, and serial number 1014985, mahogany case with Gothic molded crest above the conforming frieze continuing to fluted engaged half columns centering an astragal door with glass panels, moon face dial with Arabic chapter ring applied overall with scrolling cast brass leaf tips centering a seconds subsidiary dial, brass movement playing off nine tubes and driven by three brass weights, brass pendulum on burnished steel rod, case sides each with hinged glass panel door, case raised on frontal engaged pentagonal faceted feet, 79-1/4" h. x 23-1/2" w. overall x 16-1/2" d. ...................... **$2,587**
*James D. Julia, Inc.*

## Mid-Century Clocks

*Photos by Leslie Piña; Syroco clock photos by Ray Hanson*

Seth Thomas clock with Bakelite face, 1930................**$300-$325**

Brass and bronze Deco-era eight-day clock on marble base, French, 8" h..........................**$600-$800**

Seth Thomas "Red Apple" kitchen clock, 1930s, 8" h........ **$30-$40**

Bijou-Bazir marble Deco clock with bronze afghan hound, 14" h x 18-1/2" l................ **$2,500-$3,000**

Eight-day Art Deco clock in multiple woods with ivory inlay and design of concentric circles, 12-1/2" w x 10-1/4" h...................................... **$2,500-$3,000**

Art Deco clear glass clock with stepped glass base, silver numerals and hands, signed "Leon Hatot, Paris,"13-1/2" h................**$4,000-$5,000**

►Syroco/Lux "Waiter" clock, 6" h.................................... **$195-$250**

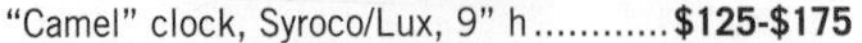

"Camel" clock, Syroco/Lux, 9" h............**$125-$175**

Syroco/Lux "Art Clock," 6-1/2" h ............ **$85-$105**

MasterCrafters circular ceramic clock, 1940s, 9" d ........ **$30-$40**

"Ship Ahoy Porthole Electric Clock" by Haddon, 8" d. Each rock of the ship marks a second. ...................................**$75-$100**

Bronze finish pot metal "Statue of Liberty" souvenir clock lamp, United Clock Corporation, 1950s, 17" h ..........................**$75-$100**

The "Kit-Cat Clock," a grinning perennial since the 1930s, 15" l. (including tail)............... **$50-$60**

A souvenir favorite, the "Fabulous Las Vegas" dice clock, 5-1/2" sq. .................................... **$25-$30**

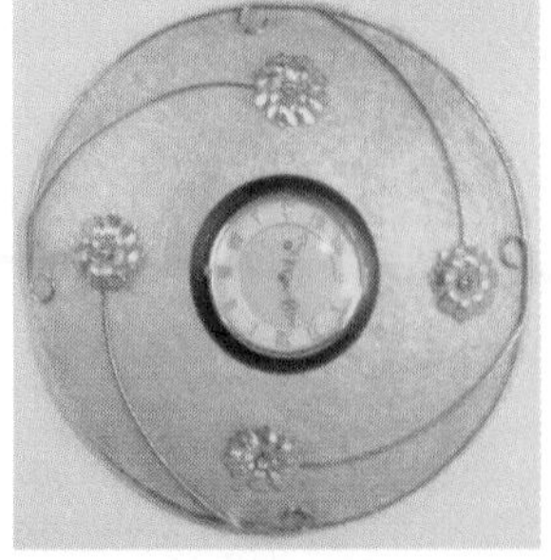

◀Spun glass, usually used by Moss for lampshades, forms the base of this wall clock, 17" d ....**$75-$100**

# Coca-Cola & Other Soda Pop Collectibles

Collectibles provide a nostalgic look at our youth and a time when things were simpler and easier to understand. Through collecting, many adults try to recapture this time loaded with fond memories.

The American soft drink industry has always been part of this collectible nostalgia phenomenon. It fits all the criteria associated with the good times, fond memories, and fun. The world of soda pop collecting has been one of the mainstays of modern collectibles since the start of the genre.

Can soda pop advertising be considered true art? Without a doubt! The very best artists in America were an integral part of that honorary place in art history. Renowned artists like Rockwell, Sundbloom, Elvgren, and Wyeth helped take a quality product and advance it to the status of an American icon and all that exemplifies the very best about America.

This beautiful advertising directly reflects the history of our country: its styles and fashion, patriotism, family life, the best of times, and the worst of times. Nearly everything this country has gone through can be seen in these wonderful images.

Organized Coca-Cola collecting began in the early 1970s. The Coca-Cola Co., since its conception in 1886, has taken advertising to a whole new level. This advertising art, which used to be thought of as a simple area of collecting, has reached a whole new level of appreciation. So much so, that it has been studied and dissected by scholars as to why it has proved to be so successful for more than 120 years.

For more information on Coca-Cola collectibles, see *Petretti's Coca-Cola Collectibles Price Guide*, 12th edition, by Allan Petretti.

Marble and onyx soda fountain made for Columbian Exposition of Chicago World's Fair, made by Liquid Carbonic Co. and exhibited at the 1893 Columbian Exposition; back bar is mostly onyx with black and green varigated marble column caps and trim; two top end panels set with stained leaded glass, showing urn flanked by wreath with ribbon adornment at base, framed by onyx surround and topped with double-layered arch with centered accent keystone; top panels of back bar have eight inset green and gold glass tile inlay patterns; mirrors are trimmed with molded bronze; back bar has eight ornate brass light fixtures. Bottom section of back bar has Liquid Carbonic Co. plaque and five evenly spaced steel doors in nickel finish with detailed hinges and hardware. Top counter of back bar is matched for color and graining and was replaced in the 1970s; front counter is mostly onyx with black and green marble trim and features 10 reeded flat columns and two alabaster fountain dispensers with three spigots each; dispensers are topped with stained and leaded glass fruit and foliate shades; shades are not the same era as the rest of the soda fountain. Coca-Cola lettering on two large central mirrors is a re-creation of lettering and wording found in a turn-of-the-century photo; counter 3' 6" h. x 21' 2" l., back bar 10' h. x 19' 9" l. .......... **$4,475,000**

# Coca-Cola

The Schmidt Museum of Coca-Cola Memorabilia held the second auction of its entire stock in March 2012 at the museum in Elizabethtown, Kentucky. The first Coca-Cola auction, held in September 2011, set a new benchmark for a Coca-Cola memorabilia sale by bringing in more than $3 million for 650 items, with several pieces going for more than $100,000 each.

The sale topper in the September 2011 auction was a mosaic, leaded-glass globe from the 1920s featuring Coca-Cola's script logo. It went for more than $150,000 – five times the pre-sale assessed value.

The centerpiece of the March 2012 auction was a soda fountain manufactured by the Liquid Carbonic Co. for the 1893 Chicago Columbian Exhibition. Made of marble and onyx with exquisite veining, the soda fountain is extremely ornate. It's actually two pieces – a customer counter and a back bar. With each piece 24 feet in length, it is among the largest items in the museum.

"This is a piece of history that goes beyond Coke memorabilia," said Larry Schmidt, head of the family-owned museum. The bar sold for a record $4.4 million, making it quite possibly the most valuable Coca-Cola collectible on the planet.

The Schmidt family's connection to Coca-Cola goes back to 1901, when Frederick Schmidt became one of the first Coke bottlers in the country by opening a plant in Louisville. For four generations, the Schmidts ran bottling operations in Kentucky and southern Indiana. Their passion for collecting Coke memorabilia began nearly 40 years ago and led to the world's largest privately held collection of its type. Altogether, there are some 80,000 items worth as much as $10 million. In 2011 the family announced it would close its museum and sell everything with proceeds going to a charitable foundation being set up by the family.

*All Coca-Cola images courtesy Richard Opfer Auctioneering, Inc.*

Coca-Cola neon building clock and sign, rare, mid-to-late 1930s, piece adorned the Piqua, Ohio bottling plant, photograph of installation on building is included; clock face, hands, and silver bezel and trim are metal; rest of sign embossed porcelain with extensive neon tubing and highlights; much of neon tubing replaced; porcelain is all original with a few small chips, nicks, and small areas of weather staining; likely the only example of its kind in existence, 14' x 7' ..............**$50,000**

1943 Coca-Cola Santa cut-out easel back sign, great graphics, soiled and rougher than average, some bends, surface scratches, medium stains, edge wear, original easel on back, 16" x 12" ........................................**$160**

1941 Coca-Cola serving tray, light border soiling, clean face, one or two small surface marks; some raised spots and light roughness on face of tray ....................**$375**

1930s Coca-Cola porcelain sign, extremely good condition; minimal surface marks and wear; high relief on the lettering, 3' x 5' .............................. **$7,500**

Drink A Bottle of Coca-Cola Delicious and Refreshing

Circa 1910 Coca-Cola canvas banner, strong colors, some minor stains on left one to two feet and extreme outer edge borders, clean and bright, light to moderate wear, 16" x 11' 6" ............................... **$4,000**

1930 Coca-Cola paper poster, dry mounted to heavy stock board, few minor ripples, light soiling, few minor marks, light wear overall, 10" x 14" .......... **$250**

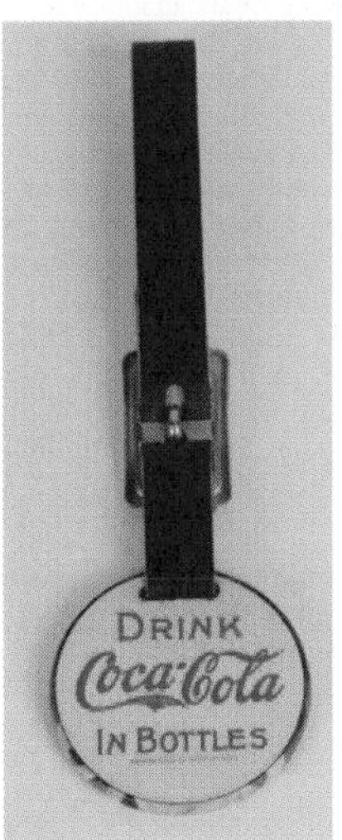


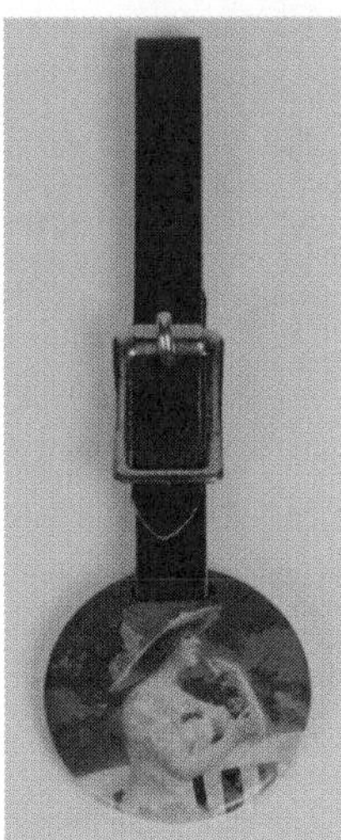

Circa 1912 Coca-Cola celluloid watch fob, strong example with miniscule surface marks and wear, few small depressions front and back, one small slit at bottom of piece when held upside down, little to no fading, staining or discoloration, 1-1/2" dia. . **$4,750**

Scarce Coca-Cola four seasons window display, 1922, considered by collectors to be one of the most attractive displays the company ever produced. Some soiling, staining, and normal expected overall wear and small marks, a few small nail holes and surface marks that have been closed and retouched, all four fold lines have been supported, and a few top edge points have been rebuilt and restored as well. 61" x 29-1/2"................................................... **$6,000**

1940s Coca-Cola Masonite cut-out sign, large scale graphics, light wear, some surface scratches, scuffs, a few minor color chips on bottom 2", a few minor edge chips and small tack holes around the perimeter, 48" x 48" ......................................................... **$475**

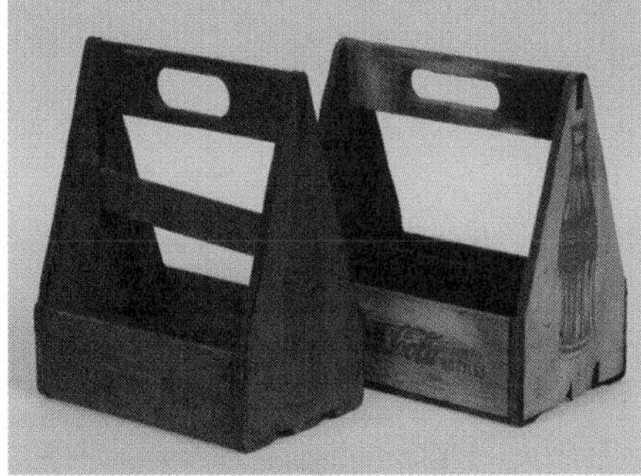

Two Coca-Cola 1930s-1940s wooden bottle carriers, both with Christmas bottles on each end, good stencils all around, natural toned carrier is slightly darkened and soiled, other carrier missing a bottom slat or two..................................................... **$120**

Leaded glass Coca-Cola globe, late teens to early 1920s, very rare, a few panels have cracks that are closed, textured and marbled red and green glass with white "Coca-Cola" logo on each side of globe, piece sits atop a bronze-colored tall lamp base, 31" h., 12-1/2" dia. ............................... **$50,000**

Coca-Cola brass script cut-out driver's hat logo, 1920s-1930s, original three threaded posts on back of piece that protrude 1/2" for attachment to driver's hat, appears to be solid brass, little to no wear, 1-1/4" x 4" ............... **$500**

1901 Coca-Cola paper poster matted and framed under conservation glass; original top and bottom strip and cloth hanger; faint stain lightly impacts left eye; few minor surface marks and small closed edge tears, vivid color on enameled and lightly textured paper, 15" x 20" ...................... **$32,500**

1907 Coca-Cola pocket mirror, slight fading, slightly bumpy surface, light to moderate surface wear and marks, 2-3/4" x 1-3/4" ... **$475**

Circa 1894 rare Coca-Cola hand fan, non-advertising side features good colors with feathered bird; advertising side makes references to tired nerves and brain; fan states that Coca-Cola cures headaches; used by Seth Fowle and Sons in Boston; light wear, minor edge bends, a few small light stains and light soiling, 12" x 8-1/2" ......................... **$5,000**

1950s Coca-Cola clock radio, slight fading on top of piece, radio does not play but clock works; case appears to have been repainted 20 years ago, grille cloth may have been replaced and has fallen away a bit, light soiling, a few small color chips and nicks in random areas, 9-1/2" x 12" x 8-1/2" d. ........................... **$475**

# Other Soda Pop Collectibles

Wool's Cherry Cheer syrup dispenser, rare pumpkin color.......................................................$26,000

Pepsi-Cola bottle carriers, two wood and one metal, with bottles, 12" t.........................................$250

Cloverdale nine-inch disc, Mission beverages door push, and B-1 Lemon-Lime Soda tin sign, largest 16" x 3" ..........................................................$210

◀Clock, electric, "Say Pepsi Please," working, 15" dia. .............................................................$400

Moxie cola tin car, rare, red version dated 1917, two-sided advertising toy with classic Moxie Man on horse in car, 8" l..........................$1,100

7UP aluminum round picnic cooler, circa 1940s to 1950s, made by Faris, 17-1/2" t.......$60

Dr. Pepper tray, tin with cat scene, 2-1/2" dia.. **$168**

Sunspot soda oval celluloid sign, circa 1950s, 12" l. ............................................................ **$110**

Dr. Pepper sign, embossed tin, circa 1960s, 54" x 18" ............................ **$330**

Dr. Pepper whistle, metal and wood with paper label on exterior, circa 1930s, 2-1/4" t............ **$72**

Grapette soda embossed tin sign, circa 1950s, wood graining on face, 16" x 27"............................ **$100**

Mit-Che Soda metal sign, 15-1/2" x 23-1/2".... **$100**

Barq's Rootbeer thermometer, tin, circa 1950s, 25-3/4" x 10"........... **$330**

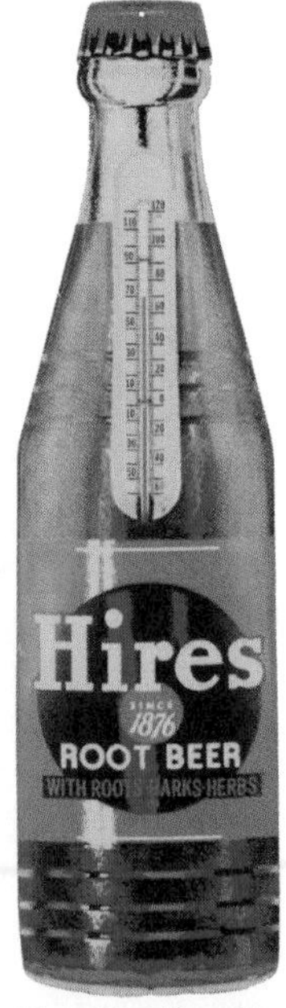


Hires Root Beer thermometer, tin, die-cut bottle form, 20-1/2" t. .................... **$400**

Royal Crown Cola bottle carrier, original embossed aluminum with six Royal Crown Cola bottles, 10-1/4" x 8" ...................... **$218**

Green Spot soda tin over cardboard easel sign, 14" x 11"... **$60**

Cool Air Orange Crush dispenser, metal bottom and plastic top, 21" t. ..................................... **$330**

Orange-Julep embossed tin sign, circa 1920-1930, 27-3/4" x 9-3/4" ............................................................................... **$228**

7UP dial thermometer, circa 1950s, plastic, metal, and glass, 13-3/4" dia........................ **$500**

Sprite Indianapolis 500-style model car, original box by Testors, circa 1950s-1960s, 12-1/2" l. ........................................................ **$85**

Cherry Smash syrup dispenser with original pump, 15-1/2" t. ..................................... **$4,200**

◄R.C. Cola and Perry's embossed tin signs, largest 11" x 27-1/2" ......................................... **$132**

# Make Mine Moxie

A Moxie museum in Union, Maine, houses a 30-foot-tall wooden Moxie bottle once used as a soda stand and other historical Moxie artifacts. This is an annex to the Matthews Museum of Maine Heritage, which is located at the Union Fairgrounds.

Every summer, "all things Moxie" are celebrated at the Moxie Festival in Lisbon Falls, Maine. (www.moxiefestival.com)

Moxie Fans: President Calvin Coolidge favored Moxie, and Boston Red Sox slugger Ted Williams endorsed it on radio and signs.

Moxie originated as a patent medicine called "Moxie Nerve Food," which was created around 1876 by Dr. Augustin Thompson of Union, Maine.

As of May 10, 2005, Moxie is the official soft drink of Maine.

The neologism "moxie" has entered popular American usage with the meaning "courage, daring, and energy," as in, "This guy's got moxie!" The new word was due to extensive advertising.

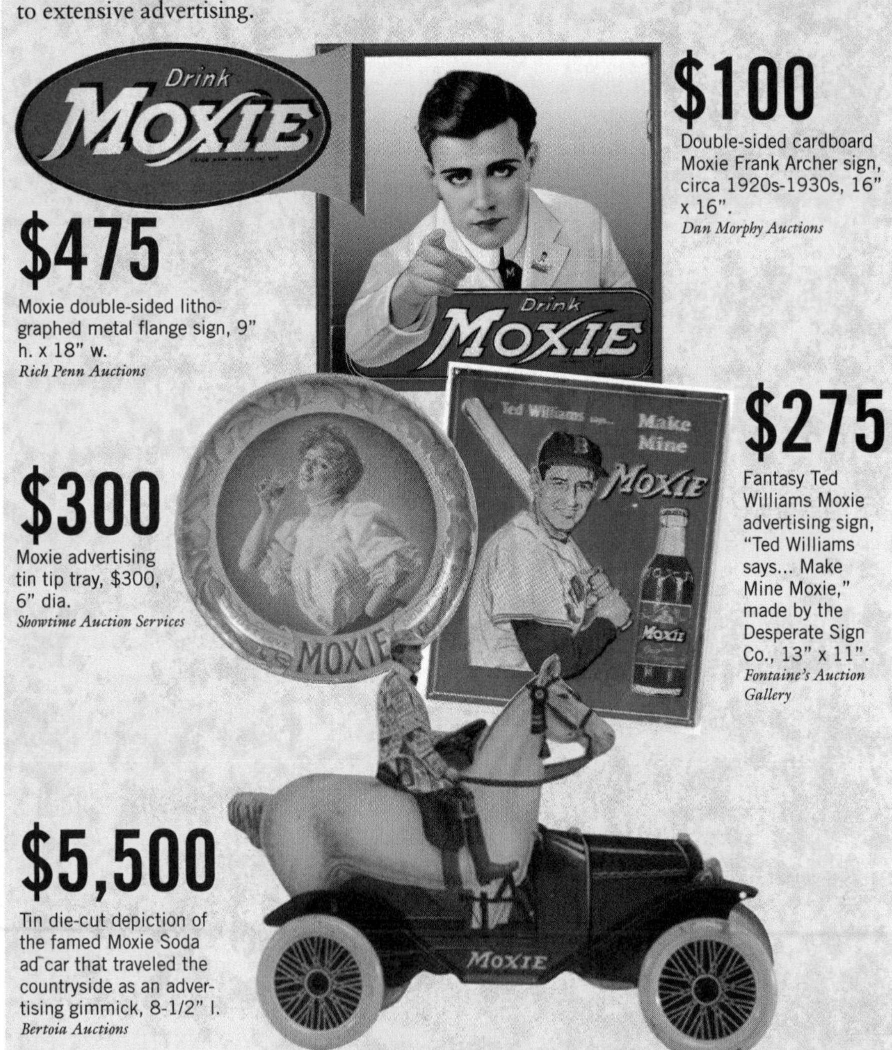


**$100**

Double-sided cardboard Moxie Frank Archer sign, circa 1920s-1930s, 16" x 16".
*Dan Morphy Auctions*

**$475**

Moxie double-sided lithographed metal flange sign, 9" h. x 18" w.
*Rich Penn Auctions*

**$275**

Fantasy Ted Williams Moxie advertising sign, "Ted Williams says... Make Mine Moxie," made by the Desperate Sign Co., 13" x 11".
*Fontaine's Auction Gallery*

**$300**

Moxie advertising tin tip tray, $300, 6" dia.
*Showtime Auction Services*

**$5,500**

Tin die-cut depiction of the famed Moxie Soda ad car that traveled the countryside as an advertising gimmick, 8-1/2" l.
*Bertoia Auctions*

# Coins & Paper Money

The worst U.S. economic crises since the Great Depression has made for uncertainty in every sector of the nation's economy, including the market for collectible coins. For the most part, however, numismatic collectibles held their own against these challenges, particularly scarce and rare issues among traditional material. Precious-metals prices form the base values for any coins containing one of the metals, such as gold and silver.

Coin and paper money prices can be as volatile as the stock market. Although some coins and notes remain stable for years, others skyrocket during a period of popularity and then plummet when they fall out of fashion. The listings presented here are guides to retail values — the approximate prices collectors can expect to pay when purchasing coins from a dealer. Because the law of supply and demand ultimately rules, the final decision about a coin's value lies with the buyer and seller.

In most cases, the grades listed represent the conditions and corresponding values collectors will most likely encounter for a particular series in the market.

Coins and paper money are not shown to scale in this chapter. Most coins have been enlarged to show more detail, all paper money has been reduced to fit the pages. Thus, do not rely on the size of the photos for identification. Instead, focus on the information stamped or printed on the coins or bills, and the captions and listings accompanying them.

### Paper Money

The U.S. government did not issue paper money until the Civil War. During the Revolutionary War, the states and Continental Congress printed so much paper money to finance their expenses that its value evaporated and it became nearly worthless. As a result, when the Constitution was adopted, it specified, "No state shall ... make anything but gold and silver coin a tender in payment of debts."

When the federal government finally did issue paper money, its use was limited. The first federal paper money, demand notes, even bore interest. Most federal paper money over the following century was redeemable in gold or silver.

Almost all U.S. paper currency bears a date, but this is not necessarily the year it was actually printed. It is the year of the act authorizing the series or the year the series went into production. The signature combinations on bank notes can often be used to date them. Originally paper money was larger than current issues. Until 1928, notes were about 7-1/2" x 3-1/8". Beginning with Series 1928 (released in 1929), U.S. paper money changed to 6-1/8" x 2-5/8". The fractional notes of the Civil War were smaller than current notes but varied in size.

## U.S. Coins

1792 Silver Center Cent, Liberty faces right with hair flowing behind, obverse periphery reads LIBERTY PARENT OF SCIENCE & INDUSTRY with 1792 just below the bust. Reverse has a wreath tied with a ribbon at the bottom; ONE CENT is within. Around the rim is UNITED STATES OF AMERICA with the fraction 1/100 below. Struck in copper with a silver plug in the center, coin is noted as the first coin struck inside the Philadelphia Mint. ............ **$1,150,000**

1825 Half Cent with Classic Head ............ **$55-$110**

1828 Large Cent with Coronet .............. **$35-$90**

1840 Large Cent with Braided Hair ................ **$30-$35**

1882 Bronze Indian Head Cent .................. **$5-$20**

1902 Bronze Indian Head Cent ...............**$2.50-$10**

1922 Plain (No D) Lincoln Cent with Wheat Ears Reverse ...... **$1,700-$11,000**

1863 Silver Three-Cent Piece with Double Border Around Star......... **$400-$480**

1865 Nickel Three-Cent Piece ................... **$18-$35**

1896 Liberty Nickel ......**$40-$100**

1913D Buffalo Nickel ......**$20-$65**

1939 Jefferson Nickel .....**25¢-$1**

2005D Jefferson Nickel with Bison Reverse .......... **$1**

1863 Seated Liberty Half Dime with Legend on Obverse ....... **$250-$400**

1877 Seated Liberty Dime with Legend on Obverse .................. **$20-$25**

1898S Barber Dime ....... **$35-$80**

1916D Mercury Dime ..... **$3,850-$13,200**

1964 Roosevelt Dime .......... **$2-$2.25**

1873 Seated Liberty Quarter, Open 3, with Motto Above Eagle ............ **$45-$120**

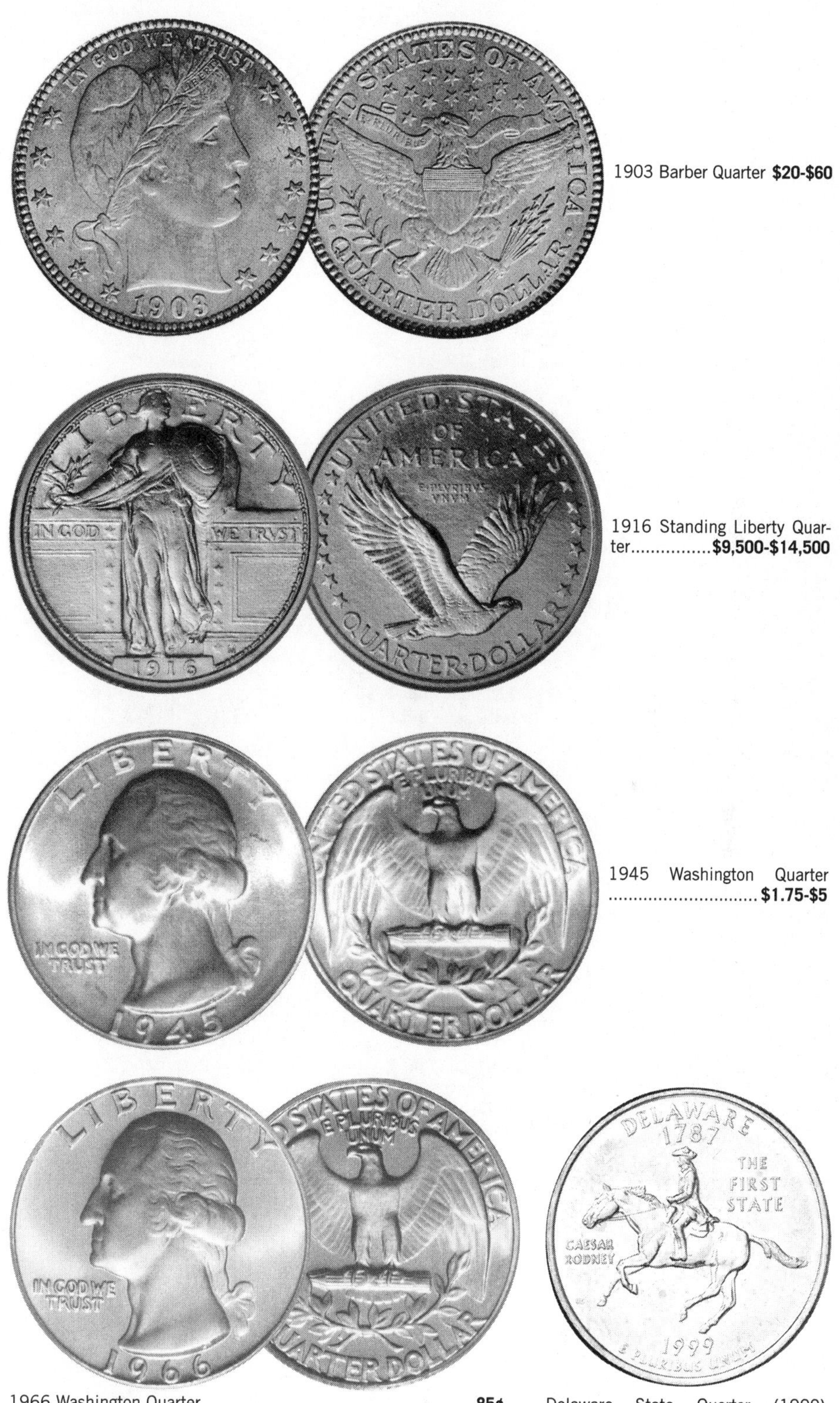


1903 Barber Quarter **$20-$60**

1916 Standing Liberty Quarter................**$9,500-$14,500**

1945 Washington Quarter ..............................**$1.75-$5**

1966 Washington Quarter.................................................. **85¢**

Delaware State Quarter (1999) ......................................**$1.25-$1.50**

1858S Seated Liberty Half Dollar with Arrows Removed From Date ......................**$50-$110**

1921D Walking Liberty Half Dollar .................**$550-$2,200**

1976D Kennedy Half Dollar with Bicentennial Reverse ....................**$1**

1871 Seated Liberty Dollar with Motto Above Eagle...........**$330-$500**

1892S Morgan Dollar ............... **$135-$34,500**

1974D Eisenhower Dollar............................ **$7**

2002P Sacagawea Dollar............................ **$2**

George Washington Presidential Dollar .... **$2**

1911D Gold $2.50 with Indian Head ............. **$2,500-$5,000**

1850 Gold $20 with Liberty Head ..............**$1,235-$1,325**

1903 Gold $20 with Liberty Head **$960-$975**

1992S Half-Dollar Commemorative Olympics ........................... **$8.50**

# U.S. Paper Money

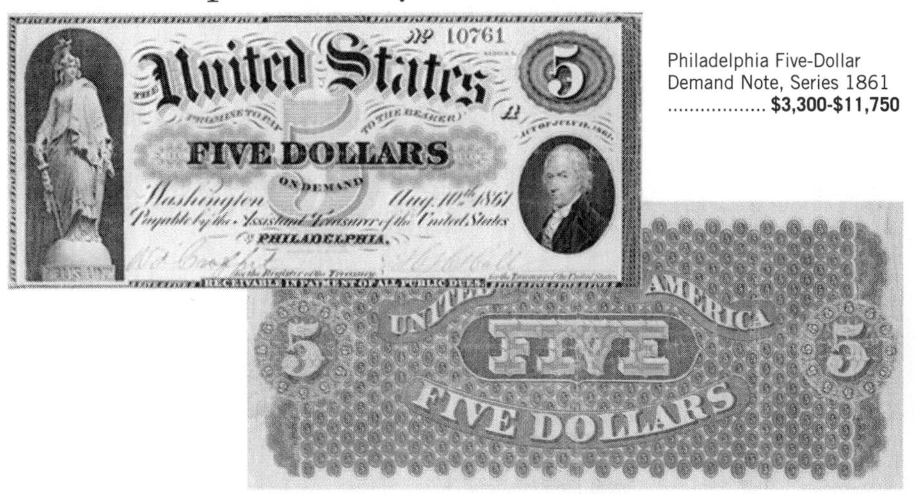

Philadelphia Five-Dollar Demand Note, Series 1861 .................. **$3,300-$11,750**

$50 National Bank Note, Third Charter **$5,500-$6,000**

$10 Large-Size United States Note, Series 1901 ........................ **$900-$2,900**

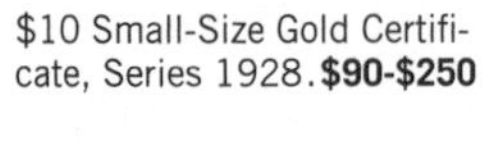

$10 Small-Size Gold Certificate, Series 1928. **$90-$250**

$2 Large-Size Silver Certificate, Series 1896 **$850-$3,000**

$10 Small-Size Silver Certificate, Special Yellow Seal, Series 1934A.......**$60-$300**

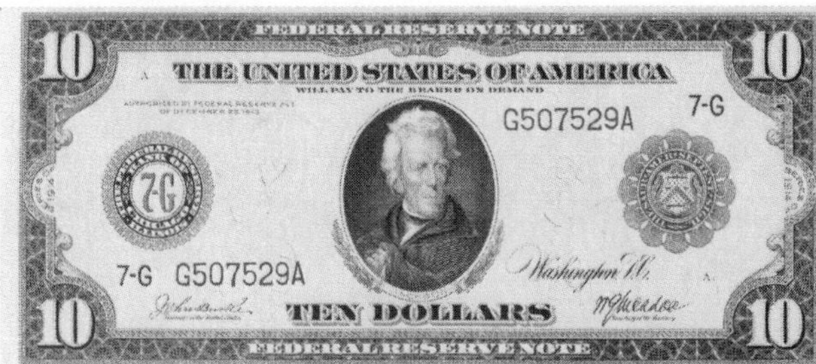

$10 Large-Size Federal Reserve Note, Red Seal, Series 1914 .............. **$750-$1,500**

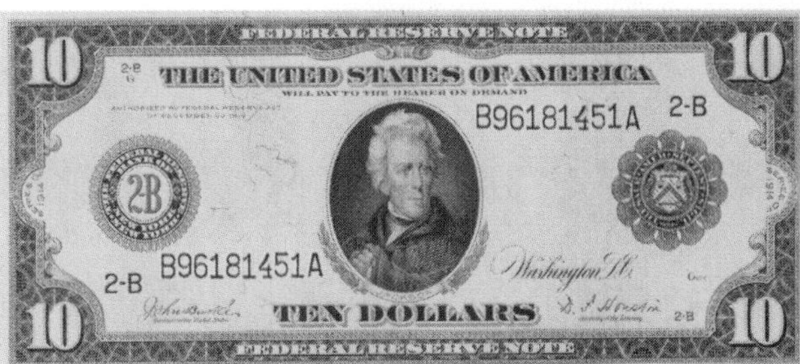

$10 Large-Size Federal Reserve Note, Blue Seal, Series 1914 ....... **$100-$225**

$5 Small-Size Federal Reserve Note, Green Seal, Series 1928A ....... **$50-$100**

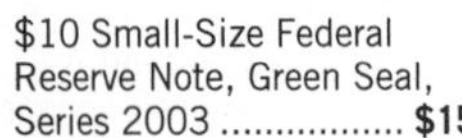

$10 Small-Size Federal Reserve Note, Green Seal, Series 2003 ................. **$15**

$50 Small-Size Federal Reserve Note, Green Seal, Series 1969A ........................**$150**

$1 Large-Size Federal Reserve Bank Note, Series 1918 .................**$125-$250**

# Comics

Superman's first appearance has started a new club all its own, closing at $2.16 million Nov. 30, 2011. *Action Comics* #1 (Jun 38), CGC-graded 9.0, and previously part of actor Nicolas Cage's collection, set a new record for online auction firm ComicConnect.com.

This particular copy of the comic book that started comics' Golden Age had been stolen several years ago but was recovered earlier in 2011 from a storage locker and later graded and consigned to ComicConnect.com.

While *Action* #1 now appears to have the top spot again with more than a half-million dollars of value separating it from its closest competitor, there's another copy of the book, CGC-graded 8.5, that ComicConnect.com sold in 2010 for $1.5 million.

It's the fourth comic book sold by ComicConnect.com in the $1 million+ range. In addition to the 8.5 copy, the firm first set a record in 2010 with the $1 million sale of a CGC 8.0 copy of *Action* #1. A year later, ComicConnect sold the first Silver Age comic book to exceed $1 million — a CGC-graded 9.6 copy of *Amazing Fantasy* #15 (Aug 62) — for $1.1 million March 7, 2011.

In February 2012, *Heritage Comic Auctions*' Signature Sale included the sale of more than 300 Golden Age comics for more than $3.5 million. Purchased between 1938 and 1941, The Billy Wright Collection had been consigned to Heritage by Wright's great-nephew, Michael Rorrer, who acquired them after the death of his great-aunt. Billy Wright kept the comics for more than 60 years before his death in 1994.

"This is just one of those collections that all the guys in the business think don't exist any more," Heritage Managing Director of Comics Lon Allen said.

So, does that mean all old comics are worth big bucks? Not necessarily. We're hearing reports of folks attempting to cash in a box of comics from the late 1980s or early 1990s, telling dealers that "they're old." While more than 20 years does seem old to the average person, unfortunately, comics of that vintage aren't in high demand and the supply of high-quality back issues is still there. Most dealers won't even look at a box of that vintage or will offer very little, if anything, for it.

Another market that has gone softer in the past few years is comics of the 1950s, especially Westerns. At one point, almost any comic book with a photo cover depicting a movie or TV star could sell to not only comics collectors but collectors of that star's memorabilia. With that group aging itself out of the market or finishing its sets, demand has dropped precipitously.

Comics dealer Steve Mortensen of Miracle Comics (*www.miraclecomics.com*) offered this advice: "Perhaps the greatest collecting skill a person can have is knowing when to buy and when to sell. It's important to be as knowledgeable as you can be on the subject you're collecting. There's lots of money to be had in the details — such as knowing which variants are worth money, the quantities in print runs, and how to grade comics. Selling is harder in some ways for us hoarders. I have my stock of inventory that I've already mentally parted with kept separate from my personal collection. From a business point of view, it is better to keep the two apart, of course — for tax reasons but also for keeping a sense of order."

## Values

Comics have been avidly collected for years. Prices for scarce, early issues of a particular series are often higher than for later issues. However, key events (the first appearance of a character, a creator's first work, or other factors) can also affect value. Prices listed below show a range for copies from "Good" to "Near Mint" condition. "Near Mint" means a nearly perfect copy, whereas "Good" is applied to a copy that's complete but is worn, with visible defects. Note the wide difference between the prices because of condition.

***Brent Frankenhoff, Editor, Comics Buyer's Guide***

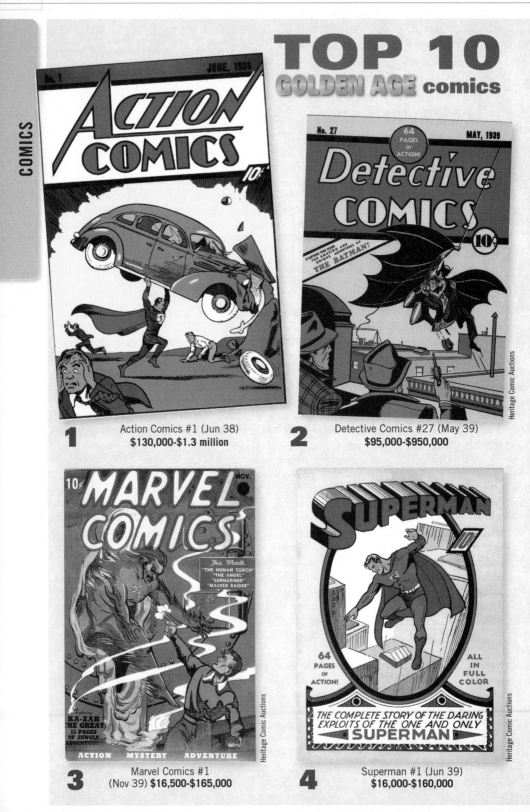

# TOP 10 GOLDEN AGE comics

**1** Action Comics #1 (Jun 38)
**$130,000-$1.3 million**

Heritage Comic Auctions

**2** Detective Comics #27 (May 39)
**$95,000-$950,000**

Heritage Comic Auctions

**3** Marvel Comics #1
(Nov 39) **$16,500-$165,000**

Heritage Comic Auctions

**4** Superman #1 (Jun 39)
**$16,000-$160,000**

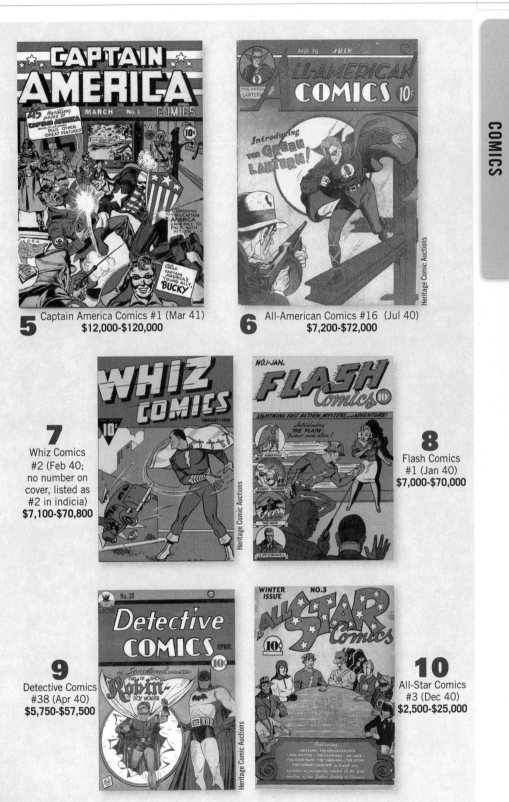

COMICS

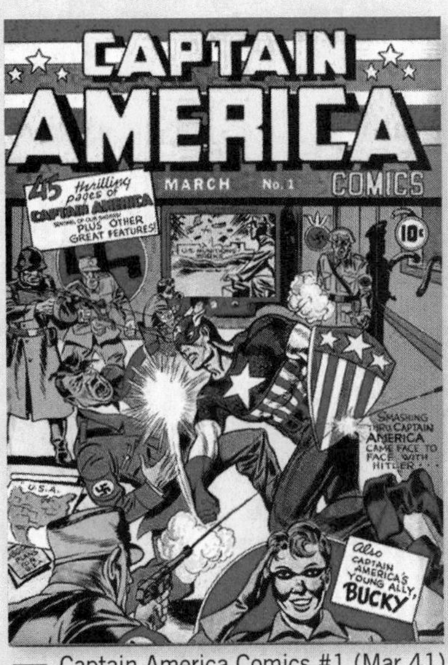


**5** Captain America Comics #1 (Mar 41)
**$12,000-$120,000**

Heritage Comic Auctions

**6** All-American Comics #16 (Jul 40)
**$7,200-$72,000**

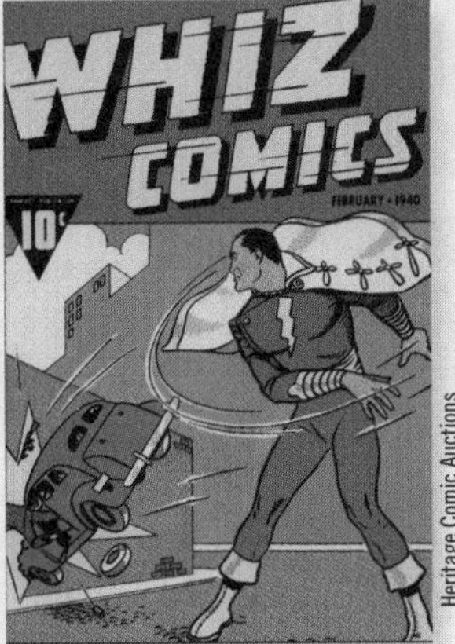


Heritage Comic Auctions

**7**
Whiz Comics #2 (Feb 40; no number on cover, listed as #2 in indicia)
**$7,100-$70,800**

**8**
Flash Comics #1 (Jan 40)
**$7,000-$70,000**

Heritage Comic Auctions

**9**
Detective Comics #38 (Apr 40)
**$5,750-$57,500**

**10**
All-Star Comics #3 (Dec 40)
**$2,500-$25,000**

# TOP 10 SILVER AGE comics

**1** Amazing Fantasy #15 (Aug 62)
**$3,200-$32,000**

**2** Showcase #4 (Oct 56)
**$2,800-$27,500**

Heritage Comic Auctions

**3** Amazing Spider-Man #1 (Mar 63)
**$2,700-$27,100**

**4** Fantastic Four #1 (Nov 61)
**$1,600-$15,600**

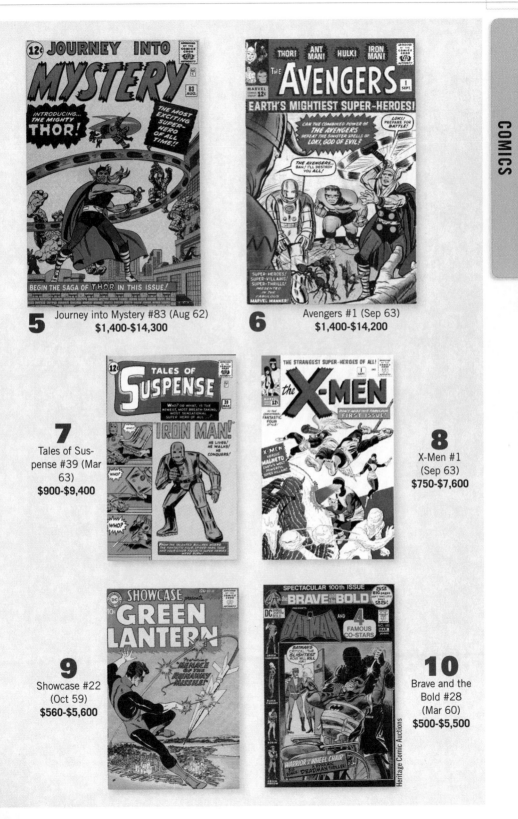

**5** Journey into Mystery #83 (Aug 62)
**$1,400-$14,300**

**6** Avengers #1 (Sep 63)
**$1,400-$14,200**

**7**
Tales of Suspense #39 (Mar 63)
**$900-$9,400**

**8**
X-Men #1
(Sep 63)
**$750-$7,600**

**9**
Showcase #22
(Oct 59)
**$560-$5,600**

**10**
Brave and the Bold #28
(Mar 60)
**$500-$5,500**

Heritage Comic Auctions

# TOP 10 BRONZE AGE comics

1 Incredible Hulk #181 (Nov 74)
**$275-$2,2825**

Heritage Comic Auctions

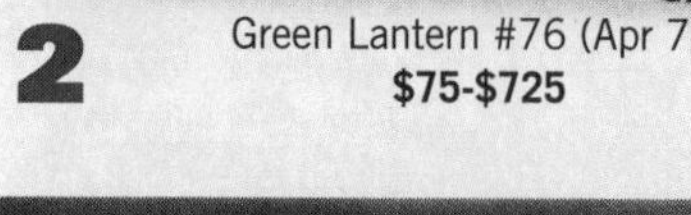

2 Green Lantern #76 (Apr 70)
**$75-$725**

Heritage Comic Auctions

3 X-Men #94 (Aug 75)
**$75-$725**

Heritage Comic Auctions

4 Cerebus #1 (Dec 77)
**$70-$700**

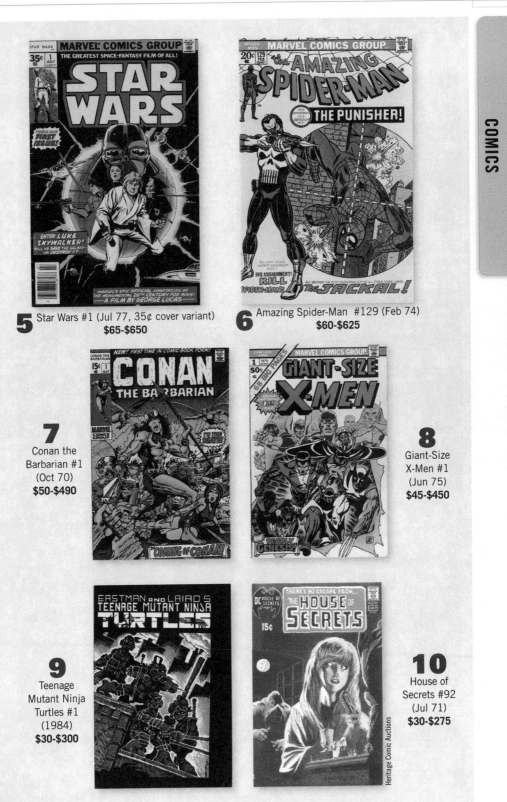

**5** Star Wars #1 (Jul 77, 35¢ cover variant)
**$65-$650**

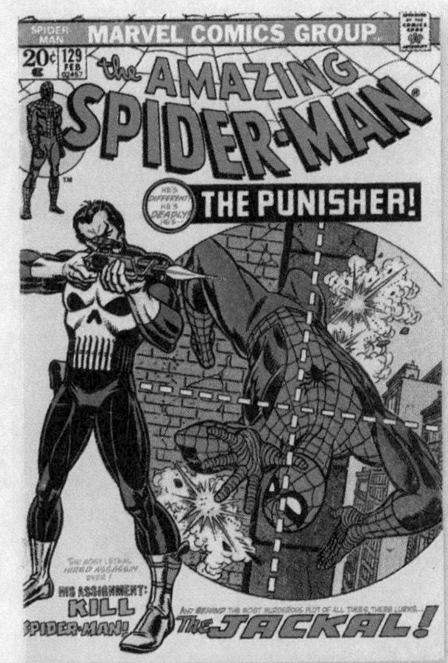


**6** Amazing Spider-Man #129 (Feb 74)
**$60-$625**

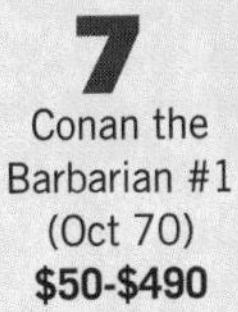

**7**
Conan the Barbarian #1 (Oct 70)
**$50-$490**

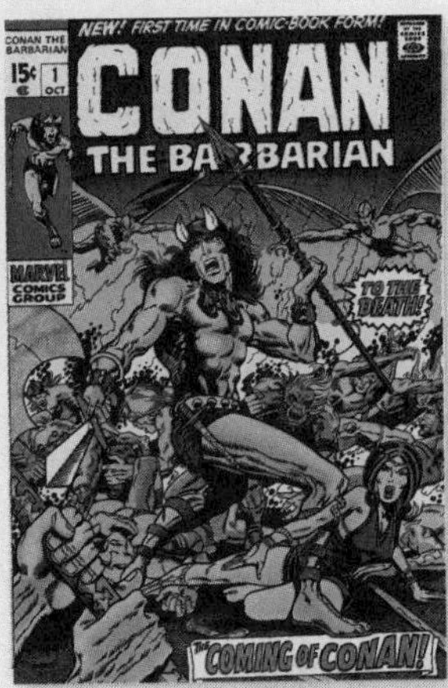


**8**
Giant-Size X-Men #1 (Jun 75)
**$45-$450**

**9**
Teenage Mutant Ninja Turtles #1 (1984)
**$30-$300**

Heritage Comic Auctions

**10**
House of Secrets #92 (Jul 71)
**$30-$275**

Abbott and Costello Comics #15 (Dec 52) ........................ **$8-$80**

Action Comics #500 (Oct 79) .................................**75¢-$7.50**

Adventures of Baron Munchausen #1 (Jul 89) ..................... **25¢-$2**

Adventures of Rex the Wonder Dog #28 (Aug 56).................. **$7-$70**

Albedo #4 (Jul 85) ......**$1.50-$15**

All Star Batman & Robin the Boy Wonder #7 (Nov 07) ....**25¢-$2.50**

Amazing Spider-Man #500 (Dec 03................................ **50¢-$4**

Angel: After the Fall #3 (Jan 08) ................................**35¢-$3.50**

Animal Antics #17 (Dec 48) ....................................... **$8-$80**

Animaniacs #1 (May 95) **25¢-$2.50**

Archie #601 (Nov 09)...... **50¢-$5**

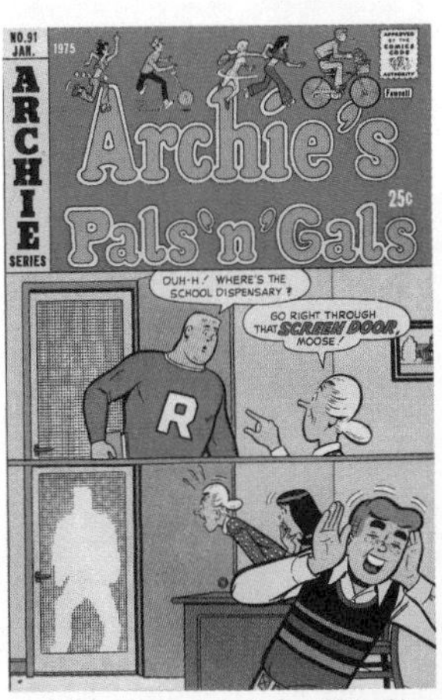

Archie's Pals 'n' Gals #91 (Jan 75) ............................ **$1-$9.50**

Avengers #100 (Jun 72). **$10-$95**

Babe, Darling of the Hills #10 (Mar 49)........................ **$5-$50**

Baseball Thrills #3 (Sum 52) .................................**$30-$300**

Batman #134 (Sep 60) . **$20-$185**

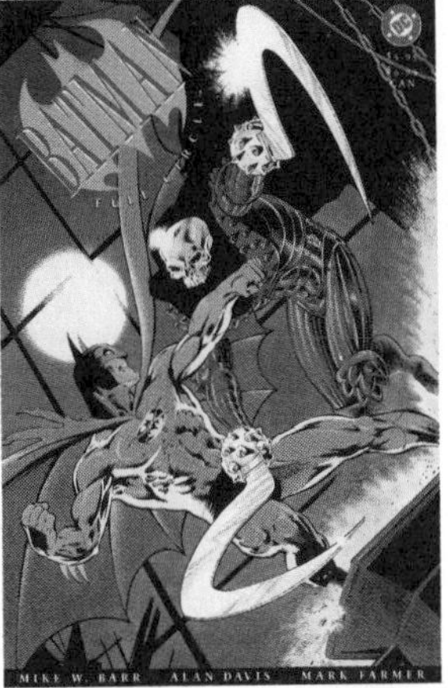

Batman: Full Circle (1991) .................................**30¢-$3.25**

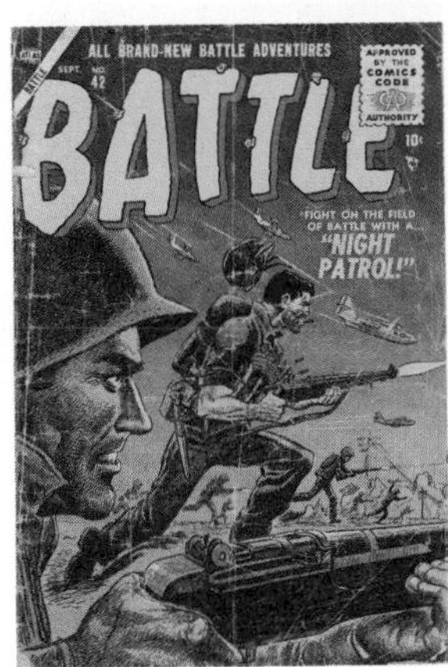

Battle #42 (Sep 55) ........ **$3-$32**

Blitzkrieg #1 (Feb 76)...... **$3-$32**

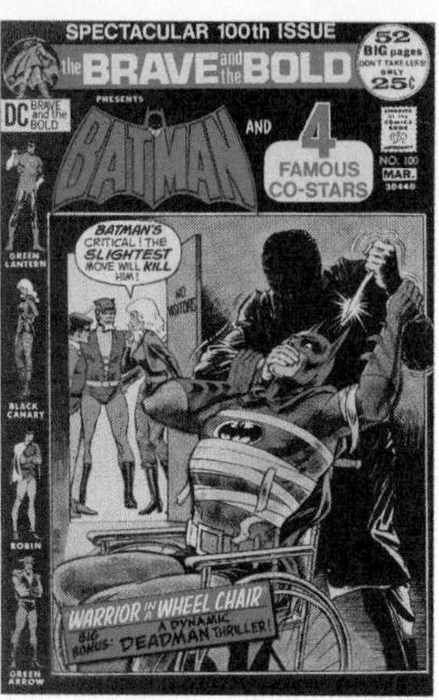


Brave and the Bold #100 (Mar 72) ..........................**$2.75 -$27**

Buckaroo Banzai #2 (Feb 85) ..................................... **25¢-$2**

Bugs Bunny #38 (Sep 54) **$4-$40**

Captain Marvel Adventures #72 (May 47)......................**$15-$125**

Captain America #100 (Apr 68)...........................................**$35-$350**
*Heritage Comic Auctions*

Cartoon Kids #1 (1957)... **$3-$28**

CyberForce #3/Gold cover (Mar 94) ................................ **25¢-$3**

Daredevil #154 (Sep 78).... **$1-$8**

Date with Judy #54 (Sep 56) ..................................**$1.50-$15**

DC Special #21 (May 76) ..................................**$1.25-$12**

Deadpool #1 (Nov 08) **35¢-$3.75**

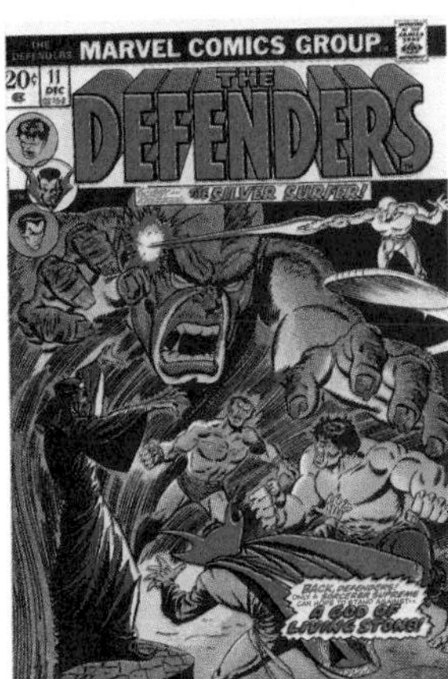

Defenders #11 (Dec 73) .. **$3-$28**

Dennis the Menace (Giants) #8 (Win 60)......................... **$5-$50**

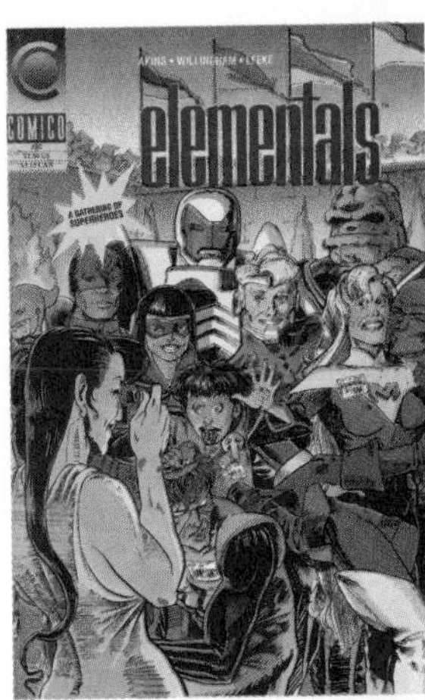

Elementals (Vol. 2) #20 (Oct 91) ..................................**25¢-$1.25**

COMICS

Detective Comics #230 (Apr 56) ...**$160-$1,625**

Fantastic Four #26 (May 64) ....................................**$60-$600**

Felix the Cat #16 (Sep 50)**$6-$60**

Fighting American #1 (Oct 66) ....................................**$4.25-$42**

Four Color #1073 (Grandma Duck's Farm Friends, Mar 60) .............................. **$12.50-$125**

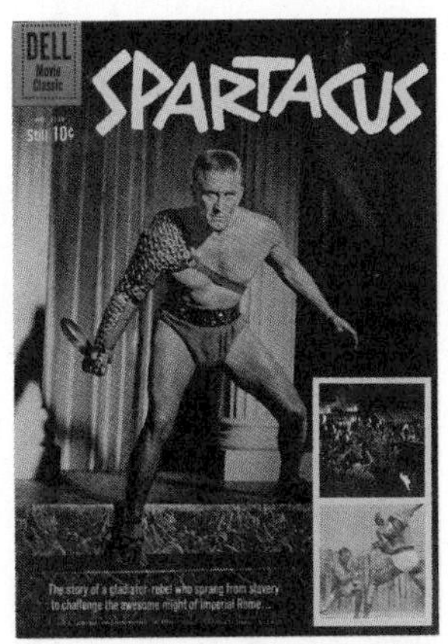


Four Color #1139 (Spartacus, Nov 60) ........................ **$16.50-$165**

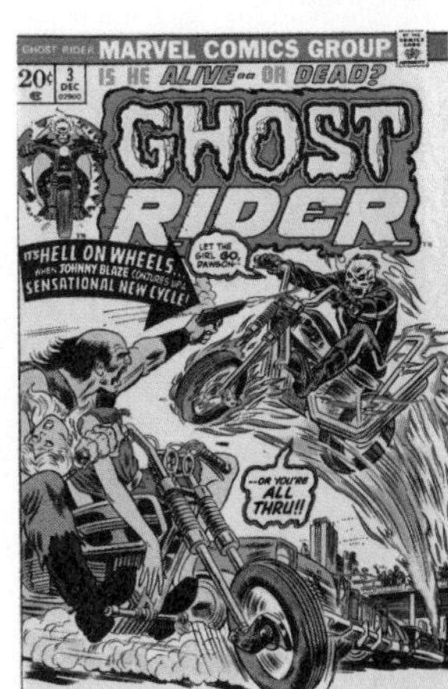


Ghost Rider #3 (Dec 73) **$2.50-$26**

G.I. Combat #250 (Feb 83) .................................... **60¢-$6**

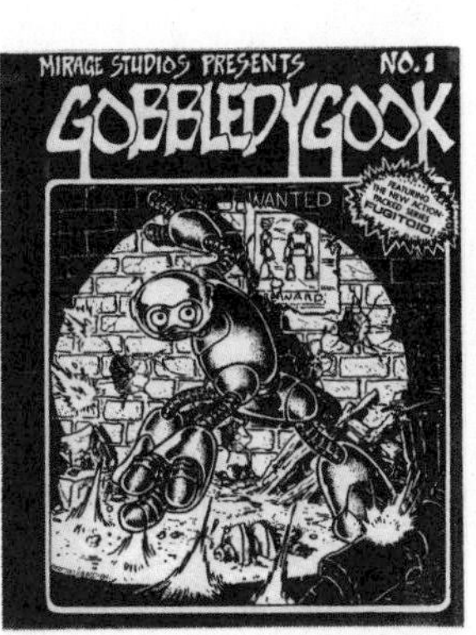


Gobbledygook #1 (1984) **$10-$110**

Ha Ha Comics #90 (Jul 53) ..................................**$1.50-$16**

Hot Stuff #93 (Oct 69) .... **75¢-$8**

Incredible Hulk #324 (Oct 86) .................................... **50¢-$5**

John Carter Warlord of Mars #15 (Aug 78)......................... **40¢-$4**

Jingle Jangle Comics #19 (Feb 46) ................................ **$5-$50**

Jughead as Captain Hero #3 (Feb 67) ................................ **$1-$10**

Kull the Conqueror #1 (Jun 71) ....................................... **$4-$38**

Little Lulu #154 (Apr 61) ................................ **$2.50-$25**

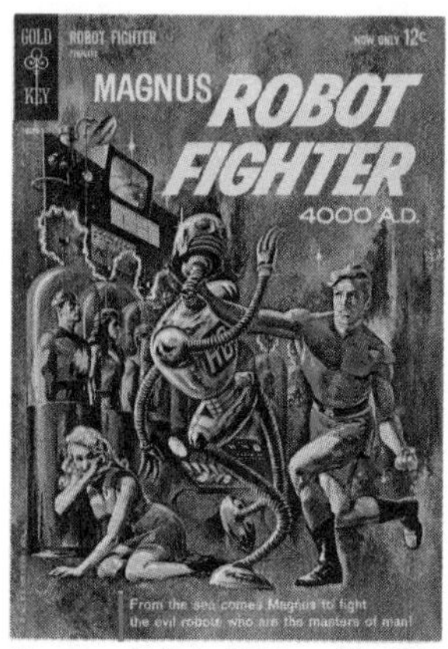

Magnus Robot Fighter #1 (Feb 63) ............................**$35-$330**

Marvel Super Heroes Secret Wars #8 (Dec 84)................**$1.50-$16**

Miracleman #4 (Dec 85) **75¢-$8**

New Funnies #169 (Mar 51) ...................................**$2.50-$26**

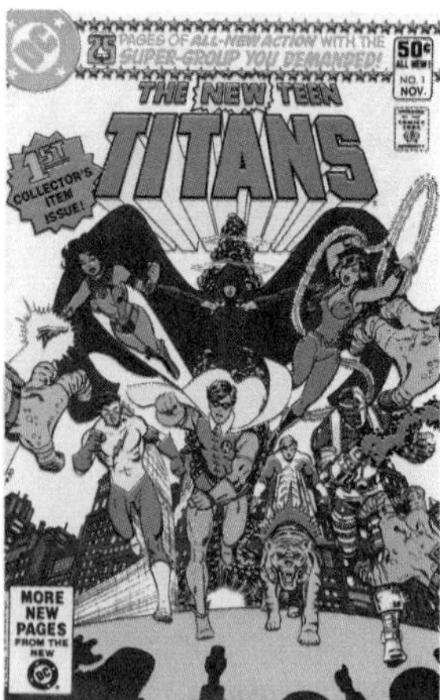

New Teen Titans #1 (Nov 80) ........................................ **$1-$9**

Our Army at War #160 (Nov 65) ....................................$1.50-$14

Power Pack #1 (Aug 84) ....................................25¢-$1.75

Primer #3 (1982)............ $4-$40

Rangers Comics #49 (Oct 49) ....................................$12-$120

Scribbly #9 (Feb 50) ....$30-$310

Shazam! #1 (Feb 73)....... $3-$35
*Heritage Comic Auctions*

Spider-Man #1 (Aug 90) .. 50¢-$5

Treasure Chest of Fun and Fact Vol. 16 #2 (Sep 60)......... $2-$20

Uncanny X-Men #180 (Apr 84) ...........................................50¢-$5

COMICS

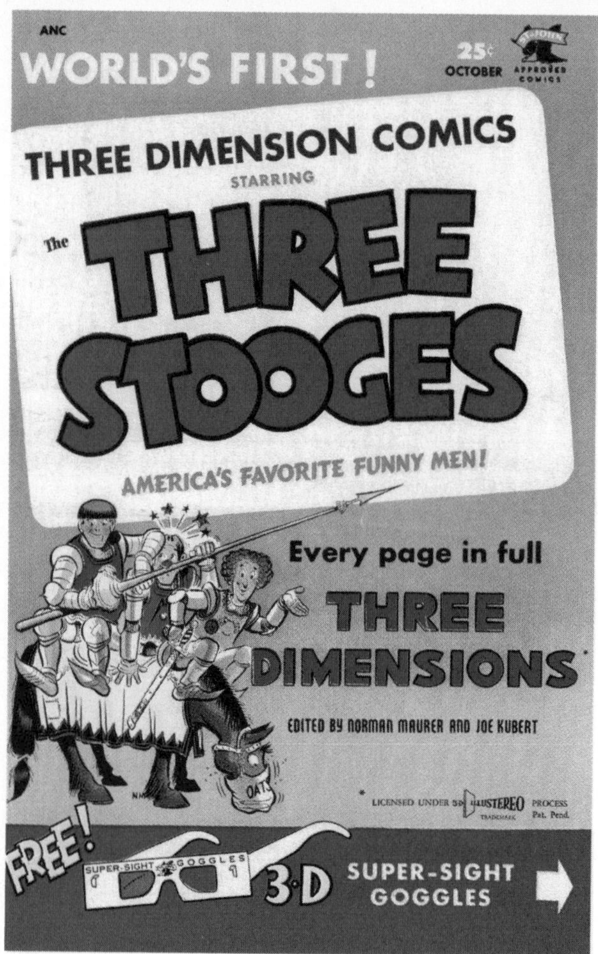

Three Stooges #2 (Oct 53) ..................................................**$30-$300**
*Heritage Comic Auctions*

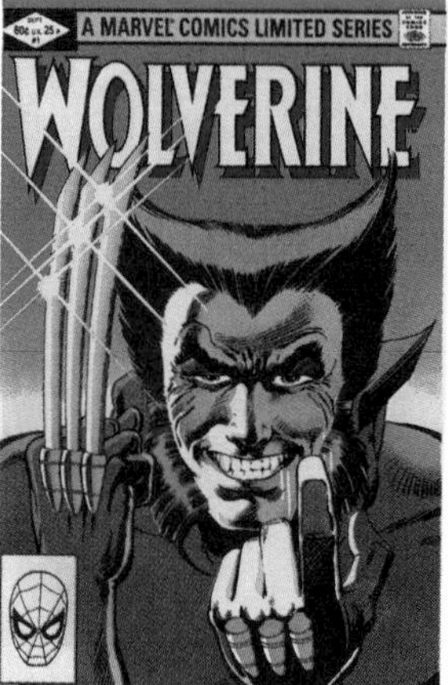

Walking Dead #1 (Oct 03) **$4-$40**



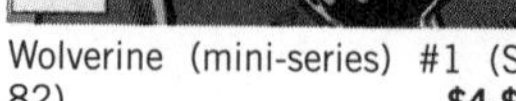

Wolverine (mini-series) #1 (Sep 82) ................................ **$4-$45**

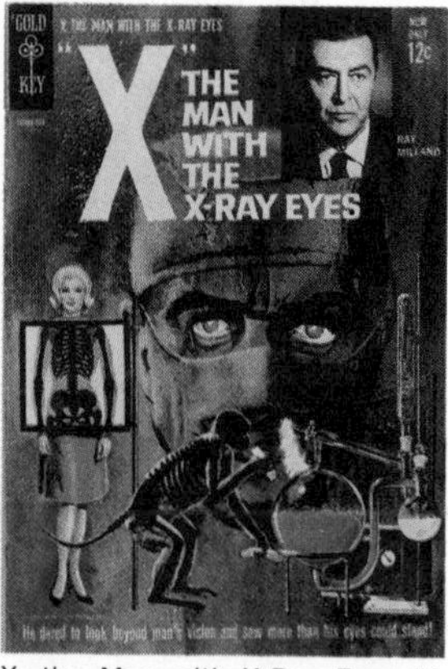


X, the Man with X-Ray Eyes #1 (Jun 63) .......................... **$8-$80**

Yosemite Sam #45 (Jul 77) .................................**$1.50-$15**

Zot! #1 (Apr 84)..........**35¢-$3.75**

# Cookie Jars

Cookie jars evolved from the elegant British biscuit jars found on Victorian-era tables. These 19th century containers featured bail handles, and were often made of sterling silver and cut crystal.

As the biscuit jar was adapted for use in America, it migrated from the dining table to the kitchen and, by the late 1920s, it was common to find a green-glass jar (or pink or clear), often with an applied label and a screw-top lid, on kitchen counters in the typical American home.

During the Great Depression—when stoneware was still popular, but before the arrival of widespread electric refrigeration—cookie jars in round and barrel shapes arrived. These heavy-bodied jars could be hand-painted after firing. This decoration was easily worn away by eager hands reaching for Mom's bakery. The lids of many stoneware jars typically had small tapering finials or knobs that also contributed to cracks and chips.

The golden age of cookie jars began in the 1940s and lasted for less than three decades, but the examples that survive represent an exuberance and style that have captivated collectors.

It wasn't until the 1970s that many collectors decided—instead of hiding their money in cookie jars—to invest their money in cookie jars. It was also at this time that cookie jars ceased to be simply storage vessels for bakery and evolved into a contemporary art form. And it's because of this evolution from utility to art that—with some exceptions—we have limited the scope of this section to jars made from the 1930s to the early 1970s.

The Brush Pottery Co. of Zanesville, Ohio, produced one of the first ceramic cookie jars in about 1929, and Red Wing's spongeware line from the late 1920s also included a ridged, barrel-shaped jar. Many established potteries began adding a selection of cookie jars in the 1930s.

The 1940s saw the arrival of two of the most famous cookie jars: Shawnee's Smiley and Winnie, two portly, bashful little pigs who stand with eyes closed and heads cocked, he in overalls and bandana, she in flowered hat and long coat. And a host of Disney characters also made their way into American kitchens.

In the 1950s, the first television-influenced jars appeared, including images of Davy Crockett and Popeye. This decade also saw the end of several prominent American potteries (including Roseville) and the continued rise of imported ceramics.

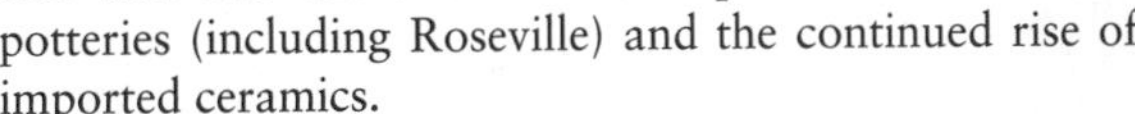

A new collection of cartoon-inspired jars was popular in the 1960s, featuring characters drawn from the Flintstones, Yogi Bear, Woody Woodpecker, and Casper the Friendly Ghost. Jars reflecting the race for space included examples from McCoy and American Bisque. This decade also marked the peak production era for a host of West Coast manufacturers, led by the twin brothers Don and Ross Winton.

For more information on cookie jars, see *Warman's Cookie Jars Identification and Price Guide* by Mark F. Moran.

Little Red Riding Hood by Metlox, 12-3/4" t., 1960s, with original silver foil label, "Made in California–Poppytrail Pottery by Metlox," also marked on bottom, "Made in Poppytrail Calif. USA."............**$1,800+**

Cooky attributed to Abingdon, 9-1/4" t., late 1950s, unmarked. ....................................... **$100+**

Little Bo Peep by Abingdon, 11-3/4" t., late 1940s, impressed mark on bottom, "694.".... **$300+**

Circus Dog, Italian, with bank in base, 11-1/2" t., late 1950s, impressed mark, "Italy." Found in other colors.................. **$2,000+**

◀Locomotive by Abingdon, 11-1/2" l., 1950s, ink-stamped, "Abingdon USA," and impressed, "651." ............................ **$225+**

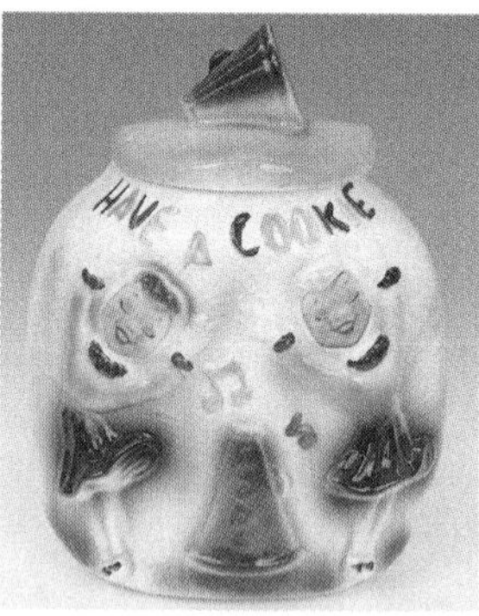


Cheerleaders with flasher faces by American Bisque, 11" t., 1950s, marked on reverse "Corner Cookie Jar 802 USA." ................. **$500+**

◀Baby Elephant by American Bisque, with heavy gold trim, 11-3/4" t., 1950s, unmarked. **$250+**

Blackboard Girl by American Bisque, stamped "DON'T FORGET!" on the front, hand-lettered under glaze "Try Mom's Cookies" on the back, 13-1/4" t., 1950s, large raised mark "U.S.A." and ink-stamped "Patent Pending U.S.A."............................ **$375+**

Cow Jumped Over the Moon with flasher face by American Bisque, 11" t., 1940s, marked on the back "806 USA." (Found with other color combinations.) ........**$2,000+**

Kitten on Beehive by American Bisque, 11-1/4" t., 1950s, raised mark on reverse, "U.S.A." ...**$70+**

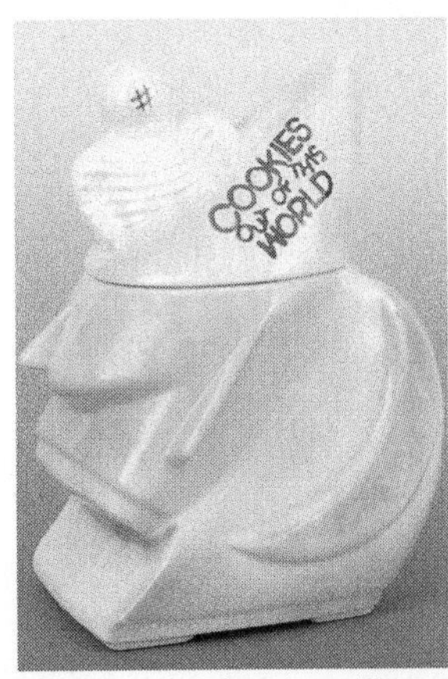


Spaceship by American Bisque, with stencil, "Cookies Out of This World," 10-3/8" t., late 1950s, raised mark on back, "U.S.A." ......................................**$700+**

Professor Ludwig Von Drake by American Bisque, 9" t., 1961, marked on top of mortar board "Ludwig V Drake" and on back, "Copyright (symbol) Walt Disney Productions USA 1961.".....**$1,500+**

Lady with Squeezebox by Brayton Laguna, late 1940s, inscribed inside lid and on bottom, "Marie" and "2," one of only two known...............................................**$2,000+**

◀Rudolph the Red-Nosed Reindeer by American Bisque, made for Sears, 9-1/4" t., 1940s (?), impressed mark on back, "RLM Copyright (symbol)." .........................**$550+**

Balloon Boy by Brush, one of the company's last production jars, 11" t., 1971, unmarked, also found with paper label, "W56." .................................... **$1,000+**

Cow with Cat Finial by Brush, 12-1/2" l., 1950s, raised mark, "Brush USA" in an artist's palette, and "W10." Prices vary widely depending on colors used, from about $200 for typical tan and yellow to near $2,000 for purple or blue combinations, or with gold trim. ............ **$200-$2,000**

Littl* Red "Ridding"-hood by Brush, 10-1/2" t., late 1950s, with misspelled words "Little" and "Riding." ...................... **$1,000+**

Hillbilly Frog by Brush, about 13" t., unmarked, 1968. ...... **$3,500+**

Lovebirds by California Cleminsons, 9-1/4" t., 1950s, ink-stamped on bottom, "The California Cleminsons–Hand Painted–Copyright (symbol)." ......... **$275+**

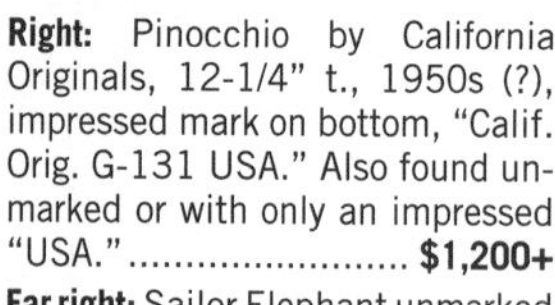

**Right:** Pinocchio by California Originals, 12-1/4" t., 1950s (?), impressed mark on bottom, "Calif. Orig. G-131 USA." Also found unmarked or with only an impressed "USA." ......................... **$1,200+**

**Far right:** Sailor Elephant unmarked but known to be Cardinal. The Cardinal catalog sheet from 1961 included a picture of several jars that had been thought to be American Bisque. This Sailor Elephant, who has "SS Cookie" in black letters on his hat, was one of them. ...................................... **$200+**

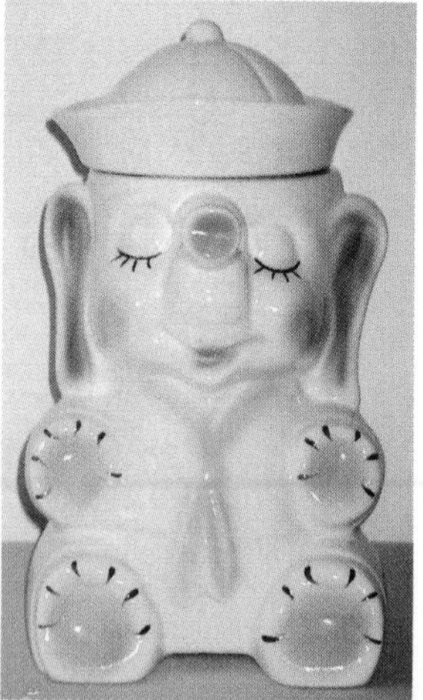

Li'l Angel by DeForest, 12-1/4" t., 1950s, with original label on shoulder and applied flower decal inside, impressed mark on bottom, "DeForest of California Copyright (symbol) 1957." ....... **$600+**

Gim-me by Helen Hutula, 10-1/2" t., 1940s, marked on bottom, "Helen's Gim-me Original–Helen Hutula Originals." .......... **$1,500+**

Jack-o'-Lantern by McCoy, also comes with orange lid, late 1950s, McCoy USA mark........ **$550-$650**

Strawberry Pie with Ice Cream by Doranne of California, 9-1/4" t., 1960s, impressed mark, "USA J55." ................................ **$150**

Little Red Riding Hood by Hull, with open basket, with transfer-decorated flowers, 13" t., 1940s, marked on the bottom, "967 Hull Ware Little Red Riding Hood—Patent Applied For USA." .. **$400+**

Gingerbread Boy by Gilner, 10-1/4" t., late 1950s, impressed mark, "Gilner." ................. **$150+**

Sheriff by Lane, 11-3/4" t., marked "Copyright 1950 Lane & Co. Los Angeles." (May also have hand-written artist initials on base.) .............................. **$400+**

Quaker Oats, 1970, unmarked, not many McCoy examples, jar was later made by another company. ......................... **$500-$600**

◀Donald Duck by Leeds China, airbrush decoration, 13" t., 1940s, unmarked. ............ **$500+**

Little Red Riding Hood by Metlox, 12-3/4" t., 1960s, with original silver foil label, "Made in California–Poppytrail Pottery by Metlox," also marked on bottom, "Made in Poppytrail Calif. USA."... **$1,800+**

Basketball: This is a McCoy jar that was not produced. There are at least three around, and two are decorated very differently.. **$4,000**

Donald Duck by Metlox, 11-3/4" t., late 1950s, unmarked, made for distribution to Disney executives, very rare.............. **$5,000+**

**Far right:** Black Chef by Pearl China, marked in gold on front, "Cooky," 10-1/4" t., 1940s, stamped on bottom, "Pearl (in a seashell) China Co. Hand decorated 22 Kt. Gold U.S.A." and impressed, "639." (A companion to the Chef was a Mammy jar, same marks, $900+.)................ **$600+**

Washtub Mammy attributed to Metlox, 11" t., late 1940s (?), unmarked........................ **$1,800+**

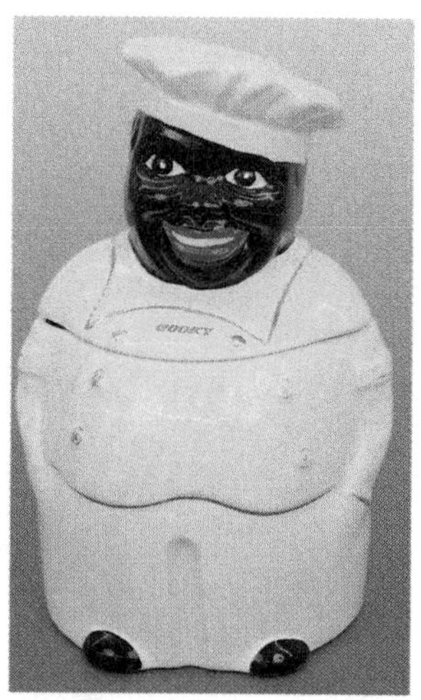

Carousel by Pfaltzgraff, lid 9-1/2" w., 1950s, unmarked..................................................... **$500+**

Derby Dan Muggsy by Pfaltzgraff, 8-1/2" t., 1950s, marked, "Derby Dan Muggsy–The Pfaltzgraff Pottery Co., York, Pa.–Designed by Jessop." .............. **$500+**

Howdy Doody by Purinton, 9-1/4" t., 1950s, unmarked......... **$700+**

Dancing Peasants "munch" jar by Red Wing, in the most common white with cold-paint decoration, 6-5/8" t., early 1940s, unmarked....... **$50+**

Drummer Boy by Red Wing, all original, 9" t., early 1960s, faint mark. ...................................... **$800+**

Dutch Girl by Regal China, 10-3/4" t., 1940s, unmarked. (Also found in predominant pale blue, yellow, and orange. $1,000+) .......................... **$800+**

Frightened Alice in Wonderland by Regal China, 13-1/4" t., late 1950s, marked "Walt Disney Productions Copyright (symbol) Alice in Wonderland." **$4,000+**

Peek-a-Boo by Regal China, 11-1/2" t., marked "Peek-A-Boo Copyright Van Telligen." .............. **$950**

Frosty the Snowman by Robinson Ransbottom, 14" t., 1960. **$325+**

Freesia green cookie jar by Roseville, 4"-8", several small chips on bottom ring, raised mark. ................................**$275-$300**

Jo Jo the Clown by Shawnee, 9-1/4" t., 1940s, raised mark, "Shawnee U.S.A." and an impressed "12." .................**$600+**
With gold tri ................ **$1,200+**

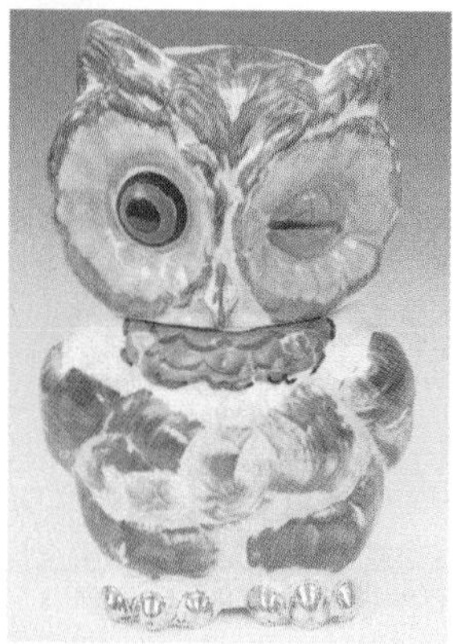
Owl by Shawnee, with gold trim, 11-1/2" t., late 1940s, impressed mark, "U.S.A." ................ **$500+**

Clock, 10-1/4" t., attributed to Starnes, factory hole in bottom, 1950s, unmarked............ **$175+**

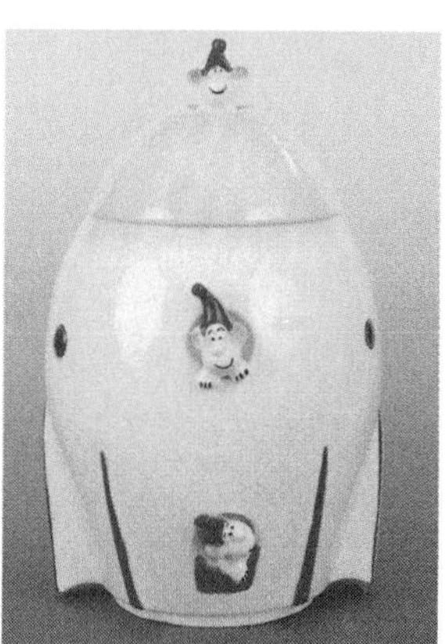
Spaceship with Martians by Sierra-Vista, 13" t., late 1950s, impressed mark, "Sierra-Vista Copyright (symbol) 57 Pasadena Cal. USA." ...................... **$400+**

Rooster by Twin Winton, in wood tone, 11-1/2" t., 1960s, marked on back, "Twin Winton Copyright (symbol) '60." ................. **$150+**

Cat (with tail finial) by Ungemach, 10-1/2" t., 1950s, impressed mark, "U.S.A." on the back. ..................................... **$225+**

Peter Peter Pumpkin Eater by Vallona-Starr, 8-1/4" t., marked "Vallona-Starr Design Patent Copyright 49 California."... **$300+**

# Country Store Collectibles

Those looking to add an extra layer of authenticity to their kitchen collecting often specialize in artifacts from actual "general" or "country" stores, a staple in any town of any size, from the mid-1800s well into the 1940s.

The country store was a natural expansion of the pioneer trading post, which provided early settlers with a bit of everything, from foodstuffs to farm implements, in exchange for items offered in trade. By the mid-1800s, the retail version of this concept, the country store, emerged. A multitude of must-have products, available in exchange for cash (or "credit," until harvest time), became the norm.

For many years, it was the storekeeper who filled your order, often knowing in advance just what you needed. Baking powder? Buggy whips? Shotguns? Sarsaparilla? The general store had it all, and the general storekeeper remembered exactly where it all was located. That personal touch lasted until 1916 when Clarence Saunders opened his first Piggly Wiggly, pioneering the self-serve concept.

The general store was the hub of the community, filling not only shopping needs, but social needs as well. Store hours were flexible to suit busy schedules. Farm wives looked forward to socializing with friends on weekly evenings in town. Storekeepers became integral parts of the community, solidifying their indispensability by taking on additional tasks, such as undertaker or postmaster, and making their facilities available for community-minded endeavors.

Typical of these establishments was The Shimer Store, which opened in southeastern Minnesota in 1870. The owner's daughter, Ruth Shimer, offered these recollections:

"Groceries were kept in the back, with dry goods in the front. A large coffee mill ground by hand many pounds of coffee. Sugar came in 100-pound bags and was dumped into a big barrel, to be sacked up as wanted. Eggs were brought in 30-dozen cases, every egg having to be candled before being shipped to Chicago. A big register from a one-lung furnace heated the store, and it was around this that many yarns were told.

"Ready-to-wear clothes hadn't hit the market then, so bolts of yard goods and other commodities came from Marshall Field's in Chicago. High-button shoes, overshoes, overalls, and a case of pretty handkerchiefs and ribbons were always on display."

Country store collectibles include, of course, the varied items sold there. In addition to dry goods, sewing paraphernalia, and colorfully labeled food and tobacco tins, there are products unique to the times. "Miracle elixirs" were ominpresent, and bottles once filled

Stool, shoe salesman's stool, early 1900s, classic old oak seat for shoe salesman, with metal frame..... **$70**

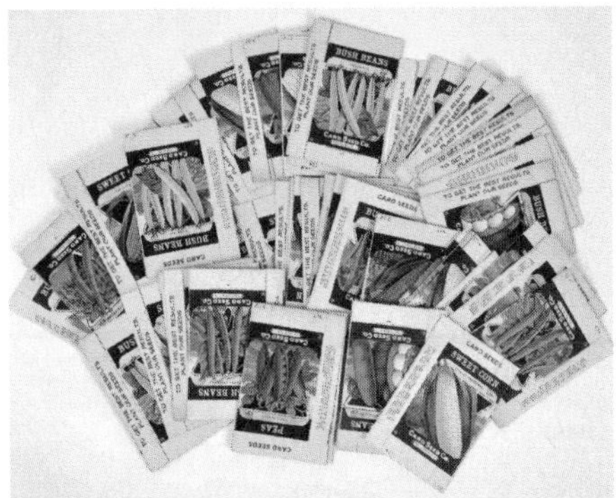

More than 150 old 3-oz. cardboard seed boxes, variety of peas, beans, and other vegetables, flat and easy to set up, 5-1/2" x 3-3/4" ea. .......................... **$90**

with such products as "Merchants Gargling Oil and Liniment For Man Or Beast" continue to attract collectors.

Even more in demand are country store trappings: authentic packaging, advertising, and furnishings. These range from the still-readily identifiable, such as sugar bags, pickle barrels, and cheese boxes, to items with long-vanished original purposes: razor strop cases, collar boxes, and ribbon cabinets. Also popular are store premiums. Some came direct from the manufacturer, such as tobacco silks, small ribbons tucked inside cigarette packaging, featuring demure pin-ups. Others relate to a specific store, such as calendars and postcards.

Country store artifacts were never intended for a long shelf life. Due to age and usage, they are often difficult to find in pristine condition. While professional restoration is available, working particularly well on tin advertising signs, it can be costly, and may actually result in diminished value. In many cases, these collectibles are best appreciated "as is" – fascinating remnants of a bygone age.

*All images courtesy Dan Morphy Auctions*

Mazda lamps light bulb display, General Electric, Art Deco design, glass on both sides, display has been rewired to light with one bulb attached inside body of display, 12-3/4" t. ........................................**$1,050**

Rice's Seeds display stand, early 1900s, embossed tin sign on collapsible fold-up telescoping seed display, all original, complete with legs ................................**$350**

Vegetable remedy countertop display, H.D. Beach Co. Coshocton, O. die-cut tin image of lady behind full display of tablets, F.J. O'Neill's Vegetable Remedy tablet display, 13" x 9" ............**$600**

Chicos Spanish peanuts counter dispenser, glass with original tin lid and tin strip across bottom, 11-1/2" t..........................**$460**

Seven oil product tins including Singer Sewing Machine Oil tin, Farmers Pride High Grade Oil, Shulife for waterproofing shoes cone top-shape tin with screw top, rare Magnet Oil, one pint Hollingshead's Neats Foot, pre-1900 Boston Coach-Axle Oil manufactured by Standard Oil Co. ........................................ **$140**

Ruby Bands rubber band display case, Eberhard Faber rubber band display/dispenser for six sizes of rubber bands, advertising on lid, inside lid and side panels, back has large picture of Mongol Pencils, 15-1/4" l. .................................................................. **$320**

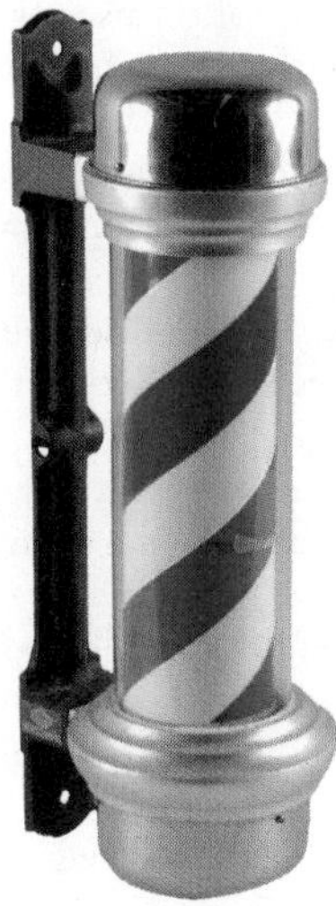

Electric barber pole, not operational, outside bottom and top plates have been replaced, 27-1/2" t. .......................... **$200**

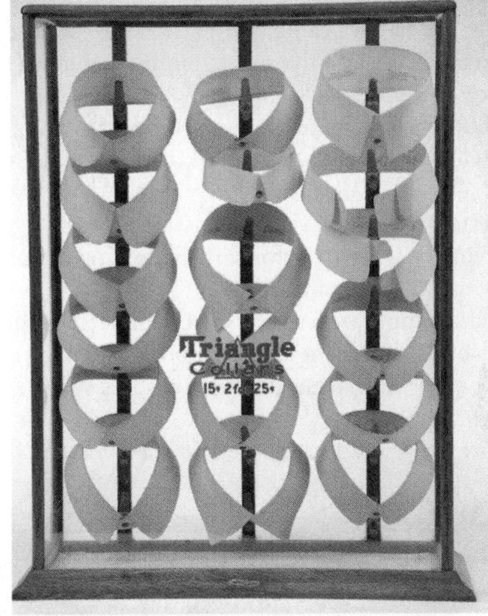


Triangle Collars store display, original decal name on collar case, some original collars included, 25-1/2" t.. **$520**

Ten-pound tin for Borden's Meadow Brand Malted Milk, early tin with screw-top lid printed on all sides,10-1/2" t. ............... **$70**

Bright Western Union Telegraph and Cable Blanks porcelain sign attached to original wood counter holder, included are original Western Union Blanks and materials, 9" x 9-1/2". ................ **$520**

# Decoys

The origin of the decoy in America lies in early American history, pre-dating the American pioneer by at least 1,000, perhaps 2,000 years. In 1924, at an archeological site in Nevada, the Lovelock Cave excavations yielded a group of 11 decoys preserved in protective containers. The careful manner of their storage preserved them for us to enjoy an estimated 1,000 to 2,000 years later.

When the first settlers came to North America, their survival was just as dependent upon hunting wild game for food as it was for the Indians. They began to fashion likenesses of their prey out of different materials, ultimately finding that wood was an ideal raw material. Thus the carving of wildfowl decoys was born out of necessity for food.

Historical records indicate wooden decoys were in general use as early as the 1770s, but it seems likely that they would have been widely used before then.

Until the middle of the 1800s, there was not sufficient commercial demand for decoys to enable carvers to make a living selling them, so most decoys were made for themselves and friends. Then the middle of the 19th century saw the birth of the market gunners. During the market-gunning period, many carvers began making a living with their decoys, and the first factory-made decoys came into existence. The huge numbers of decoys needed to supply the market hunters and the rising numbers of hunters for sport or sustenance made commercial decoy carving possible.

The market hunters and other hunters killed anything that flew. This indiscriminate destruction of wildfowl was the coup de grace for many bird species, rendering them extinct.

The United States Congress, with the passage of the Migratory Bird Treaty Act in 1918, outlawed the killing of waterfowl for sale. Following the passage of the 1918 act came the demise of the factory decoys of the day.

Today a few contemporary carvers carry on their tradition. They produce incredibly intricate, lifelike birds. What these contemporary carvings represent is that decoy carving is one of the few early American folk arts that has survived into our modern times and is still being pursued.

For more information on decoys, see *Warman's Duck Decoys* by Russell E. Lewis.

## TRADITIONAL CARVERS

TOP! LOT!

Elmer Crowell's Preening Pintail drake, carved in 1915, is known as Crowell's finest and is the only known example. It was made for Crowell's friend, Dr. John C. Phillips of Beverly, Mass., for whom Crowell ran a gunning stand at the turn of the 20th century. .......... **$801,500**
*Guyette & Schmidt, Inc.*

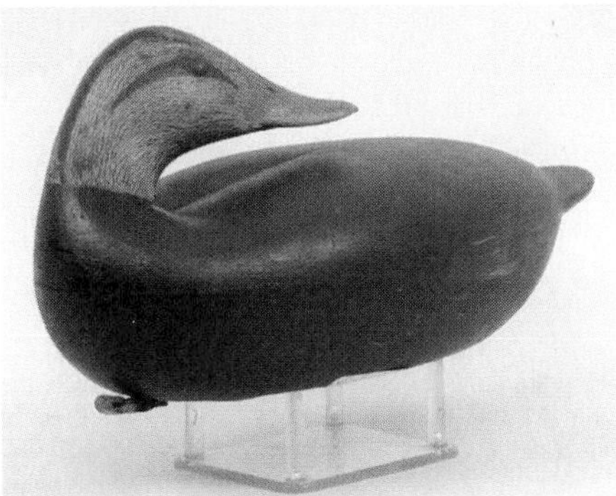

Albert Laing, Stratford, Conn. (1811-1886), carved this Black Duck in the mid- to late- 19th century. This exceptional hollow-carved bird began life as a Canvas-back by Albert Laing and it was then later converted to a Black Duck by Shang Wheeler also of Stratford, Conn. It is an old working repaint by Wheeler that comes from the Shelburne Museum collection and is so stamped. ................................ **$35,000-$40,000**
*Guyette & Schmidt, Inc.*

Capt. Ed Phillips (1901-1964), Cambridge, Md., made this Pintail drake, circa first quarter of the 20th century. This rare decoy with lifted head and an extended tail sprig is in original paint with minor wear; underside of the body has a small old touchup. ................. **$10,500**
*Guyette & Schmidt, Inc.*

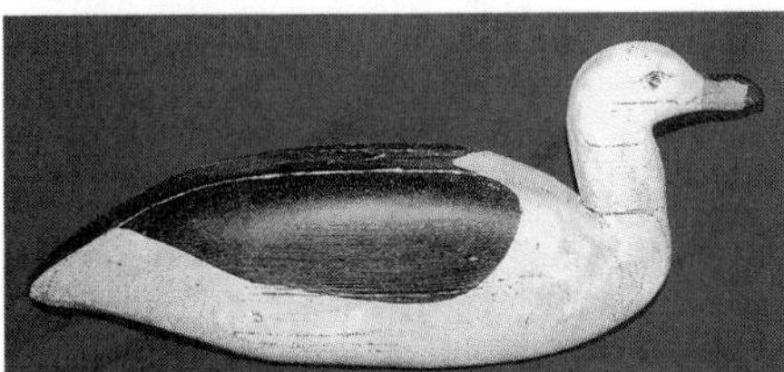

Oversized (27" long) great Black-backed Gull is by an unknown Cape Cod carver, circa 1900.......... **$3,500**
*Hank and Judy Norman Collection*

R. Madison Mitchell Bufflehead drake with original keel that dates from the late 1940s or early 1950s. ................................................................ **$400**
*Pitt Collection*

The Caines Brothers, Georgetown, S.C., made this very rare Mallard drake, circa turn of the 19th to 20th century. Carved with a peg placed to support a fragile bill, it has raised wings, tack eyes, working second coat of paint believed to have also been done by the Caines, and slight damage to the bill. .......... **$35,000**
*Guyette & Schmidt, Inc.*

Blue Goose, of wood with glass eyes and original paint, carved by C. C. Roberts and J. J. Rheinschmidt for relatives, employees, and friends, circa 1930s. This is one of only 200 decoys made by these famed fishing lure makers (makers of the Robert's Mud Puppy)..................................................... **$3,000**
*Lewis Collection*

This Brant is attributed to Nathan Cobb, Jr., circa last quarter of the 19th century. It has solid body technique, black glass eyes, original inserted hardwood bill, old working repaint. Provenance: consigned by Alma Fitchett of Northampton County and found with the rig at Smith Gun Club. Southern Decoys shows the exact decoy........................................ **$16,000**
*Guyette & Schmidt, Inc.*

Coot carved by Xavier Bourg (1901-1984) of Larose, La., circa 1950. ....................................... **$1,500**
*Hank and Judy Norman Collection*

Elmer Crowell's Canada Goose, made using the slat body technique common to this area, is a very large goose measuring approximately 42" from bill to tail. It has an oval stamp under the tail, original paint and is strong structurally.......................... **$5,500-$6,000**
*Guyette & Schmidt, Inc.*

Ward Brothers Green-wing Teal drake, made in 1936, is in original paint.........................**$16,000-$18,000**
*Griff Evans Collection*

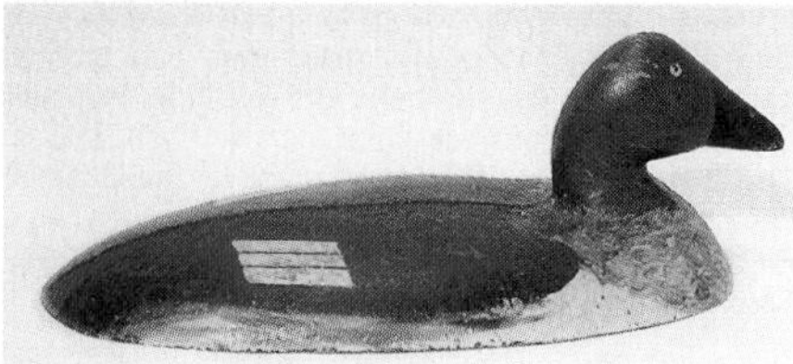

Rare Richard Tilghman Goldeneye hen sink box decoy was made of iron in the 1920s in Talbot County, Md., and is in original paint. .................... **$3,000-$4,000**
*Griff Evans Collection*

Very rare summer plumage Old Squaw drake was the very last one of these made by the Ward Brothers in 1977..........................................**$25,000-$30,000**
*Pitt Collection*

Delaware River Bluewing Teal hen is circa first quarter of the 20th century. It has raised wing tips and original paint. .................................................. **$1,000**
*Guyette & Schmidt, Inc.*

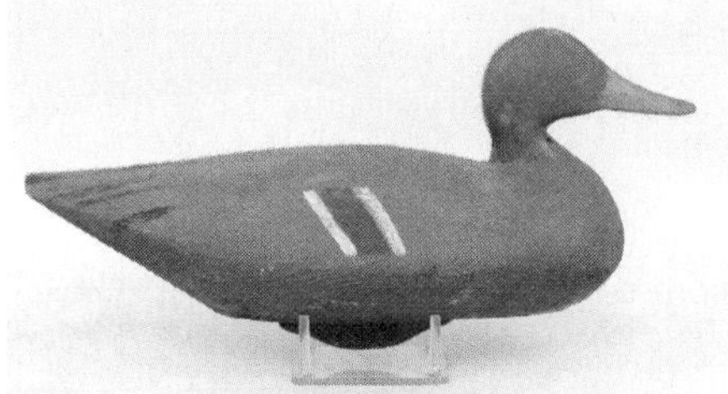

Ned Burgess, Churches Island, N.C., carved this Mallard hen. It is very rare, created in the early 20th century. It has original paint and a small dent in back. It is featured in Southern Decoys...................**$21,000**
*Guyette & Schmidt, Inc.*

Late 1800s Red-breasted Merganser hen, by an unknown carver, is from Long Island or New Jersey. It has original paint............ **$6,000**
*Guyette & Schmidt, Inc.*

Rare and early Delaware River Pintail drake dates to the last quarter of the 19th century to early 20th century. By an unknown maker, it has hollow carving, "V" primaries and inserted hardwood tail, similar to work by John English. It has original paint with very minor touchup. ............................**$27,500**
*Guyette & Schmidt, Inc.*

Golden Plover by William Bowman, Lawrence, Long Island, N.Y., circa 1880. ........................... **$25,000**
*Hank and Judy Norman Collection*

►Harry V. Shourds Yellowlegs made in 1910, Tuckerton, N.J. The original paint decoy was formerly in the Somers Headley Collection. .............. **$4,000-$5,000**
*Griff Evans Collection*

Flying Snow Goose by an unknown upstate New York carver, circa 1920s. ................................ **$12,000**
*Hank and Judy Norman Collection*

Green-wing Teal hen by William Hart, Belleville, Ontario. Hart lived from 1875-1949 and was a superb carver. This is a hollow carved swimming hen with original paint, some professional repair to the neck and a tiny tail chip and a great cocked head to the decoy. ............................................................ **$55,000**
*Guyette & Schmidt, Inc.*

Rare Widgeon drake, Premier Grade, produced by the Mason factory early in the 20th century has original paint, several tiny dents, with original newspaper wrapping visible. ............ **$55,000**
*Guyette & Schmidt, Inc.*

Mason "snake-head" Pintail drake, in Standard Grade with glass eyes, very rare configuration .................................... **$32,000**
*Pitt Collection*

## FACTORY DECOYS

This is an Evans Double Blue, Blue-wing Teal. **$4,000**
*Pitt Collection*

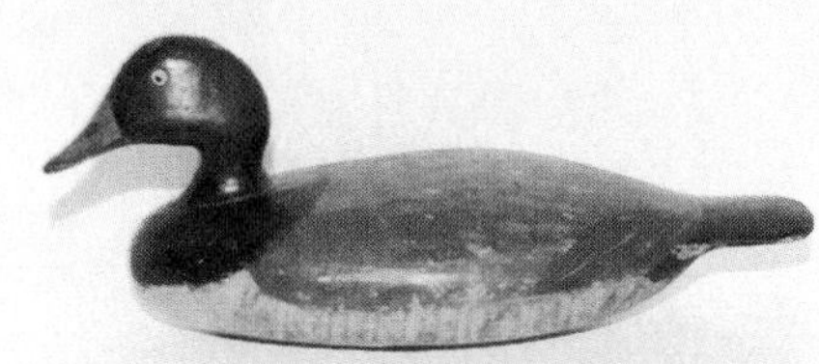
Rare Redhead drake by Harvey Stevens, circa 1890. Note the comb painting on sides and back.... **$6,000**
*Hank and Judy Norman Collection*

Mason Premier grade Widgeon drake circa 1915. ........ **$11,000**
*Hank and Judy Norman Collection*

Challenge Grade Peterson Black Duck, circa late 1800s, is rare, with original paint, small dents and cracks. ........ **$5,000**
*Guyette & Schmidt, Inc.*

Mason Standard Grade glass eyed White-wing Scoter used as a confidence decoy........ **$800-$1,200**
*Pitt Collection*

Dodge Widgeon drake with original paint, circa 1890s. ........ **$2,500**
*Pitt Collection*

Canvasback "snake-head" drake in Mason Premier Grade........ **$15,000+**
*Pitt Collection*

# Disney

Collectibles that feature Mickey Mouse, Donald Duck, and other famous characters of cartoon icon Walt Disney are everywhere. They can be found with little effort at flea markets, garage sales, local antiques and toys shows, and online as well as through auction houses and specialty catalogs.

Of the Disney toys, comics, posters, and other items produced from the 1930s through the 1960s, prewar Disney material is by far the most desirable.

Boxed running Mickey on Pluto, scarce 5" celluloid by Modern Toys, Occupied Japan, with original box with paper label ... **$3,125**
*Bonhams*

Collection of World of Disney postage stamps, binders with various first day stamps from various counties. Stamps depict events within Disney and Disney World Space Exploration, Calvary Olympics, Disney Classics Fairy Tales, post-1970s era collectibles. .................................. **$6,875**
*Bonhams*

Disney characters card set, "Walt Disney Cartooning Cards," each with a color picture of a different Disney character including Dumbo, Lady and the Tramp, Pinocchio and Mickey Mouse, the back of each with instructions on how to draw the character, 1959, complete set of 18 cards.... **$278**

Donald Duck and Goofy toy, windup tin, Donald & Goofy Duet, large Goofy standing on a large drum with a small Donald on a drum in front of him, 1946, Marx, Goofy missing one arm, replaced ears, 10-1/4" h. ................ **$201**

Donald Duck windup tin toy walker by Schuco, original colorful box with one inside flap missing, ca. 1950s, 6" h....................... **$480**

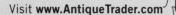

Lionel #1536 Mickey Mouse Circus, scarce boxed 1930s-era train with clockwork engine, Mickey "stoker" accompanied by three lithographed circus cars, track, composition Mickey conductor, tickets, tent and other paper components (cut out).... **$5,250**
*Bonhams*

Minnie Mouse toy, windup tin, "Minnie Mouse Knitter," Minnie sitting in rocking chair knitting, colorful, Line Mar, Japan, 1950s, mechanism works but skips, 6-1/2" h. ................................................... **$288**

Pluto toy, pull-type with bell, lithographed paper on wood figure of a racing Pluto pulling a four-wheeled platform with bell, three small lithographed cardboard figures of Mickey Mouse are detached from the platform and one is missing, early 1930s, overall 20-1/2" l. .......... **$1,898**

►Scarce 1935 Mickey Lunch Kit by Handy, depicts Silly Symphonies graphics with early pie-eyed Mickey and characters, contains actual internal "kit" ......................................................................**$2,000**
*Bonhams*

Sleeping Beauty movie cel, forest landscape with a small figure of Briar Rose walking with basket, gouache on celluloid applied to airbrushed background, 1959, 1-1/2" x 3" ........................ **$837**

Ferdinand the Bull toy, key-wind tin, walking Ferdinand with fabric flowers in his mouth, marked "Japan - Walt Disney Productions," 1938, all original with box, 5-1/2" l., 4" h...................................... **$360**

►Snow White & the Seven Dwarfs dolls, Snow White in stockinet with painted features, black mohair wig and wearing a velvet and silk dress with the hem silk screened with images of the Dwarfs, made by Ideal, the seven Dwarfs in jointed composition with molded shoes and felt outfits and hats with their names, made by Knickerbocker, 1930s, Dwarfs 9" h., Snow White 15-1/2" h., the set ........................... **$1,610**

# Dolls

I am always asked, "Is the doll market dead?" or told, "The doll market is dead!" so I decided to step back and watch the market for several months via shows, auctions, and online.

What I found might surprise you in both a good and not so good way. Our weak economy has definitely taken its toll on buyers and sellers. Travel is expensive, and dealers hesitate to travel long distances if shows are not well attended. Good advertising is expensive, and the amount of money promoters are able to spend on advertising is determined by the number of dealers supporting a show. It is a typical "catch 22" with no winners.

There is an upside to this predicament. Since December 2011, I have been a participant in five doll and toy shows. The attendance has been good and the dealers have been selling, but the show demographics have changed. No longer are shows attracting dealers from long distances. Buyers seem to come from a 100-mile radius. Advertising is concentrated in local fliers and newspapers, at antique shops, and on local TV. Dealers and buyers can attend and return home in one day, keeping costs down.

What items are drawing the most interest? In the modern and vintage area, dolls from the 1950s and 1960s have a strong following. Many dolls from this period had extensive wardrobes, and dresses and accessories for dolls such as Revlon, Cissy, the Chatty Cathy family, the Barbie family, Ginny, Muffy, or any fashion dolls are in great demand. During this period, children played with their dolls, so finding them in excellent condition or finding their accessories is a difficult search.

Most dolls from this period were made of hard plastic or vinyl. Hard plastic dolls tend to fade, and many vinyl dolls get sticky. Coloring is important—a faded 1950s doll or a sticky Barbie doll will often have trouble finding a home. The same is true for clothes that have been washed or are missing tags.

Many dolls of this period also were mechanical in some way. Some "grew" hair, walked, talked, or had pull-string eye movements. Collectors want these mechanisms to be in working order, and if you have the original box, that is even better. High prices are paid for mint condition dolls of this period, but played-with dolls in poor condition bring almost nothing.

Raggedy Ann by Volland, early model with shoe button eyes and original brown yarn hair, painted features with black outlined nose (light soil on face), red and white striped stockings and black shoes, original cotton dress in unusual pattern and pantaloons, white apron may be a vintage replacement, 15-1/2" t. ....... **$750**
*Morphy Auctions*

In the more modern area, ball-jointed dolls (BJD) with multiple joints and reborn babies have attracted a new group of collectors. At the International Doll Expo (IDEX) in Orlando, Florida, there were babies that were so real that you had to touch them to see if they would move. BJDs have articulated bodies that even have jointed fingers and toes. Many also exhibit a new face look that is reminiscent of "Avatar" characters or wide-eyed street waifs.

Quality antique dolls remain strong in the market. "Quality" is the key word. In the days when collectors' buying was limited to what they saw in shops or at shows, they bought what was available. The Internet now gives collectors access to an international doll market 24 hours a day. With this supply, collectors can pick and choose. Advanced collectors want the best that is available, and they are willing to wait for it. Damaged items or very ordinary items are left behind or have to be priced very inexpensively. Rare German, English, and French dolls in perfect condition do not remain available long.

Another area of antique doll collecting that remains strong is clothing, shoes, wigs, and accessories. During the 1960s and 1970s, many collectors went through a period of wanting their dolls to look like new. Old clothes were tossed aside for new, bright outfits, and wigs were

replaced with synthetics. Often, bodies were painted to cover wear and eyes were set stationary to keep them from falling out. Now we are trying to undo those bad choices. It is difficult work and, at times, the damage cannot be undone. That is why we see very ordinary dolls with significant problems left behind or priced very low.

What does the future hold? I know one thing: Doll collectors are going to continue to buy. It is in our blood, and a poor economy will not stop us. It might keep us from driving hundreds of miles to a show, but it will not keep us from turning on our computers. It will also not keep us from supporting shows in our area and the dealers who continue to participate in these shows. Being able to see what you are buying and talk to the person you are dealing with is still the best way.

***Sherry Minton***

*Sherry Minton has served as president of three clubs belonging to the United Federation of Doll Clubs, Inc. She is a senior member of the American Society of Appraisers with a designated specialty in dolls and toys. Minton can be contacted at dollypictures@aol.com.*

*Images courtesy Frasher's Doll Auctions unless otherwise noted.*

Embroidered Naugahyde doll, 20" l...................................... **$400**

Composition "Patsy Ann" by Effanbee, socket head on five-piece jointed body, blonde mohair wig, sleep eyes, painted and applied lashes, single-stroke brows, closed mouth, plump cheeks, wears tagged light blue organdy dress over cotton slip with attached panty, matching bonnet, blue leatherette shoes, Effanbee gold metal heart bracelet, all-original circa 1930 doll, marks: Effanbee © Patsy Ann, 19"............... **$150**

◄Poured wax figure in dome, well-detailed stylized wax figure with painted features, wax hair and coronet, pink wax dress with gilt trim, posed atop wooden base covered in wax greenery and flowers, wax-covered tree trunk with wax leaves at back, gold cross in left hand, wax lamb on left side, wooden base, glass dome, 12" dome, 9-1/2" display.......... **$225**

French bisque Bebe Teteur by Leon Casimir Bru, bisque swivel head on bisque shoulder plate, inset brown paperweight eyes with spiral threading, dark eyeliner, mauve-blushed eyelids, painted lashes, brush-stroked and feathered brows, pierced ears, open mouth, shaded and accented lips, blonde mohair wig over cork pate, Bru kid body with slender torso, Chevrot hinged upper legs, wooden lower legs, kid arms with bisque forearms, white cotton and eyelet dress, white leather shoes, original rubber mechanism inside head, nursing wing screw back of head, circa 1886, sturdy body, arms not original to body, marks: Bru Jne 6T (head and shoulder plate), 18"...................... **$4,250**

Composition Princess Elizabeth by Alexander Doll Co., composition socket head on five-piece jointed body, brown sleep eyes, painted and applied lashes, amber eye shadow, tapered brows, open mouth, upper teeth, blonde human hair wig, sheer pink formal over pink cotton slip, cotton panty, silver leatherette shoes, silver tiara, circa 1930s, tagged costume, marks: Madame Alexander Princess Elizabeth dress tag, 15" .................................... **$200**

Fine porcelain shoulder head by Dressel & Kister, glazed porcelain shoulder head with oval face, slender throat, light brown sculpted hair loosely waved from face, captured at crown into arrangement of curls and braid encircled by gilt-edged aqua ribbon, painted facial features, brown eyes, deeply sculpted eyelids, painted lower lashes, red and black upper eyeliner, feathered brows, closed mouth, marks: Blue Dressel and Kister mark inside shoulder plate, 3-1/2" ............................... **$500**

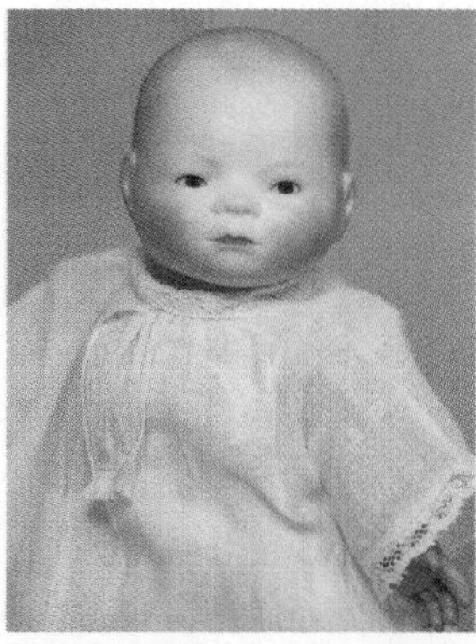

German bisque Bye-Lo baby in original gown, solid dome bisque head, flange neck, painted hair, brown sleep eyes, painted lashes, tinted brows, closed mouth, cloth bent-limb body with Bye-Lo stamp on chest, celluloid hands, white batiste gown tagged Bye-Lo Baby, marks: Copr. Grace S. Putnam, 8" head circumference ............ **$200**

German bisque character boy by Kley & Hahn, solid-dome bisque socket head, molded and painted blonde hair, brown sleep eyes, painted lashes, feathered brows, open/closed mouth with modeled detail between accented lips, composition fully jointed toddler body with slant hips, antique costume of blue velvet knee pants, red sweater and cap, blue-white cotton stockings, and black leatherette shoes, original finish, marks: 525 K & H, 16"....... **$600**

**Above left:** "Golliwog," by R. John Wright, first Collector's Club Edition, 1996-1998 Premiere Club Exclusive, all-felt, fully jointed, painted googly eyes, smiling mouth, black mohair wig, felt costume, leather shoes, original paper label #626/ plus certificate of authenticity, released in 1996, one of 1,526 models produced, 11"................... **$225**

**Above right:** "Miss Golli" R. John Wright, Collectors Club Edition, 1996-1998 Premiere Club Exclusive, all-felt, fully jointed, painted googly eyes, smiling mouth, black mohair wig, felt costume, leather shoes, original paper label #008/ plus certificate of authenticity, second Premier Club Exclusive, released in 1997, one of 849 models produced, 11".... **$300**

# Shirley Temple Dolls

Shirley Temple by Ideal, 1957, all original, 17" ............................... **$50**

In the midst of the Great Depression, when people needed an escape from the worries of their everyday lives, a darling child danced and sang her way into the hearts of a nation. Child star Shirley Temple began her film career in 1932 at the age of three, and in 1934, found international fame in "Bright Eyes,"a feature film designed specifically for her talents.

Master doll artist Bernard Lipfert created the charming Shirley Temple doll to the specifications of Ideal, Morris Mitchtom, the founder of Ideal Toys, and Shirley's mother, Mrs. Gertrude Temple in 1934. Mrs. Temple's approval was obtained only after more than 28 molds were rejected.

Mollye Goldman designed Shirley Temple outfits from 1934 to 1936. The result was one of the world's best-selling dolls. At least four markings were used on the original Shirley Temple composition dolls. The first prototypes were marked "Cop./ Ideal/N & T Co." on the head only. The second dolls, mostly 18 inches and 22 inches, were marked "Shirley Temple" with the familiar "Ideal" within a diamond trademark below.

Finally, the most commonly found Shirley Temple was marked with a size number in inches. Take note, there are also genuine unmarked Shirley Temple dolls. Ideal's version of the Shirley Temple doll was produced from 1934 to 1939. They were reissued in 1957 with a vinyl head, hard plastic body and marked "Ideal Doll/ST – (size number)" on the back of the head and ST – (size number)" on the shoulder and came with a gold plastic pin with "Shirley Temple" written in script.

Her life filled with a successful movie career, three children and a lifetime of service to various corporation boards, ambassadorships and charitable foundations, Shirley Temple turned 84 on April 23, 2012.

Source: *200 Years of Dolls, 4th edition*, by Dawn Herlocher

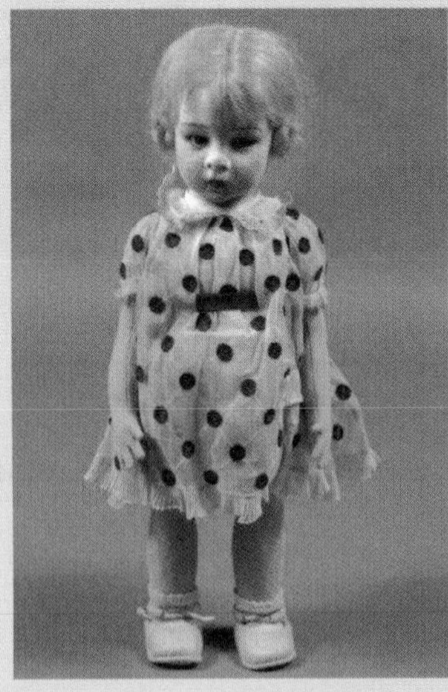

Felt Shirley Temple by Lenci, Italian, 20th c., brown eyes and felt clothes, signed on bottom of one foot, face slightly discolored, shoe laces are broken, 22" h. ...................... **$650**

All-original Shirley Temple with trunk and wardrobe, composition socket head, five-piece jointed body, sleep eyes, applied and painted lashes, feathered brows, open mouth, upper teeth, dimples, blonde mohair wig in original set, tagged NRA red and white dimity dress, cotton slip and panty, leatherette shoes, rayon socks, Shirley pin; original travel trunk with hangers, two original playsuits and tagged blue/white dotted dress with matching hat, all-original, small bit of faint craze, marks: Shirley Temple 13, 13" t...................... **$650**

Shirley Temple character doll by Ideal, mid-20th c., mint in original box, including original dress with Ideal label, pink bow in curly hair with hairpins intact, two pairs of shoes, additional pink satin dress with gold plate Shirley Temple name tag, Shirley Temple labeled handbag and folding cardboard display tag, box has original cardboard divider 12-1/2 l. overall.................. **$100**

Shirley Temple by Ideal all composition doll, sleep eyes, original plaid dress, original wig, shoes and socks, metal pin back button "My Friend Shirley Temple," head marked Shirley Temple Ideal 20, body marked Shirley Temple, 20" t................. **$300**

Shirley Temple composition doll, composition socket head, five-piece jointed body, original blonde mohair wig, sleep eyes, applied and painted eyelashes, open mouth, upper teeth, dimples, original red "music note" dress, cotton panty, white leatherette shoes, marks: Shirley Temple (head and body), 22"......................... **$250**

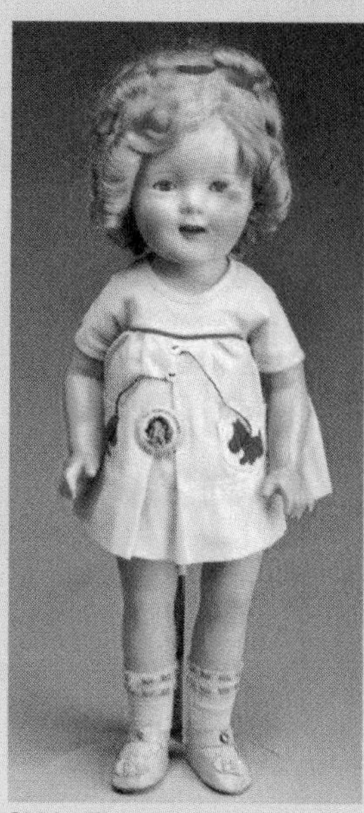

Shirley Temple by Ideal, all composition doll with sleep eyes, original tagged dress with Scottie dogs, original wig set, shoes and socks, metal pin that says "Shirley Temple, the world's darling," 19" t.................... **$750**

Bru Jne Bebe with classic face, pressed bisque swivel head on kid-edged bisque shoulder plate with modeled bosom and shoulder blades, blue paperweight inset eyes, dark eyeliner, painted lashes, mauve blushed eye shadows, brushstroked and multi-feathered brows with sculpted shaping, closed mouth with outlined shaded lips, tiny tongue tip, pierced ears, original blonde mohair wig over cork pate, slender-shaped kid body, scalloped edge collarette, Chevrot hinged wooden lower legs, bisque lower arms with sculpted hands, pale blue silk brocade and ivory lace frock with fitted bodice, shirred blue silk bonnet, antique undergarments, French white leather boots, deep paperweight eyes, professional repair to left fingers, marks: Bru Jne 7 (head and shoulder plate), 20" ...**$20,000**

Early model Jumeau Bebe known as "portrait" with original boutique label, pressed bisque socket head with elongated facial modeling, almond-shaped blue paperweight eyes with rose-blushed eyelids, dark eyeliner, painted lashes, brush-stroked and multi-feathered brows, closed mouth with modeled white space between shaded and accented lips, slightly upturned lip corners, separately modeled and applied pierced ears, blonde mohair wig over cork pate, composition and wooden eight-loose-ball-jointed body with straight wrists, costumed in antique early rose silk frock with wire-framed matching silk bonnet with lace trim, dark leather French-style shoes, circa 1880, original body with shop label, original finish, marks: 10 (incised); body: Jumeau Medaille d'or Paris stamp and original boutique label, 23"........................**$6,500**

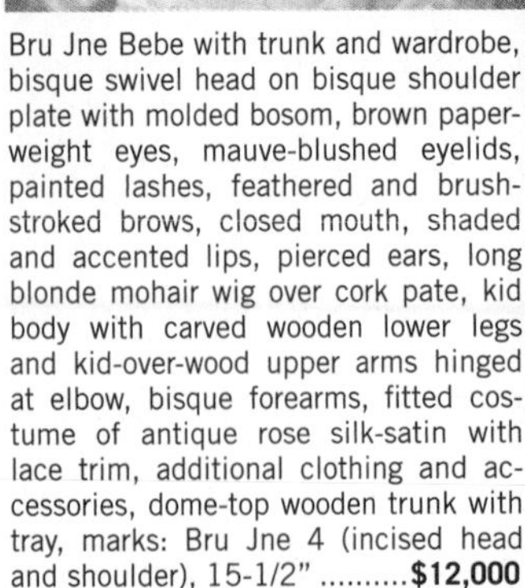

Bru Jne Bebe with trunk and wardrobe, bisque swivel head on bisque shoulder plate with molded bosom, brown paperweight eyes, mauve-blushed eyelids, painted lashes, feathered and brushstroked brows, closed mouth, shaded and accented lips, pierced ears, long blonde mohair wig over cork pate, kid body with carved wooden lower legs and kid-over-wood upper arms hinged at elbow, bisque forearms, fitted costume of antique rose silk-satin with lace trim, additional clothing and accessories, dome-top wooden trunk with tray, marks: Bru Jne 4 (incised head and shoulder), 15-1/2" ..........**$12,000**

# Drugstore and Pharmacy Items

The old-time corner drugstore, once a familiar part of every American town, has now given way to a modern, efficient pharmacy. With the streamlining and modernization of this trade, many of the early tools and store adjuncts have been outdated and now fall in the realm of "collectibles." Listed here are some of the tools, bottles, display pieces and other emphemera once closely associated with the druggist's trade.

Apothecary storage jar, covered, free-blown clear cylindrical jar with two applied cobalt blue bands around the body, high domed clear cover with cobalt blue rim band and hollow blown knob finial, pontil scar, ca. 1850, 11" h. ... **$532**

Apothecary show bottle, blown bulbous ovoid ruby glass body with tapering cylindrical neck and flaring rim, raised on an applied clear pedestal and round foot, original clear hollow-blown stopper, probably American, ca. 1870-90, 10" h. .............................. **$504**

Apothecary show globe with original stopper, Art Deco style, a large clear glass teardrop-shaped globe with a stepped shoulder, short cylindrical neck and tall oblong stopper, fitted in cast- and polished aluminum three-footed stand, American, ca. 1920-35, 18-1/8" h. ........... **$420**

Apothecary jar with fitted lid, cobalt blue-glazed pottery, cylindrical with waisted neck, wide gold banner printed in black "Pulv. Lapis P.," probably English, ca. 1860-80, 6-5/8" h. ............ **$448**

Balance scales, brass, central shaft with the balance arm suspending a fixed tray on one side and a suspended small tray on the other, on a rectangular wooden base, with five weights, crossbar marked "W and T Avery Lt. - To Weigh 2 lb.," minor scuffing, 19th c., 10-3/4 x 20", 22" h. .................................................................................. **$259**

Countertop display jar, square tall clear glass with a wide mouth with fitted mushroom-style stopper, the front with a large rectangular label-under-glass reading "Dr. D. Jayne's Sanative Pills for Constipation, Biliousness, Sick Headache, Etc. - Sugar-Coated - 25 Cents," ca. 1880-95, 8" h. ......................................................................... **$1,456**

Drug bottle, "C.W. Snow and Co., Druggists (design of eagle with shield and mortar and pestle), Syracuse, N.Y.," square with tooled lip, ca. 1885-95, deep cobalt blue, 8-1/4" h. .................................... **$468**

Drug bottle, "Jacob's Pharmacy (motif of eagle on mortar and pestle) Atlanta GA," tooled mouth, "W.T. Co. U.S.A." on smooth base, 70% original label for "Strychnine Sulphate," ca. 1885-1910, amber, 2-1/2" h. ........................................................................... **$77**

Drug bottle, rectangular with sloping shoulder, embossed "Jozeau" and "Pharmacien" on opposite ends, rolled lip, pontil-scarred base, ca. 1840-1855, deep olive green, 4-1/2" h. ................................ **$165**

Pill roller, walnut device on a brass base with a star stamp and a separate two-handled device which glides along top, 19th c., 12" h. ........ **$220**

Apothecary storage jar, porcelain, cylindrical with ringed white base and rim, domed cover with small air holes and button finial, the sides and cover in dark moss green, the base hand-painted with a gilt crown and scrolls above a red-bordered white banner reading "Leeches," early, 9-1/2" h. .................. **$5,980**

Drug bottle, narrow rectangular with beveled sides, embossed "Maximo M. Dia - Druggist - Ybor City, Fla.," tooled lip, "W.T. and Co. U.S.A." on smooth base, ca. 1890-1910, cobalt blue, 5-1/8" h..... **$190**

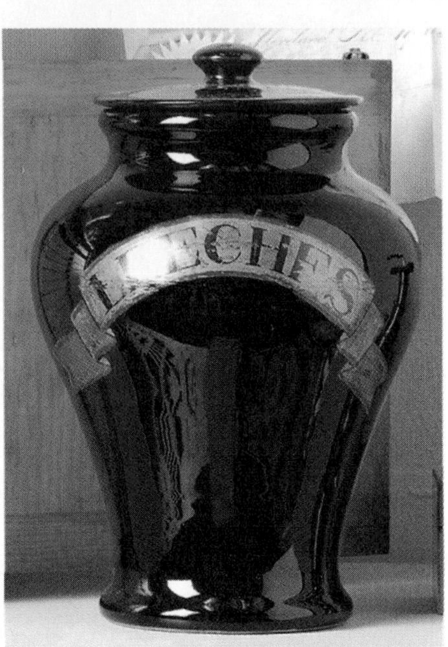

Apothecary storage jar, pottery, wide baluster-form body with flattened disk cover with small pierced holes and knob finial, deep cobalt blue glaze with an arched red-bordered gold banner reading "Leeches," impressed "Royal Doulton England," label probably repainted, late 19th-early 20th c., 9-1/2" h..... **$8,625**

Apothecary storage jar, earthenware, wide baluster-form body with a flaring round foot, fluted band around the lower body and short flaring neck with flattened inset cover with small pierced holes and knob finial, leaf-molded loop shoulder handles, sea green at the bottom and top with the white center area hand-painted with leafy scrolls and a large sea green banner decorated in gold with the word "Leeches," impressed "Alcock" mark, England, some damage on lid, late 19th-early 20th c., 13-1/2" h. ............................................................. **$8,625**

# Figurines

## Holt-Howard

The 1950s was a time of expansion. New homes were cropping up everywhere, affording people the luxury of space (both indoors and out). As a result, many families now had full-size kitchens, dining rooms, and dens to display their cherished belongings and collectibles. Best of all, barbecue grills were popping up everywhere, which created a market for condiment jars of all kinds. Americans now needed portable containers and jars to transport condiments and other goodies outdoors to picnic tables and grill areas.

During the late 1950s, with almost perfect timing, Holt-Howard developed a new concept in deep-glazed ceramics called "Pixiewares." These containers included covered condiment jars featuring whimsical pixie heads on top.

Due to the huge success of Pixiewares, other novelty companies such as Davar, Lefton, Lipper & Mann, and Napco all began to copy Holt-Howard's style. While each company made creative condiment jars, the Davar Company practically copied the Pixieware copyrighted design. Although many other companies' jars were different, they were all competing for sales around the same time — the 1950s and early 1960s. Today, many of these condiment jars have also become highly collectible and some are commanding top dollar at antiques and collectibles shows.

### Signatures and Stickers

Holt-Howard marked and copyright dated most of its collectibles with an ink stamp. However, certain tiny pieces were not marked because of a lack of space, so a foil sticker was sometimes applied instead. These items may have just read "HH" or nothing at all.

On Holt-Howard collectibles made abroad, the word "Japan" was included as part of the ink backstamp or printed on the foil label. Occasionally, Holt-Howard used numeric identification codes such as 6128L or 6457 to identify its merchandise.

Foil labels were used on many Holt-Howard items, especially on collectibles from the late 1950s and early 1960s. The label color schemes included black and gold, silver and gold, and red and gold. Most Pixieware pieces had the black and gold label. The Christmas collectibles usually had the red and gold version of this label, but during the early 1960s, the rectangular silver and gold foil label was also used.

For more information on Holt-Howard, see *Price Guide to Holt-Howard Collectibles*, second edition, by Walter Dworkin.

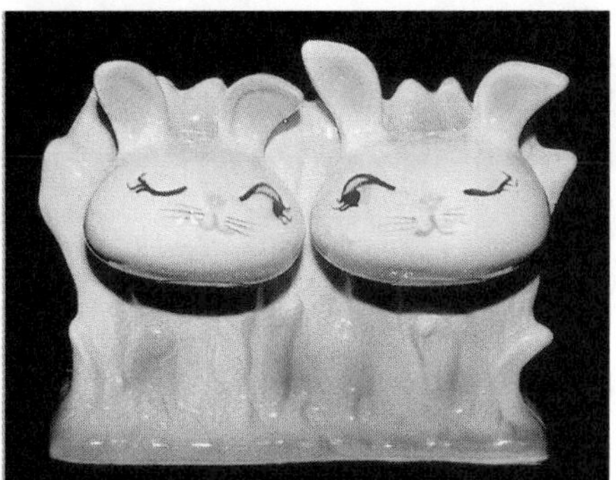

Winking Wabbits shakers ............... **$58-$68 for set**
*Collection of and photo by Darline Comisky*

Party Pretzel Pixies hors d' oeuvres dishes
Small size ............................................. **$190-$200**
Large size ................................................. **$275+**
*Patrick Haggerty collection, photo by Christine Whalon*

Peanut Butter Pat ................................ **$650-$675**
*Dworkin collection, photo by Van Blerck Photography*

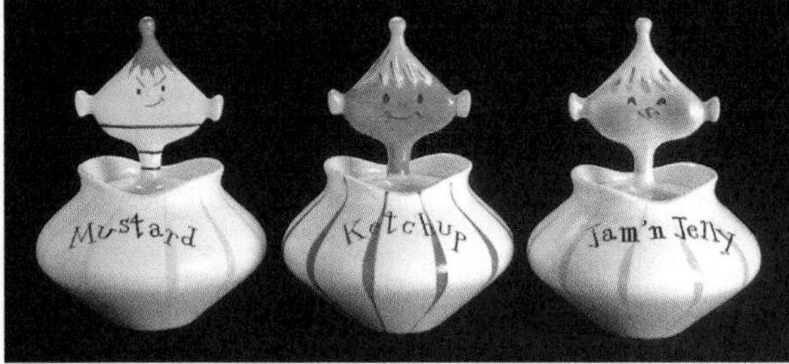


Mustard, ketchup and Jam 'n Jelly ................................ **$70-$80 each**
*Dworkin collection, photo by Van Blerck Photography*

Sam 'n Sally salad set (oil and vinegar cruets)........ **$175-$185 each**
*Dworkin collection, photo by Van Blerck Photography*

Salty and Peppy salt and pepper shakers ..................**$330-$350 for set**
*Dworkin collection, photo by Van Blerck Photography*

Flat Head Salad Dressings (Russian, French, Italian) ................................................. **$130-$140 each**
*Dworkin collection, photo by Van Blerck Photography*

Round Head Salad Dressings (Russian, French, Italian) ............................................ **$120-$130 each**
*Dworkin collection, photo by Van Blerck Photography*

Hanging Pixie planter........ **$450+**
*Dworkin collection, photo by Van Blerck Photography*

Party Pixie cheese spreaders.................................. **$20-$39 set of four**
*Dworkin collection, photo by Brenner Lennon Photo Productions*

Rudy's cookie jar .................................... **$39-$49**
*Dworkin collection, photo by Brenner Lennon Photo Productions*

Justa Flirt ............................................... **$12-$18**
*Dworkin collection, photo by Brenner Lennon Photo Productions*

Kissing Pups.................................. **$18-$28 for set**
*Dworkin collection, photo by Brenner Lennon Photo Productions*

Panda Bears................................... **$12-$18 for set**
*Dworkin collection, photo by Brenner Lennon Photo Productions*

Holly Elf Girls................................ **$35-$45 for set**
*Dworkin collection, photo by Brenner Lennon Photo Productions*

Merry Mice..................................... **$38-$48 for set**
*Dworkin collection, photo by Brenner Lennon Photo Productions*

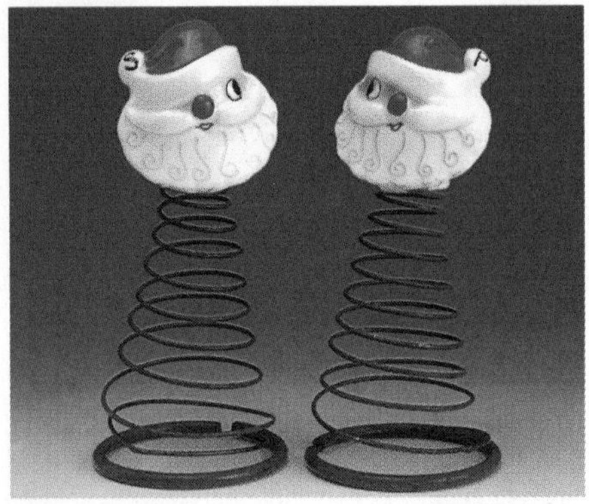

Rock 'n Roll Santa salt and peppers .. **$75-$85 for set**
*Dworkin collection, photo by Van Blerck Photography*

Bell Bottom Gobs salt and peppers.... **$48-$58 for set**
*Collection of and photo by Darline Comisky*

His and Hers Clips **$125-$135 each**
*Collection of and photo by Darline Comisky*

Paid and To Be Paid Clips ............................. **$75-$85 each**
*Collection of and photo by Darline Comisky*

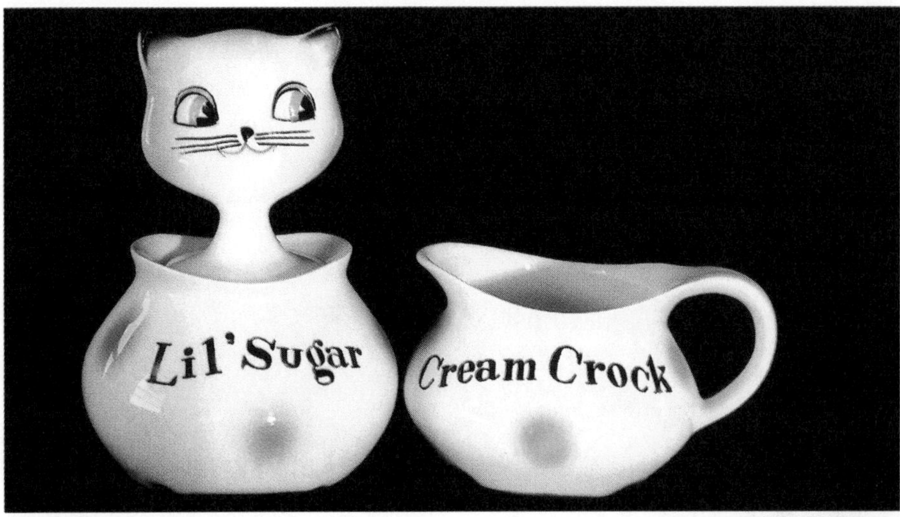


Cozy Kittens Cream Crock and Lil' Sugar.......................................................................**$225-$235 for set**
*Collection of and photo by Darline Comisky*

Cozy Kittens Merry Measure....................... **$75-$85**
*Dworkin collection, photo by Brenner Lennon Photo Productions*

Cozy Kittens cottage cheese crock............. **$50-$60**
*Dworkin collection, photo by Brenner Lennon Photo Productions*

Cozy Kittens caddy .................................. **$55-$60**
*Dworkin collection, photo by Brenner Lennon Photo Productions*

Cozy Kittens butter dish ..........................**$95-$105**
*Dworkin collection, photo by Brenner Lennon Photo Productions*

Cozy Kittens soap shaker .......................... **$75-$85**
*Dworkin collection, photo by Brenner Lennon Photo Productions*

Cozy Kittens Winky-Blinky "Meow" mug with squeaker ................................................ **$30-$40**
*Collection of and photo by Jason Wormington and John Frownfelter*

"My Fair Lady" head vase/candleholder ................................ **$85-$95**
*Dworkin collection, photo by Van Blerck Photography*

Pitcher, 32 oz. ............................................................ **$55-$65**
Pitcher, 12 oz. ............................................................ **$35-$45**
*Collection of and photo by Darline Comisky*

Small salt and pepper set ............................................................ **$10-$15**
Large salt and pepper set ............................................................ **$20-$30**
*Dworkin collection, photo by Brenner Lennon Photo Productions*

Snack tray and cup . **$23-$28 for set**
*Collection of and photo by Darline Comisky*

Cookie jar ............................................... **$95-$110**
*Collection of and photo by Darline Comisky*

Kitchen Cubs notepad holder.................. **$120-$130**
*Dworkin collection, photo by Brenner Lennon Photo Productions*

Recipe card holder......... **$60-$70**
*Collection of and photo by Darline Comisky*

Combination Polar Bears thermal egg cups with matching salt and pepper................. **$75-$85 for set**
*Dworkin collection, photo by Walter Dworkin*

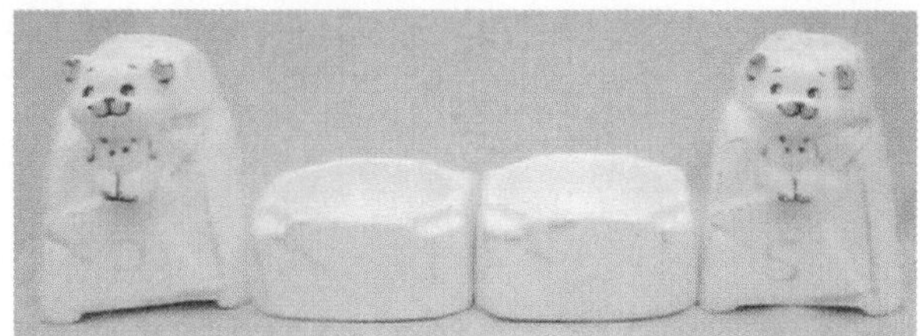

Merry Maids International all-purpose holders.................................................................. **$28-$33 each**
*Collection of and photo by Marion Howard*

Clown thermometer switch plate .................................... **$28-$38**
*Collection of and photo by Marion Howard*

Merry Mouse "Stinky Cheese Crock"...................................... **$50-$60**
Shakers ...................................................................................... **$38-$48**
*Dworkin collection, photo by Brenner Lennon Photo Productions*

Merry Mouse "Match Mouse"..................... **$75-$85**
*Dworkin collection, photo by Brenner Lennon Photo Productions*

Puss and Poodle diamond-shaped jar....... **$120-$130**
*Collection of and photo by Judy Yates*

Jeeves martini shaker set................................................ **$185+ for set**
*Dworkin collection, photo by Brenner Lennon Photo Productions*

Daisy 'Dorables bookend wall pocket planter............... **$38-$48**
*Collection of and photo by Darline Comisky*

Dandy-Lion-with-Crown bobbing bank............ **$135+**
*Dworkin collection, photo by Brenner Lennon Photo Productions*

Dandy-Lion-with-Hat bobbing bank................ **$150+**
*Collection of and photo by Darline Comisky*

Li'L Old Lace floral vases candle-holders.................. **$28-$38 each**
*Dworkin collection, photo by Brenner Lennon Photo Productions*

Moo Cow salt and peppers ........................... **$38-$48 for set**
*Dworkin collection, photo by Brenner Lennon Photo Productions*

Golfer ashtray ........................................ **$95-$110**
*Collection of and photo by Darline Comisky*

Puppy hot plate ........................................ **$55-$65**
*Collection of and photo by Darline Comisky*

Chickadee Sharpen Hold 'Em set ...... **$75-$85 for set**
*Dworkin collection, photo by Brenner Lennon Photo Productions*

Bride and Groom shadowbox candleholders ........................................ **$28-$38 for set**
*Dworkin collection, photo by Brenner Lennon Photo Productions*

"Wee Wings" candle rings ................ **$55-$65 for set**
*Dworkin collection, photo by Brenner Lennon Photo Productions*

Pelican Pete tape dispenser/storage container ........................................ **$70-$80**
*Dworkin collection, photo by Brenner Lennon Photo Productions*

Mallard pen set ........................................ **$38-$48**
*Dworkin collection, photo by Brenner Lennon Photo Productions*

# Hummel Figurines & Collectibles

The Goebel Company of Oeslau, Germany, first produced M.I. Hummel porcelain figurines in 1934, having obtained the rights to adapt the beautiful pastel sketches of children by Sister Maria Innocentia (Berta) Hummel. Every design by the Goebel artisans was approved by the nun until her death in 1946. Goebel produced these charming collectibles until Sept. 30, 2008. Manufaktur Rödental GmbH resumed production in 2009.

For more information on M.I. Hummel collectibles, see *The Official M.I. Hummel Price Guide* by Heidi Ann von Recklinghausen.

## Hummel Trademarks

Since 1935, there have been several changes in the trademarks on M.I. Hummel items. In later years of production, each new trademark design merely replaced the old one, but in the earlier years, frequently the new design trademark would be placed on a figurine that already bore the older style trademark.

### THE CROWN MARK (TMK-1): 1934-1950

The Crown Mark (TMK-1 or CM), sometimes referred to as the "Crown-WG," was used by Goebel on all of its products in 1935, when M.I. Hummel figurines were first made commercially available. The letters WG below the crown in the mark are the initials of William Goebel, one of the founders of the company. The crown signifies his loyalty to the imperial family of Germany at the time of the mark's design, around 1900. The mark is sometimes found in an incised circle.

Another Crown-type mark is sometimes confusing to collectors; some refer to it as the "Narrow Crown" and others the "Wide Ducal Crown." This mark was introduced by Goebel in 1937 and used on many of its products.

Often, the Crown Mark will appear twice on the same piece, more often one mark incised and the other stamped. This is, as we know, the "Double Crown."

When World War II ended and the United States Occupation Forces allowed Goebel to begin exporting, the pieces were marked as having been made in the occupied zone.

These marks were applied to the bases of the figurines, along with the other markings, from 1946 through 1948. They were sometimes applied under the glaze and often over the glaze. Between 1948 and 1949, the U.S. Zone mark requirement was dropped, and the word "Germany" took its place. With the partitioning of Germany into East and West, "W. Germany," "West Germany," or "Western Germany" began to appear most of the time instead.

*Incised Crown Mark*

*Stamped Crown Mark*

*Wide Ducal Crown Mark*

### THE FULL BEE MARK (TMK-2): 1940-1959

In 1950, Goebel made a major change in its trademark. The company incorporated a bee in a V. It is thought that the bumblebee part of the mark was derived from a childhood nickname of Sister Maria Innocentia Hummel, meaning bumblebee. The bee flies within a V, which is the first letter of the German word for distributing company, Verkaufsgesellschaft.

There are actually 12 variations of the Bee marks to be found on Goebel-produced M.I. Hummel items.

The Full Bee mark, also referred to as TMK-2 or abbreviated FB, is the first of the Bee marks to appear. The mark evolved over nearly 20 years until the company began to modernize it. It is sometimes found in an incised circle.

The very large bee flying in the V remained until around 1956, when the bee was reduced in size and lowered into the V. It can be found incised, stamped in black, or stamped in blue, in that order, through its evolution.

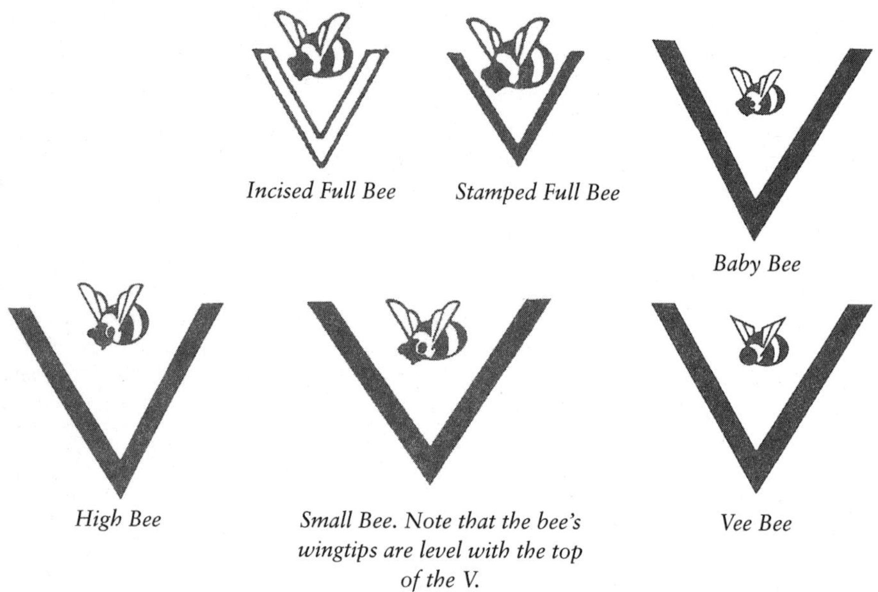

*Incised Full Bee* *Stamped Full Bee* *Baby Bee*

*High Bee* *Small Bee. Note that the bee's wingtips are level with the top of the V.* *Vee Bee*

## THE STYLIZED BEE (TMK-3): 1958-1972

A major change in the way the bee is rendered in the trademark made its appearance in 1960. The Stylized Bee (TMK-3), sometimes abbreviated as Sty-Bee, as the major component of the trademark appeared in three basic forms through 1972. The first two are both classified as the Stylized Bee (TMK-3), but the third is considered a fourth step in the evolution, the Three Line Mark (TMK-4).

**The Large Stylized Bee:** This trademark was used primarily from 1960 through 1963. The color of the mark will be black or blue. It is sometimes found inside an incised circle. When you find the Large Stylized Bee mark, you will normally find a stamped "West" or "Western Germany" in black elsewhere on the base, but not always.

**The Small Stylized Bee:** This mark is also considered to be TMK-3. It was used concurrently with the Large Stylized Bee from about 1960 and continued in this use until about 1972. The mark is usually rendered in blue, and it too is often accompanied by a stamped black "West" or "Western Germany." Collectors and dealers sometimes refer to the mark as the One Line Mark.

*Large Stylized Bee*

*Small Stylized Bee*

## THE THREE LINE MARK (TMK-4): 1964-1972

*Three Line Mark*

This trademark is sometimes abbreviated 3-line or 3LM in print. The trademark used the same stylized V and bee as the others, but also included three lines of wording beside it. This major change appeared in blue.

## THE LAST BEE MARK (TMK-5): 1972-1979

Developed and occasionally used as early as 1970, this major change was known by some collectors as the Last Bee Mark because the next change in the trademark no longer incorporated any form of the V and the bee. However, with the reinstatement of a bee in TMK-8 with the turn of the century, TMK-5 is not technically the "Last Bee" any longer. The mark was used until about mid-1979. There are three minor variations in the mark shown in the illustration. Generally, the mark was placed under the glaze from 1972 through 1976 and is found placed over the glaze from 1976 through 1979.

*Last Bee Mark*

## THE MISSING BEE MARK (TMK 6): 1979-1991

*Missing Bee Mark*

The transition to this trademark began in 1979 and was complete by mid-1980. Goebel removed the V and bee from the mark altogether, calling it the Missing Bee. In conjunction with this change, the company instituted the practice of adding to the traditional artist's mark the date the artist finished painting the piece.

## THE HUMMEL MARK (TMK-7): 1991-1999

*Hummel Mark*

In 1991, Goebel changed the trademark once again. This time, the change was not only symbolic of the reunification of the two Germanys by removal of the "West" from the mark, but very significant in another way. Until then, Goebel used the same trademark on virtually all of its products. The mark illustrated here was for exclusive use on Goebel products made from the paintings and drawings of M.I. Hummel.

## THE MILLENNIUM BEE (TMK-8): 2000-2008

*Millennium Bee Mark*

Goebel decided to celebrate the beginning of a new century with a revival in a bee-adorned trademark. Seeking once again to honor the memory of Sister Maria Innocentia Hummel, a bumblebee, this time flying solo without the V, was reinstated into the mark in 2000 and ended in 2008. Goebel stopped production of the M.I. Hummel figurines on Sept. 30, 2008.

## THE MANUFAKTUR RÖDENTAL MARK (TKM-9): 2009-PRESENT

Manufaktur Rödental purchased the rights to produce M.I. Hummel figurines from Goebel in 2009. This trademark signifies a new era for Hummel figurines while maintaining the same quality and workmanship from the master sculptors and master painters at the

Rödental factory. This trademark has a full bee using yellow and black for the bumblebee, which circles around the words "Original M.I. Hummel Germany" with the copyright sign next to M.I. Hummel. Manufaktur Rödental is underneath the circle with a copyright sign.

For purposes of simplification, the various trademarks have been abbreviated in the list below.

Generally speaking, earlier trademarks are worth more than later trademarks.

*Manufaktur Rödental Mark*

| Trademark | Abbreviations | Dates |
|---|---|---|
| Crown | TMK-1 | 1934-1950 |
| Full Bee | TMK-2 | 1940-1959 |
| Stylized Bee | TMK-3 | 1958-1972 |
| Three Line Mark | TMK-4 | 1964-1972 |
| Last Bee | TMK-5 | 1972-1979 |
| Missing Bee | TMK-6 | 1979-1991 |
| Hummel Mark | TMK-7 | 1991-1999 |
| Millennium Bee/Goebel Bee | TMK-8 | 2000-2008 |
| Manufaktur Rödental Mark | TMK-9 | 2009-present |

Hum 1: Puppy Love, trademarks 1-6 .... **$125-$2,400**

► Hum 2: Little Fiddler, trademarks 1-8.. **$110-$2,000**

Hum 3: Book Worm, trademarks 1-8..... **$200-$2,500**

Hum 4: Little Fiddler, trademarks 1-8 .. **$200-$1,200**
*The left piece features the doll face with pale hands and face, different head position, and lack of neckerchief.*

Hum 5: Strolling Along, trademarks 1-6.................. **$150-$350**

Hum 6: Sensitive Hunter, trademarks 1-8............... **$125-$1,200**

Hum 7: Merry Wanderer, trademarks 1-8. **$200-$25,000**

Hum 9: Begging His Share, trademarks 1-7. **$150-$550**

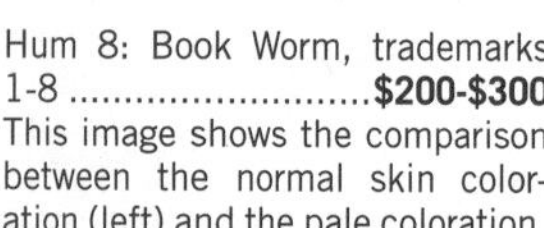

Hum 8: Book Worm, trademarks 1-8 ........................... **$200-$300**
This image shows the comparison between the normal skin coloration (left) and the pale coloration.

Hum 10: Flower Madonna, trademarks 1-7 .................. **$200-$575**

Hum 11: Merry Wanderer, trademarks 1-8 .................. **$100-$575**

Hum 12: Chimney Sweep, trademarks 1-8 .................... **$99-$450**

Hum 14/A and 14/B: Book Worm bookends, trademarks 1-7 .. **$350-$800**

Hum 13: Meditation, trademarks 1-8 .......................... **$99-$2,750**

Hum 15: Hear Ye, Hear Ye, trademarks 1-8 .................. **$125-$650**

Hum 16: Little Hiker, trademarks 1-8 ........................... **$140-$500**

Hum 18: Christ Child, trademarks 1-7 ............................... **$125-$250**

◀ Hum 17: Congratulations, trademarks 1-7 .................. **$200-$2,000**

Hum 20: Prayer Before Battle, trademarks 1-8 ....................... **$200-$450**

Hum 21: Heavenly Angel, trademarks 1-8. **$125-$800**

Hum 22: Angel With Bird holy water font, trademarks 1-8......... **$50-$275**

Hum 24: Lullaby candleholder, trademarks 1-7 ....................... **$150-$900**

Hum 26: Child Jesus holy water font, trademarks 1-7 ................. **$40-$400**

Hum 23: Adoration, trademarks 1-8 ...................................... **$250-$900**

Hum 25: Angelic Sleep candleholder, trademarks 1-6 ...................................................... **$150-$450**

Hum 27: Joyous News, trademarks 1-7.... **$225-$750**

Hum 28: Wayside Devotion, trademarks 1-8 .............. **$275-$1,100**

Hum 29: Guardian Angel holy water font (closed edition), trademarks 1-3 .............. **$800-$1,400**

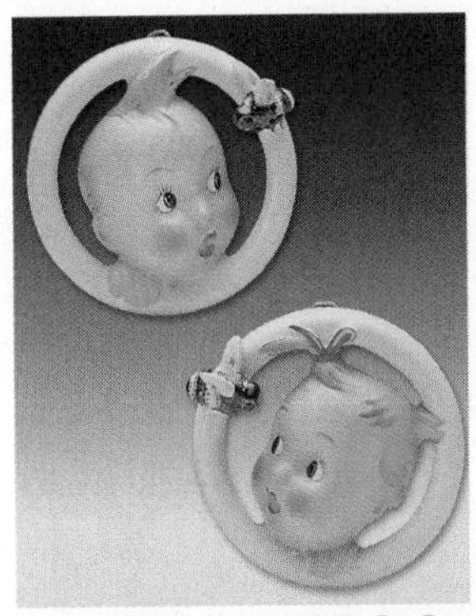

Hum 30/A and Hum 30/B: Ba-Bee Rings wall plaques, trademarks 1-8 ........................ **$220-$1,400**

Hum 31: Advent Group candleholder, trademark 1 ............................................................ **$12,000**

Hum 34: Singing Lesson ashtray, trademarks 1-6 ............................................................ **$125-$350**

Hum 32: Little Gabriel, trademarks 1-7 .............. **$150-$1,300**

Hum 33: Joyful ashtray, trademarks 1-6 .................. **$125-$350**

▶ Hum 35: Good Shepherd holy water font, trademarks 1-8 .................................. **$50-$350** (yellow lamb and green grass)

Hum 36: Child With Flowers holy water font, trademarks 1-8 ..................................**$50-$200**

Hum 37: Herald Angels candleholder, trademarks 1-6..........**$150-$300**

Hum 38, Hum 39, and Hum 40: Angel Trio candleholders, trademarks 1-8 ............................**$70-$350 each**

Hum 42: Good Shepherd, trademarks 1-7...............**$195-$5,500**

Hum 43: March Winds, trademarks 1-8....................**$55-$400**

Hum 47: Goose Girl, trademarks 1-8 ...........................**$120-$780**

Hum 44/A and 44/B: Culprits and Out of Danger table lamps, trademarks 1-6 ................................................................ **$195-$450 each**

Hum 48: Madonna plaque, trademarks 1-6 ................. **$55-$1,200**

Hum 49: To Market, trademarks 1-8 ........................ **$110-$1,020**

Hum 50: Volunteers, trademarks 1-8 ............................ **$140-$900**

Hum 51: Village Boy, trademarks 1-8 ................................ **$55-$690**

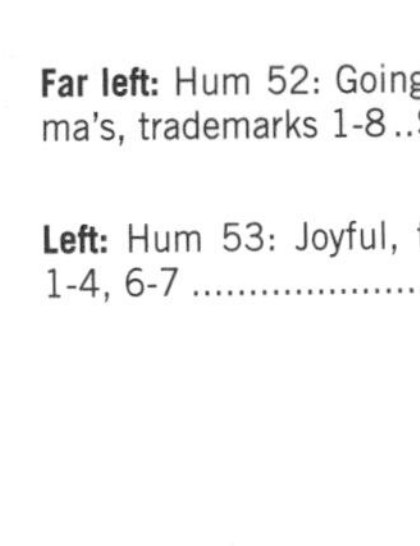

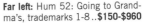

**Far left:** Hum 52: Going to Grandma's, trademarks 1-8 .. **$150-$960**

**Left:** Hum 53: Joyful, trademarks 1-4, 6-7 ........................ **$85-$270**

Hum III/53: Joyful candy box, trademarks 1-7...........**$120-$510**

Hum 54: Silent Night candleholder, trademarks 1-7..........**$220-$9,000**

Hum 55: Saint George, trademarks 1-7...............**$210-$1,800**

Hum 57: Chick Girl, trademarks 1-8...........................**$110-$630**

Hum III/57: Chick Girl candy box, trademarks 1-7 .................................**$105-$510**

Hum 58: Playmates, trademarks 1-8 ...........................**$115-$600**

Hum 59: Skier, trademarks 1-8...............**$140-$515**

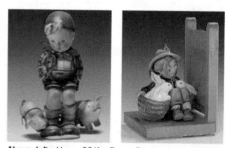

**Above left:** Hum 60/A: Farm Boy and Hum 60/B: Goose Girl bookends, trademarks 1-6 ......**$250-$760**
**Above right:** Hum 61/A: Playmates and Hum 61/B: Chick Girl bookends, trademarks 1-6.......**$250-$760**

►Hum 62: Happy Pastime ashtray, trademarks 1-6 ..............................................................**$95-$390**

# Lady Head Vases

"Lady head vases," also known as "lady head planters" or simply "head vases," reached their zenith of popularity in the 1950s and '60s, when florist shops found them a novel and inexpensive means of boosting sales. Flower overstock (which would normally be discarded) was gathered in small bouquets and used to adorn the hats of these ceramic figural novelties. Although initially a floral industry sideline, head vases quickly became collectible in their own right as consumers became attracted to their imaginative styling and seemingly infinite variations.

The term "lady head vase" was a natural identifier, since many of the most popular early vases depict beauties of the Gay '90s era decked out in large picture hats with openings in the crown (the better to display their floral bounty). Thanks to public demand, however, head vases soon celebrated every theme and nationality: clowns, children, Disney and nursery rhyme characters, holiday figures, Orientals, Asians, Africans, and favorites from television and the movies. With the introduction of male figures, the "lady head" label became somewhat inaccurate. Although often just a companion piece, the gentlemen sometimes branched out on their own in depictions ranging from cowboys to Howdy Doody.

The function of a head vase also expanded. Variations included "umbrella girls," each holding an umbrella in an upraised hand; head vase lamps; and figures with jewelry and other accent pieces added after firing.

Due to import restrictions during World War II, the United States initially led the parade of head vase production. Domestic firms such as Ceramic Arts Studio, Betty Lou Nichols, Dorothy Kindell, Royal Copley, Florence, and many more all turned their talents, at one time or another, to head vase design. Head vases can even be found bearing the marks of such unlikely producers as Van Briggle and Roseville.

The opening of overseas markets in the early 1950s eventually reduced U.S. head vase manufacture to a trickle, as imports, many from Japan, cornered the market. Unhampered by copyrights, these mass-produced vases often directly imitated their United States counterparts, but at a lower cost (and quality).

Originality resurfaced, however, with the ongoing consumer appetite for variety. The 1960s fad for bouffant hairdos, for instance, resulted in a seemingly endless series of head vases that abandoned hats entirely; the floral opening was placed directly in the hair or as part of a bow or headband.

As new celebrities took center stage, they also found themselves achieving head vase immortality. A weeping Jacqueline Kennedy (complete with miniature figures of her

Top view of an unmarked head vase, jeweled "spaghetti" trim surrounds the floral opening, 4-3/4" h. .................................. **$50-$60**

Unmarked head-and-hand vase, black with floral trim, 6" h. .................................. **$65-$85**

Napco "ribbon lady," 4" h. .................................. **$55-$65**

children) remains one of the most in-demand head vases, as are those celebrating such timeless personalities as Marilyn Monroe and Lucille Ball. By the early 1970s, head vases, along with many other mid-century figural ceramics, began to fade from the popular consciousness. If thought of at all, they were regarded as dime-store relics of an earlier time. In recent years there's been a head vase renaissance, due largely to the efforts of such authors as Maddy Gordon, Kathleen Cole, David Barron, and, most notably, the Head Hunters Collectors Association.

Each year, the Head Hunters sponsor a convention with thousands of head vases available for purchase; avid collectors are kept happy year-round with a quarterly newsletter. The Head Hunters have also championed the cause of new head vase production, with the annual release of a limited edition convention commemorative.

Today, collectors worldwide are once again appreciating the artistry and whimsical imagination that went into head vase creation. Whether put to their original use, stuffed with netting, used as pencil or eyeglass holders, or simply left unadorned, ceramic head vases retain the same appeal they held in the 1950s.

Hedi Schoop's cherub heads, 9" h, 8" h. ........ **$125-$150 ea.**

"Yulan & Shen," Oriental pair by Florence Ceramics, 7-1/2" h. ........ **$175-$200 ea.**

Wall pocket head by Kaye of Hollywood, 5-3/4" h. ........ **$100-$125**

Exotic Dorothy Kindell head vases, 5-1/2" h.; 7" h. ........ **$100-$125 ea.**

"Marie the Maid" and "The Little Chef" wall pocket heads by Cleminsons of California, 7-1/2" h., 7" h. "Marie" was originally filled with potholders. .......................................................... **$50-$75 each**

Head vase by Kathi Urbach for Ucagco, with textured finish on headdress and collar, 6" h. ....... **$100-$125**

"Bonnie" and "Barbie," two "hat girls" by Betty Harrington for Ceramic Arts Studio, 7" h. **$125-$150 ea.**

A Van Briggle head, with characteristic "Anna Van Briggle" drip glaze, 11" h. ..................... **$200-$225**

The Madonna's hands encircle the flower opening on this Hermione head; wire hair was Hermione's signature style, 5-3/4" h. ............................... **$175-$200**

"Valerie" by Betty Lou Nichols, 5-1/4" h. **$150-$175**

Japanese copy of Betty Lou's "Valerie," 6-1/4" h. ................................................................ **$25-$35**

"Sven & Svea," a 1950 Ceramic Arts Studio pair, came with instructions on where to place the flowers, 6" h., 5-3/4" h. ..........................**$350-$400/pr.**

Lefton imports, the Gay '90s winking man and partner. Woman, 6-1/4" h.; man, 6" h. ..........................**$120-$140/pr.**

The red-headed half of this unmarked couple is popularly referred to as "Lucy" (although her companion bears little resemblance to "Ricky"), 6-1/2" h., 6-1/4" h. ................ **$90-$110/pr.**

"Celeste 1944 — On the Air Flair," designed by Debby Kaspari for "Cameo Girls," 7-1/2" h. .................................. **$75-$100**

Debby Kaspari's "Cameo Girl," "Abigail 1954 — Let's Rock," displays the latest Elvis hit, 6" h. .... **$75-$100**

"Sasha 1964—Perfect Match." This "Cameo Girl" was designed by Debby Kaspari as a commemorative for the 2004 Head Vase Collectors Convention, 5-1/4" h. ............................................ **$300-$325**

FIGURINES

# Lladró

"Clown with Concertina" (#1027G/M) was first issued in the mid-1960s and retired in 1993. It was sculpted by Salvador Furió..... **$800-$875**

Lladró figurines—distinctive, elegant creations often glazed in the trademark colors of blue and white—hail from a Spanish company founded by three brothers nearly 60 years ago.

Juan, José, and Vicente Lladró began producing ceramic sculptures in their parents' home near Valencia, Spain in the mid-1950s. By 1955 they had established their own retail shop where they sold some of their earliest wares. In 1958 they moved to a factory in the town of Tavernes Blanques.

The 1960s were a decade of such strong growth and development, the Lladró company enlarged its facilities seven times before finally breaking ground for a new factory in 1967. This factory/office building complex, known as the City of Porcelain, was inaugurated in October 1969.

The 1970s were marked by Lladró's consolidation in the American market. In 1974, the first blue emblem—a bellflower and an ancient chemical symbol—appeared on the sculptures.

Lladró's success continued into the 1980s, and in 1985, the Lladró Collectors Society was launched. It lasted for more than 15 years. During the 1990s the Lladró brothers received several awards for their creations, which were exhibited in several cities throughout the world, and the company continued expanding. In 2001, the Lladró Collectors Society gave way to Lladró Privilege, a customer loyalty program.

Today Lladró—still headquartered at the City of Porcelain—employs 2,000 people and markets its creations in more than 100 countries across the globe.

*All photos courtesy Lladró USA, Inc.*

"Sad Harlequin" (#4558G) was issued in the mid-1960s and retired in 1993. It was sculpted by Fulgencio García......... **$800-$900**

"A Basket of Goodies" (#4501G) was one of Lladró's earliest issues, available from the mid-to-late 1960s through 1985. .**$450-$500**

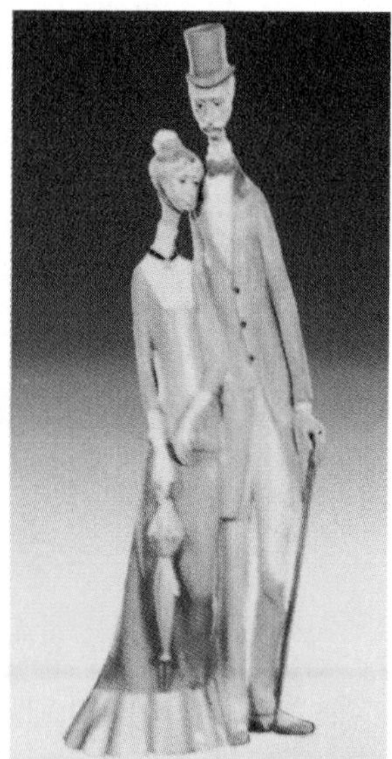

"Old Folks" (#1033G/M) was issued in the mid-to-late 1960s and retired in 1985..... **$1,600-$1,700**

"Happy Travelers" (#4652G) was issued in the late 1960s and retired in 1978. ...... **$1,100-$1,150**

"Beggar" (#1094G/M) was issued in the late 1960s and retired in 1981 ........................ **$800-$850**

"Afghan" (#1069G/M) was first issued in the mid-to-late 1960s and retired in 1985. A later standing dog produced only in a glazed version (#1282G) was issued in 1974 and retired in 1985.
#1069G/M: ................ **$700-$750**
#1282G: .................. **$550-$600**

"Waiting Backstage" (#4559G/M), in Lladró's older elongated style, was issued in the mid-to-late 1960s and retired in 1993. .............................. **$875-$900**

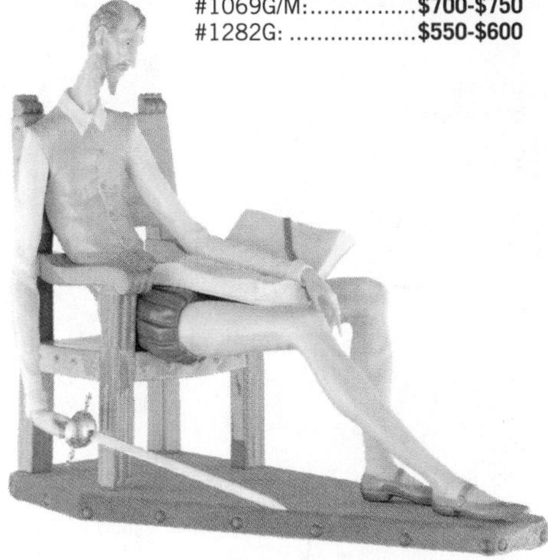

"Don Quixote" (#1030G/M), sculpted by Salvador Furió, was first issued in the mid-to-late 1960s. The matte version was retired in 1991.
Matte ............................................ **$1,700-$1,800**
Glazed ...................................................... **$1,800**

"Boy with Book" (#1024G/M) was issued in 1969 and retired in 1971 ........... **$1,000-$1,100**

"Little Green Grocer" (#1087G/M) was issued in the late 1960s and retired in 1981...........**$350-$425**

"Giraffe Group" (#1005G) was only available in 1969 and 1970. ...........................**$1,700-$1,775**

"Two Women Carrying Water Jugs" (#1014G/M), first issued in the late 1960s, was retired in 1985. ................................**$475-$750**
Matte version .........**$950-$1,000**

"Peruvian Group" (#4610G) was issued in the late 1960s and was retired in 1970..... **$1,400-$1,500**

"Woodcutter" (#4656G) was issued in the late 1960s and retired in 1978.....................**$800-$900**

▼"Antique Auto" (#1146G) was issued in 1971 in an edition size of 750. It has sold at auction for as much as $7,000-$10,500. ...........................**$5,500-$5,800**

"Hunters" (#1048G/M) was issued in the late 1960s and retired in 1985............... **$1,750-$1,950**

"Shepherdess with Goats" (#1001G/M) has the first non-decimal serial number in the Lladró collection. The figure was available from the late 1960s through 1978. ...........**$750-$900 glazed or matte**

"Hebrew Student" (#4684G/M), a popular older Lladró, was issued in 1970 and retired in 1985. It was sculpted by Juan Heurta. ................................ **$600-$625**

"Dog Playing Guitar" (#1152G) is part of a series of cartoon figures in a hound dog band. Issued in 1971 and retired in 1978, each dog band piece is valued at **$700-$800**

"Girl with Hens" (#1103G/M), one of several Lladró figurines in Dutch costume, was issued in 1971 and retired in 1981. ................................ **$450-$500**

"Little Girl with Goat" (#4812G/M) was issued in 1972 and retired in 1988......................... **$400-$600**

"Platero and Marcellino" (#1181G) was issued in 1971 and retired in 1989......................... **$350-$400**

"Three Graces" (#2028) was a limited edition of 500 available from 1971 to 1976 and was retired in 1977. It was sculpted by Fulgencio García... **$3,500-$4,500**

"Othello and Desdemona" (#1145) was one of the first-ever limited editions in the regular porcelain formula. Its edition size was 750, and it sold out by 1973. It was sculpted by Alfredo Ruiz. ........ **$2,500-$3,000**

"Oriental Horse" (#2030) was a Gres limited edition of 350 and was available from 1971 to 1983. ....................................................**$9,500-$10,000**

An early limited edition, "The Forest" (#1243G) was first issued in 1973 in an edition size of 500 and sold out by 1976. It was sculpted by Antonio Ballester. ..................................................... **$6,400-$6,500**

"Bird on Cactus" (#1303G) was issued in 1974 and retired in 1983...................... **$900-$1,000**

"Santa Claus with Toys" (#4905G) was issued in 1974 and retired in 1978. Its companion piece, #4904, is the same Santa holding an empty sack empty. ............ **$1,200-$1,400**

"Friendship" (#1230G/M), issued in 1972, was sold until 1991, when it was retired. ....**$400-$425**

"Cinderella" (#4828G/M) was issued in 1972 and retired in 1998........................**$275-$300**

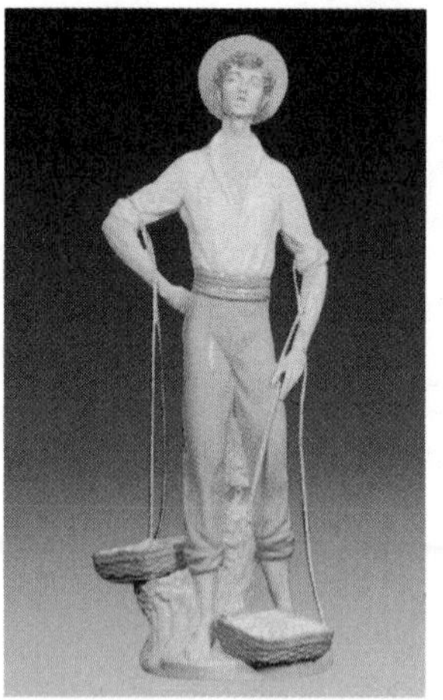

"Fisherman" (#4802G/M) was issued in 1972 and retired in 1979........................**$800-$850**

"Pharmacist" (#4844G/M) was issued in 1973 and retired in 1985. It is the earlier of two Lladró pharmacist figurines.... **$1,700-$1,800**

"Lady at Dressing Table" (#1242G) was released in 1973 and retired in 1978. ............... **$3,600-$3,700**

►"Ducks at the Pond" (#1317), a limited edition of 1,200, it was issued in 1974 and retired in 1984. .................................................**$10,000-$10,500**

"Playing Cards" (#1327) in the Gres porcelain formula was issued in 1976. ................ **$8,700-$8,800**

"The Hunt" (#1308) was produced in an edition of 750 and sold from 1974 to 1984. .... **$7,400-$7,450**

"Car in Trouble" (#1375) was issued in an edition size of 1,500 in 1978 and was retired in 1987. ..................................................... **$7,000-$7,100**

"Spring Birds" (#1368G) was issued in 1978 and retired in 1990............................... **$3,200-$3,400**

An example of "Olympic Puppet" (#4968G) sold for $3,800 at the first Lladró auction ever conducted. The piece was issued in 1977 and retired in 1983. **$800-$900**

"Sad Chimney Sweep" (#1253G) was issued in 1974 and retired in 1983...... **$1,200-$1,250**

"Minstrel" (#4927G) was available on the retail market from 1974 to 1980. ................................... **$1,450-$1,475**

"The Race" (#1249G) was issued in 1974 and retired in 1988. It was sculpted by Julio Fernandez. .......... **$2,500-$2,550**

"Little Troubadour" (#1314G) was issued in 1974 and retired in 1979. ................................ **$1,400-$1,450**

"Soccer Players" (#1266G) was limited to an edition of 500 in 1974 and was retired in 1986. It was sculpted by Fulgencio García..... **$10,000-$10,500**

◄"Scottish Lass" (#1315G) was available from 1974 through 1979. ................................ **$2,400-$2,500**

"Thoughts" (#1272G) was issued in 1974 and retired in 1998. ................................. **$3,000-$3,500**

"Impossible Dream" (#1318G) was a limited edition of 1,000 first issued in 1976. .......... **$3,000-$3,200**

"The Astronomy Lesson" (#1355G) was available for only two years, 1978 and 1979. ....... **$5,400-$5,500**

►"Allegory of Peace" (#1202G), limited to an edition size of only 150, was available from 1972-1973. .................................................**$10,000-$10,500**

"At the Circus" (#5052G) was issued in 1980 and retired in 1985. ............. **$1,400-$1,500**

"Hunter with Dog" (#5002G/M) had a short retail life from 1978-1979. .. **$1,600-$1,700**

"Coquetry" (#4995G), one of many Lladró women figurines in period costume, was available only in 1978 and 1979. ...... **$700-$800**

"Pearl Mermaid" (#1348G) was issued in 1978 and retired in 1983................................ **$1,900-$1,950**

"The Gossips" (#4984G) was sold from 1978 through 1985. It was sculpted by José Roig. ...... **$900-$1,000**

Very hard to find, "Chestnut Seller" (#1373G) was on the retail market from 1978-1981. It was sculpted by Salvador Furió. ................................ **$1,850-$1,950**

"The Harpist" (#6312G) was issued in 1996 and retired in 1999. ............................................ **$950**

"Garden Party" (#1578) was issued in 1988 in an edition size of 500. It sold out in 1999. ............ **$7,300-$7,400**

"Oriental Forest" (#6396G), issued in 1997, was retired in 2001. .. **$900-$1,100**

The enormous "Cinderella's Arrival" (#1785G), issued in 1994, was produced in a limited edition of 1,500. **$26,400**

"Afternoon Promenade" (#7636) was the Lladró Society figurine for 1995......................... **$300-$350**

"Destination Big Top" (#6245G), an event piece, was issued and retired in 1996. ............**$450-$500**

"Daddy's Little Sweetheart" (#6202G) was first issued in 1995 and retired in 2009. ...**$800-$825**

"Guardian Angel" (#6352G) was a time-limited edition available to Lladró Society members only in 1997................... **$2,000-$2,200**

"A Quiet Moment" (#6384G) was issued in 1997 and retired in 1999.........................**$400-$450**

"Enchanted Lake" (#7679G) was issued in 1998 as a limited edition of 4,000 worldwide for Lladró Society members only. It was retired in 1999. ...... **$1,600-$1,700**

# Precious Moments

The Precious Moments line of collectibles began more than 30 years ago when artist Sam Butcher and his partner, Bill Biel, started a greeting card company called Jonathan & David Inc. in Grand Rapids, Michigan. They prepared a line of cards and posters with teardrop-eyed children and inspirational messages, called Precious Moments, for the Christian Booksellers Association convention in 1975.

Around that time, Eugene Freedman, then president and CEO of Enesco Corporation, spotted Butcher's artwork and thought the drawings would translate well into figurines. Japanese sculptor Yasuhei Fujioka transformed one of Butcher's drawings into three-dimensional form, and this piece was called Love One Another. Everyone was so pleased with the resulting figurine that 20 more drawings were given to the sculptor, and in 1979, 21 Precious Moments figurines (called the "Original 21") were introduced to the public. Made of porcelain bisque painted pastel colors, the figurines and their inspirational messages were an immediate hit with the public.

You Can't Run Away From God E0525, 1983 .................................... **$85-$155**

Since 1979, more than 1,500 Precious Moments figurines have been produced. Each year approximately 25 to 40 new items are released and 12 to 20 existing pieces are retired or suspended from production.

Today the Precious Moments collection includes figurines, ornaments, plates, bells, musicals, picture frames, and a whole host of giftware and home décor items. Enesco Corporation produced the line until 2005. Precious Moments Inc., based in Carthage, Missouri, currently oversees the distribution of Precious Moments products.

For more information on Precious Moments, see *Warman's Field Guide to Precious Moments Collectibles* by Mary Sieber.

## ORIGINAL 21

Come Let Us Adore Him E2011
God Loveth a Cheerful Giver E1378
God Understands E1379B
He Careth For You E1377B
He Leadeth Me E1377A
His Burden is Light E1380G
Jesus is Born E2012
Jesus is the Answer E1381
Jesus is the Light E1373G
Jesus Loves Me (two figurines) E1372B and E1372G
Love is Kind E1379A
Love Lifted Me E1375A
Love One Another E1376
Make a Joyful Noise E1374G
O, How I Love Jesus E1380B
Praise the Lord Anyhow E1374B
Prayer Changes Things E1375B
Smile, God Loves You E1373B
Unto Us a Child is Born E2013
We Have Seen His Star E2010

## PRODUCTION MARKS

A symbol or mark is found on the bottom of each Precious Moments collectible, indicating the year it was produced. Enesco Corporation began putting these marks on Precious Moments pieces starting in 1981. Figurines produced before mid-1981 have no marks and are referred to as "no mark" pieces.

The earliest marks are often the most difficult to locate and, as a result, are continually sought after by collectors. They often have a higher secondary market value as well.

1981 Triangle
1982 Hourglass
1983 Fish
1984 Cross
1985 Dove
1986 Olive branch
1987 Cedar tree
1988 Flower
1989 Bow and arrow
1990 Flame
1991 Vessel
1992 G clef
1993 Butterfly
1994 Trumpet
1995 Ship
1996 Heart
1997 Sword
1998 Eyeglasses
1999 Star
2000 Cracked egg
2001 Sandal
2002 Cross in heart
2003 Crown
2004 Three-petal flower
2005 Loaf of bread
2006 House
2007 Hammer
2008 Sylized PM heart
2009 Sheaf of wheat
2010 Tree

Baby's First Picture E2841, Baby's First series, 1984.................. **$110**

Be Not Weary in Doing Well E3111, 1979..............**$65-$185**

Blessed Are the Peacemakers E3107, 1980..............**$60-$105**

Blessings From My House to Yours E0503, 1983.......................**$70**

But Love Goes On Forever E3115, 1979...........................**$40-$100**

Dawn's Early Light PM831, Precious Moments Collectors' Club, 1983....................................**$40**

Eggs Over Easy E3118, 1980 ....................................**$60-$120**

The End is in Sight E9253, 1982 ....................................**$55-$100**

Get Into the Habit of Prayer 12203, 1984........................**$49**

God Bless Our Home 12319, 1985.............................................. **$77**

God is Love E5213, 1980 ....................................**$55-$120**

God Loveth a Cheerful Giver E1378, 1979, one of the Original 21 figurines............................................................................. **$798**

God's Speed E3112, 1980 ....................................$50-$105

He Watches Over Us All E3105, 1980............................ $50-$70

The Heavenly Light E5637, Nativity series, 1981............. $35-$65

**Right:** His Burden is Light E1380G, 1979, one of the Original 21 figurines ..... **$85-$160**

**Far right:** His Sheep Am I E7161, Nativity series, 1982....... **$60-$70**

How Can Two Work Together Except They Agree E9263, 1983...... **$175**

I Believe in Miracles E7156, 1982............................ **$50-$75**

I Get a Kick Out of You E2827, 1984 .......................................... **$185**

Isn't He Precious E5379, Nativity series, 1984 ........................ **$36**

Jesus Loves Me E9278, 1983 .......................................... **$35**

Jesus Loves Me E1372B, 1979 .................................. **$30-$81**

Jesus Loves Me E1372G, 1979, one of the Original 21 figurines .................................. **$45-$130**

**Far left:** Let Love Reign E9273, 1982 .................. **$105-$245**

**Left:** Let Us Call the Club to Order E0303, 1982 .............. **$45-$50**

The Lord Bless You and Keep You E3114, 1980 ........ **$50-$75**

Love Cannot Break a True Friendship E4722, 1980 ........ **$85-$130**

Love is Kind E5377, 1984.... **$32**

Love is Sharing E7162, 1982 ........ **$105-$130**

Loving is Sharing E3110B, 1980 ........ **$50-$120**

**Right:** Love Lifted Me E1375A, 1979, one of the Original 21 figurines ........... **$60-$140**

**Far right:** Love One Another E1376, 1979, one of the Original 21 figurines..... **$50-$120**

Make a Joyful Noise E1374G, 1979, one of the Original 21 figurines.................................. **$100**

Mother Sew Dear E3106, 1980 .................................... **$35-$55**

Nobody's Perfect E9268, 1982 .................................... **$60-$85**

May Your Christmas Be Warm E2348, 1982**$120-$155**

Our First Christmas Together E2377, 1982........ **$69**

O, How I Love Jesus E1380B, 1979, one of the Original 21 figurines............................**$85-$140**

Onward Christian Soldiers E0523, 1983........ **$55-$95**

The Perfect Grandpa E7160, 1982 ........................................... **$65-$80**

Praise the Lord Anyhow E1374B, 1979, one of the Original 21 figurines.......................... **$65-$110**

The Purr-Fect Grandma E3109, 1980........................... **$35-$75**

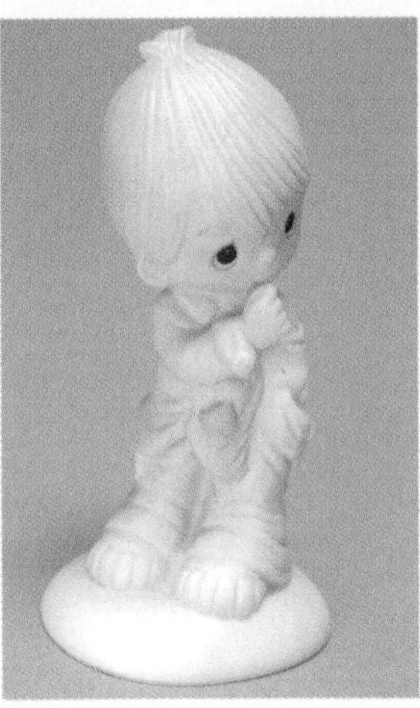

Smile, God Loves You E1373B, 1979, one of the Original 21 figurines........................... **$40-$95**

Sharing Our Season Together E0501, 1983..... **$116**

We're In It Together E9259, 1982 .................... **$55**

Wishing You a Season Filled With Joy E2805, 1980 ............. **$80-$120**

You Have Touched So Many Hearts E2821, 1984....................... **$47**

# Royal Doulton Figurines

Doulton & Company, Ltd., was founded in Lambeth, London, in about 1858. It operated there until 1956 and often incorporated the words "Doulton" and "Lambeth" in its marks. Pinder, Bourne & Company Burslem was purchased by the Doultons in 1878 and in 1882 became Doulton & Company Ltd. It added porcelain to its earthenware production in 1884. The "Royal Doulton" mark has been used since 1902 by this factory, which is still in operation. Character jugs and figurines are commanding great attention from collectors at the present time.

John Doulton, the founder, was born in 1793. He became an apprentice at the age of 12 to a potter in south London. Five years later he was employed in another small pottery near Lambeth. His two sons, John and Henry, subsequently joined their father in 1830 in a partnership he had formed with the name of Doulton & Watts. Watts retired in 1864 and the partnership was dissolved. Henry formed a new company that traded as Doulton and Company.

In the early 1870s the proprietor of the Pinder Bourne Company, located in Burslem, Staffordshire, offered Henry a partnership. The Pinder Bourne Company was purchased by Henry in 1878 and became part of Doulton & Company in 1882.

With the passage of time, the demand for the Lambeth industrial and decorative stoneware declined whereas demand for the Burslem manufactured and decorated bone china wares increased.

Tiger on a rock, brown, grey rock, HN 2639, 1952-92, 10-1/4" x 12" ............................. $1,150

Doulton & Company was incorporated as a limited liability company in 1899. In 1901 the company was allowed to use the word "Royal" on its trademarks by Royal Charter. The well known "lion on crown" logo came into use in 1902. In 2000 the logo was changed on the company's advertising literature to one showing a more stylized lion's head in profile.

Today Royal Doulton is one of the world's leading manufacturers and distributors of premium grade ceramic tabletop wares and collectibles. The Doulton Group comprises Minton, Royal Albert, Caithness Glass, Holland Studio Craft and Royal Doulton. Royal Crown Derby was part of the group from 1971 until 2000 when it became an independent company. These companies market collectibles using their own brand names.

## ANIMALS & BIRDS

Bird, Bullfinch, blue and pale blue feathers, red breast, HN 2551, 1941-46, 5-1/2" h............ **$80**

Dog, Airedale Terrier, K 5, 1931-55, 1-1/4 x 2 -1/4" ............................................................ **$275**

Dog, Bulldog, HN 1044, brown and white, 1931-68, 3-1/ 4" h. ................................................ **$250**

Dog, Bulldog Puppy, K 2, seated, tan with brown patches, 1931-77, 2" ................................. **$85**

Dog, Irish Setter, Ch. "Pat O'Moy," reddish brown, HN 1054, 1931-60, 7-1/2" h. .................. **$725**

Dog, Labrador, standing, black, DA 145, 1990-present, 5" h. .................................................. **$55**

Dog, Springer Spaniel, "Dry Toast," white coat with brown markings, HN 2517, 1938-55, 3-3/4" **$175**

Dogs, Cocker Spaniels sleeping, white dog with brown markings and golden brown dog, HN 2590, 1941-69, 1-3/4" h. .......................................... **$105**

Duck, Drake, standing, green, 2-1/2" ................ **$50**

Duck, Drake, standing, white, HN 806, 1923-68, 2-1/ 2" h. ............................................... **$105**

Horses, Chestnut Mare and Foal, chestnut mare with white stockings, fawn-colored foal with white stockings, HN 2522, 1938-60, 6-1/2" h............. **$695**

Kitten, on hind legs, light brown and black on white, HN 2582, 1941-85, 2-3/4" ......................... **$75**

Monkey, Langur Monkey, long-haired brown and white coat, HN 2657, 1960-69, 4-1/2" h. ........... **$255**

Penguin, grey, white and black, green patches under eyes, K 23, 1940-68, 1-1/2" h. .................. **$170**

Tiger, crouching, brown with dark brown stripes, HN 225, 1920-36, 2 x 9-1/2" ........................ **$575**

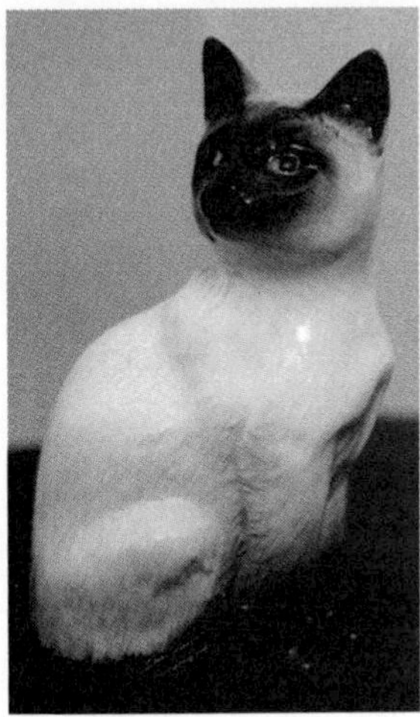
Cat, Siamese, seated, glossy cream and black, DA 129, 4" h. .......... **$30**

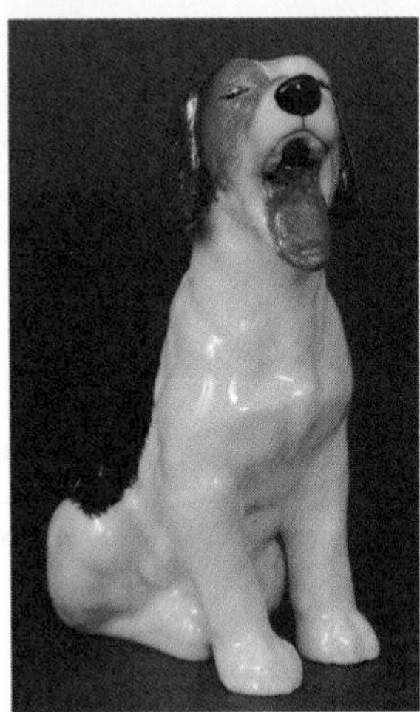
Dog, character dog yawning, white with brown patches over ears and eyes, black patches on back, HN 1099, 1934-85, 4" h. .......... **$75**

Elephant, trunk in salute, grey with black, HN 2644, 1952- 85, 4-1/4" .......... **$175**

Pony, Shetland pony (woolly Shetland mare), glossy brown, DA 47, 1989 to present, 5-3/4" .......... **$45**

Dog, bulldog, HN 1074, standing, white and brown, 1932- 85, 3-1/4" .......... **$195**

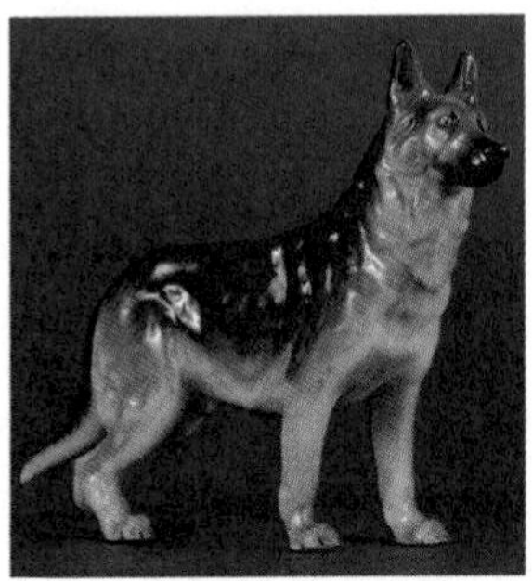
Dog, Alsatian, "Benign of Picardy," dark brown, HN 1117, 1937-68, 4-1/2" .......... **$250**

Dog, Pekinese, Ch. "Biddee of Ifield," golden with black highlights, HN 1012, 1931-85, 3" .......... **$95**

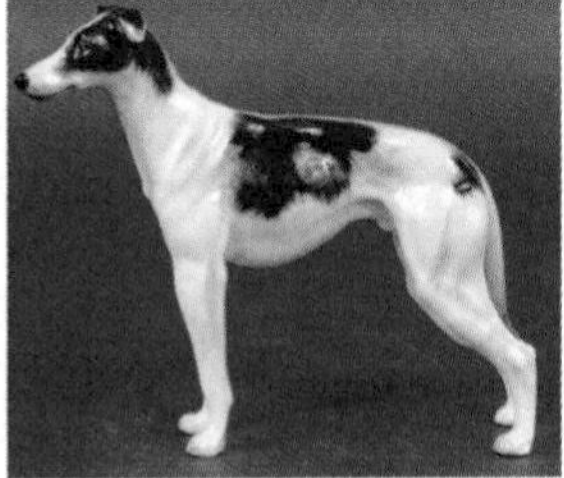

Dogs, terrier puppies in a basket, three white puppies with light and dark brown markings, brown basket, HN 2588, 1941-85, 3" h. .......... **$105**

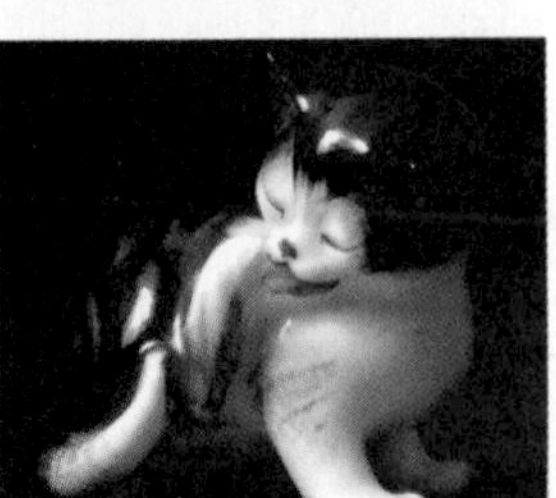

**Above left:** Dog, Scottish terrier, Ch. "Albourne Arthur," black, HN 1015, 1931-60, 5" .......... **$315**

**Above:** Dog, greyhound, white with dark brown patches, HN 1077, 1932-55, 4-1/2" .......... **$575**

**Left:** Kitten, licking hind paw, brown and white, HN 2580, 2-1/4" .......... **$75**

## BUNNYKINS FIGURINES

Airman, DB 199, limited edition of 5000, 1999 **$75**
Astro, Music Box, DB 35, white, red, blue, 1984-89 ........ **$300**
Aussie Surfer, DB 133, gold and green outfit, white and blue base, 1994 ........ **$115**
Banjo Player, DB 182, white and red striped blazer, black trousers, yellow straw hat, 1999, limited edition of 2,500 ........ **$150**
Be Prepared, DB 56, dark green and grey, 1987-96 ........ **$60**
Bedtime, DB 63, second variation, red and white striped pajamas, 1987, limited edition ........ **$425**
Bogey, DB 32, green, brown and yellow, 1984-92 ........ **$150**
Boy Skater, DB 152, blue coat, brown pants, yellow hat, green boots and black skates, 1995-98.... **$45**
Busy Needles, DB 10, white, green and maroon, 1973-88 ........ **$75**
Carol Singer, DB 104, dark green, red, yellow and white, 1991, UK backstamp, limited edition of 700 ........ **$250**
Cavalier, DB 179, red tunic, white collar, black trousers and hat, yellow cape, light brown boots, 1998, limited edition of 2,500 ........ **$265**
Choir Singer, DB 223, white cassock, red robe, 2001, RDICC exclusive ........ **$45**
Cinderella, DB 231, pink and yellow, RDICC exclusive, 2001 ........ **$70**
Clown, DB 129, white costume with red stars and black pom-poms, black ruff around neck, 1992, limited edition of 250 ........ **$1,500**
Cowboy, DB 201, 1999, limited edition of 2,500 ........ **$125**
Cymbals, DB 25, red, blue and yellow, from the Oompah Band series, 1984-90 ........ **$115**
Day Trip, DB 260, two Bunnykins in green sports car, 2002, limited edition of 1,500 ........ **$175**
Dodgem Car Bunnykins, DB 249, red car, 2001, limited edition of 2,500 ........ **$175**
Dollie Bunnykins Playtime, DB 80, white and yellow, 1988, by Holmes, limited edition of 250 ...... **$225**
Double Bass Player, DB 185, green and yellow striped jacket, green trousers, yellow straw hat, 1999, limited edition of 2,500 ........ **$150**
Drum-Major, DB 109, dark green, red and yellow, Oompah Band series, 1991, limited edition of 200 ........ **$525**
Drummer, DB 89, blue trousers and sleeves, yellow vest, cream and red drum, Royal Doulton Collectors Band series, 1990, limited edition of 250 ........ **$525**
Drummer, DB 108, dark green and red, white drum, Oompah Band series, 1991, limited edition of 200 ........ **$525**
Eskimo, DB 275, yellow coat and boots, orange trim, Figure of the Year, 2003 ........ **$65**
Federation, DB 224, blue, Australian flag, limited edition of 2,500 ........ **$165**
Fisherman, DB 170, blue hat and trousers, light yellow sweater, black Wellingtons, 1997-2000 .... **$45**
Fortune Teller, DB 218, red, black and yellow, white ball, 2000 ........ **$65**
Gardener, DB 156, brown jacket, white shirt, grey trousers, light green wheelbarrow, 1996-98..... **$50**
Goalkeeper, DB 120, yellow and black, 1991, limited edition of 250 ........ **$650**
Grandpa's Story, DB 14, burgundy, grey, yellow, blue and green, 1975-83 ........ **$350**

Bath Night, DB 141, tableau RDICC exclusive, limited edition of 5,000, 2001 ........ **$160**

Halloween, DB 132, orange and yellow pumpkin, 1993-97 ........ **$80**
Harry the Herald, DB 115, yellow and dark green, 1991, Royal Family series, limited edition of 300 ........ **$1,000**
Hornpiper, DB 261, brown, 2003 Special Event. **$43**
Jack and Jill, DB 222, tableau, brown pants, yellow and white dress, 2000 ........ **$125**
Jogging, Music Box, DB 37, yellow and blue, 1987-89 ........ **$275**
Judy, DB 235, blue and yellow, 2001, limited edition of 2,500 ........ **$180**
King John, DB 91, purple, yellow and white, Royal Family series, 1990, limited edition of 250... **$550**
Liberty Bell, DB 257, green and black, 2001, limited edition of 2,001 ........ **$125**
Little John, DB 243, brown cloak, 2001 ........ **$60**
Master Potter, DB 131, blue, white, green and brown, 1992-93, RDICC Special ........ **$250**
Minstrel, DB 211, 1999, limited edition of 2,500 ........ **$105**
Mountie, DB 135, red jacket, dark blue trousers, brown hat, 1993, limited edition of 750 ....... **$800**
Mr. Bunnykins at the Easter Parade, DB 18, red, yellow and brown, 1982-93 ........ **$85**
Mrs. Bunnykins at the Easter Parade, DB 19, pale blue and maroon, 1982-96 ........ **$75**
Old Balloon Seller, DB 217, multicolored, 1999, limited edition of 2,000 ........ **$195**
Oompah Band, DB 105, 106, 107, 108, 109, green, 1991, limited edition of 250, the set ........ **$2,750**
Out for a Duck, DB 160, white, beige and green, 1995, limited edition of 1,250 ........ **$315**
Piper, DB 191, green, brown and black, 1999, limited edition of 3,000 ........ **$150**
Prince Frederick, DB 48, green, white and red, Royal Family series, 1986-90 ........ **$125**
Princess Beatrice, DB 93, yellow and gold, Royal Family series, 1990, limited edition of 250... **$465**
Ringmaster, DB 165, black hat and trousers, red jacket, white waistcoat and shirt, black bow tie, 1996, limited edition of 1,500 ........ **$500**
Rock and Roll, DB 124, white, blue and red, 1991, limited edition of 1,000 ........ **$395**

Bride, DB 101, cream dress, grey, blue and white train, 1991 to 2001 ..... **$45**

Collector, DB 54, brown, blue and grey, 1987, RDICC ..... **$550**

Footballer, DB 119, red, 1991, limited edition of 250 ..... **$650**

Magician, DB 159, black suit, yellow shirt, yellow table cloth with red border, 1998, limited edition of 1,000 ..... **$695**

Mystic, DB 197, green, yellow and mauve, 1999 ..... **$55**

Sweetheart, DB 174, white and blue, pink heart, 1997, limited edition of 2,500 ..... **$205**

Sands of Time, DB 229, yellow, 2000, limited order period of three months ..... **$60**

Saxophone Player, DB 186, navy and white striped shirt, blue vest, black trousers, 1999, limited edition of 2,500 ..... **$180**

Scotsman (The), DB 180, dark blue jacket and hat, red and yellow kilt, white shirt, sporran and socks, black shoes, 1998, limited edition of 2,500.. **$185**

Sousaphone, DB 86, blue uniform and yellow sousaphone, Oompha Band series, 1990, limited edition of 250 ..... **$500**

Susan, DB 70, white, blue and yellow, 1988-93 ..... **$125**

Tally Ho!, DB 12, burgundy, yellow, blue, white and green, 1973-88 ..... **$105**

Touchdown, DB 29B (Boston College), maroon and gold, 1985, limited edition of 50 ..... **$2,000**

Touchdown, DB 99 (Notre Dame), green and yellow, 1990, limited edition of 200 ..... **$625**

Tyrolean Dancer, DB 246, black and white, 2001 ..... **$60**

Will Scarlet, DB 264, green and orange, 2002 ... **$60**

Wizard, DB 168, brown rabbit, purple robes and hat, 1997, limited edition of 2,000 ..... **$400**

# Twin Winton

Cute, whimsical and charged with animated energy, Twin Winton's early animal figures are arguably the most overlooked collectibles of any of the great California pottery companies. Although most recognized for its wood-tone stained cookie jars, Twin Winton's animals were what sustained and built the company 16 years before a single cookie jar was produced. Little has been written on these adorable critters.

Twin Winton produced more than 200 different animal figurines, ranging from a fierce-looking bulldog to an ostrich dressed in his Sunday best. And they aren't all little, and they aren't all figurines.

But what's truly amazing about the animals is that they were designed and produced by a couple of 17-year-old twin brothers named Don and Ross Winton (thus the name Twin Winton), who were just trying to help their dad make ends meet during the height of the Great Depression in 1936.

The animals, some of which resembled characters made famous by Walt Disney Studios, also caught the attention of Disney's attorneys, who put the kibosh on production until Walt Disney himself stepped into the picture. Recognizing their talent and discovering it was the family's sole source of income, he pulled his bulldogs off the boys, and production resumed. Don, the eldest twin, would later design hundreds of pieces for Disney that were sold worldwide from Disney stores.

The first animals produced were small figurines depicting woodland creatures — bunnies, chipmunks, deer, raccoons, squirrels, and skunks. By the time the boys formed a partnership with Helen Burke in 1937, under the name Burke Winton, more animals had been added to the lineup, and some had grown in height from a diminutive 2" to a whopping 11" tall. One year later, the Wintons amicably ended their partnership with Burke and opened their first commercial factory under the name Twin Winton Studios. They were now 19 years old.

When Hitler invaded Poland in 1939, Don designed a 3-1/2 inch skunk dressed in full regalia depicting Germany's despicable tyrant. Later he designed three more axis leader caricatures — the Mussolini Skunk, the Goering Pig, and the Tojo Rat. These are the rarest of the animals and are sought after by World War II and Anti Axis collectors, as well as diehard Twin Winton collectors, and they don't come cheap. You can expect to pay upwards of $250. When the Japanese bombed Pearl Harbor, and America entered World War II. By early 1942, both Don and Ross had entered military service, and the plant was closed. It remained closed until June 1946 when they returned to Pasadena and reopened at a new location and under a new name: Twin Winton Ceramics. They also had a new partner, older brother Bruce.

Facial expression and energetic animation are hallmarks of Twin Winton's animals. Pictured here is a rare Running Squirrel on Rocket Log................ **$150**

In April 1953, Bruce bought Twin Winton from his brothers, and production of the animals ceased. Ross went on to pursue other interests, while Don remained as Twin Winton's sole designer on a freelance basis until it closed its doors in 1976.

For the next 50 years and until his death in 2007, Don worked as a freelance designer. Perhaps you don't recognize Don Winton's name, but you will recognize some of his designs. The Mickey Mouse telephone? He designed it for Disney. He also designed the Emmy award, the John Wooden Award trophy, and the Academy of Country Music Award. Both the Richard Nixon and Ronald Reagan Presidential libraries commissioned his work, and Don's bust of President Reagan, which sits on the veranda facing the Berlin Wall exhibit, is seen by millions of visitors to the Ronald Reagan Library each year.

***Brian Parkinson***

This pair of bunny shakers shows a Twin Winton worker had nearly mastered the decorating technique.......................................................... **$75**

Cute and whimsical, this Squirrel with Hammer ($100+) is obviously not impressed with the look-alike chipmunk produced by Robert Simmons Ceramics. Look-alikes abound, but most are clearly marked by the same era competing pottery companies that produced them. The chipmunk pictured here is marked "B&S," which was the mark used by Robert Simmons when he was in partnership with Helen Burke (Burke-Simmons), the same Helen Burke who partnered with Don and Ross Winton (Burke-Winton) in 1937.

Factory workers were taught how to decorate the animals, and shaker sets produced by the workers in training are hard to find. Raccoon-styled shakers......... **$75**

These hard-to-find Axis leader caricatures were designed by Don Winton after Hitler invaded Poland in 1939. Pictured (from left) are the Tojo Rat, Hitler Skunk, and Goering Pig. A Benito Mussolini skunk also was created... **$250 ea.**

**Right:** The fourth caricature in Twin Winton's World War II series depicts Italy's dictator Benito Mussolini as a skunk........... **$250**

**Far right:** The first Twin Winton animals were small figurines depicting woodland creatures, but it wasn't long before more animals were added to the Twin Winton lineup, including this fierce-looking bulldog.......................... **$80**

# Fine Art

Today's art market is truly a global market currently estimated to be worth $56.5 billion. After being dominated by Chinese and Asian buyers in 2010 and 2011, the 2012 fine art market recorded the entrance of major buyers from Russia and the Middle East in dramatic fashion. Christie's, the world's largest seller of fine art works, recorded record sales in 2012. America's super rich are still investing in fine art, most notably Edvard Munch's "The Scream," which sold in May 2012 for $120 million, the priciest artwork ever sold at auction. Leon Black, the New York billionaire, added the painting to his landmark collection of priceless art.

Fine art remains a solid investment, however, turning a profit should never be the predominate reason for purchasing fine art.

*Eric Bradley*

Cizhou glazed stoneware pillow with incised slip decoration, Northern Song dynasty, bean shape with forward slanting top surface decorated with a tiger, cream colored slip to sides incised with floral decoration on impressed fish roe ground, 10-1/2" l. .................................**$25,000**

*Bonhams*

Pair of hexagonal porcelain garden seats with underglaze blue and celadon glaze decoration, Republic period, each with reeded walls molded as bamboo stalks covered in a celadon glaze surrounding reserve panels of flowers and birds, bats and reticulated cash roundels painted in underglaze blue under a colorless glaze, bats and cash design repeating on the top, 18-1/2" h. .....................**$18,750**

*Bonhams*

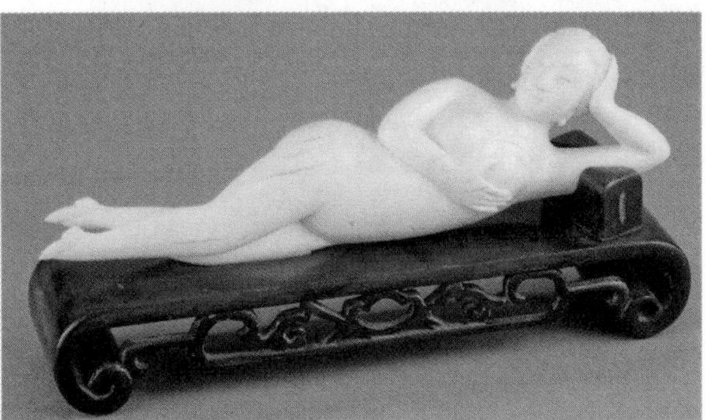

Chinese carved ivory female doctor's model, 20th c., 9-5/8", wooden base 9-3/4" l. ....... **$1,625**

Oil on canvas, artist unknown (19th c.), "Mme. Dubusly," 1835, 29" h. x 23-1/2" w. ............ **$650**

Oil on canvas, artist unknown (French, 19th c.), "Blessing the Ladies," 32" h. x 23" w... **$1,000**

Oil on canvas, manner of Jean-Auguste-Dominique Ingres (French, 1780-1867), "Bathing Women," mounted on masonite, 25-3/4" h. x 21-1/4" w. .................. **$2,200**

Oil on canvas, Sarath Yatawara (Sri Lankan, b. 1949), "The Canal, Venice," signed Sarath Yatawara, 36" h. x 60" w. ....................................................... **$20**

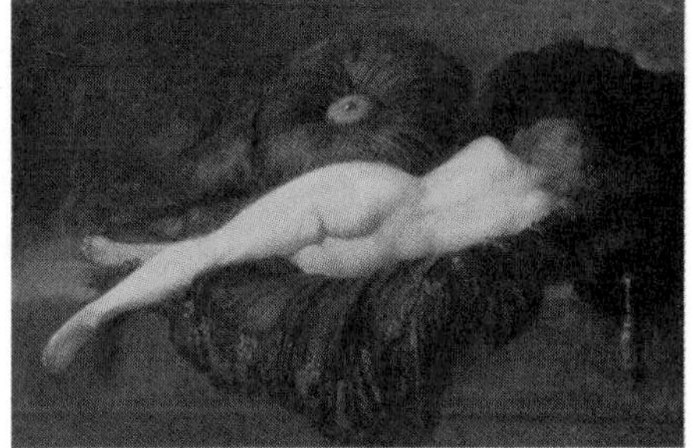

Oil on canvas, Albert Joseph Penot (French, 1862-1930), "Reclining Nude," signed A. Penot, 14-3/4" h. x 22" w.............................................. **$4,600**

Oil on canvas, Frank Boggs (American, 1855-1926), "L'Opera," 25-1/2" h. x 31-3/4" w. ............. **$4,600**

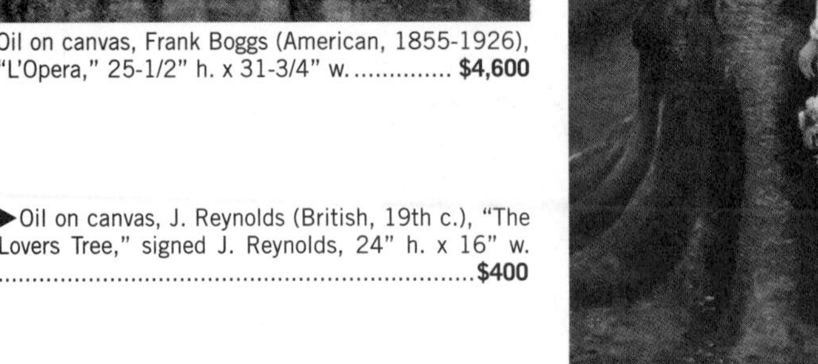

►Oil on canvas, J. Reynolds (British, 19th c.), "The Lovers Tree," signed J. Reynolds, 24" h. x 16" w. ............................................................ **$400**

Oil on board, Tom Lovell (American, 1909-1997), "The Raven Followers," 1975, signed lower left Tom Lovell NWA, 19" h. x 32" w. .................... **$131,450**

Oil on canvas, William Robinson Leigh (American, 1866-1955), "Renegade at Bay," 1941, signed and dated lower left: W.R. Leigh 1941, 24" h. x 29" w. ........................................................ **$388,375**

Crayon on paper, Bob Kuhn (b. 1920), "Moose Drawing," signed "Kuhn" lower right, 8" h. x 11" w. **$4,313**

Set of four Chinese hanging scrolls, "Abstract Landscape," attributed to Liu Kuo-sung (Liu Guosong, b. 1932), ink and color on paper, last bears signature in Chinese "Liu Guosong [Liu Kuosung]," dated "yi jiu liu qi" (=1967), followed by one artist seal, painting: 55-1/2" h. x 29" w./29.3" w./28.1" w./28.9" w. ........................................................ **$30,000**

Oil on canvas, Maynard Dixon (American, 1875-1946), "Calico Hills" (Virgin Valley, Nevada; No.350), 1927, signed, inscribed, and dated lower right: Maynard Dixon / Virgin Valley, Nev. 1927, 16" h. x 20-1/4" h. ........................................ **$95,600**

Oil on canvas, Ogden M. Pleissner (1905-1983), "The Rapids," signed "Pleissner" lower left, 30" h. x 40" w. ................................................ **$345,000**

Lithograph, Samuel A. Kilbourne (1836-1881), "Leaping Brook Trout, 13-7/8" h. x 20" w........ **$173**

Carved wood on plaque, "Striped Bass," originating from South Yarmouth, Mass. ........................ **$1,725**

FINE ART

TOP! LOT!

Planter, jade carving of rare and immense size, detailed, planter depicts complex rendering of a continuous image around the body of a bat above a dragon holding aloft a flaming pearl, and of other mythical creatures amidst clouds, rim is heavily carved in overlapping cloud details and of a creature's scaly body with bifurcated tail with central interior with a medallion carving to repeat the figural dragon carving, 27" d. x 16" h. **$22,500**

TOP! LOT!

Oil on canvas William Robinson Leigh (American, 1866-1955), "Home, Sweet Home," 1932, signed W.R. Leigh 1932, 40" w. x 60" w. .......... **$1.1 million**

TOP! LOT!

Urn, Frank Lloyd Wright, executed by James A. Miller and Brother, Chicago, 1899, from the Edward C. Waller House, River Forest, Illinois, the spherical copper vessel having a slightly flared rim over repoussé panels of interlocking geometric decoration centered with a circular medallion, raised on four conforming square legs, galvanized tin liner with loop handles, marked E.C. Waller in pencil, formerly of the Ralph Esmerian Collection, New York, New York, 18" h. x 19" d. ............................ **$690,000**
*Leslie Hindman Auctioneers*

# Sculpture-Bronze

Bronze is an alloy of copper, tin, and traces of other metals. It has been used since Biblical times not only for art objects but also for utilitarian wares. After a slump in the Middle Ages, the use of bronze was revived in the 17th century and continued to be popular until the early 20th century.

A signed bronze commands a higher market price than an unsigned one.

Bronze sculpture with mirror, "Moon Dance," by Alice Riordan (American, 20th c.), signed "Alice Riordan" upon base, 24-3/4" h. x 21-1/2" w. x 10-3/4" d. overall ..................................... **$1,000**
*Clars Auction Gallery*

Bronze Buddhist guardian figure, China, Ming Dynasty (1368-1644), standing on a rock formation in a military uniform depicting lion heads on breast plates, sleeves, and headpiece, inlaid with hardstone beads, his left hand raised, his right holding a sword, 14-1/4" h. ............ **$6,000**
*Skinner, Inc.*

Bronze sculpture, "Evening," by Alice Riordan (American, 20th c.), signed "Alice Riordan" upon sitter's dress, 23" h. x 8-1/2" w. x 11" d. overall ................. **$1,000**
*Clars Auction Gallery*

Bronze sculpture, "Nature Revealing Herself to Science" by Louis Ernest Barrias (French, 1841-1905), foundry mark "Susse Freres (Paris)" lower left bottom, 22-1/2" h. x 9-1/2" w. x 5-3/4" d., overall, 24-1/2" h. x 9-7/8" w. x 7-3/8" d. with marble base ...................................**$24,885**
*Clars Auction Gallery*

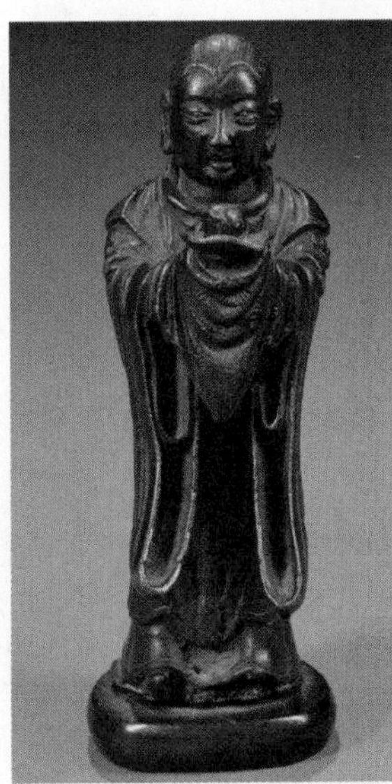

Bronze monk, China, Ming Dynasty (1368-1644), cast as a standing figure of a monk holding a bo in both hands, wood stand, 4-7/8" h. .......................... **$900**
*Skinner, Inc.*

Bronze sculpture, "The Dance," 1908, Bessie Potter Vonnoh (American, 1872-1955), signed "Bessie Potter Vonnoh" lower back base, edition inscribed "No. XXXV" lower back base, foundry inscription "Roman Bronze Works N. Y." lower side base, 12" h. x 11-1/2" w. x 5-3/4" d. overall ....... **$16,000**
*Clars Auction Gallery*

Bronze sculpture depicting two Cossacks on horseback, Lanceray, Eugene (Russian, 1848-1886), signed, approximately 11" h. x 13-1/2" w. x 7" d..........**$23,000**
*Bunte Auction Services, Inc.*

Gilded bronze of a flapper on marble base, Demetre H. Chiparus (Romanian 1886-1947), signed on base, of the period, 17" h. .................................... **$1,500**
*Kaminski Auctions*

French patinated gilt bronze and ivory figural grouping, Demetre H. Chiparus (Romanian, 1886-1947), three children at play on naturalistic ground, onyx base, circa 1920, marks: CHIPARUS, 7-1/2" h. ......................**$13,750**
*Heritage Auction Galleries*

Bronze sculpture atop marble base, "The Epic Battle" by Dan Bodelson (American, b. 1949), signed "Bodelson" at right side, 9-3/4" h. x 19" w. x 12" d. overall ........................ **$1,200**
*Clars Auction Gallery*

French patinated bronze sculpture, "The Favorite," Demetre H. Chiparus (Romanian, 1886-1947), harem girl with fitted robes and veil adjusting her headpiece as she leans back, marble base, circa 1920, marks: CHIPARUS, 15-3/4" h. ...................... **$5,625**
*Heritage Auction Galleries*

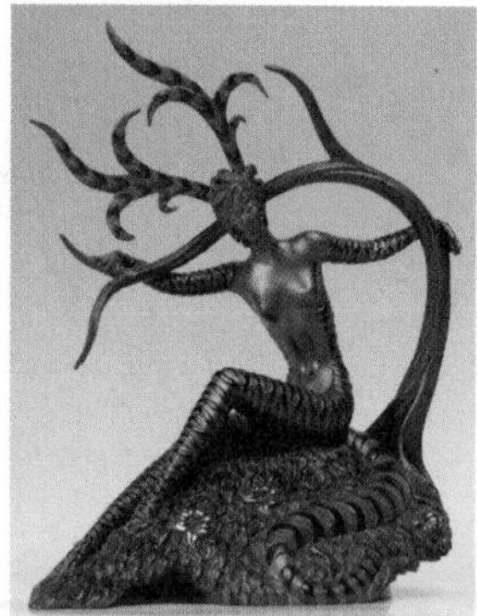

Bronze sculpture, "The Hunting," Erte (Russian/French, 1892-1990), incised signature, foundry stamp "Fine Art Acquisitions," dated 1985, numbered 85 of 375, 13" h. .................... **$3,250**
*Burchard Galleries Inc.*

Bronze sculpture, "Ibis," Erte (Russian/French, 1892-1990), incised signature, foundry mark "RKP Int. Corp," dated 1980, numbered 75 of 300, 15-1/2" h. ...................................... **$3,750**
*Burchard Galleries Inc.*

Bronze sculpture, "Faubourg St. Honore," Romain De Tirtoff Erte (Russian, 1892-1990), edition 110/375, signed on the back of coat, raised on a marble base, 20" h. x 12" w. x 8-1/2" d...... **$2,000**
*Susanin's Auctions*

Bronze sculpture atop marble base, "Poseidon," after Antoine Louis Barye (French, 1796-1875), signed "Masier," an early 20th c. casting, 13" h. x 6" w. x 5-1/2" d. overall............. **$1,000**
*Clars Auction Gallery*

Bronze sculpture, "Lovers and Idol," Erte (Russian/French, 1892-1990), incised signature, "Chalk and Vermillion and Sevenarts" foundry mark 1988, numbered 248 of 375, 18" h., 20-1/4" with beveled marble pedestal.............................. **$3,750**
*Burchard Galleries Inc.*

Bronze sculpture, "Diana," 1854, by Elkington Mason & Co. (British, 19th century), inscribed and dated "Executed by Elkington Mason & Co 1854" lower right base, 68" h. x 21-1/2" w. x 18-1/2" d. overall ..........................**$16,000**
*Clars Auction Gallery*

►Bronze sculpture, "Ribbon Dancer," 1990, by Jiang Tiefeng (Chinese/American, b.1938), signed lower back center, 27" h. x 22" w. x 15" d. overall .. **$1,600**
*Clars Auction Gallery*

Patinated bronze sculpture, "Navajo Women" by Doug Hyde (American, b. 1946), signed " D. Hyde," numbered edition "3/15," 13" h. x 8" w. x 3-1/2" d. overall ..................................... **$1,700**
*Clars Auction Gallery*

Bronze statue of an Imperial German World War I period flag bearer, unsigned, German officer holding his regiment's standard aloft. The officer's equipment on his belt includes a binocular case and pistol holster. In his left hand he clutches his sword with sword knot and hangers visible. Finely detailed uniform with officers' shoulder boards, leather leggings, and spiked helmet. 15-1/4" t., 18" overall on unpolished granite base.............................. **$2,629**
*Heritage Auction Galleries*

La Laitière, alternatively titled "Milkmaid and Grazing Cow," 1887, Isidore Jules Bonheur (French, 1827-1901), signed "I BONHEUR," foundry stamped "PEYROL ÉDTEUR" [sic] on the reverse of the base, dark brown patina, 12-7/8" x 6-3/4" x 17" ... **$4,750**
*Skinner, Inc.*

Russian parcel gilt bronze figural group, Nikolai Alexandrov Lieberich (1828-1883), depicting a hunter, his two hounds and horse, the hunter holding a fox by its hind leg and one of the hounds biting at its scruff, another fox is draped across the back of the saddle on the horse, raised on a naturalistic rectangular base with rounded corners, signed and dated 1861, 13-1/2" w. ................................................ **$22,000**
*Leslie Hindman Auctioneers*

◀Figural bronze, "The Jewish Carter," Leonid Vladimirovich Posen (Russian, 1849-1921), peasant boy and carter on wagon reading Bible, signed "Sculp. Posen Fabr. C.F. Woerfel St. Petersburg," 22-1/4" ............................................................. **$80,000**
*Rago Arts and Auction Center*

Bronze sculpture, "Indian on Horseback" by Alexander Phimster Proctor (American, 1860-1950), signed/inscribed "Phimster Proctor/1898 Gold Medal/Paris Exposition/1900" lower right base, 48" h. x 28" w. x 9" d. overall **$21,000**
*Clars Auction Gallery*

◀Bronze sculpture, "La Fantasia Arabe" by Prosper LeCourtier (French, 1855-1924), signed "Lecourtier" lower back left, 32-1/4" h. x 25" w. x 10-1/2" d., 33-3/4" h. x 21-3/8" w. x 10-3/4" d. overall with marble base ........................................... **$13,000**
*Clars Auction Gallery*

# Folk Art

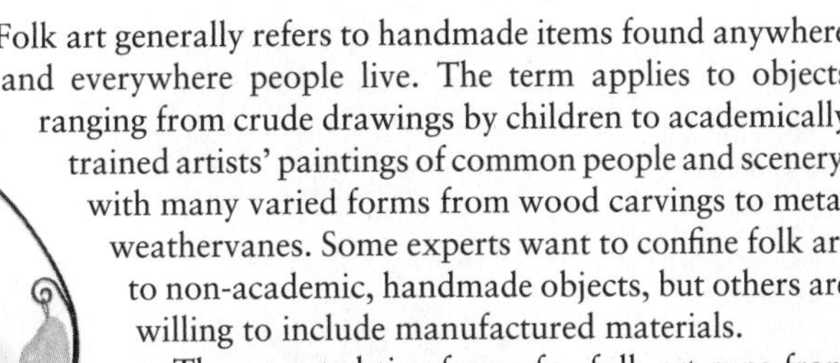

Folk art generally refers to handmade items found anywhere and everywhere people live. The term applies to objects ranging from crude drawings by children to academically trained artists' paintings of common people and scenery, with many varied forms from wood carvings to metal weathervanes. Some experts want to confine folk art to non-academic, handmade objects, but others are willing to include manufactured materials.

The accepted timeframe for folk art runs from its earliest origins up to the mid-20th century.

English painted iron and tin partridge in a pear tree ornament, 27" h., 26" w. .................................................... **$2,607**
*Pook & Pook, Inc.*

## Wallpaper Boxes

Two wallpaper boxes, 19th c., one with a light green ground, the other with floral decorations on a pink ground, 2-1/8" h. and 1-3/4" h. **$830**
*Pook & Pook, Inc.*

Two round wallpaper boxes, 19th c., together with a hexagonal wallpaper box, all having floral decorations, 2-3/4" h., 2-1/4" h., and 1-1/2" h. ............... **$1,778**
*Pook & Pook, Inc.*

Two oval wallpaper boxes, 19th c., together with a round wallpaper box, all with floral decoration on a white ground, 2-1/2" h., 2" h., and 1-3/4" h. ................. **$593**
*Pook & Pook, Inc.*

Three oval wallpaper boxes, 19th c., one with a recessed top and one with a pincushion top, 4-1/2" h., 3-5/8" h., 2-3/4" h................................ **$790**
*Pook & Pook, Inc.*

Oval box, 19th c., with floral decor, 2-1/2" h., 4-5/8" w................................................ **$1,304**
*Pook & Pook, Inc.*

Oval wallpaper box, 19th c., with orange and yellow floral decorations on a light blue ground, 6-5/8" h., 12-3/4" w................................................. **$830**
*Pook & Pook, Inc.*

Wallpaper hatbox, 19th c., decorated with a man in a chariot pulled by a lion, 12" h., 17-3/4" w. ............................................................... **$304**
*Pook & Pook, Inc.*

# General Folk Art

Folk art carved and painted model of a log cabin, 16" h., 32" w., 20-1/2" d. ....................................**$533**
*Pook & Pook, Inc.*

Wood cod fish weathervane, 20th c., 37-1/2" l. .................**$296**
*Pook & Pook, Inc.*

Folk art chip carved frame, 19th c., with love bird crest, 9" x 5"...............................................**$456**
*Pook & Pook, Inc.*

Redware bride's basket, 19th c., probably French, with rope twist handle, floral decoration, 10" h. ..........................................**$300**
*Pook & Pook, Inc.*

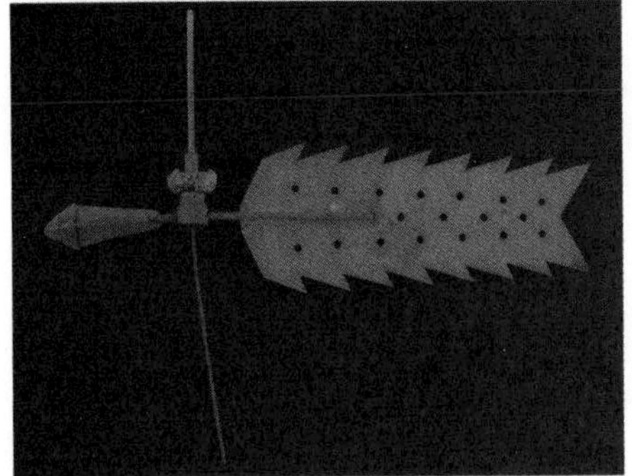

Tin and iron arrow weathervane directional, early 20th c., 28-1/2" l. ..........................................**$207**
*Pook & Pook, Inc.*

Painted sheet iron horse weathervane, early 20th c., 21-1/4" h., 28" w. .................. **$213**
*Pook & Pook, Inc.*

Sheet iron horse weathervane, 19th c., retaining an old white surface, 23-1/2" h., 44" w. ................ **$2,015**
*Pook & Pook, Inc.*

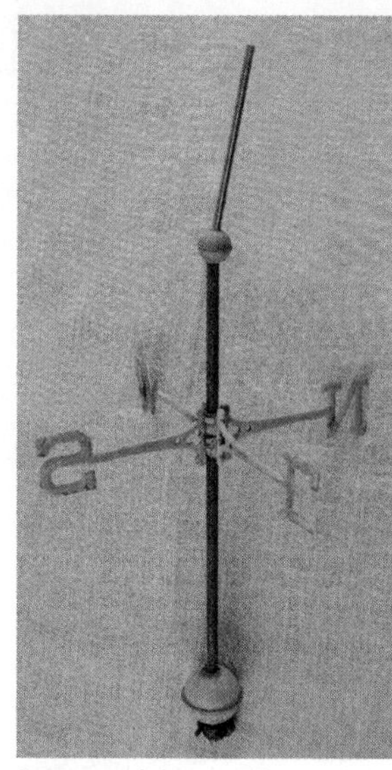

Copper and iron weathervane directionals, 19th c., 46" h...... **$89**
*Pook & Pook, Inc.*

Figure, polychrome carved bird, American, 19th c., with applied carved agate eyes, copper feet, mounted on a wall bracket, overall 26-1/4" h. ................ **$1,896**
*Skinner, Inc.*

Painted tin cockerel weathervane, mid 18th c., 21-1/2" h. ...... **$770**
*Pook & Pook, Inc.*

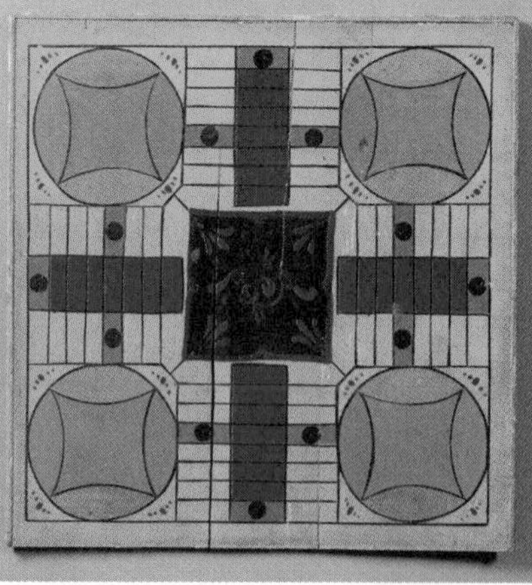

Game board, Parcheesi, American, late 19th c., square wooden panel with polychrome-painted playing field, the "Home" area at center with black-painted scrolled foliage on a red ground, the board composed of two thin wide square panels sandwiched together, surrounded by a thin applied molding, 20-1/4" square. ................. **$3,081**
*Skinner, Inc.*

Hollow body copper rooster weathervane, ca. 1900, 33" h., 36" w. ........................................ **$237**
*Pook & Pook, Inc.*

# 10 Things You Didn't Know About MEMORY JUGS

1. Researchers show memory jugs originated in Africa's Bakongo culture, which influenced slave communities in America. The culture believed the spirit world was turned upside down, and that they were connected to it by water. They decorated graves with water bearing items (shells, pitchers, jugs or vases), which would help the deceased through the watery world to the afterlife. Items were broken to release the loved one's spirit so as to make the journey.

*Appalachian History*

2. A surge of interest in memory jugs took place during the late 19th century as "scrapbooking" Victorians sought to keep their mementos in one place.

3. Jugs are often found coated in a thick layer of lacquer or gold paint to further glorify the recipient.

4. Memory jugs are also called forget-me-not jugs, memory vessels, mourning jugs, spirit jars, ugly jugs, whatnot jars, and whimsy jars.

*Encyclopedia of American Folk Art*

5. The matrix used to hold objects in place include mortar, plaster, and river clay or windowpane putty.

6. Most makers did not sign their work, however it is possible to date a memory jug by determining its under-structure or identifying the type of adhesive used.

7. A grass-roots revival of "memory jug making" swept through Appalachia and the African-American south in the 1950s and 1960s. *Appalachian History*

8. A revival of memory jug art is taking place in contemporary "found object sculptures." *Ohio Folk, www.ohiofolk.com*

9. Values for memory objects range from $20 for simple forms and adornments to as much as $3,000 for elaborate examples with provenance.

10. Other objects decorated with mementos: high-button shoes, cigar boxes, lamps, transistor radios, teapots, and even duck decoys.

*Ames Gallery of Berkeley, Calif., www.AmesGallery.com*

This American memory jug, 10" high, circa 1900, plastered with shards of metal, china, and clay objects along with toys and shells, sold for $50 by Cowan's Auctions, Inc., on May 22, 2010.

This set of three memory jugs sold for $500 during a May 2010 auction by Slotin Folk Art of Gainesville, Georgia.

# The Franklin Mint

The ads were a Sunday supplement staple: limited edition collectibles of every type, from dolls to die-cast cars, coins to Civil War commemoratives, "available only through this advance invitation." The supplier was The Franklin Mint, which began stoking and satisfying the collecting urge in 1964.

Founded by Joseph Segal and originally headquartered in Pennsylvania, The Franklin Mint first specialized in exactly what its name implied: the private minting of commemorative medallions and coins of gold, silver, and other precious metals. Usually, subscribers agreed to purchase an entire set; shipments (and invoices) were then sent monthly. Themes focused on topics that could conveniently be shoehorned into an ongoing series: famous personages, important historical events, and other iconic images from popular culture.

Among the many and varied collectibles released by The Franklin Mint over the years were plates, plaques, figurines, decorative knives, and even games. These ranged from one-of-a-kind Monopoly sets to a re-creation of the three-dimensional chess set popularized on television's "Star Trek."

The limited edition guarantee was achieved in one of several ways: Sometimes only a pre-specified number of the collectibles were minted (the original molds then "destroyed forever"). An edition could also be time-limited, with a strictly enforced closing date for purchase reservations. Still other editions were subscriber-limited: Reservations ended when a fixed number of pre-orders had been placed. The goal, however, always remained the same: exclusivity. While the quality of the item was emphasized, even more heavily stressed was the fact that production would soon cease, making it unattainable, and therefore more desirable. The aura of exclusivity was carried through in the actual products received, with individualized stampings indicating a specific issue number in the series.

Releases by The Franklin Mint were geared to reach the widest audience possible. To achieve that goal the company directed its promotional efforts toward ads in inexpensive general interest magazines and in direct mailings. A purchase from The Franklin Mint was a virtual guarantee of ongoing future offers.

In addition to its array of object collectibles, The Franklin Mint also oversaw such unique projects as the "Franklin Library" and "The 100 Greatest Classical Recordings of All Time." The Library, in operation from 1973-2000, released innumerable editions of literary classics, all in "fine library bindings." The "Greatest Recordings" of the 1970s and 1980s were just that: recorded performances by renowned musical organizations, including the New York Philharmonic and the NBC Symphony, under such acclaimed conductors as Bernstein and Toscanini. Elegance was emphasized: Each two-record release came in a bound case, and the records themselves were red vinyl.

Plate, Princess Diana portrait, 8" dia. .......................................**$5**

The Franklin Mint enterprise was acquired by Warner Communications in 1980, then sold to API (aka Roll International) in 1985, and later to The Morgan Mint, and a series of private investors. Now Manhattan-based, The Franklin Mint capitalizes on its reputation with the release of new collectibles as well as the re-release of past favorites, revised for today's generation.

The value of any collectibles issued by The Franklin Mint has never been in their rarity. Even though these were limited editions, the "limited" quantity was invariably quite high. Values on the secondary market are, in most cases, at or well below original purchase price. This, of course, makes them an ideal acquisition for those wishing to quickly (and inexpensively) amass a collection of die-cast luxury autos, for example, or tribute memorabilia, celebrating such personalities as the late Diana, Princess of Wales. The most important factor for consideration in their purchase is the immediate appeal, whether visual or sentimental. That perceived individual value might be considerable; any value as a possible investment for the future may prove considerably less, however.

Book set, World's Greatest Novels, 132 books in 114 volumes, leather-bound limited editions, silk page markers, gilt edges.................................... **$4,750**

Car figures, 11 sterling miniature automobiles, 64 troy oz. ................................................... **$1,400**

Ingots, sterling silver, 1973 and 1974 Franklin Mint Silver Bank Ingots, sterling silver 1000 grains, 50 ingots in each presentation case, total of 100 ingots, each set 104 oz, total weight 208 oz........... **$5,000**

Coin set, World's Great Casinos, Proof condition in sterling silver............................................. **$350**

Figurine set, wildlife, lot of 10, mid-1970s, tallest 4-1/2" h. ................................................... **$120**

English cottage, highly detailed Cotswold cottage with thatched roof, original furnishings and accessories, four rooms and landscaped garden, 22-1/2" h. x 27" w. x 17" d. ............................................................ **$550**

Figurines, set of nine butterflies, "Butterflies of the World": The Lilac Tree Nymph, Tiger Swallowtail, The Tiger, Malachite, Adonis Blue, The Royal Assyrian, Owl, Tufted Jungle King, and Monarch, with original boxes and brochures ........ **$40**

Figures, Revolutionary War Continental soldiers, lot of 13, mid-1970s, each approximately 4" h. ........ **$160**

Figurines, Faberge for Franklin Mint, "Sapphire Garden," eight gold-toned and enameled eggs depicting florals, birds, and butterflies, glass dome top, 6" ........ **$40**

Japanese sterling silver medallion, sculpted by T Matsuoka, 1972, 6.53 troy oz. ........ **$150**

Figurine, barn owl, designed by George McMonigle, porcelain, 10-1/4" h., 1987, with wooden base and certificate of authenticity ........ **$30**

Figure, Daum Patte D'Verre and crystal cockatoo, signed Daum on base, 1987, 13" h. x 5-1/2" w. ........ **$300**

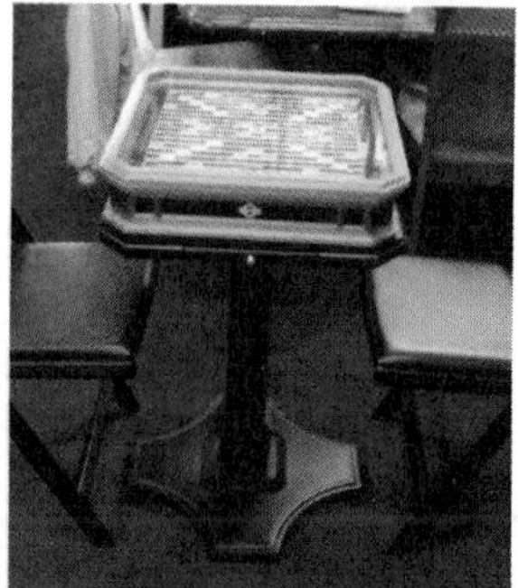

Game table, Deluxe Scrabble Collector's edition with 24kt gold embellished tiles, board and chairs are hardwood mahogany stained, 18" sq., on lazy susan ........ **$500**

Leaded glass table lamp decorated with fuchsia flowers, designed by Paul Crist for the Franklin Mint, 1987, 22-1/2" h., shade 16" dia. .......... **$150**

Liberty brass mantel clock, 13" x 7-1/2" x 6-1/2" .......... **$1,000**

Paperweight set of 12, Baccarat, for The Franklin Mint, crystal sulphide, circa 1977, Queen Elizabeth I, Simon Bolivar, Julius Caesar, Charlemagne, Napoleon Bonaparte, Peter the Great, Joan of Arc, Abraham Lincoln, George Washington, Louis XV, Sir Winston Churchill, and Alexander the Great, all signed, 2-7/8" d... **$450**

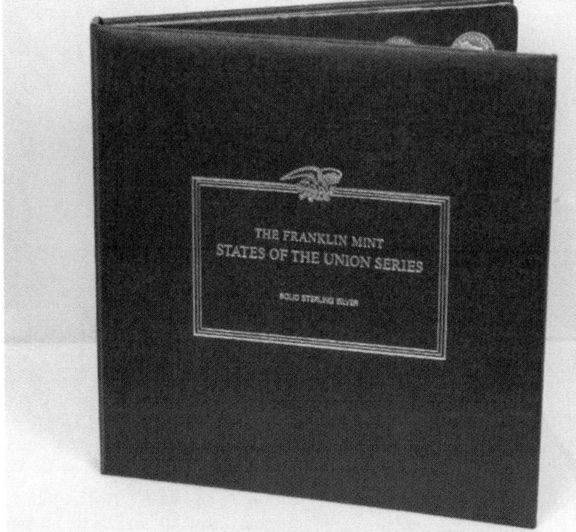


Medals, States of the Union Series, set of 50 sterling silver medals depicting each of the United States' 50 states, "The Franklin Mint States of the Union Series" marked WBL5 and LW155VX, each medal weighs .41 oz. .......... **$600**

Pocket watch, rainbow trout commemorative, limited edition, created by wildlife artist Rick Fields, commissioned by the National Fish and Wildlife Foundation, lid bears an illustration of a trout crafted to capture the look of scrimshaw, face displays a portrait of two rainbow trout, accents of 24 karat gold on the spring-action lid, frame, stem and bail .......... **$60**

Plate, John Wayne "American Legend" by Robert Tanenbaum, 8-1/4" dia. .......... **$75**

Presentation egg, silver gilt, opens to reveal green enameled interior base with detachable brooch modeled as a spray of flowers on two leafs, each set with a diamond, cased. Hallmarked Franklin Mint Birmingham 1977, numbered 77, 3" h., 5.9 troy oz. ............... **$400**

1946 Red McCormick Farmall "A" tractor, Franklin Mint Precision Models, original tag, 9" l. ........................................ **$10**

"The Wyeth Bowl" featuring artwork inspired by Andrew Wyeth, signed, 12-3/4" dia., with original box and paperwork................ **$30**

Set of 12 replica sheriffs' badges, sterling silver, with display case, circa 1980, total sterling weight approximately 7 oz., case 16" w. x 20" h., average badge is 3" w. ........................................ **$250**

Plate, Princess Diana represented as a white rose, 8" dia. ........... **$5**

"Indigo Iris Vase" (with detail), 1987.................................. **$40**

Spoon set of 12, "The Twelve Days of Christmas," sterling silver, in original presentation box, 5-1/8" h., 11.3 troy oz. ................................................ **$350**

Sterling silver Bicentennial bowl with applied border featuring George Washington, Mayflower, Abraham Lincoln, Western settlers, Roosevelt, John F. Kennedy, astronauts, flapper, and other quintessential American icons. The underside reads "The Franklin Mint Bicentennial Bowl / Crafted Especially for / Sue A. Mc Cutcheon / Number 137 of 750 / Solid Sterling Silver / Lined with 24KT. Gold / 1976." Housed in original presentation box, 7" x 14", 171.684 troy oz. ......................................................... **$5,000**

# Furniture

## Antique

Furniture collecting has been a major part of the world of collecting for more than 100 years. It is interesting to note how this marketplace has evolved.

In past decades, 18th century and early 19th century furniture was the mainstay of the American furniture market, but in recent years there has been a growing demand for furniture manufactured since the 1920s. Factory-made furniture from the 1920s and 1930s, often featuring Colonial Revival style, has seen a growing appreciation among collectors. It is well made and features solid wood and fine veneers rather than the cheap compressed wood materials often used since the 1960s. Also much in demand in recent ears is furniture in the Modernistic and Mid-Century taste, ranging from Art Deco through quality designer furniture of the 1950s through the1970s (see "Modern Furniture" later in this section).

These latest trends have offered even the less well-heeled buyer the opportunity to purchase fine furniture at often reasonable prices. Buying antique and collectible furniture is no longer the domain of millionaires and museums.

Today more furniture is showing up on Internet sites, and sometimes good buys can be made. However, it is important to deal with honest, well-informed sellers and have a good knowledge of what you want to purchase.

As in the past, it makes sense to purchase the best pieces you can find, whatever the style or era of production. Condition is still very important if you want your example to continue to appreciate in value in the coming years. For 18th century and early 19th century pieces, the original finish and hardware are especially important as it is with good furniture of the early 20th century Arts & Crafts era. These features are not quite as important for most manufactured furniture of the Victorian era and furniture from the 1920s and later. However, it is good to be aware that a good finish and original hardware will mean a stronger market when the pieces are resold. Of course, whatever style of furniture you buy, you are better off with examples that have not had major repair or replacements. On really early furniture, repairs and replacements will definitely have an impact on the sale value, but they will also be a factor on newer designs from the 20th century.

Whatever your favorite furniture style, there are still fine examples to be found. Just study the history of your favorites and the important points of their constrcution before you invest heavily. A wise shopper will be a happy shopper and have a collection certain to continue to appreciate as time marches along.

For more information on furniture, see *Antique Trader Furniture Price Guide* by Kyle Husfloen.

Delaware Valley Queen Anne maple and poplar corner chair, ca. 1750. .......................................... **$486**
*Pook & Pook, Inc.*

Rare Chippendale carved mahogany reverse serpentine bureau, Charlestown or Boston, Massachusetts, c. 1760-'70, the overhanging shaped top with molded edge above a conformingly shaped cockbeaded case of four graduated drawers flanked by fluted lambrequin corners, on a molded base with conformingly shaped ogee bracket feet, original fire-gilt rococo brasses and escutcheons, refinished, 33-1/4" h., case 34-1/4" w. x 18-1/2" d., top 41" w. x 21-1/2" d. ........................................................**$94,800**

*Skinner, Inc.*

Queen Anne walnut fan-carved scroll-top high chest of drawers, probably Boston, century 1760-'80, brasses appear to be original, old refinish, 84" h. x 38-3/4" w. x 21" d. ....................................**$14,220**

*Skinner, Inc.*

Chippendale mahogany carved gaming table with drawer, Boston or Charlestown, century 1770-'90, the rectangular folding top with squared corners opens to playing surface of early green wool baize bordered by gold-tooled leather, on a conformingly shaped skirt with thumb-molded drawer joined by cabriole legs with acanthus-carved knees and claw-and-ball feet, original brass, old refinish, 30" h., top 34-1/2" w. x 16-1/2" d. ................................................**$14,220**

*Skinner, Inc.*

Chippendale mahogany block-front bureau table, Boston, century 1760-'80, the molded top above a conforming cockbeaded case of long drawer with a carved valance drawer and hinged tombstone door, opening a removable box shelved interior, with three flanking graduated drawers on conformingly shaped bracket feet centering a drop pendant, brasses appear to be original, refinished, 28-1/2" h., case 31" w. x 21" d. Provenance: Family history relates that this bureau table was first owned by Rev. William Cooper of Boston, who was the minister at the Battle Street Church in Boston from 1716 until his death in 1743, and became president of Harvard College in 1737. The bureau table has descended in the family to its current owner. ...........................................**$14,220**

*Skinner, Inc.*

Chippendale carved mahogany tilt-top tea table, possibly Salem, Massachusetts, late 18th century, on a birdcage support, the vase- and ring-turned spiral carved post on a tripod cabriole leg base with leaf-carved knees and elongated claw-and-ball feet, old surface, 28-3/4" h., 29-3/4" dia... **$1,541**
*Skinner, Inc.*

Cherry Candlestand, probably New England, late 18th century, the circular beaded top on a vase and ring-turned support and tripod base of cabriole legs ending in pad feet, refinished, 26" h., 14-3/4" dia., cleat and underside of top both branded "L. Porter.". **$1,126**
*Skinner, Inc.*

Federal mahogany upholstered lolling chair, attributed to Joseph Short, Newbury, Massachusetts, century 1795, mellow surface, 43" h., seat 15-1/2" h. ... **$9,480**
*Skinner, Inc.*

Chippendale mahogany upholstered footstool, probably Massachusetts, late 18th century, upholstered in 18th century floral crewel work, 22" h. x 17" w. x 14-1/2" d. Provenance: James Russell Lowell, Boston.............. **$711**
*Skinner, Inc.*

Chippendale carved walnut drop-leaf dining table, Pennsylvania, c. 1760-'80, the rectangular top on cabriole legs ending in claw-and-ball feet, joined by a deeply arched skirt with conformingly shaped knee returns, refinished, 28" h. x 46" w. x 48-1/2" d. (open)................**$3,200**
*Skinner, Inc.*

Set of four Chippendale cherry side chairs, New England, late 18th century, upholstered slip seats on beaded legs, old surface, 39-1/4" h., seat 18" h..... **$3,851**

Queen Anne cherry carved scroll-top high chest of drawers, probably Connecticut, mid-18th century, replaced brasses, refinished, height without finials 79-3/4", 20-1/2" d. 37-1/2" w. Note: A handwritten label on the backboard reports family history of the piece. Among the names mentioned is Elizabeth Hoag Arnold. ........................................... **$33,180**
*Skinner, Inc.*

▼Pair of Federal mahogany carved and flame birch inlaid card tables, Joshua Cumston, Saco, Maine, c. 1810-'15, old refinish, 29-3/4" h. x 36" w. x 17-1/2" d. Note: A handwritten label on the underside reads: "Two card tables made by Joshua Cumston, uncle of Charles M. Cumston." Provenance: These tables have descended in the family since the late 19th century to their current owner. ............................... **$28,440**
*Skinner, Inc.*

Mahogany tray-top table, probably Newport, Rhode Island, c. 1795-1800, the rectangular top with applied molded edge on a straight beaded skirt with drawer continuing to square tapering beaded legs, mellow surface, 29-1/2" h., top 32" w. x 9-3/4" d. ........................................................ **$4,740**
*Skinner, Inc.*

Rare Federal mahogany inlaid chamber table, Portsmouth, New Hampshire, 1795-1805, the top on a bow-fronted case of three drawers bordered by stringing and crossbanding, joining square double-tapering legs inlaid with leafy vines and stringing and ending in cuffs, brasses appear to be original, refinished, 32-3/4" h. x 35" w. x 21" d. ...................... **$17,775**
*Skinner, Inc.*

Low-back windsor armchair, Newport, Rhode Island, c. 1765-'70, with fine vase- and ring-turnings and cross-stretchers, refinished, 30" h., seat 17" h............. **$948**
*Skinner, Inc.*

Queen Anne maple tea table, southern New England, mid-18th century, the overhanging oval top on block-turned tapering legs ending in pad feet joined by a cut-out apron, old refinish, 26-3/4" h. x 26-1/4" w. x 34-1/4" d.... **$2,370**
*Skinner, Inc.*

Federal cherry Pembroke table, Rhode Island, c. 1790, overhanging oval drop-leaf top with slightly beveled edge, on conforming beaded skirt joining molded square tapering legs, old brass bail pull, old refinish, 27-1/4" h. x 32" d., closed 20-1/2" w.. **$948**
*Skinner, Inc.*

Federal mahogany and mahogany veneer inlaid sideboard, probably Massachusetts, c. 1795, the central drawer above two hinged doors with quarter-fan inlay, flanked by two drawers, old replaced brasses, refinished, 42-1/2" h. x 65" w. x 27-1/2" d. ....... **$2,370**
*Skinner, Inc.*

Extremely rare string-inlaid Federal mahogany partner's desk, Middle Atlantic states, c. 1800, with central short drawer flanked by three graduated drawers, the other side with central short drawer flanked by hinged doors, all on square tapering legs ending in brass cap casters, replaced brass pulls, refinished, 29" h. x 50-3/4" w. x 34-1/2" d. Provenance: Christie's, Tower sale, 1989; descendent of original owner. ...................................................... **$7,703**

Six gilt and paint-decorated Regency armchairs, England, c. 1815-'20, each chair with painted tablets depicting still lifes of fruit, with cane seats, original surface, 33" h., seat15" h. ....................................... **$9,480**
*Skinner, Inc.*

Federal Mahogany inlaid bowfront corner chamberstand, probably Baltimore, Maryland, c. 1800, the folding hinged top opens to reveal a well, the case below with hinged door and drawer, 32" h. x 29" w. x 20-1/2" d. ................ **$3,555**

*Skinner, Inc.*

William & Mary maple gate-leg table, probably Massachusetts, early 18th century, the oval overhanging drop-leaf top above a cockbeaded apron with a deep drawer on block-, vase-, and ring-turned legs and stretchers, on turned feet, refinished, 28-1/2" h. x 44 d. x 51-1/2" w. ........................................................ **$593**

*Skinner, Inc.*

High fan-back braced Windsor armchair, Nantucket, c. 1790-1800, with scroll-carved crest terminals, knuckle handholds, and saddle seat, late 19th century, black-painted surface with gilt striping over original blue or green, 41" h., seat 15-1/2" h. ..................................... **$2,370**

*Skinner, Inc.*

Black-painted bow-back Windsor side chair, attributed to William Seaver and James Frost, Boston, c. 1800-'02, the back with eight bamboo-turned spindles above the seat and similarly turned legs joined by curved stretcher with oval medallions, old black paint, 39" h., seat 18" h. ........... **$711**

*Skinner, Inc.*

Blue-painted braced bow-back Windsor side chair, probably Providence, Rhode Island, area, c. 1790-'95, old surface, 36-1/2" h., seat 17" h. .................. **$551**

*Skinner, Inc.*

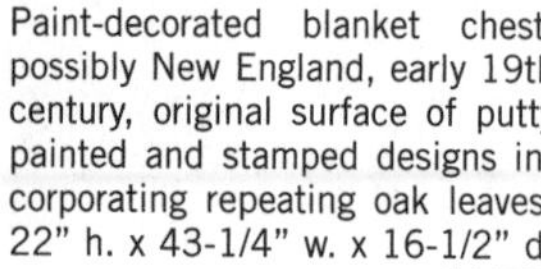

Paint-decorated blanket chest, possibly New England, early 19th century, original surface of putty painted and stamped designs incorporating repeating oak leaves, 22" h. x 43-1/4" w. x 16-1/2" d. ..................................... **$4,740**

Walnut and ash sack-back Windsor chair, Pennsylvania, late 18th century, carved knuckle handholds, vase- and ring-turnings, and shaped saddle seat, 37-1/2" h., seat 16" h. .................. **$593**
*Skinner, Inc.*

Tiger maple carved sack-back Windsor chair, New England, c. 1790, the bowed crest rail above seven spindles and knuckle handholds, on a saddle seat, and vase- and ring-turned legs joined by swelled stretchers, refinished, 35-1/2" h., seat 17" h..... **$1,541**
*Skinner, Inc.*

Federal paint-decorated chamber stand, probably Maine, early 19th century, the gallery with shaped sides above a single drawer and medial shelf joining delicate square tapering legs, original surface of white paint and smoke decoration, top 31-1/2" h. x 20" w. x 16" d....................... **$2,607**
*Skinner, Inc.*

Faux bois paint-decorated washstand, possibly Pennsylvania, c. 1840, height to top of gallery 41", 33" w. x 16" d.................. **$356**
*Skinner, Inc.*

Blue-painted pine chest over two drawers, New England, late 18th century, old turned wooden pulls, original surface, 41-1/2" h. x 45" w. x 20" d... **2,963**
*Skinner, Inc.*

Light blue-painted pine chest over drawer, New England, c. 1800, on bracket feet, old blue paint over earlier blue-green, old oval brass pulls, 32" h. x 42-1/2" w. x 18-3/4" d. ................**$2,015**
*Skinner, Inc.*

◀Federal red-stained maple one-drawer stand, New Hampshire, early 19th century, with single veneered drawer on four square tapering legs joining a shaped gallery, old surface, 28-1/2" h. x 15-3/4" w. x 15-1/2" d.......................................................................**$1,778**
*Skinner, Inc.*

Putty-painted six-board blanket chest, New England, early 19th century, original mustard-brown surface centering the initials "EC," 27-1/2" h. x 49" w. x 21-1/2" d. .................................................. **$711**
*Skinner, Inc.*

Fanciful folk art inlaid tilt-top table, coastal New England, probably Maine, c. 1850-'70, the shaped top inlaid with a variety of woods centering a mariner's compass flanked by ivory hearts, with shaped and scrolled inlaid support, on inlaid platform with scrolled legs, old surface, 29" h. x 20" w. x 14" d......... **$1,778**
*Skinner, Inc.*

Poplar two-part glazed corner cupboard, Middle Atlantic states, early 19th century, the top section with molded cornice above a hinged scratch-beaded glazed door incorporating three Gothic arches, opening to four grooved shelves, on a base with two hinged doors all resting on bracket feet, refinished, interior painted turquoise blue, 85" h. x 42-1/2" w. x 23" d. to corner. .................................................. **$1,778**
*Skinner, Inc.*

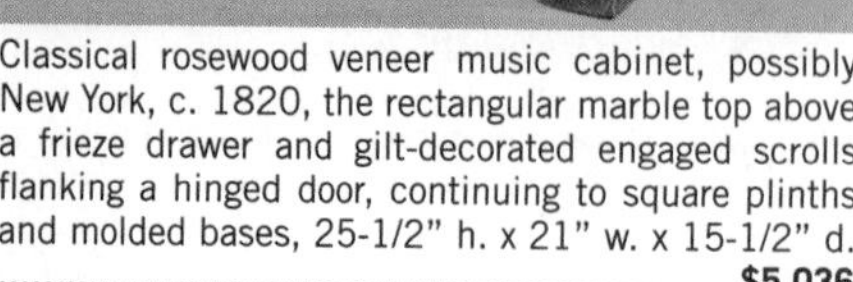

Classical rosewood veneer music cabinet, possibly New York, c. 1820, the rectangular marble top above a frieze drawer and gilt-decorated engaged scrolls flanking a hinged door, continuing to square plinths and molded bases, 25-1/2" h. x 21" w. x 15-1/2" d. ............................................................... **$5,036**
*Skinner, Inc.*

Federal tiger maple slant-lid desk, attributed to Asa Loomis, Shaftsbury, Vermont, c. 1815-'20, replaced pulls, 43" h. x 41-1/4" w. x 19" d. Provenance: Originally belonged to Lemuel Buck and descended in his family, Shaftsbury, Bennington County, Vermont, until approximately 1992.................................. **$6,518**
*Skinner, Inc.*

Classical carved mahogany and mahogany veneer sofa, possibly made by Nahum Parker, Middlebury, Vermont, c. 1825-'35, with circular arms terminating in lyre clock facades, 35" h. x 84" w. x 20-1/2" d. Note: This sofa is one of four of its kind known. Two of the others are at the Sheldon Museum in Middlebury and at the Equinox Hotel in Manchester, Vermont. ....**$3,851**
*Skinner, Inc.*

Paint-decorated sideboard, attributed to the Loomis workshop, Shaftsbury, Vermont, c. 1825-'40, the rectangular top above two short drawers and long drawer, with two recessed hinged doors below flanked by ring-turned swelled pilasters continuing to turned feet, 48-3/4" h. x 49" w. x 20" d................. **$2,489**
*Skinner, Inc.*

Painted pine chest of drawers, probably Massachusetts, c. 1700-1720, the single arch-molded case of two short drawers and four graduated long drawers on turned turnip feet, replaced engraved teardrop pulls, old black over earlier paint, 43-1/4" h. x 38-1/4" w. x 20-1/4" d. ...............................................**$10,073**
*Skinner, Inc.*

Child's brown-painted poplar blanket chest over drawer, probably Connecticut, early 18th century, with double-arch molded case, single drawer, on cut-out ends and valanced skirt, old wooden pulls, old surface, 24-3/4" h. x 27" w. x 12-1/2" d.....**$13,035**
*Skinner, Inc.*

Maple and pine tavern table, New England, 18th century, the oval top on a base with straight beaded skirt and beaded stretchers joining the block-, vase-, and ring-turned legs, refinished, 23-1/2" h., 33-1/2" w., 26" d. ........................................................ **$474**
*Skinner, Inc.*

Black-painted carved bannister-back side chair, probably Massachusetts, early 18th century, with Prince of Wales cresting, block-, vase-, and ring-turned stiles topped by turned ball finials, above the rush seat on block-, vase-, and ring-turned front legs joined to the slightly raking rear legs by bulbous-turned stretchers, old black-painted surface, 46-1/2" h., seat 16-1/2" h. ........... **$9,480**
*Skinner, Inc.*

Black-painted carved maple cane-back side chair, New England, early 18th century, the carved cresting above the molded back flanked by block-, vase-, and ring-turned stiles, on beaded trapezoidal seat, and four similarly turned legs joined by stretchers, 49-1/4" h., seat 18-1/4" h. ............ **$368**
*Skinner, Inc.*

Painted roundabout chair, New England, mid-18th century, with shaped backrest continuing to scrolled chamfered arms, on vase- and ring-turned stiles continuing to legs and double stretchers, old black painted surface over earlier red, 30" h., seat 16-1/2" h. **$563**
*Skinner, Inc.*

Red-painted pine step-back cupboard, New England, early 18th century, on trestle feet, old wrought iron H-L hinges, old surface, 66-3/4" h., 35-1/2" w., 19" d................................. **$3,555**
*Skinner, Inc.*

◀Chippendale carved mahogany block-front slant-lid desk, coastal Massachusetts, c. 1760-'75, the blocked lid opens to an amphitheater interior of blocked and shaped drawers and valanced compartments flanking a secret compartment with carved prospect door, on conformingly blocked case and bracket feet, old replaced brasses, old refinish, 41-1/4" h., 39" w., 20" d. Provenance: Papers found within the desk indicate a history in the Durfee family of the Tiverton, Rhode Island, area. ..**$20,145**

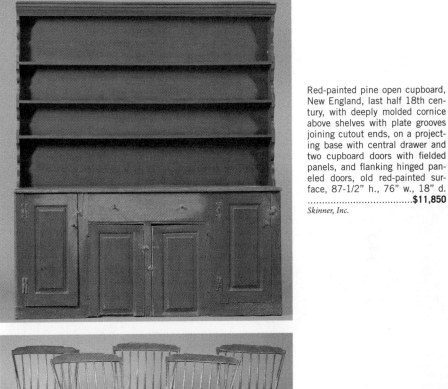

Red-painted pine open cupboard, New England, last half 18th century, with deeply molded cornice above shelves with plate grooves joining cutout ends, on a projecting base with central drawer and two cupboard doors with fielded panels, and flanking hinged paneled doors, old red-painted surface, 87-1/2" h., 76" w., 18" d. ....................................**$11,850**
*Skinner, Inc.*

Set of five painted step-down Windsor side chairs, New England, c. 1810, with bamboo turnings, old worn mustard grain-painted surface, 34-3/4" h., seat 17" h. ........................................**$368**
*Skinner, Inc.*

Set of six paint-decorated and gilt fancy chairs, probably Portsmouth, New Hampshire, 1815-'25, original surface, approximately 33-1/2" h., seat 16-18" h.................................. **$2,133**
*Skinner, Inc.*

English wrought iron garden bench, 19th century, 40-1/2" h., 73-1/2" w., together with a pair of matching chairs.................................................. **$4,740**
*Pook & Pook, Inc.*

Chippendale mahogany easy chair, ca. 1790, with square tapering molded front legs. .................. **$830**
*Pook & Pook, Inc.*

Pennsylvania painted blanket chest, dated 1795, the front inscribed Hanaden Bitsch, with decorated panels on a blue ground, two drawers, and straight bracket feet, 27-1/2" h., 49" w. ................. **$1,007**
*Pook & Pook, Inc.*

New England maple and poplar painted chair table, ca. 1800, with a round tilting top and base with a lift lid compartment, retaining its original red stained surface, 29-1/2" h., 47-1/2" dia. Provenance: Harry Hartman. .................................................. **$3,318**
*Pook & Pook, Inc.*

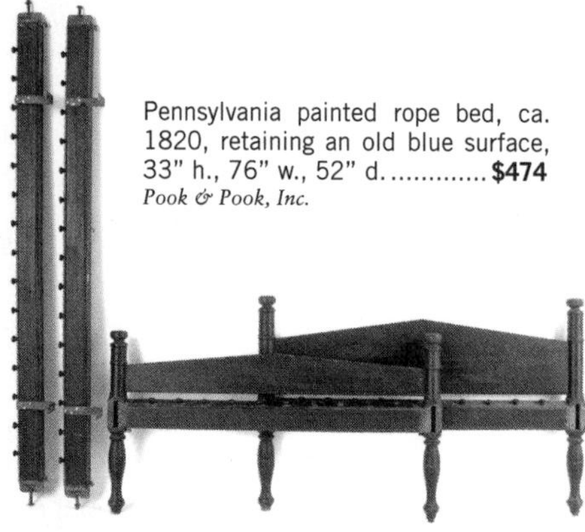

Pennsylvania painted rope bed, ca. 1820, retaining an old blue surface, 33" h., 76" w., 52" d. ............. **$474**
*Pook & Pook, Inc.*

►Continental painted miniature blanket chest, dated 1846, 10-1/2" h., 17" w. ................. **$533**
*Pook & Pook, Inc.*

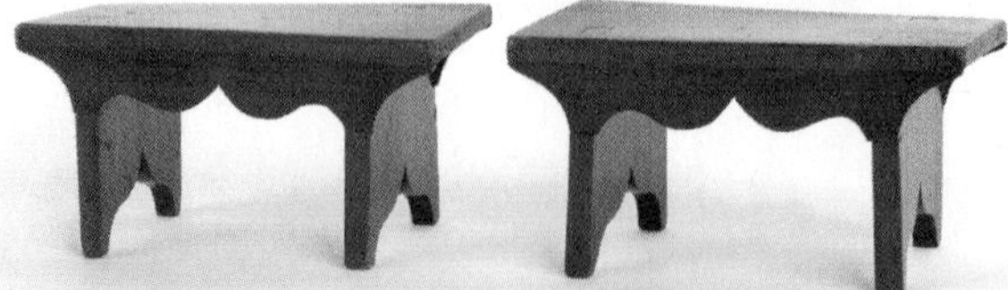

Pair of miniature stools, 19th century, 3-1/2" h., 6-3/4" w. Provenance: Descended in the Pomeroy family. ............................... **$593**
*Pook & Pook, Inc.*

Maryland or Virginia painted pine miniature blanket chest, early 19th century, the lid and front decorated with tulip trees, flanking segmented circles, 8-1/2" h., 14" w. ............................................... **$21,330**

*Pook & Pook, Inc.*

Diminutive painted pine two-part wall cupboard, mid-19th century, retaining its original blue/green surface, 73" h., 29-1/4" w. .................................... **$2,252**

*Pook & Pook, Inc.*

►Pennsylvania painted blanket chest, early 19th century, with orange sponge decoration, 29-1/2" h., 51" w. ....................................................... **$652**

*Pook & Pook, Inc.*

French Empire mahogany dressing table, early 19th century, with mirror and ormolu mounts, 59" h., 37-1/2" w. ................................................... **$790**

*Pook & Pook, Inc.*

New York painted pine chest, 19th century, with a lift lid and two cupboard doors, retaining an orange grain decorated surface, 37" h., 36-1/2" w. .......... **$2,844**

*Pook & Pook, Inc.*

Berks County, Pennsylvania painted dower chest, late 18th century, inscribed Matlena Dordner, the lid and case decorated with columnar panels with tulips and pinwheels, 24-1/2" h., 47-1/2" w. ............... **$3,159**
*Pook & Pook, Inc.*

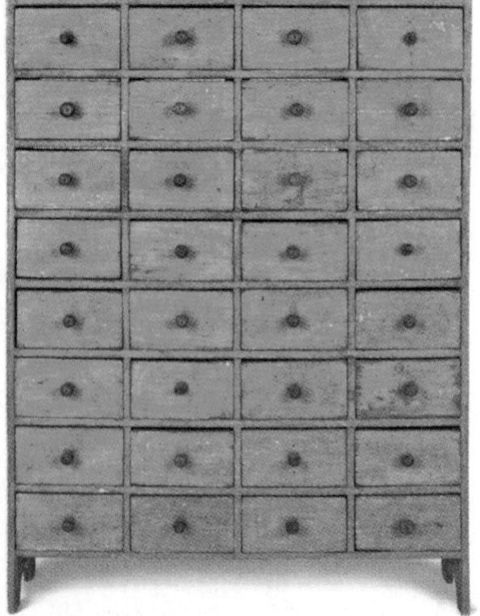

Painted pine apothecary cupboard, early 19th century, retaining an old beige surface, 62" h., 47" w. ............................................................ **$3,792**
*Pook & Pook, Inc.*

Virginia painted walnut, cherry, and pine dower chest, dated 1830, with stylized hearts flanking a wheel above three drawers, 30-1/2" h., 47-1/2" w. Provenance: Sumpter Priddy. ............................ **$4,977**
*Pook & Pook, Inc.*

Lancaster County, Pennsylvania poplar hanging cupboard, late 18th century, with original wrought iron trefoil hinges and scalloped sides, 33-3/4" h., 22-1/2" w. ..................................................... **$1,458**
*Pook & Pook, Inc.*

New England painted Sheraton dressing table, ca. 1825, with stenciled grape decoration on a yellow ground, 40" h., 31-1/4" w................................ **$948**
*Pook & Pook, Inc.*

Pennsylvania or Maryland Windsor bench, ca. 1790, with a low back, knuckle hand grips, and bulbous lower stretchers, retaining an old red painted surface, 31-1/2" h., 84" w. This bench is pictured in Santore The Windsor Style in America, plate 206. .......**$18,000**
*Pook & Pook, Inc.*

New England painted pine valuables chest, ca. 1800, with an eight-drawer interior, retaining an old ivory surface with black pinstriping, 18" h., 14-1/4" w. .................... **$2,370**
*Pook & Pook, Inc.*

Unusual Pennsylvania Sheraton painted pine wash stand, ca. 1820, retaining an old red surface, 34-3/4" h., 19" w. ...................................... **$2,133**
*Pook & Pook, Inc.*

Miniature Pennsylvania painted plank seat chair, mid-19th century, retaining a vibrant yellow surface, 16" h. .................... **$1,067**
*Pook & Pook, Inc.*

George III mahogany wing chair, ca. 1780. ....................... **$1,659**
*Pook & Pook, Inc.*

Massachusetts Hepplewhite mahogany lolling chair, ca. 1805, with line inlay and flame birch inlaid panels..... **$8,888**
*Pook & Pook, Inc.*

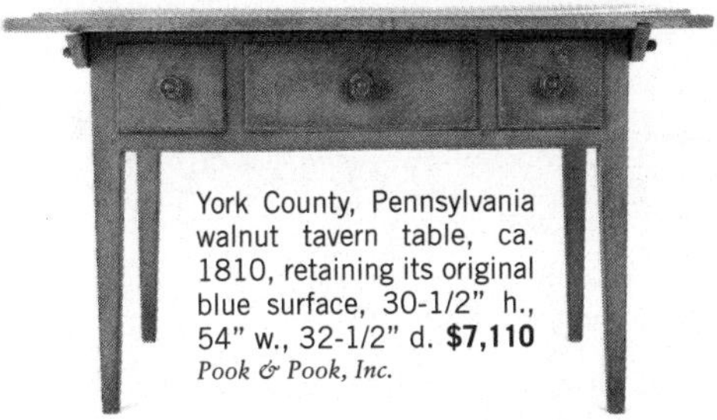

York County, Pennsylvania walnut tavern table, ca. 1810, retaining its original blue surface, 30-1/2" h., 54" w., 32-1/2" d. **$7,110**
*Pook & Pook, Inc.*

◀Pennsylvania painted pine jelly cupboard, early/mid-19th century, retaining its original vibrant red and orange grained surface, 58" h., 45" w... **$10,665**
*Pook & Pook, Inc.*

New England painted pine blanket chest, ca. 1810, with bootjack ends, retaining its original green and ochre decoration, 24-1/2" h., 42" w. ............ **$1,659**
*Pook & Pook, Inc.*

Pennsylvania painted blanket chest, early 19th century, retaining its original smoke decorated surface and red feet, 25-1/4" h., 36" w. ..................... **$770**
*Pook & Pook, Inc.*

Pennsylvania painted poplar wardrobe, mid-19th century, retaining an old faux curly maple surface, 79" h., 44" w. ................................................. **$593**
*Pook & Pook, Inc.*

Pennsylvania or Ohio painted blanket chest, ca. 1825, retaining its original red and green surface, 23-1/2" h., 35" w. ...................................... **$652**
*Pook & Pook, Inc.*

Rare Delaware Valley Queen Anne tiger maple miniature blanket chest, ca. 1755, 12-1/2" h., 25-1/2" w. ........................................................ **$4,029**
*Pook & Pook, Inc.*

Pine open pewter cupboard, 18th century, 73-1/2" h., 53-3/4" w. ......................................... **$1,033**
*Pook & Pook, Inc.*

American cast iron garden settee in laurel pattern, second half 19th century, rounded back comprised of repeating panels of cast laurel leaves within twigwork frames continuing to downswept arms terminating in winged Griffin supports centering a semi-circular seat cast with scrolling vinery, 33" h. x 45-1/2" w. x 31" d. .......... **$1,092**
*James D. Julia, Inc.*

Ohio/Indiana painted bentwood field cradle, canoe-shape body suspended from a sleigh-form frame with two iron wheels, stenciled lettering on interior includes Ohio and Indiana and "Patent Oct. 17th 76," original salmon-painted surface with stenciled and striped decorations, fourth quarter 19th century, 27-1/2" h., 47-1/2" l. .......... **$345**
*Jeffrey S. Evans & Associates*

Pennsylvania poplar two-part corner cupboard, 19th century, 84-1/2" h., 44" w. .......... **$1,778**
*Pook & Pook, Inc.*

►Ebonized humidor on stand, 20th century, 26" h., 19-1/4" w. .......... **$178**
*Pook & Pook, Inc.*

Continental painted pine blanket chest, early 19th century, 25" h., 53" w. .......... **$207**
*Pook & Pook, Inc.*

Pennsylvania cherry cradle, early 19th century, with heart cutouts, 22-1/2" h., 40-1/2" w. .......... **$119**
*Pook & Pook, Inc.*

# Modern

Modern design is everywhere, evergreen and increasingly popular. Modernism has never gone out of style. Its reach into the present day is as deep as its roots in the past. Just as it can be seen and felt ubiquitously in the mass media of today – on film, television, in magazines and department stores – it can be traced to the mid-1800s post-Empire non-conformity of the Biedermeier Movement, the turn of the 20th century anti-Victorianism of the Vienna Secessionists, the radical reductionism of Frank Lloyd Wright and the revolutionary post-Depression thinking of Walter Gropius and the Bauhaus school in Germany.

"The Modernists really changed the way the world looked," said John Sollo, a partner in Sollo Rago Auction of Lambertville, N.J. Sollo's partner in business, and one of the most recognizable names in the fie ld, David Rago, takes Sollo's idea a little further by saying that Modernism is actually more about the names behind the design than the design itself, at least as far as buying goes.

No discussion of Modern can be complete, however, without examining its genesis and enduring influence. Modernism is everywhere in today's pop culture. Austere Scandinavian furniture dominates the television commercials that hawk hotels and mutual funds. Post-war American design ranges across sitcom set dressings to movie sets patterned after Frank Lloyd Wright houses and Hollywood Modernist classics set high in the hills.

You have to look at the dorm rooms of college students and the apartments of young people whose living spaces are packed with the undeniably Modern mass-produced products of IKEA, Target, Design Within Reach and the like.

There can be no denying that the post-World War II manufacturing techniques and subsequent boom led to the widespread acceptance of plastic and bent plywood chairs along with low-sitting coffee tables, couches and recliners.

"The modern aesthetic grew out of a perfect storm of post-war optimism, innovative materials and an incredible crop of designers," said Lisanne Dickson, director of 1950s/ Modern Design at Treadway-Toomey.

"I think that the people who designed the furniture were maybe ahead of society's ability to accept and understand what they were doing," Sollo said. "It's taken people another 30 to 40 years to catch up to it."

There are hundreds of great Modern designers, many of whom worked across categories – furniture, architecture, fine art, etc. – and many contributed to the work of other big names without ever seeking that glory for themselves.

***Noah Fleisher***

For more information on Modernism, see *Warman's Modernism Furniture & Accessories Identification and Price Guide* by Noah Fleisher.

*All images courtesy Los Angeles Modern Auctions (LAMA) unless otherwise noted.*

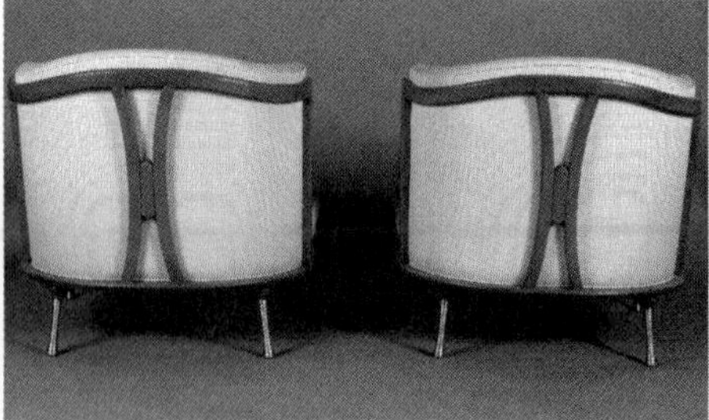

Pair mid-century birch and upholstered tub-back chairs, American, 20th century, 29" h. x 31" w. x 26" d. ............ **$800**

*Stefek's Auctioneers & Appraisers*

Mid-century Naugahyde upholstered swivel chair along with a stool, American, 20th century..**$200**
*Stefek's Auctioneers & Appraisers*

Curtis Jere (American, 20th century) abstract tree, aluminum and patinated metal, signed on base, dated "71," 45" h............. **$700**
*Stefek's Auctioneers & Appraisers*

Mid-century teak desk, Danish, 20th century, rectangular top over two banks of three drawers, 29" h. x 54" w. x 29" d.......................... **$275**
*Stefek's Auctioneers & Appraisers*

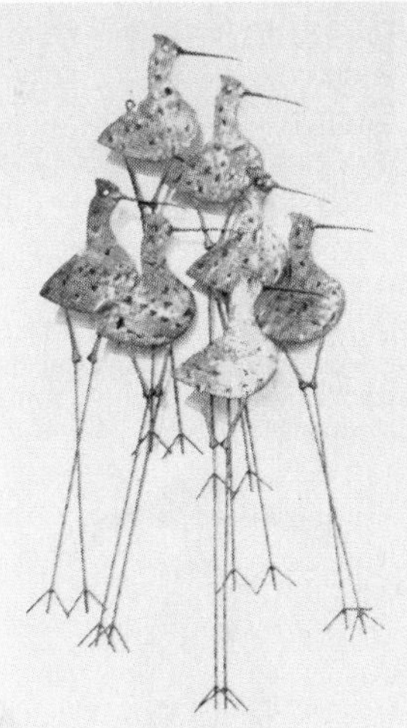

Curtis Jere (American, 20th century) patinated metal wall sculpture depicting sand pipers, signed on front, 29" x 15"............ **$175**
*Stefek's Auctioneers & Appraisers*

Pair of arm pull-up chairs, designed by Paul McCobb, manufactured by Custom Craft, 1955, from the Planner Group, maple frame with brown leather, 34-1/2" x 24-1/2" x 25"........................................... **$3,125**

Buffet, Paul McCobb design, 1961, manufactured by Lane, wood and rattan, from the Delineator Group, 32" x 72-1/2" x 17-1/2" .......................... **$2,500**

Group of chairs (10), directional, Paul McCobb design, 1955, 7000 Series chairs, each armchair 35" x 24" x 22-1/2"; each side chair 34" x 18-1/2" x 20" .......................... **$2,250**

Pair of nightstands (2), Paul McCobb design, manufactured by Calvin, Grand Rapids, Mich., c. 1950s, from the Irwin Collection, "Calvin, Paul McCobb Irwin Collection" label, each 24-1/4" x 22" x 20" . **$1,500**

Pair of "The" chairs, Hans Wegner design, 1949, manufactured by Johannes Hansen, oak with brown leather seat, Model No. JH 501, marked "Johannes Hansen/Copenhagen, Denmark," 30" x 24-3/4" x 20-1/2" .......................... **$1,500**

Fruit tray tables, Jens Quistgaard design, c. 1956, manufactured by Dansk, teak, each 17-1/4" x 19-1/2" d. .......................... **$938**

◄Valet or bachelor's chair, Hans. J. Wegner design, 1953, manufactured by Johannes Hansen, Model No. JH-540, 37-1/2" x 20" x 21". **$10,000**

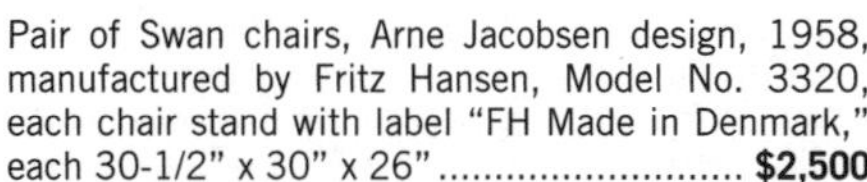

Pair of Swan chairs, Arne Jacobsen design, 1958, manufactured by Fritz Hansen, Model No. 3320, each chair stand with label "FH Made in Denmark," each 30-1/2" x 30" x 26" .......................... **$2,500**

Eva chairs (4), Bruno Mathsson design, 1934, manufactured by Dux, birch frame with woven fabric seat, each stamped "Bruno Mathsson Design Made in Sweden," each 33-1/4" x 23" x 25-1/2" ........... **$2,813**

Side table, Bruno Mathsson design, 1961, manufactured by Karl Mathsson, retains "Bruno Mathsson/Karl Mathsson Firma" label and marked "Made in Sweden," 13-3/4" x 20-1/2" x 20-1/2" ......................................... **$938**

Lamino lounge chair, Ynve Ekstrom design, c. 1960, manufactured by Swedese, stamped "Swedese Yngve Ekstrom," chair: 41" x 27-1/4" x 32"; ottoman: 18-3/4" x 23-1/4" x 18-1/2" ............................**$2,500**

Dining suite, Alvar Aalto design, c. 1935, manufactured by Artek, "Scandinavian Furniture, NY" label on the extension, comprised of a dining table, extension table and six chairs. Table: 28" x 59" x 29-1/2"; each chair: 30" x 16" x 17"; extension: 28" x 29-1/2" x 29-1/2" .................................................... **$2,250**

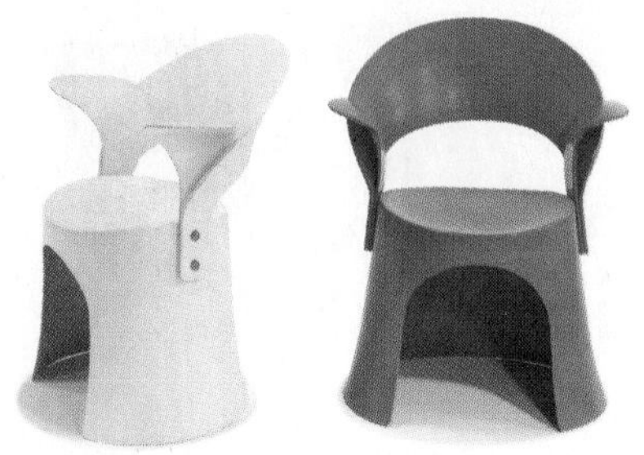

Pair of chairs, Nanna Ditzel design, 1969, manufactured by Odense, fiberglass, Model No. OD 5301-2, each: 29-1/2" x 24-1/2" x 21-1/2" ............. **$1,125**

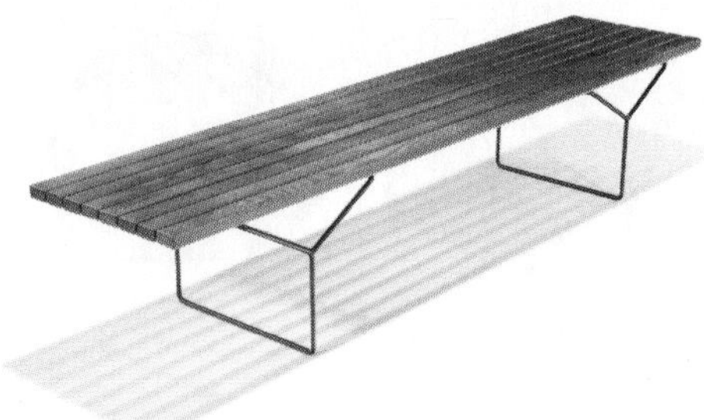

Slat bench, Harry Bertoia design, 1952, manufactured by Knoll International, wood slats with black lacquered steel rod legs, Model No. 400-82, retains Knoll International label, 15-1/4" x 82" x 18-1/4" ................................................................ **$2,250**

Pair of armchairs, Jens Risom design, 1948, manufactured by Knoll International, Model No. 652U, 30" x 24-1/4" x 28"........................ **$2,500-$3,500**

Womb chair and ottoman, Eero Saarinen design, 1948, manufactured by Knoll, Model No. 70, chair: 34-1/2" x 38-1/2" x 38"; ottoman: 16" x 19-1/2" x 17-1/2"..................................................... **$1,250**

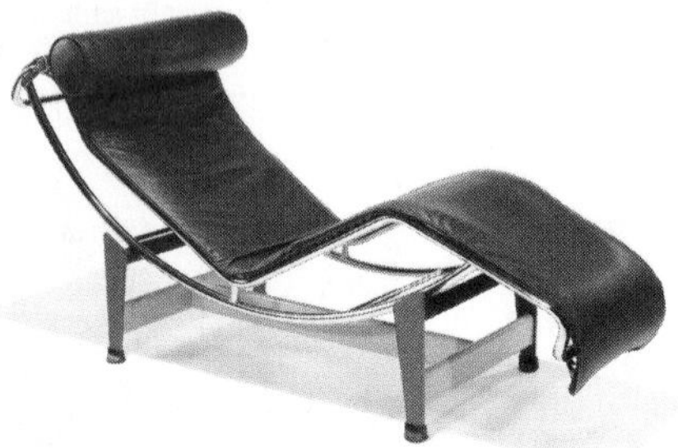

Chaise longue, Le Corbusier design, 1928, manufactured Cassina (this example 1978), Model No. LC4, sold with Cassina Masters Collection catalog, 34" x 24-1/2" x 63"............................... **$1,500-$2,000**

Chaise lounge, Marcel Breuer design, 1935-36, 32" x 25-3/8" x 52" ............................. **$4,000-$6,000**

Curved lattice back chair, Charles Rennie Mackintosh design, 1904, manufactured by Cassina, designed 1904; this example manufactured 1973, ebonized ash wood with fabric upholstered cushion, Model No. Willow 1; 46-3/4" x 37" x 16-1/4", literature: *Cassina: The Masters Collection*, sales catalog, no date, pg. 40 ....................................................... **$1,125**

Lounge chair and ottoman, Charles and Ray Eames design, 1956, manufactured by Herman Miller, black leather and rosewood, Model No. 670 & 671, chair: 32-3/4" x 33-1/4" x 32"; ottoman: 15-1/4" x 25-1/2" x 21" .......... **$4,375**

Coffee table, Milo Baughman design, c. 1955, manufactured by Glenn of California, walnut, lacquered Masonite, glass, metal,14-1/8" x 47-5/8" x 29-3/4" .......... **$8,750**

Butterfly table, Dan Cooper design, c. 1942, manufacturer unknown, plywood with lacquered top, 14" x 22" x 20" .......... **$1,250**

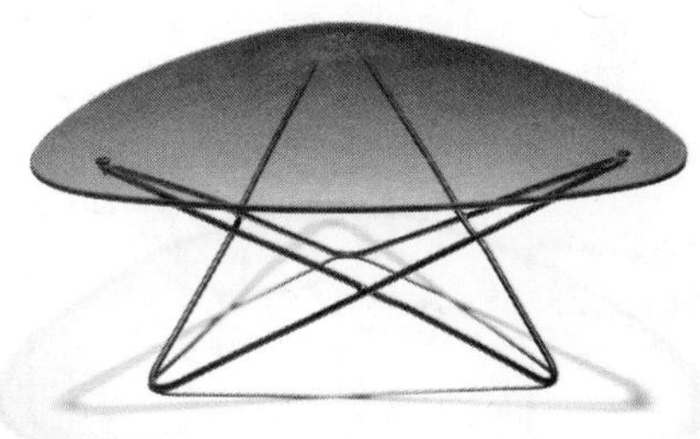

Atomic coffee table, attributed to Pierre Guariche, c. 1955, manufacturer unknown, glass top, painted steel base, brass fittings, 13-1/2" x 34" x 34-1/2" .......... **$2,250**

Lounge chair and ottoman, Frank O. Gehry design, 1972, manufactured by Easy Edges, corrugated cardboard, 29" x 23-3/4" x 61" .......... **$3,750**

◄Work chair, Odelberg Olsen design, circa 1949, manufactured by Knoll, Model No. T60, enameled metal and plywood, adjustable, 31" x 15" x 18-1/2" .......... **$2,500-$3,500**

Antony chair, Jean Prouvé design, 1954, metal and molded plywood with vinyl cover, 33-1/2" x 19-1/2" x 27-1/2" ..................................................**$47,500**

Minguren II side table, George Nakashima design, c. 1970, American black walnut, 18" x 29-1/2" x 30-1/2" ...................................................**$12,500**

Lounge chair and ottoman, Walter Lamb design, 1953, manufactured by Brown Jordan, bronze and yacht cord, Model Nos. C-5700 and C-5706, chair: 29-3/4" x 24" x 27-1/2"; ottoman: 20-1/4" x 23-1/4" x 18"............................................ **$2,813**

Pair of chairs (left arm and right arm), George Nakashima design, c. 1955, manufactured by Studio, this example made after 1962, American black walnut, each with black marker inscription of the family name "Schiller," each 32-3/4" x 32" x 28" .**$13,750**

Dining set (table and five chairs), Walter Lamb design, c. 1953, manufactured by Brown Jordan, bronze, glass and plastic cord, table: 28" x 48-1/2" dia.; each chair: 32" x 18-1/2" x 21-1/2" ...................................... **$5,000**

Coffee table, T.H. Robsjohn-Gibbings design, c. 1950s, manufactured by Widdicomb, retains "Widdicomb designed by T.H. Robsjohn Gibbings" label, 15-1/4" x 60" x 23" ..................................................... **$2,000-$3,000**

Side table, Sam Maloof design, manufactured in studio c. 1950, cork top, burn stamped "Maloof California" in the drawer, 14-1/2" x 29-3/4" x 29-3/4" .......... **$7,500**

Custom cabinet, Sam Maloof design, c. 1965, walnut, stamped verso, custom designed for Edward Fickett, 36-1/4" x 51-1/2" x 20-3/4".......... **$11,875**

Custom dining table, Sam Maloof design, manufacturing in studio c. 1958, walnut, 28-1/2" x 72" dia. .......... **$30,000-$50,000**

Chaise longue, Tommi Parzinger design, possibly manufactured by Charak Modern, 1940s, wood frame with fabric upholstery, 30" x 67" x 26-1/2" .......... **$7,500**

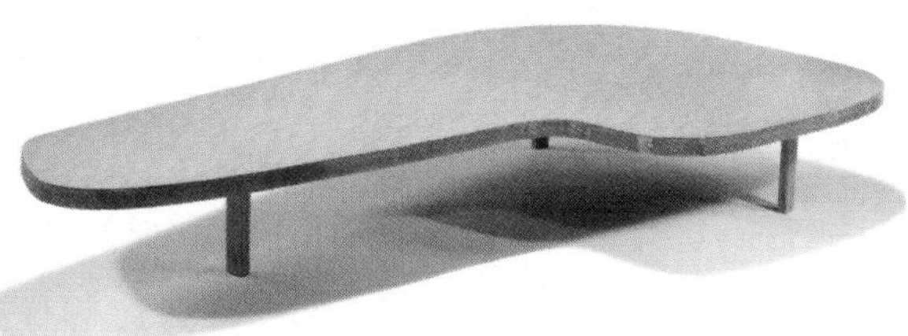

Custom coffee table, Rodney Walker design, executed c. 1950, wood with Formica laminate top, pictured in the September 1952 issue of *House Beautiful* in the Walker family home on Mulholland Drive in Los Angeles, 10" x 80" x 42-1/4" .......... **$6,875**

Double marshmallow sofa, George Nelson design, 1956, custom manufacturing, one of two examples custom ordered for the reception of Consolidated Edison, New York, 30" x 104" x 31-3/4" ........... **$80,000-$100,000**

Six panel screen, Charles and Ray Eames design, 1956, manufactured by Herman Miller, Model No. FSW-6, 34-1/4" x 60" ..... **$6,250**

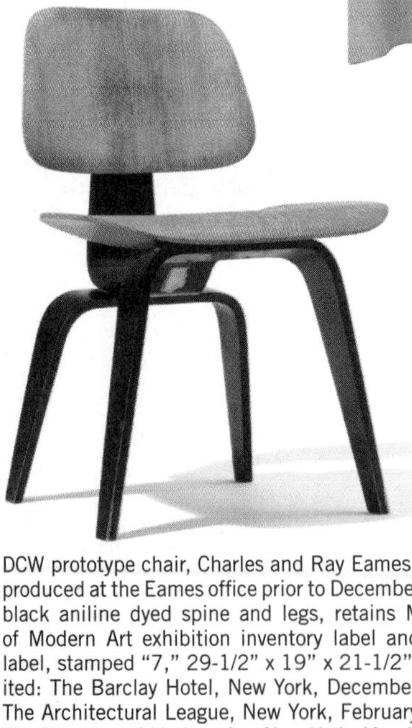

DCW prototype chair, Charles and Ray Eames design, produced at the Eames office prior to December 1945, black aniline dyed spine and legs, retains Museum of Modern Art exhibition inventory label and Evans label, stamped "7," 29-1/2" x 19" x 21-1/2". Exhibited: The Barclay Hotel, New York, December 1945; The Architectural League, New York, February 1946; The Museum of Modern Art, New York, March 1946. ............................................ **$100,000-$150,000**

Dining chair, Charles and Ray Eames design, 1945-'46, manufactured by Herman Miller, red aniline dye birch seat and back rest; black aniline dye legs and spine, Model No. DCW, 28-1/2" x 19-1/2" x 21-1/2" ............................................................ **$2,125**

Child's chair, Charles and Ray Eames design, 1945, manufactured by Evans Molded Plywood Division, produced for only one year, a total of approximately 5,000 chairs and stools were made, 14-1/2" x 14-1/2" x 11" ...**$8,750**

Rocking chair, Charles and Ray Eames design, 1950-'53, manufactured by Zenith Plastics and Herman Miller, Model No. RAR with parchment fiberglass armshell, 26-1/2" h. x 25" w. x 29-1/2" d. ...................... **$2,813**

Stacking dining chairs (4), Hans J. Wegner design, 1952, manufactured by Fritz Hansen, Model No. 4103, each 29" x 21" x 18-1/2" ...................................... **$3,500**

Chaise longue, Poul Kjaerholm design, 1965, manufactured by Fritz Hansen, brushed stainless steel and wicker, Model No. PK 24, 34-1/2" x 26" x 54-1/2".....................**$6,875**

Butterfly stool, Sori Yanagi design, 1956, manufactured by Tendo Co., Ltd., bent rosewood with metal rod, retains "Made in Japan" label, 15-3/4" x 16-1/2" x 12-1/4".......................... **$3,000-$5,000**

Storage unit, Charles and Ray Eames design, 1950, manufactured by Herman Miller, Model No. ESU-200-C, 32-1/4" x 47" x 16".......................**$10,000**

►Arabesque lounge chair, Folke Jansson design, 1955, manufactured by Wingrantz Mobelindustri, 29-1/4" x 28" x 33"........................ **$5,000-$7,000**

Lounge chair (two views), Ray Komai design, 1949, manufactured by J.G. Furniture Company, Model No. 939, 29" x 21-1/2" x 22"................ **$1,500-$2,000**

Heart cone chair, Verner Panton design, 1958, manufactured by Plus-Linje, Denmark, Model No. K3, 35-1/2" x 39-1/2" x 25"............................ **$5,313**

Wire cone chair, Verner Panton design, 1958, manufactured by Plus-Linje, Denmark, Model No. K2, 29-1/2" x 25-1/4" x 23"............................ **$2,500**

Peacock chair, Verner Panton design, c. 1950s, manufactured by Plus-Linje, Denmark, from the Wire Collection series, 16" x 37-1/2" dia.................. **$4,375**

Time-Life stools (2), Ray Eames design, 1960, manufactured by Herman Miller, solid walnut, Model No. 412, each 15" x 13" diameter .................... **$4,063**

◀Miniature chest cabinet, George Nelson design, 1952, manufactured by Herman Miller, wood with porcelain pulls and rubber feet on steel base, Model No. 5511 (from the Thin Edge Group), 32" x 20-1/4" x 14" .......................................................**$11,563**

Gazelle dining table, Dan Johnson design, 1958, made in Italy for Dan Johnson Studio, walnut with glass top, 30-1/2" x 71" x 39" ...................**$10,000**

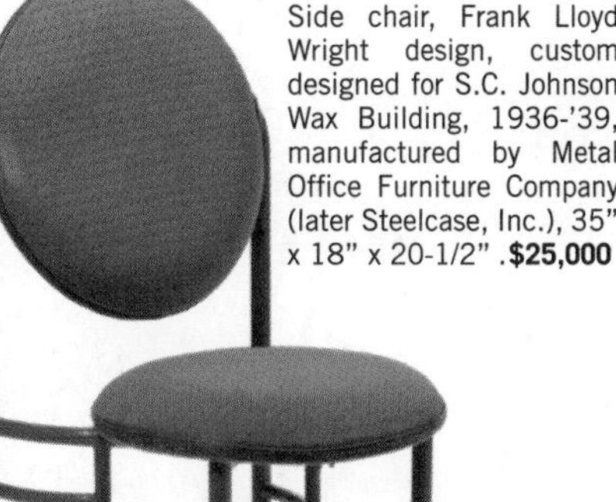

Side chair, Frank Lloyd Wright design, custom designed for S.C. Johnson Wax Building, 1936-'39, manufactured by Metal Office Furniture Company (later Steelcase, Inc.), 35" x 18" x 20-1/2" .**$25,000**

Lounge chair, Frank Lloyd Wright design, 1940-'41, custom designed for the Robert Wynn House, 29" x 24-1/2" x 23"........................................... **$8,125**

Stacking stool, Florence Knoll design, 1941-45, manufactured by Knoll, Model No. 75WR, retains Knoll label, 18" x 14" diameter ..............................**$800-$1,200**

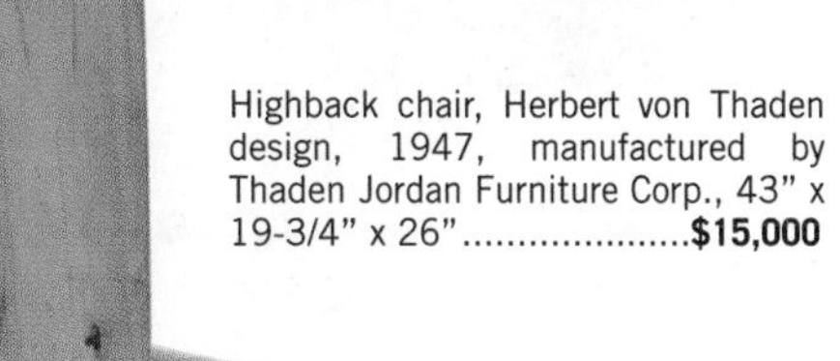

Highback chair, Herbert von Thaden design, 1947, manufactured by Thaden Jordan Furniture Corp., 43" x 19-3/4" x 26"......................**$15,000**

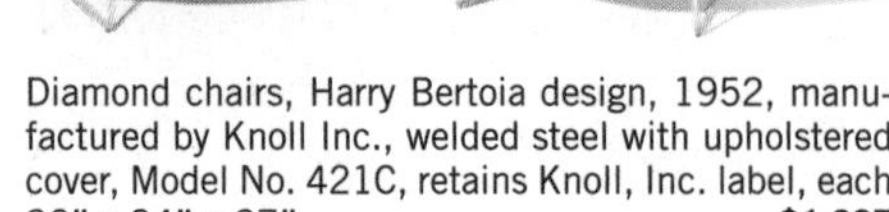

Diamond chairs, Harry Bertoia design, 1952, manufactured by Knoll Inc., welded steel with upholstered cover, Model No. 421C, retains Knoll, Inc. label, each 30" x 34" x 27" .......................................... **$1,625**

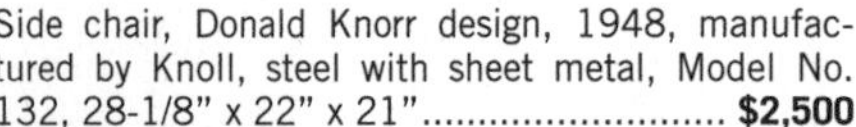

Side chair, Donald Knorr design, 1948, manufactured by Knoll, steel with sheet metal, Model No. 132, 28-1/8" x 22" x 21" ........................... **$2,500**

Lady chair and ottoman, John Risley, c. 1965, manufactured by Luger Manufacturing Corp. for Raymor, enameled steel, 40-1/2" x 25-1/2" x 55" ..........................**$2,813**

Lounge armchair, Jens Risom design, 1943, manufactured by Knoll, 28-3/4" x 24" x 27" .. **$1,500-$2,000**

Step table, Greta Grossman design, c. 1952, manufactured by Glenn of California, walnut frame and lower shelf with thermoset plastic upper shelves and black iron legs with round walnut tips, Model No. 6226, 24-1/4" x 31" x 18" ......................... **$9,375**

Chair with Jack Lenor Larsen "Primavera" fabric upholstery, American Modern design, 1960s, manufacturing unknown, plastic and upholstered cushions, 34" x 32" x 32" .............................. **$2,000-$3,000**

# Garden Antiques

Garden antiques and décor include period and vintage garden and architectural elements used to decorate porches, patios, balconies, and any other outdoor location. They include items made of iron, copper, and other metals; terra cotta and stone statuary; tables, chairs, fountains, sundials, birdbaths, urns; and architectural ornaments such as finials, obelisks, and gates.

Pair of European terra cotta deer, 19th c., reclining buck and standing doe, 19-3/4" h. x 27" w. and 23" h. x 18" w. .............................. **$563**
*Pook & Pook, Inc.*

Pair of aggregate lawn whippets, early 20th c., 30-3/4" h. ..... **$533**
*Pook & Pook, Inc.*

Terra cotta lion lawn ornament, 29" h. .................................. **$356**
*Pook & Pook, Inc.*

Cast iron stag lawn ornament, 19th c., probably Fiske, 60" h. x 53" w. ............................ **$1,304**
*Pook & Pook, Inc.*

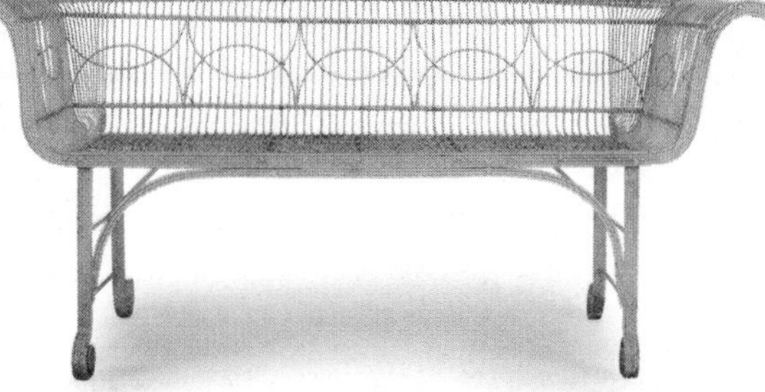

►Wrought iron and wire garden bench, 19th c., 30-1/2" h. x 69" w. .................................. **$3,792**
*Pook & Pook, Inc.*

Nine cast iron architectural stars, largest 9" w. ........................ **$30**
*Pook & Pook, Inc.*

Pair of antique English cast iron garden chairs, each with a Diana the Huntress back decoration, open arms and wood plank seat, supported on sabre-style legs, 34" h. x 22-1/2" w. x 21" d. ........................... **$2,400**
*Kame Auctions*

Pair of cast iron recumbent lion lawn ornaments, 19th c., 12" h. x 26" w. ............................ **$3,081**
*Pook & Pook, Inc.*

Group of four bird feeders, Stan Bitters design, manufactured by Hans Sumpf, c. 1960, porous low-fire clay with cord, largest pieces A: 1-1/2" x 10-1/2"; B: 5-1/2" x 6"; C: 7" x 7"; D: 5" x 7-1/2" ........ **$1,625**

Pair of antique garden statues, cherubs with grapes, 3' h. .......................................................... **$425**
*California Auctioneers*

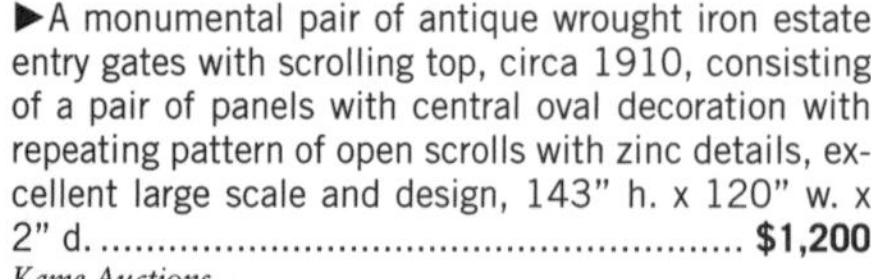

►A monumental pair of antique wrought iron estate entry gates with scrolling top, circa 1910, consisting of a pair of panels with central oval decoration with repeating pattern of open scrolls with zinc details, excellent large scale and design, 143" h. x 120" w. x 2" d. ...................................................... **$1,200**
*Kame Auctions*

Antique wrought iron garden gate with geometric Art Deco designs around scroll, decorated central circles, circa 1910, 53" h. x 55" w. ........................... **$275**

*Kame Auctions*

Rare and unusual 19th c. cast iron fencing, eight sections with Neoclassical decorations, circa 1880, includes 10 cast iron posts with stylized ball finials, 31" h. x 61" w. ........................................ **$6,000**

*Kame Auctions*

Pair of Classical style urns, probably cast lead, with round bodies adorned with egg and dart bands, each with two figural cherub handles atop lion masks with rings, early 20th c., 12" h. Urns do not appear to have been used outside. Provenance: Private Nashville, Tennessee collection. ............................. **$425**

*Case Antiques, Inc.*

Cast iron garden armillary sphere with painted copper, iron, and aluminum rings and arrow, supported by the figure of Atlas, 20th c., 28" h. x 27" w. x 16-1/2" d. Provenance: Private Nashville, Tennessee collection. ..................................................... **$375**

*Case Antiques, Inc.*

Heavy cast iron figural birdbath, support in the form of a standing female, birdbath has small iron bird perched on the edge, needs refinishing, 28-1/2" h. to top of bird x 15.75" w. at widest point, 49 lbs. ............................. **$110**

*Auctions Neapolitan*

American Victorian cast iron garden urn with ornate handle over bulbous bowl, applied floral wreath, circa 1870, raised on stepped socle and plinth, 45" h. x 36" w. x 24" d. .................. **$950**

*Kame Auctions*

◀Bronze figural garden sculpture statue/flower pot of two boys, 42" h. ..................................... **$900**

*Victorian Casino Antiques*

GLASS

# Glass

## Art Glass Baskets

Popular novelties, these ornate glass baskets of glass were usually handcrafted of free-blown or mold-blown glass. They were made in a wide spectrum of colors and shapes. Pieces were highlighted with tall applied handles and often applied feet; however, fancier ones might also carry additional appliquéd trim.

The Depression-era glassware researchers have many accurate sources, including company records, catalogs, magazine advertisements, oral and written histories from sales staff, factory workers, etc. The dates included in the introductions are approximate as are some of the factory locations. When companies had more than one factory, usually only the main office or factory is listed.

Victorian art glass basket, bulbous gourd-shaped body with flaring ruffled rim, quilted yellow and white exterior, pink interior, clear applied handle, 10-1/2" h. x 7-1/2" .................. **$200-$400**
*Fontaine's Auction Gallery*

Amberina glass basket vase, six legs, ruffled rim and painted design, 7-3/4" h. .................. **$150**
*Tory Hill Auctions*

Ambra Verde Murano glass basket form vase, 8-1/2" h. x 11-1/2" l. x 6-1/4" dia......................... **$500**
*Main Auction Galleries*

Two Italian glass baskets, one with purple and internal silver fleck decoration, lacking one arm, the other of twisted form with pink to amber decoration, height of tallest 8" . **$100**
*Leslie Hindman Auctioneers*

Victorian bowl in white cased glass with pink glass interior and amber ruffled rim, basket in white cased glass with pink interior and amber rim and handle, both unmarked; bowl 8-1/2" dia., basket 8-1/2" h.......... **$25**
*Cowan's Auctions*

◄End of Day art glass basket, c. 1890, possibly by Kralik, with applied clear twisted handle, 7-1/2" h. x 4-3/4" w. x 4" dia...................... **$50**
*Crescent City Auction Gallery*

# Baccarat

Baccarat glass has been made by Cristalleries de Baccarat, France, since 1765. The firm has produced various glassware of excellent quality as well as paperweights. Baccarat's Rose Tiente is often referred to as Baccarat's Amberina.

Baccarat art glass pink bangle bracelet and red heart necklace ..................................................... **$192**
*Heritage Auction Galleries*

Baccarat cut crystal and figural gilt bronze centerpiece with associated bowl, France, circa 1900, marks to bronze: Baccarat (logo), 10" .......... **$10,158**
*Heritage Auction Galleries*

Pair of Baccarat style cut crystal three-light candelabra, 20th c., round footed base and lobed stem, prisms from two arms and central candleholder, 19-1/2" x 12-3/4" ........................................ **$900**
*Heritage Auction Galleries*

◀ Twelve Baccarat cut glass wine glasses, cranberry cut to clear cups atop a faceted stem and scalloped cut glass foot, each signed "Baccarat" on the top of the foot, 8-1/4" t. Provenance: From the collection of Dorothy-Lee Jones. .................................... **$3,162**
*James D. Julia, Inc.*

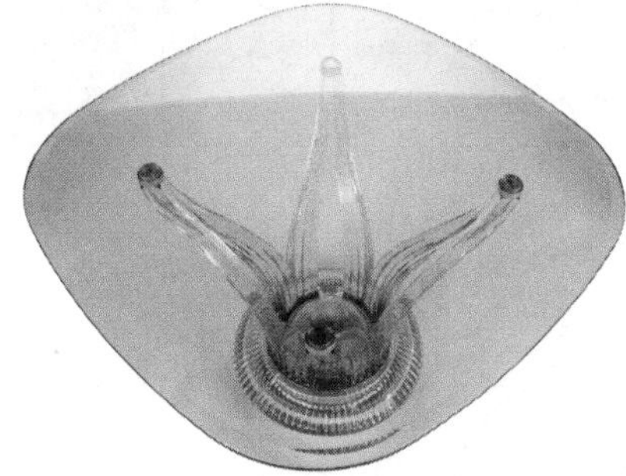

Baccarat glass center table, France, 20th c., 29-1/2" x 48" x 48" .................................................... **$5,000**
*Heritage Auction Galleries*

Red textured glass vase with red acid-etched overlay and applied gilt enamel in vine motif, circa 1900, marks: Depose, 10" .. **$896**
*Heritage Auction Galleries*

Baccarat tall crystal vase with gilt monkey frieze, France, 20th c., engraved Baccarat 22/50, red label: Baccarat, 19-1/8" ..... **$2,988**
*Heritage Auction Galleries*

Clear glass vase with red acid-etched overlay in sunflower motif, circa 1900, 8" h. ............... **$717**
*Heritage Auction Galleries*

Cased Baccarat glass perfume with tripod stand, gilt decoration holding red glass decanter with green glass stopper, metal star-form finial, in original red case, St. Petersburg, 20th c., stamped Baccarat, France, 16-1/2" x 19-1/2" .............**$1,625**
*Heritage Auction Galleries*

Pair of Baccarat cut crystal and gilt bronze figural epergnes, France, circa 1900, marks to bronze: Baccarat (logo), 22" ..................**$11,353**
*Heritage Auction Galleries*

◀Baccarat gilt and patinated bronze and glass bull's head designed by Chaumet, the House of Chaumet for Baccarat, Baccarat, France, circa 1950, bull's head titled Feria with gilt and patinated bronze horns, eyes, ears and nose, and original fitted case, letter of authentication included, marks: Baccarat, Feria, Piece Unique, Chaumet, 10-1/2" x 11" x 14" ........................................................................................**$7,500**
*Heritage Auction Galleries*

# Bride's Baskets

These berry or fruit bowls were popular late Victorian wedding gifts, hence the name. They were produced in a variety of quality art glass wares and sometimes were fitted in ornate silver plate holders.

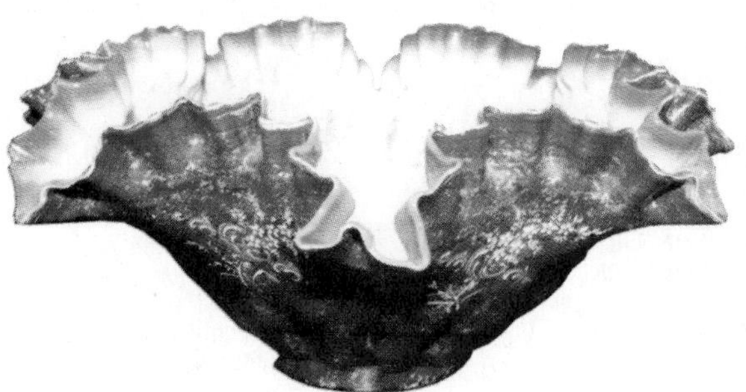

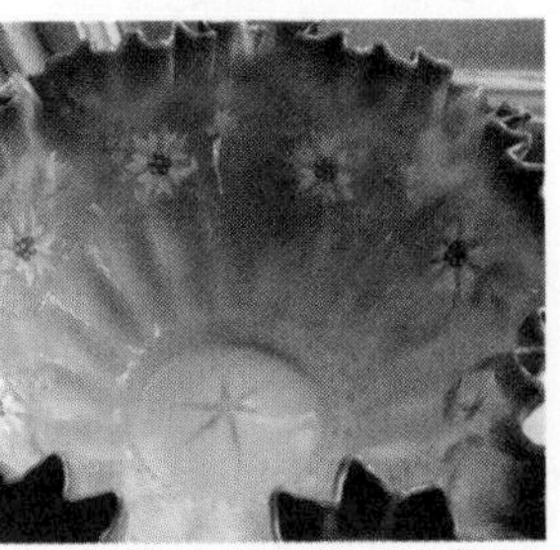

Bride's bowl with floral painted interior on white pinched edge and brown/green pattern outside, 5" h. x 11-1/2" dia. .......... **$650**
*Bob Courtney Auctions*

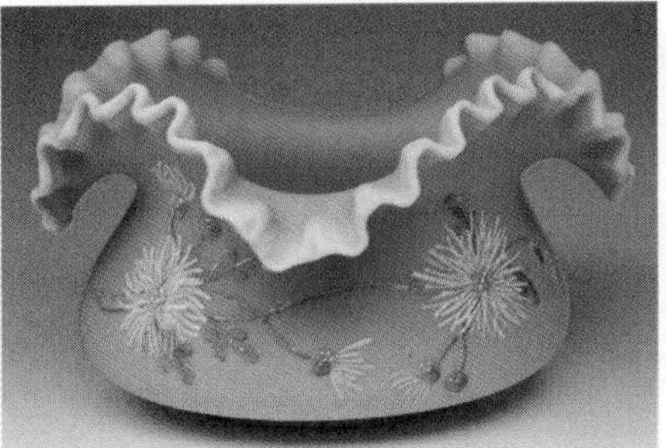

Mt. Washington decorated Burmese bride's bowl, plush finish, deep peach coloring with full-round polychrome spider mums decoration, boldly ruffled crimped rim, polished pontil mark, Mt. Washington Glass Co., fourth quarter 19th c., 5-1/4" h. overall, 9-1/2" dia. overall rim, 4-3/4" dia. base fitter. . **$747**
*Jeffrey S. Evans & Associates*

Cased satin glass bride's bowl, shaded rose interior with enamel and gilt decorations, crimped and ruffled rim, ground pontil mark, fourth quarter 19th c., 3-1/2" h., 11-1/4" dia. rim, 3-7/8" dia. base... **$103**
*Jeffrey S. Evans & Associates*

Delaware/Four-Petal flower bride's baskets, green with gilt decoration, boat-shaped example fitted in a Wm. Rogers quadruple-plate frame and a child's round example fitted in a silver-plate frame, early 20th c., 10-7/8" h. overall, 7-1/4" x 11-3/4", and 6-3/4" h. overall, bowl 4-1/4" dia. overall. .......... **$80**
*Jeffrey S. Evans & Associates*

Delaware/Four-Petal flower bride's baskets, green with gilt decoration boat-shaped example fitted in a Wm. Rogers quadruple-plate frame and a similar cranberry with gilt decoration example, without a stand, early 20th c., 10" h. overall and 4" h, 7" x 11-3/4". .......... **$103**
*Jeffrey S. Evans & Associates*

Early Fenton art glass bride's basket, hand-painted blue glass interior, white glass exterior, glass measures 9-1/2" dia., silver plate basket frame is unmarked, 12" h. x 11" dia. .......................... **$200**
*Burchard Galleries, Inc.*

Victorian art glass bride's basket in WMF cherubic figural silver plate holder, decorated large cranberry glass bowl, silver marked MF and WMF in hive, 11" dia., stand is 8-1/2" h. ........................ **$275**
*Burchard Galleries, Inc.*

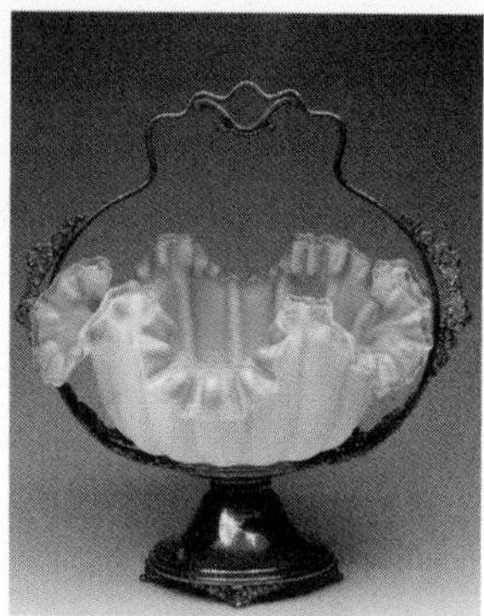

Victorian cased-glass bride's basket, cased opal with pink to yellow/green interior, colorless applied crimped rim, satin finish, polished pontil mark, fitted in a Victor Silver Co. quadruple-plate frame with floral decoration, late 19th/early 20th c., 13-1/4" h. overall, bowl 5-1/4" h., 11-1/2" dia. .................................. **$172**
*Jeffrey S. Evans & Associates*

Victorian opalescent bride's basket, vaseline opalescent with applied vaseline crimped rim, quilted diamond pattern, fitted in a pedestal stand with stamped foot and cast-brass handle, late 19th/early 20th c., 13" h. overall, bowl 2-3/4" h. overall, 9" dia....... **$161**
*Jeffrey S. Evans & Associates*

Victorian decorated bride's basket, sapphire blue with white enamel and gilt decoration, fitted in a tripartite Pairpoint Mfg. Co. weighted quadruple-plate stand, late 19th/early 20th c., 11" h., 8-1/2" dia. ........................................ **$316**
*Jeffrey S. Evans & Associates*

Victorian cased-cranberry bride's basket, tooled and ruffled rim, polished pontil mark, fitted in an Acme Silver Plate Co. quadruple-plate stand, late 19th/early 20th century, 12-1/2" h. overall, 9-1/2" dia. overall. ............. **$207**
*Jeffrey S. Evans & Associates*

Victorian art glass bride's basket, peach glass with applied amber rim, 10" dia., silver plate stand is attributed to Pairpoint, 12-1/2" w. overall ...................................................................................... **$275**
*Burchard Galleries, Inc.*

# Cambridge

The Cambridge Glass Co. was founded in Ohio in 1901. Numerous pieces are now sought, especially those designed by Arthur J. Bennett, including Crown Tuscan. Other productions included crystal animals, "Black Amethyst," "blanc opaque," and other types of colored glass. The firm was finally closed in 1954. It should not be confused with the New England Glass Co., Cambridge, Massachusetts.

Cambridge Crown Tuscan compote, pink opaque glass with flying nude figure with seashell on her back, hand painted with clusters of pink roses and leaves with purple flowers and gilt trim, on a spherical stem with a round foot, 9-1/2" h. x 12" w. x 7" d. ........................................................**$400-$650**
*Fontaine's Auction Gallery*

Pair Cambridge Crown Tuscan compotes, pink opaque glass with figural standing nude woman forming the stem on a round platform, holding a scallop shell tray above her head, 7-1/2" h. x 7" dia. .........**$500-$700**
*Fontaine's Auction Gallery*

►Six-piece Cambridge etched lemonade set, rose glass with engraved and gilt decoration, lidded pitcher (11" h. x 6-3/4") and five glasses (5-1/4"h.). .....**$100**
*Burchard Galleries, Inc.*

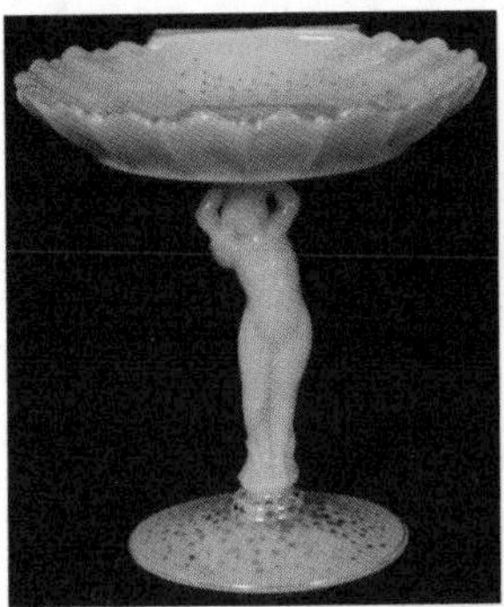

Cambridge Crown Tuscan compote (detail at right), pink opaque glass of figural standing nude woman forming the stem on a round platform with gilt decoration and holding a scallop shell tray above her head, tray is decorated with a single yellow rose, 5-1/2" h. x 5-1/4" dia... **$150-$200**
*Fontaine's Auction Gallery*

Cambridge Glass Co. light amber barrel decanter set with four glasses ...............................**$45**
*Hewlett's Auctions*

Cambridge glass three-light candelabras, pair, floral design with cut pinwheel designs on oval base, 8" h., 7" w. .......... **$35**
*DuMouchelles*

◀Cambridge Crown Tuscan vase, pink opaque glass vase in the form of a nautilus shell, hand painted with monotone clusters of roses and leaves with gold trim, 8-1/2" h. x 9-1/2" w. x 6" d. .......... **$250-$400**
*Fontaine's Auction Gallery*

Cambridge Glass draped lady figural flower frog, six holes in scalloped base, cut glass bowl with rolled edges and silver rim .......... **$150**
*Rago Arts & Auction Center*

20th c. Cambridge Japonica art glass vase, American Depression-era serpentine-shaped mold blown art glass vase by Cambridge Glass Co., deep cranberry-hued glass with enameled stylized blossoms, from the Japonica line, maker marked Japonica with a C in a triangle, 8-3/4" h. x 5-1/2" w. x 4" dia. base... **$2,000**
*Great Gatsby's Antiques and Auctions*

Cambridge Crown Tuscan candlesticks, pink opaque glass with figural standing nude woman forming the stem on a round platform, holding a candle above her head, 9" h. x 4" dia. .......... **$200-$400**
*Fontaine's Auction Gallery*

Cambridge Crown Tuscan vase, pink opaque glass vase in the form of a snail shell, hand painted with clusters of pink roses and purple flowers with gold trim, 8-1/2" h. x 8" w. x 5" d. .......... **$250-$350**
*Fontaine's Auction Gallery*

Cambridge Glass Co. Crown Tuscan and gold-etched Portia pattern, 6-1/4" t. vase, crown mark and Tuscan and C in triangle marks on base .......... **$40**
*B.S. Slosberg, Inc. Auctioneers*

# Carnival Glass

Carnival glass is what is fondly called mass-produced iridescent glassware. The term "carnival glass" has evolved through the years as glass collectors have responded to the idea that much of this beautiful glassware was made as giveaway glass at local carnivals and fairs. However, more of it was made and sold through the same channels as pattern glass and Depression glass. Some patterns were indeed giveaways, and others were used as advertising premiums, souvenirs, etc. Whatever the origin, the term "carnival glass" today encompasses glassware that is usually pattern molded and treated with metallic salts, creating that unique coloration that is so desirable to collectors.

Carnival glass is iridized glassware that is created by pressing hot molten glass into molds, just as pattern glass had evolved. Some forms are hand finished, while others are completely formed by molds. To achieve the marvelous iridescent colors that carnival glass collectors seek, a process was developed where a liquid solution of metallic salts was put onto the still hot glass form after it was unmolded. As the liquid evaporated, a fine metallic surface was left which refracts light into wonderful colors. The name given to the iridescent spray by early glassmakers was "dope."

Many of the forms created by carnival glass manufacturers were accessories to the china American housewives so loved. By the early 1900s, consumers could find carnival glassware at such popular stores as F. W. Woolworth and McCrory's. To capitalize on the popular fancy for these colored wares, some other industries bought large quantities of carnival glass and turned them into "packers." This term reflects the practice where baking powder, mustard, or other household products were packed into a special piece of glass that could take on another life after the original product was used. Lee Manufacturing Co. used iridized carnival glass as premiums for its baking powder and other products, causing some early carnival glass to be known by the generic term "Baking Powder Glass."

Classic carnival glass production began in the early 1900s and continued about 20 years, but no one really documented or researched production until the first collecting wave struck in 1960.

It is important to remember that carnival glasswares were sold in department stores as well as mass merchants rather than through the general store often associated with a young America. Glassware by this time was mass-produced and sold in large quantities by such enterprising companies as Butler Brothers. When the economics of the country soured in the 1920s, those interested in purchasing iridized glassware were not spared. Many of the leftover inventories of glasshouses that hoped to sell this mass-produced glassware found their way to wholesalers who in turn sold the wares to those who offered the glittering glass as prizes at carnivals, fairs, circuses, etc. Possibly because this was the last venue people associated the iridized glassware with, it became known as "carnival glass."

For more information on carnival glass, see *Warman's Carnival Glass Identification and Price Guide,* 2nd edition, by Ellen T. Schroy.

Imperial Grape wine decanter, purple, 12"................**$250-$350**

## Carnival Glass Companies

Much of vintage American carnival glassware was created in the Ohio valley, in the glasshouse-rich areas of Pennsylvania, Ohio, and West Virginia. The abundance of natural materials, good transportation, and skilled craftsmen that created the early American pattern glass manufacturing companies allowed many of them to add carnival glass to their production lines. Brief company histories of the major carnival glass manufacturers follow:

### *Cambridge Glass Company (Cambridge)*

Cambridge Glass was a rather minor player in the carnival glass marketplace. Founded in 1901 as a new factory in Cambridge, Ohio, it focused on producing fine crystal tablewares. What carnival glass it did produce was imitation cut-glass patterns.

Colors used by Cambridge include marigold, as well as few others. Forms found in carnival glass by Cambridge include tablewares and vases, some with its trademark "Near-Cut."

### *Diamond Glass Company (Diamond)*

This company was started as the Dugan brothers (see Dugan Glass Company) departed the carnival glass-making scene in 1913. However, Alfred Dugan returned and became general manager until his death in 1928. After a disastrous fire in June of 1931, the factory closed.

### *Dugan Glass Company (Dugan)*

The history of the Dugan Glass Company is closely related to Harry Northwood (see Northwood Glass Company), whose cousin, Thomas Dugan, became plant manager at the Northwood Glass Company in Indiana, Pennsylvania, in 1895. By 1904, Dugan and his partner W. G. Minnemayer bought the former Northwood factory from the now defunct National Glass conglomerate and opened as the Dugan Glass Company. Dugan's brother, Alfred, joined the company and stayed until it became the Diamond Glass Company in 1913. At this time, Thomas Dugan moved to the Cambridge Glass Company, later Duncan and Miller and finally Hocking, Lancaster. Alfred left Diamond Glass, too, but later returned.

Understanding how the Northwood and Dugan families were connected helps collectors understand the linkage of these three companies. Their productions were similar; molds were swapped, retooled, etc.

Colors attributed to Dugan and Diamond include amethyst, marigold, peach opalescent, and white. The company developed deep amethyst shades, some almost black.

Forms made by both Dugan and Diamond mirrored what other glass companies were producing. The significant contribution by Dugan and later Diamond were feet – either ball or spatula shapes. They are also known for deeply crimped edges.

### *Fenton Art Glass Company (Fenton)*

Frank Leslie Fenton and his brothers, John W. Fenton and Charles H. Fenton, founded this truly American glassmaker in 1905 in Martins Ferry, Ohio. Early production was of blanks, which the brothers soon learned to decorate themselves. They moved to a larger factory in Williamstown, West Virginia.

By 1907, Fenton was experimenting with iridescent glass, developing patterns and the metallic salt formulas that it became so famous for. Production of carnival glass continued at Fenton until the early 1930s. In 1970, Fenton began to reissue carnival glass, creating new colors and forms as well as using traditional patterns.

Persian Medallion flat plate, blue, 9" dia., Fenton........... **$400-$700**
Outstanding example (rare) **$1,500**

Colors developed by Fenton are numerous. The company developed red and Celeste blue in the 1920s; a translucent pale blue, known as Persian blue, is also one of its more distinctive colors, as is a light yellow-green color known as vaseline. Fenton also produced delicate opalescent colors including amethyst opalescent and red opalescent. Because the Fenton brothers learned how to decorate their own blanks, they also promoted the addition of enamel decoration to some of their carnival glass patterns.

Forms made by Fenton are also numerous. What distinguishes Fenton from other glassmakers is its attention to detail and hand finishing processes. Edges are found scalloped, fluted, tightly crimped, frilled, or pinched into a candy ribbon edge, also referred to as 3-in-1 edge.

(For a special spotlight on Fenton-made carnival glass, see page 499.)

### *Imperial Glass Company (Imperial)*

Edward Muhleman and a syndicate founded the Imperial Glass Company at Bellaire, Ohio, in 1901, with production beginning in 1904. It started with pressed glass tableware patterns as well as lighting fixtures. The company's marketing strategy included selling to important retailers of its day, such as F. W. Woolworth and McCrory and Kresge, to get glassware into the hands of American housewives. Imperial also became a major exporter of glassware, including its brilliant carnival patterns. During the Depression, it filed for bankruptcy in 1931, but was able to continue on. By 1962, it was again producing carnival glass patterns. By April 1985, the factory was closed and the molds sold.

Colors made by Imperial include typical carnival colors such as marigold. It added interesting shades of green, known as helios, a pale ginger ale shade known as clambroth, and a brownish smoke shade.

Forms created by Imperial tend to be functional, such as berry sets and table sets. Patterns vary from wonderful imitation cut glass patterns to detailed florals and naturalistic designs.

### *Millersburg Glass Company (Millersburg)*

John W. Fenton started the Millersburg Glass Company in September 1908. Perhaps it was the factory's more obscure location or the lack of business experience by John Fenton, but the company failed by 1911.

The factory was bought by Samuel Fair and John Fenton, and renamed the Radium Glass Company, but it lasted only a year.

Colors produced by Millersburg are amethyst, green, and marigold. Shades such as blue and vaseline were added on rare occasions. The company is well known for its bright radium finishes.

Forms produced at Millersburg are mostly bowls and vases. Pattern designers at Millersburg often took one theme and developed several patterns from it. Millersburg often used one pattern for the interior and a different pattern for the exterior.

### *Northwood Glass Company (Northwood)*

Englishman Harry Northwood founded the Northwood Glass Company. He developed his glass formulas for carnival glass, naming it "Golden Iris" in 1908. Northwood was one of the pioneers of the glass manufacturers who marked his wares. Marks range from a full script signature to a simple underscored capital N in a circle. However, not all Northwood glassware is marked.

Colors that Northwood created were many. Collectors prefer its pastels, such as ice blue, ice green, and white. It is also known for several stunning blue shades. The one color that Northwood did not develop was red.

Forms of Northwood patterns range from typical table sets, bowls, and water sets to whimsical novelties, such as a pattern known as Corn, which realistically depicts an ear of corn.

Good Luck, bowl, ribbed exterior, ruffled, sapphire, Northwood ........ **$2,100**

### *United States Glass Company (US Glass)*

In 1891, a consortium of 15 American glass manufacturers joined together as the United States Glass Company. This company was successful in continuing pattern glass production, as well as developing new glass lines. By 1911, it had begun limited production of carnival glass lines, often using existing pattern glass tableware molds. By the time a tornado destroyed the last of its glass factories in Glassport in 1963, it was no longer producing glassware.

Colors associated with US Glass are marigold, white, and a rich honey amber.

Forms tend to be table sets and functional forms.

### *Westmoreland Glass Company (Westmoreland)*

Started as the Westmoreland Specialty Company, Grapeville, Pennsylvania, in 1889, this company originally made novelties and glass packing containers, such as candy containers. Researchers have identified its patterns being advertised by Butler Brothers as early as 1908. Carnival glass production continued into the 1920s. In the 1970s, Westmoreland, too, begin to reissue carnival glass patterns and novelties. However, this ceased in February of 1996 when the factory burned.

Colors originally used by Westmoreland were typical carnival colors, such as blue and marigold.

Forms include tablewares and functional forms, containers, etc.

Acorn vase, maybe US Glass or possibly Millersburg, vaseline, only one known in this color..........**$11,000**

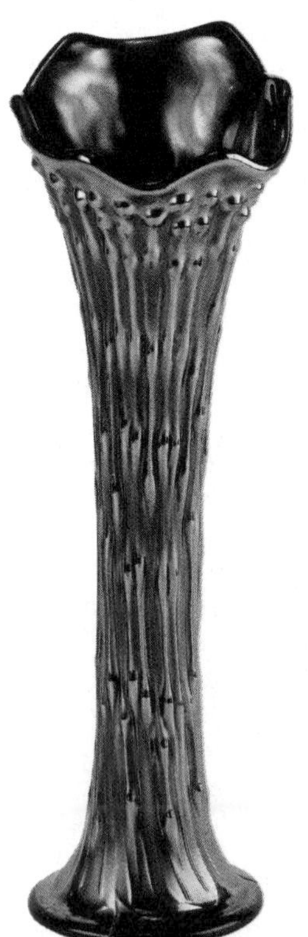

April Showers vase, black amethyst, 12" h., Fenton ..........**$80-$150**

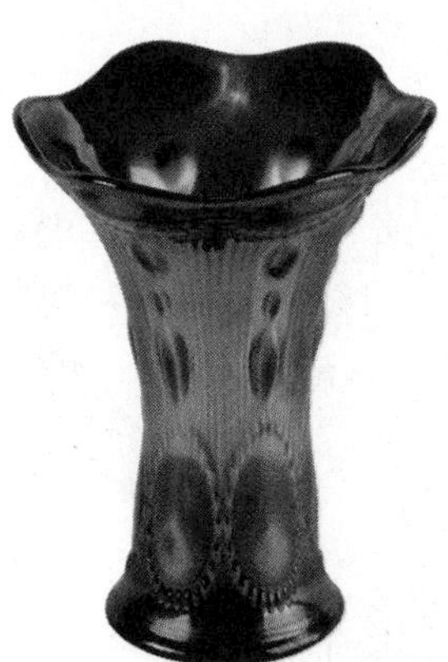

Beaded Bullseye squat vase, purple, 7" h., Imperial.....**$250-$350 (scarce)**

Beaded Bullseye vase, electric purple, 8-3/4", Imperial ................................**$150-$250**
Outstanding example .......... **$450**

Big Basketweave vase, white, 10" h, Dugan-Diamond.............. **$500**

Big Butterfly tumbler, one of four known, green, U.S. Glass.**$10,000**

Blackberry Block ruffled-top tankard, blue, 11" h., Fenton ........................... **$1,500-$1,800**

Blackberry Wreath green spittoon, Millersburg...................... **$5,200**

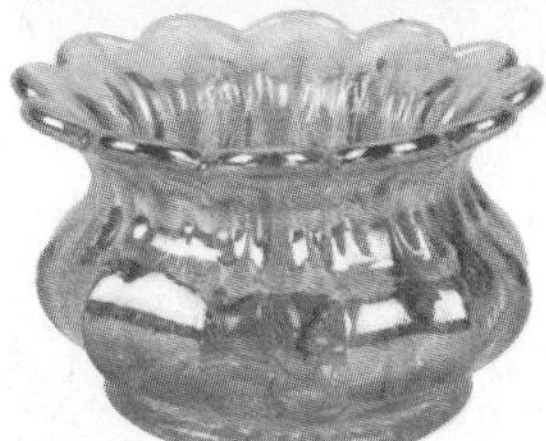

Blackberry Wreath spittoon, whimsey, marigold, Millersburg.... **$700**

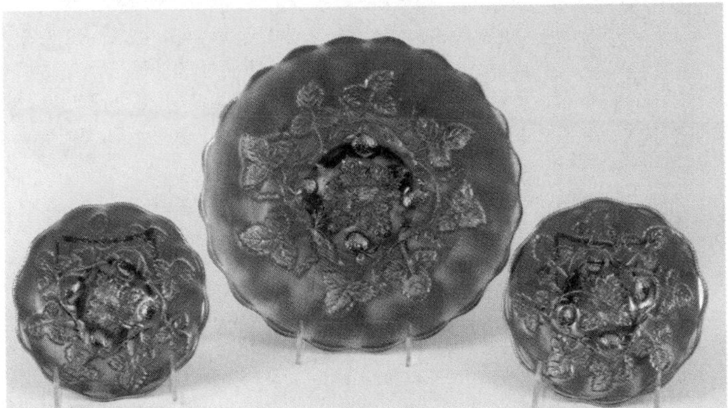

Millersburg Blackberry Wreath chop plate, 11"; and two Blackberry Wreath plates, 6-1/2". All are amethyst and rare.
Chop plate ...... **$20,000-$25,000**
Small plates ................**$2,500 ea.**

Blueberry pitcher by Fenton, blue............**$650-$950**
Outstanding example ................................. **$3,500**

Blueberry ruffled-top tankard, blue, 10" h., Fenton
.................................................... **$1,000-$1,400**
Outstanding example ................................. **$4,500**

Bouquet water pitcher and six tumblers (one shown), marigold, Fenton .......................................... **$265**

Broken Arches punch cup, purple, 2-1/4" h., Imperial ........................................................ **$40-$70**

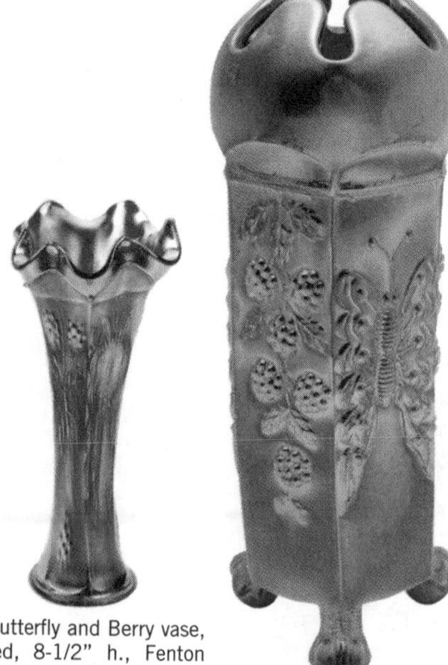

Butterfly and Berry vase, red, 8-1/2" h., Fenton ............... **$900-$1,200**

Butterfly and Berry fernery, turned in, amethyst, Fenton ......................................................... **$1,000**

◄Butterfly and Berry hatpin holder, blue, rare, Fenton ......................................................... **$1,300**

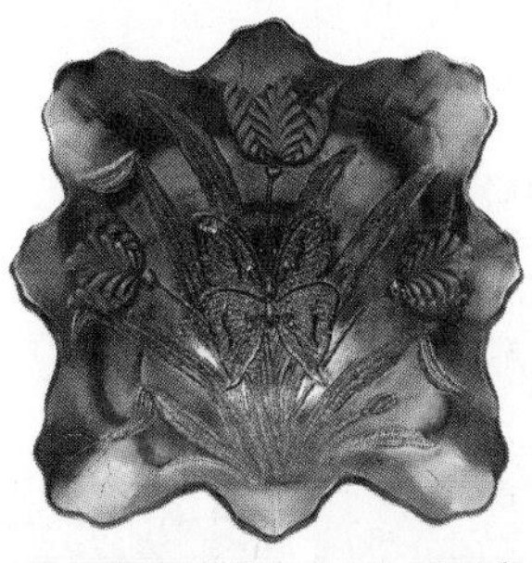
Butterfly and Tulip bowl, electric purple, square, 11" dia.... **$1,200**

Butterfly and Fern water pitcher and six tumblers, amethyst, Fenton ........................................**$1,050**

Butterfly and Tulip square-ruffled bowl, purple, footed, 11" d dia., Dugan ................. **$1,200-$3,500**

Captive Rose plate, emerald green, rare, Fenton, 9"....... **$600-$1,800**
Outstanding example ....... **$8,000**

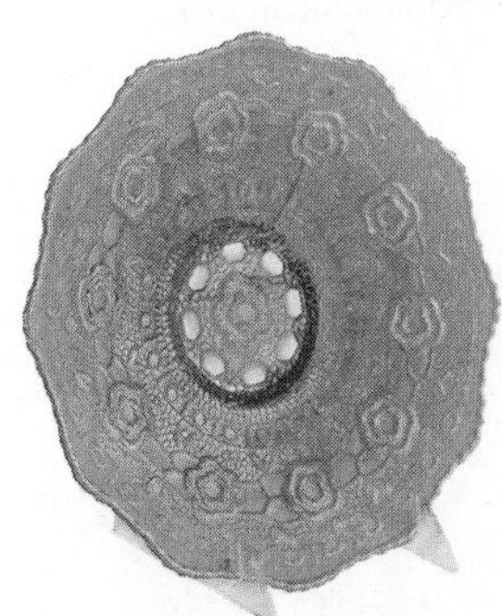
Captive Rose flat plate, green, 9" dia., Fenton ............ **$900-$1,500**
Outstanding example ....... **$4,500**

Captive Rose bowl with 3-in-1 edge, electric blue, Fenton .. **$500**

Captive Rose plate with great detail, amethyst, Fenton, 9".... **$575**

Farmyard ruffled bowl, purple, Dugan ............................**$5,500-$8,000**
Outstanding example ..........................................................**$12,500**

Fentonia water pitcher and one tumbler, blue, Fenton........................................................ **$875**

Fluffy Peacock water pitcher and six tumblers, amethyst.................................................... **$1,050**

Good Luck bowl, 8-1/2", ruffled/ ribbed, ice blue, Northwood ........................... **$4,000-$4,800**

Good Luck bowl with pie crust edge, emerald green, 8-1/2", Northwood ..............**$750-$1,100**
Outstanding example ....... **$2,800**

Good Luck plate, electric blue, 9", Northwood ........... **$4,500-$5,500**
Outstanding example ....... **$8,000**

Good Luck, bowl, ribbed exterior, ruffled, sapphire, Northwood ..................................... **$2,100**

Imperial Grape punch bowl, base and six cups, electric purple ..................................... **$1,700**

Imperial Grape stemmed wine, marigold, 4" h. ............... **$20-$35**

Imperial Grape wine decanter, purple, 12" ................ **$250-$350**

Morning Glory, vase, 5", squatty, smoke, Imperial .................. **$165**

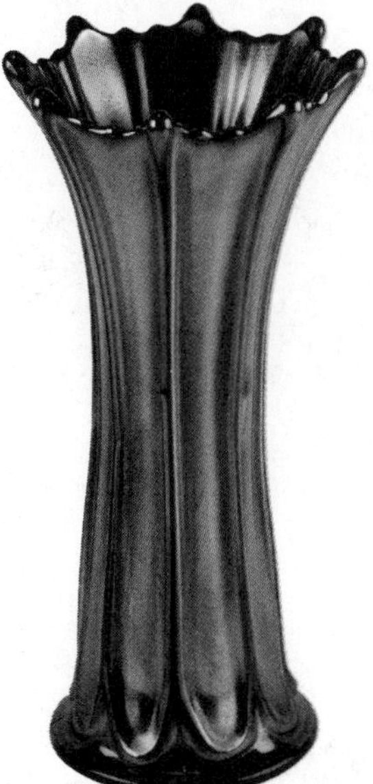
Morning Glory vase, purple, 12-1/2" h., Imperial ... **$500-$800**

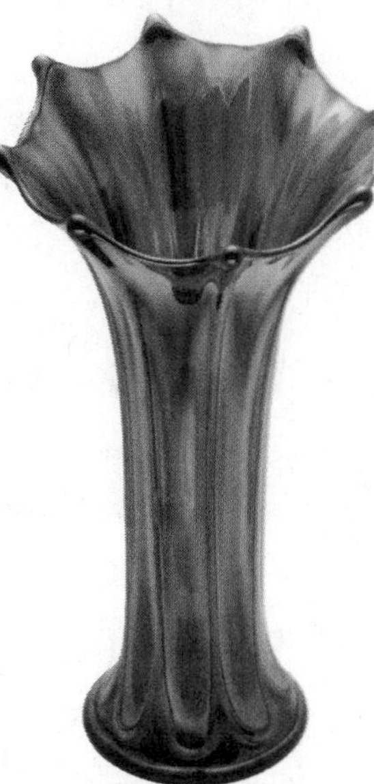
Morning Glory funeral vase, blue, one of only three perfect examples known in this color, Imperial, rare ........................... **$8,000-12,500**

Peacocks on the Fence ruffled bowl, electric blue, 8-1/2", Northwood ................................ **$400**

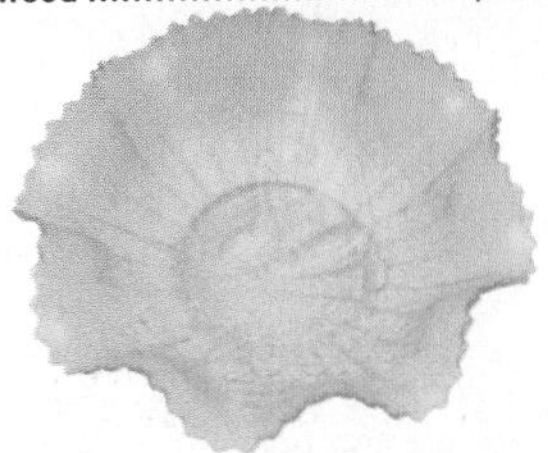
Peacocks on the Fence ruffled bowl with ribbed back, ice green, 8-1/2", Northwood .............. **$850**

Peacocks on the Fence plate, blue, unbelievable color, Northwood .............................. **$2,100**

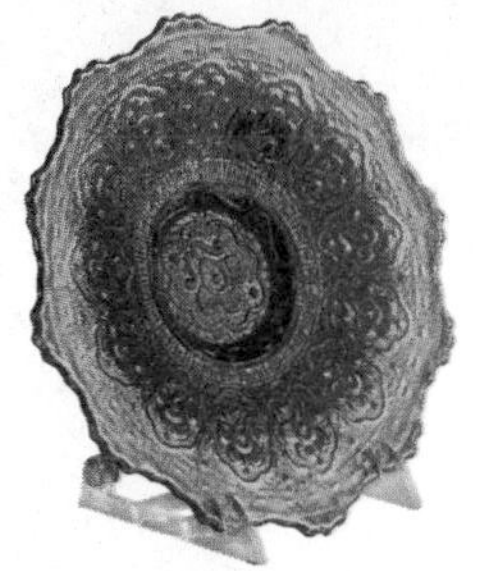
Persian Medallion flat plate, green, 6-3/4", Fenton . **$400-$600**
Outstanding example ....... **$1,700**

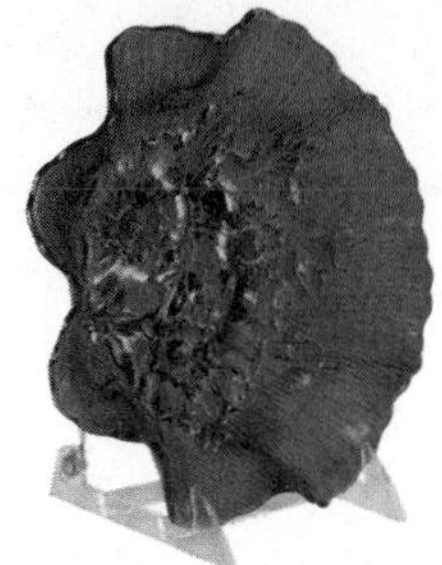
Poppy Show bowl, eight ruffles, blue, 8-1/2" dia., Northwood ............................... **$700-$1,100**
Outstanding example ....... **$2,500**

Ripple vase, electric purple with electric highlights, 12" h. with 3-3/8" base, Imperial .**$100-$300**

Peacocks on the Fence bowl, pie crust edge, ribbed, ice blue, Northwood .................... **$2,000**

Poppy Show plate, white, 9" dia., Northwood .............. **$700-$1,100**

Ripple mid-size vase, teal, 11-1/4" h., with a 3-7/8" base, Imperial, rare .............**$275-$500**

Rose Show plate, pastel marigold, 9" dia., Northwood ........................... **$1,200-$1,800**

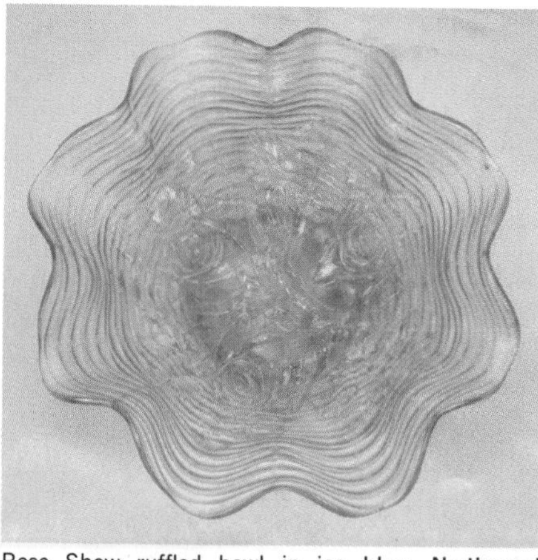

Rose Show ruffled bowl in ice blue, Northwood ........................................................ **$1,300**

►Strawberry Scroll blue pitcher, Fenton ...................................................... **$1,700-$2,500**
Outstanding example ................................. **$3,500**

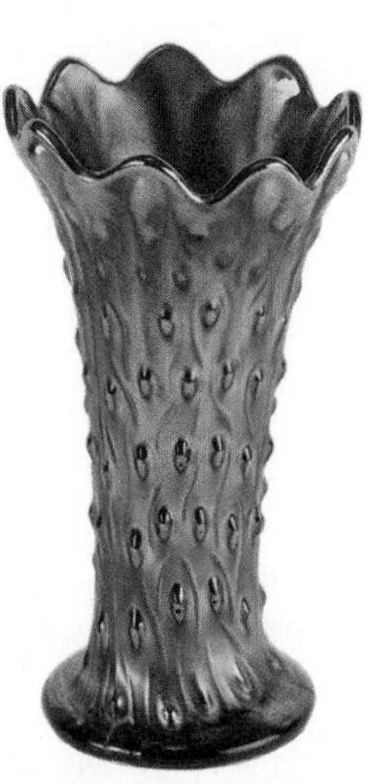

Tree Trunk standard vase, purple, 8", Northwood.............**$80-$150**

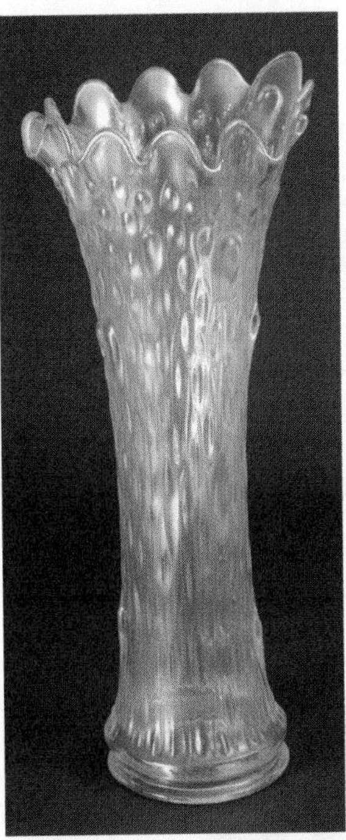

Tree Trunk white funeral vase, 17", Northwood.... **$4,000-$5,000**

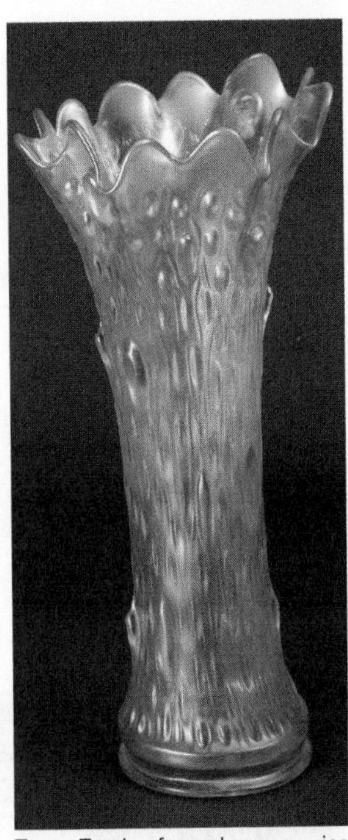

Tree Trunk funeral vase, ice green, 18", Northwood; there are only a handful of these vases known, making it very rare ........................**$23,000-$26,000**

Tree Trunk vases from left: squatty, ice blue, 7"; ice blue, 11", Northwood ............................. **$400 ea.**

Strawberry Scroll marigold pitcher and tumbler, Fenton. Pitcher.................................. **$2,100-$4,000**
Tumbler.................................................. **$30-$80**

GLASS

# Central Glass

From the 1890s until its closing in 1939, the Central Glass Co. of Wheeling, West Virginia, produced colorless and colored handmade glass in all the styles then popular. Decorations from etchings with acid to hand-painted enamels were used.

The popular "Depression" era colors of black, pink, green, light blue, ruby red and others were all produced. Two of its 1920s etchings are still familiar today, one named for the then-president of the United States and the other for the governor of West Virginia: Harding and Morgan patterns.

From high end art glass to mass-produced plain barware tumblers, Central Glass Works was a major glass producer throughout the period.

Central No. 775/Pressed Diamond blue celery vase and compote on high standard, Central Glass Co., fourth quarter 19th c., 6-7/8" h. and 6-1/2" h., 7-1/2" d. .................................................... **$69**
*Jeffrey S. Evans & Associates*

Log Cabin butter dish, colorless, Central Glass Co., fourth quarter 19th c., 5-3/4" h. overall, 4-1/8" x 5-7/8" ......................................................... **$184**
*Jeffrey S. Evans & Associates*

Pair of Log Cabin covered compotes, colorless, Central Glass Co., fourth quarter 19th c., 9" h. overall, 4-1/4" x 6" ................................ **$374**
*Jeffrey S. Evans & Associates*

Log Cabin water pitcher, colorless, Central Glass Co., fourth quarter 19th c., 8-1/2" h. overall .... **$288**
*Jeffrey S. Evans & Associates*

# Consolidated Glass

The Consolidated Lamp & Glass Co. of Coraopolis, Pennsylvania, was founded in 1894. For a number of years it was noted for its lighting wares but also produced popular lines of pressed and blown tableware. Highly collectible glass patterns of this early era include the Cone, Cosmos, Florette and Guttate lines.

Lamps and shades continued to be good sellers, but in 1926 a new "art" line of molded decorative wares was introduced. This "Martelè" line was developed as a direct imitation of the fine glassware being produced by Renè Lalique of France, and many Consolidated patterns resembled their French counterparts. Other popular lines produced during the 1920s and 1930s were Dancing Nymph, the delightfully Art Deco Ruba Rombic introduced in 1928, and the Catalonian line, which debuted in 1927 and imitated 17th-century Spanish glass.

Although the factory closed in 1933, it was reopened under new management in 1936 and prospered through the 1940s. It finally closed in 1967. Collectors should note that many later Consolidated patterns closely resemble wares of other competing firms, especially the Phoenix Glass Company. Careful study is needed to determine the maker of pieces from the 1920-1940 era.

A book that will be of help to collectors is *Phoenix & Consolidated Art Glass, 1926-1980*, by Jack D. Wilson (Antique Publications, 1989).

Cosmos syrup pitcher, opaque white/milk glass with polychrome decoration, opaque white/milk glass applied handle, period lid, Consolidated Lamp & Glass Co., late 19th/early 20th c., 6-1/4" h. overall, 3-1/2" dia. overall..... **$92**
*Jeffrey S. Evans & Associates*

Florette cracker jar, cased pink, satin finish, with matching glass cover, Consolidated Lamp & Glass Co., fourth quarter 19th c., 6-3/8" h. overall, 5-3/4" dia. overall. **$57**
*Jeffrey S. Evans & Associates*

Cosmos pickle caster, opaque white/milk glass with polychrome stain, fitted in a Lexington Silver Plate Co. quadruple-plate frame, marked "11," with cover and tongs, rim of jar polished during manufacturing process, Consolidated Lamp & Glass Co., fourth quarter 19th c., 10" h. overall, jar 4" h., 4" dia. overall........... **$172**
*Jeffrey S. Evans & Associates*

◀Two Cosmos water pitchers, opaque white/milk glass with polychrome decoration, one with pink band at neck, the other with peach band and slightly darker flowers, each with opaque white/milk glass applied handle with pressed fan on upper terminal, Consolidated Lamp & Glass Co., late 19th/early 20th c., 9" h. overall, 6" dia. overall. ... **$80**
*Jeffrey S. Evans & Associates*

Cone sugar shaker, cased pink, period lid, Consolidated Lamp & Glass Co., fourth quarter 19th c., 5-1/8" h. overall................**$103**
*Jeffrey S. Evans & Associates*

Cone sugar shaker, opaque blue, period lid, Consolidated Lamp & Glass Co., fourth quarter 19th c., 5-1/8" h. overall..................**$92**
*Jeffrey S. Evans & Associates*

Cone sugar shaker, opaque green, period lid, Consolidated Lamp & Glass Co., fourth quarter 19th c., 5-1/8" h. overall..................**$80**
*Jeffrey S. Evans & Associates*

Phoenix (Consolidated) art glass vase, auberge glass with blackberry and cricket decorated body, unsigned, 18" h. ...............**$350**
*Clars Auction Gallery*

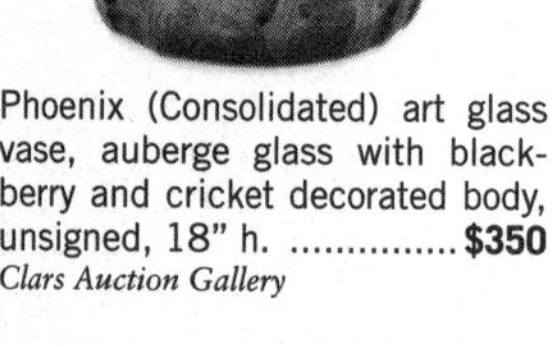

Guttate syrup pitcher, cased pink, colorless applied handle, period lid with patent date, Consolidated Lamp & Glass Co., fourth quarter 19th c., 6-3/8" h. overall. ...**$138**
*Jeffrey S. Evans & Associates*

Criss-Cross water pitcher, cranberry opalescent, tri-corner crimped rim, colorless applied handle, polished pontil mark, Consolidated Lamp & Glass Co., late 19th/early 20th c., 8-3/4" h. overall. ..........................**$2,185**
*Jeffrey S. Evans & Associates*

Two Phoenix Consolidated molded glass vases, ca. 1940; dogwood vase, 7" dia., 10-5/8" h.; polychrome parakeets feeding on berry bush, 10" dia., 8-7/8" h.; parakeets, 8-1/2" line across base ........................................**$170**
*Horst Auction Center*

Ten-piece Ruba Rombic smoky topaz glass decanter set, model nos. 823, 824, and 825, designed by Ruben Haley, circa 1928, Consolidated Lamp & Glass Co., 9-1/4" h. liquor bottle, 2-3/4" h. each whiskey glass, 11-5/8" l. tray............................................................**$6,274**
*Heritage Auction Galleries*

Art glass vases with blue owls and salmon reeds on satin custard glass base, Consolidated Lamp & Glass Co., 6" x 4-1/2" ea................ **$110**
*Dirk Soulis Auctions*

A4-9 art glass vase, Consolidated Lamp & Glass Co., 7-1/2" t. x 6-3/4" w. .................................................................................. **$80**
*Don Presley Auction*

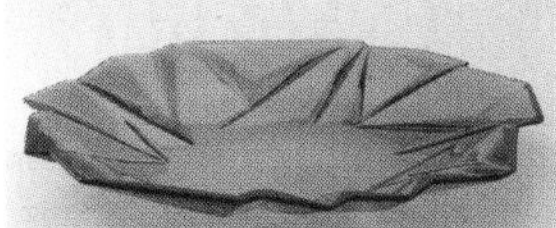

Ruba Rombic smoky topaz glass plate, model no. 809, designed by Ruben Haley, circa 1928, Consolidated Lamp & Glass Co., 15" dia. .......................................**$717**
*Heritage Auction Galleries*

Victorian red satin art glass biscuit jar, bead and puffy design, attributed to Consolidated Lamp & Glass Co., circa 1890, 6" x 9" .......................................**$125**
*Richard D. Hatch & Associates*

Victorian green satin art glass biscuit jar, bead and puffy design, attributed to Consolidated Lamp & Glass Co., circa 1890, 7" x 8" .......................................**$150**
*Richard D. Hatch & Associates*

◀Pair of Katydid vases, electrified, together with a vase, Consolidated Lamp & Glass Co., 8" **$250**
*Susanin's Auctions*

# Crackle Glass

Home decorating schemes of the mid-20th century were often distinguished by at least one piece of crackle glass. Although first produced in the 1930s, these brilliant light-catchers proved particularly popular from the 1950s onward. The lines were clean and uncluttered, and the varied shapes held visual interest. The colors, whether bold or clear, solids, shaded, or stark contrasts, made each piece the ideal complement to modern décor.

Crackle glass is a treatment, rather than a style. The "crackling" finish is created when a hot glass object is submerged in cold water; the abrupt temperature change cracks the glass. The object is then reheated, strengthening and smoothing the glass. Once the process is complete, crack lines ("crackling") remain. Because of the irregularity of the crackling, light shining on crackle glass deflects in intriguing patterns on other surfaces, flattering even the most staid environment.

Numerous companies dabbled in crackle glass production. The major manufacturers, however, were located in West Virginia: Blenko, Pilgrim, Rainbow, Bischoff, Kanawha, and Viking.

Although ostensibly vessels with a function (vases, decanters, pitchers, bowls, goblets), the overriding purpose of a crackle glass piece was decorative. Intended additions, such as flowers or beverages, not only deaden the color and play of light through the crackling, but also detract from the design simplicity of the piece.

Today's crackle glass collectors have a wealth of options to choose from. Some collect a specific shape, color, or type of vessel. Others focus on the output of a particular company, like Blenko, or the work of particular craftsmen, such as Wayne Husted and Joel Myers; their creations contributed much to the Blenko reputation. Many more, however, simply collect crackle glass to collect it. Its diverse styles and interplay of light and color continue to delight decades after its introduction.

Amber jug, Blenko #5424, Wayne Husted design, 1954, 12" h. .......................................... **$70-$90**

Bischoff turquoise decanter #478, teardrop stopper, 13" h. .................................................. **$60-$70**

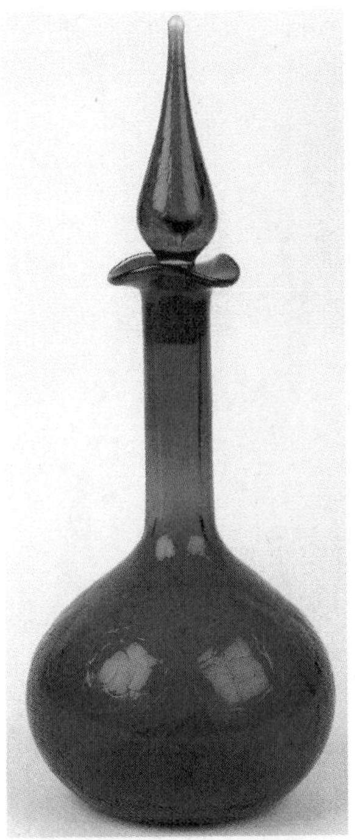
Blenko ruby decanter #37, an often-copied design, 13-1/2" h. .................................. **$50-$60**

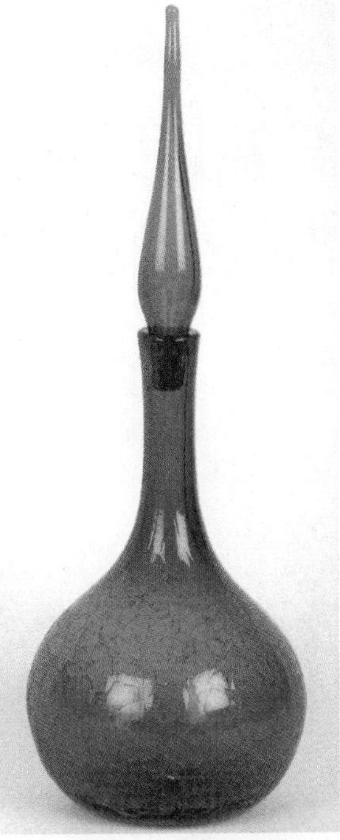
Blenko honey decanter, #627-L, Wayne Husted design, 1962, 18" h................................ **$75-100**

Blenko tangerine decanter #657 M, Joel Myers design, 1965, 14" h................................ **$70-$90**

Blenko pitchers, #3750-L, 5-1/2" h........... **$30-$40**
#939, Winslow Anderson design, 1950, 14" h ........................................................ **$60-$70**

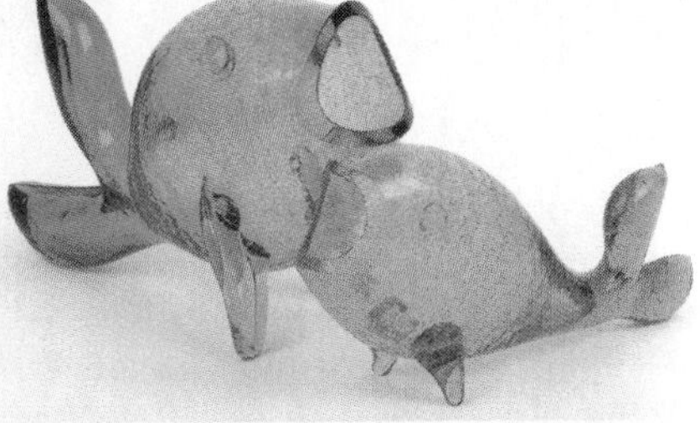
Fish vases, Blenko #5433, amber, 10" l..**$100-$125**
#971 S olive green, 12-1/2" l.................... **$50-$60**

Footed bowl, Blenko #468 L, crystal with turquoise foot, 13" d.............................................. **$70-$90**

◄Blenko three-cup mugs, "Blenko Blue" ........................................................ **$30-$40 ea.**

Gold martini pitcher, Bischoff #308, 8-3/4" h. ....... **$25-$35**

▼Gurgle bottle, Rainbow #9761, bubble stopper, 8-1/2" h. ................ **$50-$60**

Honey crackle pitcher, Blenko #976, Winslow Anderson design, 1950, 19-1/2" h. ......... **$75-$100**

◀Pilgrim beaker vase #72, turquoise, 10" h. ............... **$40-$50**

Kanawha pitchers, Amberina, tallest 14" h. ........................................................ **$35-$45 ea.**

Pilgrim bent decanter, 1950, 14" h. .......... **$70-$90**

Vase, Blenko #6833-LT, lemon with tangerine spiral trim, Joel Myers design, 1968, 10-1/4" h .................................. **$60-$80**

Rainbow decanters #933 and #315, Amberina, flame stoppers, 13-1/2" h.................... **$50-$70**
16-1/2" h.................... **$75-$100**

Rainbow miniature window pitchers, yellow and Amberina, 5-3/4" h............................ **$15-$20 ea.**

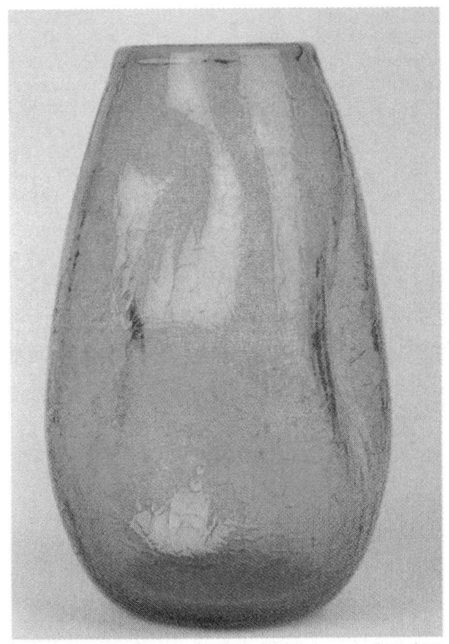

Pilgrim "dented" vase #60, 9-1/2" h.......... **$50-$60**

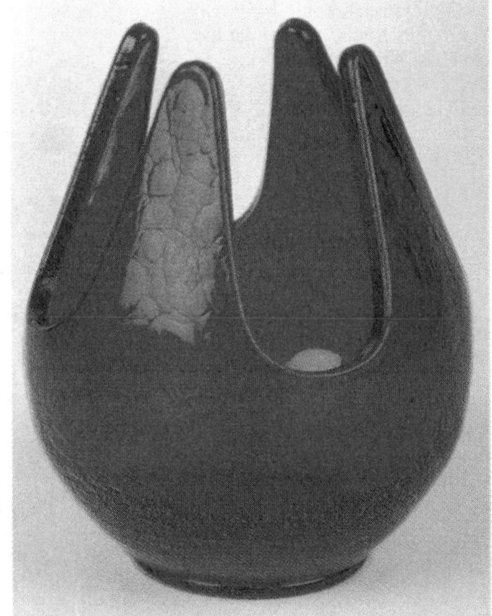

Viking patio light, 5" h.............................. **$25-$35**

GLASS

# Cranberry Glass

Gold was added to glass batches to give cranberry glass its color on reheating. It has been made by numerous glasshouses for years and is currently being reproduced. Both blown and molded articles were produced. A less expensive type of cranberry glass was made with the substitution of copper for gold.

Inverted Thumbprint pickle caster, deep cranberry with full-round polychrome decoration, fitted in an Acme Silver Co. quadruple-plate frame, marked "345," with cover and tongs, rim of jar polished during manufacturing process, fourth quarter 19th c., 11-3/4" h. overall, jar 5" h., 4" dia. overall. .............................. **$316**
*Jeffrey S. Evans & Associates*

Inverted Thumbprint pickle caster, cranberry, fitted in a Reed and Barton silver-plate frame, marked "1200," with cover and pick, rim of jar polished during manufacturing process, fourth quarter 19th c. 12-3/4" h. overall, jar 5" h., 3-3/4" dia. overall. ............. **$195**
*Jeffrey S. Evans & Associates*

Inverted Thumbprint pickle caster, shaded cranberry with full-round polychrome decoration, fitted in a Rockford Silver Plate Co. quadruple-plate frame, marked "662," a second partially legible mark "? JEWELERS SIL. CO. QUADRUPLE" with "N.R.J.A." centered over a triangle, above this mark is impressed "S.C.LEVY," with cover, tongs, and fork, rim of jar polished during manufacturing process, fourth quarter 19th c., 10" h. overall, jar 4-1/4" h., 3-1/4" dia. overall. .............................. **$218**
*Jeffrey S. Evans & Associates*

Cranberry art glass bowl, vertically ribbed body with lightly ruffled rim, bowl decorated with three applied clear glass feet that curve upward to form a tree limb with applied leaves and flowers, bowl is unsigned but attributed to Stevens & Williams, 5-1/4" h. x 7" dia. **$201**
*James D. Julia, Inc.*

Inverted Thumbprint pickle caster, cranberry with polychrome decoration, fitted in an Adelphia Silver Plate Co. quadruple-plate frame, with cover and tongs, rim of jar polished and gilded during manufacturing process, fourth quarter 19th c., 12-3/4" h. overall, jar 4-1/2" h., 3-1/4"dia. .......... **$258**
*Jeffrey S. Evans & Associates*

Diamond-Optic pickle caster, rubina with full-round polychrome floral decoration, fitted in a Derby Silver Co. quadruple-plate frame, with cover and tongs, rim of jar polished during manufacturing process, fourth quarter 19th c., 11-1/2" h. overall, jar 4-1/4" h., 3-1/4" dia. overall. ............. **$345**
*Jeffrey S. Evans & Associates*

Venetian Diamond sugar shaker, deep cranberry, period lid, Hobbs, Brockunier & Co., fourth quarter 19th c., 4-3/4" h. overall. ... **$115**
*Jeffrey S. Evans & Associates*

Medallion Sprig sugar shaker, rubina, period lid, West Virginia Glass Co, fourth quarter 19th c., 4-3/4" h. overall................ **$207**
*Jeffrey S. Evans & Associates*

Rustic-Optic pickle caster, rubina with full-round white and gilt floral decoration, fitted in a Homan Silver Plate Co. quadruple-plate frame, with cover and tongs, rim of jar polished during manufacturing process, fourth quarter 19th c., 10-1/8" h. overall, jar 4-1/2" h., 4" dia. overall. .............. **$258**
*Jeffrey S. Evans & Associates*

Inverted Thumbprint pickle caster, deep cranberry, fitted in a Middletown Plate Co. silver-plate frame, marked "350," with cover and tongs, rim of jar polished during manufacturing process, fourth quarter 19th c., 9-1/2" h. overall, jar 4-3/4" h., 4" dia. overall.**$115**
*Jeffrey S. Evans & Associates*

Pair of cranberry and enameled glass lusters, Continental, 20th c., 13-1/2" h. .................... **$325**
*Stefek's Auctioneers & Appraisers*

Cranberry pickle caster, polychrome and gilt decoration, fitted in a Forbes Silver Co. silver-plate stand, with cover and tongs, fourth quarter 19th c., 10-7/8" h. overall, jar 4-3/4" h., 3-1/4" dia. overall. .................................... **$230**
*Jeffrey S. Evans & Associates*

Inverted Thumbprint pickle caster, cranberry with full-round white and gilt floral decorations, fitted in a Derby Silver Co. quadruple-plate frame, marked "149," with cover and tongs, rim of jar polished during manufacturing process, fourth quarter 19th c., 11-3/8" h. overall, jar 4-5/8" h., 3-1/2" dia. overall. .................................... **$218**
*Jeffrey S. Evans & Associates*

Inverted Thumbprint pickle caster, deep cranberry with full-round polychrome decoration, fitted in a James W. Tufts triple-plate frame, marked "2362," with cover and tongs, jar with polishing to rim, possibly post production, fourth quarter 19th c., 11-3/4" h. overall, jar 4-3/4" h., 3-1/2" dia. overall. .................................... **$287**
*Jeffrey S. Evans & Associates*

Pair of cranberry lusters with prisms, Bohemian, gilt decorated borders with enamel embellishments and 10 hanging prisms, 15" h. x 6-1/2" dia. .......... **$850**
*Fontaine's Auction Gallery*

Pair of cranberry cut glass decanters with elongated stoppers and gilt trim, 9" h. ........................... **$325**
*Fontaine's Auction Gallery*

# Custard Glass

"Custard glass," as collectors call it today, came on the American scene in the 1890s, more than a decade after similar colors were made in Europe and England. The Sowerby firm of Gateshead-on-Tyne, England had marketed its patented "Queen's Ivory Ware" quite successfully in the late 1870s and early 1880s.

There were many glass tableware factories operating in Pennsylvania and Ohio in the 1890s and early 1900s, and the competition among them was keen. Each company sought to capture the public's favor with distinctive colors and, often, hand-painted decoration. That is when "custard glass" appeared on the American scene.

The opaque yellow color of this glass varies from a rich, vivid yellow to a lustrous light yellow. Regardless of intensity, the hue was originally called "ivory" by several glass manufacturers who also used superlative sounding terms such as "Ivorina Verde" and "Carnelian." Most custard glass contains uranium, so it will "glow" under a black light.

The most important producer of custard glass was certainly Harry Northwood, who first made it at his plants in Indiana, Pennsylvania, in the late 1890s and, later, in his Wheeling, West Virginia, factory. Northwood marked some of his most famous patterns, but much early custard is unmarked. Other key manufacturers include the Heisey Glass Co., Newark, Ohio; the Jefferson Glass Co., Steubenville, Ohio; the Tarentum Glass Co., Tarentum, Pennsylvania; and the Fenton Art Glass Co., Williamstown, West Virginia.

Custard glass fanciers are particular about condition and generally insist on pristine quality decorations free from fading or wear. Souvenir custard pieces with events, places, and dates on them usually bring the best prices in the areas commemorated on them rather than from the specialist collector. Also, collectors who specialize in pieces such as cruets, syrups, or salt and pepper shakers will often pay higher prices for these pieces than would a custard collector.

Key reference sources include William Heacock's *Custard Glass from A to Z*, published in 1976 but not out of print, and the book *Harry Northwood: The Early Years*, available from Glass Press. Heisey's custard glass is discussed in Shirley Dunbar's *Heisey Glass: The Early Years* (Krause Publications, 2000), and Coudersport's production is well-documented in Tulla Majot's book, *Coudersport's Glass 1900- 1904* (Glass Press, 1999).

*James Measell*

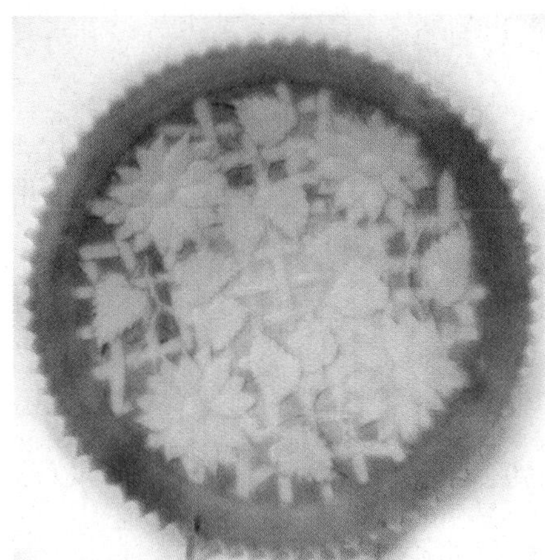

Rare Northwood custard glass Poinsettia pattern footed compote, center dish with floral and leaf pattern raised over a blue decorated surface, stands on three scrolling feet. 9" dia. .............................. **$250**
*Fontaine's Auction Gallery*

Northwood custard glass Chrysanthemum fruit bowl, shallow flake on edge of foot, unmarked, 10-1/2" l., 4-1/2" h. .......................................................... **$30**
*Central Street Antiques and Auction*

Custard glass Beaded Circle with floral enamel, seven-piece water set, great color.................... **$600**
*Strawser Auction Group*

Custard glass Intaglio pattern seven-piece berry set, nice color...................................................... **$100**
*Strawser Auction Group*

Custard glass Beaded Circle pattern with floral enamel four-piece table set, butter keeper, creamer, sugar, and spooner, great color........................ **$600**
*Strawser Auction Group*

Single Victorian custard glass lustre, raised gilt tulip and foliate motif, 14" h......................... **$50**
*DuMouchelles*

Northwood custard glass Inverted Fan and Feather pattern seven-piece berry set with good color, ca. 1900 ........................................... **$160**
*Strawser Auction Group*

Northwood custard glass Argonaut covered sugar and two bowls, bases decorated with green seaweed and gold shells, cover to sugar (rare) has gold shell finial, signed in script, "Ca.1900. Made-Indiana, Pa."...................... **$250**
*Phoebus Auction Gallery*

# Cut Glass

Cut glass is made by grinding decorations into glass by means of abrasive-carrying metal or stone wheels. An ancient craft, it was revived in 1600 by Bohemians and spread through Europe to Great Britain and America.

American cut glass came of age at the Centennial Exposition in 1876 and the World Columbian Exposition in 1893. America's most significant output of h.-quality glass occurred from 1880 to 1917, a period now known as the Brilliant Period. Glass from this period is the most eagerly sought glass by collectors.

Colorless cut glass compote, America, 19th c., with scalloped rim, diamond and faceted bands, octagonal faceted shaft on round stepped base with cut rays on bottom, 7-5/8", 8-1/2" dia. ............................ **$184**
*Skinner, Inc.*

Two early cut glass bottles with wide bodies, rounded shoulders, and narrow, slightly flaring necks. Bottles cut and etched with stylized floral designs and flower baskets, all with gilded outlines, matching glass stoppers, signed on the underside with etched crown and entwined initials "EH," 6-1/2" t. Provenance: From the collection of Dorothy-Lee Jones. ............... **$575**
*James D. Julia, Inc.*

William Fritsche cut crystal vase with detailed palm trees carved against applied bulbous knobs, bottom carved to depict waves of water with billowing clouds carved around top, signed on underside "Webb" and "1674" and on side "W. Fritsche," 8-1/4" t. x 10" dia. Provenance: From the collection of Dorothy-Lee Jones....................................................... **$8,050**
*James D. Julia, Inc.*

Unger Bros. silver and cut glass vanity jar with cupids kissing, Unger Bros., Newark, New Jersey, circa 1900, marks: (UB intertwined) STERLING, FINE, 925; 3" h., 16.4 oz. .................................... **$215**
*Heritage Auction Galleries*

Three cut glass items. 1) Footed Libbey bowl with strawberry pattern surrounding the sides, signed on underside "Libbey," 10" dia. 2) Bowl with cut strawberries, stems, and leaves with rolled rim, unsigned. 3) Lead crystal pitcher with allover deeply cut pattern of raspberries, stems, and leaves, finished with applied crystal notched handle, unsigned, 9" t. Provenance: From the collection of Dorothy-Lee Jones. ..........**$632**

*James D. Julia, Inc.*

Cut glass decanter with five glasses, Fan and Nailhead diamond pattern with faceted neck, spout, and matching original stopper, decanter accompanied by five matching glasses, all with a star cut base, decanter is 11-1/2" t. Provenance: From the collection of Dorothy-Lee Jones................................ **$1,265**

*James D. Julia, Inc.*

Hunt Glass Co. Royal pattern cut glass bowl, oval form with scalloped rim, 4-1/2" h. x 11" x 8-1/2" ............................................................... **$250**

*Fontaine's Auction Gallery*

Three cut glass bowls. 1) Libbey bowl with vertical cutting and diamond cut design around rim, signed on interior with "Libbey" insignia. 2) Bowl with hobstar design and scalloped rim. 3) Bowl with notched fan design with hobstar panels and scalloped rim; ranging from 8" to 9-1/4" dia. Provenance: From the collection of Dorothy-Lee Jones...................... **$460**

*James D. Julia, Inc.*

Two large cut glass vases with deep all over cutting, one with pedestal foot, taller vase is 14-1/2". Provenance: From the collection of Dorothy-Lee Jones. ............................................................... **$826**

*James D. Julia, Inc.*

American cut glass and silver footed compote, T.G. Hawkes & Co., Corning, New York, circa 1950, marks: HAWKES, STERLING, 28 PWT; 4-3/8" x 5-3/8" dia., .91 troy oz. ................................................. **$40**

*Heritage Auction Galleries*

Signed Hawkes cut glass bowl, signature on base, 7" dia, 3-1/2" h. .......................................... **$75-$125**

*Fontaine's Auction Gallery*

Hawkes cut glass compote with round foot and applied stem; bowl has wide flaring rim that rolls over at the ends with a fancy cut border, signed Hawkes on the base, 5" h. x 14" dia. ........................ **$150-250**

*Fontaine's Auction Gallery*

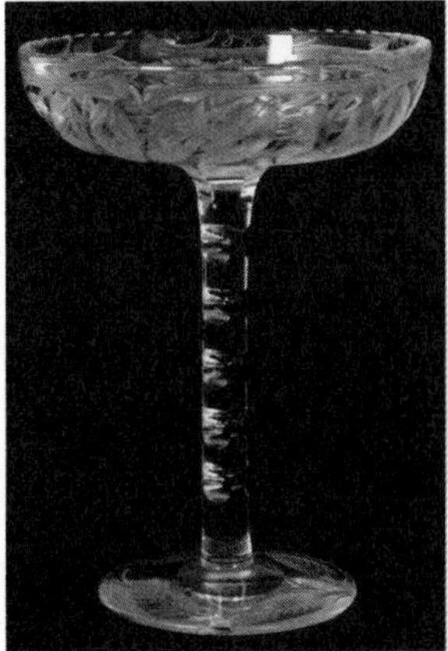

Intaglio cut fruit compote with shallow bowl, cut with leafy branch wrapping around with a cluster of grapes, pears, and oranges, on a long stem with notched pattern and round foot cut with more leaves around an orange, 8-1/28" h. x 6" ............................... **$150**

*Fontaine's Auction Gallery*

Twelve cut glass plates decorated with patterns of carved fruits, two plates each, including raspberries, grapes, peaches, pears, cherries, and strawberries, unsigned, each 8-1/2" dia. Provenance: From the collection of Dorothy-Lee Jones. ........................................ **$632**

*James D. Julia, Inc.*

Signed J. Hoare large cut glass vase, signed "J. Hoare – Corning – 1853," 18-1/2" h. ........ **$1,000**

*Fontaine's Auction Gallery*

**Right:** Rose cut wine glass used by George and Martha Washington during the presidency and afterwards at Mount Vernon, descended by Martha Washington's will to her granddaughter, Eleanor Parke Lewis and sold at an1891 auction held by Thomas Birch's and Sons, Philadelphia. It next surfaced in a 1950 auction at Parke-Bernet in New York, and has been privately held since then. 4" h. ................................ **$14,340**

*Heritage Auction Galleries*

**Far right**: German cut glass pitcher, silver handle, lid, and spout, beaded border and engraved shield-form decoration, beaded finial to lid, maker unidentified, circa 1900, marks: (half sun ray), (crescent moon and crown), 800, H; 10-1/8" h., 39.3 oz. ........... **$438**

*Heritage Auction Galleries*

Pair of George IV cut glass decanters with stoppers, panel of cut diamonds, stepped tapering necks, England, circa 1825, unmarked, 8-1/4" h............ **$167**
*Heritage Auction Galleries*

Victorian cut glass pilgrim-form flagon and decanter each with stopper, footed, England, circa 1840, unmarked, 12-1/2" h....................................... **$359**
*Heritage Auction Galleries*

Unger Bros. large silver and cut glass Indian head vanity jar, Unger Bros., Newark, New Jersey, circa 1905, marks: (UB intertwined) STERLING, FINE, 925; 3-1/4" h., 16.2 oz.............................. **$657**
*Heritage Auction Galleries*

Silver and cut glass "rock crystal" three-handled loving cup with everted silver rim with repoussé grapevine decoration, Tiffany & Co., New York, New York, circa 1890, marks: TIFFANY & CO., MAKERS STERLING SILVER, 8-3/4" h., 95.6 oz................ **$2,500**
*Heritage Auction Galleries*

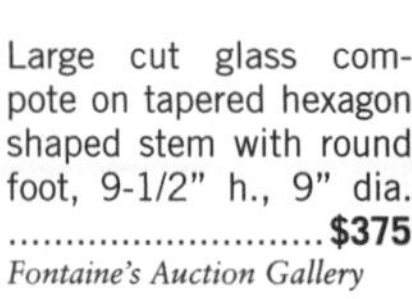

Large cut glass compote on tapered hexagon shaped stem with round foot, 9-1/2" h., 9" dia. ............................**$375**
*Fontaine's Auction Gallery*

# Czechoslovakian

The country of Czechoslovakia, including the glassmaking region of Bohemia, was not founded as an independent republic until after the close of World War I in 1918. The new country soon developed a large export industry, including a wide range of brightly colored and hand-painted glasswares such as vases, tableware, and perfume bottles. Fine quality cut crystal or Bohemian-type etched wares were also produced for the American market. Some Bohemian glass carries faint acid-etched markings on the base.

With the breakup of Czechoslovakia into two republics, the wares produced between World War I and II should gain added collector appeal.

Set of five Czech figural glass coupes, 9-1/2" h. **$140**
*Michaan's Auction Gallery*

Czech glass fruit basket lamp, Bohemian, glass beaded basket with fruit lid, 11" h. x 11" w..... **$850**
*Cowan's Auctions, Inc.*

Czech Art Deco Modernist glass vase, handled bottle form with abstract decoration, signed HEM, 8-3/4" h.............................................................. **$550**
*Leslie Hindman Auctioneers*

Czech Art Deco malachite pressed art glass Ingrid vase, square cut corner rim on vasiform body, relief decorated with nude figures and vertical geometric devices, 9-3/8" h........................................... **$250**
*Skinner, Inc.*

Pair of Moser smoke-colored vases, Czech Republic, 1960s, octagonal shape that graduates up in size from the base, color resembles fine smoky quartz, #1: 12" h. x 6-1/2" l. x 6-1/2" w.; #2: 10" h. x 5-1/2" l. x 5-1/2" w. .................................................. **$80**
*Louis J. Dianni, LLC Auctions*

►Czech Art Deco agate glass vase with continuous band of nudes in relief with a faceted circular foot, 5-1/8" h. .................................................. **$150**
*Leslie Hindman Auctioneers*

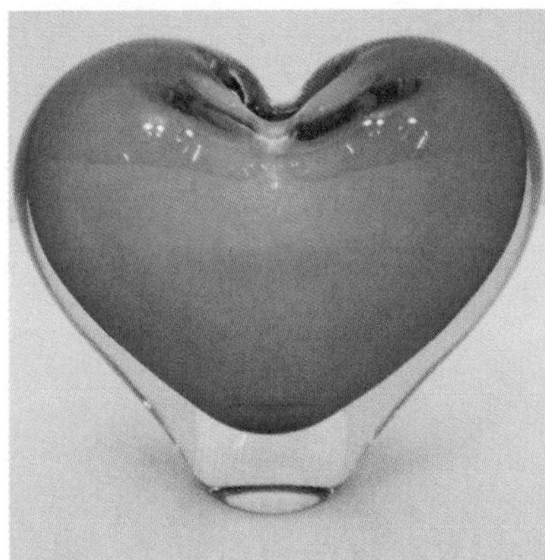

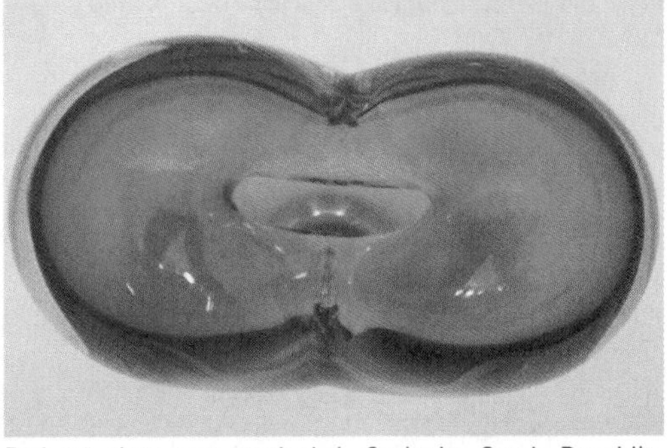

Red art glass vase marked J. Svoboda, Czech Republic, 6-1/2" x 8" thick.................................................. **$40**
*The Gap Auction*

1920s Czech chrome glass airplane atomizer, enameled glass, chromed metal fittings, original hose and ball, 7-1/2"....... **$3,000**
*Perfume Bottles Auction*

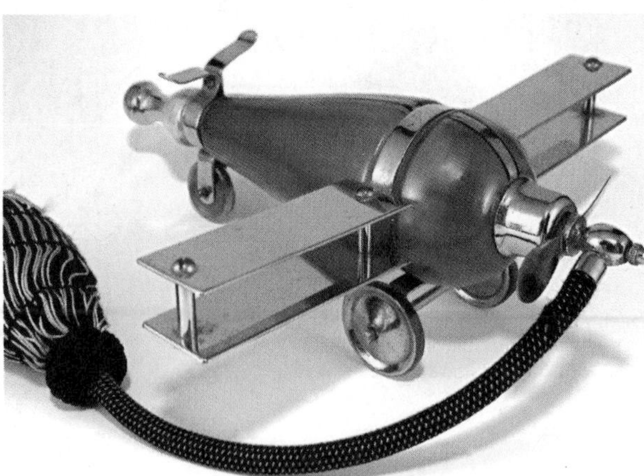

Czech art glass gold iridescent vase, deep orange color with pink highlights, signed on base "Czecho" over "Slovakia" in oval, 8" h. ................................ **$200**
*Fontaine's Auction Gallery*

Czech Austrian 1920s scenic landscape cameo glass vase, unsigned, 7-1/4" h. ................ **$130**
*Dirk Soulis Auctions*

Curt Schlevogt Czech art glass Ingrid vase, mold cast lapis glass showing four panels of women in various stages of dress and dance, 9-1/2" h. .......................... **$110**
*Burchard Galleries Inc.*

Loetz Czech iridescent hand blown yellow art glass vase with coiled overlay design depicting a snake, approx. 10" h. x 6-1/2" dia........................................................................................................ **$750**
*Elite Decorative Arts*

# Daum Nancy

Daum Nancy fine glass, much of it cameo, was made by Auguste and Antonin Daum, who founded a factory in 1875 in Nancy, France. Most of their cameo and enameled glass was made from the 1890s into the early 20th century.

Cameo glass is made by carving into multiple layers of colored glass to create a design in relief. It is at least as old as the Romans.

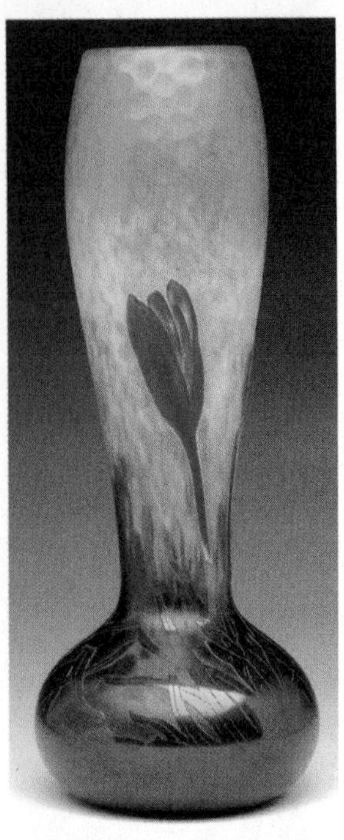

Daum Nancy crocus vase decorated with four cameo and wheel-carved crocus flowers, three in orange and one in deep purple, all against a blue shading to mottled yellow and frosted background, entire background also has subtle martele; signed on underside with engraved "Daum Nancy" with Cross of Lorraine, 11-3/4" t., from a private Long Island, New York collection....................... **$12,075**

*James D. Julia, Inc.*

Daum Nancy vase with cameo spring scene of budding trees with green grass meadows and hills in the background, all set against a mottled light blue ground, trees are enameled in browns and tans with hints of yellow; signed on side with black enamel "Daum Nancy" with Cross of Lorraine and initials "FG," 9-1/2" t., from a private Long Island, New York collection.............................. **$7,475**

*James D. Julia, Inc.*

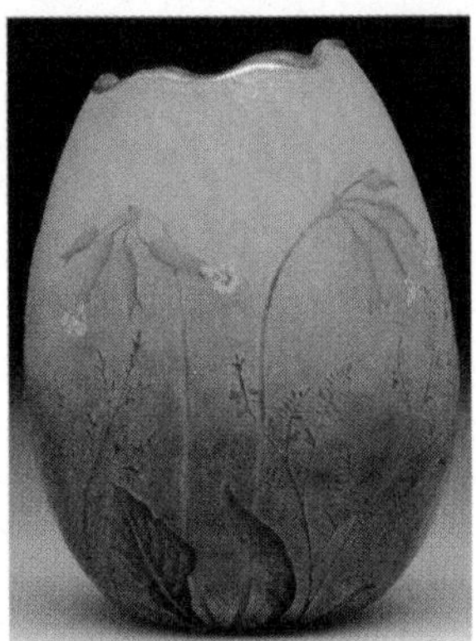

Daum vase in rare broken egg form with gilded cameo flowers, stems, and leaves against a purple shading to green background, cameo decoration is enameled with gold flowers and green leaves and stems; signed on underside in gold "Daum Nancy" with the Cross of Lorraine, 4" t. ............. **$5,750**

*James D. Julia, Inc.*

▶Daum Nancy cameo vase with winter scene decoration of barren trees against a yellow shading to orange background, trees are enameled to depict the brown bark and are highlighted with areas of snow against the bark, forest floor is enameled in white depicting the snowy ground and drifts; signed on underside "Daum Nancy" with Cross of Lorraine, 6-1/4" t.**$5,175**

*James D. Julia, Inc.*

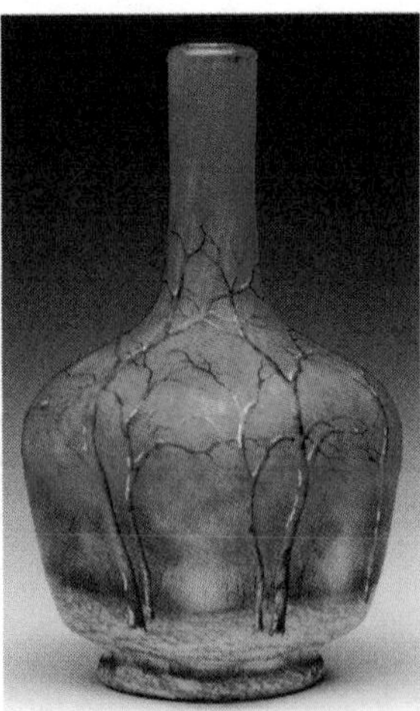

Daum Nancy creamer with cameo decoration of vitrified autumn-colored leaves and black berries, cameo decoration is set against a mottled green and cream background and is finished with an applied striated green glass handle; signed on side in cameo "Daum Nancy" with Cross of Lorraine, 5-3/4" t., from a private Long Island, New York collection. **$2,070**

*James D. Julia, Inc.*

Daum Nancy miniature vase with acid-etched and enamel winter decoration with barren trees and snow around the foot as well as accenting trees, black spotted enameled top rim; enamel signature on underside "Daum Nancy" with the Cross of Lorraine, 2-1/4" t. **$1,725**
*James D. Julia, Inc.*

Daum Nancy vase features acid cut cameo decoration of flowers, stems, and leaves set against a mottled green shading to cream background with areas of mottled orange internal decoration, flowers enameled in shades of pink with brown stems and leaves; vase features pinched sides and is signed on side in cameo "Daum Nancy" with Cross of Lorraine, 5-1/2" t., from a private Long Island, New York collection................ **$4,140**
*James D. Julia, Inc.*

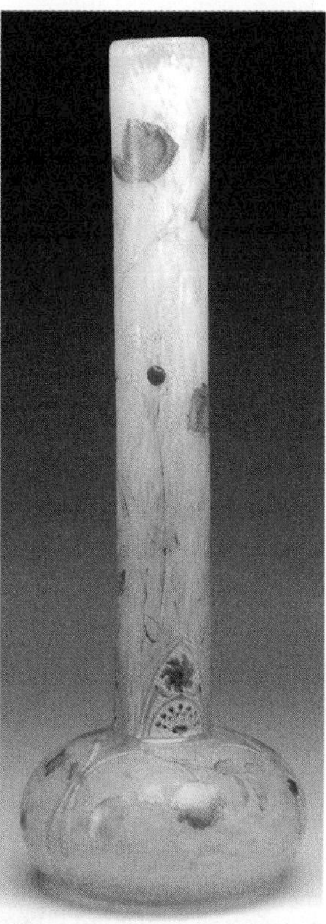

Daum Nancy vase features cameo and enamel roses, stems, and leaves against an acid textured background of mottled yellow shading to cream, each rose enameled in shades of pink and red while the leaves and stems are highlighted with gold gilding; vase is further decorated with a cameo and enameled butterfly and dragonfly and is finished with random applied green and red cabochons; signed on bottom in gold "Daum Nancy" with Cross of Lorraine, 25" t., from a private Long Island, New York collection. ....... **$13,800**
*James D. Julia, Inc.*

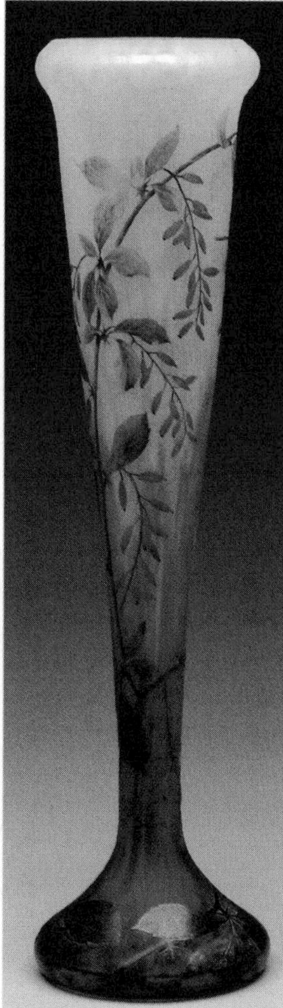

Daum Nancy vase decorated with cameo flowers, stems, and leaves against a mottled orange shading to yellow and cream background, cameo decoration enameled with red berries, green and brown leaves, and brown stems; signed on side in cameo "Daum Nancy France" with Cross of Lorraine, 17-1/4" t....................... **$4,600**
*James D. Julia, Inc.*

◀Daum Nancy vase with deep green cameo floral decoration surrounding the four slightly square sides, all set against an overall martele background of purple and opalescent shading to green at top and bottom; signed on underside with engraved and gilt "Daum Nancy" with Cross of Lorraine, 5-3/4" t., from a Private Long Island, New York collection. **$3,680**
*James D. Julia, Inc.*

Daum Nancy vase of a grove of barren trees with enamel bark, ground and forks of the trees are enameled with white snow, all set against an acid textured background of brown shading to mottled orange; signed on underside with black enameled "Daum Nancy" with Cross of Lorraine, 10" t., from a private Long Island, New York collection. ........ **$6,325**
*James D. Julia, Inc.*

French vase has mottled purple glass body blown into the Majorelle wrought-iron cage, vase is signed on underside "Daum Nancy" with the Cross of Lorraine and "Majorelle," 9-1/2" t. **$2,300**
*James D. Julia, Inc.*

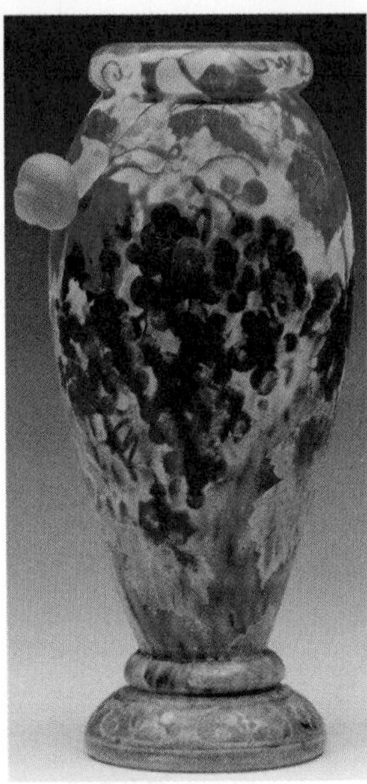

Daum Nancy vase has cameo decoration of grapevines, leaves, and grape clusters done in green, gray, and purple vitrified glass against a mottled brown shading to yellow background, further adorned with an applied snail and several applied cabochon grapes; signed on underside with etched "Daum Nancy" with the Cross of Lorraine, 10-1/8" t., from a private Long Island, New York collection. **$12,650**
*James D. Julia, Inc.*

Daum Nancy vase with cameo decoration of large orange poppies encircling the vase set against an orange shading to yellow shading to mottled orange background, vase is finished with a mottled green foot; signed on side in cameo "Daum Nancy" with Cross of Lorraine, 8-1/4" t. ....... **$2,185**
*James D. Julia, Inc.*

Daum Nancy boudoir lamp with detailed acid-etched cameo flowers, stems, and leaves in deep brown against a frosted background with hints of yellow internal decoration; shade has matching cameo pattern with a background of mottled brown shading to cream and yellow shading to peach; lamp is signed on foot of base with conjoined initials "DN" with the Cross of Lorraine, 11-3/4" t.......... **$7,000-$10,000**
*James D. Julia, Inc.*

Daum Nancy vase decorated with cameo berries, stems, and leaves against an internally decorated background of mottled brown shading to yellow, cameo decoration enameled with red berries and green leaves and stems; signed on the side in cameo "Daum Nancy" with Cross of Lorraine, 7" w. x 4-1/4" t., from a private Long Island, New York collection. **$2,760**
*James D. Julia, Inc.*

Daum Nancy miniature pillow vase has enamel decoration on front of a bird standing on a rock pulling a weed from a pond with enameled trees and rocks surrounding the pond, backside is decorated with cameo flower, stems, and leaves, flower is enameled with orange while the stems and leaves are done in green and gold gilding, decoration is all set against an acid textured opalescent background, while the water in the pond is polished to give a pond-like reflection; signed on underside in gold "Daum Nancy" with Cross of Lorraine, 1-5/8" t. **$1,035**

*James D. Julia, Inc.*

Daum Nancy vase has internal decoration of mottled black shading to mottled fuchsia in center, squat bulbous vase finished with a short neck and slightly flaring rim; signed on side with engraved signature "Daum Nancy" and Cross of Lorraine, 6-1/4" t., from a private Long Island, New York collection. ................................ **$172**

Daum Nancy vase with vitrified cameo of impressionistic flowers, stems, and leaves in reds, browns, and greens set against a cameo background of striated vitrified glass in gray, white, and cream; signed on underside with engraved "Daum Nancy" with Cross of Lorraine as well as an engraved leaf or feather, 15-3/4" t., from a private Long Island, New York collection. ..................................... **$5,865**

*James D. Julia, Inc.*

Daum Nancy vase decorated with cameo vitrified autumn-colored leaves set against an internally decorated background of mottled yellow, green, and maroon, decorated with three applied glass insects with foil-backed bodies and engraved legs as well as a foil-backed applied cabochon, each leaf decorated with etched veins; signed on underside with engraved "Daum Nancy" with Cross of Lorraine, 11-1/4" t., from a private Long Island, New York collection. ............................ **$6,900**

*James D. Julia, Inc.*

Daum Nancy tray with cameo winter scene decoration of barren trees against a mottled yellow to orange background, trees are enameled in shades of brown with white snow highlights, while the ground is enameled with white snowdrifts; signed on underside in black "Daum Nancy" with the Cross of Lorraine, 5-1/4" sq. ............................................................................... **$3,450**

# Depression

Depression glass is the name of colorful glassware collectors generally associated with mass-produced glassware found in pink, yellow, crystal, or green in the years surrounding the Great Depression in America.

The housewives of the Depression-era were able to enjoy the wonderful colors offered in this new inexpensive glass dinnerware because they received pieces of their favorite patterns packed in boxes of soap, or as premiums given at "dish night" at the local movie theater. Merchandisers, such as Sears & Roebuck and F. W. Woolworth, enticed young brides with the colorful wares that they could afford even when economic times were harsh.

Because of advancements in glassware technology, Depression-era patterns were mass-produced and could be purchased for a fraction of what cut glass or lead crystal cost. As one manufacturer found a pattern that was pleasing to the buying public, other companies soon followed with their adaptation of a similar design. Patterns included several design motifs, such as florals, geometrics, and even patterns that looked back to Early American patterns like Sandwich glass.

As America emerged from the Great Depression and life became more leisure-oriented again, new glassware patterns were created to reflect the new tastes of this generation. More elegant shapes and forms were designed, leading to what is sometimes called "Elegant Glass." Today's collectors often include these more elegant patterns when they talk about Depression-era glassware.

Depression-era glassware is one of the best-researched collecting areas available to the American marketplace. This is due in large part to the careful research of several people, including Hazel Marie Weatherman, Gene Florence, Barbara Mauzy, Carl F. Luckey, and Kent Washburn. Their books are held in high regard by researchers and collectors today.

Regarding values for Depression glass, rarity does not always equate to a high dollar amount. Some more readily found items command lofty prices because of high demand or other factors, not because they are necessarily rare. As collectors' tastes range from the simple patterns to the more elaborate patterns, so does the ability of their budget to invest in inexpensive patterns to multi-hundreds of dollars per form patterns.

To maintain the fine tradition of extensive descriptions typically found in Warman's price guides, as much information as possible has been included as far as sizes, shapes, colors, etc. Whenever possible, the original manufacturer's language was maintained. A glossary is included to help you identify some of those puzzling names. As the patterns evolved, sometimes other usage names were assigned to pieces. Color names are also given as the manufacturers originally named them.

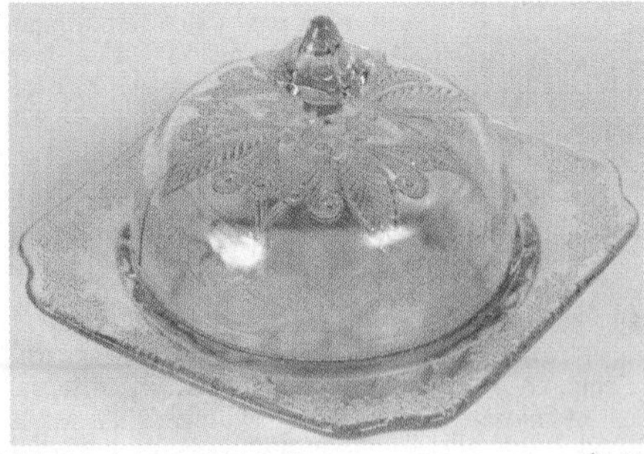

Adam, pink covered butter.............................. **$140**

American, crystal bowl, flared .......................... **$75**

The Depression-era glassware researchers have many accurate sources, including company records, catalogs, magazine advertisements, oral and written histories from sales staff, factory workers, etc. The dates included in the introductions are approximate as are some of the factory locations. When companies had more than one factory, usually only the main office or factory is listed.

For more information on Depression glass, see *Warman's Depression Glass Identification and Price Guide*, 5th Edition, or *Warman's Depression Glass Field Guide*, 4th Edition, both by Ellen T. Schroy.

American Pioneer, green plate, ........................ **$10;**
cup ........................................................ **$15;**
saucer ........................................................ **$5**

American Sweetheart, pink soup bowl ................ **$80**

Anniversary, iridescent dinner plate ................ **$8.50**

◄Aurora, cobalt blue tumbler ...................... **$27.50**

Block Optic, green sherbet ............................. **$28;**
sugar ........................................................ **$12;**
creamer ................................................ **$17.50;**
Hazel Atlas look-alike covered candy dish

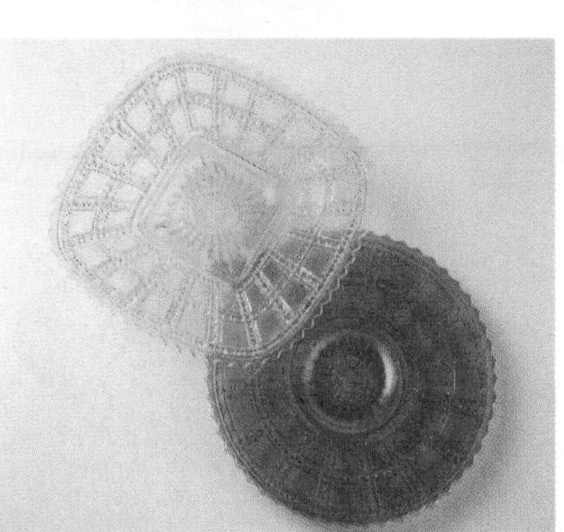

◄Beaded Block, Vaseline square plate ............ **$10;**
iridescent round plate .................................... **$20**

GLASS

By Cracky, green covered candy .................................... **$17.50**

Bowknot, green tumbler ....... **$20;** footed berry bowl ................. **$25**

Bubble, royal ruby cup ..... **$12.50**

Cameo, green 56 oz pitcher. .. **$90**

Candlewick, crystal luncheon plate, 9" d. ......................... **$18**

Coin, red candy dish with cover ........................................ **$120**

Cherry Blossom, 11" green two-handled bowl .. **$120**

Christmas Candy, crystal sugar ........................ **$15;** creamer ........................................................ **$15**

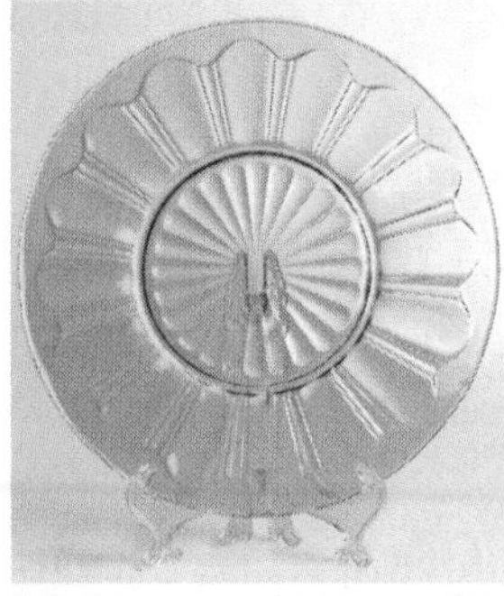
Colonial, green luncheon plate ............................................ **$8**

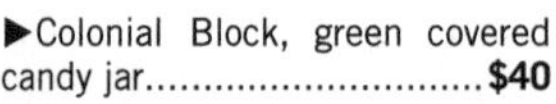

►Colonial Block, green covered candy jar............................. **$40**

Colonial Fluted, green sugar . **$10;** green creamer ..................... **$14**

Coronation, royal ruby handled berry bowl ........................... **$20**

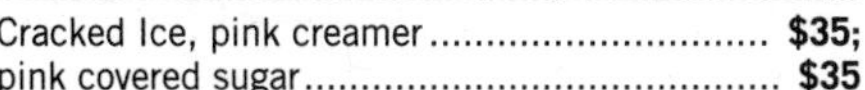

Cracked Ice, pink creamer .............................. **$35;** pink covered sugar.......................................... **$35**

Cupid, pink low pedestal-foot comport, 6-1/4" ....................................................................... **$290**

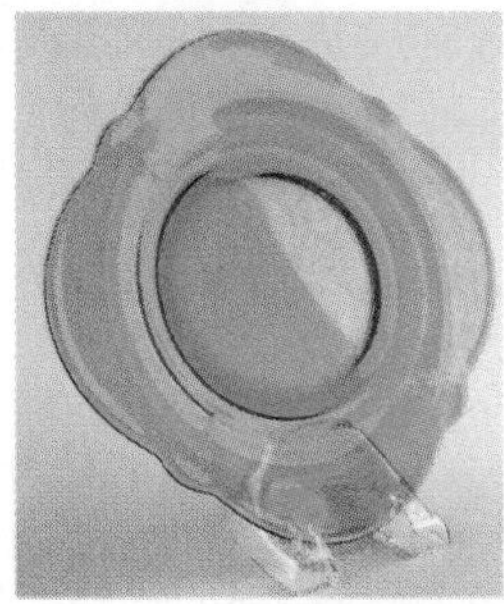

Crow's Foot, amber square plate, 8-1/2" d. ............... **$7**

Cube, green covered butter dish.. **$60**

Daisy, green luncheon plate... **$12**

Diamond Quilted, pink sugar....................... **$13.50;** pink creamer................................................. **$12**

Doric and Pansy, ultramarine child's sugar ....... **$60;** ultramarine child's creamer ............................ **$50**

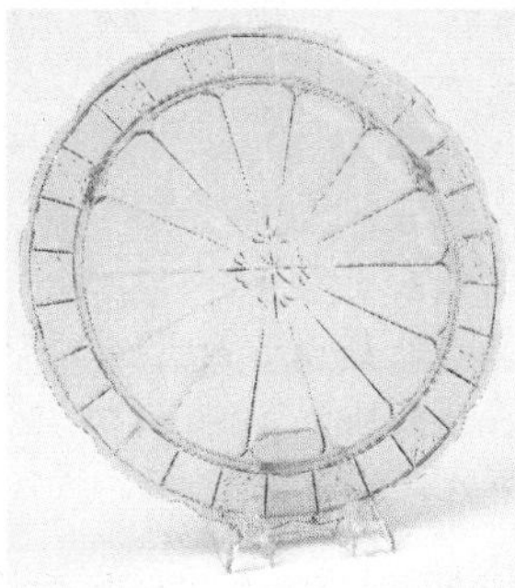

Doric, green cake plate.......... **$30**

►English Hobnail, crystal tumbler .................................... **$10**

Floral, green covered candy jar ........................................... **$45**

Floral and Diamond Band, green luncheon plate ..................... **$40**

Florentine No. 1, pink 8-1/2" salad plate ........................... **$12**

Florentine No. 2, yellow cup ...................................... **$14.50**

Flower Garden with Butterflies, blue comport, 5-7/8" h., 11" w. ........................................................ **$95**

Forest Green, oak leaf-shaped candy dish....... **$7.50;** 6-3/8" h. Harding vase.................................... **$10**

Fruits, green cup ........................................... **$15;** green saucer ...................................................... **$5**

Holiday, pink pitcher, 16 oz.............................. **$85**

Hex Optic, green cup ...................................... **$5;** green saucer ...................................................... **$4**

Homespun, pink 9-1/4" dinner plate ................. **$18**

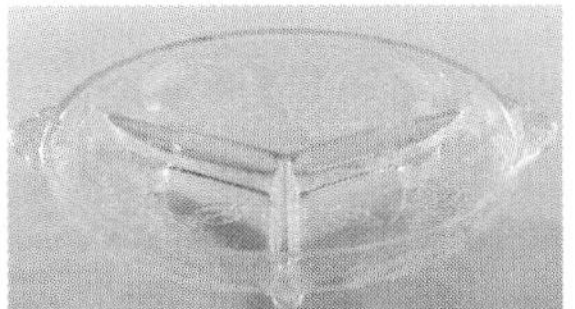

Horseshoe, yellow three-part footed relish dish .................. **$24**

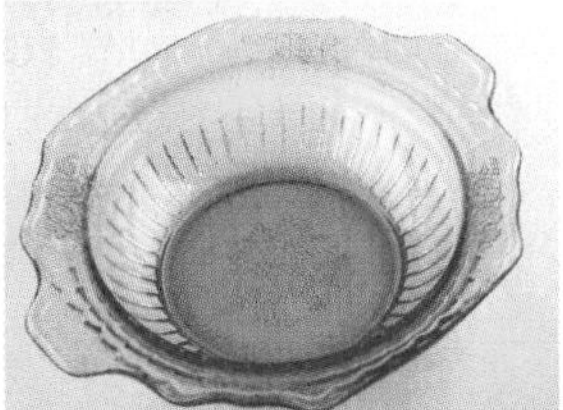

Mayfair Open Rose, ice blue handled vegetable bowl .............. **$75**

Iris, iridescent 9" vase .......... **$25**

Lincoln Inn, cobalt blue goblet ........................................... **$30**

Jamestown, brown footed pitcher ...................... **$95**

Madrid, amber sugar ...................................... **$10;** amber creamer ............................................... **$12**

Moderntone, cobalt blue sugar ......................... **$15;** cobalt blue creamer ....................................... **$15**

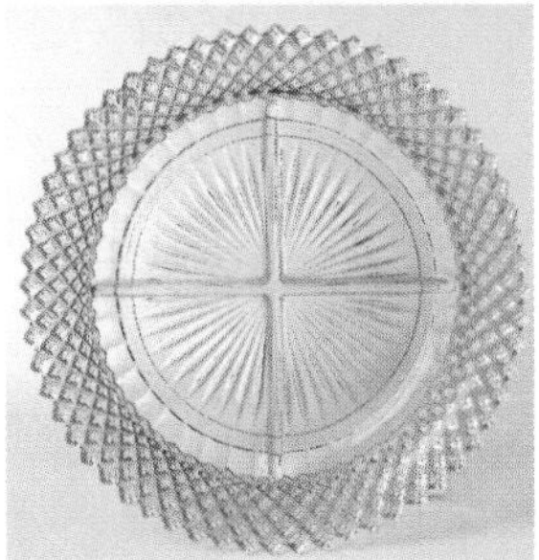

Miss America, pink relish, four parts ................................. **$40**

Moroccan, amethyst cup ... **$7.50;** amethyst saucer .................... **$3**

New Century, green dinner plate .......................................... **$24**

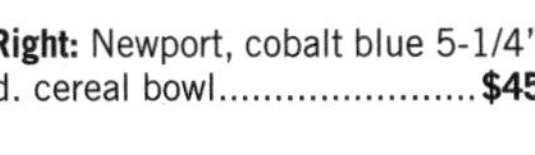

**Right:** Newport, cobalt blue 5-1/4" d. cereal bowl ....................... **$45**

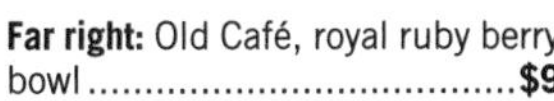

**Far right:** Old Café, royal ruby berry bowl ..................................... **$9**

Oyster and Pearl, pink relish .............................. **$35**

Petalware, pink 5-1/4" cereal bowl.................... **$15**

Patrician, amber covered butter ........................ **$95**

Pineapple & Floral, amber cream soup bowl .. **$16.50**

Pioneer, pink luncheon plate, fruit center.................................... **$8**

Princess, green covered candy ............................................ **$75**

Ring, green ice tub ............... **$20**

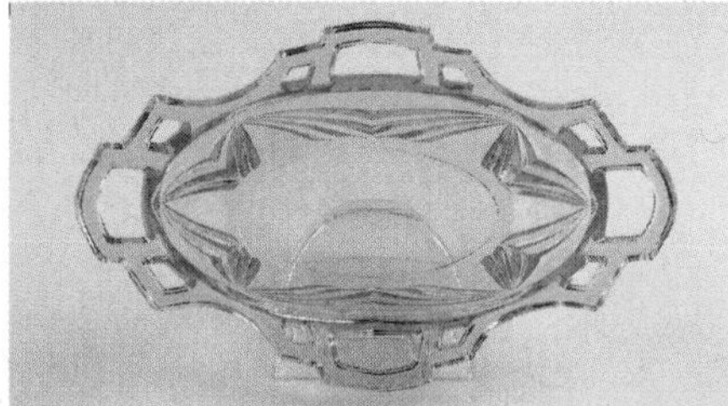
Pyramid, green pickle dish ............................... **$35**

Radiance ice blue 6" comport with ruffled edge.. **$35**

◀Queen Mary, pink 9-1/2" dinner plate ............ **$60**

Ribbon, green cup .................................... **$6.50;**
creamer ................................................ **$15**

Royal Ruby 3-1/2" h. flat tumbler with original label.................................................. **$15;**
4-1/2" h. tumbler with original label ............... **$12;**
5" h. tumbler.............................................. **$10;**
86 oz pitcher ............................................ **$35**

Rock Crystal, amber plate, 8-1/2" d.......................................**$12**

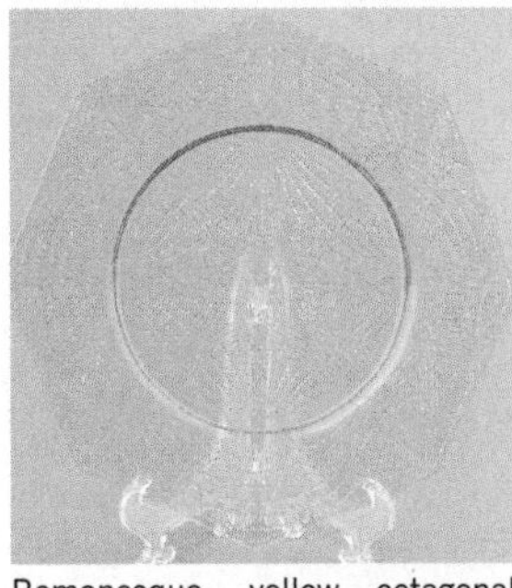
Romanesque, yellow octagonal plate, 8" d...........................**$10**

Roulette, green cup ...............**$6**

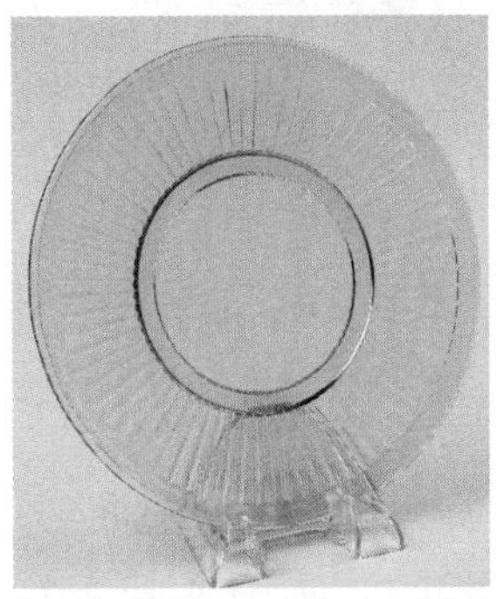
Round Robin, green luncheon plate ..................................**$12**

Sharon, pink 10-1/2" fruit bowl ................................................**$50**

S-Pattern, yellow footed sherbet........................ **$8;**
yellow 4-3/4" flat tumbler ........................... **$8.50**

Sandwich, Hocking, smooth desert gold bowl, 6-1/2" d...................................................................**$9**

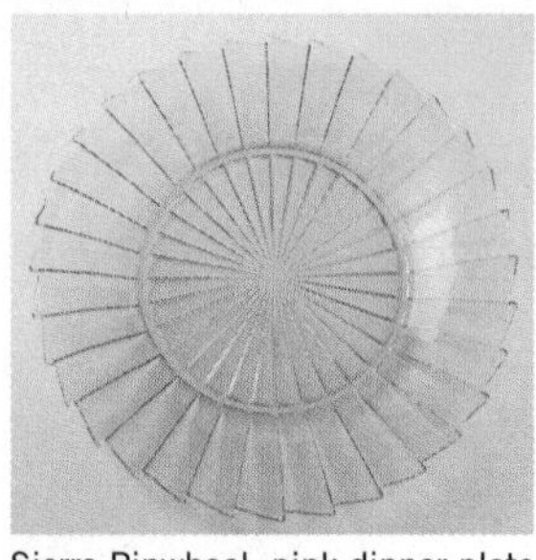

Sierra Pinwheel, pink dinner plate .......... **$25**

Sunburst, crystal candelabra, two-light .......... **$20**

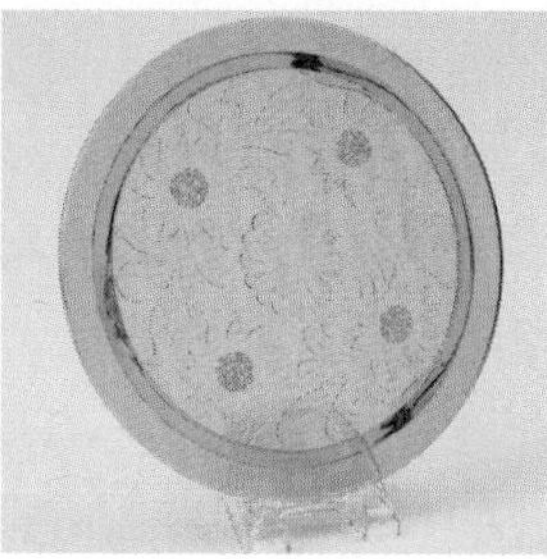

Sunflower, green cake plate. .. **$20**

Starlight, crystal cup .......... **$6;**
crystal creamer .......... **$10**

Tulip, green creamer .......... **$25**

Swirl, ultramarine 9-1/4" dinner plate .......... **$22.50;**
salt shaker .......... **$25**

Twisted Optic, green tall footed covered candy dish .......... **$60**

Tea Room, pink footed sugar .......... **$60 (without lid);**
pink footed creamer .......... **$28**

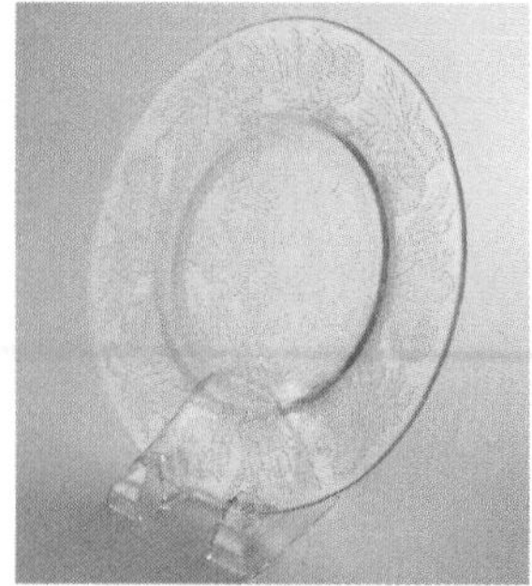

Thistle, green luncheon plate. **$24**

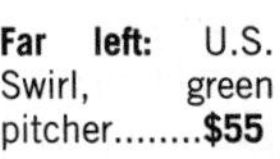

**Far left:** U.S. Swirl, green pitcher........**$55**

**Left:** Vernon, yellow tumbler.**$45**

Victory, pink creamer .................................... **$15;** pink sugar........................................................ **$15**

►Waterford, crystal 7-1/8" d. salad plate .......... **$9;** 5-1/4" h. goblet ............................................. **$18**

Windsor, pink 11-1/2" oval platter..... **..$25;** 10-1/2" oval bowl with pointed ends .. **$32;** 8-1/2" l. oval bowl.............................. **$30**

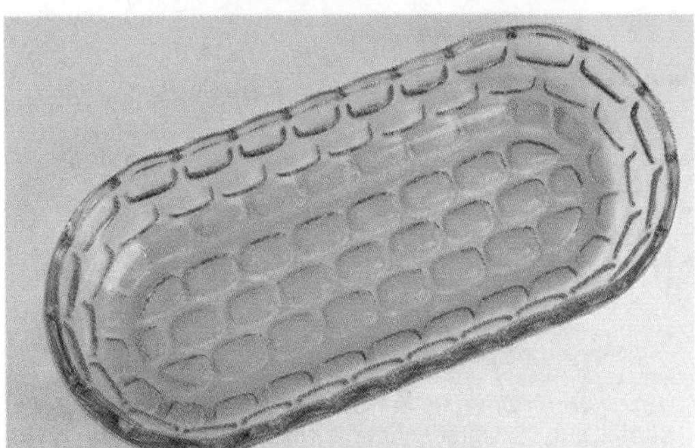

Yorktown, yellow celery tray .................**$10**

# Duncan & Miller

Duncan & Miller Glass Co., a successor firm to George A. Duncan & Sons Co., produced a wide range of pressed wares and novelty pieces during the late 19th century and into the early 20th century. During the Depression era and after, the company continued making a wide variety of more modern patterns, including mold-blown types, and also introduced a number of etched and engraved patterns. Many colors, including opalescent hues, were produced during this era, and especially popular today are the graceful swan dishes they produced in the Pall Mall and Sylvan patterns.

The numbers after the pattern name indicate the original factory pattern number. The Duncan factory was closed in 1955.

Duncan-Miller Polka Dot vase, marigold, 8-1/2" h., 5-3/4" across with 3-1/2" base .................. **$15**
*Desert West Auction Service*

Set of 12 Duncan & Miller ruby red water goblets, Georgian pattern, No. 103, 5-1/4" h. ............ **$50**
*Ivy Auctions, Inc.*

►Mardi Gras/D & M No. 42 toy four-piece table set, colorless, butter dish, covered sugar bowl, creamer, and spooner, Duncan & Miller Co., late 19th/early 20th c., 2-1/2" to 4-1/2" h............. **$173**
*Jeffrey S. Evans & Associates*

Pair of Duncan & Miller opalescent candleholders, petal-shaped with one upturned side, 2-1/2" x 7-1/2" x 6" ............ **$60**
*Dirk Soulis Auctions*

Mardi Gras/D & M No. 42 plates, set of seven, green, late 19th/first quarter 20th c., 7-7/8" dia. ....... **$161**
*Jeffrey S. Evans & Associates*

# Fenton Art Glass

The Fenton Art Glass Co. was founded in 1905 by Frank L. Fenton and his brother, John W., in Martins Ferry, Ohio. They initially sold hand-painted glass made by other manufacturers, but it wasn't long before they decided to produce their own glass. The new Fenton factory in Williamstown, W.V., opened on Jan. 2, 1907. From that point on, the company expanded by developing unusual colors and continued to decorate glassware in innovative ways.

Two more brothers, James and Robert, joined the firm. But despite the company's initial success, John W. left to establish the Millersburg Glass Co. of Millersburg, Ohio, in 1909. The first months of the new operation were devoted to the production of crystal glass only. Later iridized glass was called "Radium Glass." After only two years, Millersburg filed for bankruptcy.

Fenton's iridescent glass had a metallic luster over a colored, pressed pattern, and was sold in dime stores. It was only after the sales of this glass decreased and it was sold in bulk as carnival prizes that it came to be known as carnival glass.

Fenton became the top producer of carnival glass, with more than 150 patterns. The quality of the glass, and its popularity with the public, enabled the new company to be profitable through the late 1920s. As interest in carnival subsided, Fenton moved on to stretch glass and opalescent patterns. A line of colorful blown glass (called "off-hand" by Fenton) was also produced in the mid-1920s.

During the Great Depression, Fenton survived by producing functional colored glass tableware and other household items, including water sets, table sets, bowls, mugs, plates, perfume bottles and vases. Restrictions on European imports during World War II ushered in the arrival of Fenton's opaque colored glass, and the lines of "Crest" pieces soon followed. In the 1950s, production continued to diversify with a focus on milk glass, particularly in Hobnail patterns.

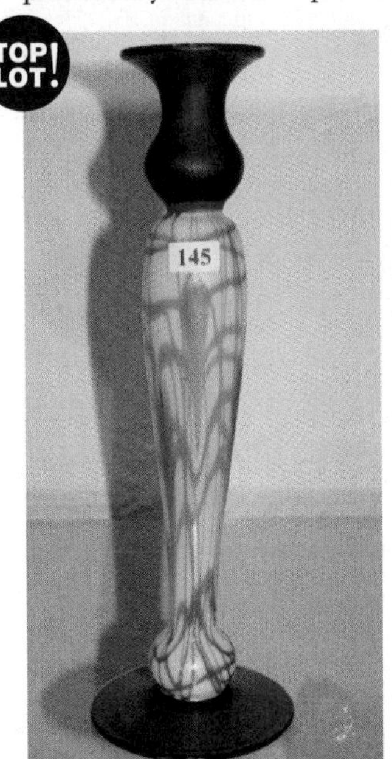

Rare antique green 12" tall off-hand candlestick with hand-applied Hanging Hearts and random threading, cobalt blue socket and cobalt blue foot............................**$2,970**

In the third quarter of Fenton's history, the company returned to themes that had proved popular to preceding generations, and began adding special lines, such as the Bicentennial series. Innovations included the line of Colonial colors that debuted in 1963, including amber, blue, green, orange and ruby. Based on a special order for an Ohio museum, Fenton in 1969 revisited its early success with "Original Formula Carnival Glass." Fenton also started marking its glass in the molds for the first time.

The star of the 1970s was the yellow and blushing pink creation known as Burmese, which remains popular today. This was followed closely by a menagerie of animals, birds, and children. In 1975, Robert Barber was hired by Fenton to begin an artist-in-residence program, producing a limited line of art-glass vases in a return to the off-hand, blown-glass creations of the mid-1920s.

In August 2007, Fenton discontinued all but a few of its more popular lines, and the company ceased production in 2011.

For more information on Fenton Art Glass, see *Warman's Fenton Glass Identification and Price Guide*, 2nd edition, by Mark F. Moran.

## 1905-1930

Persian Blue rose bowl, 1915, in Persian Medallion, with enamel decoration, 3-1/4" h. .................... **$55**

Green Opalescent covered jug and tumbler with cobalt handles in Rib Optic, part of a lemonade set that would have included six tumblers, 1920s; jug, 10" h.; tumbler, 5" h. ................ **$700+ for complete set**

Hanging Hearts and Vines off-hand footed bowl, mid-1920s, 10" d. ........................................ **$2,800+**

Crystal Opalescent pieces in Beaded Stars, circa 1910, from left: square crimp bonbon, 6-1/2" w.; bowl, 7-1/2" d. ........................................ **$45+ ea.**

Mosaic off-hand candlestick, mid-1920s, 5" h. .................... **$900+**

Ruby flared vase with wheel-cut decoration, ribbed, late 1920s, 6" h. .............................. **$200+**

◀Tangerine stretch-glass comport with dolphin handles, late 1920s, 5" h. .............................. **$160+**

▶Topaz cut candlestick with notched profile, 1920s (?), 10-1/2" h. ....................... **$100+**

## FENTON CARNIVAL GLASS

The golden era of carnival glass was from about 1905 to the mid-1920s. It is believed that by 1906 the first cheap, iridized glass to rival the expensive Tiffany creations was in production. Carnival glass was originally made to bridge a gap in the market by providing ornamental wares for those who couldn't afford to buy the fashionable, iridized pieces popular at the height of the art nouveau era. It wasn't until much later that it acquired the name "carnival glass." When it fell from favor, it was sold off cheaply to carnivals and offered as prizes. Fenton made about 150 patterns of carnival glass.

Here are some of the basic colors:

**Amethyst:** A purple color ranging from quite light to quite dark

**Aqua opalescent:** Ice blue with a milky (white or colored) edge

**Black amethyst:** Very dark purple or black in color

**Clam broth:** Pale ginger ale color, sometimes milky

**Cobalt blue (sometimes called royal blue):** A dark, rich blue

**Green:** A true green, not pastel

**Marigold:** A soft, golden yellow

**Pastel colors:** A satin treatment in white, ice blue, ice green

**Peach opalescent:** Marigold with a milky (white or colored) edge

**Red:** A rich red, rare

**Vaseline (Fenton called it topaz):** Clear yellow/yellow-green glass

Green whimsy vase in Diamond and Rib, pinched in .............. **$1,350**

Amethyst water pitcher in Butterfly and Berry **$3,000**

Marigold cup and saucer in Kittens ............ **$200**

Blue tankard in Floral and Grape Variant, candy-ribbon edge, 9-1/2" h....... **$300-$500**
Outstanding example .......................... **$900**

Blue bowl with 3-in-1 edge, Ten Mums, 9-1/2" ............................................ **$350**

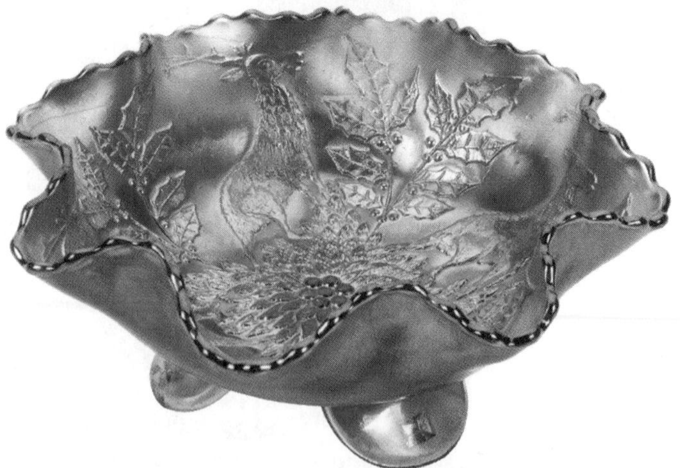

Red ruffled bowl in Stag and Holly, spatula feet, 6-1/2" d. ............ **$1,500**

## 1930-1955

Black (Ebony) covered candy dish with flower finial, 1931, 6-1/2" h. .................................... **$250+**

Blue Opalescent jug and square-top goblet in Hobnail, part of a lemonade set that would have included six tumblers, 1950s; jug, 8" h.; goblet, 5-1/2" h. ........................................................ **$500+ for complete set**

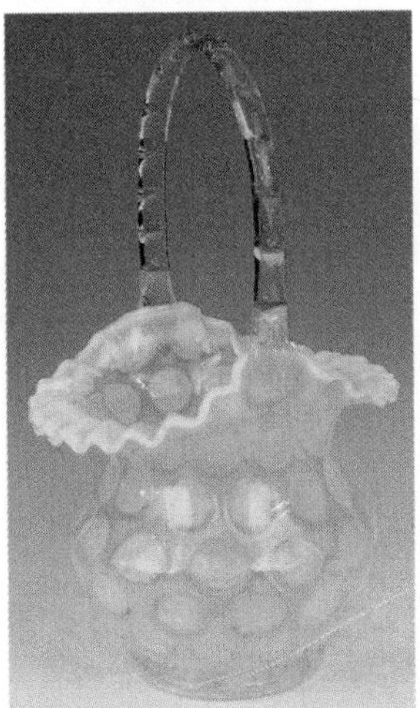

**Far left:** Topaz Opalescent basket in Coin Spot, 1930s, 12" h. ...................... **$300+**

**Left:** Cranberry Opalescent 70-ounce jug in Coin Spot, mid-1930s, 8-1/2" h. ...................... **$200+**

French Opalescent three-horn epergne in Emerald Crest/Diamond Lace, 1949-55, 11" h. .......... **$250+**

Ivy Overlay vase with applied Charleton Ivory Leaves and Needles decoration, early 1950s, 5" h. ....... **$85**

Rare experimental "Milady" vase in Kitchen Green, 1942, 11" h. ...................................... **$500+**

Ruby flared vase in Apple Tree, with raised circle where handle could have been attached to side, 1930s, 9" h., rare in this color ...................................... **$300+**

Peach Crest vase, melon form, with Charleton decoration, mid-1950s, 8" h....................... **$90+**

Dancing Ladies Mongolian Green vase, flared and ruffled, mid-1930s, 8-1/2" h........................ **$650+**

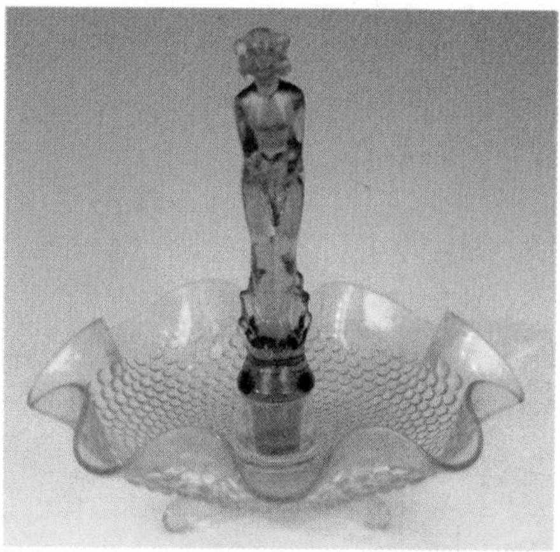

Nymph in footed bowl in Green Transparent, 1930s, 7-1/2" h. ................................................ **$275+ set**

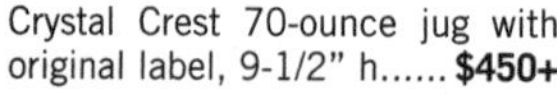

Crystal Crest 70-ounce jug with original label, 9-1/2" h...... **$450+**

## 1955-1980

Aurene Jefferson comport, one of only 75 made as a test color before the Bicentennial colors were established, circa 1973, 10-1/2" h. .................................... **$300+**

Coral baluster vase in Bubble Optic, 1961, 11" h. ............. **$275+**

Cranberry Satin apothecary jar in Daisy and Fern, made for L.G. Wright, 1950s and 1960s, 8" h. ....................................... **$350+**

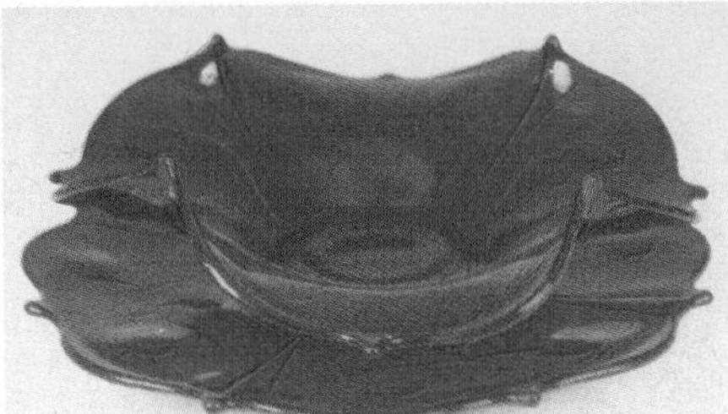

Ruby crimped bowl and platter in Pineapple, 1970s, each about 14" d. ................................. **$250+ pair**

◀Rose Overlay pieces in Corn (also called Maize), made for L.G. Wright, 1960s:
jug, 9" h. ..................................................... **$300+**
sugar shaker, 5-1/2" h. ............................... **$150+**

Cameo Opalescent covered margarine tub holder in Hobnail, 1979, 5" d. **$50+**

Goldenrod condiment set (salt, pepper, mustard and stand) in Tear Drop, late 1950s, 7" h. with handle ............................. **$350+**

Vasa Murrhina ribbed vase in Blue Mist, mid-1960s, 14" h. ...................... **$200**

Ohio's Dexter City Auction Gallery offered more than 400 lots of Fenton glass on April 21, 2012. Fenton staff members at the factory in Williamstown, West Virginia, chose items from all eras of Fenton's rich 107 years of history, and more than 250 Fenton fans attended the sale. Fenton ceased production of its collectible and giftware glass products in 2011 following a 2007 restructuring.

Favrene vase with cameo carved grapes and leaves by cameo artists Kelsey Murphy and Robert Bomkamp................................ **$797**

Rare turquoise No. 3029 8-1/4" t. offhand vase with hand-applied Hanging Vine decoration and light iridescent finish.............. **$2,090**

Sample Peach Opalescent Lily of the Valley oval basket with crystal "nicked" or bamboo handle, c. 1979................................ **$302**

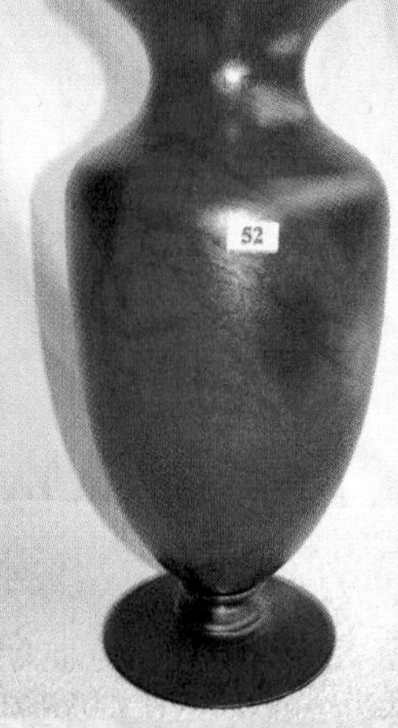


Super rare Karnak Red No. 3024 14" t. offhand Egyptian vase with hand applied Hanging Hearts and random threading and applied cobalt blue short stem and foot ...................................**$11,000**

Designer sample custard satin lamp with hand-painted Going Home decoration and hammered colonial hardware, dated "1980" and lettered "Sample M7242 GH" and signed inside "Fenton hand painted by Diane Johnson"..**$192**

Opal Satin 3" Luv Bug with hand-painted decoration designed by J. K. "Robin" Spindler........... **$412**

Dave Fetty whimsical 6-1/2" l. pig, signed "Dave Fetty 1-31-11" ....................................... **$192**

Twilight Crackle 10-1/2" t. pitcher with applied handle, c. mid-1992. ........................................ **$71**

One-of-a-kind Lotus Mist Burmese 10 " vase with tri-crimp finish and hand-painted fishing scene, designed and hand painted by J. K. "Robin" Spindler ................ **$302**

Royal Blue cornucopia candleholder with tulip finish, c. 1934 .......................................... **$88**

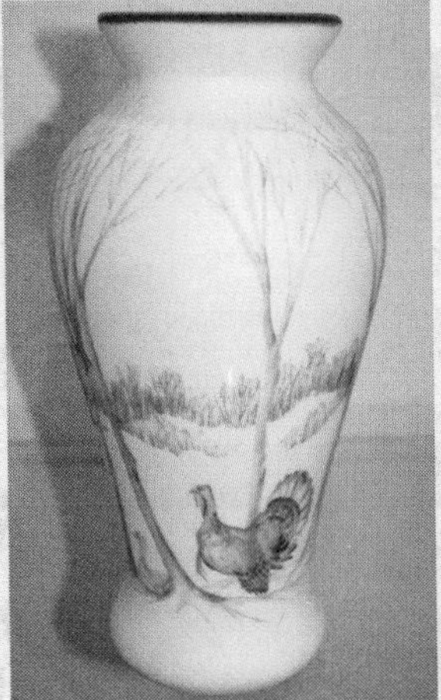

One-of-a-kind 10" vase with hand-painted woodland and wild turkeys, designed and hand painted by J. K. "Robin" Spindler .... **$550**

► Mosaic inlaid 10-1/2" t. offhand vase with hand-applied cobalt blue handles .............. **$2860**

Vasa Murrhina 8" pinch vase, Connoisseur Collection (1989), tri-crimp finish, numbered 52/2000 ....................................... **$137**

Unique cranberry spiral optic 10-1/4" vase with sand-carved portrait of young woman ...... **$467**

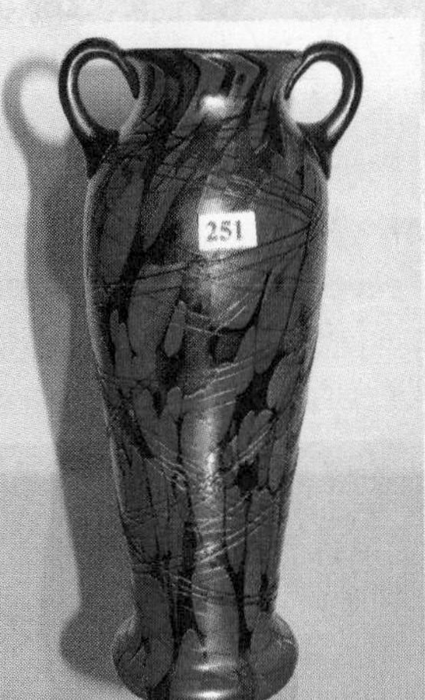

Custard satin 6-1/4" t. bell with hand-painted fawn and floral motif with "Mothers Day 1981" lettering, signed "Hand Painted Louise Piper" ................................ **$99**

Limited edition amethyst carnival covered "Reber & Co. Pie Wagon," c. 2005, made with moulds that originated at Imperial Glass in the 1950s .............................. **$115**

Sample Favrene sunfish figurine, 2-3/4" t. .......................... **$440**

Dave Fetty offhand fish, sparkling mica in its body and applied black glass fins and applied black/milk glass eyes, 8-1/2" l............... **$93**

GLASS

# Fostoria

Fostoria Glass Company, founded in 1887, produced numerous types of fine glassware over the years. Its factory in Moundsville, West Virginia, closed in 1986.

American Fostoria punch bowl, 12" dia. x 7 " t.**$140**
*Langston Auction Gallery*

American Fostoria deep dish, 9" across, 3-1/2" deep...........................................................**$20**
*Purcell Auction Gallery*

Atlanta/Square Lion goblet, colorless, Fostoria Glass Co., fourth quarter 19th century, 6" h.....**$69**
*Jeffrey S. Evans & Associates*

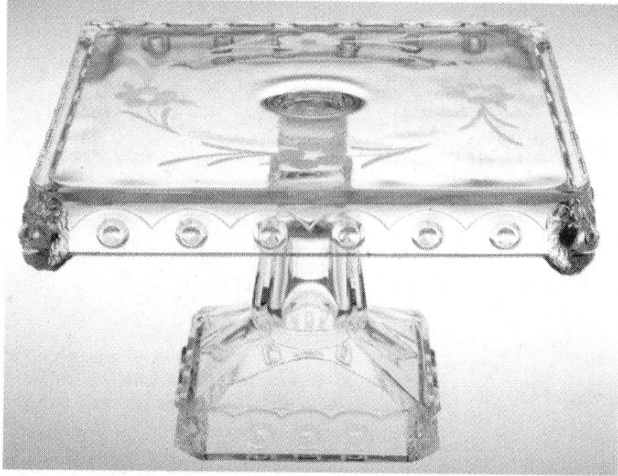

Atlanta/Square Lion cake stand, colorless, engraved floral decoration, Fostoria Glass Co., late 19th/early 20th century, 6" h., 9" sq. ...... **$115**
*Jeffrey S. Evans & Associates*

Nine etched glass goblets, Scroll & Floral decoration, signed Fostoria, 7-1/4" h. ....................**$125**
*Ames Auctioneers*

Atlanta/Square Lion covered compote, colorless, frosted finish to finial, pattern at bottom edge of bowl and edge of base, engraved floral decoration to bowl, Fostoria Glass Co., late 19th/early 20th century, 9-7/8" h. overall, 6" dia. overall .................... **$115**
*Jeffrey S. Evans & Associates*

Fostoria America low foot punch bowl with standard, 18" .......................................................... **$800**
*Mark Mattox Real Estate & Auctioneer*

Fostoria America square cake stand, 7-1/8" t... **$120**
*Mark Mattox Real Estate & Auctioneer*

Set of 14 Fostoria American stems with amethyst glass stops, clear stems: six water goblets and eight champagnes ............................ **$90**
*A-1 Auction*

Fostoria art glass bowl, 1977, heavy oval form with folded rim, opaque and transparent striations of orange, blue, green, yellow, and brown, inscribed Fostoria and dated 77 on base, 7-7/8" .... **$100**
*Skinner, Inc.*

Fostoria Chanticleer rooster figure, unsigned, 10" x 8-1/2" ....... **$240**
*Dirk Soulis Auctions*

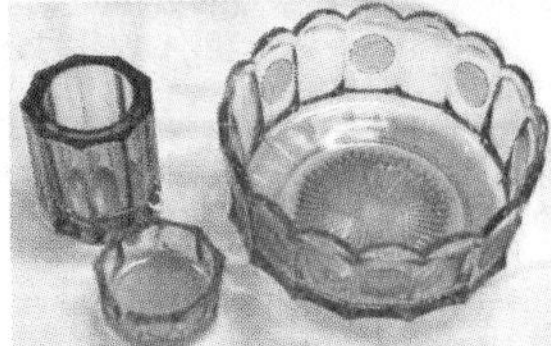

Light blue Fostoria Coin pattern glassware, 6-1/2" footed compote, 6" pitcher, 6" lidded jar, 3" salt and pepper shakers, 3-1/2" x 7-1/2" bowl, 2 x 7" lidded bowl, 4-1/2" cigarette holder with ashtray lid................................ **$60**
*Affiliated Auctions*

Fostoria June azure blue crystal 41-piece set, 1928-1944, centerpiece bowl, 12 tall sherbets, eight low sherbets, eight 5-1/4" inch parfaits, 12 3-3/4" inch oyster cocktails ............................ **$500**
*Jackson's Auction*

Fostoria Lido "elegant" glassware: 30 pieces to include 12 iced tea, 12 sherbet/champagnes, five liquor, covered candy dish ..... **$125**
*Burchard Galleries, Inc*

Fostoria stemware, 42 pieces: 11 goblets, 8-1/2", 11 champagnes, nine parfaits, 11 short pedestal water glasses, 6-1/2"; hand cut, tapered hexagonal stem, circa 1940, Fern and Flower motif .................. **$250**
*DuMouchelles*

Twelve Fostoria House of Representatives wine glasses, engraved House of Representatives medallion by Fostoria, includes six stems (8" x 3" dia.), six smaller stems (5-3/4" x 3-1/4"). Unused with original Fostoria labels still attached to base of stems, sold with original Fostoria boxes, one glass has factory error, missing part of second R on "Representatives." ....................... **$80**
*Burchard Galleries, Inc*

Fostoria Romance pattern "elegant" glass 31-piece set, mayonnaise bowl, underplate and ladle, six goblets (7-1/2"), seven champagne cocktail (5-1/2"), seven liquor cocktail (5"), and seven cordials (3-7/8"), and 8-1/2" footed pitcher .......................................... **$150**
*Burchard Galleries, Inc.*

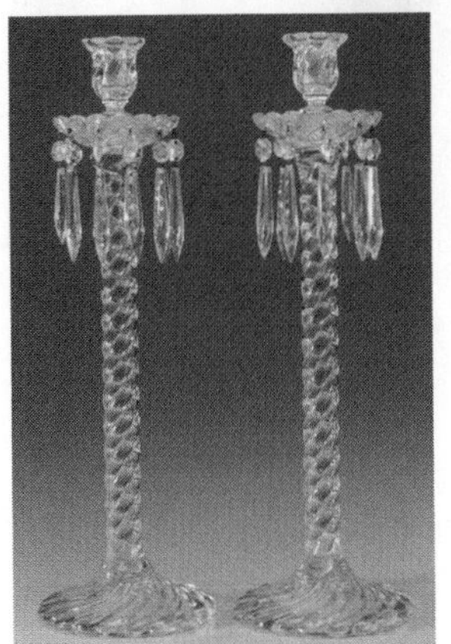

Fostoria Queen Anne candlesticks, late 19th/early 20th century, each with single socket with finely threaded mounts hung with prisms over twisted stem and swirled base, 18-1/2" ......... **$350**
*Brunk Auctions*

George Sakier Art Deco vase for Fostoria, 7-1/2" h. x 6" w.... **$100**
*Dirk Soulis Auctions*

St. Bernard covered compote, colorless and frosted, on high standard patterned stem, wafer construction, Fostoria Glass Co., late 19th/early 20th century, 8-1/2" h. overall, 6 1/4" dia. ............. **$259**

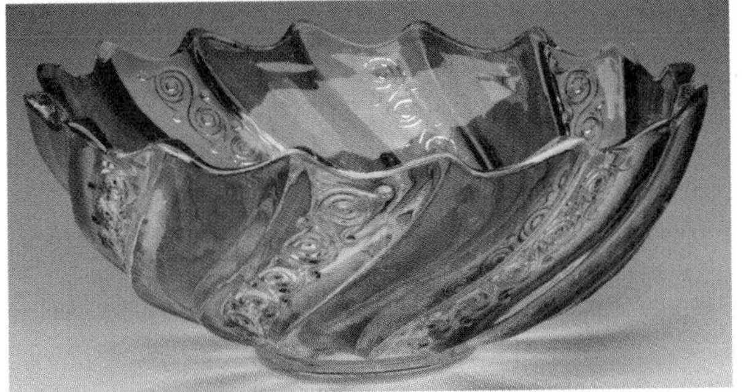

Wedding Bells – Maiden's Blush punch bowl, colorless, Fostoria Glass Co., late 19th/early 20th century, 5-3/4" h. overall, 14-3/4" dia. overall. ........... **$127**
*Jeffrey S. Evans & Associates*

# Gallé

Gallé glass was made in Nancy, France, by Emile Gallé, a founder of the Nancy School and a leader in the Art Nouveau movement in France. Much of his glass, both enameled and cameo, is decorated with naturalistic motifs. The finest pieces were made in the last two decades of the 19th century and the opening years of the 20th.

Pieces marked with a star preceding the name were made between 1904, the year of Gallé's death, and 1914.

Gallé Art Deco vase, cameo stylized flowers in amethyst and mauve against a frosted yellow background, pattern repeats itself on each of four sides of vase, signed near foot with engraved "Gallé," 4" t. Provenance: From a private Long Island collection ........ **$805**
*James D. Julia, Inc.*

Gallé cabinet vase, purple cameo flowers, stems, and leaves encircle entire vase against a frosted cream-colored background, signed on side in cameo "Gallé," 5-1/4" t. Provenance: From a private Long Island collection ......... **$632**
*James D. Julia, Inc.*

Gallé cabinet vase, brown cameo flowers, stems, and leaves against a dark salmon background, vase is signed on side in cameo "Gallé," 5-1/4" t. Provenance: From a private Long Island collection .. **$747**
*James D. Julia, Inc.*

◄Gallé cabinet vase decorated with green cameo flowers, stems, and leaves, longest stem leads up neck of vase to light blue cameo flower, leaves at bottom of vase are both cameo and engraved, signed near the foot with engraved "Gallé," 4-1/4" t. Provenance: From a private Long Island collection ........ **$747**
*James D. Julia, Inc.*

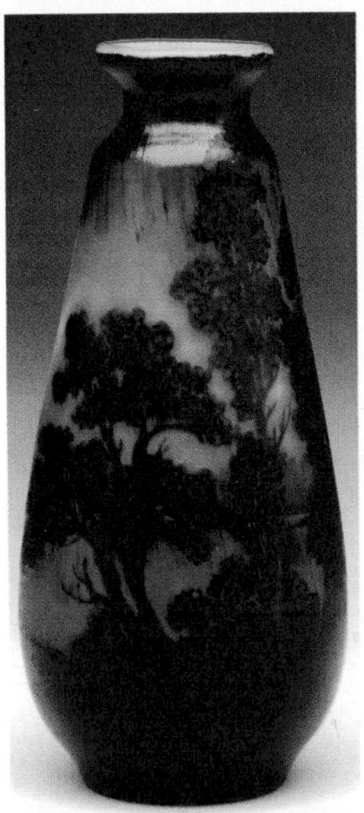

Gallé cameo and engraved vase, brown acid-cut cameo decoration of deciduous trees against a creamy orange background, leaves on trees are engraved with areas of martele, signed on the side with engraved "Gallé," 6-1/2" t. .................................... **$2,300**
*James D. Julia, Inc.*

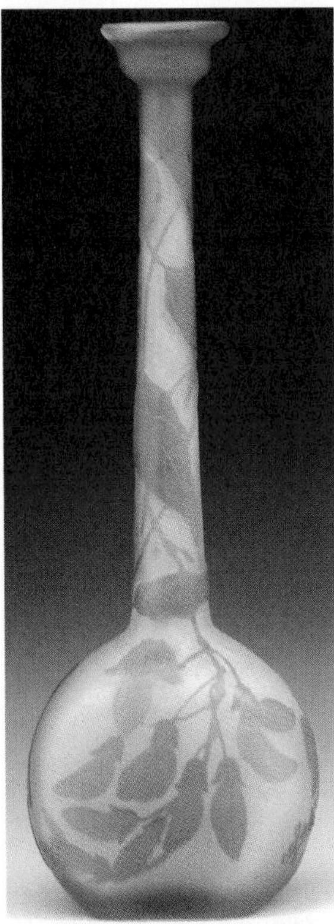

Gallé cameo banjo vase, cameo decoration of maroon seed pods, stems, and leaves against a frosted background, vase is signed on side in cameo "Gallé," 8" t. Provenance: From a private Long Island collection ................ **$805**
*James D. Julia, Inc.*

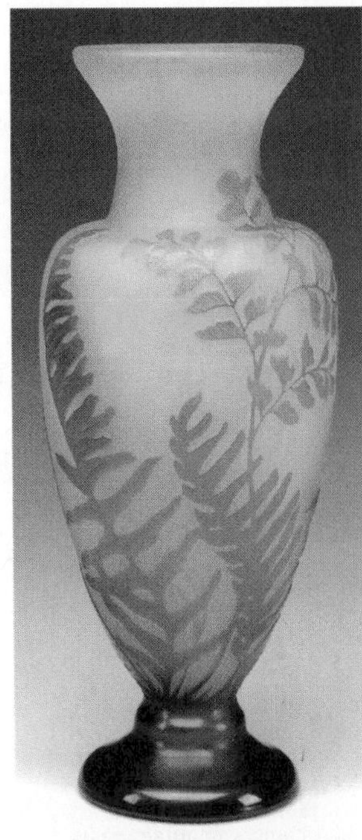

Gallé cameo fern vase, deep green cameo fern decoration against a background shading from light green to cream to yellow, vase is signed on side in cameo "Gallé," 11-1/4" t. Provenance: From a private Long Island collection ........................... **$1,500-$2,500**
*James D. Julia, Inc.*

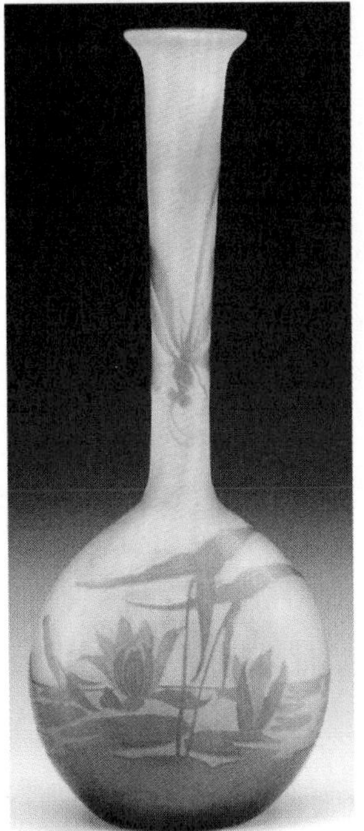

◀Gallé cameo lily pond vase, lily pads, flowers, and other aquatic vegetation set against a cream shading to light green background, neck of vase decorated with large green cameo dragonfly in flight, signed on side in cameo "Gallé," 11-1/2" t. Provenance: From a private Long Island collection .................................... **$2,300**
*James D. Julia, Inc.*

▶Monumental Gallé cameo vase decorated with deeply cut allover floral design with olive green stems and leaves and purple floral clusters, cameo design set against a frosted cream-colored background with light purple shadowing, signed on side in cameo "*Gallé," 24" t. Provenance: From a private Long Island collection .................................... **$3,422**
*James D. Julia, Inc.*

Gallé cameo mountain vase, pine trees set against a background of mountain lake and blue mountain peaks, decoration gives way to a sky of cream shading to yellow, signed on side in cameo "Gallé," 14" t. Provenance: From a private Long Island collection ...... **$4,600**
*James D. Julia, Inc.*

Gallé cameo table lamp, multi-shaded red floral and foliage design on a camphor ground, signed on the side in cameo "Gallé," shade is supported by a single socket cameo glass three-pronged base with multi-shaded red floral and foliage decoration leading to a blood red foot, signed on the side of the shade and base in cameo "Gallé," lamp is 22" t. ........................**$16,000-$20,000**
*James D. Julia, Inc.*

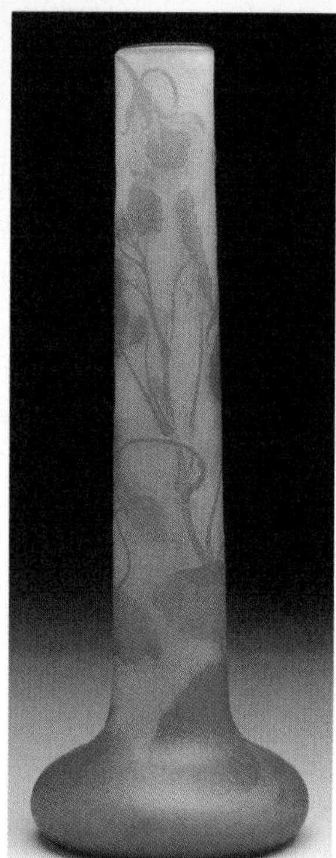

Gallé cameo vase, orange cameo flowers, stems, and leaves against a frosted background, vase signed on the side in cameo "Gallé," 17" t. Provenance: From a private Long Island collection .......................... **$2,000-$3,000**
*James D. Julia, Inc.*

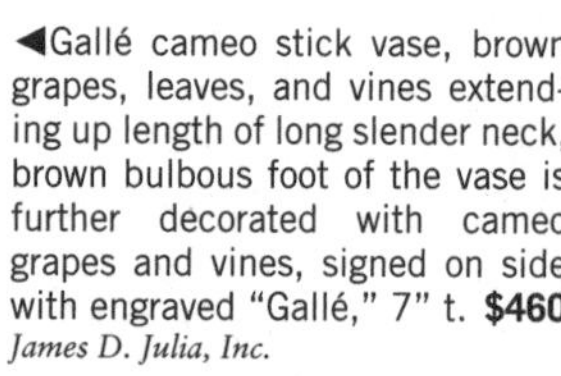

◄Gallé cameo stick vase, brown grapes, leaves, and vines extending up length of long slender neck, brown bulbous foot of the vase is further decorated with cameo grapes and vines, signed on side with engraved "Gallé," 7" t. **$460**
*James D. Julia, Inc.*

►Gallé cameo covered jar decorated with red cameo flowers, stems, and leaves all set against a frosted yellow background, highlighted with windowpane technique, domed lid is decorated with three matching red butterflies, lid and the jar signed in cameo "Gallé," 8" t. Provenance: From a private Long Island collection ..................................... **$5,750**
*James D. Julia, Inc.*

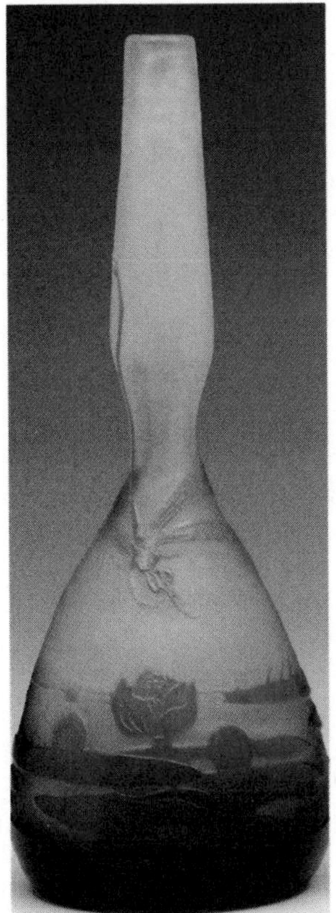

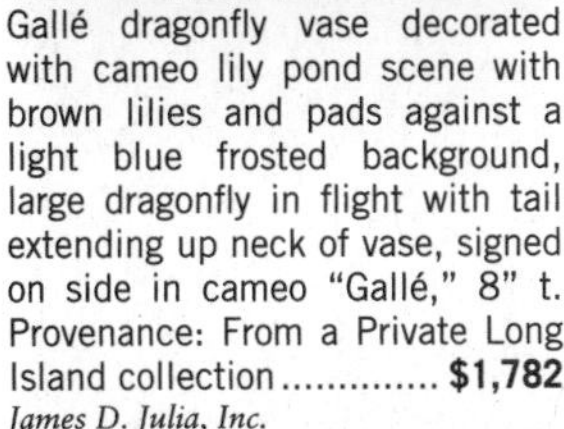

Gallé dragonfly vase decorated with cameo lily pond scene with brown lilies and pads against a light blue frosted background, large dragonfly in flight with tail extending up neck of vase, signed on side in cameo "Gallé," 8" t. Provenance: From a Private Long Island collection .............. **$1,782**
*James D. Julia, Inc.*

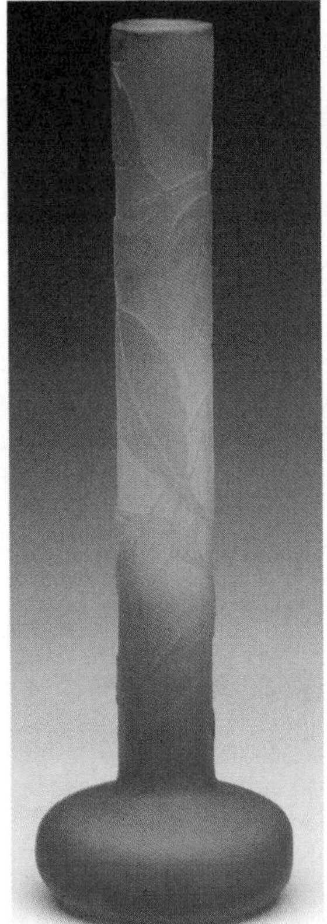

Gallé cameo stick vase, light green cameo leaves and stems descending from mouth to bulbous body of vase, cameo decoration is set against a shaded peach and cream background, signed on side in cameo "Gallé," 8-1/2" t. Provenance: From a private Long Island collection........................... **$690**
*James D. Julia, Inc.*

Gallé crocus vase, cameo decoration of brown and green leaves and stems leading to purple crocus flowers with green background petals all set against a frosted yellow background, foot of vase is purple translucent glass, signed on side with engraved "Gallé," 8-1/2" t. Provenance: From a private Long Island collection **$1,955**
*James D. Julia, Inc.*

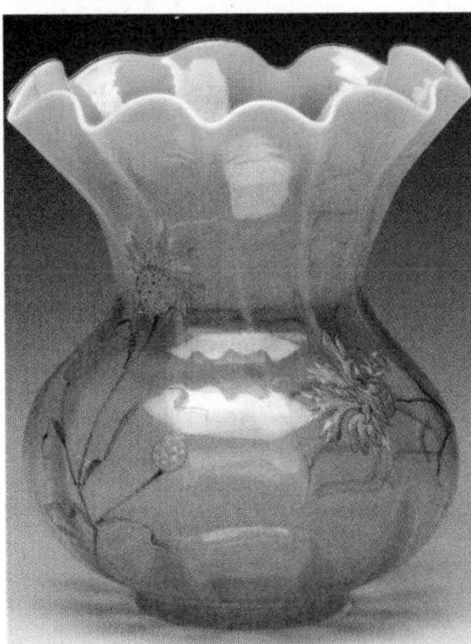

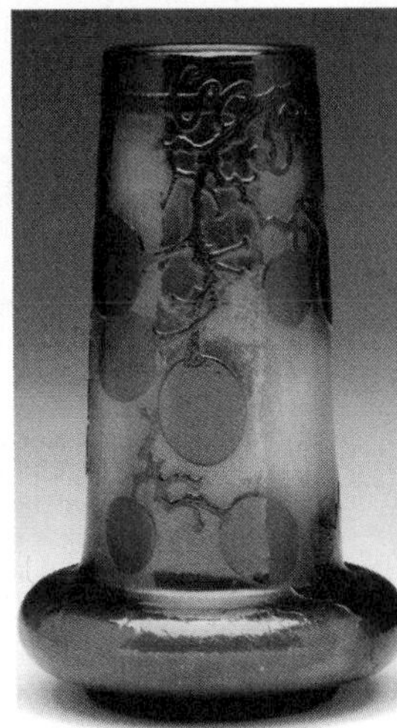

**Far left:** Gallé enameled vase, thistle decoration in mauve, white, and lavender set against a green vertically ribbed opalescent body with ruffled rim, signed on underside in brown enamel "Emile Gallé Inv" with a thistle, 6-3/8" t. Provenance: From a private Long Island collection........................**$2,070**
*James D. Julia, Inc.*

**Left:** Gallé fire-polished vase, olive green cameo decoration depicting grapes, vines, and leaves against a shaded cream and amber background, finished with a fire polish and signed on the side with ornate Oriental cameo "Gallé" signature, 7-3/4" t. Provenance: From a private Long Island collection.................. **$2,070**
*James D. Julia, Inc.*

GLASS

Gallé floral cameo vase, red cameo flowers, stems, and leaves against a frosted yellow background, primary flowers and buds done with a windowpane technique, signed on the side in cameo "Gallé," 9-3/4" t. Provenance: From a private Long Island collection...... **$4,600**
*James D. Julia, Inc.*

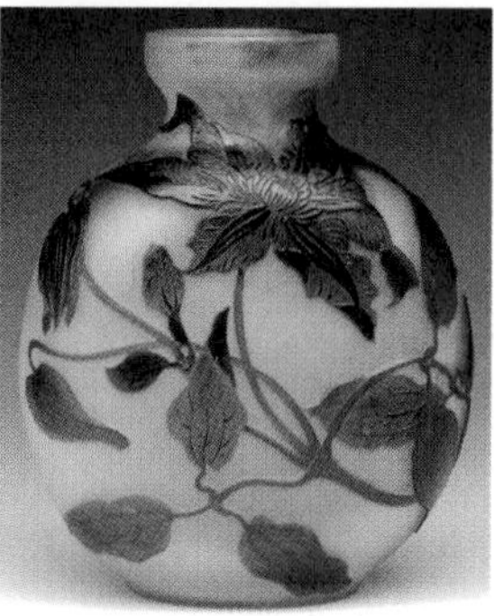

Gallé floral cameo vase, cut purple cameo flowers, stems, and leaves around vase, cameo decoration set against an acid textured cream-colored background that shades to green at the neck and mouth, signed on side in cameo "Gallé," 8" t. Provenance: From a private Long Island collection ........................... **$1,500-$2,500**
*James D. Julia, Inc.*

Gallé French cameo fire polish vase, purple and light blue clematis flowers encircle this bulbous footed vase with ground of milky white and blue, signed "Gallé" in cameo to side of vase, 4-1/2" t. ...................................... **$1,150**
*James D. Julia, Inc.*

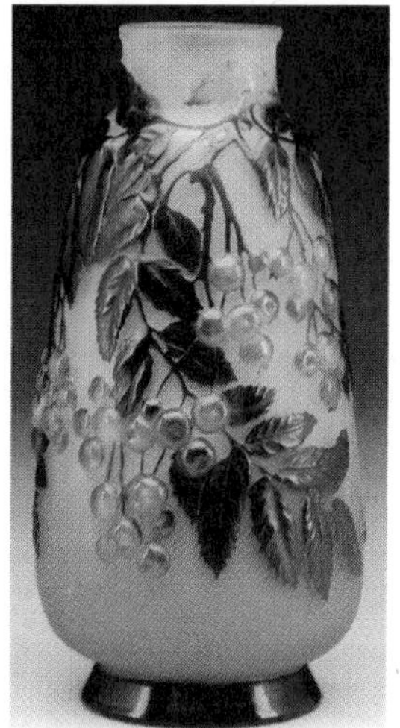

Gallé mold blown vase, translucent green cherries and opaque olive green leaves and stems against a frosted background of light brown shading to clear, signed on side in cameo "Gallé," 11-1/2" t. Provenance: From a private Long Island collection............. **$6,900**
*James D. Julia, Inc.*

Gallé French cameo dragonfly box decorated around the body of box with green and light blue water lilies against a cream shading to yellow background, matching cover, decorated with two cameo dragonflies in green and blue against a mottled background of purple, green, and cream, signed on side of box in cameo "Gallé," 5-1/2" dia. ..................... **$3,500-$5,000**
*James D. Julia, Inc.*

Gallé French cameo vase, dark olive green cameo decoration of grapes, leaves, and vines against a forest green background, rare color combination, signed on the side in cameo "Gallé," 9" t. .......................... **$2,500-$3,500**
*James D. Julia, Inc.*

Gallé four-color cameo vase decorated with purple flowers and stems with white backgrounds and green leaves set against a frosted peach-colored ground, vase signed on side in cameo "Gallé," 9-3/4" t. Provenance: From a private Long Island collection.....**$2,000-$3,000**
*James D. Julia, Inc.*

# Heisey Glass

Numerous types of fine glass were made by A.H. Heisey & Co., Newark, Ohio, from 1895. The company's trademark, an H enclosed within a diamond, has become known to most glass collectors. The company's name and molds were acquired by Imperial Glass Co., Bellaire, Ohio, in 1958, and some pieces have been reissued. The glass listed below consists of miscellaneous pieces and types.

Fancy Loop water pitcher, colorless, applied handle, A. H. Heisey & Co., fourth quarter 19th c., 9-1/4" h. ............................. **$35**
*Jeffrey S. Evans & Associates*

Various Early American Pattern Glass (EAPG) colored goblets, lot of four, amber, green with traces of gilt decoration, and vaseline, Heisey Fancy Loop, Finecut, and two Cathedral, fourth quarter 19th c., 5-1/2" to 6" h. ............................................................................. **$104**
*Jeffrey S. Evans & Associates*

Heisey No. 160/Locket on Chain cake stand, colorless, A. H. Heisey & Co., late 19th/early 20th c., 5" h., 9-1/4" dia. .................... **$115**
*Jeffrey S. Evans & Associates*

Heisey table articles, lot of five, colorless and green, some with gilt decoration, Fancy Loops individual creamer, Pineapple and Fan spooner, creamer and open sugar set, and Prince of Wales Plumes butter dish, A. H. Heisey & Co., late 19th/early 20th c., various sizes................. **$150**
*Jeffrey S. Evans & Associates*

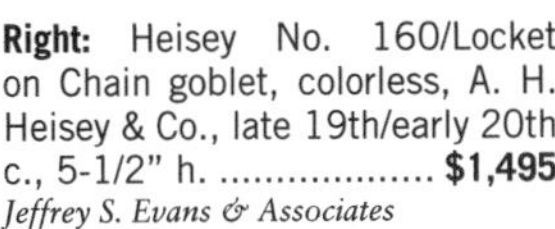

**Right:** Heisey No. 160/Locket on Chain goblet, colorless, A. H. Heisey & Co., late 19th/early 20th c., 5-1/2" h. .................. **$1,495**
*Jeffrey S. Evans & Associates*

**Far right:** Heisey No. 160/Locket on Chain wine glass, colorless, A. H. Heisey & Co., late 19th/early 20th c., 3-1/2" h................. **$35**
*Jeffrey S. Evans & Associates*

# Higgins Glass

Fused glass, an "old craft for modern tastes," enjoyed a mid-20th century revival through the work of Chicago-based artists Frances and Michael Higgins of the Higgins Glass Studio.

Although known for thousands of years, fusing had, by the 1940s, been abandoned in favor of glassblowing. A meticulous craft, fusing can best be described as the creation of a "glass sandwich." A design is either drawn with colored enamels or pieced with glass segments on a piece of enamel-coated glass. Another piece of enameled glass is placed over this. The "sandwich" is then placed on a mold and heated in a kiln, with the glass "slumping" to the shape of the mold. When complete, the interior design is fused between the outer glass layers. Additional layers are often utilized, accentuating the visual depth.

Sensing that fused glass was a marketable commodity, the Higgins opened their studio in 1948 and applied the fusing technique to a wide variety of uses: tableware, such as bowls, plates, and servers; housewares, ranging from clocks and lamps to ashtrays and candleholders; and purely decorative items, such as mobiles and jewelry. With its arresting mix of geometric and curved lines and bold use of color, Higgins glass transformed the ordinary into décor accent pieces both vibrant and exciting.

Unlike many of their contemporaries, the Higgins received national exposure thanks to an association with Chicago industrial manufacturer Dearborn Glass Company. This collaboration, lasting from 1957 through 1964, resulted in the mass marketing of "higginsware" worldwide. Since nearly every piece carried the lowercase signature "higgins," name recognition was both immediate and enduring.

The Dearborn demand for new Higgins pieces resulted in more than 75 identifiable production patterns with such buyer-enticing names as "Stardust," "Arabesque," and "Barbaric Jewels." Objects created in these patterns included ashtrays of every size (4" "Dinner Dwarfs" to 15" jumbo models), "rondelay" room dividers, and an extensive line of tableware. As evidenced by Dearborn promotional postcards, complete dining tables could literally be set with Higgins glass.

In 1965, the Higgins briefly moved their base of operations to Haeger Potteries, before opening their own studio in Riverside, Illinois, where it has been located since 1966. Although Michael Higgins died in 1999 and Frances Higgins in 2004, the studio today continues under the leadership of longtime artistic associates Louise and Jonathan Wimmer. New pieces celebrate and expand on the traditions and techniques of the past.

Higgins pieces created from 1948 until 1957 are engraved on the reverse with the signature "higgins" or the artist's complete name. A raised "dancing man" logo was added in 1951. Pieces created at Dearborn or Haeger (1957-'65) bear a gold "higgins" signature on the surface or a signature in the colorway. The marking since 1966 has been an engraved "higgins" on the reverse of an object, with the occasional addition of the artist's name. Pieces produced since the death of Frances Higgins are signed "higgins studio."

Once heralded as "an exclamation point in your decorating scheme," Higgins glass continues, nearly 60 years since its inception, to enchant collectors with its zest and variety.

References on Higgins glass include the Schiffer books Higgins: Poetry in Glass (2005) and Higgins: Adventures in Glass (1997), both by Donald-Brian Johnson and Leslie Piña. The Higgins Glass Studio is located at 33 East Quincy Street, Riverside, IL 60546, (708) 447-2787, www.higginsglass.com.

◄"Pointille" circular plate, Dearborn Glass Company, 1960s, 12-1/4" d. ............ **$200-$300**

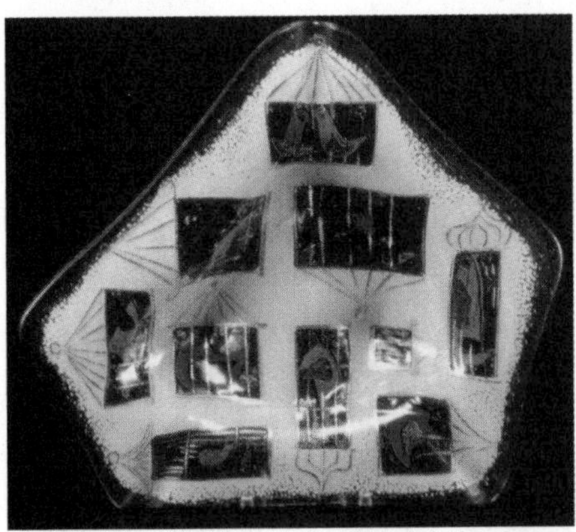

"Birdcages" ashtray on white background, Dearborn Glass Company, 1960s, 8" longest side. The pattern was also available in other colorways. ......**$300-$400**

"Birds #1" and "Birds #2" ashtrays, Dearborn Glass Company, 1960s, 9-1/2" and 10-1/2" longest sides ........................................................**$175-$250;** ........................................................ **$200-$250**

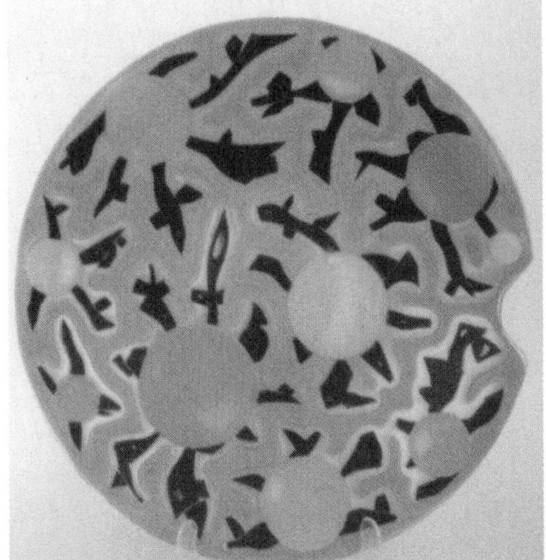

"Black Hole" platter, Michael Higgins, 24" d. The design was revamped to work around a kiln crack. ........................................................ **$3,750-$4,000**

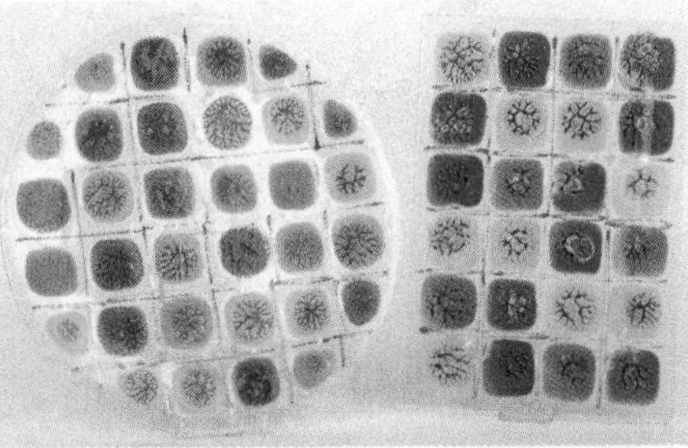

"Blot" plates, Frances Higgins, 1950s, 15" d. x 10" w. x 14" h. Because the colors are "blotted" between two pieces of glass, each design is unique. ........................................................ **$1,000-$1,250 ea.**

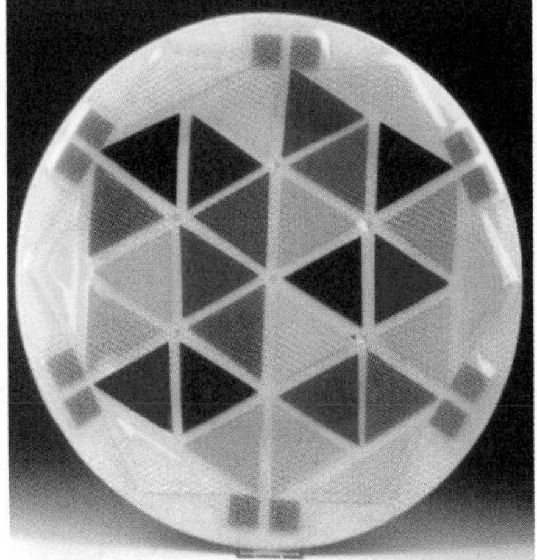

"Dimples" platter, Michael Higgins, 15" d. ........................................................ **$2,000-$2,250**

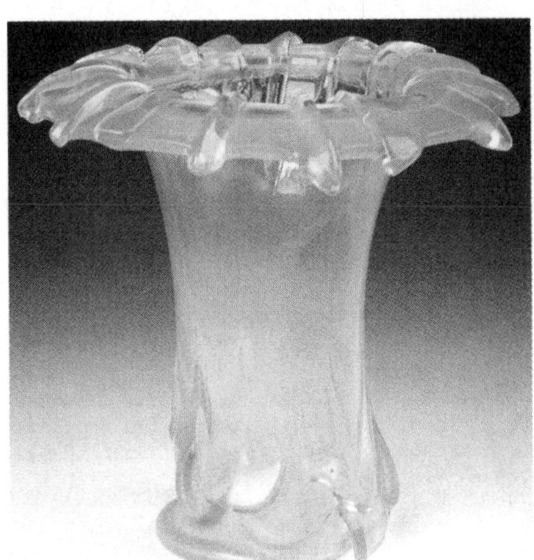

Clear plate glass "dropout," so named because the vase body "drops" in the mold when heated. A Jane Cumby design for Higgins Glass Studio, 7" h. x 8" d........................................................**$350-$400**

"Eye Over Quad" four-ply Michael Higgins glass sculpture, 1960, 11-1/2" w. x 19-1/2" h. ........................................................ **$5,000-$5,500**

"Gemspread" ashtray, Dearborn Glass Company, 1960s, 7-1/4" longest sides.................. **$275-$325**

Framed floral "flip art" plaque, Frances Higgins, 16" w. x 10" h. Actual vegetation is tapped in colored pigment, then "flipped" against the glass to create the pattern. .......................................... **$3,750-$4,000**

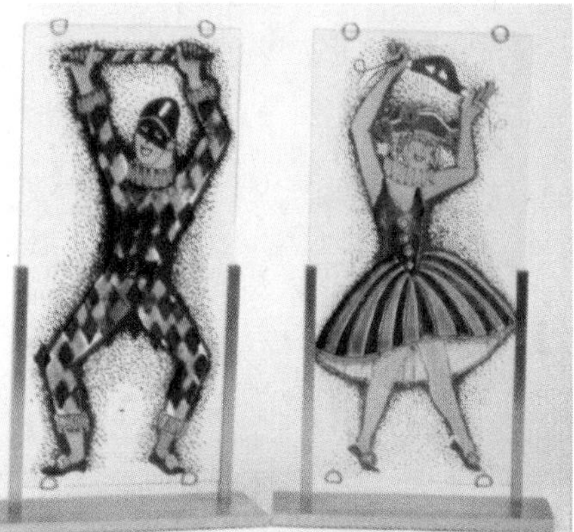

"Harlequin & Columbine" plaques on brass stands, 1950s, 7-1/2" w. x 15-1/2" h. ....... **$900-$1,000 ea.**

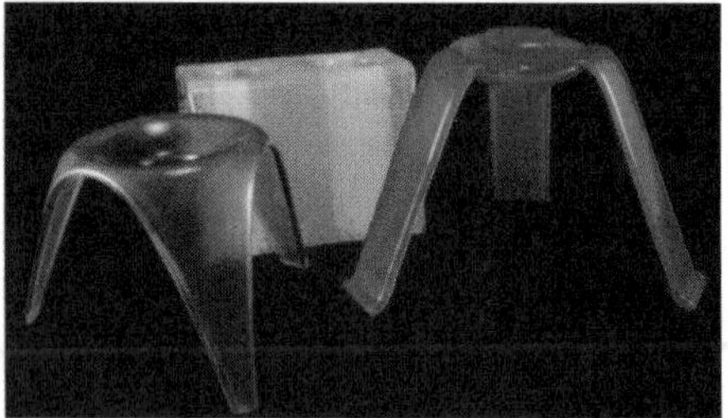

Higgins candleholder prototypes for Dearborn Glass Company, early 1960s ...................... **$500-$750 ea.**

◄"Hexagon with Cubes," framed Michael Higgins sculpture, 13-1/2" d. Both Michael and Frances Higgins used unique personal stampings to individualize sculpture frames............................. **$2,000-$2,200**

"Little Girl" plaque and ashtray, Dearborn Glass Company, 1960s, 5" x 7" .......................... **$75-$100 ea.**

Wall sculpture, 15-1/2" d. plate with 9" dangles, copper wire hangers. Jonathan Wimmer design for Higgins Glass Studio, 2011 .................... **$300-$400**

Higgins striped ashtray and cigarette box with black ceramic base, 10-1/2" longest side, 3" w. x 4-1/2" h. ...................................... **$250-$300; $450-$500**

"Waterfall Sparkler" on brass stand, Frances Higgins, 5" w. x 7" h. .................................. **$1,200-$1,300**

"Sewed Up Box," Michael Higgins, 8" l x 4-1/2" d. x 4" h. The bottom, sides, and hinged lid are all made from one folded sheet of glass. ......... **$2,500-$2,750**

◀Table lamp, on brass stand, Higgins Glass Studio, 2011, 19" h. ................................. **$1,550-$1,700**

GLASS

# Imperial

From 1902 until 1984 Imperial Glass of Bellaire, Ohio, produced hand made glass. Early pressed glass production often imitated cut glass and may bear the raised "NUCUT" mark in the interior center. In the second decade of the 1900s Imperial was one of the dominant manufacturers of iridescent or Carnival glass. When glass collecting gained popularity in the 1970s, Imperial again produced Carnival and a line of multicolored slag glass. Imperial purchased molds from closing glass houses and continued many lines popularized by others including Central, Heisey and Cambridge. These reissues may cause confusion but they were often marked.

## CANDLEWICK

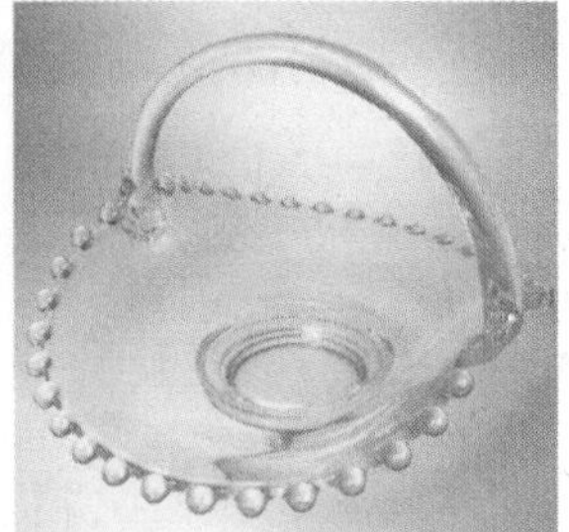

Basket, No. 400/40/0, clear, 6-1/2" l., 4-1/2" h................ **$38**

Cake stand and dome cover, No. 400/10D, beaded stem, cover made by West Virginia Glass Specialty and sold with the stand, cover 10" d., stand 11" d., 2 pcs.... **$135**

Compote, 10" h., crimped, three-bead stem, No. 400/103, clear with hand-painted pink roses & blue ribbons...................... **$260**

Cruet with stopper, No. 400/274, flat, bulbous bottom, clear, 4 oz. ........................................ **$52**

Relish dish, three-part, three-toed, No. 400/208, clear, 9" l............ **$98**

Candleholder, No. 400/40C, flower-type with crimped rim, clear, 5" h. ........................................................................ **$47**

Jam set: oval tray with two cov. marmalade jars with ladles; No. 400/1589, clear, 5 pcs. ................................................ **$125**

Punch set, punch bowl, underplate, 12 cups and ladle; No. 400/20, bowl and cups with cut Mallard pattern, 15 pcs...................... **$650**

Vase, two open beaded arms, crimped top, clear.......................... **$38**

Cream soup bowl with underplate, two-handled, No. 400/50, clear, 5" d. bowl and 6-3/4" d. underplate, 2 pcs.............................. **$75**

## CAPE COD

Candlestick, two-light, No. 160/100, crystal .................. **$85**

Finger bowl, No. 1604 1/2A, ruby, 4-1/2" d............................... **$24**

Goblet, dinner, ball stem, Azalea Pink, 11 oz. ............................................... **$17**

Pitcher, No. 160/239, clear, 60 oz............ **$95**

Plate, 16" d., cupped, No. 160/20V, clear........ **$50**

Punch set: punch bowl, underplate and twelve cups; clear, 1 gal., 14 pcs...................... **$220**

Salt and pepper shakers with original tops, original factory label, No. 160/251, clear, pr. .**$20**

Sherbet, tall, No. 1602, Verde green, 6 oz....**$15**

Sundae, No. 1602, ball stem, clear, 4" h. ..... **$7**

Tumbler, ced tea, No. 1602, amber, 6" h. .**$15**

Tom and Jerry punchbowl, footed, No. 160/200, clear.................... **$290**

Wine carafe and stopper, footed, handled, No. 160/185, crystal...**$220**

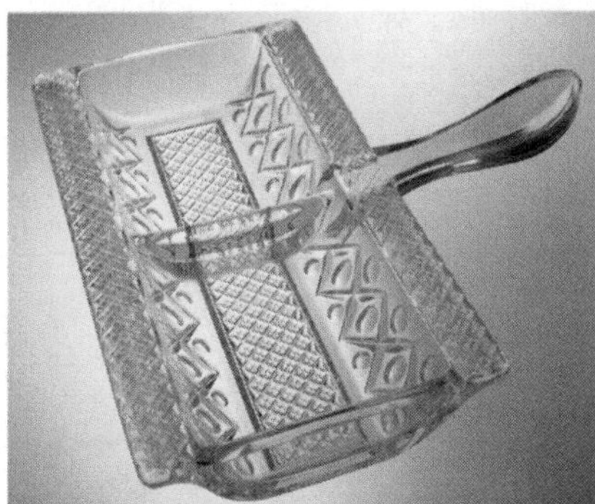

Cigarette server/relish, handled, two-part, No. 160/223, clear, 8-1/2" l.............................. **$40**

Pitcher w/ice lip, No. 160/24, clear, 60 oz., 2 qt.... **$92**

◀Pepper mill and salt shaker, chrome base and covers, No. 16/236 & 160/238, clear, pr.......................... **$55**

GLASS

## FREE-HAND WARE

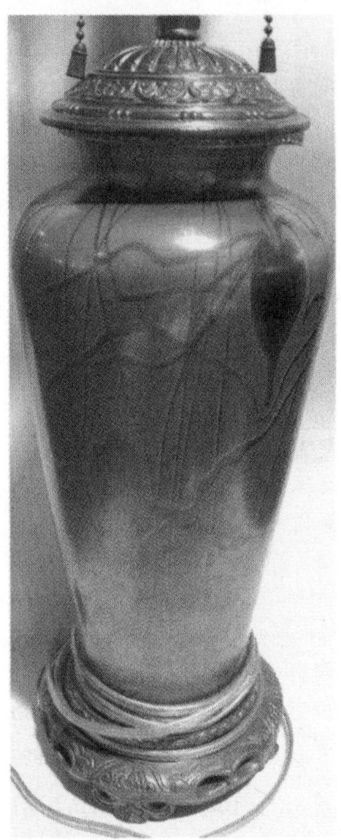

Lamp, electric, cast metal foot and cap, tapering ovoid glass body in iridescent orange with cobalt blue Hanging Hearts pattern, 10" h. ....................................... **$1,650**

Vase, flat flaring foot and tall slender gently flaring cylindrical body, iridescent cobalt blue exterior and orange interior, 8" h. ........... **$235**

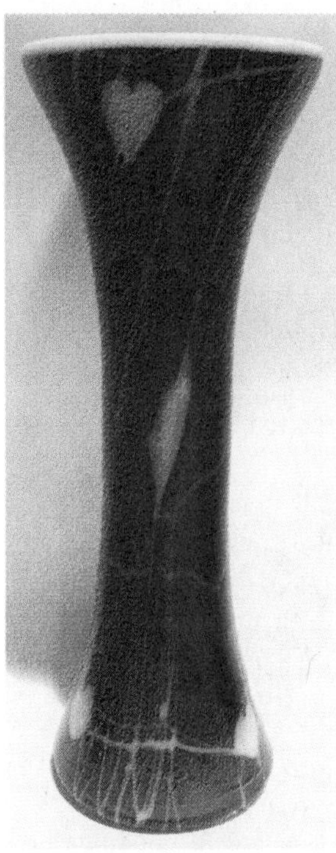

Vase, tall slender waisted shape with flaring top, iridescent cobalt blue exterior with white Hanging Heart decoration, 10-1/2" h., ....................................... **$1,175**

## MISCELLANEOUS PATTERNS & LINES

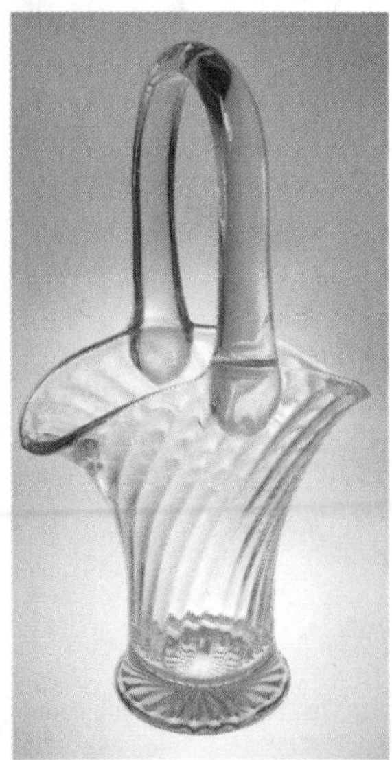

Cake plate, hexagonal with two open handles, Brocaded Daffodils etching, green, 7" w. ........................................................................ **$49**

◀Basket, Twisted Optic pattern, pale blue, 10" h. ......................... **$85**

Candlestick, single-light, Cathay Line, figural Candle Servant (female), No. 5035, clear satin ........................................ **$195**

Goblet, water, Chroma pattern No. 123, burgandy, 5-1/2" h........ **$24**

Pitcher, Reeded pattern, No. 701, green with clear applied handle .......................................... **$80**

Decanter with crystal mushroom stopper, No. 451, spherical body w/ringed foot and cylindrical neck, ruby ................................. **$120**

Epergne, one-lily, two-piece, Pattern #1950/196, Doeskin (milk glass), 9" d., 11" h............... **$78**

Plate, Beaded Block pattern, pink, 8" w. ................................. **$20**

Tumbler, footed, Parisian Provincial pattern, milk glass stem and foot, amethyst bowl, 7 oz. ..... **$22**

Vase, 8" h., pressed, trumpet-shaped, Pattern #G 505, gold on crystal ................................ **$28**

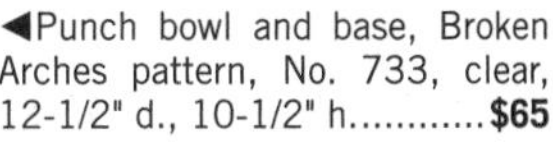

◀Punch bowl and base, Broken Arches pattern, No. 733, clear, 12-1/2" d., 10-1/2" h............ **$65**

# Lalique Glass

René Jules Lalique was born on April 6, 1860, in the village of Ay, in the Champagne region of France. In 1862, his family moved to the suburbs of Paris.

In 1872, Lalique began attending College Turgot where he began studying drawing with Justin-Marie Lequien. After the death of his father in 1876, Lalique began working as an apprentice to Louis Aucoc, who was a prominent jeweler and goldsmith in Paris.

Lalique moved to London in 1878 to continue his studies. He spent two years attending Sydenham College, developing his graphic design skills. He returned to Paris in 1880 and worked as an illustrator of jewelry, creating designs for Cartier, among others. In 1884, Lalique's drawings were displayed at the National Exhibition of Industrial Arts, organized at the Louvre.

At the end of 1885, Lalique took over Jules Destapes' jewelry workshop. Lalique's design began to incorporate translucent enamels, semiprecious stones, ivory, and hard stones. In 1889, at the Universal Exhibition in Paris, the jewelry firms of Vever and Boucheron included collaborative works by Lalique in their displays.

In the early 1890s, Lalique began to incorporate glass into his jewelry, and in 1893 he took part in a competition organized by the Union Centrale des Arts Decoratifs to design a drinking vessel. He won second prize.

Lalique opened his first Paris retail shop in 1905, near the perfume business of François Coty. Coty commissioned Lalique to design his perfume labels in 1907, and he also created his first perfume bottles for Coty.

In the first decade of the 20th century, Lalique continued to experiment with glass manufacturing techniques, and mounted his first show devoted entirely to glass in 1911.

During World War I, Lalique's first factory was forced to close, but the construction of a new factory was soon begun in Wingen-sur-Moder, in the Alsace region. It was completed in 1921, and still produces Lalique crystal today.

In 1925, Lalique designed the first "car mascot" (hood ornament) for Citroën, the French automobile company. For the next six years, Lalique would design 29 models for companies such as Bentley, Bugatti, Delage, Hispano-Suiza, Rolls Royce, and Voisin.

Lalique's second boutique opened in 1931, and this location continues to serve as the main Lalique showroom today.

René Lalique died on May 5, 1945, at the age of 85. His son, Marc, took over the business at that time, and when Marc died in 1977, his daughter, Marie-Claude Lalique Dedouvre, assumed control of the company. She sold her interest in the firm and retired in 1994.

"Ecureuil" ashtray in amber glass, circa 1931, 4-3/4" dia. (M p. 279, No. 315) ................ **$500+**

For more information on Lalique, see *Warman's Lalique Identification and Price Guide* by Mark F. Moran.

(In the descriptions of Lalique pieces that follow, you will find notations like this: "M p. 478, No. 1100." This refers to the page and serial numbers found in *René Lalique, maître-verrier, 1860-1945: Analyse de L'oeuvre et Catalogue Raisonné*, by Félix Marcilhac, published in 1989 and revised in 1994. Printed entirely in French, this book of more than 1,000 pages is the definitive guide to Lalique's work, and listings from auction catalogs typically cite the Marcilhac guide as a reference. A used copy can cost more than $500. Copies in any condition are extremely difficult to find, but collectors consider Marcilhac's guide to be the bible for Lalique.)

GLASS

"Alice" ashtray, circa 1924, in clear and frosted glass, molded R.LALIQUE, stenciled R. LALIQUE FRANCE, 4-1/3" long. (M p. 272, No. 289)...**$450-$500**

"Cerises" box, circa 1923, in red celluloid, molded R. LALIQUE, 2-1/8" square. (M p. 236, No. 73) ..............................**$900-$1,100**

"Cleones" box, circa 1921, in amber glass, molded R. LALIQUE, engraved France, 6-3/4" dia. (M p. 231, No. 9).........**$900-$1,100**

"Amiens" vase, circa 1929, in opalescent glass, wheel-cut R LALIQUE, 7-1/4" tall. (M p. 443, No. 1023) ........... **$1,700-$2,000**

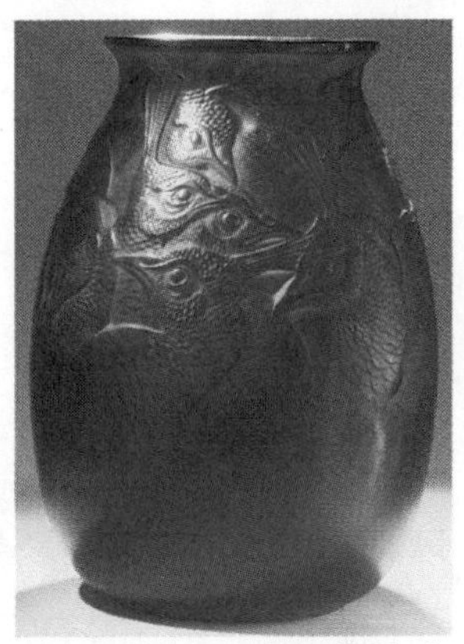

"Borrome" vase, circa 1928, in peacock blue glass vase with white patina, stenciled R. LALIQUE, 9" tall. (Ref. M p. 442, No. 1017) ........................... **$7,000-$8,000**

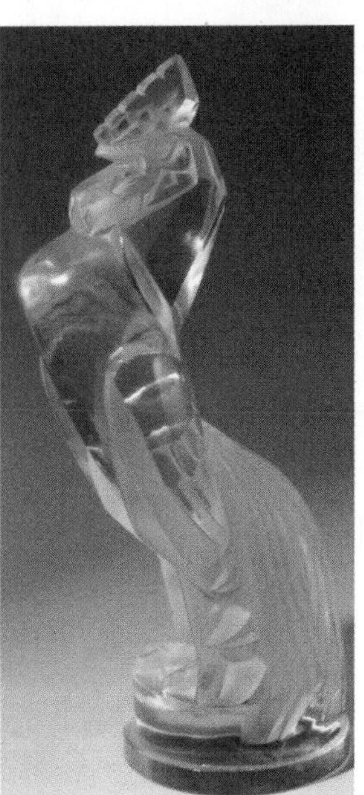

"Biches" inkwell in deep amber glass with white patina, circa 1912, base 6" square. (M p. 315, No. 427) ...................... **$2,000+**

"Chat Assis," a figure of a sitting cat, circa 1970, in clear and frosted glass, engraved Lalique France, 8-1/4" tall. ....**$650-$750**

"Dahlias" vase, circa 1919, in clear and frosted glass with sepia patina and black enamel highlights, engraved R. Lalique France, No. 928, 5" tall. (M p. 425, No. 938) ..... **$2,400-$2,600**

**Far left:** "Coeur Joie" perfume bottle for Nina Ricci, circa 1955, in clear and frosted glass, engraved Lalique France, 6" tall. ................................**$400-$500**

**Left:** "Coq Houdan" car mascot (hood ornament), circa 1929, in clear and frosted glass, wheel-cut R. LALIQUE FRANCE, 8" tall. (M p. 504, No. 1161) **$4,000-$5,000**

"Druides" vase, circa 1924, in opalescent glass with green patina, engraved R. Lalique France, 7-1/2" tall. (M p. 424, No. 937)........................ **$1,700-$1,900**

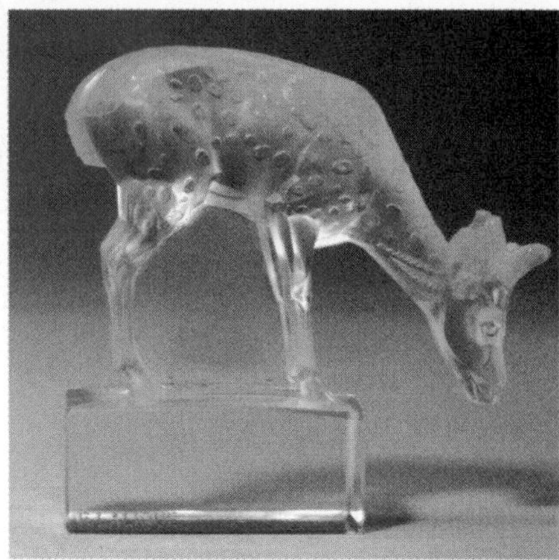

"Daim" paperweight in clear and frosted glass, molded and stenciled R. LALIQUE, 3-1/3" tall. (Ref. M p. 389, No. 1168).......................... **$900-$1,200**

"Floride" bowl, clear and green glass with black enamel details, circa 1960, engraved Lalique France, 7-1/4" dia. ........................................... **$300-$350**

◄"Fleur" bowl, circa 1912, in clear and frosted glass with sepia patina and black enamel, molded R. LALIQUE, 4-1/2" dia. (M p. 727, No. 3100) ............................................................. **$650-$750**

"Formose" vase in cased red glass with traces of white patina, circa 1924, 7-1/8" tall. (M p. 425, No. 934) ....................................................... **$5,000+**

"Fougeres" vase in charcoal gray glass, circa 1912, 7-1/1/2" tall. (M p. 422, No. 923)..............**$4,000+**

"Frise Fleurs" perfume bottle for Raquel Meller, in clear and frosted glass with enamel decoration, circa 1925, 3" tall. (M p. 947)..........................**$2,500+**

"Hirondelles" vase in cherry red glass with white patina, circa 1919, 9-1/4" tall. (M p. 414, No. 889) ..........................................................**$5,000+**

"Hirondelle" car mascot (hood ornament), circa 1928, in clear and frosted glass, molded R. LALIQUE FRANCE, 6" tall. (M p. 501, No. 1143) ................ **$1,500-$2,000**

"Irene" ashtray in bright green glass, stenciled R. LALIQUE FRANCE. (Ref. M p. 276, No. 304.) .................. **$1,200-$1,500**

►"L'Air Du Temps" display perfume bottle for Nina Ricci, circa 1960, in clear and frosted glass, sealed and with contents, 12-1/2" tall......................... **$900-$1,000**

"Malines" vase, circa 1924, in blue glass, stenciled R. LALIQUE, engraved France, 5-1/8" tall. (M p. 429, No. 957).......... **$2,000+**

"Meduse" vase in teal green glass, circa 1921, 6-7/8" tall. (M p. 428, No. 950) ...................... **$6,000+**

"Misti" perfume bottle for Piver (L.T.) in clear and frosted glass, circa 1920, 2-1/8" tall. (M p. 946, Piver (L.T.) 1)........ **$1,500+**

"Moissac" vase in yellow amber glass, wheel-cut R. Lalique France, 5-1/8" tall. (M p. 437, No. 992) ............ **$1,700-$2,000**

"Palerme" perfume bottle, circa 1926, in clear glass, molded R. LALIQUE, 4-1/2" tall. (M p. 336, No. 518) ...................**$600-$700**

"Piriac" vase, circa 1930, in blue glass, stenciled R. LALIQUE FRANCE, 7-1/4" tall. (M p. 447, No. 1043) .......... **$4,200-$4,800**

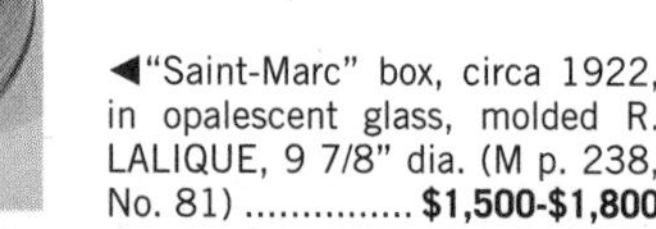

"Moyenne Violee," a statuette, circa 1912, in opalescent glass with blue patina, engraved Lalique, 5-3/8" tall. (M p. 398, No. 829) ............ **$4,800-$5,300**

◄"Saint-Marc" box, circa 1922, in opalescent glass, molded R. LALIQUE, 9 7/8" dia. (M p. 238, No. 81) .............. **$1,500-$1,800**

"Muguet" shallow dish, circa 1931, in opalescent glass, stenciled R. LALIQUE FRANCE, 11 7/8" dia. (M p. 302, No. 416)........................ **$1,800-$2,000**

"Oran" vase in opalescent glass, circa 1927, 10-1/4" tall. (M p. 439, No. 999) ........................**$20,000+**

"Sauge" vase in blue-green glass with white patina, circa 1923, 10-1/4" tall. (M p. 425, No. 935) .................................... **$2,000+**

"Taureau" paperweight in clear and frosted glass, wheel-cut R. LALIQUE FRANCE. (M p. 391, No. 1194) ............. **$900-$1,200**

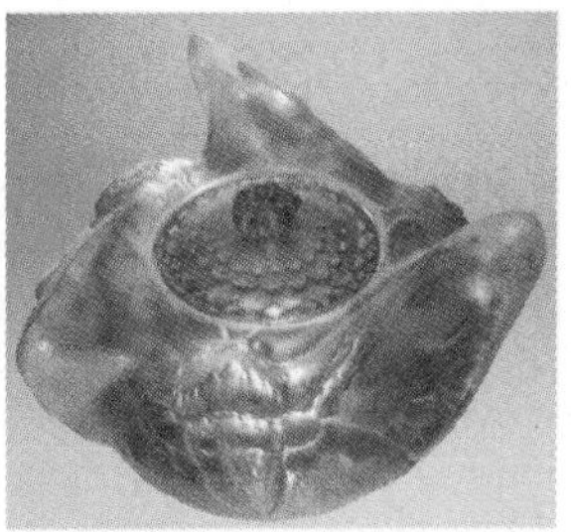

"Trois Papillons" inkwell in opalescent glass with sepia patina, circa 1912, 3-7/8" dia. (M p. 315, No. 426) ............. **$2,000+**

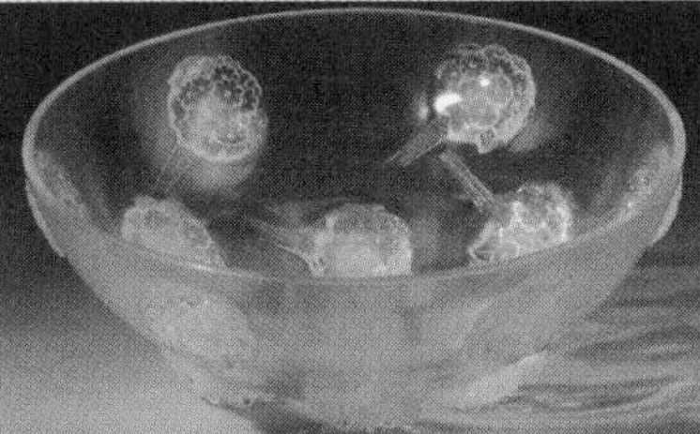

"Tournon," a center bowl, circa 1928, in opalescent glass, molded R. LALIQUE FRANCE, 12" dia. (M p. 298, No. 401) ...... **$1,100-$1,400**

**Far left:** "Vase Deux Anemones" perfume bottle in clear and frosted glass with black enamel decoration, circa 1935, 6-1/4" tall. (M p. 339, No. 530)........... **$1,500+**

**Left:** "Vezelay" ashtray, circa 1928, in clear and frosted glass with blue patina, molded R. LALIQUE, 4-1/2" dia. (M p. 270, No. 281) ................... **$225-$275**

"Serpent" vase in purple glass, circa 1924, 10-1/4" tall. (M p. 416, No. 896) ........................... **$40,000**

"Victoire" car mascot (hood ornament), circa 1928, in clear and frosted glass, molded R. LALIQUE FRANCE, 10-1/4" long, together with an original Lalique wood display mount. (M p. 502, No. 1147) ............................................. **$24,000-$26,000**

# Libbey Glass

In 1878, William L. Libbey obtained a lease on the New England Glass Co. of Cambridge, Massachusetts, changing the name to the New England Glass Works, W.L. Libbey and Son, Proprietors. After his death in 1883, his son, Edward D. Libbey, continued to operate the company at Cambridge until 1888, when the factory was closed. Edward Libbey moved to Toledo, Ohio, and set up the company subsequently known as Libbey Glass Co. During the 1880s, the firm's master technician, Joseph Locke, developed the now much desired colored art glass lines of Agata, Amberina, Peach Blow, and Pomona. Renowned for its cut glass of the Brilliant Period, the company continues in operation today as Libbey Glassware, a division of Owens-Illinois, Inc.

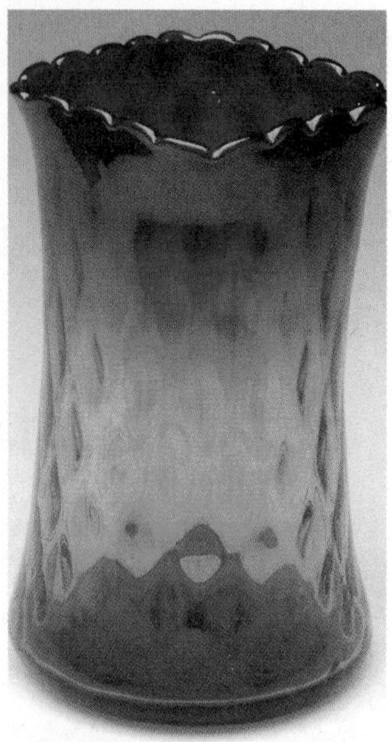

Four Amberina Optic pattern mugs/cups, Rib, Diamond and Baby Thumbprint patterns, latter with polychrome enamel decoration, each with an applied handle, W.L. Libbey & Sons and others, fourth quarter 19th c., 2-3/8" to 3-3/4" h. .................................... **$149**
*Jeffrey S. Evans & Associates*

◄Amberina Diamond-Optic celery vase, square scalloped rim and rough pontil mark, probably W.L. Libbey & Sons, late 19th/early 20th c., 6" h., 3-1/8" sq. rim .................................................... **$138**
*Jeffrey S. Evans & Associates*

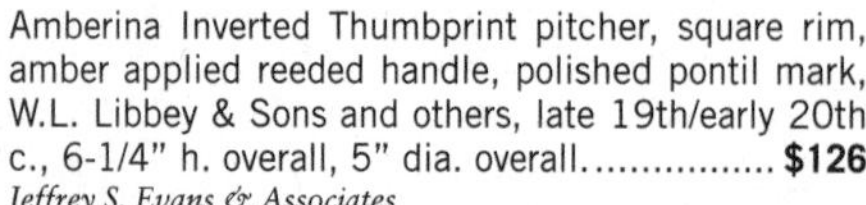

Amberina Inverted Thumbprint pitcher, square rim, amber applied reeded handle, polished pontil mark, W.L. Libbey & Sons and others, late 19th/early 20th c., 6-1/4" h. overall, 5" dia. overall ................ **$126**
*Jeffrey S. Evans & Associates*

Four Amberina Diamond-Optic punch cups, each with an amber applied reeded handle and polished pontil mark, W.L. Libbey & Sons and others, late 19th/early 20th c., 2-1/2" h., 2-1/4" dia. rim ................. **$149**
*Jeffrey S. Evans & Associates*

Libbey Amberina scent bottle, lightly ribbed body with nice color shading and finished with an Amberina dauber stopper, signed on the underside "Libbey Amberina," 8-3/8" t. .......................... **$1,380**

*James D. Julia, Inc.*

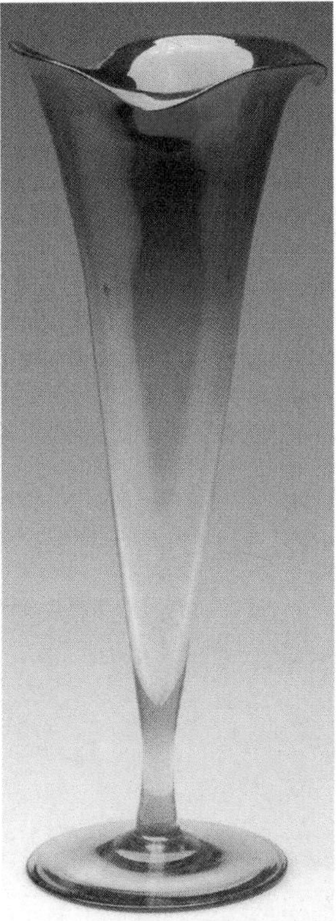

Amberina lily vase, unpatterned, two-part construction, polished pontil mark, possibly W.L. Libbey & Sons, late 19th/early 20th c., 11-3/4" h. overall, 4-1/2" dia. overall. .............................. **$184**

*Jeffrey S. Evans & Associates*

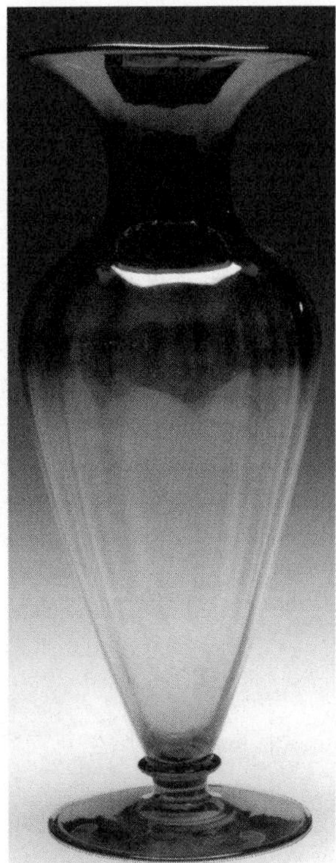

Libbey Amberina vase, vertically ribbed body with rich fuchsia top shading to amber, signed on the polished pontil "Amberina Libbey," 14-1/4" t. .............. **$1,150**

*James D. Julia, Inc.*

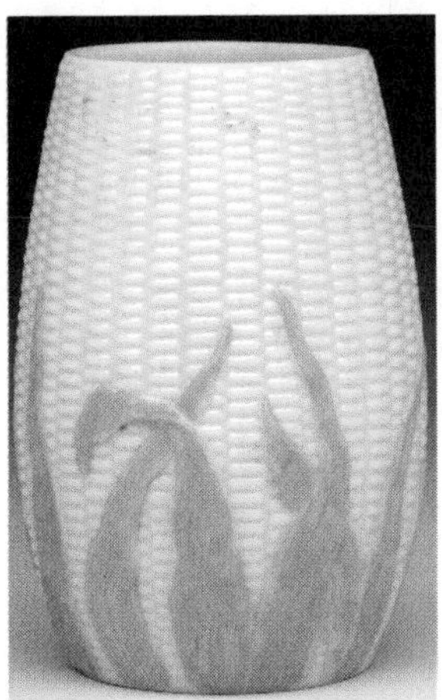

Libbey Maize pattern master berry bowl and celery vase, translucent white with green stain, Libbey Glass Co., late 19th/early 20th c., 3-3/4" h., 9" dia. overall, and 6-1/2" h, 4-1/2" dia. overall. ...................... **$57**

*Jeffrey S. Evans & Associates*

Libbey Maize pattern milk glass vase, impressed corn kernels covering the body of the vase and pressed corn husks extending upward from the foot, husks stained light green and kernels white, 6-1/2" t. .......... **$143**

*James D. Julia, Inc.*

GLASS

# Mary Gregory

Glass enameled in white with silhouette-type figures, primarily of children, is now termed "Mary Gregory" and was attributed to the Boston and Sandwich Glass Co. However, recent research has proven conclusively that this was not decorated by Mary Gregory, nor was it made at the Sandwich plant. Miss Gregory was employed by Boston and Sandwich Glass Co. as a decorator; however, records show her assignment was the painting of naturalistic landscape scenes on larger items such as lamps and shades, but never the charming children for which her name has become synonymous. Further, in the inspection of fragments from the factory site, no paintings of children were found.

It is now known that all wares collectors call "Mary Gregory" originated in Bohemia beginning in the late 19th c. and were extensively exported to England and the United States well into this c..

For further information, see *The Glass Industry in Sandwich*, Volume #4 by Raymond E. Barlow and Joan E. Kaiser, and the book *Mary Gregory Glassware*, 1880-1900 by R. & D. Truitt.

Mary Gregory Victorian decorated perfume bottles, peacock blue, Rib-Optic with enameled so-called Mary Gregory children and gilt decorations, original stoppers, 1880-1900, 8-1/2" h. overall ........................................ **$259**
*Jeffrey S. Evans & Associates*

Inverted Thumbprint pickle caster, green, with so-called Mary Gregory decoration of child sitting on stylized branch, fitted in a Van Bergh Silver Plate Co. quadruple-plate frame, marked "619L," with cover and tongs, rim of jar roughed and lightly gilded, probably during manufacturing process, fourth quarter 19th c., 10" h. overall, jar 4-1/4" h., 3-3/4" dia. overall........... **$184**
*Jeffrey S. Evans & Associates*

Rib-Optic pickle caster, ruby, with so-called Mary Gregory decoration of child pointing to bird's nest, roughed pontil mark, fitted in a Wm. Rogers Manufacturing Co. quadruple-plate frame, marked "453," with cover and tongs, rim of jar polished during manufacturing process, fourth quarter 19th c., 11" h. overall, jar 5-1/8" h., 4-1/4" dia. overall. ............. **$402**
*Jeffrey S. Evans & Associates*

Mary Gregory water set, tall pitcher and six tumblers, pitcher decorated with white enameled woman in long dress holding flower basket surrounded by large flowers, three tumblers decorated in white enamel with young boy holding his hand out, other three tumblers decorated with young girl holding her hand out, all decoration against lime green background, pitcher 14" t......................... **$201**
*James D. Julia, Inc.*

# McKee

The McKee name has been associated with glass production since 1834, first producing window glass and later bottles. In the 1850s a new factory was established in Pittsburgh, Pennsylvania, for production of flint and pressed glass. The plant was relocated in Jeanette, Pennsylvania, in 1888 and operated there as an independent company almost continuously until 1951, when it sold out to Thatcher Glass Manufacturing Co. Many types of collectible glass were produced by McKee through the years, including Depression, pattern, milk glass, and a variety of utility kitchenware items. See these categories for additional listings.

Feather milk pitcher, chocolate, probably McKee Glass Co., early 20th c., 8-1/4" h. overall, 4-1/4" dia. overall........................ **$316**
*Jeffrey S. Evans & Associates*

Pressed Charleston tumbler, fiery opalescent with excellent pooling, slightly tapered form with six lower panels and plain wide band at rim, polished pontil mark, probably McKee & Brothers, Pittsburgh, 1850-1875, 3-5/8" h., 3-3/8" dia. rim. ............................ **$184**
*Jeffrey S. Evans & Associates*

Sultan (Omn)/Wild Rose with Bow-knot pitcher, chocolate, McKee & Brothers Glass Works, early 20th c., 8" h. overall, 5" dia. overall. ........................................ **$161**
*Jeffrey S. Evans & Associates*

Pressed McKee diamond compote, bright vaseline non-lead glass, bowl with wide scallop and point rim, raised on hexagonal faceted standard stepped to a circular foot, wafer construction, McKee & Brothers, Pittsburgh, 1870-1890, 9-5/8" h.,10-1/4" dia. rim, 5-1/2" dia. foot. ................................................. **$138**
*Jeffrey S. Evans & Associates*

Pillar-molded quart bar decanter, colorless with applied blue ribbons from base to mouth, tall petticoat form with eight protruding ribs, applied wide convex neck ring, rounded bar lip ground on interior, polished pontil mark, extremely rare, attributed to the Pittsburgh area, possibly McKee & Brothers, 1850-1870, 12-1/2" h., 5" dia. base. ................. **$195**
*Jeffrey S. Evans & Associates*

# Milk Glass

Though invented in Venice in the 1500s, the opaque glass commonly known as milk glass was most popular at the end of the 19th century. American manufacturers such as Westmoreland, Fenton, Imperial, Indiana, and Anchor Hocking produced it as an economical substitute for pricey European glass and china.

After World War I, the popularity of milk glass waned, but production continued. Milk glass made during the 1930s and 1940s is often considered of lower quality than other periods because of the economic Depression and wartime manufacturing difficulties.

Milk glass has proven to be an "evergreen" collectible. When asked about milk glass, Warman's Depression Glass author and expert Ellen Schroy said, "Milk glass is great. I'm seeing a new interest in it."

"Milk glass" is a general term for opaque colored glass. Though the name would lead you to believe it, white wasn't the only color produced.

"Colored milk glasses, such as opaque black, green, or pink usually command higher prices," Schroy advises. "Beware of reproductions in green and pink. Always question a milk glass pattern found in cobalt blue. (Swirled colors are a whole other topic and very desirable.)"

The number of patterns, forms, and objects made is only limited by the imagination. Commonly found milk glass items include dishes – especially the ever-popular animals on "nests" – vases, dresser sets, figurines, lanterns, boxes, and perfume bottles.

"The milk glass made by Westmoreland, Kemple, Fenton, etc., was designed to be used as dinnerware," Schroy explains. "Much of the milk glass we see at flea markets, antique shows, and shops now is coming out of homes and estates where these 1940-1950s era brides are disposing of their settings." Schroy follows up with some practical advice: "Care should be taken when purchasing, transporting, and using this era of milk glass as it is very intolerant of temperature changes. Don't buy a piece outside at the flea market unless you can protect it well for its trip to your home. And when you get it home, leave it sit for several hours so its temperature evens out to what your normal home temperature is. It's almost a given if you take a piece of cold glass and submerge it into a nice warm bath, it's going to crack. And never, ever expose it to the high temps of a modern dishwasher."

So how do you tell the old from the new? Schroy says many times, getting your hands on it is the only way to tell: "Milk glass should have a wonderful silky texture. Any piece that is grainy is probably new." She further reveals, "The best test is to look for 'the ring of fire,' which will be easy to see in the sunlight: Hold the piece of milk glass up to a good light source (I prefer natural light) and see if there is a halo of iridescent colors right around the edge, look for reds, blues and golds. This ring was caused by the addition of iridized salts into the milk glass formula. If this ring is present, it's probably an old piece." She does caution, however, that 1950s-era milk glass does not have this tell-tale ring.

Old milk glass should also carry appropriate marks and signs, such as the "ring of fire"; appropriate patterns for specific makers are also something to watch for, such as Fenton's "Hobnail" pattern. Collectors should always check for condition issues such as damage and discoloration. According to Schroy, there is no remedy for discolored glass, and cracked and chipped pieces should be avoided, as they are prone to further damage.

*Karen Knapstein, Antique Trader*

## ONLINE RESOURCES:

Milkglass.org is an informational website. It includes historical and identification details, in addition to a collection of categorized links to milk glass items for sale on the Internet (primarily eBay).

The National Westmoreland Glass Collectors Club's mission is to promote the appreciation for the artistry and craftsmanship of Westmoreland glass and to continue the preservation of this important part of American history. (westmorelandglassclub.org)

*Courtesy Antique Helper, Apple Tree Auction Center, Dargate Auction Galleries, Jeffrey S. Evans & Associates, Ken Farmer Auctions & Appraisals, Montrie Auction & Estate Service LLC, O'Gallerie, and Pacific Galleries*

Pressed Bellflower – Single Vine molasses jug, opaque white, small-size ovoid body, applied solid handle with delicate flattened curl, plain base, original pewter hinged lid, Boston & Sandwich Glass Co. and possibly others, 1850-1870, 6" h. overall, 4-1/2" h. neck, 2-3/8" dia. base ............................... **$1,265**
*Jeffrey S. Evans & Associates*

Boar's head covered dish, opaque white/milk glass, on ribbed base, original red glass eyes, patent date on lid interior and under base, Atterbury & Co., fourth quarter 19th c., 5-1/2" h. overall, 6-1/8" x 9-3/8" overall rim................................................ **$2,185**
*Jeffrey S. Evans & Associates*

Blue milk glass condiments and frames. Set consists of two blue milk glass condiment frames with silver plated wire handles and three blue milk glass salt shakers. Each shaker has a different pressed pattern; one with stylized flowers, stems and leaves; one with an oak leaf pattern; and one with slightly diagonal vertical panels that matches one of the frames; tallest frame is 7" to top of handle............................. **$17**
*James D. Julia, Inc.*

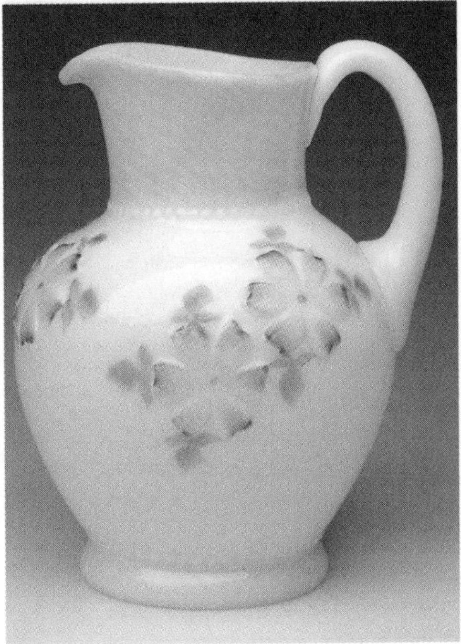

Coreopsis water pitcher, opaque white/milk glass with polychrome decoration, pale green band at rim, applied opaque white/milk glass handle, first quarter 20th c., 8-1/2" h. overall, 5-3/4" dia. overall..... **$46**
*Jeffrey S. Evans & Associates*

Fainting couch covered dish, opaque white/milk glass with original green decoration, fourth quarter 19th c., 1-3/4" h. overall, 2" x 5"........ **$259**
*Jeffrey S. Evans & Associates*

Scrolled Rib sugar shaker, opaque blue, period lid, Gillinder & Sons, late 19th/early 20th c., 4-3/8" h. overall ................................ **$80**
*Jeffrey S. Evans & Associates*

Gillinder George Washington centennial bust, opaque white/milk glass with satin finish, embossed "WASHINGTON" on the front and "CENTENNIAL EXHIBITION/GILLINDER & SONS" on reverse, Gillinder & Sons, fourth quarter 19th c., 6" h., 2-1/2" x 3-1/4" base ........................................................ **$633**
*Jeffrey S. Evans & Associates*

Franklin D. Roosevelt head vase, opaque white/milk glass, well detailed, factory polishing to opening, probably mid-20th c., 7-1/4" h. overall, base 3-7/8" x 4-1/2", opening 1-1/4" x 2-1/2" .................. **$403**
*Jeffrey S. Evans & Associates*

McKee horse covered dish, opaque white/milk glass, on split rib base, neither piece marked, McKee & Brothers, late 19th/early 20th c., 4-1/2" h. overall, 4-1/4" x 5-1/2" .......................................... **$69**

*Jeffrey S. Evans & Associates*

# Morgantown (Old Morgantown)

Morgantown, West Virginia, was the site where a glass firm named the Morgantown Glass Works began in the late 19th century, but the company reorganized in 1903 to become the Economy Tumbler Co., a name it retained until 1929. By the 1920s the firm was producing a wider range of better quality and colorful glass tableware; to reflect this fact, it resumed its earlier name, Morgantown Glass Works, in 1929. Today its many quality wares of the Depression era are growing in collector demand.

Tumbler, No. 7682 Ramona, footed iced tea, Stiegel green............... **$45**

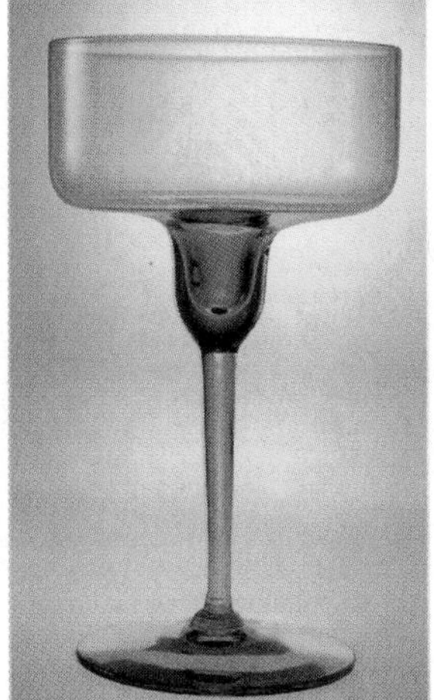

Candle/vase, Guild, No. 83 Patrician, pineapple (deep yellow), 8" h. ...................................... **$36**

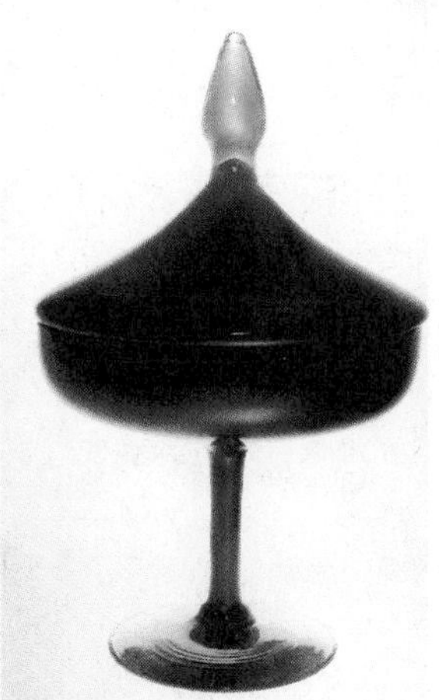

Compote, covered, 4 -7/8" h., No. 7801 Cumberland, ebony with green foot and finial..... **$475**

Goblet, Tiburon, No. 7634, blank with Westchester Rose cutting, water, Anna Rose color, 9 oz... **$48**

Morgantown cobalt Golf Ball stems: 21 pieces including eight water (6-3/4" h. x 3-1/2"), six sherbets (4-1/4" x 3-5/8"), five cordials (3-1/2" x 1-5/8"), two juice (5" h. x 2-1/2")................................... **$300**
*Burchard Galleries, Inc.*

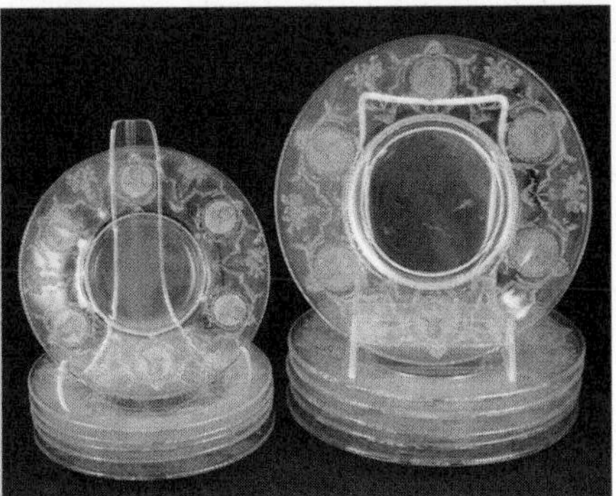

Queen Louise pattern plates, six 7-1/2", six 6"...**$225**
*William Bunch Auctions & Appraisals*

# Mt. Washington

A wide diversity of glass was made by the Mt. Washington Glass Company of New Bedford, Massachusetts, between 1869 and 1900. It was succeeded in 1900 by the Pairpoint Manufacturing Company. Throughout its history, the Mt. Washington Glass Company made different types of glass including pressed, blown, art, lava, Napoli, cameo, cut, Albertine, Peachblow, Burmese, Crown Milano, Royal Flemish, and Verona.

Amberina Diamond-Optic tumblers, set of six, each with polished pontil mark, Mt. Washington Glass Co. and others, late 19th/early 20th c., 3-3/4" h., 2-1/2" dia. **$287**
*Jeffrey S. Evans & Associates*

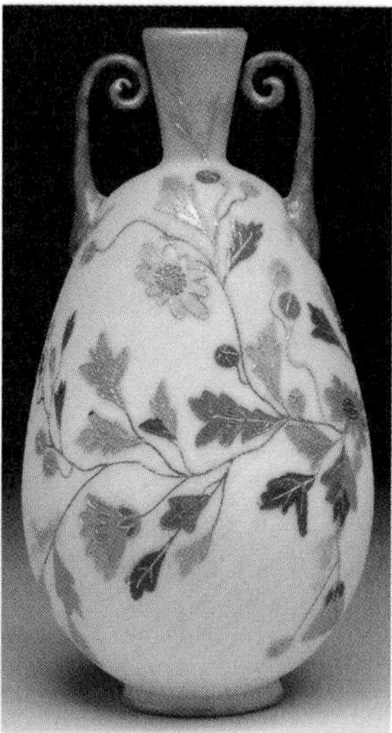

Mt. Washington Burmese decorated vase with allover flower design with gold gilt flowers, colored beaded stamen and red, green, and gold leaves, all set against a Burmese background, finished with two applied delicate curled handles, 10-1/2" t........... **$3,680**
*James D. Julia, Inc.*

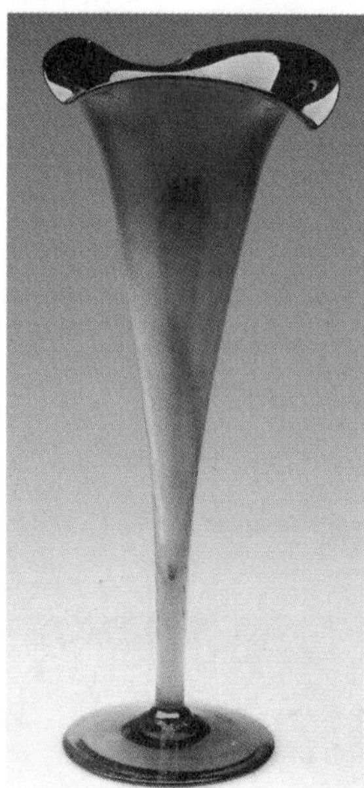

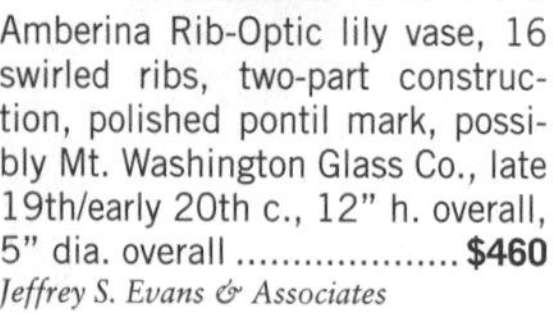

Amberina Rib-Optic lily vase, 16 swirled ribs, two-part construction, polished pontil mark, possibly Mt. Washington Glass Co., late 19th/early 20th c., 12" h. overall, 5" dia. overall ................... **$460**
*Jeffrey S. Evans & Associates*

Mt. Washington Burmese plush ribbed salt and pepper shakers, fitted in a Barbour Bros. Silver Co. silver-plate stand, two-part period lids, Mt. Washington Glass Co., fourth quarter 19th c., 7" h. overall, shakers 4" h. overall...... **$258**
*Jeffrey S. Evans & Associates*

►Mt. Washington Crown Milano marmalade jar, soft yellow with satin finish, mold-blown diamond pattern, gilt starfish decoration set with jewels, unmarked silver-plate fittings, Mt. Washington Glass Co., fourth quarter 19th c., 3" h. to rim, 5-3/4" dia. overall ....... **$546**
*Jeffrey S. Evans & Associates*

Amberina Swirl-Optic toothpick holder, square rim, polished pontil mark, Mt. Washington Glass Co. and possibly others, late 19th/early 20th c., 2-3/4" h., 1-7/8" sq. .................................. **$184**
*Jeffrey S. Evans & Associates*

Mt. Washington Crown Milano cracker jar, fired-on Burmese satin finish with polychrome floral decoration, silver-plate fittings, marked "M. W. / 4404/a," base marked "2598," Mt. Washington Glass Co., fourth quarter 19th c., 6" h. to rim, 5-1/2" dia. overall.... **$230**
*Jeffrey S. Evans & Associates*

Mt. Washington Crown Milano cracker jar, fired-on Burmese satin finish with polychrome and gilt decoration, silver-plate fittings, marked "M. W. / 1402/a," Mt. Washington Glass Co., fourth quarter 19th c., 5-5/8" h. to rim, 5-1/2" dia. overall ............ **$373**
*Jeffrey S. Evans & Associates*

Mt. Washington Crown Milano cracker jar, opal with blue shading to cream stain finish, polychrome floral decoration, silver-plate fittings, lid marked "M.W. / 3918," base with "3918 / 825," Mt. Washington Glass Co., fourth quarter 19th c., 5" h. to rim, 4-1/4" dia........................ **$207**
*Jeffrey S. Evans & Associates*

Mt. Washington Crown Milano jar, satin opaque glass with swirling ribbed design, enamel decorated with orange and gold swirling leaves and colorful beaded embellishments, signed on base Crown over C.M., silver-plated cover, stamped on the reverse M.W. 526, 5" h. x 5"............................................**$400-$600**
*Fontaine's Auction Gallery*

Mt. Washington decorated covered vase with allover decoration of raised gold outlines depicting stems and leaves swirling around body of vase, four stylized flowers outlined in black raised lines, finished with a dome lid, unsigned, 8-1/2" t. ...................... **$5,462**
*James D. Julia, Inc.*

◄Rare Mt. Washington inkwell, square black glass case with beveled edges with clear glass lip and nickel plated plunger, original paper label with instructions, patented "August 30, 1887," 3-1/4" square. Provenance: From the collection of Dorothy-Lee Jones .....................**$57**
*James D. Julia, Inc.*

Mt. Washington egg sugar shaker, opaque custard, satin finish, polychrome floral decoration, period lid, Mt. Washington Glass Co., fourth quarter 19th c., 4-1/4" h. overall .............................. **$230**
*Jeffrey S. Evans & Associates*

Mt. Washington egg sugar shaker, opal with shaded yellow ground, satin finish, polychrome floral decoration, base embossed "PAT'D," period lid, Mt. Washington Glass Co., fourth quarter 19th c., 4-1/4" h. overall ........................... **$161**
*Jeffrey S. Evans & Associates*

Mt. Washington egg sugar shaker, opal shading to pale blue, satin finish, polychrome floral decoration, period lid, Mt. Washington Glass Co., fourth quarter 19th c., 4-1/4" h. overall................. **$517**
*Jeffrey S. Evans & Associates*

Mt. Washington lava glass vase, matte black finish with colored glass shards in blue, red, green, and orange, 4-3/4" t........ **$1,610**
*James D. Julia, Inc.*

Mt. Washington tomato sugar shaker, opaque custard, satin finish, polychrome foliate decoration, ornate silver-plate two-part period lid, Mt. Washington Glass Co., fourth quarter 19th c., 2-3/4" h. overall ........................... **$316**
*Jeffrey S. Evans & Associates*

Mt. Washington mushroom flower holder decorated with white and purple flowers and orange, yellow, and brown leaves and stems connecting the decoration, unsigned, 5-1/2" dia.......................... **$345**
*James D. Julia, Inc.*

Mt. Washington tomato sugar shaker, opal with light blue shading, satin finish, polychrome floral decoration, ornate silver-plate two-part period lid, Mt. Washington Glass Co., fourth quarter 19th c., 2-5/8" h. overall................. **$172**
*Jeffrey S. Evans & Associates*

►Pressed arch vase, canary yellow, deep conical bowl with gauffered and tooled 10-petal rim, raised on a double-knop stem, hexagonal three-step standard, hexagonal base, wafer construction, Mt. Washington Glass Works, 1845-1860, 11-1/4" h., 4-3/8" dia. rim, 4-1/4" dia. base.... **$518**
*Jeffrey S. Evans & Associates*

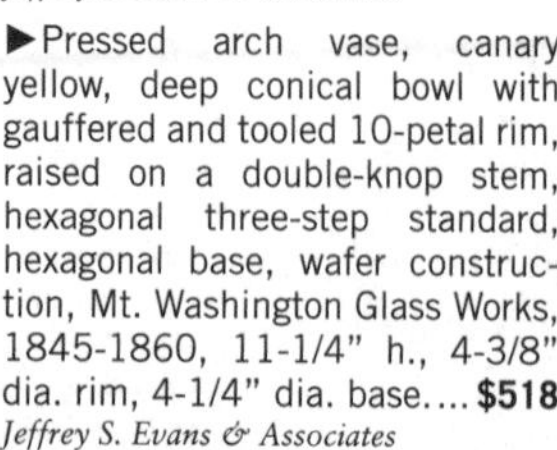

Mt. Washington Peachblow bowl, round at base and forming to square at top, ruffled rim, deep pink color graduates to white at bottom, 3-1/2" h. x 6-1/2" x 6-1/2"...................... **$400-$600**
*Fontaine's Auction Gallery*

# Nailsea

Nailsea was a glassmaking center in England where a variety of wares similar to those from Bristol, England were produced between 1788 and 1873. Today most collectors think of Nailsea primarily as a glass featuring swirls and loopings, usually white, on a clear or colored ground. This style of glass decoration, however, was not restricted to Nailsea and was produced in many other glasshouses, including some in America.

◄Pair of free-blown Marbrie Loop decorated bottles or vases, colorless with six groups of opal loopings, each elongated pyriform body with applied concave neck ring raised on an applied thick foot with rough pontil mark. Probably South Jersey or Pittsburgh area, 1840-1880, 9-1/2" h., 3-3/8" and 3-5/8" dia. feet. **$431**
*Jeffrey S. Evans & Associates*

Free-blown Marbrie Loop decorated vase, colorless with four groups of opal loopings, compressed pyriform bowl with applied shoulder ring and elongated deeply waisted neck below gauffered eight-petal rim with applied deep ruby edge, raised on an applied baluster-form solid stem and wide circular foot with rough pontil mark. Probably Pittsburgh area, 1840-1880, 9-3/4" h. overall, 5" dia. rim, 4-3/4" dia. foot. ........................................ **$748**
*Jeffrey S. Evans & Associates*

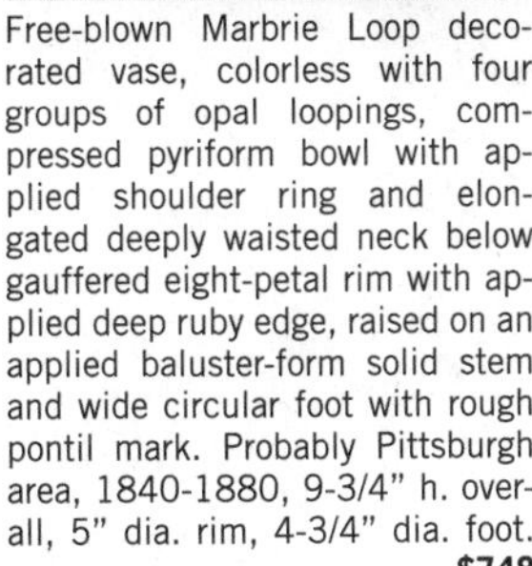

Yellow Nailsea fairy lamp, white pulled loop design against a frosted yellow background, base with rufffled rim with Clarke insert marked "Cricklite Clarke's Patent Trademark" with impressed fairy in the middle, original candle cup marked "Clarke Trademark Fairy," matching domed Nailsea shade, 6" t................................. **$690**
*James D. Julia, Inc.*

Nailsea threaded mini lamp, Nailsea body with white pulled loop design against a clear background, encircled with pink threading around the top and yellow threading around the bottom, finished with an applied shell-shaped rigaree around the body and foot, 11-3/8" t.......................... **$460**
*James D. Julia, Inc.*

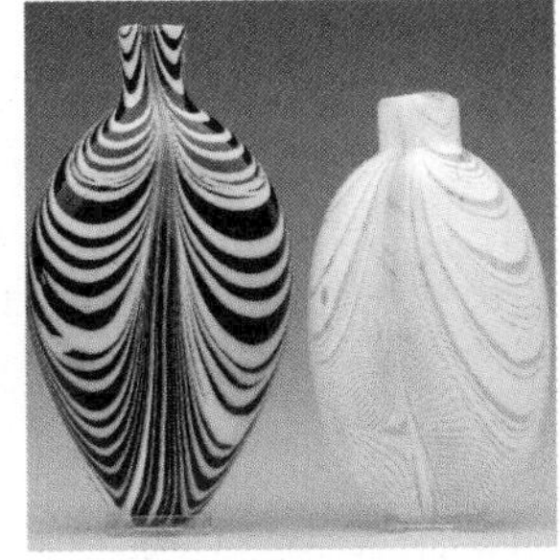

►Free-blown Marbrie Loop decorated flasks, deep amethyst and colorless, each with four groups of opal loopings, flattened ovoid and oval forms with plain mouths, rough and polished pontil marks. United States and/or England, 1840-1880, 7" h., 4" w., and 6" h., 3-1/2" w...................... **$259**
*Jeffrey S. Evans & Associates*

# New Martinsville

The New Martinsville Glass Mfg. Co. opened in New Martinsville, West Virginia, in 1901, and during its first period of production came out with a number of colored opaque pressed glass patterns. Also developed was an art glass line named "Muranese," which collectors refer to as "New Martinsville Peach Blow." The factory burned in 1907 but reopened later that year and began focusing on productions of various clear pressed glass patterns, many of which were then decorated with gold or ruby staining or enameled decoration. After going through receivership in 1937, the factory again changed the focus of its production to more contemporary glass lines and figural animals. The firm was purchased in 1944 by The Viking Glass Company (later Dalzell-Viking).

New Martinsville No. 88 / Carnation ruby-stained water pitcher, colorless with excellent gilt decoration. New Martinsville Glass Mfg. Co., first quarter 20th c., 8-1/4" h. overall ....... **$80**
*Jeffrey S. Evans & Associates*

Placid Thumbprint ruby-stained water pitcher, colorless, traces of gilt decoration at rim. New Martinsville Glass Mfg. Co., early 20th c., 8-7/8" h. overall ............................... **$57**
*Jeffrey S. Evans & Associates*

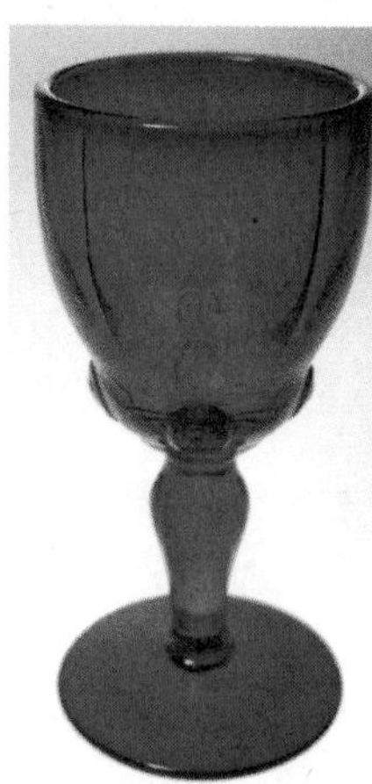

Cordial, Moondrops pattern, ruby, 3/4 oz................ **$32**

Butter dish with chrome lid, round, Moondrops pattern, cobalt blue, 6" dia. ....................................... **$120**

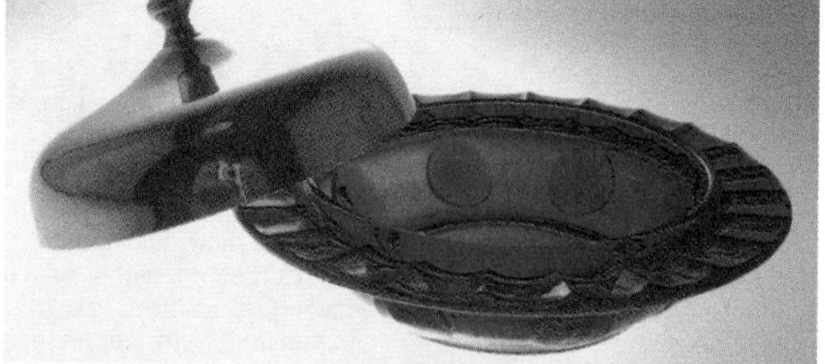

New Martinsville No. 88/Carnation ruby-stained seven-piece berry set, colorless with gilt decoration, master berry bowl and six berry dishes. New Martinsville Glass Mfg. Co., first quarter 20th c., 4" h., 8-1/4" dia. and 2" h, 4-3/4" dia. ........................ **$92**

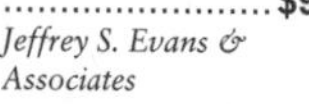

*Jeffrey S. Evans & Associates*

# Northwood Glass Co.

Northwood Glass Co. was founded by Harry Northwood, son of prominent English glassmaker John Northwood, who was famous for his expertise in cameo glass.

Harry migrated to America in 1881 and, after working at various glass manufacturers, formed the Northwood Glass Co. in 1896 in Indiana, Pennsylvania. In 1902 he created H. Northwood and Co. in Wheeling, West Virginia. After Northwood died in 1919, H. Northwood and Co. began to falter and eventually closed in 1925.

Northwood produced a wide variety of opalescent, decorated, and special effect glasses, and colors like iridescent blue and green, which were not widely seen at the time.

Alaska sugar bowl, blue opalescent, Northwood Co. and Dugan Glass Co., late 19th/early 20th c., 5-1/2" h. overall, 4-1/4" sq. ........................................ **$103**

*Jeffrey S. Evans & Associates*

Apple blossom syrup pitcher, opaque white/milk glass with polychrome decoration, opaque white/milk glass applied handle, period lid, Northwood Glass Co., late 19th/early 20th c., 6-1/4" h. overall ........................................ **$69**

*Jeffrey S. Evans & Associates*

Blown Twist wide-waist sugar shaker, green opalescent, period lid, Northwood Glass Co., late 19th/early 20th c., 4-5/8" h. overall ........................................ **$218**

*Jeffrey S. Evans & Associates*

Alaska cruet, blue opalescent, with well-fitting colorless cut-facetted stopper, Northwood Co. and Dugan Glass Co., late 19th/early 20th c., 6" h. overall, 3-1/2" dia. overall ................................ **$184**

*Jeffrey S. Evans & Associates*

Blown Twist water pitcher, cranberry opalescent, round tooled rim, colorless applied twisted-reed handle, Northwood Glass Co. and West Virginia Glass, late 19th/early 20th c., 10-1/4" h. overall ........................................ **$2,185**

*Jeffrey S. Evans & Associates*

Christmas Snowflake ribbed water pitcher, cranberry opalescent, square rim, colorless applied handle, Northwood Co. and Dugan Glass Co., late 19th/early 20th c., 9" h. overall ..................... **$1,265**

*Jeffrey S. Evans & Associates*

GLASS

Chrysanthemum Swirl pickle caster, cranberry opalescent, fitted in an Adelphia Silver Plate Co. quadruple-plate frame, marked "112," with cover and tongs, rim of jar polished during manufacturing process, Northwood Glass Co./ Buckeye Glass Co., fourth quarter 19th c., 11-1/8" h. overall, jar 4" h., 4" dia. overall ............... **$373**
*Jeffrey S. Evans & Assoc iates*

Christmas Snowflake ribbed water pitcher, cranberry opalescent, square rim, colorless applied handle, Northwood Co. and Dugan Glass Co., late 19th/early 20th c., 9" h. overall.................... **$1,150**
*Jeffrey S. Evans & Associates*

**Right:** Coinspot water pitcher, cranberry opalescent, tooled ruffled rim, colorless applied handle, possibly Jefferson Glass Co. or Northwood Glass Co., late 19th/ early 20th c., 10-3/4" h. overall ........................................ **$402**
*Jeffrey S. Evans & Associates*

**Far right:** Coinspot three-tier tankard water pitcher, cranberry opalescent, colorless applied handle, Northwood Glass Co., late 19th/ early 20th c., 11-1/4" h. overall, 6-1/4" dia. overall ............. **$517**
*Jeffrey S. Evans & Associates*

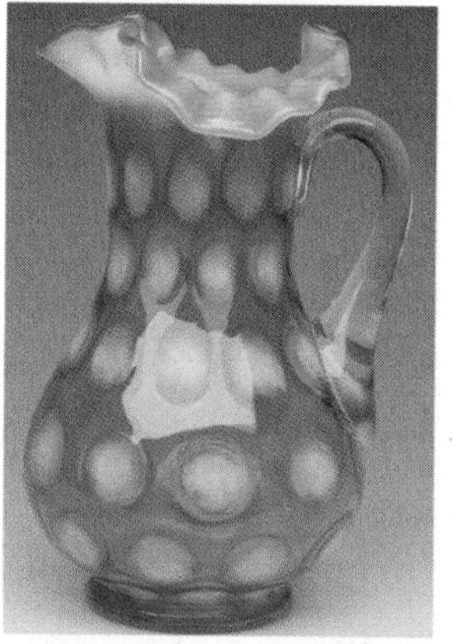

Coinspot nine-panel mold syrup pitcher, cranberry opalescent, colorless applied handle, period lid, Northwood Glass Co., late 19th/ early 20th c., 6" h. overall .. **$402**
*Jeffrey S. Evans & Associates*

Coinspot nine-panel mold syrup pitcher, green opalescent, green applied handle, period lid, Northwood Glass Co., late 19th/early 20th c., 6" h. overall .......... **$138**
*Jeffrey S. Evans & Associates*

Coinspot nine-panel mold sugar shaker, blue opalescent, period lid, Northwood Glass Co., late 19th/early 20th c., 4 5/8" h. overall .................................... **$115**
*Jeffrey S. Evans & Associates*

Chrysanthemum Swirl sugar shaker, cranberry opalescent, period lid, Northwood Glass Co./Buckeye Glass Co., late 19th/early 20th c., 4-3/4" h. overall .... **$172**
*Jeffrey S. Evans & Associates*

Chrysanthemum Swirl water pitcher, cranberry opalescent, colorless applied handle with faint pressed fan design at upper terminal, Northwood Glass Co./Buckeye Glass Co., late 19th/early 20th c., 9" h. overall.................... **$1,495**
*Jeffrey S. Evans & Associates*

Chrysanthemum Swirl spooner, cranberry opalescent, Northwood Glass Co./Buckeye Glass Co., late 19th/early 20th c., 4" h...... **$126**
*Jeffrey S. Evans & Associates*

Daisy and Fern Northwood swirl pickle caster, cranberry opalescent, fitted in a Meriden quadruple-plate frame, marked "291," with cover and tongs, rim of jar polished during manufacturing process, Northwood Glass Co., fourth quarter 19th c., 8-3/4" h. overall, jar 3-1/2" h., 3 5/8" dia. overall ............................... **$207**
*Jeffrey S. Evans & Associates*

Daisy and Fern apple blossom mold sugar shaker, blue opalescent, period lid, Northwood Glass Co., late 19th/early 20th c., 4-1/4" h. overall................. **$138**
*Jeffrey S. Evans & Associates*

Daisy and Fern Northwood Swirl mold sugar shaker, cranberry opalescent, period lid, Northwood Glass Co., late 19th/early 20th c., 4 3/8" h. overall................. **$149**
*Jeffrey S. Evans & Associates*

►Klondyke/Fluted Scroll eight-piece water set, blue opalescent, pitcher raised on three scrolled feet and seven tumblers with polished table rings, Northwood Co. and Dugan Glass Co., late 19th/early 20th c., 8" h. overall, 5" dia. overall, and 3-7/8" h., 3" dia. overall ...... **$345**
*Jeffrey S. Evans & Associates*

Klondyke/Fluted Scroll seven-piece berry set, vaseline opalescent, master berry bowl and six berry dishes, each raised on three feet, Northwood Co. and Dugan Glass Co., late 19th/early 20th c., 4" h. overall, 9" dia. overall, and 2" h. overall, 5" dia. overall..**$103**
*Jeffrey S. Evans & Associates*

Klondyke/Fluted Scroll scroll eight-piece berry set, blue opalescent, master berry bowl and seven berry dishes, each raised on three scrolled feet, Northwood Co. and Dugan Glass Co., late 19th/early 20th c., 4" h. overall, 8-1/4" dia. overall, and 2" h. overall, 5-1/4" dia. overall........................**$126**
*Jeffrey S. Evans & Associates*

**Right:** Northwood's No. 333 Leaf mold sugar shaker, canary with cranberry and opal spatter, period lid, Northwood Glass Co., fourth quarter 19th c., 3-1/2" h. ...**$460**
*Jeffrey S. Evans & Associates*

**Far right:** Netted Oak sugar shaker, opaque white/milk glass with polychrome and gilt decoration, period lid, Northwood Glass Co., late 19th/early 20th c., 4-1/4" h. overall, 3" sq. ......................**$69**
*Jeffrey S. Evans & Associates*

Northwood's No. 263 Leaf umbrella syrup pitcher, ruby/cranberry, colorless applied handle with pressed fan to upper terminal, period lid with patent date, Northwood Glass Co., fourth quarter 19th c., 6-3/4" h. overall.**$373**
*Jeffrey S. Evans & Associates*

Northwood's No. 263 Leaf umbrella sugar shaker, cased turquoise/blue, period lid, Northwood Glass Co., fourth quarter 19th c., 4-1/2" h. overall.................**$207**
*Jeffrey S. Evans & Associates*

Northwood's No. 333 Leaf mold syrup pitcher, cased opal with cranberry spatter and mica flecks, colorless applied handle, period lid with patent date, Northwood Glass Co., fourth quarter 19th c., 6" h. overall.......................**$575**
*Jeffrey S. Evans & Associates*

Paneled Sprig sugar shaker, amethyst, period lid, Northwood Glass Co., late 19th/early 20th c., 4-3/4" h. overall ........... **$195**
*Jeffrey S. Evans & Associates*

Royal Ivy syrup pitcher, rubina, colorless applied handle, period lid, Northwood Glass Co., fourth quarter 19th c., 6-1/2" h. overall. **$632**
*Jeffrey S. Evans & Associates*

Royal Ivy sugar shaker, rainbow spatter craquelle, satin finish, period lid, Northwood Glass Co., fourth quarter 19th c., 4-1/4" h. overall .............................. **$172**
*Jeffrey S. Evans & Associates*

Poinsettia tankard water pitcher, cranberry opalescent, colorless applied handle with pressed fan design at upper terminal, Northwood Glass Co., late 19th/early 20th c., 13-1/8" h. overall **$2,645**
*Jeffrey S. Evans & Associates*

Royal Ivy pickle caster, rubina with glossy finish, fitted in a Homan Silver Plate Co. quadruple-plate frame, marked "1081," with cover and fork, rim of jar polished during manufacturing process, Northwood Glass Co., fourth quarter 19th c., 8" h. overall, jar 3-3/8" h., 3-1/2" dia. overall ......... **$373**
*Jeffrey S. Evans & Associates*

►Threaded Rubina Swirl syrup pitcher, colorless applied handle with pressed fan to upper terminal, period lid, Northwood Glass Co., fourth quarter 19th c., 5" h. overall .............................. **$115**
*Jeffrey S. Evans & Associates*

Ring Neck sugar shaker, colorless with cranberry and opal spatter, period lid, Northwood Glass Co., fourth quarter 19th c., 4-3/4" h. overall ............................... **$103**
*Jeffrey S. Evans & Associates*

Royal Ivy pickle caster, rubina with satin finish, fitted in a Reed and Barton silver-plate frame, marked "930," with cover and fork, rim of jar polished during manufacturing process, Northwood Glass Co., fourth quarter 19th c., 9" h. overall, jar 3-3/8" h., 3-1/2" dia. overall .............................. **$230**
*Jeffrey S. Evans & Associates*

GLASS

# Opalescent Glass

Opalescent glass is one of the most popular areas of glass collecting. The opalescent effect was attained by adding bone ash chemicals to areas of an item while still hot and refiring the object at tremendous heat. Both pressed and mold-blown patterns are available to collectors. *Opalescent Glass from A to Z* by the late William Heacock is the definitive reference book for collectors.

Swirl opalescent pendant shade, blue, first quarter 20th c., 8" h., 4" fitter. ............................ **$103**
*Jeffrey S. Evans & Associates*

Swirling Maze water pitcher, cranberry opalescent, tooled ruffled rim, colorless applied handle. Jefferson Glass Co., late 19th/early 20th c., 11" h. overall ..... **$2,070**
*Jeffrey S. Evans & Associates*

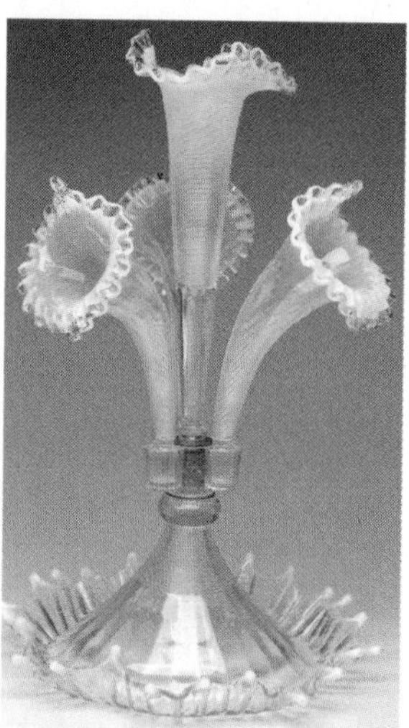

Threaded four-trumpet epergne, vaseline opalescent, base and each trumpet with tooled rim. Fenton Art Glass for L. G. Wright, 20th c., 18" h. overall, 12" dia. overall .............................. **$218**
*Jeffrey S. Evans & Associates*

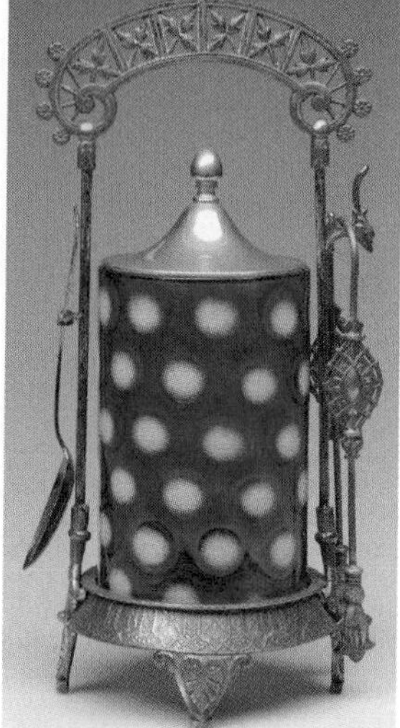

Coinspot pickle caster, cranberry opalescent, fitted in a Meriden Silver Plate Co. quadruple-plate frame, marked "094," with cover, tongs, and sterling spoon. Rim of jar polished during manufacturing process. Fourth quarter 19th c., 10-1/4" h. overall, jar 5" h., 3-1/4" dia......................... **$138**
*Jeffrey S. Evans & Associates*

Coinspot bulbous variant syrup pitcher, cranberry opalescent, slight ring at top of neck, colorless applied handle, concave base with a circle of connected coin spots centered by a 10-petal daisy, period lid with patent date, late 19th/early 20th c., 6-3/8" h. overall .............................. **$161**
*Jeffrey S. Evans & Associates*

Stars and Stripes water pitcher, cranberry opalescent, colorless applied handle with pressed fan design to upper terminal, polished pontil mark. Hobbs, Brockunier & Co., late 19th/early 20th c., 8-1/4" h. overall............. **$3,450**
*Jeffrey S. Evans & Associates*

Seaweed/Coral Reef pickle caster, blue opalescent, fitted in a Van Bergh Silver Plate Co. quadruple-plate frame, marked "2210," with cover and tongs. Rim of jar polished during manufacturing process. Hobbs, Brockunier & Co. and Beaumont Glass Co., fourth quarter 19th c., 8-1/2" h. overall, jar 3-1/2" h., 4" dia. overall **$373**
*Jeffrey S. Evans & Associates*

Opalescent hobnail pickle caster, pale Rubina opalescent, polished pontil mark and base, fitted in a Simpson, Hall & Miller frame, marked "0856," with cover, lacking tongs. Rim of jar polished during manufacturing process. Fourth quarter 19th c., 11-1/2" h. overall, jar 4-1/4" h., 3-1/2" dia. overall .............................. **$161**
*Jeffrey S. Evans & Associates*

Opalescent Swirl pickle caster, blue opalescent, fitted in a Wilcox Silver Plate Co. frame, marked "6521," with cover and tongs. Rim of jar polished during manufacturing process. Fourth quarter 19th c., 10-3/4" h. overall, jar 4" h., 3" dia. overall ............... **$345**
*Jeffrey S. Evans & Associates*

Fern sugar shaker, cranberry opalescent, period lid, late 19th/early 20th c., 5" h. overall .......... **$460**
*Jeffrey S. Evans & Associates*

▶Coinspot and Swirl syrup pitcher, blue opalescent, blue applied handle, period lid, late 19th/early 20th c., 6-1/4" h. overall............. **$126**
*Jeffrey S. Evans & Associates*

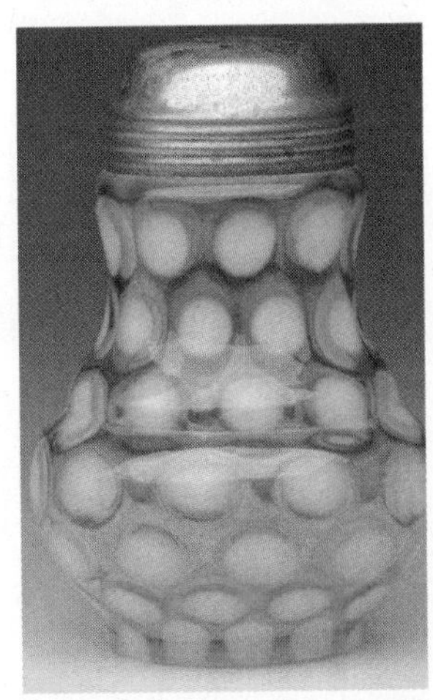

Coinspot bulbous base sugar shaker, green opalescent, period lid, late 19th/early 20th c., 4-3/4" h. overall .......................... **$115**
*Jeffrey S. Evans & Associates*

Coinspot ring neck sugar shaker, Rubina opalescent, period lid, late 19th/early 20th c., 4-3/4" h. overall .................................. **$149**
*Jeffrey S. Evans & Associates*

Coinspot nine-panel mold sugar shaker, bittersweet, period lid, late 19th/early 20th c., 4-3/4" h. overall .............................. **$172**
*Jeffrey S. Evans & Associates*

Opaline Brocade/Spanish Lace wide-waist sugar shaker, strong canary opalescent, period lid, late 19th/early 20th c., 4-3/4" h. overall .................................... **$316**
*Jeffrey S. Evans & Associates*

Ribbed Opal Lattice sugar shaker, cranberry with strong opalescence, period lid, late 19th/early 20th c., 4-1/2" h. overall .... **$138**
*Jeffrey S. Evans & Associates*

Arabian Nights water pitcher, cranberry opalescent, crimped triangular rim, colorless applied handle with pressed fan design at upper terminal. Possibly Beaumont Glass Co., late 19th/early 20th c., 9" h. overall ....**$1,610**
*Jeffrey S. Evans & Associates*

Ribbed Opal Lattice sugar shaker, cranberry opalescent, period lid, late 19th/early 20th c., 4-1/4" h. overall ............................... **$149**
*Jeffrey S. Evans & Associates*

**Right:** Coinspot WV mold water pitcher, cranberry opalescent, four-lobed rim, colorless applied handle with pressed fan design to upper terminal. West Virginia Glass Co., late 19th/early 20th c., 9-1/8" h. overall...... **$373**
*Jeffrey S. Evans & Associates*

**Far right:** Buttons and Braids water pitcher, cranberry opalescent, round crimped rim, colorless applied handle. Jefferson Glass Co./Fenton Art Glass Co., late 19th/early 20th c., 9-1/2" h. overall . **$632**
*Jeffrey S. Evans & Associates*

Drapery blown tankard water pitcher, cranberry opalescent, colorless applied handle. Early 20th c., 13-1/4" h. overall ....... **$1,092**
*Jeffrey S. Evans & Associates*

Opalescent Stripe five-bottle caster set, two colorless and one vaseline shaker, each with period lid, one of which is frozen in place, and a cranberry and blue bottle with matching possibly original colorless stoppers, fitted in a colorless opalescent and metal revolving stand, late 19th/early 20th c., 11-1/2" h. overall, 6-1/2" dia. overall ............................... **$862**
*Jeffrey S. Evans & Associates*

Drapery blown tumbler, cranberry opalescent, full height with factory-polished rim. Early 20th c., 4" h. ................................ **$258**
*Jeffrey S. Evans & Associates*

Pressed Arched Panel footed tumbler, powder blue opalescent with good resonance, small cylindrical form raised on an eight-petal foot, 1850-1880, 4" h., 2-7/8" dia. rim, 2-1/4" dia. foot. .......... **$403**
*Jeffrey S. Evans & Associates*

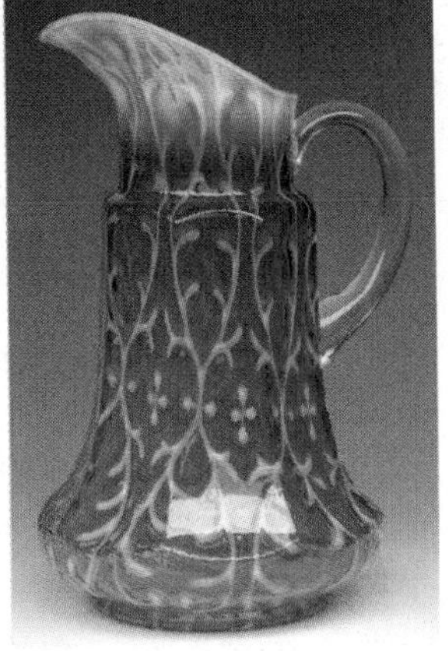

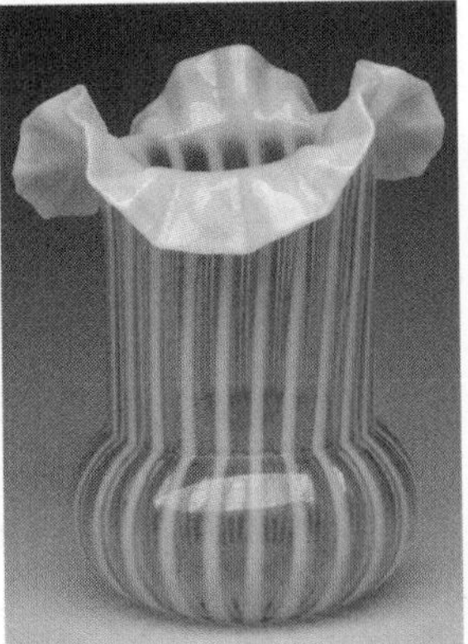

Opalescent Stripe celery vase, blue, tooled, ruffled rim, late 19th/early 20th c., 6" h. overall, 4-3/4" dia. overall ................ **$80**
*Jeffrey S. Evans & Associates*

Victorian glass basket with diagonal swirls of opalescent glass leading to a flaring, ruffled rim, finished with an applied clear glass handle, 13" to top of handle.. **$59**
*James D. Julia, Inc.*

Opaline Brocade/Spanish Lace eight-panel mold tankard water pitcher, cranberry opalescent, colorless applied handle, late 19th/early 20th c., 11-1/2" h. overall .................................... **$2,185**
*Jeffrey S. Evans & Associates*

# Pairpoint

Originally organized in New Bedford, Massachusetts, in 1880 as the Pairpoint Manufacturing Co. on land adjacent to the famed Mount Washington Glass Co., Pairpoint first manufactured silver and plated wares. In 1894, the two famous factories merged as the Pairpoint Corp. and enjoyed great success for more than 40 years. The company was sold in 1939 to a group of local businessmen and eventually bought out by one of the group, who turned the management over to Robert M. Gundersen. Subsequently, it operated as the Gundersen Glass Works until 1952 when, after Gundersen's death, the name was changed to Gundersen-Pairpoint. The factory closed in 1956. Subsequently, Robert Bryden took charge of this glassworks, at first producing glass for Pairpoint abroad and eventually, in 1970, beginning glass production in Sagamore, Massachusetts. Today the Pairpoint Crystal Glass Company is owned by Robert and June Bancroft. They continue to manufacture fine quality blown and pressed glass.

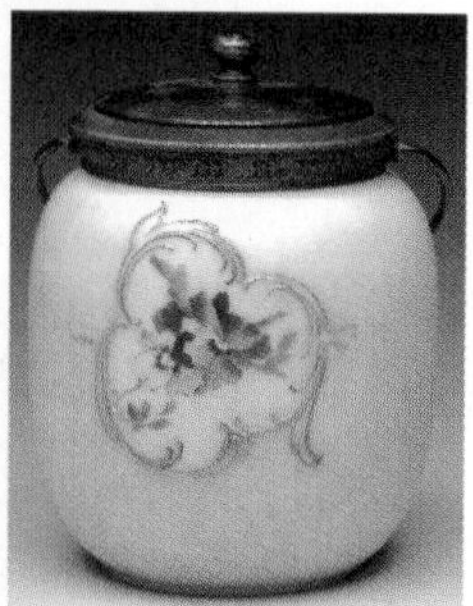

Pairpoint biscuit jar, large cartouche on front with hand-painted flowers in yellow, brown, purple, and blue surrounded by gold gilt swirling frame, smaller cartouche with two pansies on backside, light pink background, silver-plated collar, handle, and lid. Signed on the underside "Pairpoint 2586," silver-plated lid marked "MW 4404." 9-1/2" to top of handle **$400-$600**
*James D. Julia, Inc.*

Pairpoint cut glass powder jar, pearl pattern, silver plated collar and hinge, pictured in Paget's book Pairpoint Glass on page 119. 4-1/2" dia. x 2-3/4" t. ........ **$143**
*James D. Julia, Inc.*

Pairpoint biscuit jar decorated with gold water lilies and green lily pads against white shading to green background, finished with silver-plated collar, handle, and lid. Marked on the underside "Pairpoint 3913/56," lid marked "MW 4418." 8-1/2" to top of handle x 6-1/2" dia. ........... **$147**
*James D. Julia, Inc.*

Pairpoint dresser box decorated on top with gold gilt flowers and buds with green leaves and stems, edge of foot has molded floral designs highlighted with gold gilding. Signed on underside "PMC" within a diamond shape. 7" l. x 2-3/4" t............ **$230**
*James D. Julia, Inc.*

Four Pairpoint controlled bubble vases, one amber vase with controlled bubble clear spherical stem, two clear vases with blue controlled bubble spherical stems, and cobalt blue vase with clear foot and twisted spherical stem. Tallest is 13-1/2" h..... **$400-$600**
*Fontaine's Auction Galleries*

Pair of Pairpoint crystal vases, green crystal inserts with cut vertical line decoration, inserts attached to brass tripod stand with gargoyle heads and lion paw feet all resting on top of white alabaster foot. Each signed on the inside of one leg "Pairpoint C1510." 5-1/2" t............................ **$402**
*James D. Julia, Inc.*

Pairpoint creamer and sugar, hand decorated with pink and red flowers against a white glass background, raised fern design adorns foot of each piece and is highlighted with gold gilding, each piece finished with silver-plated handles, collars, and spout. Each piece numbered on bottom "2042 140." Creamer: 4-1/4" t. ...................................................... **$300-$500**
*James D. Julia, Inc.*

# Pattern Glass

Though it has never been ascertained whether glass was first pressed in the United States or abroad, the development of the glass pressing machine revolutionized the glass industry in the United States, and this country receives the credit for improving the method to make this process feasible. The first wares pressed were probably small flat plates of the type now referred to as "lacy," the intricacy of the design concealing flaws.

In 1827, both the New England Glass Co., Cambridge, Massachusetts, and Bakewell & Co., Pittsburgh, took out patents for pressing glass furniture knobs; soon other pieces followed. This early pressed glass contained red lead, which made it clear and resonant when tapped (flint). Made primarily in clear, it is rarer in blue, amethyst, olive green, and yellow.

By the 1840s, early simple patterns such as Ashburton, Argus, and Excelsior appeared. Ribbed Bellflower seems to have been one of the earliest patterns to have had complete sets. By the 1860s, a wide range of patterns was available.

In 1864, William Leighton of Hobbs, Brockunier & Co., Wheeling, West Virginia, developed a formula for "soda lime" glass that did not require the expensive red lead for clarity. Although "soda lime" glass did not have the brilliance of the earlier flint glass, the formula came into widespread use because glass could be produced cheaply.

Aquarium/No. 6405 water pitcher, green, U.S. Glass Co., late 19th/early 20th c., 9-1/4" h. overall, 4-5/8" dia. foot .................. **$230**
*Jeffrey S. Evans & Associates*

Bringing Home the Cows water pitcher, colorless, Dalzell, Gilmore & Leighton Co., fourth quarter 19th c., 10-1/2" h. overall, 4-5/8" dia. overall .............. **$632**
*Jeffrey S. Evans & Associates*

Cord and Tassel, colorless, water pitcher with applied handle and goblet, fourth quarter 19th c., 8-1/2" h. overall, 5-3/4" dia. overall, and 5-1/2" h. ............... **$115**
*Jeffrey S. Evans & Associates*

Cut Log set of four goblets, colorless, fourth quarter 19th c., 5-7/8" h. ........................................... **$80**
*Jeffrey S. Evans & Associates*

►Cut Log cake stand, colorless, wafer construction, fourth quarter 19th c., 6-5/8" h. overall, 10-1/2" dia. overall ......................................................... **$69**
*Jeffrey S. Evans & Associates*

Daisy and Button with V ornament pickle caster, vaseline, polished table ring, fitted in a Rogers & Bro. triple-plate frame, marked "4615," with cover and tongs, fourth quarter 19th c., 10-7/8" h. overall, jar 4-1/2" h., 3" dia. overall ............................... **$138**

*Jeffrey S. Evans & Associates*

Delaware/Four-Petal Flower seven-piece water set, green with gilt decoration, water pitcher and six tumblers, early 20th c., 7-1/4" h. overall, 4-1/2" dia. overall, and 3-7/8" h. 2-3/4" dia. overall ..................... **$92**

*Jeffrey S. Evans & Associates*

Deer and Oak Tree water pitcher, colorless, Dalzell, Gilmore & Leighton Co., late 19th/early 20th c., 8-3/4" h. overall, 4-1/2" dia. overall ................................. **$69**

*Jeffrey S. Evans & Associates*

Dog with rabbit in hole water pitcher, colorless, featuring a dog with rabbit in hole on each side, framed by two palm trees, Consolidated Lamp & Glass Co., late 19th/early 20th c., 9" h. overall, 4-5/8" dia. overall ................ **$69**

*Jeffrey S. Evans & Associates*

Greentown Racing Deer and Doe water pitcher, colorless, plain rim, Indiana Tumbler & Goblet Co. and Dalzell, Gilmore & Leighton Co., late 19th/early 20th c., 8-3/4" h. overall, 5" dia. overall ......... **$115**

*Jeffrey S. Evans & Associates*

TOP LOT!

Greentown rabbit on nest covered dish, red agate on a diamond and basketweave nest with very light impression to upper half, Indiana Tumbler & Goblet Co., early 20th c., 4-3/8" h. overall, 4-1/4" x 5-1/2" overall ................................................................................. **$431**

*Jeffrey S. Evans & Associates*

Hobbs' No. 323 Dew Drop/Hobbs' Hobnail No. 0 jug/creamer, ruby/cranberry, square rim, colorless applied handle, polished pontil mark, Hobbs, Brockunier & Co., fourth quarter 19th c., 4" h. overall .................................. **$103**

*Jeffrey S. Evans & Associates*

Greentown dolphin covered dish, chocolate, showing some red agate to cover, with beaded rim, Indiana Tumbler & Goblet Co., early 20th c., 4-3/8" h. overall, 7" l. overall .................................................. **$149**

*Jeffrey S. Evans & Associates*

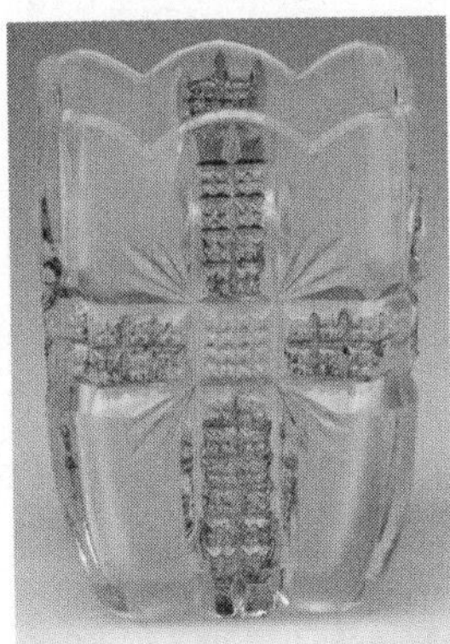

**Far left:** Klondike amber-stained toothpick holder, colorless with satin finish, Dalzell, Gilmore & Leighton Co., late 19th/early 20th c., 2-3/8" h., 1-3/4" sq. ..... **$149**

*Jeffrey S. Evans & Associates*

**Left:** Leaf and Dart water pitcher, colorless, applied handle, fourth quarter 19th c., 9-1/8" h. overall, 5-1/2" dia. overall ................ **$92**

*Jeffrey S. Evans & Associates*

Lee/Rose No. 298 cup plate, brilliant emerald green lead glass, plain rim with 68 dots underneath, extremely rare, uncertain origin, 1850-1870, 3-13/16" dia. ........................................................ **$219**

*Jeffrey S. Evans & Associates*

Lee/Rose No. 509 cup plate, brilliant peacock blue, 22 large scallops with a single point between, unlisted in AGCP, probably extremely rare, probably Eastern, possibly Boston & Sandwich Glass Co., 1840-1860, 3" dia. ...................................... **$374**

*Jeffrey S. Evans & Associates*

Lee/Rose No. 531 cup plate, light green with some yellow, 34 bull's-eye scallops, rare, possibly Boston & Sandwich Glass Co., 1835-1860, 3-5/8" dia................ **$259**
*Jeffrey S. Evans & Associates*

Lee/Rose No. 612-A cup plate, colorless, octagonal with seven even scallops between corners, rare, Midwestern, probably Pittsburgh, 1830-1850, 3-1/2" dia. ....... **$92**
*Jeffrey S. Evans & Associates*

Lee/Rose No. 677-A cup plate, blue, 44 even scallops, rare, Midwestern, 1830-1850, 3-1/4" d. ......................................... **$259**
*Jeffrey S. Evans & Associates*

Moon and Star/Palace covered compote, colorless, on high standard, wafer construction, fourth quarter 19th c., 15-1/2" h. overall, 10-1/4" dia. ................. **$207**
*Jeffrey S. Evans & Associates*

Oregon/Beaded Loop seven-piece water set, colorless, water pitcher embossed "15073" in base for the U.S. Glass Co. pattern number, and six goblets with gilt decoration, U.S. Glass Co., early 20th c., 9" h. overall, 4-3/4" dia. overall, and 6" h. ................................................... **$57**
*Jeffrey S. Evans & Associates*

Moon and Star/Palace compotes, two, colorless, covered example and open example, each on high standard, fourth quarter 19th c., 11" and 7-3/8" h. overall, 7-1/4" dia. ........................................................................ **$92**
*Jeffrey S. Evans & Associates*

Pair of covered jars, early American pressed glass in bell flower pattern against a vertically ribbed background, finished with matching lids and pedestal feet, 9" t. .......................... **$143**
*James D. Julia, Inc.*

S Repeat punch bowl base and 10 cups, apple green with gilt decoration, fourth quarter 19th c., 4" h., 4-1/4" inner dia. of top, and 2" h., 3-1/2" dia. .................... **$69**
*Jeffrey S. Evans & Associates*

Pineapple and Leaf water pitcher, colorless, featuring three circles, each centered by a well-molded pineapple on stem and separated by a branch of three leaves, 3/4" h. band of prisms atop the line above the pattern, applied handle, fourth quarter 19th c., 8-3/4" h. overall, 5-1/2" dia. overall .............................................. **$172**
*Jeffrey S. Evans & Associates*

Shrine one-gallon water pitcher, colorless, fourth quarter 19th c., 10-3/4" h. overall, 6-1/4" dia. overall ...................................................... **$57**
*Jeffrey S. Evans & Associates*

Sprig pressed glass pickle caster, blue, fitted in a Middletown Plate Co. quadruple-plate frame with figural cherubs, with cover and tongs, fourth quarter 19th c., 11-3/4" h. overall, 4-1/4" h., 3-1/8" dia. overall ............. **$230**
*Jeffrey S. Evans & Associates*

Stork and Rushes/No. 6404 water pitcher, green, U.S. Glass Co., late 19th/early 20th c., 9-3/8" h. overall, 4-1/4" dia. foot.............................. **$92**
*Jeffrey S. Evans & Associates*

GLASS

# Quezal

In 1901, Martin Bach and Thomas Johnson, who had worked for Louis Tiffany, opened a competing glassworks in Brooklyn, New York, called the Quezal Art Glass and Decorating Co. Named for the quetzal, a bird with brilliantly colored features, Quezal produced wares closely resembling those of Tiffany until the plant closed in 1925. In general, Quezal pieces are more defined than Tiffany glass, and the decorations are more visible and brighter.

Quezal

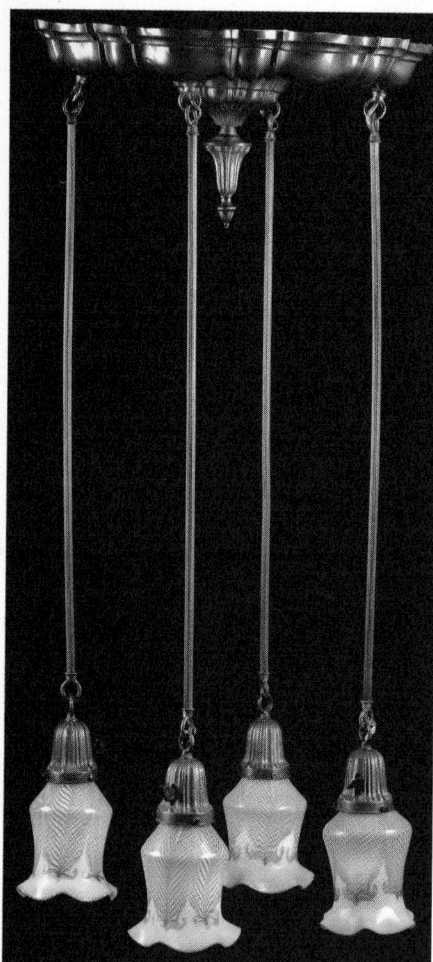

Quezal art glass four-arm chandelier, brass vertically ribbed ceiling panel supporting four solid arms, each holding a blue hooked feather art glass shade, blue hooked feather design outlined with gold iridescence all set against a cream-colored background, interior of each shade finished with bright gold iridescence, three shades signed on the fitter "Lustre Art" while the fourth is signed "Quezal," 37-1/2" t. overall ............................................................ **$2,419**
*James D. Julia, Inc.*

Quezal five-light chandelier, brass ceiling pan supports five pulled feather shades, center shade is extra large with green pulled feather design descending from the fitter with gold iridescent trim, all against a creamy white background with white, slightly iridescent interior, large shade encircled by four vertically ribbed lily shades with matching pulled feather decoration, interior of each shade is bright gold iridescence, all five shades signed on the fitter rim "Quezal," approximately 19" t. .................... **$6,900**
*James D. Julia, Inc.*

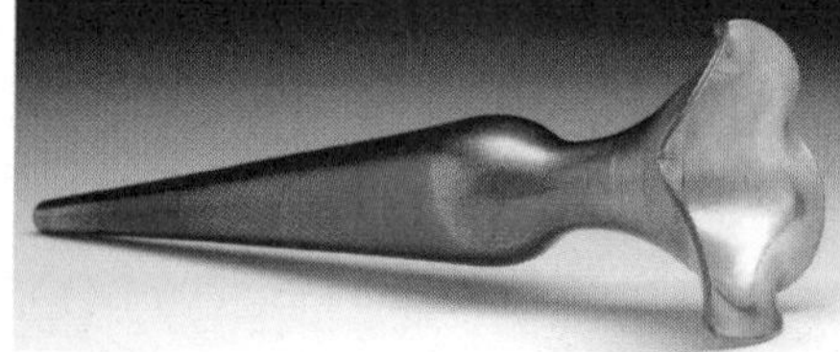

Quezal lily vase insert, blue iridescent body shading to green at the top, vase flares to a ruffled rim and is finished on the interior with bright gold iridescence, signed near the bottom of the insert with an engraved "Q," 13-1/8" t. ............................................ **$287**
*James D. Julia, Inc.*

Pair of Quezal lily shades with green pulled feather design descending from the fitter rim against a cream-colored, vertically ribbed body, pulled feather design outlined with gold iridescence, shades finished with a bright gold iridescent interior, each shade signed on inside of fitter "Quezal," 5-1/2" t. ................ **$1,265**
*James D. Julia, Inc.*

Quezal nightlight with gold finished metal base with openwork design around foot, base supports a Quezal art glass shade with gold iridescent pulled feather design with green outline against a cream-colored, vertically ribbed body, shade is finished on the interior with bright gold iridescence and signed on fitter rim "Quezal," 5-1/2" t. ....................................... **$575**
*James D. Julia, Inc.*

Pair of Quezal tulip shades, green pulled feather design against a cream, slightly iridescent background, each pulled feather is outlined with a band of gold iridescence and each shade has a white pearlescent interior, signed on fitter "Quezal," 4-1/4" t. ..... **$575**
*James D. Julia, Inc.*

Pair of Quezal sconces, heavy brass wall plates with arm extending out to support the bell-shaped shade holder, each with a Quezal lily shade with green pulled feather design descending from the fitter against a creamy white background, pulled feather design outlined with bright gold iridescence, interior of each shade is bright gold iridescent, shades are signed on the inside of fitter "Quezal," wall plates: 8-1/2" l., shades: 5-1/2" l., overall 10" l...... **$4,255**
*James D. Julia, Inc.*

GLASS

# Sandwich Glass

Numerous types of glass were produced at the Boston & Sandwich Glass Co. in Sandwich, Massachusetts, on Cape Cod, from 1826 to 1888. Founded by Deming Jarves, the company produced a wide variety of wares in differing levels of quality. The factory used free-blown, blown three mold, and pressed glass manufacturing techniques. Both clear and colored glass were used.

Jarves served as general manager from 1826-1858, and after he left, emphasis was placed on mass production. The development of a lime glass (non-flint) led to lower costs for pressed glass. Some free-blown and blown-and-molded pieces were made. By the 1880s the company was operating at a loss, and the factory closed on Jan. 1, 1888.

Beaded Grape Medallion six-piece water set, colorless, pitcher with applied handle and five goblets, each with the pattern under the foot, Boston & Sandwich Glass Co., fourth quarter 19th c., 9" h. overall and 5-3/4" h. ........................................ **$46**
*Jeffrey S. Evans & Associates*

Fifteen Sandwich glass Christmas salts in various colors including cranberry, cobalt, electric blue, amber, canary, amethyst, teal blue, deep green, and light green, all with agitator tops, 2-1/2" t. .............. **$767**
*James D. Julia, Inc.*

Large Sandwich glass covered dish, Princess Feather Medallion and Basket of Flowers patterns, produced by the Boston & Sandwich Glass Co. from about 1830 to 1845, dish is 10-1/2" x 9-3/4", with lid in place 5-1/2" t. Provenance: From the collection of Dorothy-Lee Jones. ........................................ **$977**
*James D. Julia, Inc.*

Two blown Sandwich glass bowls with pressed bases, 7" dia. bowl with etched Leaf and Vine motif on pressed four-step base and 6-1/4" dia. bowl with etched Rope and Swag motif on a pressed five-step base, 5-1/2" t. and 4-3/4" t., respectively. Provenance: From the collection of Dorothy-Lee Jones. ..................... **$230**
*James D. Julia, Inc.*

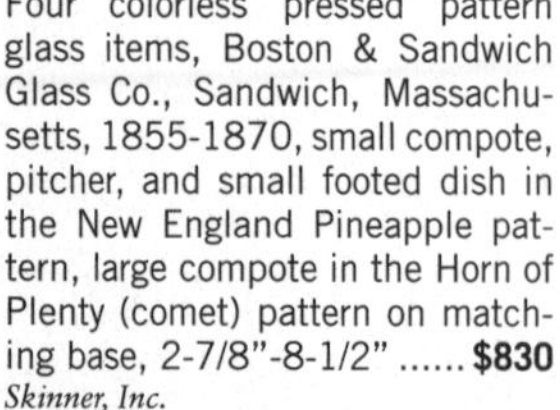

Four colorless pressed pattern glass items, Boston & Sandwich Glass Co., Sandwich, Massachusetts, 1855-1870, small compote, pitcher, and small footed dish in the New England Pineapple pattern, large compote in the Horn of Plenty (comet) pattern on matching base, 2-7/8"-8-1/2" ...... **$830**
*Skinner, Inc.*

Blue Sandwich glass bear, rare, embossed on the base "X. Bazin Philada," 3-1/2" t. ............. **$345**
*James D. Julia, Inc.*

Two black Sandwich glass bears, both lacking embossing on base, 3-3/4" t. ........................................................ **$402**
*James D. Julia, Inc.*

Cobalt whale oil lamp, Boston & Sandwich Glass Co., ca. 1850, 11" h. ............................ **$1,000**
*Pook & Pook, Inc.*

Three Sandwich glass bears, clambroth colored, largest example embossed on base "Eugene Bize & Fricke Successors to J. Hauel & Co.," second is embossed "FB Strouse N.Y.," and third is embossed "X. Bazin Philada"; tallest is 4-1/2". ........................................................ **$575**
*James D. Julia, Inc.*

Pair of cobalt glass candlesticks, Boston & Sandwich Glass Co., ca. 1850, 7-1/2" h. ................. **$516**
*Pook & Pook, Inc.*

Two Sandwich glass cup plates, very difficult to find: very rare Lee #247 in deep blue-green and unique Lee #246 in opal, 3-7/16" dia. Provenance: From the collection of Dorothy-Lee Jones......................... **$230**
*James D. Julia, Inc.*

Five Sandwich glass sugar bowls. 1) Pressed Acanthus Leaf and Shield on foot in light blue opalescent, no lid. 2) Pressed Gothic Arch in clear. 3) Pressed Gothic Arch in canary. 4) Pressed Gothic Arch in opaque starch blue. 5) Pressed Gothic Arch in amethyst; lidded sugars are 5-1/2" x 5" dia. Provenance: From the collection of Dorothy-Lee Jones...... **$1,495**
*James D. Julia, Inc.*

►Four vaseline glass candlesticks, Boston & Sandwich Glass Co., ca. 1850, 7" h. ...................... **$563**
*Pook & Pook, Inc.*

Pressed Lacy Hairpin square dish, colorless, center featuring a leaf-like quatrefoil enclosing a four-petal blossom set within a background of tiny diamonds in squares, scallop and point rim, Boston & Sandwich Glass Co., 1830-1840, 1-1/4" h., 7-3/8" x 7-3/4" ............................................................ **$2,875**
*Jeffrey S. Evans & Associates*

Pressed loop vase, brilliant sapphire blue, deep conical bowl with a gauffered seven-petal rim, raised on a ring-top hexagonal baluster-form standard and panel-top circular foot, wafer construction, Boston & Sandwich Glass Co. and probably others, 1840-1860, 10-1/2" h., 4-1/4" dia. rim, 4-1/4" dia. base......................... **$1,380**
*Jeffrey S. Evans & Associates*

Pressed Lacy Gothic Arch sugar bowl and cover, alabaster/clambroth, octagonal bowl with two different arch designs and a plain rim, raised on an eight-petal foot, fitted with a similar, darker color cover with four arch designs that is usually associated with the circular-foot variant of the pattern, Boston & Sandwich Glass Co. and Midwestern, 1840-1850, 5-1/4" h. overall, 3-5/8" h. rim, 5" dia. rim, 2-7/8" dia. foot ........... **$196**
*Jeffrey S. Evans & Associates*

Pressed Sandwich glass Star spoon holder/spill, deep electric blue, hexagonal rim and single-step foot with small rough iron pontil mark, Boston & Sandwich Glass Co. and probably others, third quarter 19th c., 5" h., 3-3/4" dia. rim, 3-1/8" dia. foot ......................................... **$460**
*Jeffrey S. Evans & Associates*

Pressed open-work dish on low foot, colorless, flared 22-scallop rim surrounding the acid-roughed center, polished table ring, Boston & Sandwich Glass Co., 1860-1870, 2-3/8" h., 5-3/4" dia. rim, 3" dia. foot .......................... **$69**
*Jeffrey S. Evans & Associates*

Pressed open-work dish on low foot, brilliant apple green, flared 22-scallop rim surrounding the acid-roughed center with worn original silver floral decoration, polished table ring, Boston & Sandwich Glass Co., 1860-1870, 2-1/4" h., 5-7/8" dia. rim, 3" dia. foot .............................. **$1,955**
*Jeffrey S. Evans & Associates*

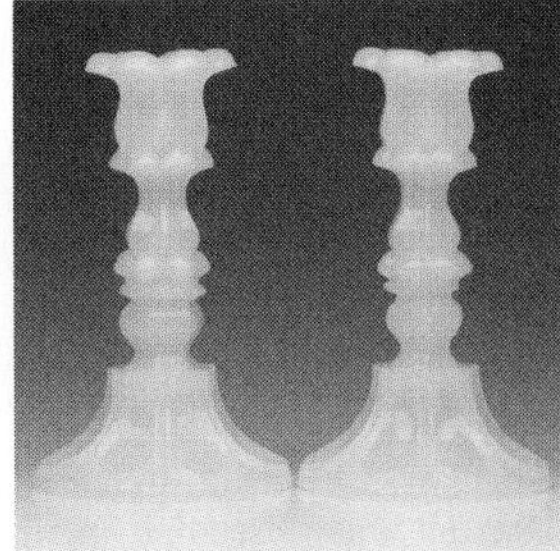

Pair of pressed Petal and Loop candlesticks, alabaster/clambroth, each six-petal socket with a hexagonal extension, raised on a hexagonal knop and seven-loop circular base with rough pontil mark, wafer construction, Boston & Sandwich Glass Co. and others, 1840-1860, 7" h., 4-1/4" dia. base ....... **$219**
*Jeffrey S. Evans & Associates*

GLASS

Pair of pressed Dolphin single-step candlesticks, opaque white, each six-petal socket with lower extension, raised on a large dolphin-form standard and square base, wafer construction, probably Boston & Sandwich Glass Co., 1845-1870, 10" h., 3-7/8" sq. base ................................ **$259**
*Jeffrey S. Evans & Associates*

Pair of pressed Dolphin double-step candlesticks, canary yellow, each thin-lipped six-petal socket with lower extension, raised on a medium dolphin-form standard and square base, wafer construction, Boston & Sandwich Glass Co., 1845-1870, 9-1/4" h., 3-1/2" sq. base ................. **$460**
*Jeffrey S. Evans & Associates*

Pressed four-printie block vase, deep brilliant cobalt blue, deep conical bowl with a gauffered six-petal rim and hexagonal-knop extension, raised on a hexagonal knop and flared base, wafer construction, Boston & Sandwich Glass Co., 1840-1860, 11-3/4" h., 4-1/2" dia. rim, 5-1/4" dia. foot ............................... **$1,495**
*Jeffrey S. Evans & Associates*

Three pressed Plume and Acorn nappies, deep amethyst and amber each with an even-scallop rim, Boston & Sandwich Glass Co., 1840-1860, 5" and 6-1/8" dia. ..................................................................... **$138**
*Jeffrey S. Evans & Associates*

# Schneider Glass

Charles Schneider's monumental glass vases are among the most dazzling of the Art Deco era. His bold use of color, combined with such techniques as mottling, flecking, streaking, and etched cameo designs, make Schneider vases stand-alone art objects.

Born in 1881 in France, Schneider studied at the Ecole des Beaux-Arts under famed glass artist Emile Galle. He then found employment, with older brother Ernest, at the Daum factory in Nancy. In 1913, the brothers opened the Cristallerie Schneider near Paris. Charles was designer, and Ernest (later aided by sister Ernestine) handled the marketing. Closed during World War I, the firm reopened in 1917 and began producing the cameo glass for which Schneider became best-known: "Le Verre Francais" ("The French Glass").

Their line included the jumbo trumpet and urn-shaped vases today's collectors associate with Schneider, as well as bowls, lamps, candlesticks, and epergnes. Vivid reds and oranges are characteristic of "Le Verre Francais," including the rich hue Schneider dubbed "tango orange." For dramatic effect, the vase foot was often in a color contrasting with the vase body. Highly stylized, acid-etched patterns of exotic vines or flowers usually decorated the outer vase layer, although, in a nod to Art Deco's "modern" emphasis, abstract geometric designs also put in an appearance.

An etched "La Verre Francais" is an immediate identifier of a Schneider piece, along with the alternate signature "Charder" (an abbreviation of CHAR-les schnei-DER). Later pieces are signed "Schneider." Vases are also sometimes found marked "Ovington," the New York store for which Schneider created commissioned works.

Schneider's heyday lasted until World War II. After the war, the firm reopened under the direction of Charles Schneider, Jr., and glass production continued in diminished form until the early 1980s. Today's collectors, however, are most interested in the eye-popping output of the 1920s and '30s.

Schneider amethyst jar vase in plum, 10" h. ..................... **$1,200-$1,500**

The bases are black, the accent color Schneider's signature tango orange, 15-3/4" h........ **$1,800-$2,000;** 18" h. ..................... **$2,200-$2,500**

Blue globe vases, 7-1/2" h. ......... **$1,500-$2,000 ea.**

Exotic cobalt blooms on terra cotta, 14" h. ................................................... **$3,000-$4,000**

Cobalt on frosted light blue, 10-1/2" h. **$900-$1,200;** 14" h. ........................................ **$1,500-$1,800**

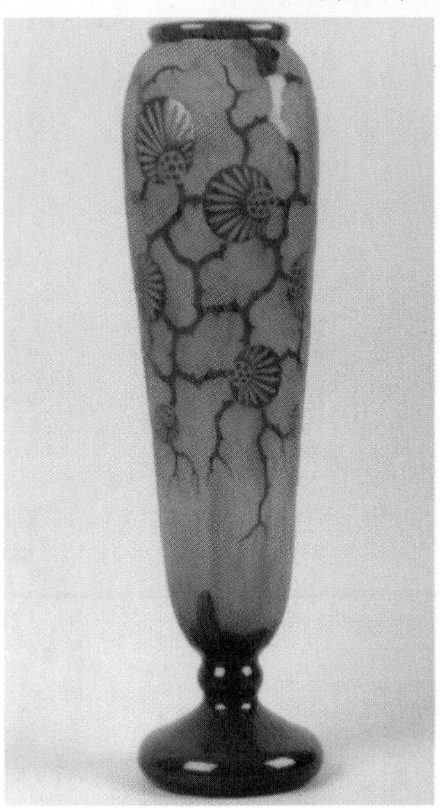

Entwined array of flowers and vines, 22-1/2" h. ...................................................... **$2,200-$2,400**

◀Schneider globe vase in tortoiseshell browns, with pattern of heart-shaped leaves, 8" h.. **$1,200-$1,500**

Grey-centered orange sunflowers on yellow, 10-1/4" h. .......................... **$1,500-$2,000**

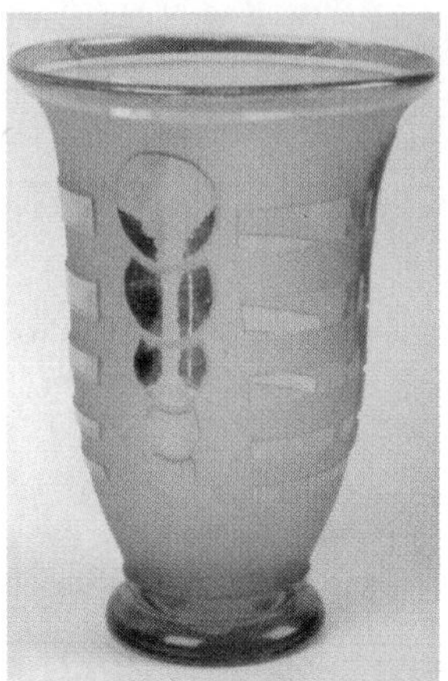

Smoky-grey Schneider, with metallic pattern of circles and bars, 12-3/4" h. ........... **$3,000-$3,500**

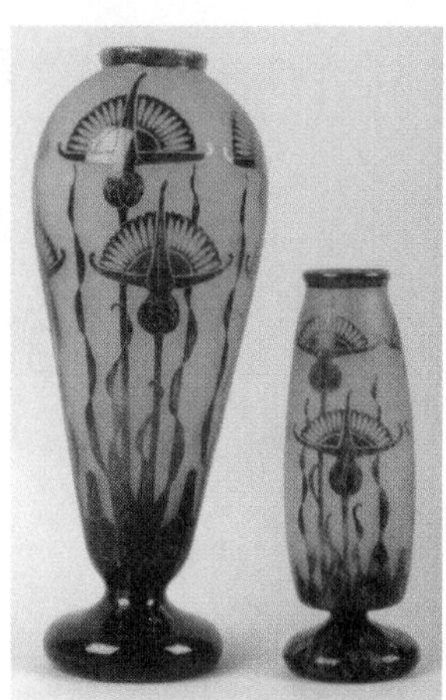

Two Schneider lotus fan vases, 19" h. ................. **$1,800-$2,000**
12" h. ................. **$1,200-$1,400**

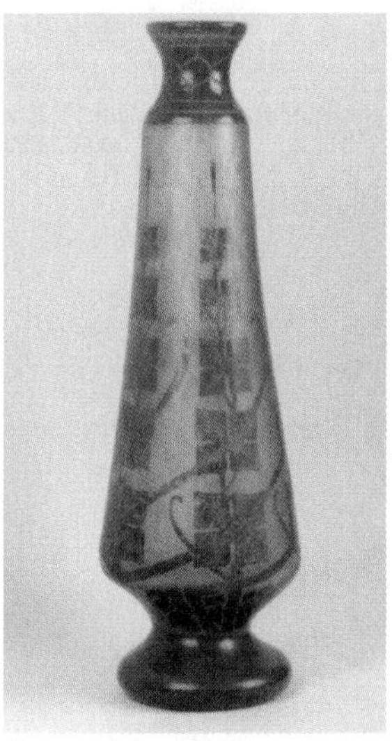

Monumental tri-color orange, green, and frosted Schneider vase, 26" h. ................. **$4,000-$6,000**

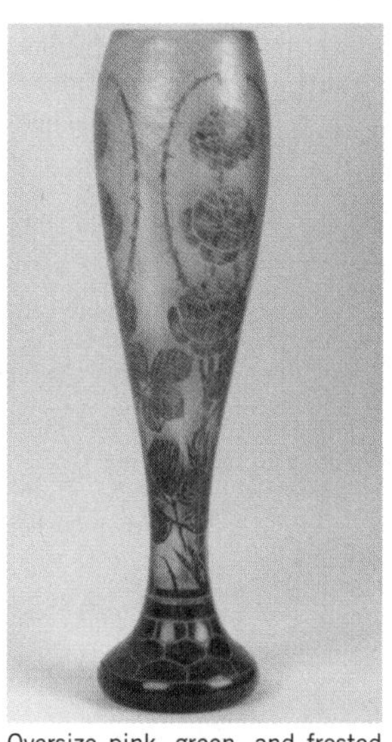

Oversize pink, green, and frosted Schneider vase with floral vine motif, 26" h......... **$4,000-$6,000**

Lilies of the valley, in red, 11-3/4" h......................... **$1,000-$1,200**
19-1/4" h. ........... **$2,000-$2,500**

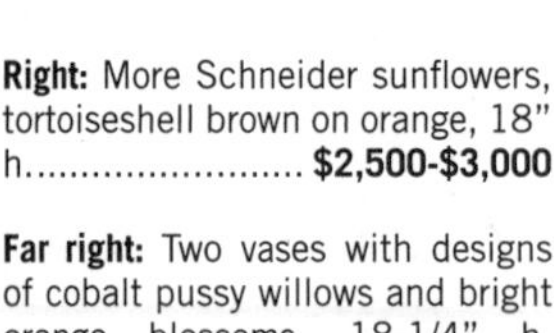

**Right:** More Schneider sunflowers, tortoiseshell brown on orange, 18" h......................... **$2,500-$3,000**

**Far right:** Two vases with designs of cobalt pussy willows and bright orange blossoms, 18-1/4" h. ...................... **$1,500-$2,000 ea.**

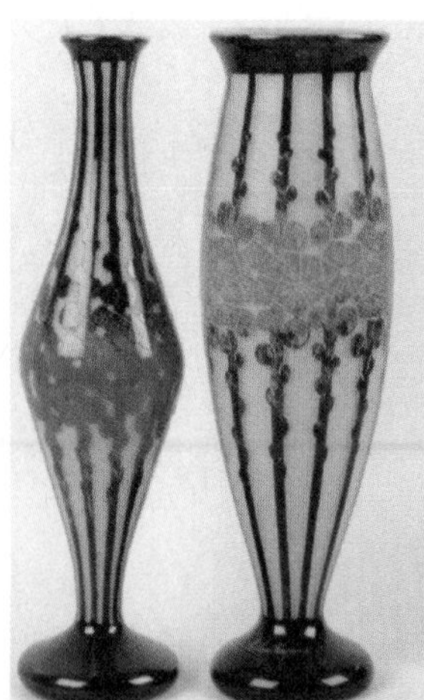

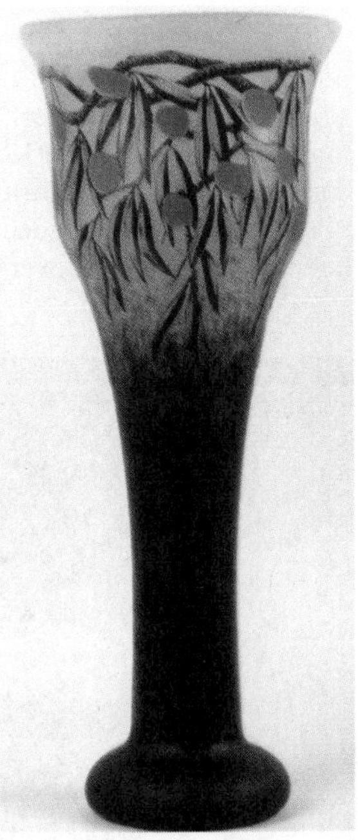
Persimmons with green and black foliage, on yellow, 23" h. .......................... **$6,000-$8,000**

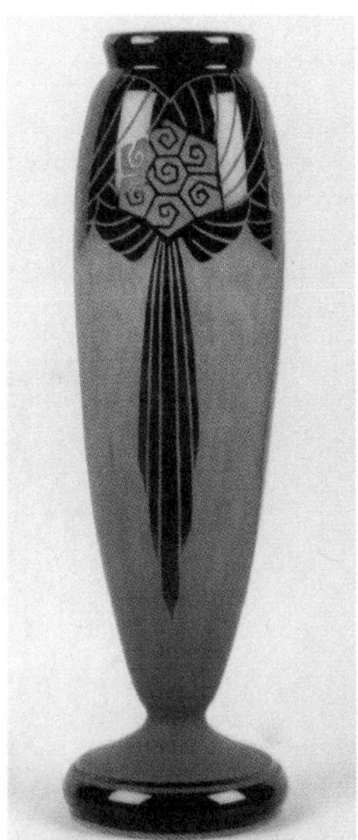
Purple floral rosettes, on orange, 21" h. ................ **$3,000-$3,500**

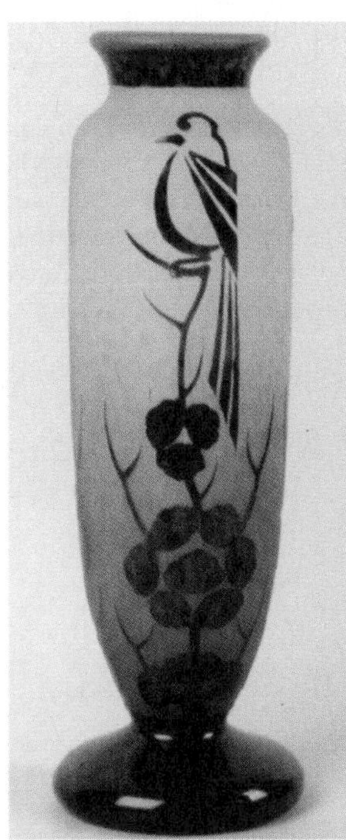
Watchful bird perched on flower, 17-1/2" h. .......... **$2,000-$2,500**

Sinuous blossoms and hanging fruit, in tones of burnt apricot, 12-1/2" h. ........................ **$1,600-$2,000;** 17-1/2" h. .................................... **$1,800-$2,200**

Three Schneider vases with circular motifs. Left: Purple-green links on white; center: interlocked blossoms on blue; right: light green hanging oranges on a darker green base; 16" h. ......................... **$2,000-$2,500;** 19-1/4" h. ..................................... **$800-$1,200;** 9-1/2" h. ........................................ **$2,000-$2,500**

GLASS

# Steuben

Frederick Carder, an Englishman, and Thomas G. Hawkes of Corning, New York, established the Steuben Glass Works in 1903 in Steuben County, New York. In 1918, the Corning Glass Co. purchased the Steuben company. Carder remained with the firm and designed many of the pieces bearing the Steuben mark. Probably the most widely recognized wares are Aurene, Verre De Soie, and Rosaline, but many other types were produced. The firm operated until 2011.

Gold iridescent art glass shade attributed to Steuben, made entirely of gold Aurene type glass with iridescent finish, unsigned, 2-1/4" fitter x 10" dia. **$1,955**
*James D. Julia, Inc.*

Steuben lead crystal vase in Strawberry Mansion pattern, cut and engraved with an eagle holding a flower spray in its beak with a garland design encircling the rim, finished with two applied "M"-shaped handles, unsigned, 12-7/8" t. ................................. **$1,725**
*James D. Julia, Inc.*

◀Green Steuben architectural plaque of kneeling nude picking grapes from a vine, unsigned, 9" w. x 9" t. ................................................................ **$862**
*James D. Julia, Inc.*

Steuben console set, green jade center bowl resting atop alabaster stem and foot, bowl finished with two applied handles with free floating alabaster rings, accompanied by matching pair of candlesticks with green jade candle cups and feet with alabaster stems, unsigned, bowl is 8-3/4" t. Provenance: From the collection of Dorothy-Lee Jones. ............. **$977**
*James D. Julia, Inc.*

Steuben Oriental Poppy decanter decorated with vertical bands of pink Oriental Poppy alternating with white opalescence, finished with matching Oriental Poppy stopper, 8-1/4" t. ............ **$1,888**
*James D. Julia, Inc.*

Rare Steuben vase blown in the form of a fish with swirling ribbed body and applied fins and eyes, vase rests atop applied stem and foot, unsigned, 12-1/2" t. **$1,782**
*James D. Julia, Inc.*

►Steuben vase with brown Aurene body decorated with blue iridescent hooked feather design descending from the lip, marked on the underside "Aurene 649," 3-1/4" t.......................... **$3,507**
*James D. Julia, Inc.*

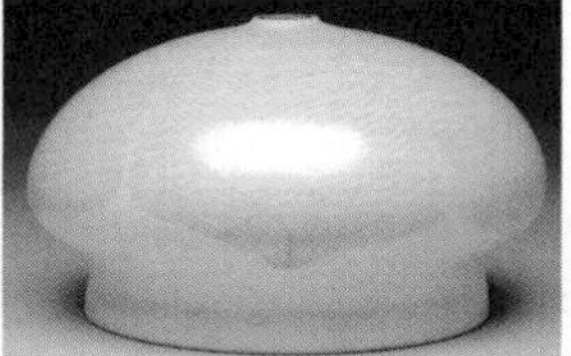

Steuben shade, yellow pulled feather design with light iridescence showing green and pink highlights, design set against an Ivrene background, interior finished in bright gold iridescence, unsigned, 10" dia............ **$1,782**
*James D. Julia, Inc.*

Steuben teared crystal candlestick, shape #7792, multiple joined sections, signed, Steuben Glass Works, Corning, N.Y., second quarter 20th c., 8-5/8" h. ...........**$172**
*Jeffrey S. Evans & Associates*

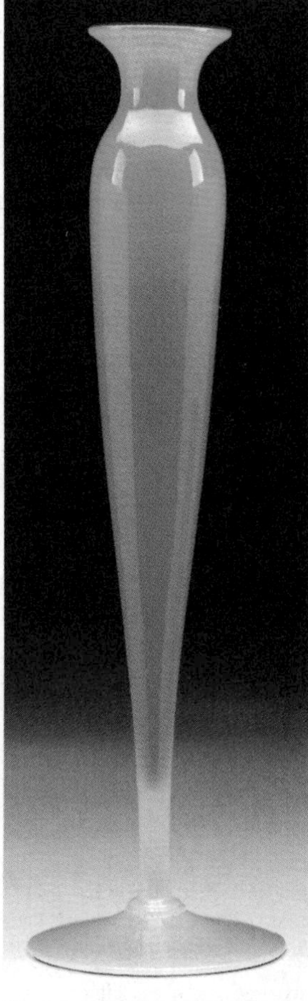

Steuben Rosaline and alabaster vase, Rosaline body with alabaster inverted saucer foot and stem, unsigned, 16-1/8" t................ **$632**
*James D. Julia, Inc.*

# Tiffany Glass

Tiffany & Co. was founded by Charles Lewis Tiffany (1812-1902) and Teddy Young in New York City in 1837 as a "stationery and fancy goods emporium." The store initially sold a wide variety of stationery items, and operated as Tiffany, Young and Ellis in lower Manhattan. The name was shortened to Tiffany & Co. in 1853, and the firm's emphasis on jewelry was established.

The first Tiffany catalog, known as the "Blue Book," was published in 1845. It is still being published today.

In 1862 Tiffany & Co. supplied the Union Army with swords, flags and surgical implements.

Charles' son, Louis Comfort Tiffany (1848-1933) was an American artist and designer who worked in the decorative arts and is best known for his work in stained glass. Louis established Tiffany Glass Co. in 1885, and in 1902 it became known as the Tiffany Studios. America's outstanding glass designer of the Art Nouveau period produced glass from the last quarter of the 19th century until the early 1930s. Tiffany revived early techniques and devised many new ones.

Tiffany Blue Favrile cabinet vase, blue iridescence at the foot shading to platinum iridescence at the shoulder and neck, signed on the bottom "L.C.T. D3473," 2-1/2" h.................................... **$805**
*James D. Julia, Inc.*

Tiffany flower form vase with pastel pink interior and white opalescent shaded exterior resting atop a clear freeform stem and foot, foot finished with a white opalescent edge, signed on the underside "LCT Favrile 1938," 5-1/4" t. .................................... **$1,725**
*James D. Julia, Inc.*

Tiffany gold Favrile pitcher with corset-shaped body with applied handle, pitcher finished with gold iridescence showing strong pink highlights, signed on the underside "LC Tiffany Favrile," 5-1/4" t. .................................... **$460**
*James D. Julia, Inc.*

Tiffany leaf and vine cabinet vase decorated with green iridescent leaves and brown iridescent vines all set against a gold Favrile iridescent background, gold iridescence shows flashes of pink and blue, signed on underside "L.C.T. Y8387," 3-1/2" t. ........... **$1,897**
*James D. Julia, Inc.*

Tiffany Studios art glass shade, vertical ribbing and deep gold with purple and blue iridescence, shade finished with a gently scalloped border, signed "L.C.T. Favrile" in rim, 2-1/4" fitter x 4-3/4" h. .**$862**
*James D. Julia, Inc.*

Tiffany Studios bell shade decorated with a translucent green pulled-feather motif with gold trim on an oyster ground, signed "L.C.T." 2-1/4" fitter rim x 4-1/2" h. Minor grinding to fitter rim .................................... **$2,530**
*James D. Julia, Inc.*

Tiffany gold Favrile cordial with a fine twisted stem and inverted saucer foot, gold iridescence on the stem and foot shows lovely flashes of lavender, signed on the underside "LCT," 5-1/2" t. . **$460**

*James D. Julia, Inc.*

Tiffany stalactite hanger, shade with gold iridescent hooked-feather design extending from the bottom of the shade, additional hooked-feather design descending from the fitter against a lighter gold iridescent background of the vertically ribbed body, interior has a light chartreuse color. Shade is unsigned and numbered "L2400," suspended from three chains attached to hooks on a center light post, which terminates to a ceiling cap with beaded rim. Bronze replacement hardware is finished in a rich brown patina with strong red and green highlights. Shade is 8" l x 6" dia. x 4-3/4" fitter, overall 24" h. ....................................... **$7,187**

*James D. Julia, Inc.*

Tiffany Studios Blue Favrile vase, classic Egyptian form with elongated neck and squared shoulder, vase begins with a platinum iridescence over neck area that recedes into a medium blue and a cobalt blue at the foot, signed "L.C. Tiffany Inc. Favrile X1421024," 5-3/4" h. .......................... **$920**

*James D. Julia, Inc.*

Tiffany Studios blown-glass six-arm candelabra made of bronze with patina finish of brown with hints of green and red, oval-shaped platform base with single center stem with three candle cups on either side, each with green blown-glass ornamentation and bobeche. In the center stem of the candlestick rests a Tiffany snuffer that is concealed when in place, signed on the underside "Tiffany Studios New York 1648," 15" x 21". .................................. **$6,900**

*James D. Julia, Inc.*

Tiffany Studios counterbalance desk lamp with pendulous turtleback tile counterweight, artichoke design stand and blue decorated damascene shade signed "L.C.T. Favrile," base is marked "Tiffany Studios New York." Shade is 8" dia., cverall 14-1/2" h. ... **$32,775**

*James D. Julia, Inc.*

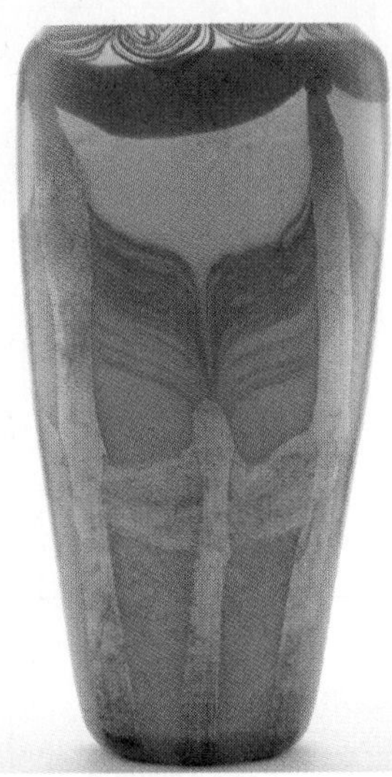

Tiffany Studios early experimental Favrile glass vase lamp base, c. 1900, engraved "X103 Louis C. Tiffany-Favrile," 14-3/4" t. **$3,585**
*Heritage Auction Galleries*

Tiffany Studios Favrile cabinet vase, round squat body with pulled handles on each side and slightly flaring mouth, gold Favrile finish shows purple and blue highlights at foot and lip, signed on the underside "L.C. Tiffany-Favrile 4014L," 2" t. .................... **$540**
*James D. Julia, Inc.*

►Tiffany Studios Favrile Lily vase, slender body, slightly flaring at the lip with saucer foot, gold iridescence shows flashes of pink and blue at the foot, signed on the underside "L.C. Tiffany Inc. Favrile 1504-7408M," 6" t. .......... **$660**
*James D. Julia, Inc.*

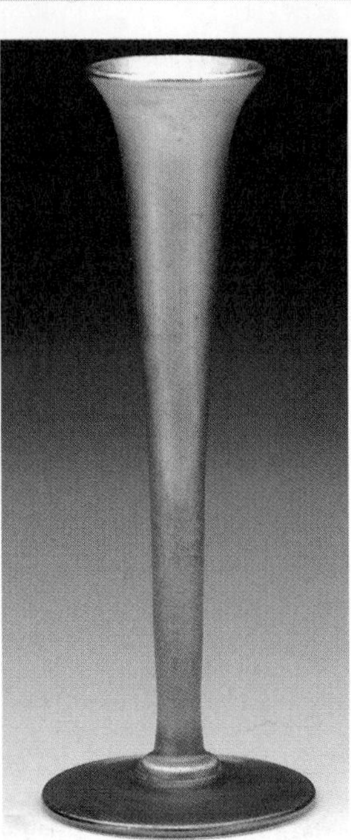

Tiffany Studios Fireball lamp, one of two known examples. Early Tiffany Studios leaded orb shade has flame design in mottled red and orange glass against a textured green and brown swirled background, flames are made up of numerous types of glass, including heavily rippled to lightly textured, shade rests atop a bronze saucer base with single socket, base is finished with rich brown patina with green highlights, shade and base unsigned, shade 12" dia., overall 15" h. .................................................................. **$48,875**
*James D. Julia, Inc.*

Tiffany Studios Favrile desk lamp, gold Favrile shade with rainbow iridescent finish with stretched edge, cased white-lined shade supported by a three-arm, leaf-decorated base with a statuary finish, top cap in patina finish, shade signed on the fitter "L.C.T. Favrile" and base is signed on the underside "Tiffany Studios New York 426." Shade is 7" dia., overall 14" t.............................................. **$4,200**
*James D. Julia, Inc.*

Tiffany Studios flower-form vase, pulled-feather design on opalescent ground with everted rim and decorated foot, engraved signature "L.C. Tiffany Favrile 539A," 11-1/4" h. .................... **$3,680**

*James D. Julia, Inc.*

Tiffany Studios Damascene table lamp, green Favrile shade with Damascene-wave pattern decoration in gold shading to platinum having eight vertical ribs, cased lined shade supported by a patinated single-socket, three-arm bronze base with elongated rib decoration over ornate root-style foot resting on four ball feet, completed with a bronze heat cap. Shade signed on the fitter rim "L.C.T.," base signed "Tiffany Studios New York 431." Shade is 9-1/2" dia. x 3-3/4" fitter, overall 19-1/2" t. ...................... **$6,612**

*James D. Julia, Inc.*

Tiffany Studios footed candy dish with applied gold iridescent border on opaque blue body and foot, scratched in "59" on the underside, 6" dia. ........................ **$60**

*James D. Julia, Inc.*

◀Tiffany Studios Lemon Leaf table lamp, heavily mottled apple-green background glass with heavily mottled maize-colored lemon-leaf band, shade signed "Tiffany Studios New York 1470," base signed "Tiffany Studios New York 531." Original patina on base and shade. Shade is 18" dia., overall 25-1/2" h. .................... **$17,250**

*James D. Julia, Inc.*

Tiffany Studios Geometric table lamp with leaded "dichroic" glass shade glass (containing multiple micro-layers of metal oxides) that shows colors of green, tan, and mauve when unlit. When lit, the glass turns a rich orange. Shade is signed "Tiffany Studios New York 1436" and rests atop an early Tiffany Studios base with an incised and slightly raised wave design. Base is finished with three attached arms to support the shade. Marked on the underside "25778." Shade is 16" dia. Overall 20" h. A few tight hairlines in the shade. Bottom of font has been drilled.................. **$15,525**

*James D. Julia, Inc.*

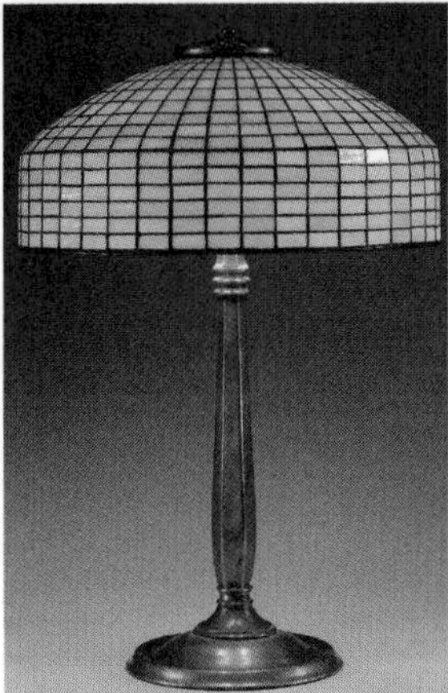

Tiffany Studios Geometric table lamp, colors of butterscotch and caramel striated with white, shade is supported by Colonial-style, four-socket base with inverted saucer foot, shade signed "Tiffany Studios NY 1469," base is marked "Tiffany Studios New York 532." Shade is 18" dia., overall 25" h. .......................... **$8,050**

*James D. Julia, Inc.*

Tiffany Studios Lily & Prism chandelier, six gold lily shades and 19 prisms in colors of oyster, gold, amber, and green with a deep iridescence over the lilies and complimentary prisms, decorated stalactite Tiffany shade with deep vertical ribbing and a hooked-feather pattern. Shade is supported by a bronze collar, three chains, and hooks. Shades are supported by a Moorish-style bronze hanging fixture with openwork at the top, medallions of roping above six lily shade holders, 19 prism hooks and a single stem for the stalactite shade. Lamp is supported by a bronze decorated ceiling cap, chain, and S hook. Stalactite shade is signed "S323" and one lily shade is signed "L.C.T. Favrile" and another is signed "L.C.T." and the remainder are unsigned. Overall 42" l. ........................ **$32,775**
*James D. Julia, Inc.*

Tiffany Studios mini flower-form vase, blue iridescent with vertical ribbing and applied foot, irregular iridescence to top quarter of the vase shading down to deep purple mirror iridescence on the foot, engraved signature "7311N 1522 L.C. Tiffany-Inc Favrile" on the underside, 6-1/4" t.......... **$2,400**
*James D. Julia, Inc.*

Tiffany Studios, nine Favrile glass tiles, circa 1900, four with molded "PAT. APPL'D. FOR," largest 4" square............................... **$1,195 all**
*Heritage Auction Galleries*

Tiffany Studios pastel creamer with bright yellow interior shading to clear, foot and body are further decorated with vertical panels of white opalescence with a shaded opalescent band surrounding the outer edge of the creamer, signed on the underside "LCT Favrile 1917," 3" t. ......**$460**
*James D. Julia, Inc.*

Tiffany Studios Nautilus lamp, natural shell shade on patina harp base with additional hook on the underside for possible wall hanging as well as five ball feet, impressed on underside "403 Tiffany Studios New York," 12-1/2" h. ..................................... **$6,900**
*James D. Julia, Inc.*

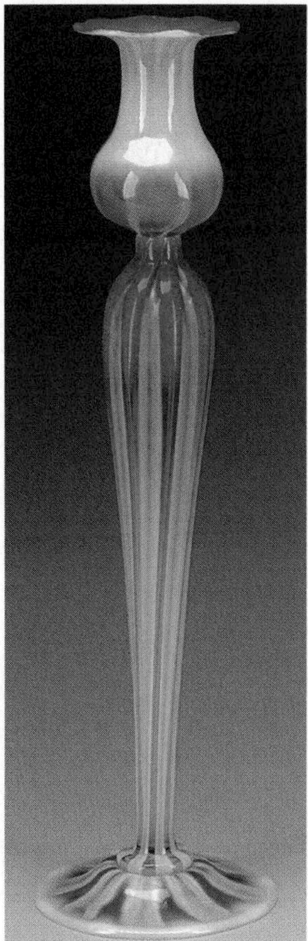

Tiffany Pastel Tulip candlestick with raspberry opalescent cup applied to blue-to-green opalescent stem with white pulled striping and applied raspberry foot with opalescent ribbing, signed on the underside "1845 L.C. Tiffany-Favrile," 16" t. **$6,612**

*James D. Julia, Inc.*

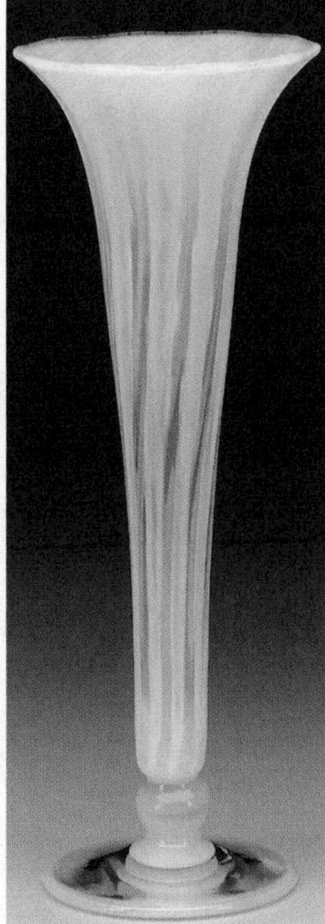

Tiffany Studios pastel vase, clear foot with white opalescent rim, foot gives way to white opalescent stem with white opalescent ribs vertically extending to the slightly flaring lip, interior of the mouth finished with a rich pastel yellow, signed on the underside "L.C. Tiffany Favrile 1886," 9-3/4" t. **$1,380**

*James D. Julia, Inc.*

Tiffany Studios Pine Needle card case constructed of green slag panels with darker striations, panels set in bronze frame with decorative pine-needle decoration overall, patina finish, signed on underside "Tiffany Studios New York 875," 4" x 3" x 1"... **$1,495**

*James D. Julia, Inc.*

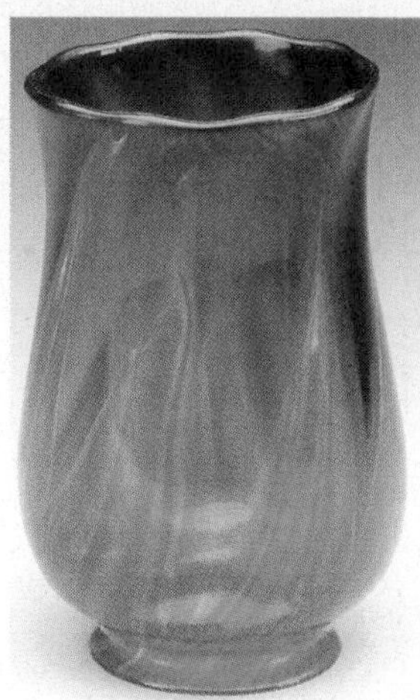

Tiffany reactive glass shade, green and orange flame design extending from the foot to near rim, smoky gray body of the shade has slightly swirling rib running vertically, shade unsigned, 5" t x 2-1/4" fitter. **$4,025**

*James D. Julia, Inc.*

◄Tiffany Studios picture frame, circa 1906, Grapevine pattern with green and white opalescent glass, easel back, 7-3/8" x 8-3/4". **$1,673**

*Heritage Auction Galleries*

Tiffany Studios Pomegranate table lamp. Shade has an allover geometric background of green striated glass with hints of blue, yellow, and white. The shade is decorated with a single band of pomegranates in fiery mottled yellow and orange glass. Shade is supported by a three-socket, three-armed Grecian urn that is supported by four flaring feet on a pedestal stand. Shade is signed on "Tiffany Studios New York" with a small early tag. Shade is 16" dia. Overall 20" h. Several spider cracks. ............................**$16,100**

*James D. Julia, Inc.*

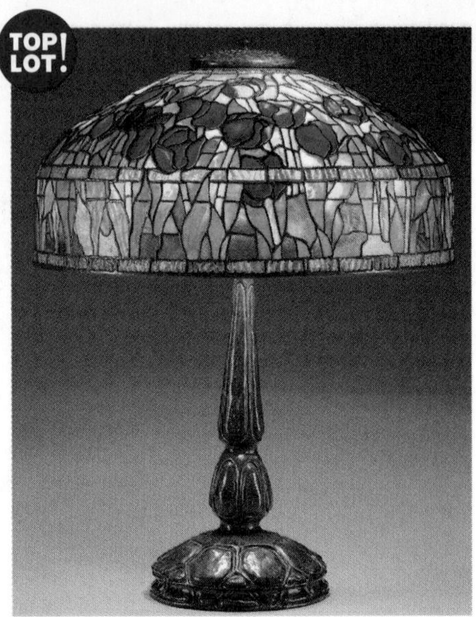


Tiffany Studios Red Tulip table lamp, shade depicts tulips in every stage of bloom, colors range from pink to purple, also shows foliage in various shades of green. Glass used is a wide variety from striated to cat's paw to rippled and finally granular. Shade is completed with three geometric bands of rippled glass in earthen hues of fiery orange with hints of green, supported by mock-turtleback three-socket base complete with riser, wheel, and top cap all in a rich patina finish. Shade signed "Tiffany Studios New York 1596," base signed "Tiffany Studios New York 587." Shade 18" dia., overall 22-1/2" h. ..**$109,250**

*James D. Julia, Inc.*

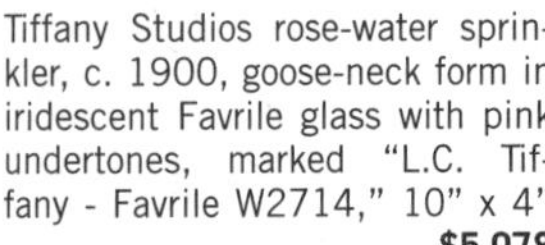

Tiffany Studios rose-water sprinkler, c. 1900, goose-neck form in iridescent Favrile glass with pink undertones, marked "L.C. Tiffany - Favrile W2714," 10" x 4" ...................................... **$5,078**

*Heritage Auction Galleries*

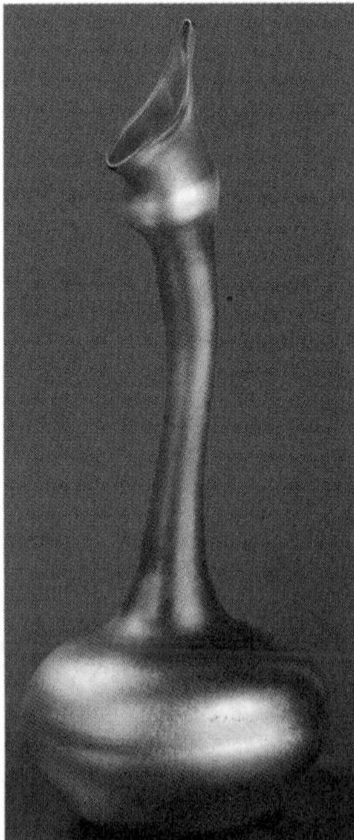

Tiffany Studios Tel El Amarna vase with applied and decorated collar, engraved "Exhibition Piece" and "6340N L.C. Tiffany – Favrile" on the underside, 5-3/4" h. .. **$5,750**

*James D. Julia, Inc.*

**Far right:** Tiffany Studios ruffled bowl. deep gold iridescent finish with magenta, blue, and pink highlights, signed on the underside "L.C.T.," 4-1/2" diameter. ......................................... **$287**

*James D. Julia, Inc.*

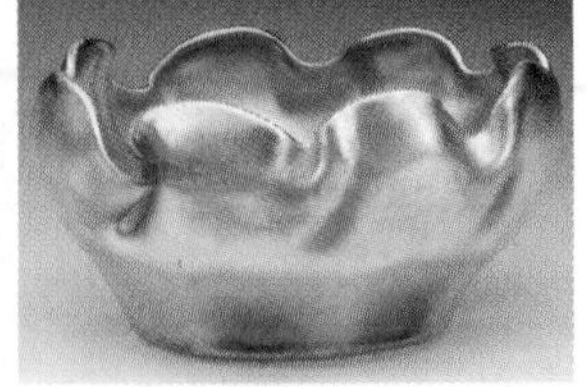

# Tiffin

A wide variety of fine glasswares were produced by the Tiffin Glass Company of Tiffin, Ohio. Beginning as a part of the large U.S. Glass Company early in the 20th century, the Tiffin factory continued making a wide range of wares until its final closing in 1984. One popular line is now called "Black Satin" and included various vases with raised floral designs. Many other acid-etched and hand-cut patterns were also produced over the years and are very collectible today. The three "Tiffin Glassmasters" books by Fred Bickenheuser are the standard references for Tiffin collectors.

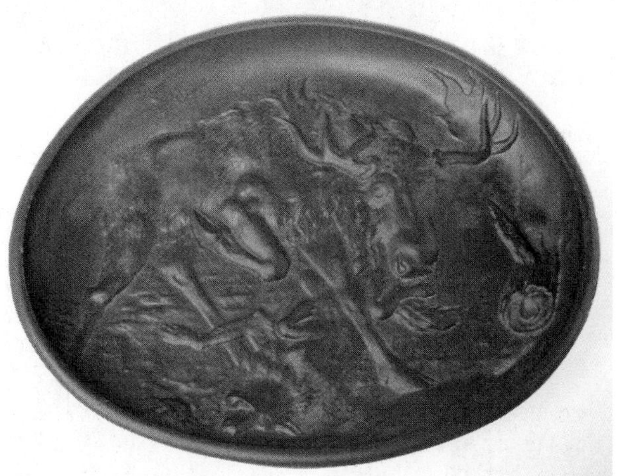

Ashtray, shallow oval form, molded stag and wolf design, Black Satin, 6" l. .................... **$55**

Atomizer, footed tall slender waisted body, blue satin, new atomizer fitting, 7" h. ............ **$120**

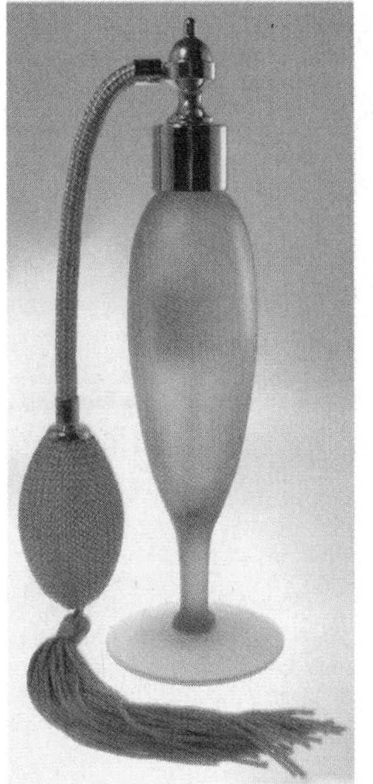

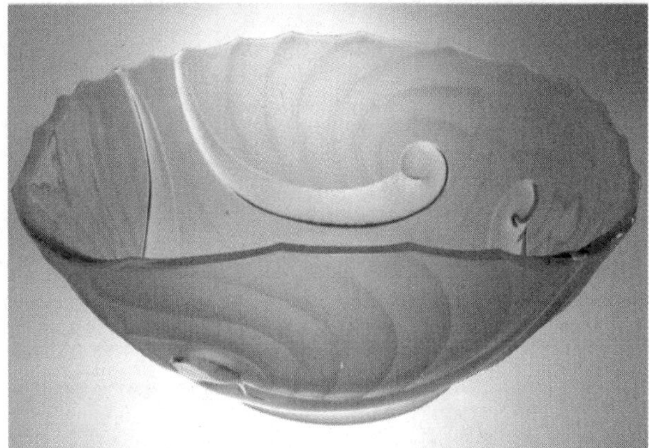

Bowl, square with flaring sides, Velva pattern, frosted blue, 9-1/2" w. .................... **$87**

◀Atomizer, round foot and slender stem with a tall slender ovoid body, amber satin, new atomizer fitting, 7" h. .................... **$115**

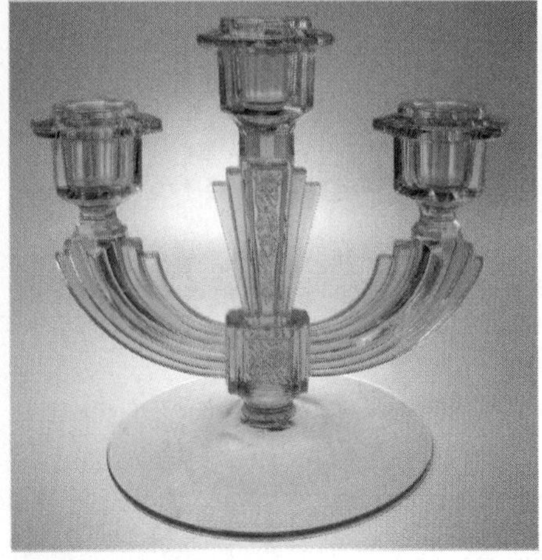

Candleholder, three-light, Art Deco style Pattern 308, sky blue, 7-1/4" w., 6-3/8" h. ........................... **$65**

Candleholders, one-light, figural stylized frogs, black satin, 5-1/2" h., pr. ..................................... **$250**

Candlestick, one-light, floral cut decoration, royal blue, pr..... **$160**

Candlestick, one-light, No. 82 with Jack Frost decoration, canary, 8-1/2" h., pr....................... **$130**

Candlesticks, one-light, figural Dolphin stem, round base, light green, 4-1/4" h., pr. ............. **$68**

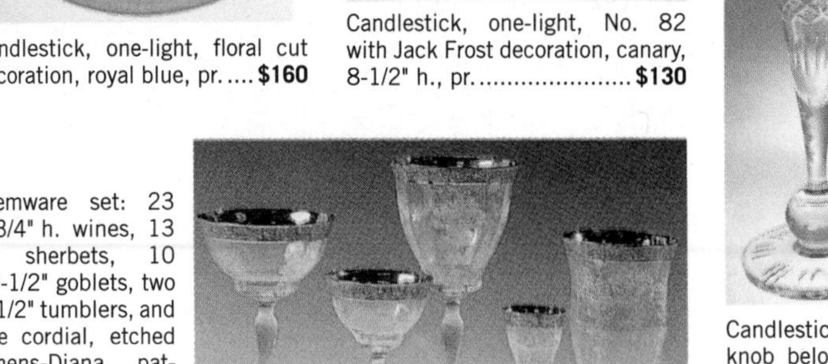

Candlesticks, round foot and large knob below the flaring stem below a ringed collar and tulip-form socket, Pattern No. 17350, clear with cut decoration, 10" h., pr. ........................................ **$145**

Stemware set: 23 4-3/4" h. wines, 13 6" sherbets, 10 10-1/2" goblets, two 5-1/2" tumblers, and one cordial, etched Athens-Diana pattern, platinum rim bands, the set..**$949**

Candlesticks, one-light, Pattern No. 151, black satin with gold band trim, 8" h., pr. ........................ **$85**

Candlesticks, one-light, Velva pattern, blue satin, 5-3/4" h., pr. ............................................. **$115**

Candlesticks, Twist Stem pattern, Pattern 315, Amberina, 8-3/4" h., pr. (with Twist Stem compote). **$95**

Compote, open, wide shallow Killarney green bowl raised on four applied clear pointed feet, Pattern No. 17430 (with Killarney green vase), 6-1/4" d., 3" h. ............................................................... **$48**

Candy jar, covered, Pattern No. 179, footed widely flaring base and wide pagoda-style cover with gold ship decoration, black satin, 6-1/2" d., 7-1/2" h. .............. **$95**

►Candy jar, covered, mold-blown, No. 6106, diamond optic ovoid body tapering to a slender stem and foot, domed cover with pointed finial, plum ......................................... **$125**

Console set: footed round bowl and pair of tall candlesticks; bowl No. 8098 and No. 300 candlesticks, royal blue with satin finish, bowl 9-1/2" dia., candlesticks 8-1/2" h., the set .................................... **$230**

Serving tray, flaring open center handle, Pattern No. 15320, black satin with gold border bands, 10-1/2" dia. ............................................. **$58**

Decanter w/original stopper, Pattern No. 17437, a clear applied foot and heavy clear swirled ribs supporting the tall slender ovoid Killarney green body, tall rounded clear stopper, 12" h. .......... **$140**

Vase, 20" h., swung-type, Green Fantasy Line, green and crystal ........................................ **$235**

►Sherbet, tall stem and deep rounded bowl, topaz stretch glass, 4-1/2" h. ............................. **$24**

Ivy ball, mold-blown, No. 6120 patt., bulbous diamond optic bowl on a tall faceted stem with faceted rings on a round foot, original label, Golden Banada ............. **$72**

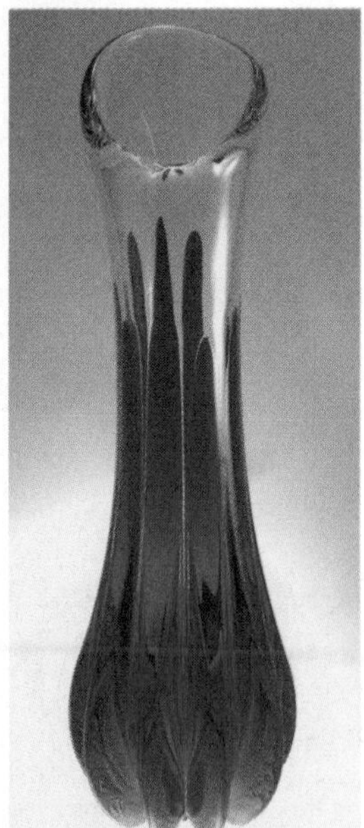

Vase, swung-type, Empress Line, ruby and crystal, 16" h., ...... **$175**

Rose bowl, spherical with wide flat mouth, Killarney green bowl with gold Melrose etching, on four applied clear pointed feet, 6-1/4" h. ....... **$250**

# Westmoreland

In 1890 Westmoreland opened in Grapeville, Pennsylvania, and as early as the 1920s was producing colorwares in great variety. Cutting and decorations were many and are generally under appreciated and undervalued. Westmoreland was a leading producer of milk glass in "the antique style." The company closed in 1984 but some of their molds continued in use by others.

Basket, English Hobnail pattern, high arched handle, clear, 5" w. ........................................ **$24**

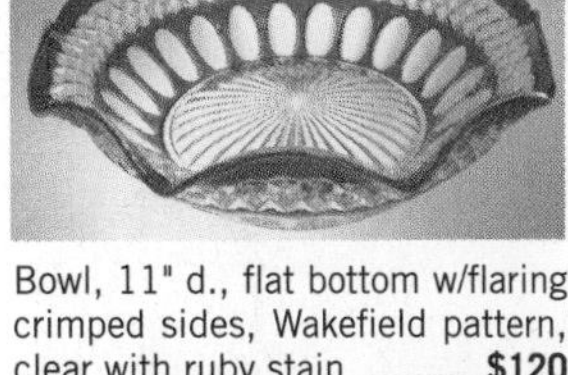

Bowl, 11" d., flat bottom w/flaring crimped sides, Wakefield pattern, clear with ruby stain ......... **$120**

Bowl, 9-1/2" dia., scalloped rim, American Hobnail pattern, blue opalescent ......................... **$50**

Cheese compote, Marguerite pattern, No. 700, pink, 4-1/2" d., 2-3/4" h. ............................ **$18**

◀Basket, English Hobnail pattern, fan-shaped body with high arched handle, milk glass, 5" w., 10" h.................................................. **$30**

Compote, hexagonal foot and tall figural dolphin stem supporting a wide shallow round bowl, milk glass with hand-painted Charlton Leaf decoration, 7" d., 7-3/4" h....................................................... **$85**

Compote, sweetmeat-type with ball stem, Della Robbia pattern, clear with ruby stain, 8" h. ........... **$125**

Compote, two-handled, tall stem, Colonial pattern, blue mist, 5-1/4" w., 6" h. ................................ **$22**

Compote, oval, pressed cut glass-style design, Pattern No. 240, clear, 6-1/2" l., 4-1/4" h. ............. **$25**

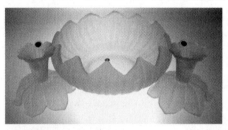

Lamp, table model, hexagonal foot and figural dolphin stem supporting a large flaring cylindrical paneled font, made to resemble an antique lamp, pink, 9-1/4" h............. **$200**

Console set: 9" dia. cupped petal-form bowl and pair of one-light 4" petal-form candleholders, Lotus pattern, original labels, pink satin, the set ........ **$95**

Tumbler, iced tea, English Hobnail patt., square foot, clear, 11 oz. .......................................... **$14**

Vase, Jack-in-the-pulpit style, Corinth pattern, amethyst carnival, 8-1/4" h......................... **$49**

Plate, openwork Forget-Me-Not pattern, black decorated in white enamel with scene of running deer, modern version of an early design, 8" dia....................... **$40**

Compote, open stem, Lotus pattern, flame red, 5-1/2" d., 3-1/2" h. .................................. **$30**

Compote, ball stem, spray-cased black, amber stain, cut to clear, 7-1/2" h., 8" dia. .............**$150**

Compote, Mother of Pearl Dolphin & Shell line, shell-shaped bowl with dolphin base, milk white, mother of pearl finish, 8" h. **$85**

Mayonnaise dish and underplate, Paneled Grape pattern, milk white,3-1/2" d., 2 pcs. ...... **$23**

Nappy, round, handled, Paneled Grape pattern, milk white, 5" d. ...................................... **$17**

Planter, Paneled Grape pattern, square, milk white, 4-1/2" w.**$40**

Puff box, covered, Paneled Grape pattern, milk white, 4-1/2" d.**$32**

Sweetmeat, covered, Old Quilt pattern, high-footed, milk white, 6-1/2" h. .......................... **$35**

Tumbler, Beaded Edge pattern, No. 64-2 fruit decoration, milk white ...................................... **$19**

# Spotlight: Glasshouse Whimsies

Every once in a while, you come across a piece of art glass that you just know must be one of a kind. Perhaps it's because of the design or the eclectic colors of the glass, but you just get this feeling that there's no other piece like it. If this is the impression you get, you may have just found yourself a glasshouse whimsy.

From witch balls to top hats, gavels to cigarette holders, whimsies are representations of glass artisans' skills and imaginations in solid form.

Glasshouse whimsies – whether they are entirely free-form or created from production glass pieces – are items made by glassworkers to show off their skills. Whimsies, often given the misnomers "end-of-day" or "lunch-hour" pieces, are known as "friggers" in England. They are non-production pieces; other than the use of factory glass, the whimsies have no connection to the glass factory.

Dale Murschell is a life-long collector who has written many articles and books on aspects of glass collecting, including the 1989 publication "Glasshouse Whimsies: An Enhanced Reference," co-written with Joyce Blake. Murschell says these one-of-a-kind glass items had to be made on the glassblowers' own time; they didn't have the leisure to amuse themselves with their creations during working hours. Pay scales were equated to the volume of the product or numbers of piecework.

At some glass houses, workers took a "turn," meaning they worked a specified length of time, possibly four hours. During that "turn," the shop had to produce a "move," which equaled a certain number of items. The number of items per "move" was determined through negotiations between the union and the company. Artisans working together enabled a shop to produce a "move" in a "turn," leaving no time for personal creations other than during a lunch break or at the end of the day.

Glass working was difficult because of the heat, the smoky, dusty air, and the pressure to complete a "move" to make the maximum wage. "The opportunity to make a useful item for home or just an attractive item for pleasure was one of the few benefits that had the owner's consent," says Murschell. Even though the glass workers had unions, they were unable to get many benefits because the glasshouse owners would stop production and close before giving in to union demands; this happened at Sandwich Glass Works of Sandwich, Masschusetts, in 1888.

Murschell notes one problem glassworkers faced when they made a whimsy was preventing someone else from taking it. The item had to cool overnight in the lehr, an oven that let the glass anneal slowly so as to prevent breakage; whoever was first to get to work the next morning had the opportunity to grab the whimsy if he was so inclined.

Ellen Schroy, author of *Warman's Depression Glass Identification and Price Guide*, says, "Glasshouse whimsies are wonderful creations: Whimsical because they often were made using the imagination of the glass blower, with materials and colors readily at hand, or so we believe."

Whimsies fuel glass enthusiasts' imaginations. "Perhaps if we had a time machine, we could travel back in time and watch how long elegant

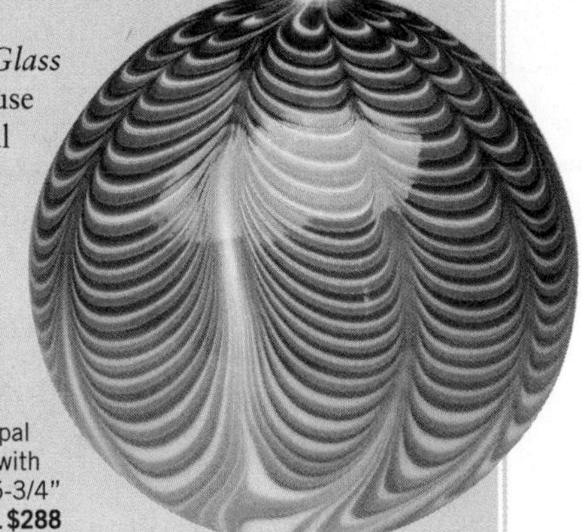

Undamaged free-blown Marbrie Loop decorated witch ball, opal with 10 groups of red and green loopings, rough pontil mark with half-inch opening, United States or Europe, 1860-1900; 5-3/4" dia. .......... **$288**
*Jeffrey S. Evans & Associates*

glass canes with stripes and swirls were blown so that they could be used in parades," Schroy continues. "Or watch as witch balls were gathered and again swirled. We could watch as the glassblowers crimped and prodded the molten gather into what they wished it to be."

In addition to witch balls, other desirable forms include chains, sock darners, bells, banks, powder horns, pipes, rolling pins, and many more items.

"Additional novelties surface each year, including witch wands, gavels, screwdrivers, pistols, and swords," Murschell says. "The pieces are unmarked, making creator identification difficult – if not impossible." The best lead to the maker would be a documentation of provenance; unfortunately, such a record is unlikely. The whimsies' color is also a clue to where the pieces may have been made.

Some whimsies are made of clear or aqua glass. Others may be of a single color like amber or cobalt blue, while others may have many colors. "Some glasshouse whimsies also incorporate bits of color called spatter; think of it as raindrops of color on a pretty blue or olive green ground," says Schroy.

According to Murschell, the whimsies of aqua color were probably made at a window glass or bottle factory. "Bottle glass was usually aqua due to the natural iron in the sand that discolored the glass," he explains. "Window glass may have been chemically treated to produce a somewhat clearer glass."

Green, amber, cobalt blue, or ruby red glass were seldom available to bottle and window glass workers. The more colorful whimsy items may have originated in larger glassworks that had several colors available.

The 19th century was the heyday for glasshouse whimsies, and it extended into the 20th century until machines finally took over production at all of the glass factories; when the machines took over, the glass was no longer accessible to the glass blowers, ending the practice.

"All glasshouse whimsies are one-of-a-kind and therefore should be judged on their own individual quality and beauty and not necessarily on their age," Murschell says. "This is especially important with glass because it is difficult to judge its age."

According to American glass specialist Jeffrey S. Evans, board member of the Museum of American Glass in West Virginia and principle of Jeffrey S. Evans & Associates, "Pieces made from known objects can be dated by the time period of the object. Blown off-hand pieces are much more difficult to assign a date. One has to be familiar with the

Free-blown Marbrie Loop decorated bellows whimsy, opal with four groups of red and blue swirled loopings, flattened chestnut form with elongated neck and tooled mouth, applied rings, rigaree straps and handles, disk under base with small rough pontil mark, 1850-1890, 11" h., 4-1/2" w. .................... **$207**
*Jeffrey S. Evans & Associates*

Three blown turtle-form whimsy paperweights, deep amber, medium green, and blue green, each with pulled and pinched head, tail and four feet, New York State and other areas, 1860-1920, 2" to 2-1/4" h., 4-3/4" to 6-1/4" l. ..................................... **$374**
*Jeffrey S. Evans & Associates*

techniques employed to make the piece and the type of glass being used. Whimsies have been made as long as there have been glassmakers."

However, there are some types of whimsies still being made today. "In today's market pretty much any seemingly whimsical object it referred to as a whimsy," says Evans.

Reproduction efforts are usually thick and clumsy. Modern art glass houses (like Murano) attempting to recreate the look of the 19th and early 20th century whimsies are usually marked. "One should have a good general knowledge of glass in order to avoid modern production pieces," Evans advises. "While these are not a big problem at the moment, this is the type of thing that can begin coming out of China at any time."

When asked how to tell a whimsy from a production piece, Evans replied, "True whimsies are objects that are produced by manipulating previously established utilitarian forms into a totally different article. Whimsies can still serve a useful purpose, or they can be strictly decorative in nature.

"Many times pieces, such as powder-horn form bottles, were actual production pieces that were being sold as novelty containers. When these were made from colorful decorated glass and raised on a standard or foot, they were often sold as mantle decorations. So technically these objects are not whimsies – although they are certainly whimsical."

Many whimsies are bought and sold at antique bottle shows, with some appearing at glass shows and auctions. Evans, whose Mount Crawford, Virginia, firm sells approximately 50 to 100 whimsies per year through its glass and lighting sales, says bottles and/or fruit jars made into hats or other forms see the most interest at auction. The most extraordinary piece he has sold is a pressed Greentown Holly Amber pattern shelf support or hat stand made by joining two compote bases top-to-top. The 9-inch-high piece brought a remarkable $8,250 (including 10 percent buyer's premium) in a Jan. 26-27, 2007 glass auction.

"A general collector should collect whimsies for fun and not investment," Evans advises. And, just like any other collectible venture, the buyer needs to be educated on the subject. He says most whimsies are fairly inexpensive and trade for less than $200. But there are some extreme examples. "Whimsies that were produced from American historical flasks would probably fetch in excess of $100,000 if one ever came on the market," he says.

***Karen Knapstein, Antique Trader***

Free-blown Marbrie Loop decorated rolling pin, pale green with three groups of ruby loopings, two pinched knob handles, one with opening and the other with a rough pontil mark, possibly South Jersey, 1850-1880, 14-1/2" l., 2" dia.............. **$219**
*Jeffrey S. Evans & Associates*

Pattern-molded horn whimsy, deep cobalt blue lead glass, displaying 12 ribs tightly swirled to the right, tooled stem and mouth, probably 19th c., 8-1/2" l., 2-5/8" dia. rim. ......................... **$288**
*Jeffrey S. Evans & Associates*

# Hallmark Keepsake Ornaments

For nearly 40 years, Hallmark Keepsake Ornaments—produced by Hallmark Cards Inc. of Kansas City, Missouri—have transformed Christmas trees everywhere into 3-D scrapbooks of memories that capture and preserve times, events, and special occasions. When the first 18 ornaments were introduced in 1973, Christmas tree decorations went from simple colored glass balls to creative and fun designs. Soon, Americans started a new tradition that changed the way they viewed ornaments. No longer were ornaments just pretty decorations for the tree. Suddenly they became unique, year-dated and available only for a limited time, making them an instant hit with collectors.

In 1973 Hallmark issued a handful of ornaments, six in ball shape and 12 made of yarn. Today the Keepsake line releases more than 200 new ornaments each year. Collectors eagerly anticipate Hallmark's Keepsake Ornament Premiere every July, where they have their first opportunity to purchase that year's new ornaments. In October Hallmark holds its Keepsake Ornament Debut, offering even more new releases. Each year Hallmark also publishes a full-color catalog, called the Dream Book, showcasing the new ornaments.

A total of more than 6,000 Hallmark ornaments have been produced since the company began issuing them in 1973, and more than 11 million U.S. households collect them.

For more information, see *Hallmark Keepsake Ornaments: Warman's Companion* by Mary Sieber.

## 1970S

Angel, 1974......................... **$29**

Angel, 1978......................... **$70**

| Ornament Title | Series | Year | Price | Value |
|---|---|---|---|---|
| 25th Christmas Together 350QX269-3 | Commemoratives | 1978 | $4 | $15 |
| Angel 125XHD78-5 | Yarn Ornaments | 1973 | $1 | $29 |
| Angel 150QX103-1 | Yarn Ornaments | 1974 | $2 | $29 |
| Angel 175QX220-2 | Cloth Doll Ornaments | 1977 | $2 | $45 |
| Angel 250QX110-1 | General Line | 1974 | $2 | $80 |
| Angel 300QX176-1 | Tree Treats | 1976 | $3 | $85 |
| Angel 350QX354-3 | Colors Of Christmas | 1978 | $4 | $50 |
| Angel 400QX139-6 | Handcrafted Ornaments | 1978 | $4 | $70 |
| Angel 450QX171-1 | Twirl-Abouts | 1976 | $4 | $100 |
| Angel 500QX182-2 | Nostalgia | 1977 | $5 | $62 |
| Angel 600QX172-2 | Yesteryears | 1977 | $6 | $70 |
| Angel Delight 300QX130-7 | Little Trimmers | 1979 | $3 | $72 |
| Angel Music 200QX343-9 | Sewn Trimmers | 1979 | $2 | $19 |
| Angel Tree Topper 900HD230-2 | Tree Topper | 1977 | $9 | $425 |
| Angels 800QX150-3 | Handcrafted Ornaments | 1978 | $8 | $200 |
| Animal Home 600QX149-6 | Handcrafted Ornaments | 1978 | $6 | $160 |
| Antique Car 500QX180-2 | Nostalgia | 1977 | $5 | $40 |
| Antique Toys Carousel 1st Ed. 600QX146-3 | Carousel Series | 1978 | $6 | $175 |
| Baby's First Christmas 250QX211-1 | General Line | 1976 | $2 | $129 |
| Baby's First Christmas 350QX131-5 | General Line | 1977 | $4 | $85 |
| Baby's First Christmas 350QX200-3 | Commemoratives | 1978 | $4 | $31 |
| Baby's First Christmas 350QX208-7 | Commemoratives | 1979 | $4 | $28 |
| Baby's First Christmas 800QX154-7 | Commemoratives | 1979 | $8 | $100 |
| Behold The Star 350QX255-9 | Decorative Ball Ornaments | 1979 | $4 | $30 |
| Bell 350QX154-2 | Christmas Expressions Collection | 1977 | $4 | $40 |
| Bell 350QX200-2 | Colors Of Christmas | 1977 | $4 | $40 |
| Bellringer 600QX192-2 | Twirl-Abouts | 1977 | $6 | $62 |
| Bellswinger 1st Ed. QX147-9 | Bellringer Series | 1979 | $10 | $170 |
| Betsey Clark (2) 350QX167-1 | General Line | 1975 | $4 | $38 |
| Betsey Clark (3) 450QX218-1 | General Line | 1976 | $4 | $60 |

| Ornament Title | Series | Year | Price | Value |
|---|---|---|---|---|
| Betsey Clark (4) 450QX168-1 | General Line | 1975 | $4 | $35 |
| Betsey Clark 1st Ed. 250XHD110-2 | Betsey Clark | 1973 | $3 | $100 |
| Betsey Clark 250QX157-1 | Adorable Adornments | 1975 | $2 | $230 |
| Betsey Clark 250QX163-1 | General Line | 1975 | $2 | $20 |
| Betsey Clark 250QX210-1 | General Line | 1976 | $2 | $45 |
| Betsey Clark 250XHD100-2 | General Line | 1973 | $2 | $45 |
| Betsey Clark 2nd Ed. 250QX108-1 | Betsey Clark | 1974 | $3 | $45 |
| Betsey Clark 3rd Ed. 300QX133-1 | Betsey Clark | 1975 | $3 | $40 |
| Betsey Clark 4th Ed. 300QX195-1 | Betsey Clark | 1976 | $3 | $60 |
| Betsey Clark 5th Ed. 350QX264-2 | Betsey Clark | 1977 | $4 | $350 |
| Betsey Clark 6th Ed. 350QX201-6 | Betsey Clark | 1978 | $4 | $40 |
| Betsey Clark 7th Ed. 350QX201-9 | Betsey Clark | 1979 | $4 | $19 |
| Bicentennial '76 Commemorative QX203-1 | Bicentennial Commemoratives | 1976 | $2 | $20 |
| Bicentennial Charmers 300QX198-1 | Bicentennial Commemoratives | 1976 | $3 | $50 |
| Black Angel 350QX207-9 | Decorative Ball Ornaments | 1979 | $4 | $25 |
| Blue Girl 125XHD85-2 | Yarn Ornaments | 1973 | $1 | $25 |
| Boy Caroler 125XHD83-2 | Yarn Ornaments | 1973 | $1 | $19 |
| Buttons & Bo (2) 350QX113-1 | General Line | 1974 | $4 | $50 |
| Buttons & Bo (4) 500QX139-1 | General Line | 1975 | $5 | $38 |
| Calico Mouse 450QX137-6 | Handcrafted Ornaments | 1978 | $4 | $50 |
| Candle 350QX203-5 | Colors Of Christmas | 1977 | $4 | $60 |
| Candle 350QX357-6 | Colors Of Christmas | 1978 | $4 | $85 |
| Cardinals 225QX205-1 | Decorative Ball Ornaments | 1976 | $2 | $30 |
| Caroler 175QX126-1 | Yarn Ornaments | 1976 | $2 | $22 |
| Charmers (2) 350QX215-1 | General Line | 1976 | $4 | $25 |
| Charmers 250QX109-1 | General Line | 1974 | $2 | $20 |
| Charmers 300QX135-1 | General Line | 1975 | $3 | $50 |
| Charmers 350QX153-5 | General Line | 1977 | $4 | $60 |
| Chickadees 225QX204-1 | Decorative Ball Ornaments | 1976 | $2 | $40 |
| Choir Boy 125XHD80-5 | Yarn Ornaments | 1973 | $1 | $27 |
| Christmas Angel 350QX300-7 | Holiday Highlights | 1979 | $4 | $100 |
| Christmas Carousel 2nd Ed. 650QX146-7 | Carousel Series | 1979 | $6 | $115 |
| Christmas Cheer 350QX303-9 | Holiday Highlights | 1979 | $4 | $40 |
| Christmas Chickadees 350QX204-7 | Decorative Ball Ornaments | 1979 | $4 | $32 |
| Christmas Collage 350QX257-9 | Decorative Ball Ornaments | 1979 | $4 | $40 |
| Christmas Eve Surprise 650QX157-9 | Handcrafted Ornaments | 1979 | $6 | $70 |
| Christmas Heart 650QX140-7 | Handcrafted Ornaments | 1979 | $6 | $45 |
| Christmas Is For Children 500QX135-9 | Handcrafted Ornaments | 1979 | $5 | $45 |
| Christmas Is Love 250XHD106-2 | General Line | 1973 | $2 | $75 |
| Christmas Mouse 350QX134-2 | Decorative Ball Ornaments | 1977 | $4 | $60 |
| Christmas Star Tree Topper QX702-3 | Tree Topper | 1978 | $8 | $40 |
| Christmas Traditions 350QX253-9 | Decorative Ball Ornaments | 1979 | $4 | $40 |
| Christmas Treat 500QX134-7 | Handcrafted Ornaments | 1979 | $5 | $42 |
| Christmas Tree 350QX302-7 | Holiday Highlights | 1979 | $4 | $50 |
| Colonial Children (2) 400QX208-1 | Bicentennial Commemoratives | 1976 | $4 | $10 |
| Currier & Ives (2) 250QX164-1 | Currier & Ives | 1975 | $2 | $40 |
| Currier & Ives (2) 350QX112-1 | Currier & Ives | 1974 | $4 | $38 |
| Currier & Ives (2) 400QX137-1 | Currier & Ives | 1975 | $4 | $40 |
| Currier & Ives 250QX209-1 | Currier & Ives | 1976 | $2 | $40 |
| Currier & Ives 300QX197-1 | Currier & Ives | 1976 | $3 | $50 |
| Currier & Ives 350QX130-2 | Currier & Ives | 1977 | $4 | $50 |
| Della Robia Wreath 450QX193-5 | Twirl-Abouts | 1977 | $4 | $42 |
| Desert 250QX159-5 | Beauty Of America Collection | 1977 | $2 | $42 |
| Disney (2) 400QX137-5 | General Line | 1977 | $4 | $55 |
| Disney 350QX133-5 | General Line | 1977 | $4 | $70 |
| Disney 350QX207-6 | General Line | 1978 | $4 | $42 |
| Dove 350QX310-3 | Holiday Highlights | 1978 | $4 | $50 |
| Dove 450QX190-3 | Handcrafted Ornaments | 1978 | $4 | $45 |

Angel, 1978, from the Colors of Christmas series .................. **$50**

Angel Delight, 1979, from the Little Trimmers series............ **$72**

The original Baby's First Christmas ornament, 1976 .......... **$129**

Baby's 1st Christmas, 1979 .. **$28**

Bellringer, 1977, from the Twirl-Abouts series........................**$62**

Betsey Clark, 1973...............**$45**
Christmas 1973, 1st in the Betsey Clark series........................**$100**

Betsey Clark, 1978, 6th in the Betsey Clark series................**$40**

Bicentennial '76 Commemorative, 1976..................................**$20**

Candle, 1978, from the Colors of Christmas series...................**$85**

Christmas Carousel, 1979, 2nd in the Carousel series..............**$115**

| Ornament Title | Series | Year | Price | Value |
|---|---|---|---|---|
| Downhill Run, The 650QX145-9 | Handcrafted Ornaments | 1979 | $6 | $120 |
| Drummer Boy 175QX123-1 | Yarn Ornaments | 1975 | $2 | $13 |
| Drummer Boy 175QX123-1 | Yarn Ornaments | 1976 | $2 | $26 |
| Drummer Boy 250QX136-3 | Little Trimmers | 1978 | $2 | $78 |
| Drummer Boy 250QX161-1 | Adorable Adornments | 1975 | $2 | $175 |
| Drummer Boy 350QX130-1 | Nostalgia | 1975 | $4 | $168 |
| Drummer Boy 350QX252-3 | Decorative Ball Ornaments | 1978 | $4 | $42 |
| Drummer Boy 350QX312-2 | Holiday Highlights | 1977 | $4 | $62 |
| Drummer Boy 400QX130-1 | Nostalgia | 1976 | $4 | $83 |
| Drummer Boy 500QX184-1 | Yesteryears | 1976 | $5 | $85 |
| Drummer Boy, The 800QX143-9 | Handcrafted Ornaments | 1979 | $8 | $75 |
| Elf 125XHD79-2 | Yarn Ornaments | 1973 | $1 | $26 |
| Elf 150QX101-1 | Yarn Ornaments | 1974 | $2 | $26 |
| Elves 250XHD103-5 | General Line | 1973 | $2 | $40 |
| First Christmas Together 350QX132-2 | Commemoratives | 1977 | $4 | $48 |
| First Christmas Together 350QX218-3 | Commemoratives | 1978 | $4 | $48 |
| For Your New Home 350QX217-6 | Commemoratives | 1978 | $4 | $25 |
| For Your New Home 350QX263-5 | Commemoratives | 1977 | $4 | $35 |
| Friendship 350QX203-9 | Commemoratives | 1979 | $4 | $25 |
| Granddaughter 350QX208-2 | Commemoratives | 1977 | $4 | $19 |
| Granddaughter 350QX211-9 | Commemoratives | 1979 | $4 | $38 |
| Granddaughter 350QX216-3 | Commemoratives | 1978 | $4 | $38 |
| Grandma Moses 350QX150-2 | General Line | 1977 | $4 | $34 |
| Grandmother 350QX252-7 | Commemoratives | 1979 | $4 | $18 |
| Grandmother 350QX260-2 | Commemoratives | 1977 | $4 | $50 |
| Grandmother 350QX267-6 | Commemoratives | 1978 | $4 | $18 |
| Grandson 350QX209-5 | Commemoratives | 1977 | $4 | $35 |
| Grandson 350QX210-7 | Commemoratives | 1979 | $4 | $40 |
| Grandson 350QX215-6 | Commemoratives | 1978 | $4 | $40 |
| Green Boy 200QX123-1 | Yarn Ornaments | 1978 | $2 | $28 |
| Green Girl 125XHD84-5 | Yarn Ornaments | 1973 | $1 | $25 |
| Green Girl 200QX126-1 | Yarn Ornaments | 1978 | $2 | $28 |
| Hallmark's Antique Card Coll. 350QX220-3 | Decorative Ball Ornaments | 1978 | $4 | $44 |
| Happy Holidays Kissing Balls QX225-1 | General Line | 1976 | $5 | $225 |
| Happy The Snowman (2) QX216-1 | General Line | 1976 | $4 | $50 |
| Heavenly Minstrel Tabletop QHD 921-9 | Table Decor | 1978 | $35 | $145 |
| Holiday Memories Kissing Ball QHD 900-3 | General Line | 1978 | $5 | $120 |
| Holiday Scrimshaw 400QX152-7 | Handcrafted Ornaments | 1979 | $4 | $135 |
| Holiday Wreath 350QX353-9 | Colors Of Christmas | 1979 | $4 | $42 |

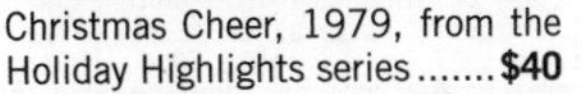

Christmas Cheer, 1979, from the Holiday Highlights series....... **$40**

Christmas Heart, 1979 ......... **$45**

Christmas is for Children, 1979 ........................................ **$45**

| Ornament Title | Series | Year | Price | Value |
|---|---|---|---|---|
| Holly & Poinsettia Ball 600QX147-6 | Handcrafted Ornaments | 1978 | $6 | $60 |
| Holly & Poinsettia Table Decor OHD320-2 | Table Decor | 1977 | $8 | $132 |
| House 600QX170-2 | Yesteryears | 1977 | $6 | $70 |
| Ice Hockey Holiday 1st Ed. 800QX141-9 | Snoopy & Friends | 1979 | $8 | $160 |
| Jack-In-The-Box 600QX171-5 | Yesteryears | 1977 | $6 | $67 |
| Joan Walsh Anglund 350QX205-9 | General Line | 1979 | $4 | $35 |
| Joan Walsh Anglund 350QX221-6 | General Line | 1978 | $4 | $40 |
| Joy 350QX132-1 | Nostalgia | 1975 | $4 | $143 |
| Joy 350QX201-5 | Colors Of Christmas | 1977 | $4 | $50 |
| Joy 350QX254-3 | Decorative Ball Ornaments | 1978 | $4 | $44 |
| Joy 350QX310-2 | Holiday Highlights | 1977 | $4 | $50 |
| Joy 450QX138-3 | Handcrafted Ornaments | 1978 | $4 | $44 |
| Light Of Christmas, The 350QX256-7 | Decorative Ball Ornaments | 1979 | $4 | $30 |
| Little Girl 125XHD82-5 | Yarn Ornaments | 1973 | $1 | $25 |
| Little Girl 175QX126-1 | Yarn Ornaments | 1975 | $2 | $22 |
| Little Miracles (4) 450QX115-1 | General Line | 1974 | $4 | $60 |
| Little Miracles (4) 500QX140-1 | General Line | 1975 | $5 | $40 |
| Little Trimmer Collection QX132-3 | General Line | 1978 | $9 | $320 |
| Little Trimmer Set QX159-9 | General Line | 1979 | $9 | $340 |
| Locomotive (Dated) 350QX127-1 | Nostalgia | 1975 | $4 | $113 |
| Locomotive 350QX356-3 | Colors Of Christmas | 1978 | $4 | $60 |
| Locomotive 400QX222-1 | Nostalgia | 1976 | $4 | $110 |
| Love 350QX258-7 | Commemoratives | 1979 | $4 | $38 |
| Love 350QX262-2 | Commemoratives | 1977 | $4 | $27 |
| Love 350QX268-3 | Commemoratives | 1978 | $4 | $60 |
| Love 350QX304-7 | Holiday Highlights | 1979 | $4 | $55 |
| Mandolin 350QX157-5 | Christmas Expressions Collection | 1977 | $4 | $40 |
| Manger Scene 250XHD102-2 | General Line | 1973 | $2 | $90 |
| Marty Links (2) 400QX207-1 | General Line | 1976 | $4 | $55 |
| Marty Links 300QX136-1 | General Line | 1975 | $3 | $50 |
| Mary Hamilton 350QX254-7 | General Line | 1979 | $4 | $28 |
| Matchless Christmas 400QX132-7 | Little Trimmers | 1979 | $4 | $39 |
| Merry Christmas (Santa) 350QX202-3 | Decorative Ball Ornaments | 1978 | $4 | $20 |
| Merry Christmas 350QX355-6 | Colors Of Christmas | 1978 | $4 | $55 |
| Merry Santa 200QX342-7 | Sewn Trimmers | 1979 | $2 | $8 |
| Mother 350QX251-9 | Commemoratives | 1979 | $4 | $18 |
| Mother 350QX261-5 | Commemoratives | 1977 | $4 | $35 |
| Mother 350QX266-3 | Commemoratives | 1978 | $4 | $40 |
| Mountains 250QX158-2 | Beauty Of America Collection | 1977 | $2 | $35 |
| Mr. & Mrs. Snowman Kissing Ball QX225-2 | General Line | 1977 | $5 | $100 |
| Mr. Claus 200QX340-3 | Yarn Ornaments | 1978 | $2 | $23 |
| Mr. Santa 125XHD74-5 | Yarn Ornaments | 1973 | $1 | $25 |
| Mr. Snowman 125XHD76-5 | Yarn Ornaments | 1973 | $1 | $24 |

Christmas is Love, 1973 ....... **$75**

Christmas Tree, 1979, from the Holiday Highlights series....... **$50**

Drummer Boy, 1976, from the Yesteryears series.................. **$85**

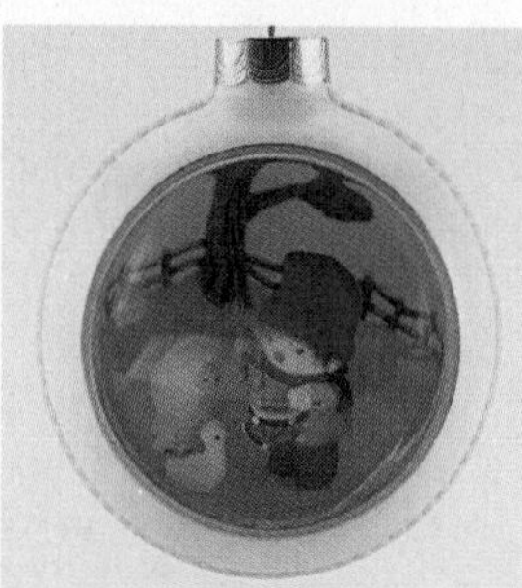
The Drummer Boy, 1979 ....... **$75**

Elves, 1973 ......................... **$40**

Granddaughter, 1978........... **$38**

Grandson, 1979.................. **$40**

Joy, 1977, from the Holiday Highlights series.......................... **$50**

| Ornament Title | Series | Year | Price | Value |
|---|---|---|---|---|
| Mrs. Claus 200QX125-1 | Yarn Ornaments | 1978 | $2 | $22 |
| Mrs. Santa 125XHD75-2 | Yarn Ornaments | 1973 | $1 | $22 |
| Mrs. Santa 150QX100-1 | Yarn Ornaments | 1974 | $2 | $22 |
| Mrs. Santa 175QX125-1 | Yarn Ornaments | 1975 | $2 | $19 |
| Mrs. Santa 175QX125-1 | Yarn Ornaments | 1976 | $2 | $19 |
| Mrs. Santa 250QX156-1 | Adorable Adornments | 1975 | $2 | $125 |
| Mrs. Snowman 125XHD77-2 | Yarn Ornaments | 1973 | $1 | $24 |
| Nativity 350QX253-6 | Decorative Ball Ornaments | 1978 | $4 | $125 |
| Nativity 350QX309-6 | Holiday Highlights | 1978 | $4 | $95 |
| Nativity 500QX181-5 | Nostalgia | 1977 | $5 | $97 |
| New Home 350QX212-7 | Commemoratives | 1979 | $4 | $24 |
| Night Before Christmas 350QX214-7 | Decorative Ball Ornaments | 1979 | $4 | $40 |
| Norman Rockwell 250QX106-1 | General Line | 1974 | $2 | $45 |
| Norman Rockwell 250QX111-1 | General Line | 1974 | $2 | $84 |
| Norman Rockwell 250QX166-1 | General Line | 1975 | $2 | $62 |
| Norman Rockwell 300QX134-1 | General Line | 1975 | $3 | $20 |
| Norman Rockwell 300QX196-1 | General Line | 1976 | $3 | $78 |
| Norman Rockwell 350QX151-5 | General Line | 1977 | $4 | $65 |
| Old Fashion Customs Kissing Ball QX225-5 | General Line | 1977 | $5 | $147 |
| Ornaments 350QX155-5 | Christmas Expressions Collection | 1977 | $4 | $45 |
| Our First Christmas Together 350QX209-9 | Commemoratives | 1979 | $4 | $68 |
| Our Twenty-Fifth Anniversary 350QX250-7 | Commemoratives | 1979 | $4 | $14 |
| Outdoor Fun 800QX150-7 | Handcrafted Ornaments | 1979 | $8 | $120 |
| Panorama Ball 600QX145-6 | Handcrafted Ornaments | 1978 | $6 | $140 |
| Partridge 450QX174-1 | Twirl-Abouts | 1976 | $4 | $100 |
| Partridge 500QX183-1 | Yesteryears | 1976 | $5 | $62 |
| Partridge In A Pear Tree 350QX351-9 | Colors Of Christmas | 1979 | $4 | $40 |
| Peace On Earth (Dated) 350QX131-1 | Nostalgia | 1975 | $4 | $93 |
| Peace On Earth 350QX311-5 | Holiday Highlights | 1977 | $4 | $60 |
| Peace On Earth 400QX223-1 | Nostalgia | 1976 | $4 | $90 |
| Peanuts (2) 400QX163-5 | Peanuts Collection | 1977 | $4 | $90 |
| Peanuts 250QX162-2 | Peanuts Collection | 1977 | $2 | $80 |
| Peanuts 250QX203-6 | Peanuts Collection | 1978 | $2 | $60 |
| Peanuts 250QX204-3 | Peanuts Collection | 1978 | $2 | $70 |
| Peanuts 350QX135-5 | Peanuts Collection | 1977 | $4 | $80 |
| Peanuts 350QX205-6 | Peanuts Collection | 1978 | $4 | $70 |
| Peanuts 350QX206-3 | Peanuts Collection | 1978 | $4 | $60 |
| Peanuts: Time To Trim 350QX202-7 | General Line | 1979 | $4 | $45 |
| Praying Angel 250QX134-3 | Little Trimmers | 1978 | $2 | $40 |
| Quail, The- 350QX251-6 | Decorative Ball Ornaments | 1978 | $4 | $40 |
| Rabbit 250QX139-5 | Decorative Ball Ornaments | 1977 | $2 | $90 |
| Raggedy Andy 175QX122-1 | Yarn Ornaments | 1975 | $2 | $40 |
| Raggedy Andy 175QX122-1 | Yarn Ornaments | 1976 | $2 | $40 |
| Raggedy Andy 250QX160-1 | Adorable Adornments | 1975 | $2 | $275 |
| Raggedy Ann & Raggedy Andy 400QX138-1 | General Line | 1975 | $4 | $65 |
| Raggedy Ann & Raggedy Andy 450QX114-1 | General Line | 1974 | $4 | $90 |
| Raggedy Ann 175QX121-1 | Yarn Ornaments | 1976 | $2 | $40 |
| Raggedy Ann 175QX121-1 | Yarn Ornaments | 1975 | $2 | $40 |
| Raggedy Ann 250QX159-1 | Adorable Adornments | 1975 | $2 | $160 |
| Raggedy Ann 250QX165-1 | General Line | 1975 | $2 | $50 |
| Raggedy Ann 250QX212-1 | General Line | 1976 | $2 | $40 |
| Ready For Christmas 650QX133-9 | Handcrafted Ornaments | 1979 | $6 | $50 |
| Red Cardinal 450QX144-3 | Handcrafted Ornaments | 1978 | $4 | $150 |
| Reindeer 300QX178-1 | Tree Treats | 1976 | $3 | $55 |
| Reindeer 600QX173-5 | Yesteryears | 1977 | $6 | $71 |
| Reindeer Chimes 450QX320-3 | Holiday Chimes | 1978 | $4 | $35 |
| Reindeer Chimes 450QX320-3 | Holiday Chimes | 1979 | $4 | $35 |

| Ornament Title | Series | Year | Price | Value |
|---|---|---|---|---|
| Rocking Horse 350QX128-1 | General Line | 1975 | $4 | $65 |
| Rocking Horse 400QX128-1 | General Line | 1976 | $4 | $170 |
| Rocking Horse 600QX148-3 | General Line | 1978 | $6 | $90 |
| Rocking Horse, The 200QX340-7 | General Line | 1979 | $2 | $20 |
| Rudolph & Santa 250QX213-1 | General Line | 1976 | $2 | $90 |
| Santa & Sleigh 350QX129-1 | Nostalgia | 1975 | $4 | $150 |
| Santa 150QX105-1 | Yarn Ornaments | 1974 | $2 | $18 |
| Santa 175QX124-1 | Yarn Ornaments | 1975 | $2 | $25 |
| Santa 175QX124-1 | Yarn Ornaments | 1976 | $2 | $24 |
| Santa 175QX221-5 | Cloth Doll Ornaments | 1977 | $2 | $35 |
| Santa 250QX135-6 | Little Trimmers | 1978 | $2 | $28 |
| Santa 250QX155-1 | Adorable Adornments | 1975 | $2 | $100 |
| Santa 300QX135-6 | Little Trimmers | 1979 | $3 | $28 |
| Santa 300QX177-1 | Tree Treats | 1976 | $3 | $100 |
| Santa 350QX307-6 | Holiday Highlights | 1978 | $4 | $80 |
| Santa 450QX172-1 | Twirl-Abouts | 1976 | $4 | $43 |
| Santa 500QX182-1 | Yesteryears | 1976 | $5 | $105 |
| Santa With Elves 250XHD101-5 | General Line | 1973 | $2 | $80 |
| Santa's Here 500QX138-7 | Handcrafted Ornaments | 1979 | $5 | $30 |
| Santa's Motorcar 1st Ed. 900QX155-9 | Here Comes Santa | 1979 | $9 | $294 |
| Schneeberg Bell 800QX152-3 | Handcrafted Ornaments | 1978 | $8 | $135 |
| Seashore 250QX160-2 | Beauty Of America Collection | 1977 | $2 | $50 |
| Shepherd 300QX175-1 | Tree Treats | 1976 | $3 | $70 |
| Skating Raccoon 600QX142-3 | Handcrafted Ornaments | 1978 | $6 | $35 |
| Skating Raccoon 650QX142-3 | Handcrafted Ornaments | 1979 | $6 | $35 |
| Skating Snowman, The 500QX139-9 | Handcrafted Ornaments | 1979 | $5 | $30 |
| Snowflake 350QX301-9 | Holiday Highlights | 1979 | $4 | $40 |
| Snowflake 350QX308-3 | Holiday Highlights | 1978 | $4 | $65 |
| Snowflake Collection (4) 500QX210-2 | Metal Ornaments | 1977 | $5 | $90 |
| Snowgoose 250QX107-1 | General Line | 1974 | $2 | $70 |
| Snowman 150QX104-1 | Yarn Ornaments | 1974 | $2 | $25 |
| Snowman 450QX190-2 | Twirl-Abouts | 1977 | $4 | $78 |
| Soldier 100XHD81-2 | Yarn Ornaments | 1973 | $1 | $16 |
| Soldier 150QX102-1 | Yarn Ornaments | 1974 | $2 | $24 |
| Soldier 450QX173-1 | Twirl-Abouts | 1976 | $4 | $45 |
| Spencer Sparrow 350QX200-7 | General Line | 1979 | $4 | $25 |
| Spencer Sparrow 350QX219-6 | General Line | 1978 | $4 | $50 |
| Squirrel 250QX138-2 | Decorative Ball Ornaments | 1977 | $2 | $95 |
| Stained Glass 350QX152-2 | Decorative Ball Ornaments | 1977 | $4 | $36 |
| Star 350QX313-5 | Holiday Highlights | 1977 | $4 | $50 |
| Star Chimes 450QX137-9 | Holiday Chimes | 1979 | $4 | $29 |
| Star Over Bethlehem 350QX352-7 | Colors Of Christmas | 1979 | $4 | $44 |
| Stuffed Full Stocking 200QX341-9 | Sewn Trimmers | 1979 | $2 | $24 |
| Teacher 350QX213-9 | Commemoratives | 1979 | $4 | $21 |
| Thimble Christmas Salute, A 2nd Ed. 400QX131-9 | Thimble Series | 1979 | $4 | $80 |
| Thimble Series-Mouse 300QX133-6 | Little Trimmers | 1979 | $3 | $100 |
| Thimble W/Mouse 1st Ed. 300QX133-6 | Thimble Series | 1978 | $3 | $120 |
| Tiffany Angel Tree Topper 1000QX703-7 | Tree Topper | 1979 | $10 | $25 |
| Toys 500QX183-5 | Nostalgia | 1977 | $5 | $67 |
| Train 500QX181-1 | Yesteryears | 1976 | $5 | $78 |
| Weather House 600QX191-5 | Twirl-Abouts | 1977 | $6 | $35 |
| Wharf 250QX161-5 | Beauty Of America Collection | 1977 | $2 | $36 |
| Winnie-The-Pooh 350QX206-7 | General Line | 1979 | $4 | $34 |
| Words Of Christmas 350QX350-7 | Colors Of Christmas | 1979 | $4 | $78 |
| Wreath 350QX156-2 | Christmas Expressions Collection | 1977 | $4 | $38 |
| Wreath 350QX202-2 | Colors Of Christmas | 1977 | $4 | $60 |
| Yesterday's Toys 350QX250-3 | Decorative Ball Ornaments | 1978 | $4 | $25 |

Norman Rockwell, 1974 ....... **$62**

Nativity, 1977, from the Nostalgia series ................................ **$97**

Peanuts: Time to Trim, 1979 . **$45**

Snowman, 1977, from the Twirl-Abouts series........................ **$78**

Santa's Motorcar, 1979, 1st in the Here Comes Santa series..... **$294**

Christmas Dreams, 1981 .......... **$110**

Gentle Blessings, 1986......... **$90**

Victorian Dollhouse, 1984, 1st in the Nostalgic Houses and Shops series ............ **$200**

Dorothy and Toto, 1994, from the Wizard of Oz Collection ......... **$43**

Starship Enterprise, 1991, from the Star Trek series ............ **$250**

## 1980S

| Ornament Title | Series | Year | Price | Value |
|---|---|---|---|---|
| Frosty Friends 10th Ed. 925QX457-2 | Frosty Friends | 1989 | $9 | $40 |
| Frosty Friends 2nd Ed. QX433-5 | Frosty Friends | 1981 | $8 | $325 |
| Frosty Friends 3rd Ed. 800QX452-3 | Frosty Friends | 1982 | $8 | $275 |
| Frosty Friends 4th Ed. 800QX400-7 | Frosty Friends | 1983 | $8 | $200 |
| Frosty Friends 5th Ed. 800QX437-1 | Frosty Friends | 1984 | $8 | $150 |
| Frosty Friends 6th Ed. 850QX482-2 | Frosty Friends | 1985 | $8 | $125 |
| Frosty Friends 7th Ed. 850QX405-3 | Frosty Friends | 1986 | $8 | $95 |
| Frosty Friends 8th Ed. 850QX440-9 | Frosty Friends | 1987 | $8 | $85 |
| Frosty Friends 9th Ed. 875QX403-1 | Frosty Friends | 1988 | $9 | $90 |
| Rocking Horse 1st Ed. 900QX422-2 | Rocking Horse | 1981 | $9 | $425 |
| Rocking Horse 2nd Ed. 1000QX502-3 | Rocking Horse | 1982 | $10 | $315 |
| Rocking Horse 3rd Ed. 1000QX417-7 | Rocking Horse | 1983 | $10 | $223 |
| Rocking Horse 4th Ed. 1000QX435-4 | Rocking Horse | 1984 | $10 | $85 |
| Rocking Horse 5th Ed. 1075QX493-2 | Rocking Horse | 1985 | $11 | $68 |
| Rocking Horse 6th Ed. 1075QX401-6 | Rocking Horse | 1986 | $11 | $58 |
| Rocking Horse 7th Ed. 1075QX482-9 | Rocking Horse | 1987 | $11 | $67 |
| Rocking Horse 8th Ed. 1075QX402-4 | Rocking Horse | 1988 | $11 | $52 |
| Rocking Horse 9th Ed. 1075QX462-2 | Rocking Horse | 1989 | $11 | $45 |

## 1990S

| Ornament Title | Series | Year | Price | Value |
|---|---|---|---|---|
| Holiday Barbie 1st In Ed. 1495QX572-5 | Holiday Barbie Collection | 1993 | $15 | $50 |
| Holiday Barbie 2nd In Ed. 1495QX521-6 | Holiday Barbie Collection | 1994 | $15 | $25 |
| Holiday Barbie 3rd In Ed. QXI505-7 | Holiday Barbie Collection | 1995 | $15 | $18 |
| Holiday Barbie 4th In Ed. QXI537-1 | Holiday Barbie Collection | 1996 | $15 | $14 |
| Holiday Barbie 5th In Ed. QXI6212 | Holiday Barbie Collection | 1997 | $15 | $13 |
| Holiday Barbie 6th & Final Ed. QXI402-3 | Holiday Barbie Collection | 1998 | $16 | $25 |

# Hooked Rugs

When collectors started taking rugs off the floor and hanging them on the wall, prices also moved in an upward direction.

Hooked rugs, which were introduced about 1830 and came into vogue in the 1850s, were crafted from homemade designs as well as from commercial patterns. They often appeal to folk art collectors who are attracted to examples with bold graphic designs as well as pictorials with a folkish flair.

Large rag hooked rugs (around 3 feet by 5 feet in size), incorporating folksy images of animals, seem to be the most popular, with late 19th and early 20th century examples in the best condition selling for between $1,000 and $3,000. But smaller, simpler rugs are still available for much less, depending on the shop or show you are browsing.

Hooked rugs made with yarn are not as sought-after as those that use shredded rags, but some yarn rugs are quite appealing and usually sell for a fraction of rag examples. Whether yarn or rag, repairs are usually not too expensive.

American hooked rug, early/mid-20th c., 8' 4" x 3' 4"................................**$474**
*Pook & Pook, Inc.*

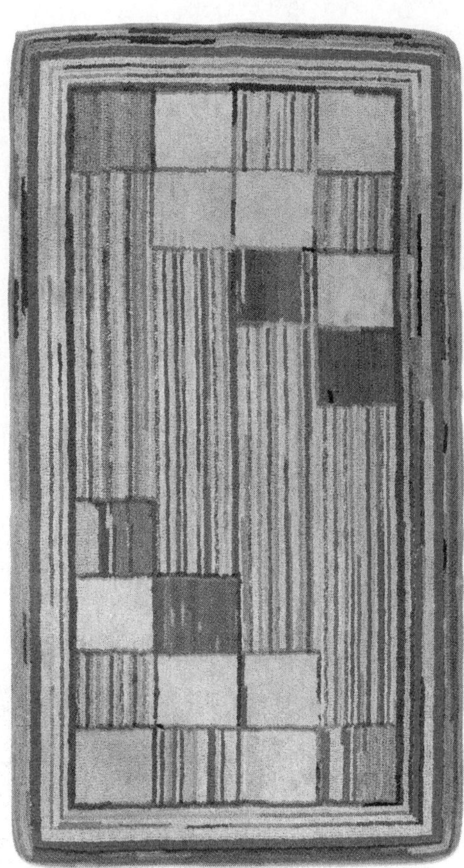

American geometric hooked rug, early 20th c. (framed), 51" x 28"....................................................**$148**
*Pook & Pook, Inc.*

Two American hooked rugs, early 20th c., 29" x 55" and 26" x 36". .......................................................................................... **$385**
*Pook & Pook, Inc.*

Three large American hooked area rugs, early 20th c., 69" x 42", 70" x 66", and 86" x 35". .................... **$356**
*Pook & Pook, Inc.*

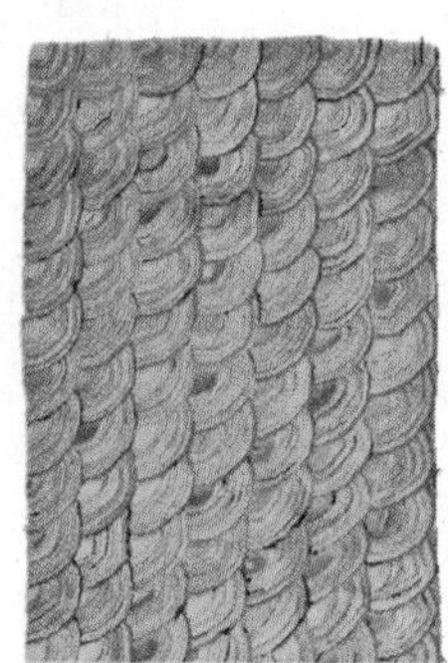

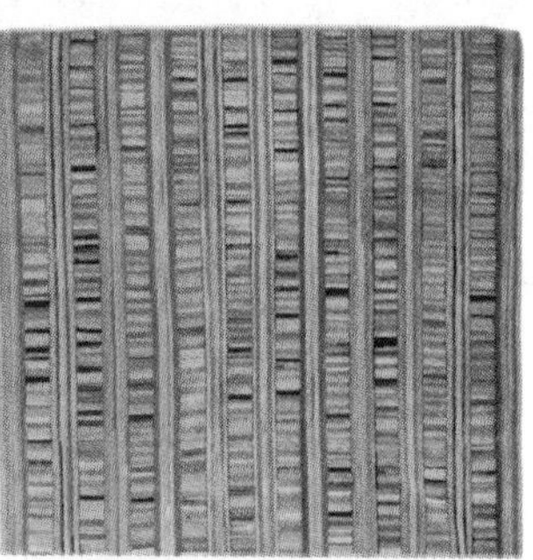

Three American hooked rugs, early 20th c., with overall geometric patterns, 46" x 29", 65" x 36", and 78" x 34". ............................... **$425**
*Pook & Pook, Inc.*

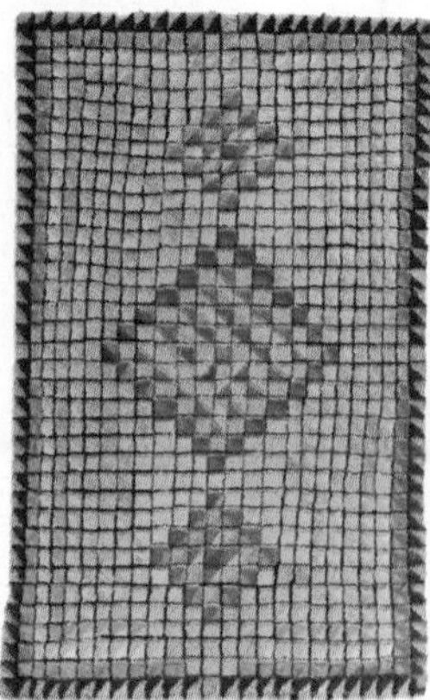

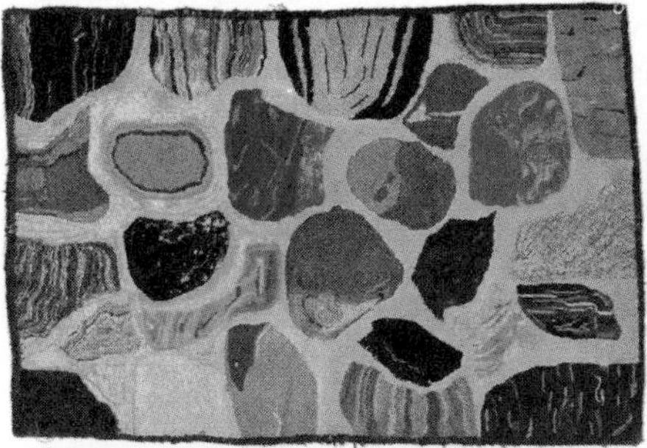

Three American hooked rugs, each 20th c., with floral decoration, 38-1/2" x 31", 36" x 22", and 24-1/2" x 34" (one shown)........................................... **$395**
*Pook & Pook, Inc.*

◀Three American hooked rugs, early/mid-20th c., largest 3' x 4' 7"........................................... **$296**
*Pook & Pook, Inc.*

American hooked rug with tiger, early 20th c., 33" x 39".............. **$89**
*Pook & Pook, Inc.*

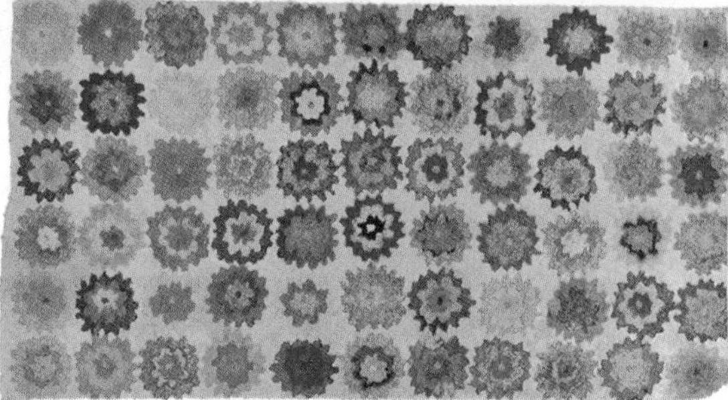

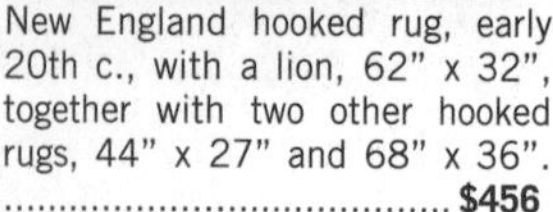

New England hooked rug, early 20th c., with a lion, 62" x 32", together with two other hooked rugs, 44" x 27" and 68" x 36". .......................................... **$456**
*Pook & Pook, Inc.*

Room-size hooked rug, mid-20th c., 11' 6" x 8' 8". .............. **$148**
*Pook & Pook, Inc.*

Large Pennsylvania hooked Domestic Zoo rug by Magdalina Briner, ca. 1870, with a multitude of animals, 45" x 115". ............................................................................................................................. **$11,850**
*Pook & Pook, Inc.*

# Illustration Art

Collectors, whether looking for a distinctive decoration for a living room or seeking a rewarding long-term investment, will find something to fit their fancy — and their budget — when they turn to illustration art. Pieces of representational art — often, art that tells some sort of story — are produced in a variety of forms, each appealing in a different way. They are created as source material for political cartoons, magazine covers, posters, story illustrations, comic books and strips, animated cartoons, calendars, and book jackets. They may be in color or in black and white. Collectible forms include:

• **Mass-market printed reproductions.** These can range from art prints and movie posters to engravings, clipped advertising art, and bookplates. While this may be the least-expensive art to hang on your wall, a few rare items can bring record prices. Heritage Auction Galleries, for example, commanded a price of $334,600 for a Universal 1935 Bride of Frankenstein poster (artist unidentified).

• **Limited-run reproductions.** These range from signed, numbered lithographs to numbered prints.

• **Tangential items.** These are hard-to-define, oddball pieces. One example is printing plates (some in actual lead; some in plastic fused to lightweight metal) used by newspapers and comic-book printers to reproduce the art.

• **Unique original art.** These pieces have the widest range of all, from amateur sketches to finished paintings. The term "original art" includes color roughs produced by a painter as a preliminary test for a work to be produced, finished oil paintings, animation cels for commercials as well as feature films, and black-and-white inked pages of comic books and strips. They may be signed and identifiable or unsigned and generic. "Illustration art" is often differentiated from "fine art," but its very pop-culture nature may increase the pool of would-be purchasers. Alberto Vargas (1896-1982) and Gil Elvgren (1914-1980) bring high prices for pin-up art; Norman Rockwell (1894-1978), James Montgomery Flagg (1877-1960), and J.C. Leyendecker (1874-1951) were masters of mainstream illustration; and Margaret Brundage (1900-1976) and Virgil Finlay (1914-1971) are highly regarded pulp artists.

Golden Fleece cover (June 1939) by Margaret Brundage ............**$7,170**

Taking a look at a specific genre, consider comic-book-related illustration art. Two of the top painters in the field were heroic-fantasy artist Frank Frazetta (1928-2010) and "Disney ducks" artist Carl Barks (1901-2000). Top dollar at Heritage for a Frazetta painting was $150,000 — but, he, too, drew roughs that bring less, when they can be found. In his "retirement," Barks licensed permission to produce and sell illustrations of "his" Disney characters, and full paintings bring six-figure prices. In 2011, Barks oil paintings from the collection of Kerby Confer commanded top prices in several Heritage auctions with the top item a painting titled "The Sport of Tycoons," which sold for $262,900. Barks also produced many sketches for fans over the years — some simply quick pencils — that obviously go for much less when they're available.

The original art for printed comic-book pages and covers can also command high prices, especially if they're from particularly rare or historic comics. A prime example of this was the record-setting price for an original art page by Frank Miller and Klaus Janson from 1986's Batman: The Dark Knight #3, which sold for $448,125. On the other hand, it is possible to get started with original-art pages as low as $10 each.

Other comics art forms include magazine cartoons and newspaper strips. Charles Addams (1912-1988) in the former category and Charles Schulz (1922-2000) in the latter have active collecting communities. Spending time with dealers at shows, browsing online auctions, and even following favorite creators on Twitter can turn up low-priced opportunities to get a collection started. Often, art that's returned to the original writers and artists is later sold by those same creators when they need space in their studios, providing excellent opportunities to get that one-of-a-kind collectible and even get it signed by the creator. Remember: Charles Schulz gave away originals of his Peanuts strips — originals that bring thousands of dollars to their owners today.

***Brent Frankenhoff and Maggie Thompson, CBGXtra.com***

*All prices and images courtesy Heritage Auction Galleries*

Al Jaffee original illustration art from Mad #232 (1982) .......... **$50**

Smilin' Jack original strip (March 30, 1966) by Zack Mosley .......... **$15**

Page 10 from Batman: The Dark Knight #3 (1986) by Frank Miller and Klaus Janson.................... **$448,125**

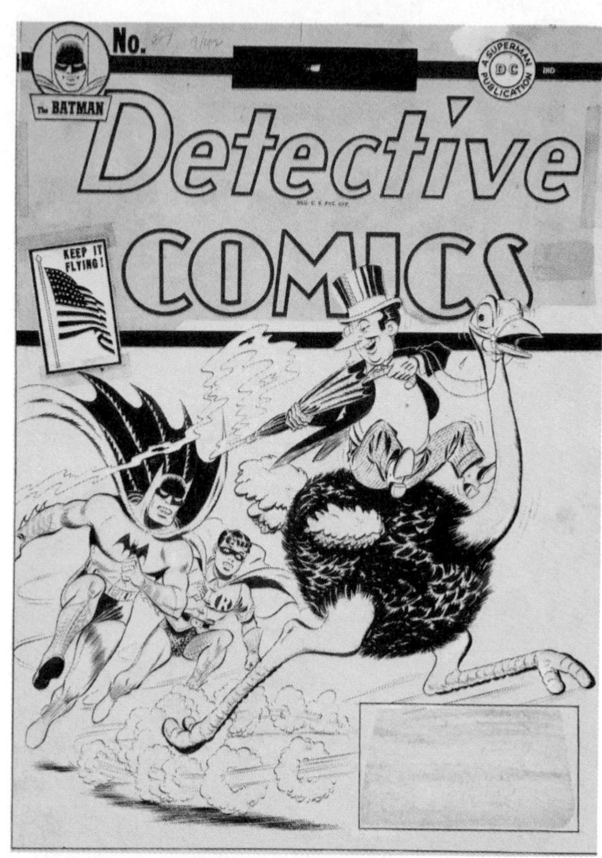


Original cover for Detective Comics #67 (1942, first cover to feature The Penguin) by Jerry Robinson from Robinson's personal collection......................**$239,000**

Preliminary study for One Against the Moon (1956) by Virgil Finlay ..........................................**$310**

"Fifty-Fifty on My Last Smoke, Bill!" watercolor and pencil on paper (undated) by James Montgomery Flagg ........................................................ **$1,553**

"Gay Nymph" (1947) original oil by Gil Elvgren ................................................. **$286,800**

"Gold Carnation" (Legacy Nude #9, 1940s), original illustration by Alberto Vargas ............**$89,625**

The New Adventures of Flash Gordon production cel with background (1979) ......................**$26**

"Lovebirds, The House of Kuppenheimer" advertising diptych (1951) by J.C. Leyendecker.............. **$155,350**

"The Band Concert" production cel (1935, thought to be the only cel from this cartoon in existence). **$44,812**

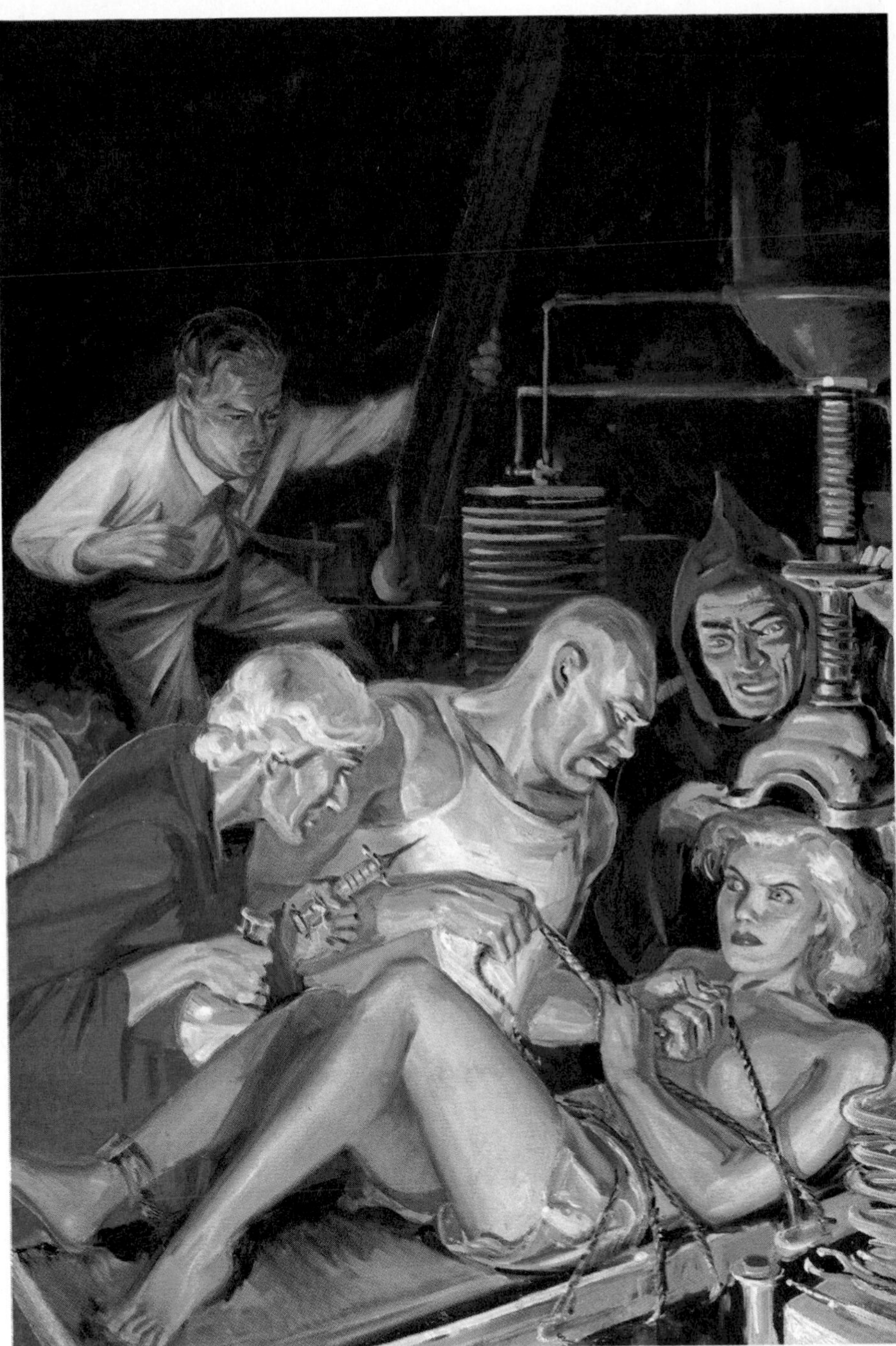

Mystery Tales cover (May 1939) by John Walter Scott ........................................ $9,560

"The Sport of Tycoons" original oil painting (1974) by Carl Barks, 27" x 24"................................ **$262,900**

"Throwing the Gun" oil cover painting for Western Story magazine (April 8, 1939) by Norman Saunders ............................................................**$20,315**

"Davy Jones" page from Undersea Agent #5 (1966) by Gil Kane.................................................. **$776**

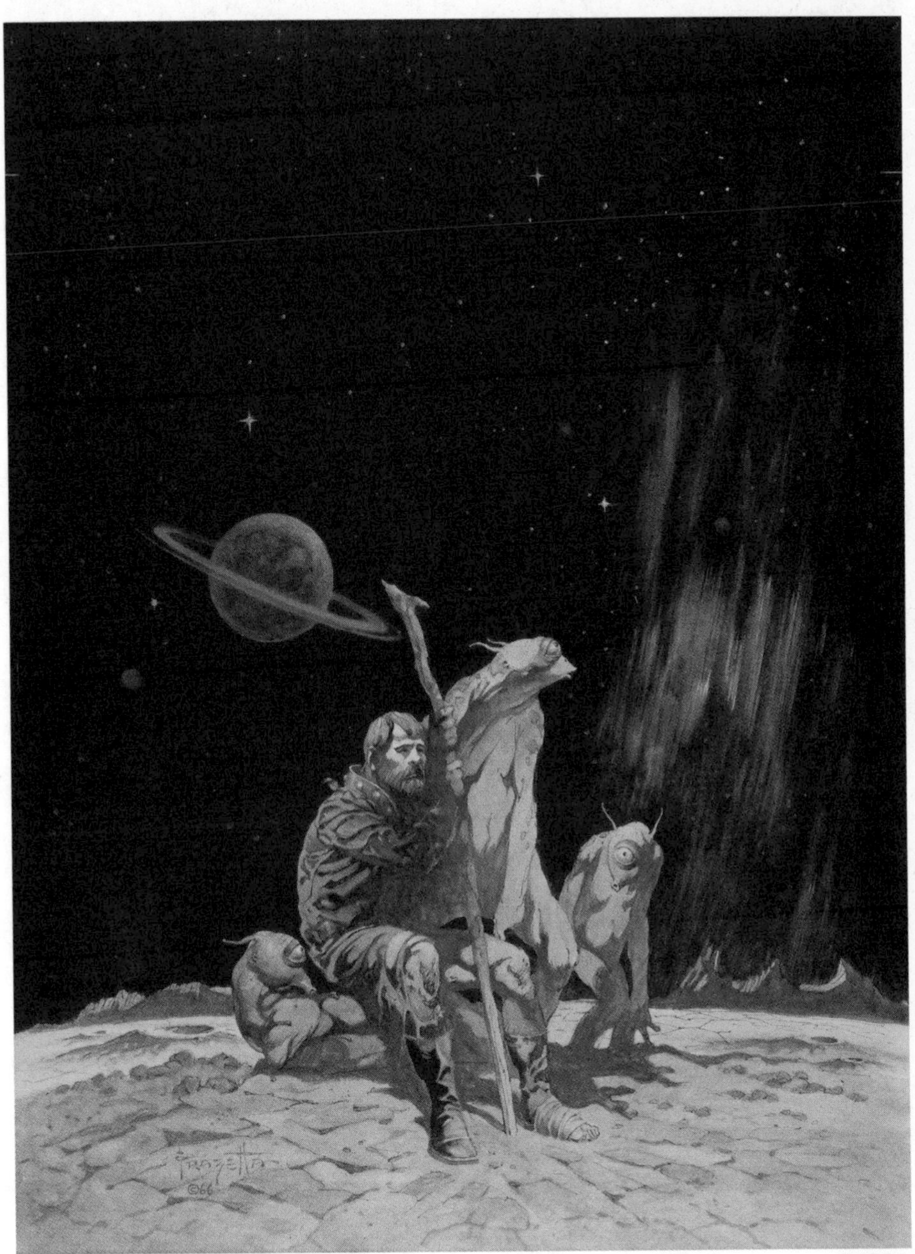


"Tomorrow Midnight" (1966), paperback cover illustration, oil on board by Frank Frazetta................. **$83,650**

Conan the Fearless paperback cover (1986) by Boris Vallejo ........................................................ **$8,365**

# Indian Artifacts (North American)

This section covers collectible items commonly referred to as American Indian artifacts. Our interest in Native American material cultural artifacts has been long-lived, as was the Indian's interest in many of our material cultural items from an early period.

During recent years, it has become commonplace to have major sales of these artifacts by at least four major auction houses, in addition to the private trading, local auctions, and Internet sales of these items.

Anthropologists have written millions of words on American Indian cultures and societies and have standardized various regions of the country when discussing these cultures. Those standard regional definitions are continued here.

We have been fascinated with the material culture of Native Americans from the beginning of our contact with their societies. The majority of these valuable items are in repositories of museums, universities, and colleges, but many items that were traded to private citizens are now being sold to collectors of Native American material culture.

Native American artifacts are now acquired by collectors in the same fashion as any material cultural item. Individuals interested in antiques and collectibles find items at farm auction sales (an especially good place for farm family collections to be dispersed), yard sales, estate sales, specialized auctions, and from private collectors trading or selling items. The most wonderful of all sources is the Internet, especially online auction sales. There is no shortage of possibilities in finding items; it is merely deciding where to place one's energy and investment in adding to one's collection.

Native American artifacts are much more difficult to locate for a variety of reasons including the following: scarcity of items; legal protection of items being traded; more vigorous collecting of artifacts by numerous international, national, state, regional, and local museums and historical societies; frailties of the items themselves, as most were made of organic materials; and a more limited distribution network through legitimate secondary sales.

However, it is still possible to find some types of Native American items through the traditional sources of online auctions, auction houses in local communities, antique stores and malls, flea markets, trading meetings, estate sales, and similar venues. The most likely items to find in the above ways would be items made of stone, chert, flint, obsidian, and copper. Most organic materials will not have survived the rigors of a marketplace unless they were recently released from some estate or collection and their value was unknown to the previous owner.

For more information on Native American collectibles, see *Warman's North American Indian Artifacts Identification and Price Guide* by Russell E. Lewis.

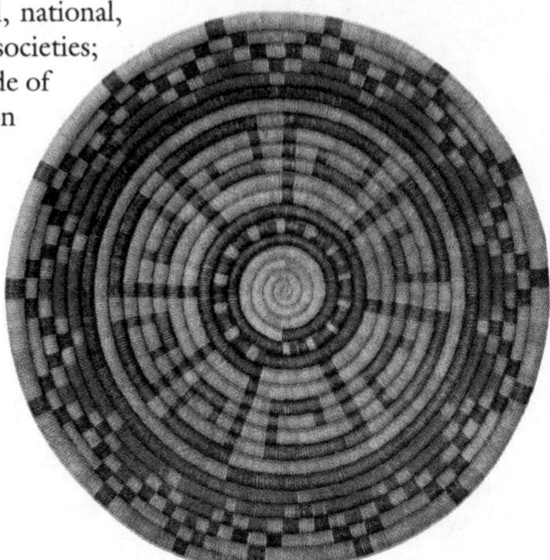

Hopi basketry bowl, circa 1940. Fine weave traditional pattern full geometric design coiled flat bowl with key and other symbols, 14-1/2" dia. ............ **$375**
*Allard Auctions*

## SOUTHWEST

Early Hopi Kachina, circa early 1900s. Fox Dancer Kachina, 9" t. .................................... **$1,200**
*Allard Auctions*

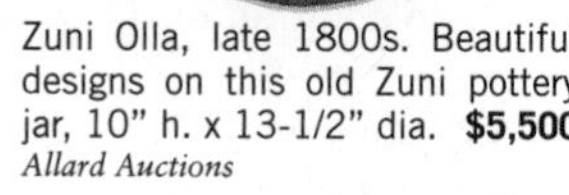

Zuni Olla, late 1800s. Beautiful designs on this old Zuni pottery jar, 10" h. x 13-1/2" dia. **$5,500**
*Allard Auctions*

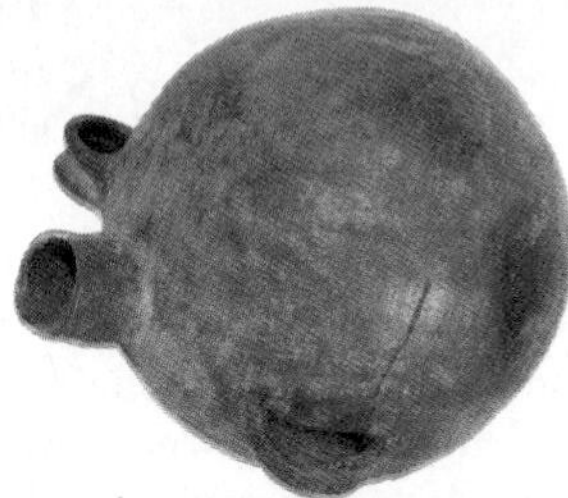

Pueblo water jar, late 1800s. Very large water jar, possibly Hopi, in excellent condition with original lugs and spout, 12" x 15" x 16-1/2". ........................ **$2,500**
*Allard Auctions*

Four Southwestern painted items, Pueblo, 20th c. Two polychrome gourd rattles and two carved and painted wood rasps with bird and animal finials, longest item is 14". Provenance: Wistariahurst Museum. ......................... **$998**
*Skinner, Inc.*

Zuni Olla, late 1800s. Rare older Zuni pottery jar covered with designs including the classic Zuni heartline deer design, etc., in polychrome, an outstanding early example, 9-1/4" h. x 13" dia. .................... **$16,000**
*Allard Auctions*

◀ Navajo weaving, late 1800s. Fine tapestry grade weaving of classic red, gold, brown, green, etc., 45" x 30". ...................................................... **$2,250**

## SOUTHEASTERN WOODLANDS

Cherokee basketry, early 1900s. Polychrome woven cane basket with bentwood handle, 10" x 14" x 15". .............................. **$300**
*Allard Auctions*

Three prehistoric painted pottery items from Smith County, Tennessee. Two jars with swirling red designs and a bowl with a human head effigy (broken and reassembled), largest is 8-1/4" h. Provenance: Wistariahurst Museum; Sherman Collection. ................................................ **$1,997**
*Skinner, Inc.*

Two prehistoric stone effigy pipes, both Southeastern.
**Right:** 6-1/2" pipe in form of human holding a large container with two handles. Provenance: Wistariahurst Museum, Sherman Collection. .................... **$11,162**

**Far right:** 5-1/2" effigy pipe in the form of a bird eating a frog. Provenance: Wistariahurst Museum, Sherman Collection. ........ **$3,818**
*Skinner, Inc.*

## NORTHEASTERN WOODLANDS

Passamaquaddy basket, circa 1900. Woven split ash basket with bentwood handles in excellent condition, a style seen throughout both the Northeast and Great Lakes regions, 9-1/2" x 9-1/2". ......... **$150**
*Allard Auctions*

Iroquois basketry, early 1900s. Two small traditional lidded treasure baskets, fully quilled floral patterns on lids, 2" x 3" each. ............ **$110**
*Allard Auctions*

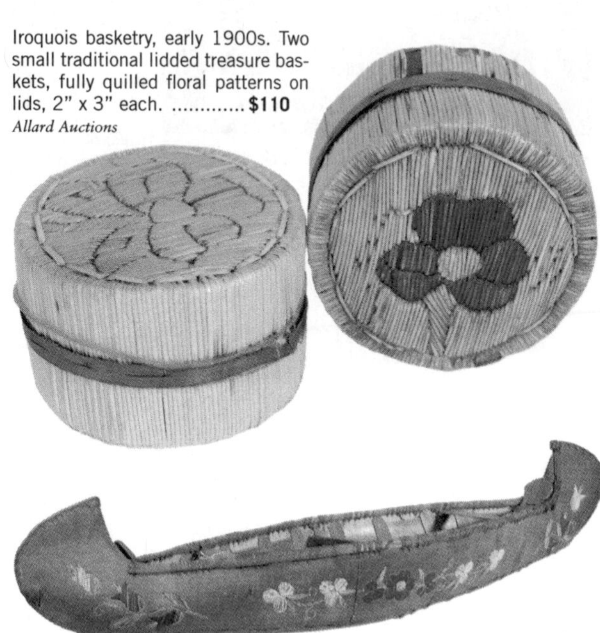

Iroquois birch bark canoe, early 1900s. Small canoe of birch bark with traditional Woodland design and style and decorated with quilled floral designs, 9" x 11" x 40". ................................ **$275**
*Allard Auctions*

## GREAT LAKES

Great Lakes wooden ladle, 19th c. Burled wooden ladle with an eagle head carved on the handle's end, 4-1/2" x 12-1/2" l. ....................................... **$110**
*Allard Auctions*

Great Lakes war club, 19th c. Carved wooden club with iron spike, nice patina, 23" long. ............ **$475**
*Allard Auctions*

Winnebago loom beaded bandolier bag, circa last quarter 19th c. Tabs have remnant silk ribbons, framed, some bead loss, 33" long. .............. **$3,055**
*Skinner, Inc.*

Huron moccasins, circa 1900. Small, early pair of buckskin child's moccasins with pinched toe, embroidered vamp and beaded trim, 4-1/2" long. ...... **$160**
*Allard Auctions*

Ojibwa man's shirt, circa 1890. Hand-dyed cotton shirt with beaded French velvet cuffs, 27" x 58".................................. **$750**
*Allard Auctions*

## PRAIRIES

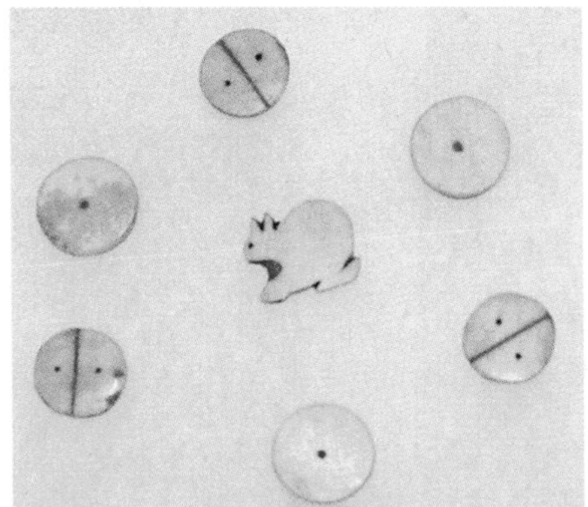

Osage dice game, 19th c. Six dice and one rabbit figure with incised markings and dyed blue and red, as shown in the "Art of the Osage, Saint Louis Art Museum," objects are approximately 1" dia. ........ **$375**
*Allard Auctions*

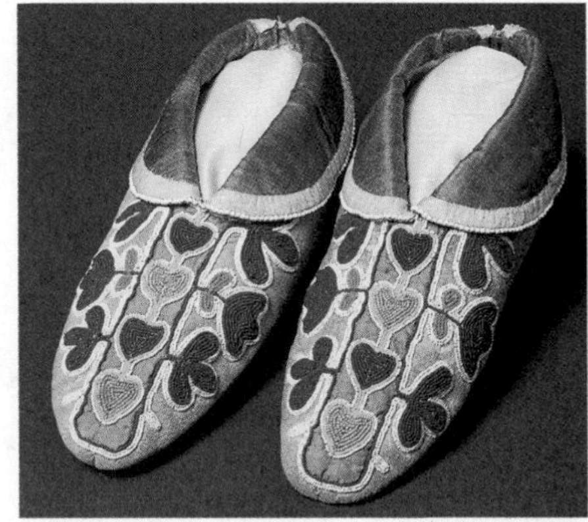

Pair of Delaware moccasins, circa second quarter 19th c. Soft soles with beaded vamps using small seed beads with green silk striped backing on the vamp, edge beaded two color silk cuffs, 8-1/4" long. Provenance: The Charles and Blanche Derby collection and by repute previously of the Mary Bremmen of Lancaster, Pennsylvania, collection and brought back from Ohawa, Kansas in 1867. .................... **$23,500**
*Skinner, Inc.*

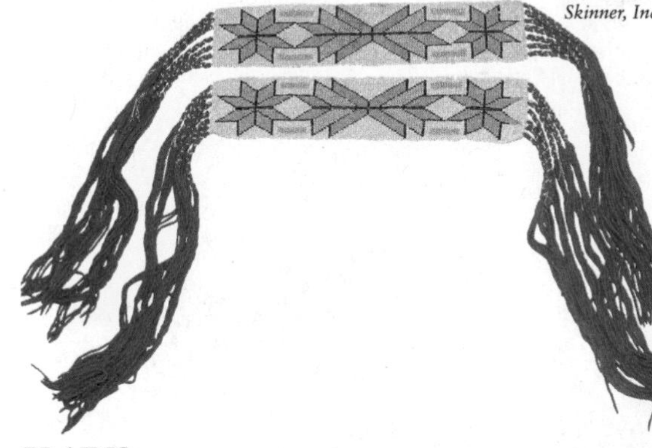

Potawatomi garters, circa 1880s. Loom woven garters with greasy yellow background and red Germantown yarn fringe, 2-1/2" x 34" l. These could also be placed in the Great Lakes Region as the Potawatomi extended into southern Michigan. .................... **$600**
*Allard Auctions*

## PLAINS

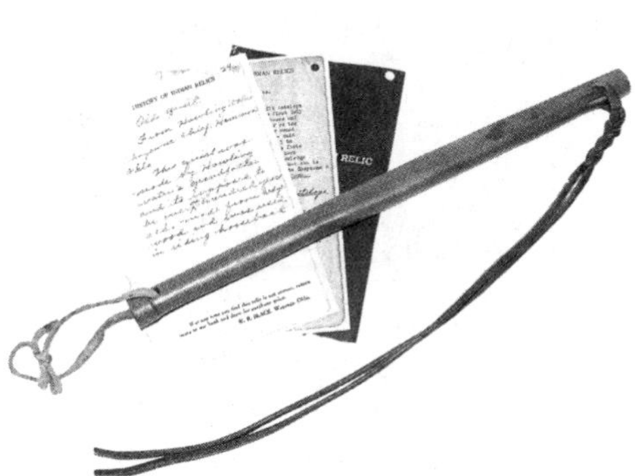

Cheyenne 1860s quirt owned by Chief Howling Waters. Hedgewood quirt with harness leather whip thongs and a buffalo hide wrist strap, 35-1/2" long. Provenance: Collected from Chief Howling Waters by W. R. Black, collection papers included. ...... **$1,100**
*Allard Auctions*

Cheyenne buffalo horn ladle. Carved buffalo horn with quilled drops, 9" x 3". Provenance: Collected from Cheyenne Bone Road by W. R. Black, Watanga, Oklahoma, includes documentation. ...................... **$275**
*Allard Auctions*

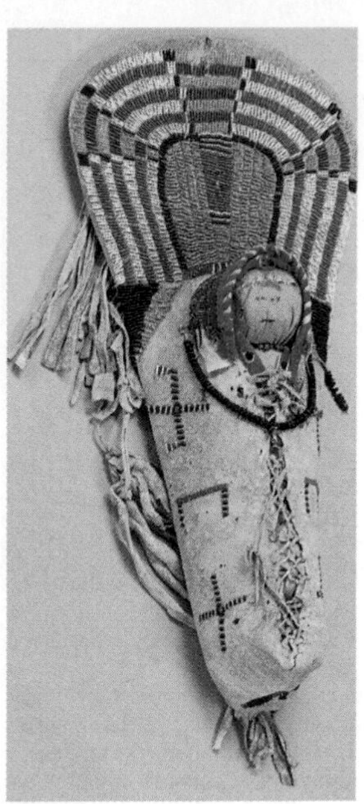

Central Plains, Ute, beaded hide cradle and cloth doll, circa last quarter 19th c. 21" h. .... **$8,812**
*Skinner, Inc.*

Sioux pipe bag, circa late 1800s/ early 1900s. All original sinew sewn native tanned buffalo hide with quilled slats and fringe, 7" x 35". .............................. **$2,750**
*Allard Auctions*

Kiowa/Apache Peyote bag, circa 1890s. An example of the early Peyote culture expandable pouch with beaded rosettes on each side and beaded balls on the draw-strings representing Peyote buttons, 2-1/2" x 5". .............. **$475**
*Allard Auctions*

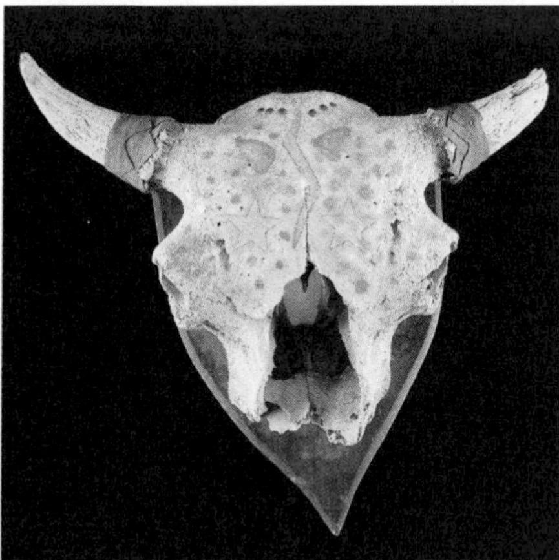

Plains buffalo "medicine" bull skull, circa 1880. Provenance from Moon collection indicates it may have belonged to a Chief Thunderbird, circa 1880. The green dots represent hail stones to call on the might of the Thunderbird. .......................... **$4,600**
*James D. Julia Auctions*

Rare Arapaho child's moccasins, circa 1880. High-top child's moccasins, sinew sewn beadwork on yellow ocher stained antelope hide, museum mounted, 5-1/2" l. x 10" h. ...................................... **$3,250**
*Allard Auctions*

## PLATEAU

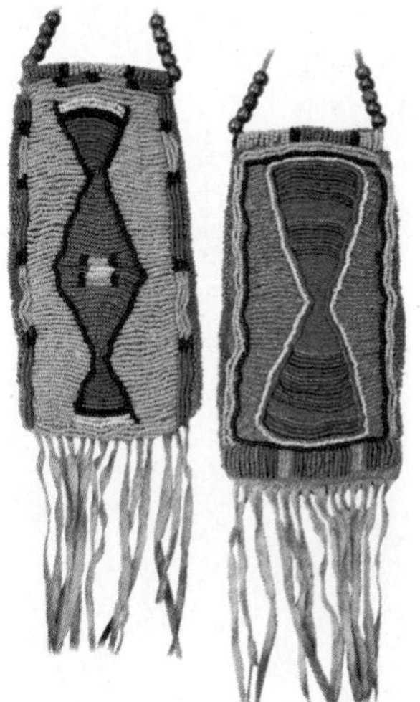

Crow fire bag, circa 1870. Rare sinew sewn fully beaded firebag, complete with striker and flint, 3-1/2" x 6 1/4". Provenance: Honnen Collection. .......... **$2,000**
*Allard Auctions*

Crow parfleche, circa 1860. Early mineral painted elk hide parfleche, 11" x 18". ......... **$550**
*Allard Auctions*

Nez Perce bag, circa 1860. Rare figured cornhusk bag with pine trees, flowers, and arrowheads, 11" x 11". ........................ **$700**
*Allard Auctions*

Blackfoot leggings, circa 1880. Mountain sheep hide leggings with beaded strips and long fringe, 30" l. x 9" w. Provenance: Richard Pohrt, Sr. collection. ........................................................................ **$3,250**
*Allard Auctions*

Piegan pipe bag, mid-19th c. Rare and early tab-top Piegan pipebag, sinew and thread sewn on mountain sheep hide with pony bead trim terminated with ocher stained fringe wrapped with coiled brass wire, 5" x 21" l. ............ **$3,250**
*Allard Auctions*

## NORTHWEST PACIFIC COASTAL

NW Coastal polychrome carved wooden mask, Nootka, circa late 19th c. Stunning colors on this articulated jaw carved cedar mask make it stand out among others. Portions of the inner headband and cloth and cedar bark strips remain, mask has some cracking, 20-1/2" h. Provenance: "...gotten from Indian agent, Mr. P. B. Ashbridge, Port Alberni, B.C. 4,20,40... It was a mask used by the chief of the Nootka tribe at ceremonial dances and is approximately 70 years old. The crown is the mark of a king or chief. Worn by the chief and this particular one was owned by the late Chief 'Maguinna'..." (from a letter by P. B. Ashbridge). ..**$17,625**
*Skinner, Inc.*

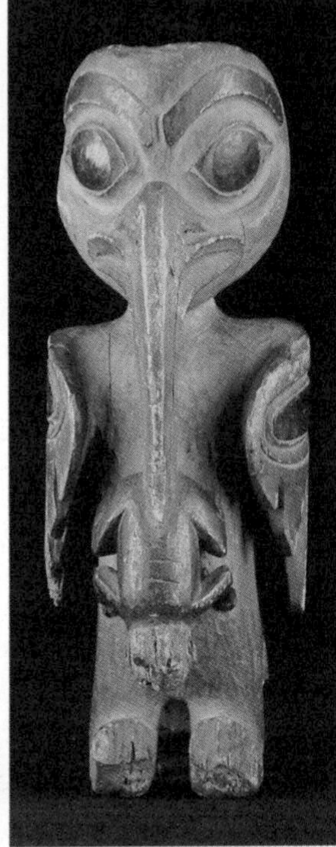

Northwest Coastal carved wooden figure, 19th c. Tlingit culture, 11" ................................ **$5,462**
*James D. Julia Auctions*

Small Nootka basket, circa 1900. Fine-weave treasure basket with lid in polychrome depicting a sea serpent, whalers, and eagle, 2" h x 3-1/2" dia. ............................ **$170**
*Allard Auctions*

Cowlitz basket, early 1900s. Classic upright basketry vessel with intricate exterior designs, some of the rim loops are missing, 7-1/2" x 7-1/2". ................ **$275**
*Allard Auctions*

NW Coastal mask, circa 1980s. Hand-carved and painted cedar mask with woven cedar bark "hair" signed by "Fred Peters," 17" x 16" x 10". This mask is clearly in the traditions shown following under Ceremonial Items. ............................................ **$300**
*Allard Auctions*

# Jewelry

Jewelry has held a special place for humankind since prehistoric times, both as an emblem of personal status and as a decorative adornment worn for its sheer beauty. This tradition continues today. We should keep in mind, however, that it was only with the growth of the Industrial Revolution that jewelry first became cheap enough so that even the person of modest means could win a piece or two.

Only since around the mid-19th century did certain forms of jewelry, especially pins and brooches, begin to appear on the general market as a mass-produced commodity and the Victorians took to it immediately. Major production centers for the finest pieces of jewelry remained in Europe, especially Italy and England, but less expensive pieces were also exported to the booming American market and soon some American manufacturers also joined in the trade. Especially during the Civil War era, when silver and gold supplies grew tremendously in the U.S., did jewelry in silver or with silver, brass or gold-filled (i.e. gold-plated or goldplate) mounts begin to flood the market here. By the turn of the 20th century all the major mail-order companies and small town jewelry shops could offer a huge variety of inexpensive jewelry pieces aimed at not only the feminine buyer but also her male counterpart.

Inexpensive jewelry of the late 19th and early 20th century is still widely available and often at modest prices. Even more in demand today is costume jewelry, well-designed jewelry produced of inexpensive materials and meant to carefully accent a woman's ensemble. Today costume jewelry of the 20th century has become one of the most active areas in the field of collecting and some of the finest pieces, signed by noted designers and manufacturers, can reach price levels nearly equal to much earlier and scarcer examples.

Jewelry prices, as in every other major collecting field, are influenced by a number of factors including local demand, quality, condition and rarity. As market prices have risen in recent years it has become even more important for the collector to shop and buy with care. Learn as much as you can about your favorite area of jewelry and keep abreast of market trends and stay alert to warnings about alterations, repairs or reproductions that can be found on the market.

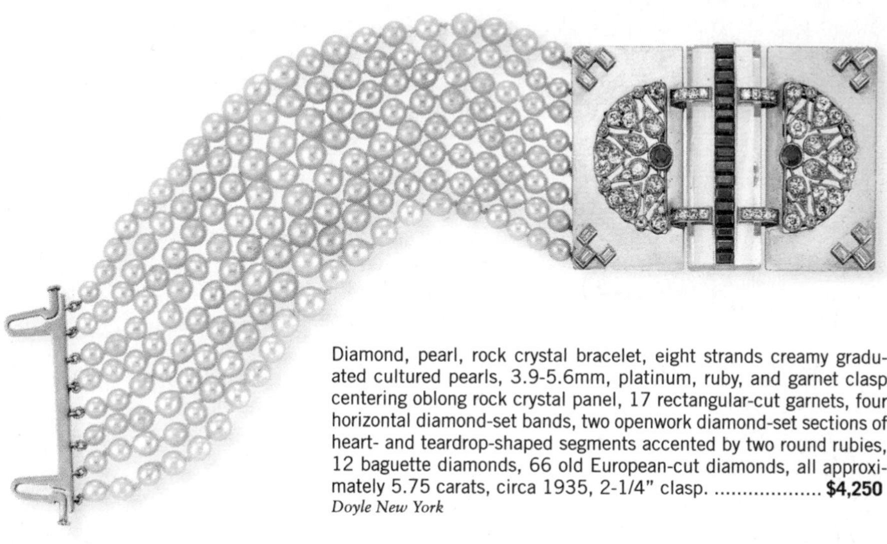

Diamond, pearl, rock crystal bracelet, eight strands creamy graduated cultured pearls, 3.9-5.6mm, platinum, ruby, and garnet clasp centering oblong rock crystal panel, 17 rectangular-cut garnets, four horizontal diamond-set bands, two openwork diamond-set sections of heart- and teardrop-shaped segments accented by two round rubies, 12 baguette diamonds, 66 old European-cut diamonds, all approximately 5.75 carats, circa 1935, 2-1/4" clasp. .................. **$4,250**
*Doyle New York*

# What's Hot in Jewelry

If current trends continue, diamonds, wristwatches, and rare gemstones will dominate the top of the antique jewelry market. The following four experts share their viewpoints.

## Nicholas Thorn, Vice President, Litchfield County Antiques, Litchfield, Conn.

"Watches were certainly our biggest seller, followed by jewelry with sapphires, diamonds, or rubies. I feel watches will continue to do well; it's so easy to see the advantage of buying watches at auction against prices one would need to pay in retail settings. It seems to me interest in rubies has been increasing over the past few years, while diamonds and sapphires have always been popular. We only do one jewelry sale per year, but [2011's] was a great success, with a sales total of $94,000 [on 102 lots]."

### *Top-Selling Auction Lots*

**Watches:** The top-selling lot was a men's Rolex Oyster Chronograph Antimagnetic wristwatch, stainless steel case, black calfskin band, which sold for $18,720 on 29 bids. A Patek Philippe 18-karat gold men's wristwatch, circa 1950-'60, square face, marked "Patek Philippe/Geneve" sold for $5,520 on 16 bids.

**Gems:** A cushion sapphire, round and baguette diamond platinum ring, the cushion sapphire approximately 6.0 carats, tripled its low estimate of $2,000 to $3,000, selling for $6,300 after 19 bids, while a vintage platinum and round twin diamond ring with two round diamonds surrounded by chip diamonds, approximate weight 1.65 carats, nearly doubled its low estimate of $2,500 to $3,500, selling for $4,380 on 13 bids.

## Jill Burgum, Graduate Gemologist, Director of Fine Jewelry, Heritage Auctions

"By far, the greatest demand and strongest prices achieved were for the sale of large diamonds, mainly those over 8.0 carats. This trend is anticipated to continue in 2012 and beyond."

### *Top-Selling Auction Lots*

1. Fancy light brownish-pink diamond, diamond, platinum ring. Marquise-shaped diamond weighing 11.74 carats, enhanced by triangle-shaped diamonds, one weighing 1.33 carats, one weighing 1.26 carats, set in platinum. It sold for $358,500 in May 2011.
2. Fancy intense yellow diamond, diamond, platinum, gold ring, custom made by Underwood's. Cut-cornered rectangular modified brilliant-cut fancy intense yellow diamond weighing 10.02 carats, set in 18-karat gold, enhanced by cut-cornered bullet-cut diamonds weighing a total of 0.92 carats, set in platinum. It sold for $179,250 in December 2011.
3. Diamond, platinum, and gold ring, marked Moyer. Marquise-shaped diamond weighing 15.16 carats, enhanced by marquise-shaped diamonds weighing a total of 2.39 carats, accented by full-cut diamonds weighing a total of 2.10 carats, set in platinum, having 18-karat gold accents. It sold for $131,450 in May 2011.

## Redge Martin, President, Clars Auction Gallery, Oakland, Calif.

"Diamond jewelry – and jewelry by well-known names: Tiffany, Rolex, Patek Philippe..." are top performing antique jewelry categories. Martin says they expect those trends to continue.

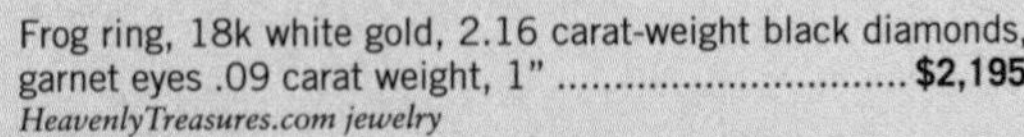

Frog ring, 18k white gold, 2.16 carat-weight black diamonds, garnet eyes .09 carat weight, 1" .............................. **$2,195**
*HeavenlyTreasures.com jewelry*

*Top-Selling Auction Lots*

1. Solitaire diamond pendant necklace, platinum, with pear-shaped modified brilliant-cut diamond weighing 10.09 carats and diamond accents on mount. Total pendant and neck chain weight 10.2 grams. Chain length 18 inches. It sold on Feb. 6, 2011 for $90,000.

2. Diamond ring, 18-karat white gold, center set with round diamond weighing 7.08 carats (GIA stating: VVS2 clarity), accented by 84 round and baguette cut diamonds weighing 3.00 carats. It sold on Nov. 13, 2011 for $60,000.

3. Gentleman's Patek Philippe Perpetual Calendar "Complicated" wristwatch, 18-karat yellow gold, mechanical automatic movement, day, date, month, leap year and moon phase indicator, 36 mm case, exhibition back, 22-karat gold router, black alligator strap with 18-karat yellow gold deployant clasp. It sold on Aug. 7, 2011 for $40,000.

## Daphne Lingon, Senior Vice President, Jewelry, Christie's New York

"Diamonds, both colorless and fancy-colored, continued to show great strength in a market where demand continues to exceed the scarce supply of rare gemstones. We expect this to continue into 2012."

1. Vivid yellow diamond, a pear-shaped fancy vivid yellow VS2 diamond of 32.77 carats. It sold for $6,578,500.

2. Diamond ring, set with cut-cornered rectangular-cut diamond weighing approximately 37.16 carats, flanked on either side by three graduated baguette-cut diamonds, mounted in platinum. It sold for $4,450,500.

3. An impressive diamond ring set with an oval-cut E color VVS2 diamond weighing approximately 46.51 carats, flanked on either side by a pear-shaped diamond weighing approximately 1.00 and 1.01 carats, mounted in platinum. It sold for $4,226,500.

## Rhonda Harness, Director of Jewelry, Michaan's Auctions, Alameda, Calif.

"The strongest items in jewelry this past year [for Michaan's] were jadeite jade; larger high-quality diamonds; anything antique and unusual in good condition; and watches. Just a few examples of unusual antique pieces included a great bear bangle bracelet in gold that looked like the front of a bear rug, with diamond eyes and platinum teeth, in the Art Nouveau style, dated Christmas 1905; an unusual modern art necklace by Vivianna Torun for Georg Jensen; and 18th century multi-gemstone brooches and paste jewelry."

*Top-Selling Auction Lots*

1. Jade, diamond, and 14-karat white gold ring, June 2011 fine jewelry sale; it sold for $25,000.

2. Diamond and platinum ring, July 2011 estate sale; it sold for $20,000.

3. Jade, diamond, and 18-karat yellow gold ring, June 2011 fine jewelry sale; it sold for $12,000.

***Kathy Flood***

*Kathy Flood is a journalist, author of* Warman's Jewelry Identification and Price Guide, *4th edition, and owner of the online antique jewelry shop ChristmasTreePins.com.*

## PEARLS

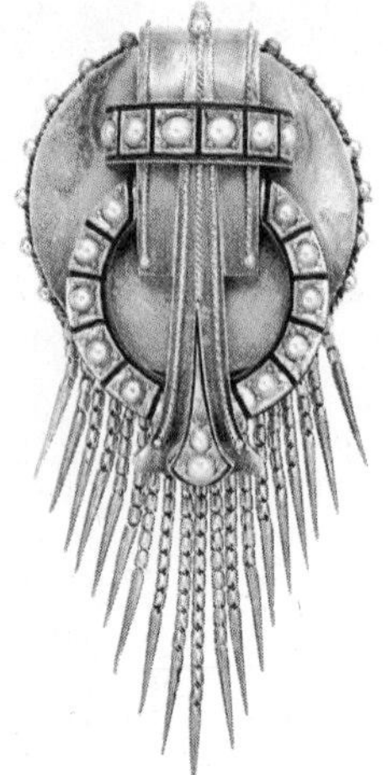

Victorian pearl, enamel, gold pendant-brooch, designed as an elaborate tassel, features half-pearls, enhanced by blue and black enamel applied on 14k yellow gold, completed by a retractable bail, pin stem and catch mechanism on the reverse, 3" x 1-3/8" ........................................ **$480**
*Heritage Auction Galleries*

Victorian Danish crucifix, 14k rose gold, the base has a punched surface for a textured effect. Rounded off into a fleur de lis at the four points, the cross culminates at the center with a starburst flower. A collection of 16 spherical and half spherical pearls are threaded down the middle, hallmark of the Netherlands. circa 1900. .... **$650**
*www.Topazery.com*

Edwardian pearl and diamond brooch, 15k bar and clasp are topped with a platinum-finished oval, encircled with 12 natural oriental pearls. Rhomboid and fleur de lis diamond accents frame the oval; 12 single-cut and rose-cut diamonds, circa 1905......... **$900**
*www.Topazery.com*

Retro cultured pearl, diamond, platinum ring, designed as an oyster shell, features a cultured pearl measuring 8.50-8.00mm, enhanced by full-cut diamonds weighing a total of approximately 1.25 carats, set in platinum, circa 1950................................ **$836**
*Heritage Auction Galleries*

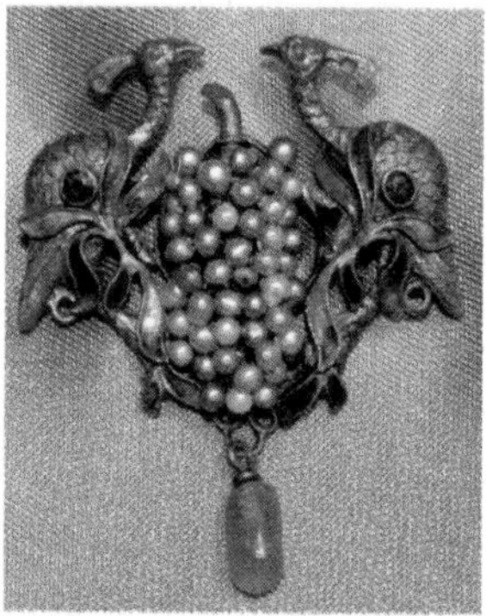

Enamel, rubies, emerald drop brooch, gilded silver; "grape cluster" set with natural American pink and lavender pearls. 1-3/4", early 20th century............ **$2,600**
*Pearl Society jewelry; Matthew Arden photo*

Edwardian diamond, pearl, white gold "jabot" (meaning an ornamental cascade of ruffles or frills), Cartier, French, features mine-, single- and rose-cut diamonds, highlighted by a pearl measuring 4.00-3.50mm, set in 18k white gold. Marked Cartier Paris, reference number 2463. French hallmarks, gross weight 7.00 grams, 3-3/8" x 1". ..................................................................**$8,365**
*Heritage Auction Galleries*

## JADEITE

Ring with intense, fine lavender 3/5" cabochon, 18k white gold, .53ct pavé-set diamonds . **$15,500**
*Mason-Kay, Inc. jewelry, Zalephoto.com, L.A.*

Double dragons simulated carved jadeite spring-hinged cuff bracelet, faux coral cabochons, emeralds and diamonds, fancy cast 22k gold-plated metal, 3-1/2" wide, signed © KJL, 1960s. **$240**
*Kenneth Jay Lane jewelry*

Walter Lampl enameled sterling circus tent brooch, gold wash over sterling tent, roof finely enameled, polychrome colors. Two 20mm carved roosters, one amethyst, one jade, wired to small shelf so birds tremble slightly, appearing to peck at ground; marked Sterling by Lampl, 2-1/4", 1940s. ... **$400**
*Milky Way Jewels; Rocky Day photo*

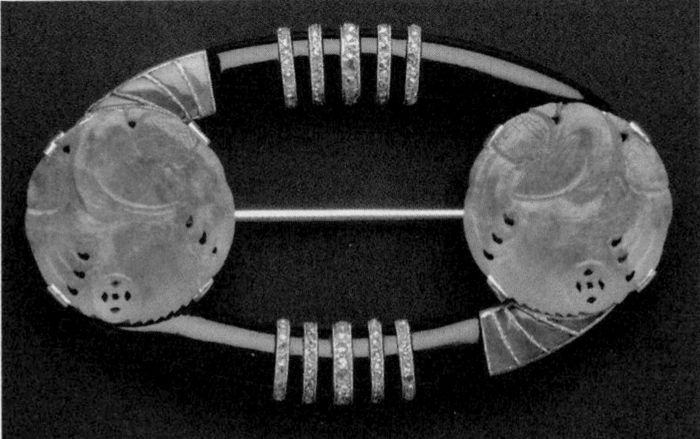

Art Deco jadeite, onyx, diamond brooch, Boucheron, Paris, composed of two pierced, carved jadeite disks joined by arched onyx plaques highlighted by rose-cut diamond bands, accented by buff-top jadeites, platinum mount, 3", signed Boucheron Paris, no. 2794; 1923. ...... **$41,475**
*Skinner Inc.*

Animal bracelet, two dragon heads, white mutton-fat nephrite jade bangle, nine carved balls as tails, mouths hold pearl; very rare; 2-1/2" diameter, 19th century. ...................................... **$2,000**

Cartier Pendulette, jadeite, diamond, coral and MOP dial carved with bird and leaf motif, framed by faceted coral beads and green jadeite ring, engraved with no. 200, signed, circa 1949, including Cartier box. ............... **$13,000**
*Skinner Inc.*

Jadeite, ruby, and diamond ring, set with three pear-shape jadeite cabochons, bezel and bead-set with ruby and diamond melee in 14 karat gold mount ................................ **$2,100**
*Skinner, Inc.*

## 10 Things You Didn't Know About

# JADEITE

1. A single-strand necklace of 63 jadeite beads recently sold at Christie's for $2.9 million.
2. Besides varying hues of green, jade colors include lavender, black, ice, and shades of yellow-brown-orange.
3. Jade is assigned as the modern 35th wedding anniversary gift.
4. Fashionable Chinese women often mix fine jadeite with simulated-jade costume pieces because, while jade is mysterious, it's not to be taken too seriously.
5. Decorative hinges or connectors often serve to restore broken jade bangles or ones with flaws and cracks. They also appear on low-quality jade for export.
6. Gem jade is mined in Burma, not China.
7. Old-stock jadeite can be found in areas across America, made available by descendants of Chinese immigrants.
8. When possible, purchase jadeite from family collections, which often feature more old-stock jade.
9. Some people prefer buying jadeite to gold as an investment.
10. The key question to ask a dealer when buying is not "Is this real jade?" but rather, "Is this untreated 'A' jadeite from Burma?" If the answer is yes, ask to have that in writing.

*Kathy Flood*

## CAMEOS

Eos (also called Aurora) with the genius of light on her back, ushering in the new morning. Italian, 18k fancy etched gold brooch mount, finely carved in high relief, 2-3/4", circa 1870.......... **$2,250**
*Jewelry Camelot Cameos and Antiques*

Coral cameo habille of Athena Parthenos, Italian, late 19th century, well carved after a work by the Greek sculptor Phidias. Athena's helmet is adorned with a sphinx and horse and is inset with a diamond. She wears her aegis (breastplate) complete with head of Medusa. Set in gold pendant mount, 2-1/8"................. **$2,500**
*Camelot Cameos and Antiques jewelry; Kerry Davidson photo*

Exquisitely carved high relief hardstone cameo of the "Madonna" set in an equally fine 18k gold, pearl and black enamel brooch mount. Italian, circa 1880, 2"..... **$3,750**
*Camelot Cameos and Antiques jewelry; Kerry Davidson photo*

Historical cameo representing the high esteem and affection of the Italian people for Giuseppe Garibaldi, military hero of the Italian Risorgimento (rebirth) that resulted in the unification of Italy. Italian, circa 1861-1862, finely carved from lava in high relief to depict Cupid (god of love) holding up a picture of Garibaldi, 2", gold brooch mount................. **$1,450**
*Camelot Cameos and Antiques jewelry; Kerry Davidson photo*

Cameo connoisseurs had their eyes fixed on a piece of glyptic grandeur auctioned by Skinner in 2009, an antique sardonyx and amethyst brooch, the work of Roman master Domenico Calabresi. In three layers, depicting Mars in a chariot drawn by two horses, with images of warring figures driven over clouds, the stone was set within a frame of circular-cut amethysts and purple rhinestones, all in 14k gold and silver mount, signed "(C)ALABRE(SI)." Estimated at ............**$800 to $1,200**
The cameo hammered down at .................................. **$13,035**
*Skinner Inc.*

Seed pearl cameo, 14k gold, molded glass, enamel, diamond, seed pearls, depicting an Elizabethan lady within blue enamel foliate frame set with diamond melee and pearls, 2".................. **$415**
*Skinner Inc.*

Cameo, Psyche and Eros, ultra-rare, see Psyche's wedding veil. The cameo has wonderful Victorian shading, 15k gold setting (tested), c-clasp with a trombone closure pin, 2-1/2", 1850. **$1,595**
*CameoHeaven.com*

Antique 18k gold, hardstone cameo brooch, "The Abduction of Proserpine," three-layer sardonyx cameo depicting Pluto hit by Cupid's arrow carrying off Proserpine in chariot of four horses, titled in French on the reverse, signed, in original fitted velvet box; 2-1/16", Tiffany & Co. ..**$8,000**
*Skinner Inc.*

JEWELRY

## GEORGIAN/VICTORIAN/EDWARDIAN

Victorian pierced locket with rose-cut diamonds and rubies, 14k gold.............................. **$2,800**
*Steve Fishbach Collection jewelry; Linda Lombardo photo*

Bohemian garnet necklace and brooch in low-karat gold setting, 1880s, 14-1/2" with 3-1/2" drop............................ **$3,500**
*Steve Fishbach Collection jewelry; Linda Lombardo photo*

Victorian Etruscan two-color gold earrings on wires, circa 1880s, 1-3/4"........................... **$1,800**
*Steve Fishbach Collection jewelry; Linda Lombardo photo*

European 18k gold, amethyst, rose diamond and purple enamel necklace, circa 1890s, 24" with chain............................ **$6,500**
*Steve Fishbach Collection jewelry; Linda Lombardo photo*

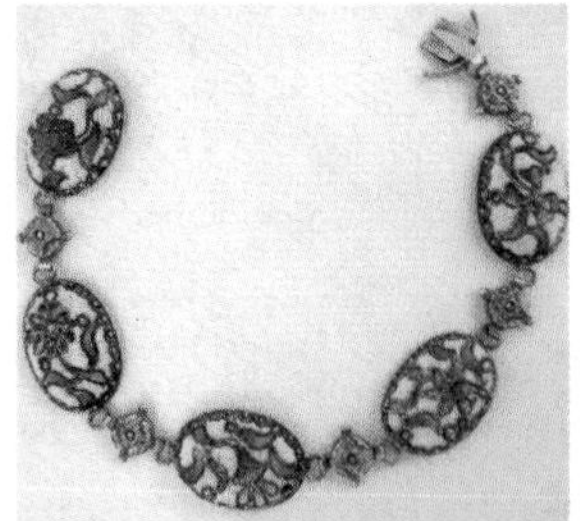

Bow brooch, silver face, gold back, turquoise and natural pearls, 1880s, 5"..................... **$3,500**
*Steve Fishbach Collection jewelry; Linda Lombardo photo*

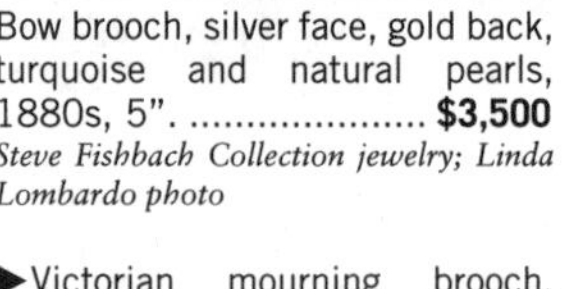

►Victorian mourning brooch, antique jet, varied shapes (diamonds, ovals, rounds), English, unmarked, 4", late 1800s... **$350**

◄Italian micro-mosaic bracelet in silver gilt setting, circa 1890, 7". ........................................ **$700**
*Steve Fishbach Collection jewelry; Linda Lombardo photo*

Triple-strand woven hairwork watch chain, yellow gold-filled fittings with hearts, 1860s-1880s, 13"................................ **$250**
*Linda Lombardo jewelry and photo, Worn to Perfection on Ruby Lane*

Rashistan Indian necklace, 22k gold, circa 1900, 17"...... **$6,500**
*Steve Fishbach Collection jewelry; Linda Lombardo photo*

## ART NOUVEAU

W.S. Hadaway enamel on silver ship pendant, 2" drop, circa 1900, English. ................ **$7,465**
*Didier Antiques London jewelry; Adam Wide photo*

Dorrie Nossiter comet brooch, pink tourmalines and pearl, 1920s, 2-1/3", British. ............... **$2,735**
*Didier Antiques London jewelry; Adam Wide photo*

Earrings, pearl and 18k gold, Art Nouveau style, pendant-type, the top designed as an open flower and leaves centered by a small European-cut diamond and suspending a foliate designed gold framework enclosing a rounded blister pearl, European hallmarks, late 19th/early 20th century, each 2-5/8" l. ......................... **$4,994**

Bar pin, garnet, amethyst and 14k gold, Arts & Crafts style, long oblong form centered by a cabochon amethyst flanked by rose- cut garnets bezel-set among leaves and berries, signed, early 20th century. .... **$650**

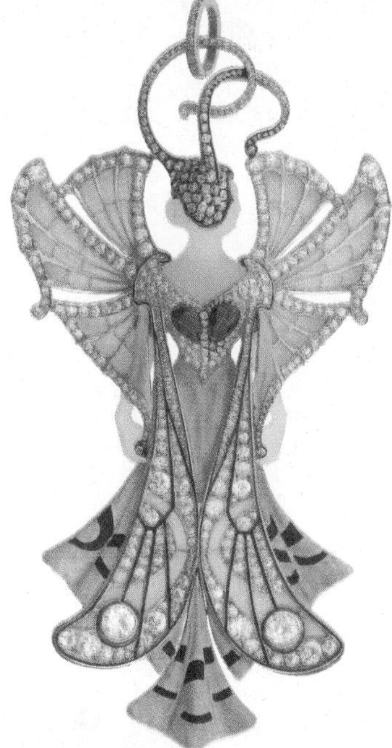

Art Nouveau pendant, snakes headdress, gold, enamel, rubies; original, "Sylvia," circa 1900 Paris, out of Maison Vever.......................... **Price unknown**
*Les Arts décoratifs, Paris/Jean Tholance. All rights reserved.*

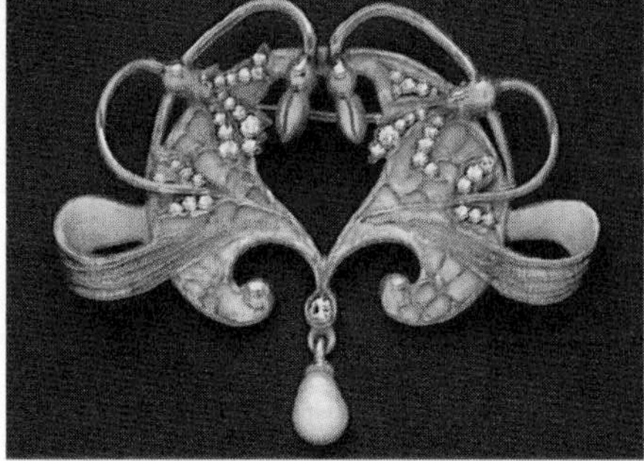

Pin, diamond, enamel and 18k gold, Art Nouveau style, designed as a pair of large scrolled leaves enameled in bluish green and framed by looping leaves and arching blossoms and buds bead-set with single-cut diamond, suspending a freshwater pearl drop, early 20th century. ........................................... **$2,250**

Choker, gem-set 14k yellow gold, Art Nouveau style, composed of openwork looped and serpentine links highlighted with seed pearls, diamonds, rubies, sapphires or turquoise, joined by trace link chains, American hallmark, late 19th/early 20th century, 13" l. ............................................................. **$3,800**

## ART DECO

Art Deco winged dress clip, Egyptian influence, also converts to necklace pendant, 10 faceted oval emerald crystals, graduated chain fringe, deeply carved casting, bronze-finished base metal, 1930s, 4", stamped Reinad. ........................................ **$200**

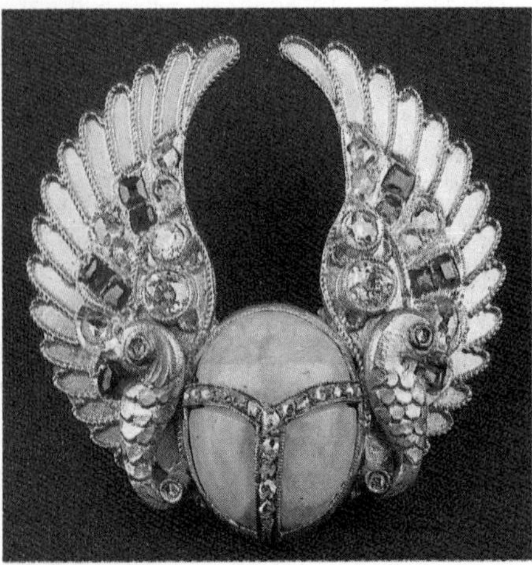

Egyptian Revival scarab brooch, gem-set 14k gold, designed as winged scarab, oval amazonite cabochon forms body enclosed by thin diamond-set bands, flanked by small S-scroll snakes, tall curved feathered gold wings bezel-set with old European-cut diamonds, step-cut rubies, European assay marks, possibly Austrian. ........................................ **$4,230**

Pagoda earrings, chalcedony, coral, marcasite, onyx, each designed as a shaped chalcedony tablet suspended from marcasite pagoda with coral bead accents, cabochon onyx tops, silver mounts, hallmark of Theodor Fahrner, circa 1930. ................ **$3,000 pair**

Art Deco necklace, pink crystal demilune stones, 1940s, unsigned, 16". ................................ **$150**

Art Deco bracelet, jadeite, diamond, ruby, composed of jadeite pis, each centering a pyramidal-cut ruby joined by geometric single-cut diamond links, platinum and gold mount, 7-3/8", maker's mark MvPc with man carrying rifle; guarantee stamps, at Boucheron Paris, 1926. ........................................ **$33,180**

*Skinner Inc.*

## PLASTICS

Jelly lilypad brooch, Lucite and enameled base metal, very rare, signed Leo Glass, 4-1/8", late 1930s. ........................ **$2,000+**

*Dr. Thomas Portzline collection; Carolyn Louise Newhouse photo*

Dagger brooch, well carved, painted black Bakelite, gold brass trim, 4", 1930s, unsigned. ........................ **$450**

Jelly Pekinese brooch, Lucite and base metal, rare, by Trifari, 3-1/8", 1942........................ **$2,000+**

*Dr. Thomas Portzline collection; Carolyn Louise Newhouse photo*

Jelly acorn necklace, Lucite and metal, rare, signed Mazer, 16", mid-1940s. ..................... **$800-$1,000**

*Dr. Thomas Portzline collection; Carolyn Louise Newhouse photo*

Jelly frog brooch, Lucite and enameled base metal, extremely rare, signed Sandor, 3-1/2", 1938-42. ........................ **$5,000+**

*Dr. Thomas Portzline collection; Carolyn Louise Newhouse photo*

Vintage bangle, detailed, highly carved root-beer Bakelite bangle, unusual clasp allows bracelet to open and fit many wrist sizes, rare, 1930s. ...... **$900**

JEWELRY

## SILVER

Rare unisex sterling mask pendant, among first in solid metal by Peter Macchiarini, signed P. Macchiarini and dated 1947, 1-5/8"........................ **$4,000**
*Michael Zarou jewelry; Shirley Byrne photo*

Ivory sterling set, rare Ming's Honolulu carved, painted ivory shell ginger brooch and earrings, marked Ming's and S/S, 1950-73; pin 3", earrings 1-3/4". ...........................................................**$1,000 set**
*Joanne Valentine jewelry and photo, AlmostAntiquesHawaii.com*

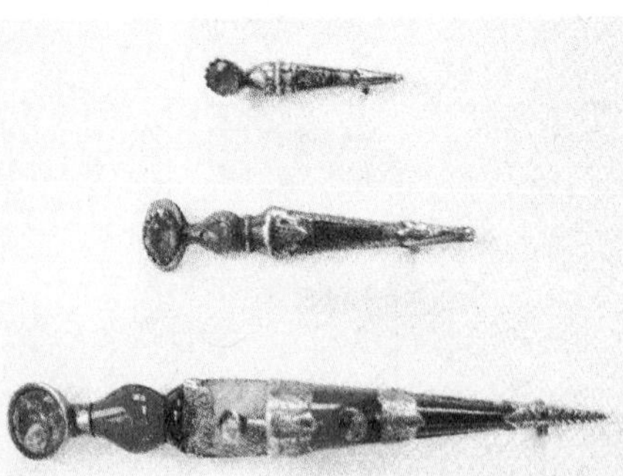

Ivory sterling set, rare Ming's Honolulu carved, painted ivory shell ginger brooch and earrings, marked Ming's and S/S, 1950-73; pin 3", earrings 1-3/4". ...........................................................**$1,000 set**
*Joanne Valentine jewelry and photo, AlmostAntiquesHawaii.com*

Arts & Crafts open cuff bracelet, American, silver (tested), abstract floral pattern, 1939, signed by artist Mabel S. Nicoll with date (April 1939)...... **$150+**

Sterling bracelet, Victorian hinged silver bangle chased with scrolls on front and sides, inlaid with Montrose (blue/gray) agate, unsigned, 2-3/4", mid-to-late 19th century. ..................................... **$450**

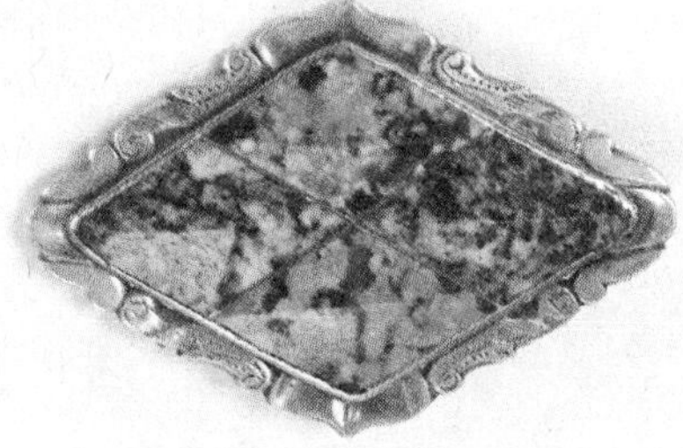

Diamond-shaped pendant/brooch with bezel-set pyramid-cut granite stones, colors of Aberdeen (gray) and Peterhead (pink), silver frame with slate back, also attributed to M. Rettie & Sons, 2-5/8", circa 1850. ................................................................ **$325**

Stag head brooch, cast-silver, garnet eyes, 1" faceted cairngorm bezel-mounted between antlers, unsigned, 2-7/8", mid-Victorian era. ............................. **$450**

## RHINESTONES

Unsigned earrings, have been attributed to Christian Dior, green glass drops and clear and green chatons, and clear navettes, 2-1/2" long...............**$175-$225**

DeLizza & Elster coral gold stippled cabochon set in peach from the early 1960s. Necklace, pin, bracelet and earrings; price depends on color. ....................................................................**$1,500-$2,500+ set**

DeLizza & Elster large pink sunburst pin in light rose....**$95-$115**

DeLizza & Elster bracelet with blue and black beads that look like seed pods but are called "nugget beads," from the early 1960s, the set was called "Elegance."...........................................................**$250-$300**

Jomaz bracelet with flawed emerald glass stones and clear navettes and baguettes, signed Jomaz, 7" x-1/2"...................................**$200-$250**

Unsigned Vendome adjustable ring with flawed emerald glass cabochon and clear chatons, has the patented squared-off shank that takes the ring from a size 5 to a size 8, patent mark is on inside of shank. ...................**$175-$225**

Jomaz faux opal ring with clear chatons, size 8, 7/8" tall, signed Jomaz..........................**$95-$125**

►Unsigned red flower pin with clear navettes and chatons, all red stones are open-backed, 3-1/4" x 1-1/4".......................... **$75-$95**

Rare Zoe Coste bracelet with black and clear Lucite stones, signed "Zoe Coste Made in France." 7-1/4" x 2"........................................................ **$175-$195**

Miriam Haskell green glass flower brooch with pearl and rhinestone headpins, along with green and clear chatons, and a green glass leaf. Marked Miriam Haskell, 2-1/4" x 1-3/4"........................ **$200-$250**

Mazer brooch with aquamarine baguettes and square, chaton and baguette clear rhinestones, signed MAZER, 2-3/4" x 1-7/8"............................ **$250-$300**

Unsigned brooch has a rose gold and gold washed appearance with amethyst and ruby glass stones, 2-3/4" x 2-1/8". ............................................ **$100-$150**

Les Bernard circle pin with matching earrings with colored glass cabochons and marcasites, pin and one earring are marked Les Bernard, pin 1-1/2" diameter, earrings 7/8".................................... **$95-$125 set**

Rhinestones get their name from stones found in the Rhine. Though colored glass stones have been around since the 13th or 14th centuries, today's glass stone gets its name from the colorful quartz pebbles that were found in the river that begins at the Rheinwaldhorn Glacier in the Swiss Alps and flows north and east for 820 miles, through Germany. These glass pebbles were used in jewelry making until their scarcity prompted a search for something similar but more readily available. The name "rhinestone" came to mean any cut glass used in jewelry.

## FIGURALS

Rose-in-hand fur clip, enameled pot metal two-pronged pin clip, metallic teal-green leaf color typical of Austrian work; woman's enameled hand with painted nails features Art Nouveau-style bracelet; unsigned,1938-42, 3"..**$125**

Dove duo, pair of pistachio or metallic-butterscotch enameled sterling pins with rhinestone accents, signed Sterling R. DeRosa, from DeRosa's Tick Tack Toe series of scatter pins, 1-1/4", 1949. ........................................**$250**

Flower brooch with carved-Lucite leaves, pavé-set crystal chaton, faceted, point-tipped Lucite ball set into tube-like claws on high-quiver spring for lots of movement. Unsigned, looks like work of Boucher or Mazer, 4-1/4", 1939-42..................................**$750+**

Forbidden Fruit pins, scarcer design motifs, maize and bunch of carrots, orange acrylic, orange rhinestones, Austrian, unsigned, 1950s-60s......... **$100-$150 each**

*Marjorie Chester jewelry; Durrell Godfrey photo*

Water lily brooch, huge gold-plated flower with tendril, purple-black pearlescent enamel, ruby-rose rhinestones, signed Eisenberg Original, 3", 1940s..... **$500**

Fool's Scepter pin clip, twist-pattern post and articulated leaf-like cap and collar points enameled metallic green, tipped with ruby cabochon beads, post finished with larger glass bead; silvered pot metal; unsigned, sometimes marked Boucher; 1938-42, 2-5/8"......................**$100-$150**

Mechanical pelican pin, gilded, enameled pot metal, pavé-set rhinestone wing; pushing on head feather plume raises top of beak to reveal one fish; second fish dangles as charm from beak; 1940-42; unsigned; 3". ................................................................................ **$500+**

JEWELRY

# Spotlight on Christmas Tree Pins

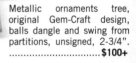

Metallic ornaments tree, original Gem-Craft design, balls dangle and swing from partitions, unsigned, 2-3/4". ............................... **$100+**

Polka-dots tree, multicolor rhinestones on skinny trunk, original 1950-60s Gem-Craft, signed Craft, 2-5/8" ............................... **$100+**

Teepee tree, original Gem-Craft design, similar, one with scalloped edges, the other with more stones, both unsigned, 1960s, 2-3/4". ............................... **$50 ea.**

Rhinestones, original vintage design by Alfeo Verrecchia at Gem-Craft, Austrian coloration, japanned setting, 1950s-60s, 2-1/4"................... **$250**

Teepee tree, original Gem-Craft design, similar, one with scalloped edges, the other with more stones, both unsigned, 1960s, 2-3/4". ............................... **$50 ea.**

# Kitchenwares

## Vintage

In today's world of multi-use kitchen equipment, a slicer that isn't also a dicer will soon be out with the trash. Many of the earliest kitchen implements, however, were single-task items, inventively designed for purposes no longer routine. That specialization only increases the collecting appeal of "kitchenabilia." The challenge lies not only in finding such items, but also in identifying them. Among the job-specific vintage kitchen items that might leave modern chefs baffled: vinegar measures; butter paddles (and molds and stamps); preserving jars; cherry pitters; pudding sticks; pie lifters; and sugar nippers!

Other early kitchen items had purposes defined by the demands of an individual household. Before the days of pre-packaging, homemakers supplied their own containers for food storage, relying on what was affordable and readily at hand. Assorted crocks, jars, tins, and boxes were put to a variety of kitchen uses and repurposed as needed. Unless specifically marked (or identifiable by comparison), original intended functions can only be guessed at. Here, the collecting appeal revolves around such intangibles as design; material utilized (some collectors specialize in toleware, for example, others copper or cast-iron); color; and individual taste.

Many subsets of kitchenabilia are easily recognizable and have avid fans. Among the most popular: coffeepots (and related items, such as coffee mills); egg beaters; churns; kettles; kitchen scales; spoon holders; reamers; trivets; and rolling pins. As with other "daily use" items, vintage kitchen items will show their age; this only adds to their authenticity.

Only the most determined (or curious) actually put early kitchenabilia to use today. For the most part, these are display collectibles. A wall dotted with examples of peelers, graters, and skillets, or shelves accented with graniteware coffee pots and copper tea kettles add to a kitchen's charm, artifacts of a simpler (if much more labor-intensive) age.

Cake mold, man on safety bicycle, 11-1/2" h... **$125**
*Copake Auction*

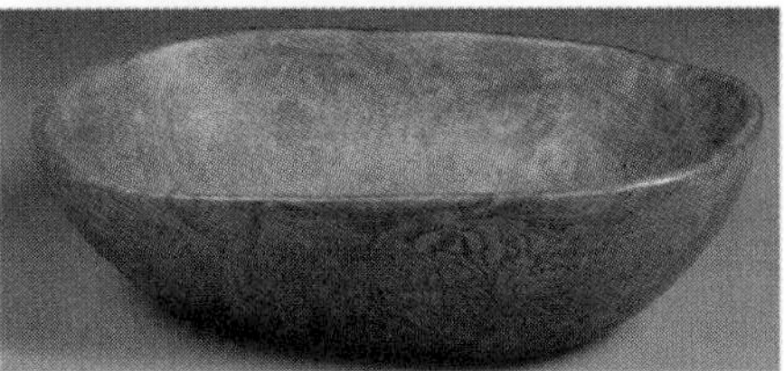

Carved burl bowl, New England, 19th c., slightly irregular oblong shape with rounded sides, old dry work surface, 4-1/2" h. x 18" w. x 13" d............. **$1,304**
*Skinner, Inc.*

►Early corn muffin mold with fish motif, 15-1/4" l............................................................ **$125**
*Copake Auction*

Blue painted tabletop butter churn, square with rounded bottom, handled removable lid, interior paddle worked by side crank handle, 15-1/2" h. x 12-1/2" x 15" base ..................................... **$236**
*James D. Julia, Inc.*

Cast iron ball of string dispenser, hinged at bottom, painted black, 5-1/2" h. ................................ **$385**
*Skinner, Inc.*

Large relief-carved butter stamp, America, 19th c., round tub-size stamp with turned handle, centered with large fruit and leaf, chip-carved borders, 9-1/2" dia. ....................................................... **$1,067**
*Skinner, Inc.*

Paint-decorated tinware dome-top trunk, America, early 19th c., hinged lid on trunk with wire handle, painted with white band on front with red and green leaves over red, green, and yellow floral spray, on an asphaltum ground, 7" h. x 9-3/4" w. x 6-1/2" d. . **$830**
*Skinner, Inc.*

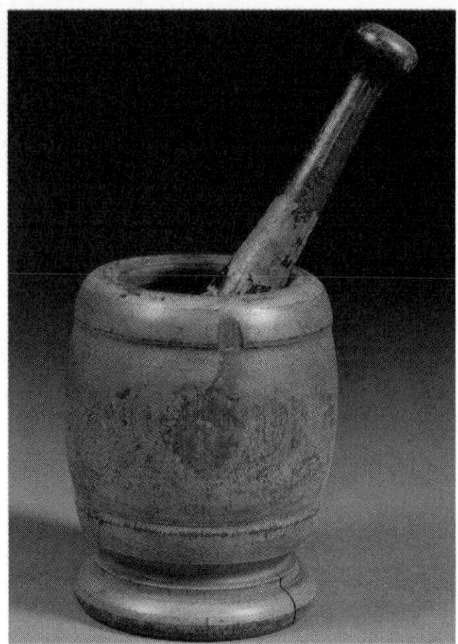

Mustard-painted turned wooden mortar with porcelain and wood pestle, America, 19th c., mortar 6-5/8" h., pestle 9-3/4" l. ........................................... **$178**
*Skinner, Inc.*

Wrought-iron upright broiler, easel style with straight horizontal cross members and front ledge, upper member topped with ram's horn ornament, 18th c., 13-1/2" h. overall, 13-1/4" d. ....................... **$230**
*Jeffrey S. Evans & Associates*

Wrought-iron broiler, meandering members welded to revolving flat ring attached through handle by rivet, handle displays hanging loop and is split to form the front legs, late 18th/early 19th c., 3-1/2" h. overall, 23-1/4" l. overall, 7-1/2" d. .......................... **$161**
*Jeffrey S. Evans & Associates*

Pewter coffeepot, Roswell Gleason, Dorchester, Massachusetts, 1821-1871, baluster-form pot with hinged lid, round molded base, black-painted handle, impressed "R. GLEASON" in circle on base, 10-3/4" h. ............ **$237**
*Skinner, Inc.*

Pewter flagon, Oliver Trask, Beverly, Massachusetts, c. 1830, lighthouse form with molded fillets, double-scroll handle with molded thumb-piece, impressed maker's mark "O.TRASK" on base, 11-3/4" h................. **$711**
*Skinner, Inc.*

Red-painted and decorated tinware coffeepot, America, early 19th c., lighthouse form with hinged lid and gooseneck spout, decorated with bands of white, yellow, and green stylized leaves and fruit, on red ground, 9-3/4" h. ..................................... **$2,133**
*Skinner, Inc.*

Pine and oak kneading table, early 18th c. Thick pine five-board top, each seam with butterfly tenon above the square frieze and joined by sliding brackets attached to top and frieze. Top slides above frieze, opening to compartmented well revealing original receptacle for a lock, now absent. The underside of top displays area where original lock engaged the top to prevent it from opening. Square frieze section of dovetailed construction decorated on three sides with scrolled fielded panels above a molded plinth, joined on dowels to a shaped and scalloped trestle base with scalloped and shaped edges joined by square trusses fixed by wedges centering a decorative panel with molded edges and pierced heart. Trestle base fitted with a single drawer with canted sides conforming to the shape of table. Drawer front decorated with a pair of scrolled fielded panels. Whole constructed with exposed dovetails. Drawer retains original iron strap backing for original pull, now absent. Base of feet is joined by flat mortised shelf-like stretchers. 30" h. x 41-1/2" l. x 35-1/2" d. Provenance: Purchased by current owner from a family in Brooklyn Heights, New York in middle of 20th c. ...**$805**
*James D. Julia, Inc.*

Wrought-iron toaster with six supports attached to upper and lower cross members, arched legs ending in penny feet, attached to long rod with wooden handle, first half 19th c., 9" h. overall, 35-1/2" l. overall, 12" w. overall .................................................... **$196**
*Jeffrey S. Evans & Associates*

Wrought-iron wall rack, ornate design, five hooks, 19th c., 11-1/4" h. overall, 20-1/4" l. overall..**$1,725**
*Jeffrey S. Evans & Associates*

Tinware man and woman cookie cutters, America, 19th c., shaped figures on rectangular tin panel with handle, 6-1/4" x 3-3/4" .......................................... **$148**
*Skinner, Inc.*

Treen commercial butter mold, tall rectangular form with two handles and central plunger, grape and acorn design, original natural surface, late 19th/early 20th c., 11-1/2" h., 2-1/4" x 3-1/2" mold....... **$184**
*Jeffrey S. Evans & Associates*

Steel table-top sugar nippers, turned wooden handle and brass standard, raised on walnut molded-edge base with line inlay, first half 19th c., 6" h., 3-1/2" x 11" base. ................................................... **$259**
*Jeffrey S. Evans & Associates*

Small enterprise coffee mill, stencil-decorated and painted, marked on wheel "ENTERPRISE M'F'G. CO. PHILADELPHIA U.S.A.," base additionally marked with manufacturer's name, bottom drawer mounted with porcelain knob, painted and stenciled surfaces original, 12-1/2" h. x 10-1/4" w. overall....................................... **$690**
*James D. Julia, Inc.*

◀Red-painted chip-carved pine spoon rack, America, late 18th/early 19th c., pierced rosette finial on backboard, three-tier rack decorated with chip-carved rosettes and zigzags, each tier with four spoon slots, 20-1/2" h. x 10" w. .................................. **$1,896**
*Skinner, Inc.*

## Modern

The diverse area of kitchenware/household objects offers a world of collecting opportunities. Your interests may lead you to antique rarities more than 100 years old or to items of more recent manufacture. Any and all territory should be considered fair game. As with other collectibles, your primary motivation should be your individual likes and preferences.

There is a great deal of interest in kitchenware and related items from 35 to 60 years old; these objects rekindle old memories and represent a different, less-complicated era for many.

The items here represent a broad spectrum of kitchen items and cooking activities. These include just about every task you would want to try to master in your kitchen of yesteryear. There are gadgets of all types and all sorts of accessories, sets, holders, and miscellaneous gizmos. Most of the items are non-electrical and small in scale.

For more information on kitchen collectibles, see *Spiffy Kitchen Collectibles* or *Warman's Kitschy Kitchen Collectibles Field Guide*, both by Brian S. Alexander.

Acme Rotary Mincer, stainless steel blade with wood handle, "For mincing, cutting noodles, etc.," in red or green with instructions, boxed, 1935 .................... **$22-$25**

Alumode Gingerbread House Mold, mentions Woman's Day article on box, with cardboard sleeve, 1950s, Aluminum Specialty Co. .................... **$22-$25**

Androck Flour Sifter, three screens, "Hand-I-Sift," red and white "Pantry Pattern" design with bakery items, 1950s .......................................... **$25-$30**

Arthur Godfrey Barbecue, with charcoal inside, "The charcoal pit for broiling your food," with cardboard insert, 1950s, Marc Mfg. Co., Chicago........ **$28-$35**

Cake cover, metal, yellow lid with apple design. Same pattern was used on canister sets, flour sifters, etc., 1940s-1950s........................................... **$22-$25**

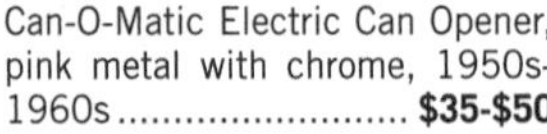

Can-O-Matic Electric Can Opener, pink metal with chrome, 1950s-1960s .......................... **$35-$50**

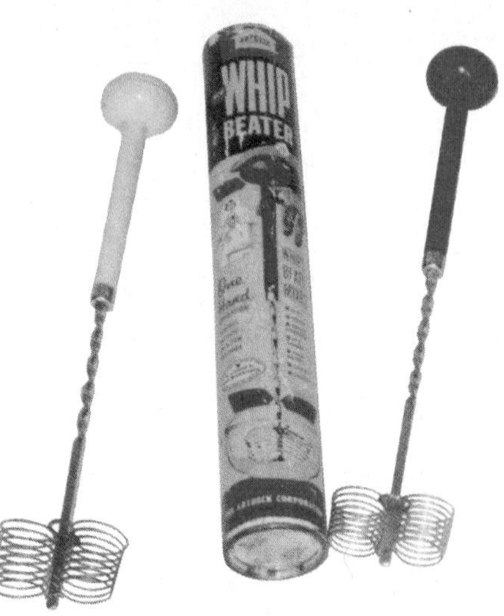


Artbeck Whip Beater, with plastic knob, "Whips, beats, mixes, one hand operation," with tube carton, 1954, Arthur Beck Co., Chicago................. **$15-$18**

Cake cover, locking copper-tone aluminum, square with wooden handle, boxed, has tag, 1950s Mirro Aluminum............................................... **$30-$35**

Canister set, three-piece styrene plastic, "The smart set for smart kitchens. The first and only canister set with a window, a feature to gladden any woman's heart," boxed, 1950s, Janetware Plastic Products, Aurora, Ill....... **$40-$45**

Dazey Mix-er-ator, with graduations and mixing directions, 1950s, Dazey Corp., St. Louis .................................. **$20-$25**

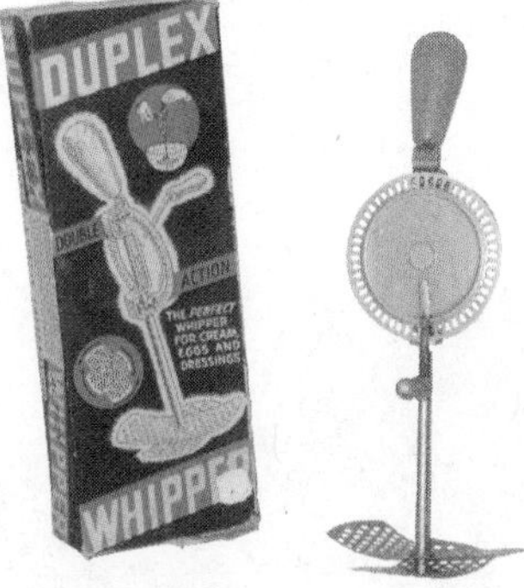


Duplex Whipper, metal with green wood handle, "Double action for cream, eggs, and dressings," boxed, 1930s-1940s..... **$40-$45**

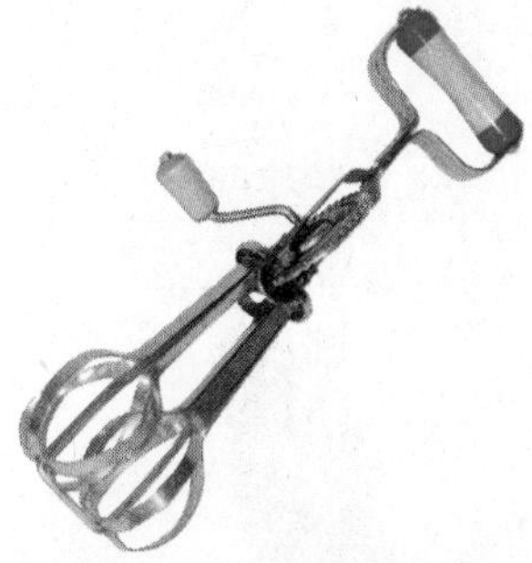

Eggbeater, natural and red wooden handle, "Another Androck Product," 1940s-1950s. ...... **$22-$25**

Eggbeater, with green Bakelite side handle, 1940s, Worlbeater, Los Angeles.................. **$30-$35**

Gadget Master Hot Vegetable Tongs, metal, "No more burned fingers, a star in any kitchen," boxed, 1950s, Popiel Bros, Chicago............................ **$18-$22**

Ekco non-spatter Egg Beater and Bowl Set (quart), A&J with 1923 patent date .................. **$40-$45**

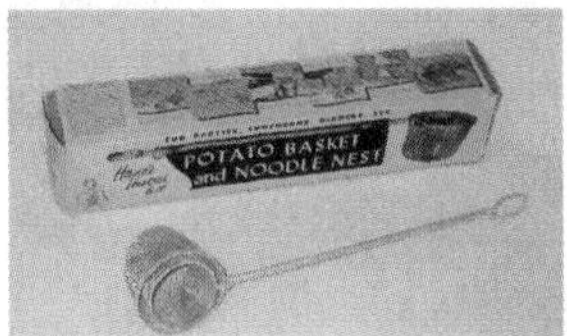


"Handi Hostess" Potato Basket and Noodle Nest, "Makes a delicious potato basket for parties, luncheons," boxed, 1951, Bonley Products Co., Chicago.... **$18-$22**

Kit Cat Klock, styrene plastic, battery-operated with moving eyes and tail, 1950s, California Clock Co., San Juan Capistrano, Calif. .................................. **$35-$50**

Krispy Krust Rolling Pin, chrome, with catalin plastic handles and ball bearings, 1940s, Buffalo Toy and Tool Works, Buffalo, N.Y. .................................... **$40-$45**

Longhorn Meat Markers, 12 metal cooking level markers, boxed, 1950s, Bar & Barbecue Products, Los Angeles, Calif. ......... **$15-$18**

Mirro Spring-Form Pan, aluminum, "Clampless, for Tortes, Cakes, Desserts," boxed, 1950s, Mirro Aluminum, Manitowoc, Wis. .................................... **$20-$25**

Ohio Baster, for roast meat and fowl, in cardboard tube, 1950s, Ohio Thermometer Co., Springfield, Ohio..................... **$18-$22**

Plastic cookie cutters, eight-piece set with figural animal shapes, boxed, 1940s, Hutzler Mfg. Co., Long Island City, N.Y........................................ **$35-$40**

Roasting pan, metal, "Easy to clean, completely seamless, surehold handles," with label, 1950s, Bake King, Chicago Metallic Mfg. Co., Lake Zurich, Ill.......................................................... **$18-$20**

Rudolph the Red Nosed Reindeer Cake and Mold Pan Set, eight pieces, copyright 1939, Robert L. May, boxed, 1950s, Bake King, Chicago Metallic Mfg. Co., Chicago ............................ **$45-$55**

Rooster measuring spoon and hot pad holder, styrene plastic, with spoons, 1950s ............. **$22-$25**

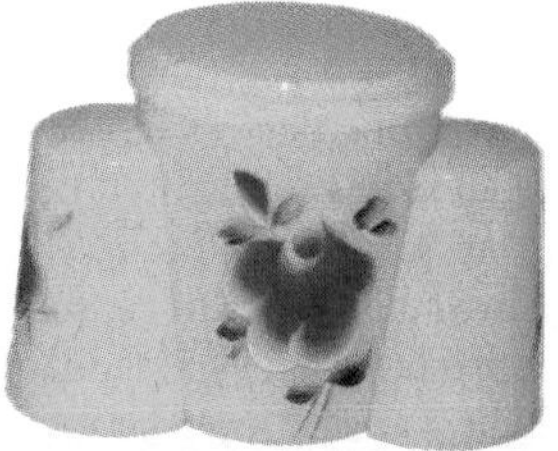

Salt and pepper shakers with sugar container, three-piece styrene plastic set with hand-painted flower decoration, 1950s, Plastic Novelties Inc., Los Angeles ................................... **$22-$25**

Skotch O' Matic Hot or Cold Jug, metal and plastic, half-gallon, "Press the bulb, it serves a drink, a delight to use!," boxed, 1950s, Hamilton-Skotch Corp., Hamilton, Ohio ............................ **$30-$35**

Spud Spikes, set of six, aluminum, "Exclusive knife edge, bake potatoes fast," with card sleeve, 1950s, Monarch Die Casting, Santa Monica, Calif. ...... **$18-$20**

Swans Down Cake Pan, "Swans Down cake flour makes better cakes," 1920s ............. **$25-$30**

◄Tater Baker, metal with plastic handle, "Bakes potatoes, warms buns and leftovers on top of stove," boxed, 1950, The Everedy Co., Frederick, Md. ........ **$25-$28**

Wonderlier Bowl Set, five sizes in pastel shades with lids, 1950s-1960s ......................... **$45-$50**

Tupperware Tumblers, 2 oz. "Midgets" with seals, set of six in pastel shades, 1950s-1960s......................................................... **$12-$15**
Plastic Spice Rack, styrene plastic, non Tupperware, 1950s..... **$12-$15**

# Lighting Devices

Lighting devices have been around for thousands of years, and antique examples range from old lanterns used on the farm to high-end Tiffany lamps. The earliest know type of lamp was the oil lamp, which was patented by Aimé Argand in 1784 and mass-produced starting in the 19th century. Around 1850 kerosene became a popular lamp-burning fluid, replacing whale oil and other fluids. In 1879 Thomas A. Edison invented the electric light, causing fluid lamps to lose favor and creating a new field for lamp manufacturers. Decorative table and floor lamps with ornate glass lampshades reached their height of popularity from 1900-1920, due to the success of Tiffany and other Arts and Crafts lamp makers, such as Handel.

## Early Lighting

Amethyst pressed three-printie block glass whale oil lamp, Boston & Sandwich Glass Co., Sandwich, Massachusetts, 1840-1860, on octagonal standard and square base, 9-3/4" h. .................... **$533**
*Skinner, Inc.*

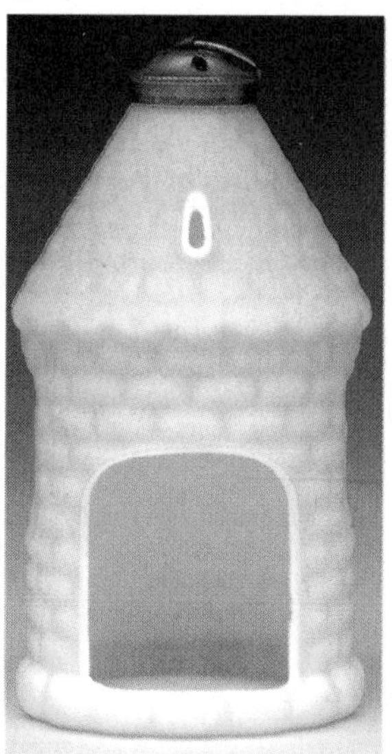

Blue satin mini lantern formed in the shape of a round stone building with peaked roof. White milk glass shading to blue at the top. Lantern is finished with a brass heat cap and ring. Unsigned. 6" h. ....................................... **$59**
*James D. Julia, Inc.*

Bradley & Hubbard "Little B & H" footed finger lamp, nickel plated, impressed on shoulder "THE B & H," refill cap embossed "B & H," period slip burner and a marked MacBeth No. 4 chimney. Fourth quarter 19th century. 4-5/8" h. to top of collar, 3-7/8" dia. base. ....................................... **$149**
*Jeffrey S. Evans & Associates*

Blue satin fairy lamp, ruffled base shading from light to dark blue with white interior. Base is complete with Clarke insert signed "S. Clarke Patent Trademark Fairy." Insert is complete with candle cup also signed. Lamp is finished with a ruffled fairy lamp shade shading from light to medium blue. 5-3/4" t. ......... **$115**
*James D. Julia, Inc.*

Cricklite five-light fairy lamp, porcelain figural stand of a classical woman in gold robes with an amphora in her hand and a water jug on her head, marked on the underside "Royal Worcester Made in England 2/125 Trade Mark Cricklite." Atop the porcelain figure is a brass five-arm lamp spider that supports five fairy lamps with clear pressed glass lamp cups and Burmese shades. Each lamp cup is marked in the bottom "Cricklite Clarkes Trade Mark." Each lamp ring is impressed on the interior "Clarkes Trade Mark Cricklite." 34" t................ **$7,475**
*James D. Julia, Inc.*

Cut panel composite stand lamp, cranberry font, brass stem attached to a painted black Veritas ceramic base, underside embossed "Veritas Lamp Works," metal connector, period No. 3 collar. Period No. 3 set-up consisting of a Hinks Duplex Patent burner, chimney, and a dark to light cranberry shade with swirled branches and hobnails, gauffered top. Late 19th/early 20th century. 14-1/4" h. to top of collar, 7-1/4" dia. base. Shade 8-3/4" h., 5-1/2" dia. fitter........................... **$287**
*Jeffrey S. Evans & Associates*

Eason footed finger lamp, blue opalescent font, colorless base with molded handle and embossed petal to lower terminal, No. 1 Taplin-Brown collar, period No. 1 slip burner and chimney. Fourth quarter 19th century. 5-1/4" h. to top of collar, 4-1/4" dia. base.... **$805**
*Jeffrey S. Evans & Associates*

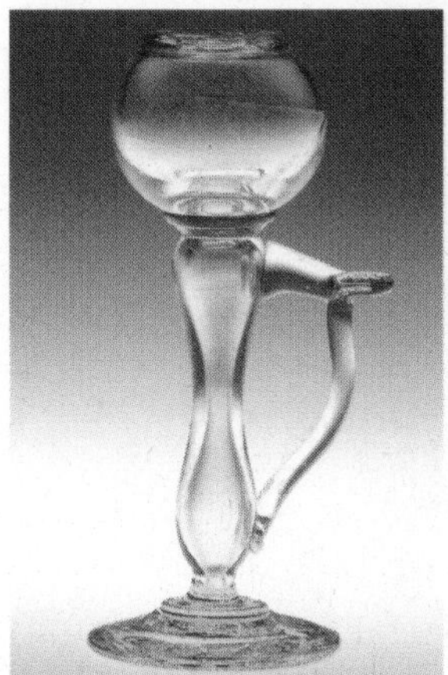

Free-blown lacemaker's lamp, colorless, globular font with thick top edge, raised on a hollow hourglass-form stem with applied handle and a broad circular foot. 19th century. 8-1/4" h., 3-1/2" dia. foot.............................. **$81**
*Jeffrey S. Evans & Associates*

Five small free-blown colorless glass lamps with pressed glass bases, attributed to the Boston & Sandwich Glass Co., Sandwich, Massachusetts, 1830-1835, one with round font on a square stepped base, one with round font on a scalloped circular base, one with a bulb font on a stepped quatrefoil base, one with a round font on a stepped quatrefoil base, and one with a round font on a cup plate base, all with drop-in whale-oil burners, 3- 7/8"-7-1/4" h.......................................... **$948**
*Skinner, Inc.*

Eight colorless free-blown glass lamp items, possibly the Boston Sandwich & Glass Co., Sandwich, Massachusetts, 1825-1835, comprising four small hand lamps with applied handles and drop-in tin whale oil burners, one ribbed; three small sparking lamps, one with drop-in tin whale oil burner, the other with pewter burners, and a lamp filler with cover and remnants of gilt decoration, 1-7/8"-5-3/4" h........................ **$1,541**
*Skinner, Inc.*

Green and mustard-painted tin fluid burning lamp, third quarter 19th century, removable conical shade over lamp stand with handle, saucer base, and well on shaft supporting a molded colorless glass sparking lamp with a threaded pewter single tube camphene burner with cap, overall 10-3/4" h. ........................ **$474**

*Skinner, Inc.*

Hanging library lamp, cranberry opalescent hobnail umbrella shade, dark to light pink opalescent hobnail font holder with brass liner, brass drop-in font with side-fill cap. Frame featuring stamped and cast-brass elements with butterflies, horizontal spring tension mechanism, ceiling mount with patent date for suspension device, fitted with 29 colorless period prisms. Late 19th/early 20th century. 78" h. extended, 40" unextended, shade 6-1/4" h., 14" dia. fitter. ............................ **$1,092**

*Jeffrey S. Evans & Associates*

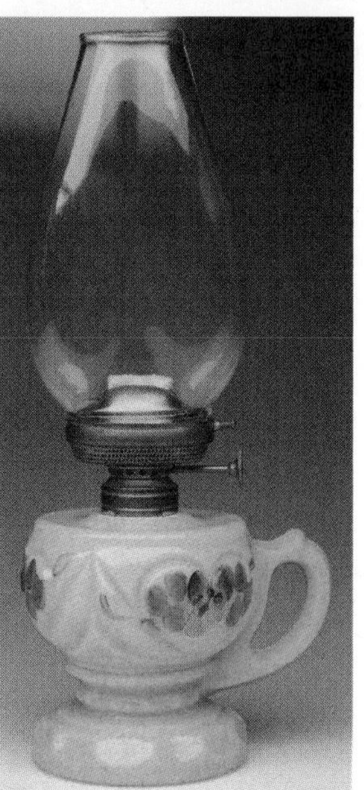

Heart footed finger lamp, opaque green with floral polychrome decoration on hearts, opaque green molded handle, No. 1 Taplin-Brown collar, period H. B. & H. Pinafore lip burner and chimney. Tarentum Glass Co. Fourth quarter 19th century. 4-3/4" h. to top of collar, 3-3/4" dia. base. ...... **$218**

*Jeffrey S. Evans & Associates*

Hobbs' Coral Reef/Seaweed finger lamp, ruby opalescent/cranberry opalescent, colorless applied handle, No. 1 Taplin-Brown collar, period No. 0 slip burner and chimney with beaded top. Hobbs, Brockunier & Co. and Beaumont Glass Co., fourth quarter 19th century. 2-1/2" h. to top of collar, 3-3/8" dia. base................ **$690**

*Jeffrey S. Evans & Associates*

Hobbs' Coral Reef/Seaweed stand lamp, ruby opalescent/cranberry opalescent font, colorless beehive stem and ribbed base, No. 2 Taplin-Brown collar, period No. 2 slip burner. Hobbs, Brockunier & Co. and Beaumont Glass Co., late 19th/early 20th century. 9" h. to top of collar, 4-1/4" square base. ........................................ **$690**

*Jeffrey S. Evans & Associates*

**Tip:** Do not store oil lamp fluid in glass bases. Bases may be cleaned with soap and water and air dried for a day or two before new oil is added.

Hobbs' Coral Reef/Seaweed stand lamp, sapphire opalescent/blue opalescent font, colorless beehive stem and ribbed base, No. 1 Miller oval band collar, period No. 1 slip burner and chimney with beaded top. Hobbs, Brockunier & Co. and Beaumont Glass Co., late 19th/early 20th century. 8-1/2" h. to top of collar, 3-3/4" square base. ................................ **$345**

*Jeffrey S. Evans & Associates*

Hobbs' No. 326 Windows/Coin Dot stand lamp, sapphire opalescent/blue opalescent font, colorless base, No. 1 Taplin-Brown collar, period No. 0 slip burner and chimney with scalloped top. Hobbs, Brockunier & Co. Fourth quarter 19th century. 6-1/2" h. to top of collar, 3-5/8" dia. base. .......................................... **$517**

*Jeffrey S. Evans & Associates*

Hulsebus II, Fig. 385/Daisy miniature lamp, cranberry, swirled rib font mounted on an embossed circular base, light cranberry matching patterned ball chimney-shade, period collar, period string burner with thumbwheel embossed "DAISY lamp." Late 19th/early 20th century. 10-1/2" h. to top of shade, 3-3/4" dia. base....... **$431**

*Jeffrey S. Evans & Associates*

◀L. G. Wright Honeycomb stand lamp, cranberry opalescent pyriform font, opaque white base, brass connector, period No. 2 collar, matching patterned shade with crimped and folded rim, electrified burner, factory drilled hole in base of font, base not drilled, non-period chimney. L. G. Wright Glass Co. Mid-20th century. 24" h. overall to top of shade, 14" h. to top of collar, 5-1/2" square base. ................................ **$230**

*Jeffrey S. Evans & Associates*

▶L. G. Wright Coin Dot miniature lamp, cranberry opalescent, matching patterned dark cranberry umbrella shade with factory polished rims, period collar. L. G. Wright Glass Co. Mid-20th century. 6-5/8" h. to top of shade, 3-3/4" h. to top of collar, 2" dia. base. ................................ **$138**

*Jeffrey S. Evans & Associates*

Inverted Thumbprint and Fan Base stand lamp, colorless opalescent font, amber base, No. 2 Taplin-Brown collar, period No. 2 slip burner, colorless opalescent Inverted Thumbprint shade. Fourth quarter 19th century. 10" h. to top of collar, 5-1/4" dia. base; shade 5-3/4" h., 4" dia. fitter. .................................... **$460**

*Jeffrey S. Evans & Associates*

L. G. Wright Honeycomb stand lamp, cranberry opalescent square-form font with embossed lobes, opaque white base, brass screw connector, period No. 1 collar, period No. 1 slip burner and chimney. L. G. Wright Glass Co. Mid-20th century. 9-3/4" h. to top of collar, 5-1/4" dia. base.... **$115**
*Jeffrey S. Evans & Associates*

Pewter adjustable doctor's lens lamp, early 19th century, with round font with wick channel, swivel-adjustable lens, on a round base, the underside marked "JD," 5-1/4" h. ........................... **$652**
*Skinner, Inc.*

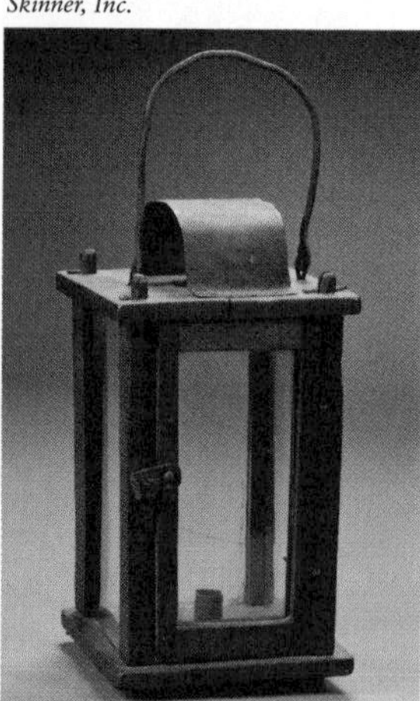

L. G. Wright Thumbprint miniature lamp, cranberry, matching patterned umbrella shade, period collar. L. G. Wright Glass Co. Mid-20th century. 7" h. to top of shade, 3-3/4" h. to top of collar, 2" dia. base. ...................... **$103**
*Jeffrey S. Evans & Associates*

Pierced tin and glass lantern, New England, late 18th/early 19th century, with three round colorless bull's-eye glass windows, hinged door, 13-1/2" h. ............. **$1,185**
*Skinner, Inc.*

Early pine candle lantern, American, late 18th/early 19th century, with bent iron rod hanger, tin chimney, pegged, through-tenon construction, with likely original glass, wire-hinged door with iron latch,11-1/2" h. ................. **$948**
*Skinner, Inc.*

Paint-decorated wood and tin lantern, "R.B. Ostrom, Manufacturer, Angola, NY, Patented March 14th 1865 by D.L. Jaques," rectangular case with glazed panels on three sides with wire guards, the top and rear lined with tin panels, the rear panel with access to brass kerosene font, painted green with red-stenciled floral borders, yellow-stenciled maker's mark on top, studded with white glass bosses, 9-3/4" h., 5-1/2" w., 8-1/2" l. ............................ **$326**
*Skinner, Inc.*

Pewter whale oil work lamp with two magnifying lenses, American, early 19th century with whale oil burners on font fitted with slots for magnifying lens, on a round weighted base, 8-3/4" h...... **$711**
*Skinner, Inc.*

Pair of E.W. Smith, Beverly, Massachusetts pewter whale oil lamps, 8-1/4" h.................. **$652**
*Pook & Pook, Inc.*

Princess Feather stand lamp, cobalt blue, No. 2 Ebling collar, period No. 2 slip burner and chimney. Late 19th/early 20th century. 9-5/8" h. to top of collar, 5-3/4" square base........................ **$149**
*Jeffrey S. Evans & Associates*

Plume and Atwood brass "Harvard" single-arm student lamp, horizontal tank, adjustable center shaft, weighted base, period central draft burner with thumbwheel embossed "PA HARVARD," cast brass shade holder together by association, cased lemon yellow ball shade, non-period chimney. Fourth quarter 19th century. 20-3/4" h. overall, 5-1/4" dia. base; shade 5-7/8" h., 2-3/4" dia. fitter.............................. **$1,495**
*Jeffrey S. Evans & Associates*

◀Punched tin and glass candle lantern, 18th century, with ring handle, two hinged doors, removable double candle holder tray, supported on conical feet, 20-1/2" h., 5" w., 9" l..... **$1,659**
*Skinner, Inc.*

▶Smith I, Fig. 326 opaque glass miniature peg lamp, opaque white with cherub transfer decoration, candlestick base with some opalescence and polychrome floral decoration, later ball form shade with similar cherub decoration and peach shading to top, period No. 1 collar, period burner. Possibly Pairpoint Glass Co. Late 19th/early 20th century. 14-1/2" h. to top of chimney-shade, 3-1/2" square base........................ **$126**
*Jeffrey S. Evans & Associates*

Pressed hexagonal candlestick, opaque white above opal opaque, urn-form socket with knop extension raised on a flared hexagonal base featuring two bands of four rings on stem and a band of four rings repeated under the foot, wafer construction. A very rare combination. Probably Midwestern. 1840-1860. 7-1/2" h., 4-1/4" DOA base........................... **$138**
*Jeffrey S. Evans & Associates*

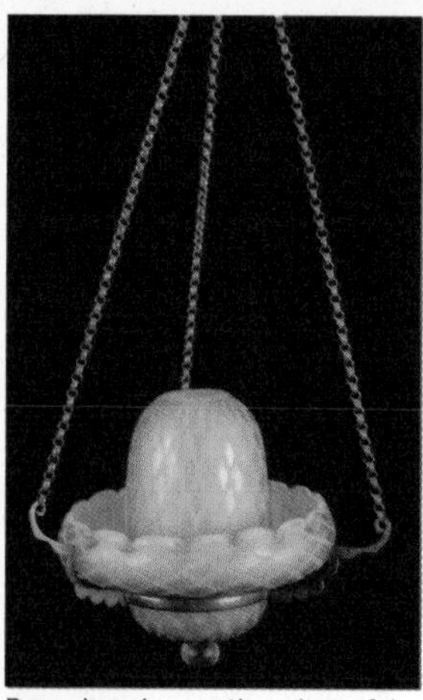

Rare hanging satin glass fairy lamp, butterscotch satin diamond-quilted pattern shading to salmon at the base finished with a frosted clear glass knob. Shade is signed "Clarkes Patent Fairy." Base rests in a brass three-arm hanging fixture and is complete with original insert marked "Cricklite Clarkes Trade Mark" with a fairy in the center. Lamp is finished with a matching satin diamond-quilted shade. Base is marked in the bottom interior "Clarkes Patent Fairy." 19" l., 6-1/2" dia. **$3,105**
*James D. Julia, Inc.*

Sultan (Omn)/Wild Rose with Festoon stand lamp, colorless font, chocolate base, No. 1 Taplin-Brown collar. McKee Glass Co. Early 20th century. 8-3/8" h. to top of collar, 4-1/4" dia. base. ........................................ **$230**
*Jeffrey S. Evans & Associates*

Three colored glass cut overlay peg lamps and four brass candlesticks, Boston & Sandwich Glass Co., Sandwich, Massachusetts, 1840-1860, the peg lamps with ruby, green, and blue cut to clear cylindrical fonts with notched pegs, accompanied by a pair and two single brass candlesticks, of peg lamps to top of collars 5-3/8" h., candlestick 6- 5/8" h. . **$1,007**
*Skinner, Inc.*

Unpatterned stand lamp, pink alabaster pyriform font, opaque white base with worn gilt decoration, brass connector, No. 1 fine line collar. Third quarter 19th century. 8-1/4" h. to top of collar, 3-1/2" square base....................... **$172**
*Jeffrey S. Evans & Associates*

Thousand Eye variant stand lamp, apple green, brass connector, No. 2 Taplin-Brown collar. Late 19th/early 20th century. 13-3/4" h. to top of collar, 6-5/8" dia. base. ........................................ **$218**
*Jeffrey S. Evans & Associates*

Victorian satin finish parlor lamp, ruby, embossed with cherub faces and scrolls, matching patterned ball shade, cast metal base embossed "300" to underside, font holder with a metal lining and brass drop-in font, Plume and Atwood "Royal" burner. Late 19th/early 20th century. 24-1/4" height overall, lamp 13-1/4" h. to top of collar, shade 9-1/2" h., 4-1/8" dia. fitter.......................... **$862**
*Jeffrey S. Evans & Associates*

# Electric Lighting

American leaded glass table lamp attributed to Unique, red poinsettia flowers encircling skirt against a green background of randomly shaped panels. Shade rests on Handel tree trunk base with rich brown finish and is unsigned. Base is impressed on the underside "Handel." Shade 20" dia. Lamp 24-1/2" t. .............................................. **$3,450**
*James D. Julia, Inc.*

American leaded glass table lamp, shade of small scalloped panels constructed in butterscotch hues, glass used is heavily textured. Irregular border shade supported by three-socket base with brown patina finish. Platform base decorated with roped coil design and completed with top cap, finial, and three-acorn pull chains. Unsigned. Shade 18" dia. Lamp 24" t. ........................................................... **$1,610**
*James D. Julia, Inc.*

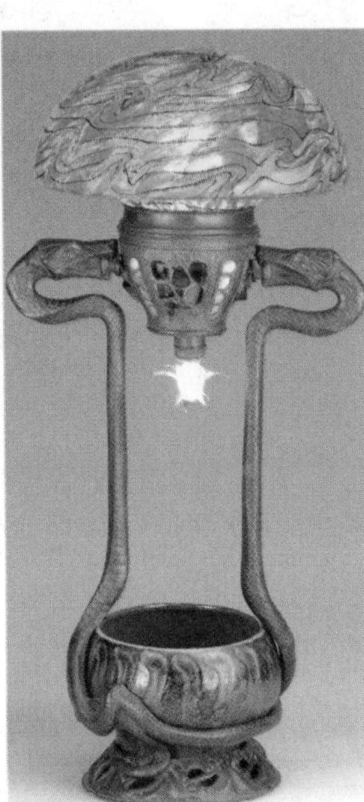

**Far left:** American leaded glass floor lamp, grape clusters, leaves, and vines encircle skirt, set against a green and brown striated background. Shade rests on cast metal floor base with impressed ship design and openwork vines decorating the foot, which supports a square shaft adorned with a two-handle connector in the middle, complete with two-socket cluster. Shade 22-1/4" dia. Lamp 60" t. ...**$1,180**
*James D. Julia, Inc.*

**Left:** Austrian table lamp, two bronze snakes climbing from openwork base around a pottery bowl extending to support the bronze shade holder set with purple and turquoise chunk jewels. Lamp topped with a mushroom-shaped blue and green iridescent swirling shade with strong purple highlights. Shade unsigned. Pottery bowl is marked "Hollosino Ware Austria" and "N21074." Shade 11" dia. x 5" fitter. Lamp 29" t. .........**$4,312**
*James D. Julia, Inc.*

American leaded floral table lamp attributed to Unique, white floral pattern encircling long skirt of shade with irregular border, set against a green leafy background, while top is done in geometric panels with light green shaded glass. Shade unsigned and rests on simple spun bronze stick base with three-light cluster and matching heat cap. Base is unsigned. Shade 16" dia. Lamp 23-1/2" t........ **$1,610**
*James D. Julia, Inc.*

Contemporary Porcelli Studios leaded lamp, floral bouquet inspired by the paintings of Jan van Huysum. Shade depicts all-over floral bouquet of numerous types of flowers in blue, purple, lavender, and yellow against a shaded green background. Shade rests atop decorative bronze base with impressed berry and leaf design around the foot and shoulder, topped with a four-socket cluster and finished with a mottled green patina. Shade 22" dia. Lamp 25-1/2" t.......**$11,500**
*James D. Julia, Inc.*

Large Chicago mosaic leaded table lamp, stylized floral design with six flowers surrounding top with variegated pink and yellow leaves and red stems, irregular border decorated with alternating white lilies and pink flowers with long slender leaves all set against a light green background. Shade rests on tall tree trunk base with three-light cluster finished with brown patina. Shade 25-1/4" dia. Lamp 28" t.................. **$2,990**
*James D. Julia, Inc.*

TOP LOT!

Duffner & Kimberly peony table lamp, shaded red glass and green leaves against a striated green and brown background, shade rests atop a bronze base with stylized acanthus leaf decoration, base finished with brown patina with subtle green highlights and is signed near the socket cluster with applied round tag "Duffner & Kimberly Co. New York." Shade 24-1/4" dia. Lamp 32" t. ......................................**$40,250**
*James D. Julia, Inc.*

Durand King Tut electric table lamp, original gilt-brass mounts and two-socket fixture. Vineland Flint Glass Works, 1924-1931. 22" h. overall, 5-3/4" h. glass insert..... **$373**
*Jeffrey S. Evans & Associates*

Durand Moorish crackle lamp base, red and white crackle glass body with silvery-blue iridescence within the crackling. Glass section of the base rests atop a brass cylinder and is finished with a brass cap, riser, and double sockets. 27" to top of finial.............. **$460**
*James D. Julia, Inc.*

◀Gilt-brass and marble astral lamp with wheel-cut shade, American, 19th century, tooled ruffled rim on vasiform frosted glass shade with wheel-cut flowers and foliage set on a brass ring on font and fluted brass columnar standard, square stepped white marble base, electrified, overall 23" h. ......**$533**
*Skinner, Inc.*

▶Gilt-brass and marble astral lamp, American, early 19th century, wheel-cut acid-finish shade with floral and fruiting vine supported on brass ring above a fluted column on a brass-mounted square, stepped marble base, with prisms, electrified, converted to a three-socket fixture, top rim of shade ground, 30-1/2" h..... **$474**
*Skinner, Inc.*

Rare Pairpoint lamp base, glass body decorated with seagull in flight and stormy skies over sea. Base rests on a turned wooden foot and is finished with a metal cap, ribbed riser and three-socket cluster. Signed on the underside "Pairpoint D3000." 25" t. ......... **$575**
*James D. Julia, Inc.*

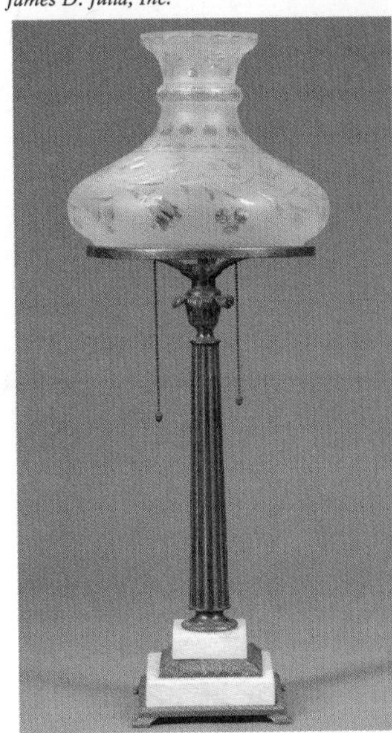

Handel chandelier, light blue wisteria flowers against a dark blue background with interspersed leaves of light mint green, openwork top cast with branches all leading to the cast hook, illuminated with a four-socket cluster. Shade complete with a bronze "S" hook and short length of chain for hanging. Signed on the interior with applied metal tag "Handel." 18" dia. x 20" to top of hook. ............................................................**$13,800**
*James D. Julia, Inc.*

Handel desk lamp, loaf-shaped shade with reverse-painted decoration of pink flowers with shaded green leaf background, exterior with chipped ice finish, shade supported by a bronze tone two-arm base. Base has a ribbed stem and quatrefoil foot. Pictured in the book Handel Lamps: Painted Shades & Glassware by DeFalco, Hibel & Hibel, page 210. Lamp signed "Handel" and numbered "6760." 13-1/2" t. **$2,530**
*James D. Julia, Inc.*

Handel scenic table lamp, reverse-painted shade featuring fall trees with orange and yellow leaves alongside tall evergreens with rolling hills and stormy sky in the background. Shade rests on a vertically ribbed Handel base with dark brown patina and three-light cluster. Shade signed "Handel 7111" and artist initial "M." Base is unsigned. Shade 17-7/8" dia. Lamp 23" t. From a private Long Island Collection. **$4,312**
*James D. Julia, Inc.*

Handel metal overlay lamp, design of grape clusters, leaves, and vines surrounding skirt with andom geometric brickwork overlay design highlighting bent panels. Metal overlay is backed by green slag glass; grapes and leaves are enameled. Shade rests on a Handel base with copper finish and impressed panels of floral design on the foot and stem. Lamp has a three-socket cluster. Shade 18" dia. Lamp 25" t. .. **$2,530**
*James D. Julia, Inc.*

Lamb Bros leaded lamp, geometric top half of shade, skirt is bent panels with metal overlay fleur de lis design. Shade rests on cast metal base with brass plated finish and two-socket cluster, marked with a decal on the riser "Lamb Bros & Greene Lamb Lamps Are Best Nappanee Ind." Shade 14-1/4" dia. Lamp 20" t..... **$460**

*James D. Julia, Inc.*

Pairpoint nautical table lamp, Bombay shade with reverse painted New Bedford harbor scene, trimmed on bottom and top in light brown and further decorated with six seashells. Shade rests on a brass plated base decorated around the shoulder with fruit baskets and sea serpents. Shade signed "The Pairpoint Corp'n." Base is signed on the underside "Pairpoint D3055" along with the Pairpoint logo. Shade 19-3/4" dia. Lamp 24-1/2" t. ........................... **$3,800-$4,200**

*James D. Julia, Inc.*

Pairpoint Puffy three-color lamp, closed top puffy shade with pink, red, and white azaleas against a green leafy background. Shade rests on a Pairpoint floral base with two-socket cluster and gold finish. Base is signed on underside "Pairpoint Mfg. Co. 3095" as well as Pairpoint logo. Shade signed on the exterior rim in gold "Patent Appl'd For." Shade 12" dia. with 10" fitter, lamp 19" t .....................................**$16,100**

*James D. Julia, Inc.*

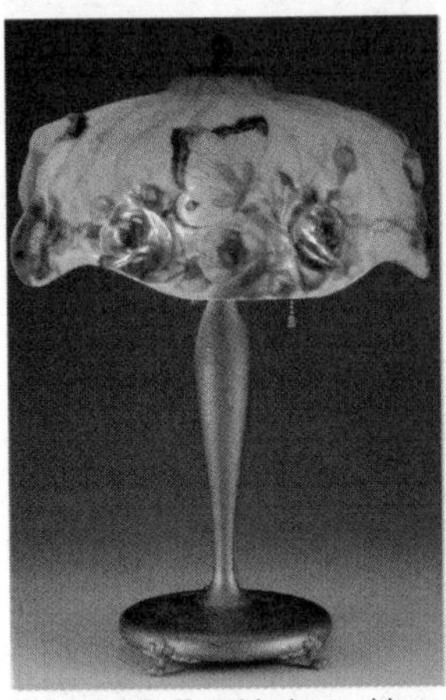

Pairpoint Puffy table lamp, blown out design of various flowers surrounding bottom rim of shade. Flying above each cluster of flowers is a butterfly, all set against a creamy white background with green shadowing. Shade rests on a simple Pairpoint base with four paw feet and gold finish. Shade signed "The Pairpoint Corp'n" and "Patented July 9-1907." Base is signed on the underside "Pairpoint 3047-1/2 12 Made in USA" along with the Pairpoint logo. Shade 14" dia. Lamp 20-1/2" t. ..................................... **$2,875**

*James D. Julia, Inc.*

Pairpoint reverse-painted scenic lamp, Carlisle shade with scenic view of tall trees extending the length of shade and outlining castles in background with small fishing boat and peasant fisherman. Signed on the interior in gold "The Pairpoint Corp'n" with artist initials. Shade rests atop a copper plated urn-shaped base with double handles and three-socket cluster. Base is signed on underside "Pairpoint D3027 Made in USA" along with the Pairpoint logo. Shade 20-3/4" dia. Lamp 25-1/2" t........................ **$1,150**

*James D. Julia, Inc.*

Pairpoint reverse-painted table lamp, Exeter shade with four scenic panels depicting forest scenes in the four seasons, each panel separated by Art Deco design, top of shade decorated with half circle panels mirroring panel below. Shade artist signed "H Fisher" and rests on a brass plated base with squared foot and bulbous ribbed body leading to a three-socket cluster. Base is signed on the underside "Pairpoint D3050" and the Pairpoint logo. Shade 17" dia. Lamp 22" t. ............. **$1,652**

*James D. Julia, Inc.*

Pair of Bohemian glass table lamps, total 38" h. ............. **$119**
*Pook & Pook, Inc.*

Pair of tole canister lamps in Oriental taste, mid-19th century England, used for tea transport and storage, numbered 4 and 5, one decorated with a figure smoking a pipe in front of a tea crate within gilt decorated borders on black ground, second showing a figure dressed in tunic carrying two bundles suspended from a yoke. Now mounted as lamps. Canister 16" h. Lamp 24" h. .................. **$575**
*James D. Julia, Inc.*

Tiffany Moorish double student lamp, twisted wire Moorish decoration on bronze base that supports two bronze overlay shades with blown out green glass inserts. Lamp complete with chimneys. Shades are marked on the side "D1022." Base is unsigned. Shades are 10" dia. Lamp 29" t. ............. **$14,160**
*James D. Julia, Inc.*

Tiffany Studios 10-light lily lamp, favrile glass gold shades have vertical ribbing and fluted rims, shades supported by bronze lily base with gold dore finish. The 10 stems extend upwards from a lily pad base of three-dimensional styling, which shows various stages of buds along with the lily pads. All 10 shades are signed "LCT Favrile." Base is signed on the underside "Tiffany Studios New York 381." 20-1/2" t. ..................................... **$21,850**
*James D. Julia, Inc.*

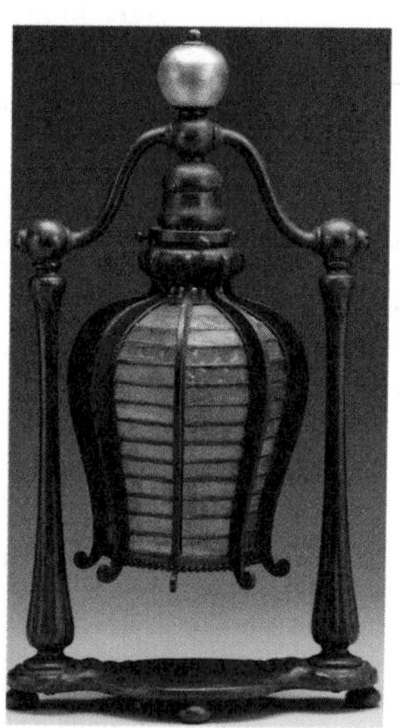

Tiffany octopus lamp with eight bronze tentacles descending from the fitter, area between each tentacle filled with geometric panels of amber, slightly opalescent glass. Shade suspended from base with two pillars supporting an arched top from which the shade hangs. Top of arch adorned with a gold favrile finial. Base is finished with rich brown patina with green and red highlights. Shade unsigned. Signed on the underside of the base "Tiffany Studios New York 448." 18-1/2" t. ..... **$21,275**
*James D. Julia, Inc.*

Tiffany pendant lamp, green shade with rolled lip and vertical coloration lines with light iridescence showing flashes of green and purple. Shade suspended by three chains attaching it to the single arm pendant drop. Hardware is finished in unusual silver patina. Shade 11" t. Approx. 27-1/2" l. overall. **$2,300**
*James D. Julia, Inc.*

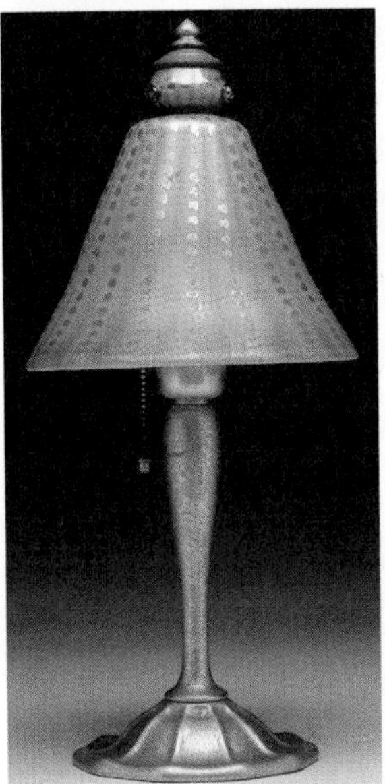

Tiffany Studios Arabian lamp, gold dore bronze base supports butterscotch shade with platinum iridescent vertical zipper design, top of shade finished with three applied blue iridescent puntis. Shade unsigned. Base is signed "Louis C. Tiffany Furnaces Inc. Favrile" with the Tiffany logo. 14-1/4" t. .......................... **$3,500-$4,500**

*James D. Julia, Inc.*

Tiffany Studios arrowroot table lamp, fully leaded shade depicts an artistic rendering of arrowroot plant's life cycle; spring green panels, mottled with darker green and white shaped together, between and below each root are white flowers with yellow centers. Finishing the shade are geometric bands to top and bottom rims, conical shaped shade supported by a single stem bronze base with inverted saucer foot resting atop five ball feet. Three sockets, riser, wheel and pierced top cap finish the lamp. Entire lamp has desirable green brown patina finish with red accents. Shade signed "Tiffany Studios New York" and the base is signed "Tiffany Studios New York 384." Shade 20" dia. Lamp 25" t. ............................... **$51,750**

*James D. Julia, Inc.*

Tiffany Studios crocus table lamp, mottled yellow and cream crocus blossoms with olive green stems all set against a mottled green background. Shade finished with textured amber border on bottom lip. Shade rests on torpedo base with medium brown patina with green and red highlights. Lamp finished with three-socket cluster having Bryant sockets. Shade signed "Tiffany Studios New York." Base is signed with applied round bronze tag "Tiffany Studios New York 444." Shade 16" dia. Lamp 21-1/2" t. ............**$17,700**

*James D. Julia, Inc.*

Tiffany Studios bronze harp table lamp with a Steuben gold iridescent shade with Steuben stencil, the base marked "Tiffany Studios, New York, 27361," 13-1/4" h......**$948**

*Pook & Pook,, Inc.*

▶Tiffany counterbalance floor lamp, green pulled feather shade with gold iridescence outlining the pulled feather design set against a cream-colored background. Shade has white interior and is signed "LCT Favrile." Supported by a Tiffany counterbalance floor lamp base with five lily pad feet and finished in a rich brown patina. Base is signed "Tiffany Studios New York." Shade 10" dia. Lamp 53" t. ......... **$3,450**

*James D. Julia, Inc.*

**Right:** Tiffany Studios adjustable double student lamp with long riser, adjustable height arms supporting two vertically ribbed gold favrile tulip shades; base has brown patina. Shades signed "LCT Favrile." Base signed "Tiffany Studios New York 23574" and Tiffany Glass & Decorating Co. logo. 19" t.......... **$5,750**
*James D. Julia, Inc.*

**Far right:** Leaded floral table lamp, six leaded panels with green background panels, pink flowers; bronze-colored base with impressed loop design at foot, vertically ribbed stem, three-socket cluster. Unsigned. Shade 20-1/2" dia. Lamp 24-3/4" t. ....... **$3,737**
*James D. Julia, Inc.*

## MOSS LAMPS

Floor lamp, No. 2293, "Leaning Lena," butterfly Plexiglas angled standard, 4' 7" h. ......**$275-$300**

Floor lamp, No. 2317, marble pattern plexiglass, Decoramic Kilns figurine "Cocktail Girl," 5' h. ................................**$600-$625**

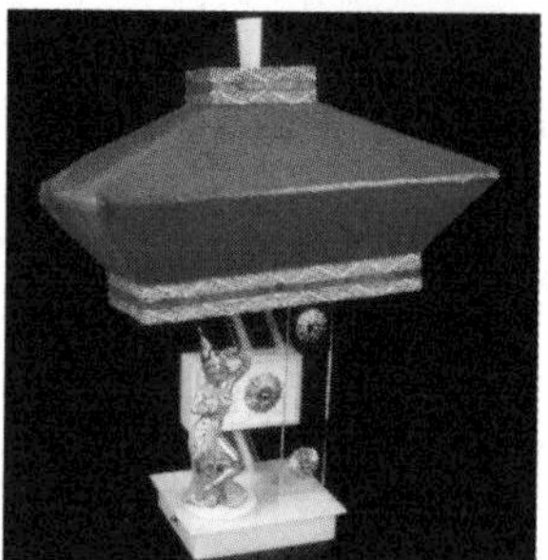

Partner lamp, No. XT 815, no clock, deLee Art female "Siamese Dancer" figurine, 2' 11" h. ................................**$200-$225**

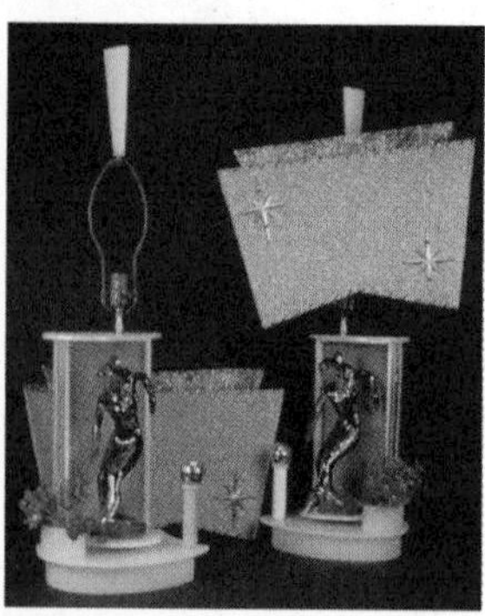

Table lamp, No. XT 835, Johanna "Black Luster Dancer" figurine, 3' h., each (ILLUS. of two) ................................**$125-$150**

Table lamp, No. T 731, Decoramic Kilns "Prom Girl" figurine, 3' 7-1/2" h. ...............**$300-$325**

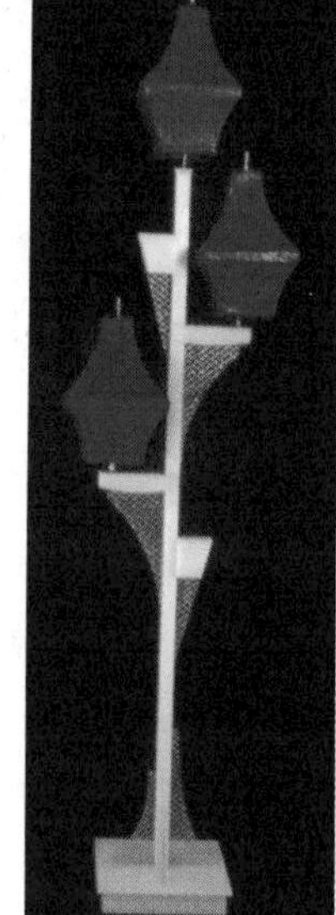

Floor lamp, No. 2328, triple red pagoda-style shade, 6' 5-1/2" h. ................................**$400-$425**

# Lionel Trains

Few brand names have the instantaneous recognition that Lionel enjoys as it enters its second century. Young or old, male or female, it seems almost everyone identifies the name with toy trains. In fact, to many people the two are synonymous.

The firm bears the middle name of its founder, Joshua Lionel Cohen, the son of immigrants, who was born August 25, 1877. The young Cohen, a clever inventor and shameless self-promoter with a clear head for business, formed the firm with Harry Grant on September 5, 1900. Their first business was with the U.S. Navy, producing fuses for mines.

With the Navy work completed, Cohen began tinkering, trying to find a product to keep he and his partner busy and his new firm afloat. A motor he developed for a less-than-successful fan was installed under a gondola car. The car was placed on a circle of steel rails connected to dry cell batteries, and in 1901 the age of Lionel Electric Trains began.

As originally conceived, the "train"—still only a motorized gondola car—was to be an animated window display for shopkeepers to use promoting other products. Immediately, though, it was apparent that there was more interest in the displays than the goods they held, and the transition from merchandising aid to retail product was made.

In 1902, in addition to the gondola car, Lionel offered a miniature trolley, the first step towards realism. Like the gondola, the trolley ran on two-rail 2 7/8-inch gauge track. The first catalog was produced in 1902 and orders poured in.

In 1906, Lionel began producing trains that rolled on "standard gauge" track, and in 1915 this was supplemented by the smaller "0-gauge" trains. Though Lionel made forays into other sizes, namely 00 and, three attempts at HO, it was to be 0-gauge where Lionel rose to notoriety. It is also the predominate size of trains produced after WWII and the subject of this chapter.

During 1909, Lionel first used the slogan "Standard of the World," but it would be many years before the bold statement would become fact.

While toy train production continued in Lionel's plant during World War I, alongside were defense products — after all, the company was born making signaling and navigational devices. This type of relationship continued as long as The Lionel Corporation was in the manufacturing business, during both war and peacetime.

World War II brought a halt to Lionel's toy production, with toy train production ending in June 1942. The Lionel plant, like countless others throughout the country, became totally devoted to manufacturing military products. The complete cessation of train production for three years provided Lionel the opportunity to completely revamp

3535 Operating Security Car with rotating searchlight.
*See page 662.*

its line. When production resumed in the fall of 1945, not only was standard gauge not mentioned, but the 0-gauge trains had totally newly designed trucks and couplers that were incompatible with the previous models and a newly designed plastic-bodied gondola car. Over the next few years, plastics would increasingly replace metal in Lionel's products.

The late 1940s and 1950s were Lionel's glory years, with the Irvington plant churning out thousands of trains in dozens of models and hundreds of paint schemes.

Some of the features Lionel Trains are known for were introduced prior to WWII. Die-cast boilers, electrical reversing mechanisms dubbed "E-units," and the whistle all predate WWII. However, the postwar era brought about many more innovations. "Real railroad knuckle couplers" debuted in 1945, smoke was added the next year to many steam locomotives, America's favorite milk man first unloaded the milk car in 1947, and the famed Santa Fe F3 streamlined diesel took to Lionel's rails in 1948 Though it was untouted until 1950, Magnetraction, which magnetized the wheels of locomotives, was introduced in 1949.

For a short time in the early 1950s, The Lionel Corporation was the largest toy manufacturer in the world. But increasing competition from television and slot cars (though Lionel manufactured slot cars as well — something it had done as far back as 1912), and the public's fascination with travel by jet or car made toy trains somewhat blasé. By the 1960s, the company's fortunes had begun to change and there was increased emphasis on diversification.

Through the 1960s Lionel continued its unsuccessful diversification efforts as its profits, and the quantity and quality of its trains, spiraled downward.

Ultimately, in 1969, The Lionel Toy Corporation (as it was renamed in 1965) exited the toy train business by licensing the name and selling the tooling to the Fundimensions Division of General Mills. Some production was moved immediately, and by the mid-1970s Lionel trains were no longer present in the huge Hillside plant.

With the exception of 1967, Lionel trains have been, and are still, in production every year since 1945 (trains were available even in the bleak 1967). Today's Lionel trains have elaborate paint schemes and sophisticated electronics undreamed of during the postwar heyday. Many of today's trains are manufactured as a collectible, to be displayed, or operated, but rarely are they played with. Contrary to what one may think by glancing at the prices in vintage catalogs, Lionel trains were always expensive, high-quality toys. They were built to last a lifetime and many have. Now that the baby boomers have reached adulthood, many of childhood's financial constraints are lifted — the toys of youthful dreams are at last within grasp.

## Collecting

Toy train collectors are their own fraternity, eagerly welcoming new buffs with a sincere interest in toy trains. Avail yourself of this knowledge base and friendship, whether you are an experienced collector or a rookie, and something can always be learned. There is no substitute for experience in this hobby, as in any other. No book, no matter how complete, contains all the answers. Thousands of words and the best illustrations cannot equal the experience gained by holding a piece in your own hands. There is no finer place for an enthusiast than in the home of a friend and fellow collector. The piece that is not for sale can be examined unhurried and questions answered honestly. It is excellent preparation for seeking an item in the marketplace.

The advent of Internet auctions has been a boon for collectors in remote areas. But for those in more populous areas, there is no substitute for shopping in the company of fellow collectors in hobby shops and train shows. Examining an item personally, with the counsel of more experienced collectors, is especially important when purchasing expensive, often repaired, or forged items.

Enthusiasts have been collecting toy trains perhaps as long as the trains have been produced. In the United States, the largest and oldest collectors group is the Train Collector's Association, or TCA. Founded in 1954 in Yardley, Pennsylvania, the group has grown to more than 31,000 members. An annual convention is held at various locations around the country each summer. Smaller, regional divisions and chapters dot the nation. Twice each year, one such group, the Eastern Division, hosts the largest toy train show in the world. The York Fairgrounds, in York, Pennsylvania, becomes a veritable Mecca for the toy train buff, with several buildings encompassing tens of thousands of square feet are full of toy trains for sale or trade. Members of the TCA agree to abide by a code of conduct, assuring fair and honest dealings between members. The nationally recognized Grading Standards were developed by the TCA.

The TCA headquarters is located in its Toy Train Museum and can be reached at:

The Train Collectors Association
P.O. Box 248
300 Paradise Lane
Strasburg, PA 17579
(717) 687-8623
www.traincollectors.org

The second-oldest organization is the Toy Train Operating Society, formed on the West Coast in 1966. It is similar in style and purpose to the TCA. Traditionally, the bulk of the TTOS members and events have been in the West, but the group has been gradually spreading eastward. The TTOS can be contacted at:

Toy Train Operating Society
P.O. Box 6710
Fullerton, CA 92834
(714) 449-9391
www.ttos.org

One of the first, and certainly the largest, Lionel-specific clubs is the Lionel Collector's Club of America. Founded August 1, 1970, by Jim Gates of Des Moines, Iowa, the organization has grown steadily since. The club was founded on the idea that collectors and operators of Lionel trains need an organization of their own. The clubs' mailing address is:

LCCA Business Office
P.O. Box 529
Peru, IL 61354-0529
www.lionelcollectors.org

The youngster of these groups is the Lionel Operating Train Society, or LOTS. Founded in 1979 by Larry Keller of Cincinnati, this club's purpose is to provide a national train club for operators of Lionel trains and accessories. Like the others, it publishes magazines, swap lists, and a membership directory. LOTS can be reached at:

LOTS Business Office
6376 West Fork Road
Cincinnati, OH 45247-5704
(513) 598-8240
www.lots-trains.org

**Price Key: VG=Very Good, Ex=Excellent, LN=Like New,**

**Rarity = Scale from 1-8 with 8 being the hardest to find.**

## STEAM LOCOMOTIVES

221 (Type III): In 1947, the color of the body casting changed to black. All black-bodied 221 locomotives came with nickel-rimmed black drivers.VG ......... **$50**
Ex ......... **$85**
LN ......... **$150**
Rarity 2

246 (Type II): In 1960, the 246 began to use the later body mold tooling that did not include the see-through cowcatcher. Concurrently, the earlier smooth-bottom 246-100 motor was replaced by the redesigned motor (part no. 246-200), which had a rippled bottom. This new motor was retained by a new pin, part number 246-12, which was simply driven into place. VG ......... **$20**
Ex ......... **$35**
LN ......... **$60**
Rarity 2

665 (Type II): The 1966 production came with white heat-stamped cab numbering. VG ......... **$175**
Ex ......... **$275**
LN ......... **$350**
Rarity 3

671 RR (Type II): On other versions, the cab itself was rubber-stamped with the legend "671" and a tiny "RR" beneath the number. VG ......... **$225**
Ex ......... **$375**
LN ......... **$500**
Rarity 6

238 (Type I): Initial 1963 production was made using the old made-for-die-casting tooling with thick running boards. VG ......... **$100**
Ex ......... **$170**
LN ......... **$300**
Rarity 5

665 (Type I): 1950s locomotives had their numbers applied by rubber-stamping. Over time the white numbers were stamped in two different sizes, but neither seems to be harder to find or more desirable than the other. VG ......... **$175**
Ex ......... **$275**
LN ......... **$350**
Rarity 3

671 (Type III): The bulk of the locomotives had a gold-trimmed red keystone decal with the number "6200" applied to the boiler front keystone. VG **$135**
Ex ......... **$190**
LN ......... **$325**
Rarity 3

685 (Type II): Most of the production came with white heat-stamped cab numbering. VG.................. **$200**
Ex.......................................................... **$310**
LN.......................................................... **$450**
Rarity 5

1050: This uncataloged 0-4-0 locomotive was produced only in 1959. The same tool was used to produce the 1050 boiler that previously had been used to produce the 1001 boiler. The molded plastic body was left unpainted, with its number heat-stamped in white beneath the cab window. Its plastic motor would propel the locomotive forward only, and even though it had an operating headlight, it did not have a headlight lens. The locomotive came with a 1050T slope-back tender. VG .....**$150**
Ex.......................................................... **$210**
LN.......................................................... **$400**
Rarity 6

2016 (Type II): A few of these locomotives were produced with the number rubber-stamped in white. VG.......................................................... **$150**
Ex.......................................................... **$275**
LN.......................................................... **$425**
Rarity 5

736 (Type IV): From 1957 through 1960, the 736 had its number heat-stamped in white, using a smaller typeface than that used previously. Sometime during this period, flagstaff application became intermittent, finally disappearing altogether. The collector roller assembly, previously attached with two small fillister-head screws, was changed to a shorter unit, similar to the one used on GP-7 diesels, and was retained by one large round-head screw. VG ........ **$200**
Ex.......................................................... **$315**
LN.......................................................... **$450**
Rarity 4

1061 (Type III): In 1969, as the fortunes of Lionel reached the lowest point, the cab number of the 1061 was not heat-stamped, rather, the 1061 number was printed in white on a piece of black paper. This piece of paper was then glued to the side of the cab. In less than Excellent condition, this locomotive is almost worthless, but is quite valuable in Excellent and Like New condition. VG ...................................... **$150**
Ex.......................................................... **$250**
LN.......................................................... **$350**
Rarity 7

1110 (Type II): Later in the 1949 production run, the reverse lever began to be made of fiber, and spoked drive wheels replaced the Baldwin disc wheels. VG. **$10**
Ex.......................................................... **$25**
LN.......................................................... **$50**
Rarity 1

2029 (Type I): From 1964 through 1967, the common 2029 was available. VG ........................... **$55**
Ex.......................................................... **$80**
LN.......................................................... **$150**
Rarity 4

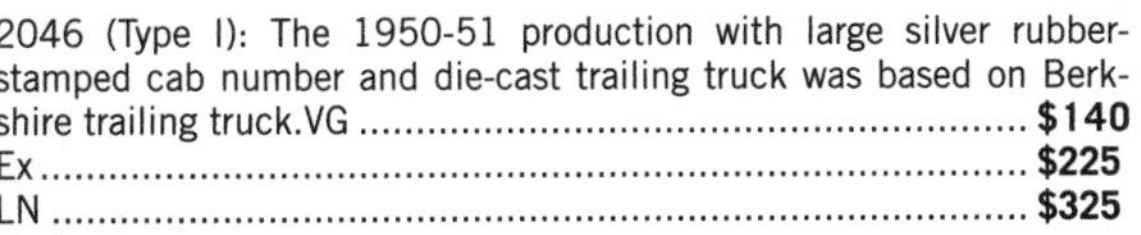

2046 (Type I): The 1950-51 production with large silver rubber-stamped cab number and die-cast trailing truck was based on Berkshire trailing truck.VG ........................................................ **$140**
Ex.......................................................... **$225**
LN.......................................................... **$325**
Rarity 3

## DIESEL LOCOMOTIVES

204 SANTA FE: The retooled ALCO was offered in the A-A powered and dummy set in 1957. One of the more attractive schemes was the blue and yellow freight colors of the Santa Fe railway. These bodies were painted dark with wide yellow painted upper stripe and cab roof, and yellow heat-stamped lettering. Narrow red and yellow stripes ran along the lower body, and the Santa Fe herald on the nose was a decal. These units were more elaborate both in decoration and mechanically than the 202, and had a three-position E-unit and two-axle Magnetraction and operating headlights. Each A unit had a coupler both front and rear. The 204 dummy unit, item 204T, was the only "cheap" ALCO A dummy to include an operating headlight. VG .......... **$100**
Ex .......... **$190**
LN .......... **$325**
Rarity 4

218 SANTA FE (Type I): Provided as A-A units, the earliest runs had pilots with a small ledge under the front coupler and red and yellow nose decals. VG...... **$100**
Ex .......... **$165**
LN .......... **$275**
Rarity 3

600 MKT (Type I): The initial production had its sheet-metal frame painted gray, and the platform railings were painted yellow and the steps were blued steel. VG .......... **$400**
Ex .......... **$600**
LN .......... **$950**
Rarity 6

616 SANTA FE (Type III): A third variation was built using body molding in which both the E-unit and bell slots were plugged. VG .......... **$200**
Ex .......... **$350**
LN .......... **$550**
Rarity 6

210 TEXAS SPECIAL: Also produced only in 1958 were these ALCO A-A units lettered "Texas Special." The actual Texas Special was a passenger train jointly operated by the St. Louis-San Francisco (Frisco) and Missouri-Kansas-Texas (Katy) railroads. The 210 bodies had a lower body panel painted white. The "Texas Special" lettering was heat-stamped in red on this panel, and a white star was heat-stamped on the nose. The powered unit included two-axle Magnetraction, a three-position E-unit, and operating headlight. VG .......... **$75**
Ex .......... **$200**
LN .......... **$300**
Rarity 4

224 UNITED STATES NAVY: In 1960, the Navy moved from the sea to the rails with this A-B ALCO diesel set. White heat-stamped lettering adorned the sides of the painted blue plastic bodies and a wide ledge reinforced the pilot beneath the non-operating front coupler. A three-position E-unit controlled the power truck, which featured two-axle Magnetraction, and an operating headlight showed the way down the track. VG .......... **$150**
Ex .......... **$250**
LN .......... **$425**
Rarity 6

614 ALASKA RAILROAD (Type I): The earliest production had the "BUILT BY / LIONEL" placard near the nose outlined in yellow. This is a very scarce variation, but one that is often fraudulently duplicated. VG .......... **$325**
Ex .......... **$525**
LN .......... **$900**
Rarity 7

626 BALTIMORE AND OHIO: Produced only in 1957, the colorful Baltimore and Ohio 44-ton switcher had an unpainted blue body trimmed with a painted yellow stripe and yellow heat-stamped lettering. It had headlight lens and operating couplers at each end, and an ornamental horn and ornamental bell. The frame and end railings were painted yellow, and an operating headlight was installed at one end. Whereas the actual GE 44-ton locomotives were powered by twin Caterpillar diesel engines, this model was powered with a single-axle Magnetraction power truck, controlled through a lever-down three-position E-unit. VG ............... **$250**
Ex ............................................................. **$450**
LN ............................................................. **$750**
Rarity 6

2033 UNION PACIFIC: The third A-A ALCO set offered by Lionel during 1952-54 was another edition of the Union Pacific. These units were painted silver and had black heat-stamped lettering. Unlike the earlier UP units, the 2033 did not have a gray roof or black pinstripes. Both units had two-piece ornamental horns, window shells, operating headlights and operating coil couplers on the front. The number "2033" was formed into their illuminated number boards. The die-cast frames were painted silver, and blued steel steps were staked to them at the rear. The powered unit housed a three-position lever-down E-unit and an operating horn, and its power truck had Magnetraction. Locomotives produced in 1953 and later have a dime-sized bump added to the roof of the body between the first and second porthole. This was done to prevent warping of the body that was prevalent in the earlier models. There is no difference in value associated with either version, although it is expected that both locos of a pair match. VG **$175**
Ex ............................................................. **$300**
LN ............................................................. **$550**
Rarity 3

2353 SANTA FE (Type II): Beginning in 1954, a bump was added behind the roof vents to mask a sink mark caused by the molding process. Also in 1954, the pilot casting was revised, eliminating the "notch" on its lower surface. The notch had been intended to reduce the tendency for short circuits caused by the pilot striking the center rail while traversing uneven track. VG ............. **$350**
Ex ............................................................. **$700**
LN ........................................................... **$1,350**
Rarity 4

2023 UNION PACIFIC (Type III): These units were identical to the Type II units except, rather than painted truck side frames, they were black-oxide coated. VG ................................ **$225**
Ex ............................................................. **$400**
LN ............................................................. **$600**
Rarity 5

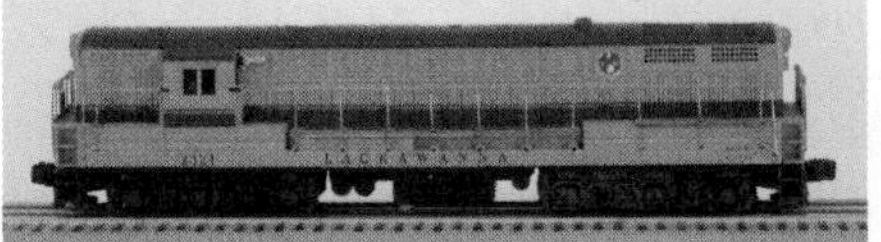


2321 LACKAWANNA (Type I): The Train Masters produced in 1954 had roofs painted maroon, inverted L-shaped headlight brackets and engraved battery covers. VG .................................................. **$575**
Ex ............................................................. **$875**
LN ........................................................... **$1,450**
Rarity 6

2334 NEW YORK CENTRAL (Type III): Some of the units used red "GM" decals that were intended for Santa Fe F-3 production. VG .. **$375**
Ex ............................................................. **$700**
LN ........................................................... **$1,500**
Rarity 5

2339 WABASH: This 1957 GP7 road switcher looked just like the 2337, but it was upgraded with operating couplers. VG ................**$210**
Ex................ **$325**
LN ............................................................. **$550**
Rarity 5

2365 CHESAPEAKE AND OHIO: The body of this EMD GP7 was painted blue with yellow heat-stamped markings. Cosmetically, it had an ornamental horn on each side, and headlight and marker light lenses. Mechanically, it had an operating headlight in each end, Magnetraction, non-operating plastic couplers and a three-position lever-down E-unit. The 2365 was cataloged during 1962-63. VG............................ **$200**
Ex ............................................................. **$350**
LN ............................................................. **$575**
Rarity 4

## CABOOSES

1007 LIONEL LINES (Type I): The most common version of this car had an unpainted body molded of red plastic. VG........................**$2**
Ex.........................................**$5**
LN.......................................**$8**
Rarity 2

3535 OPERATING SECURITY CAR WITH ROTATING SEARCHLIGHT: During 1960-61, this multi-featured car was available. On the roof of the offset unpainted red superstructure, which itself was derived from the 520 electric body, was a twin 40m Bofors anti-aircraft cannon borrowed from the Pyro military loads. On the other end of the unpainted black plastic body was mounted a small blued-steel deck with a vibrator-operated rotating searchlight installed. There was no lettering whatsoever on the body, but the superstructure was heat-stamped "AEC" "SECURITY CAR" and "3535" in white. VG.............................**$75**
Ex...................................**$125**
LN..................................**$200**
Rarity 4

6017 LIONEL LINES (Type III): Some cars were finished in a semi-gloss Tuscan paint. VG..........**$50**
Ex.....................................**$85**
LN..................................**$125**
Rarity 6

2357 LIONEL-SP (Type IV): The most desirable version of the 2357 had a pure red body and smokejack. VG...................**$250**
Ex..................................**$475**
LN.................................**$850**
Rarity 8

6017 LIONEL LINES: Listed in the Lionel Service Manual as a 6017-85, this 1958 cupola-type caboose was numbered only "6017" in its black heat-stamped reversible markings. Its chemically blackened frame was attached to its light gray painted body with tabs. AAR-type trucks were used, with an operating coupler being provided on the "front" truck. It did not have illumination, window inserts, smokejack, ladders or battery boxes. VG......................**$15**
Ex......................................**$35**
LN....................................**$60**
Rarity 3

6027 ALASKA RAILROAD: This caboose was produced only in 1959 as part of the Alaska and Alaska railroad-themed merchandise. It used a cupola-type body that was painted dark blue. Its markings, including the Alaska Railroad Eskimo figure, were heat-stamped in yellow. Cars with white markings are chemically altered fakes. The body was tab-mounted to a chemically blackened frame. AAR-type trucks were used, with an operating coupler provided on the "front" truck. It did not have illumination, window inserts, smokejack, ladders or battery boxes. VG............................**$40**
Ex.....................................**$75**
LN..................................**$125**
Rarity 5

2419 D. L. & W: The first wrecking car Lionel produced was this 1946-47 Delaware, Lackawanna and Western specimen. It had a die-cast frame, two molded plastic toolboxes and a molded plastic cab, all painted light gray. A tall black die-cast smokejack was mounted on the cab, and a 2419-23 brake wheel and vertical post assembly were mounted on each end of the frame, along with wire handrails. The staple-end trucks were fitted with coil-type couplers. The markings, including the "Lionel Lines" on the frame, were heat-stamped in black. Cars produced in 1947 can be distinguished by the blanked-out remnants of stake pockets being visible on the underside. This is a result of the 2411 flat car using the same frame. VG..............**$25**
Ex......................................**$40**
LN....................................**$65**
Rarity 3

6119 D.L.&W.: This Delaware, Lackawanna and Western caboose, produced in 1955-56, introduced the inexpensive, sheet metal frame-equipped work caboose. Rather than the two toolboxes of previous wrecking cars, this and subsequent cars were provided with an unpainted red open tool compartment. Its cab was also unpainted red plastic and it was decorated with white heat-stamped lettering. The short die-cast smokejack installed on this caboose was originally developed for the bay window caboose. The sheet metal frame was painted black with white heat-stamped serif lettering. Bar-end trucks were installed, as well as one magnetic coupler. VG.........................**$12**
Ex......................................**$25**
LN....................................**$50**
Rarity 3

6119-125 RESCUE: This uncataloged "work caboose" was manufactured in 1964 for inclusion in outfit X 924-0680. This outfit was assembled exclusively for J.C. Penney. This car was also included in uncataloged outfit 19351-500, but its inclusion in this set was probably an effort by Lionel to rid itself of overrun. Though similar to the 6824 Rescue Caboose, this car did not have a number stamped on it at all, nor did it include the stretcher, air tank and tool compartment insert of the Rescue Caboose. Its cab and tool compartment moldings were unpainted olive drab plastic, and what markings were on the plastic components were heat-stamped in white. A short smokejack was mounted on its roof. The car ALWAYS had a chemically blackened frame that was rubber-stamped "LIONEL" in white serif lettering. It rode on AAR trucks and had one coupler, which was operating. The stock number of this car was given in the Lionel Service Manual. VG....................................**$100**
Ex....................................**$185**
LN....................................**$300**
Rarity 4

6167 LIONEL LINES (Type I): The bulk of these cars had two couplers. Some had one fixed and one operating coupler; others had two fixed couplers. VG....................**$4**
Ex....................................**$7**
LN....................................**$12**
Rarity 1

6427 LIONEL LINES: From 1954 through 1960, the N5c porthole caboose was again offered in Lionel Lines markings. Its Tuscan-painted body had white heat-stamped lettering, including the number "64273". This illuminated caboose had bar-end trucks and one coupler. VG..............**$20**
Ex....................................**$35**
LN....................................**$55**
Rarity 3

6357 LIONEL (Type I): These cabooses were usually equipped with black die-cast smokejacks. They were painted in various shades of Tuscan and maroon, although neither color nor shade has any bearing on the value of this piece. VG **$15**
Ex....................................**$25**
LN....................................**$45**
Rarity 4

6657 RIO GRANDE (Type I): Most cars had a body molded with slots in the roof overhang to accept ladders, which were not installed. VG....................................**$75**
Ex....................................**$135**
LN....................................**$250**
Rarity 5

6517/1966 TCA: Also produced in 1966 were 700 bay window cabooses commissioned by the Train Collectors Association as commemoratives of their 1966 Santa Monica, Calif., convention. Construction details were the same as Lionel's other bay window cabooses. The body of this car was painted orange, and the markings were white rubber-stampings. VG....................................**$75**
Ex....................................**$135**
LN....................................**$250**
Rarity 4

6824 U.S.M.C: The 1805 Gift Pack, offered in 1960, included this work-type caboose. In fact, that was the only way it was offered by Lionel. The cab, tool compartment, tool compartment insert and frame were all painted olive drab. The markings were all done in white: "U.S.M.C." rubber-stamped on the sheet-metal frame and "RESCUE UNIT", "6824" and two crosses heat-stamped on the plastic components. The First-Aid Medical Car had a short black die-cast smokejack, a blue rubber figure with painted hands and face, a white plastic air tank, and two white plastic stretchers with red cross markings. It was equipped with AAR trucks, and the front truck had an operating coupler.VG....................................**$125**
Ex....................................**$225**
LN....................................**$350**
Rarity 7

## PASSENGER CARS

400 BALTIMORE AND OHIO: The first replica of a RDC produced by Lionel was this rendition of an RDC-1 offered from 1956 through 1958. It featured a silver-painted plastic body with blue heat-stamped lettering; The unit was further decorated with passenger silhouettes in the windows and a "BUDD / RDC-1" nameplate near the end. Mechanically, the 400 had Magnetraction on both axles of the powered truck, an operating horn, three-position E-unit and three-lamp interior illumination. Operating couplers were provided at each end.
VG......**$150**
Ex......**$250**
LN......**$350**
Rarity 3

2440 PULLMAN (Type I): The 1946 production had silver rubber-stamped lettering and a box without the Toy Manufacturers Association logo. VG......**$25**
Ex......**$50**
LN......**$90**
Rarity 3

2541 PENNSYLVANIA / ALEXANDER HAMILTON: The Congressional observation car in 1955 and 1956 was the Alexander Hamilton. VG......**$125**
Ex......**$225**
LN......**$325**
Rarity 5

2552 CANADIAN PACIFIC / SKYLINE 500: The Skyline 500 is the Vista Dome for the 1957 Canadian Pacific outfit. With three of these cars in each outfit, the Skyline 500 is the easiest of the CP cars to find.
VG......**$150**
Ex......**$250**
LN......**$375**
Rarity 5

2625 IRVINGTON (Type I): Those cars produced from 1946 through 1948 had plain window strips and the wires for the interior illumination were plainly visible beneath the car. The white heat-stamped markings included the words "Lionel Lines" above the window. This was positioned so that the first "L" in "LIONEL LINES" was located to the left of the first window in the center window group. VG......**$125**
Ex......**$250**
LN......**$425**
Rarity 3

## CATALOGS AND PAPER PRODUCTS

**THE LIONEL LINE for Christmas 1945**

**Flash! This is a quick picture of available LIONEL merchandise for Christmas 1945. It's only the beginning, of course! Some sensational suprises on the way for 1946.**

**FEATURING THE *NEW* REMOTE CONTROL REAL RAILROAD KNUCKLE COUPLERS, DIE CAST TRUCKS, AND *SOLID* STEEL WHEELS**

1945 Consumer Catalog: Lionel rushed an outfit on the market to meet the pent-up demand for trains caused by the war years. Only one type of outfit was available in 1945, and Lionel knew it could not meet the demand. Nevertheless, a four-page 8 1/2 x 11-inch brochure was produced extolling the return of Lionel trains, with new features, too. The company hoped to continue fanning the flames of desire among consumers until production could meet demand. The strategy worked. Ex ........................................ **$150**
LN ........................................................... **$225**
Rarity 8

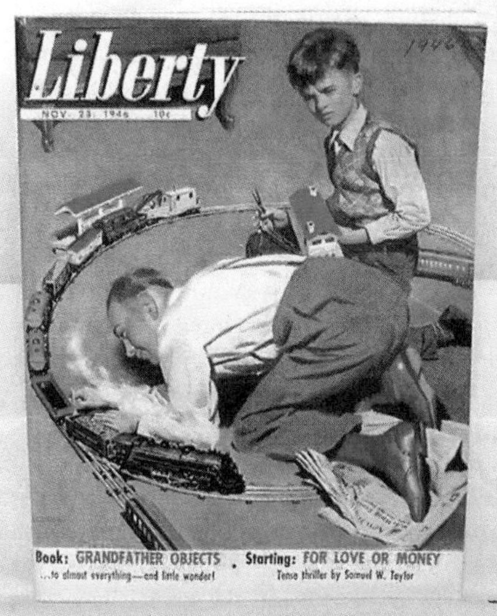


1946 Liberty Magazine: Lionel, concerned about distribution problems for its catalog, took out one of the most expensive advertisements of anyone up to that time. A 16-page insert, duplicating the consumer catalog, was put in the Nov. 23, 1946, edition of Liberty magazine. Ex................................................ **$100**
LN ........................................................... **$200**
Rarity 7

1959 Advance Catalog: 8 1/2 x 10 7/8, 44-page vertical format catalog. Ex ................................ **$25**
LN .................................... **$40**
Rarity 5

1960 Advance Catalog: 8 1/2 x 11, 60-page vertical format catalog. Ex ................................ **$20**
LN .................................... **$30**
Rarity 4

1963 Consumer Catalog: 8 3/8 x 10 7/8, 56-page vertical format catalog printed with full-color cover. Includes slot cars and science products. Ex .................. **$7**
LN ..................................... **$12**
Rarity 3

# Lunch Boxes

The human urge to collect is primal. There are a myriad of reasons why a person decides to collect this or that; those reasons number as many as people on the planet. When it comes to the antiques and collectibles market, though, there is usually one driving factor that pushes people into it: nostalgia.

There is little that is stronger in people who were kids in the 1950s, '60s and '70s than the sense of nostalgia for those decades past. The '50s-'70s represented a time in American life that was decidedly simpler in terms of technology, television and society. It was also in these decades that lunch boxes saw their heyday.

"It's going back into your childhood," said Joe Soucy. "Lunch boxes conjure up memories in your mind. A lot of times I've seen people go after what they had when they were a kid or they go after the ones that their mother wouldn't buy them when they were a kid."

The other avenue that leads collectors to the pursuit of lunch boxes, said Soucy, is an attraction to the artwork of the boxes.

That may seem, at first, a bit comical, but the artwork on the best of lunch boxes is a true testament to the artistic styles and design philosophies of the time in which they were produced. Some can be quite striking, with bold color choices. In this way, many transcend their origins as simple lunch boxes and become a form of industrial pop art.

"If you focus on it, the art really is nice," said Soucy. "It locks in a time period of this country that's no longer there. Life was a lot simpler then."

If you are considering getting into the lunch box game these days, the ways for you to approach the hobby are numerous. There's the old school approach, which is simply getting out and beating the bushes at antique shows, yard sales, consignment shops and flea markets. It's still a viable method to build a collection, said Soucy, but not necessarily the way that the majority of people are doing it these days.

The way that most people are doing it should be fairly obvious to anyone who's bought anything online in the past decade: eBay. There you can find a wide array of boxes from the 1950s through 1985, when metal lunch boxes went out of production.

18 Wheeler, Aladdin,1978 ............................ **$175**

High and low end lunch boxes mix freely in the online marketplace, and buyers of all stripes discover quickly what fair market value is.

"On eBay," said Soucy, "no matter how rare or common something is, it will find its fair market value."

Whether you're a seasoned veteran or neophyte lunch box collector, the good news is that, in today's market with a soft economy, it's more than ever a buyer's market.

As in most collecting areas, people will pay a premium for high-profile character boxes, while prices on lesser characters, and what he calls more common and non-character boxes go down.

"Today I see that condition is a

really important factor in what people are buying, along with major character items," he said. "Something from a TV series, like the Brady Bunch or The Waltons, these boxes still have a good market value."

The "common" boxes, like plaids, floral patterns or non-character boxes, which normally might sell for anywhere between $75 and $150, are where collectors can use the current drop-off in prices to bolster their collections for when the economy, and the lunch box market, come back around.

There is a truism that applies to all levels of collecting, whether it's lunch boxes, fine art, costume jewelry or Matchbox cars.

"Good is always good," said Soucy, "and it will always be good. In lunch boxes, super stuff like Underdog, Rocky and Bullwinkle or Dudley Do-Right, if condition is there, the price is very substantial. Strong character items will usually hold their value."

The number of collectors that can usually go after the top-of-the-line character boxes, however, is limited. The majority of collectors who pursue their hobby part-time can't go after the 1954 Superman lunch box in near-mint to mint condition. Most of them can acquire the minor character boxes or the more common boxes, especially in today's market.

Take, for instance, a box that might have brought $150 two years ago: A collector looking at that same box today on eBay, or consigned through a dealer, may well be able to pick it up for around $50. In a short time, combined with a little bit of patience, a substantial collection can be put together and significant value realized as long as he or she can wait out the soft market.

"In terms of the minor boxes," Soucy said, "there's usually a very slight fluctuation in those values; they may waffle a little bit, but they won't nosedive."

There's also a distinct possibility of finding a rare box for very little, which is so much a trend as it is dumb luck. As Soucy says, it is always possible, as was the case when a Rocky and Bullwinkle prototype lunch box appeared on eBay in May of 2008.

"It's in the top 10 of the rarest boxes made," he said. "To date only five of this same box have surfaced."

It turned out that the seller wasn't aware of what he had, and listed it with the "Buy It Now" feature for a mere $185. A lucky collector, who also didn't necessarily know what he was looking at, bought it at the arranged price. It turns out, for the $185 investment, the collector walked away with a $3,000 box.

That, however, is the exception to the rule. For the most part, the current market supports the low-end boxes and prices, and buyers would be smart to focus on the lower end of the market, where boxes that are toward the bottom of their price fluctuation can be had for a virtual song. It's in this way that solid collections are put together, and capital stocked to make the big deals when they come along.

Along with guides and talking with collectors like Soucy who have a vested interest in seeing the hobby flourish, if you are interested in collecting lunch boxes you should take your time, do your research and watch how various sales pan out. The availability, like so many other areas of the market, is not what it was 10 or 15 years ago. Most attics and basements have been cleaned out and very few spectacular finds are to be had for rock bottom prices.

Getting into the open market and seeing what's available on the floors of shows and shops is a good education, especially when coupled with a digital approach via eBay. In this way, even the collector with absolutely no experience can get a quick degree in lunch box collecting and start assembling their own collection within a few weeks.

For more information on lunch boxes, see *Warman's Lunch Boxes Field Guide* by Joe Soucy.

***Noah Fleisher***

Adam-12, Aladdin, 1973 .............................. **$450**

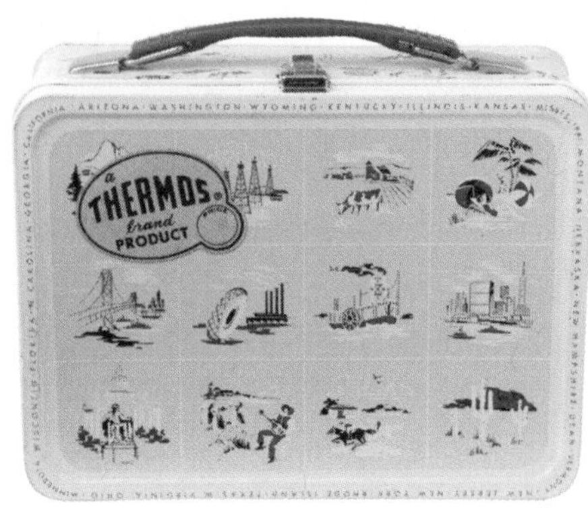


Americana, American Thermos, 1958............. **$425**

Archies, The, Aladdin, 1969.......................... **$325**

Atom Ant, King Seeley Thermos, 1966 ........... **$360**

Barbie & Midge, American Thermos, Canada, 1960s......................................................... **$250**

Battlestar Galactica, Aladdin, 1978 ................ **$275**

Bionic Woman, The, Aladdin, 1977-78............ **$275**

Bugaloos, Aladdin, 1971............................... **$425**

Casey Jones, this is the only metal dome box Universal ever made, Universal, 1960....................... **$650**

Chitty Chitty Bang Bang, King Seeley Thermos, 1969.......................................................... **$400**

Cracker Jack, Aladdin, 1979 .......................... **$150**

Dick Tracy, Aladdin, 1967 ............................. **$450**

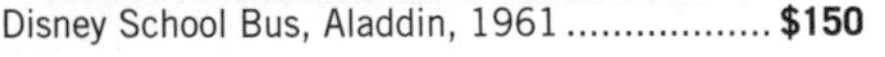
Disney School Bus, Aladdin, 1961 .................. **$150**

Dr. Seuss, Aladdin, 1970 ................................ **$525**

Dukes of Hazzard, The, Aladdin, 1980 ............ **$225**

E.T., Aladdin, 1982 ....................................... **$125**

Emergency!, Aladdin, 1973 ............................ **$350**

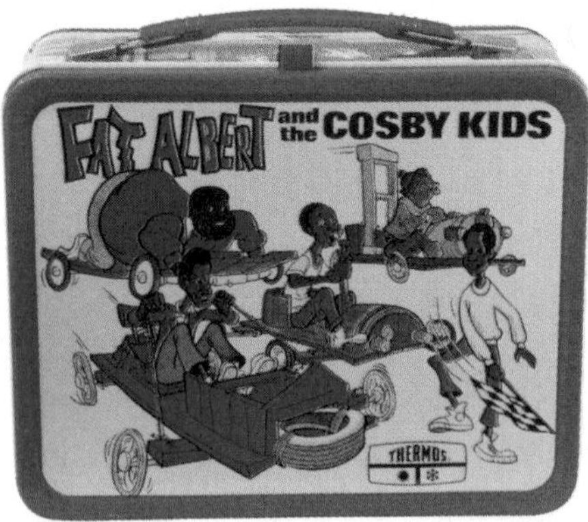


Fat Albert and the Cosby Kids, King Seeley Thermos, 1973.......................................................... **$120**

Frosted Flakes a.k.a. Tony the Tiger, Aladdin, 1969.......................................................... **$450**

G.I. Joe, King Seeley Thermos, 1967 ............. **$425**

Gene Autry, Universal, 1954........................ **$1,850**

Get Smart, King Seeley Thermos, 1966........... **$725**

Happy Days, King Seeley Thermos, 1977......... **$300**

Hee Haw, King Seeley Thermos, 1971............. **$300**

Hopalong Cassidy, Aladdin, 1950, the very first pictured box ........ **$550**

Indiana Jones and the Temple of Doom, King Seeley Thermos, 1984 ........ **$150**

James Bond XX, Ohio Arts, 1969 ........ **$300**

Johnny Lightning, Aladdin, 1970 ........ **$250**

King Kong, King Seeley Thermos, 1977 ........ **$250**

KISS, King Seeley Thermos, 1977 ........ **$400**

Man From U.N.C.L.E., The, King Seeley Thermos, 1966.......... **$850**

NFL, Universal, 1962 .................................... **$350**

Planet of the Apes, Aladdin, 1974 .................. **$525**

Rifleman, The, Aladdin, 1961......................... **$675**

Snoopy Dome, blue cup in Snoopy's hand, King Seeley Thermos .................................................. **$450**

Superman, front of box, Adco, 1954 ........ **$16,500**

Star Wars: Return of the Jedi, King Seeley Thermos, 1983........................................................ **$150**

Trigger, American Thermos, 1956 .................. **$700**

Universal Movie Monsters, Aladdin, 1979........ **$400**

Waltons, The, Aladdin, 1973 ......................... **$325**

# Maps & Globes

Map collecting is slowly growing in visibility thanks to recent discoveries and sales of historically important maps. In 2010, a rare copy of George Washington's own map of Yorktown sold for more than $1.1 million. And a copy of "Theatrvm civitatvm et admirandorvm Italiae" (Theater of the Cities and Wonders of Italy), published in 1663 by the atlas maker Joan Blaeu of Amsterdam, was exhibited with much fanfare during the 2012 San Francisco Antiquarian Book Print and Paper Fair. It's asking price: $75,000.

Top of the market aside, map collecting remains a surprisingly affordable hobby when one considers most made in the early 19th century are hand-colored and represent the cutting edge scientific knowledge at the time. Most examples from the last 400 years are available for less than $500, and engravings depicting America or its states may be owned for less than $150. Larger maps are usually worth more to collectors.

*All images courtesy Heritage Auction Galleries*

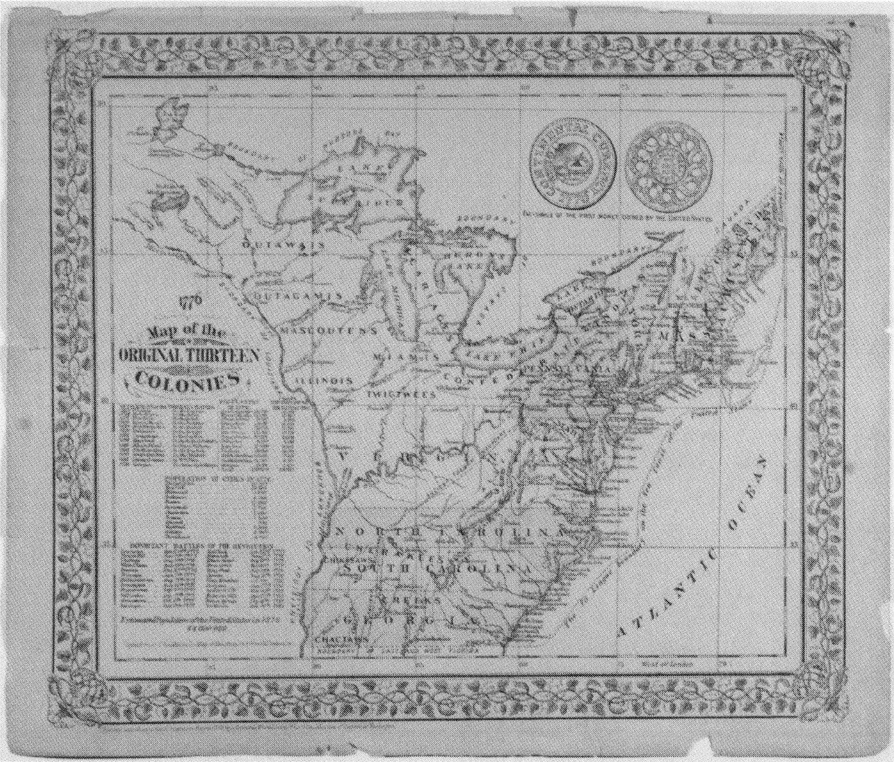


Map titled "1776 Map of the Original Thirteen Colonies," Washington: S. Augustus Mitchell, 1878. Toning to edges with chipping and tears to edges. 12-1/5" x 15-1/4" ........ **$125**

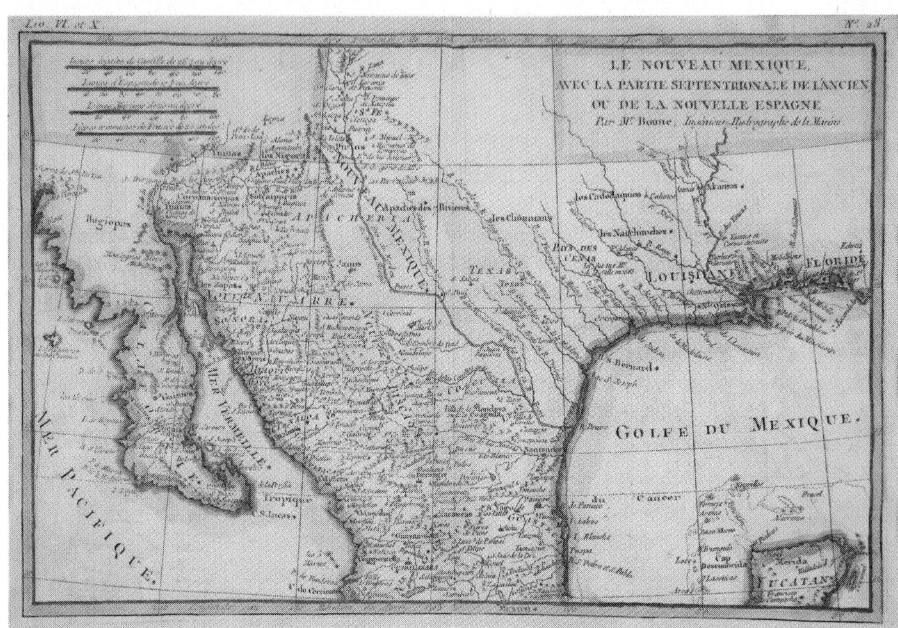


Map by Rigobert Bonne (1727-1795), hand-colored engraving from Atlas de Toutes les Parties Connues du Globe Terrestre by Raynal and Bonne. Geneva: 1780. Titled "Le Nouveau Mexique, Avec La Partie Septentrionale De L'Ancien, ou De La Nouvelle Espagne," the map depicts the Southwest with Baja California, Northern Mexico, Texas, Louisiana, and their waterways, excellent condition, visible area of print measures 8-3/4" x 12-1/2", matted and framed to a measurement of 15-1/2" x 21-3/4" ....................................................**$418**

Traveling globe, cased, Late George III, published by Newton Son & London, England, circa 1830-1838, terrestrial pocket globe in simulated fish skin case lined with celestial gores, marks: NEWTON'S NEW & IMPROVED TERRESTRIAL POCKET GLOBE, 3", case is 4" in diameter ........................................ **$6,572**

Chein globe bank (J. Chein & Co., circa 1950s), has Hawaii listed as the "Hawaiian Islands" (Hawaii would not become a state until 1959) ...............**$19**

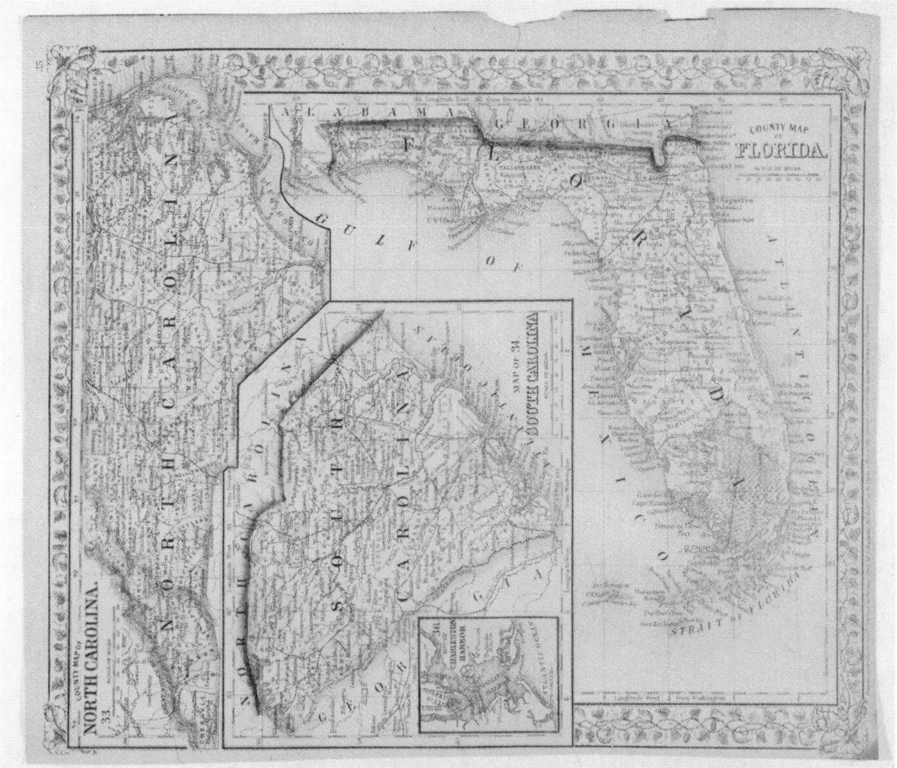

Map published by S. Augustus Mitchell, 1867, partially hand-colored county maps of Florida, North Carolina, and South Carolina, 12-1/4" x 14-1/2", removed from a larger volume .................................................. **$16**

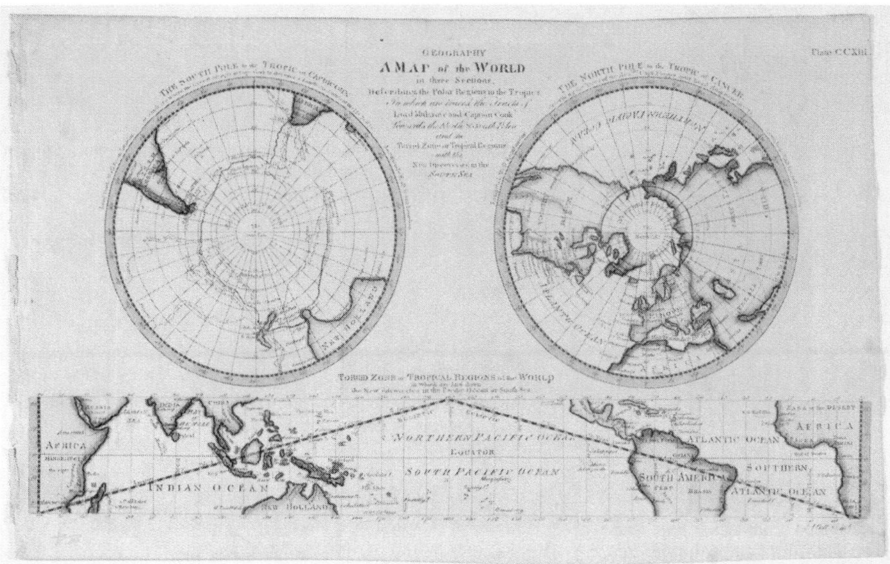


Map engraved by A. Bell, [N.p., n.d., ca. 1710] "Geography A Map of the World in Three Sections, Describing the Polar Regions to the Tropics," hand-colored map of the world with views from the top of each pole and the Torrid Zone, taken from an unknown book, 17-1/2" x 10-1/2" ............................................................**$262**

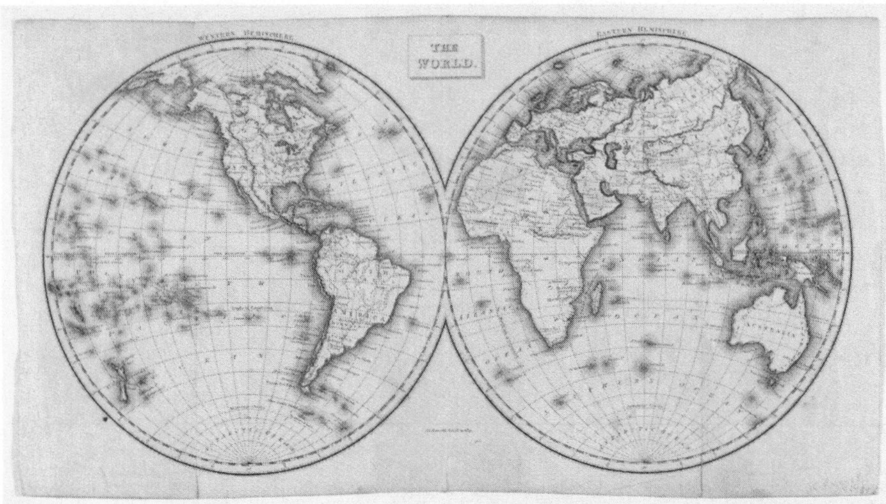


Map, J. C. Russell, London circa 1820, engraved world map with hand-coloring, 8-1/2" x 15-3/4" .......... **$69**

Ivory globe compass cane, the knob carved as a globe, hinged top lifts to reveal compass under glass window, brass collar and hardwood shaft, 35-1/4" overall length of cane.............................. **$2,031**

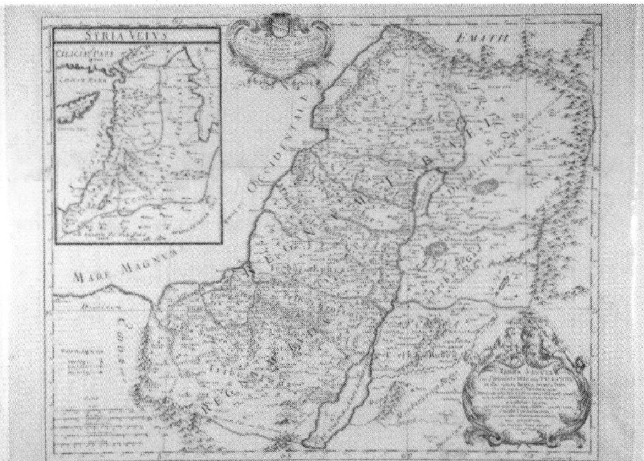


Map engraved by Georgius Widman and published by Gulielmo Sanson. "Engraved Map of the Terra Sancta (Holy Lands)," 1679, 24-1/2" x 19", country borders hand-colored, removed from a larger volume ........ **$262**

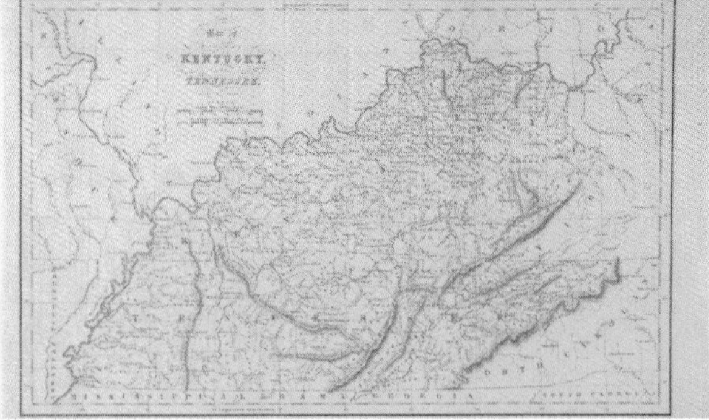


Map engraved by Fenner Sears & Co., depicting Kentucky and Tennessee, circa 1831, 16-3/4" x 11", London: I.T. Hinton and Simpkin & Marshall, June 1, 1831, removed from a larger volume ................. **$50**

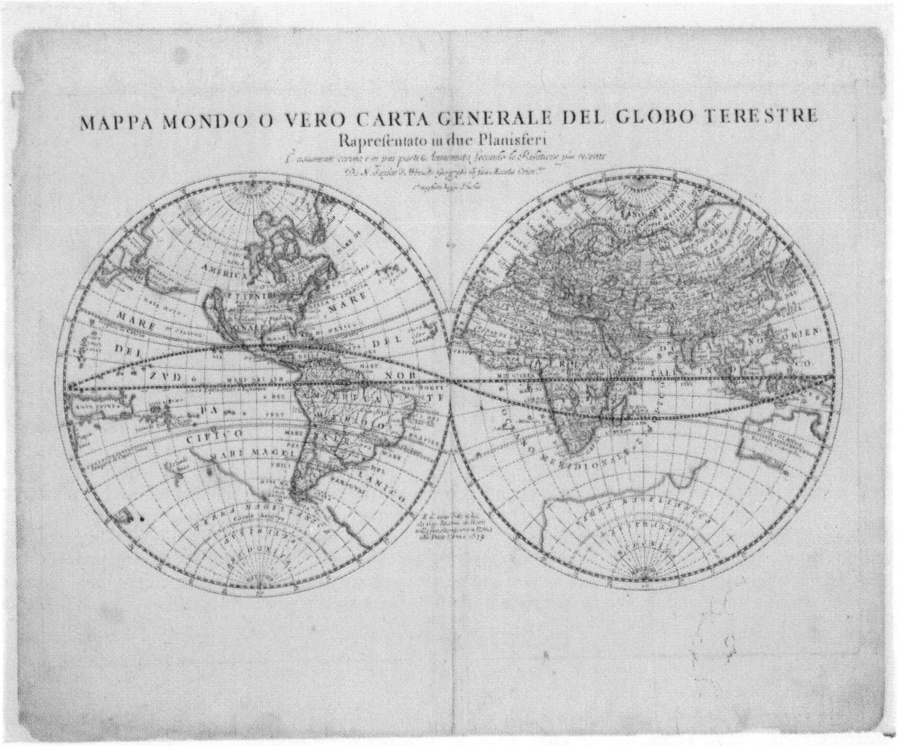

Map by Nicolas Sanson d'Abbeville, titled "Mappa Mondo o Vero Carta Generale del Globo Terestre." Roma: 1674. Italian edition of the original French map of 1651. Hand-colored map depicting the world in two hemispheres. 19" x 24" .......... **$531**

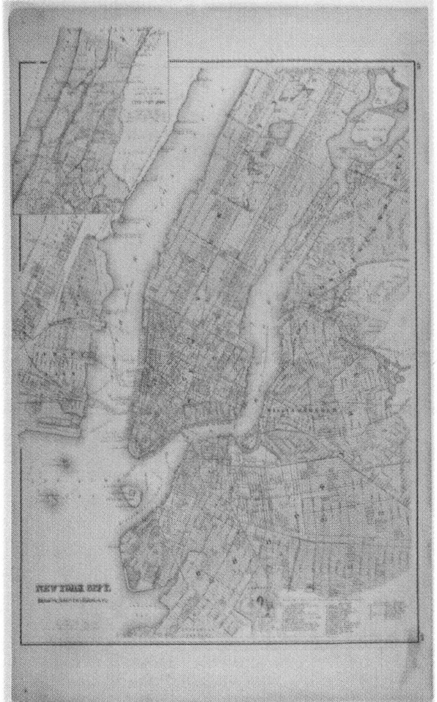

Map, New York City, including Brooklyn, Jersey City, and Hoboken, circa 1890, 27-1/2" x 17-1/4" .. **$143**

Globe, Rand McNally & Co. globe on stand, 49" high .......... **$2,607**

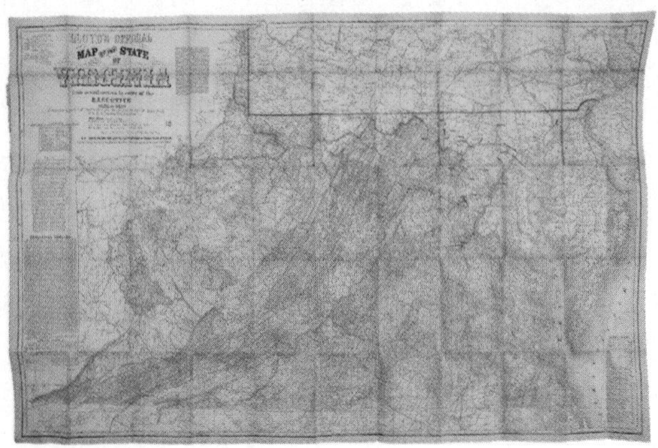

Map by J. T. Lloyd, "Lloyd's Official Map of the State of Virginia." New York: J. T. Lloyd, 1862. 46" by 30". A large linen-backed folding map first issued in 1861, then 1862, and last issued in 1863 taken from Boye's map of 1828 and extensively revised. Each county is in color. This version was intended for use by Union military officers and bears the printed notation, "This is the only map used to plan campaigns in Virginia by Gen. McClellan." The map is mounted in embossed brown cloth covers measuring 4-1/2" x 7-1/4", and the front board is titled in gold "Lloyd's $100,000 Topographical Map of Virginia." This copy has contemporary ink notations on the front pastedown indicating battles and movements corresponding to marks on the map, probably made by a soldier mustered into an Ohio regiment; front board detached and missing spine. ...............**$1,000**

Map by Abraham Ortelius, titled "Thraciae Veteris Typus," circa 1624, hand-colored copper engraved map, 19" x 14" ..........**$143**

# Oddities & Curiosities

These collectibles fall in the "weird and wonderful" category of unusual items.

Bicycle and automobile badges, collection of 33, variety of stamped and die struck emblems, most having been flattened from their original rounded shape, including Kansas AAA Motor Club "Chiropractic Member," plus Dentist Member; plus stamped spec and logo plates for Nonpareil Bicycle Wks, Yale Consolidated Mfg, LaMarne, State Farm Mutual, Racycle, Westing Arrow, Excelsior Supply Co., Beatrice No 45 Creamery, Davis Sewing Machine Co., Packard, Monark, KW Master Vibrator and more. Also a large shield-shaped plaque of "The Postmaster Creed," 8-1/4" x 7" ............. **$275**

Carved cherry barber chair with dog's heads carved at the arms' terminals, incised line decoration and matching foot rest with ornate iron casting, no maker's marks, 44" x 24" x 29" ................ **$300**

Box, one-of-a-kind footrest, covered in bottle caps from Schlitz, Country Club, Brunswick Orange Soda, and others, 7-1/4" x 13 x 12-1/2" ............................ **$110**

Fly trap, three-footed amber glass base, "patent applied for" around rim, clear glass dome, 6-1/2" x 6-1/2" with dome .............. **$200**

Carl Worner diorama whimsy bottle of a meat market, American, probably early 20th c., signed "Carl Worner/Hanan/a/Main" in pencil on reverse, carved and painted wood and paper, foil, depicting meat market with sign above the counter reading "Choicest and best/Meat at the Lowest Prices," with butchers and customer mounted in a glass bottle with glass stopper, 11-1/2" h. ...................................... **$5,333**

*Skinner, Inc.*

Horse taxidermy mount, Trigger, made famous as being cowboy actor Roy Rogers' pet and sidekick .................................**$266,500**

Lantern, Halloween-motif in foot form, papier-maché, highly detailed, huge open grinning mouth, large protruding nose, individual comical faces on each toe, likely one of a kind, 7-1/2" ......**$10,350**
*Dan Morphy Auctions*

Lantern, railroad-style with unusual elongated clear glass globe, 13" h. x 6" w. .................... **$200**

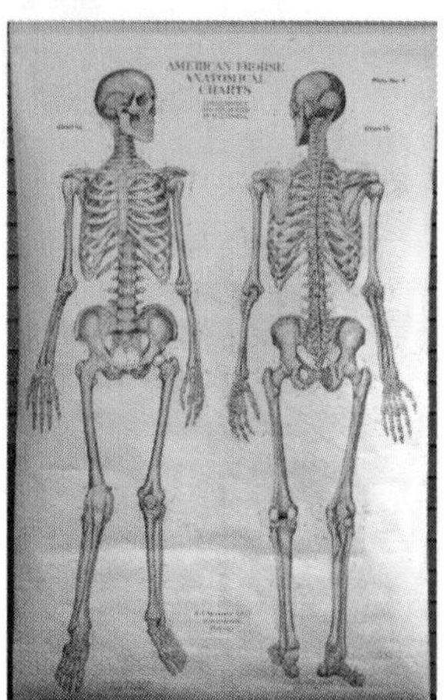

Medical charts, five World War I-era pull-down diagrams in wooden frame, includes American Frohse Anatomical Chart of the nervous and circulatory systems, hair, viscera of chest and abdomen, skeletal and musculature systems, edited and augmented by Dr. Max Blodel, average size 70" x 41" ........................................ **$300**

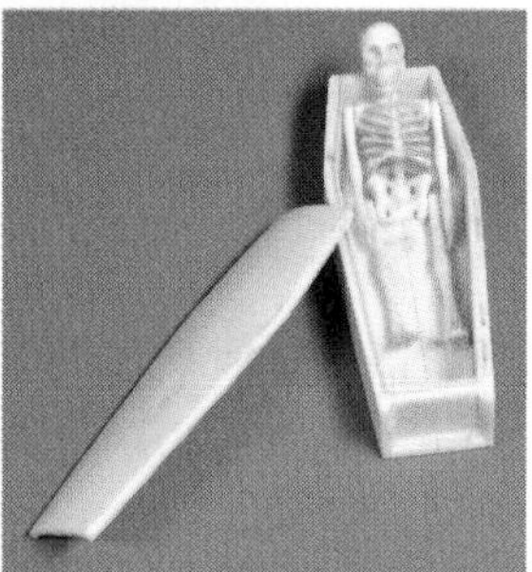

Miniature carved ivory coffin with skeleton figure, 19th c., pegged construction, coffin with lift-off lid, containing an articulated skeleton figure, 4-1/2" l., 4" ..... **$889**
*Skinner, Inc.*

Napoleonic prisoner-of-war bone and straw-work spinning jenny, Britain, late 18th/early 19th c., mechanized model with eight figures and two dogs, polychrome painted details, upper and lower wood platforms with applied geometric straw-work designs, 7-3/8" h. x 5-3/4" w. x 3" d. Provenance: From the collection of Wright Ludington, founder of the Santa Barbara Museum. Note: This prisoner-of-war artifact was made by a French prisoner, incarcerated by the British under dismal conditions, using primitive tools............................................................**$16,590**
*Skinner, Inc.*

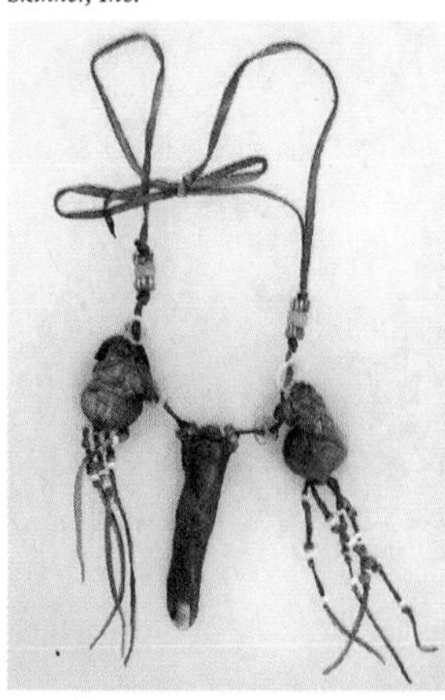

◀ Necklace, Cree or Crow trophy necklace, 1775-1830, assembled from Caucasian finger and testicles, strung on buckskin with glass trade beads and carved bone buttons, testicles wrapped in buckskin sacks, worn by the warrior as a talisman to receive the strength of his conquered enemy, likely one of a kind ...............................................................**$3,500**
*Empire Estates & Auctions*

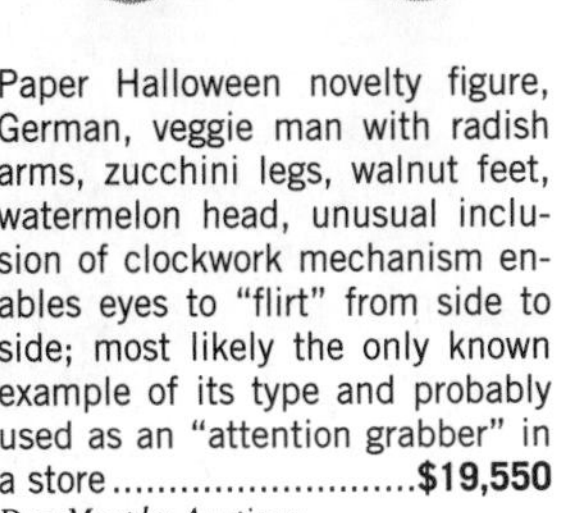

Paper Halloween novelty figure, German, veggie man with radish arms, zucchini legs, walnut feet, watermelon head, unusual inclusion of clockwork mechanism enables eyes to "flirt" from side to side; most likely the only known example of its type and probably used as an "attention grabber" in a store ........................... **$19,550**
*Dan Morphy Auctions*

Steamer trunk, made by Goyard, circa 1900, signed Goyard Aine, Monte Carlo, Biarritz, Paris, decorated with original decals from Cunard White Star, Pullman Golden Arrow, France, Italy, and England's Victoria Station, 22" h. x 32" w. x 19" d. Note: This trunk was purchased at a Califorina rummage sale for $20 and sold through Clars Auction Gallery........ **$5,629**

Prisoner calligraphic exercise depicting the Lord's Prayer, reportedly Pennsylvania, c. 1855, 18-1/4" x 14-1/2". Provenance: Estate of Susan Parrish....... **$711**
*Skinner, Inc.*

Roman bronze cavalry parade helmet, circa late 1st/2nd c. A.D. ................................ **$3,631,750**
*Christie's*

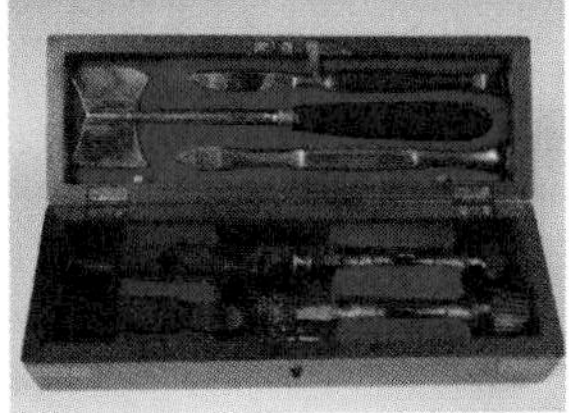

Surgical kit with two trephines, single wooden grip and matching brush, inside lid has Hey's saw, scalpel, and lenticular knife, inside box with "L.V. Helmold Surgical Instrument Maker..." tag, circa 19th c., box 2" x 3" x 9-1/4" ............................... **$850**

Rare c. 1870s Ice Velocipede, possibly one-of-a-kind bicycle built for ice riding, wooden-spoked wheel with metal rim (with four studs for traction), metal pan seat, brake assembly, wooden tiller (broken), on unusual platform base with wrought iron runners, 50" wheel. Provenance: Given to (and deaccessioned from) a private museum by Alan Jones, c. 1928. Used on the Passaic River, N.J., and said to be built by Mr. Sanford after whom Sanford Avenue in Trenton was named.........**$10,750**

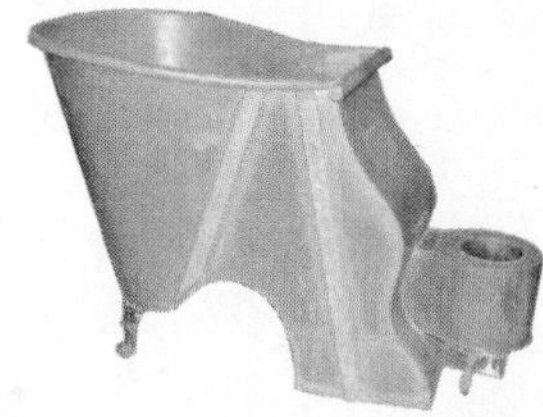

"Slipper-shaped" brothel bathtub with front load coal heater, 52" x 34-1/2" x 26", rare and possibly one of a kind.................. **$4,500**

Wall sconce, pair of triple font wall sconces with crimp decoration, tin, 8-1/2" h. x 12" w. ........ **$900**

# Paperweights

Although paperweights had their origin in ancient Egypt, it was in the mid-19th century that this art form reached its zenith. The finest paperweights were produced between 1834 and 1855 in France by the Clichy, Baccarat, and St. Louis factories. Other weights made in England, Italy, and Bohemia during this period rarely match the quality of the French weights.

In the early 1850s, the New England Glass Co. in Cambridge, Massachusetts, and the Boston and Sandwich Glass Co. in Sandwich, Massachusetts, became the first American factories to make paperweights.

Popularity peaked during the classic period (1845-1855) and faded toward the end of the 19th century. Paperweight production was rediscovered nearly a century later in the mid-1900s. Baccarat, St. Louis, Perthshire, and many studio craftsmen in the United States and Europe still make contemporary paperweights.

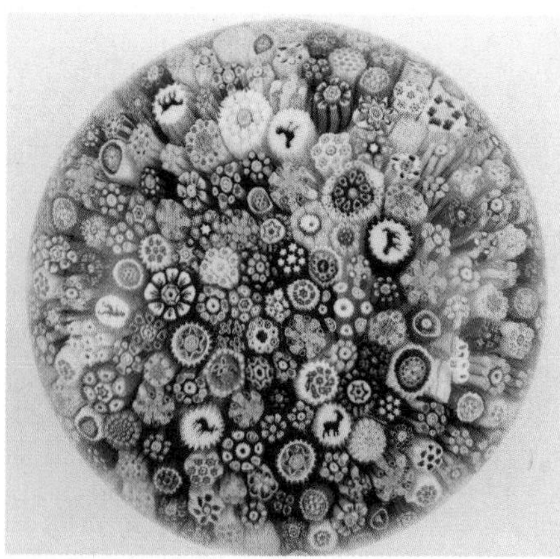

Antique Baccarat close pack paperweight, millefiori with complex canes including six gridel canes of a horse, rooster, dog, goat, deer, and monkey. Also has "B 1848" signature/date cane. 3-3/4" dia. x 2-1/2" t. Provenance: Barry Schultheiss Collection... **$6,325**
*James D. Julia, Inc.*

►Antique Baccarat paperweight chalice, four panels of loosely packed millefiori canes with white spiral latticino connector and loosely packed millefiori canes on foot, cut flutes on foot and stem with applied gold gilding around base of foot, rim, and edge of panels, chalice comes with velvet-lined presentation case. 6-3/4" t. Provenance: Applewhaite-Abbott Collection sold at Sotheby's, Oct. 21, 1952, then the Hida Takayama Museum of Art sale at Sotheby's, Dec. 19, 2002 to the Barry Schultheiss Collection ............................................................**$12,650**
*James D. Julia, Inc.*

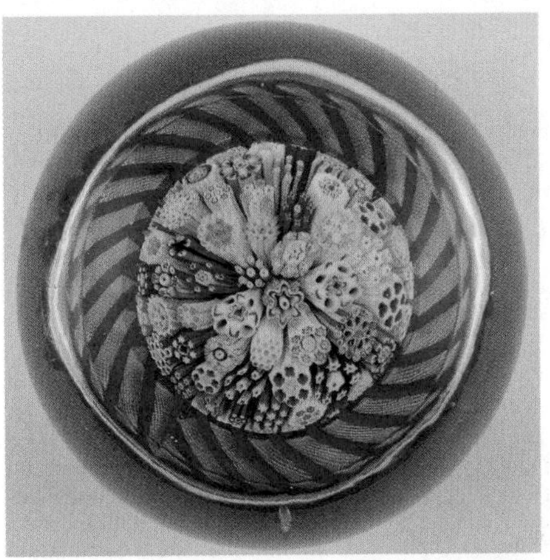

Antique Baccarat mushroom paperweight, close pack millefiori with blue and white torsade and star cut base. 3" dia. x 2" t. Provenance: Barry Schultheiss Collection ................................................ **$1,035**

*James D. Julia, Inc.*

Antique Baccarat paperweight with handle, close pack millefiori with "B 1847" signature/date cane and silhouette cane of monkey, applied gold washed metal handle. 2-1/2" dia. x 2-3/8" t. to top of handle. Provenance: Barry Schultheiss Collection......... **$460**

*James D. Julia, Inc.*

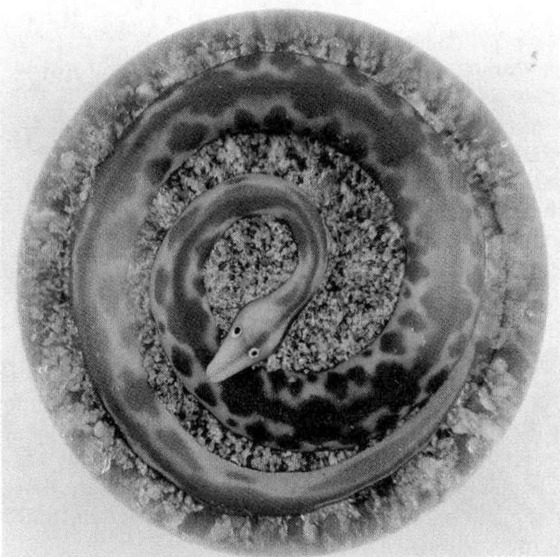

Rare antique Baccarat snake paperweight with brown spatters and beady eyes rests on a rock ground with two complete coils. 3" dia. x 2-1/8" t.**$5,000-$7,000**

*James D. Julia, Inc.*

Antique St. Louis dahlia paperweight, yellow central stamen surrounded by five tiers of blue striped petals and eight green leaves, star cut base. 3" dia. x 2-1/4" t. ........................................................**$16,100**

*James D. Julia, Inc.*

Antique Baccarat primrose paperweight, blue and white primrose blossom with green leaves and stem on clear ground with a star cut base. 2-1/2" dia. x 1-1/2" t. Provenance: Dorothy-Lee Jones Collection .......................... **$690**

*James D. Julia, Inc.*

Antique Baccarat spill vase, close pack millefiori paperweight with four silhouette canes of dog, goat, rooster, and squirrel, "B 1848" signature/date canes, clear crystal vase mounted atop the paperweight with an engraved floral, leaf, and vine decoration with applied ruby edge. 5-1/4" t. Provenance: Barry Schultheiss Collection ................................ **$4,887**

*James D. Julia, Inc.*

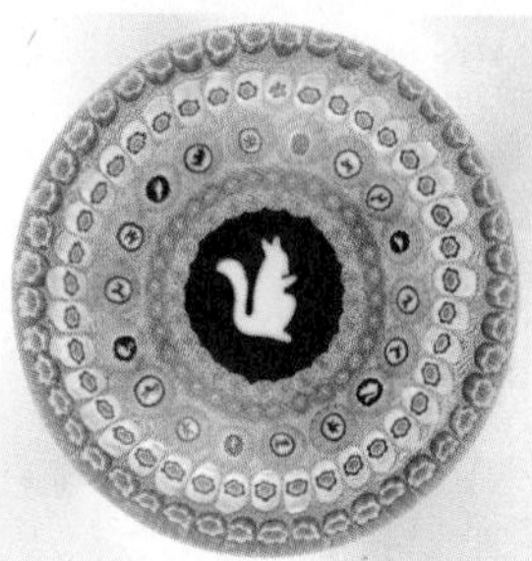

Baccarat squirrel gridel paperweight, large silhouette of white squirrel on black ground surrounded by five concentric millefiori rings including a ring of 18 additional silhouettes, signed with "B 1972" signature/date cane and also signed on underside with acid etched Baccarat insignia, numbered "485." 3" dia. x 2-3/8" t. Provenance: Barry Schultheiss Collection .......................... **$345**
*James D. Julia, Inc.*

Clichy millefiori newel post, green and white millefiori cane surrounded by two concentric rings of millefiori canes including 16 pink and white roses, eight circlets of millefiori canes and a garland of pink and green rose canes surrounding design. Included in design is a circlet of 10 rose canes. Original metal hardware. 3-3/4" dia. x 6-1/2" t. Provenance: Barry Schultheiss Collection.....**$10,350**
*James D. Julia, Inc.*

►Contemporary St. Louis carpet ground paperweight, open concentric millefiori canes on a white stardust carpet ground, signed on the underside with an "SL 1982" signature/date cane. 3" dia. x 2" t. Provenance: Barry Schultheiss Collection .......................... **$747**
*James D. Julia, Inc.*

Caithness/Whitefriars paperweight scent bottle, two purple pansy blossoms surrounded by a garland of pink and white millefiori canes on translucent blue ground, 15 side facets and signed on underside in script "Whitefriars Pansy P.B. Caithness Scotland 37-50." Stopper has a matching lamp worked single purple pansy blossom. 5-3/8" t. Provenance: Barry Schultheiss Collection......... **$472**
*James D. Julia, Inc.*

Clichy swirl paperweight, green, white, and red central millefiori cane surrounded by swirls of white, blue, and green. 3" dia. x 2" t. .............................. **$4,025**
*James D. Julia, Inc.*

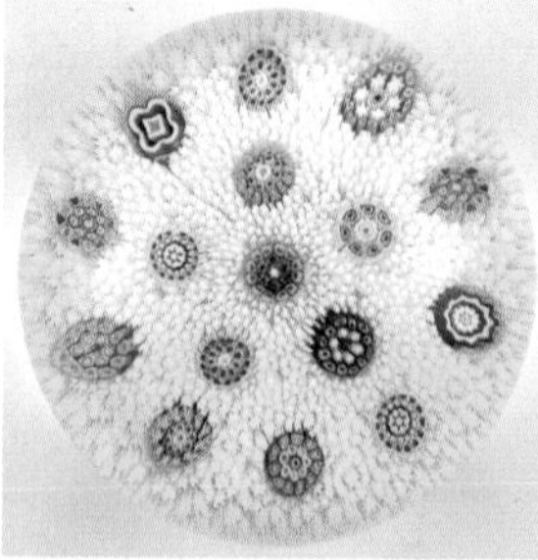

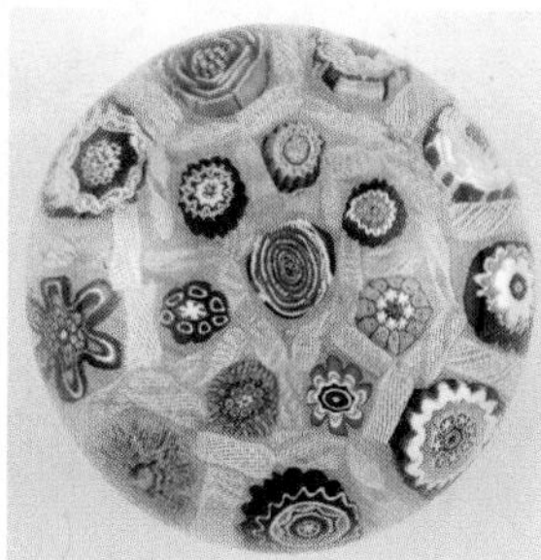

Clichy Chequer paperweight, central rose cane surrounded by 16 complex millefiori canes including white/red and blue rose canes, all canes are separated by white latticino twists. 2-3/4" dia. x 2-1/4" t. Provenance: Barry Schultheiss Collection. ..................... **$2,012**
*James D. Julia, Inc.*

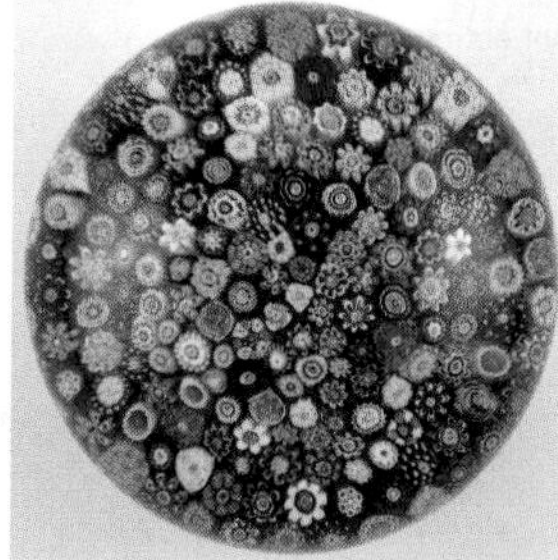

Clichy millefiori paperweight, close pack millefiori canes including six pink and green rose canes, four white rose canes, one purple and one green rose cane, design rests in a white stave basket. 2-7/8" dia. Provenance: Barry Schultheiss Collection......... **$805**
*James D. Julia, Inc.*

Daniel Salazar Magnum crane compound paperweight with four layers of decoration including two white cranes and blue irises against a white and blue marine background, signed in script on underside "Daniel Salazar 121867 Lundberg Studios 1992 Happy 50th Birthday." 4-1/2" dia. x 4-1/4" t. Provenance: Barry Schultheiss Collection......... **$517**
*James D. Julia, Inc.*

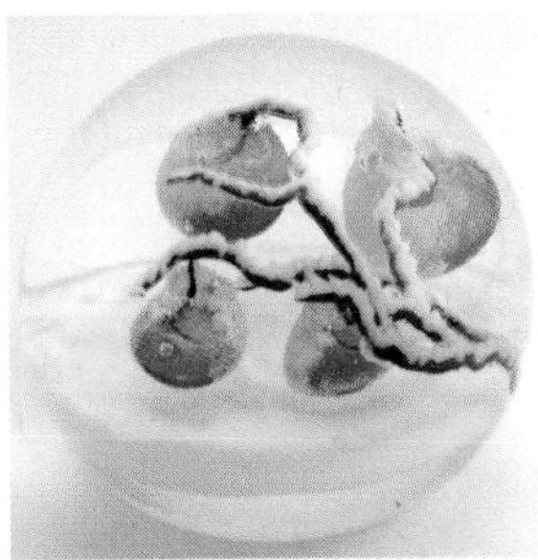

Daniel Salazar snow-covered fruit paperweight, orange fruit with green leaves hang from a snow-covered branch, signed on underside with a lamp worked "DS" and also signed in script "Lundberg Studios 1999 050468 Daniel Salazar." 3-1/2" dia. x 3-1/8" t. Provenance: Barry Schultheiss Collection ........................ **$236**
*James D. Julia, Inc.*

Debbie Tarsitano floral bouquet paperweight, 13 lamp worked flower blossoms, some of which are comprised of latticino twist petals, and four ladybugs rest on opaque blue ground with colored shreds, signed with a "DT" signature cane and cut in a cross-hatch basket pattern. 3-1/2" dia. x 2-1/2" t. Provenance: Barry Schultheiss Collection...... **$1,150**
*James D. Julia, Inc.*

Jim Brown paperweight knife, complex millefiori canes comprise the handle of this jack knife, unsigned. 3-1/2" l. closed. Provenance: Barry Schultheiss Collection ..........**$402**
*James D. Julia, Inc.*

Delmo Tarsitano paperweight, green overlay salamander on a rock ground with white flower growing behind a rock, early blue dahlia made by Debbie Tarsitano, signed "DT" on an internal cane. 3-1/4" dia...................... **$1,035**
*James D. Julia, Inc.*

Ken Rosenfeld orb paperweight, two-sided bouquet with multiple floral blossoms in colors of pink, purple, yellow, and blue along with green leaves and stems, unsigned. 3-3/8" dia. Provenance: Barry Schultheiss Collection......... **$805**
*James D. Julia, Inc.*

Loren stump glass paperweight, two butterflies hover over an orange-petaled flower with brown leaves encased in a gold-covered egg, nude winged fairy sits atop the egg amongst applied flowers and leaves, unsigned. 4" t. Provenance: Barry Schultheiss Collection ............................. **$2,300**
*James D. Julia, Inc.*

◄Pair of French stalagmite stem paperweights/mantle ornaments, each featuring free-form sulphide lumps covered with polychrome and opal glass, raised on waisted base with rough pontil mark. Possibly Clichy or Alsace/Lorraine. Fourth quarter 19th century. 10-3/4" h., 3" and 3-1/4" dia. base. ............................... **$488**
*Jeffrey S. Evans & Associates*

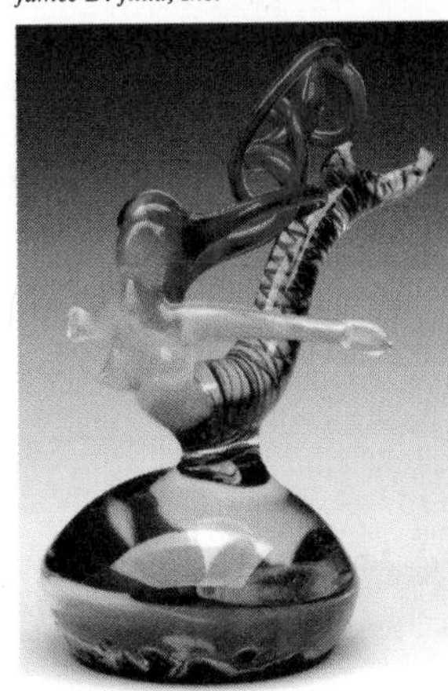

►Milon Townsend mermaid paperweight, lamp worked mermaid with flowing red hair and blue latticino tail rests atop blue, aqua mottled paperweight base, signed on underside "Mermaid Friggers Milon Townsend 2001." 3-3/4" t. Provenance: Barry Schultheiss Collection ........................... **$86**
*James D. Julia, Inc.*

St. Louis "Modernity" millefiori and lamp work paperweight, six millefiori cane and rod clusters centered amongst green leaves, multiple side flutes and signed with an "SL 2002" signature/date cane, numbered on the underside "12/125." 3" dia. x 3-1/4" t. Provenance: Barry Schultheiss Collection .......................... **$977**
*James D. Julia, Inc.*

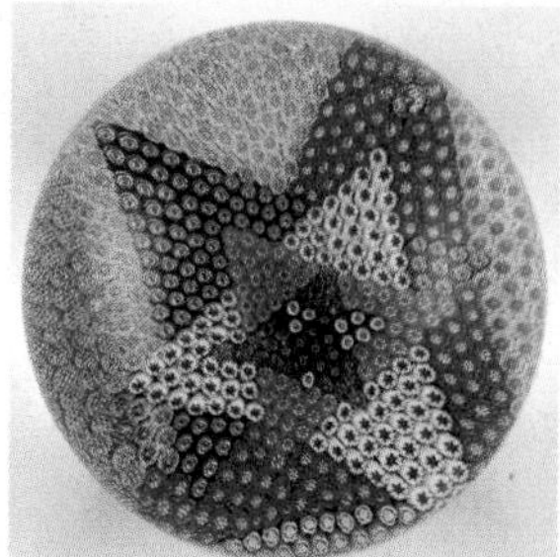

St. Louis Pattern millefiori paperweight, carpet ground interlocking diamond-shaped millefiori patterns in colors of red, white, blue, and chartreuse, signed with signature/date cane "SL 1996." 3" dia. x 2-1/4" t. Provenance: Barry Schultheiss Collection...... **$1,121**
*James D. Julia, Inc.*

St. Louis multicolored swirl paperweight, five swirls of white, blue, green, red, and chartreuse with a central signature/date cane "SL 1971." 3" dia. x 2-1/8" t. Provenance: Barry Schultheiss Collection .................................. **$402**
*James D. Julia, Inc.*

St. Louis paperweight wafer dish, close concentric millefiori paperweight base with a translucent green bowl and white spiral latticino edge, signed with "SL 1983" signature/date cane. 4-1/4" dia. x 4" t. Provenance: Barry Schultheiss Collection. ................. **$1,437**
*James D. Julia, Inc.*

Large St. Louis upright bouquet paperweight with multiple flower blossoms in blue, pink, white, chartreuse, and orange with green leaves, all over multiple facets and signed with an "SL 1991" signature/date cane, also signed in script on underside "Saint Louis." 3" dia. x 3-7/8" t. Provenance: Barry Schultheiss Collection..**$805**
*James D. Julia, Inc.*

St. Louis upright floral bouquet paperweight, seven flower blossoms with millefiori cane centers in colors of red, blue, white, orange, and chartreuse on a bed of green lamp worked leaves resting on a spiral latticino pad, entire design surrounded by a red and white twist torsade, signed with an "SL 1971" signature/date cane. 3" dia. x 2-1/2" t. Provenance: Barry Schultheiss Collection **$345**
*James D. Julia, Inc.*

Two American pressed glass paperweights. 1) Mt. Washington antique clear paperweight with pressed dog's face in base. 2) Mt. Washington antique clear paperweight with pressed figure of sleeping baby in the base. 3-1/4" dia. and 4-3/4" l., respectively.......................... **$200-300**
*James D. Julia, Inc.*

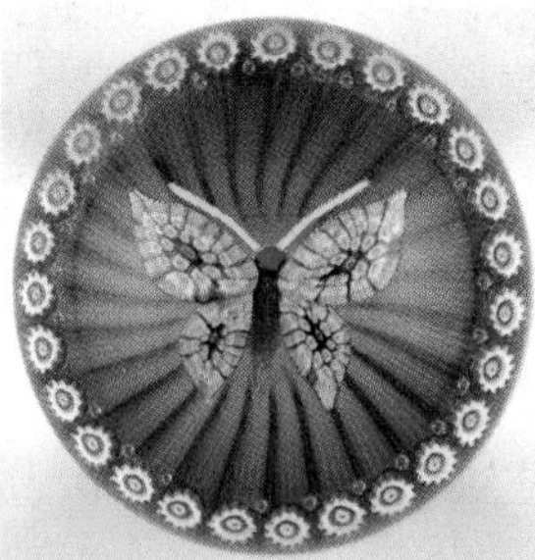

William Manson butterfly paperweight, blue and white butterfly with green aventurine body hovers over a gold and white basket, signed on the underside "WM/80" and numbered "71/250." 2-3/4" dia. x 2-1/4" t. Provenance: Barry Schultheiss Collection......... **$236**
*James D. Julia, Inc.*

# Perfume Bottles

Although the human sense of smell isn't nearly as acute as that of many other mammals, we have long been affected by the odors in the world around us. Science has shown that scents or smells can directly affect our mood or behavior.

No one knows for certain when humans first rubbed themselves with some plant or herb to improve their appeal to other humans, usually of the opposite sex. However, it is clear that the use of unguents and scented materials was widely practiced as far back as Ancient Egypt.

Some of the first objects made of glass, in fact, were small cast vials used for storing such mixtures. By the age of the Roman Empire, scented waters and other mixtures were even more important and were widely available in small glass flasks or bottles. Since that time glass has been the material of choice for storing scented concoctions, and during the past 200 years some of the most exquisite glass objects produced were designed for that purpose.

It wasn't until around the middle of the 19th century that specialized bottles and vials were produced to hold commercially manufactured scents. Some aromatic mixtures were worn on special occasions, while many others were splashed on to help mask body odor. For centuries it had been common practice for "sophisticated" people to carry on their person a scented pouch or similar accoutrement, since daily bathing was unheard of and laundering methods were primitive.

Commercially produced and brand name perfumes and colognes have really only been common since the late 19th and early 20th centuries. The French started the ball rolling during the first half of the 19th century when D'Orsay and Guerlain began producing special scents. The first American entrepreneur to step into this field was Richard Hudnut, whose firm was established in 1880. During the second half of the 19th century most scents carried simple labels and were sold in simple, fairly generic glass bottles. Only in the early 20th century did parfumeurs introduce specially designed labels and bottles to hold their most popular perfumes. Coty, founded in 1904, was one of the first to do this, and they turned to Rene Lalique for a special bottle design around 1908. Other French firms, such as Bourjois (1903), Caron (1903), and D'Orsay (1904) were soon following this trend.

Perfume bottle and stopper, "Sirene" pattern by Lalique, the perfume bottle in clear and frosted glass with a blue patina, clear flattened upright disk shape molded with the swirled figure of a siren trimmed in blue, matching mushroom stopper, first documented example with conforming stopper, molded "R. Lalique," French, ca. 1927, 5" h. ............................................... **$57,000**

People collect two kinds of perfume bottles—decorative and commercial. Decorative bottles include any bottles sold empty and meant to be filled with your choice of scent. Commercial bottles are any that were sold filled with scent and usually have the label of the perfume company.

The rules of value for perfume bottles are the same as for any other kind of glass—rarity, condition, age, and quality of glass.

For more information on perfume bottles, see *Antique Trader Perfume Bottles Price Guide* by Kyle Husfloen.

Cologne bottle and stopper, cut and engraved clear glass, squatty bulbous shape with a tall neck and sterling silver-coated mushroom stopper, in the Rock Crystal style, signed by Hawkes, sterling by Gorham, American, ca. 1900 ........................... **$1,000-$1,250**

Cologne bottle and stopper, squatty cobalt blue glass shape with four projecting tiered oval panels below a curved shoulder and short flaring neck, ornately trimmed with gilt flower and leaf sprigs, large squared mushroom stopper, possibly Bohemia, ca. 1900-'20, 4-2/3" h....**$150-$175**

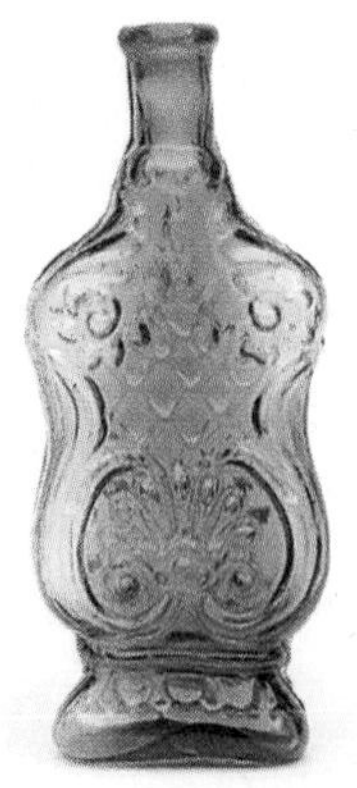

Perfume atomizer with fittings, pate de verre, upright flat-bottomed tapering ovoid shaped with a mottled pale green ground molded with dark blue and green violets, gilt metal fittings, signed by Argy Rousseau, French, ca. 1920s 5-1/2" h.... **$1,500-$3,000**

Rare Coty perfume bottle and stopper, "L'Effleur," upright rectangular clear and frosted Lalique glass bottle molded in center panel with an Art Nouveau female above waves, brown patina, probably first collaboration with Lalique, ca. 1908, 4-1/3" h................**$4,500-$4,750**

Cologne bottle, mold-blown sapphire blue glass, flattened corseted shape with palmette scrolled acanthus with cross-hatching, inward rolled mouth, pontil scar, American, ca. 1840-60, 5-3/4" h.................. **$2,128**

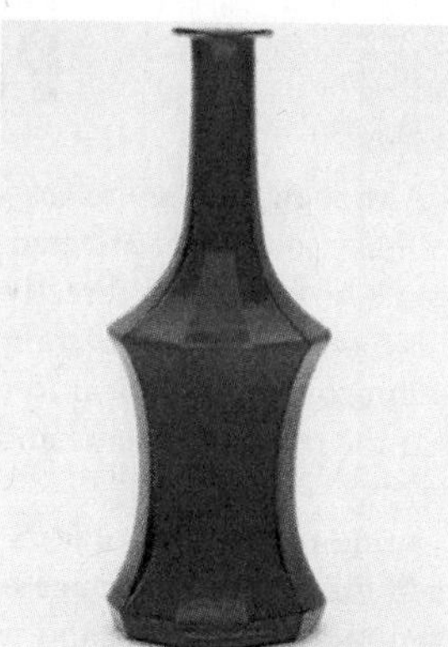

Cologne bottle, cobalt blue mold-blown glass, tall paneled and waisted sides with an angled shoulder to the long paneled neck with a flattened rim, smooth base, Boston and Sandwich Glass Co., mid-19th c., 7" h........... **$1,456**

Perfume atomizer with fittings, Wave Crest glass in the Helmschmeid Swirl mold, shaded pink to white ground hand-painted overall with tiny blue blossoms on leafy stems, by C.F. Monroe Co., American, ca. 1898, 5-1/2" h. ................................**$750-$900**

Perfume bottle and stopper, clear cut crystal bottle in the shape of a cross-form military medal, the center cut with a fine diamond point design, French, ca. 1840-50, 2-3/4" h.............**$450-$550**

Perfume bottle and powder box, porcelain, figural, designed as a lady in 18th c. dress in yellow with green trim, her upper body lifts off to expose the powder box, her upper body forms the perfume bottle topped by a small metal crown-form stopper, German, ca. 1930s, 7-1/4" h. .......................... **$525**

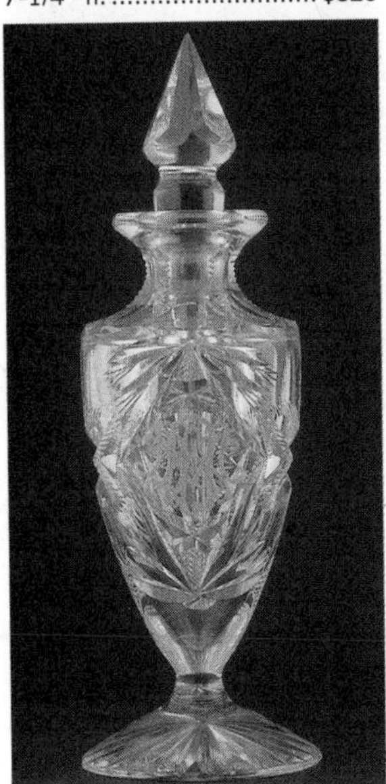

Perfume bottle and stopper, clear cut glass, pedestal base with tall elaborately cut ovoid body and flared neck, pointed cut stopper with long dauber, engraved monogram on side, signed by Libbey, American, ca. 1900, 7-3/4" h. .................. **$750-$850**

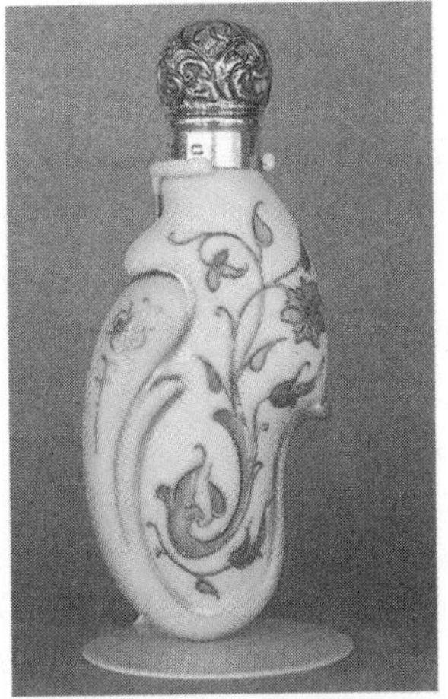

Perfume bottle and stopper, asymmetrical scroll-molded porcelain bottle in cream hand-painted with delicate flowering leafy stems issuing from a blue scroll, heavy gold trim, répoussé sterling silver hinged cap, English, Royal Worcester, late 19th c., 4" h. ....................................... **$500**

Perfume bottle and stopper, boule-shaped deep red shaded to pink cased glass bottle enclosed in gold netting, glossy finish, Thomas Webb & Sons, with sterling silver collar and hinged cap with hallmarks for London, 1885-86, 3-1/4" h. ............**$750-$900**

Perfume bottle and stopper, blown heavy clear glass encasing yellow and white narcissus and dark green leaves, clear blown ovoid stopper, signed "Steven Lundberg Studios 1980," 4" h...**$450-$550**

Perfume bottle and stopper, arched and facet-cut peach crystal bottle with a large round flat clear stopper etched with a kneeling female nude and large blossoms, signed, Czechoslovakian, ca. 1930s, 6-1/2" h. .......... **$400**

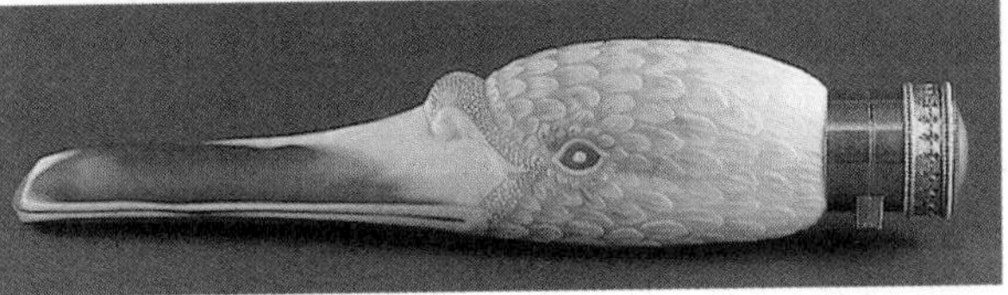

Perfume bottle and stopper, cameo glass, figural swan's head cameo bottle in blue cased in white and cameo carved, sterling silver overcap on inner glass stopper, cap marked by Keller, Thomas Webb, English, ca. 1885, 9-1/3" l. ................................................. **$9,000-$12,000**

Perfume bottle and stopper, clear crystal in a long low form with a gently curved and ribbed bottom, the wide shoulder and neck trimmed with enameled gilt-metal filigree trimmed with red jewels, tall clear oblong stopper etched with a large cockatoo on a flowering vine, ending in dauber stub, metal tag marked "Czechoslovakia," ca. 1920s, 5-3/4" h. ........................... **$1,000-$1,500**

Perfume bottle and stopper, bulbous tapering ovoid pink mother-of-pearl satin glass in the Diamond Quilted pattern, trimmed with gilt flowers, sterling silver collar and hinged répoussé cap with glass inner stopper, English, ca. 1880, 4-7/8" h..... **$750-$850**

Perfume bottle and stopper, boule-shaped body with short flared neck and ball-shaped stopper, gold iridescent Tiffany Favrile glass with an overall green hearts and vines decoration, signed, American, ca. 1920s, 4-1/4" h......... **$750-$900**

Perfume bottle and stopper, cut-overlay glass in clear cased in white and turquoise blue, rounded notch-cut base tapering to six cut oval panels each enameled with flowers or leaves below tall cut neck panels with matching decoration, panel-cut and enameled acorn-shaped stopper, French, ca. 1870-'80, 4-1/4" h. ........... **$253**

Perfume bottle and stopper, cylindrical cobalt blue glass bottle with rounded shoulders and short cylindrical neck, the upper half of the body covered in gold forming points and further highlighted with raised gilt stylized florals, the lower body decorated with delicate gold flowers, gold-covered knob stopper, Bohemian, ca. 1865, 5-1/4" h. .................. **$350-$450**

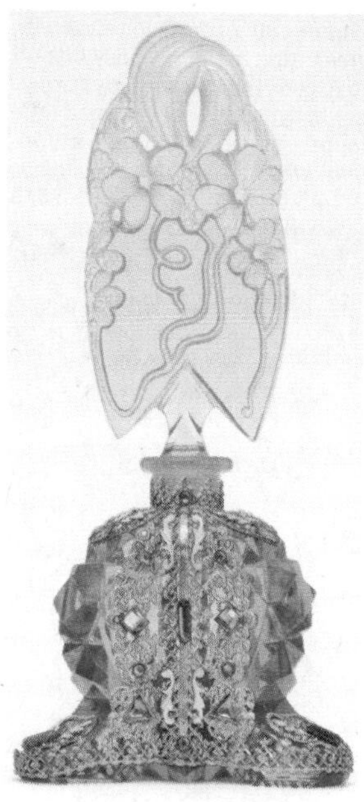

Perfume bottle and stopper, dark blue flattened bulbous bottle flaring at the base, wrapped with a filigree metal base band and a fancy enameled and jeweled filigree side panel, tall flattened and pointed blue openwork stopper etched with large stylized flowers, with dauber stub, metal tag reading "Czechoslovakia," 1920s, 8-1/2" h. ............ **$1,900-$2,400**

Perfume bottle and stopper, flattened oval crystal bottle with notch-cut sides and enclosing a sulphide bust of Napoleon, decorative silver cap, French, ca. 1840-'50, 3-1/4" l. ......... **$2,000**

Perfume bottle and stopper, flattened ovoid fancy silver-gilt body with a stippled background highlighted with delicate designs in enamels colored red, blue, and white, matching ball-form cap, hallmarked, Russian, ca. 1880, 3" h. .................. **$1,750-$2,000**

Perfume bottle and stopper, flattened ruby red pitcher-form bottle, flattened round bottle mounted on a round sterling silver foot and a silver collar, spouted neck, cover and S-scroll handle, English, London hallmarks for 1872, 4-1/2" h. ................................ **$400-$500**

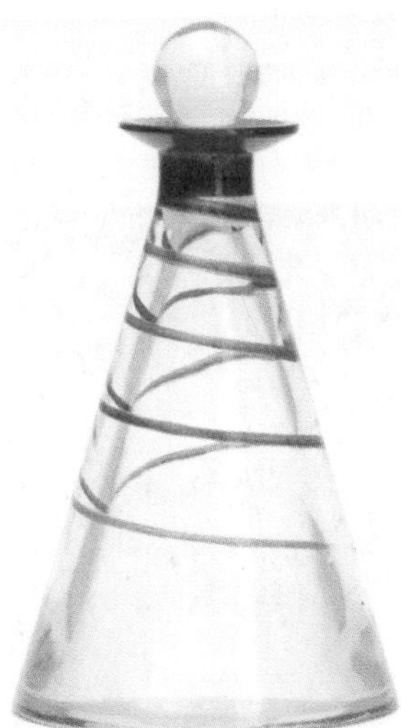

Perfume bottle and stopper, "Jasmin" by Mury, a Baccarat bottle in a conical form, clear glass with an enameled cobalt blue spiral down the sides, flared rim, clear ball stopper, French, ca. 1917, 4" h. .......................... **$1,500-$2,200**

Perfume bottle and stopper, "Hop 6010" by Pascall, figural clear glass candlestick-style telephone with a metal head and handle, metal bicycle bell ringer, bottom molded "C.T.G.," French, 1920s, 6-1/2" h. .................. **$550-$950**

Rare early perfume bottle and stopper, "L'Effleur" by Coty, a Lalique bottle in clear and frosted glass with a black patina, upright flattened rectangular shape with a rectangular panel molded with a mermaid among swirling waves, clear faceted ball stopper, applied "Lalique" glass label, first collaboration between Coty and René Lalique, French, ca. 1908, 4-1/2" h. ............ **$3,600-$4,500**

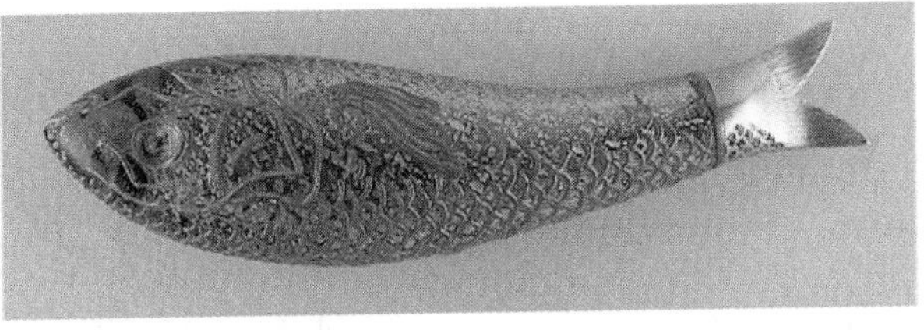

◀Perfume bottle and stopper, novelty fish shape composed of clear glass over mica chips and trimmed with gold enamel details, unmarked silver tail forming the stopper, Stevens and Williams, English, ca. 1880, 5-1/2" l. ................................ **$600-$750**

Perfume bottle and stopper, low arched and faceted black glass body mounted with a filigree neck band joined to a filigree metal panel centered by a long oval pink jewel, the tall openwork frosted clear stopper molded with flowers and complete with dauber, stenciled oval "Made in Czechoslovakia" and an "Irice" label, 1920s, 6" h. .......................... **$1,800**

Perfume bottle and stopper, "Orchis," a Lalique bottle in clear and frosted glass with a light rose patina, upright flattened rectangular shape with an overall etched design of stylized flowers on the sides, with label, molded "R. Lalique," ca. 1927, 3-5/8" h. .................................... **$2,520**

Perfume bottle and stopper, small oblong crystal deeply cut overall with a diamond design, silver screw-on cap and glass inner stopper, damage to inner lip, Irish, probably Cork, ca. 1820, 3-1/8" h. .................. **$300-$400**

Perfume bottle and stopper, squatty round tapering bottle in swirled blue and white latticino glass, matching blown bulbous stopper, probably by St. Louis, French, ca. 1870s, 5-1/2" h. .................. **$450-$600**

Perfume bottle and stopper, tall slender green pilgrim bottle-shaped Steuben glass body raised on a swirled Cintra and mica-flecked ball stem and an amber foot, swirled Cintra and mica-flecked ball stopper with long dauber, American, ca. 1920s, 11-3/4" h. .......... **$2,500-$3,500**

Perfume bottle and stopper, squatty translucent Verre de Soie Steuben eight-lobed glass with a pointed jade green stopper with dauber, American, unsigned, 4-1/2" h. .......................... **$600**

Perfume bottle and stopper, pink crystal bottle in a long narrow shape with angled shoulders, oval frosted pink stopper with a pierced design of draped nudes, with dauber, mounted on a four-footed gilt-metal base with green enameling and a large green jewel, marked in intaglio "Hoffman," Czechoslovakian, 1920s, 6" h. .......................... **$1,600-$2,000**

Perfume bottle and stopper, "Roses" by D'Orsay, clear and frosted Lalique bottle with sepia patina, footed spherical bottle with a short neck and tall figural stopper, molded "Lalique" with extended "L," some interior residue, stopper frozen, French, ca. 1912, 4" h. ................... **$3,360**

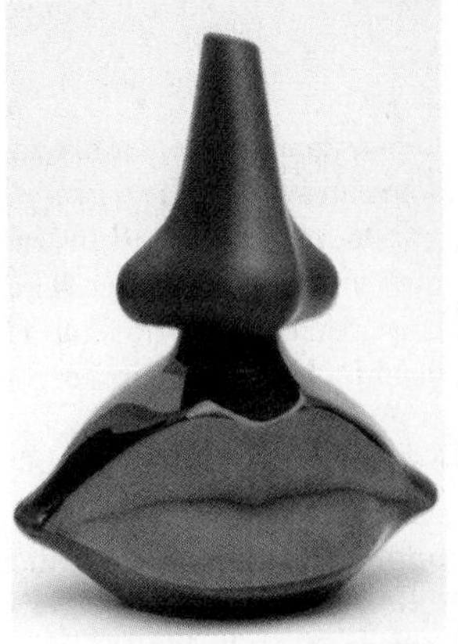

Perfume bottle and stopper, "Salvador Dali" black (dark blue) glass factice bottle designed as a pair of full lips below a tall nose forming the stopper, based on Dali's 1981 painting "Apparition du Visage de l'Aphrodite de Cinde dans un Payage," French, ca. 1983, 12-1/2" h. ...................... **$1,200**

Perfume bottle and stopper, pale amethyst crystal, narrow long ovoid shape with sharply tapering paneled sides with a small neck and a pointed stopper, resting on a narrow gilt-metal band trimmed with white enamel, metal stamped "Austria," ca. 1920s, 7" h. .......................... **$1,500-$2,000**

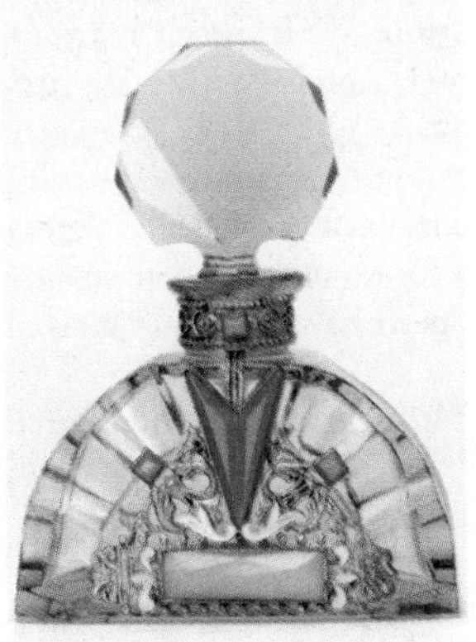

Perfume bottle and stopper, pale purple arched and fanned bottle fitted with filigree metal decorated with enamel and jewels, flat plain fanned stopper with dauber, stenciled "Czechoslovakia" and with metal tag reading "Czechoslovakia, Aristo," 1920s, 3-1/4" h. ....................................... **$840**

Perfume bottle and stopper, "Sirene" pattern by Lalique, the perfume bottle in clear and frosted glass with a blue patina, clear flattened upright disk shape molded with the swirled figure of a siren trimmed in blue, matching mushroom stopper, first documented example with conforming stopper, molded "R. Lalique," French, ca. 1927, 5" h. ................... **$57,000**

# Petroliana

Petroliana covers a broad range of gas station collectibles from containers and globes to signs and pumps and everything in between.

The items featured in this section are organized by type and have been selected at the high end of the market. The focus is on the top price items, not to skew the values, but to emphasize the brands and types that are the most desirable. Some less valuable items have been included to help keep values in perspective.

As with all advertising items, factors such as brand name, intricacy of design, color, age, condition, and rarity drastically affect value.

Beware of reproduction and fantasy pieces. For collectors of vintage gas and oil items, the only way to avoid reproductions is experience: making mistakes and learning from them; talking with other collectors and dealers; finding reputable resources (including books and websites), and learning to invest wisely, buying the best examples one can afford.

Marks can be deceiving, paper labels and tags are often missing, and those that remain may be spurious. Adding to the confusion are "fantasy" pieces, globes that have no vintage counterpart, and that are often made more for visual impact than deception.

How does one know whether a given piece is authentic? Does it look old, and to what degree can age be simulated? What is the difference between high-quality vintage advertising and modern mass-produced examples? Even experts are fooled when trying to assess qualities that have subtle distinctions.

There is another important factor to consider. A contemporary maker may create a "reproduction" sign or gas globe in tribute of the original, and sell it for what it is: a legitimate copy. Many of these are dated and signed by the artist or manufacturer, and these legitimate copies are highly collectible today. Such items are not intended to be frauds.

But a contemporary piece may pass through many hands between the time it leaves the maker and wind up in a collection. When profit is the only motive of a reseller, details about origin, ownership, and age can become a slippery slope of guesses, attribution, and—unfortunately—fabrication.

As the collector's eye sharpens, and the approach to inspecting and assessing petroliana improves, it will become easier to buy with confidence. And a knowledgeable collecting public should be the goal of all sellers, if for no other reason than the willingness to invest in quality.

For more information about petroliana, consult *Warman's Gas Station Collectibles* by Mark Moran.

*Photo acknowledgments to Aumann Auctions, Rich Gannon, George Simpson, and John Hudson*

## CONTAINERS

**Right:** Ace Wil-Flo Motor Oil quart tin can, excellent condition, small dents around top. ............ **$175+**

**Far right:** Aristo Motor Oil one-gallon tin, fair to good condition, dent in back.................... **$250+**

Bisonoil Motor Oil quart tin can, near mint........................**$300+**

Harley-Davidson Motorcycle five-gallon rocker can, poor to fair condition, overall wear, paint drips on reverse........... **$2,250+**

Opaline Motor Oil (Sinclair, striped) one-gallon tin, good condition. ............................**$300+**

Standard Stations Inc. copper swing-spout one-gallon oil can, with embossed "Property of Standard Stations Inc.," good condition, wear and small dents. **$125+**

Fleetwood Aero Craft Motor Oil quart tin can, very good condition, has blemish in display and light rust around bottom...........**$400+**

Indian Oil Valvoline Oil Company one-gallon flat tin can, excellent condition, light wear. .... **$4,800+**

Richlube Motor Oil five-quart tin can, excellent condition, no top. .................................... **$100+**

Golden Penn tin quart can, excellent condition, open on bottom. ......................................**$300+**

Magnolia one-gallon oil can, paper label, excellent condition. ..**$400+**

Power-lube Motor Oil five-gallon rocker can, display side excellent condition, reverse side fair.**$2,100+**

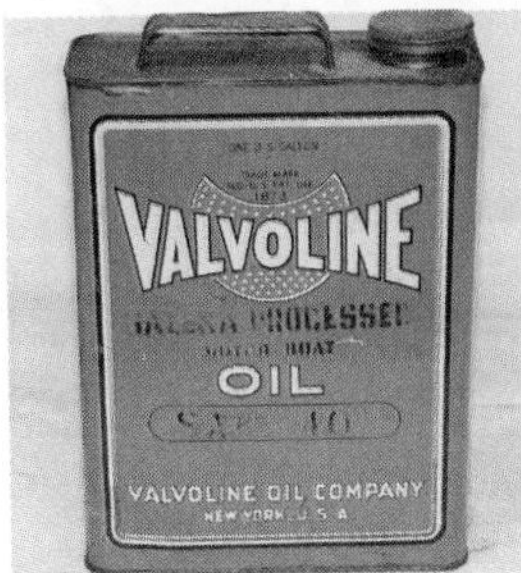

Valvoline Motor Oil one-gallon tin can (early design), display side excellent condition, reverse fair to good..............................**$150+**

◀Texaco Spica Oil pint can, excellent condition..............**$100+**

## GLOBES

Associated Gasoline "More Miles to the Gallon" globe, 15" lenses in high-profile metal globe, minor paint flaking around edge of one lens, reverse has small spot of paint loss, body repainted....... **$1,800+**

Beacon Gasoline globe 13-1/2" lenses in gill glass body, light scratches to field, ring and base repainted..................... **$3,000+**

Bull's Head Products globe 16-1/2" lenses in high-profile metal body, both lenses have been professionally restored (less than 15 percent).................. **$1,700+**

**Right:** Globe (with map) globe, 13-1/2" lenses in a gill body with metal base, light scratches..... **$1,600+**

**Far right:** Green Streak globe 15" lenses in high-profile body, display side excellent condition, reverse very good. .................. **$2,750+**

Hudson Ethyl with logo, 13" lenses in an orange ripple gill body, body cracked with paint loss around base...................................................... **$3,250+**

Magnolia Gasoline globe 16-1/2" lenses in high-profile metal body, lenses very good condition, body repainted................................................ **$2,750+**

Marathon globe 15" lenses in a high-profile metal body, display side excellent condition, small scratches on reverse....... **$2,100+**

Midland globe 13-1/2" lenses, in a white plastic body. ......... **$200+**

Mobilgas Ethyl globe 15" lenses in high-profile body, excellent condition. ............................ **$575+**

Oriole Gas globe 15" lenses in high-profile metal body, reverse has scratches. ............... **$4,500+**

Shell globe (West Coast), 15" single lens in high-profile body, lenses very good condition, body good original paint......... **$2,500+**

Standard Gasoline (California) globe, 15" lenses in a high-profile metal body, near mint. ... **$1,200+**

Spur Gas Gasoline globe 13-1/2" single lens in red ripple body, excellent condition. ....................................................................**$4,200+**

Texaco Ethyl (black T) globe, 15" lenses, in a high-profile metal body. ........................... **$2,000+**

Union 76 globe 15" single lens in high-profile body, very good condition. .............................. **$700+**

## SIGNS

Chevron Gasoline porcelain pump plate with hallmark, near mint, 15" x 12". **$1,600+**

Golden West Oil Company porcelain pump plate, new old stock. **$900+**

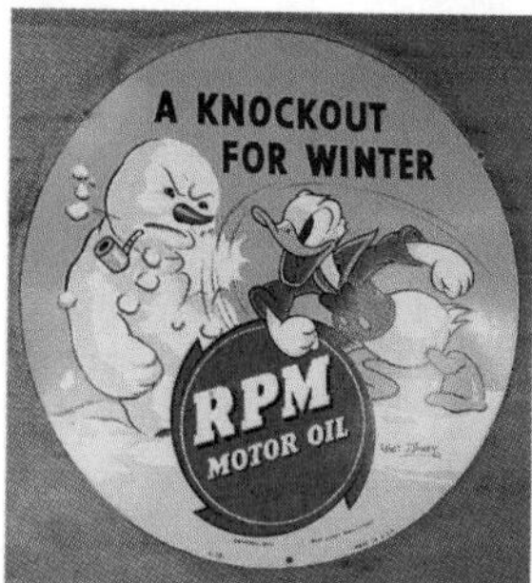


RPM Motor Oil 1940 Walt Disney Donald Duck sign, near mint, 24" diameter. **$7,000+**

**Right:** Standard Heating Oils single-sided porcelain die-cut sign, very good condition, scratches in field, quarter-size chip lower left, dime-size chip upper right, 30" x 40". **$500+**

**Far right:** Wil-Flo Motor Oil double-sided tin oval sign, 17" x 23", display side restored, reverse total loss. **$3,100+**

Douglas Aviation Regular single-sided tin pump sign, near mint, 18" x 12-1/2". **$1,500+**

Pan-Am Motor Oils single-sided porcelain Lubster sign, excellent condition, 15" diameter. **$1,150+**

Shell Gasoline porcelain pump plate (red background), near mint, 12" x 12". **$2,600+**

Esso Oil Drop Girl die-cut single-sided tin sign, dated 1965, near mint, 15" x 5". **$450+**

Indian Motorcycle Motor Oil bevel-edge single-sided tin easel sign, excellent condition-plus, light wear, glossy, 9-1/2" x 13". **$1,600+**

Sinclair Pennsylvania (black dinosaur) porcelain pump plate, fair to good condition, with repaired quarter-size chip in center, minor edge wear, 11" diameter. **$800+**

# Postcards

In the first half of the 20th century, postcards were cheap, often one cent and rarely more than five cents on the racks. Worldwide exchanges were common, making it possible to gain huge variety without being rich.

Those days are gone forever, but collectors today are just as avid about their acquisitions. What postcards are bestsellers today? The people most likely to have the pulse of the hobby are dealers who offer thousands of cards to the public every year.

Ron Millard, longtime owner of Cherryland Auctions, and Mary L. Martin, known for running the largest store in the country devoted exclusively to postcards, have offered some insights into the current state of the market. Both dealers have taken a son into their business, a sure sign of the confidence they have in the future of postcard collecting.

Real photo postcards of the early 1900s are highly rated by both dealers. Martin, who sells at shows as well as through her store, reports that interest in rare real photos is "increasing faster than they can be bought."

Millard, whose Cherryland Auctions feature 1,800 lots closing every five weeks, indicates that real photos seem to be "holding steady with prices actually rising among the lower-end real photos as some people shy from paying the huge prices they have been bringing ... Children with toys and dolls have been increasing and also unidentified but interesting U.S. views."

Cherryland bidders have also been focused on "advertising cards, high-end art cards, Halloween, early political and baseball postcards." Movie stars, other famous people and transportation, especially autos and zeppelins, also do very well. Lower-priced cards with great potential for rising in value include linen restaurant advertising, "middle range" holidays, and World War I propaganda.

Millard also cites vintage chromes, especially advertising, is "really starting to take off with many now bringing $10 to $15. (These were $1 cards a few years ago.)"

At one time, foreign cards were largely ignored by collectors, but online sales have broadened the international market. In Millard's experience, "The sky is the limit on any China related." A few months ago Cherryland had a huge influx of new bidders from Australia, and the number from Asia is also increasing.

Martin sees hometown views as the most popular category, with real photo social history, dressed animals, and Halloween also in high demand. She reports: "We see a lot of interest in military right now, and I don't believe it has really peaked yet." Social history from the 1950s and '60s also does well. She's encouraged by the number of new and younger collectors at postcard shows.

Will anyone want your postcards when you're ready to sell? It's a valid question, and our two experts have good advice for anyone with a sizeable accumulation, say 500 or more postcards.

Auctions are one good option, both for direct purchases and consignments. Millard is always looking for quality postcards to offer collectors worldwide. His firm can handle collections of any size from small specialized to giant accumulations, and is willing to travel for large consignments. Active buying is a necessity for dealers to keep their customers supplied, which

Real photo postcards can reach high prices without an identified location. These kids on a pedal car would interest toy collectors. ..... **$75**
*Cherryland Auctions*

should reassure collectors that their cards will have a ready market. Contact Millard at CherrylandAuctions@charter.net or www.Cherrylandauctions.com.

Martin suggests that collectors go back to some of the dealers who sold them cards when they're ready to sell. Her firm is always willing to buy back good quality cards. She also sees reputable auction houses as a good avenue, and strongly suggests, "They should never be sold as a very large group if they can be broken down into different subject matter or topics." Martin can be contacted at marymartinpostcards@gmail.com.

Both experts agree there's an active demand for quality collections. That would exclude postcards in poor condition, a caution for collectors expanding their holdings. Look for the best and pass up damaged and dirty cards.

Billions of postcards were produced in the last century on practically every topic imaginable. As collections become more specialized, new subjects are sure to attract attention. Many outstanding collections were put together with moderate expense by people who were among the first to recognize the value of a new collecting area.

As an example of an area yet to be fully explored, the photographers who made postcards possible haven't been widely collected in their own right. Many were anonymous, but some, like Bob Petley, famous for Western views as well as comic humor, have attracted collectors' attention. The Tucson Post Card Exchange Club has made a specialty of gathering and listing the output of its "favorite son." No doubt there are fresh, new specialties just waiting to be discovered.

Postcard collectors love history, appreciate fine art, enjoy humor, and above all, are imaginative. There's every indication that today's favorite topics will be joined by new and exciting ones in the future.

***Barbara Andrews***

*Barbara Andrews has contributed postcard articles to* Antique Trader *for more than 35 years.*

Advertising postcard, Harry's Cafe, Minneapolis, Minnesota, showing staff, used 1945...................... **$25**
*Cherryland Auctions*

Advertising postcard, Jack Dempsey, Great Northern Hotel, New York City, 1946, used same year ...... **$33**
*Cherryland Auctions*

Advertising postcard, Successful Farming publication, Des Moines, Iowa, with rewards including Hamilton hunting rifle, etc. .......... **$36**
*Cherryland Auctions*

Advertising postcard, Wilson Meat Co., Chicago, with Clydesdales Team in front of World's Fair Building **$18**
*Cherryland Auctions*

Artist signed postcard, Bessie Pease Gutmann, copyright 1907, "The Happy Family," many dolls...... **$35**
*Cherryland Auctions*

Artist signed postcard, Chilton Longley, S.H. & Co. publisher, series No. 421, colorful .................... **$26**
*Cherryland Auctions*

Linen cards have come into their own in recent years, especially good topics; '39 Buick ...................... **$35**
*Cherryland Auctions*

Postcard, alligator border, Langsdorf # S 613, Livery Parade, Hotel Ormond, Florida.......................... **$40**
*Cherryland Auctions*

Postcard, Christmas, Early Quality series with doll and fantasy pine cones.................................... **$26**
*Cherryland Auctions*

Hold to the light die-cut postcard, purple-suited Santa, artist signature, Mailick....................... **$155**
*Cherryland Auctions*

Postcard, cowboy actors Roy Rogers, Gabby Hayes, and Dale Evans, photograph ............................ **$38**
*Cherryland Auctions*

Postcard, fantasy cats, artist signed, Ellam, Raphael Tuck publisher, Breakfast in Bed series 9321..... **$42**
*Cherryland Auctions*

Postcard, 3-1/2" x 5-1/2", c. early 1900s, likely made in England. Nighttime image of Santa on snow-covered moonlit street carrying satchel with toys and holding small Christmas tree with candles while knocking on door with two children inside. When card is held to light, candles on Christmas tree appear to glow as does heart carving on door, light inside house, and moon and windows in background. Reverse side has text poem in English with handwritten note dated December 1905. .... **$115**

Postcard, 3-1/2" x 5-1/2", c. 1910, image of Santa Claus handing large block of chocolate to little girl with angel wings while other children with angel wings carry baskets of apples from house in background. When card is held to light, iron grate in rock and windows in background appear to glow as does moon and apple images near bottom of front. Card is postally used....................................................................... **$170**

Postcards, each 2-1/2" x 5-1/2", c. 1910. Images include boy smoking pipe with actual applied small "Coney Island" felt pennant, Luna Park, beach scene with girl in early swimsuit on piling about to dive into ocean, and two embossed cards showing people on beach with sea life borders. Four are postally used, sent to same recipient. All were sent from apparent business owner with one including text, "Great crowds are coming & I am very busy but well. It is no fun to handle several thousand people of all nationality at a amusement place."............. **$115**

Postcards, each 3-1/2" x 5-1/2". First is copyright 1911 with image of girl dressed as a witch looking over her shoulder as ghouls watch her from behind jack-o-lantern. Second card is copyright 1912 with image of woman holding jack-o-lantern who is smoking a pipe and other jack-o-lantern who is smoking a cigar with Halloween candles smoking nearby. First card has pencil note on reverse, second card is postally used. .......... **$175**

Postcard, Halloween, boys pulling cart with jack-o-lanterns............ **$37**
*Cherryland Auctions*

Postcard, 3-1/2" x 5-1/2", c. 1910, made in Germany. Image of snow-covered Santa with sack of toys on his back warming his hands at fireplace hearth as boy and girl watch with Christmas tree in background. Top has text, "A Merry Christmas." When card is held to light, hearth and candles on tree glow as do a few things in Santa's sack as well as buttons on his coat. Card is postally unused but has ink note on reverse.. **$115**

Postcard, Halloween, John Winsch, copyright 1914, witch in outer space and red goblin .. **$100**
*Cherryland Auctions*

Postcard, fantasy mermaids, Wagner series, Raphael Tuck publisher, Series 694, "The Rhine Gold".... **$50**
*Cherryland Auctions*

Postcard, 3-1/2" x 5-1/2", "FIRST PARADE IN N.E. STATES / OF KU KLUX KLAN. / FIRST DAYLIGHT PARADE IN U.S.A. / AT MILO. ME. 9/3/23." Photo credit "BY THE CLEMENT STUDIO. MILO." Very crisp/clean image of large number of hooded Klansmen walking across bridge, town/river in background, unused. ........................................................ **$170**

Postcard, 3-1/2" x 5-1/2", by Providence Novelty Co. (Rhode Island) with "COPYRIGHT 1907 BY T.R. GAINES, N.Y." On Teddy Roosevelts's shoulder, at left: "THE TEDDY BEAR SAYS: Mr. President, I feel blue / And I scarce know what to do / For I have been told to-day / That a third term you won't stay. / Tell me quickly it's absurd, / This rumor that I just have heard, / For if to run you don't agree, / My finish I can plainly see." On Roosevelt's shoulder, at right: "THE LITTLE DOLLY SAYS: Dear Mr. President be firm, / And don't accept a third term, / Teddy bears for years, you know, / Have caused us dolls lots of woe, / Please don't run 'twill end this fad / And make every dolly glad. / We'll forgive the harm you've done / If you promise not to run." Unused ............................................... **$170**

Postcard, Gen. U.S. Grant, published in Japan, art card, published by American Tourist Party Welcome Committee of Nagasaki, illustrated, signed letter, 1879............................................................. **$80**
*Cherryland Auctions*

Postcard, Pennsylvania, Punxsutawney large letter linen, Ground Hog Day related .......................... **$28**
*Cherryland Auctions*

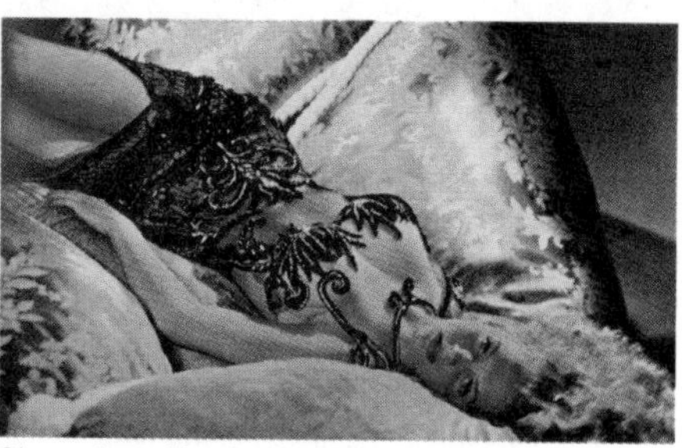

Six-card set, Esquire Magazine, copyright 1945, Hurrell Girls #13, complete with wrapper ............... **$60**
*Cherryland Auctions*

The interest is antique farm machinery carries over on this real photo, although the location isn't identified. ........................................................... **$30**
*Cherryland Auctions*

Postcard, World War II, U.S. publisher, Kirtland Field, Albuquerque, New Mexico, large letter greeting .. **$10**
*Cherryland Auctions*

William Jennings Bryan campaign card, third run for president, used Nov. 2, 1908 .......................... **$55**
*Cherryland Auctions*

Taft novelty card .......................................... **$125**
*Cherryland Auctions*

William Jennings Bryan novelty campaign postcard, pull donkey's tail and see the next president .... **$125**
*Cherryland Auctions*

TOP LOT!

Postcard, 3-3/8" x 5-1/4" mat finish postcard with image of crowd in small roof-covered grandstand and in automobiles watching baseball game played in Randolph, Wisconsin. Black batter at far right has just hit ball with runner heading toward second base and white player heading back towards first base. Crowd appears to be mostly white except for apparent manager standing at left side watching the game. A sharp image, postally unused. The Chicago Union Giants were founded by partners Frank Leland and W. S. Peters in 1887. Each man then operated a Chicago Giants team under his own name. Frank Leland combined the Chicago Unions and the Columbia Giants to form the Chicago Union Giants in 1901. By 1905 they had become the Leland Giants. This historic card dates to the period of about 1904 to 1912. From the Richard Merkin Collection and comes with Hake's certificate of authenticity. ........................................................................................ **$3,600**

# Posters

A poster is a large, usually printed placard, bill, or announcement, often illustrated, that is posted to advertise or publicize something. It can also be an artistic work, often a reproduction of an original painting or photograph, printed on a large sheet of paper.

Vintage posters are usually between 20 and 50 years old and must be original and not copies or newer reproductions.

The value of a vintage poster is determined by condition, popularity of the subject matter, rarity, artistic rendering, and the message it conveys.

The Three Stooges in Three Little Beers (Columbia, 1935). One sheet, 27" x 41" Many Stooge aficionados consider this short, Three Little Beers, to be one of the group's best films and also one of its earliest. One sheets from this period are the hardest to find for the comedy trio, and this is the only known copy of this poster. It is from the personal collection of Moe Howard and was acquired after his death from his daughter Joan. The poster has been restored, and the issues addressed include wear to the vertical fold, which included some slight paper loss in the top cross fold as well along the top fold and the other two center cross fold points. From the Joan Howard Maurer Collection. Linen. ..................................... **$59,750**
*Heritage Auction Galleries*

The 39 Steps (Gaumont, 1935). One sheet, 27" x 41" The 39 Steps was one of director Alfred Hitchcock's first major international successes, and many of the stylistic and thematic elements that would become integral parts of his later work can be seen in this important picture. Robert Donat stars as Richard Hannay, an innocent bystander to the murder of a secret agent. When he is accused of the crime, Hannay is on the run from the police as he tries to find the real killers. Madeleine Carroll plays Pamela, who reluctantly is trapped into helping Hannay. The secret to all of the twisting mysteries lies with Mr. Memory and the man with a missing finger. Professional restoration has addressed condition issues including pinholes in the corners, a small missing top left corner, a tear in the bottom border slightly into the background, and small chips and tears in the top, bottom, and left border. Linen..................... **$17,925**
*Heritage Auction Galleries*

The Adventures of Robin Hood (Warner Brothers, 1938). One sheet, 27" x 41" From the classic title painted on a shield, to the colorful image of the dashing Errol Flynn loosing an arrow while "Maid Marian" (Olivia de Havilland) is tucked safely behind him, this poster stands out as one of the defining moments in Hollywood's storied history. This always elusive poster has been linenbacked, and there has been some color touchup in the image area. There were surface abrasions and small chips in the borders. Linen... **$9,560**
*Heritage Auction Galleries*

Anna Christie (MGM, 1930). One sheet, 27" x 41" "Gif me a vhisky, ginger ale on the side, and don't be stingy, baby." These, the first words uttered by Greta Garbo in her inaugural sound film, electrified audiences and confirmed the actress would have no trouble succeeding where other silent era stars had failed. MGM mounted a massive ad campaign to promote Anna Christie with the legendary ad line, "Garbo talks!" In fact, Garbo's English was so good by the time she appeared in this film, she had to add an accent in several retakes to sound more like the Swedish Anna. Based on the play by Eugene O'Neill (and filmed once before in 1923), the film follows a young woman trying to hide her past (prostitution) from her newly found father (George F. Marion), as well as the Irish sailor (Charles Bickford) she has fallen for. This richly colored stone litho captivates, as Garbo, a woman with dark secrets, meets the viewer's gaze. Rare and superb quality — only pinholes in the corners, a tear in the right border, and touch up to fold wear. Artwork rendered by William Galbraith Crawford. Linen................................................**$38,838**
*Heritage Auction Galleries*

◄Footlight Parade (Warner Brothers, 1933). One sheet, 27" x 41" This classic film stars Joan Blondell, Ruby Keeler, Dick Powell, and James Cagney. Cagney must put on a series of "prologues" in order to raise money for his next show. The rehearsals, sabotage, and back stage dramas culminate in a climax featuring the Harry Warren and Al Dubin hit numbers "By a Waterfall," "Honeymoon Hotel," and "Shanghai Lil." The extremely rare one sheet has been professionally restored to address some chipping in the borders, crossfold separations with some minor paper loss, and creases in the top left. Linen. .............. **$47,800**
*Heritage Auction Galleries*

Wanted The Phantom, 11" x 14" Stiff paper printed on front with image of Batman. In 1943 Columbia released both Batman & Phantom serials. Text at bottom reads "Keep Your Eyes Open For The Phantom. A Master Of Disguise, The Phantom May Be Eluding You Every Day. The Reward For The Phantom's Capture Is Great." Scattered light handling wear with a few light creases, overall bright and clean. Rare. .............. **$3,827**
*Hakes Americana & Collectibles*

▼The Cat Girl (American International, 1957). Insert, 14" x 36", horror Starring Barbara Shelley, Robert Ayres, Kay Callard, Paddy Webster, and Ernest Milton. Directed by Alfred Shaughnessy. An unrestored poster with bright color and a clean overall appearance. It may have general signs of use, such as slight fold separation and fold wear, pinholes, or very minor tears. There are very small tape stains in the bottom corners. Folded. ............................. **$108**
*Heritage Auction Galleries*

Circus poster (Russell Brothers, 1937). 28" x 42", and date and place snipe, 9" x 27", miscellaneous Fierce and exotic, two tigers crouch and bellow on this colorful circus poster. Unrestored poster with good color and an overall very presentable appearance. It may have tears with tape on the verso, edge and fold wear, slight paper loss, minor stains, and/or some fold separation. Folded........ **$359**
*Heritage Auction Galleries*

Circus poster (Hagenbeck-Wallace, 1930s). 28" x 41", miscellaneous Lovely poster depicting acrobatic women on the rings and featuring Jeanette May, known for her "aerial ballet." An unrestored poster with good color and an overall very presentable appearance. It may have tears, edge and fold wear, slight paper loss, minor stains, and/or some fold separation. There are remnants from a date and place snipe attached to the bottom edge. Tape on the verso. ................................ **$176**
*Heritage Auction Galleries*

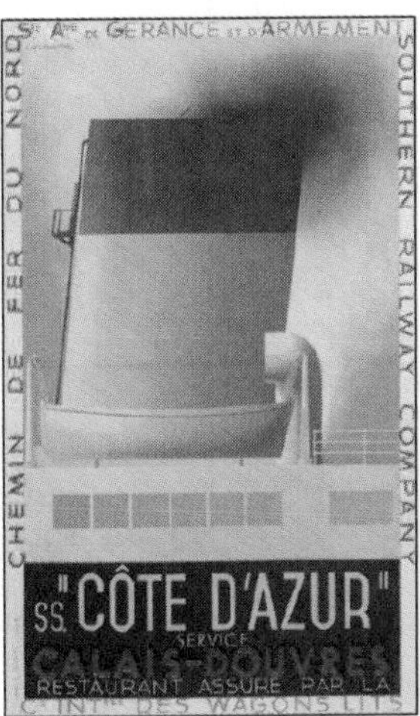


S.S. "Côte D'azur"/Chemin De Fer Du Nord (A. M. Cassandre [Adolphe Mouron, 1901-1968], 1931). 39" x 24-1/2", L. Danel, Lille. Cote d'Azur is the last of Cassandre's "chimney series." He depicts the boat from the side, cutting off the prow and the stern and focusing only on the center, with the funnel, lifeboat, airshaft, and railing. Cassandre runs the typography around the outside of the image. Restored losses, restoration, repaired tears and overpainting in margins and image; vertical and horizontal folds..............**$16,000**
*Swann Auction Galleries*

Death Valley Manhunt (Republic, 1943). One sheet, 27" x 41", western. Starring Wild Bill Elliott, George "Gabby" Hayes, Anne Jeffreys, Weldon Heyburn, Herbert Heyes. Directed by John English. An unrestored poster that displays signs of use. May include light edge or fold wear, slight fold separations, very minor paper loss, pinholes, or unobtrusive stains. Folded. ...... **$84**
*Heritage Auction Galleries*

Cunard Line/New York (designer unknown, circa 1905). 39" x 24", Wm. Strain & Sons, Belfast. The Slavonia foundered and sank off the Azores on June 10, 1909, the first ship to ever send an S.O.S. distress message by Morse code. Two German ships, North German Lloyd's Prinzess Irene and Hamburg America's Batavia were able to safely rescue all 410 passengers. This exceptional nocturnal image stands out not only for the painterly way in which the subject is presented but also the unusual positioning of the ship. The unknown artist presents the ship slightly askew from head on. Repaired tear through image; restoration and minor restored losses in margins and corners..... **$4,600**
*Swann Auction Galleries*

►Hula (Paramount, 1927). One sheet, 27" x 41", Style A. Clara Bow stars as Hula Calhoun, a free spirit who falls for the proper and married English gentleman, Anthony Haldance (Clive Brook). Victor Fleming directs this light romantic tale set in Hawaii. The opening sequence features Hula skinny-dipping when she comes to the rescue of Anthony. This stone litho image of the It girl has been professionally restored to address chips that are mainly limited to the border area, with one in the title and one in the image. There was a tear in the left side of the blue background and fold wear, but hese issues are no longer apparent. Linen. ................**$13,145**
*Heritage Auction Galleries*

Cunard Line/Liverpool - New - York - Boston [Lusitania], Odin Rosenvinge [1880-1957], circa 1907). 39-3/4" x 24-3/4", Turner & Dunnett Lithos, Liverpool. An extremely rare and beautiful poster advertising transatlantic travel on the legendary Lusitania. Although the ship's name does not appear on the bow of the vessel illustrated, it is known to be the Lusitania because of her profile (with her signature four smokestacks) and the white stripe along the top edge of her bow. This poster predates the Lusitania's maiden voyage (Sept. 7, 1907), as she was never in regular service with this white stripe in place. The top of her bow was only painted white for her trials. This is one of very few posters for the Lusitania, which entered into popular culture and immortality when she was sunk by German torpedoes on May 7, 1915. Unobtrusive vertical and horizontal folds; minor restoration at edges. ....................**$9,000**
*Swann Auction Galleries*

MASH (20th Century Fox, 1970). One sheet, 27" x 41", and lobby cards (8), 11" x 14", "Gives a Damn" style, comedy. Starring Donald Sutherland, Elliott Gould, Tom Skerritt, Sally Kellerman, Robert Duvall, Roger Bowen, Rene Auberjonois, Fred Williamson, David Arkin, Jo Ann Pflug, Gary Burghoff, Michael Murphy, and John Schuck. Directed by Robert Altman. Original poster style used at the world premier. The use of the word "damn" was in reference to the Ratings Administration citing problems with every use of the word in the movie. An unrestored poster and lobby cards with an overall very presentable appearance. They may have tears, slight paper loss, pinholes, minor stains, edge wear, color fading, toning, small corner bumps or bends and/or some fold separation. A snipe has been removed from the poster's right side, leaving a rectangular section that is not toned. There is one duplicate lobby card. Archival tape on poster's verso. Folded. ........................................................ **$448**
*Heritage Auction Galleries*

Moon Over Miami (20th Century Fox, 1941). One sheet, 27" x 41", Style B. Don Ameche and pin-up star Betty Grable star in this romantic musical. The gorgeous and always rare one sheet features Grable in one of her most iconic pin-up shots, fashioned after artist Alberto Vargas. The poster is in excellent condition and has had professional restoration to address light edge wear at the left, a small chip and tear in the lower left corner, and a minor tear in the top border. Linen. ........................... **$14,938**
*Heritage Auction Galleries*

The Most Dangerous Game (RKO, 1932). Half sheet, 22" x 28" One of the rarest and most desirable half sheets from the 1930s horror genre, this is the only known existing style of this half sheet from RKO's Most Dangerous Game. Shipwrecked on a remote island, a group of innocent survivors are imprisoned and forced to become human prey by a deranged big-game hunter, tired of "ordinary" prey. Based on Richard Connell's famous story, the film was shot on the same sets and produced by the same people (Willis O'Brien and Ernest B. Schoedsack) as 1933's King Kong. The poster pictures the evil Count Zaroff (Leslie Banks) and his two helpless victims – Fay Wray and Joel McCrea. Original paper from this elusive title has always been hard to find. Prior to restoration, the poster had pinholes into the interior on the right side, corner and bottom border chips, small tears on the left and right borders, and a crease on the right side. Rolled. ................................................................................ **$31,070**
*Heritage Auction Galleries*

Panama Lady (RKO, 1939). One Sheet, 27" x 41", drama. Starring Lucille Ball, Allan Lane, Steffi Duna, Evelyn Brent, Donald Briggs, Bernadene Hayes, Abner Biberman, William Pawley, Earle Hodgins. Directed by Jack Hively. An unrestored poster that displays signs of use. May include light edge or fold wear with small tears, slight fold separations, minor paper loss in the top border, and pinholes. Folded. .................... **$120**
*Heritage Auction Galleries*

New 20th Century Limited (Leslie Ragan [1897-1972], 1938). 40" x 26-1/2" ...................... **$19,200**
*Swann Auction Galleries*

The Outlaw (United Artists, 1946). Insert, 14" x 36", Western. Starring Jane Russell, Jack Beutel, Thomas Mitchell, Walter Huston, Mimi Aguglia, Joe Sawyer, Gene Rizzi, John Howard, and Ben Johnson. Directed by Howard Hughes and Howard Hawks. An unrestored poster with good color and an overall very presentable appearance. It may have tears, pinholes, edge wear, creasing, slight paper loss, minor stains, and/or some fold separation. Folded. ........................................ **$568**
*Heritage Auction Galleries*

Share/Jewish Relief Campaign (Alfred F. Burke [dates unknown], circa 1915). 40" x 29-3/4", Sackett & Wilhelms Corp., Brooklyn. Alfred F. Burke's Share/Jewish Relief Campaign is an allegorical figure of America offering her bounty, a tray laden with bread and fruits, to four desperate Jewish refugees dressed in tatters. In the background, the New York skyline, a symbol of the prosperous and secure New World, beneath an optimistic orange and yellow sky. One of the finest and rarest of the World War I Judaic posters. Repaired tears, creases and abrasions in margins and image; restored losses and restoration in margins, some affecting image. . **$4,200**
*Swann Auction Galleries*

Raiders of the Lost Ark (Paramount, 1981). One sheet, 27" x 41", adventure. Starring Harrison Ford, Karen Allen, Paul Freeman, Ronald Lacey, John Rhys-Davies, Denholm Elliott, Alfred Molina, Wolf Kahler, and William Hootkins. Directed by Steven Spielberg. An unrestored poster that displays signs of use. May include light edge or fold wear, slight fold separations, very minor paper loss, pinholes, or unobtrusive stains. Richard Amsel artwork. Folded. ............................... **$114**
*Heritage Auction Galleries*

Rugby League Cup Final (Herry-Perry [Heather Perry, 1893-1965], 1933). 10" x 13" The London Transport Museum refers to this kind of small format poster as a panel poster. They were "produced for display in Underground car interiors, as well as on the inside and outside of buses and trams. Because they did not have to fit a standard frame or wall space, they are smaller than other poster formats and vary slightly in size." Creases in lower left corner; rounded corners as issued. . **$3,000**
*Swann Auction Galleries*

Southern Pacific (Maurice Logan [1886-1977], two posters, 1928). Approximately 23" x16" ea. Group includes Crater Lake and Old Missions. Condition varies. .... **$5,400**
*Swann Auction Galleries*

# Spotlight: World War I Propaganda Posters

American illustrator James Montgomery Flagg (1877-1960) used Lord Kitchener as inspiration for his famous recruiting poster, "I Want You for U.S. Army." Flagg worked for many popular magazines in the early 20th century and would contribute 46 posters to the war effort. His most recognizable and influential was his Kitchener-derived poster, featuring a white-haired, serious Uncle Sam with pointed finger. Flagg's creation first appeared on the cover of Leslie's Weekly in July 6, 1916, under the title "What Are You Doing For Preparedness?" More than four million copies were printed between 1917 and 1918 as the United States entered the war and began sending troops overseas.

All branches of the military were recruiting for enlistment. Flagg's "The Navy Needs You" (1918) and "Be a U.S. Marine" (1918) competed for the doughboy's place in history. His navy poster shows a sailor tapping the shoulder of a civilian, dressed in suit and tie, holding a newspaper, imploring "Don't Read American History—Make It," with the spirit of Columbia hovering above. Flagg makes powerful use of guilt and the promise of a place in history to urge men to join. "Be a Marine" shows a uniformed Marine with clenched fist, superimposed on Old Glory with his sidearm raised for action. Swann Galleries (New York) sold both posters in their August 2008 sale for $1,400 and $750, respectively.

Wake Up America Day (James Montgomery Flagg [1870-1960], 1917). 41" x 28" A patriotic young lady is running, with a lantern in one hand and a flag in the other, to warn the populace of the impending conflagration of World War I. Before the United States officially entered the war, private groups of concerned citizens took it upon themselves to begin preparing America for the upcoming battle. Artist James Montgomery Flagg was responsible for two of these images. This, the rarer of the two, is a departure from the artist's usual style and represents his "only attempt at modernity." ............................................. **$8,400**
*Swann Auction Galleries*

Many government agencies called on the American public to pitch in for the war effort. To spur the production of coal, the U.S. Fuel Administration commissioned Whitehead's 1918 "Mine More Coal." With its call to "Stand By the Boys in the Trenches," the image depicts a soldier and a coal miner, standing side-by-side atop a pile of coal and the thorny barbed-wired ground zero of the trench, the miner with an axe and the soldier with a bayonet, both at the ready. The message was a bold reminder that citizen and soldier had a role to play in winning the war. The poster was included in Swann's 2008 sale, fetching $425.

Magazine illustrator Harrison Fisher (1875-1934), whose stylized images of the "Fisher Girl" and the "American Girl"

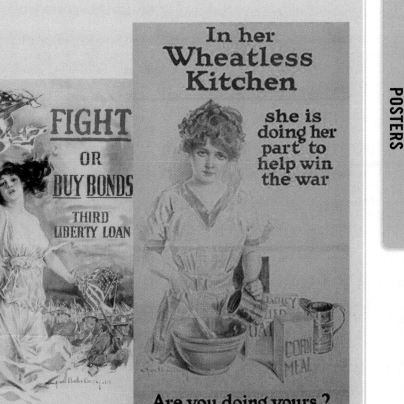


World War I propaganda poster by Howard Chandler Christy (Forbes, 1918). Third Liberty Loan poster, 20" x 30", Fight or Buy Bonds, war. Howard Chandler Christy was so good at illustrating iconic women in uniquely styled poster art, that they soon became known as "Christy Girls." He used some of these images to sell war bonds during World War I. His lovely art was instrumental in raising countless millions for the war effort. An unrestored poster with good color and an overall presentable appearance, it may have tears, pinholes, edge wear, wrinkling, slight paper loss, and minor stains. Rolled................................**$837**
*Heritage Auction Galleries*



In Her Wheatless Kitchen (Howard Chandler Christy [1873-1952], 1918). 78" x 40", Alpha Litho Co., New York. As part of the conservation effort during World War I, Americans, "in addition to meat and eggs ... were urged to cut back on wheat, the single most vital food item, and to eat corn and barley instead, which were in good supply." "In Her Wheatless Kitchen" exemplifies the extent the public supported the war effort. The poster was released in 1918 by the Alpha Litho Co, New York. .......................... **$2,200**
*Swann Auction Galleries*

became models of feminine beauty in the early 20th century, created a popular poster called "I Summon You In Comradeship in the Red Cross." The title was taken from a quote by President Woodrow Wilson; the image shows a young girl clutching an American flag with the Red Cross and U.S. Capitol in the background. The 30" x 40" lithograph from the collection of the American Red Cross sold at Heritage Auction's February 2010 sale for $310.

*Mary Manion*

*Mary Manion is associate director of Landmarks Gallery and Restoration Studio in Milwaukee, Wis. A columnist for* Antique Trader *since 2006, Manion is a member of the New England Appraisers Association.*

# Quilts

Each generation made quilts, comforters and coverlets, all intended to be used. Many were used into oblivion and rest in quilt heaven, but for myriad reasons, some have survived. Many of them remain because they were not used but stored, often forgotten, in trunks and linen cabinets.

A quilt is made up of three layers: the top, which can be a solid piece of fabric, appliquéd, pieced, or a combination; the back, which can be another solid piece of fabric or pieced; and the batting, which is the center layer, which can be cotton, wool, polyester, a blend of poly and cotton, or even silk. Many vintage quilts are batted with an old blanket or even another old, worn quilt.

The fabrics are usually cotton or wool, or fine fancy fabrics like silk, velvet, satin, and taffeta. The layers of a true quilt are held together by the stitching, or quilting, that goes through all three layers and is usually worked in a design or pattern that enhances the piece overall. The term "quilt" has become synonymous with bedcover to many people, and we include tied quilts, comforters and quilt tops, none of which are true quilts in the technical description.

Quilts made from a seemingly single solid piece of fabric are known as wholecloth quilts, or if they are white, as whitework quilts. Usually such quilts are constructed from two or more pieces of the same fabric joined to make up the necessary width. They are often quilted quite elaborately, and the seams virtually disappear within the decorative stitching. Most wholecloth quilts are solid-colored, but prints were also used. Whitework quilts were often made as bridal quilts and many were kept for "best," which means that they have survived in reasonable numbers.

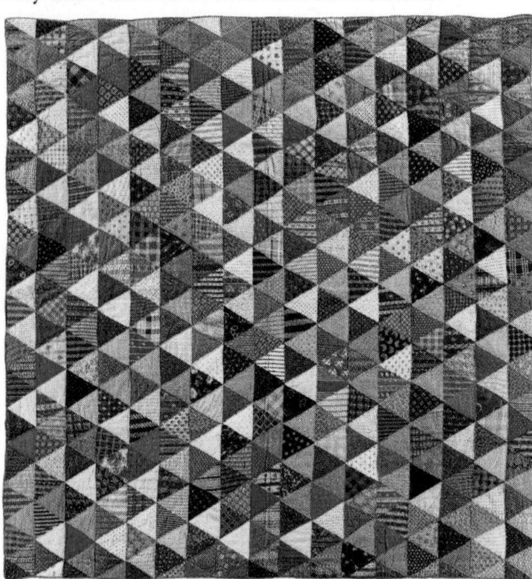

1,000 PYRAMIDS
C 1875
Maker unknown. Pennsylvania.
Multicolored cotton solids, prints, stripes, plaids and checks; almost a charm quilt but with a few repeated fabrics; some triangles pieced. Green, black and orange print back; and overdyed green binding. .................................. **$1,750-$2,000**

Wholecloth quilts were among the earliest type of quilted bedcovers made in Britain, and the colonists brought examples with them according to inventory lists that exist from colonial times. American quiltmakers used the patterns early in the nation's history, and some were carried with settlers moving west across the Appalachians.

Appliqué quilts are made from shapes cut from fabric and applied, or appliquéd, to a background, usually solid-colored on vintage quilts, to make a design. Early appliqué quilts dating back to the 18th century were often worked in a technique called broderie perse, or Persian embroidery, in which printed motifs were cut from a piece of fabric, such as costly chintz, and applied to a plain, less expensive background cloth.

## PATCHWORK QUILTS

ANVIL ON POINT
C 1875
Maker unknown. United States.
Cotton shirtings, browns, paisleys, florals, double pinks; double pink setting squares; half-blocks on three sides; brown floral cotton print border. Cream muslin back; pale orange and red cotton print binding. Hand quilted fans. Unused; unwashed. .................................................................. **$1,000-$1,500**

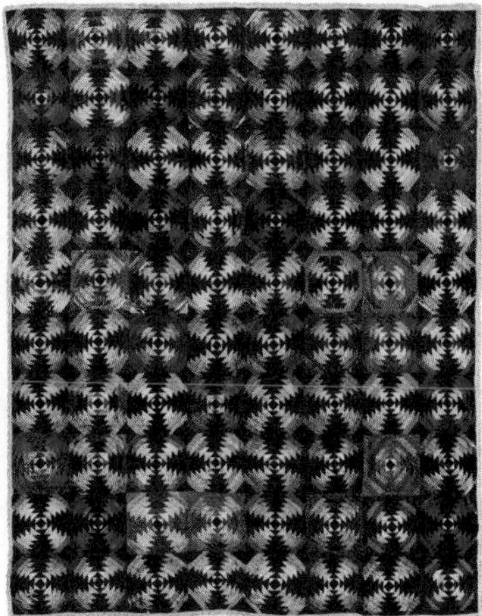

PINEAPPLE LOG CABIN
C 1900
Maker unknown. United States.
Multicolored silks and velvets, mainly black with bright colors; pink silk border with pink eyelet edging. Some shattering of silk fabrics. ........................................ **$600-$750**

Appliqué was popular in the 1800s, and there are thousands of examples, from exquisite, brightly colored Baltimore Album quilts made in and around Baltimore between circa 1840 and 1860, to elegant four-block quilts made later in the century. Many appliqué quilts are pictorial—with floral designs the predominant motif. In the 20th century, appliqué again enjoyed an upswing, especially during the Colonial Revival period, and thousands were made from patterns or appliqué kits that were marketed and sold from 1900 through the 1950s.

Pieced or patchwork quilts are made by cutting fabric into shapes and sewing them together to make a larger piece of cloth. The patterns are usually geometric, and their effectiveness depends heavily on the contrast of not just the colors themselves, but of color value as well. Patchwork became popular in the United States in the early 1800s.

Colonial clothing was almost always made using cloth cut into squares or rectangles, but after the Revolutionary War, when fabric became more widely available, shaped garments were made, and these garments left scraps. Frugal housewives, especially among the westward-bound pioneers, began to use these cutoffs to put together blocks that could then be made into quilts. Patchwork quilts are by far the most numerous of all vintage-quilt categories, and the diversity of style, construction and effect that can be found is a study all its own.

Dating a quilt is a tricky business unless the maker included the date on the finished item, and unfortunately for historians and collectors, few did. The value of a particular example is affected by its age, of course, and educating yourself about dating methods is invaluable. There are several aspects that can offer guidelines for establishing a date. These include fabrics; patterns; technique; borders; binding; batting; backing; quilting method; and colors and dyes.

The quilts shown here were made in the United States, with a few from England, almost all pre-1950s. For more information on quilts, see *Warman's Vintage Quilts Identification and Price Guide* by Maggi McCormick Gordon.

BARN RAISING LOG CABIN
C 1900
Maker unknown. United States. Multicolored wool and silk logs, in light rows strips of red alternating with light fabrics; centers pieced light and dark. Brown-and-gray wool plaid back; black binding. Tied to the back. Some shattered silks. .......................... **$400-$600**

BEAR'S PAW
C 1890
Maker unknown. Wisconsin. Multicolored cotton prints and solids, mainly shirtings, set on point; alternating with gray cotton spacers; multicolored pieced cotton diamonds border. Thin cotton batting. Print back (faded); back-to-front self-binding. Hand quilted. ................................. **$400-$600**

BURGOYNE SURROUNDED
C 1880
Maker unknown. United States. Blue and white microprints on muslin background. Muslin back; muslin binding. Hand-quilted crosshatch. .......... **$1,000-$1,500**

CAROLINA LILY
C 1850
Maker unknown. United States.
Solid red cotton flowers, green-on-cream cotton print stems and leaves, cream cotton background; hand pieced flowers and leaves with appliquéd stems; pieced border in four strips of red/cream/red/cream cotton solids on opposite sides. Cream cotton back; green print binding. Crosshatch and outline quilting. ...................................................... **$2,000-$3,000**

CHIPS AND WHETSTONES WITH DOUBLE IRISH CHAIN
C 1850
Maker unknown. Believed to have been made by a slave on a plantation near Pennington Gap, Virginia. Red, green and white cotton solids on white background for blocks; blue and white microdot cotton prints for chains. Cream back; blue microdot binding. Heavy hand quilting. ........................ **$2,000-$3,000**

CHINTZ STRIPPY
Dated 1841 in ink
Maker Mary Raymond? Signature is faded and only partially legible. Mt.??, Ohio.
Faded chintz strips alternating with muslin strips. Cotton batting. Muslin back; muslin binding. Closely worked, hand-quilted diagonal lines on chintz, leafy vine on muslin. Some staining on back. **1,500-$2,000**

COURTHOUSE STEPS LOG CABIN
1930s
Maker unknown. Virginia.
Red, yellow, pink and green cotton solids for logs; pieced centers of two triangle squares; hand pieced; turquoise border. Green cotton back; back-to-front self-binding. Hand-quilted diamond grid. ........................................................ **$750-$1,000**

DOUBLE BROKEN STAR WITH FEATHERED EDGES
C 1930
Maker unknown. United States.
Gold, blue, yellow, green, red and blue cotton solids on white background; unique edging on two opposite sides; machine pieced. Cotton batting. White cotton back; white cotton binding on top and bottom, and straight edges on both sides, red cotton bias binding on the feathered pointed edges. Hand quilted. ...................................................... **$1,500-$2,500**

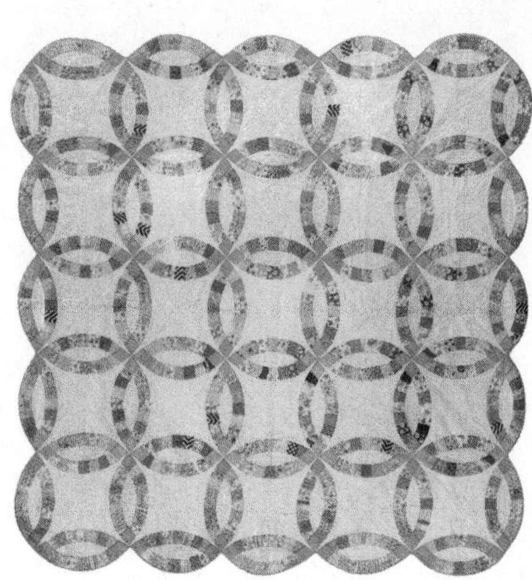

DOUBLE WEDDING RING
C 1920
Maker unknown; made for the owner's grandmother's wedding. Midwestern United States. Multicolored cotton scraps; pink connectors; muslin centers and melons; outer rings form scalloped border. Muslin back; pink cotton binding. Hand-quilted floral motif in centers; possibly an Eastern Star symbol in the melons. Some staining on the back. ......... **$250-$400**

DRUNKARD'S PATH SET SQUARE WITH SPACERS
C 1920
Maker unknown. Iowa.
Blue cotton microdots and white cotton, traditional blocks set square with blue cotton microdot spacers. White, blue microdot, white cotton triple borders. Muslin back, new white binding. .......... **$750-$1,000**

GRANDMOTHER'S FLOWER GARDEN
Pre-1924
Maker Aletta Belle Anderson Stephenson of Mason City, Iowa, grandmother of the owner.
Multicolored cotton prints and solids with green "paths;" green borders of pieced hexagons, top and bottom edges straight, opposite sides following the shape of the blocks. Green back; knife-edge binding. .......... **$400-$600**

EIGHT-POINT SUNBURST STARS
C 1860
Maker unknown. Northern Wisconsin.
Multicolored cotton prints and solids with cream muslin on gray-blue background for pieced sunburst stars; double pink zigzag sashing; green cotton inner border (faded), double pink cotton outer border. Muslin back; double pink cotton binding. Hand quilted. .......... **$750-$1,000**

FOUR-PATCH FRAME QUILT
C 1930
Maker unknown. United States.
Multicolored cotton solids and prints assembled in four-patch blocks joined to make strips for frames; center rectangle with five-pieced frames and six white cotton frames. Muslin back; muslin binding. Hand quilted. Skillful piecing and quilting; well washed. .......... **$400-$600**

LONE STAR
C 1875
Maker unknown: professional Mennonite quiltmaker. York, Pa. Red, pinks, yellow, green and orange cotton solids on bright, rose pink background; yellow/green/pink mitered triple border. Striking double pink cotton back; green cotton binding. Hand-quilted outline, crosshatch and cables. ........................... **$1,500-$2,000**

OCEAN WAVES
C 1935
Maker unknown. United States. Multicolored cotton prints and solids, mainly greens, blues, purples, grays and cream; green cotton inner border, cream cotton outer border. Muslin back; green cotton binding. Hand quilted. **$400-$600**

STRING-PIECED FOUR-POINT STARS
C 1900
Maker unknown. United States. Multicolored cotton scraps; hourglass centers with four string-pieced points; white cotton diamond spacers. Coarse white cotton back; back-to-front self-binding. Hand-quilted outline. ................................**$250-$400**

## Quilt Care

Never dry clean an antique quilt. Air the quilt outside on a sunny day to restore freshness. Vacuum with a nylon stocking over the end of a vacuum hose and hold the hose slightly above the top of the quilt. If the quilt has beading, embroidery or appliqué, do not vacuum. Try cold distilled water and a mild liquid detergent and add half cup vinegar to the water to both brighten colors and soften the quilt to clean spots.

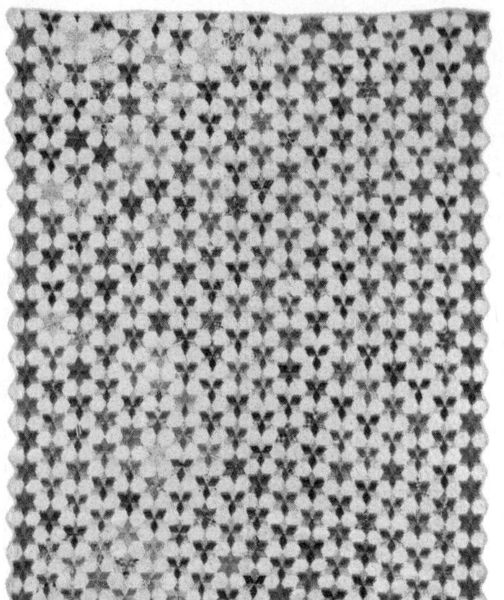

TOUCHING SIX-POINT STARS
C 1910
Maker unknown. United States.
Multicolored cotton prints including many indigo colors set to make six-point stars; white cotton spacer hexagons. Pink with white polka dot cotton back; pink binding. Hand quilted outline. ............ **$750-$1,000**

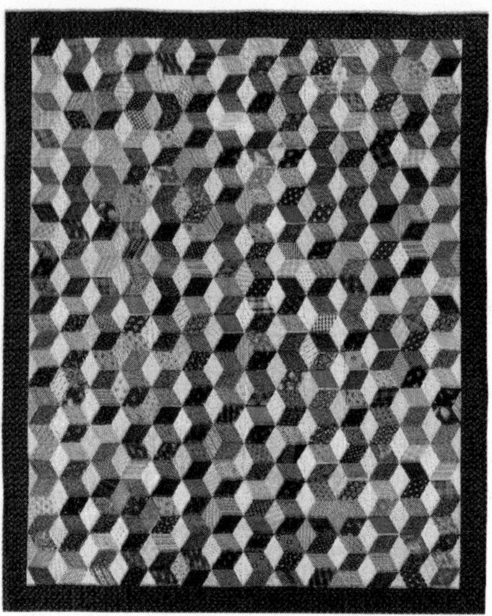

TUMBLING BLOCKS
C 1875 (top)
Maker unknown. Quilted by Carol Brown, 2002.
Multicolored 19th-century cotton prints and solids; hand pieced; new brown cotton print border. New brown on cream cotton microprint back; brown print binding. Machine quilted........................ **$600-$750**

TURKEY TRACKS
C 1860
Maker unknown. United States.
Green, cream and cheddar cotton solids in blocks set on point; green cotton diagonal sashing; green cotton border, scalloped on the inner edge. Cream cotton back; cream cotton binding. Hand-quilted crosshatch in blocks, running feather in sashing and border. Pattern also known as Bible Tulip........... **$1,000-$1,250**

TURKEY TRACKS FRIENDSHIP QUILT
Dated 1842 and 1844
Maker unknown. Probably Minnesota.
Turkey red and white cotton blocks; white sashing; 72 names signed in ink, 15 locations listed; hand pieced. Cotton batting. Muslin back; cotton twill tape binding. Hand-quilted crosshatch, parallel lines and motifs, clamshell on sashing............. **$2,000-$3,000**

VARIABLE STAR
C 1865
Maker unknown. Frederick, Maryland.
Multicolored cotton prints with cream background for star blocks, mainly reds, browns and greens, some stripes; orange cotton print spacers. Muslin back; double pink binding. Hand-quilted parallel lines in star blocks, crosshatch on spacers........ **$750-$1,000**

WHITEWORK QUILT
C 1825
Maker unknown. Philadelphia, Pennsylvania.
White cotton medallion-style with four-poster cut-outs in two corners; hand quilted rings and cables in center surrounded by pairs of doves touching beaks and with hand-embroidered eyelet eyes; birds are framed with stitched "broderie anglaise" embroidery, then a frame of crosshatch, then a wide border of more broderie anglaise with swags and floral motifs. ....................................................... **$3,000-$5,000**

## APPLIQUÉ QUILTS

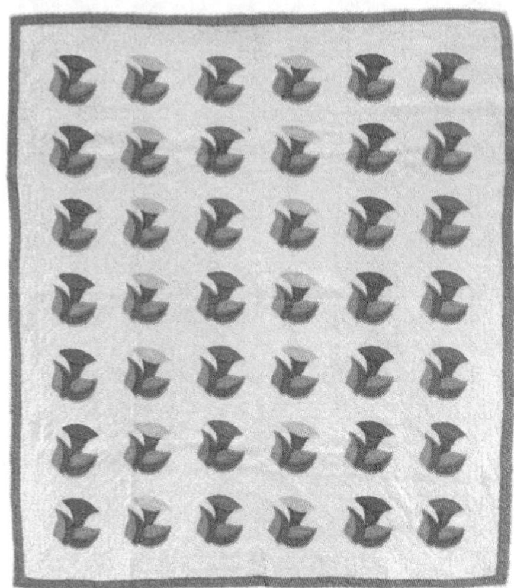

ART DECO TULIPS
1930s
Maker unknown. Mid-Atlantic United States.
Pink, yellow, orange, purple and green cotton solids hand appliquéd on white background; white and orange borders. White cotton back; back-to-front self-binding. Probably a kit. .......................... **$400-$600**

CAESAR'S CROWN
1870s
Maker unknown. United States or Britain.
Red, yellow and green cotton prints hand appliquéd on white English linen background; red and green swag border. White cotton back; white binding. Elaborate quilting. Never washed. ............. **$2,000-$3,000**

FOUR-BLOCK CHARIOT WHEEL
C 1870
Maker unknown. United States.
Red, yellow and green faded to blue-gray cottons hand appliquéd to white background; red/yellow/red/white border. Muslin back; brown binding; may be later than the top. Hand quilted close crosshatch and outline on the blocks, parallel lines on the border. ........................................................ **$2,000-$3,000**

LANCASTER ROSE FOUR-BLOCK
Dated 1915 (on back binding)
Maker unknown. United States, probably Midwest.
Solid pink, rose, faded green and orange cottons hand appliquéd to white background; pink, rose and green cotton triple borders. Cotton batting. White cotton back; back-to-front self-binding. Hand quilted crosshatch, spaced one inch apart. .............. **$750-$1,000**

LAUREL LEAVES
C 1860
Maker unknown. United States.
Green and red cotton prints hand appliquéd on white background; red horizontal and white vertical sashing between blocks; white inner and green outer borders. White back; red binding. Heavy hand quilting. ........................................................ **$750-$1,000**

OAK LEAF AND REEL
Dated 1844
Maker unknown. Signed "ES". Minnesota.
Dotted blue and white cotton hand appliquéd to white background; small blue star flowers throughout; blue hand appliquéd oak trees along edges. White back; front to back self-binding. Outline hand quilting. ........................................................ **$2,000-$3,000**

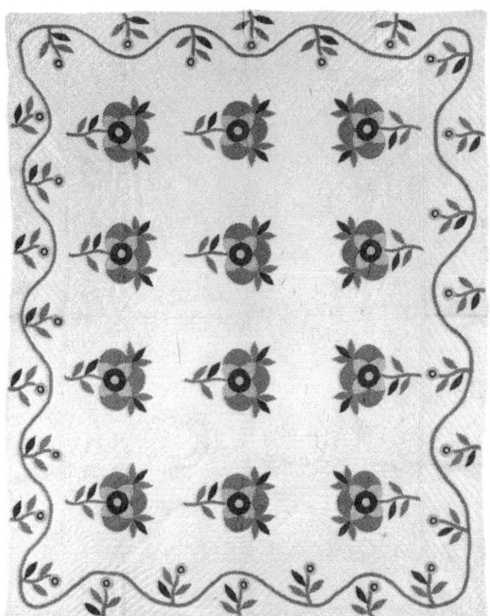

POMEGRANATE
C 1860
Maker unknown. United States.
Red, pink and green cotton prints hand appliquéd on white cotton whole-cloth background; vine border is green cotton print with flowers made from yo-yos in light and dark red and yellow; blocks are set on point with white spacers. White cotton back; white binding. Hand quilted outlines on motifs, feather wreaths in spacers, and parallel lines in border...... **$750-$1,000**

WHIG ROSE
C 1850
Maker unknown. United States.
Red, green and cheddar cotton prints and solids hand appliquéd on white cotton background; red inner and green outer borders; blocks set on point with white cotton sashing. Red-microprint binding. Hand quilted: crosshatch on blocks, running feather on sashing, cable on green border.......... **$1,500-$2,000**

## EMBELLISHED QUILTS

BALTIMORE ALBUM-STYLE CROSS-STITCH KIT QUILT
C 1970
Maker unknown. United States, possibly Midwest.
Cross-stitch on white cotton ground, bright floss in typical Baltimore colors; pink and red sawtooth embroidered border; machine pieced. White cotton back; back to front self-binding. Hand quilted, overall grid.**$600-$750**

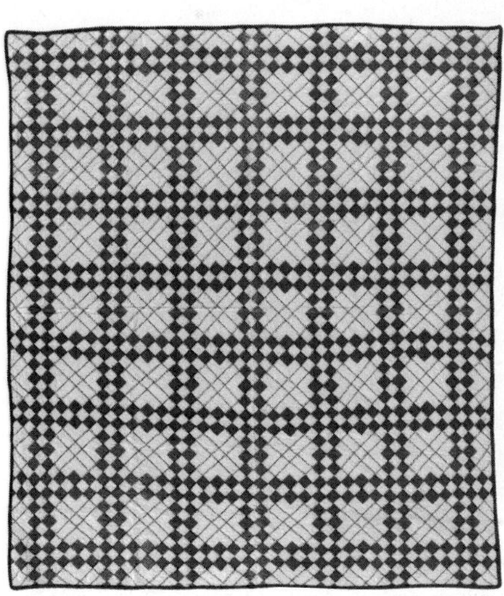

DOUBLE IRISH CHAIN WITH CROSS-STITCH QUILTING
C 1900 (top). Back, binding, and quilting 1970s.
Maker Ira Hosto Zoelzer, age 12-14, grandmother of the owner. Wisconsin.
Embroidered penny squares with typical flowers, bird, etc., and many words; dated "April 11 1915," thought by owner to be the maker's birthday; yellow setting squares and border. Knife-edge binding. ............................................................ **$400-$600**

SILK CRAZY QUILT
C 1890
Maker unknown. Probably central New York.
Dressmaking silks, taffetas, brocades and velvets crazy-pieced on 22 foundation blocks; strip-pieced fans on two opposite corner blocks; excellent decorative stitching worked with silk floss; border pieced from thin strips of similar fabrics; crazy-pieced corner blocks. Black silk binding................ **$1,500-$2,000**

CONTAINED CRAZY QUILT
C 1880
Maker unknown. United States.
Mainly velvets crazy-pieced on 30 foundation blocks; good decorative stitching. Beige silk back; black silk binding.......................................... **$1,500-$2,000**

CONTAINED CRAZY QUILT
C 1885
Maker unknown. Three Bridges, New Jersey.
Assorted dressmaking scraps crazy-pieced on foundation blocks and strips; one corner fan; dated partly by a Stevengraph ribbon of a foxhunting scene, excellent decorative stitching with a brown velvet border. Pre-quilted satin comforter back; knife-edge binding.
.................................................... **$2,000-$3,000**

CRAZY QUILT THROW
C 1890
Maker unknown. Probably Wisconsin.
Dressmaking scraps, mainly silks and velvets, crazy-pieced on nine foundation blocks and embellished with ribbon-work flowers; excellent decorative stitching. Cotton back. Black polyester binding added later. ............................................ **$1,000-$1,500**

# Railroad Collectibles

For more than 180 years, railroads have been a part of our lives. The railroad has been equal parts responsible for the growth of nations as well as the gist for myth, legend, and song.

Railroads are also a wonderful area for collecting, offering many specialties. We will concentrate on full-size operations for the scope of this section. One can approach vintage railroad collectibles on many levels, but the first decisions need to be about the scope – collect things from one railroad, or collect things of one type from many railroads.

The first scope would be to select "your" railroad to collect. It could be the line that served the area where you grew up, the line that serves or served the area where you now live, or a railroad on which a parent or grandparent worked. For me, that choice was the Pennsylvania Railroad, as my grandparents and several other relatives worked at Sunnyside Yards in Queens, New York, or in New York-Washington passenger service as train crew members.

With the railroad line selected, one then has to choose what to collect. Common items such as public timetables, tickets, and employee passes can be had with a limited budget.

A bit more money allows expanding a collection to include employee timetables and publications, annual reports, stationery, stocks and bonds, lanterns, switch locks, keys, uniforms, buttons and badges, blueprints and calendars, or dining car service items. At an even higher price range, station signs, locomotive bells, whistles, and builder's plates can be had.

If your collecting preference leans to items, then nice collections can be made from acquiring a number of similar items. Dining car items such as silver service knives, forks, spoons or coffee pots, or china dinner or dessert plates, cups and saucers (which come in many patterns) can make an extensive collection and consume many hours in researching and hunting for items.

Many of these specialties have good reference books, and a collector should always do research by buying a reference and learning about the field before spending hard-earned money on a collection; a few hours spent in research is well worth the money saved by avoiding reproductions (and the disappointment of being fooled).

PRR Conductor silvered lapel pin, or Trainman gilt pin, vertical locking clasp pin on back... **$15**
Two locking pins on back........................... **$10**

Photographs – either contemporary publicity photos or those taken by rail fans – always make a nice addition to a collection if they show the collected items when they were in revenue use.

Best of all, enjoy your collection in your hobby room, as railroad items make nice display items and often lead to good stories. Visit a museum where you can appreciate the full-size equipment many of us do not have the room for, and the display items preserved by the collectors of the past.

*George Cuhaj*

*George Cuhaj is editor of the* Standard Catalog of World Coins *and* Standard Catalog of World Paper Money *for Krause Publications and has been a railroad enthusiast for more than 40 years.*

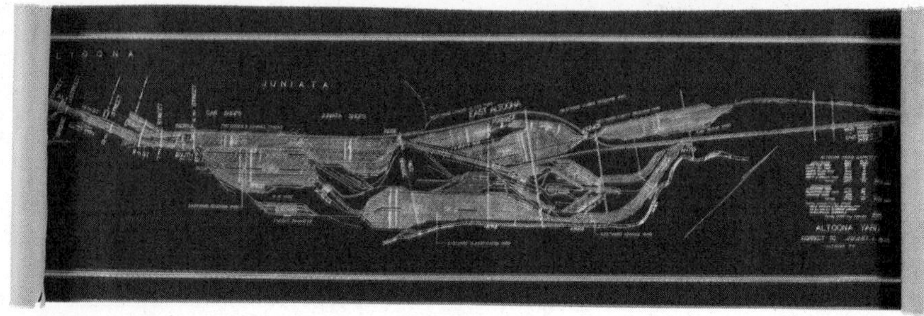

Blueprints: Locomotives, stations, tracks, other buildings (value depending on size, condition and interest), $40-$100. This particular blueprint shows Altoona and Juniata shops along the PRR, and is over 50" l........................................ **$60-$75**

New York Central Railroad bonds, Grand Central Terminal vignette image........................ **$5-$10**
New York Central bond signed by Railroad President Chauncey DePew........................ **$15-$20**

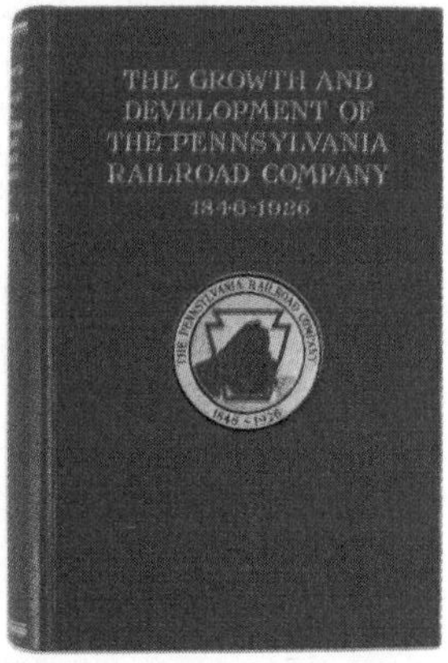


Book, *The Growth and Development of the Pennsylvania Railroad Company 1946-1926* ........................ **$60-$75**

Bronze paperweight, Trans-continental Rail-Air Service, 1928 ........................ **$80-$125**

Printed calendar, missing month pads........................ **$35-$50**

Pennsylvania Railroad Conductor hat badge ........................ **$45-$60**

Employee band cap for the Pennsylvania Railroad for one of the railroad's shops or yards........................ **$50-$75**

Full headrest from the Pennsylvania Railroad's Congressional Limited, circa 1940s........................ **$15-$25**

Vintage glass insulator with original wire .......................... **$3-$5**

Black and white photo of Pennsylvania Railroad's GG1 locomotive at Newark Station, 3" x 5" . **$3-$5**

Long Island Railroad conductor uniform jacket, Long Island buttons and hat. The LIRR was a wholly owned subsidiary of the Pennsylvania Railroad from 1904-1964. Gray colors date from the late 1950s.
Jacket and hat.............................................................**$100-$140**
Trousers...................................................................... **add $50**

Hand lantern, kerosene, Pennsylvania Railroad keystone marked frame, Pennsylvania System raised on the tall glass globe, comes in several colors: clear, amber, green, red and blue **$75-$150**

End marker lamp with mounting bracket, railroad mark on frame, CNR for Canadian National Railroad .........................**$200-$250** (Switch lamps have four large reflectors and no mounting bracket, ...............................**$200-$250)**

Lantern, short round clear globe PRR Keystone etched..... **$60-$75**

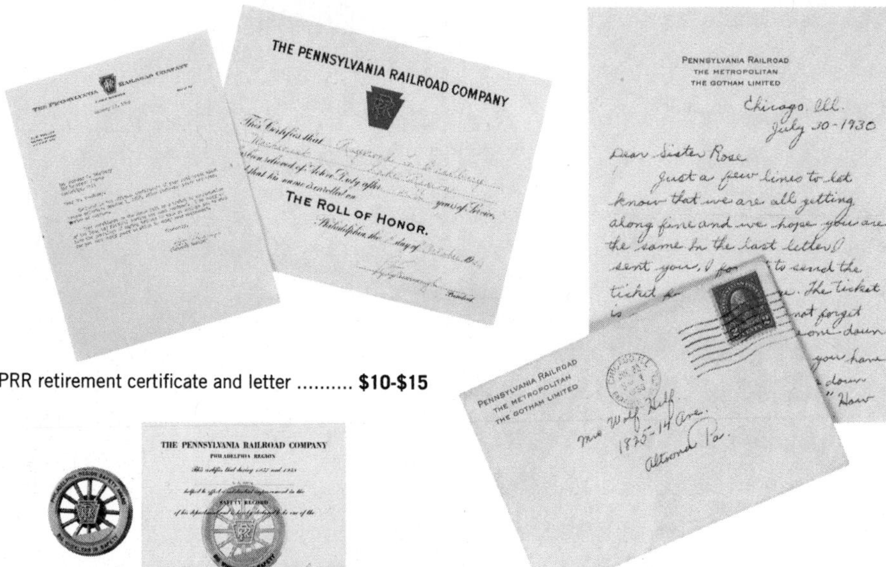


PRR retirement certificate and letter .......... **$10-$15**

Safety award, issued to employees of the Philadelphia region circa 1957-58 along with brass paperweight, 3-1/2" dia. and 8" x 10" certificate ........... **$40-$60**

A letter written en route on official PRR train stationary in 1930................................................ **$3-$7**

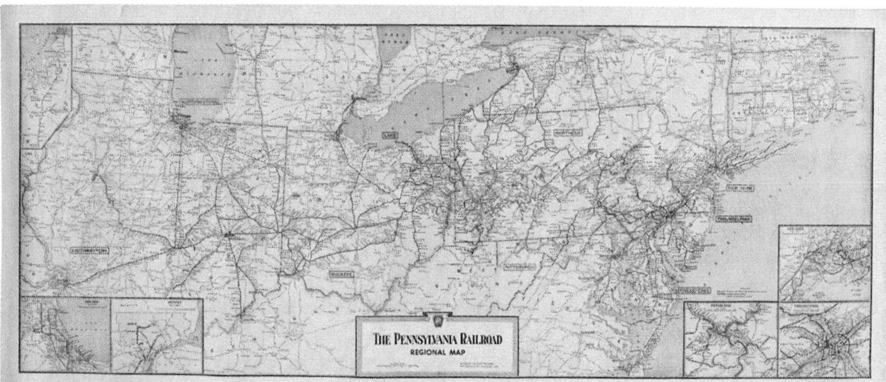


System map, 1964, 20" x 60" ................................................................................................**$35-50**
Not pictured: System map, 1940s, 20" x 60" ..........................................................................**$60-75**

Station flag, "Pennsylvania Railroad Serves the Nation," maroon background, white keystone with view of steam train on the Rockville bridge stone viaduct over the Susquehanna River just outside of Harrisburg, Pa., wool, 1940s slogan ..........................**$300-$400**

# Records

A lot has happened in the 140-odd years since the first functional phonograph debuted. In the 1870s, early recordings were made on tin foil cylinders and played back on phonographs. American inventor Thomas Edison improved the technology when he patented wax-coated cylinders in 1886. By 1908, Edison's cylinders faced increasing competition from the now-familiar flat discs we call records.

Record sizes and playback speeds varied: 7-inch, 10-inch, 12-inch records all were available, and speeds typically ranged from 74 to 82 revolutions per minute. To make a recording, performers would gather around a large acoustic horn. The sound energy from the performance was channeled through the horn, and the signal was inscribed on a master cylinder. This technique was known as acoustical recording.

By 1925, the advent of microphones and amplifiers made electrical recording methods a reality. Records were louder and clearer. As electric-powered record players and amplifiers became the norm, a playback rate of 78 RPM was chosen as the industry standard — a speed that worked with electrical infrastructure in place both in the United States (110 volts/60 Hz) and abroad (220 volts/50 Hz). Ironically, 78 RPM records weren't actually referred to as 78s until much later, when the term was used to help distinguish among 78, 45, 33-1/3 and 16-2/3 RPM records.

Early records were fashioned from hard rubber. By 1898, mass production began for records containing shellac, a resin secreted by beetles. Shellac records were incredibly brittle; dropping one was pretty much a death sentence for the disc. In 1904, the first "unbreakable" records hit the market. Made of cardboard core discs coated with celluloid, an early form of unbreakable plastic, these records suffered from a lot of surface noise during playback. They didn't catch on with consumers.

RCA introduced the first commercially available vinyl records in 1930: 12-inch, 33-1/3 RPM "program transcription" discs. These records boasted less surface noise and greater strength than shellac records, but the format, which was introduced in the middle of the Great Depression, was a commercial failure.

After World War II, 7-inch 45s and 12-inch LPs challenged the 78's dominance. Both of these formats used narrower grooves, sometimes referred to as microgrooves, and a smaller stylus for playback. Columbia's 33-1/3 LP made its debut in 1948; it boasted up to 30 minutes of playback time.

RCA rolled out 45 RPM records in 1949. Made of polystyrene or vinyl, each 45 had a large hole to accommodate its placement on a record changer. This allowed listeners to stack up several 45s on top of a changer, where discs could then drop and be played one at a time. (The little record with the big hole also was perfect for jukeboxes.) Many music lovers had to buy spindle-size adapters or snap-in inserts, sometimes called "spiders," in order to play 45s on their record players.

By the late 1950s, 45 RPM records were outselling 78s. Most U.S. record labels stopped pressing popular music on 78s by the early 1960s, although the format hung on for a few more years abroad and in select uses, including children's records. As the new industry standard for shorter-duration recordings, 45s were either singles, which offered one song per side, or extended-play records that could contain up to three songs per side.

Even though stereo recording technology had been around since its invention by EMI's Alan Blumlein in 1931, it didn't become a key factor in playback until much later. In 1958, the first two-channel records were issued by Audio Fidelity and Pye in the United States and the United Kingdom, respectively. For a while, records were offered in both monaural and stereo formats, because stereo records couldn't be played on monophonic systems. But most record companies abandoned mono recordings by the close of the 1960s. Although stereo eventually became the industry standard, many collectors prefer mono records, and labels recently have reissued classic albums in mono format due to consumer demand.

Post-World War II Americans wanted to be able to take their music with them, and automakers paid attention. In 1956, Chrysler, DeSoto, Dodge, and Plymouth offered optional in-car phonographs made by Columbia that could play 45s and 7-inch, 16-2/3 RPM records. These systems had a lot of drawbacks, not the least of which included bumpy roads that made records skip during playback. Inspired by radio station technology that used cartridge tapes, inventors came out with magnetic tape recording technology known as the Lear Jet Stereo 8, or 8-track, in the early 1960s. By the 1966 model year, Ford offered 8-track tape players as an option available on select models of its cars.

If two is better than one, four must be better than two, right? That was the philosophy behind the four-track quadraphonic playback system, which arrived in 1971 with the promise of providing an incredible listening experience. But the technology, which was the forerunner to Surround Sound, never took off. Quadraphonic records typically cost at least $1 more than their stereo counterparts. Quadraphonic recordings also required a custom audio system for playback. The record labels were divided on the quadraphonic technology that was in use, so listeners who bought a quadraphonic sound system were very limited as to which label's recordings were compatible.

In the 1970s and 1980s, recording companies experimented with different ways of producing records, including new mastering techniques that promised even better sound, and portability continued to be a driving force for music lovers. Cassette tapes, which emerged around the same time as 8-tracks, grew in popularity during the 1970s and reached their peak in the 1980s, thanks to boom boxes, in-car tape decks, and Sony's Walkman individual portable cassette players.

By the 1990s, 8-track tapes and vinyl records had basically been phased out, and cassette tapes were facing the same threat in the United States that 78s and cylinders had before them: obsolescence. The new technology known as the compact disc was gaining ground, thanks to its ability to fit the contents of a 12-inch, two-sided vinyl record on a single-sided polycarbonate disc that measured just 4-3/4 inches in diameter.

Sound recordings managed to get even smaller with the advent of digital music players, the best known of which is Apple's iPod. Introduced in 2001, the player was touted by Apple CEO Steve Jobs as a way to put "1,000 songs in your pocket," thanks to the cassette-tape-sized player's hard drive that stored downloadable MP3 music files, and later video and other multimedia files. The iPod and other MP3 players literally sounded the death knell for the Sony Walkman. The company halted production and sales in Japan of the portable cassette players in spring 2010 after 30 years and more than 200 million units sold. Chinese makers continued to manufacture Sony Walkmans for sale in Asia and the Middle East. Production also is continuing — for now — on Sony's Discman portable CD player.

If you look to car stereos, it's clear what automakers see as the future of music. CD players are basically standard equipment along with an AM/FM radio, and most new cars come with at least the option for an MP3 port, if not with a digital music system in place. Sales of digital recordings have exploded to the tune of 1.41 billion digital singles and albums sold in 2011 vs. 248 million vinyl and CD singles and albums, according to RIAA statistics.

But don't count vinyl records out just yet. Sales of vinyl singles, EPs, and LPs began to bounce back in 2008 as a new generation of music lovers and collectors discovered the format. That year, sales hit 2.9 million units shipped — the most that the format had seen since 1998. Just three years later, vinyl record sales had nearly doubled to reach 5.9 million units sold. Longtime fans tout the "warmth" of the sound that vinyl provides, and many credit the format's less-compressed audio as providing a listening experience superior to that of CDs or MP3s.

*Susan Sliwicki, Editor, Goldmine magazine, www.goldminemag.com*

The Ad Libs, "New York in the Dark" b/w "Human," 45 RPM single, A.G.P. Records, AGP 101, 1968................................**$100**

Al Green, "Back Up Train," 33-1/3 stereo LP, Hot Line, HLS-1500S, 1967. Name is misspelled as Al Greene on the album cover. ...**$80**
Mono version........................**$50**

Aretha Franklin, "Don't Cry, Baby" b/w "Without The One You Love," 45 RPM single with picture sleeve, Columbia, 4-42456, 1962....**$30**

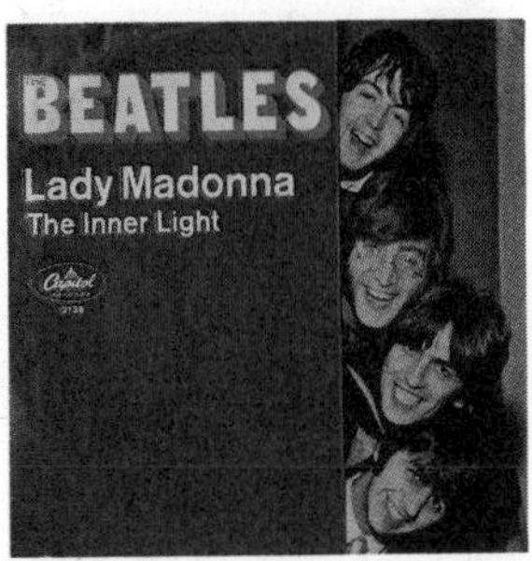


The Beatles, "Lady Madonna" / "The Inner Light," 45 RPM single with picture sleeve, Capitol Records, 2138, 1968.............**$100**

The Beatles, "Help"/"I'm Down," 45 RPM single with picture sleeve, Capitol Records, 5476, 1965.................................**$75**

The Beach Boys, "Four By The Beach Boys" 45 RPM EP with picture sleeve. Features "Little Honda," "Wendy," "Don't Back Down," and "Hushabye," Capitol Records, R-5267, 1964........**$60**

The Beach Boys, "I Get Around"/"Don't Worry Baby," 45 RPM single with picture sleeve, Capitol Records, 5174, 1964 ..........................................**$40**

Bill Haley with Haley's Comets, "Farewell – So Long – Goodbye" b/w "Rock The Joint," 45 RPM single, Essex Records, 399, 1955.................................**$75**

Bob Seger and the Silver Bullet Band, "Night Moves," 12-inch picture disc, Capitol Records, 1977.................................**$40**

**Far left:** Bruce Springsteen, "Santa Claus is Comin' to Town" (same on both sides), 45 RPM single with picture sleeve, Columbia, AE7 1332, 1981........................**$25**
Without picture sleeve...........**$20**

**Left:** Buchanan and Goodman, "The Flying Saucer Part 1" b/w "The Flying Saucer Part 2," 45 RPM single, Luniverse Records, 101, 1956..........................**$50**

Buddy Holly, "That'll Be the Day," 33-1/3 RPM LP, Decca, DL 8707, 1958.............................. **$1,500**

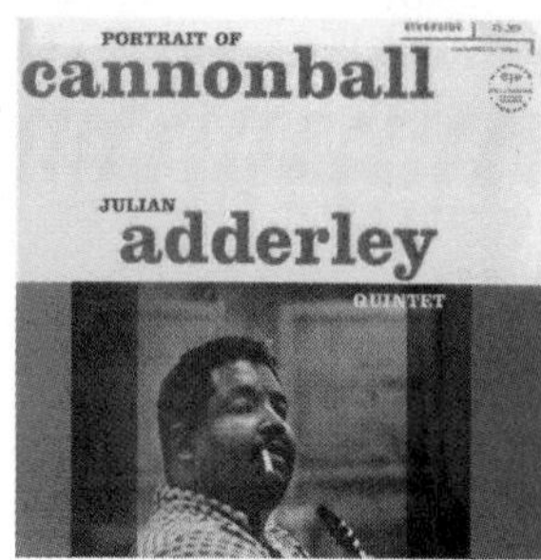


Cannonball Adderley, "Portrait of Cannonball," 33-1/3 RPM LP, Riverside, RLP 12-269, 1958, Mono................................ **$100**

Connie Francis, "My Happiness" b/w "Never Before," 45 RPM with pink picture sleeve, MGM, K12738, 1958 .................... **$30**
Mono version........................ **$20**
With white picture sleeve....... **$40**

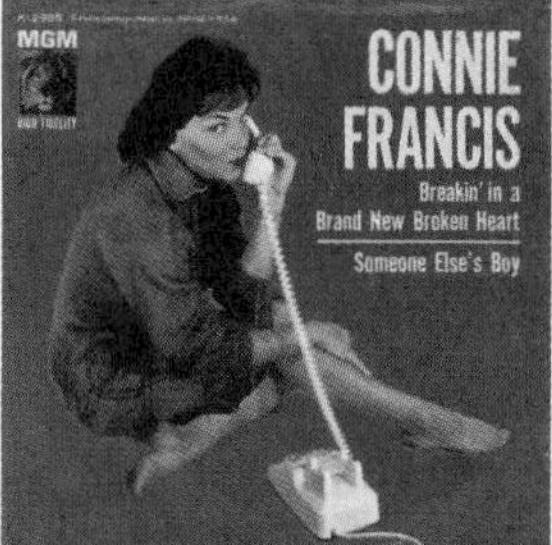


Connie Francis, "Breaking in a Brand New Broken Heart" / "Someone Else's Boy," 45 RPM single with picture sleeve, MGM, K12995, 1961 .................... **$20**

Cream, "Wheels of Fire," two 33-1/3 LPs. Mobile Fidelity, 2-066, audiophile vinyl, 1980.......... **$90**

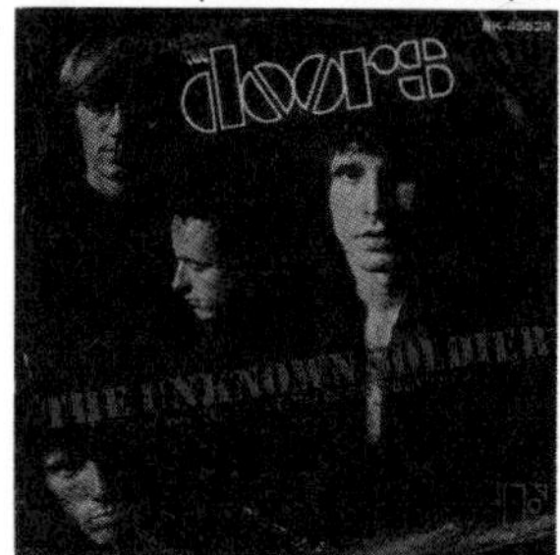


The Doors, "The Unknown Soldier" / "We Could Be So Good Together," 45 RPM single with picture sleeve, Elektra Records, EK-45628, 1968 ................ **$30**

Duane and Gregg Allman, "Morning Dew" b/w "Morning Dew," 45 RPM single, Bold Records, 200, 1973. Red vinyl, DJ copy, mono ............................................ **$30**

Ellie Pop, "Ellie Pop," 33-1/3 RPM LP, Mainstream, S-6115, 1968................................ **$125**

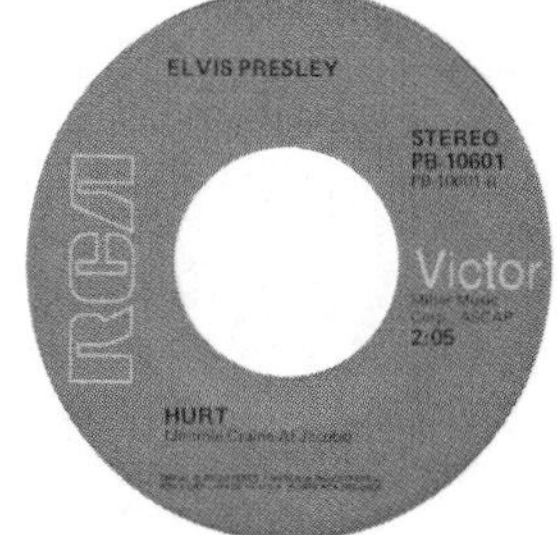


Elvis Presley, "Hurt" b/w "For the Heart," 45 RPM single, RCA Victor, PB-10601, 1976.......... **$100** (Second pressings, which are very rare, have the 1976-1988 "dog near top" black label.)

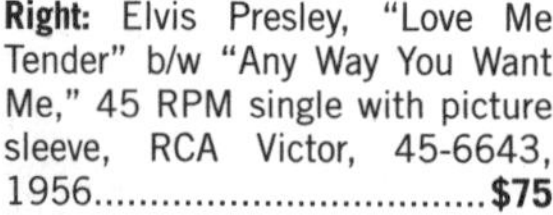

**Right:** Elvis Presley, "Love Me Tender" b/w "Any Way You Want Me," 45 RPM single with picture sleeve, RCA Victor, 45-6643, 1956................................. **$75**

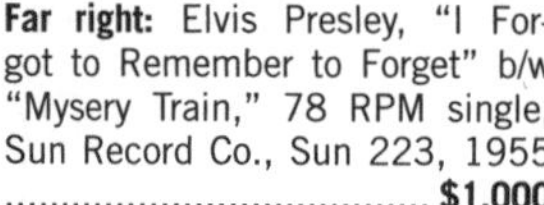

**Far right:** Elvis Presley, "I Forgot to Remember to Forget" b/w "Mysery Train," 78 RPM single, Sun Record Co., Sun 223, 1955 ...................................... **$1,000**

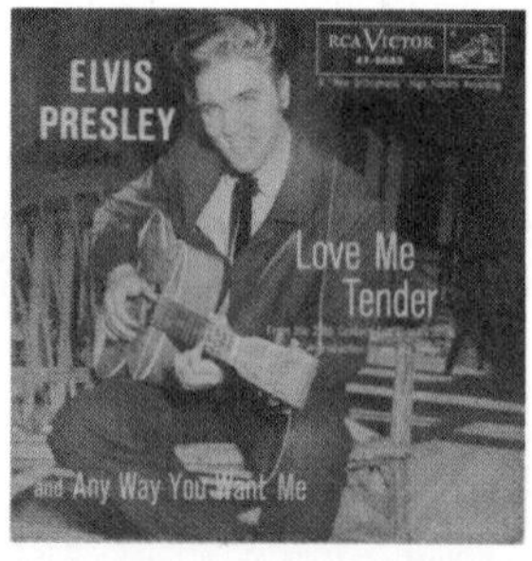

Elvis Presley, "Baby Let's Play House" / "I'm Left, You're Right, She's Gone," 78 RPM single, Sun Record Co., Sun 217, 1955 ....................................... **$1,500**

Elvis Presley with The Jordanaires, "Too Much" b/w "Playing For Keeps," 45 RPM single with picture sleeve, RCA Victor, 47-6800, 1957 .................................. **$90**

Frank Sinatra, "A Baby Just Like You" / "Christmas Mem'ries," 45 RPM single with picture sleeve, blue printing released with promo copies only, 1975 ................ **$40**

Red and black printed picture sleeve released with stock copies: ........................................... **$20**

Single only .......................... **$10**

**Far left:** Fugazi, "Song #1" / "Joe #1" / "Break In," 45 RPM single, green vinyl, limited pressing of 1,200, Sub Pop, SP52, 1989 **$65**

**Left:** The Fugs, "The Village Fugs Sing Ballads of Contemporary Protest, Point of View and General Dissatisfaction," 33-1/3 RPM LP, Broadside Records, 304, 1965 ........................................... **$400**

With insert ......................... **$500**

Gene Pitney, "Every Breath I Take" b/w "Mr. Moon, Mr. Cupid, and I," 45 RPM single with picture sleeve, Musicor, MU 1011, 1961 ................................. **$25**

Grand Funk Railroad, "E Pluribus Funk," 33-1/3 LP with round cover designed to look like a coin, Capitol, SW-853, 1971 ......... **$50**

The Grateful Dead, "U.S. Blues" b/w "Loose Lucy," 45 RPM single with picture sleeve, Grateful Dead Records, GD45-03, 1974...... **$25**

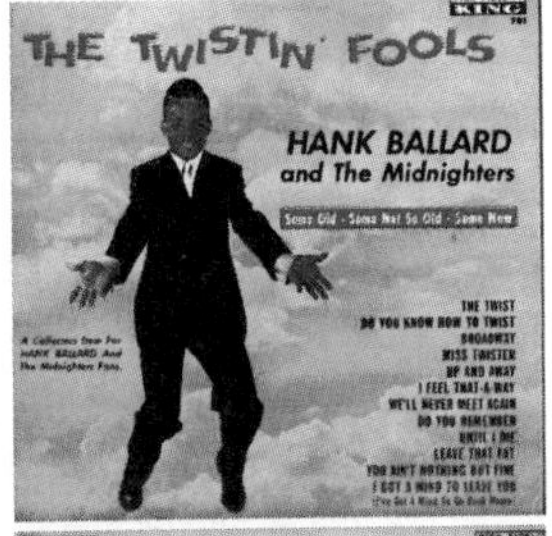

**Far left:** Hank Ballard, "The Twistin' Fools," 33-1/3 RPM LP, King Records, King 781, Mono, 1962 ........................................ **$100**

**Left:** Hendrix Band of Gypsys, "Stepping Stone"/"Izabella," 45 RPM single, Reprise 0905, 1970 ........................................ **$100**

The Isley Brothers, "This Is the End" b/w "Don't Be Jealous," 45 RPM single, Cindy, C-3009, with Cindy printed in shadow print, 1958................................**$150**
Same 45 single with Cindy appearing in regular print:.........**$75**

Martha and The Vandellas, "Come and Get These Memories"/ "Jealous Lover," 45 RPM single, Gordy Records, 7014, 1963..........**$30**

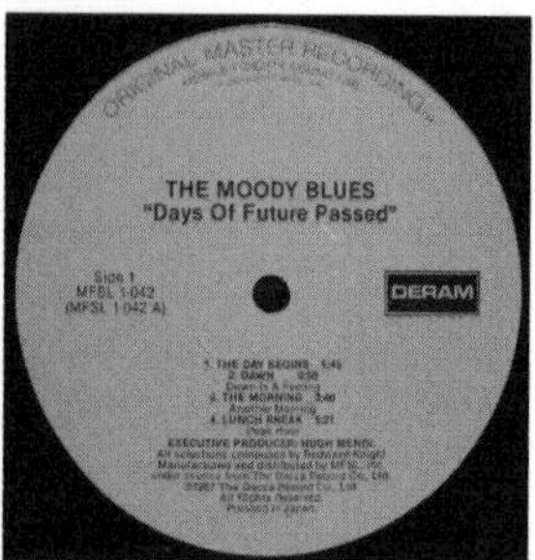


Moody Blues, "Days of Future Passed," 33-1/3 RPM LP, remastered, audiophile vinyl, Mobile Fidelity Sound Lab, MFSL 1-042, 1980................................**$60**

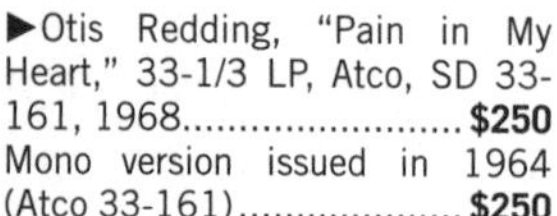

►Otis Redding, "Pain in My Heart," 33-1/3 LP, Atco, SD 33-161, 1968........................**$250**
Mono version issued in 1964 (Atco 33-161)...................**$250**

James Brown, "Please, Please, Please" b/w "Why Do You Do Me," 45 RPM single, Federal Records, 45-12258, 1956................**$48**

The Monkees, "The Monkees," jukebox mini LP, small hole, plays at 33-1/3 RPM, 1966. Features "Theme From The Monkees," "I Wanna Be Free," "Take a Giant Step," "Last Train to Clarksville," "Saturday's Child" and "Tomorrow's Gonna Be Another Day." .......................................**$150**

Nick Drake, "Fruit Tree," four-disc set of 33-1/3 LPs, Hannibal, HNBX-5302, 1986............**$170**

KISS, "The Originals" three-disc set of 33-1/3 LPs featuring "Kiss," "Hotter Than Hell" and "Dressed To Kill." Casablanca, NBLP 7032, tan Casablanca label with desert scene, 1976......**$100**
Other variations:
Three LP set with tan Casablanca label with desert scene, as well as a booklet, six KISS cards, and a KISS Army sticker, 1976.....**$150**
Three LP set, features tan labels with desert scene that read "Casablanca Record and FilmWorks"; "Second Printing" marked on cover; includes the booklet, cards and sticker........................**$100**
Three LP set features tan labels with desert scene that read "Casablanca Record and FilmWorks" and "Second Printing" marked on cover.................................**$50**

The Monkees, "Last Train to Clarksville" b/w "Take a Giant Step," 45 RPM single with picture sleeve, Colgems, 66-1001, 1966 .........................................**$30**
This is one of several picture sleeves for this release. Other known versions:
Same image, except it is in color, with "Ask for The Monkees LP Album" on the bottom of Side 1 and "Write to Monkees Fan Club" on Side 2...............................**$20**
Same black and white photo with a red strip at the bottom that reads "Ask for The Monkees LP Album" in white.............................**$25**

Pete Seeger, "Pete Seeger Sings and Answers Questions," 33-1/3 LP, at the Ford Hall Forum in Boston, Mass., Folkways, FH 5702, 1968 .............................. **$25**

Pink Floyd, "Arnold Layne" b/w "Candy and a Currant Bun," 45 RPM promotional single with picture sleeve, Tower, 333, 1967 .............................. **$700**

Without picture sleeve ......... **$200**

The Police, "Roxanne"/"Can't Stand Losing You," 45 RPM badge-shaped picture disc, A&M Records, AM-2096/AM-2147, 1979 .............................. **$10**

Queen, "Keep Yourself Alive" / "Son and Daughter," 45 RPM single, Elektra, EK-45863, 1973 .............................. **$25**

Ricky Nelson, "I Got a Feeling"/ "Lonesome Town," 45 RPM single with picture sleeve. Imperial Records, X5545, 1958 ............ **$70**

Red vinyl version (no picture sleeve) .............................. **$600**

Regular black vinyl single without the picture sleeve ................ **$30**

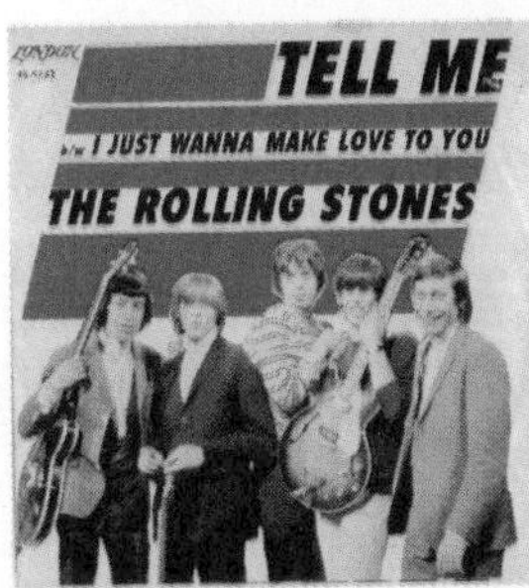


The Rolling Stones, "Tell Me" b/w "I Just Wanna Make Love to You," 45 RPM single with picture sleeve, London, 45-9682, 1964 .............................. **$175**

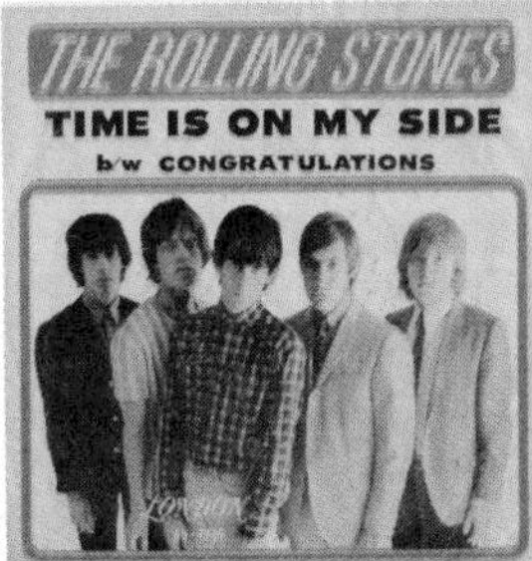


The Rolling Stones, "Time is on My Side" b/w "Congratulations," 45 RPM single with picture sleeve, London, 45-9708, 1964 .............................. **$100**

Other variations:

DJ copy with orange swirl label .............................. **$75**

Regular 45 RPM single with white, purple, and blue label: .......... **$30**

Regular 45 RPM single with blue swirl label ........................... **$10**

Selena Y Los Dinos, "Muñequito De Trapo, 33-1/3 RPM LP, GP, LP-1005, 1986 ...................... **$300**

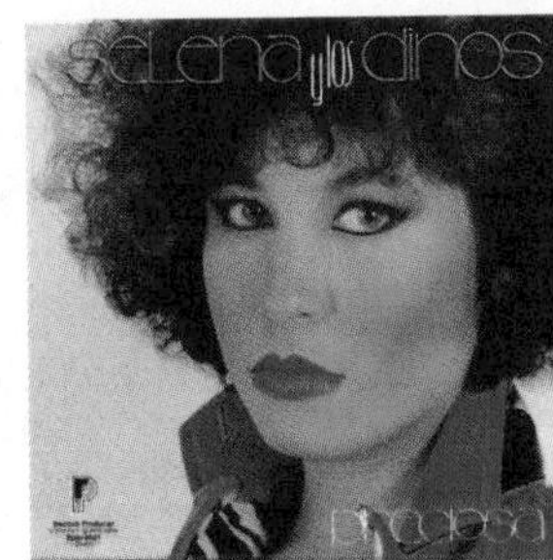


Selena Y Los Dinos, "Preciosa," 33-1/3 RPM LP, RP LP 8801, 1988 .............................. **$150**

# MARKET WATCH: Top 20 Record Sales on eBay

Values for records — much like those for other collectibles — are dependent on a mix of factors, including condition, rarity and overall desirability.

Here's a snapshot of some of the most valuable records that have changed hands via recent eBay auctions. The next time you're out garage-saling or thrift-store hunting, keep your eyes peeled. You never know when you might find a valuable record someone else has overlooked.

(Note: Any images shown are the same ones that appeared with the seller's description of the lot.)

***Susan Sliwicki, Editor, Goldmine magazine, www.goldminemag.com***

**20.** Bob Dylan, "Blood on the Tracks," test pressing, $8,000. This unreleased VG+/NM test pressing of Bob Dylan's "Blood on the Tracks" features five songs with alternate takes to the ones that appeared on the final album. Only three other copies are believed to exist.

**19.** The C.O.D.'s, "She's Fire"/ "It Must Be Love" 45, $8,100. Northern Soul records have been a staple of collectors for years. So-named for the region in Britain where these songs were popular at dance clubs — rather than the region in which they were recorded — these American soul songs were pressed by under-the-radar artists for equally under-the-radar labels (at least, to uninitiated collectors). The music typically resembles Motown, Chicago, or New York soul. This VG copy of Kellmac 1010 was cut by the Chicago-based group The C.O.D.'s for the Chicago-based Kellmac label.

**18.** The Combinations, "Like I Never Did Before" / "What 'Cha Gonna Do," 45 RPM, $8,500. The Combinations recorded a couple of 45s for the Kellmac label. This one — a VG+ copy of Kellmac 1011 pressed in 1966 — is typically harder to find and tends to draw stronger prices than Kellmac 1007.

**17.** Queen, "The Works," LP, $9,000. This Columbian red vinyl pressing of EMI 11964 earned visual grades of NM for the cover and VG++ for the vinyl.

**16.** Old Funeral, "Grim Reaping Norway," LP, $9,100. This Mint condition first pressing copy on the Hearse Records label (HR 001) was one of just 200 pressed.

**15.** Led Zeppelin, "The Final Option," limited edition 70-record box set with hard case, $9,500. The hand-pressed, heavyweight black and white splattered vinyl records in this limited-edition set (No. 40 of 150) were never played.

**14.** Billy Nichols, "Would You Believe," LP, $9,700. This NM 1968 psych-pop album issued on The Immediate label was withdrawn before it ever hit the streets due to problems with the label; it is estimated that only 100 promotional copies were pressed. Featured musicians include Small Faces' Steve Marriot, Humble Pie drummer Jerry Shirley, and John Paul Jones of Led Zeppelin fame.

**13.** Mutilation, "Vampires of Black Imperial Blood," LP, $10,000. This EX-condition black metal LP with a NM cover was remastered and released in 1999 by End All Life Productions. It is numbered 45 of 100.

**12.** $10,000 — Nirvana, "Nevermind," LP, $10,000. Ordinarily, NM copies of "Nevermind" (DGC-24425) are valued at roughly $30. But this signed copy, which came with a COA but no condition grades — was obtained backstage by the seller, directly from Kurt Cobain, in 1993.

**11.** Maitreya Kali, "Apache/Inca," LP, $10,101. Only three copies of this psychedelic-rock set (CF-2777) are known to exist. This copy has NM discs and an EX+ condition gatefold cover. Beach Boy Mike Love is credited with singing on the song "Salesman" on the Apache record.

**10.** Dark, "Dark Round the Edges," LP, $10,607. Just because something was made in small quantities is no guarantee that buyers will go bonkers. This EX-condition copy of SIS-0102, which was one of a handful made via SIS Studios in 1972, proved the exception to the rule. This privately pressed prog-rock record is purported to be the U.K.'s rarest vinyl album.

**9.** Elvis Presley, "That's All Right" / "Blue Moon of Kentucky" 45 RPM, $10,987. This Mint, unplayed copy of Sun 209, complete with its original brown stock paper sleeve, came from the personal collection of Sun Records Promotion Manager Cecil Scaife, who had received a box of 25 copies directly from Sam Phillips back in the 1950s. Honorable mention: Another copy of this 1954 pressing from the same source sold for $10,000.

**8.** Annelies Schmidt, "Six Suites Pour Violoncelle Solo," three-LP box set, $11,212. This nicely kept classical set pressed on the French Ducretet Thomson label (300 C 045/044/045) earned grades of EX+/NM for the records and EX for the cover and sleeves.

**7.** The Beatles, "From Me to You," EP, $11,367. This VG-condition, French-pressed EP on the Odeon label (SOE 3739) features the Fab 4 in a rare "police/sandwich" cover" that was withdrawn after only a few were made.

**6.** Robert Johnson, "Me and the Devil Blues" / "Little Queen of Spades," 78 RPM, $12,100. This NM copy of Vocalion 01408 was touted as being in "near perfect" condition — not bad for something that's been around for nearly 75 years.

**5.** The Beatles, "Please Please Me" / "Ask Me Why," 45 RPM, $12,500. This VG+ copy of Parlophone 4983 commands top dollar for a very special reason: John Lennon, Paul McCartney, George Harrison, and Ringo Starr signed it during a publicity session at Brian Epstein's NEMS record shop. Only three such copies are known to exist.

**4.** The Beatles, "Please Please Me," LP, $15,845. First-pressing stereo copies of PCS 3042 bearing the black and gold label are among the most-sought by Beatles collectors. It is estimated that only 900 of these first-pressing records on the Parlophone label exist. This particular copy was described to be in a very pristine NM condition. Other copies of PCS 3042 sold during the period under study include: $13,601.21 (NM); $13,396.61 (EX+); $12,932.23 (NM-); $9,848.70 (NM-); and $8,238.88 (EX-)

**3.** Sex Pistols, "God Save the Queen" / "No Feelings," 45 RPM, $16,921. This original pressing of AMS 7284 came with a letter of provenance tracing it back to A&M Records. The record graded EX; the sleeve graded VG.

**2.** The Beatles, "Love Me Do" / "P.S. I Love You," 45 RPM, $17,234. This EX-condition promotional disc on the Parlophone label (4949), completed with the EMI Top Pop sleeve, is believed to be one of only 250 copies pressed in 1962 to promote The Beatles. Paul McCartney's songwriting credit on both labels is misspelled as "McArtney." A VG+/VG also copy sold for $9,788.13.

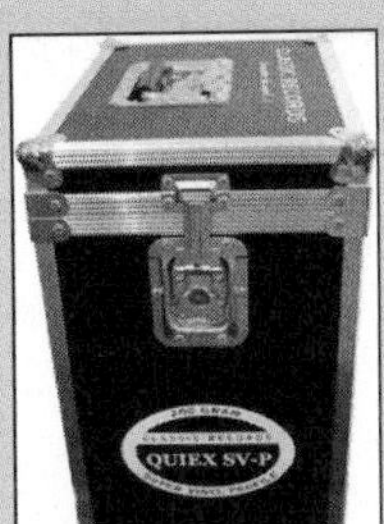


**1.** Led Zeppelin, 45 RPM test pressing road case, $17,999. Limited edition (No. 4 of 5). Factory-sealed, 48-disc set of 200-gram 45 RPM test pressings on the Classic Records/Atlantic label.

The Valentines, "Lily Maebelle" b/w "Falling For You," 45 RPM single, Rama, RR-171, 1955 ........................................ **$200**

The Who, "Anyway, Anyhow, Anywhere" b/w "Anytime You Want Me," 45 RPM single, Decca, 31801, 1965....................... **$50**

The Who, "Happy Jack" b/w "Whiskey Man," 45 RPM single with picture sleeve, Decca 32114, 1967.................................. **$50**

**Right:** X, "Adult Books" b/w "We're Desperate," 45 RPM single with picture sleeve, Dangerhouse, D88, 1978. Authentic sleeves are black, white, and yellow; photocopies in black and white exist and have no collector value.... **$60**
Red-label single ................... **$40**

**Far right:** The Yardbirds, "Heart Full of Soul" b/w "Steeled Blues," 45 RPM single with picture sleeve, Epic, 5-9823, 1965 .. **$50**
Single (no picture sleeve) ...... **$15**

## Goldmine's Record Grading Guide

Record grading uses both objective and subjective factors. Our advice: Look at everything about a record — its playing surface, the label, the record's edges, the cover and/or sleeve — under a strong light. If you're in doubt, assign the record a lower grade. Many dealers grade records, sleeves, or covers and sometimes even labels separately. The grades listed below are common to vinyl records, including EPs, 45s, LPs and 12-inch singles. More grading tips may be found at Goldminemag.com.

**MINT (M):** Perfect in every way. Often rumored, but rarely seen. Never played, and often still factory sealed. Never use Mint as a grade unless more than one person agrees that a record or sleeve truly is in this condition. Mint price is best negotiated between buyer and seller.

**NEAR MINT (NM OR M-):** Nearly perfect. Looks and sounds like it just came from a retail store and was opened for the first time. Jackets and sleeves are free of creases, folds, markings, or seam splits. Records are glossy and free of imperfections. Many dealers won't use a grade higher than NM, implying that no record or sleeve is ever truly perfect.

**VERY GOOD PLUS (VG+) or EXCELLENT (E):** Except for a few minor things ⊠ slight warps, scuffs, or scratches that don⊠t affect playback, ring wear on the labels, a turned up corner, cut-out hole, or seam split on the sleeve or cover ⊠ this record would be NM. Most collectors, especially those who want to play their records, are happy with a VG+ record, especially if it⊠s toward the high end of the grade (VG++ or E+). Worth 50 percent of NM value.

**VERY GOOD (VG):** Many of the imperfections found on a VG+ record are more obvious on a VG record. Surface noise, groove wear, and light scratches can be found on VG records. You may find stickers, tape or writing on labels, sleeves, and covers, but no more than two of those three problems. VG records are among the biggest bargains in record collecting. Worth 25 percent of a NM record.

**GOOD (G), GOOD PLUS (G+), or VERY GOOD MINUS (VG-):** Expect a lot of surface noise, visible groove wear and scratches on the vinyl, as well as more defects and repairs to labels, sleeves, and covers. Unless the record is unusually rare, G/G+ or VG- records are worth 10 to 15 percent of the NM value.

**POOR (P) and FAIR (F):** Records are cracked, impossibly warped, or skip and/or repeat when an attempt is made to play them. Covers and sleeves are heavily damaged, if they even exist. Unless they are incredibly rare, P and F records sell for 0 to 5 percent of the NM value (if they sell at all).

# Samplers

Samplers: The name says it all. Avid seamstresses of the 1400s had no pattern books to turn to. Instead, when running across a unique stitch or pattern, the custom was to sew a small example of the new find on a piece of fabric: in other words, a "sampler."

The term is drawn from the Latin exemplum ("an example to be followed"). Over the years, these samplers, their designs quickly and randomly worked in the cloth, served as treasured three-dimensional reference guides. The conscientious needleworker used them to perfect her skill, while at the same time continuing to bolster her sampler collection.

The 1500s gave rise to "band samplers." Fabric was costly, and these very narrow cloth bands of six to nine inches were closely covered with stitchery, incorporating numerous styles and types of ornamentation, such as the use of metallic and multicolored threads. "Spot samplers" were popular in the 1600s. In this version, stitched motifs on silk were made to be cut out and used as ornamentation.

Since the first pattern book appeared in 1523, samplers had progressed past the point of serving as a means of sharing and preserving new patterns. Instead, the creation of a sampler became an art form in itself, an enduring exhibition of sewing expertise.

Early samplers were the province of skilled adult seamstresses. However, by the 1700s, the ability to successfully embroider a sampler was considered the mark of a girl's growing maturity. The pattern was no longer random. Instead, a variety of nature images (trees, fruits, flowers, birds, and animals) were now worked into a carefully planned overall picture. In its new incarnation, the sampler was viewed as an excellent learning tool. That educational aim is evidenced by the array of alphabet samplers, number samplers, almanac samplers, and even map samplers brought into being by their youthful embroiderers.

By the 1800s, the needle art was often accompanied by a stitched verse. Those verses drew heavily on the sort of Biblical quotations, moral platitudes, and uplifting poetry considered suitable for impressionable young minds. Personalization also played an important role, with the name of the maker and the date often stitched into the design, and even at times incorporated into the verse.

Needlework sampler, "Sarah Somers was born in Danvill in the County of Caledonia and the State of Vt/Dec the 3 aged 13," 1834, silk threads on a linen ground with rows of alphabets over Sarah's statistics and unfinished panel with birds perched on shrubs and fence, surrounded on three sides with a geometric vine design, 17-1/2" x 16-1/2", later frame. Note: Sarah Somers was born in Danvill Township, Vermont, on Dec. 3, 1821, the daughter of William and Sarah (Potter) Somers. ............... **$711**
*Skinner, Inc.*

With the growing availability of printed pattern books, the sampler format became increasingly more regimented; full designs proved easy to emulate, with only slight variations. Originality took the form of new themes suited to the locale. In the United States, patriotic and homespun images (eagles, farm scenes, and liberty bells) proved favorites. Church sewing circles specialized in Biblical figurals.

Collectors of samplers focus on such measurable factors as age of the work; overall design; skill of execution; and use of color. Signed samplers are in high demand, with signed-and-dated samplers among the most desirable. Condition also plays an important role, particularly if the sampler is intended for display. However, if the sampler is a unique one, any age-related damage can be outweighed by its rarity. For a vintage sampler with damage, only professional restoration is recommended, and only if absolutely necessary; incompetent work will decrease the sampler's value.

Large needlework sampler, "Abigail Walker AE't 11 Y/1796," possibly Quincy, Massachusetts, area, silk threads on a linen ground with rows of alphabets over a pious verse and borders of ladies, birds in a tree, potted flowering plants, enclosed on three sides with a sawtooth border and a wide geometric chain border with stylized flower motifs, 21" x 15-1/2", later molded wood frame. .................................. **$1,126**
*Skinner, Inc.*

Needlework Adam and Eve sampler, "Ann Goodson Age 13 Years 1807," probably England, silk threads on a wool gauze ground with central Adam and Eve figures flanking the Tree of Knowledge of Good and Evil with serpent, scene with house, figures, and farm animals on a hill, animals, flowers, crowns, trees, sun and moon motifs, surrounded by a geometric flowering vine, 17" x 12-1/2", period molded giltwood frame. ........................................................ **$830**
*Skinner, Inc.*

Needlework Adam and Eve sampler, "Hannah Frenchs...Aged 8 May 16 1802," probably Massachusetts, silk threads on a linen ground with bands of alphabets over a pious verse, figures of Adam and Eve and the Tree of Knowledge of Good and Evil with serpent, flanked by baskets, plants, birds, and animals, 17" x 13-1/2", later frame. ......................... **$1,126**
*Skinner, Inc.*

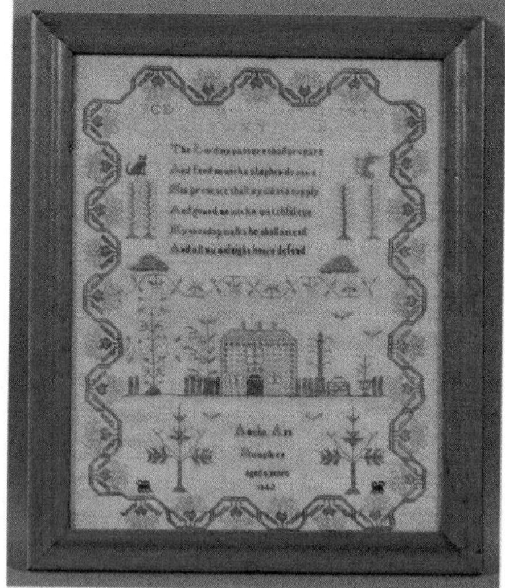

Needlework sampler, "Amelia Ann Humphrey aged 9 years 1842," probably England, silk threads on a linen ground with rows of alphabets over a pious verse flanked by trees, cat, and squirrel, above a brick house flanked by a fence, flowering trees, dog figures, enclosed in a geometric carnation floral vine, 16-1/4" x 13-1/2", period bird's-eye maple frame......... **$474**
*Skinner, Inc.*

Needlework sampler, "Clara Barnes Aged 6 Years Finish'd December 4th 1828," probably England, silk threads on a linen/wool ground with rows of stars, potted plants, baskets of fruit, and birds over a large tree with perching bird flanked by a tower, castle, fence, animals, and baskets of fruit enclosed in a geometric floral vine, 17-1/4" x 13", period maple frame. ..**$504**

*Skinner, Inc.*

Needlework sampler, "Emily Cone Aged 12 Years 1837," England, silk threads on a linen/wool ground with a large house flanked by trees, flowers, and birds over a pious verse, with three borders depicting crowns, urns, flowers, and baskets of fruit, birds, potted plants, and flowering vegetation, enclosed in a geometric flowering vine, 17" x 12-1/4", later wood frame. ........................................................**$385**

*Skinner, Inc.*

Small needlework sampler, "Dolly Woodis," probably Massachusetts, late 18th/early 19th c., silk threads on a linen ground with rows of alphabets above bands of flowers and geometric designs, 8-1/4" x 7-1/4", unframed. Provenance: The sampler was found in the 1970s in the home of a relative of Mary Elizabeth Sawyer (Mary of the nursery rhyme "Mary Had a Little Lamb") of Sterling, Massachusetts (Sterling was once part of Lancaster). ........................................ **$889**

*Skinner, Inc.*

Needlework sampler, "Elizabeth Forfitt her work/ Stony Stratford Sep'tr ye 29th 1749," England, silk threads on a linen/wool ground with rows of alphabets over three pious verses and a carnation blossom flanked by butterflies and flowers, enclosed in a vine with anchors and flower blossoms, 13-3/4" x 12-1/4"........................................................ **$444**

*Skinner, Inc.*

Needlework sampler, "Rebecca Whites Sampler worked in the twelfth year of her age 1797," possibly Lancaster, Massachusetts, silk threads on a linen ground with rows of alphabets over a large potted flower, flanked by baskets of fruit and flowers and enclosed on three sides with a sawtooth border and wide geometric flowering vine, 17-1/2" x 11-3/4", unframed. Note: This sampler is possibly the work of Rebecca White (b. April 10, 1785), the first child of nine born to Joseph and Rebecca (Hoar) White of Lancaster, Massachusetts. The sampler was found in the 1970s in the home of a relative of Mary Elizabeth Sawyer (Mary of the nursery rhyme "Mary Had a Little Lamb") of Sterling, Massachusetts (Sterling was once part of Lancaster). The name "Mary L. Sawyer" is inscribed on a paper label stitched to upper left corner of sampler.................................................. **$1,185**
*Skinner, Inc.*

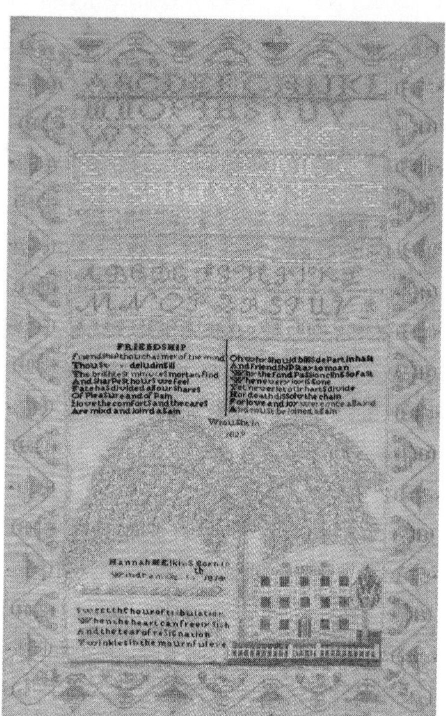


Needlework mourning sampler, "Hannah M. Elkins Born in Windham/O-- --th 1814/Wrought in 1829," Maine, silk threads on a linen ground with alphabets, "Friendship," mourning verses over a large weeping willow and Federal house with fenced yard, enclosed in a geometric flowering border, 25-3/4" x 26-3/4", later tiger maple veneer frame. Note: An Internet search found Hannah M. Elkins is buried at the Mayberry Cemetery in Windham, Maine. She died Aug 25, 1844, at the age of 29 years, 10 months...... **$1,067**
*Skinner, Inc.*

Needlework family record sampler, probably New York, early 19th c., silk threads on a linen ground with rows of alphabets above vital statistics of Isaac Lake and Margaret Robins and their six children, surrounded by a geometric flowering vine, 18" x 16-1/2", bird's-eye maple veneer frame. Note: Genealogy records indicate Isaac Lake was born in May 1805 and is buried in the Hillside Cemetery on Staten Island. He married Margaret Robins on Nov. 20, 1824, they had nine children, and six of their names are stitched on this sampler.................. **$356**
*Skinner, Inc.*

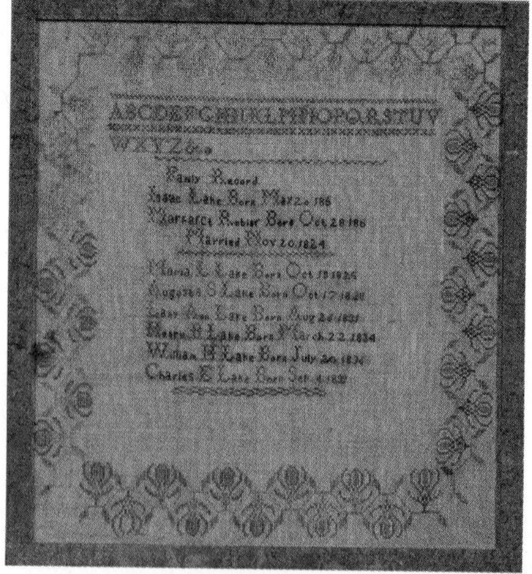

Needlework sampler, "MARTHA BRADLEY BORN JANUARY THE 31 IN Ye YEAR 1774 AGD TWELVE YEARS," Dracut, Massachusetts, 1786, silk threads on a linen ground, with rows of alphabets over signature lines, surrounded by solid-stitched floral borders on three sides and lower geometric border (background linen toned), 13" x 10-1/2", unframed. Note: Martha Bradley was the daughter of Amos and Elesebeth Bradley of Dracut, Massachusetts.......................................................................................................**$7,110**

*Skinner, Inc.*

Needlework family record, "Wraught by Mary Ann Hobbs In the 12 year of her age 1832," Livermore, Androscoggin County, Maine, silk threads on a linen ground with rows of alphabets over arched columns ornamented with hearts, birds, and flowers, vital statistics of Josiah Hobbs (b. 1787) and Sarah Walker (b. 1788), married on Feb. 18, 1813, and their two children, William (b. 1814) and Mary Ann (b. 1821), with geometric and floral borders, 17-1/4" x 17-1/2", later mahogany veneer frame. Note: According to History of the Town of Livermore Maine..., by Ira Thompson Monroe, 1928, Colonel Josiah Hobbs (1788-1855) married Sarah Walker (1788-1872) and resided in Livermore, Maine. Hobbs was prominent in town affairs. The couple had two children, William (1815-1896) and Mary Ann (1821-1886). Mary Ann married Sonanus Briggs (1823-1902), also of Livermore, and together they had five children...........................**$889**

*Skinner, Inc.*

# Silver

Silver is a precious metal used to make ornaments, jewelry, tableware, utensils, silverware, and currency coins. It is a favorite medium for visual arts because of its bright white color.

Sterling silver (standard silver) is an alloy made of silver and copper and is harder than pure silver. It is used in the creation of sterling silver flatware (silverware) and various other tableware, such as tea services, trays and salvers, goblets, water and wine pitchers, candlesticks, and centerpieces. Coin silver is slightly less pure than sterling.

Sheffield silver, or Old Sheffield Plate, is a fusion method of silver-plating that was used from the mid-18th century until the mid-1880s, when the process of electroplating silver was introduced. An electroplated silver item is shaped and formed from a base metal and then coated with a thin layer of silver.

From the 17th century to the mid-19th century, English silversmiths set the styles that inspired the rest of the world. The work from this period exhibits the highest degree of craftsmanship. English silver is actively collected in the American antiques marketplace. Fine examples of Irish and Scottish silver, as well as Continental silver, are also popular with collectors.

Silversmithing in America goes back to the early 17th century in Boston and New York and the early 18th century in Philadelphia. Boston artisans were influenced by the English styles, New Yorkers by the Dutch. American manufacturers began to switch to the sterling standard about the time of the Civil War.

American, basket, touch of R&W Wilson, Philadelphia, 19th century, 4-1/4" h. x 11" d., approximately 28.7 troy oz. ........................................... **$1,400**
*Pook & Pook, Inc.*

American, punch ladle, Captain William Richardson (1757-1809), Richmond, rounded-end handle, hallmarked with two raised spread-wing eagles and "W.R." in rectangle, "M" monogram, light dents to bowl, late 18th or early 19th century, 12-1/4" l. ........................................... **$1,760**
*Green Valley Auctions*

American, coin silver pitcher, classical, presentation, John B. Jones, Boston, 1782-1854, the c. 1830 pitcher with double scroll cast handle, rectangular in section with applied leaf on top, bands of gadrooning on rim, middle and base, marked "J.B. Jones" on base, the side engraved with the names of five generations of males by the name of Dexter residing in or around Boston, 9-3/4" h., approximately 31 troy oz., subtle dents and several pinhead size pits on bulbous area........................................... **$1,185**
*Skinner Inc.*

American, coin silver tea service, three pieces, Peter Chitry, New York, early 19th century, comprising a teapot, covered sugar bowl and creamer, oval lobed bodies with fruit-form finials, shaped serpent spout, an anthemion leaf and grapevine borders on stepped oval bases, marked "P. Chitry" on bases, 7-1/4" to 9-1/2" h., approximately 55 troy oz.; together with a later plated, similarly formed, unmarked teapot and a plated rectangular tray with engraved scrolled floral and foliate design marked "Wm. Rogers 4090," teapot 9-3/4", tray 14" x 22-1/2", handles are hollow, the bases all have several small dents around them, wear to the plated pieces, the tray has surface wear. .......... **$1,896 all**

*Skinner Inc.*

American, pitcher, bearing touch of James Thomson, New York, c. 1835, 39.5 oz total wt, 13-1/2" h. .......... **$1,040**

*Pook & Pook, Inc.*

American, coin silver, tea service, three pieces, two teapots, 11-1/2" h., creamer 8-1/2" h., Philadelphia, by J.E. Caldwell & Co., approximately 70.4 troy oz. .......... **$1,160**

*Pook & Pook, Inc.*

American, serving bowl, Tiffany & Co., Art Deco, footed, marked "23356," approximately 47.10 oz, 12-1/2" d., 4-1/4" h. .......... **$1,150**

*Pook & Pook, Inc.*

American, salver, leaf tip and dart border, center flat-chased, floral sprays in oval reserves, scrolling, three scroll feet, Tiffany & Co., 28 oz, c. 1855, 12" d. .......... **$1,005**

*Sloans & Kenyon Auctioneers and Appraisers*

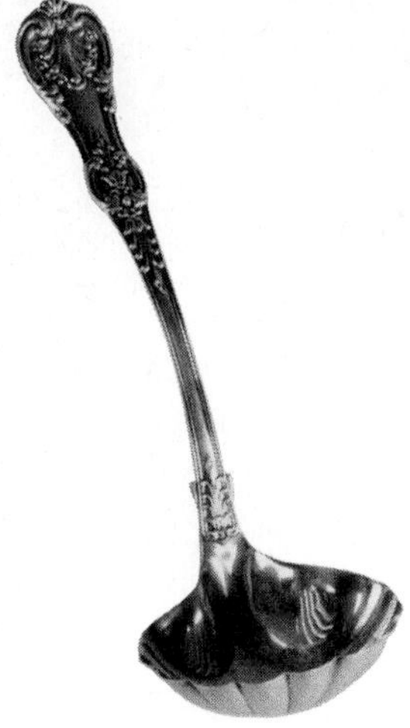

American, sterling ladle, English King pattern, Tiffany & Co., late 19th century, 11 oz., 4 dwt, 12-1/2" l. ........................ **$1,420**
*Sloans & Kenyon Auctioneers and Appraisers*

American, probably Massachusetts, porringer, second quarter 18th century, round bowl with domed center, pierced keyhole-pattern handle with "A+B to D+A & M+W" engraved on the back of handle (an inscription on a tag attached to the handle reads: "Andrew Bowditch of Salem Mass. to Daniel Appleton and Mary Williams Boston"), 1-1/2" h., 4-1/4" d., 6-3/4" l., approximately 4 troy oz., several soft dents to bulbous area of bowl, rim a little out of round. ............................... **$651**
*Skinner Inc.*

American, silver repousse creamer, Andrew Ellicott Warner, 1786-1870, Baltimore, the sides chased and embossed with chinoiserie motifs including pagodas, boat scenes, and dense scrolled foliage, a shield-shaped cartouche below spout, angled ribbed handle with grape cluster terminals, marked "A.E.WARNER" in serrated rectangle, and 11 and an underlined 8, 5-3/4" h., approximately 13 troy oz............ **$2,251**
*Skinner Inc.*

American, sterling, bun warmer, three hinged doors, three silver gilt interior compartments with pierced covers, exterior with floral repoussé design, fruit basket finial, 62 oz., 9-3/4" h..... **$2,715**
*Sloans & Kenyon Auctioneers and Appraisers*

American, sterling tea service, five pieces, coffeepot 9" h., teapot, creamer, covered sugar, and waste bowl, grapevine decorated silver-plated tray, approximately 65.3 troy oz .................................... **$1,520**
*Pook & Pook, Inc.*

American, sterling, hammered, cup, Theodore Pond, inscribed SYLVIA, stamped POND/KWONESHE/HAND WROUGHT STERLING, 2-1/2" x 3-1/2" **$600**
*David Rago Auctions, Inc.*

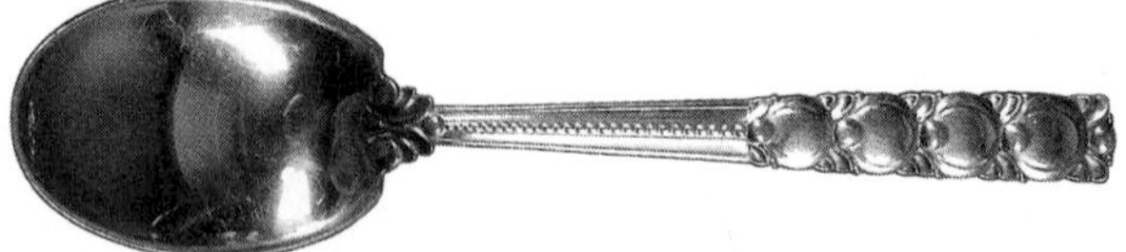

American, sterling serving spoon, overlapping stylized apple stem, gold-washed bowl, Tiffany & Co., Art Deco first half 20th century, 4 troy oz, 9-5/8" l. ........................................................................ **$470**
*Skinner, Inc.*

American, sterling presentation cup, oviform, circular foot, overturned pierced rim, scrolls and arabesques, engraved "From the Lunch Club, Boston," silver-plated liner, 32 oz, 8 dwt, c. 1920, 8" h.. ....... **$500**
*Sloans & Kenyon Auctioneers and Appraisers*

American, sterling, presentation pitcher, squat ovoid, short spout, scroll handle, applied acanthus bands, engraved with presentation inscription dated 1889, 34 troy oz, 1886, 6-1/2" h............................. **$500**
*Skinner, Inc.*

American, sterling presentation tray, oval, two handles, plain molded border, "Presented by the Board of Governers, New York Stock Exchange, to William McChesney Martin Jr., engraved signatures including Felix Rohatyn, James C. Kellogg, Will R. Salomon, San W. Lufkin, and others, 127 oz, 6 dwt, Tiffany & Co., c. 1970......................... **$2,950**
*Sloans & Kenyon Auctioneers and Appraisers*

American, sterling coffee set, Shreve, coffeepot, sugar bowl, creamer, six demitasse cups with Lenox porcelain liners, saucers, and two 4-1/2" glass lined cordials, all monogrammed "S"; six fine Lebolt demitasse spoons in assorted floral patterns, in original box, marked........... **$1,680**
*David Rago Auctions, Inc.*

American, sterling, repousse Monteith-style bowl, chased and embossed, floral sprays, rocaille shells, stippled ground, trefoil rim, domed foot, base underside monogrammed, S. Kirk and Son, Baltimore, 1880-1890, 7-1/8" h. x 8-7/8" d. ............... **$2,350**
*Skinner, Inc.*

American, Tiffany, vase, three handles, 44 troy oz, 6-1/4 PTS, 6" d., 8-1/2" h. ......................... **$1,800**
*David Rago Auctions, Inc.*

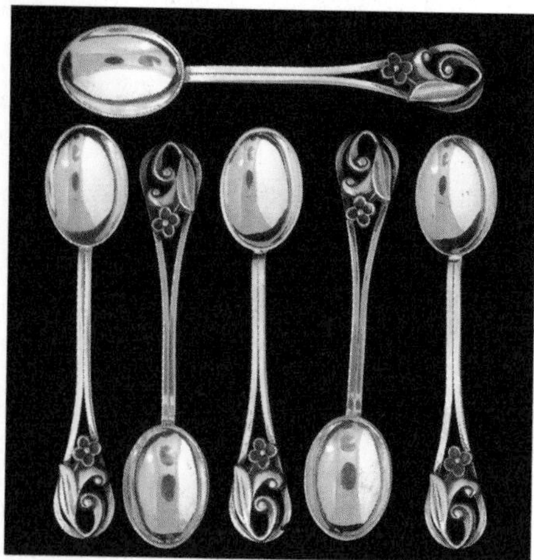

Continental, Denmark, Georg Jensen, demitasse spoons, sterling, set of six ............................ **$225**
*David Rago Auctions, Inc.*

Continental, centerpiece, oval, foliate scroll and shell feet, sides pierced with guilloches, hung with ribbon-tied berried laurel swags between bands of vitruvian scrolls, pierced anthemion, open double scroll handles, fitted with silver-plated liner, crowned A, crowned P and crowned fleur-de-lis marks, 27 oz, 14" h. ...................................................... **$1,100**
*Sloans & Kenyon Auctioneers and Appraisers*

American, water pitcher, presentation type, Tiffany & Co., 1875-91 mark, baluster body, repoussè and chased with Bacchanal couple, medallions framed by scrolling grape vines and acanthus leaf tips, centering presentation tablet inscription "Monmouth Park, July 12th 1879, Three Quarter Dash, Gentlemen Riders Won By Mr. W. C. Sanford's, Brg. Kadi by Lexington, Owner," wrapped anthemion-form handle rising from bacchanal mask, 38 oz 4 dwt., 8-3/4" h. .................................... **$5,350**
*Sloans & Kenyon Auctioneers and Appraisers*

Continental, Denmark, Georg Jensen, pitcher, No. 385, sterling, ivory handle ..................... **$4,250**
*David Rago Auctions, Inc.*

Continental, Denmark, Georg Jenson, two sterling hand-hammered bowls, raised on leaf and ball feet, price for pair, 12 t.o., 5" d., 2-3/4" h.......................................................................................**$1,900**

*David Rago Auctions, Inc.*

Continental, German silver centerpiece and mirrored plateau, plateau with elaborate scrolling, reticulated border, medallions, interspersed along border with German inscriptions, centerpiece cast with similar scrolls, sides with carotouche bearing German inscription, 12 Februar 1872-1897, metal insert included, 51 oz weighable silver, 25" l. plateau ..........................................................................................**$4,130**

*Sloans & Kenyon Auctioneers and Appraisers*

**Above left:** Continental, covered cup, Baroque style, likely Austro-Hungarian, English import marks for London 1901, tapering baluster-form body, attenuated vertical lobes, rounded ends, lid, taverner finial, quatrefoil pierced rim, trefoil-cut cardwork stem, spreading foot spherical lobes, mid-19th century, 16" h., approximately 34 troy oz. ..................**$1,115**

*Skinner, Inc.*

**Left:** Continental footed cup and cover, Baroque style, cast with masques, fruit and strapwork, 17 oz, 4 dwt, c1860, 15-1/2" h. ..................**$825**

*Sloans & Kenyon Auctioneers and Appraisers*

English, caudle cup, George I, base body with reeding and fluting, chased and embossed with cartouche, cherub mask, engraved with two monograms, dated 1718, lobed waistband, serpentine handles, Joseph Clare, London, 1718, 4-3/8", 10 troy oz..................................**$3,055**

*Skinner, Inc.*

English silver dessert dishes, pair, touch of William Burwash, cast grapevine rim, 3-1/4" h., 11" d., approx. 53.2 oz total wt.......................................................... **$1,755**
*Pook & Pook, Inc.*

English, George V salver, flaring stepped serpentine rim, four feet, Mappin & Webb, Sheffield, 41 oz., 4 dwt., 1933, 14-1/4" d. ............................. **$1,300**
*Sloans & Kenyon Auctioneers and Appraisers*

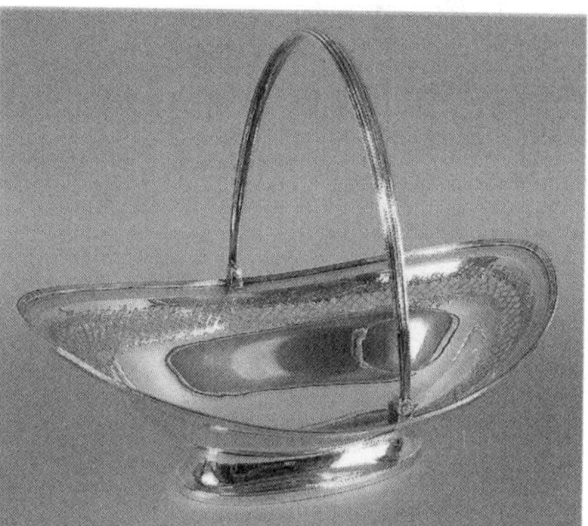

English, Georgian, basket, bearing the touch of Thomas Robins, c. 1804, 25.6 oz total wt, 13-1/4" l............................................................ **$1,955**
*Pook & Pook, Inc.*

English, Georgian silver, covered sugar, touch of Samuel Taylor, floral repousse decoration, 1762-1763, 5-1/4" h., 13.2 oz. total wt. .................................... **$645**
*Pook & Pook, Inc.*

English, Georgian, tankard, touch of Hester Bateman, dome lid, scrolled handle, heart terminal, 1787-1788, 8" h., approximately 26.3 oz total wt.............. **$4,210**
*Pook & Pook, Inc.*

English, teapot, George III, partly fluted baluster-shaped body, wood handle, Thomas and James Phipps III, London, 1819, 6-1/2" h...................................... **$355**
*Sloans & Kenyon Auctioneers and Appraisers*

# Tools

Tool collecting is nearly as old as tools themselves. Certainly it was not long after Stone Age man used his first stone tool that he started watching for that special rock or piece of bone. Soon he would have been putting tools away just for the right time or project. The first tool collector was born!

Since earliest man started collecting tools just for the right time or project, many other reasons to collect have evolved. As man created one tool, he could then use that tool to make an even better tool.

Very quickly toolmakers became extremely skilled at their craft, and that created a new collecting area – collecting the works of the very best makers. In time toolmakers realized that tools were being purchased on the bases of the quality of workmanship alone. With this realization an even more advanced collector was born as toolmakers began making top-of-the-line tools from special materials with fine detailing and engraving. These exquisite tools were never intended for use but were to be enjoyed and collected. Many of the finest tools were of such quality that they are considered works of art.

So many tools exist in today's world that many tool collectors focus on one special category. Some of the most popular categories to collect fall into the general areas of: function, craft or trade, personal connection, company or brand, patents, and investments.

For more information on tools, see *Antique Trader Tools Price Guide* by Clarence Blanchard.

## BRACES & BITS

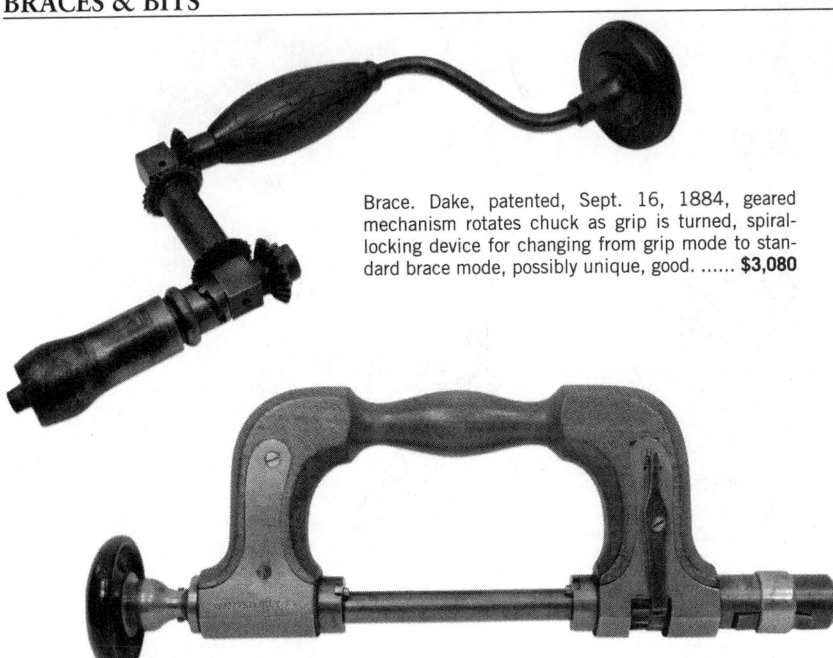

Brace. Dake, patented, Sept. 16, 1884, geared mechanism rotates chuck as grip is turned, spiral-locking device for changing from grip mode to standard brace mode, possibly unique, good. ...... **$3,080**

Brace. Henry W. Porter patent, June 9, 1857, West Earl, Lancaster County, Pa., beech brace, rosewood pad, first U.S. patent for a ratcheting brace, removable iron shaft runs from top crank to bottom crank, clip top and bottom holds shaft in place, lever alongside lower crank controls ratchet direction, slip-ring chuck, little use, fine. .......... **$17,050**

Brace. Pilkington, Pedigor & Storr, beech, brass stem, ebony head, ivory ring, lever chuck, all proper marks, even patina on brass, good.............................. **$1,265**

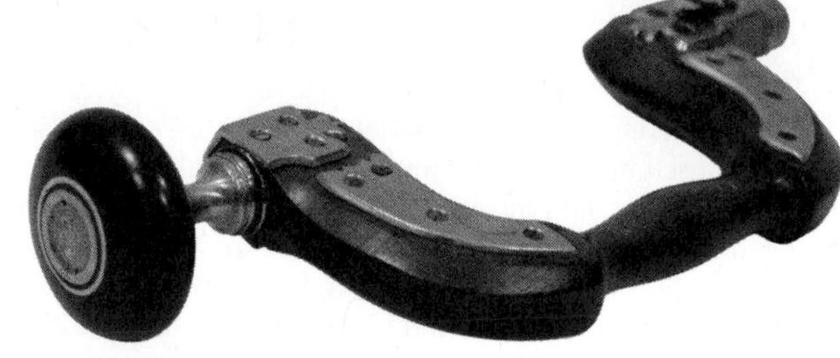

Framed brace. William Marples, c. 1872, ebony, ivory ring, fine+.................................................. **$385**

## DRILLS

Bench drill press. Goodell-Pratt Co., holds breast drill, screws to bench with tripod base, auto advance, fine......................... **$385**

Pistol-grip hand drill. Stanley No. 610, second Sweet Hart, type 1, no bit caddy, hand and gear wheel redesigned before production began, possibly unique, japanning and paint 95%, fine. .............................. **$770**

Lens drill for eyeglasses. For drilling screw holes in lens, bench mounted, hand cranked, gold and black finishes 95%, includes set of old glasses for demonstrating drill, fine. .................................................... **$126**

## EDGED TOOLS

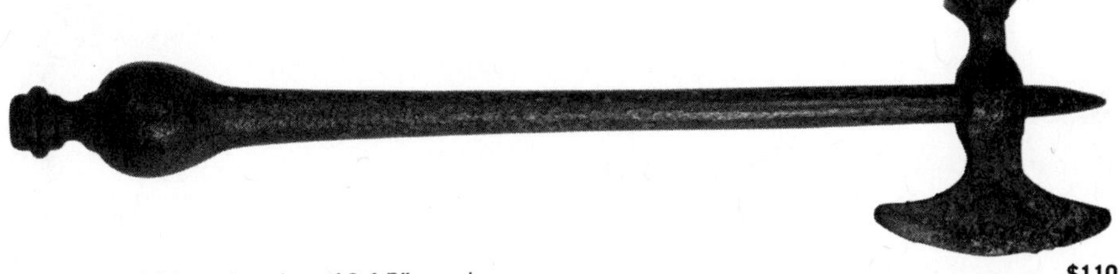

Ax. Possibly 16th century, iron, 10-1/2", good.......... **$110**

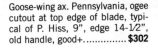

Goose-wing ax. Pennsylvania, ogee cutout at top edge of blade, typical of P. Hiss, 9", edge 14-1/2", old handle, good+.......... **$302**

Drawshave. Stanley, fine...... **$825**

Mortise chisels. Atkin & Son, set of eight, 1/8" to 5/8", unused, fine.......... **$1,595**

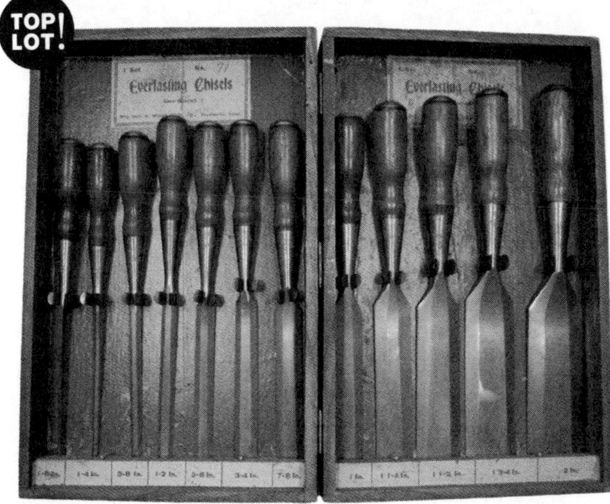


Everlasting chisels. C.E. Wood Tool Co. No. 71, Plantsville, Conn., set of 12, unused, original oak box, fine.......... **$13,750**

## HAMMERS & MALLETS

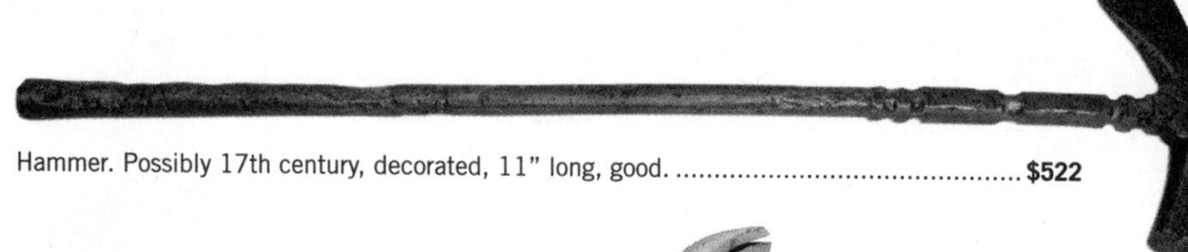

Hammer. Possibly 17th century, decorated, 11" long, good. .......................................... $522

Hammer. 18th century, possibly earlier, ring design, turned wood handle possibly original, one claw broken, good................................................ $302

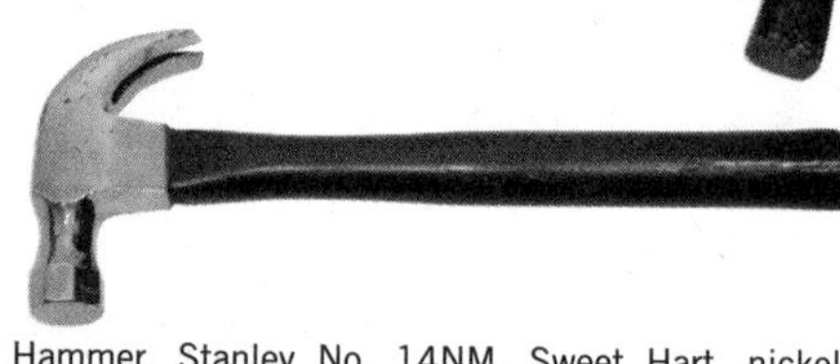

Hammer. Stanley No. 14NM, Sweet Hart, nickel-plated, mahogany handle, plating 97%, face may never have been struck, price on end of handle ($2.10), fine. ............................................. $632

## LEVELS & INCLINOMETERS

Combination inclinometer level. Valentine, dial marked "Made in Oldham," walnut, level vial, 9", brass plate and sole, good+. ........................... $385

Corner level. Davis & Cook, japanning 90% and bright, fine................. $935

Inclinometer. Champion, Philadelphia, R.I. Frambes patent, Sept. 2, 1884, graduating plumb and level, pendulum-type dial with graduated scale, slide locks pendulum in place, bevel glass face, hang hole, 16", good.................................................... $1,760

Inclinometer. Davis Level & Tool Co., 12", machining marks on rails 99%, japanning 96%, fine. ...................................... $220

Level. Fitchburg Level Co., Webb patent, Dec. 7, 1886, 12", one dry vial, japanning 85%, good+. ...................................... $143

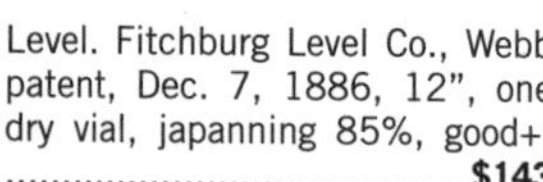

Machinist's level. Stanley No. 45, early eagle trademark, early carryover from the Hall & Knapp, sold iron w/ brass top plate, acorn finials, 8-1/2", fine....... $605

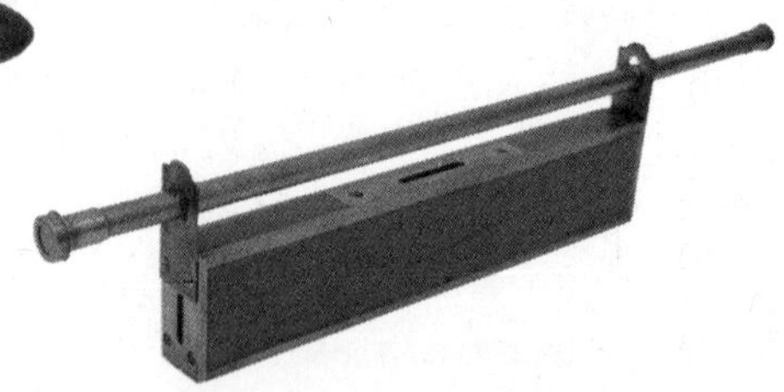

►Sighting level. Stratton Brothers, brass bound, rosewood level, brass sighting tube on top, brass escutcheon for tripod on bottom, base level 10", good+. . $220

## PLANES, ROUTERS, & SCRAPERS

Beading plane. Union No. 44, handled, 1⁄4", no rust, good. .......................................................... **$2,420**

Bench plane. F.M. Bailey patent, April 16, 1889, No. 4 size, marked on iron, fine. ........................... **$962**

Bench plane. Union No. XO, smoother, No. 1 size, vertical post adjustment, japanning 90%, fine. .... **$3,630**

Block plane. Henry Foss patent, Feb. 6, 1877, No. 2, adjustable cutter and mouth, rosewood palm rest on end of two-piece cap, japanning 95%, good.. **$4,180**

Bench plane. L. Bailey patent, July 13, 1858, No. 1 size, marked on adjuster nut, vertical post, one of only two known, tote has couple of edge chips and hairline crack, solid back lever cap has two minor chips, japanning 90%, good+. ................................**$28,600**

Bench plane. Stanley, Sweet Hart, original box with some minor wear, label scuffed on one corner and faded, fine. ................................................ **$4,400**

Block plane. Stanley No. 120 prototype, Stanley Model Shop No. 58, folded steel body Traut & Richards patent, Oct. 5, 1875, Liberty Bell adjustment Traut & Richards patent, April 18, 1876, lever cap redesigned Bailey patent, rosewood button, cap possibly early knuckle-cap design, unused, some dirt, fine. ............................................................ **$742**

Patented plane. Foster turntable plane, smoother, frog rotates to adjust the angle of the iron, japanning 96%, wood fine, marked "101" and "Jan. 20, 07" in the bed, fine. ............................................ **$2,200**

Carriage maker's plow plane. S. Courcelles No. 110A, Paris, fruitwood, brass plate with maker mark on side, screw arm, 6-1/2", good+. .............................. **$165**

Combination plane. Preston, bull nose, fenced rabbet, chamfer, three fences (one rabbet, two chamfer), plating 96%, wood box with slide lid, fine ............................................................. **$1,210**

Corner-rounding plane. Stanley No. 144 1/4, patent applied for, japanning 94%, fine. .................... **$715**

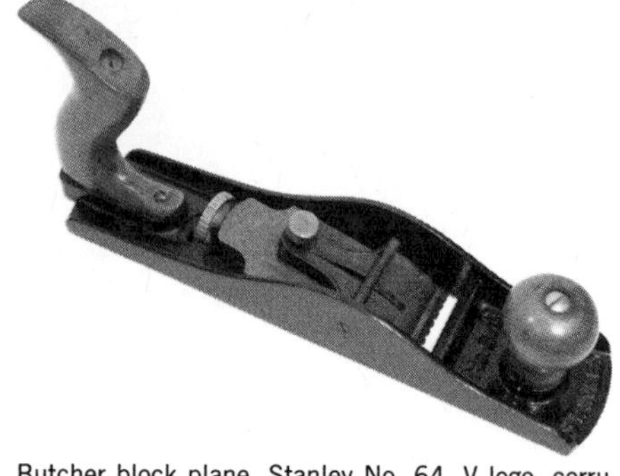

Butcher block plane. Stanley No. 64, V logo, corrugated cutter, japanning 100%, fine+. ........... **$2,860**

Circular plane. L. Bailey No. 13, first type manufactured by Bailey before March 28, 1871, patent, 1867 Bailey patent-date stamp on cutter and cap, Bailey 1858 and 1867 patent-date stamps on solid adjuster nut, banjo spring on lever cap, japanning 98%, fine ................................................................. **$1,870**

Crown molder. I. Walton, double stamped by maker, yellow birch, round top wedge and iron, offset tote, 3-3/4" wide, 12" long, fine, ........................ **$3,300**

Dovetail plane. Stanley No. 444, four cutters in original box, both spur blocks, color instructions, plating 99%, original box, labels nearly full, fine. ..... **$1,870**

Infill plane. Norris No. 1A, early type, adjustable panel, "Patent Adjustable" on screw cap, dovetailed, rosewood infill, gunmetal cap, 17-1/2", Norris iron 2-1/2", fine. .................................................. **$880**

Jack plane. Sandusky No. 13SC, semisteel, new, original box near mint, fine. ........................ **$3,080**

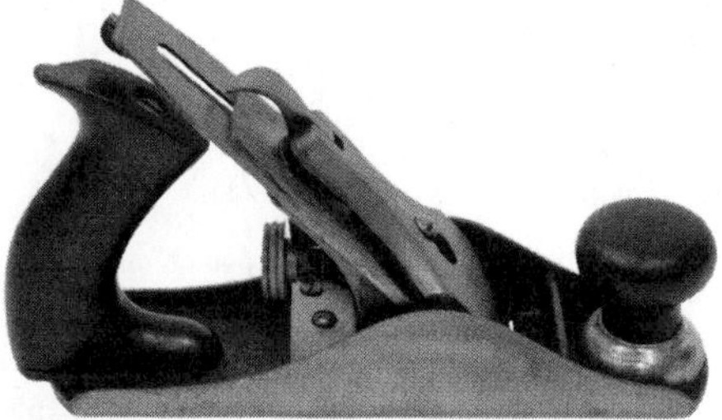

Infill plane. Carter, London, modern, blade and cap marked, gunmetal jointer, steel sole, dark rosewood infill, dovetailed, Cupid's bow dovetails, 281/2" long, iron 2-1/2", two made, fine. ......................... **$5,500**

Jack plane. Challenge, patented, Sept. 11, 1883, body and handle cast as one unit, adjustable cutter (screw) passes through slot in body, 15", japanning 90%, good ............................................................ **$2,915**

Panel-raiser plane. E. Clark, Middleboro, yellow birch, fenced, stopped, round top skew wedge, fine. **$2,860**

Plane. C. Jensen, patented, May 14, 1872, marked with "C. Jensen" and patent date, double bodies adjust on two threaded rods, slitter adjusts to width, fence on one side for filletster work, few thread chips, small chip at one adjustment washer, fine..... **$2,200**

◀ Plane. O. Longval, oiler, patented, March 22, 1892, modified Stanley No. 4, double set of oiling ports, front knob behind frog oilers, top of knob marked "Pat. Apl'd For. O Longval," some roughness on top of tote, good+.................................... **$577**

Plane. W.S. Loughborogh, Rochester, N.Y., patented May 10, 1859, filletster plane, marked on side of handle, complete, good+. . **$3,190**

Plane. "The Phillips Plough Plane Co. Boston. Patented Aug. 31, 1867. Cast by the Metallic Compression Casting Co. No. 46 Congress St. Boston" engraved on skate, rosewood, bronze, three known, probably special casting manufactured for presentation, fine.............................**$39,600**

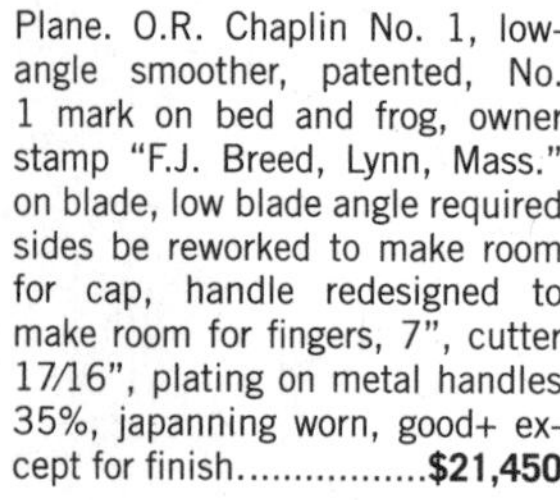

Plane. O.R. Chaplin No. 1, low-angle smoother, patented, No. 1 mark on bed and frog, owner stamp "F.J. Breed, Lynn, Mass." on blade, low blade angle required sides be reworked to make room for cap, handle redesigned to make room for fingers, 7", cutter 17/16", plating on metal handles 35%, japanning worn, good+ except for finish................**$21,450**

Plane. Stanley No. 41, Miller patent, hook type, oval trademark, perfect tote, filletster bed missing nicker, japanning 90%, good+. ....................................**$18,150**

Plane. Metallic Plane Co., patented, adjustable filletster, early cast-iron fence held to body w/ single screw, complete, good+ .................................... **$1,705**

Plane. Ohio Tool Co., smoother, Morris patent, waffle bottom, cast-iron body, beech infill, Ohio Tool Co. iron 2-1/4" wide, good. .................................... **$1,650**

Plane. Rodier patent, smoother, wavy sides and sole, cam adjusts pitch of frog for depth of cut, 9-1/2", japanning 90%, fine. .................................... **$1,155**

## RULES, SQUARES, & GAUGES

Bevel square. St. Johnsbury Tool Co., double blades, rosewood and brass handle with locking screw in base, blades 6", good. ................................ **$1,265**

Boxwood rule. Stanley, marked with "Rule & Level Co." trademark and "Special", special rope caliper, wide English type, graduated to 4" in English layout, traces of original finish, fine............................ **$990**

Combination marking gauge. O. Brown & T.F. Berry, patented, July 7, 1868, six-sided, brass slides on five sides, boxwood set screws lock five slides in place, few chips in slide tracks, good. .................... **$3,190**

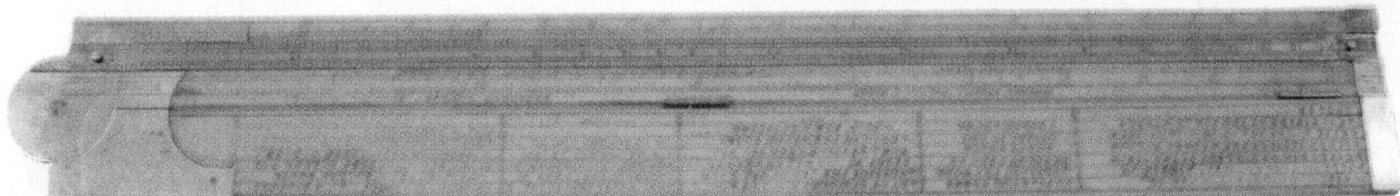

Ivory rule. William Slater, Bolton (designer), Aston & Mander, London (makers), cotton spinner's rule, gunther's slide, tables and instructions for cotton spinning, including revolution of spindles, counts of yarn, draught of mules, two-fold, 2', German silver, arch joint, edge marked, light yellowing, good+. ...............................**$715**

Mortise gauge. J.L. Pringle patent, Oct. 29, 1907, patent assigned to Union Manufacturing Co., Stanley acquired Union and dropped this tool, twist-locking stem w/ mortise slide, four marking points, slitting knife, fine. ............................................... **$2,640**

Roller slide rule. Thatcher calculating instrument, manufactured by K&E, large size, wood case, tables and scales nearly perfect, photocopies of patent and manuals, fine. .............................................. **$935**

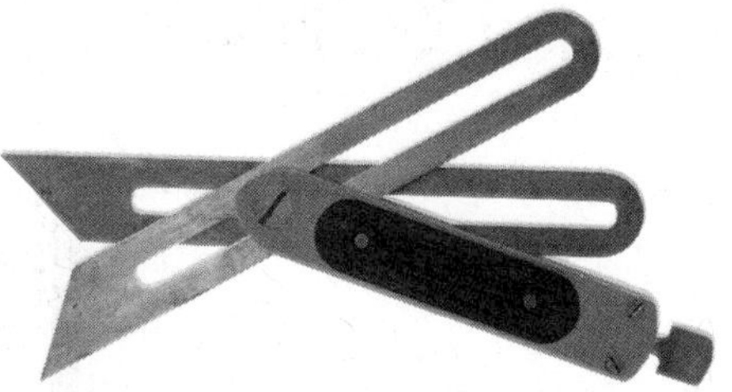

Square. St. Johnsbury Tool Co., patented, June 14, 1870, double-bladed bevel, locking screw at end of brass handle, rosewood infill, 6", good+........... **$935**

Slitting gauge. Kinney patent, May 26, 1880, rotary, adjustment wheel below handle controls notched cutter wheel, plating 90%, fine. ........................ **$3,740**

Tape rule. Stanley No. 7566, advertising, The Stanley Works, Bed Fasts Furniture & Cabinet Hardware, New Britain, Conn., fine+. .......................................... **$242**

Trammels. Heavy cast brass, star on one side, slash on other, steel points, 9", fine. ................... **$330**

◀Traveler. Wood spoke wheel, red paint, yellow and black pinstriping, turned wood handle, 23", good+. ................................................ **$308**

## SAWS

Handsaw, Henry Disston No. 43, combination saw, rule, square, level and scribe. ...................... **$1,815**

Handsaw, Woodrough & McParlin, with carved panther head. .................................................. **$2,310**

Saw, wrought iron and hardwood, possibly for stair work. ............................................................ **$193**

Ice saw, Henry Disston & Sons. ........................................ **$132**

Saw, turning, with chain and gear mechanism. ....................... **$187**

## MULTI-TOOLS

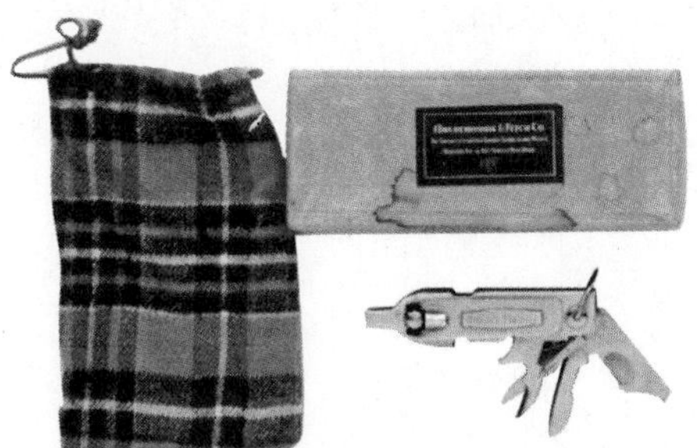

Walton's Thumb multi-tool sold by Abercrombie & Fitch, marked as made by Hank Roberts, one of the first multi-tools offered, with tweezers, scissors, bottle opener, etc. Marked with serial number A17787, this stainless-steel tool comes complete with plaid bag and very good plus-condition box with A&F label. .......................................................... **$200**

Multi-tool, cast iron, functions as pry bar, hammer, hook, and wrench, 6-1/4" l. ............................. **$62**

19th c. multi-wrench, embossed "MOORE & KLING, BOSTON MASS," 8-1/4" l. .................. **$45**

W.H. Thayer cast iron universal tool, household combination tool has multiple applications as a holder for hot items in the kitchen, meat tenderizer, and trivet signed W. H. Thayer and patent date May 24, 1881, 5-3/4" l. ............. **$140**
*William Bunch Auctions & Appraisals*

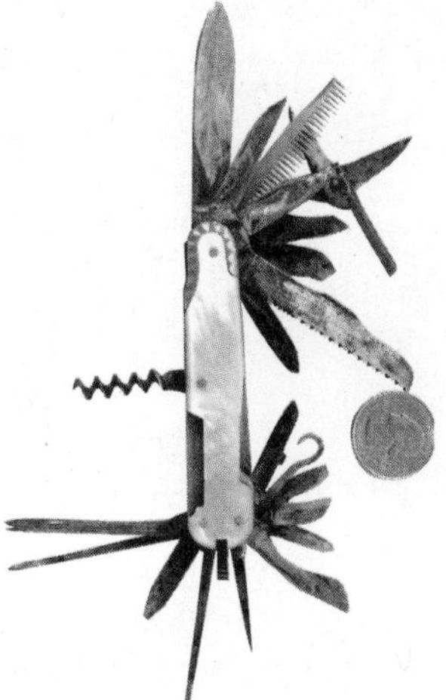

Multi-tool pocket knife, made by A. Feist & Co., Germany, featuring 21 blades with tweezers and toothpick plus moustache comb, triangular awl, scissors, saw, corkscrew, fingernail file and nail cleaner, sewing needle, screwdrivers, and other sundry blades. Large blade is marked "A. FEIST & CO. SOLINGEN" on one side and "GERMANY" on reverse, mother-of-pearl handle, 3-1/4" l. when closed, 1" w., circa 19th c.. ............................. **$565**

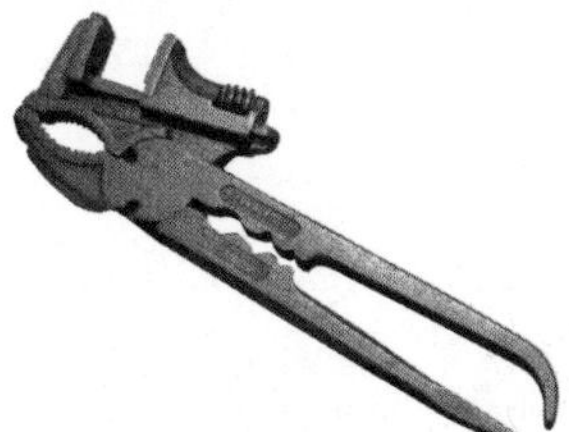

Multi-tool, embossed "Never Stall," combination adjustable wrench, pliers, crimping tool, screwdriver, vise and more..... **$10**

Multi-tool featuring glass cutter, bottle opener, screwdriver and pry, 5-3/4" l. ............................. **$10**

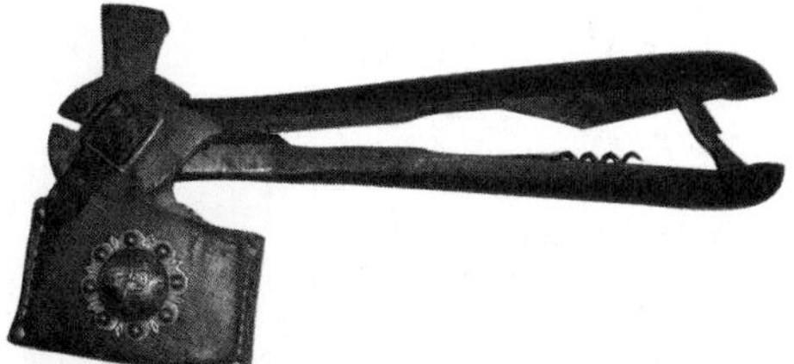

Haynes-Bates Mfg. Co. combination multi-tool hammer/corkscrew, patent granted July 4, 1905. Multi-tool is hammer/axe/hatchet with knife, two blades, corkscrew, bottle-cap opener, screwdriver, and wrench hidden inside. ............................................. **$892**

# 10 Things You Didn't Know About John Deere Collectibles

1. Vintage John Deere advertising literature from the mid-1800s includes the personal signature of one of its late presidents, Charles Deere, who signed all advertising and promotional literature.

2. A great resource devoted to sharing news and community among John Deere collectors is The Plowshare, a quarterly newsletter. Subscribe at JohnDeere.com, http://www.deere.com/en_US/attractions/plowshare/index.html, or 815-652-4551.

3. John Deere (Deere & Company) is opening a new tractor and engine museum in Waterloo, Iowa, by mid-2012.

4. John Deere was at the forefront of the nation's bicycle craze of the late 1800s with the Deere Leader, Deere Roadster, and the Moline Special. Originally priced at $50 in the 1900s, today the limited number of these bicycles, many made with wooden wheels, are valued at $1,800 to $3,000 each.

5. "Nothing Runs Like a Deere" was first used in John Deere snowmobile ads in the 1970s before becoming the mantra for all things Deere.

6. A series of John Deere video games allows players to plant crops, raise livestock, manage fields, and even buy farming equipment.

7. As an episode of the History Channel's hit show "American Pickers" demonstrated, one of the most sought-after of all Deere gear are owner and operator manuals – truly evergreen Deere.

8. John Deere is among the most popular brands people choose for a tattoo.

9. In addition to establishing his company, John Deere's founder also served as president of the National Bank of Moline, Ill., library director, and Moline's mayor.

10. Vintage John Deere matchbooks can fetch anywhere from $20 to $125.

*Toni Rahn*

A Vindex John Deere 'D' tractor, circa 1928, sold for **$2,000** at the November 2008 Bertoia Auction in Vineland, New Jersey.
*LiveAuctioneers*

# Toys

The American antique toy market remains one of the bright spots among collecting categories. Longtime collectors are deciding it's time to pass decades' worth of accumulation to a new generation, and those fine collections continue to lead the market. Wonderful objects are now available to own and collectors are digging deep for rare items: The first offering of the Dick Claus collection of antique toy boats sold for $1.8 million in May 2012. In February 2011 pop culture collectors set Hake's Americana & Collectibles Auction No. 202 as the highest-grossing auction in the company's 45-year history.

As collectors are increasingly drawn to rarity, it means a softening in values among low-end and mid-range items. Some auction houses are starting to offer group lots like never before in an effort to sell lesser-quality items. Luckily, lots like these offer newcomers a chance to own an instant collection of toys without having to scour a dozen flea markets in the process. This trend shows no signs of slowing in 2013 and beyond. This serves as a lesson to toy collectors: Pay close attention to trends in pop culture and take note of your rarest items. If you are serious about building an investment-grade collection of antique toys, then research your next purchase, pass on the common stuff, and spend your money buying the best examples you can afford.

*Eric Bradley*

Action figure, Superman Kresge carded figure, 1972, made by Mego, original first issue blister card contains 8" t. posable figure in polyester suit with nylon trunks, item No. 1300, comes with custom acrylic case, mint from the Benjamin Holcomb collection with a signed COA. .................... **$948**
*Hakes Americana*

Cast toy, Early American cast iron toy in burnt orange trimmed in olive green, gold and black lettering with private label Abraham Straus, pulled by two dray horses and driver, 1895, American, 16" l. ............... **$4,375**
*Bonhams*

Model, "Apollo Lunar Module," circa 1960s, manufactured by Precise Models, Inc. for Grumman, two-piece injection-molded plastic model made prior to the Apollo 11 moon landing, module removes from base and separates into ascent and descent stages with numerous tiny projecting parts, 6-1/4" t. module on 10-1/4" base ..................... **$345**
*Hakes Americana*

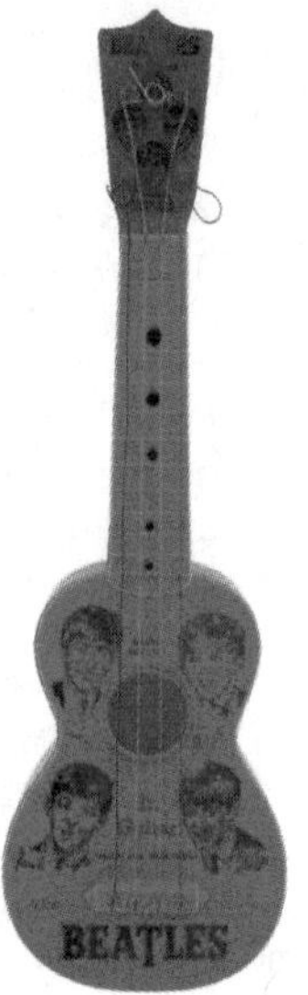


Toy guitar, "The Beatles Jr. Guitar," copyright 1964, made by Mastro, hard plastic toy with all original strings and four-page slick paper instruction folder, 14-1/2" l. .................................... **$290**
*Hakes Americana*

"Betty Boop" wood jointed figure, circa 1930s, made by Cameo, standing 7" high, head has applied decal face and leatherette-like curls, rare ................. **$1,222**
*Hakes Americana*

Action figures, set of boxed figures from the "Bonanza" television series, depicting Ben, Hoss, and Little Joe Cartwright, 1966, made by American Character, figures are 8" t., boxes measure 3-3/4" x 10-3/4" x 2". Accessory pieces still in original bags ........................................... **$759**
*Hakes Americana*

Toy ring, for Buck Rogers Solar Scouts "repeller ray ring," 1936, used as a Cream of Wheat and newspaper premium, at ring's center of the rocket ship on face is an emerald green faceted stone, mint, scarce. .................. **$2,530**
*Hakes Americana*

Pull toy, "Buddy Bronc" by Fisher Price, 1938, No. 430, wooden with applied paper labels on two sides, Buddy goes up and down, clicking noise is produced, toy was only made for one year, 3-1/2" x 8-3/8" x 8" t. overall, mint condition .................................. **$313**
*Hakes Americana*

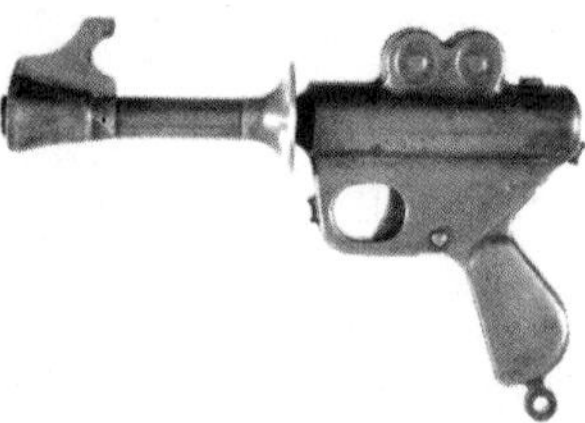

Toy pistol, "Buck Rogers Rocket Pistol XZ-31," 1934, made by Daisy, gun style was produced in two sizes, larger 9-2/5" long variety shown here, working example in fine condition producing a loud pop when fired .................. **$306**
*Hakes Americana*

►Wind-up toy, "The Climbing Fireman," Marx, circa 1930s, legs move up and down allowing fireman to climb ladder, accompanied by heavily worn box, 7-3/4" . **$158**
*Hakes Americana*

Tinplate clockwork "Eppie Hogg in Auto," made by Nifty.......................................................... **$6,900**
*Bertoia Auctions*

Pull toy, highly unusual German squeak toy on wheels, late 19th c., with a mother and two chicks feeding, 10-1/2" h., 11" w. Provenance: Collection of Elie Nadelman; Lincoln Kirsteins.............. **$5,214**
*Pook & Pook, Inc.*

"Howdy Doody Marionette," cloth/wood/composition, circa 1948-1950, made by Peter Puppet Playthings Inc., and copyright Bob Smith, 3-1/4" by 5-1/2" x 15-3/4" with 17" box with lid containing instructions for using "Unitrol" (one-piece controller) included. ................................................................ **$158**
*Hakes Americana*

Hubley Ingersoll Rand cast-iron truck..........**$13,800**
*Bertoia Auctions*

Bing "King Edward" clockwork painted-tin gunboat ................................................................ **$8,625**
*Bertoia Auctions*

Wind-up toy, "Marx Big Parade," circa 1920s, tin litho street scene includes soldiers marching under bridges marked with patriotic decorations with reviewing stand and skyscrapers in background, 24" l. ................................................................ **$340**
*Hakes Americana*

Wind-up, German articulated lithographed row toy, first part 20th c., toy depicts lithographed crew, clockwork action.............. **$3,125**
*Bonhams*

Wind-up toy, "Li'l Abner and His Dogpatch Band," 1946, made by Unique Art Mfg. Co. and copyright United Features Syndicate, Inc., tin litho toy with built-in key, consists of piano unit and four separate figures that attach to it, figures are of Abner, Daisy Mae seated in front of the piano, Pappy Yokum as drummer, and Mammy Yokum on piano top holding baton. All figures move when wound, including Abner who dances, 5" x 9" overall, 8" t. .................. **$505**
*Hakes Americana*

Distler Mickey Mouse Hurdy Gurdy with miniature dancing Minnie Mouse ................................ **$8,050**
*Bertoia Auctions*

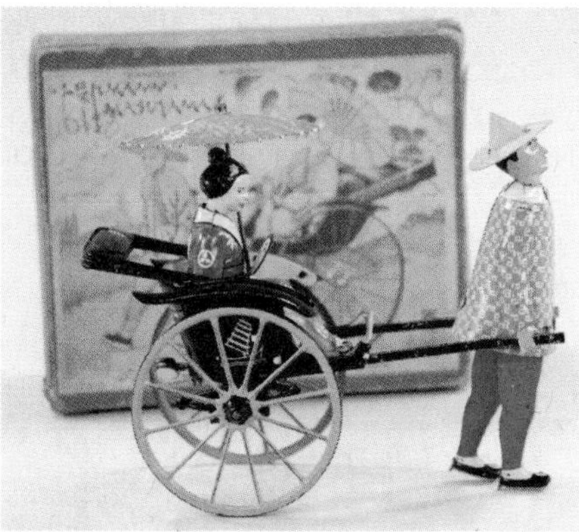

Lehmann tinplate wind-up "Masuyama" ....... **$6,900**
*Bertoia Auctions*

Wind-up toy, Mickey and Minnie Mouse on motorcycle, 1930, made by Tipp & Co., Germany, example is complete and all original with no restoration, highly detailed including Tipp logo on the gas tank, visible motor, tires marked "Dunlop Cord/935x135," considered to be the most desirable Disney toy, not only coveted by collectors of Disneyana but motorcycle and wind-up collectors; fewer than 10 of this toy are known in all original condition, 2-1/2" x 9-1/2" x 6-1/2" t. .................................................. **$28,750**
*Hakes Americana*

"Mickey Mouse Circus" pull toy, circa 1931, distributed by Borgfeldt, features a pair of 4" t. wood figures of Mickey and Minnie, each complete with string tail, between them is Wienie, a dachshund that appeared in several early shorts including "Plane Crazy." Figures are attached to a tin litho platform base with wood wheels, and as toy moves forward, the figures do somersaults, 4-1/4" x 11" x 6" t. ...................... **$747**
*Hakes Americana*

Wind-up toy, "Mickey Mouse No. 2 Paddle Boat," circa 1930s, 12" l. boat with wood hull with metal top and metal strip on bottom for balance in water, tin litho Mickey figure from the waist up holding metal oars, rare .............. **$4,174**
*Hakes Americana*

Toy lantern, depicting Mickey Mouse's pet Pluto the dog, circa 1950s, made by Line Mar, mostly tin litho battery operated with glass mid-section containing the original light bulb, eyes are plastic, tongue, tail and ears are rubber, 6-3/4" t. ....................... **$94**
*Hakes Americana*

Mickey Mouse "Roly-Poly" figure, circa 1930s, made of celluloid, weighted bottom, interior has bell that rings as toy move about, movable arms, 3-3/4" t. ............ **$126**
*Hakes Americana*

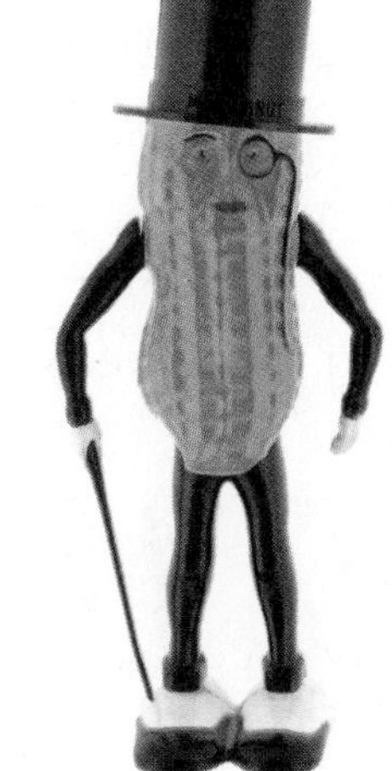

Wind-up toy, "Mr. Peanut" walking figure, circa 1950s, tall hard plastic with built-in key on back, 8-1/2" .............................. **$285**
*Hakes Americana*

Blocks, "New Animal ABC" boxed set of alphabet blocks, circa late 1880s, made in Germany by unknown maker, 9" x 14-1/8" x 1-1/4", wood box covered with paper labels has litho lid art of two tigers in poster design, box contains 26 wood blocks, front of each has image of animal or bird with its name matching letter on block, each measuring 1-7/8" x 2-1/8" ........................................................................ **$361**
*Hakes Americana*

Motorcycle toy, "Policeman on Motorcycle," circa 1950s, made by Masudaya Toys, Japan, tin litho battery-operated toy travels in a circle as the headlight lights up. After traveling a short distance, it comes to a stop and the policeman is designed to swing his right leg up and over the cycle and dismount. He then gets back on and continues forward. 4-1/2" x 11-1/2" x 8" ...................... **$423**
*Hakes Americana*

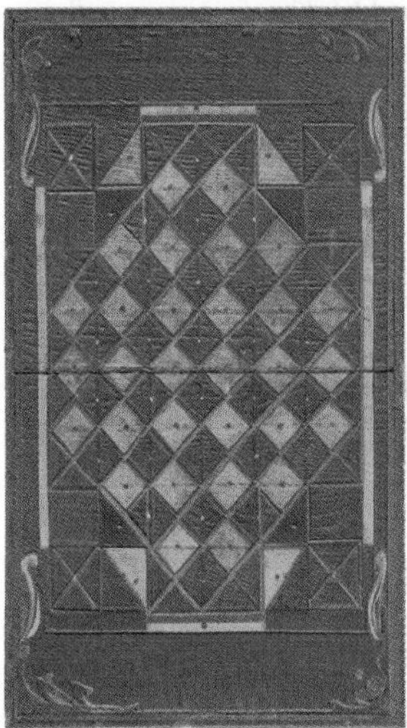

Painted double-sided game board, early 20th c., 20" x 11-1/2".. **$577**
*Pook & Pook, Inc.*

Painted double-sided pine game board, late 19th c., 13" x 13" ........................................ **$237**
*Pook & Pook, Inc.*

►Rattles, set of two jester baby rattles, late 19th c., one with a painted tin face, 19" h., the other composition with a squeaker, 13-1/2" h. ......................... **$326**
*Pook & Pook, Inc.*

PEZ candy dispenser depicting Pinocchio and Jiminy Cricket pair, circa 1960s, made by Pez in Austria and marked as such on stems, 3.9 stem on red hat Pinocchio, 3.4 on Jiminy. Pinocchio is later "B" style with black plastic hair while earlier versions had painted hair. .................................. **$168**
*Hakes Americana*

Wind-up toy, war bomber, circa late 1940s, made by Marx, plane has plated engine front and props and realistic depictions of machine gunners, working with the two guns mounted on wings emit sparks as plane moves forward, 18" w. x 13" l. .................. **$728**
*Hakes Americana*

Sturditoy pressed-steel U.S. Mail truck .............................. **$7,475**
*Bertoia Auctions*

Wind-up toy, "Tut Tut" figure produced 1903-1935, made by Lehmann, tin litho with built-in key, toy works and car travels around changing direction as a bellows mechanism produces sound as if the man is blowing the horn, 6-3/4", mostly original with some paint touchups, classic Lehmann toy. ..................... **$600**

# The Classic Superman Wind-Up Toy

In just two short years since his debut in Action Comics No. 1, the comic book character Superman was quickly used to sell toys to pre-World War II children. One of the more popular win-up toys is the Superman Roll Over Plane. The clockwork mechanism allows for the plane to travel forward a short distance before the Superman figure flips the plane over 360 degrees and then repeats this cycle. The tin lithographed toy was issued with four different colored planes: gold, blue, red, and the very scarce silver coloration. The red version (not pictured here) is often found priced at $750 in very good to excellent condition. A silver version once sold on eBay for $4,100.

Wind-up toy, Superman Roll Over Plane, gold version, 1940, Superman Inc. on Superman's cape, tin litho toy with built-in key, primarily gold body, 5-1/2" x 6" x 3-1/2" ............ **$84**
*Hakes Americana*

Wind-up toy, Superman Roll Over Plane, blue version, 1940, Superman Inc. on Superman's cape, tin litho toy with built-in key, this has primarily blue body, 5-1/2" x 6" x 3-1/2" .................................. **$2,024**
*Hakes Americana*

# 10 Things You Didn't Know About Board Games

1. The oldest backgammon game was discovered in 2004 in the Burnt City in Sistan-Baluchistan province in southeastern Iran. The 5,000-year-old game is called Nard in Persian.

2. Mancala (similarly Wari, Gabata, Hus) was first played without a board; players used holes made in the sand or soil and played with pebbles or seeds. Mancala is a game of mathematical skill and may be the oldest game in existence.

3. George S. Parker founded Parker Brothers in Salem, Massachusetts, in 1883 at the tender age of 16. The company was the first to specialize in games offering simple fun rather than emphasizing morals or values.

4. Milton Bradley is often credited with launching the board game industry in the United States. He set up his first color lithography shop in Springfield, Massachusetts, in 1860.

5. There have been hundreds of versions of Monopoly produced, including locally themed Monopoly games. The exact number of variations is unknown because Milton Bradley/Hasbro licenses the design rights to smaller companies for custom versions. It is licensed in 103 countries for 37 languag

Though missing the game pieces, this Buck Rogers Game of the 25th Century A.D. sold for **$200** at Dan Morphy Auctions' Jan 29, 2011 sale. Made by Lutz and Sheinkman, marked "1934 Steven Slesinger New York," the lot included the game board and the box top with a couple of side aprons detached but present.

6. Bingo started in 1530 in Italy. It is related to a lotto game named Lo Giuoco del Lotto d Italia. New York toy salesman Edwin S. Lowe transformed the popular carnival game Beano (named for the dried beans used to cover a numbered grid) to the recognizable bingo.

7. Eleanor Abbott (while recuperating from polio in the 1940s) invented games to help sick children deal with endless hours of bed rest. She invented Candy Land for children who had not yet learned to read. The game has been continually produced since 1949.

8. In 2005, French artist/jeweler Bernard Maquin directed 30 craftsmen who spent 4,500 hours (and a total of $500,000) creating the Royal Diamond Chess set. The gold, platinum, and jewel-encrusted set carries a retail price tag of $7.8 million.

This list was inspired by the Donal Markey toy auction, in which an early hand-painted wood Monopoly game board was estimated to sell for **$3,500** to **$4,500**, but sold for **$23,000**.

9. The world's largest board game is The War Game: World War II, by Jeffry Stein of Burbank, California. The board measures 6 feet, 5 inches long by 3 feet, 2 inches wide and weighs 13.8 pounds.

10. The fastest time to complete Operation was 21.87 seconds. The feat was achieved by Maharoof Decibels of India at the Guinness World Records Pavilion in Dubai on Nov. 28, 2008.

***Karen Knapstein***

*Sources: Strong Museum of Play (www.museumofplay.org); LiveAuctioners.com, Iranian Cultural Heritage News Agency; wikianswers.com; bingohistory.org; most-expensive.net; www.ccgs.com; www.guinnessworldrecords.com.*

# 10 Things You Didn't Know About Japanese Toys & Robots

1. Toys were being made in Japan before World War II broke out, but it was after the war ended that Japan seized the opportunity to use industries like toy manufacturing to strengthen its struggling economy.

2. The first toy robot (a windup) is believed to be Japan's Robot Lilliput – believed by some to have been made as early as 1938, while others think it was in the post-war1940s. This was quickly followed by the unveiling of the more well-known Atomic Robot Man. This robot was given out at the New York Sci-fi convention in 1950.

3. A mid-century Masudaya Target Robot, in excellent condition, sold for $23,600 at auction (double pre-auction estimates).

4. The design of many Japanese robots of the 1950s was significantly influenced by the world's fascination with space exploration at the peak of the Space Race.

5. For collectors, toy robots bring their own challenge of authentication – as many robots made in Japan have an American company logo – which doesn't accurately identify who made it.

6. In 1950, prior to the electronics and toy push, only 1 percent of products imported to the United States were made in Japan. In 2010, 6.4 percent of U.S. imports came from Japan – with automobiles topping the list.

7. Japan's toy robot makers were "going green" long before it became the movement it is today – and at the time it was out of economic necessity that they used tin cans cast off by plants to make smaller toy robots.

8. An ultra active and superbly informative forum dedicated to Japanese toy robots is robotjapan.proboards.com

9. One of the pioneer companies of Japanese toy robot production was the Tokyo Toy Industry Group.

10. Japanese toy makers were the first to use battery-operated motors in their toys, taking toys beyond clockwork operation.

*Toni Rahn*

Standing 12 inches high, this robot, marked "Made in Japan," has a host of special features. As the spaceman walks, his chest pops down and a video action screen appears, then closes. In working condition, it was offered at **$125** at a July 2010 sale by Premier Auction Galleries of Willoughby, Ohio.
*Artfact.com*

This tin plate circa 1960s Robotank-Z space robot is fully functional with flashing lights and retracting machine guns. In mint condition with original box, the robot is marked "Made by T.N. Made in Japan." It sold for **$478** in the March 1, 2011 sale by Mullock's Specialist Sporting Auctioneers.
*Artfact.com*

# Valentines

According to legend, the first Valentine greeting was sent by St. Valentine himself. Actually, there are at least three "St. Valentines," each clamoring to be recognized as the day's patron saint, but here's the most romantic story:

A 3rd century clergyman, this Valentine was imprisoned for performing marriages in defiance of Emperor Claudius II, who'd decreed that all men of military age must remain single. While in prison, Valentine fell in love with his jailer's daughter, declaring his feelings in a note signed "from your Valentine." Since Valentine was eventually beheaded, the story lacks a happy ending, but nonetheless, a tradition was born.

The oldest-known written valentine dates from 1415, a poem the Duke of Orleans sent to his wife, while imprisoned in the Tower of London. Shortly thereafter, King Henry V began sending valentines to his favorite, Catherine of Valois, although Henry hired a professional poet to do the actual writing.

By the 1700s, kings and dukes weren't the only ones dispensing valentines. Each Feb. 14, handwritten "Valentine" messages made their way across all levels of society, often accompanied by small gifts. The dawn of mass printing and inexpensive postal rates meant that, by the early 1800s, just about anyone who wanted to could send (and, hopefully, receive) a valentine.

In the 1840s, ready-made valentines swept the United States, thanks to Esther A. Howland (now hailed by grateful retailers as the "Mother of the Valentine"). Her creations were quite lavish, incorporating ribbon, lace, and colorful bits of material.

Nowadays, the Greeting Card Association notes that over one billion valentines are sent annually, vs. 2.5 billion Christmas cards; 85 percent of all valentines are purchased by women.

Valentines are increasingly popular with today's collectors, who enjoy their colorful visuals, whimsical themes, and, in some cases, varied functions (for instance, pop-up or moving-part valentines). Displayed singly or framed in a montage, vintage valentines add a touch of retro charm to any décor, and are guaranteed to rekindle plenty of nostalgic memories.

**Unillustrated Price Listings**

"A Valentine's Wish," lace heart, foil arrow, white ribbon, 1950s .......... **$10-$12**
Candy box heart, dogs in top hats, 1939 .......... **$10-$12**
Cupid, 1908 postcard .......... **$10-$15**
Cupid and lady, 1908 postcard .......... **$10-$12**
Kids at clothesline, "Just Hanging Around," 1939 .......... **$5-$10**
"Mother" bear cub storybook valentines, 1950s .......... **$10-$12**
Sailor/tramp, "I'll Knot Let You Say No," 1940s .......... **$10-$12**

Aviation-themed child's valentine, 1930s.... **$15-$20**

"Comic Dutch" 1913 postcard, city of origin (Hastings, Nebraska) stamped in .......... **$15-S20**

Black cat, single-sheet child's valentine, 1930s ................ **$5-$10**

Bluebirds on heart, 1940s .................................... **$10-$15**

Girl at mailbox, 1940s ..... **$15-20**

Jean Harlow illustration, 1930s .................................... **$15-$20**

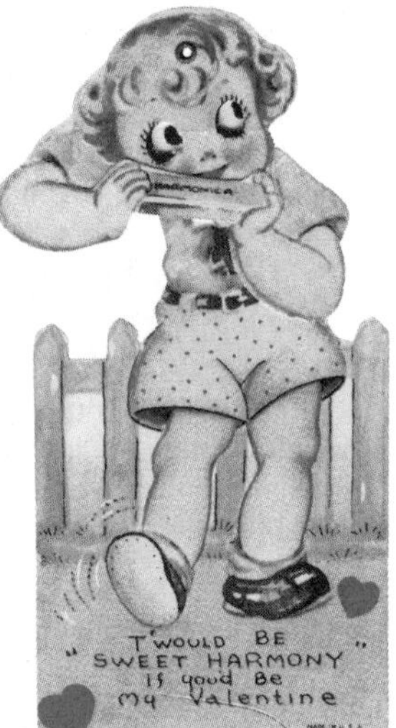

Harmonica player "mechanical" valentine, moving arms and eyes, 1930s .......................... **$15-$20**

"Pal in the Service," shield motif, 1940s .......................... **$10-$15**

"V for Victory," 1940s.... **$10-$15**

Soda fountain sweethearts, 1914 postcard ....................... **$10-$15**

# Vintage Fashion Accessories

Throughout history, women have adorned themselves with the likes of found objects to create a look or style that is unique to them. Carryall bags and footwear were made from the hides of last night's dinner. It was quickly discovered that the head needed to be protected from the elements, so a good fur pelt became the most ideal source for warmth. In the tropics, raffia or straw hats were fashioned to shield one from the sun.

It was only a matter of time before these utilitarian items would be artistically adapted by the individual wearer, and fashion had begun.

Fashion changes over the next couple millennia were insignificant compared to the past couple of centuries. People were generally clothed in full-length garb with little variation in accessorizing.

It wasn't until the industrial revolution that we had the ability to mass produce items that would affect the buying and selling of fashionable frills. The more a machine could crank out, the less pricey these items became.

Of course, the best hats and shoes continue to be those of the handmade variety, but these goods are justifiably costly and may not be affordable to all. Mass production allows the manufacturer to lower the cost of their goods to the consumer since there is an exceedingly unlimited supply.

Men and women alike utilize the availability of accessories to express their individuality. A businessman carefully chooses his tie so as not to offend his clients, whereas a salesman might choose a loud, showy one to attract customers. A woman of this same status might have a chic designer handbag on her arm or perhaps drape a graceful scarf around her neck.

Some of us prefer to pile on the accoutrements as part of our daily costume with the likes of a pillbox hat, leather gloves, "Vera" designer scarf, or cinch belt. But no matter what your style or mode of fashion, your options are practically limitless when it comes to enhancing your modern or vintage attire.

For more information on vintage fashion, see *Warman's Handbags Field Guide* by Abigail Rutherford, *Vintage Fashion Accessories* by Stacy LoAlbo, and *Warman's Shoes Field Guide* by Caroline Ashleigh.

## EYEWARE

For many years, eyewear was regarded as a necessary evil, with the emphasis on serviceability rather than style. By the mid-20th century, however, consumers were in the mood for something more flattering. In 1930, eyeglasses made their debut in a major New York fashion show, and 1939 saw the arrival of the "Harlequin" frame. This Altina Sanders creation, predecessor of the upswept "cat-eyes" of the 1950s, was the recipient of an America Design award

Then, following World War II, cellulose acetate emerged as an inexpensive, workable frame component, leading to 1948's introduction of the first molded frame. Finally, eyeglass designers could let their imaginations run wild.

Eyewear advertising soon focused on the appeal of glasses as a desirable fashion accessory. Different eye fashions were now specifically geared for work, for play, for dress, and for everything in between. Bausch & Lomb ran an entire campaign based on the premise that "one pair of glasses is

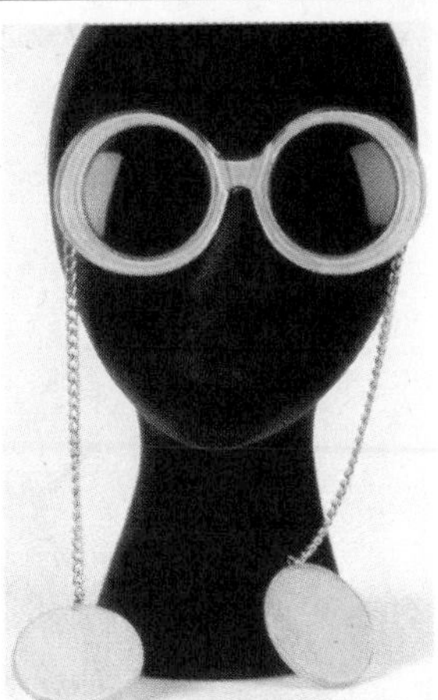

"Earring Chains," yellow or black and white check, 1960s **$120-$160**

not enough," and 1954's "Miss Beauty in Glasses" declared "modern frames for various occasions are as much a part of fashion today as shoes, hats, or jewelry."

Short-lived eyeglass innovations included "radio glasses," which came with a built-in transistor radio; "headband glasses"; "earring glasses"; "eyelash glasses" – even "awning glasses" equipped with mini-shades to ward off raindrops.

Achieving a longer lifespan was the "cat-eye." Although its swooping brow edges were almost uniformly unflattering, the style remains firmly identified with the 1950s. Variations included the "double cat-eye," the "triple cat-eye," and even versions with yellow, blue, or green lenses.

Also popular were "highbrows," among the most imaginative (and most expensive) of eyewear designs. Liberally dotted with rhinestones, pearls, and other decorative accents, highbrows came in a variety of fanciful shapes. Some were built up like sparkling tiaras; others took on the form and patterning of colorful butterflies, or had brow edges reminiscent of soaring bird wings.

Vintage eyeglass frames continue to grow in popularity. Their revival began as far back as the late 1960s, when "The Outasight Co." capitalized on the hippie look by marketing round metal frames from the late 1800s as "the original granny glasses." More recently, those with an eye for recycled fashion acquire period frames, then have the original lenses replaced with a new prescription, or restyled as sun glasses. Today, eyewear of the 1950s and '60s continues to make an extravagant fashion statement all its own.

A comprehensive overview of collectible eyewear is included in *Specs Appeal: Extravagant 1950s & 1960s Eyewear* by Leslie Piña and Donald-Brian Johnson (Schiffer Publishing Ltd., 2001).

*Photos courtesy Dr. Leslie Piña*

"Anne Marie" rhinestone unibrow sunglasses, French ....................................................... **$110-$120**

Glasses, "Highbrow" style, purple with purple lenses, crosshatching with rhinestone decoration.**$300- $400**

Frames, "Highbrow" style with black and rhinestone plumes on clear plastic, by Frame France **$600-$650**

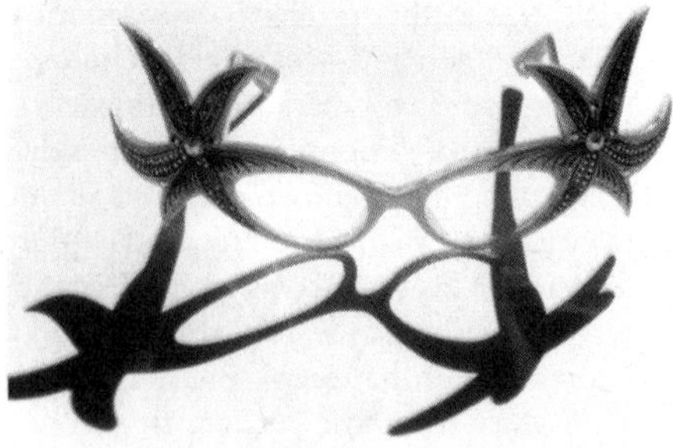

Frames, large star flowers on brow edges with rhinestone decoration .................................... **$300-$400**

Glasses, novelty, "Eyelash" design with fringed brow ........ **$350-$375**

Lorgnette, black with rhinestone decoration **$70-$80**

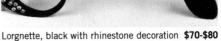

Highbrows, feather shape, black with rhinestone decoration ........ **$275-$300**

Schiaparelli sunglasses, clear yellow-gold frame, fruit clusters ........ **$230-$250**

Sunglasses, "headband" design, tortoiseshell frames ........ **$250-$275**

Sunglasses, novelty, one circular lens, one oval ........ **$35-$50**

Tura, floral vine temples ........ **$275-$325**

## HANDBAGS

The handbag is a 20th-century phenomenon, which, according to Caroline Cox, author of The Handbag: An Illustrated History, parallels "women's status vis-a-vis men" and is directly related to "the increase in woman's social mobility and independence." Today's handbags are not only a useful way to carry necessary items, but also act as a vital extension of a woman's body and a means of self-expression. Whether the purse is a work of art or utilitarian, it makes an enduring statement about its owner and the time period in which it was designed. Furthermore, the handbag has drastically changed women's lives and reflects women's growing sense of empowerment.

14k mesh bag, early 20th century, 5" x 5" ........ **$3,000-$5,000**
*Leslie Hindman Auctioneers*

1930s Bakelite-framed horny crocodile bag with braided handle and claws ........ **$450**
*Vintage with a Twist*

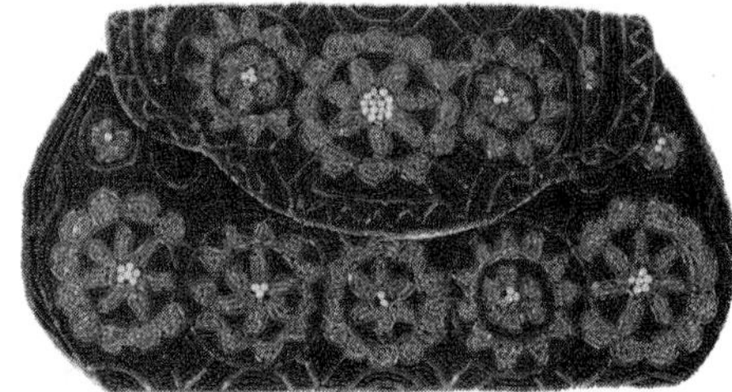

Beaded, French, early 20th century, 7-1/2" x 4" ........ **$200-$400**
*Leslie Hindman Auctioneers*

1940s bamboo frame with floral cloth and felt flowers handbag ........ **$62**
*Bonnie Allen of Somerville Center Antiques*

1940s bag made in France for George Baring, Paris, of kidskin suede with genuine hand-carved conch shell cameos imbedded in the black enameled frame ........ **$395**
*What Once Was*

Beaded, Swedish, early 20th century, 3" x 5"...............**$100-$200**
*Leslie Hindman Auctioneers*

Beaded, early 20th century, 7" x 8"...........................**$100-$200**
*Leslie Hindman Auctioneers*

Circa 1840 Berlin wirework change purse probably for a chatelaine, rare, showing some age ........................................**$295**
*What Once Was*

Chanel, 2.55 bag, mid-20th century, 10" x 6"...............**$3,000-$5,000**
*Leslie Hindman Auctioneers*

A 1920s envelope-style enameled flat mesh handbag with rose center...................................**$225**

Charles S. Kahn, Lucite and faux tortoiseshell box bag, mid-20th century, 3-1/2" x 8" x 4" ................................**$275-$325**
*Incogneeto*

Crocodile purse, mid-20th century, 7" x 6"...............**$400-$600**
*Leslie Hindman Auctioneers*

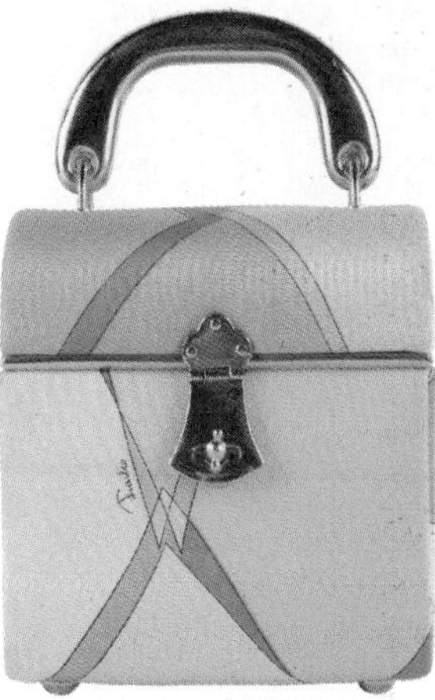

Emilio Pucci, mid-20th century, 5" x 5-1/2"................**$400-$600**
*Leslie Hindman Auctioneers*

Early 1940s Lefaye blue carnival glass beaded bag with flower outline in relief ....................... **$155**

Enid Collins, Love Box bag, mid-20th century, 8-1/2" x 5-1/2" x 4" ............................ **$200-$400**
*Leslie Hindman Auctioneers*

Florida Handbags, Lucite, mid-20th century, 7" x 5-1/4" ................................ **$300-$500**
*Wright*

1940s gray swirled plastic clutch bag with Art Deco rhinestone design.................................. **$110**
*Kitsch 'n' Wear*

Genuine Persian lamb fur purse from the 1940s.................... **$78**
*Kitsch 'n' Wear*

Gucci, Ostrich, mid-20th century, 7" x 9-1/2"............. **$800-$1,200**
*Leslie Hindman Auctioneers*

1950s hard plastic box bag with rhinestone-studded top ....... **$148**
*Kitsch 'n' Wear*

Hard-to-find pink 1950s Bellestone lizard skin boxy handbag ................................. **$195**
*Incogneeto*

Hermes, Kelly, crocodile, mid-20th century, 14" x 10-1/2" ........................**$10,000-$15,000**
*Leslie Hindman Auctioneers*

Late 1940s Aztec-theme loomed carpet purse..........................**$68**
*Kitsch 'n' Wear*

Lucille de Paris, alligator, mid-20th century, 9" x 9-1/2" ..................................**$300-$500**
*Leslie Hindman Auctioneers*

Magnificent frame on this 1930s cobalt blue swag beaded on knit handbag in superior condition .......................................**$375**
*Incogneeto*

Jacomo, lizard, mid-20th century, 9" x 5"**$200-$400**
*Leslie Hindman Auctioneers*

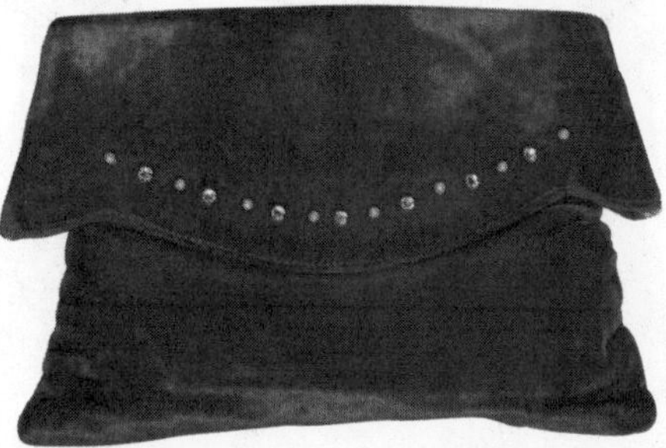

Late 1940s crimson velvet clutch with rhinestone and pearl embellishments.......................................**$48**
*Kitsch 'n' Wear*

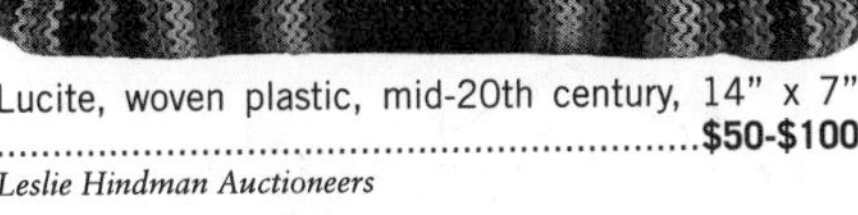

Lucite, woven plastic, mid-20th century, 14" x 7" ..........................................................**$50-$100**
*Leslie Hindman Auctioneers*

Woven cigarette pack purse, mid-century, 5" x 8" ..........................................................**$125-$175**
*Incogneeto*

◄ Whiting and Davis, 14k, mid-20th century, 4" x 9" ....................**$1,000-$1,500**
*Leslie Hindman Auctioneers*

Whiting and Davis, 14k, mid-20th century, 3" x 3"...........**$1,000-$1,500**
*Leslie Hindman Auctioneers*

Mesh bag, early 20th century, 4" x 5" ............................... **$50-$100**
*Leslie Hindman Auctioneers*

► Midas, elephant, mid-20th century, 13" x 13" ..... **$400-$600**
*Leslie Hindman Auctioneers*

Midas, poodle, mid-20th century, 10" x 8" .................... **$150-$250**
*Leslie Hindman Auctioneers*

► Nettie Rosenstein, leopard fur, mid-20th century, 14-1/2" x 11" .............................. **$800-$1,200**
*Leslie Hindman Auctioneers*

Mid-1930s black leather hand-braided "softee" purse with linen lining and back handstrap ................................................................ **$150**
*Vintage with a Twist*

## HATS

Amazingly designed mix of brown feathers, cut felt leaves, and brown netting, 1930s ......... **$125**

Borsalino fur felt fedora, 1940s ........................................ **$110**

Flocked velvet 1960s floppy hat from Bamberger's ................. **$66**

Late '30s black wool felt hat with unusual rolled up crown design ........................................... **$95**

Lovely 1950s custom-made brown Persian lamb hat ................ **$110**

Lovely 1930s kelly green wool felt Ida May hat with feather........ **$78**

*Rhona Ferling*

A 1940s Platinum Beaver fur felt fedora................................ **$110**

Plum satin and velour Coronet Exclusive late '50s lampshade hat ........................................... **$58**

*Rhona Ferling*

A 1940s women's version of a men's straw hat .................... **$65**

Victorian-style wide-brimmed velvet hat from Henri Bendel's in New York with wispy brown ostrich feathers, satin bow and gold flower buds ................. **$175**

Wonderfully woven straw 1940s hat with red and green feathers ............................................... **$155**

## SHOES

Alfred Ruby Inc. Detroit/New York, silk floral-design evening slippers with amber rhinestone buckle and black satin heel, circa 1940s.......................... **$100**
*Rebecca L'Ecuyer*

Black satin marabou boudoir slippers, circa 1950s ............................................................... **$45**
*Rebecca L'Ecuyer*

**Right:** Hand embroidered black satin evening slippers with T-strap, button closure and silver Louis heel, early 20th century ........................................ **$800**
*Rebecca L'Ecuyer*

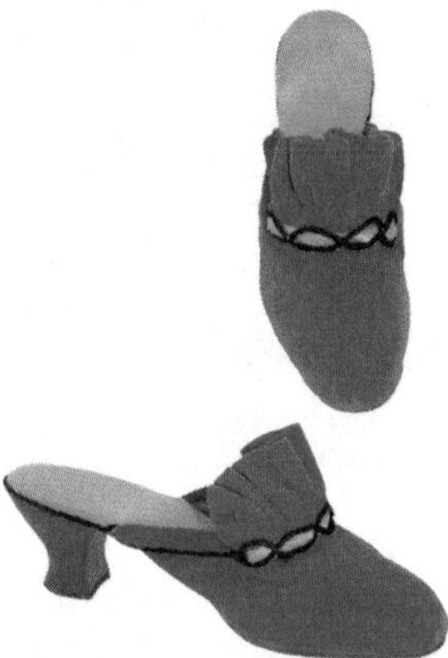

Beautiful French handmade pink velvet mules with black braid trim and Louis heel, c. 1935...... **$245**
*Vintage with a Twist*

Bold blue leather '30s heels with intricate detail across the vamp and cute bows................... **$150**
*Kitsch 'n' Wear*

Classic alligator leather platform shoes from the 1940s......... **$225**

Huge 1970s leather platform shoes in autumn shades by Nina ......................................... **$295**

Late 1920s chocolate brown shoes, with leather strip detailing across the vamp and silk grosgrain ribbon ties ......................... **$155**
*Incogneeto*

Early '20s dance shoes with a swirled bit of genuine snakeskin and a "Louis"-shaped heel .. **$175**

Green lizard skin (sometimes referred to as baby alligator) biscuit-toe pumps from the 1940s.. **$195**
*Incogneeto*

Paputsi of Greece, black leather woven cage lace-up brogues, circa 1940s ............................... **$200**
*Rebecca L'Ecuyer*

Lucite slingbacks from the '50s have pink leather heels and decorations .............................. **$125**

Pristine Victorian black leather "granny" boots ................... **$175**

Saks Kay Shoe Salon, red suede wedge sandals, Detroit, circa 1940s ......................................... **$100**
*Rebecca L'Ecuyer*

◀Gainsborough, pink suede ankle strap platform sandals, circa 1940s ......................................... **$200**
*Rebecca L'Ecuyer*

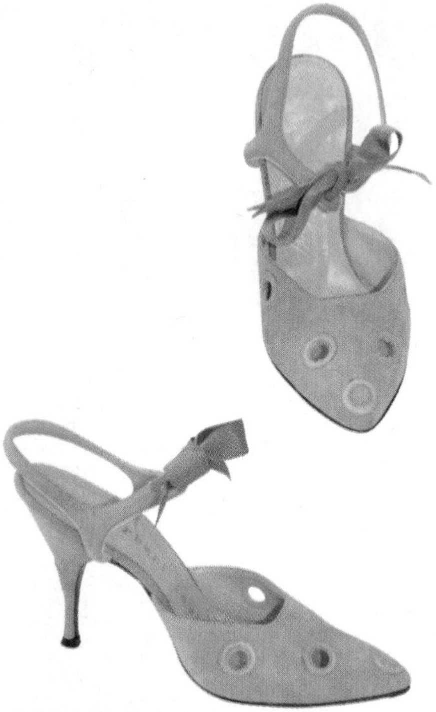

Late '50s Schiaparelli aqua satin shoes with embedded rhinestones ............................................ **$150**

Violet suede slingback shoes, circa 1960 from Herbert Levine.................................................. **$235**
*Vintage with a Twist*

1940s suede platform peep-toe shoes with multicolored metal studs in a swirled Art Deco pattern.. **$350**
*Incogneeto*

Woven raffia sandals with applied flower detail and cork heels. Made in Italy, circa 1940s .............**$60**
*Rebecca L'Ecuyer*

## BELTS & BUCKLES

A 1920s buckle is brass patterned to look like snakeskin............ **$85**

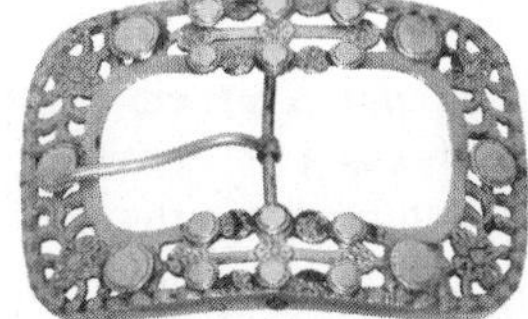

Decorative sterling silver buckle from the early part of last century ........................................ **$150**

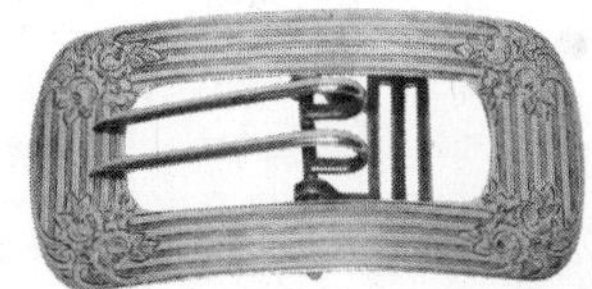

Another sterling silver belt buckle from the early part of last century ........................................ **$150**

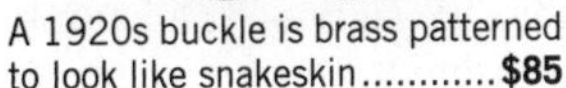

Hammered brass buckle set with glass stones from the Victorian period .................................. **$125**

End of day Bakelite 1920s belt with silver filigree panels ............. **$175**

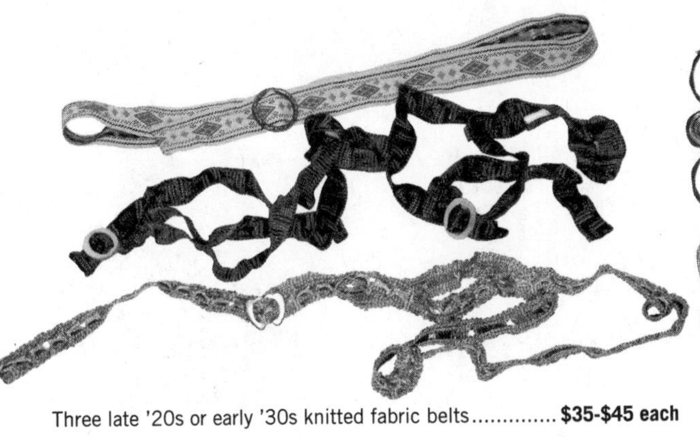

Three late '20s or early '30s knitted fabric belts............. **$35-$45 each**

Scrolls of gold-toned metal linked together to make this 1960s belt ........................................ **$72**

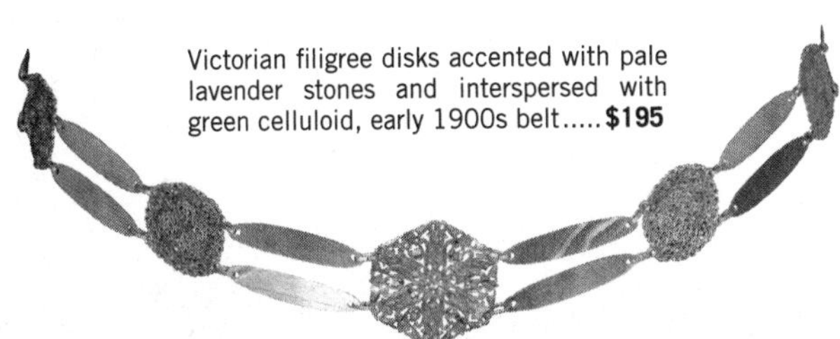

Victorian filigree disks accented with pale lavender stones and interspersed with green celluloid, early 1900s belt..... **$195**

# Watches

Collecting timepieces is not a new fad, but one enjoyed by men and women, the young and old alike. Essentially, there is something for everyone. Whether you collect by maker, by style or by the type of movement, you can find things for any budget.

Most everyone has a watch. They were given as graduation gifts from high school or college, something that was handed down to you from a family member, or potentially a gift received from a company you work for. By collecting watches, not only do you have a fun collectible, but it also has function.

Over the last 100+ years, millions of watches have been produced. Some were made for the masses, others made in very small quantities for a select few. There are dealers that specialize in watches, but they can also be found at flea markets, garage sales, auctions, on the Internet and at antique shops. Collecting creates an opportunity for you to have a watch for every occasion. You can have a watch to wear to work, one when out on the town, another one to use while participating in sports, and finally, an everyday watch.

The values placed on the watches illustrated in this section are market value, representing what they have recently sold for privately or at auction. Values can fluctuate due to numerous variables. How a watch is sold, where it is sold, and the condition all play a big role in the value.

The Internet has helped collectors identify watches worn by their favorite celebrity, worn on the moon, in a car race, in their favorite action film, etc.

One of the not-so-positive aspects of Internet collecting is the sheer volume of reproductions out there posing as authentic watches. They turn up everywhere, with links to professionally designed Web sites offering the best of the best for a discount, or up for bid on an Internet auction. You must keep in mind the old saying, "If it looks to good to be true, it probably is."

For more information on watches, see *Warman's Watches Field Guide* by Reyne Haines.

A. Lange & Söhne 18K yellow gold, power reserve, contemporary (two views)........ **$12,000**
*James F. Dicke II*

Audemars Piguet Royal Oak, modern, stainless steel, 18K gold octagonal bezel secured with screws ........ **$2,600**
*Heritage Auction Galleries*

Baume et Mercier Automatic, circa 1975, 18K yellow gold, synthetic sapphire in crown... **$1,150**
*Heritage Auction Galleries*

Blancpain Fifty Fathoms "Aqua Lung 1000 Feet," Ref. 3500, late 1950s. Center-seconds, antimagnetic, self-winding, water-resistant stainless steel, with wide bezel ............................ **$4,500**
*Antiquorum Auctioneers*

Breitling "Navitimer – Automatic," Ref. 1806, 1970s. Octagonal, self-winding, water-resistant, stainless steel with round-button chronograph, registers, telemeter, slide-rule, date, winding crown at 9 and the chronograph pushers at 2 and 4 o'clock, and a stainless steel Breitling link bracelet ............**$3,000**
*Antiquorum Auctioneers*

Benrus platinum, white gold and diamonds, manual wind............................................................**$1,220**
*Leslie Hindman Auctioneers*

Bulova lady's cocktail, 18.75mm, gold filled, 15 jewel manual wind, 1950s .............................. **$125**
*Derek Dier, WatchesToBuy.com*

Cartier Pasha Golf, Ref. 30010, 1980s. Center seconds, 18K yellow gold quartz with five pushers and four digital registers to add up golf strokes, and an 18K yellow gold Cartier deployant clasp ...................................**$17,500**
*Antiquorum Auctioneers*

Cartier Santos, stainless steel ..................................... **$1,500**
*Leslie Hindman Auctioneers*

Bulova enamel bezel, manual wind, sub second, 14K yellow gold.........................................................**$500**
*Charlie Cleves – Cleves and Lonnemann Jewelers*

Concord "Saratoga," lady's, 18K gold and diamonds, Roman numeral indicators, quartz movement, diamond melee bezel. .................................. **$1,500**
*Skinner Inc.*

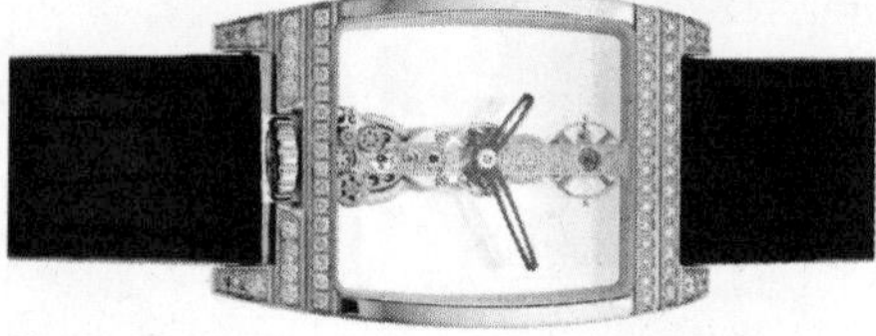

Corum "Golden Bridge," 18K white gold, skeletonized back, pavé diamond lugs, double row of diamonds top and bottom, sapphire crystals, manual wind, circa 2006 ....................................... **$9,850**
*Heritage Auction Galleries*

Corum 18K yellow gold, manual wind .... **$1,450**
*Leslie Hindman Auctioneers*

Paul Ditisheim 14K pink gold, rubies and diamonds, manual wind, circa 1930 ............................ **$1,500**
*Heritage Auction Galleries*

►Gruen Early diver's, sterling case, manual wind, luminescent numbers ...................................... **$600**
*Charlie Cleves – Cleves and Lonnemann Jewelers*

Franck Muller "Crazy Hours," circa 2000, 18K rose gold, tonneau case, sapphire crystal, back marked "Master of Complications, No. 51,7851, Crazy Hours" ....................................**$13,145**
*Heritage Auction Galleries*

Gilbert James Bond 007 novelty, 60mm, plastic and metal, 1960s ........................................ **$900**
*Derek Dier, WatchesToBuy.com*

Gallet "Up Down" single-button chronograph in stainless steel. ......................................... **$450**
*Chris Miller*

Glycine lady's, manual wind, platinum with diamonds ......... **$1,000**
*Charlie Cleves – Cleves and Lonnemann Jewelers*

Elgin U.S. Military, in sterling silver with enamel dial, circa 1920s. .............................. **$325**
*Tim and Reyne Haines*

Gruen Precision, fancy lugs, black dial, diamond markers, manual wind, 10K gold filled .......... **$200**
*Charlie Cleves – Cleves and Lonnemann Jewelers*

Gruen doctor's, 877 movement, duo dial, black enamel Roman numerals, manual wind, 14K white gold filled ....................... **$3,000**
*Charlie Cleves – Cleves and Lonnemann Jewelers*

Gruen "Hunter," manual wind, flip top shown open and closed ..... **$800**
*Charlie Cleves – Cleves and Lonnemann Jewelers*

Gruen lady's Precision, 14K white gold with diamonds, manual wind ........................................................................................ **$300**
*Charlie Cleves – Cleves and Lonnemann Jewelers*

Gübelin stainless steel, manual wind, black dial, gold bar markers **$125**
*Phil Lucas*

Hamilton Electric, calendar (day), "Masterpiece Line," circa 1971, 10K yellow gold filled........................................................................ **$50**
*Phil Lucas*

Hamilton platinum and diamonds, manual wind, circa 1950 ......**$1,500**
*Leslie Hindman Auctioneers*

►Hamilton Pacer, gold filled, yellow center, white lugs, back inscribed, circa 1958........................................................................ **$500**
*Heritage Auction Galleries*

Heuer Monaco, 40mm, stainless steel, Valjoux 7740 movement ....................................... **$5,000**
*Derek Dier, WatchesToBuy.com*

Ingersoll manual wind, white dial, gold numerals, yellow gold plated ........................................... **$40**
*Tim and Reyne Haines*

Illinois lady's, Edgewaters, 14K white gold filled, manual wind . **$75**
*Charlie Cleves – Cleves and Lonnemann Jewelers*

Illinois New Yorker, manual wind, stainless steel, sub second at 6 ........................................................ **$350**
*Phil Lucas*

Jaeger-LeCoultre 18K gold, 35mm, manual wind with teardrop lugs................................ **$2,500**
*Derek Dier, WatchesToBuy.com*

Jules Jurgensen 14K yellow gold and diamonds, manual wind..**$650**
*Leslie Hindman Auctioneers*

Longines Comet, stainless steel, manual wind, circa 1970 . **$1,250**
*Phil Lucas*

LeCoultre lady's, manual wind, fancy lugs, 14K yellow gold filled ......................................................... **$175**
*Tim and Reyne Haines*

Omega Constellation, pie-pan, kite marker dial, 24 jewel automatic, stainless steel, 1958 .......... **$400**
*Derek Dier, WatchesToBuy.com*

Omega Seamaster, No. 34687672, Ref. ST 176.005, circa 1972. Self-winding, water-resistant, stainless steel with round-button chronograph, 12-hour and 60-minute registers, 24-hour indication, date and a stainless steel Omega link bracelet with deployant clasp .............. **$2,000**
*Antiquorum Aucti oneers*

Omega lady's, gold and opal bracelet, circa 1975, 14K yellow gold, scalloped bezel, manual wind.............................. **$2,100**
*Heritage Auction Galleries*

Patek Philippe for Tiffany Circa 1955, with rare Masonic dial ................................... **$3,000**
*Heritage Auction Galleries*

Rolex stainless steel, manual wind, chronograph, circa 1966 ...................................**$23,000**
*Heritage Auction Galleries*

Rolex Oyster Perpetual, day/date, Ref. 1803, in 1972. Center seconds, self-winding, water-resistant, 18K pink gold with day and date and an 18K pink gold Rolex clasp ...........................**$17,500**
*Antiquorum Auctioneers*

Rolex Chronograph, pre-Daytona, black dial, Ref. 6238, 1960s. Water-resistant, stainless steel with round-button chronograph, registers, tachometer, stainless steel riveted Rolex Oyster bracelet with deployant clasp.........................................**$50,000**
*Antiquorum Auctioneers*

Rolex Steve McQueen Oyster Perpetual, date, Explorer II, Ref. 1655, in 1979. Center seconds, self-winding, water-resistant, stainless steel with date, special 24-hour bezel, large white arrow 24-hour hand and a stainless steel Rolex Oyster bracelet. Accompanied by a fitted box, hangtag and instruction booklets ........**$17,500**
*Antiquorum Auctioneers*

Tiffany & Co. Art Deco lady's, platinum, silver-tone dial with Arabic numeral indicators.............. **$700**
*Skinner Inc.*

Universal Genève Manual wind, square dial, sub second, 18K yellow gold............................ **$500**
*Charlie Cleves – Cleves and Lonnemann Jewelers*

Royce Professional Marine, diver's, 46mm, anodized steel, automatic, 1970s.................. **$2,000**
*Derek Dier, WatchesToBuy.com*

Tiffany & Co. Calendar by Movado, circa 1940s, 14K yellow gold, beveled lugs, two-tone dial, Arabic numerals and markers, subsidiary seconds, case and movement signed Movado, dial signed Tiffany & Co............................... **$1,400**
*Heritage Auction Galleries*

Ulysee Nardin "1846" marine chronometer, circa 2000, stainless steel, No. 1564, back inscribed with Nardin gold medal dates and world locations, coin edge on the bezel, screw-down crown, automatic movement ..................................... **$3,300**
*Heritage Auction Galleries*

Seiko Lordmatic, 39mm, stainless steel, 25 jewel automatic .... **$250**
*Derek Dier, WatchesToBuy.com*

Tudor Oyster, Ref. 7159/0, case made by Rolex, 1972. Water-resistant, stainless steel with date, round-button chronograph, register, tachometer and a stainless steel Rolex Oyster bracelet **$9,000**
*Antiquorum Auctioneers*

Vacheron Constantin "Gerard Mercator 1594 – 1994", platinum, circa 1994......................**$18,500**
*Heritage Auction Galleries*

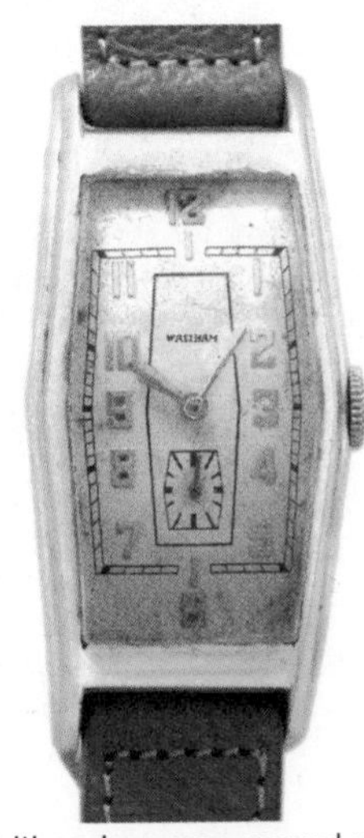

Waltham long case, manual wind, gold applied numerals, yellow gold filled, cir ca 1930s, 48mm.. **$500**
*Charlie Cleves – Cleves and Lonnemann Jewelers*

Wakmann stainless steel triple-date chronograph, 37mm, Valjoux 723, manual wind, 1960s .**$1,695**
*Derek Dier, WatchesToBuy.com*

Vacheron Constantin for LeCoultre "Mystery Dial," diamond numbers and hands, 14K white gold ........**$3,000**
*Charlie Cleves – Cleves and Lonnemann Jewelers*

Van Cleef & Arpels 18K yellow gold and diamond, circa 1940s.........................................................**$6,000**
*Leslie Hindman Auctioneers*

Wittnauer lady's, 14K pink gold, manual wind with diamonds and rubies................................**$250**
*Charlie Cleves – Cleves and Lonnemann Jewelers*

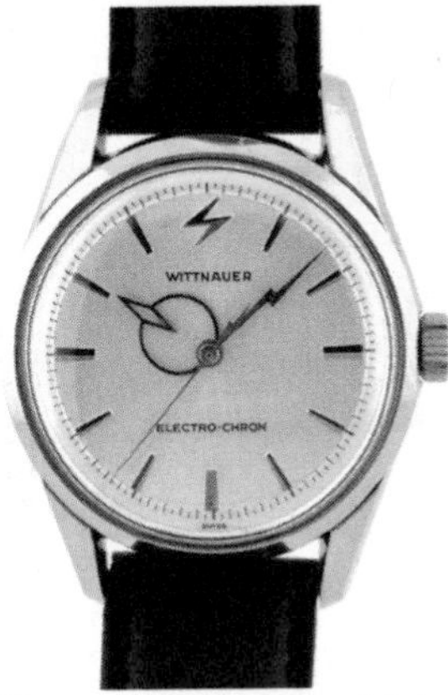

Wittnauer Electro Chron, stainless steel, 35mm, 1960s........... **$900**
*Derek Dier, WatchesToBuy.com*

Zodiac Sea Wolf, 17 jewel, automatic with uncommon bezel..**$950**
*Derek Dier, WatchesToBuy.com*

Agassiz, World Time, circa 1945, 14k..................... **$5,000-$7,000**
*Antiquorum Auctioneers*

Ball, 16 size official railroad standard, 21J RR, gold-fill case.......................... **$400-$900**

Dudley Masonic, circa late 1940s, 12 size, third model, display back, yellow gold-fill...... **$1,500-$2,500**

Elgin, circa 1910, 18 size 17J hunter case, diamond, sapphire, and ruby.............. **$3,000-$3,500**
*Antiquorum Auctioneers*

Elgin/Montgomery dial RR, 6 size 21J, gold-filled, incorrect bow ................................. **$225-$495**

Gruen, Veri Thin, circa 1920, gold-fill, 17J, pentagon shape, fancy enamel detail .... **$195-$495**

Elgin, circa 1919, note sub-seconds at 3:00, 15J 16 size, white gold-fill/metal dial......... **$65-$175**

Hamilton, circa 1919, 992 Time King, 21J 16 size....... **$295-$595**

Hamilton, 4992B, GCT (Greenwich Civil Time), circa 1942, 22J, chrome case/24-hour black dial ................................. **$395-$595**

Dueber Hampden, circa 1918, 12 size 7J, base metal case **$90-$290**

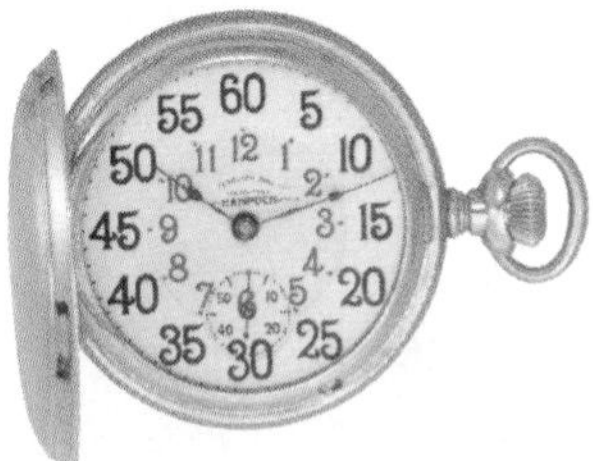

Hampden, John Hancock model, circa 1910, 18 size 21J gold-fill hunter case Ferguson dial ........................... **$2,000-$2,400**

*Antiquorum Auctioneers*

E. Howard & Co., Boston, circa 1870s, N size (approx. 18 size), transition period pendant set, 18k hunter case.......... **$1,500-$2,800**

Hebdomas, Swiss, exposed balance, silver and Niello case, fancy dial ........................... **$395-$595**

Illinois, circa 1880, 18 size, silver, very rare floral dial **$595-$995**

Illinois Autocrat, circa 1924, gold-fill, 17J 12 size... **$195-$395**

E. Ingraham, master, approx. 18 size dollar watch, metal dial ..................................... **$40-$75**

Ingersoll, Reliance, circa 1894, 16 size 7J, nickel......... **$50-$100**

Lemania-Swiss, chronograph, circa 1930s, black military dial, chrome case............... **$495-$895**

**Far left:** Rockford Watch Co., circa 1904, unusual red dial, 16 size 15J ........................... **$2,000-$2,500**

*Antiquorum Auctioneers*

**Left:** South Bend Watch Co., OF Montgomery dial RR ... **$250-$500**

Swiss Frenia, hand-painted blister-type metal dial pin, lever pin set, gold-plated case.....**$75-$175**

Swiss Pearlham, cylinder movement, enamel blister type dial, base metal case............**$95-$150**

Swiss Roskopf, gun metal, pin lever pin set....................**$75-$150**

Vacheron & Constantin-Swiss, presentation watch circa 1949, rare aluminum case..... **$1,500-$2,500**

Waltham, Model 1883, circa 1888, gold-fill open face 18 size, fancy dial-bird scene...**$400-$700**

American Waltham, circa 1890s, 18 size, nickel case, fancy dial ..................................**$250-$550**

Waltham, Vanguard up-down indicator, circa 1926, 23J RR ..............................**$600-$1,100**

Waterbury Watch Co., Addison Series N, circa 1890s, duplex escapement, silver case..... **$75-$95**

Zenith Swiss, unusual alarm pocket watch, PS circa 1910s, nickel case-enamel dial, missing hand .........................**$300-$450**

# World War II Collectibles

In the 65 years since the end of World War II, veterans, collectors, and history buffs have eagerly bought, sold and traded the "spoils of war." Actually, souvenir collecting began as soon as troops set foot on foreign soil. Soldiers from every nation involved in the greatest armed conflict mankind has known eagerly sought items which would remind them of their time in the service, validate their presence during the making of history, and potentially generate income when they returned home. Such items might also be bartered with fellow soldiers for highly prized or scarce goods. Helmets, medals, Lugers, field gear, daggers, and other pieces of war material filled parcels, which were mailed home or stuffed into the duffel bags of soldiers who gathered them.

As soon as hostilities ended in 1945, the populations of the defeated nations quickly realized that they could make money by selling souvenirs to their former enemies. This was particularly true in Germany and Japan, which hosted large contingents of occupying U.S. soldiers and troops from other Allied nations. The flow of war material increased. Values became well established. For instance, a Luger was worth several packs of cigarettes, a helmet, just one. A Japanese sword was worth two boxes of K-rations, and an Arisaka bayonet was worth a chocolate Hershey bar.

Over the years, these values have remained proportionally consistent. Today, that "two-pack" Luger might be worth $4,000 and that one-pack helmet $1,000. The Japanese sword might fetch $1,200 and the Arisaka bayonet $85. Though values have increased dramatically, demand has not slackened. In fact, World War II collecting is the largest segment of the militaria hobby. Demand for homefront collectibles grows each year as well, as our focus on the era's sheet music will attest.

The value of military items resides in variation. Whether it is a difference in manufacturing technique, material or markings, the nuances of an item will determine its true value. Do not expect 20 minutes on the Internet—or even glancing through this section—to teach these nuances. Collectors are a devoted group. They have spent years and hundreds, if not thousands, of dollars to establish the critical knowledge base that enables them to navigate through the hobby. This basic information may be used to assist in acquiring the necessary foundation of price negotiations.

Whether an individual is hoping to sell military items or to buy, chances are there is a military collector living in close proximity. Check your local classifieds. Advanced collectors will often run "Military Items Wanted" ads in local newspapers and classified ad Web sites. Even those hoping to buy items may call these people and initiate a conversation that will lead to subsequent deals.

Militaria shows take place throughout the U.S., Europe, and Japan. Ranging from just a dozen dealers to more than 2,000, these shows are still the best source of fresh material for the devoted collector.

For more information on World War II collectibles, see *Warman's World War II Collectibles Identification and Price Guide* by Michael E. Haskew.

Collectors call this style the "1st Ranger Battalion Special Knife" though it was, most likely, an Australian-made fighting knife. ............................................ **$600-$700**
*www.advanceguardmilitaria.com*

9th Air Force senior pilot's Ike jacket with bullion insignia .................................................. **$330-$413**
*www.advanceguardmilitaria.com*

36th Division first sergeant's Class A tunic ............................................................ **$25-$41**
*www.advanceguardmilitaria.com*

AAF P-51 Ace's identified group that included the flyer's A-2 jacket, flight gear, documents, and even his gun camera.......................................... **$9,975**
*www.advanceguardmilitaria.com*

An A-2 jacket with a painted squadron insignia immediately skyrockets in value. ...................... **$1,238-$2,145**
*www.advanceguardmilitaria.com*

A-3 aviator's parachute........................... **$200-$300**
*www.advanceguardmilitaria.com*

Afrika korps field binoculars ......................................**$165**
*Mohawk Arms Inc. Militaria Auctions*

Argentine Model 30 sun helmet ..............................**$200-$300**
*Peter Suciu*

Army combat drawstring rucksack ..........................................**$40**
*Mohawk Arms Inc. Militaria Auctions*

Australian jungle hat...**$350-$450**
*Charles D. Pautler*

Army tropical issue M43 cap ..............................**$895-$1,350**
*Charles D. Pautler*

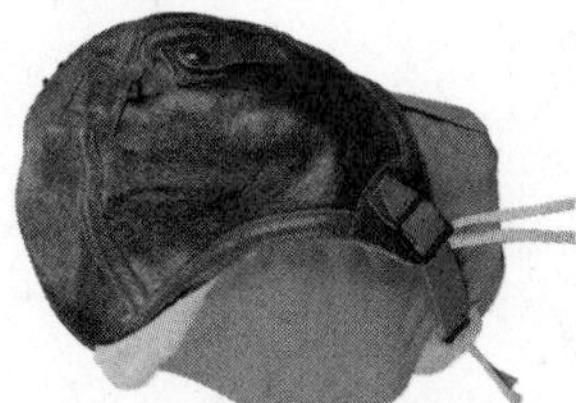

B-6 fleece flight helmet fitted with ANB-H-1 receivers......**$250-$325**
*www.advanceguardmilitaria.com*

Army gas mask...................**$105**
*Mohawk Arms Inc Militaria Auctions*

Army khaki leggings....... **$15-$25**
*Charles D. Pautler*

Belgian Sacic pattern gas mask ...................................**$65-$95**
*www.advanceguardmilitaria.com*

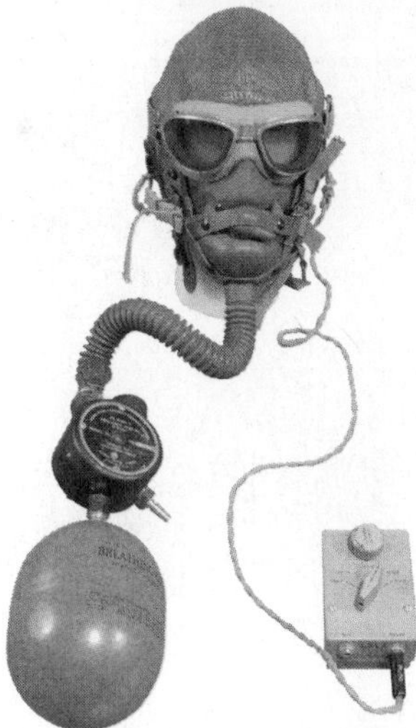

A-11 leather flight helmet, type R-14 earphone receivers and A-14 demand oxygen mask..**$650-$750**

Boxed dinner K-ration in the 1943-style blue and tan camouflaged carton................................**$135-$175**
*John F. Graf collection*

Belgian carabiner's uniform and equipment ........................................................... **$743-$990**
*www.advanceguardmilitaria.com*

British auxiliary territorial service bush jacket ........................................................... **$165-$248**
*www.advanceguardmilitaria.com*

Combat medic's kit ............... **$90**
*Mohawk Arms Inc. Militaria Auctions*

Eastern Front winter sentry boots ......................................... **$125**
*Mohawk Arms Inc. Militaria Auctions*

Enameled canteen, cup and cover ................................ **$100-$165**
*www.advanceguardmilitaria.com*

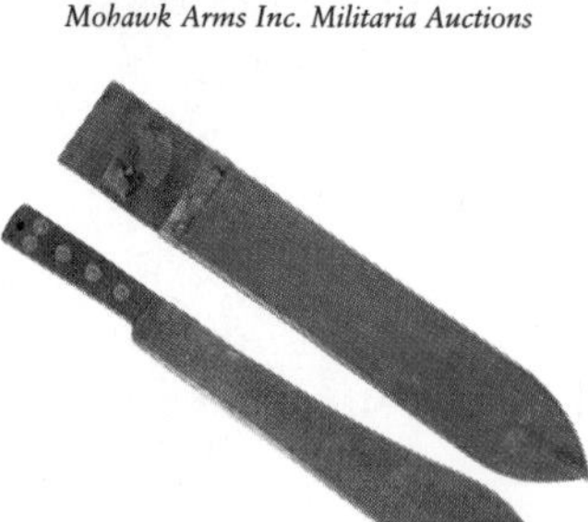

British machete and 1943-dated leather scabbard......... **$100-$150**
*www.advanceguardmilitaria.com*

Finnish officer's Model 1936 wool field cap .................... **$175-$300**
*www.advanceguardmilitaria.com*

Two different field phones are seen here: early-war and late-war versions of the EE-8 A. **$100-$200 ea.**
*Charles D. Pautler*

Commonly known as the "tanker's jacket," the official designation noted that it was a "winter combat jacket." .............................................. **$215-$322**
*Charles D. Pautler*

Like any piece of flight gear, the presence of squadron insignia adds significantly to the garment's value. Navy M-422A jacket with a patch for bomber squadron VPB 102 ............................................ **$1,275**
*www.advanceguardmilitaria.com*

Generally, an Enfield No. 4 Mk I would sell for $150-$400. Fitted as a sniper rifle with original No. 15 Mk I wooden storage case like this example ........ **$4,000-$6,000**
*Rock Island Auction Co.*

Browning M2 .50 caliber machine gun ............................................... **$26,000-$32,000**
*Private collection*

German General Assault Badge, 75 engagements.... **$3,000-$4,000**
*Hermann Historical OHG*

Civil Service Honor Award, I Class.............. **$40-$50**
*www.advanceguardmilitaria.com*

Czechoslovakian Medal for Merit, First Class ...................... **$40-$50**
*George S. Cuhaj*

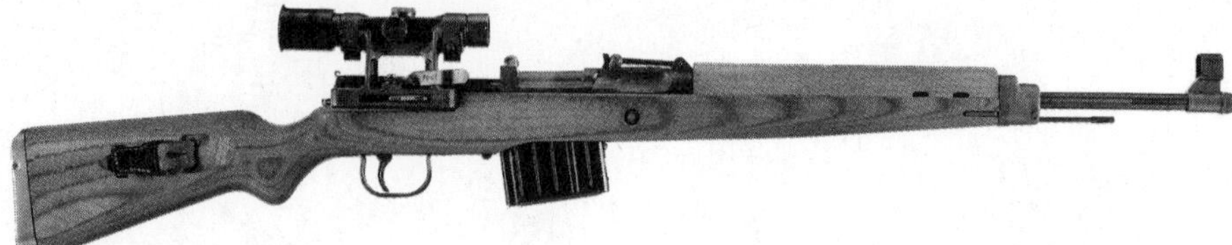

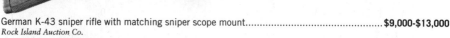

German K-43 sniper rifle with matching sniper scope mount................................................ **$9,000-$13,000**
*Rock Island Auction Co.*

German Proficiency Badge of the SS in bronze ....... **$6,500-$7,500**
*Hermann Historica OHG*

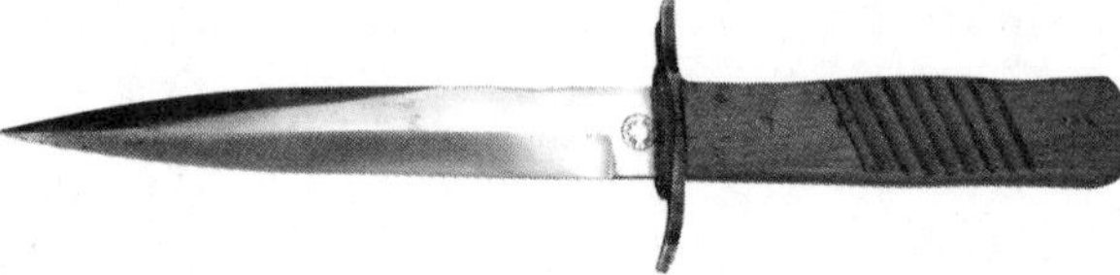

German soldier's fighting knife........................................... **$150-$250**
*www.advanceguardmilitaria.com*

Hitler Youth sport shirt........ **$125**
*Mohawk Arms Inc. Militaria Auctions*

Hungarian Occupation of North Transylvania Medal ........ **$25-$35**
*www.advanceguardmilitaria.com*

Honorable Railroad Worker, Type III ................................ **$65-$85**
*Colin R. Bruce II*

This grouping belonged to a Canadian women's army corps corporal. ............................................ **$650**
*www.advanceguardmilitaria.com*

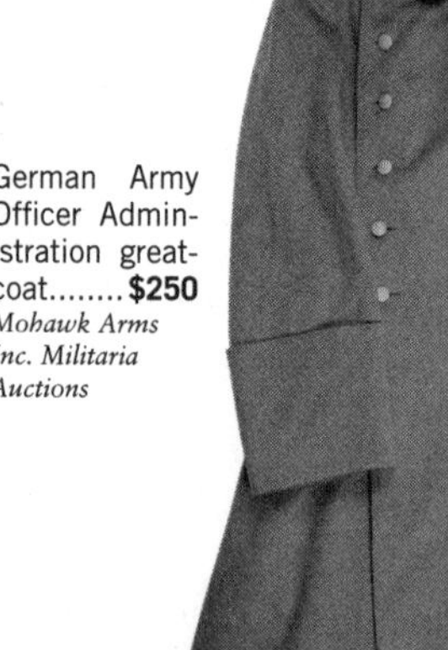

German Army Officer Administration greatcoat........ **$250**
*Mohawk Arms Inc. Militaria Auctions*

Japanese army cold weather vest ........................... **$248-$289**
*www.advanceguardmilitaria.com*

Japanesee navy seaman's cap with "Imperial Japanese Navy" katana ................................ **$400-$550**
*www.advanceguardmilitaria.com*

Kriegsmarine enlisted belt plate ................................ **$200-$265**
*www.advanceguardmilitaria.com*

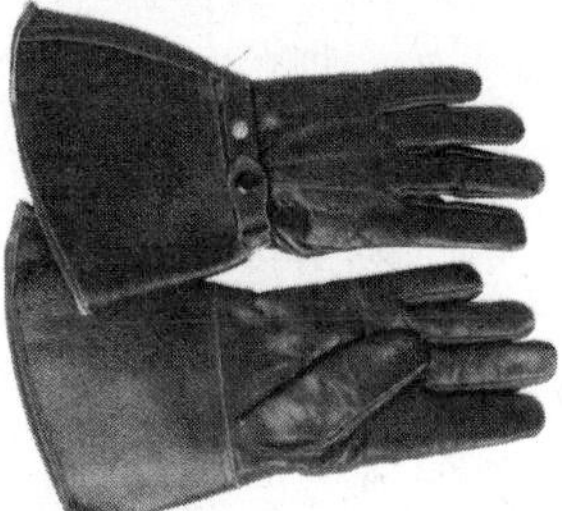

Leather motorcyclist's gloves .................................... **$35-$50**
*Camp Ripley Museum*

►Lifebuoy soap............. **$10-$15**
*Charles D. Pautler*

Japanese army leading private's tropical tunic...................... **$150**
*Mohawk Arms Inc. Militaria Auctions*

Japanese Order of the Rising Sun, 5th Class ................... **$400-$450**
*Colin R. Bruce II*

Luftwaffe enlisted man's field cap ................................ **$275-$395**
*Camp Ripley Museum*

Japanese Kamikaze headband ................................ **$300-$450**
*www.advanceguardmilitaria.com*

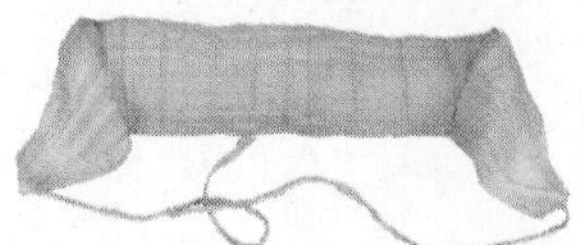

Japanese soldier's "Thousand Stitch" belt ................ **$225-$300**
www.advanceguardmilitaria.com

Japanese Type 90 army helmet with cover and camouflage net .............................. **$700-$1,100**
*Camp Ripley Museum*

Japanese winter flight suit ........................................ **$500**
*Mohawk Arms Inc. Militaria Auctions*

Kriegsmarine Walther double-barrel Model SLD flare pistol.............................................. **$800-$1,400**
*www.advanceguardmilitaria.com*

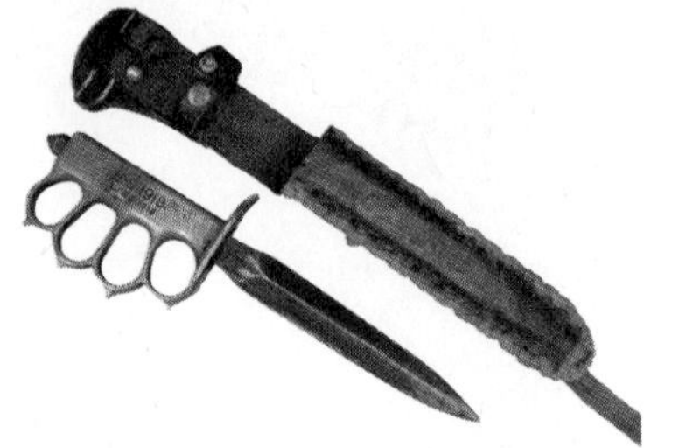

M1918 pattern trench knife .................**$450-$600**
*www.advanceguardmilitaria.com*

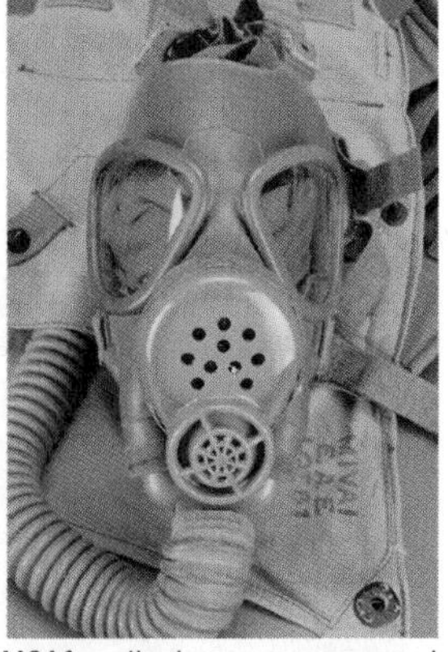

M3A1 diaphragm gas mask .................................. **$65-$95**
*www.advanceguardmilitaria.com*

Army wehrpass ............**$60-$100**
*Charles D. Pautler*

Rumanian Anti-Communist Campaign Medal ................. **$20-$30**
*www.advanceguardmilitaria.com*

Pattern of 1940 bread bag with shoulder sling............**$100-$150**
*www.advanceguardmilitaria.com*

Russian shovel captured and reissued by the Finnish army, with hanger......................**$100-$150**
*www.advanceguardmilitaria.com*

Sake cup, Imperial Guard 4th Regiment..................... **$30-$50**
*www.advanceguardmilitaria.com*

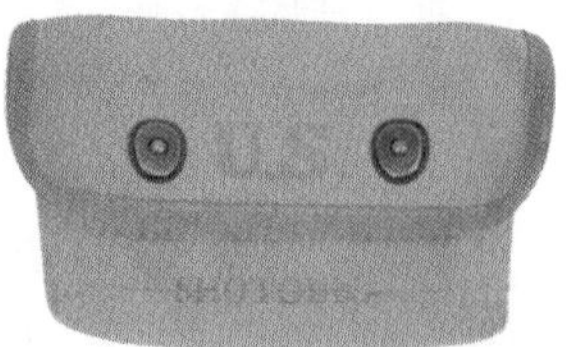

Shotgun ammo pouch for attaching to web belt ..........**$250-$300**
*www.advanceguardmilitaria.com*

Stamped steel Heere belt plate on black leather belt........**$100-$175**
*Camp Ripley Museum*

Referred to as "transitional," this German Model 1916 helmet has a single army decal ...............................**$450-$650**
*Charles D. Pautler*

Model 1928 Bersaglieri sun helmet.........**$500-$750**
*Peter Suciu*

Navy Rising Sun flag.......................................**$500**
*Mohawk Arms Inc. Militaria Auctions*

Officer's canteen...................**$80**
*Mohawk Arms Inc. Militaria Auctions*

NSKK Haupttruppfuhrer greatcoat
.........................................**$400**
*Mohawk Arms Inc. Militaria Auctions*

Uniform of an identified major general in the ROA
....**$9,900-$12,705**
*Hermann Historica OHG*

Order of the Red Banner, Type I
.................................**$300-$400**
*Colin R. Bruce II*

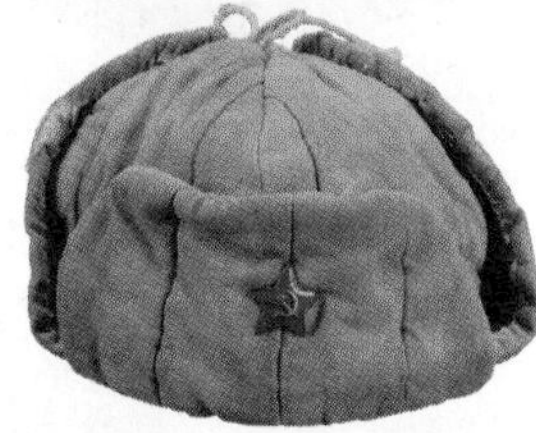

The padded material belies that this cap was made from a discarded Russian winter coat, or telogreika...................**$150-$225**
*www.advanceguardmilitaria.com*

▼Overseas cap for an enlisted parachute infantryman ..**$85-$165**
*Camp Ripley Museum*

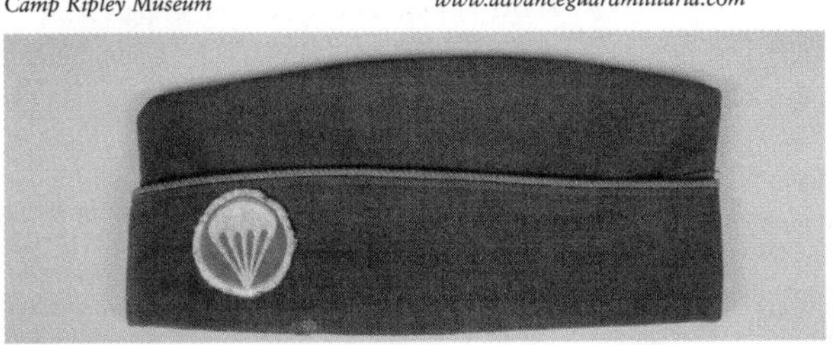

Norway War Participant's Medal
...................................**$75-$85**
*Fred Borgmann*

Who hasn't fantasized about owning their own Sherman tank? It is possible, but it will cost more than ........................................ **$100,000!**

Third Reich military stein .... **$350**
*Mohawk Arms Inc. Militaria Auctions*

This Spanish colonel's 1914 pattern tunic has been altered to conform to the 1926 regulations ................................**$248-$314**
*www.advanceguardmilitaria.com*

Tunic for a French collaborationist serving in the German Organization Todt ....................**$627-$743**
*www.advanceguardmilitaria.com*

Soviet army general's parade uniform ................................**$400**
*Mohawk Arms Inc. Militaria Auctions*

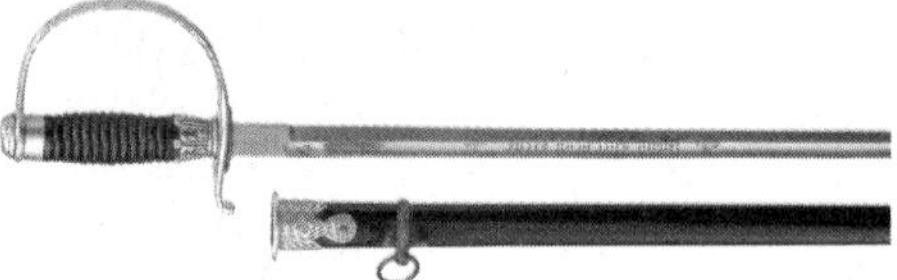

Sword for an SS Unterfuehrer ........... **$1,500-$2,500**
*Hermann Historica OHG*

Union Switch & Signal Co. M1911A1 pistol... **$2,000-$3,000**
*Rock Island Auction Co.*

Wool puttees ....... **$50-$75**
*www.advanceguardmilitaria.com*

The white fatigue hat is probably the most recognizable of U.S. World War II naval headgear. ......................................**$5-$10**
*Charles D. Pautler*

United Kingdom 1939-45 Star ..................................... **$10-$15**
*Colin R. Bruce II*

Waffen SS Deutschland M43 combat tunic......................... **$7,935**
*Manion's International Auction House*

◄ Waffen SS visor cap for a medical officer ............ **$3,000-$3,650**
*Hermann Historica OHG*

U.S. Army officer's visor cap .................................**$85-$195**
*Charles D. Pautler*

U.S. "Boonie" style OD fatigue hat.............................. **$45-$55**
*Charles D. Pautler*

U.S. Navy Colt Service Model Ace with original box and accessories. A factory letter states that this was one of a group of 45 pistols shipped to the Naval Supply Depot, Sewall's Point, Va., on Dec. 1, 1942...............**$15,000-$20,000**
*Rock Island Auction Co.*

Waffen SS Model 42 single decal helmet................ **$2,000-$3,500**
*Charles D. Pautler*

U.S. Army Purple Heart with Oak Leaf cluster signifying an additional receipt of the award ..................................**$75-$100**
*www.advanceguardmilitaria.com*

Waffen SS panzer wraparound ...................................... **$1,800**
*Mohawk Arms Inc. Militaria Auctions*

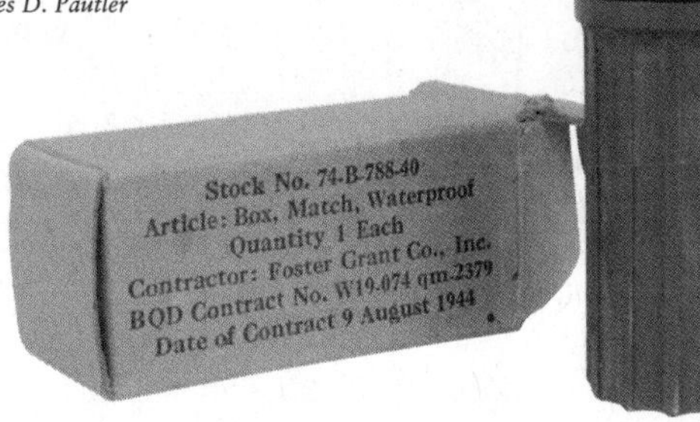


▲ Waterproof match safe in original carton ..................... **$20-$30**
*Charles D. Pautler*

# 1940s Sheet Music

Music often helps define an era, and nowhere is that more evident than in the songs of World War II. 1940s sheet music offers a unique window into this particular aspect of United States history, colorfully illustrating many of the themes and concerns of primary importance to wartime Americans.

Patriotic tunes are the melodies most regularly identified with World War II. Many, such as "We Did It Before and We Can Do It Again," served as musical morale boosters. Day-to-day military life received its due as well, in songs ranging from the humorous "Ten Little Soldiers on a Ten Day Leave" to the inspirational "Say a Pray'r for the Boys Over There" to the heartrending Bob Wills' "White Cross on Okinawa," which concludes, "there's a White Cross tonight on Okinawa, and a Gold Star in some Mother's home."

Life on the home front was also fair game for '40s songwriters, offering a glimpse of domestic demands during wartime. Victory Gardens, for instance, were celebrated in "Up to Her Heart In Victory" while assembly line workers were the subject of many songs, including "On the Swing Shift," "Milkman, Keep Those Bottles Quiet," and "Rosie the Riveter."

The "girl back home" was often featured, whether rhapsodizing about her dreamboat in "He Wears a Pair of Silver Wings" or proclaiming "He's 1-A in the Army and He's A-1 in My Heart." One of the most poignant girl-back-home songs, "P.S. I Love You," by Gordon Jenkins and Johnny Mercer, actually made its debut in 1934. Wartime separations gave new meaning to such lyrics as "Dear, I thought I'd drop a line—the weather's cool, the folks are fine. I'm in bed each night at nine. P.S. I love you."

Whether clever, corny, or downright silly, '40s novelty tunes were guaranteed day-brighteners. Some had a military theme ("The Canteen Bounce"). Others poked barbed fun at the enemy ("Der Fuehrer's Face," introduced by Donald Duck!). "The Machine Gun Bounce" even made use of nonsense syllables, with its hilarious vocal "ack-acks."

If you're collecting for the song itself, regardless of condition, paper shows often offer "as is" 1940s sheet music for as little as $1 per copy, less if purchased in bargain bundles. For the general range of World War II sheet music, however, expect to pay $5-$15 per song, $15-$25 for specific "personality" numbers, and $25-$35 for tunes featuring a particularly popular performer, or covers bearing the artist's autograph. Pristine, uncirculated sheet music, sometimes found at estate sales and music store clearances, also falls in the higher price range.

"He's My Uncle" by Lew Pollack and Charles Newman, 1940 ................................**$15-$20**

"Johnny Zero" by Vee Lawnhurst and Mack David, 1943...**$5-$10**

"Let's Bring New Glory to Old Glory" by Harry Warren and Mack Gordon, 1942 ................ **$5-$10**

Minor creasing is to be expected, and will not detract from visual appeal. Be on the lookout, however, for crumpled or crumbling edges, water spotting, or original owner signatures that encroach on the central image. These are defects which the asking price should reflect.

To preserve intrinsic value, interior pages should be kept with the cover, and only the minimum necessary repairs should be made, never on the cover, and never with glue. Since light will eventually fade the original colors, sheet music should not be displayed in direct sun.

On display, sheet music covers make vibrant wall accents, whether framed individually, or in a thematic collage. Much of the cover art is eye-catching, relying heavily on a red-white-and-blue color spectrum. For collectors as well as historians, World War II sheet music provides a grand look back at the hopes, trials, and ultimate triumphs of "the greatest generation."

"The Machine Gun Song" by Al Hoffman, Mann Curtis and Jerry Livingston, 1943.........**$20-$25**

"Mr. and Mrs. America" by Ray Henderson and Paul Webster, 1939........................**$20-$25**

"(There'll Be a) Hot Time in the Town Of Berlin When the Yanks Go Marching In" by Sgt. Joe Bushkin and Pvt. John De Vries, Frank Sinatra cover, 1943 ..................................**$20-$25**

"Three Little Sisters" by Vic Mizzy and Irving Taylor, 1942 ................................**$10-$15**

"We Did It Before And We Can Do It Again," Cliff Friend and Charlie Tobias, 1941....**$20-$25**

"When the Lights Go on Again (All Over The World)," by Eddie Seiler, Sol Marcus, and Bennie Benjemen, 1942 ..........**$5-$10**

"White Cross on Okinawa" by Bob Wills, Cliff Sundin, and "Cactus Jack," 1945 **$10-$15**

# Special Contributors and Advisors

The following collectors, dealers, sellers and researchers have supported the *Antique Trader Antiques & Collectibles Price Guide* with their pricing and contacts for nearly 30 years. Many continue to serve as a valuable resource to the entire collecting hobby, while others have passed away. We honor all contributors past and present as their hard work and passion lives on through this book.

Andre Ammelounx
Mannie Banner
Ellen Bercovici
Sandra Bondhus
James R. and Carol S. Boshears
Bobbie Zucker Bryson
Emmett Butler
Dana Cain
Linda D. Carannante
David Chartier
Les and Irene Cohen
Amphora Collectors International
Marion Cohen
Neva Colbert
Marie Compton
Susan N. Cox
Caroline Torem-Craig
Leonard Davis
Bev Dieringer
Janice Dodson
Del E. Domke
Debby DuBay
Susan Eberman
Joan M. George
Roselyn Gerson
William A. and Donna J. Gray
Pam Green
Linda Guffey
Carl Heck
Alma Hillman
K. Robert and Bonne L. Hohl
Ellen R. Hill
Joan Hull
Hull Pottery Association
Louise Irvine
Helen and Bob Jones
Mary Ann Johnston
Donald-Brian Johnson
Dorothy Kamm
Edwin E. Kellogg
Madeleine Kirsh
Vivian Kromer
Curt Leiser
Gene Loveland
Mary McCaslin
Pat Moore
Reg G. Morris
Craig Nissen
Joan C. Oates
Margaret Payne
Gail Peck
John Petzold
Dr. Leslie Piña
Arlene Rabin
John Rader, Sr.
Betty June Wymer
LuAnn Riggs
Tim and Jamie Saloff
Federico Santi
Peggy Sebek
Steve Stone
Phillip Sullivan
Mark and Ellen Supnick
Tim Trapani
Jim Trautman
Elaine Westover
Kathryn Wiese
Laurie Williams
Nancy Wolfe

# Contributors by Subject

**Advertising Items:** Donald-Brian Johnson
**Baseball:** Tom Bartsch
**Bottles:** Brent Frankenhoff
**Christmas Collectibles:** Donald-Brian Johnson
**Clocks:** Karen Knapstein/ Donald-Brian Johnson
**Cloisonné:** Arlene Rabin
**Coins:** Brent Frankenhoff
**Compacts & Vanity Cases:** Roselyn Gerson
**Country Store:** Donald-Brian Johnson/Eric Bradley
**Disney Collectibles:** Eric Bradley
**Eyewear:** Donald-Brian Johnson
**Franklin Mint:** Donald-Brian Johnson/Eric Bradley
**Holt Howard:** Brent Frankenhoff
**Jewelry (Costume):** Kathy Flood
**Kitchenwares:**
Kitchenware (vintage): Donald-Brian Johnson
**Kitchenware (modern):**
**Lady Head vases:** Donald-Brian Johnson
**Lighting:** Carl Heck
**Lighting Devices:**
**Early Lighting:** Donald-Brian Johnson
**Lionel Trains:** Brent Frankenhoff
**Lunchboxes:** Brent Frankenhoff
**Moss Lamps:** Donald-Brian Johnson
**Nativity Sets:** Donald-Brian Johnson
**Plant Waterers:** Bobbie Zucker Bryson
**Pop Culture Collectibles:** Dana Cain and Emmett Butler
**Ribbon Dolls:** Bobbie Zucker Bryson
**Samplers:** Donald-Brian Johnson/Karen Knapstein
**Steins:** Andre Ammelounx
**Valentines:** Donald-Brian Johnson
**Vintage Clothing:** Nancy Wolfe and Madeleine Kirsh
**Watches:** Brent Frankenhoff
**World War II:** Brent Frankenhoff

## CERAMICS

**Abingdon:** Elaine Westover
**American Painted Porcelain:** Dorothy Kamm
**Amphora-Teplitz:** Les and Irene Cohen
**Bauer Pottery:** James Elliott-Bishop
**Belleek (American):** Peggy Sebek
**Belleek (Irish):** Del Domke
**Blue & White Pottery:** Steve Stone
**Blue Ridge Dinnerwares:** Marie Compton and Susan N. Cox
**Brayton Laguna Pottery:** Susan N. Cox
**Buffalo Pottery:** Phillip Sullivan
**Caliente Pottery:** Susan N. Cox
**Catalina Island Pottery:** James Elliott-Bishop
**Ceramic Arts Studio of Madison:** Donald-Brian Johnson
**Clarice Cliff Designs:** Laurie Williams
**Cleminson Clay:** Susan N. Cox
**deLee Art:** Susan N. Cox
**Doulton/Royal Doulton:** Reg Morris, Louise Irvine and Ed Pascoe
**East Liverpool Potteries:** William and Donna J. Gray
**Flow Blue:** K. Robert and Bonne L. Hohl
**Franciscan Ware:** James Elliott-Bishop/ Eric Bradley
**Frankoma Pottery:** Susan N. Cox
**Fulper Pottery:** Eric Bradley
**Gonder Pottery:** James R. and Carol S. Boshears
**Haeger:** Donald-Brian Johnson
**Hall China:** Marty Kennedy
**Haviand:** Eric Bradley
**Hedi Schoop:** Donald-Brian Johnson
**Harker:** William A. and Donna J. Gray
**Hull:** Joan Hull
**Ironstone:** General - Bev Dieringer; Tea Leaf - The Tea Leaf Club International
**Limoges:** Eric Bradley
**Majolica:** Michael Strawser
**McCoy:** Craig Nissen
**Mettlach:** Andre Ammelounx
**Noritake:** Tim Trapani
**Old Ivory:** Alma Hillman
**Pacific Clay Products:** Susan N. Cox
**Phoenix Bird & Flying Turkey:** Joan Collett Oates
**Pierce (Howard) Porcelains:** Susan N. Cox
**Quimper:** Sandra Bondhus
**Red Wing:** Gail Peck
**Royal Bayreuth:** Mary McCaslin
**Rozart Pottery:** Susan N. Cox
**R.S. Prussia:** Mary McCaslin
**Russel Wright Designs:** Kathryn Wiese
**Schoop (Hedi) Art Creations:** Susan N. Cox
**Shawnee:** Linda Guffey
**Shelley China:** Mannie Banner; David Chartier; Bryand Goodlad; Edwin E. Kellogg; Gene Loveland andCurt Leiser
**Stoneware and Spongeware:** Bruce and Vicki Waasdorp
**Vernon Kilns:** Pam Green
**Warwick China:** John Rader, Sr.
**Zeisel (Eva) Designs:** Kathryn Wiese
**Zsolnay:** Federico Santi/ John Gacher

## GLASS

**Animals:** Helen and Bob Jones
**Cambridge:** Karen Knapstein
**Carnival Glass:** Jim and Jan Seeck
**Central Glass Works:** Karen Knapstein
**Consolidated Glass:** Karen Knapstein
**Crackle Glass:** Donald-Brian Johnson
**Depression Glass:** Ellen Schroy
**Duncan & Miller:** Karen Knapstein
**Fenton:** Helen and Bob Jones
**Fostoria:** Karen Knapstein
**Heisey:** Karen Knapstein
**Higgins Glass:** Donald-Brian Johnson
**Imperial:** Karen Knapstein
**Morgantown:** Karen Knapstein
**New Martinsville:** Helen and Bob Jones
**Opalescent Glass:** James Measell
**Paden City:** Helen and Bob Jones
**Phoenix Glass:** Helen and Bob Jones
**Schneider Glass:** Donald-Brian Johnson
**Wall Pocket Vases:** Bobbie Zucker Bryson
**Westmoreland:** Karen Knapstein

# PRICING, IDENTIFICATIONS AND IMAGES PROVIDED BY:

## LIVE AUCTION PROVIDERS

AuctionZip
113 West Pitt St., Suite C
Bedford, PA 15522
(814) 623-5059
www.auctionzip.com

Artfact, LLC.
38 Everett St.
Suite 101
Allston, MA 02134
(617) 746-9800
www.artfact.com

LiveAuctioneers LLC
2nd floor
220 12th Ave.
New York, NY 10001
www.liveauctioneers.com

## AUCTION HOUSES

Allard Auctions, Inc.
P.O. Box 1030
St. Ignatius, MT 59865
(406) 745-0500
(800) 314-0343
www.allardauctions.com

American Bottle Auctions
2523 J St., Suite 203
Sacramento, CA 95816
(800) 806-7722
americanbottle.com

American Pottery Auction
Vicki and Bruce Waasdorp
P.O. Box 434
Clarence, NY 14031
(716) 759-2361
www.antiques-stoneware.com

Antique Helper Auction House
2764 East 55th Place
Indianapolis, IN 46220
(317) 251-5635
www.antiquehelper.com

Apple Tree Auction Center
1616 West Church St.
Newark, OH 43055-1540
(740) 344-4282
www.appletreeauction.com

Artingstall & Hind Auctioneers
9312 Civic Center Drive
# 104
Beverly Hills, CA 90210
(310) 424 5288
www.artingstall.com

Auction Team Breker's
Otto-Hahn-Str. 10
50997 Köln (Godorf), Germany
02236 384340
www.breker.com

Bonhams
7601 W. Sunset Boulevard
Los Angeles CA 90046
323-850-7500
www.bonhams.com

Brunk Auctions
P.O. Box 2135
Asheville, NC 28802
(828) 254-6846
www.brunkauctions.com

Charlton Hall Auctioneers
912 Gervais St.
Columbia, SC 29201
www.charltonhallauctions.com

Cherryland Postcard Auctions
Ronald & Alec Millard
P.O. Box 427
Frankfort, MI 49635
231-352-9758
CherrylandPostcards.com

Christie's New York
20 Rockefeller Plaza
New York, NY 10020
www.christies.com

Cincinnati Art Galleries
225 East Sixth St.
Cincinnati, OH 45202
www.cincinnatiartgalleries.com

Dargate Auction Galleries
326 Munson Ave.
McKees Rocks, PA 15136
(412) 771-8700
dargate.com

Frasher's Doll Auction
2323 S. Mecklin Sch. Rd.
Oak Grove, MO 64075
816-625-3786

Fontaines Auction Gallery
1485 W. Housatonic St.
Pittsfield, MA 01210
www.fontainesauction.net

Garth's Arts & Antiques
P.O. Box 369
Delaware, OH 43015
(740) 362-4771
www.garths.com

Glass Works Auctions
Box 180
East Greenville, PA 18041
(215) 679-5849
www.glswrk-auction.com

Guyette & Schmidt, Inc.
P.O. Box 522
West Farmington, ME 04922
www.guyetteandschmidt.com

Ken Farmer Auctions and Appraisals
105 Harrison St.
Radford, VA 24141
(540) 639-0939
www.kfauctions.com

Hake's Americana & Collectibles
P.O. Box 12001
York, PA 17402
(717) 434-1600
www.hakes.com

Norman Heckler & Company
79 Bradford Corner Rd.
Woodstock Valley, CT 06282
www.hecklerauction.com

Heritage Auction Galleries
3500 Maple Ave.
Dallas, TX 75219-3941
800-872-6467
www.ha.com

Jackson's International Auctioneers & Appraisers
2229 Lincoln St.
Cedar Falls, IA 50613
jacksonsauction.com

James D. Julia, Inc.
P.O. Box 830
203 Skowhegan Road
Fairfield, ME 04937
(207) 453-7125
jamesdjulia.com

Jeffrey S. Evans & Assoc.
2177 Green Valley Lane
Mount Crawford, VA 22841
(540) 434-3939
www.jeffreysevans.com

John Moran Auctioneers
735 West Woodbury Rd.
Altadena, CA 91001
(626) 793-1833
www.johnmoran.com

Los Angeles Modern Auctions
16145 Hart St.
Van Nuys, CA 91406
(323) 904-1950
www.lamodern.com

Legend Numismatics
P.O. Box 9
Lincroft, NJ 07738
(800) 743-2646
www.legendcoin.com

Leslie Hindman Auctioneers
1338 West Lake St.
Chicago, IL 60607
(312) 280-1212
www.lesliehindman.com

Matthews Auctions
111 South Oak St.
Nokomis, IL 62075-1337
(215) 563-8880
www.matthewsauctions.com

McMasters-Harris Auction Company
P.O. Box 755
Cambridge, OH 43725
www.mcmastersharris.com

Dan Morphy Auctions
2000 N. Reading Rd.
Denver, PA 17517
(717) 335-3435
morphyauctions.com

Neal Auction Company
4038 Magazine St.
New Orleans, LA 70115
(504) 899-5329
www.nealauctions.com

New Orleans Auction Gallery
1330 St. Charles Ave.
New Orleans, LA 70130
www.neworleansauction.com

O'Gallerie: Fine Arts, Antiques and Estate Auctions
228 Northeast 7th Ave.
Portland, OR 97232-2909
(503) 238-0202
www.ogallerie.com

Pacific Galleries Auction House and Antique Mall
241 South Lander St.
Seattle, WA 98134
(206) 441-9990
www.pacgal.com

Past Tyme Pleasures
39 California Ave., Suite 105
Pleasanton, CA 94566
www.pasttyme1.com

Pook & Pook, Inc.
463 East Lancaster Ave.
Downingtown, PA 19335
(610) 269-4040
info@pookandpook.com
www.pookandpook.com

Rago Art & Auction Center
333 No. Main St.
Lambertville, NJ 08530
www.ragoarts.com

Rock Island Auction Co.
7819 42 St. West
Rock Island, IL 61201
(800) 238-8022
www.rockislandauction.com

Seeck Auction Company
Jim and Jan Seeck
P.O. Box 377
Mason City, IA 50402
www.seeckauction.com

Skinner, Inc.
357 Main St.
Boston, MA 01740
617-350-5400
www.skinnerinc.com

Sloans & Kenyon Auctioneers and Appraisers
7034 Wisconsin Ave.
Chevy Chase, MD 20815
(301) 634-2330
www.sloansandkenyon.com

Sotheby's New York
1334 York Ave.
New York, NY 10021
(212) 606-7000
www.sothebys.com

Specialists of the South, Inc.
544 E. Sixth St.
Panama City, FL 32401
(850) 785-2577
www.specialistsofthesouth.com

Stanley Gibbons
399 Strand,
London
WC2R 0LX
England
Tel: +44 (0)207 836 8444
www.stanleygibbons.com

Stefek's Auctioneers & Appraisers
18450 Mack Ave.
Grosse Pointe Farms, MI 48236
(313) 881-1800
www.stefeksltd.com

Stephenson's Auctioneers & Appraisers
1005 Industrial Blvd.
Southampton, Pa 18966
(215) 322-6182
www.stephensonsauction.com

Stevens Auction Company
301 North Meridian St.
Aberdeen, MS 39730-2613
(662) 369-2200
www.stevensauction.com

Strawser Majolica Auctions
P.O. Box 332
Wolcottville, IN 46795
www.strawserauctions.com

Swann Auction Galleries
104 E 25th St., # 6
New York, NY 10010-2999
(212) 254-4710
www.swanngalleries.com

Theriault's – the doll masters
PO Box 151
Annapolis, MD 21404
(800) 638-0422
www.theriaults.com

John Toomey Gallery
818 North Blvd.
Oak Park, IL 60301

Treadway Gallery, Inc.
2029 Madison Rd.
Cincinnati, OH 45208
www.treadwaygallery.com

Whiterell's Art & Antiques
300 20th St.
Sacramento, CA 95811
(916) 446-6490
witherells.com

## ADDITIONAL PHOTOGRAPHS AND RESEARCH PROVIDED BY:

45cat.com, an online archive dedicated to the magic of the vinyl seven inch single; Belleek Collectors International Society, www.belleek.ie/collectors-society; CAS Collectors, www.cascollectors.com & www.ceramicartstudio.com; International Perfume Bottle Association, www.perfumebottles.org; National Assn. of Warwick China & Pottery Collectors; popsike.com, Rare Records Auction Results; Red Wing Collectors Society, www.redwingcollectors.org and Tea Leaf Club International, www.tealeafclub.com.

# Index